sociology

sociology

13th edition

Richard T. Schaefer

DePaul University

dedication

To my granddaughter, Tillie, and her parents, Peter and Margaret, for a wonderful life together.

The McGraw·Hill Companies

Connect
Learn
Succeed™

Published by McGraw-Hill, an imprint of The McGraw-Hill Companies, Inc., 1221 Avenue of the Americas, New York, NY 10020. Copyright © 2012, 2010, 2008, 2007, 2005, 2003, 2001, 1998, 1995, 1992, 1989, 1986, 1983. All rights reserved. Printed in the United States of America. No part of this publication may be reproduced or distributed in any form or by any means, or stored in a database or retrieval system, without the prior written consent of The McGraw-Hill Companies, Inc., including, but not limited to, in any network or other electronic storage or transmission, or broadcast for distance learning.

This book is printed on acid-free paper.

2 3 4 5 6 7 8 9 0 DOW/DOW 1 0 9 8 7 6 5 4 3 2

ISBN: 978-0-07-802666-9
MHID: 0-07-802666-0

Executive Editor: *Gina Boedeker*
Marketing Manager: *Patrick Brown*
Development Editor: *Meghan Campbell*
Production Editor: *Holly Paulsen*
Manuscript Editor: *Margaret Moore*
Design Managers: *Andrei Pasternak, Allister Fein*
Text Designer: *Andrei Pasternak*
Cover Designer: *Allister Fein*
Photo Research Coordinator: *Nora Agbayani*
Photo Research: *Toni Michaels/PhotoFind, LLC*
Buyer: *Tandra Jorgensen*
Media Project Managers: *Jennifer Barrick, Andrea Helmbolt*
Digital Product Manager: *Jocelyn Spielberger*
Composition: *10/12 Minion by Laserwords Private Limited*
Printing: *45# New Era Thin Plus, R. R. Donnelley & Sons*

Vice President Editorial: *Michael Ryan*
Publisher: *William Glass*
Editorial Director: *William Glass*
Director of Development: *Dawn Groundwater*

Cover: See page 539 for cover image credits.

Credits: The credits section for this book begins on page 535 and is considered an extension of the copyright page.

Library of Congress Cataloging-in-Publication Data has been applied for.

The Internet addresses listed in the text were accurate at the time of publication. The inclusion of a website does not indicate an endorsement by the author or McGraw-Hill, and McGraw-Hill does not guarantee the accuracy of the information presented at these sites.

www.mhhe.com

about the author

Richard T. Schaefer: Professor, DePaul University
B.A. Northwestern University
M.A., Ph.D. University of Chicago

Growing up in Chicago at a time when neighborhoods were going through transitions in ethnic and racial composition, Richard T. Schaefer found himself increasingly intrigued by what was happening, how people were reacting, and how these changes were affecting neighborhoods and people's jobs. His interest in social issues caused him to gravitate to sociology courses at Northwestern University, where he eventually received a BA in sociology.

"Originally as an undergraduate I thought I would go on to law school and become a lawyer. But after taking a few sociology courses, I found myself wanting to learn more about what sociologists studied, and fascinated by the kinds of questions they raised." This fascination led him to obtain his MA and PhD in sociology from the University of Chicago. Dr. Schaefer's continuing interest in race relations led him to write his master's thesis on the membership of the Ku Klux Klan and his doctoral thesis on racial prejudice and race relations in Great Britain.

Dr. Schaefer went on to become a professor of sociology, and now teaches at DePaul University in Chicago. In 2004 he was named to the Vincent DePaul professorship in recognition of his undergraduate teaching and scholarship. He has taught introductory sociology for over 35 years to students in colleges, adult education programs, nursing programs, and even a maximum-security prison. Dr. Schaefer's love of teaching is apparent in his interaction with his students. "I find myself constantly learning from the students who are in my classes and from reading what they write. Their insights into the material we read or current events that we discuss often become part of future course material and sometimes even find their way into my writing."

Dr. Schaefer is the author of the ninth edition of *Sociology: A Brief Introduction* (McGraw-Hill, 2011), *Sociology in Modules* (McGraw-Hill, 2011), and of the fifth edition of *Sociology Matters* (McGraw-Hill, 2012). He is also the author of *Racial and Ethnic Groups,* now in its thirteenth edition (2012), and *Race and Ethnicity in the United States,* seventh edition, both published by Pearson. Together with William Zellner, he coauthored the ninth edition of *Extraordinary Groups,* published by Worth in 2011. Dr. Schaefer served as the general editor of the three-volume *Encyclopedia of Race, Ethnicity, and Society,* published by Sage in 2008. His articles and book reviews have appeared in many journals, including *American Journal of Sociology; Phylon: A Review of Race and Culture; Contemporary Sociology; Sociology and Social Research; Sociological Quarterly;* and *Teaching Sociology.* He served as president of the Midwest Sociological Society in 1994–1995.

Dr. Schaefer's advice to students is to "look at the material and make connections to your own life and experiences. Sociology will make you a more attentive observer of how people in groups interact and function. It will also make you more aware of people's different needs and interests—and perhaps more ready to work for the common good, while still recognizing the individuality of each person."

brief contents

contents

PART 1
The Sociological Perspective

PART 2
Organizing Social Life

PART 3
Social Inequality

PART **4**
Social Institutions

PART 5
Changing Society

22 Social
Change in the Global
Community   482

chapter opening excerpts

Every chapter in this textbook begins with an excerpt from one of the works listed here. These excerpts convey the excitement and relevance of sociological inquiry and draw readers into the subject matter from each chapter.

boxed features

RESEARCH TODAY

SOCIOLOGY IN THE GLOBAL COMMUNITY

SOCIOLOGY ON CAMPUS

TAKING SOCIOLOGY TO WORK

TRENDSPOTTING

social policy sections

maps

summing UP tables

preface

Sociology leads students to move beyond their intuitive understanding of the social world and to instead examine society by applying a sociological perspective to contemporary issues, events, and everyday life. Combining balanced coverage of theory with current research findings, examples that students can easily relate to, and abundant learning aids, the new edition continues to encourage the development of a sociological imagination that students can use in class and take with them on campus, in their careers, and into their communities.

Introducing ...

McGraw Hill connect™ | SOCIOLOGY

This edition of *Sociology* is available to instructors and students in traditional print format, as well as online with an integrated e-Book, interactive activities, videos, and an adaptive learning system that generates a study plan specifically designed to address each student's strengths and weaknesses. These online tools and resources, collectively called *Connect Sociology,* make managing assignments easier for instructors and learning and studying more engaging and efficient for students.

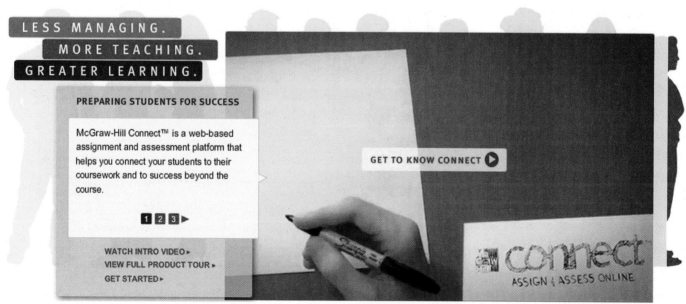

LESS MANAGING.
MORE TEACHING.
GREATER LEARNING.

PREPARING STUDENTS FOR SUCCESS

McGraw-Hill Connect™ is a web-based assignment and assessment platform that helps you connect your students to their coursework and to success beyond the course.

1 2 3 ▶

WATCH INTRO VIDEO ▸
VIEW FULL PRODUCT TOUR ▸
GET STARTED ▸

GET TO KNOW CONNECT ▶

connect
ASSIGN | ASSESS ONLINE

Taking Sociology with You
in College

Thinking Critically: These questions, appearing at the end of each section, prompt students to review and reflect on the content.

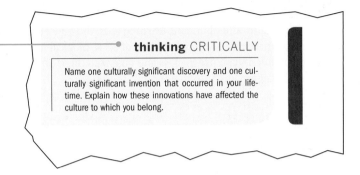

thinking CRITICALLY

Name one culturally significant discovery and one culturally significant invention that occurred in your lifetime. Explain how these innovations have affected the culture to which you belong.

LearnSmart: An adaptive learning system designed to help students learn faster, study more efficiently, and retain more knowledge for greater success.

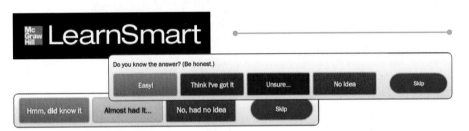

Chapter-Opening Excerpts: Each chapter opens with a lively excerpt from the writing of sociologists and others working in related fields, clearly conveying the excitement and relevance of sociological inquiry.

66 I was made in America. My *Jingle These* Christmas boxers were made in Bangladesh.

I had an all-American childhood in rural Ohio. My all-American blue jeans were made in Cambodia.

I wore flip-flops every day for a year when I worked as a SCUBA diving instructor in Key West. They were made in China.

One day while staring at a pile of clothes on the floor, I noticed the tag of my favorite T-shirt: "Made in Honduras."

I read the tag. My mind wandered. A quest was born.

Where am I wearing? It seems like a simple question with a simple answer. It's not.

The question inspired the quest that took me around the globe. It cost me a lot of things, not the least of which was my consumer innocence. Before the quest, I could put on a piece of clothing without reading its tag and thinking about Arifa in Bangladesh or Dewan in China, about their children, their hopes and dreams, and the challenges they face.

Where am I wearing? This isn't so much a question related to geography and clothes, but about the people who make our clothes and the texture of their lives. This quest is about the way we live and the way *they* live; because when it comes to clothing, others make it, and we have it made. And there's a big, big difference. . . .

Where am I wearing? This isn't so much a question related to geography and clothes, but about the people who make our clothes and the texture of their lives.

Workers flood the narrow alley beside the Delta Apparel Factory in San Pedro Sula, Honduras. They rush to catch one of the many waiting buses at the highway. Merchants hoping to part them from a portion of their daily earnings—$4 to $5—fight for their attention. Vehicles push through the crowd. A minivan knocks over a girl in her midtwenties and then runs over her foot. She curses, is helped to her feet, and limps onto a waiting bus.

The buildings behind the fence are shaded in Bahamian pastels and very well kept. The shrubs have been recently shaped, and the grass trimmed. In the bright Honduran sun, they seem as pleasant as a factory can get.

The lady at Delta Apparel, based in Georgia, giggled at me on the phone when I told her my plans. She was happy to tell me that their Honduran factory was located in the city of Villanueva just south of San Pedro Sula. She even wished me good luck.

Now that I'm in Honduras, the company doesn't think it's very funny.

I stand among the chaos overwhelmed. A thousand sets of eyes stare at me; perhaps they recognize my T-shirt. The irony that this is Tattoo's tropical paradise wore off long ago—somewhere between the confrontation with the big-bellied guards at the factory gate who had guns shoved down their pants like little boys playing cowboy and the conversation with the tight-lipped company representative who failed to reveal much of anything about my T-shirt or the people who assembled it. There was no way I was getting onto the factory floor. All I learned was that eight humans of indiscriminate age and sex stitched my shirt together in less than five minutes—not exactly information that required traveling all the way to Honduras to obtain. 99

(Timmerman 2009:xiii–xiv, 14) Additional information about this excerpt can be found on the Online Learning Center at www.mhhe.com/schaefer13e.

SOCIOLOGY ON CAMPUS

3-4 A Culture of Cheating?

On November 21, 2002, after issuing several warnings, officials at the U.S. Naval Academy seized the computers of almost 100 midshipmen suspected of downloading movies and music illegally from the Internet. Officers at the school may have taken the unusually strong action to avoid liability on the part of the U.S. government, which owns the computers students were using. But across the nation, college administrators have been trying to restrain students from downloading pirated entertainment for free. The practice is so widespread, it has been slowing down the high-powered computer networks colleges and universities depend on for research and admissions.

Illegal downloading is just one aspect of the growing problem of copyright violation, both on campus and off. Now that college students can use personal computers to surf the Internet, most do their research online. Apparently, the temptation to cut and paste passages from website postings and pass them off as one's own is irresistible to many.

Surveys done by the Center for Academic Integrity show that from 1999 to 2005, the percentage of students who approved of this type of plagiarism rose from 10 percent to 41 percent. At the same time, the percentage who considered cutting and pasting from the Internet to be a serious form of cheating fell from 68 percent to 23 percent. Perhaps the worst form of Internet plagiarism is the purchase of entire papers from other writers. Increasingly, the websites that sell essays to

students are based in other countries, including India, Ukraine, Nigeria, and the Philippines.

The Center for Academic Integrity estimates that at most schools, more than 75 percent of the students engage in some form of cheating.

The Center for Academic Integrity estimates that at most schools, more than 75 percent of the students engage in some form of cheating. Students not only cut passages from the Internet and paste them into their papers without citing the source; they share questions and answers on

exams, collaborate on assignments they are supposed to do independently, and even falsify the results of their laboratory experiments.

To address what they consider an alarming trend, many schools are rewriting or adopting new academic honor codes. Observers contend that the increase in student cheating reflects widely publicized instances of cheating in public life, which have served to create an alternative set of values in which the end justifies the means. When young people see sports heroes, authors, entertainers, and corporate executives exposed for cheating in one form or another, the message seems to be "Cheating is okay, as long as you don't get caught."

LET'S DISCUSS

1. Do you know anyone who has engaged in Internet plagiarism? What about cheating on tests or falsifying laboratory results? If so, how did the person justify these forms of dishonesty?
2. Even if cheaters aren't caught, what negative effects does their academic dishonesty have on them? What effects does it have on students who are honest? Could an entire college or university suffer from students' dishonesty?

Sources: Argetsinger and Krim 2002; Bartlett 2009; Center for Academic Integrity 2006; R. Thomas 2003; Toppo 2011; Zernike 2002.

orientation. Soon, however, it took on a global meaning—especially after 9/11, as Americans wondered, "Why do they hate us?" Through 2000, global studies of public opinion had reported favorable views of the United States in countries as diverse as Morocco and Germany. But by 2003, in the wake of the U.S. invasion of Iraq, foreign opinion of the United States had become quite negative (J. Hunter 1991; Kohut ...

occupations of the early 21st century as a "clash of civilizations." According to this thesis, cultural and religious identities, rather than national or political loyalties, are becoming the prime source of international conflict. Critics of this thesis point out that conflict over values is nothing new; only our ability to create havoc and violence has grown. Furthermore, ... of a clash of "civilizations" disguises the sharp d...

THINKING ABOUT MOVIES

Brokeback Mountain

In the rural West, two men struggle to reconcile their social roles with their personal identities.

Frozen River

Two working-class women overcome racial prejudice to form an unlikely friendship.

When the Levees Broke

Spike Lee directs this documentary about the devastating social costs of Hurricane Katrina.

25

Taking Sociology with You
in Your Career

NEW!

Taking Sociology with You: These critical thinking questions and reflection prompts at the end of each chapter encourage students to apply the material that they have just read to their daily lives.

Taking Sociology to Work: These boxes underscore the value of an undergraduate or community college degree in sociology by profiling individuals who majored in sociology and now use its principles in their work.

Use Your Sociological Imagination: These short, thought-provoking sections encourage students to apply the sociological concepts they have learned to the world around them.

RESEARCH TODAY

1-1 Looking at the Gulf Coast Oil Spill from Four Sociological Perspectives

The Gulf Coast oil spill, which began on April 20, 2010, dominated the national news in the United States for much of that year. Like other disasters, the huge spill had social effects that can be analyzed from the four major sociological perspectives.

SWIMMING WATER QUALITY STATUS
HEALTH ADVISORY:
THE PUBLIC IS ADVISED NOT TO SWIM IN THESE WATERS DUE TO THE PRESENCE OF OIL-RELATED CHEMICALS

Functionalist View

In evaluating the effects of the Gulf Coast oil spill, functionalists would stress society's supportive function. For example:

- Functionalists might expect a revitalization of the environmental movement, as happened in the early 1900s after the damming of the Hetch Hetchy Valley just outside Yosemite, and later in the 1990s, after massive wildfires swept through the Everglades.

- Functionalists might note full employment in selected occupations, such as the manufacture of containment booms, even when jobs in other industries were scarce.

- Functionalists would observe that churches and other charities along the Gulf Coast provided both spiritual and material support to households affected by the spill.

- Functionalists would not be surprised that because offshore oil drilling is an integral part of the Gulf Coast economy, the governor of Louisiana strongly opposed a moratorium on deep-sea drilling, despite questions about its safety.

Conflict View

Because conflict theorists see the social order in terms of conflict or tension between competing groups, they would emphasize the coercion and exploitation that underlies relations between the oil companies and Gulf Coast communities:

- The oil industry, conflict theorists would note, is a form of big business, in which profits are more important than workers' health and safety.

- Conflict theorists would emphasize the often-overlooked effect of the spill on minority groups living in inland communities, including Vietnamese Americans, Native American tribal groups, and African Americans. These groups, which were living a marginal existence before the spill, endured particularly significant economic setbacks after the spill.

- Conflict theorists would note that although news outlets tend to focus on oil spills that affect wealthy industrial countries, often the worst spills afflict communities in disadvantaged developing nations, such as Nigeria.

Feminists would note that during times of economic upheaval and dislocation, women bear a disproportionate share of the burden in their role as caregivers.

Feminist View

Feminists would note that during times of economic upheaval and dislocation, such as the Gulf Coast oil crisis, women bear a disproportionate share of the burden in their role as caregivers:

- As family wage earners leave home to seek work elsewhere, women with children or elderly dependents are left to cope as best they can.

- With time, the physical separation these families experience may turn into marital separation.

Interactionist View

Interactionists would examine the Gulf Coast oil spill on the micro level, by focusing on how it shaped personal relations and day-to-day social behavior:

- Interactionists would note that difficult times often strengthen ties among neighbors and family members.

- At the same time, stressful events can contribute to social breakdowns, including divorce or even suicide—a pattern researchers observed in the aftermath of the *Exxon Valdez* oil spill in 1989.

Despite their differences, functionalists, conflict theorists, feminists, and interactionists would all agree that disasters like the Gulf Coast oil spill are a worthy subject for sociological study.

LET'S DISCUSS

1. Which of the four sociological perspectives seems most useful to you in analyzing the Gulf Coast oil crisis? Why?
2. For many people, the worldwide economic crisis that began in 2008 had disastrous personal consequences. Use the four sociological perspectives to analyze what happened to you, your family, and your community during the Great Recession.

Sources: Capriccioso 2010; Freudenburg and Gramling 2010; Greenemeier 2010; Jopling and Morse 2010; Liptak 2010; Molotch 1970; Samuels 2010; N. Wallace 2010.

APPENDIX Careers in Sociology

For the past two decades the number of U.S. college students who have graduated with a degree in sociology has risen steadily (Figure 1-2, page 22). In this appendix we'll consider some of the options these students have after completing their undergraduate education.

How do students first learn about the sociological perspective on society? Some may take a sociology course in high school. Others may study sociology at community college, where 40 percent of all college students in the United States are enrolled. Indeed, many future sociology majors first develop their sociological imaginations at a community college.

An undergraduate degree in sociology doesn't just serve as excellent preparation for future graduate work in sociology. It also provides a strong liberal arts background for entry-level positions in business, social services, foundations, community organizations, not-for-profit groups, law enforcement, and many government jobs. A number of fields—among them marketing, public relations, and broadcasting—now require investigative skills and an understanding of the diverse groups found in today's multiethnic and multinational environment. Moreover, a sociology degree requires accomplishment in oral and written communication, interpersonal skills, problem solving, and critical thinking—all job-related skills that may give sociology graduates an advantage over those who pursue more technical degrees.

Consequently, while few occupations specifically require an undergraduate degree in sociology, such academic training can be an important asset in entering a wide range of occupations. To emphasize this point, a number of chapters in this book highlight a real-life professional who describes how the study of sociology has helped in his or her career. For example, in Chapter 6 a Taking Sociology to Work box explains how a college graduate uses her training

in sociology in managing a small business that she started. And in Chapter 17, another Taking Sociology to Work box shows how a recent graduate uses the skill set he acquired as a sociology major in his role as a government analyst.

Figure 1-3 on page 22 summarizes the sources of employment for those with BA or BS degrees in sociology. It shows that the areas of nonprofit organizations, education, business, and government offer major career opportunities for sociology graduates. Undergraduates who know where their career interests lie are well advised to enroll in sociology courses and specialties best suited to those interests. For example, students hoping to become health planners would take a class in medical sociology; students seeking employment as social science research assistants would focus on courses in statistics and methods. Internships, such as placements at city planning agencies and survey research organizations, afford another way for sociology students to prepare for careers. Studies show that students who choose an internship placement have less trouble finding jobs, obtain better jobs, and enjoy greater job satisfaction than students without internship placements. Finally, students should expect to change fields during their first five years of employment after graduation—for example, from sales and marketing to management (American Sociological Association 2009; Salem and Grabarek 1986; Spalter-Roth and Van Vooren 2010).

Many college students view social work as the field most closely associated with sociology. Traditionally, social workers received their undergraduate training in sociology and allied fields such as psychology and counseling. After some practical experience, social workers would generally seek a master's degree in social work (MSW) to be considered for supervisory or administrative positions. Today, however, some students choose (where it is available) to pursue a bachelor's degree in social work (BSW). This degree prepares graduates for direct ser-

Taking Sociology with You

into the Community

espon... ...oking
e. That is, how
rs feel about
he research-
te statistics
okers feel
ns.
ce of edu-
ts that not
educational
hat is one of
y. Since edu-
me, we may
rspective to
What impact
nder have? Is
degree likely
n with similar
tbook we will
nd variables.
e impact that
while control-
nder and race.

the process of
gh a review
led a prob-
her it pays to
l degree). We
her studies of

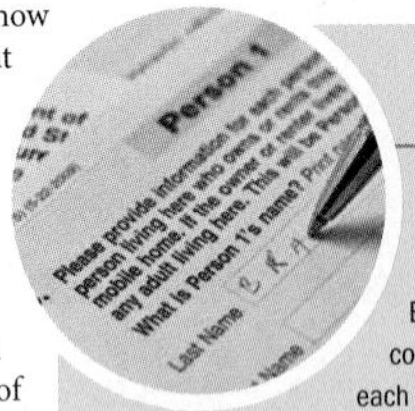

TREND SPOTTING

Overcounting and Undercounting in the U.S. Census

Every 10 years, as required by the Constitution, the U.S. government conducts a census to determine how many congressional representatives each state is allowed. Besides determining the states' political power, these data are used for a myriad of other purposes, from distributing federal aid to education to researching the market for breakfast cereal.

Despite concerns about government intrusion into people's private lives, U.S. citizens are relatively compliant with the head count. About three-quarters of households fill out and return the form or answer face-to-face questions from a census worker. Other industrial countries have much less success than the United States. Because of strong concerns about privacy, for example, the Netherlands has not had a door-to-door census since 1971.

With detailed knowledge of three out of every four households in the United States, census workers can use statistical techniques to estimate data for the other quarter. Still, officials have long recognized that the count is more likely to miss certain groups of people than others. This tendency, called *undercounting*, applies especially to low-income people, non-English speakers, and the homeless. Those who have good reason to avoid census workers, such as illegal immigrants and families who crowd together in inadequate housing, also swell the ranks of the undercounted.

Recently, however, concern has been growing about *overcounting*, or the tendency to count some people twice. College students who live at school rather than at home with their parents, "snowbirds" (retirees who move to warmer climes during the winter), active military personnel, and children whose parents share their custody all are likely to be overcounted.

Census officials estimate that the 2000 Census undercounted 10.2 million people and overcounted 11.6 million. In a nation of over 300 million people, a population count that is off by a net figure of a million or so may not seem much of a problem. However, the error biases the count ... racial and socioeconomic groups. Whites, homeowners, and the edu- ... renters

NEW!

Trendspotting: These notes alert students to trends on their campuses and in their communities, viewed through a sociological lens.

Sociology in the Global Community: These boxes provide a global perspective on topics such as stratification, marriage, and the women's movement.

SOCIOLOGY IN THE GLOBAL COMMUNITY

1-2 Your Morning Cup of Coffee

When you drink a cup of coffee, do you give much thought to where the coffee beans came from, or do you think more about the pleasure you get from the popular beverage? Coffee certainly is popular—as an import, it is second only to petroleum, the most traded commodity in the world.

Although the coffee trade has been globalized, the customs of coffee drinking still vary from place to place. Starbucks, which now has 4,500 locations outside the United States, has over 1,000 locations in Europe. Managers find that in European countries, where the coffeehouse culture originated, 80 percent of their customers sit down to drink their coffee. In the United States, 80 percent of Starbucks' customers leave the store immediately, taking their coffee with them.

Today, the coffee trade relies on the exploitation of cheap labor. Coffee is a labor-intensive crop: there is little that technology can do to ease the coffee picker's burden. The typical coffee picker works in a developing nation near the equator, receiving for a day's wages an amount that matches the price of a single cup of coffee in North America.

The typical coffee picker works in a developing nation near the equator, receiving for a day's wages an amount that matches the price of a single cup of coffee in North America.

In the 1940s, advocacy groups began to promote the sale of certified *fair trade coffee*, which gives a living wage to those who harvest the crop, allowing them to become economically self-sufficient. But as of late 2009, fair trade coffee accounted for only 2.5 percent of the coffee that was bought and sold in the United States. Recently, a similar movement has begun to promote fair trade in the global clothing industry, reported on by Kelsey Timmerman in his book *Where Am I Wearing?*

Ecological activists have drawn attention to what they see as the coffee industry's contribution to the trend toward global warming. The need to make room for more coffee fields, they charge, has encouraged the destruction of rain forests. The same criticism can be aimed at much of the consumption in industrial nations. Of all the products that emerge from developing nations, however, few have as singular a place in many people's daily ritual as that morning cup of joe. The drink in your hand is your tangible link to rural workers in some of the poorest areas of the world.

LET'S DISCUSS

1. Do you enjoy coffee? Would you willingly pay more for a cup of coffee if you knew that the worker who picked the beans would benefit from the higher price?
2. The coffee trade has been blamed for perpetuating social inequality and global warming. Can you think of any positive effects of the coffee trade? Who benefits most from this economic activity?

Sources: Adamy 2008; Fieser 2009; Jaffee 2007; Luttinger and Dicum 2006; E. Marx 2009; Pendergrast 1999; Ritzer 2011:218–227.

of wealth, prestige, or power. For example, the disparity between what coffee bean pickers in developing nations are paid and the price you pay for a cup of coffee underscores global inequality (see Box 1-2). Kelsey Timmerman's research among foreign garment workers uncovered some other aspects of global inequality. And the impact of Hurricane Katrina on residents of the Gulf Coast drew attention to social inequality in the United States. Predictably, the people who were hit the hardest by the massive storm were the poor, who had the greatest difficulty evacuating ...

attract more attention and financial support than do, say, the merits of a needle exchange program for low-income inner-city residents. Yet today more than ever, sociology seeks to better understand the experiences of all people.

Sociologists have noted, for example, that the huge tsunami that hit South Asia in 2004 affected men and women differently. When the waves hit, mothers and grandmothers were at home with the children; men were outside working, where they were more likely ... disast...

Social Policy Sections:
The end-of-chapter Social Policy sections play a critical role in helping students to think like sociologists. These sections apply sociological principles and theories to important social and political issues currently being debated by policymakers and the general public. Take the Issue with You questions prompt students to consider their own experiences and thoughts regarding the issue.

social policy and Organizations

The State of the Unions Worldwide

How many people do you know who belong to a labor union? Chances are you can name a lot fewer people than someone could 50 years ago. In 1954 unions represented 39 percent of workers in the private sector of the U.S. economy; in 2010 they represented only 11.9 percent—the lowest share in more than 70 years. As Figure 6-1 shows, the decline in unionization is common to virtually all industrial nations. What has happened to diminish the importance of organized labor? Have unions outlived their usefulness in a rapidly changing global economy that is dominated by the service sector?

Looking at the Issue

Labor unions consist of organized workers who share either the same skill (as in electronics) or the same employer (as in the case of postal employees). Unions began to emerge during the Industrial Revolution in England, in the 1700s. Groups of workers banded together to extract concessions from employers (for example, safer working conditions, a shorter workweek), as well as to protect their positions.

Historically, labor unions have engaged in restrictive practices that are regarded today as discriminatory. They frequently tried to protect their jobs by limiting entry to their occupation based on

gender, race, ethnicity, citizenship, age, and sometimes rather arbitrary measures of skill levels. Today we see less of this protection of special interests, but individual labor unions are still the target of charges of discrimination, as are employers (J. Rosenfeld 2010).

The power of labor unions varies widely from country to country. In some countries, such as Britain and Mexico, unions play a key role in the foundation of governments. In others, such as Japan and Korea, their role in politics is very limited, and even their ability to influence the private sector is relatively weak. In the United States, unions can sometimes have a significant influence on employers and elected officials, but their effect varies dramatically by type of industry and even region of the country (S. Zimmerman 2008c).

Few people today would dispute the fact that union membership is declining. Among the reasons for the decline are the following:

1. **Changes in the type of industry.** Manufacturing jobs, the traditional heart of the labor union, have declined, giving way to postindustrial service jobs.

2. **Growth in part-time jobs.** Between 1982 and 1998 the number of temporary jobs in the United States rose 577 percent, while total employment increased only 41 percent. Only in ⟨allow tempo⟩

---

casestudy Culture at Walmart

By some measures, Walmart is the largest corporation in the world. By other measures, it is the world's 14th largest economy. Indeed, the Bentonville, Arkansas–based retailer's annual revenue—over one-third of a trillion dollars—surpasses the total value of goods and services produced in many countries, such as Sweden.

Walmart's rise to the status of an economic superpower has not been without criticism. To keep prices low, the corporation pays store clerks as little as possible and has determinedly shut out labor organizers who seek to better their wages. Recently, the debate has expanded to include health care benefits. Given Walmart's wage levels, a large proportion of employees simply cannot afford health insurance, even if the corporation offers it. Also, Walmart has been noted for its lack of commitment to equal opportunity: very few women occupy managerial positions at the company (Barbaro 2008).

Although U.S. consumers have embraced Walmart's "everyday low prices," the reaction has not been as positive in countries where consumers hold different cultural values. The company, now located in 15 countries, has not been an unqualified success abroad. Consider the following missteps in three very different countries. In 2006, the company sold all its facilities in South Korea, where its warehouse-style stores were not appreciated by shoppers accustomed to more elegant surroundings. Today,

Walmart is learning not to impose its corporate culture on foreign customers and employees. No longer do managers plan to sell golf clubs in Brazil, where the game is rarely played, or ice skates in Mexico, where skating rinks are hard to find. More important, the corporate giant has begun to study the culture and social patterns of potential customers (Landler and Barbaro 2006; Saporito 2007; Walmart 2010; A. Zimmerman and Nelson 2006).

Walmart also pulled out of Germany, due in part to its failure to adjust to the national culture. German shoppers, accustomed to no-nonsense, impersonal service, found Walmart employees' smiling, outgoing style off-putting. The company's "ten-foot attitude"—a salesperson who comes within 10 feet of a customer must look the person in the eye, greet the person, and ask if he or she needs help—simply did not play well there. Food shoppers, used to bagging their own groceries, were turned off by Walmart's practice of allowing clerks to handle their purchases. Furthermore, German employees, who had grown up in a culture that accepts workplace romances, found the company's prohibition against on-the-job relationships bizarre.

Today, rather than risk another mistake abroad, Walmart is considering buying Massmart, a retailer with 288 existing stores in Africa. Time will tell whether the proposed takeover is welcomed, or Walmart is again rejected as the "Beast of Bentonville," as critics in Germany and South Africa called it (Stewart 2010)

Case Studies: Applying a sociological lens, our case studies evaluate both the local and the global community—from culture at Walmart and online virtual worlds to stratification in Mexico and capitalism in China.

Maps: Mapping Life Nationwide and Mapping Life Worldwide maps show the prevalence of social trends in the United States as well as in the global community.

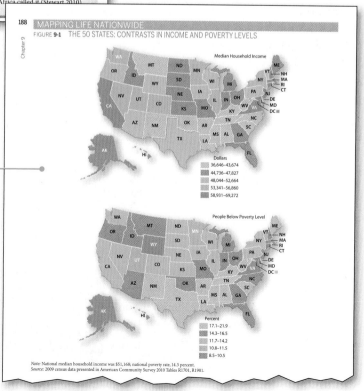

188 MAPPING LIFE NATIONWIDE
FIGURE **9-1** THE 50 STATES: CONTRASTS IN INCOME AND POVERTY LEVELS

Chapter 9

Median Household Income

Dollars
36,646–43,674
44,736–47,827
48,044–52,664
53,341–56,860
58,931–69,272

People Below Poverty Level

Percent
17.1–21.9
14.3–16.5
11.7–14.2
10.8–11.5
8.5–10.5

Note: National median household income was $51,168; national poverty rate, 14.3 percent.
Source: 2009 census data presented in American Community Survey 2010 Tables R1701, R1901.

Chapter 1: Understanding Sociology

- Opening excerpt from *Where Am I Wearing? A Global Tour to the Countries, Factories, and People that Make Our Clothes*, by Kelsey Timmerman

- Discussion of how researchers in the different social sciences would study the effects of the 2010 earthquake in Haiti, with photo
- Thinking Critically exercise on social and cultural capital
- Research Today box, "Looking at the Gulf Coast Oil Spill from Four Sociological Perspectives," with photo
- Emphasis on the theme "Taking Sociology with You" in the last two sections, Applied and Clinical Sociology and Developing a Sociological Imagination

Chapter 2: Sociological Research

- Revised double Mapping Life Nationwide map, "Educational Level and Household Income in the United States"
- Discussion of nonrespondents to the Current Population Survey
- Trendspotting box, "Overcounting and Undercounting in the U.S. Census"
- Discussion of the need to adjust survey questions in response to changes in society
- Coverage of ethnography as a major research design, and observation as one component of ethnography, with cartoon
- Coverage of content analysis of gender stereotyping in children's coloring books and of television coverage of men's versus women's sports
- Section, "The Data-Rich Future"
- Discussion of epidemiologists' use of Google topic searches in tracking the spread of the H1N1 virus
- Revised figure, "Median Age of First Sex"
- Revised figure, "People Who Favor Legalization of Marijuana by Gender and Age, 2010"
- Discussion of the vastly increased amount of data now available to sociologists and its ethical implications

Chapter 3: Culture

- Sociology in the Global Community box, "Cultural Genocide"
- Expanded discussion of the increasing popularity of sushi in the United States
- Use of official responses to the invention of electronic cigarettes as an illustration of culture lag
- Coverage of countercultural patriot militia groups

- Trendspotting box, "Linguistic Isolation"
- Discussion of parental teaching of heterosexuality as the norm for young children
- Figure, "Torture Values by Country"
- Discussion of the "clash of civilizations" thesis

Chapter 4: Socialization

- Trendspotting box, "Multiple Births"
- Discussion of how the recent recession has affected the presentation of the self among the unemployed
- Research Today box, "*Rum Springa*: Raising Amish Children"
- Figure, "The New Normal: The Internet at Home"

Chapter 5: Social Interaction and Social Structure

- Taking Sociology to Work box, "Danielle Taylor, Account Manager, Cash Cycle Solutions"
- Research Today box, "Social Networks and Obesity," with figure
- Trendspotting box, "The Growth of Online Societies"
- Discussion of how social networks served as a morale booster for the unemployed during the recent economic downturn
- Case study, "Second Life," with Use Your Sociological Imagination exercise
- Social Policy section, "Media Concentration"

Chapter 6: Groups and Organizations

- Use Your Sociological Imagination exercise
- Discussion of small-group behavior among the Chilean miners trapped below ground in 2010, with photo
- Key term coverage of focus groups, with photo
- Trendspotting box, "Joining Up: Voluntary Associations in the United States"
- Discussion of Toyota's recent organizational restructuring following a series of recalls
- Summing Up table, "Telecommuting: The Pros and Cons"
- Taking Sociology to Work box, "Sarah Levy, Owner, Sarah's Pastries & Candies"
- Discussion of recent attempts by state and local governments to curtail government workers' retirement benefits and their right to collective bargaining

Chapter 7: The Mass Media

- Chapter-opening excerpt from *Mix It Up: Popular Culture, Mass Media, and Society* by David Grazian
- Discussion of the use of the Internet and social media to fuel anti-government protests during the 2011 upheavals in Egypt, Tunisia, and Bahrain, with cartoon

- Discussion of the Department of Homeland Security's monitoring of social media sites for rescue and relief purposes following the 2010 earthquake in Haiti
- Discussion of media coverage of obesity as a health problem
- Research Today box, "Diversity in Reality Television"
- Discussion of differences in media portrayals of male and female professional golfers
- Discussion of the differential impact of online gaming on male and female adolescents
- Trendspotting box, "Internet Dropouts"
- Discussion of audience segmentation in the two major political parties' placement of television advertisements during the 2010 midterm elections
- Discussion of how the arrival of television in Brazil's Amazon region created a new social norm, with photo
- Social Policy section on the right to privacy, including a discussion of online tracking and the compilation and sale of personal profiles

Chapter 8: Deviance, Crime, and Social Control

- Chapter-opening excerpt from *Cop in the Hood: My Year Policing Baltimore's Eastern District,* by Peter Moskos
- Trendspotting box, "Incarceration Nation"
- Subsection on hate crime, with figure, "Categorization of Reported Hate Crimes"
- Social Policy section on the death penalty, with Mapping Life Worldwide map, "Death Penalty Status by Country"

Chapter 9: Stratification and Social Mobility in the United States

- Chapter-opening excerpt from "Is It Now a Crime to Be Poor?" by Barbara Ehrenreich
- Discussion of the crime of trafficking in humans in the subsection on slavery, with table, "Human Trafficking Report"
- Key term treatment of conspicuous consumption
- Expanded discussion of income inequality in the United States, with figure, "Mean Household Income by Quintile"
- Trendspotting box, "Women as Wage Earners"
- Discussion of the effect of the recent economic recession, compounded by federal and state tax policies, on income inequality

- Discussion of the federal government's new Supplemental Poverty Measure (SPM)
- Discussion of the possibility that the recent economic recession may swell the underclass
- Discussion of the reversal of the trend in which young men earn more than their fathers
- Discussion of the cost of attending community college in the Sociology on Campus box, "Social Class and Financial Aid"

- Social Policy section, "Executive Compensation," with cartoon

Chapter 10: Global Inequality

- Trendspotting box, "Feeding the World"
- Sociology in the Global Community box, "Income Inequality: A Global Perspective"
- Figure, "Multinational Corporations Compared to Nations"
- Sociology in the Global Community box, "Stratification in Brazil," with figure, "Income by Race, Brazil and the United States"
- Discussion of the shrinking social safety net in European countries

Chapter 11: Racial and Ethnic Inequality

- Discussion of the 2010 census finding that the majority of all children ages three and under are now either Hispanic or non-White
- Discussion of the finding that in 2009, Asian American men earned slightly more income than White men
- Trendspotting box, "Members of the Board"
- Discussion of France's expulsion of the ethnic Roma (Gypsies) beginning in 2009, with photo
- Coverage of secession as a pattern of intergroup relations
- Figure, "Spectrum of Intergroup Relations"
- Discussion of recent census data on the segregation of U.S. cities
- Discussion of the federal government's recent settlement of Native Americans' lawsuit for recovery of lease payments for public use of tribal lands
- Subsection on Asian Indians
- Subsection on Filipino Americans
- Figure, "Arab American Religious Affiliations"
- Research Today box, "Latinos in the Voting Booth"
- Subsection on Central and South Americans
- Discussion of the perception of race relations as a zero-sum game
- Coverage of Arizona's law empowering police to detain without authorization people they suspect of being illegal immigrants

Chapter 12: Stratification by Gender

- Opening excerpt from "Skating Femininity: Gender Maneuvering in Women's Roller Derby," by Nancy J. Finley
- Subsection on gender and human sexuality
- Discussion of gender inequality in housework among both the rich and the poor, with figure, "Gender Inequality in Housework"
- Discussion of research showing small-investor bias against female members of corporate boards of directors

- Trendspotting box, "Working Mothers"
- Research Today box, "Give Me a Male Boss, Please"
- Updated Social Policy section, "The Battle over Abortion from a Global Perspective," with discussion of the controversy over "womb lynchings"

Chapter 13: Stratification by Age

- Chapter-opening excerpt from *Shock of Gray* by Ted C. Fishman
- Two Thinking Critically exercises
- Discussion of the projected rise in the median age of the world's population
- Research Today box, "Native Americans and Death"
- Figure, "Percentage of U.S. Population in Selected Age Groups, 1970–2050"
- Trendspotting box, "Job Wanted—Over 65"

Chapter 14: The Family and Intimate Relationships

- Chapter-opening excerpt from *The Marriage-Go-Round: The State of Marriage and the Family in America Today,* by Andrew J. Cherlin
- Trendspotting box, "Cougars on the Rise"
- Updated discussion of Internet romance
- Statistics on interracial and interethnic marriages in the United States
- Discussion of the impact of new media technologies, including the Internet, on the practice of polygyny in Turkey and Morocco
- Sociology in the Global Community box, "Family Life, Italian Style: Thirty-Something and Living with Mom"
- Discussion of the foreign perspective on international adoption
- Updated discussion of state law regarding adoption by unmarried and gay and lesbian couples
- Use Your Sociological Imagination exercise
- Updated Research Today box, "Divorce and Military Deployment," with photo
- Updated discussion of the cost of raising children as a consideration in marriage without children
- Updated discussion of public opinion of gay marriage, with Mapping Life Nationwide map, "Gay Marriage by State"

Chapter 15: Religion

- Chapter-opening excerpt from *Toying with God: The World of Religious Games and Dolls,* by Niki Bado-Fralick and Rebecca Sachs Norris
- Trendspotting box, "None of the Above:

The Nonreligious"
- Figure, "Test Your Religious Knowledge"
- Discussion of the socialization function of religion
- Use Your Sociological Imagination exercise
- Research Today box, "Wicca: Religion or Quasi-Religion?"

Chapter 16: Education

- Chapter-opening excerpt from *The Death and Life of the Great American School System,* by Diane Ravitch
- Figure, "Annual Median Earnings by Educational Level"
- Trendspotting box, "Rising College Enrollment among Racial and Ethnic Minorities, Women"
- Figure, "Tuition Costs, 1976–2009"
- Taking Sociology to Work box, "Diane Belcher, Assistant Director of Volunteer Services, New River Community College"
- Discussion of the immigration to the United States of families from countries where homeschooling is prohibited by law
- Social Policy section on charter schools, with Mapping Life Nationwide map, "Charter Schools"

Chapter 17: Government and Politics

- Chapter-opening excerpt from *Is Voting for Young People?* By Martin P. Wattenberg
- Sociology in the Global Community box, "Sovereignty in the Aloha State"
- Trendspotting box, "Democracy on the Rise?"
- Discussion of the nation-state perspective on the supposed socioeconomic benefits of war
- Taking Sociology to Work box, "Joseph W. Drummond, Management Analyst, U.S. Army Space and Missile Defense Command"

- Updated and expanded coverage of terrorism, including (a) factors that facilitate its development and (b) cyberattacks

- Updated discussion of the role of the Internet in politics, including social media sites

- Updated Social Policy section on campaign financing, including discussion of the 2010 Supreme Court decision in *Citizens United v. Federal Election Commission*

Chapter 18: The Economy and Work

- Chapter-opening excerpt from *The Fair Trade Revolution,* edited by John Bowes, with key term treatment of *fair trade*

- Trendspotting box, "Occupational Growth and Decline"

- Expanded coverage of the informal economy, including a cross-national comparison

- Dedicated section on the U.S. economy, with subsection on offshoring

- Social Policy section, "Microfinancing," including (a) research on the sophisticated use of financial tools by poor families in developing nations and (b) criticisms of microfinancing

Chapter 19: Health and the Environment

- Chapter-opening excerpt from *Shopping Our Way to Safety: How We Changed from Protecting the Environment to Protecting Ourselves,* by Andrew Szasz

- Mapping Life Nationwide map, "Percentage of Children without Health Insurance"

- Discussion of the Patient Protection and Affordable Care Act (2010)

- Trendsetting box, "Medical Technology and Telemedicine"

- Research Today box, "Health Care, Retail Style"

- Discussion of the Tea Party movement's objection to health care reform

- Subsection on ecological modernization, with key term treatment

- Coverage of the globalization of the environmental justice movement

- Coverage of the BP Gulf oil spill of 2010

- Discussion of the problem of water scarcity and its role in promoting armed conflict

- Figure, "Are U.S. Teens Green Enough?"

Chapter 20: Population, Communities, and Urbanization

- Chapter-opening excerpt from *Aerotropolis: The Way We'll Live Next,* by John Kasarda and Greg Lindsay

- Figure, "Population Growth Rate in Selected Countries"

- Trendspotting box, "Urbanization and Its Costs"

- Discussion of the *decoupling* of agriculture and small rural communities

- Figure, "Change in Population by County, 2000–2010"

Chapter 21: Collective Behavior and Social Movements

- Chapter-opening excerpt from *The Global Grapevine: Why Rumors of Terrorism, Immigration, and Trade Matter,* by Gary Alan Fine and Bill Ellis

- Trendspotting box, "Gun Control: The Public Speaks"

- Discussion of the mobilization of social movements by institutional insiders

Chapter 22: Social Change in the Global Community

- Chapter-opening excerpt from *I Live in the Future and Here's How It Works: Why Your World, Work, and Brain Are Being Creatively Disrupted,* by Nick Bilton

- Discussion of the vested interests that opposed cancellation of NASA's Constellation project

- Trendspotting box, "Longer Life Spans, More Social Change"

- Case study, "Social Change in Dubai"

- Discussion of the use of cell phones to improve agriculture in developing countries, as an alternative to biotechnology

- Discussion of the role of migrants in facilitating global trade and development in the Social Policy section on transnationals

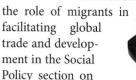

Teaching and Learning with *Sociology*

The complete content of *Sociology* is available to instructors and students in traditional print format, as well as online with integrated and time-saving tools that involve students personally, critically, and actively.

The online tools, collectively called *Connect Sociology*, make managing assignments easier for instructors, and make learning and studying more motivating and efficient for students.

- **LearnSmart.** An adaptive learning system designed to help students learn faster, study more efficiently, and retain more knowledge for greater success.

- **Real-time Reports.** These printable, exportable reports show how well each student (or section) is performing on each course segment. Instructors can use this feature to spot problem areas *before* they crop up on an exam.

- **Learning Objectives.** Every assignment and every course resource can be sorted by learning objective, with point-and-click flexibility. Instructors can use this feature to customize the content and course materials to meet the particular needs of their syllabus.

- **Assignable and assessable activities.** Instructors can deliver assignments and tests easily online, and students can practice skills that fulfill learning objectives at their own pace and on their own schedule.

- **Instructor's Manual.** The Instructor's Manual provides sociology instructors with detailed chapter outlines and summaries, learning objectives, additional lecture ideas, class discussion topics, essay questions, topics for student research, critical thinking questions, video resources, and additional readings. The Instructor's Manual also features a special section on service learning resources and suggestions.

- **PowerPoint Slides.** These slides include bulleted lecture points, figures, and maps. They can be used as is or modified to meet the needs of individual instructors.

- **Student Study Guide.** This resource includes a detailed list of key points, key terms and their definitions, true or false self-quizzes, multiple-choice quizzes, fill-in-the-blank questions, and social policy questions.

- **Test Bank.** This collection includes multiple-choice, true or false, and essay questions for every chapter. Questions test recall of important factual information, application of theoretical perspectives, and understanding of key sociological concepts. McGraw-Hill's computerized EZ Test allows the instructor to create customized exams using the publisher's supplied test items or the instructor's own questions.

ⓣegrity campus

Tegrity Campus is a service that makes class time available all the time by automatically capturing every lecture in a searchable format for students to review when they study and complete assignments.

With a simple one-click start-and-stop process, you capture all computer screens and corresponding audio. Students replay any part of any class with easy-to-use browser-based viewing on a PC or Mac.

With Tegrity Campus, students quickly recall key moments by using Tegrity Campus's unique search feature. This search helps students efficiently find what they need, when they need it across an entire semester of class recordings.

Help turn all your students' study time into learning moments immediately supported by your lecture. To learn more about Tegrity, watch a two-minute Flash demo at http://tegritycampus.mhhe.com

CourseSmart
Learn Smart. Choose Smart.

Visit coursesmart.com to purchase registration codes for this exciting new product.

CourseSmart offers thousands of the most commonly adopted textbooks across hundreds of courses from a wide variety of higher education publishers. It is the only place for faculty to review and compare the full text of a textbook online, providing immediate access without the environmental impact of requesting a printed exam copy. At CourseSmart, students can save up to 50% off the cost of a printed book, reduce their impact on the environment, and gain access to powerful Web tools for learning, including full text search, notes and highlighting, and e-mail tools for sharing notes among classmates. Learn more at www.coursesmart.com

Acknowledgments
Author Acknowledgments

Since 1999, Elizabeth Morgan has played a most significant role in the development of my introductory sociology books. Fortunately for me, in the 13th edition, Betty has once again been responsible for the smooth integration of all changes and updates.

I deeply appreciate the contributions to this book made by my editors. Development editor Meghan Campbell assisted me to make this edition even better than its predecessors. Dawn Groundwater served as director of development.

I have received strong support and encouragement from Gina Boedeker, executive editor, and Holly Paulsen, production editor. Additional guidance and support were provided by Patrick Brown, marketing manager; Brittany Pogue-Mohammed, editorial coordinator; Andrei Pasternak and Allister Fein, design managers; Nora Agbayani, photo research coordinator; Toni Michaels, photo researcher; Judy Brody, text permissions editor; and Margaret Moore, copyeditor. At DePaul University, assistance has been provided by student workers Jessica Chiarella and Kathleen Tallmadge.

This edition continues to reflect many insightful suggestions made by reviewers of the twelve hardcover editions and the nine paperback brief editions. I have also benefited in earlier editions from the creative ideas of Rhona Robbin, Thom Holmes, and Jinny Joyner.

Finally, I would like to thank Peter D. Schaefer, Marymount Manhattan College, for developing the end-of-chapter sections, "Thinking about Movies."

As is evident from these acknowledgments, the preparation of a textbook is truly a team effort. The most valuable member of this effort continues to be my wife, Sandy. She provides the support so necessary in my creative and scholarly activities.

I have had the good fortune to introduce students to sociology for many years. These students have been enormously helpful in spurring on my sociological imagination. In ways I can fully appreciate but cannot fully acknowledge, their questions in class and queries in the hallway have found their way into this textbook.

Richard T. Schaefer
www.schaefersociology.net
schaeferrt@aol.com

Academic Reviewers

This current edition has benefited from constructive and thorough evaluations provided by sociologists from both two-year and four-year institutions.

Dennis Anderson, *Butler Community College*
Felecia Cantwell, *New Mexico State University*
Heather Griffiths, *Fayetteville State University*
Craig R. Humphrey, *Pennsylvania State University*
Love Mills-Byrd, *Cincinnati State Technical and Community College*
Dan Muhwezi, *Butler Community College*
Hence Parson, *Hutchinson Community College*
Shanta Sharma, *Henderson State University*
Robert Shirilla, *Cuyahoga Community College*
Tomecia Sobers, *Fayetteville Technical Community College*
Brandy Trainor, *Rowan University*
Deidre Tyler, *Salt Lake Community College*
Sally Vyain, *Ivy Technical Community College*

Connect Consultants

The creation of *Connect Sociology* has been a highly collaborative effort. Thank you to the following for their guidance, insight, and innovative suggestions.

James Bazan, *Central Piedmont Community College*
Scott Brooks, *University of California, Riverside*
Susan Cody-Rydzewski, *Georgia Perimeter College*
Russell Davis, *University of West Alabama*
Shelly Dutchin, *Western Technical College*
Isaac Eberstein, *Florida State University*
Tammie Foltz, *Des Moines Area Community College*
John Gannon, *College of Southern Nevada*
Thomas Kersen, *Jackson State University*
Melinda Messineo, *Ball State University*
Tommy Sadler, *Union University*
Theresa Schrantz, *Tarrant County College*
Sharon Wettengel, *Tarrant County College*

Connect Contributors

These instructors contributed their time, thought, and creativity to make our vision for *Connect Sociology* a reality. Thank you to the following content authors.

Heather Griffiths, *Fayetteville State University*
Linda Lombard, *Embry-Riddle Aeronautical University*
Cheryl North, *Tarrant County College*
Denise Shuster, *Owens Community College*
Rachel Stehle, *Cuyahoga Community College*
Brandy Trainor, *Rowan University*
Sally Vyain, *Ivy Tech Community College*
Marie Wallace, *Pima Community College*

Symposia Attendees

Every year McGraw-Hill conducts several Introductory Sociology symposia for instructors from across the country. These events offer a forum for instructors to exchange ideas and experiences with colleagues they might not have the chance to meet otherwise. They also provide an opportunity for members of the McGraw-Hill team to learn about the needs and challenges of the Introductory Sociology course for both instructors and students. The feedback we have received has been invaluable and contributed—directly and indirectly—to this edition of *Sociology:*

Douglas Adams, *University of Arkansas*
Isaac Addai, *Lansing Community College*
Robert Aponte, *Purdue University*
David Arizmendi, *South Texas College*
Sergio Banda, *Fullerton College*
John Batsie, *Parkland College*
James Bazan, *Central Piedmont Community College*
Janice Bending, *University of Cincinnati*
Scott Brooks, *University of California, Riverside*
Elaine Cannon, *El Camino College*
Nina Chapman, *Golden West College*
Margaret Choka, *Pellissippi State Tech College*
Rodney Clayton, *Central Community College*
Susan Cody-Rydzewski, *Georgia Perimeter College*
Charles Combs, *Sinclair Community College*
Lisa Coole, *Bridgewater College*
Carolyn Corrado, *University of Albany*
Larry Curiel, *Cypress College*
Scott Davis, *Treasure Valley Community College*
Aimee Dickinson, *Lorain County Community College*
Joe Donnermeyer, *Ohio State University*
Brian Donovan, *University of Kansas*
Gianna Durso-Finley, *Mercer County Community College*
Shelly Dutchin, *Western Technical College*
Ike Eberstein, *Florida State University*
Samuel Echevarria-Cruz, *Austin Community College*
John Ehle, *Northern Virginia Community College*
David Embrick, *Loyola University*
Kathryn Feltey, *University of Akron*
Tammie Foltz, *Des Moines Area Community College*
John Gannon, *College of Southern Nevada*
Sergio Gomez, *Chaffey College*

Kyra Greene, *San Diego State University*
Mike Greenhouse, *Middlesex County College*
Bram Hamovitch, *Lakeland Community College*
Carl Hand, *Valdosta State University*
Garrison Henderson, *Tarrant County College*
Peter Iadicola, *Indiana University–Purdue University Indianapolis*
Laura Jamison, *Parkland College*
Paul Ketchum, *University of Oklahoma*
Steve Keto, *Kent State University*
Brian Klocke, *State University of New York Plattsburgh*
Jodie Lawston, *DePaul University*
Jason Leiker, *Utah State University*
Joe Lengermann, *University of Maryland*
David Liu, *Harrisburg Area Community College*
David Locher, *Missouri Southern State University*
Michael Loukine, *Northern Michigan University*
Jean Lynch-Brandon, *Lansing Community College*
Lori Maida, *Westchester Community College*
Farshad Malek-Ahmadi, *Naugatuck Valley Community College*
Karen McCue, *Central New Mexico Community College*
Messineo Melinda, *Ball State University*
Kelly Mosel-Talavera, *Texas State University–San Marcos*
Frank Mossadeghi, *Palm Beach Community College*
Cheryl North, *Tarrant County College*
Pat O'Brien, *Elgin Community College*
Jacob Oni, *Cape Cod Community College*

Robert Orrange, *Eastern Michigan University*
Diane Owsley, *Elizabeth Community College*
Kevin Payne, *Park University*
Lisa Pellerin, *Ball State University*
Paul C. Price, *Pasadena City College*
Richard Rosell, *Westchester Community College*
Alan Rudy, *Central Michigan University*
Terri Schrantz, *Tarrant County Community College–Southeast*
Barbara Seiter, *Raritan Valley Community College*
Michelle Smith, *Lakeland Community College*
Rachael Stehle, *Cuyahoga Community College*
Lawrence Stern, *Collin College*
Rose Suggett, *Southeast Community College*
Richard Sweeny, *Modesto Junior College*
Margaret Taylor, *Greenville Technical College*
Baishakhi Banerjee Taylor, *Duke University*
Michelle Stewart Thomas, *Mt. San Antonio College*
Ruth Thompson-Miller, *Texas A&M University*
Ronald Thrasher, *Oklahoma State University*
Vu-Duc Vuong, *DeAnza College*
Marie L. Wallace, *Pima Community College*
Sharon Wettengel, *Tarrant County College*
Amanda White, *St. Louis Community College*
Susan Williams, *Kansas State University*
John Zipp, *University of Akron*

sociology

No matter where you're going—to work, to study abroad, or just on vacation—you can take sociology and its insights with you.

Understanding Sociology 1

66 I was made in America. My *Jingle These* Christmas boxers were made in Bangladesh.

I had an all-American childhood in rural Ohio. My all-American blue jeans were made in Cambodia.

I wore flip-flops every day for a year when I worked as a SCUBA diving instructor in Key West. They were made in China.

One day while staring at a pile of clothes on the floor, I noticed the tag of my favorite T-shirt: "Made in Honduras."

I read the tag. My mind wandered. A quest was born.

Where am I wearing? It seems like a simple question with a simple answer. It's not.

The question inspired the quest that took me around the globe. It cost me a lot of things, not the least of which was my consumer innocence. Before the quest, I could put on a piece of clothing without reading its tag and thinking about Arifa in Bangladesh or Dewan in China, about their children, their hopes and dreams, and the challenges they face.

Where am I wearing? This isn't so much a question related to geography and clothes, but about the people who make our clothes and the texture of their lives. This quest is about the way *we* live and the way *they* live; because when it comes to clothing, others make it, and we have it made. And there's a big, big difference. . . .

Where am I wearing? This isn't so much a question related to geography and clothes, but about the people who make our clothes and the texture of their lives.

Workers flood the narrow alley beside the Delta Apparel Factory in San Pedro Sula, Honduras. They rush to catch one of the many waiting buses at the highway. Merchants hoping to part them from a portion of their daily earnings—$4 to $5—fight for their attention. Vehicles push through the crowd. A minivan knocks over a girl in her midtwenties and then runs over her foot. She curses, is helped to her feet, and limps onto a waiting bus.

The buildings behind the fence are shaded in Bahamian pastels and very well kept. The shrubs have been recently shaped, and the grass trimmed. In the bright Honduran sun, they seem as pleasant as a factory can get.

The lady at Delta Apparel, based in Georgia, giggled at me on the phone when I told her my plans. She was happy to tell me that their Honduran factory was located in the city of Villanueva just south of San Pedro Sula. She even wished me good luck.

Now that I'm in Honduras, the company doesn't think it's very funny.

I stand among the chaos overwhelmed. A thousand sets of eyes stare at me; perhaps they recognize my T-shirt. The irony that this is Tattoo's tropical paradise wore off long ago—somewhere between the confrontation with the big-bellied guards at the factory gate who had guns shoved down their pants like little boys playing cowboy and the conversation with the tight-lipped company representative who failed to reveal much of anything about my T-shirt or the people who assembled it. There was no way I was getting onto the factory floor. All I learned was that eight humans of indiscriminate age and sex stitched my shirt together in less than five minutes—not exactly information that required traveling all the way to Honduras to obtain. 99

(Timmerman 2009:xiii–xiv, 14) Additional information about this excerpt can be found on the Online Learning Center at www.mhhe.com/schaefer13e.

In his book *Where Am I Wearing? A Global Tour to the Countries, Factories, and People that Make Our Clothes,* journalist Kelsey Timmerman recounts his travels to the countries where his jeans, T-shirts, and flip-flops—the uniform of today's young adult—were made. From Honduras to Bangladesh, from Cambodia to the United States, he tracked down the factories and befriended the seamstresses who labored there. Though owners were reluctant to allow him on the factory floor, they couldn't prevent him from visiting workers' homes and families. Timmerman found that both inside and outside the factory, garment workers lived in what would be considered substandard conditions in the United States. He argues that global apparel companies should take responsibility for conditions at their suppliers' factories, even if those factories are located halfway around the world (Fairtrade Foundation 2010).

Timmerman's book focuses on an unequal global economy, which is a central topic in sociology. His investigative work, like the work of many other journalists, is informed by sociological research that documents the existence and extent of inequality around the world. Social inequality has a pervasive influence on human interactions and institutions. Certain groups of people control scarce resources, wield power, and receive special treatment.

Although it might be interesting to know how one individual, like Kelsey Timmerman or a foreign factory worker, is affected by social inequality, sociologists consider how entire groups of people are affected by such factors, and how society itself might be altered by them. Sociologists, then, are not concerned with what one individual does or does not do, but with what people do as members of a group or in interaction with one another, and what that means for individuals and for society as a whole. For example, sociologists have considered how, together, college students have taken sociology with them, organizing to confront the sportswear companies that underpay the overseas workers who create their team uniforms and T-shirts proclaiming their school pride (Esbenshade 2008; Silverstein 2010).

As a field of study, sociology is extremely broad in scope. You will see throughout this book the range of topics sociologists investigate—from suicide to TV viewing habits, from Amish society to global economic patterns, from peer pressure to genetic engineering. Sociology looks at how others influence our behavior; how major social institutions like the government, religion, and the economy affect us; and how we ourselves affect other individuals, groups, and even organizations.

How did sociology develop? In what ways does it differ from other social sciences? This chapter will explore the nature of sociology as both a field of inquiry and an exercise of the "sociological imagination." We'll look at the discipline as a science and consider its relationship to other social sciences. We'll meet four pioneering thinkers—Émile Durkheim, Max Weber, Karl Marx, and W. E. B. DuBois—and examine the theoretical perspectives that grew out of their work. We'll note some of the practical applications for sociological theory and research. Finally, we'll see how sociology helps us to develop a sociological imagination. For those students interested in exploring career opportunities in sociology, the chapter closes with a special appendix.

What Is Sociology?

"What has sociology got to do with me or with my life?" As a student, you might well have asked this question when you signed up for your introductory sociology course. To answer it, consider these points: Are you influenced by what you see on television? Do you use the Internet? Did you vote in the last election? Are you familiar with binge drinking on campus? Do you use alternative medicine? These are just a few of the everyday life situations described in this book that sociology can shed light on. But as the opening excerpt indicates, sociology also looks at large social issues. We use sociology to investigate why thousands of jobs have moved from the United States to developing nations, what social forces promote prejudice, what leads someone to join a social movement and work for social change, how access to computer technology can reduce social inequality, and why relationships between men and women in Seattle differ from those in Singapore.

Sociology is, simply, the scientific study of social behavior and human groups. It focuses on social relationships; how those relationships influence people's behavior; and how societies, the sum total of those relationships, develop and change.

The Sociological Imagination

In attempting to understand social behavior, sociologists rely on a particular type of critical thinking. A leading sociologist, C. Wright Mills, described such thinking as the **sociological imagination**—an awareness of the relationship between an individual and the wider society, both today and in the past (Mills [1959] 2000a). This awareness allows all of us (not just sociologists) to comprehend the links between our immediate, personal social settings and the remote, impersonal social world that surrounds and helps to shape us. Kelsey Timmerman certainly used a sociological imagination when he studied foreign garment workers.

A key element in the sociological imagination is the ability to view one's own society as an outsider would, rather than only from the perspective of personal experiences and cultural biases. Consider something as simple as sporting events. On college campuses in the United States, thousands of students cheer well-trained football players. In Bali, Indonesia, dozens of spectators gather around a ring to cheer on roosters trained in cockfighting. In both instances, the spectators debate the merits of their favorites and bet on the outcome of the events. Yet what is considered a normal sporting event in one part of the world is considered unusual in another part.

The sociological imagination allows us to go beyond personal experiences and observations to understand broader public issues. Divorce, for example, is unquestionably a personal hardship for a husband and wife who split apart. However, C. Wright Mills advocated using the sociological imagination to view divorce not as simply an individual's personal problem but rather as a societal concern. Using this perspective, we can see that an increase in the divorce rate actually redefines a major social institution—the family. Today's households frequently include stepparents and half-siblings whose parents have divorced and remarried. Through the complexities of the blended family, this private concern becomes a public issue that affects schools, government agencies, businesses, and religious institutions.

The sociological imagination is an empowering tool. It allows us to look beyond a limited understanding of human behavior to see the world and its people in a new way and through a broader lens than we might otherwise use. It may be as simple as understanding why a roommate prefers country music to hip-hop, or it may open up a whole different way of understanding other populations in the world. For example, in the aftermath of the terrorist attacks on the United States on September 11, 2001, many citizens wanted to understand how Muslims throughout the world perceived their country, and why. From time to time this textbook will offer you the chance to exercise your sociological imagination in a variety of situations.

use your sociological *imagination*

You are walking down the street in your city or hometown. In looking around you, you can't help noticing that half or more of the people you see are overweight. How do you explain your observation? If you were C. Wright Mills, how do you think you would explain it?

Sociology and the Social Sciences

Is sociology a science? The term **science** refers to the body of knowledge obtained by methods based on systematic observation. Just like other scientific disciplines, sociology involves the organized, systematic study of phenomena (in this case, human behavior) in order to enhance understanding. All scientists, whether studying mushrooms or murderers, attempt to collect

Sociology is the scientific study of social behavior and human groups.

on? They study the influence that society has on people's attitudes and behavior and the ways in which people interact and shape society. Because humans are social animals, sociologists examine our social relationships with others scientifically. The range of the relationships they investigate is vast, as the current list of sections in the American Sociological Association suggests (Table 1-1).

Let's consider how different social scientists would study the impact of the earthquake that hit Port-au-Prince, the capital of Haiti, in 2010. Historians would stress Haiti's past economic exploitation as a colony of France and its resulting poverty today. Economists would discuss ways to rebuild Haiti's economy, perhaps by diversifying it. Environmental ecologists would treat Haiti and its neighbor, the Dominican Republic, as a single ecosystem—the island of Hispaniola. Psychologists would study individual cases of emotional stress caused by the traumatic event. And political scientists would study the short-term prospects for the nation's governance, which might include trustee status under the United Nations.

What approach would sociologists take? They might consider the possibility of reversing Haitians' generation-long migration from the countryside to the capital city, by making life in rural areas more sustainable. They might study the use of new media, such as Twitter, to funnel donations to charities. They might conduct short- and long-term research on the adoption of

precise information through methods of study that are as objective as possible. They rely on careful recording of observations and accumulation of data.

Of course, there is a great difference between sociology and physics, between psychology and astronomy. For this reason, the sciences are commonly divided into natural and social sciences. **Natural science** is the study of the physical features of nature and the ways in which they interact and change. Astronomy, biology, chemistry, geology, and physics are all natural sciences. **Social science** is the study of the social features of humans and the ways in which they interact and change. The social sciences include sociology, anthropology, economics, history, psychology, and political science.

These social science disciplines have a common focus on the social behavior of people, yet each has a particular orientation. Anthropologists usually study past cultures and preindustrial societies that continue today, as well as the origins of humans. Economists explore the ways in which people produce and exchange goods and services, along with money and other resources. Historians are concerned with the peoples and events of the past and their significance for us today. Political scientists study international relations, the workings of government, and the exercise of power and authority. Psychologists investigate personality and individual behavior. So what do *sociologists* focus

The earthquake that hit Haiti in January 2010 may have lasted only a few minutes, but the social impact on the small, impoverished island nation will last many years. This "temporary" tent city shelters 375,000 people whose homes were destroyed, and for whom there is still no permanent housing, as of June 2011.

Aging and the Life Course	Environment and Technology	Peace, War, and Social Conflict
Alcohol, Drugs, and Tobacco	Ethnomethodology and Conversation Analysis	Political Economy of the World-System
Altruism, Morality, and Sociology	Evolution, Biology, and Sociology	Political Sociology
Animals and Society	Family	Population
Asia and Asian America	Global and Transnational Sociology	Race, Gender, and Class
Body and Embodiment	History of Sociology	Racial and Ethnic Minorities
Children and Youth	Human Rights	Rationality and Society
Collective Behavior and Social Movements	International Migration	Religion
Communication and Information Technologies	Labor and Labor Movements	Science, Knowledge, and Technology
Community and Urban Sociology	Latino/a Sociology	Sex and Gender
Comparative and Historical Sociology	Law	Sexualities
Crime, Law, and Deviance	Marxist Sociology	Social Psychology
Culture	Mathematical Sociology	Sociological Practice and Public Sociology
Disability and Society	Medical Sociology	Teaching and Learning
Economic Sociology	Mental Health	Theory
Education	Methodology	
Emotions	Organizations, Occupations, and Work	

The range of sociological issues is very broad. For example, sociologists who belong to the Animals and Society section of the ASA may study the animal rights movement; those who belong to the Sexualities section may study global sex workers or the gay, bisexual, and transgendered movements. Economic sociologists may investigate globalization or consumerism, among many other topics.
Source: American Sociological Association 2011.

Think about It

Which of these topics do you think would interest you the most? Why?

Haitian orphans by U.S. families, many of them White. Or they might evaluate current and potential U.S. policy toward Haitian immigrants, refugees, and deportees.

Sociologists would take a similar approach to studying episodes of extreme violence. In April 2007, just as college students were beginning to focus on the impending end of the semester, tragedy struck on the campus of Virginia Tech. In a two-hour shooting spree, a mentally disturbed senior armed with semi-automatic weapons killed a total of 32 students and faculty at Virginia's largest university. Observers struggled to describe the events and place them in some social context. For sociologists in particular, the event raised numerous issues and topics for study, including the media's role in describing the attacks, the presence of violence in our educational institutions, the gun control debate, the inadequacy of the nation's mental health care system, and the stereotyping and stigmatization of people who suffer from mental illness.

Besides doing research, sociologists have a long history of advising government agencies on how to respond to disasters. Certainly the poverty of the Gulf Coast region complicated the huge challenge of evacuation in 2005. With Katrina bearing down on the Gulf Coast, thousands of poor inner-city residents had no automobiles or other available means of escaping the storm. Added to that difficulty was the high incidence of disability in the area. New Orleans ranked second among the nation's 70 largest cities in the proportion of people over age 65 who are disabled—56 percent. Moving wheelchair-bound residents

to safety requires specially equipped vehicles, to say nothing of handicap-accessible accommodations in public shelters. Clearly, officials must consider these factors in developing evacuation plans (Bureau of the Census 2005b).

Sociological analysis of the disaster did not end when the floodwaters receded. Long before residents of New Orleans staged a massive anticrime rally at City Hall in 2007, researchers were analyzing resettlement patterns in the city. They noted that returning residents often faced bleak job prospects. Yet families who had stayed away for that reason often had trouble enrolling their children in schools unprepared for an influx of evacuees. Faced with a choice between the need to work and the need to return their children to school, some displaced families risked sending their older children home alone. Meanwhile, opportunists had arrived to victimize unsuspecting homeowners. And the city's overtaxed judicial and criminal justice systems, which had been understaffed before Katrina struck, had been only partially restored. All these social factors led sociologists and others to anticipate the unparalleled rise in reported crime the city experienced in 2006 and 2007 (Jervis 2008; Kaufman 2006).

Throughout this textbook, you will see how sociologists develop theories and conduct research to study and better understand societies. And hyou will be encouraged to use your sociological imagination to examine the United States (and other societies) from the viewpoint of a respectful but questioning outsider.

Sociology and Common Sense

Sociology focuses on the study of human behavior. Yet we all have experience with human behavior and at least some knowledge of it. All of us might well have theories about why people become homeless, for example. Our theories and opinions typically come from common sense—that is, from our experiences and conversations, from what we read, from what we see on television, and so forth.

In our daily lives, we rely on common sense to get us through many unfamiliar situations. However, this commonsense knowledge, while sometimes accurate, is not always reliable, because it rests on commonly held beliefs rather than on systematic analysis of facts. It was once considered common sense to accept that the earth was flat—a view rightly questioned by Pythagoras and Aristotle. Incorrect commonsense notions are not just a part of the distant past; they remain with us today.

Contrary to the common notion that women tend to be chatty compared to men, for instance, researchers have found little difference between the sexes in terms of their talkativeness. Over a five-year period they placed unobtrusive microphones on 396 college students in various fields, at campuses in Mexico as well as the United States. They found that both men and women spoke about 16,000 words per day (Mehl et al. 2007).

Similarly, common sense tells us that in the United States today, military marriages are more likely to end in separation or divorce than in the past due to the strain of long deployments in Iraq and Afghanistan. Yet a study released in 2007 shows no significant increase in the divorce rate among U.S. soldiers over the past decade. In fact, the rate of marital dissolution among members of the military is comparable to that of nonmilitary families. Interestingly, this is not the first study to disprove the widely held notion that military service strains the marital bond. Two generations earlier, during the Vietnam era, researchers came to the same conclusion (Call and Teachman 1991; Karney and Crown 2007).

Like other social scientists, sociologists do not accept something as a fact because "everyone knows it." Instead, each piece of information must be tested and recorded, then analyzed in relation to other data. Sociologists rely on scientific studies in order to describe and understand a social environment. At times, the findings of sociologists may seem like common sense, because they deal with familiar facets of everyday life. The difference is that such findings have been *tested* by researchers. Common sense now tells us that the earth is round, but this particular commonsense notion is based on centuries of scientific work that began with the breakthroughs made by Pythagoras and Aristotle.

thinking CRITICALLY

What aspects of the social and work environment in a fast-food restaurant would be of particular interest to a sociologist? How would the sociological imagination help in analyzing the topic?

What Is Sociological Theory?

Why do people commit suicide? One traditional commonsense answer is that people inherit the desire to kill themselves. Another view is that sunspots drive people to take their lives. These explanations may not seem especially convincing to contemporary researchers, but they represent beliefs widely held as recently as 1900.

Sociologists are not particularly interested in why any one individual commits suicide; they are more concerned with identifying the social forces that systematically cause some people to take their own lives. In order to undertake this research, sociologists develop a theory that offers a general explanation of suicidal behavior.

We can think of theories as attempts to explain events, forces, materials, ideas, or behavior in a comprehensive manner. In sociology, a **theory** is a set of statements that seeks to explain problems, actions, or behavior. An effective theory may have both explanatory and predictive power. That is, it can help us to see the relationships among seemingly isolated phenomena, as well as to understand how one type of change in an environment leads to other changes.

The World Health Organization (2010) estimates that almost a million people die from suicide every year. More than a hundred years ago, a sociologist tried to look at suicide data scientifically. Émile Durkheim ([1897] 1951) developed a highly original theory about the relationship between suicide and social factors. Durkheim was primarily concerned not with the personalities of individual suicide victims, but rather with suicide rates and how they varied from country to country. As a result, when he looked at the number of reported suicides in France, England, and Denmark in 1869, he also noted the total population of each country in order to determine the rate of suicide in each nation. He found that whereas England had only 67 reported suicides per million inhabitants, France had 135 per million and Denmark had 277 per million. The question then became "Why did Denmark have a comparatively high rate of reported suicide?"

Durkheim went much deeper into his investigation of suicide rates. The result was his landmark work *Suicide,* published in 1897. Durkheim refused to accept unproved explanations regarding suicide, including the beliefs that inherited tendencies or cosmic forces caused such deaths. Instead, he focused on social factors, such as the cohesiveness or lack of cohesiveness of religious, social, and occupational groups.

Durkheim's research suggested that suicide, although it is a solitary act, is related to group life. He found that people without religious affiliations had a higher suicide rate than those who were affiliated; the unmarried had much higher rates than married people; and soldiers had a higher rate than civilians. In addition, there seemed to be higher rates of suicide in times of peace than in times of war and revolution, and in times of economic instability and recession rather than in times of prosperity. Durkheim concluded that the suicide rates of a society reflected the extent to which people were or were not integrated into the group life of the society.

Émile Durkheim, like many other social scientists, developed a theory to explain how individual behavior can be understood within a social context. He pointed out the influence of groups and societal forces on what had always been viewed as a highly personal act. Clearly, Durkheim offered a more *scientific* explanation for the causes of suicide than that of inherited tendencies or sunspots. His theory has predictive power, since it suggests that suicide rates will rise or fall in conjunction with certain social and economic changes.

Of course, a theory—even the best of theories—is not a final statement about human behavior. Durkheim's theory of suicide is no exception. Sociologists continue to examine factors that contribute to differences in suicide rates around the world and to a particular society's rate of suicide. They have observed that in Las Vegas, for example, the chances of dying by suicide are strikingly high—twice as high as in the United States as a whole. Noting Durkheim's emphasis on the relationship between suicide and social isolation, researchers have suggested that Las Vegas's rapid growth and constant influx of tourists have undermined the community's sense of permanence, even among longtime residents. Although gambling—or more accurately, losing while gambling—may seem a likely precipitating factor in suicides there, careful study of the data has allowed researchers to dismiss that explanation. What happens in Vegas may stay in Vegas, but the sense of community cohesiveness that the rest of the country enjoys may be lacking (Wray et al. 2008).

thinking CRITICALLY

Can you think of any other explanation for the high suicide rate in Las Vegas? Does that explanation agree with Durkheim's theory?

The Development of Sociology

People have always been curious about sociological matters—how we get along with others, what we do for a living, whom we select as our leaders. Philosophers and religious authorities of ancient and medieval societies made countless observations about human behavior. They did not test or verify those observations scientifically; nevertheless, their observations often became the foundation for moral codes. Several of these early social philosophers correctly predicted that a systematic study of human behavior would emerge one day. Beginning in the 19th century, European theorists made pioneering contributions to the development of a science of human behavior.

Early Thinkers

Auguste Comte The 19th century was an unsettling time in France. The French monarchy had been deposed in the revolution of 1789, and Napoleon had suffered defeat in his effort to conquer Europe. Amid this chaos, philosophers considered how society might be improved. Auguste Comte (1798–1857), credited with being the most influential of the philosophers of the early 1800s, believed that a theoretical science of society and a systematic investigation of behavior were needed to improve society. He coined the term *sociology* to apply to the science of human behavior.

Writing in the 1800s, Comte feared that the excesses of the French Revolution had permanently impaired France's stability. Yet he hoped that the systematic study of social behavior would eventually lead to more rational human interactions. In Comte's hierarchy of the sciences, sociology was at the top. He called it the "queen," and its practitioners "scientist-priests." This French theorist did not simply give sociology its name; he presented a rather ambitious challenge to the fledgling discipline.

Harriet Martineau Scholars learned of Comte's works largely through translations by the English sociologist Harriet Martineau (1802–1876). But Martineau was a pathbreaker in her own right: she offered insightful observations of the customs and social practices of both her native Britain and the United States. Martineau's book *Society in America* ([1837] 1962) examined religion, politics, child rearing, and immigration in the young nation. It gave special attention to social class distinctions and to such factors as gender and race. Martineau ([1838] 1989) also wrote the first book on sociological methods.

Martineau's writings emphasized the impact that the economy, law, trade, health, and population could have on social problems. She spoke out in favor of the rights of women, the emancipation of slaves, and religious tolerance. Later in life, deafness did not keep her from being an activist. In Martineau's ([1837] 1962) view, intellectuals and scholars should not simply offer observations of social conditions; they should *act* on their convictions in a manner that will benefit society. That is why Martineau conducted research on the nature of female employment and pointed to the need for further investigation of the issue (Deegan 2003; Hill and Hoecker-Drysdale 2001).

Harriet Martineau, an early pioneer of sociology who studied social behavior both in her native England and in the United States, proposed some of the methods still used by sociologists.

Herbert Spencer Another important early contributor to the discipline of sociology was Herbert Spencer (1820–1903). A relatively prosperous Victorian Englishman, Spencer (unlike Martineau) did not feel compelled to correct or improve society; instead, he merely hoped to understand it better. Drawing on Charles Darwin's study *On the Origin of Species,* Spencer applied the concept of evolution of the species to societies in order to explain how they change, or evolve, over time. Similarly, he adapted Darwin's evolutionary view of the "survival of the fittest" by arguing that it is "natural" that some people are rich while others are poor.

Spencer's approach to societal change was extremely popular in his lifetime. Unlike Comte, Spencer suggested that since societies are bound to change eventually, one need not be highly critical of present social arrangements or work actively for social change. This viewpoint appealed to many influential people in England and the United States who had a vested interest in the status quo and were suspicious of social thinkers who endorsed change.

Émile Durkheim

Émile Durkheim made many pioneering contributions to sociology, including his important theoretical work on suicide. The son of a rabbi, Durkheim (1858–1917) was educated in both France and Germany. He established an impressive academic reputation and was appointed one of the first professors of sociology in France. Above all, Durkheim will be remembered for his insistence that behavior must be understood within a larger social context, not just in individualistic terms.

To give one example of this emphasis, Durkheim ([1912] 2001) developed a fundamental thesis to help explain all forms of society. Through intensive study of the Arunta, an Australian tribe, he focused on the functions that religion performed and underscored the role of group life in defining what we consider to be religion. Durkheim concluded that like other forms of group behavior, religion reinforces a group's solidarity.

Another of Durkheim's main interests was the consequences of work in modern societies. In his view, the growing division of labor in industrial societies, as workers became much more specialized in their tasks, led to what he called "anomie." **Anomie** refers to the loss of direction felt in a society when social control of individual behavior has become ineffective. Often, the state of anomie occurs during a time of profound social change, when people have lost their sense of purpose or direction. In a period of anomie, people are so confused and unable to cope with the new social environment that they may resort to suicide.

Durkheim was concerned about the dangers that alienation, loneliness, and isolation might pose for modern industrial societies. He shared Comte's belief that sociology should provide direction for social change. As a result, he advocated the creation of new

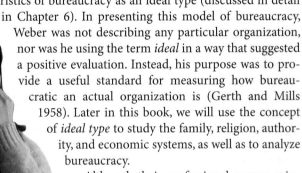

social groups—mediators between the individual's family and the state—that would provide a sense of belonging for members of huge, impersonal societies. Unions would be an example of such groups.

Like many other sociologists, Durkheim did not limit his interests to one aspect of social behavior. Later in this book we will consider his thinking on crime and punishment, religion, and the workplace. Few sociologists have had such a dramatic impact on so many different areas within the discipline.

Max Weber

Another important early theorist was Max Weber (pronounced VAY-ber). Born in Germany, Weber (1864–1920) studied legal and economic history, but gradually developed an interest in sociology. Eventually, he became a professor at various German universities. Weber taught his students that they should employ ***verstehen*** (pronounced fair-SHTAY-en), the German word for "understanding" or "insight," in their intellectual work. He pointed out that we cannot analyze our social behavior by the same type of objective criteria we use to measure weight or temperature. To fully comprehend behavior, we must learn the subjective meanings people attach to their actions—how they themselves view and explain their behavior.

For example, suppose that a sociologist was studying the social ranking of individuals in a fraternity. Weber would expect the researcher to employ *verstehen* to determine the significance of the fraternity's social hierarchy for its members. The researcher might examine the effects of athleticism or grades or social skills or seniority on standing within the fraternity. He or she would seek to learn how the fraternity members relate to other members of higher or lower status. While investigating these questions, the researcher would take into account people's emotions, thoughts, beliefs, and attitudes (L. Coser 1977).

We also owe credit to Weber for a key conceptual tool: the ideal type. An **ideal type** is a construct or model for evaluating specific cases. In his works, Weber identified various characteristics of bureaucracy as an ideal type (discussed in detail in Chapter 6). In presenting this model of bureaucracy, Weber was not describing any particular organization, nor was he using the term *ideal* in a way that suggested a positive evaluation. Instead, his purpose was to provide a useful standard for measuring how bureaucratic an actual organization is (Gerth and Mills 1958). Later in this book, we will use the concept of *ideal type* to study the family, religion, authority, and economic systems, as well as to analyze bureaucracy.

Although their professional careers coincided, Émile Durkheim and Max Weber never met and probably were unaware of each other's existence, let alone ideas. Such was not true of the work of Karl Marx. Durkheim's thinking about the impact of the division of labor in industrial societies was related to Marx's writings, while Weber's concern for a

FIGURE **1-1**   CONTRIBUTORS TO SOCIOLOGY   11

Understanding Sociology

	Émile Durkheim 1858–1917	Max Weber 1864–1920	Karl Marx 1818–1883	W. E. B. DuBois 1868–1963
Academic training	Philosophy	Law, economics, history, philosophy	Philosophy, law	Sociology
Key works	1893—*The Division of Labor in Society* 1897—*Suicide: A Study in Sociology* 1912—*Elementary Forms of Religious Life*	1904-1905—*The Protestant Ethic and the Spirit of Capitalism* 1921—*Economy and Society*	1848—*The Communist Manifesto* 1867—*Das Kapital*	1899—*The Philadelphia Negro* 1903—*The Negro Church* 1903—*Souls of Black Folk*

value-free, objective sociology was a direct response to Marx's deeply held convictions. Thus, it is not surprising that Karl Marx is viewed as a major figure in the development of sociology, as well as several other social sciences (Figure 1-1).

Karl Marx

Karl Marx (1818–1883) shared with Durkheim and Weber a dual interest in abstract philosophical issues and the concrete reality of everyday life. Unlike them, however, Marx was so critical of existing institutions that a conventional academic career was impossible. He spent most of his life in exile from his native Germany.

Marx's personal life was a difficult struggle. When a paper he had written was suppressed, he fled to France. In Paris, he met Friedrich Engels (1820–1895), with whom he formed a lifelong friendship. The two lived at a time when European and North American economic life was increasingly dominated by the factory rather than the farm.

While in London in 1847, Marx and Engels attended secret meetings of an illegal coalition of labor unions known as the Communist League. The following year they prepared a platform called *The Communist Manifesto,* in which they argued that the masses of people with no resources other than their labor (whom they referred to as the *proletariat*) should unite to fight for the overthrow of capitalist societies. In the words of Marx and Engels:

> The history of all hitherto existing society is the history of class struggles. . . . The proletarians have nothing to lose but their chains. They have a world to win. WORKING MEN OF ALL COUNTRIES, UNITE! (Tucker 1978:473, 500).

After completing *The Communist Manifesto,* Marx returned to Germany, only to be expelled. He then moved to England, where he continued to write books and essays. Marx lived there in extreme poverty; he pawned most of his possessions, and several of his children died of malnutrition and disease. Marx

clearly was an outsider in British society, a fact that may well have influenced his view of Western cultures.

In Marx's analysis, society was fundamentally divided between two classes that clashed in pursuit of their own interests. When he examined the industrial societies of his time, such as Germany, England, and the United States, he saw the factory as the center of conflict between the exploiters (the owners of the means of production) and the exploited (the workers). Marx viewed these relationships in systematic terms; that is, he believed that a system of economic, social, and political relationships maintained the power and dominance of the owners over the workers. Consequently, Marx and Engels argued that the working class should overthrow the existing class system. Marx's influence on contemporary thinking has been dramatic. His writings inspired those who would later lead communist revolutions in Russia, China, Cuba, Vietnam, and elsewhere.

Even apart from the political revolutions that his work fostered, Marx's significance is profound. Marx emphasized the *group* identifications and associations that influence an *individual's* place in society. This area of study is the major focus of contemporary sociology. Throughout this textbook, we will consider how membership in a particular gender classification, age group, racial group, or economic class affects a person's attitudes and behavior. In an important sense, we can trace this way of understanding society back to the pioneering work of Karl Marx.

W. E. B. DuBois

Marx's work encouraged sociologists to view society through the eyes of those segments of the population that rarely influence decision making. In the United States, some early Black sociologists, including W. E. B. DuBois (1868–1963), conducted research that they hoped would assist in the struggle for a racially egalitarian society. DuBois (pronounced doo-BOYSS) believed that knowledge was essential in combating prejudice and achieving tolerance and justice. Sociologists, he contended, needed to draw on scientific principles to study social problems such as those experienced by Blacks in the United States. To separate opinion from fact, he advocated basic research on the lives of Blacks. Through his in-depth studies of urban life, both White and Black, in cities such as Philadelphia and Atlanta, DuBois ([1899] 1995) made a major contribution to sociology.

Like Durkheim and Weber, DuBois saw the importance of religion to society. However, he tended to focus on religion at the community level and the role of the church in the lives of its members ([1903] 2003). DuBois had little patience with theorists such as Herbert Spencer, who seemed content with the status quo. He believed that the granting of full political rights to Blacks was essential to their social and economic progress.

Because many of his ideas challenged the status quo, DuBois did not find a receptive audience within either the government or the academic world. As a result, he became increasingly involved with organizations whose members questioned the established social order. In 1909 he helped to found the National Association for the Advancement of Colored People, better known today as the NAACP (Wortham 2008).

DuBois's insights have been lasting. In 1897 he coined the term **double consciousness** to refer to the division of an individual's identity into two or more social realities. He used the term to describe the experience of being Black in White America. Today, an African American holds the most powerful office in the nation, President of the United States. Yet for millions of African Americans, the reality of being Black in the United States typically is not one of power (DuBois [1903] 1961).

Twentieth-Century Developments

Sociology today builds on the firm foundation developed by Émile Durkheim, Max Weber, Karl Marx, and W. E. B. DuBois. However, the field certainly has not remained stagnant over the past hundred years. While Europeans have continued to make contributions to the discipline, sociologists from throughout the world and especially the United States have advanced sociological theory and research. Their new insights have helped us to better understand the workings of society.

Charles Horton Cooley Charles Horton Cooley (1864–1929) was typical of the sociologists who came to prominence in the early 1900s. Born in Ann Arbor, Michigan, Cooley received his graduate training in economics but later became a sociology professor at the University of Michigan. Like other early sociologists, he had become interested in this new discipline while pursuing a related area of study.

Cooley shared the desire of Durkheim, Weber, and Marx to learn more about society. But to do so effectively, he preferred to use the sociological perspective to look first at smaller units— intimate, face-to-face groups such as families, gangs, and friendship networks. He saw these groups as the seedbeds of society, in the sense that they shape people's ideals, beliefs, values, and social nature. Cooley's work increased our understanding of groups of relatively small size.

Jane Addams In the early 1900s, many leading sociologists in the United States saw themselves as social reformers dedicated to systematically studying and then improving a corrupt society. They were genuinely concerned about the lives of immigrants in the nation's growing cities, whether those immigrants came from Europe or from the rural American South. Early female sociologists,

Jane Addams (right) was an early pioneer both in sociology and in the settlement house movement. She was also an activist in the campaign for women's right to vote, as this photograph shows.

in particular, often took active roles in poor urban areas as leaders of community centers known as *settlement houses*. For example, Jane Addams (1860–1935), a member of the American Sociological Society, cofounded the famous Chicago settlement, Hull House.

Addams and other pioneering female sociologists commonly combined intellectual inquiry, social service work, and political activism—all with the goal of assisting the underprivileged and creating a more egalitarian society. For example, working with the Black journalist and educator Ida Wells-Barnett, Addams successfully prevented racial segregation in the Chicago public schools. Addams's efforts to establish a juvenile court system and a women's trade union reveal the practical focus of her work (Addams 1910, 1930; Deegan 1991; Lengermann and Niebrugge-Brantley 1998).

By the middle of the 20th century, however, the focus of the discipline had shifted. Sociologists for the most part restricted themselves to theorizing and gathering information; the aim of transforming society was left to social workers and activists. This shift away from social reform was accompanied by a growing commitment to scientific methods of research and to value-free interpretation of data. Not all sociologists were happy with this emphasis. A new organization, the Society for the Study of Social Problems, was created in 1950 to deal more directly with social inequality and other social problems.

Robert Merton Sociologist Robert Merton (1910–2003) made an important contribution to the discipline by successfully combining theory and research. Born to Slavic immigrant parents in Philadelphia, Merton won a scholarship to Temple University.

He continued his studies at Harvard, where he acquired his lifelong interest in sociology. Merton's teaching career was based at Columbia University.

Merton (1968) produced a theory that is one of the most frequently cited explanations of deviant behavior. He noted different ways in which people attempt to achieve success in life. In his view, some may deviate from the socially approved goal of accumulating material goods or the socially accepted means of achieving that goal. For example, in Merton's classification scheme, *innovators* are people who accept the goal of pursuing material wealth but use illegal means to do so, including robbery, burglary, and extortion. Although Merton based his explanation of crime on individual behavior that has been influenced by society's approved goals and means, it has wider applications. His theory helps to account for the high crime rates among the nation's poor, who may see no hope of advancing themselves through traditional roads to success. Chapter 8 discusses Merton's theory in greater detail.

Merton also emphasized that sociology should strive to bring together the *macro-level* and *micro-level* approaches to the study of society. **Macrosociology** concentrates on large-scale phenomena or entire civilizations. Émile Durkheim's cross-cultural study of suicide is an example of macro-level research. More recently, macrosociologists have examined international crime rates (see Chapter 8) and the stereotype of Asian Americans as a "model minority" (see Chapter 11). In contrast, **microsociology** stresses the study of small groups, often through experimental means. Sociological research on the micro level has included studies of how divorced men and women disengage from significant social roles (see Chapter 5); of how conformity can influence the expression of prejudiced attitudes (see Chapter 8); and of how a teacher's expectations can affect a student's academic performance (see Chapter 16).

Pierre Bourdieu Increasingly, scholars in the United States have been drawing on the insights of sociologists in other countries. The ideas of the French sociologist Pierre Bourdieu (1930–2002) have found a broad following in North America and elsewhere. As a young man, Bourdieu did fieldwork in Algeria during its struggle for independence from France. Today, scholars study Bourdieu's research techniques as well as his conclusions.

Bourdieu wrote about how capital in its many forms sustains individuals and families from one generation to the next. To Bourdieu, *capital* included not just material goods, but cultural and social assets. **Cultural capital** refers to noneconomic goods, such as family background and education, which are reflected in a knowledge of language and the arts. Not necessarily book knowledge, cultural capital refers to the kind of education that is valued by the socially elite. Though a knowledge of Chinese cuisine is culture, for example, it is not the prestigious kind of culture that is valued by the elite. In the United States, immigrants—especially those who arrived in large numbers and settled in ethnic enclaves—have generally taken two or three generations to develop the same level of cultural capital enjoyed by more established groups. In comparison, **social capital** refers to the collective benefit of social networks, which are built on reciprocal trust. Much has been written about the importance of family and friendship networks in providing people with an opportunity to advance. In his emphasis on cultural and social capital, Bourdieu's work extends the insights of early social thinkers such as Marx and Weber (Bourdieu and Passerson 1990; Field 2008).

Today sociology reflects the diverse contributions of earlier theorists. As sociologists approach such topics as divorce, drug addiction, and religious cults, they can draw on the theoretical insights of the discipline's pioneers. A careful reader can hear Comte, Durkheim, Weber, Marx, DuBois, Cooley, Addams, and many others speaking through the pages of current research. Sociology has also broadened beyond the intellectual confines of North America and Europe. Contributions to the discipline now come from sociologists studying and researching human behavior in other parts of the world. In describing the work of these sociologists, it is helpful to examine a number of influential *theoretical perspectives,* also known as *approaches* or *views.*

thinking CRITICALLY

What kinds of social and cultural capital do you possess?

Major Theoretical Perspectives

Sociologists view society in different ways. Some see the world basically as a stable and ongoing entity. They are impressed with the endurance of the family, organized religion, and other social institutions. Other sociologists see society as composed of many groups in conflict, competing for scarce resources. To still other sociologists, the most fascinating aspects of the social world are the everyday, routine interactions among individuals that we sometimes take for granted. These three views, the ones most widely used by sociologists, are the functionalist, conflict, and interactionist perspectives. Together, these approaches will provide an introductory look at the discipline.

Functionalist Perspective

Think of society as a living organism in which each part of the organism contributes to its survival. This view is the **functionalist perspective**, which emphasizes the way in which the parts of a society are structured to maintain its stability.

Talcott Parsons (1902–1979), a Harvard University sociologist, was a key figure in the development of functionalist theory. Parsons was greatly influenced by the work of Émile Durkheim, Max Weber, and other European sociologists. For more than four decades, he dominated sociology in the United States with his advocacy of functionalism. Parsons saw any society as a vast network of connected parts, each of which helps to maintain the system as a whole. His approach, carried forward by German sociologist Niklas Luhmann (1927–1998), holds that if an aspect of social life does not contribute to a society's stability or survival—if it does not serve some identifiably useful function or promote value consensus among members of society—it will not be passed on from one generation to the next (Joas and Knöbl 2009; Knudsen 2010).

Let's examine an example of the functionalist perspective. Many Americans have difficulty understanding the Hindu prohibition against slaughtering cows (specifically, zebu). Cattle browse unhindered through Indian street markets, helping themselves to oranges and mangoes while people bargain for the little food they can afford. What explains this devotion to the cow in the face of human deprivation—a devotion that appears to be dysfunctional?

The simple explanation is that cow worship is highly functional in Indian society, according to economists, agronomists, and social scientists who have studied the matter. Cows perform two essential tasks: plowing the fields and producing milk. If eating their meat were permitted, hungry families might be tempted to slaughter their cows for immediate consumption, leaving themselves without a means of cultivation. Cows also produce dung, which doubles as a fertilizer and a fuel for cooking. Finally, cow meat sustains the neediest group in society, the *Dalit*, or untouchables, who sometimes resort to eating beef in secrecy. If eating beef were socially acceptable, higher-status Indians would no doubt bid up its price, placing it beyond the reach of the hungriest.

Manifest and Latent Functions A college catalog typically states various functions of the institution. It may inform you, for example, that the university intends to "offer each student a broad education in classical and contemporary thought, in the humanities, in the sciences, and in the arts." However, it would be quite a surprise to find a catalog that declared, "This university was founded in 1895 to assist people in finding a marriage partner." No college catalog will declare this as the purpose of the university. Yet societal institutions serve many functions, some of them quite subtle. The university, in fact, *does* facilitate mate selection.

Robert Merton (1968) made an important distinction between manifest and latent functions. **Manifest functions** of institutions are open, stated, and conscious functions. They involve the intended, recognized consequences of an aspect of society, such as the university's role in certifying academic competence and excellence. In contrast, **latent functions** are unconscious or unintended functions that may reflect hidden purposes of an institution. One latent function of universities is to hold down unemployment. Another is to serve as a meeting ground for people seeking marital partners.

Dysfunctions Functionalists acknowledge that not all parts of a society contribute to its stability all the time. A **dysfunction** refers to an element or process of a society that may actually disrupt the social system or reduce its stability.

Cows (zebu), considered sacred in India, wander freely through this city, respected by all who encounter them. The sanctity of the cow is functional in India, where plowing, milking, and fertilizing are far more important to subsistence farmers than a diet that includes beef.

We view many dysfunctional behavior patterns, such as homicide, as undesirable. Yet we should not automatically interpret them in this way. The evaluation of a dysfunction depends on one's own values, or as the saying goes, on "where you sit." For example, the official view in prisons in the United States is that inmate gangs should be eradicated because they are dysfunctional to smooth operations. Yet some guards have come to view prison gangs as a functional part of their jobs. The danger posed by gangs creates a "threat to security," requiring increased surveillance and more overtime work for guards, as well as requests for special staffing to address gang problems (G. Scott 2001).

Conflict Perspective

Where functionalists see stability and consensus, conflict sociologists see a social world in continual struggle. The **conflict perspective** assumes that social behavior is best understood in terms of tension between groups over power or the allocation of resources, including housing, money, access to services, and political representation. The tension between competing groups need not be violent; it can take the form of labor negotiations, party politics, competition between religious groups for new members, or disputes over the federal budget.

Throughout most of the 1900s, the functionalist perspective had the upper hand in sociology in the United States. However, the conflict approach has become increasingly persuasive since the late 1960s. The widespread social unrest resulting from battles over civil rights, bitter divisions over the war in Vietnam, the rise of the feminist and gay liberation movements, the Watergate political scandal, urban riots, and confrontations at abortion clinics have offered support for the conflict approach—the view that our social world is characterized by continual struggle between competing groups. Currently, the discipline of sociology accepts conflict theory as one valid way to gain insight into a society.

The Marxist View As we saw earlier, Karl Marx viewed struggle between social classes as inevitable, given the exploitation of workers that he perceived under capitalism. Expanding on Marx's work, sociologists and other social scientists have come to see conflict not merely as a class phenomenon but as a part of everyday life in all societies. In studying any culture, organization, or social group, sociologists want to know who benefits, who suffers, and who dominates at the expense of others. They are concerned with the conflicts between women and men, parents and children, cities and suburbs, Whites and Blacks, to name only a few. Conflict theorists are interested in how society's institutions—including the family, government, religion, education, and the media—may help to maintain the privileges of some groups and keep others in a subservient position. Their emphasis on social change and the redistribution of resources makes conflict theorists more radical and activist than functionalists (Dahrendorf 1959).

The Feminist View Sociologists began embracing the feminist perspective only in the 1970s, although it has a long tradition in many other disciplines. The **feminist view** sees inequity in gender as central to all behavior and organization. Because it focuses clearly on one aspect of inequality, it is often allied with the conflict perspective. Proponents of the feminist view tend to focus on the macro level, just as conflict theorists do. Drawing on the work of Marx and Engels, contemporary feminist theorists often view women's subordination as inherent in capitalist societies.

Some radical feminist theorists, however, view the oppression of women as inevitable in *all* male-dominated societies, whether capitalist, socialist, or communist.

An early example of this perspective (long before the label came into use by sociologists) can be seen in the life and writings of Ida Wells-Barnett (1862–1931). Following her groundbreaking publications in the 1890s on the practice of lynching Black Americans, she became an advocate in the women's rights campaign, especially the struggle to win the vote for women. Like feminist theorists who succeeded her, Wells-Barnett used her analysis of society as a means of resisting oppression. In her case, she researched what it meant to be Black, a woman in the United States, and a Black woman in the United States (Giddings 2008; Wells-Barnett 1970).

Feminist scholarship has broadened our understanding of social behavior by extending the analysis beyond the male point of view. Consider sports, for example. Feminist theorists consider how watching or participating in sports reinforces the roles that men and women play in the larger society:

- Although sports generally promote fitness and health, they may also have an adverse effect on participants' health. Men are more likely to resort to illegal steroid use (among body-builders and baseball players, for example); women, to excessive dieting (among gymnasts and figure skaters, for example).

- Gender expectations encourage female athletes to be passive and gentle, qualities that do not support the emphasis on competitiveness in sports. As a result, women find it difficult to enter sports traditionally dominated by men, such as Indy or NASCAR.

- Although professional women athletes' earnings are increasing, they typically trail those of male athletes.

Ida Wells-Barnett explored what it meant to be female and Black in the United States. Her work established her as one of the earliest feminist theorists.

use your sociological *imagination*

You are a sociologist who takes the conflict perspective. How would you interpret the practice of prostitution? How would your view of prostitution differ if you took the functionalist perspective? The feminist perspective?

Interactionist Perspective

Workers interacting on the job, encounters in public places like bus stops and parks, behavior in small groups—all these aspects of microsociology catch the attention of interactionists. Whereas functionalist and conflict theorists both analyze large-scale, society-wide patterns of behavior, theorists who take the **interactionist perspective** generalize about everyday forms of social interaction in order to explain society as a whole. Today, given rising concern over the cost and availability of gas, interactionists have begun to study a form of commuter behavior called "slugging." To avoid driving to work, commuters gather at certain preappointed places to seek rides from complete strangers. When a driver pulls into the parking area or vacant lot and announces his destination, the first slug in line who is headed for that destination jumps in. Rules of etiquette have emerged to smooth the social interaction between driver and passenger: neither the driver nor the passenger may eat or

The Marxist view asks "Who benefits, who suffers, and who dominates?"

	Functionalist	Conflict	Interactionist
View of Society	Stable, well integrated	Characterized by tension and struggle between groups	Active in influencing and affecting everyday social interaction
Level of Analysis Emphasized	Macro	Macro	Micro, as a way of understanding the larger macro phenomena
Key Concepts	Manifest functions Latent functions Dysfunctions	Inequality Capitalism Stratification	Symbols Nonverbal communication Face-to-face interaction
View of the Individual	People are socialized to perform societal functions	People are shaped by power, coercion, and authority	People manipulate symbols and create their social worlds through interaction
View of the Social Order	Maintained through cooperation and consensus	Maintained through force and coercion	Maintained by shared understanding of everyday behavior
View of Social Change	Predictable, reinforcing	Change takes place all the time and may have positive consequences	Reflected in people's social positions and their communications with others
Example	Public punishments reinforce the social order	Laws reinforce the positions of those in power	People respect laws or disobey them based on their own past experience
Proponents	Émile Durkheim Talcott Parsons Robert Merton	Karl Marx W. E. B. DuBois Ida Wells-Barnett	George Herbert Mead Charles Horton Cooley Erving Goffman

smoke; the slug may not adjust the windows or radio or talk on a cell phone. The presence of the slugs, who get a free ride, may allow the driver to use special lanes reserved for high-occupancy vehicles (Slug-Lines.com 2008).

Interactionism (also referred to as *symbolic interactionism*) is a sociological framework in which human beings are viewed as living in a world of meaningful objects. Those "objects" may include material things, actions, other people, relationships, and even symbols. Interactionists see symbols as an especially important part of human communication (thus the term *symbolic interactionism*). Symbols have a shared social meaning that is understood by all members of a society. In the United States, for example, a salute symbolizes respect, while a clenched fist signifies defiance. Another culture might use different gestures to convey a feeling of respect or defiance. These types of symbolic interaction are classified as forms of **nonverbal communication**, which can include many other gestures, facial expressions, and postures (Masuda et al. 2008).

Manipulation of symbols can be seen in dress codes. Schools frown on students who wear clothes displaying messages that appear to endorse violence or drug and alcohol consumption. Businesses stipulate the attire employees are allowed to wear on the job in order to impress their customers or clients. In 2005, the National Basketball Association (NBA) adopted a new dress code for the athletes who play professional basketball—one that involved, not the uniforms they wear on court, but the clothes they wear off court on league business. The code requires "business casual attire" when players are representing the league. Indoor sunglasses, chains, and sleeveless shirts are specifically banned (Crowe and Herman 2005:A23).

While the functionalist and conflict approaches were initiated in Europe, interactionism developed first in the United States. George Herbert Mead (1863–1931) is widely regarded as the founder of the interactionist perspective. Mead taught at the University of Chicago from 1893 until his death. As his teachings have become better known, sociologists have expressed greater interest in the interactionist perspective. Many have moved away from what may have been an excessive preoccupation with the macro (large-scale) level of social behavior and have redirected their attention toward behavior that occurs in the micro (small-scale) level.

Erving Goffman (1922–1982) popularized a particular type of interactionist method known as the **dramaturgical approach**, in which people are seen as theatrical performers. The dramaturgist compares everyday life to the setting of the theater and stage. Just as actors project certain images, all of us seek to present particular features of our personalities while we hide other features. Thus, in a class, we may feel the need to project a serious image; at a party, we may want to look relaxed and friendly.

The Sociological Approach

Which perspective should a sociologist use in studying human behavior? Functionalist? Conflict? Interactionist? Feminist? We simply cannot squeeze all sociological thinking into three or four theoretical categories—or even ten, if we include several other productive approaches. However, by studying the three major frameworks, we can better grasp how sociologists seek to explore social behavior. Table 1-2 summarizes these three broad approaches to sociological study.

Although no one approach is correct by itself, and sociologists draw on all of them for various purposes, many sociologists tend to favor one particular perspective over others. A sociologist's theoretical orientation influences his or her approach to a research problem in important ways—including the choice of what to study, how to study it, and what questions to pose (or not to pose). See Box 1-1 for an example of how researchers would study the 2010 Gulf Coast oil spill from different sociological perspectives.

RESEARCH TODAY

The Gulf Coast oil spill, which began on April 20, 2010, dominated the national news in the United States for much of that year. Like other disasters, the huge spill had social effects that can be analyzed from the four major sociological perspectives.

Functionalist View

In evaluating the effects of the Gulf Coast oil spill, functionalists would stress society's supportive function. For example:

- Functionalists might expect a revitalization of the environmental movement, as happened in the early 1900s after the damming of the Hetch Hetchy Valley just outside Yosemite, and later in the 1990s, after massive wildfires swept through the Everglades.

- Functionalists might note full employment in selected occupations, such as the manufacture of containment booms, even when jobs in other industries were scarce.

- Functionalists would observe that churches and other charities along the Gulf Coast provided both spiritual and material support to households affected by the spill.

- Functionalists would not be surprised that because offshore oil drilling is an integral part of the Gulf Coast economy, the governor of Louisiana strongly opposed a moratorium on deep-sea drilling, despite questions about its safety.

Conflict View

Because conflict theorists see the social order in terms of conflict or tension between competing groups, they would emphasize the coercion and exploitation that underlies relations between the oil companies and Gulf Coast communities:

- The oil industry, conflict theorists would note, is a form of big business, in which profits are more important than workers' health and safety.

- Conflict theorists would emphasize the often-overlooked effect of the spill on minority groups living in inland communities, including Vietnamese Americans, Native American tribal groups, and African Americans. These groups, which were living a marginal existence before the spill, endured particularly significant economic setbacks after the spill.

SWIMMING WATER QUALITY STATUS
HEALTH ADVISORY:
THE PUBLIC IS ADVISED NOT TO SWIM IN THESE WATERS DUE TO THE PRESENCE OF OIL-RELATED CHEMICALS

- Conflict theorists would note that although news outlets tend to focus on oil spills that affect wealthy industrial countries, often the worst spills afflict communities in disadvantaged developing nations, such as Nigeria.

Feminists would note that during times of economic upheaval and dislocation, women bear a disproportionate share of the burden in their role as caregivers.

Feminist View

Feminists would note that during times of economic upheaval and dislocation, such as the Gulf Coast oil crisis, women bear a disproportionate share of the burden in their role as caregivers:

- As family wage earners leave home to seek work elsewhere, women with children or elderly dependents are left to cope as best they can.

- With time, the physical separation these families experience may turn into marital separation.

Interactionist View

Interactionists would examine the Gulf Coast oil spill on the micro level, by focusing on how it shaped personal relations and day-to-day social behavior:

- Interactionists would note that difficult times often strengthen ties among neighbors and family members.

- At the same time, stressful events can contribute to social breakdowns, including divorce or even suicide—a pattern researchers observed in the aftermath of the Exxon *Valdez* oil spill in 1989.

Despite their differences, functionalists, conflict theorists, feminists, and interactionists would all agree that disasters like the Gulf Coast oil spill are a worthy subject for sociological study.

LET'S DISCUSS

1. Which of the four sociological perspectives seems most useful to you in analyzing the Gulf Coast oil crisis? Why?
2. For many people, the worldwide economic crisis that began in 2008 had disastrous personal consequences. Use the four sociological perspectives to analyze what happened to you, your family, and your community during the Great Recession.

Sources: Capriccioso 2010; Freudenburg and Gramling 2010; Greenemeier 2010; Jopling and Morse 2010; Liptak 2010; Molotch 1970; Samuels 2010; N. Wallace 2010.

Whatever the purpose of sociologists' work, their research will always be guided by their theoretical viewpoints. For example, sociologist Elijah Anderson (1990) embraces both the interactionist perspective and the groundbreaking work of W. E. B. DuBois. For 14 years Anderson conducted fieldwork in Philadelphia, where he studied the interactions of Black and White residents who lived in adjoining neighborhoods. In particular, he was interested in their public behavior, including their eye contact—or lack of it—as they passed one another on the street. Anderson's research tells us much about the everyday social interactions of Blacks and Whites in the United States, but it does not explain the larger issues behind those interactions. Like theories, research results illuminate one part of the stage, leaving other parts in relative darkness.

thinking CRITICALLY

Relate the toys on display in your local store to issues of race, class, and gender.

Taking Sociology with You

You've seen how sociologists employ the major sociological perspectives in their research. How does sociology relate to *you,* your own studies, and your own career? In this section you'll learn about *applied* and *clinical sociology,* two growing fields that allow sociology majors and those with advanced degrees in sociology to apply what they have learned to real-world settings. You'll also see how to develop your sociological imagination, one of the keys to thinking like a sociologist. See the appendix at the end of this chapter for more information on careers in sociology.

Applied and Clinical Sociology

Many early sociologists—notably, Jane Addams, W. E. B. DuBois, and George Herbert Mead—were strong advocates for social reform. They wanted their theories and findings to be relevant to policymakers and to people's lives in general. For instance, Mead was the treasurer of Hull House, where he applied his theory to improving the lives of those who were powerless (especially immigrants). He also served on committees dealing with Chicago's labor problems and public education. Today, **applied sociology** is the use of the discipline of sociology with the specific intent of yielding practical applications for human behavior and organizations. By extension, Michael Burawoy (2005), in his presidential address to the American Sociological Association, endorsed what he called *public sociology,* encouraging scholars to engage a broader audience in bringing about positive outcomes. In

effect, the applied sociologist reaches out to others and joins them in their efforts to better society.

Often, the goal of such work is to assist in resolving a social problem. For example, in the past 50 years, eight presidents of the United States have established commissions to delve into major societal concerns facing our nation. Sociologists are often asked to apply their expertise to studying such issues as violence, pornography, crime, immigration, and population. In Europe, both academic and government research departments are offering increasing financial support for applied studies.

One example of applied sociology is the growing interest in community health care. Rather than focusing on social problems, sociologists and others have begun to emphasize the assets a community can offer its residents. For example, sociologist P. Rafael Hernández-Arias developed the Community Health Assets and Needs Assessment (CHANA) to study four low-income immigrant communities on the South Side of Chicago. The idea was to identify existing resources that could be used to address residents' health needs, from medical clinics to fresh produce markets. CHANA showed that from one neighborhood to another, and even within a single neighborhood, the resources available to residents varied considerably. One community had plenty of sources for fresh produce; another, next to none. One had sixteen social service organizations; another, just two. The number of health clinics and doctors' offices also varied widely. Hernández-Arias is sharing the data from CHANA with community activists and with Chicago's Department of Public Health, in an effort both to maximize existing resources and to develop new ones (Velásquez and Hernández-Arias 2009).

Growing interest in applied sociology has led to such specializations as *medical sociology* and *environmental sociology.* The former includes research on how health care professionals and patients deal with disease. To give one example, medical sociologists have studied the social impact of the AIDS crisis on families, friends, and communities (see Chapter 19). Environmental

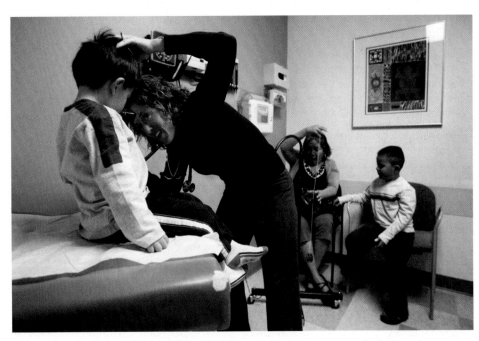

A Latino family visits a community medical center in Lakewood, Colorado. Increasingly, applied sociologists are becoming interested in the existing assets a community has to offer, from health clinics to fresh produce markets and social service organizations.

sociologists examine the relationship between human societies and the physical environment. One focus of their work is the issue of "environmental justice" (see Chapter 19), raised when researchers and community activists found that hazardous waste dumps are especially likely to be situated in poor and minority neighborhoods (M. Martin 1996).

The growing popularity of applied sociology has led to the rise of the specialty of clinical sociology. Louis Wirth (1931) wrote about clinical sociology more than 75 years ago, but the term itself has become popular only in recent years. While applied sociology may simply evaluate social issues, **clinical sociology** is dedicated to facilitating change by altering social relationships (as in family therapy) or restructuring social institutions (as in the reorganization of a medical center).

Today, both the positive and negative aspects of globalization are receiving increased scrutiny from sociologists.

Applied sociologists generally leave it to policymakers to act on their evaluations. In contrast, clinical sociologists take direct responsibility for implementation and view those with whom they work as their clients. This specialty has become increasingly attractive to graduate students in sociology because it offers an opportunity to apply intellectual learning in a practical way. A shrinking job market in the academic world has made such alternative career routes appealing.

Applied and clinical sociology can be contrasted with **basic**, or **pure, sociology**, which seeks a more profound knowledge of the fundamental aspects of social phenomena. This type of research is not necessarily meant to generate specific applications, although such ideas may result once findings are analyzed. When Durkheim studied suicide rates, he was not primarily interested in discovering a way to eliminate suicide. In this sense, his research was an example of basic rather than applied sociology.

Developing a Sociological Imagination

In this book, we will be illustrating the sociological imagination in several different ways—by showing theory in practice and in current research; by thinking globally; by exploring the significance of social inequality; by speaking across race, gender, and religious boundaries; and by highlighting social policy throughout the world.

Theory in Practice We will illustrate how the major sociological perspectives can be helpful in understanding today's issues, from capital punishment to the AIDS crisis. Sociologists do not necessarily declare, "Here I am using functionalism," but their research and approaches do tend to draw on one or more theoretical frameworks, as will become clear in the pages to follow.

Research Today Sociologists actively investigate a variety of issues and social behavior. We have already seen that research can shed light on the social factors that affect suicide rates. Sociological research often plays a direct role in improving people's

lives, as in the case of increasing the participation of African Americans in diabetes testing. Throughout the rest of the book, the research performed by sociologists and other social scientists will shed light on group behavior of all types.

Thinking Globally Whatever their theoretical perspective or research techniques, sociologists recognize that social behavior must be viewed in a global context. **Globalization** is the worldwide integration of government policies, cultures, social movements, and financial markets through trade and the exchange of ideas. Although public discussion of globalization is relatively recent, intellectuals have been pondering both its negative and positive social consequences for a long time. Karl Marx and Friedrich Engels warned in *The Communist Manifesto* (written in 1848) of a world market that would lead to production in distant lands, sweeping away existing working relationships.

Today, developments outside a country are as likely to influence people's lives as changes at home. For example, though much of the world was already in recession by September 2001, the terrorist attacks on New York and Washington, D.C., caused an immediate economic decline, not just in the United States, but throughout the world. One example of the massive global impact was the downturn in international tourism, which lasted for at least two years. The effects have been felt by people far removed from the United States, including African game wardens and Asian taxi drivers. Some observers see globalization and its effects as the natural result of advances in communications technology, particularly the Internet and satellite transmission of the mass media. Others view it more critically, as a process that allows multinational corporations to expand unchecked. We examine the impact of globalization on our daily lives and on societies throughout the world in Box 1-2 and throughout this book (Fiss and Hirsch 2005).

The Significance of Social Inequality Who holds power? Who doesn't? Who has prestige? Who lacks it? Perhaps the major theme of analysis in sociology today is **social inequality**, a condition in which members of society have differing amounts

SOCIOLOGY IN THE GLOBAL COMMUNITY

1-2 Your Morning Cup of Coffee

When you drink a cup of coffee, do you give much thought to where the coffee beans came from, or do you think more about the pleasure you get from the popular beverage? Coffee certainly is popular—as an import, it is second only to petroleum, the most traded commodity in the world.

Although the coffee trade has been globalized, the customs of coffee drinking still vary from place to place. Starbucks, which now has 4,500 locations outside the United States, has over 1,000 locations in Europe. Managers find that in European countries, where the coffeehouse culture originated, 80 percent of their customers sit down to drink their coffee. In the United States, 80 percent of Starbucks' customers leave the store immediately, taking their coffee with them.

Today, the coffee trade relies on the exploitation of cheap labor. Coffee is a labor-intensive crop: there is little that technology can do to ease the coffee picker's burden. The typical coffee picker works in a developing nation near the equator, receiving for a day's wages an amount that matches the price of a single cup of coffee in North America.

The typical coffee picker works in a developing nation near the equator, receiving for a day's wages an amount that matches the price of a single cup of coffee in North America.

In the 1940s, advocacy groups began to promote the sale of certified *fair trade coffee*, which gives a living wage to those who harvest the crop, allowing them to become economically self-sufficient. But as of late 2009, fair trade coffee accounted for only 2.5 percent of the coffee that was bought and sold in the United States. Recently, a similar movement has begun to promote fair trade in the global clothing industry, reported on by Kelsey Timmerman in his book *Where Am I Wearing?*

Ecological activists have drawn attention to what they see as the coffee industry's contribution to the trend toward global warming. The need to make room for more coffee fields, they charge, has encouraged the destruction of rain forests. The same criticism can be aimed at much of the consumption in industrial nations. Of all the products that emerge from developing nations, however, few have as singular a place in many people's daily ritual as that morning cup of joe. The drink in your hand is your tangible link to rural workers in some of the poorest areas of the world.

LET'S DISCUSS

1. Do you enjoy coffee? Would you willingly pay more for a cup of coffee if you knew that the worker who picked the beans would benefit from the higher price?
2. The coffee trade has been blamed for perpetuating social inequality and global warming. Can you think of any positive effects of the coffee trade? Who benefits most from this economic activity?

Sources: Adamy 2008; Fieser 2009; Jaffee 2007; Luttinger and Dicum 2006; E. Marx 2009; Pendergrast 1999; Ritzer 2011:218–227.

---

of wealth, prestige, or power. For example, the disparity between what coffee bean pickers in developing nations are paid and the price you pay for a cup of coffee underscores global inequality (see Box 1-2). Kelsey Timmerman's research among foreign garment workers uncovered some other aspects of global inequality. And the impact of Hurricane Katrina on residents of the Gulf Coast drew attention to social inequality in the United States. Predictably, the people who were hit the hardest by the massive storm were the poor, who had the greatest difficulty evacuating before the storm and have had the most difficulty recovering from it.

Some sociologists, in seeking to understand the effects of inequality, have made the case for social justice. W. E. B. DuBois ([1940] 1968:418) noted that the greatest power in the land is not "thought or ethics, but wealth." As we have seen, the contributions of Karl Marx, Jane Addams, and Ida Wells-Barnett also stressed this belief in the overarching significance of social inequality, and by extension, social justice. In this book, social inequality will be the central focus of Chapters 9 and 10, and sociologists' work on inequality will be highlighted throughout.

Speaking across Race, Gender, and Religious Boundaries

Sociologists include both men and women, who come from a variety of ethnic, national, and religious origins. In their work, sociologists seek to draw conclusions that speak to all people— not just the affluent or powerful. Doing so is not always easy. Insights into how a corporation can increase its profits tend to attract more attention and financial support than do, say, the merits of a needle exchange program for low-income inner-city residents. Yet today more than ever, sociology seeks to better understand the experiences of all people.

Sociologists have noted, for example, that the huge tsunami that hit South Asia in 2004 affected men and women differently. When the waves hit, mothers and grandmothers were at home with the children; men were outside working, where they were more likely to become aware of the impending disaster. Moreover, most of the men knew how to swim, a survival skill that women in these traditional societies usually do not learn. As a result, many more men than women survived the catastrophe— about 10 men for every 1 woman. In one Indonesian village typical of the disaster area, 97 of 1,300 people survived; only 4 were women. The impact of this gender imbalance will be felt for some time, given women's primary role as caregivers for children and the elderly (BBC News 2005).

Social Policy throughout the World One important way we can use a sociological imagination is to enhance our understanding of current social issues throughout the world. Beginning with Chapter 2, each chapter will conclude with a discussion of a contemporary social policy issue. In some cases, we will examine a specific issue facing national governments. For example, government funding of child care centers will be discussed in Chapter 4, Socialization and the Life Course; global immigration in Chapter 11, Racial and Ethnic Inequality; and charter schools in

Chapter 16, Education. These Social Policy sections will demonstrate how fundamental sociological concepts can enhance our critical thinking skills and help us to better understand current public policy debates taking place around the world.

In addition, sociology has been used to evaluate the success of programs or the impact of changes brought about by policymakers and political activists. For example, Chapter 10, Global Inequality, includes a discussion of research on the effectiveness of welfare programs. Such discussions underscore the many practical applications of sociological theory and research.

Sociologists expect the next quarter of a century to be perhaps the most exciting and critical period in the history of the discipline. That is because of a growing recognition—both in the United States and around the world—that current social problems must be addressed before their magnitude overwhelms human societies. We can expect sociologists to play an increasing role in government by researching and developing public policy alternatives. It seems only natural for this textbook to focus on the connection between the work of sociologists and the difficult questions confronting policymakers and people in the United States and around the world.

thinking CRITICALLY

What issues facing your local community would you like to address with applied sociological research? Do you see any global connections to these local issues?

APPENDIX Careers in Sociology

For the past two decades the number of U.S. college students who have graduated with a degree in sociology has risen steadily (Figure 1-2). In this appendix we'll consider some of the options these students have after completing their undergraduate education.

How do students first learn about the sociological perspective on society? Some may take a sociology course in high school. Others may study sociology at community college, where 40 percent of all college students in the United States are enrolled. Indeed, many future sociology majors first develop their sociological imaginations at a community college.

An undergraduate degree in sociology doesn't just serve as excellent preparation for future graduate work in sociology. It also provides a strong liberal arts background for entry-level positions in business, social services, foundations, community organizations, not-for-profit groups, law enforcement, and many government jobs. A number of fields—among them marketing, public relations, and broadcasting—now require investigative skills and an understanding of the diverse groups found in today's multiethnic and multinational environment. Moreover, a sociology degree requires accomplishment in oral and written communication, interpersonal skills, problem solving, and critical thinking—all job-related skills that may give sociology graduates an advantage over those who pursue more technical degrees.

Consequently, while few occupations specifically require an undergraduate degree in sociology, such academic training can be an important asset in entering a wide range of occupations. To emphasize this point, a number of chapters in this book highlight a real-life professional who describes how the study of sociology has helped in his or her career. For example, in Chapter 6 a Taking Sociology to Work box explains how a college graduate uses her training in sociology in managing a small business that she started. And in Chapter 17, another Taking Sociology to Work box shows how a recent graduate uses the skill set he acquired as a sociology major in his role as a government analyst.

Figure 1-3 summarizes the sources of employment for those with BA or BS degrees in sociology. It shows that the areas of nonprofit organizations, education, business, and government offer major career opportunities for sociology graduates. Undergraduates who know where their career interests lie are well advised to enroll in sociology courses and specialties best suited to those interests. For example, students hoping to become health planners would take a class in medical sociology; students seeking employment as social science research assistants would focus on courses in statistics and methods. Internships, such as placements at city planning agencies and survey research organizations, afford another way for sociology students to prepare for careers. Studies show that students who choose an internship placement have less trouble finding jobs, obtain better jobs, and enjoy greater job satisfaction than students without internship placements. Finally, students should expect to change fields during their first five years of employment after graduation—for example, from sales and marketing to management (American Sociological Association 2009; Salem and Grabarek 1986; Spalter-Roth and Van Vooren 2010).

Many college students view social work as the field most closely associated with sociology. Traditionally, social workers received their undergraduate training in sociology and allied fields such as psychology and counseling. After some practical experience, social workers would generally seek a master's degree in social work (MSW) to be considered for supervisory or administrative positions. Today, however, some students choose (where it is available) to pursue a bachelor's degree in social work (BSW). This degree prepares graduates for direct service positions, such as caseworker or group worker.

Many students continue their sociological training beyond the bachelor's degree. More than 250 universities in the United States have graduate programs

Did you know that as a student at Princeton University, Michelle Obama majored in sociology? She used that degree as a stepping-stone to Harvard law school. Read her senior thesis at www.politico.com/news/stories/0208/8642.html.

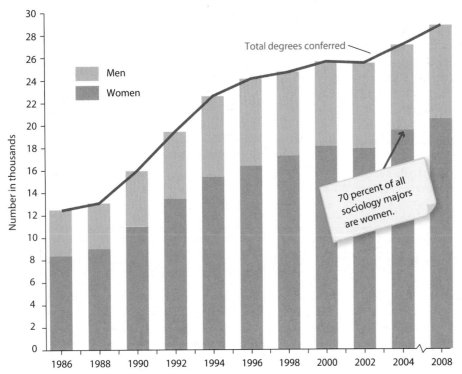

FIGURE **1-2** SOCIOLOGY DEGREES CONFERRED IN THE UNITED STATES BY GENDER

Men

Women

Total degrees conferred

70 percent of all sociology majors are women.

Number in thousands

Source: National Center for Education Statistics 2010:Table 275 on p. 413.

engage in four to seven years of intensive work, including the time required to complete the dissertation. Yet even this effort is no guarantee of a job as a sociology professor.

The good news is that over the next 10 years, the demand for instructors is expected to increase because of high rates of retirement among faculty from the baby boom generation, as well as the anticipated slow but steady growth in the college student population in the United States. Nonetheless, anyone who launches an academic career must be prepared for considerable uncertainty and competition in the college job market (American Sociological Association 2009).

Of course, not all people who work as sociologists teach or hold doctoral degrees. Take government, for example. The Census Bureau relies on people with sociological training to interpret data for other government agencies and the general public. Virtually every agency depends on survey research—a field in which sociology students can specialize—in order to assess everything from community needs to the morale of the agency's workers. In addition, people with sociological training can put their academic knowledge to effective use in probation and

in sociology that offer PhD and/or master's degrees. These programs differ greatly in their areas of specialization, course requirements, costs, and the research and teaching opportunities available to graduate students. About 71 percent of the graduates are women (American Sociological Association 2005, 2010).

Higher education is an important source of employment for sociologists with graduate degrees. About 83 percent of recent PhD recipients in sociology seek employment in colleges and universities. These sociologists teach not only majors who are committed to the discipline but also students hoping to become doctors, nurses, lawyers, police officers, and so forth (American Sociological Association 2005).

Sociologists who teach in colleges and universities may use their knowledge and training to influence public policy. For example, sociologist Andrew Cherlin (2003) has commented on the debate over proposed federal funding to promote marriage among welfare recipients. Citing the results of two of his studies, Cherlin questioned the potential effectiveness of such a policy in strengthening low-income families. Because many single mothers choose to marry someone other than the father of their children—sometimes for good reason—their children often grow up in stepfamilies. Cherlin's research shows that children who are raised in stepfamilies are no better off than those in single-parent families. He sees government efforts to promote marriage as a politically motivated attempt to foster traditional social values in a society that has become increasingly diverse.

For sociology graduates who are interested in academic careers, the road to a PhD (or doctorate) can be long and difficult. This degree symbolizes competence in original research; each candidate must prepare a book-length study known as a dissertation. Typically, a doctoral student in sociology will

FIGURE **1-3** OCCUPATIONS OF GRADUATING SOCIOLOGY MAJORS

Other, including public relations 11.1%

Research 5.7%

Education 8.1%

Services 8.3%

Sales, marketing 10.1%

Social services 26.5%

Administrative, clerical support 15.8%

Management 14.4%

Note: Based on a national survey conducted in early 2007 of 1,800 sociology majors who graduated in 2005.
Source: Spalter-Roth and Van Vooren 2008a, p. 3.

parole, health sciences, community development, and recreational services. Some people working in government or private industry have a master's degree (MA or MS) in sociology; others have a bachelor's degree (BA or BS).

Currently, about 15 percent of the members of the American Sociological Association use their sociological skills outside the academic world, whether in social service agencies or in marketing positions for business firms. Increasing numbers of sociologists with graduate degrees are employed by businesses, industry, hospitals, and nonprofit organizations. Studies show that many sociology graduates are making career changes from social service areas to business and commerce. For an undergraduate major, sociology is

excellent preparation for employment in many parts of the business world (Spalter-Roth and Van Vooren 2008b).

Whether you take a few courses in sociology or complete a degree, you will benefit from the critical thinking skills developed in this discipline. Sociologists emphasize the value of being able to analyze, interpret, and function within a variety of working situations—an asset in virtually any career. Moreover, given rapid technological change and the expanding global economy, all of us will need to adapt to substantial social change, even in our own careers. Sociology provides a rich conceptual framework that can serve as a foundation for flexible career development and assist you in taking advantage of new employment opportunities.

Connect Learn Succeed™

For more information on career opportunities for individuals with a background in sociology, visit the Online Learning Center at www.mhhe.com/schaefer13e. Go to "Student Edition," and in the section titled "Course-wide Content," click on "Web Resources." Then click on "Career Opportunities," which will provide you with numerous links to sites offering career advice and information.

MASTERING THIS CHAPTER

Summary

Sociology is the scientific study of social behavior and human groups. This chapter examines the nature of sociological theory, the founders of the discipline, theoretical perspectives in contemporary sociology, practical applications for sociological theory and research, and ways to exercise the *sociological imagination.*

1. The **sociological imagination** is an awareness of the relationship between an individual and the wider society. It is based on the ability to view our own society as an outsider might, rather than from the perspective of our limited experiences and cultural biases.

2. In contrast to other **social sciences,** sociology emphasizes the influence that groups can have on people's behavior and attitudes and the ways in which people shape society.

3. Knowledge that relies on common sense is not always reliable. Sociologists must test and analyze each piece of information they use.

4. Sociologists employ **theories** to examine relationships between observations or data that may seem completely unrelated.

5. Nineteenth-century thinkers who contributed sociological insights included Auguste Comte, a French philosopher; Harriet Martineau, an English sociologist; and Herbert Spencer, an English scholar.

6. Other important figures in the development of sociology were Émile Durkheim, who pioneered work on suicide; Max Weber, who taught the need for insight in intellectual work; Karl Marx, who emphasized the importance of the economy and social conflict; and W. E. B. DuBois, who advocated the usefulness of basic research in combating prejudice and fostering racial tolerance and justice.

7. In the 20th century, the discipline of sociology was indebted to the U.S. sociologists Charles Horton Cooley and Robert Merton, as well as to the French sociologist Pierre Bourdieu.

8. **Macrosociology** concentrates on large-scale phenomena or entire civilizations; **microsociology** stresses the study of small groups.

9. The **functionalist perspective** emphasizes the way in which the parts of a society are structured to maintain its stability.

10. The **conflict perspective** assumes that social behavior is best understood in terms of conflict or tension between competing groups.

11. The **feminist view,** which is often allied with the conflict perspective, sees inequity in gender as central to all behavior and organization.

12. The **interactionist perspective** is concerned primarily with fundamental or everyday forms of interaction, including symbols and other types of **nonverbal communication.**

13. Sociologists make use of all four perspectives, since each offers unique insights into the same issue.

14. **Applied** and **clinical sociology** apply the discipline of sociology to the solution of practical problems in human behavior and organizations. In contrast, **basic sociology** is sociological inquiry that seeks only a deeper knowledge of the fundamental aspects of social phenomena.

15. This textbook makes use of the sociological imagination by showing theory in practice and in current research; by thinking globally; by focusing on the significance of social inequality; by speaking across race, gender, and religious boundaries; and by highlighting social policy around the world.

Key Terms

Anomie The loss of direction felt in a society when social control of individual behavior has become ineffective. (page 10)

Applied sociology The use of the discipline of sociology with the specific intent of yielding practical applications for human behavior and organizations. (18)

Basic sociology Sociological inquiry conducted with the objective of gaining a more profound knowledge of the fundamental aspects of social phenomena. Also known as *pure sociology.* (19)

Clinical sociology The use of the discipline of sociology with the specific intent of altering social relationships or restructuring social institutions. (19)

23

Conflict perspective A sociological approach that assumes that social behavior is best understood in terms of tension between groups over power or the allocation of resources, including housing, money, access to services, and political representation. (14)

Cultural capital Noneconomic goods, such as family background and education, which are reflected in a knowledge of language and the arts. (13)

Double consciousness The division of an individual's identity into two or more social realities. (12)

Dramaturgical approach A view of social interaction in which people are seen as theatrical performers. (16)

Dysfunction An element or process of a society that may disrupt the social system or reduce its stability. (14)

Feminist view A sociological approach that views inequity in gender as central to all behavior and organization. (14)

Functionalist perspective A sociological approach that emphasizes the way in which the parts of a society are structured to maintain its stability. (13)

Globalization The worldwide integration of government policies, cultures, social movements, and financial markets through trade and the exchange of ideas. (19)

Ideal type A construct or model for evaluating specific cases. (10)

Interactionist perspective A sociological approach that generalizes about everyday forms of social interaction in order to explain society as a whole. (15)

Latent function An unconscious or unintended function that may reflect hidden purposes. (14)

Macrosociology Sociological investigation that concentrates on large-scale phenomena or entire civilizations. (13)

Manifest function An open, stated, and conscious function. (14)

Microsociology Sociological investigation that stresses the study of small groups, often through experimental means. (13)

Natural science The study of the physical features of nature and the ways in which they interact and change. (6)

Nonverbal communication The sending of messages through the use of gestures, facial expressions, and postures. (16)

Science The body of knowledge obtained by methods based on systematic observation. (5)

Social capital The collective benefit of social networks, which are built on reciprocal trust. (13)

Social inequality A condition in which members of society have differing amounts of wealth, prestige, or power. (19)

Social science The study of the social features of humans and the ways in which they interact and change. (6)

Sociological imagination An awareness of the relationship between an individual and the wider society, both today and in the past. (5)

Sociology The scientific study of social behavior and human groups. (5)

Theory In sociology, a set of statements that seeks to explain problems, actions, or behavior. (8)

Verstehen The German word for "understanding" or "insight"; used to stress the need for sociologists to take into account the subjective meanings people attach to their actions. (10)

TAKING SOCIOLOGY with you

1. Research! Find out who makes the sports apparel sold at your school's bookstore. What can you learn (perhaps from a company website) about where such products are manufactured and what the working conditions are?

2. In what ways have you been affected by the recent spate of home mortgage foreclosures? Has the widespread loss of home ownership made you and others more aware of the problem of homelessness, or has it pushed the issue out of sight?

3. Consider some group or organization that you participate in. Using Robert Merton's concepts, list its manifest and latent functions.

Self-Quiz

Read each question carefully and then select the best answer.

1. Sociology is
   a. very narrow in scope.
   b. concerned with what one individual does or does not do.
   c. the systematic study of social behavior and human groups.
   d. an awareness of the relationship between an individual and the wider society.

2. Which of the following thinkers introduced the concept of the sociological imagination?
   a. Émile Durkheim
   b. Max Weber
   c. Karl Marx
   d. C. Wright Mills

3. Émile Durkheim's research on suicide suggested that
   a. people with religious affiliations had a higher suicide rate than those who were unaffiliated.
   b. suicide rates seemed to be higher in times of peace than in times of war and revolution.
   c. civilians were more likely to take their lives than soldiers.
   d. suicide is a solitary act, unrelated to group life.

4. Max Weber taught his students that they should employ which of the following in their intellectual work?
   a. anomie
   b. *verstehen*
   c. the sociological imagination
   d. microsociology

5. Robert Merton's contributions to sociology include
   a. successfully combining theory and research.
   b. producing a theory that is one of the most frequently cited explanations of deviant behavior.
   c. an attempt to bring macro-level and micro-level analyses together.
   d. all of the above

6. Which sociologist made a major contribution to society through his in-depth studies of urban life, including both Blacks and Whites?
   a. W. E. B. DuBois
   b. Robert Merton
   c. Auguste Comte
   d. Charles Horton Cooley

7. In the late 19th century, before the term *feminist view* was even coined, the ideas behind this major theoretical approach appeared in the writings of
   a. Karl Marx.
   b. Ida Wells-Barnett.
   c. Charles Horton Cooley.
   d. Pierre Bourdieu.

8. Thinking of society as a living organism in which each part of the organism contributes to its survival is a reflection of which theoretical perspective?
   a. the functionalist perspective
   b. the conflict perspective
   c. the feminist perspective
   d. the interactionist perspective

9. Karl Marx's view of the struggle between social classes inspired the contemporary
   a. functionalist perspective.
   b. conflict perspective.
   c. interactionist perspective.
   d. dramaturgical approach.

10. Erving Goffman's dramaturgical approach, which postulates that people present certain aspects of their personalities while obscuring other aspects, is a derivative of what major theoretical perspective?
   a. the functionalist perspective
   b. the conflict perspective
   c. the feminist perspective
   d. the interactionist perspective

11. While the findings of sociologists may at times seem like common sense, they differ because they rest on _____ analysis of facts.

12. Within sociology, a(n) _____ is a set of statements that seeks to explain problems, actions, or behavior.

13. In _____ _____'s hierarchy of the sciences, sociology was the "queen," and its practitioners were "scientist-priests."

14. In *Society in America*, originally published in 1837, English scholar _____ _____ examined religion, politics, child rearing, and immigration in the young nation.

15. _____ _____ adapted Charles Darwin's evolutionary view of the "survival of the fittest" by arguing that it is "natural" that some people are rich while others are poor.

16. Sociologist Max Weber coined the term _____ _____ in referring to a construct or model that serves as a measuring rod against which actual cases can be evaluated.

17. In *The Communist Manifesto*, _____ _____ and _____ _____ argued that the masses of people who have no resources other than their labor (the proletariat) should unite to fight for the overthrow of capitalist societies.

18. _____ _____, an early female sociologist, cofounded the famous Chicago settlement house called Hull House and also tried to establish a juvenile court system.

19. The university's role in certifying academic competence and excellence is an example of a(n) _____ function.

20. The _____ _____ draws on the work of Karl Marx and Friedrich Engels in that it often views women's subordination as inherent in capitalist societies.

THINKING ABOUT **MOVIES**

Brokeback Mountain

In the rural West, two men struggle to reconcile their social roles with their personal identities.

Frozen River

Two working-class women overcome racial prejudice to form an unlikely friendship.

When the Levees Broke

Spike Lee directs this documentary about the devastating social costs of Hurricane Katrina.

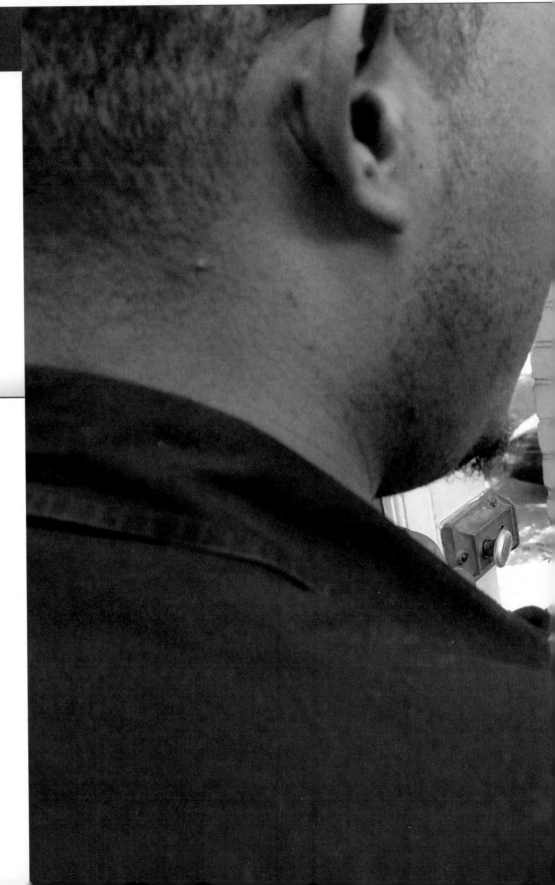

▶ INSIDE

A U.S. census worker introduces herself to the householder she is about to interview. Note the handheld electronic device she carries to record and transmit data. The census is a survey, one of the many methods sociologists, governments, and businesses use to collect data.

26

Sociological Research 2

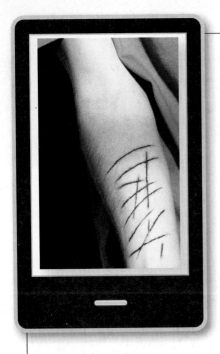

“ Long a subterranean topic, the deliberate, non-suicidal destruction of one's own body tissue emerged from obscurity in the 1990s and began to spread dramatically. . . . Although a range of behaviors may be considered self-injurious, . . . we focus here on . . . self-cutting, burning, branding, scratching, picking at skin or reopening wounds, biting, head banging, hair pulling (trichotillomania), hitting (with a hammer or other object), and bone breaking.

. . .

This analysis draws on eighty in-depth interviews conducted in person and on the telephone. Participants ranged in age from sixteen to their mid-fifties, with more women (sixty-five) than men (fifteen), nearly all Caucasian.

In addition, beginning in 2001–2002, we began to explore the Web sites and public postings of self-injurers. We joined several Internet self-injury groups as overt researchers and became active participants in group discussions. Because of the intimate nature of virtual communication . . . , we formed several deep and enduring relationships with people in different friendship circles that lasted for years, and we discussed with people the features of their ordinary lives and rallied around them during their many crises. We worked, with others, on the difficulties of supporting people who were disembodied and distant. Together with them, we learned to discern the seriousness of people's suicidal threats, their claims of abstinence,

Some reported that they hung out with "the wrong crowd" and acted out or were drawn into countercultural groups such as Goths. They were nihilists who delighted in showing off by burning or cutting themselves.

their presentation of different personas under different pseudonyms in different groups, and the consequences of flame wars. We networked through bulletin boards, MySpace, and the hundreds of self-injury–related Web Usenet support groups.

. . .

We . . . found a growing number of self-injurers who belonged to alternative youth subcultures. Some reported that they hung out with "the wrong crowd" and acted out or were drawn into countercultural groups such as Goths. They were nihilists who delighted in showing off by burning or cutting themselves. Natalie, a twenty-two-year-old college student, reflected back on her junior high school friends:

Eighth grade was the point at which I really started getting sociable, identifying with this alternative subculture. It wasn't like I hung out with the freaks and the rejects and, like, the outcasts. I definitely was in the subculture of the stoners and the punks, and we hung out on the bridge and I started smoking and doing drugs and, um, at that point I associated with more people who also hurt themselves.

. . .

Some self-injurers rooted their unhappiness in peer social situations. Rachel, a twenty-three-year-old college student with an intact, happy family, blamed her friends for driving her to self-injure:

It happened the first time when my group turned against me for some reason. They alienated me for a week straight, they started rumors about me. I didn't go to any activities that week and I didn't even go to school. I was so sad, it just started. I was crying and so upset and couldn't stop crying, and I just took a coat hanger, and that's how it started.

. . .

Many people continued self-injuring, either continuously or intermittently, into adulthood. Contrary to extant knowledge, roughly two-thirds of the "regulars" we encountered on the Internet were older than twenty-five, and half were older than thirty-five. . . . ”

(P. Adler and P. Adler 2007:537–538, 540, 541, 544, 545, 547) Additional information about this excerpt can be found on the Online Learning Center at www.mhhe.com/schaefer13e.

This description of the covert practice of self-injury is taken from Patricia Adler and Peter Adler's extensive research on the little-known behavior and its social underpinnings. Over a six-year period, the Adlers conducted lengthy, emotionally intense interviews with self-injurers, becoming friends with many. They met others in virtual space, through Internet-based support groups and web postings. "Rather than remaining strictly detached from our subjects, we became involved in their lives, helping them and giving voice to their experiences and beliefs," the Adlers admit (2007:542).

The Adlers' work on self-injury reflects all three major sociological approaches. For self-injurers, who rarely come into contact with others like themselves, the Internet functions as a meeting place, a refuge from their self-imposed social isolation. As conflict theorists would point out, their unconventional

behavior marginalizes them, preventing them from receiving assistance even when they would welcome it. Interactionists would recognize the critical nature of self-injurers' interpersonal contacts, in person and often online. And feminist theorists would look for gender differences in self-injurers' behavior.

Though many people would like to ignore the phenomenon of self-injury, believing that those who practice it will eventually "grow out of it," the Adlers' research allows us to consider it intelligently and scientifically, within the social context. Self-injurers, the Adlers found, are a diverse group, whose behavior is carefully planned and considered. Surprisingly, members often begin to injure themselves in the company of others rather than in secret. They have recently begun to coalesce as a subculture (2007:559–560).

Effective sociological research can be quite thought-provoking. It may suggest many new questions that require further study, such as why we make assumptions about people who engage in atypical behaviors like self-injury. In some cases, rather than raising additional questions, a study will simply confirm previous beliefs and findings. Sociological research can also have practical applications. For instance, research results that disconfirm accepted beliefs about marriage and the family may lead to changes in public policy.

This chapter will examine the research process used in conducting sociological studies. How do sociologists go about setting up a research project? How do they ensure that the results of the research are reliable and accurate? Can they carry out their research without violating the rights of those they study?

We will first look at the steps that make up the scientific method used in research. Then we will take a look at various techniques commonly used in sociological research, such as experiments, observations, and surveys. We will pay particular attention to the ethical challenges sociologists face in studying human behavior, and to the debate raised by Max Weber's call for "value neutrality" in social science research. We will also examine feminist methodology and the role technology plays in research today. Though sociological researchers can focus on any number of subjects, in this chapter we will concentrate on two in particular: the relationship of education to income and the controversial subject of human sexuality. The Social Policy section that closes the chapter considers the difficulties and the challenges in researching human sexuality.

Whatever the area of sociological inquiry and whatever the perspective of the sociologist—whether functionalist, conflict, feminist, interactionist, or any other—there is one crucial requirement: imaginative, responsible research that meets the highest scientific and ethical standards.

What Is the Scientific Method?

" Like all of us, sociologists are interested in the central questions of our time: Is the family falling apart? Why is there so much crime in the United States? Is the world falling behind in its ability to feed a growing population? Such issues concern most people, whether or not they have academic training. However, unlike the typical citizen, the sociologist has a commitment to use the **scientific method** in studying society. The scientific method is a systematic, organized series of steps that ensures maximum objectivity and consistency in researching a problem.

Many of us will never actually conduct scientific research. Why, then, is it important that we understand the scientific method? The answer is that it plays a major role in the workings of our society. Residents of the United States are constantly bombarded with "facts" or "data." A television news report informs us that "one in every two marriages in this country now ends in divorce," yet Chapter 14 will show that this assertion is based on misleading statistics. Almost daily, advertisers cite supposedly scientific studies to prove that their products are superior. Such claims may be accurate or exaggerated. We can better evaluate such information—and will not be fooled so easily—if we are familiar with the standards of scientific research. These standards are quite stringent, and they demand as strict adherence as possible.

The scientific method requires precise preparation in developing useful research. Otherwise, the research data collected may not prove accurate. Sociologists and other researchers follow five basic steps in the scientific method: (1) defining the problem, (2) reviewing the literature, (3) formulating the hypothesis, (4) selecting the research design and then collecting and analyzing data, and (5) developing the conclusion (Figure 2-1). We'll use an actual example to illustrate the workings of the scientific method.

Defining the Problem

Does it "pay" to go to college? Some people make great sacrifices and work hard to get a college education. Parents borrow money for their children's tuition. Students work part-time jobs or even

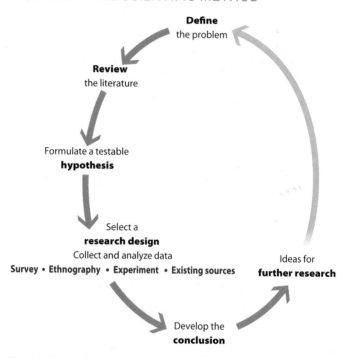

FIGURE **2-1** THE SCIENTIFIC METHOD

Define the problem

Review the literature

Formulate a testable **hypothesis**

Select a **research design**
Collect and analyze data
Survey • Ethnography • Experiment • Existing sources

Ideas for **further research**

Develop the **conclusion**

The scientific method allows sociologists to objectively and logically evaluate the data they collect. Their findings can suggest ideas for further sociological research.

take full-time positions while attending evening or weekend classes. Does it pay off? Are there monetary returns for getting that degree?

The first step in any research project is to state as clearly as possible what you hope to investigate—that is, *define the problem*. In this instance, we are interested in knowing how schooling relates to income. We want to find out the earnings of people with different levels of formal schooling.

Early on, any social science researcher must develop an operational definition of each concept being studied. An **operational definition** is an explanation of an abstract concept that is specific enough to allow a researcher to assess the concept. For example, a sociologist interested in status might use membership in exclusive social clubs as an operational definition of status. Someone studying prejudice might consider a person's unwillingness to hire or work with members of minority groups as an operational definition of prejudice. In our example, we need to develop two operational definitions—education and earnings—in order to study whether it pays to get an advanced educational degree. We'll define *education* as the number of years of schooling a person has achieved and *earnings* as the income a person reports having received in the past year.

Initially, we will take a functionalist perspective (although we may end up incorporating other perspectives). We will argue that opportunities for more earning power are related to level of schooling and that schools prepare students for employment.

Reviewing the Literature

By conducting a *review of the literature*—relevant scholarly studies and information—researchers refine the problem under study, clarify possible techniques to be used in collecting data, and eliminate or reduce avoidable mistakes. In our example, we would examine information about the salaries for different occupations. We would see if jobs that require more academic training are better rewarded. It would also be appropriate to review other studies on the relationship between education and income.

The review of the literature would soon tell us that many factors besides years of schooling influence earning potential. For example, we would learn that the children of rich parents are more likely to go to college than those of poor parents, so we might consider the possibility that rich parents may later help their children to secure better-paying jobs.

We might also look at macro-level data, such as state-by-state comparisons of income and educational levels. In one macro-level study based on census data, researchers found that in states whose residents have a relatively high level of education, household income levels are high as well (Figure 2-2). This finding suggests that schooling may well be related to income, though it does not speak to the micro-level relationship we are interested in. That is, we want to know whether *individuals* who are well educated are also well paid.

Formulating the Hypothesis

After reviewing earlier research and drawing on the contributions of sociological theorists, the researchers may then *formulate the hypothesis*. A **hypothesis** is a speculative statement about the relationship between two or more factors known as variables. Income, religion, occupation, and gender can all serve as variables in a study. We can define a **variable** as a measurable trait or characteristic that is subject to change under different conditions.

Researchers who formulate a hypothesis generally must suggest how one aspect of human behavior influences or affects another. The variable hypothesized to cause or influence another is called the **independent variable**. The other variable is termed the **dependent variable** because its action *depends* on the influence of the independent variable. In other words, the researcher

It seems reasonable that these graduates of Fort Bethold Community College on the Fort Bethold Reservation, North Dakota, will earn more income than high school graduates. How would you go about testing that hypothesis?

believes that the independent variable predicts or causes change in the dependent variable. For example, a researcher in sociology might anticipate that the availability of affordable housing (the independent variable, *x*) affects the level of homelessness in a community (the dependent variable, *y*).

Our hypothesis is that the higher one's educational degree, the more money one will earn. The independent variable that is to be measured is the level of education. The variable that is thought to depend on it—income—must also be measured.

Identifying independent and dependent variables is a critical step in clarifying cause-and-effect relationships. As shown in Figure 2-3 on page 32, **causal logic** involves the relationship between a condition or variable and a particular consequence, with one event leading to the other. For instance, being less integrated into society may be directly related to, or produce a greater likelihood of, suicide. Similarly, the time students spend reviewing material for a quiz may be directly related to, or produce a greater likelihood of, getting a high score on the quiz.

A **correlation** exists when a change in one variable coincides with a change in the other. Correlations are an indication that causality *may* be present; they do not necessarily indicate causation. For example, data indicate that people who prefer to watch televised news programs are less knowledgeable than those who read newspapers and newsmagazines. This correlation between people's relative knowledge and their choice of news media seems to make sense, because it agrees with the common belief that television dumbs down information. But the correlation between the two variables is actually caused by a third variable, people's relative ability to comprehend large amounts of information. People with poor reading skills are much more likely than others to get their news from television, while those who are more educated or skilled turn more often to the print media. Though television viewing is *correlated* with lower news comprehension, then, it does not *cause* it.

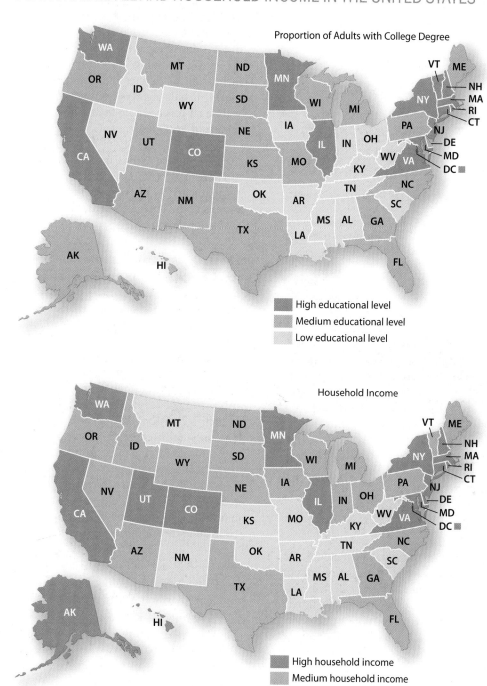

Notes: Cutoffs for high/medium and medium/low educational levels in 2009 were 29.7 percent and 24.5 percent of the population with a college degree, respectively; median for the entire nation was 27.9 percent. Cutoffs for high/medium and medium/low household income levels in 2009 were $53,900 and $43,000, respectively; national median household income was $51,618 in 2009.
Source: American Community Survey 2010: Tables R1502, R1901.

Sociologists seek to identify the *causal* link between variables; the suspected causal link is generally described in the hypothesis (Neuman 2009).

Collecting and Analyzing Data

How do you test a hypothesis to determine if it is supported or refuted? You need to collect information, using one of the research designs described later in the chapter. The research design guides the researcher in collecting and analyzing data.

Selecting the Sample   In most studies, social scientists must carefully select what is known as a sample. A **sample** is a selection from a larger population that is statistically representative of that population. There are many kinds of samples, but the

FIGURE **2-3** CAUSAL LOGIC

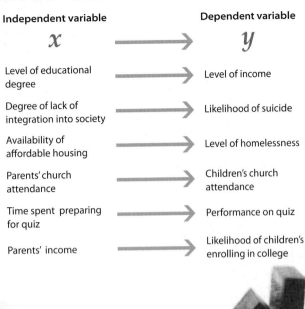

Independent variable	Dependent variable
x	y
Level of educational degree	Level of income
Degree of lack of integration into society	Likelihood of suicide
Availability of affordable housing	Level of homelessness
Parents' church attendance	Children's church attendance
Time spent preparing for quiz	Performance on quiz
Parents' income	Likelihood of children's enrolling in college

Think about It

Identify two or three dependent variables that might be influenced by this independent variable: number of alcoholic drinks ingested.

one social scientists use most frequently is the random sample. In a **random sample**, every member of an entire population being studied has the same chance of being selected. Thus, if researchers want to examine the opinions of people listed in a city directory (a book that, unlike the telephone directory, lists all households), they might use a computer to randomly select names from the directory. The results would constitute a random sample. The advantage of using specialized sampling techniques is that sociologists do not need to question everyone in a population (Igo 2007).

In some cases, the subjects researchers want to study are hard to identify, either because their activities are clandestine or because lists of such people are not readily available. How do researchers create a sample of illegal drug users, for instance, or of women whose husbands are at least 10 years younger than they are? In such cases, researchers employ what are called *snowball* or *convenience samples*—that is, they recruit participants through word of mouth or by posting notices on the Internet. With the help of special statistical techniques, researchers can draw conclusions from such nonrandom samples.

It is all too easy to confuse the careful scientific techniques used in representative sampling with the many *nonscientific* polls that receive much more media attention. For example,

website viewers are often encouraged to register their views on headline news or political contests. Such polls reflect nothing more than the views of those who happened to visit the website and took the time, perhaps at some cost, to register their opinions. These data do not necessarily reflect (and indeed may distort) the views of the broader population. Not everyone has access to a computer on a regular basis, or the means and/or inclination to register their opinions. Even when these techniques include answers from tens of thousands of people, they will be far less accurate than a carefully selected representative sample of 1,500 respondents.

For the purposes of our research example, we will use information collected in the Current Population Survey conducted by the Bureau of the Census. Each year, the Census Bureau surveys approximately 77,000 households across the United States. Technicians at the bureau then use the data to estimate the nation's entire population.

Ensuring Validity and Reliability The scientific method requires that research results be both valid and reliable. **Validity** refers to the degree to which a measure or scale truly reflects the phenomenon under study. A valid measure of income depends on the gathering of accurate data. Various studies show that people are reasonably accurate in reporting how much money they earned in the most recent year. If a question is written unclearly, however, the resulting data might not be accurate.

For example, respondents to an unclear question about income might report their parents' or spouse's income instead of their own. **Reliability** refers to the extent to which a measure produces consistent results. Some people may not disclose accurate information, but most do. In the Current Population Survey, some people refuse to give their income, or even to participate. Periodically, the Census Bureau follows up with a personal visit to nonrespondents, to ensure that their data do not differ significantly from data obtained from those who do cooperate (Bureau of the Census 2004b).

Developing the Conclusion

Scientific studies, including those conducted by sociologists, do not aim to answer all the questions that can be raised about a particular subject. Therefore, the conclusion of a research study represents both an end and a beginning. It terminates a specific phase of the investigation but should also generate ideas for future study.

Supporting Hypotheses In our example, we find that the data support our hypothesis: People with more formal schooling *do* earn more money than others. Those with a high school diploma earn more than those who failed to complete high school, but those with an associate's degree earn more than high school graduates. The relationship continues through more advanced levels of schooling, so that those with graduate degrees earn the most.

The relationship is not perfect, however. Some people who drop out of high school end up with high incomes, whereas some with advanced degrees earn modest incomes, as shown in Figure 2-4. A successful entrepreneur, for example, might not have much formal schooling, while a holder of a doctorate may choose to work for a low-paying nonprofit institution.

Think about It

What kinds of knowledge and skills do people with an associate's degree or higher possess, compared to those with a high school education or less? Why would employers value those kinds of knowledge and skills?

Sociologists are interested in both the general pattern that emerges from their data and exceptions to the pattern.

Sociological studies do not always generate data that support the original hypothesis. Many times, a hypothesis is refuted, and researchers must reformulate their conclusions. Unexpected results may also lead sociologists to reexamine their methodology and make changes in the research design.

Controlling for Other Factors A **control variable** is a factor that is held constant to test the relative impact of an independent variable. For example, if researchers wanted to know how adults in the United States feel about restrictions on smoking in public places, they would probably attempt to use a respondent's smoking behavior as a control variable. That is, how do smokers versus nonsmokers feel about smoking in public places? The researchers would compile separate statistics on how smokers and nonsmokers feel about antismoking regulations.

Our study of the influence of education on income suggests that not everyone enjoys equal educational opportunities, a disparity that is one of the causes of social inequality. Since education affects a person's income, we may wish to call on the conflict perspective to explore this topic further. What impact does a person's race or gender have? Is a woman with a college degree likely to earn as much as a man with similar schooling? Later in this textbook we will consider these other factors and variables. That is, we will examine the impact that education has on income while controlling for variables such as gender and race.

In Summary: The Scientific Method

Let us briefly summarize the process of the scientific method through a review of the example. We *defined a problem* (the question of whether it pays to get a higher educational degree). We *reviewed the literature* (other studies of the relationship between education and income) and *formulated a hypothesis* (the higher one's educational degree, the more money one will earn). We *collected and analyzed the data,* making sure the

FIGURE 2-4 IMPACT OF A COLLEGE EDUCATION ON INCOME

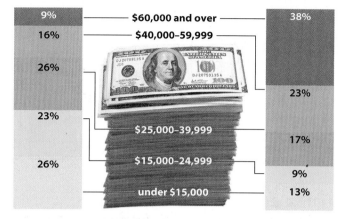

High school diploma or less — Associate's degree or more

High school diploma or less	Income	Associate's degree or more
9%	$60,000 and over	38%
16%	$40,000–59,999	23%
26%	$25,000–39,999	17%
23%	$15,000–24,999	9%
26%	under $15,000	13%

Source: Author's analysis of DeNavas-Walt et al. 2010, Detailed Table PINC-03.

Forty-nine percent of people with a high school diploma or less (left) earn under $25,000 a year, while only 25 percent earn $40,000 or more. In contrast, only 22 percent of those with an associate's degree or higher (right) earn less than $25,000, while 61 percent earn $40,000 or more.

TREND SPOTTING

Overcounting and Undercounting in the U.S. Census

Every 10 years, as required by the Constitution, the U.S. government conducts a census to determine how many congressional representatives each state is allowed. Besides determining the states' political power, these data are used for a myriad of other purposes, from distributing federal aid to education to researching the market for breakfast cereal.

Despite concerns about government intrusion into people's private lives, U.S. citizens are relatively compliant with the head count. About three-quarters of households fill out and return the form or answer face-to-face questions from a census worker. Other industrial countries have much less success than the United States. Because of strong concerns about privacy, for example, the Netherlands has not had a door-to-door census since 1971.

With detailed knowledge of three out of every four households in the United States, census workers can use statistical techniques to estimate data for the other quarter. Still, officials have long recognized that the count is more likely to miss certain groups of people than others. This tendency, called *undercounting,* applies especially to low-income people, non-English speakers, and the homeless. Those who have good reason to avoid census workers, such as illegal immigrants and families who crowd together in inadequate housing, also swell the ranks of the undercounted.

Recently, however, concern has been growing about *overcounting,* or the tendency to count some people twice. College students who live at school rather than at home with their parents, "snowbirds" (retirees who move to warmer climes during the winter), active military personnel, and children whose parents share their custody all are likely to be overcounted.

Census officials estimate that the 2000 Census undercounted 10.2 million people and overcounted 11.6 million. In a nation of over 300 million people, a population count that is off by a net figure of a million or so may not seem much of a problem. However, the error biases the count toward or against particular racial and socioeconomic groups. Whites, homeowners, and the educated are more likely than others to show up twice in the census. Blacks, Hispanics, and renters are more likely not to show up. Given the growing importance of accuracy in the nation's population count, this problem looms large for those who must interpret the 2010 Census.

Doonesbury

Think about It
What would constitute a less biased question for a survey on smoking?

sample was representative and the data were valid and reliable. Finally, we *developed the conclusion*: the data do support our hypothesis about the influence of education on income.

thinking CRITICALLY

What might be the effects of a college education on society as a whole? Think of some potential effects on the family, government, and the economy.

Major Research Designs

An important aspect of sociological research is deciding *how* to collect the data. A **research design** is a detailed plan or method for obtaining data scientifically. Selection of a research design is often based on the theories and hypotheses the researcher starts with (Merton 1948). The choice requires creativity and ingenuity, because it directly influences both the cost of the project and the amount of time needed to collect the data. Research designs that sociologists regularly use to generate data include surveys, ethnography, experiments, and existing sources.

Surveys

Almost all of us have responded to surveys of one kind or another. We may have been asked what kind of detergent we use, which presidential candidate we intend to vote for, or what our favorite television program is. A **survey** is a study, generally in the form of an interview or questionnaire, that provides researchers with information about how people think and act. As anyone who watches the news during presidential campaigns knows, surveys have become a staple of political life.

When you think of surveys, you may recall seeing online polls that offer instant results. Although such polls can be highly interesting, they reflect only the opinions of those who visit the website and choose to respond online. As we have seen, a survey must be based on precise, representative sampling if it is to genuinely reflect a broad range of the population. Box 2-1 describes the challenges of conducting a public opinion survey over the telephone.

In preparing to conduct a survey, sociologists must not only develop representative samples; they must also exercise great care in the wording of questions. An effective survey question must be simple and clear enough for people to understand. It must also be specific enough so that there are no problems in interpreting the results. Open-ended questions ("What do you think of the programming on educational television?") must be carefully phrased to solicit the type of information desired. Surveys can be indispensable sources of information, but only if the sampling is done properly and the questions are worded accurately and without bias.

In wording questions, researchers must also pay careful attention to changes in society. In December 2010, officials at the Bureau of Labor Statistics recognized the effects of an extended recession by changing a decades-old practice. In the past, multiple-choice questions about how long a respondent had been unemployed had ended with a maximum of "99 weeks or over." By the end of 2010, joblessness had become so chronic that the bureau increased the number of choices, ending with "290 weeks or longer."

There are two main forms of the survey: the **interview**, in which a researcher obtains information through face-to-face, telephone, or online questioning, and the **questionnaire**, in which the researcher uses a printed or written form to obtain information from a respondent. Each of these has its own advantages. An interviewer can obtain a higher response rate, because people find it more difficult to turn down a personal request for an interview than to throw away a written questionnaire. In addition, a skillful interviewer can go beyond written questions and probe for a subject's underlying feelings and reasons. On the other hand, questionnaires have the advantage of being cheaper, especially in large samples.

RESEARCH TODAY

2-1 Surveying Cell Phone Users

"Can you hear me now?" This question, familiar to cell phone callers everywhere, could be used to characterize a debate among researchers in sociology. Until recently, calling people on the telephone was a common way for survey takers to reach a broad range of people. Though not everyone owns a telephone—particularly not low-income people—researchers managed to account for that relatively small portion of the population in other ways.

However, the fact that many people now have a cell phone but no landline presents a serious methodological problem to scholars who depend on surveys and public opinion polling. As of 2009, one in six adults in the United States could be reached only by cell phone, and the proportion was rising. Among those under 30, the abandonment of landlines was nearly three times as common. These cell phone subscribers are more likely than others to be male and to earn a modest income.

Scholars are reluctant to rely only on landline-based surveys. They are concerned about the potential for misleading results, such as underestimates of the prevalence of health problems. For example, 38 percent of cell phone-only households have a binge drinker, compared to only 17 percent of landline households. And 28 percent of cell phone-only households do not have health insurance, compared to 14 percent of landline households.

Unfortunately, surveying cell phone users has its own problems. In general, cell phone users are more likely than landline users to screen incoming calls or ignore them.

As of 2009, one in six adults in the United States could be reached only by cell phone, and the proportion was rising.

And studies show that because cell phone users often take calls while they are involved in other activities, they are much more likely to break off a call midsurvey than someone who is speaking on a landline. Thus, it takes an average of nine calls to a working cell phone number to complete one survey, compared to five calls to a working landline number. Furthermore, federal law requires that calls to cell phones be hand-dialed; the use of automatic dialers, a standard tool of survey firms, is illegal. Survey takers have also found that calling cell phone numbers means they will reach a higher proportion of nonadults than when calling landline numbers. Finally, there are some ethical issues involved in randomly dialing cell phone users, who may be driving a motor vehicle or operating dangerous machinery when they answer.

Researchers are taking steps to stay abreast of technological change. For example, they are making allowances for people who communicate without any kind of telephone, using their personal computers and the Internet. And by drawing on historical data that suggest what kinds of people tend to adopt other wireless technologies, researchers are projecting which people are likely to abandon their landlines in the near future.

LET'S DISCUSS

1. Are you a cell phone-only user? If so, do you generally accept calls from unknown numbers? Aside from underestimating certain health problems and distorting the degree of support for certain politicians, what other problems might result from excluding cell phone-only users from survey research?
2. Apply what you have just learned to the task of surveying Internet users. Which of the problems that arise during telephone surveys might also arise during Internet surveys? Might Internet surveys involve some unique problems?

Sources: Blumberg and Luke 2007; David Brown 2009; Harrisinteractive 2008; Keeter and Kennedy 2006; Lavrakas et al. 2007.

Why do people have sex? A straightforward question, but until recently it was rarely investigated scientifically, despite its significance to public health, marital counseling, and criminology. In a study published in 2007, researchers interviewed nearly 2,000 undergraduates at the University of Texas at Austin. To develop the question for the interview, they first asked a random sample of 400 students to list all the reasons why they had ever had sex. The explanations were highly diverse, ranging from "I was drunk" to "I wanted to feel closer to God." The team then asked another sample of 1,500 students to rate the importance of each of the 287 reasons given by the first group. Table 2-1 ranks the results. Nearly every reason was rated most important by at least some respondents. Though there were some gender differences in the replies, there was significant consensus between men and women on the top 10 reasons (Meston and Buss 2007).

Studies have shown that the characteristics of the interviewer have an impact on survey data. For example, female interviewers tend to receive more feminist responses from female subjects than do male interviewers, and African American interviewers tend to receive more detailed responses about race-related issues from African

TABLE **2-1** TOP REASONS WHY MEN AND WOMEN HAD SEX

Reason	Men	Women
I was attracted to the person	1	1
It feels good	2	3
I wanted to experience the physical pleasure	3	2
It's fun	4	8
I wanted to show my affection to the person	5	4
I was sexually aroused and wanted the release	6	6
I was "horny"	7	7
I wanted to express my love for the person	8	5
I wanted to achieve an orgasm	9	14
I wanted to please my partner	10	11
I realized I was in love	17	9
I was "in the heat of the moment"	13	10

Source: Meston and Buss 2007:506.

American subjects than do White interviewers. The possible impact of gender and race indicates again how much care social research requires (D. W. Davis and Silver 2003).

The survey is an example of **quantitative research**, which collects and reports data primarily in numerical form. Most of the survey research discussed so far in this book has been quantitative. While this type of research can make use of large samples, it can't offer great depth and detail on a topic. That is why researchers also make use of **qualitative research**, which relies on what is seen in field and naturalistic settings, and often focuses on small groups and communities rather than on large groups or whole nations. The most common form of qualitative research is ethnography, or observation, which we consider next. Throughout this book you will find examples of both quantitative and qualitative research, since both are used widely. Some sociologists prefer one type of research to the other, but we learn most when we draw on many different research designs and do not limit ourselves to a particular type of research.

Ethnography

Investigators often collect information or test hypotheses through firsthand studies. **Ethnography** is the study of an entire social setting through extended systematic fieldwork. **Observation,** or direct participation in closely watching a group or organization, is the basic technique of ethnography. However, ethnographic research also includes the collection of historical information and the conduct of in-person interviews. Although ethnography may seem a relatively informal method compared to surveys or experiments, ethnographic researchers are careful to take detailed notes while observing their subjects.

In some cases, the sociologist actually joins a group for a period, to get an accurate sense of how it operates. This approach is called *participant observation*. In Barbara Ehrenreich's widely read book, *Nickel and Dimed: On (Not) Getting By in America,* the author was a participant observer. Disguising herself as a divorced, middle-aged housewife without a college degree, Ehrenreich set out to see what life was like for low-wage workers. Her book chronicles her own and others' experiences trying to make ends meet on a minimum wage (Ehrenreich 2001).

During the late 1930s, in a classic example of participant-observation research, William F. Whyte moved into a low-income Italian neighborhood in Boston. For nearly four years he was a member of the social circle of "corner boys" that he describes in *Street Corner Society.* Whyte revealed his identity to these men and joined in their conversations, bowling, and other leisure-time activities. His goal was to gain greater insight into the community that these men had established. As Whyte (1981:303) listened to Doc, the leader of the group, he "learned the answers to questions I would not even have had the sense to ask if I had been getting my information solely on an interviewing basis." Whyte's work was especially valuable, since at the time the academic world had

little direct knowledge of the poor, and tended to rely for information on the records of social service agencies, hospitals, and courts (P. Adler et al. 1992).

The initial challenge that Whyte faced—and that every participant observer encounters—was to gain acceptance into an unfamiliar group. It is no simple matter for a college-trained sociologist to win the trust of a religious cult, a youth gang, a poor Appalachian community, or a circle of skid row residents. It requires a great deal of patience and an accepting, nonthreatening type of personality on the part of the observer.

Ethnographic research poses other complex challenges for the investigator. Sociologists must be able to fully understand what they are observing. In a sense, then, researchers must learn to see the world as the group sees it in order to fully comprehend the events taking place around them. This raises a delicate issue. If the research is to be successful, the observer cannot allow the close associations or even friendships that inevitably develop to influence the subjects' behavior or the conclusions of the study. Even while working hard to gain acceptance from the group being studied, the participant observer *must* maintain some degree of detachment.

Recently, the issue of detachment became a controversial one for social scientists embedded with the U.S. military in

Sergeant Britt Damon, a social scientist on the U.S. Army Human Terrain Team, chats with Afghani children during a search operation. The participation of social scientists in the Army program, which some see as a violation of scholarly detachment, has proved controversial.

Afghanistan and Iraq. Among other studies, the academicians participated in the creation of the Army's Human Terrain System, a $4 million effort to identify the customs, kinship structures, and internal social conflicts in the two countries. The intention was to provide military leaders with information that would help them to make better decisions. Although the idea of scholars cooperating in any way with soldiers struck many people as inappropriate, others countered that the information they developed would help the military to avoid needless violence and might even facilitate the withdrawal of troops from the region (Glenn 2007; Human Terrain System 2010).

Experiments

When sociologists want to study a possible cause-and-effect relationship, they may conduct experiments. An **experiment** is an artificially created situation that allows a researcher to manipulate variables.

In the classic method of conducting an experiment, two groups of people are selected and matched for similar characteristics, such as age or education. The researchers then assign the subjects to one of two groups: the experimental or the control group. The **experimental group** is exposed to an independent variable; the **control group** is not. Thus, if scientists were testing a new type of antibiotic, they would administer the drug to an experimental group but not to a control group.

In some experiments, just as in observation research, the presence of a social scientist or other observer may affect the behavior of the people being studied. Sociologists have used the term **Hawthorne effect** to refer to the unintended influence that observers of experiments can have on their subjects. The term originated as the result of an experiment conducted at the Hawthorne plant of the Western Electric Company during the 1920s and 1930s. Researchers found that *every* change they made in working conditions—even reduced lighting—seemed to have a positive effect on workers' productivity. They concluded that workers had made a special effort to impress their observers. Though the carefully constructed study did identify some causes for changes in the workers' behavior that did not have to do with their being observed, the term *Hawthorne effect* has become synonymous with a placebo or guinea pig effect (Franke and Kaul 1978).

thinking CRITICALLY

How would you go about setting up an experiment to measure the effect of TV watching on schoolchildren's grades?

Use of Existing Sources

Sociologists do not necessarily need to collect new data in order to conduct research and test hypotheses. The term **secondary analysis** refers to a variety of research techniques that make use of previously collected and publicly accessible information and data. Generally, in conducting secondary analysis, researchers use data in ways that were unintended by the initial collectors of information. For example, census data are compiled for specific uses by the federal government but are also valuable to

marketing specialists in locating everything from bicycle stores to nursing homes. And Social Security registrations, originally meant for government use in administering the nation's retirement system, have been used to track cultural trends in the naming of newborn children (Box 2-2).

Sociologists consider secondary analysis to be *nonreactive*—that is, it does not influence people's behavior. For example, Émile Durkheim's statistical analysis of suicide neither increased nor decreased human self-destruction. Researchers, then, can avoid the Hawthorne effect by using secondary analysis.

There is one inherent problem, however: the researcher who relies on data collected by someone else may not find exactly what is needed. Social scientists who are studying family violence can use statistics from police and social service agencies on *reported* cases of spouse abuse and child abuse, but how many cases are not reported? Government bodies have no precise data on *all* cases of abuse.

Many social scientists find it useful to study cultural, economic, and political documents, including newspapers, periodicals, radio and television tapes, the Internet, scripts, diaries, songs, folklore, and legal papers (Table 2-2). In examining these

TABLE **2-2** EXISTING SOURCES USED IN SOCIOLOGICAL RESEARCH

Most Frequently Used Sources
Census data
Crime statistics
Birth, death, marriage, divorce, and health statistics

Other Sources
Newspapers and periodicals
Personal journals, diaries, e-mail, and letters
Records and archival material of religious organizations, corporations, and other organizations
Transcripts of radio programs
Videotapes of motion pictures and television programs
Web pages, blogs, and chat rooms
Song lyrics
Scientific records (such as patent applications)
Speeches of public figures (such as politicians)
Votes cast in elections or by elected officials on specific legislative proposals
Attendance records for public events
Videos of social protests and rallies
Literature, including folklore

summingup

Think about It

Which of these sources do you access to collect information?

2-2 What's in a Name?

Sociologists can learn a great deal using available information. For example, every year the Social Security Administration receives thousands of registrations for newborn babies. Using these data, we can identify some cultural trends in the popularity of children's names.

As the accompanying figure shows, for example, John has been an extremely popular boy's name for over a century. In 2009 about 4,000 babies were named John, making it the 26th most popular boy's name that year. Though less than half as many babies were named Juan in 2009, that name has been gaining in popularity in recent generations, reflecting the growing impact of the Latino population in the United States.

In 2009 about 4,000 babies were named John, making it the 26th most popular name that year.

The public data contained in name registries also reveal a trend toward "American-sounding" names among immigrants to the United States. In Italy, for example, Giuseppe is a very popular boy's name. Among Italian immigrants to the United States, the English form of Giuseppe, Joseph, is the 3rd most popular boy's name, though it ranks only 11th among non-Italian immigrants. The pattern of selecting names that will allow children to fit in is not uniform, however.

Popularity of John versus Juan

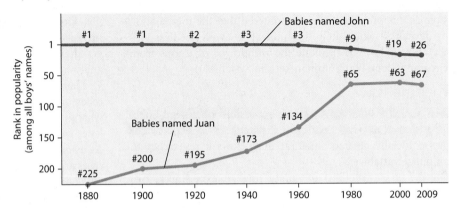

Source: Baby Name Wizard 2010.

In some immigrant groups, parents tend to favor names that symbolize their ethnicity. For example, Kelly is popular among Irish Americans, even though it isn't a traditional girl's name in Ireland. Thus, the available data on newborns' names allow sociologists to detect cultural trends that reflect changing group identities.

Records kept by the Social Security Administration also reveal some regional variations in names. Given the large Hispanic population in Texas, we probably should not be surprised to find that Juan ranks 9th as a name for baby boys in that state. In states like Alabama, Delaware, and Mississippi, however, John is on the top 10 list.

LET'S DISCUSS

1. Visit www.babynamewizard.com on the Internet, and click on "NameVoyager." According to this website, how popular is your first name? Is it becoming more or less fashionable over time?

2. Using the Name Mapper feature at www.babynamewizard.com, find out how popular your name is in the state where you were born. Is your name even more popular in some other states?

Sources: Baby Name Wizard 2010; S. Levitt and Dubner 2006; Lieberson 2000.

---

sources, researchers employ a technique known as **content analysis**, which is the systematic coding and objective recording of data, guided by some rationale.

Content analysis can be revealing. We might think that in the 21st century, blatant favoritism in media representations of men versus women is a thing of the past. However, research suggests otherwise. An analysis of hundreds of characters in children's coloring books shows that males are more likely than females to be shown taking an active role. Gender-stereotyped behavior dominates, with only 3 percent of males engaged in stereotypically female behavior, and only 6 percent of females engaged in stereotypically male behavior (Fitzpatrick and McPherson 2010).

Similarly, despite women's participation in all sports, content analysis of televised sports coverage shows that even when a men's sport is out of season (for example, men's basketball in late summer), it gets more coverage than women's sports in season (for example, women's basketball in July). Furthermore, coverage of female cheerleaders and athletes' wives exceeds coverage of the female athletes who compete in sports (Messner and Cooky 2010).

Table 2-3 summarizes the major research designs, along with their advantages and limitations.

use your sociological *imagination*

Imagine you are a legislator or government policymaker working on a complex social problem. What might happen if you were to base your decision on faulty research?

Ethics of Research

A biochemist cannot inject a drug into a human being unless it has been thoroughly tested and the subject agrees to the shot. To do otherwise would be both unethical and illegal. Sociologists, too, must abide by certain specific standards in conducting research, called a **code of ethics**. The professional society of the discipline, the American Sociological Association (ASA), first published the society's *Code of Ethics* in 1971 and revised it most recently in 1997. It puts forth the following basic principles:

1. Maintain objectivity and integrity in research.

2. Respect the subject's right to privacy and dignity.

TABLE **2-3** MAJOR RESEARCH DESIGNS

summing**up** 39

Method	Examples	Advantages	Limitations
Survey	Questionnaires Interviews	Yields information about specific issues	Can be expensive and time-consuming
Ethnography	Observation	Yields detailed information about specific groups or organizations	Involves months if not years of labor-intensive data
Experiment	Deliberate manipulation of people's social behavior	Yields direct measures of people's behavior	Ethical limitations on the degree to which subjects' behavior can be manipulated
Existing sources/ Secondary analysis	Analysis of census or health data Analysis of films or TV commercials	Cost-efficiency	Limited to data collected for some other purpose

3. Protect subjects from personal harm.

4. Preserve confidentiality.

5. Seek informed consent when data are collected from research participants or when behavior occurs in a private context.

6. Acknowledge research collaboration and assistance.

7. Disclose all sources of financial support (American Sociological Association 1997).

These basic principles probably seem clear-cut. How could they lead to any disagreement or controversy? Yet many delicate ethical questions cannot be resolved simply by reading these seven principles. For example, should a sociologist who is engaged in participant-observation research always protect the confidentiality of subjects? What if the subjects are members of a religious cult allegedly involved in unethical and possibly illegal activities? What if the sociologist is interviewing political activists and is questioned by government authorities about the research?

Because most sociological research uses *people* as sources of information—as respondents to survey questions, subjects of ethnography, or participants in experiments—these sorts of questions are important. In all cases, sociologists need to be certain they are not invading their subjects' privacy. Generally, they do so by assuring subjects of anonymity and by guaranteeing the confidentiality of personal information. In addition, research proposals that involve human subjects must now be overseen by a review board, whose members seek to ensure that subjects are not placed at an unreasonable level of risk. If necessary, the board may ask researchers to revise their research designs to conform to the code of ethics.

We can appreciate the seriousness of the ethical problems researchers confront by considering the experience of sociologist Rik Scarce, described in the next section. Scarce's vow to protect his subjects' confidentiality got him into considerable trouble with the law.

Confidentiality

Like journalists, sociologists occasionally find themselves subject to questions from law enforcement authorities because of knowledge they have gained in the course of their work. This uncomfortable situation raises profound ethical questions.

In May 1993, Rik Scarce, a doctoral candidate in sociology at Washington State University, was jailed for contempt of court. Scarce had declined to tell a federal grand jury what he knew—or even whether he knew anything—about a 1991 raid on a university research laboratory by animal rights activists. At the time, Scarce was conducting research for a book about environmental protesters and knew at least one suspect in the break-in. Curiously, although he was chastised by a federal judge, Scarce won respect from fellow prison inmates, who regarded him as a man who "wouldn't snitch" (Monaghan 1993:A8).

The American Sociological Association supported Scarce's position when he appealed his sentence. Scarce maintained his silence. Ultimately the judge ruled that nothing would be gained by further incarceration, and Scarce was released after serving 159 days in jail. In January 1994, the U.S. Supreme Court declined to hear Scarce's case on appeal. The Court's failure to consider his case led Scarce (2005) to argue that federal legislation is needed to clarify the right of scholars and members of the press to preserve the confidentiality of those they interview.

Conflict of Interest

Sometimes disclosing all the sources of funding for a study, as required in principle 7 of the ASA's *Code of Ethics*, is not a sufficient guarantee of ethical conduct. Especially in the case of both corporate and government funding, money given ostensibly for the support of basic research may come with strings attached. Accepting funds from a private organization or even a government agency that stands to benefit from a study's results can call into question a researcher's objectivity and integrity (principle 1). The controversy surrounding the involvement of social scientists in the U.S. Army's Human Terrain System is one example of this conflict of interest.

Another example is the Exxon Corporation's support for research on jury verdicts. In 1989, the Exxon oil tanker *Valdez* hit a reef off the coast of Alaska, spilling more than 11 million gallons of oil into Prince William Sound. Five years later a federal court ordered Exxon to pay $5.3 billion in damages for the accident. Exxon appealed the verdict and began approaching legal scholars, sociologists, and psychologists who might be willing to study jury deliberations. The corporation's objective was to develop academic support for its lawyers' contention that the punitive judgments in such cases result from faulty deliberations and do not have a deterrent effect.

Some scholars have questioned the propriety of accepting funds under these circumstances, even if the source is disclosed. In at least one case, an Exxon employee explicitly told a

TAKING SOCIOLOGY TO WORK

Dave Eberbach, **Research Coordinator, United Way of Central Iowa**

As a research specialist, Dave Eberbach uses his training in sociology to work for social change. Eberbach looks for small pockets of poverty that are generally hidden in state and county statistics. By zeroing in on conditions in specific neighborhoods, he empowers state and local agencies that work on behalf of the disadvantaged.

Eberbach, who is based in Des Moines, Iowa, was hired to establish a "data warehouse" of social statistics for the local United Way. Part of his job has been to demonstrate to agencies how the information in the database can be of use to them. "We have moved most of our data presentations away from charts and graphs, and on to maps of the county, the city, and the neighborhood," he explains. "This allows people to truly 'see' the big picture."

When Eberbach entered Grinnell College in 1985, he had already taken a sociology course and knew that the subject interested him. Still, he could not have foreseen all the practical uses he might have had for what he learned. "Never assume that you'll never need to know something (including statistics)," he advises. "Life has a funny way of bringing things around again."

At Grinnell, Eberbach benefited from the presence of several visiting professors who exposed him to a variety of cultural and racial perspectives. His personal acquaintance with them complemented the concepts he was learning in his sociology classes. Today, Eberbach draws on his college experiences at the United Way, where his work brings him into contact with a diverse group of people.

Sociology has also helped Eberbach in his chosen specialty, research. "I believe that I am a better 'data person' because of my sociology background," he claims. "The human context for data is as important and can get lost or misdirected by pure statistics," he explains. "My sociology background has helped me ask the appropriate questions to make effective change in our community."

LET'S DISCUSS

1. Do you know what you want to be doing 10 years from now? If so, how might a knowledge of statistics help you in your future occupation?
2. What kinds of statistics, specifically, might you find in the United Way's data warehouse? Where would they come from?

A floating containment barrier (or boom) encircles the Exxon oil tanker *Valdez* after its grounding on a reef off the coast of Alaska. Exxon was found negligent in the environmental disaster and was ordered to pay $5.3 billion for the cleanup. But the corporation's executives spent $1 million to fund academic research that lawyers used to reduce the penalty to $500 million. We will have to see how research results are used or abused to resolve damage claims arising from BP's 2010 oil spill in the Gulf of Mexico.

sociologist that the corporation offers financial support to scholars who have shown the tendency to express views similar to its own. An argument can also be made that Exxon was attempting to set scholars' research agendas with its huge war chest. Rather than funding studies on the improvement of cleanup technologies or the assignment of long-term environmental costs, Exxon chose to shift scientists' attention to the validity of the legal awards in environmental cases.

The scholars who accepted Exxon's support deny that it influenced their work or changed their conclusions. Some received support from other sources as well, such as the National Science Foundation and Harvard University's Olin Center for Law, Economics, and Business. Many of their findings were published in respected academic journals after review by a jury of peers. Still, at least one researcher who participated in the studies refused monetary support from Exxon to avoid even the suggestion of a conflict of interest.

Exxon has spent roughly $1 million on the research, and at least one compilation of studies congenial to the corporation's point of view has been published. As ethical considerations require, the academics who conducted the studies disclosed Exxon's role in funding them. Nevertheless, the investment appears to have paid off. In 2006, drawing on these studies, Exxon's lawyers succeeded in persuading an appeals court to reduce the corporation's legal damages from $5.3 to $2.5 billion. In 2008 Exxon appealed that judgment to the Supreme Court, which further reduced the damages to $500 million. The final award, which is to be shared by about 32,000 plaintiffs, will result in payments of about $15,000 to each person (Freudenburg 2005; Liptak 2008).

Value Neutrality

The ethical considerations of sociologists lie not only in the methods they use and the funding they accept, but also in the way they interpret their results. Max Weber ([1904] 1949) recognized that personal values would influence the questions that sociologists select for research. In his view, that was perfectly acceptable, but under no conditions could a researcher allow his or her personal feelings to influence the *interpretation* of data. In Weber's phrase, sociologists must practice **value neutrality** in their research.

As part of this neutrality, investigators have an ethical obligation to accept research findings even when the data run counter to their personal views, to theoretically based explanations, or to widely accepted beliefs. For example, Émile Durkheim challenged popular conceptions when he reported that social (rather than supernatural) forces were an important factor in suicide.

Although some sociologists believe that neutrality is impossible, ignoring the issue would be irresponsible. Let's consider what might happen if researchers brought their own biases to the investigation. A person investigating the impact of intercollegiate sports on alumni contributions, for example, might focus only on the highly visible revenue-generating sports of football and basketball and neglect the so-called minor sports, such as tennis or soccer, which are more likely to involve women athletes. Despite the early work of W. E. B. DuBois and Jane Addams, sociologists still need to be reminded that the discipline often fails to adequately consider all people's social behavior.

In her book *The Death of White Sociology* (1973), Joyce Ladner called attention to the tendency of mainstream sociology to treat the lives of African Americans as a social problem. More recently, feminist sociologist Shulamit Reinharz (1992) has argued that sociological research should be not only inclusive but also open to bringing about social change and to drawing on relevant research by nonsociologists. Both Ladner and Reinharz maintain that researchers should always analyze whether women's unequal social status has affected their studies in any way. For example, one might broaden the study of the impact of education on income to consider the implications of the unequal pay status of men and women. The issue of value neutrality does not mean that sociologists can't have opinions, but it does mean that they must work to overcome any biases, however unintentional, that they may bring to their analysis of research.

Sociologist Peter Rossi (1987) admits to having liberal inclinations that direct him to certain fields of study. Yet in line with Weber's view of value neutrality, Rossi's commitment to rigorous research methods and objective interpretation of data has sometimes led him to controversial findings that are not necessarily supportive of his liberal values. For example, his measure of the extent of homelessness in Chicago in the mid-1980s fell far below the estimates of the Chicago Coalition for the Homeless. Coalition members bitterly attacked Rossi for hampering their social reform efforts by minimizing the extent of homelessness. Rossi (1987:79) concluded that "in the short term, good social research will often be greeted as a betrayal of one or another side to a particular controversy."

thinking CRITICALLY

If you were planning to do research on human sexuality, which of the seven principles in the ASA's *Code of Ethics* would particularly concern you? What ethical problems might arise in such a study, and how would you attempt to prevent them?

Feminist Methodology

Of the four theoretical approaches to sociology introduced in Chapter 1, the feminist perspective has had the greatest impact

Feminist theorists see the global trafficking of sex workers as one sign of a close relationship between the two supposedly separate worlds of industrial nations and the developing nations that depend on them.

on the current generation of social researchers. How might this perspective influence research? Although researchers must be objective, their theoretical orientation may influence the questions they ask—or, just as important, the questions they fail to ask. Until recently, for example, researchers frequently studied work and the family separately. Yet feminist theorists see the two spheres of activity as being closely integrated. Similarly, work and leisure, paid and unpaid domestic work may be seen not as two separate spheres, but as two sides of the same coin.

Feminist theorists have also drawn researchers' attention to their tendency to overlook women in their studies. For most of the history of sociology, researchers conducted studies of male subjects or male-led groups and organizations and then generalized their findings to all people. For many decades, for example, ethnographic studies of urban life focused on street corners, neighborhood taverns, and bowling alleys—places where men typically congregated. Although researchers gained some valuable insights in this way, they did not form a true impression of city life, because they overlooked the areas where women were likely to gather, such as playgrounds, grocery stores, and front stoops. These are the arenas that the feminist perspective focuses on.

The feminist perspective has also had an impact on global research. To feminist theorists, the traditional distinction between industrial nations and developing nations overlooks the close relationship between these two supposedly separate worlds. Feminist theorists have called for more research on the special role that immigrant women play in maintaining their households; on the use of domestic workers from less developed nations by households in industrial nations; and on the global trafficking of sex workers (Cheng 2003; Cooper et al. 2007; Sprague 2005).

Feminist researchers tend to involve and consult their subjects more than other researchers, and they are more oriented toward seeking change, raising the public consciousness, and influencing policy. They are particularly open to a multidisciplinary approach, such as making use of historical evidence or legal studies (T. Baker 1999; Lofland 1975; Reinharz 1992).

thinking CRITICALLY

Even if women are represented in a study, could the researcher's gender influence the data that are collected? If so, how, and how might the problem be prevented?

The Data-Rich Future

Advances in technology have affected all aspects of our lives, and sociological research is no exception. Massive increases in available data have allowed sociologists to undertake research that was virtually impossible just a decade ago. In the recent past, only people with grants or major institutional support could work easily with large amounts of data. Now anyone with a computer can access huge amounts of data and learn more about social behavior. Moreover, data from foreign countries are sometimes as available as information from the United States.

In the latter part of 2009, the world experienced an intense burst of influenza initially referred to as "swine flu," but later identified as the H1N1 flu strain. How did medical researchers track the virus's spread across a nation, much less the world? Epidemiologists typically rely on reports that originate in doctors' offices and are funneled through government agencies. Data collection is a time-consuming process, with many days passing between the detection of symptoms and the publication of official statistics. However, public health researchers found a way to track contagious diseases using Google. By monitoring the topics people search for and compensating for the relative access to computers in different countries (high in Sweden and low in Nigeria, for example), they can monitor the spread of disease almost in real time (Dukić et al. 2011).

Similarly, in the past sociologists had to rely on victims' complaints or police reports to understand crime patterns. Now they are beginning to access real-time, geocoded (that is, location-specific) incident reports. These new data will offer sociologists much more information, which they can interpret and relate to other aspects of the social environment (G. King 2011).

One ethical concern raised by all these data involves individual privacy. Sociologists now have access to information about people's real estate transactions, campaign contributions, online product purchases, and even travel along toll ways. What steps should they take to protect the privacy of the individuals whose data they

Carnegie Mellon University's Data Truck lets researchers go where their subjects are—from nightclubs to marathon races. Equipped with the latest technology, the truck allows social scientists to enter the responses to their community surveys into their databases on site. It also gives them access to online social networks in the area, and even lets them videotape street activity.

are using? This is not an academic question. Today, 87 percent of the people in the United States can be personally identified given only their gender, date of birth, and ZIP code (G. King 2011).

We have seen that researchers rely on a number of tools, from time-tested observational research and use of existing sources to the latest in computer technologies. The Social Policy section that follows will describe researchers' efforts to survey the general population about a controversial aspect of social behavior: human sexuality. This investigation was complicated by its potential social policy implications. Because in the real world, sociological research can have far-reaching consequences for public policy and public welfare, each of the following chapters in this book will close with a Social Policy section.

thinking CRITICALLY

Male sociologists once overlooked women in their studies of city life. What other groups could easily be overlooked in today's research, and why?

social**policy** and Sociological Research

Studying Human Sexuality

Looking at the Issue

Is sex only as far away as your cable box? The latest content analysis of sexual content on television shows that more than two-thirds of all TV shows include some sexual content—up from about half of all shows seven years earlier (Figure 2-5). Yet a national survey showed that only 17 percent of parents use electronic means, such as the V-chip, to block TV content that may be inappropriate for children. Media

representations of sexual behavior are important, because surveys of teens and young adults tell us that television is one of their top sources of information and ideas about sex. TV has more influence on young people's conceptions of sex than schools, parents, or peers (Kaiser Family Foundation 2007).

In this age of devastating sexually transmitted diseases, there is no time more important to increase our scientific understanding of

FIGURE **2-5** PERCENTAGE OF TELEVISION SHOWS THAT CONTAIN SEXUAL CONTENT

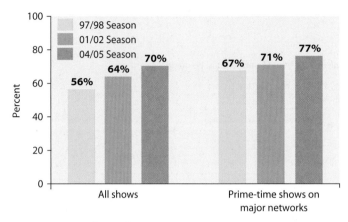

Source: Kaiser Family Foundation 2005:4.

human sexuality. As we will see, however, this is a difficult topic to research because of all the preconceptions, myths, and beliefs people bring to the subject of sexuality. How does one carry out scientific research on such a controversial and personal topic?

Applying Sociology

Sociologists have little reliable national data on patterns of sexual behavior in the United States. Until the 1990s, the only comprehensive study of sexual behavior was the famous two-volume *Kinsey Report,* prepared in the 1940s (Kinsey et al. 1948, 1953; see also Igo 2007). Although the *Kinsey Report* is still widely quoted, the volunteers interviewed for the report were not representative of the nation's adult population.

In part, we lack reliable data on patterns of sexual behavior because it is difficult for researchers to obtain accurate information about this sensitive subject. Moreover, until AIDS emerged in the 1980s, there was little scientific demand for data on sexual behavior, except for specific concerns such as contraception. And even though the AIDS crisis has reached dramatic proportions (as will be discussed in Chapter 19), government funding for studies of sexual behavior is still controversial and therefore difficult to obtain.

The controversy surrounding research on human sexual behavior raises the issue of value neutrality (see page 40), which becomes especially delicate when one considers the relationship of sociology to the government. The federal government has become the major source of funding for sociological research. Yet Max Weber urged that sociology remain an autonomous discipline and not become unduly influenced by any one segment of society. According to Weber's ideal of value neutrality, sociologists must remain free to reveal information that is embarrassing to the government, or for that matter, supportive of government institutions.

Initiating Policy

In 1987 the National Institute of Child Health and Human Development sought proposals for a national survey of sexual behavior. Sociologists responded with various plans that a review panel of scientists approved for funding. However, in 1991, the U.S. Senate voted to forbid

funding any survey of adult sexual practices. Despite the vote, sociologists developed the National Health and Social Life Survey (NHSLS) to better understand the sexual practices of adults in the United States. The researchers raised $1.6 million of *private* funding to make their study possible (Laumann et al. 1994a, 1994b).

The authors of the NHSLS believe that their research is important. They argue that data from their survey allow interest groups to more easily address public policy issues such as AIDS, sexual harassment, welfare reform, sex discrimination, abortion, teenage pregnancy, and family planning. Moreover, the research findings help to counter some commonsense notions. For instance, contrary to the popular beliefs that women regularly use abortion for birth control and that poor teens are the most likely socioeconomic group to have abortions, researchers found that three-fourths of all abortions are the first for the woman, and that well-educated and affluent women are more likely to have abortions than poor teens (Sweet 2001).

The usefulness of the NHSLS in addressing public policy issues has proved influential. As Figure 2-6 shows, scholars around the world are now studying human sexual behavior in an effort to reduce the occurrence of HIV/AIDS.

Take the Issue with You

1. Do you see any merit in the position of those who oppose government funding for research on sexual behavior? Explain your reasoning.

2. Exactly how could the results of research on human sexual behavior be used to control sexually transmitted diseases?

3. Compare the issue of value neutrality in government-funded research to the same issue in corporate-funded research. Are concerns about conflict of interest more or less serious in regard to government funding?

FIGURE **2-6**   MEDIAN AGE OF FIRST SEX

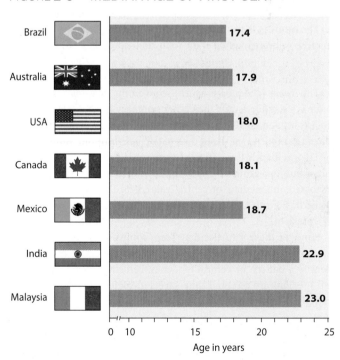

Source: Durex 2007.

APPENDIX | Using Statistics and Graphs

In their effort to better understand social behavior, sociologists rely heavily on numbers and statistics. For example, how have attitudes toward the legalization of marijuana changed over the past 40 years? A quick look at the results of 12 national surveys shows that while support for legalization of the drug has increased, it remains relatively weak (Figure 2-7).

Using Statistics

The most common summary measures used by sociologists are percentages, means, modes, and medians. A **percentage** is a portion of 100. Use of percentages allows us to compare groups of different sizes. For example, if we were comparing financial contributors to a town's Baptist and Roman Catholic churches, the absolute numbers of contributors in each group could be misleading if there were many more Baptists than Catholics in the town. By using percentages, we could obtain a more meaningful comparison, showing the proportion of persons in each group who contribute to churches.

The **mean**, or *average,* is a number calculated by adding a series of values and then dividing by the number of values. For example, to find the mean of the numbers 5, 19, and 27, we add them together (for a total of 51), divide by the number of values (3), and discover that the mean is 17.

The **mode** is the single most common value in a series of scores. Suppose we were looking at the following scores on a 10-point quiz:

10 10 9 9 8 8 7 7 7 6 5

The mode—the most frequent score on the quiz—is 7. While the mode is easier to identify than other summary measures, it tells sociologists little about all the other values. Hence, you will find much less use of the mode in this book than of the mean and the median.

The **median** is the midpoint or number that divides a series of values into two groups of equal numbers of values. For the quiz just discussed, the median, or central value, is 8. The mean, or average, would be 86 (the sum of all scores) divided by 11 (the total number of scores), or 7.8.

Some of these statistics may seem confusing at first. But think how difficult it is to comb through an endless list of numbers to identify a pattern or central tendency. Percentages, means, modes, and medians are essential time-savers in sociological research and analysis.

Reading Graphs

Tables and figures (that is, graphs) allow social scientists to display data and develop their conclusions more easily. In 2010, the Gallup poll interviewed 1,025 people in the United States, age 18 and over. Each respondent was asked, "Do you think the use of marijuana should be made legal, or not?" Without some type of summary, there is no way that analysts could examine the hundreds of individual responses to this question and reach firm conclusions. One type of summary sociologists use, a **cross-tabulation**, shows the relationship between two or more variables. Through the cross-tabulations presented graphically in Figure 2-8, we can quickly see that older people are less likely to favor the legalization of marijuana than younger people, and that women are less supportive of legalization than men.

Graphs, like tables, can be quite useful to sociologists. And illustrations are often easier for the general public to understand, whether in newspapers or in PowerPoint presentations. Still, as with all data, we need to be careful how they are presented.

FIGURE **2-7** CHANGING ATTITUDES TOWARD THE LEGALIZATION OF MARIJUANA

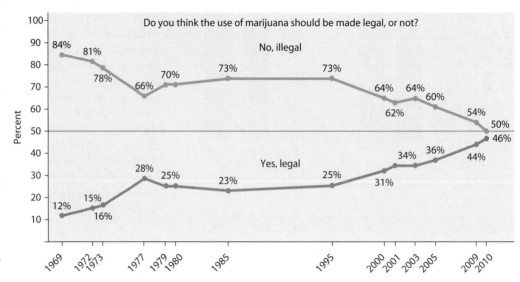

Source: Gallup 2010; see Mendes 2010 in references.

FIGURE **2-8** PEOPLE WHO FAVOR LEGALIZATION OF MARIJUANA BY GENDER AND AGE, 2010

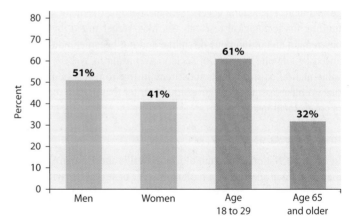

Source: Gallup 2010; see Mendes 2010 in references.

APPENDIX II Writing a Research Report

Let's say you have decided to write a report on cohabitation (unmarried couples living together). How do you go about doing the necessary library research? Students must follow procedures similar to those used by sociologists in conducting original research. For your first step you must define the problem that you wish to study—perhaps in this case, how much cohabitation occurs and what its impact is on later marital happiness. The next step is to review the literature, which generally requires library research.

Finding Information

The following steps will be helpful in finding information:

1. Check this textbook and other textbooks that you own. Don't forget to begin with the materials closest at hand, including the website associated with this textbook, www.mhhe.com/schaefer13e.

2. Use the library catalog. Computerized library systems now access not only the college library's collection but also books and magazines from other libraries, available through interlibrary loans. These systems allow you to search for books by author or title. You can use title searches to locate books by subject as well. For example, if you search the title base for the keyword *cohabitation,* you will learn where books with that word somewhere in the title are located in the library's stacks. Near these books will be other works on cohabitation that may not happen to have that word in the title. You may also want to search other, related keywords, such as *unmarried couples.*

3. Investigate using computerized periodical indexes if they are available in your library. *Sociological Abstracts* online covers most sociological writing since 1963. In 2011, a search of just this one database found more than 2,632 documents having either *cohabitation* or *unmarried couples* as keywords. Some dealt with laws about cohabitation, while others focused on trends in other countries. If you limited your topic to same-sex couples, you would find 301 citations. Other electronic databases cover general-interest periodicals (*Time, Ms., National Review, Atlantic Monthly,* and so forth), reference materials, or newspapers. These electronic systems may be connected to a printer, allowing you to produce a printout complete with bibliographic information, and sometimes even complete copies of articles.

4. Examine government documents. The U.S. government, states and cities, and the United Nations publish information on virtually every subject of interest to social science researchers. Publications of the Census Bureau, for example, include tables showing the number of unmarried couples living together and some social characteristics of those households.

5. Use newspapers. Major newspapers publish indexes annually or even weekly that are useful in locating information about specific events or issues. Lexis-Nexis is an electronic index to U.S. and international newspapers.

6. Ask people, organizations, and agencies concerned with the topic for information and assistance. Be as specific as possible in making requests. You might receive very different information on the issue of cohabitation from talking with marriage counselors and with clergy from different religions.

7. If you run into difficulties, consult the instructor or the reference librarian at your college library.

A word of caution: be extremely careful in using the Internet to do research. Much of the information on the Internet is simply incorrect—even if it looks authoritative, is accompanied by impressive graphics, or has been widely circulated. Unlike the information in a library, which must be screened by a highly qualified librarian, "information" on the Internet can be created and posted by anyone with a computer. Check the sources for the information and note the Web page sponsor. Is the author qualified to write on the subject? Is the author even identified? Is the Web page sponsor likely to be biased? Whenever possible, try to confirm what you have read on the Internet through a well-known, reputable source or organization. If the accuracy of the information could be affected by how old it is, check the date on which the page or article was created or updated. Used intelligently, the Internet is a wonderful tool that offers students access to many of the reliable print sources noted earlier, including government documents and newspaper archives extending back over a century.

Writing the Report

Once you have completed all your research, you can begin writing the report. Here are a few tips:

- Be sure the topic you have chosen is not too broad. You must be able to cover it adequately in a reasonable amount of time and a reasonable number of pages.

- Develop an outline for your report. You should have an introduction and a conclusion that relate to each other, and the discussion should proceed logically throughout the paper. Use headings within the paper if they will improve clarity and organization.

- Do not leave all the writing until the last minute. It is best to write a rough draft, let it sit for a few days, and then take a fresh look before beginning revisions.

- If possible, read your paper aloud. Doing so may be helpful in locating sections or phrases that don't make sense.

Remember that you *must* cite all information you have obtained from other sources, including the Internet. Plagiarism is a serious academic offense, for which the penalties are severe. If you use an author's exact words, it is essential that you place them in quotation marks. Even if you reworked someone else's ideas, you must indicate the source of those ideas.

MASTERING THIS CHAPTER

Summary

Sociologists are committed to the use of the *scientific method* in their research efforts. In this chapter we examined the basic principles of the scientific method and studied various techniques used by sociologists in conducting research.

1. There are five basic steps in the **scientific method:** defining the problem, reviewing the literature, formulating the hypothesis, collecting and analyzing the data, and developing the conclusion.

2. Whenever researchers wish to study abstract concepts, such as intelligence or prejudice, they must develop workable **operational definitions.**

3. A **hypothesis** states a possible relationship between two or more variables.

4. By using a **sample,** sociologists avoid having to test everyone in a population.

5. According to the scientific method, research results must possess both **validity** and **reliability.**

6. An important part of scientific research is devising a plan for collecting data, called a **research design.**

7. The two principal forms of **survey** research are the **interview** and the **questionnaire.**

8. **Ethnography** allows sociologists to study certain behaviors and communities that cannot be investigated through other research methods.

9. When sociologists wish to study a cause-and-effect relationship, they may conduct an **experiment.**

10. Sociologists also make use of existing sources in **secondary analysis** and **content analysis.**

11. The *Code of Ethics* of the American Sociological Association calls for objectivity and integrity in research, confidentiality, and disclosure of all sources of financial support.

12. Max Weber urged sociologists to practice **value neutrality** in their research by ensuring that their personal feelings do not influence their interpretation of data.

13. Technology plays an important role in sociological research, whether it be a computer database or information obtained from the Internet.

14. Despite failure to obtain government funding, researchers developed the National Health and Social Life Survey (NHSLS) to better understand the sexual practices of adults in the United States.

Key Terms

Causal logic The relationship between a condition or variable and a particular consequence, with one event leading to the other. (page 30)

Code of ethics The standards of acceptable behavior developed by and for members of a profession. (38)

Content analysis The systematic coding and objective recording of data, guided by some rationale. (38)

Control group The subjects in an experiment who are not introduced to the independent variable by the researcher. (37)

Control variable A factor that is held constant to test the relative impact of an independent variable. (33)

Correlation A relationship between two variables in which a change in one coincides with a change in the other. (30)

Cross-tabulation A table or matrix that shows the relationship between two or more variables. (44)

Dependent variable The variable in a causal relationship that is subject to the influence of another variable. (30)

Ethnography The study of an entire social setting through extended systematic fieldwork. (36)

Experiment An artificially created situation that allows a researcher to manipulate variables. (37)

Experimental group The subjects in an experiment who are exposed to an independent variable introduced by a researcher. (37)

Hawthorne effect The unintended influence that observers of experiments can have on their subjects. (37)

Hypothesis A speculative statement about the relationship between two or more variables. (30)

Independent variable The variable in a causal relationship that causes or influences a change in another variable. (30)

Interview A face-to-face, telephone, or online questioning of a respondent to obtain desired information. (34)

Mean A number calculated by adding a series of values and then dividing by the number of values. (44)

Median The midpoint or number that divides a series of values into two groups of equal numbers of values. (44)

Mode The single most common value in a series of scores. (44)

Observation A research technique in which an investigator collects information through direct participation by closely watching a group or community. (36)

Operational definition An explanation of an abstract concept that is specific enough to allow a researcher to assess the concept. (29)

Percentage A portion of 100. (29)

Qualitative research Research that relies on what is seen in field or naturalistic settings more than on statistical data. (36)

Quantitative research Research that collects and reports data primarily in numerical form. (36)

Questionnaire A printed or written form used to obtain information from a respondent. (34)

Random sample A sample for which every member of an entire population has the same chance of being selected. (32)

Reliability The extent to which a measure produces consistent results. (32)

Research design A detailed plan or method for obtaining data scientifically. (34)

Sample A selection from a larger population that is statistically representative of that population. (31)

Scientific method A systematic, organized series of steps that ensures maximum objectivity and consistency in researching a problem. (29)

Secondary analysis A variety of research techniques that make use of previously collected and publicly accessible information and data. (37)

Survey A study, generally in the form of an interview or questionnaire, that provides researchers with information about how people think and act. (34)

Validity The degree to which a measure or scale truly reflects the phenomenon under study. (32)

Value neutrality Max Weber's term for objectivity of sociologists in the interpretation of data. (40)

Variable A measurable trait or characteristic that is subject to change under different conditions. (30)

TAKING SOCIOLOGY with you

1. Think about a job you are interested in. How can you see yourself using research techniques—surveys, observation, experiments, or existing sources—in that occupation?

2. How can a sociologist genuinely maintain value neutrality while studying a group that he or she finds repugnant (for example, a White supremacist organization, a satanic cult, or a group of convicted rapists)?

3. New technologies have benefited sociological research by facilitating surveys and statistical analysis. Can you think of any potential drawbacks these new technologies might have for sociological investigation?

Self-Quiz

Read each question carefully and then select the best answer.

1. The first step in any sociological research project is to
   a. collect data.
   b. define the problem.
   c. review previous research.
   d. formulate a hypothesis.

2. An explanation of an abstract concept that is specific enough to allow a researcher to measure the concept is a(n)
   a. hypothesis.
   b. correlation.
   c. operational definition.
   d. variable.

3. The variable hypothesized to cause or influence another is called the
   a. dependent variable.
   b. hypothetical variable.
   c. correlation variable.
   d. independent variable.

4. A correlation exists when
   a. one variable causes something to occur in another variable.
   b. two or more variables are causally related.
   c. a change in one variable coincides with a change in another variable.
   d. a negative relationship exists between two variables.

5. Through which type of research technique does a sociologist ensure that data are statistically representative of the population being studied?
   a. sampling
   b. experiments
   c. ethnography
   d. control variables

6. In order to obtain a random sample, a researcher might
   a. administer a questionnaire to every fifth woman who enters a business office.
   b. examine the attitudes of residents of a city by interviewing every 20th name in the city's telephone book.
   c. study the attitudes of registered Democratic voters by choosing every 10th name found on a city's list of registered Democrats.
   d. do all of the above.

7. A researcher can obtain a higher response rate by using which type of survey?
   a. an interview
   b. a questionnaire
   c. representative samples
   d. ethnographic techniques

8. In the 1930s, William F. Whyte moved into a low-income Italian neighborhood in Boston. For nearly four years, he was a member of the social circle of "corner boys" that he describes in *Street Corner Society*. His goal was to gain greater insight into the community established by these men. What type of research technique did Whyte use?
   a. experiment
   b. survey
   c. secondary analysis
   d. participant observation

9. When sociologists want to study a possible cause-and-effect relationship, they may engage in what kind of research technique?
  a. ethnography
  b. survey research
  c. secondary analysis
  d. experiment

10. Émile Durkheim's statistical analysis of suicide was an example of what kind of research technique?
  a. ethnography
  b. observation research
  c. secondary analysis
  d. experimental research

11. Unlike the typical citizen, the sociologist has a commitment to the use of the _____ method in studying society.

12. A(n) _____ is a speculative statement about the relationship between two or more factors known as variables.

13. _____ refers to the degree to which a measure or scale truly reflects the phenomenon under study.

14. In order to obtain data scientifically, researchers need to select a research _____.

15. If scientists were testing a new type of toothpaste in an experimental setting, they would administer the toothpaste to a(n) _____ group, but not to a(n) _____ group.

16. The term _____ _____ refers to the unintended influence that observers of experiments can have on their subjects.

17. Using census data in a way unintended by its initial collectors would be an example of _____ _____.

18. Using _____ _____, researchers conducted a study of gender-stereotyped behavior in children's coloring books.

19. The American Sociological Association's *Code of* _____ requires sociologists to maintain objectivity and integrity and to preserve the confidentiality of their subjects.

20. As part of their commitment to _____ neutrality, investigators have an ethical obligation to accept research findings even when the data run counter to their personal views or to widely accepted beliefs.

_____

THINKING ABOUT **MOVIES**

And the Band Played On

In the early years of the AIDS crisis, researchers employ the scientific method to understand how the disease is transmitted.

An Inconvenient Truth

In this documentary about global warming, Al Gore argues that certain social groups are already paying the price for climate change.

Kinsey

A researcher struggles with the ethical challenges of studying human sexual behavior.

► INSIDE

In Africa, Maasai tribesmen ride bicycles through Masai Mara National Park in Kenya. Shared learned behavior—what we call culture—can move across international borders to become part of other societies.

" Nacirema culture is characterized by a highly developed market economy which has evolved in a rich natural habitat. While much of the people's time is devoted to economic pursuits, a large part of the fruits of these labors and a considerable portion of the day are spent in ritual activity. The focus of this activity is the human body, the appearance and health of which loom as a dominant concern in the ethos of the people. While such a concern is certainly not unusual, its ceremonial aspects and associated philosophy are unique.

The fundamental belief underlying the whole system appears to be that the human body is ugly and that its natural tendency is to debility and disease. Incarcerated in such a body, man's only hope is to avert these characteristics through the use of the powerful influences of ritual and ceremony. Every household has one or more shrines devoted to this purpose. The more powerful individuals in the society have several shrines in their houses and, in fact, the opulence of a house is often referred to in terms of the number of such ritual centers it possesses. Most houses are of wattle and daub construction, but the shrine rooms of the more wealthy are walled with stone. Poorer families imitate the rich by applying pottery plaques to their shrine walls.

The focal point of the shrine is a box or chest which is built into the wall. In this chest are kept the many charms and magical potions without which no native believes he could live.

While each family has at least one such shrine, the rituals associated with it are not family ceremonies but are private and secret. The rites are normally only discussed with children, and then only during the period when they are being initiated into these mysteries. I was able, however, to establish sufficient rapport with the natives to examine these shrines and to have the rituals described to me.

The focal point of the shrine is a box or chest which is built into the wall. In this chest are kept the many charms and magical potions without which no native believes he could live. These preparations are secured from a variety of specialized practitioners. The most powerful of these are the medicine men, whose assistance must be rewarded with substantial gifts. However, the medicine men do not provide the curative potions for their clients, but decide what the ingredients should be and then write them down in an ancient and secret language. This writing is understood only by the medicine men and by the herbalists who, for another gift, provide the required charm.

The charm is not disposed of after it has served its purpose, but is placed in the charm-box of the household shrine. As these magical materials are specific for certain ills, and the real or imagined maladies of the people are many, the charm-box is usually full to overflowing. The magical packets are so numerous that people forget what their purposes were and fear to use them again. While the natives are very vague on this point, we can only assume that the idea in retaining all the old magical materials is that their presence in the charm-box, before which the body rituals are conducted, will in some way protect the worshipper. "

(*Miner 1956:503–504*) Additional information about this excerpt can be found on the Online Learning Center at www.mhhe.com/schaefer13e.

In this excerpt from his journal article "Body Ritual among the Nacirema," anthropologist Horace Miner casts his observant eye on the intriguing rituals of an exotic culture. If some aspects of this culture seem familiar to you, however, you are right, for what Miner is describing is actually the culture of the United States ("Nacirema" is "American" spelled backward). The "shrine" Miner writes of is the bathroom; he correctly informs us that in this culture, one measure of wealth is how many bathrooms one's home has. In their bathroom rituals, he goes on, the Nacirema use charms and magical potions (beauty products and prescription drugs) obtained from specialized practitioners (such as hair stylists), herbalists (pharmacists), and medicine men (physicians). Using our sociological imaginations, we could update Miner's description of the Nacirema's charms, written in 1956, by adding tooth whiteners, anti-aging creams, Waterpiks, and hair gel.

When we step back and examine a culture thoughtfully and objectively, whether it is our own culture in disguise or another less familiar to us, we learn something new about society. Take Fiji, an island in the Pacific where a robust, nicely rounded body has always been the ideal for both men and women. This is a society in which "You've gained weight" traditionally has been considered a compliment, and "Your legs are skinny," an insult. Yet a recent study shows that for the first time, eating disorders have been showing up among young people in Fiji. What has happened to change their body image? Since the introduction of cable television in 1995, many Fiji islanders, especially young women, have begun to emulate not their mothers and aunts, but the small-waisted stars of television programs currently airing there, like *Grey's Anatomy* and *Desperate Housewives*. Studying culture in places like Fiji, then, sheds light on our society as well (A. Becker 2007; Fiji TV 2010).

In this chapter we will study the development of culture around the world, including the cultural effects of the worldwide trend toward globalization. We will see just how basic the study of culture is to sociology. Our discussion will focus both on general cultural practices found in all societies and on the wide variations that can distinguish one society from another. We will define and explore the major aspects of culture, including language, norms, sanctions, and values. We will see how cultures develop a dominant ideology, and how functionalist and conflict theorists view culture. We'll also see what can happen when a major corporation ignores cultural variations. Then, in the Social Policy section, we will look at the conflicts in cultural values that underlie current debates over bilingualism.

What Is Culture?

Culture is the totality of learned, socially transmitted customs, knowledge, material objects, and behavior. It includes the ideas, values, and artifacts (for example, DVDs, comic books, and birth control devices) of groups of people. Patriotic attachment to the flag of the United States is an aspect of culture, as is a national passion for the tango in Argentina.

Sometimes people refer to a particular person as "very cultured" or to a city as having "lots of culture." That use of the term *culture* is different from our use in this textbook. In sociological terms, culture does not refer solely to the fine arts and refined intellectual taste. It consists of *all* objects and ideas within a society, including slang words, ice-cream cones, and rock music. Sociologists consider both a portrait by Rembrandt and the work of graffiti spray painters to be aspects of culture. A tribe that cultivates soil by hand has just as much culture as a people that relies on computer-operated machinery. Each people has a distinctive culture with its own characteristic ways of gathering and preparing food, constructing homes, structuring the family, and promoting standards of right and wrong.

The fact that you share a similar culture with others helps to define the group or society to which you belong. A fairly large number of people are said to constitute a **society** when they live in the same territory, are relatively independent of people outside their area, and participate in a common culture. Metropolitan Los Angeles is more populous than at least 150 nations, yet sociologists do not consider it a society in its own right. Rather, they see it as part of—and dependent on—the larger society of the United States.

A society is the largest form of human group. It consists of people who share a common heritage and culture. Members of the society learn this culture and transmit it from one generation to the next. They even preserve their distinctive culture through literature, art, video recordings, and other means of expression.

Sociologists have long recognized the many ways in which culture influences human behavior. Through what has been termed a tool kit of habits, skills, and styles, people of a common culture construct their acquisition of knowledge, their interactions with kinfolk, their entrance into the job market—in short, the way in which they live. If it were not for the social transmission of culture, each generation would have to reinvent television, not to mention the wheel (Swidler 1986).

Having a common culture also simplifies many day-to-day interactions. For example, when you buy an airline ticket, you know you don't have to bring along hundreds of dollars in cash. You can pay with a credit card. When you are part of a society, you take for granted many small (as well as more important) cultural patterns. You assume that theaters will provide seats for the

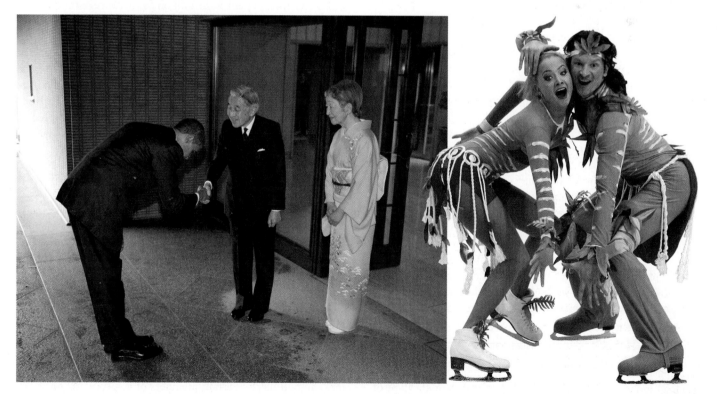

Navigating cultural differences can be a challenge. During a visit to Tokyo, President Obama was criticized for his deep bow to Emperor Akihito. And at the 2010 Winter Olympics, Russian ice dancers Domnina and Shabalin were criticized for their interpretation of Aboriginal dress. Favored to win, they took only third place.

audience, that physicians will not disclose confidential information, and that parents will be careful when crossing the street with young children. All these assumptions reflect basic values, beliefs, and customs of the culture of the United States.

Today, when text, sound, and video can be transmitted around the world instantaneously, some aspects of culture transcend national borders. The German philosopher Theodor Adorno and others have spoken of the worldwide **culture industry** that standardizes the goods and services demanded by consumers. Adorno contends that globally, the primary effect of popular culture is to limit people's choices. Yet others have shown that the culture industry's influence does not always permeate international borders. Sometimes the culture industry is embraced; at other times, soundly rejected (Adorno [1971] 1991:98–106; Horkheimer and Adorno [1944] 2002).

Cultural Universals

All societies have developed certain common practices and beliefs, known as **cultural universals.** Many cultural universals are, in fact, adaptations to meet essential human needs, such as the need for food, shelter, and clothing. Anthropologist George Murdock (1945:124) compiled a list of cultural universals, including athletic sports, cooking, dancing, visiting, personal names, marriage, medicine, religious ritual, funeral ceremonies, sexual restrictions, and trade.

The cultural practices Murdock listed may be universal, but the manner in which they are expressed varies from culture to culture. For example, one society may let its members choose their marriage partners; another may encourage marriages arranged by the parents.

Not only does the expression of cultural universals vary from one society to another; within a society, it may also change dramatically over time. Each generation, and each year for that matter, most human cultures change and expand.

Ethnocentrism

Many everyday statements reflect our attitude that our culture is best. We use terms such as *underdeveloped, backward,* and *primitive* to refer to other societies. What "we" believe is a religion; what "they" believe is superstition and mythology.

It is tempting to evaluate the practices of other cultures on the basis of our perspectives. Sociologist William Graham Sumner (1906) coined the term **ethnocentrism** to refer to the tendency to assume that one's culture and way of life represent the norm or are superior to all others. The ethnocentric person sees his or her group as the center or defining point of culture and view all other cultures as deviations from what is "normal." Westerners who think cattle are to be used for food might look down on India's Hindu religion and culture, which view the cow as sacred. Or people in one culture may dismiss as unthinkable the mate selection or child-rearing practices of another culture. In sum, our view of the world is dramatically influenced by the society in which we were raised.

Conflict theorists point out that ethnocentric value judgments serve to devalue groups and to deny equal opportunities. Functionalists, on the other hand, point out that ethnocentrism serves to maintain a sense of solidarity by promoting group pride. Denigrating other nations and cultures can enhance our patriotic feelings and belief that our way of life is superior. Yet this type of social stability is established at the expense of other peoples. In extreme cases, ethnocentrism can lead to the destruction of an entire culture. Box 3-1 describes several instances of what social scientists have termed *cultural genocide.*

Ethnocentrism is hardly limited to citizens of the United States. Visitors from many African cultures are surprised at the disrespect that children in the United States show their parents. People from India may be repelled by our practice of living in the same household with dogs and cats. Many Islamic fundamentalists in the Arab world and Asia view the United States as corrupt, decadent, and doomed to destruction. All these people may feel comforted by membership in cultures that in their view are superior to ours.

Cultural Relativism

While ethnocentrism means evaluating foreign cultures using the familiar culture of the observer as a standard of correct behavior, **cultural relativism** means viewing people's behavior from the perspective of their own culture. It places a priority on understanding other cultures, rather than dismissing them as "strange" or "exotic." Unlike ethnocentrists, cultural relativists employ the kind of value neutrality in scientific study that Max Weber saw as so important.

Cultural relativism stresses that different social contexts give rise to different norms and values. Thus, we must examine practices such as polygamy, bullfighting, and monarchy within the particular contexts of the cultures in which they are found. Although cultural relativism does not suggest that we must unquestioningly accept every cultural variation, it does require a serious and unbiased effort to evaluate norms, values, and customs in light of their distinctive culture.

Consider the practice of children marrying adults. Most people in North America cannot fathom the idea of a 12-year-old girl marrying. The custom, which is illegal in the United States, is common in West Africa and South Asia. Should the United States respect such marriages? The apparent answer is no. In 2006 the U.S. government spent $623 million to discourage the practice in many of the countries with the highest child-marriage rates (Figure 3-1, page 56).

From the perspective of cultural relativism, we might ask whether one society should spend its resources to dictate the norms of another. However, federal officials have defended the government's actions. They contend that child marriage deprives girls of education, threatens their health, and weakens public health efforts to combat HIV/AIDS (Jain and Kurz 2007; B. Slavin 2007).

Sociobiology and Culture

While sociology emphasizes diversity and change in the expression of culture, another school of thought, sociobiology, stresses the universal aspects of culture. **Sociobiology** is the systematic study of how biology affects human social behavior. Sociobiologists assert that many of the cultural traits humans display, such as the almost universal expectation that women will be nurturers and men will be providers, are not learned but are rooted in our genetic makeup.

Sociobiology is founded on the naturalist Charles Darwin's (1859) theory of evolution. In traveling the world, Darwin had noted small variations in species—in the shape of a bird's beak, for example—from one location to another. He theorized that over hundreds of generations, random variations in genetic makeup had helped certain members of a species to survive in a particular environment. A bird with a differently shaped beak might have been better at gathering seeds than other birds, for

SOCIOLOGY IN THE GLOBAL COMMUNITY

3-1 Cultural Genocide

Usually, the term **genocide** refers to the deliberate, systematic killing of an entire people or nation. However, social scientists have long recognized another form of genocide, called *cultural genocide*, in which a nation's culture is eliminated even though the people live on.

Cultural genocide refers to the systematic destruction of a group's culture. Social scientists have used the term to describe one nation's efforts to suppress another nation's language. Japan's attempt to eliminate the Korean people's language, history, and even

names during its occupation of Korea in the early 20th century is one example. However, the term also applies to government efforts to eliminate indigenous peoples' traditions. Australia, Canada, New Zealand, and the United States illustrate this second form of cultural genocide.

Agents of the U.S. government took American Indian children from their parents' homes and sent them to be raised in families far from their native culture.

In the United States, government officials encouraged White families to "adopt" indigenous children and raise them in the dominant culture. Agents of the U.S. government took American Indian children from their parents' homes and sent them to be raised in families far from their native culture. Sometimes the children were removed with their parents' permission, but often they were taken against their parents' will. Government officials assumed that

the supposed benefit of familiarizing the children with the dominant culture would outweigh and ultimately excuse the personal and cultural losses the children experienced.

Inevitably, the forced removal of generations of American Indian children from their families led to the near extinction of their culture. Only in 1968, following political pressure by Native Americans, did Congress call a halt to the program. Under the Indian Child Welfare Act (ICWA), even if a family agrees to a child's removal from the home, the tribe must also agree. In placing children for adoption and foster care, social workers must give priority first to the child's extended family, then to members of the child's tribe, and finally to all American Indian families.

LET'S DISCUSS

1. Can you imagine being taken from your parents' home by a government agent and moved to a different family with a different culture? How would you react?
2. What might be the long-term consequences of American Indian children's removal from their families, besides the destruction of their culture?

Sources: Cantzler 2008; National Indian Child Welfare Association 2010.

---

instance. In reproducing, these lucky individuals had passed on their advantageous genes to succeeding generations. Eventually, given their advantage in survival, individuals with the variation began to outnumber other members of the species. The species was slowly adapting to its environment. Darwin called this process of adaptation to the environment through random genetic variation *natural selection.*

Sociobiologists apply Darwin's principle of natural selection to the study of social behavior. They assume that particular forms of behavior become genetically linked to a species if they contribute to its fitness to survive (van den Berghe 1978). In its extreme form, sociobiology suggests that *all* behavior is the result of genetic or biological factors, and that social interactions play no role in shaping people's conduct.

Sociobiologists do not seek to describe individual behavior on the level of "Why is Fred more aggressive than Jim?" Rather, they focus on how human nature is affected by the genetic composition of a *group* of people who share certain characteristics (such as men or women, or members of isolated tribal bands). In general, sociobiologists have stressed the basic genetic heritage that *all* humans share and have shown little interest in speculating about alleged differences between racial groups or nationalities. A few researchers have tried to trace specific behaviors, like

criminal activity, to certain genetic markers, but those markers are not deterministic. Family cohesiveness, peer group behavior, and other social factors can override genetic influences on behavior (Guo et al. 2008; E. Wilson 1975, 1978).

Some researchers insist that intellectual interest in sociobiology will only deflect serious study of the more significant influence on human behavior, the social environment. Yet Lois Wladis Hoffman (1985), in her presidential address to the Society for the Psychological Study of Social Issues, argued that sociobiology poses a valuable challenge to social scientists to better document their research. Interactionists, for example, could show how social behavior is not programmed by human biology, but instead adjusts continually to the attitudes and responses of others.

Certainly most social scientists would agree that there is a biological basis for social behavior. But there is less support for the extreme positions taken by certain advocates of sociobiology. Like interactionists, conflict theorists and functionalists believe that people's behavior rather than their genetic structure defines social reality. Conflict theorists fear that the sociobiological approach could be used as an argument against efforts to assist disadvantaged people, such as schoolchildren who are not competing successfully (Freese 2008; Machalek and Martin 2010; E. Wilson 2000).

MAPPING LIFE WORLDWIDE

FIGURE **3-1**   COUNTRIES WITH HIGH CHILD MARRIAGE RATES

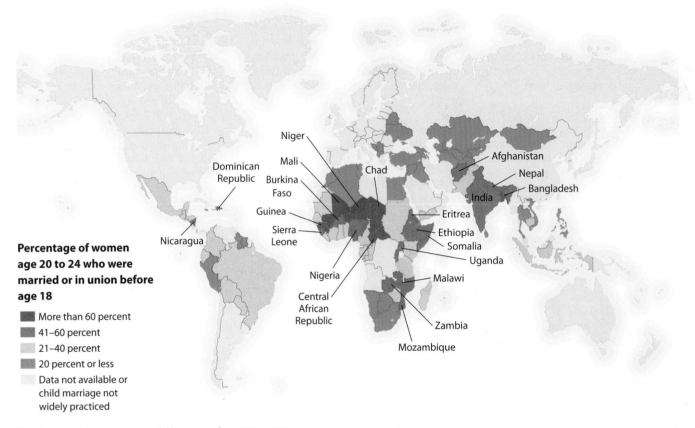

Percentage of women age 20 to 24 who were married or in union before age 18

- More than 60 percent
- 41–60 percent
- 21–40 percent
- 20 percent or less
- Data not available or child marriage not widely practiced

Note: Data are the most recent available, ranging from 1987 to 2006.
Source: UNICEF 2010.
In 21 countries, 40 percent or more of the women under 18 are married.

thinking CRITICALLY

Select three cultural universals from George Murdock's list (page 54) and analyze them from a functionalist perspective. Why are these practices found in every culture? What functions do they serve?

Development of Culture around the World

We've come a long way from our prehistoric heritage. The human species has produced such achievements as the novels of Leo Tolstoy, the art of Pablo Picasso, and the films of Ang Lee. A decade into the new millennium, we can transmit an entire book around the world via the Internet, clone cells, and prolong lives through organ transplants. We can peer into the outermost reaches of the universe or analyze our innermost feelings. In this section we will examine two of the social processes that make these remarkable achievements possible: innovation and the diffusion of culture through globalization and technology.

Innovation

The process of introducing a new idea or object to a culture is known as **innovation.** Innovation interests sociologists because of the social consequences of introducing something new. There are two forms of innovation: discovery and invention. **Discovery** involves making known or sharing the existence of an aspect of reality. The finding of the structure of the DNA molecule and the identification of a new moon of Saturn are both acts of discovery. A significant factor in the process of discovery is the sharing of newfound knowledge with others. In contrast, an **invention** results when existing cultural items are combined into a form that did not exist before. The bow and arrow, the automobile, and the television are all examples of inventions, as are Protestantism and democracy.

use your sociological *imagination*

If you grew up in your parents' generation—without computers, e-mail, MP3 players, and cell phones—how would your daily life differ from the one you lead today?

3-2 Life in the Global Village

Imagine a "borderless world" in which culture, trade, commerce, money, and even people move freely from one place to another. Popular culture is widely shared, whether it be Japanese sushi or U.S. running shoes, and the English speaker who answers questions over the telephone about your credit card account is as likely to be in India or Ireland as in the United States. In this world, even the sovereignty of nations is at risk, challenged by political movements and ideologies that span nations.

What caused this great wave of cultural diffusion? First, sociologists take note of advances in communications technology. Satellite TV, cell phones, the Internet, and the like allow information to flow freely across the world, linking global markets. In 2008, this process reached the point where consumers could view videos on handheld devices and surf the Internet on their wireless cell phones, shopping online at Amazon.com, eBay, and other commercial websites from cars, airports, and cafeterias. Second, corporations in the industrial nations have become multinational, with both factories and markets in developing countries. Business leaders welcome the opportunity to sell consumer goods in populous countries such as China. Third, these multinational firms have cooperated with global financial institutions, organizations, and governments to promote free trade—unrestricted or lightly restricted commerce across national borders.

Globalization is not universally welcomed. Many critics see the dominance of "businesses without borders" as benefiting the rich, particularly the very wealthy in industrial countries, at the expense of the poor in less developed nations. They consider globalization to be a

Even James Bond movies and Taylor Swift may be seen as threats to native cultures.

successor to the imperialism and colonialism that oppressed Third World nations for centuries.

Another criticism of globalization comes from people who feel overwhelmed by global culture. Embedded in the concept of globalization is the notion of the cultural domination of developing nations by more affluent nations. Simply put, people lose their traditional values and begin to identify with the culture of dominant nations. They may discard or neglect their native languages and dress as they attempt to copy the icons of mass-market entertainment and fashion. Even James Bond movies and Taylor Swift may be seen as threats to native cultures, if they dominate the media at the expense of local art forms. As Sembene Ousmane, one of Africa's most prominent writers and filmmakers, noted, "[Today] we are more familiar with European fairy tales than with our own traditional stories" (World Development Forum 1990:4).

Globalization has its positive side, too. Many developing nations are taking their place in the world of commerce and bringing in much needed income. The communications revolution helps people to stay connected and gives them access to knowledge that can improve living standards and even save lives.

LET'S DISCUSS

1. How are you affected by globalization? Which aspects of globalization do you find advantageous and which objectionable?
2. How would you feel if the customs and traditions you grew up with were replaced by the culture or values of another country? How might you try to protect your culture?

Sources: Dodds 2000; Giddens 1991; Hirst and Thompson 1996; D. Martin et al. 2006; Ritzer 2004; Sernau 2001; Tedeschi 2006.

Globalization, Diffusion, and Technology

The recent emergence of Starbucks, the worldwide chain of coffeehouses, is just one illustration of the rapidly escalating trend toward globalization (see Chapter 1). While people in Asia are beginning to enjoy coffee, people in North America are discovering sushi. Some have become familiar with the *bento box,* a small lunchbox that is often used to serve sushi. A trademark Japanese cuisine, sushi has evolved from a once-exotic dish in the United States to a mainstream food commonly found in supermarket refrigerators. Yet its move across the Pacific has changed the delicacy. Americans tend to treat sushi as a take-out or menu item. The authentic way to eat sushi is to sit at a bar and engage the chef in conversation about the day's catch before choosing which fish or shellfish to eat.

More and more cultural expressions and practices are crossing national borders and having an effect on the traditions and customs of the societies exposed to them. Sociologists use the term **diffusion** to refer to the process by which a cultural item spreads from group to group or society to society. Diffusion can occur through a variety of means, among them exploration, military conquest, missionary work, and the influence of the mass media, tourism, and the Internet (Box 3-2). It has also been hastened by the spread of the fast-food restaurant.

Sociologist George Ritzer coined the term *McDonaldization of society* to describe how the principles of fast-food restaurants, developed in the United States, have come to dominate more and more sectors of societies throughout the world (see Chapter 5). For example, hair salons and medical clinics now take walk-ins. In Hong Kong, sex selection clinics offer a menu of items, from fertility enhancement to methods of increasing the likelihood of having a child of the desired sex. And religious groups—from evangelical preachers on local stations or websites to priests at the Vatican Television Center—use marketing techniques similar to those that are used to sell Happy Meals.

The fictional Spider-Man first appeared in comic books in the United States in 1962. Since then, the superhero's image and the legends surrounding him have circled the globe through the process of cultural diffusion. In this photograph, taken at a fairground in Iran, a girl enjoys a Spider-Man ride.

SOCIOLOGY IN THE GLOBAL COMMUNITY

3-3 Cultural Survival in Brazil

When the first Portuguese ships landed on the coast of what we now know as Brazil, more than 2 million people inhabited the vast, mineral-rich land. The natives lived in small, isolated settlements, spoke a variety of languages, and embraced many different cultural traditions.

Today, over five centuries later, Brazil's population has grown to more than 180 million, only about 500,000 of whom are indigenous peoples descended from the original inhabitants. Over 200 different indigenous groups have survived, living a life tied closely to the land and the rivers, just as their ancestors did. But over the past two generations, their numbers have dwindled as booms in mining, logging, oil drilling, and agriculture have encroached on their land and their settlements.

Many indigenous groups were once nomads, moving around from one hunting or fishing ground to another. Now they are hemmed in on the reservations the government confined them to, surrounded by huge farms or ranches whose owners deny their right to live off the land. State officials may insist that laws restrict the development of indigenous lands, but indigenous peoples tell a different story. In Mato Grosso, a heavily forested state near the Amazon River, loggers have been clear-cutting the land at a rate that alarms the Bororo, an indigenous group that has lived in the area for centuries. According to one elder, the Bororo are now confined to six small reservations of about 500 square miles—much less than the area officially granted them in the 19th century.

> *In Mato Grosso, a heavily forested state near the Amazon River, loggers have been clear-cutting the land at a rate that alarms the Bororo.*

In the face of dwindling resources, indigenous groups like the Bororo struggle to maintain their culture. Though the tribe still observes the traditional initiation rites for adolescent boys, members are finding it difficult to continue their hunting and fishing rituals, given the scarcity of game and fish in the area. Pesticides in the runoff from nearby farms have poisoned the water they fish and bathe in, threatening both their health and their culture's survival.

LET'S DISCUSS

1. Compare the frontier in Brazil today to the American West in the 1800s. What similarities do you see?
2. What does society lose when indigenous cultures die?

Sources: Brazier and Hamed 2007; Chu 2005.

McDonaldization is associated with the melding of cultures, through which we see more and more similarities in cultural expression. In Japan, for example, African entrepreneurs have found a thriving market for hip-hop fashions popularized by teens in the United States. Similarly, the familiar Golden Arches of McDonald's can be seen around the world. Yet corporations like McDonald's have had to make some adjustments of their own. Until 2001, McDonald's ran its overseas operations from corporate headquarters in suburban Chicago. After a few false starts, executives recognized the need to develop the restaurant's menus and marketing strategies overseas, relying on advice from local people. Now, at over 3,700 restaurants in Japan, customers can enjoy the Mega Tamago Burger—beef, bacon, and fried egg with special sauces. In India, patrons who don't eat beef can order a double chicken-patty sandwich known as the Maharaja Mac. And in Austria, the locals' love of coffee, cake, and conversation has inspired the McCafé (Hughlett 2008; Ritzer 2002, 2011).

Technology in its many forms has increased the speed of cultural diffusion and broadened the distribution of cultural elements. Sociologist Gerhard Lenski has defined **technology** as "cultural information about the ways in which the material resources of the environment may be used to satisfy human needs and desires" (Nolan and Lenski 2009:357). Today's technological developments no longer await publication in journals with limited circulation. Press conferences, often carried simultaneously on the Internet, trumpet the new developments.

Technology not only accelerates the diffusion of scientific innovations but also transmits culture. The English language and North American culture dominate the Internet and World Wide Web. Such control, or at least dominance, of technology influences the direction of cultural diffusion. For example, websites cover even the most superficial aspects of U.S. culture but offer little information about the pressing issues faced by citizens of other nations. People all over the world find it easier to visit electronic chat rooms about the latest reality TV shows than to learn about their own governments' policies on day care or infant nutrition.

Sociologist William F. Ogburn (1922) made a useful distinction between the elements of *material* and *nonmaterial culture*. **Material culture** refers to the physical or technological aspects of our daily lives, including food, houses, factories, and raw materials. **Nonmaterial culture** refers to ways of using material objects, as well as to customs, beliefs, philosophies, governments, and patterns of communication. Generally, the nonmaterial culture is more resistant to change than the material culture. Consequently, Ogburn introduced the term **culture lag** to refer to the period of maladjustment when the nonmaterial culture is still struggling to adapt to new material conditions. For example, in 2010, manufacturers introduced electronic cigarettes, battery-powered tubes that turn nicotine-laced liquid into a vapor mist. The innovation soon had officials at airlines (which ban smoking) and the Food and Drug Administration scrambling to respond to the latest technology (Kesmodel and Yadron 2010).

Resistance to technological change can lead not only to culture lag, but to some real questions of cultural survival (Box 3-3).

thinking CRITICALLY

Name one culturally significant discovery and one culturally significant invention that occurred in your lifetime. Explain how these innovations have affected the culture to which you belong.

When a society's nonmaterial culture (its values and laws) does not keep pace with rapid changes in its material culture, people experience an awkward period of maladjustment called culture lag. The transition to nuclear power generation that began in the second half of the 20th century brought widespread protests against the new technology, as well as serious accidents that government officials were poorly prepared to deal with. Tensions over the controversial technology have not run as high in some countries as in others, however. France, where this nuclear power plant is situated, generates 78 percent of all its electricity through nuclear power. The technology is not as controversial there as in the United States and Canada, which generate less than 20 percent of their electricity through nuclear reaction.

Cultural Variation

Each culture has a unique character. Inuit tribes in northern Canada, wrapped in furs and dieting on whale blubber, have little in common with farmers in Southeast Asia, who dress for the heat and subsist mainly on the rice they grow in their paddies. Cultures adapt to meet specific sets of circumstances, such as climate, level of technology, population, and geography. Thus, despite the presence of cultural universals such as courtship and religion, great diversity exists among the world's many cultures. Moreover, even *within* a single nation, certain segments of the populace develop cultural patterns that differ from the patterns of the dominant society.

Subcultures

Rodeo riders, residents of a retirement community, workers on an offshore oil rig—all are examples of what sociologists refer to as *subcultures.* A **subculture** is a segment of society that shares a distinctive pattern of customs, rules, and traditions that differs from the pattern of the larger society. In a sense, a subculture can be thought of as a culture existing within a larger, dominant culture. The existence of many subcultures is characteristic of complex societies such as the United States.

Members of a subculture participate in the dominant culture while engaging in unique and distinctive forms of behavior. Frequently, a subculture will develop an **argot,** or specialized language, that distinguishes it from the wider society. Athletes who play *parkour,* an extreme sport that combines forward running with fence leaping and the vaulting of walls, water barriers, and even moving cars, speak an argot they devised especially to describe their feats. Parkour runners talk about doing *King Kong vaults*—diving arms first over a wall or grocery cart and landing in a standing position. They may follow this maneuver with

a *tic tac*—kicking off a wall to overcome some kind of obstacle (Tschorn 2010).

Such argot allows insiders—the members of the subculture—to understand words with special meanings. It also establishes patterns of communication that outsiders can't understand. Sociologists associated with the interactionist perspective emphasize that language and symbols offer a powerful way for a subculture to feel cohesive and maintain its identity.

In India, a new subculture has developed among employees at the international call centers established by multinational corporations. To serve customers in the United States and Europe, the young men and women who work there must be fluent speakers of English. But the corporations that employ them demand more than proficiency in a foreign language; they expect their Indian employees to adopt Western values and work habits, including the grueling pace U.S. workers take for granted. In return they offer perks such as Western-style dinners, dances, and coveted consumer goods. Significantly, they allow employees to take the day off only on U.S. holidays, like Labor Day and Thanksgiving—not on Indian holidays like Diwali, the Hindu festival of lights. While most Indian families are home celebrating, call center employees see only each other; when they have the day off, no one else is free to socialize with them. As a result, these employees have formed a tight-knit subculture based on hard work and a taste for Western luxury goods and leisure-time pursuits.

Another shared characteristic among some employees at Indian call centers is their contempt for the callers they serve. In performing their monotonous, repetitive job day after day, hundreds of thousands of these workers have come to see the faceless Americans they deal with as slow, often rude customers. Such shared understandings underpin this emerging subculture (Bhagat 2007; Gentleman 2006).

Functionalist and conflict theorists agree that variation exists within cultures. Functionalists view subcultures as variations of particular social environments and as evidence that differences can exist within a common culture. However, conflict theorists suggest that variations often reflect the inequality of social arrangements within a society. A conflict theorist would view the challenges to dominant social norms by African

Employees of an international call center in India socialize after their shift has ended. Call center employees, whose odd working hours isolate them from others, tend to form tight-knit subcultures.

American activists, the feminist movement, and the gay rights movement as reflections of inequity based on race, gender, and sexual orientation. Conflict theorists also argue that subcultures sometimes emerge when the dominant society unsuccessfully tries to suppress a practice, such as the use of illegal drugs.

Countercultures

By the end of the 1960s, an extensive subculture had emerged in the United States, composed of young people turned off by a society they believed was too materialistic and technological. This group included primarily political radicals and hippies who had dropped out of mainstream social institutions. These young men and women rejected the pressure to accumulate cars, homes, and an endless array of material goods. Instead, they expressed a desire to live in a culture based on more humanistic values, such as sharing, love, and coexistence with the environment. As a political force, this subculture opposed the United States' involvement in the war in Vietnam and encouraged draft resistance (Flacks 1971; Roszak 1969).

When a subculture conspicuously and deliberately opposes certain aspects of the larger culture, it is known as a **counterculture.** Countercultures typically thrive among the young, who have the least investment in the existing culture. In most cases, a 20-year-old can adjust to new cultural standards more easily than someone who has spent 60 years following the patterns of the dominant culture (Zellner 1995).

In the last decade, counterterrorism experts have become concerned about the growth of ultraconservative militia groups in the United States. Secretive and well armed, members of these countercultural groups tend to be antigovernment, and they often tolerate racism in their midst. Watchdogs estimate that

127 militias are operating in the United States today (Southern Poverty Law Center 2010).

Culture Shock

Anyone who feels disoriented, uncertain, out of place, or even fearful when immersed in an unfamiliar culture may be experiencing **culture shock.** For example, a resident of the United States who visits certain areas in China and wants local meat for dinner may be stunned to learn that the specialty is dog meat. Similarly, someone from a strict Islamic culture may be shocked by the comparatively provocative dress styles and open displays of affection common in the United States and various European cultures.

All of us, to some extent, take for granted the cultural practices of our society. As a result, it can be surprising and even disturbing to realize that other cultures do not follow our way of life. The fact is, customs that seem strange to us may be considered normal and proper in other cultures, which may see our social practices as odd.

use your sociological *imagination*

You arrive in a developing African country as a Peace Corps volunteer. What aspects of a very different culture do you think would be the hardest to adjust to? What might the citizens of that country find shocking about your culture?

Counterculture in uniform. Members of the militia group Ohio Defense Force engage in paramilitary exercises imagining they are destroying a threatening Muslim stronghold in the United States.

Role of Language

Language is one of the major elements of culture that underlie cultural variations. It is also an important component of cultural capital. Recall from Chapter 1 that Pierre Bourdieu used the term *cultural capital* to describe noneconomic assets, such as family background and past educational investments, which are reflected in a person's knowledge of language and the arts.

Members of a society generally share a common language, which facilitates day-to-day exchanges with others. When you ask a hardware store clerk for a flashlight, you don't need to draw a picture of the instrument. You share the same cultural term for a small, portable, battery-operated light. However, if you were in England and needed this item, you would have to ask for an electric torch. Of course, even within the same society, a term can have a number of different meanings. In the United States, *pot* signifies both a container that is used for cooking and an intoxicating drug. In this section we will examine the cultural influence of language, which includes both the written and spoken word and nonverbal communication.

Language: Written and Spoken

Seven thousand languages are spoken in the world today—many more than the number of countries. For the speakers of each one, whether they number 2,000 or 200 million, language is fundamental to their shared culture.

The English language, for example, makes extensive use of words dealing with war. We speak of "conquering" space, "fighting" the "battle" of the budget, "waging war" on drugs, making a "killing" on the stock market, and "bombing" an examination; something monumental or great is "the bomb." An observer from an entirely different and warless culture could gauge the importance that war and the military have had in our lives simply by recognizing the prominence that militaristic terms have in our language. Similarly, the Sami people of northern Norway and Sweden have a rich diversity of terms for snow, ice, and reindeer (Haviland et al. 2008; Magga 2006).

Language is, in fact, the foundation of every culture. **Language** is an abstract system of word meanings and symbols for all aspects of culture. It includes speech, written characters, numerals, symbols, and nonverbal gestures and expressions. Because language is the foundation of every culture, the ability to speak other languages is crucial to intercultural relations. Throughout the Cold War era, beginning in the 1950s and continuing well into the 1970s, the U.S. government encouraged the study of Russian by developing special language schools for diplomats and military advisers who dealt with the Soviet Union. And following September 11, 2001, the nation recognized how few skilled translators it had for Arabic and other languages spoken in Muslim countries. Language quickly became a key not only to tracking potential terrorists, but also to building diplomatic bridges with Muslim countries willing to help in the war against terrorism.

Language does more than simply describe reality; it also serves to *shape* the reality of a culture. For example, most people in the United States cannot easily make the verbal distinctions concerning snow and ice that are possible in the Sami culture. As a result, they are less likely to notice such differences.

The **Sapir-Whorf hypothesis,** named for two linguists, describes the role of language in shaping our interpretation of reality. According to Sapir and Whorf, because people can conceptualize the world only through language, language *precedes* thought. Thus, the word symbols and grammar of a language organize the world for us. The Sapir-Whorf hypothesis also holds that language is not a given. Rather, it is culturally determined, and it encourages a distinctive interpretation of reality by focusing our attention on certain phenomena (Sapir 1929).

For decades, the Navajo have referred to cancer as *lood doo na'dziihii.* Now, through a project funded by the National Cancer Institute, the tribal college is seeking to change the phrase. Why? Literally, the phrase means "the sore that does not heal," and health educators are concerned that tribal members who have been diagnosed with cancer view it as a death sentence. Their effort to change the Navajo language, not easy in itself, is complicated by the Navajo belief that to talk about the disease is to bring it on one's people (Fonseca 2008).

A native speaker trains instructors from the Oneida Nation of New York in the Berlitz method of language teaching. Many Native American tribes are taking steps to recover their seldom-used languages, realizing that language is the essential foundation of any culture. Their efforts are helping to reverse the cultural genocide they endured in the past.

TREND SPOTTING

Linguistic Isolation

In 2006, a severe winter storm hit the northwest United States, knocking out electrical power in many communities. Residents turned on their generators, some without heeding warnings about the risk of carbon monoxide poisoning. Although local media ran public service announcements about the need for adequate ventilation of the generators, six people died and several others fell ill from exposure to carbon monoxide. Investigators later determined that the victims had been unable to understand the English-only warnings. In response to the discovery, the *Seattle Times* took the unprecedented step of publishing the front-page story in six languages: English, Vietnamese, Chinese, Spanish, Russian, and Somali.

Although most immigrants can communicate effectively in English, language does isolate a small percentage of them. Social scientists use the term *linguistic isolation* to refer to households in which all members age 14 and older speak a non-English language and at the same time do not speak English very well. They have found that the proportion of the U.S. population that is linguistically isolated has been increasing steadily, from 3.2 percent in 2000 to 8.6 percent in 2008.

Studies show that those who are linguistically isolated are cut off from many public services. For example, public health professionals find that even after controlling for education and income, members of linguistically isolated households are less likely than others to receive adequate health care, or even to participate in basic health screening. And as the 2006 power outage in the Northwest showed, in some cases linguistic isolation can be deadly.

Similarly, feminists have noted that gender-related language can reflect—although in itself it does not determine—the traditional acceptance of men and women in certain occupations. Each time we use a term such as *mailman, policeman,* or *fireman,* we are implying (especially to young children) that these occupations can be filled only by males. Yet many women work as *mail carriers, police officers,* and *firefighters*—a fact that is being increasingly recognized and legitimized through the use of such non-sexist language.

Language can shape how we see, taste, smell, feel, and hear. It also influences the way we think about the people, ideas, and objects around us. Language communicates a culture's most important norms, values, and sanctions. That's why the decline of an old language or the introduction of a new one is such a sensitive issue in many parts of the world (see the Social Policy section at the end of this chapter).

Using American Sign Language, a form of nonverbal communication, a football coach discusses a play with his team. The Silent Warriors, four-time national champions and the pride of the Alabama School for the Deaf, have defeated both hearing and nonhearing teams.

Nonverbal Communication

If you don't like the way a meeting is going, you might suddenly sit back, fold your arms, and turn down the corners of your mouth. When you see a friend in tears, you may give a quick hug. After winning a big game, you probably high-five your teammates. These are all examples of *nonverbal communication,* the use of gestures, facial expressions, and other visual images to communicate.

We are not born with these expressions. We learn them, just as we learn other forms of language, from people who share our same culture. This statement is as true for the basic expressions of happiness and sadness as it is for more complex emotions, such as shame or distress (Fridlund et al. 1987).

Like other forms of language, nonverbal communication is not the same in all cultures. For example, sociological research done at the micro level documents that people from various cultures differ in the degree to which they touch others during the course of normal social interactions. Even experienced travelers are sometimes caught off guard by these differences. In Saudi Arabia, a middle-aged man may want to hold hands with a partner after closing a business deal. In Egypt, men walk hand in hand in the street; in cafés, they fall asleep while lounging in each other's arms. These gestures, which would shock an American businessman, are considered compliments in those cultures. The meaning of hand signals is another form of nonverbal communication that can differ from one culture to the next. In Australia, the thumbs-up sign is considered rude (Passero 2002; Vaughan 2007).

A related form of communication is the use of symbols to convey meaning to others. **Symbols** are the gestures, objects, and words that form the basis of human communication. The thumbs-up gesture, a gold star sticker, and the smiley face in an e-mail are all symbols. Often deceptively simple, many symbols are rich in meaning and may not convey the same meaning in all social contexts. Around someone's neck, for example, a cross can symbolize religious reverence; over a grave site, a belief in everlasting life; or set in flames, racial hatred.

thinking CRITICALLY

Do you agree with Sapir and Whorf's hypothesis that language precedes thought? What kind of evidence might you cite to refute their hypothesis? Could language shape our interpretation of reality without preceding thought?

Norms and Values

"Wash your hands before dinner." "Thou shalt not kill." "Respect your elders." All societies have ways of encouraging and enforcing what they view as appropriate behavior while discouraging and punishing what they consider to be inappropriate behavior. They also have a collective idea of what is good and desirable in life—or not. In this section we will learn to distinguish between the closely related concepts of norms and values.

Norms

Norms are the established standards of behavior maintained by a society. For a norm to become significant, it must be widely shared and understood. For example, in movie theaters in the United States, we typically expect that people will be quiet while the film is shown. Of course, the application of this norm can vary, depending on the particular film and type of audience. People who are viewing a serious artistic film will be more likely to insist on the norm of silence than those who are watching a slapstick comedy or horror movie.

One persistent social norm in contemporary society is that of heterosexuality. Children are socialized to accept this norm from a very young age. Overwhelmingly, parents describe adult romantic relationships to their children exclusively as heterosexual relationships. That is not necessarily because they consider same-sex relationships unacceptable, but more likely because they see heterosexuality as the norm in marital partnerships. According to a national survey of mothers of three- to six-year-olds, one in five mothers teaches her young children that homosexuality is wrong. The same survey showed that parenting reflects the dominant ideology, in which homosexuality is treated as a rare exception. Most parents assume that their children are heterosexual; only one in four had even considered whether his or her child might grow up to be gay or lesbian (K. Martin 2009).

Types of Norms Sociologists distinguish between norms in two ways. First, norms are classified as either formal or informal. **Formal norms** generally have been written down and specify strict punishments for violators. In the United States, we often formalize norms into laws, which are very precise in defining proper and improper behavior. Sociologist Donald Black (1995) has termed **law** "governmental social control," meaning that laws are formal norms enforced by the state. Laws are just one example of formal norms. The requirements for a college major and the rules of a card game are also considered formal norms.

In contrast, **informal norms** are generally understood but not precisely recorded. Standards of proper dress are a common example of informal norms. Our society has no specific punishment, or *sanction*, for a person who comes to school, say, wearing a monkey suit. Making fun of the nonconforming student is usually the most likely response.

Norms are also classified by their relative importance to society. When classified in this way, they are known as *mores* and *folkways*. **Mores** (pronounced "*MOR*-ays") are norms deemed highly necessary to the welfare of a society, often because they embody the most cherished principles of a people. Each society demands obedience to its mores; violation can lead to severe penalties. Thus, the United States has strong mores against murder, treason, and child abuse, which have been institutionalized into formal norms.

Folkways are norms governing everyday behavior. Folkways play an important role in shaping the daily behavior of members of a culture. Society is less likely to formalize folkways than mores, and their violation raises comparatively little concern. For example, walking up a down escalator in a department store challenges our standards of appropriate behavior, but it will not result in a fine or a jail sentence.

Acceptance of Norms People do not follow norms, whether mores or folkways, in all situations. In some cases, they can evade a norm because they know it is weakly enforced. It is illegal for U.S. teenagers to drink alcoholic beverages, yet drinking by minors is common throughout the nation. (In fact, teenage alcoholism is a serious social problem.)

In some instances, behavior that appears to violate society's norms may actually represent adherence to the norms of a particular group. Teenage drinkers are conforming to the standards of their peer group when they violate norms that condemn underage drinking. Similarly, business executives who use shady accounting techniques may be responding to a corporate culture that demands the maximization of profits at any cost, including the deception of investors and government regulatory agencies.

Norms are violated in some instances because one norm conflicts with another. For example, suppose that you live in an apartment building and one night hear the screams of the woman next door, who is being beaten by her husband. If you decide to intervene by ringing their doorbell or calling the police, you are violating the norm of minding your own business, while following the norm of assisting a victim of violence.

Acceptance of norms is subject to change as the political, economic, and social conditions of a culture are transformed. Until the 1960s, for example, formal norms throughout much of the United States prohibited the marriage of people from different racial groups. Over the past half century, however, such legal prohibitions were cast aside. The process of change can be seen today in the increasing acceptance of single parents and growing support for the legalization of marriage between same-sex couples (see Chapter 14).

When circumstances require the sudden violation of long-standing cultural norms, the change can upset an entire population. In Iraq, where Muslim custom strictly forbids touching by strangers for men and especially for women, the war that began in 2003 has brought numerous daily violations of the norm. Outside important mosques, government offices, and other facilities likely to be targeted by terrorists, visitors must now be patted down and have their bags searched by Iraqi security guards. To reduce the discomfort caused by the procedure, women are searched by female guards and men by male guards. Despite that

use your sociological *imagination*

You are a high school principal. What norms would you want to govern the students' behavior? How might those norms differ from norms appropriate for college students?

thinking CRITICALLY

In the United States, is the norm of heterosexuality a formal norm or an informal norm? Would you categorize it with mores or folkways? Explain your reasoning.

concession, and the fact that many Iraqis admit or even insist on the need for such measures, people still wince at the invasion of their personal privacy. In reaction to the searches, Iraqi women have begun to limit the contents of the bags they carry or simply to leave them at home (Rubin 2003).

Sanctions

Suppose a football coach sends a 12th player onto the field. Imagine a college graduate showing up in shorts for a job interview at a large bank. Or consider a driver who neglects to put any money into a parking meter. These people have violated widely shared and understood norms. So what happens? In each of these situations, the person will receive sanctions if his or her behavior is detected.

Sanctions are penalties and rewards for conduct concerning a social norm. Note that the concept of *reward* is included in this definition. Conformity to a norm can lead to positive sanctions such as a pay raise, a medal, a word of gratitude, or a pat on the back. Negative sanctions include fines, threats, imprisonment, and stares of contempt.

Table 3-1 summarizes the relationship between norms and sanctions. As you can see, the sanctions that are associated with formal norms (which are written down and codified) tend to be formal as well. If a college coach sends too many players onto the field, the team will be penalized 15 yards. The driver who fails to put money in the parking meter will receive a ticket and have to pay a fine. But sanctions for violations of informal norms can vary. The college graduate who goes to the bank interview in shorts will probably lose any chance of getting the job; on the other hand, he or she might be so brilliant that bank officials will overlook the unconventional attire.

The entire fabric of norms and sanctions in a culture reflects that culture's values and priorities. The most cherished values

TABLE **3-1** NORMS AND SANCTIONS

Norms	Sanctions	
	Positive	Negative
Formal	Salary bonus	Demotion
	Testimonial dinner	Firing from a job
	Medal	Jail sentence
	Diploma	Expulsion
Informal	Smile	Frown
	Compliment	Humiliation
	Cheers	Bullying

will be most heavily sanctioned; matters regarded as less critical will carry light and informal sanctions.

Values

Though we each have a personal set of values—which may include caring or fitness or success in business—we also share a general set of values as members of a society. Cultural **values** are these collective conceptions of what is considered good, desirable, and proper—or bad, undesirable, and improper—in a culture. They indicate what people in a given culture prefer as well as what they find important and morally right (or wrong). Values may be specific, such as honoring one's parents and owning a home, or they may be more general, such as health, love, and democracy. Of course, the members of a society do not uniformly share its values. Angry political debates and billboards promoting conflicting causes tell us that much.

In Iraq, a female member of the U.S. Army searches a covered Muslim woman. The searches, which are necessary to prevent terrorist attacks, violate a Muslim norm that forbids touching by strangers.

FIGURE 3-2 LIFE GOALS OF FIRST-YEAR COLLEGE STUDENTS IN THE UNITED STATES, 1966–2010

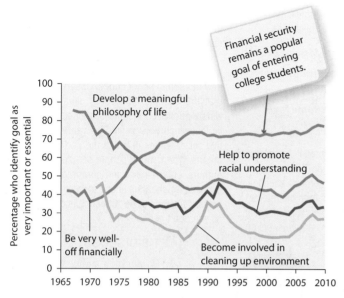

Sources: Pryor et al. 2007, 2010.

Think about It

Why do you think values have shifted among college students in the past few decades? Which of these values is important to you?

Values influence people's behavior and serve as criteria for evaluating the actions of others. The values, norms, and sanctions of a culture are often directly related. For example, if a culture places a high value on the institution of marriage, it may have norms (and strict sanctions) that prohibit the act of adultery or make divorce difficult. If a culture views private property as a basic value, it will probably have stiff laws against theft and vandalism.

The values of a culture may change, but most remain relatively stable during any one person's lifetime. Socially shared, intensely felt values are a fundamental part of our lives in the United States. Sociologist Robin Williams (1970) has offered a list of basic values. It includes achievement, efficiency, material comfort, nationalism, equality, and the supremacy of science and reason over faith. Obviously, not all 309 million people in this country agree on all these values, but such a list serves as a starting point in defining the national character.

Each year more than 200,000 entering college students at nearly 300 of the nation's four-year colleges fill out a questionnaire about their values. Because this survey focuses on an array of issues, beliefs, and life goals, it is commonly cited as a barometer of the nation's values. The respondents are asked what values are personally important to them. Over the past half century, the value of "being very well-off financially" has shown the strongest gain in popularity; the proportion of first-year college students who endorse this value as "essential" or "very important" rose from 42 percent in 1966 to 77.4 percent in 2010 (Figure 3-2).

In contrast, the value that has shown the most striking decline in endorsement by students is "developing a meaningful

philosophy of life." While this value was the most popular in the 1967 survey, endorsed by 85 percent of the respondents, it had fallen to seventh place on the list by 2010, when it was endorsed by less than 47 percent of students entering college.

During the 1980s and 1990s, support for values having to do with money, power, and status grew. At the same time, support for certain values having to do with social awareness and altruism, such as "helping others," declined. According to the 2010 nationwide survey, only 41.6 percent of first-year college students stated that "influencing social values" was an "essential" or "very important" goal. The proportion of students for whom "helping to promote racial understanding" was an essential or very important goal reached a record high of 46 percent in 1992, then fell to 33.8 percent in 2010. Like other aspects of culture, such as language and norms, a nation's values are not necessarily fixed.

Whether the slogan is "Think Green" or "Reduce Your Carbon Footprint," students have been exposed to values associated with environmentalism. How many of them accept those values? Poll results over the past 40 years show fluctuations, with a high of nearly 46 percent of students indicating a desire to become involved in cleaning up the environment. By the 1980s, however, student support for embracing this objective had dropped to around 20 percent or even lower (see Figure 3-2). Even with recent attention to global warming, the proportion remains level at only 27.3 percent of first-year students in 2010.

Recently, cheating has become a hot issue on college campuses. Professors who take advantage of computerized services that can identify plagiarism, such as the search engine Google, have been shocked to learn that many of the papers their students hand in are plagiarized in whole or in part. Box 3-4 examines the shift in values that underlies this decline in academic integrity.

Another value that has begun to change recently, not just among students but among the public in general, is the right to privacy. Americans have always valued their privacy and resented government intrusions into their personal lives. In the aftermath of the terrorist attacks of September 11, 2001, however, many citizens called for greater protection against the threat of terrorism. In response, the U.S. government broadened its surveillance powers and increased its ability to monitor people's behavior without court approval. In 2001, shortly after the attacks, Congress passed the Patriot Act, which empowers the FBI to access individuals' medical, library, student, and phone records without informing them or obtaining a search warrant.

Antiterrorism campaigns, especially efforts to acquire information from suspected terrorists, have fueled debate about yet another value, freedom from torture. In the past few years, the use of torture to obtain information has become controversial around the world. As Figure 3-3 on page 67 shows, public opinion regarding the use of torture varies dramatically from one country to another.

Global Culture War

For almost a generation, public attention in the United States has focused on **culture war,** or the polarization of society over controversial cultural elements. Originally, in the 1990s, the term referred to political debates over heated issues such as abortion, religious expression, gun control, and sexual

SOCIOLOGY ON CAMPUS

3-4 A Culture of Cheating?

On November 21, 2002, after issuing several warnings, officials at the U.S. Naval Academy seized the computers of almost 100 midshipmen suspected of downloading movies and music illegally from the Internet. Officers at the school may have taken the unusually strong action to avoid liability on the part of the U.S. government, which owns the computers students were using. But across the nation, college administrators have been trying to restrain students from downloading pirated entertainment for free. The practice is so widespread, it has been slowing down the high-powered computer networks colleges and universities depend on for research and admissions.

Illegal downloading is just one aspect of the growing problem of copyright violation, both on campus and off. Now that college students can use personal computers to surf the Internet, most do their research online. Apparently, the temptation to cut and paste passages from website postings and pass them off as one's own is irresistible to many.

Surveys done by the Center for Academic Integrity show that from 1999 to 2005, the percentage of students who approved of this type of plagiarism rose from 10 percent to 41 percent. At the same time, the percentage who considered cutting and pasting from the Internet to be a serious form of cheating fell from 68 percent to 23 percent. Perhaps the worst form of Internet plagiarism is the purchase of entire papers from other writers. Increasingly, the websites that sell essays to students are based in other countries, including India, Ukraine, Nigeria, and the Philippines.

The Center for Academic Integrity estimates that at most schools, more than 75 percent of the students engage in some form of cheating.

The Center for Academic Integrity estimates that at most schools, more than 75 percent of the students engage in some form of cheating. Students not only cut passages from the Internet and paste them into their papers without citing the source; they share questions and answers on

exams, collaborate on assignments they are supposed to do independently, and even falsify the results of their laboratory experiments.

To address what they consider an alarming trend, many schools are rewriting or adopting new academic honor codes. Observers contend that the increase in student cheating reflects widely publicized instances of cheating in public life, which have served to create an alternative set of values in which the end justifies the means. When young people see sports heroes, authors, entertainers, and corporate executives exposed for cheating in one form or another, the message seems to be "Cheating is okay, as long as you don't get caught."

LET'S DISCUSS

1. Do you know anyone who has engaged in Internet plagiarism? What about cheating on tests or falsifying laboratory results? If so, how did the person justify these forms of dishonesty?
2. Even if cheaters aren't caught, what negative effects does their academic dishonesty have on them? What effects does it have on students who are honest? Could an entire college or university suffer from students' dishonesty?

Sources: Argetsinger and Krim 2002; Bartlett 2009; Center for Academic Integrity 2006; R. Thomas 2003; Toppo 2011; Zernike 2002.

---

orientation. Soon, however, it took on a global meaning—especially after 9/11, as Americans wondered, "Why do they hate us?" Through 2000, global studies of public opinion had reported favorable views of the United States in countries as diverse as Morocco and Germany. But by 2003, in the wake of the U.S. invasion of Iraq, foreign opinion of the United States had become quite negative (J. Hunter 1991; Kohut et al. 2005, 2007).

In the past 20 years, extensive efforts have been made to compare values in different nations, recognizing the challenges in interpreting value concepts in a similar manner across cultures. Psychologist Shalom Schwartz has measured values in more than 60 countries. Around the world, certain values are widely shared, including benevolence, which is defined as "forgiveness and loyalty." In contrast, power, defined as "control or dominance over people and resources," is a value that is endorsed much less often (Hitlin and Piliavin 2004; S. Schwartz and Bardi 2001).

Despite this evidence of shared values, some scholars have interpreted the terrorism, genocide, wars, and military occupations of the early 21st century as a "clash of civilizations." According to this thesis, cultural and religious identities, rather than national or political loyalties, are becoming the prime source of international conflict. Critics of this thesis point out that conflict over values is nothing new; only our ability to create havoc and violence has grown. Furthermore, speaking of a clash of "civilizations" disguises the sharp divisions that exist within large groups. Christianity, for example, runs the gamut from Quaker-style pacifism to certain elements of the Ku Klux Klan's ideology (Berman 2003; Huntington 1993; Said 2001).

thinking CRITICALLY

Do you believe that the world is experiencing a clash of civilizations rather than of nations, as some scholars assert? Why or why not?

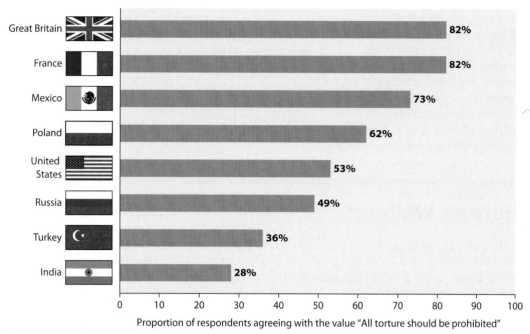

FIGURE **3-3** TORTURE VALUES BY COUNTRY

Country	%
Great Britain	82%
France	82%
Mexico	73%
Poland	62%
United States	53%
Russia	49%
Turkey	36%
India	28%

Proportion of respondents agreeing with the value "All torture should be prohibited"

Source: World Public Opinion 2008.

Culture and the Dominant Ideology

Functionalist and conflict theorists agree that culture and society are mutually supportive, but for different reasons. Functionalists maintain that social stability requires a consensus and the support of society's members; strong central values and common norms provide that support. This view of culture became popular in sociology beginning in the 1950s. It was borrowed from British anthropologists who saw cultural traits as a stabilizing element in a culture. From a functionalist perspective, a cultural trait or practice will persist if it performs functions that society seems to need or contributes to overall social stability and consensus.

Conflict theorists agree that a common culture may exist, but they argue that it serves to maintain the privileges of certain groups. Moreover, while protecting their self-interest, powerful groups may keep others in a subservient position. The term **dominant ideology** describes the set of cultural beliefs and practices that helps to maintain powerful social, economic, and political interests. This concept was first used by Hungarian Marxist Georg Lukacs (1923) and Italian Marxist Antonio Gramsci (1929), but it did not gain an audience in the United States until the early 1970s. In Karl Marx's view, a capitalist society has a dominant ideology that serves the interests of the ruling class.

From a conflict perspective, the dominant ideology has major social significance. Not only do a society's most powerful groups and institutions control wealth and property; even more important, they control the means of producing beliefs about reality through religion, education, and the media. Feminists would also argue that if all a society's most important institutions tell women they should be subservient to men, that dominant ideology will help to control women and keep them in a subordinate position. Table 3-2 summarizes the major sociological perspectives on culture.

A growing number of social scientists believe that it is not easy to identify a core culture in the United States. For support, they point to the lack of consensus on national values, the diffusion of cultural

TABLE **3-2** SOCIOLOGICAL PERSPECTIVES ON CULTURE summing**up**

	Functionalist Perspective	Conflict Perspective	Feminist Perspective	Interactionist Perspective
Cultural Variation	Subcultures serve the interests of subgroups; ethnocentrism reinforces group solidarity	Countercultures question the dominant social order; ethnocentrism devalues groups	Cultural relativism respects variations in the way men and women are viewed in different societies	Customs and traditions are transmitted through inter-group contact and through the media
Norms	Reinforce societal standards	Reinforce patterns of dominance	Reinforce roles of men and women	Are maintained through face-to-face interaction
Values	Are collective conceptions of what is good	May perpetuate social inequality	May perpetuate men's dominance	Are defined and redefined through social interaction
Culture and Society	Culture reflects a society's strong central values	Culture reflects a society's dominant ideology	Culture reflects society's view of men and women	A society's core culture is perpetuated through daily social interactions
Walmart	Provides goods and services to customers	Opposes labor unions; slow to provide employee health benefits, promote women	Limits role of women in leadership	History of insensitivity to cultural variations in store-customer relationships

Chapter 3

traits, the diversity within our culture, and the changing views of young people (look again at Figure 3-2). Yet there is no way of denying that certain expressions of values have greater influence than others, even in as complex a society as the United States.

How one views a culture—whether from an ethnocentric point of view or through the lens of cultural relativism—can have serious consequences in business, as the following case study on Walmart demonstrates. It also has important implications for social policy. Should a nation accommodate non-native-language speakers by sponsoring bilingual programs, for example? We'll take a close look at this controversial issue in the Social Policy section.

thinking CRITICALLY

Look around your campus. Do the people you see suggest that the United States has a core culture with a dominant ideology, or a diverse culture with differing values and ideologies? What about the city or town where your college or university is located—does it suggest the same conclusion?

casestudy Culture at Walmart

By some measures, Walmart is the largest corporation in the world. By other measures, it is the world's 14th largest economy. Indeed, the Bentonville, Arkansas–based retailer's annual revenue—over one-third of a trillion dollars—surpasses the total value of goods and services produced in many countries, such as Sweden.

Walmart's rise to the status of an economic superpower has not been without criticism. To keep prices low, the corporation pays store clerks as little as possible and has determinedly shut out labor organizers who seek to better their wages. Recently, the debate has expanded to include health care benefits. Given Walmart's wage levels, a large proportion of employees simply cannot afford health insurance, even if the corporation offers it. Also, Walmart has been noted for its lack of commitment to equal opportunity: very few women occupy managerial positions at the company (Barbaro 2008).

Although U.S. consumers have embraced Walmart's "everyday low prices," the reaction has not been as positive in countries where consumers hold different cultural values. The company, now located in 15 countries, has not been an unqualified success abroad. Consider the following missteps in three very different countries. In 2006, the company sold all its facilities in South Korea, where its warehouse-style stores were not appreciated by shoppers accustomed to more elegant surroundings. Today,

Walmart is learning not to impose its corporate culture on foreign customers and employees. No longer do managers plan to sell golf clubs in Brazil, where the game is rarely played, or ice skates in Mexico, where skating rinks are hard to find. More important, the corporate giant has begun to study the culture and social patterns of potential customers (Landler and Barbaro 2006; Saporito 2007; Walmart 2010; A. Zimmerman and Nelson 2006).

Walmart also pulled out of Germany, due in part to its failure to adjust to the national culture. German shoppers, accustomed to no-nonsense, impersonal service, found Walmart employees' smiling, outgoing style off-putting. The company's "ten-foot attitude"—a salesperson who comes within 10 feet of a customer must look the person in the eye, greet the person, and ask if he or she needs help—simply did not play well there. Food shoppers, used to bagging their own groceries, were turned off by Walmart's practice of allowing clerks to handle their purchases. Furthermore, German employees, who had grown up in a culture that accepts workplace romances, found the company's prohibition against on-the-job relationships bizarre.

Today, rather than risk another mistake abroad, Walmart is considering buying Massmart, a retailer with 288 existing stores in Africa. Time will tell whether the proposed takeover is welcomed, or Walmart is again rejected as the "Beast of Bentonville," as critics in Germany and South Africa called it (Stewart 2010).

socialpolicy and Culture

Bilingualism

Looking at the Issue

All over the world, nations face the challenge of how to deal with minorities who speak a different language from that of mainstream culture. Because languages know no political boundaries, minority languages are common. In India, for example, Hindi is the most widely spoken language, while English is used widely for official purposes. Yet 18 other languages are officially recognized in this nation of about 1 billion people.

Throughout the world, then, schools must deal with incoming students who speak many languages. **Bilingualism** refers

to the use of two languages in a particular setting, such as the workplace or schoolroom, treating each language as equally legitimate. Thus, a teacher of bilingual education may instruct children in their native language while gradually introducing them to the language of the host society. If the curriculum is also bicultural, children will learn about the mores and folkways of both the dominant culture and the subculture.

To what degree should schools in the United States present the curriculum in a language other than English? This issue has prompted a great deal of debate among educators and

FIGURE **3-4** PERCENTAGE OF PEOPLE WHO SPEAK A LANGUAGE OTHER THAN ENGLISH AT HOME, BY STATE

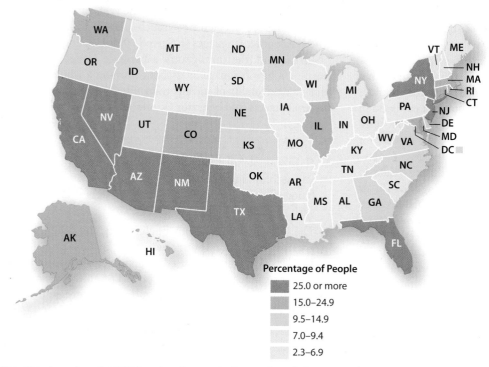

Percentage of People

- 25.0 or more
- 15.0–24.9
- 9.5–14.9
- 7.0–9.4
- 2.3–6.9

Note: Data drawn from the 2009 American Community Survey of people five years and over. National average was 20.0 percent.
Source: American Community Survey 2010:Table R1601.

Recent decades have seen challenges to this pattern of forced obedience to the dominant ideology. Beginning in the 1960s, active movements for Black pride and ethnic pride insisted that people regard the traditions of all racial and ethnic subcultures as legitimate and important. Conflict theorists explain this development as a case of subordinated language minorities seeking opportunities for self-expression. Partly as a result of these challenges, people began to view bilingualism as an asset. It seemed to provide a sensitive way of assisting millions of non-English-speaking people in the United States to *learn* English in order to function more effectively within the society.

The perspective of conflict theory also helps us to understand some of the attacks on bilingual programs. Many of them stem from an ethnocentric point of view, which holds that any deviation from the majority is bad. This attitude tends to be expressed by those who wish to stamp out foreign influence wherever it occurs, especially in our schools. It does not take into account that success in bilingual education may actually have beneficial results, such as decreasing the number of high school dropouts and increasing the number of Hispanics in colleges and universities.

policymakers. According to the Bureau of the Census, 59 million U.S. residents over age five—that's about 20 percent of the population—spoke a language other than English as their primary language at home in 2009 (Figure 3-4). Indeed, 32 other languages are each spoken by at least 200,000 U.S. residents (Shin and Bruno 2003).

Do bilingual programs help the children of these families to learn English? It is difficult to reach firm conclusions because bilingual programs in general vary so widely in their quality and approach. They differ in the length of the transition to English and in how long they allow students to remain in bilingual classrooms. Moreover, results have been mixed. In the years since California effectively dismantled its bilingual education program, reading and math scores of students with limited English proficiency rose dramatically, especially in the lower grades. Yet a major overview of 17 studies, done at Johns Hopkins University, found that students who are offered lessons in both English and their home languages make better progress than similar students who are taught only in English (R. Slavin and Cheung 2003).

Applying Sociology

For a long time, people in the United States demanded conformity to a single language. This demand coincided with the functionalist view that language serves to unify members of a society. Little respect was granted to immigrants' cultural traditions; a young person would often be teased about his or her "funny" name, accent, or style of dress.

Initiating Policy

Bilingualism has policy implications largely in two areas: efforts to maintain language purity and programs to enhance bilingual education. Nations vary dramatically in their tolerance for a variety of languages. China continues to tighten its cultural control over Tibet by extending instruction of Mandarin, a Chinese dialect, from high school into the elementary schools, which will now be bilingual along with Tibetan. In contrast, nearby Singapore establishes English as the medium of instruction but allows students to take their mother tongue as a second language, be it Chinese, Malay, or Tamil.

One bilingual hot spot is Québec, the French-speaking province of Canada. The Québécois, as they are known, represent 83 percent of the province's population, but only 25 percent of Canada's total population. A law implemented in 1978 mandated education in French for all Québec's children except those whose parents or siblings had learned English elsewhere in Canada. While special laws like this one have advanced French in the province, dissatisfied Québécois have tried to form their own separate country. In 1995, the people of Québec indicated their preference of remaining united with Canada by only the narrowest of margins (50.5 percent). Language and language-related cultural areas both unify and divide this nation of 33 million people (*The Economist* 2005b; R. Schaefer 2011).

Policymakers in the United States have been somewhat ambivalent in dealing with the issue of bilingualism. In 1965, the Elementary and Secondary Education Act (ESEA) provided for bilingual, bicultural education. In the 1970s, the federal government took an active role in establishing the proper form for bilingual programs. However, more recently, federal policy has been less supportive of bilingualism, and local school districts have been forced to provide an increased share of funding for their bilingual programs. Yet bilingual programs are an expense that many communities and states are unwilling to pay for and are quick to cut back. In 1998, voters in California approved a proposition that all but eliminated bilingual education: it requires instruction in English for 1.4 million children who are not fluent in the language.

In the United States, repeated efforts have been made to introduce a constitutional amendment declaring English as the nation's official language. As of 2011, 30 states had declared English their official language—an action that is now more symbolic than legislative in its significance.

Public concern over a potential decline in the use of English appears to be overblown. In reality, most immigrants and their offspring quickly become fluent in English and abandon their mother tongue. Nevertheless, many people are impatient with those immigrants who continue to use their mother tongue. The release in 2006 of *"Nuestro Himno,"* the Spanish-language version of the "Star-Spangled Banner," produced a strong public reaction: 69 percent of those who were surveyed on the topic said the anthem should be sung only in English. In reaction against the Spanish version, at least one congressman defiantly sang the national anthem in English—with incorrect lyrics. And the proprietor of a restaurant in Philadelphia posted signs advising patrons that he would accept orders for his famous steak sandwiches only in English. Throughout the year, passions ran high as policymakers debated how much support to afford people who speak other languages (J. Carroll 2006; U.S. English 2010).

In the end, the immigrant's experience is not only about learning a new language. It is about learning a whole new culture—a new totality of socially transmitted customs, knowledge, material objects, and behavior (Viramontes 2007).

Take the Issue with You

1. Have you attended a school with students for whom English is a second language? If so, did the school set up a special bilingual program? Was it effective? What is your opinion of such programs?

2. The ultimate goal of both English-only and bilingual programs is for foreign-born students to become proficient in English. Why should the type of program students attend matter so much to so many people? List all the reasons you can think of for supporting or opposing such programs. What do you see as the primary reason?

3. Besides bilingualism, can you think of another issue that has become controversial recently because of a clash of cultures? If so, analyze the issue from a sociological point of view.

MASTERING THIS CHAPTER

Summary

Culture is the totality of learned, socially transmitted customs, knowledge, material objects, and behavior. This chapter examines social practices common to all cultures, variations that distinguish one culture from another, and the basic elements that make up a culture.

1. A shared culture helps to define the group or **society** to which we belong.

2. Anthropologist George Murdock compiled a list of **cultural universals,** or common practices found in every culture, including marriage, sports, cooking, medicine, and sexual restrictions.

3. People who assume that their culture is superior to others engage in **ethnocentrism.** In contrast, **cultural relativism** is the practice of viewing other people's behavior from the perspective of their own culture.

4. Culture is constantly expanding through the process of **innovation,** which includes both **discovery** and **invention.**

5. **Diffusion**—the spread of cultural items from one place to another—has fostered globalization. Still, people resist ideas that seem too foreign, as well as those they perceive as threatening to their values and beliefs.

6. In a sense, a **subculture** can be thought of as a small culture that exists within a larger, dominant culture. **Countercultures** are subcultures that deliberately oppose aspects of the larger culture.

7. **Language,** an important element of culture, includes speech, written characters, numerals, and **symbols,** as well as gestures and other forms of nonverbal communication. Language both describes culture and shapes it.

8. Sociologists distinguish between **norms** in two ways, classifying them as **formal** or **informal** and as **mores** or **folkways.**

9. The formal norms of a culture will carry the heaviest **sanctions;** informal norms will carry light sanctions.

10. The **dominant ideology** of a culture is the set of cultural beliefs and practices that help to maintain powerful social, economic, and political interests.

11. The social policy of **bilingualism** calls for the use of two languages, treating each as equally legitimate. It is supported by those who want to ease the transition of non-native-language speakers into a host society, but opposed by those who adhere to a single cultural tradition and language.

Key Terms

Argot Specialized language used by members of a group or subculture. (page 59)

Bilingualism The use of two languages in a particular setting, such as the workplace or schoolroom, treating each language as equally legitimate. (68)

Counterculture A subculture that deliberately opposes certain aspects of the larger culture. (60)

Cultural genocide The systematic destruction of a group's culture. (55)

Cultural relativism The viewing of people's behavior from the perspective of their culture. (54)

Cultural universal A common practice or belief found in every culture. (54)

Culture The totality of learned, socially transmitted customs, knowledge, material objects, and behavior. (53)

Culture industry The worldwide media industry that standardizes the goods and services demanded by consumers. (54)

Culture lag A period of maladjustment when the nonmaterial culture is still struggling to adapt to new material conditions. (58)

Culture shock The feeling of surprise and disorientation that people experience when they encounter cultural practices that are different from their own. (60)

Culture war The polarization of society over controversial cultural elements. (65)

Diffusion The process by which a cultural item spreads from group to group or society to society. (57)

Discovery The process of making known or sharing the existence of an aspect of reality. (56)

Dominant ideology A set of cultural beliefs and practices that helps to maintain powerful social, economic, and political interests. (67)

Ethnocentrism The tendency to assume that one's culture and way of life represent the norm or are superior to all others. (54)

Folkway A norm governing everyday behavior whose violation raises comparatively little concern. (63)

Formal norm A norm that has been written down and that specifies strict punishments for violators. (63)

Genocide The deliberate, systematic killing of an entire people or nation. (55)

Informal norm A norm that is generally understood but not precisely recorded. (63)

Innovation The process of introducing a new idea or object to a culture through discovery or invention. (56)

Invention The combination of existing cultural items into a form that did not exist before. (56)

Language An abstract system of word meanings and symbols for all aspects of culture; includes gestures and other nonverbal communication. (61)

Law Governmental social control. (63)

Material culture The physical or technological aspects of our daily lives. (58)

Mores Norms deemed highly necessary to the welfare of a society. (63)

Nonmaterial culture Ways of using material objects, as well as customs, beliefs, philosophies, governments, and patterns of communication. (58)

Norm An established standard of behavior maintained by a society. (62)

Sanction A penalty or reward for conduct concerning a social norm. (64)

Sapir-Whorf hypothesis A hypothesis concerning the role of language in shaping our interpretation of reality. It holds that language is culturally determined. (61)

Society A fairly large number of people who live in the same territory, are relatively independent of people outside their area, and participate in a common culture. (53)

Sociobiology The systematic study of how biology affects human social behavior. (54)

Subculture A segment of society that shares a distinctive pattern of customs, rules, and traditions that differs from the pattern of the larger society. (59)

Symbol A gesture, object, or word that forms the basis of human communication. (62)

Technology Cultural information about the ways in which the material resources of the environment may be used to satisfy human needs and desires. (58)

Value A collective conception of what is considered good, desirable, and proper—or bad, undesirable, and improper—in a culture. (64)

TAKING SOCIOLOGY with you

1. Locate ethnocentrism. For two days, bearing in mind what sociologists mean by *ethnocentrism,* systematically record the places where you see or hear evidence of it.

2. Document a subculture. For two days, record the norms, values, sanctions, and argot evident in a subculture you are familiar with.

3. Analyze popular culture. For two days, record whatever evidence of the dominant culture you see on the Internet or in literature, music, movies, theater, television programs, and sporting events.

Self-Quiz

Read each question carefully and then select the best answer.

1. Which of the following is an aspect of culture?
   a. a comic book
   b. the patriotic attachment to the flag of the United States
   c. slang words
   d. all of the above

2. People's adaptations to meet the needs for food, shelter, and clothing are examples of what George Murdock referred to as
   a. norms.
   b. folkways.
   c. cultural universals.
   d. cultural practices.

3. What term do sociologists use to refer to the process by which a cultural item spreads from group to group or society to society?
    a. diffusion
    b. globalization
    c. innovation
    d. cultural relativism

4. The appearance of Starbucks coffeehouses in China is a sign of what aspect of culture?
    a. innovation
    b. globalization
    c. diffusion
    d. cultural relativism

5. Which of the following statements is true according to the Sapir-Whorf hypothesis?
    a. Language simply describes reality.
    b. Language does not transmit stereotypes related to race.
    c. Language precedes thought.
    d. Language is not an example of a cultural universal.

6. Which of the following statements about norms is correct?
    a. People do not follow norms in all situations. In some cases, they evade a norm because they know it is weakly enforced.
    b. In some instances, behavior that appears to violate society's norms may actually represent adherence to the norms of a particular group.
    c. Norms are violated in some instances because one norm conflicts with another.
    d. all of the above

7. Which of the following statements about values is correct?
    a. Values never change.
    b. The values of a culture may change, but most remain relatively stable during any one person's lifetime.
    c. Values are constantly changing; sociologists view them as being very unstable.
    d. all of the above

8. Which of the following terms describes the set of cultural beliefs and practices that help to maintain powerful social, economic, and political interests?
    a. mores
    b. dominant ideology
    c. consensus
    d. values

9. Terrorist groups are examples of
    a. cultural universals.
    b. subcultures.
    c. countercultures.
    d. dominant ideologies.

10. What is the term used when one places a priority on understanding other cultures, rather than dismissing them as "strange" or "exotic"?
    a. ethnocentrism
    b. culture shock
    c. cultural relativism
    d. cultural value

11. _____ are gestures, objects, and/or words that form the basis of human communication.

12. _____ is the process of introducing a new idea or object to a culture.

13. The bow and arrow, the automobile, and the television are all examples of _____ .

14. Sociologists associated with the _____ perspective emphasize that language and symbols offer a powerful way for a subculture to maintain its identity.

15. "Put on some clean clothes for dinner" and "Thou shalt not kill" are both examples of _____ found in U.S. culture.

16. The United States has strong _____ against murder, treason, and other forms of abuse that have been institutionalized into formal norms.

17. From a(n) _____ perspective, the dominant ideology has major social significance. Not only do a society's most powerful groups and institutions control wealth and property; more important, they control the means of production.

18. Countercultures (e.g., hippies) are typically popular among the _____, who have the least investment in the existing culture.

19. A person experiences _____ when he or she feels disoriented, uncertain, out of place, even fearful when immersed in an unfamiliar culture.

20. From the _____ perspective, enthocentrism serves to maintain a sense of solidarity by promoting group pride.

THINKING ABOUT MOVIES

Smoke Signals

Members of the Coeur d'Alene Indian tribe hold to their own norms and values.

Sugar

A baseball player from the Dominican Republic copes with culture shock after being drafted into the U.S. Major Leagues.

The Wrestler

Through his sport's subculture, a professional wrestler who has passed his prime travels away from the mainstream.

A *father teaches* his daughter to ride a bike. Around the world, the family is the most important agent of socialization.

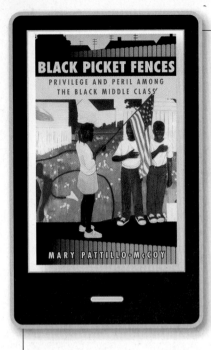

BLACK PICKET FENCES

PRIVILEGE AND PERIL AMONG THE BLACK MIDDLE CLASS

MARY PATTILLO-McCOY

" Charisse . . . is sixteen and lives with her mother and younger sister, Deanne, across the street from St. Mary's Catholic Church and School. Charisse's mother is a personnel assistant at a Chicago university, and is taking classes there to get her bachelor's degree. Mr. Baker is a Chicago firefighter. While her father and mother are separated, Charisse sees her father many times a week at the afterschool basketball hour that he supervises at St. Mary's gym. He and Charisse's mother are on very good terms, and Charisse has a loving relationship with both parents. Mr. Baker is as active as any parent could be, attending the father/daughter dances at Charisse's high school, never missing a big performance, and visiting his daughters often.

Charisse and her sister are being raised by the neighborhood family in addition to their biological parents. "We [are] real close. Like all our neighbors know us because my dad grew up over here. Since the '60s." Charisse is a third-generation Grovelandite just like Neisha Morris. Her grandparents moved into Groveland with Charisse's then-teenage father when the neighborhood first opened to African Americans. . . . Now Charisse is benefiting from the friends her family has made over their years of residence in Groveland, especially the members of St. Mary's church, who play the role of surrogate parents. When Charisse was in elementary school at St. Mary's, her late paternal grandmother was the school secretary, and so the Baker girls were always under the watchful eye of their grandmother as well as the staff, who were their grandmother's friends. And in the evenings Charisse's mother would bring her and her sister to choir practice, where they accumulated an ensemble of mothers and fathers.

After St. Mary's elementary school, Charisse went on to St. Agnes Catholic High School for girls, her father's choice. St. Agnes is located in a suburb of Chicago and is a solid, integrated Catholic school where 100 percent of the girls graduate and over 95 percent go on to college. . . .

Most of Charisse's close friends went to St. Mary's and now go to St. Agnes with her, but her choice of boyfriends shows modest signs of rebellion. . . . Many of Charisse's male interests are older than she, and irregularly employed—although some are in and out of school. She meets many of them hanging out at the mall. One evening, members of the church's youth choir sat around talking about their relationships. Charisse cooed while talking about her present boyfriend, who had just graduated from high school but did not have a job and was uncertain about his future. But in the middle of that thought, Charisse spontaneously changed her attentions to a new young man that she had just met. "Charisse changes boyfriends like she changes her clothes," her sister joked, indicating the impetuous nature of adolescent relationships.

While these young men are not in gangs or selling drugs, many of them do not seem to share Charisse's strong career goals and diligence in attaining them. Some of them would not gain the approval of her parents. However, this full list of boyfriends has not clouded Charisse's focus. "

Charisse is a third-generation Grovelandite just like Neisha Morris. Her grandparents moved into Groveland with Charisse's then-teenage father when the neighborhood first opened to African Americans.

(Pattillo-McCoy 1999:100–102) Additional information about this excerpt can be found on the Online Learning Center at www.mhhe.com/schaefer13e.

This excerpt from *Black Picket Fences: Privilege and Peril among the Black Middle Class* describes the upbringing of a young resident of Groveland, a close-knit African American community in Chicago. The author, sociologist Mary Pattillo-McCoy, became acquainted with Charisse while living in the Groveland neighborhood, where she was doing ethnographic research. Charisse's childhood is similar to that of other youths in many respects. Regardless of race or social class, a young person's development involves a host of influences, from parents, grandparents, and siblings to friends and classmates, teachers and school administrators, neighbors and churchgoers—even youths who frequent the local mall. Yet in some ways, Charisse's development is specifically influenced by her race and social class. Contact with family and community members, for instance, has undoubtedly prepared her to deal with prejudice and the scarcity of positive images of African Americans in the media (W. Wilson et al. 2006).

Sociologists, in general, are interested in the patterns of behavior and attitudes that emerge *throughout* the life course, from infancy to old age. These patterns are part of the lifelong process of **socialization**, in which people learn the attitudes, values, and behaviors appropriate for members of a particular culture. Socialization occurs through human interactions that begin in infancy and continue through retirement. We learn a great deal from those people most important in our lives—immediate family members, best friends, and teachers. But we also learn from people we see on the street, on television, on the Internet, and in films and magazines. From a microsociological perspective, socialization helps us to discover how to behave "properly" and what to expect from others if we follow (or challenge) society's norms and values. From a macrosociological perspective, socialization provides for the transmission of a culture from one generation to the next and thereby for the long-term continuance of a society.

Socialization also shapes our self-images. For example, in the United States, a person who is viewed as "too heavy" or "too short" does not conform to the ideal cultural standard of physical attractiveness. This kind of unfavorable evaluation can significantly influence the person's self-esteem. In this sense, socialization experiences can help to shape our personalities. In everyday speech, the term **personality** is used to refer to a person's typical patterns of attitudes, needs, characteristics, and behavior.

How much of a person's personality is shaped by culture, as opposed to inborn traits? In what ways does socialization continue

into adulthood? Who are the most powerful agents of socialization? In this chapter we will examine the role of socialization in human development. We will begin by analyzing the interaction of heredity with environmental factors. We will pay particular attention to how people develop perceptions, feelings, and beliefs about themselves. The chapter will also explore the lifelong nature of the socialization process, as well as important agents of socialization, among them the family, schools, peers, the media, and technology. Finally, the Social Policy section will focus on the socialization experience of group child care for young children.

The Role of Socialization

What makes us who we are? Is it the genes we are born with, or the environment in which we grow up? Researchers have traditionally clashed over the relative importance of biological inheritance and environmental factors in human development—a conflict called the *nature versus nurture* (or *heredity versus environment*) debate. Today, most social scientists have moved beyond this debate, acknowledging instead the *interaction* of these variables in shaping human development. However, we can better appreciate how heredity and environmental factors interact and influence the socialization process if we first examine situations in which one factor operates almost entirely without the other (Homans 1979).

Social Environment: The Impact of Isolation

In the 1994 movie *Nell*, Jodie Foster played a young woman hidden from birth by her mother in a backwoods cabin. Raised without normal human contact, Nell crouches like an animal, screams wildly, and speaks or sings in a language all her own. This movie was drawn from the actual account of an emaciated 16-year-old boy who appeared mysteriously in 1828 in the town square of Nuremberg, Germany (Lipson 1994).

Isabelle and Genie: Two Cases Some viewers may have found the story of Nell difficult to believe, but the painful childhood of Isabelle was all too real. For the first six years of her life, Isabelle lived in almost total seclusion in a darkened room. She had little contact with other people, with the exception of her mother, who could neither speak nor hear. Isabelle's mother's parents had been so deeply ashamed of Isabelle's illegitimate birth that they kept her hidden away from the world. Ohio authorities finally discovered the child in 1938, when Isabelle's mother escaped from her parents' home, taking her daughter with her.

When she was discovered at age six, Isabelle could not speak; she could merely make various croaking sounds. Her only communications with her mother were simple gestures. Isabelle had been largely deprived of the typical interactions and socialization experiences of childhood. Since she had seen few people, she showed a strong fear of strangers and reacted almost like a wild animal when confronted with an unfamiliar person. As she became accustomed to seeing certain individuals, her reaction changed to one of extreme apathy. At first, observers believed that Isabelle was deaf, but she soon began to react to nearby sounds. On tests of maturity, she scored at the level of an infant rather than a six-year-old.

Specialists developed a systematic training program to help Isabelle adapt to human relationships and socialization. After a few days of training, she made her first attempt to verbalize. Although she started slowly, Isabelle quickly passed through six years of development. In a little over two months she was speaking in complete sentences. Nine months later she could identify both words and sentences. Before Isabelle reached age nine, she was ready to attend school with other children. By age 14 she was in sixth grade, doing well in school, and emotionally well adjusted.

Yet without an opportunity to experience socialization in her first six years, Isabelle had been hardly human in the social sense when she was first discovered. Her inability to communicate at the time of her discovery—despite her physical and cognitive potential to learn—and her remarkable progress over the next few years underscore the impact of socialization on human development (K. Davis 1940, 1947).

Unfortunately, other children who have been locked away or severely neglected have not fared so well as Isabelle. In many instances, the consequences of social isolation have proved much more damaging. For example, in 1970 a 14-year-old Californian named Genie was discovered in a room where she had been confined since age 20 months. During her years of isolation, no family member had spoken to her, nor could she hear anything other than swearing. Since there was no television or radio in her home, she had never heard the sounds of normal human speech. One year after beginning extensive therapy, Genie's grammar resembled that of a typical 18-month-old. Though she made further advances with continued therapy, she never achieved full language ability. Today Genie, now in her late 50s, lives in a home for developmentally disabled adults. Figure 4-1 shows a sketch Genie made of her teacher five years after she was discovered (Curtiss 1977, 1985; W. Johnson 2009; Rymer 1993).

Isabelle's and Genie's experiences are important to researchers because there are only a few cases of children reared in total isolation. Unfortunately, however, there are many cases of children raised in extremely neglectful social circumstances. In the 1990s, public attention focused on infants and young children from orphanages in the formerly communist countries of Eastern Europe. In Romanian orphanages, babies once lay in their cribs for 18 to 20 hours a day, curled against their feeding bottles and receiving little adult care. Such minimal attention continued for the first five years of their lives. Many of them were fearful of human contact and prone to unpredictable antisocial behavior.

This situation came to light as families in North America and Europe began adopting thousands of the children. The adjustment

This sketch was made in 1975 by Genie—a girl who had been isolated for most of her 14 years, until she was discovered by authorities in 1970. In her drawing, her linguist friend (on the left) plays the piano while Genie listens. Genie was 18 when she drew this picture.
Source: Curtiss 1977:274.

problems for about 20 percent of them were often so dramatic that the adopting families suffered guilty fears of being ill-fit adoptive parents. Many of them have asked for assistance in dealing with the children. Slowly, efforts are being made to introduce the deprived youngsters to feelings of attachment that they have never experienced before (Groza et al. 1999; Craig Smith 2006).

Increasingly, researchers are emphasizing the importance of the earliest socialization experiences for children who grow up in more normal environments. We now know that it is not enough to care for an infant's physical needs; parents must also concern themselves with children's social development. If, for example, children are discouraged from having friends even as

toddlers, they will miss out on social interactions with peers that are critical for emotional growth.

Primate Studies Studies of animals raised in isolation also support the importance of socialization in development. Harry Harlow (1971), a researcher at the primate laboratory of the University of Wisconsin, conducted tests with rhesus monkeys that had been raised away from their mothers and away from contact with other monkeys. As was the case with Isabelle, the rhesus monkeys raised in isolation were fearful and easily frightened. They did not mate, and the females who were artificially inseminated became abusive mothers. Apparently, isolation had had a damaging effect on the monkeys.

A creative aspect of Harlow's experimentation was his use of "artificial mothers." In one such experiment, Harlow presented monkeys raised in isolation with two substitute mothers—one cloth-covered replica and one covered with wire that had the ability to offer milk. Monkey after monkey went to the wire mother for the life-giving milk, yet spent much more time clinging to the more motherlike cloth model. It appears that the infant monkeys developed greater social attachments from their need for warmth, comfort, and intimacy than from their need for milk.

While the isolation studies just discussed may seem to suggest that heredity can be dismissed as a factor in the social development of humans and animals, studies of twins provide insight into a fascinating interplay between hereditary and environmental factors.

use your sociological *imagination*

What events in your life have had a strong influence on who you are?

The Influence of Heredity

Identical twins Oskar Stohr and Jack Yufe were separated soon after their birth and raised on different continents, in very different cultural

Despite the striking physical resemblance between these identical twins, there are undoubtedly many differences between them. Research points to some behavioral similarities between twins, but little beyond the likenesses found among nontwin siblings.

settings. Oskar was reared as a strict Catholic by his maternal grandmother in the Sudetenland of Czechoslovakia. As a member of the Hitler Youth movement in Nazi Germany, he learned to hate Jews. In contrast, his brother Jack was reared in Trinidad by the twins' Jewish father. Jack joined an Israeli kibbutz (a collective settlement) at age 17 and later served in the Israeli army. When the twins were reunited in middle age, however, some startling similarities emerged: They both wore wire-rimmed glasses and mustaches. They both liked spicy foods and sweet liqueurs, were absentminded, flushed the toilet before using it, stored rubber bands on their wrists, and dipped buttered toast in their coffee (Holden 1980).

The twins also differed in many important respects: Jack was a workaholic; Oskar enjoyed leisure-time activities. Oskar was a traditionalist who was domineering toward women; Jack was a political liberal who was much more accepting of feminism. Finally, Jack was extremely proud of being Jewish, whereas Oskar never mentioned his Jewish heritage (Holden 1987).

Oskar and Jack are prime examples of the interplay of heredity and environment. For a number of years, the Minnesota Twin Family Study has been following pairs of identical twins reared apart to determine what similarities, if any, they show in personality traits, behavior, and intelligence. Preliminary results from the available twin studies indicate that *both* genetic factors *and* socialization experiences are influential in human development. Certain characteristics, such as temperaments, voice patterns, and nervous

habits, appear to be strikingly similar even in twins reared apart, suggesting that these qualities may be linked to hereditary causes. However, identical twins reared apart differ far more in their attitudes, values, chosen mates, and even drinking habits; these qualities, it would seem, are influenced by environmental factors. In examining clusters of personality traits among such twins, researchers have found marked similarities in their tendency toward leadership or dominance, but significant differences in their need for intimacy, comfort, and assistance.

Researchers have also been impressed with the similar scores on intelligence tests of twins reared apart in *roughly similar* social settings. Most of the identical twins register scores even closer than those that would be expected if the same person took a test twice. At the same time, however, identical twins brought up in *dramatically different* social environments score quite differently on intelligence tests—a finding that supports the impact of socialization on human development (Joseph 2004; Kronstadt 2008a; McGue and Bouchard 1998; Minnesota Center for Twin and Family Research 2010).

We need to be cautious in reviewing studies of twin pairs and other relevant research. Widely broadcast findings have often been based on preliminary analysis of extremely small samples. For example, one study (not involving twin pairs) was frequently cited as confirming genetic links with behavior. Yet the researchers had to retract their conclusions after they increased the sample and reclassified two of the original cases. After those changes, the initial findings were no longer valid.

Critics add that studies of twin pairs have not provided satisfactory information concerning the extent to which separated identical twins may have had contact with each other, even though they were raised apart. Such interactions—especially if

TREND SPOTTING

Multiple Births

The birth of identical twins or triplets is a rare event—only about 1 in every 250 births. Recently, however, multiple births have increased dramatically. There is some evidence that fertility treatments may be contributing to the increase, as they did with Kate and Jon Gosselin's sextuplets, born in 2004, and the Suleman octuplets, born in 2009. However, multiple births in general seem to be on the rise. Over the quarter century from 1980 to 2006, the birthrate for triplets and other multiples, identical or not, increased more than fourfold, from 37 to 153 of every 100,000 births.

they were extensive—could call into question the validity of the twin studies. As this debate continues, we can certainly anticipate numerous efforts to replicate the research and clarify the interplay between heredity and environmental factors in human development (Horgan 1993; Plomin 1989).

thinking CRITICALLY

What might be some ethical concerns regarding research on environmental influences on people's behavior?

The Self and Socialization

We all have various perceptions, feelings, and beliefs about who we are and what we are like. How do we come to develop them? Do they change as we age?

We were not born with these understandings. Building on the work of George Herbert Mead (1964b), sociologists recognize that our concept of who we are, the *self,* emerges as we interact with others. The **self** is a distinct identity that sets us apart from others. It is not a static phenomenon, but continues to develop and change throughout our lives.

Sociologists and psychologists alike have expressed interest in how the individual develops and modifies the sense of self as a result of social interaction. The work of sociologists Charles Horton Cooley and George Herbert Mead, pioneers of the interactionist approach, has been especially useful in furthering our understanding of these important issues.

Sociological Approaches to the Self

Cooley: Looking-Glass Self In the early 1900s, Charles Horton Cooley advanced the belief that we learn who we are by interacting with others. Our view of ourselves, then, comes not only from direct contemplation of our personal qualities but also from our impressions of how others perceive us. Cooley used the phrase **looking-glass self** to emphasize that the self is the product of our social interactions.

The process of developing a self-identity or self-concept has three phases. First, we imagine how we present ourselves to others—to relatives, friends, even strangers on the street. Then we imagine how others evaluate us (attractive, intelligent, shy, or strange). Finally, we develop some sort of feeling about ourselves, such as respect or shame, as a result of these impressions (Cooley 1902; M. Howard 1989).

A subtle but critical aspect of Cooley's looking-glass self is that the self results from an individual's "imagination" of how others view him or her. As a result, we can develop self-identities based on *incorrect* perceptions of how others see us. A student may react strongly to a teacher's criticism and decide (wrongly) that the instructor views the student as stupid. This misperception may be converted into a negative

self-identity through the following process: (1) the teacher criticized me, (2) the teacher must think that I'm stupid, (3) I *am* stupid. Yet self-identities are also subject to change. If the student receives an A at the end of the course, he or she will probably no longer feel stupid.

Mead: Stages of the Self George Herbert Mead continued Cooley's exploration of interactionist theory. Mead (1934, 1964a) developed a useful model of the process by which the self emerges, defined by three distinct stages: the preparatory stage, the play stage, and the game stage.

The Preparatory Stage During the *preparatory stage,* children merely imitate the people around them, especially family members with whom they continually interact. Thus, a small child will bang on a piece of wood while a parent is engaged in carpentry work, or will try to throw a ball if an older sibling is doing so nearby.

As they grow older, children become more adept at using symbols, including the gestures and words that form the basis of human communication. By interacting with relatives and friends, as well as by watching cartoons on television and looking at picture books, children in the preparatory stage begin to understand symbols. They will continue to use this form of communication throughout their lives.

The Play Stage Mead was among the first to analyze the relationship of symbols to socialization. As children develop skill in communicating through symbols, they gradually become more aware of social relationships. As a result, during the play stage, they begin to pretend to be other people. Just as an actor "becomes" a character, a child becomes a doctor, parent, superhero, or ship captain.

Mead, in fact, noted that an important aspect of the play stage is role-playing. **Role taking** is the process of mentally assuming the perspective of another and responding from that imagined viewpoint. For example, through this process a young child will gradually learn when it is best to ask a parent for favors. If the parent usually comes home from work in a bad mood, the child will wait until after dinner, when the parent is more relaxed and approachable.

Children imitate the people around them, especially family members they continually interact with, during the *preparatory* stage described by George Herbert Mead.

TABLE **4-1** MEAD'S STAGES OF THE SELF summing**up** 81

Socialization

Stage	Self Present?	Definition	Example
Preparation	No	Child imitates the actions of others.	When adults laugh and smile, child laughs and smiles.
Play	Developing	Child takes the role of a single other, as if he or she were the other.	Child first takes the role of doctor, then the role of patient.
Game	Yes	Child considers the roles of two or more others simultaneously.	In game of hide-and-seek, child takes into account the roles of both hider and seeker.

The Game Stage   In Mead's third stage, the *game stage,* the child of about age eight or nine no longer just plays roles but begins to consider several tasks and relationships simultaneously. At this point in development, children grasp not only their own social positions but also those of others around them—just as in a football game the players must understand their own and everyone else's positions. Consider a girl or boy who is part of a scout troop out on a weekend hike in the mountains. The child must understand what he or she is expected to do but must also recognize the responsibilities of other scouts as well as the leaders. This is the final stage of development under Mead's model; the child can now respond to numerous members of the social environment.

Mead uses the term **generalized other** to refer to the attitudes, viewpoints, and expectations of society as a whole that a child takes into account in his or her behavior. Simply put, this concept suggests that when an individual acts, he or she takes into account an entire group of people. For example, a child will not act courteously merely to please a particular parent. Rather, the child comes to understand that courtesy is a widespread social value endorsed by parents, teachers, and religious leaders.

Table 4-1 summarizes the three stages of self outlined by George Herbert Mead.

Mead: Theory of the Self   Mead is best known for his theory of the self. According to Mead (1964b), the self begins at a privileged, central position in a person's world. Young children picture themselves as the focus of everything around them and find it difficult to consider the perspectives of others. For example, when shown a mountain scene and asked to describe what an observer on the opposite side of the mountain might see (such as a lake or hikers), young children describe only objects visible from their vantage point. This childhood tendency to place ourselves at the center of events never entirely disappears. Many people with a fear of flying automatically assume that if any plane goes down, it will be the one they are on. And who reads the horoscope section in the paper without looking at their own horoscope first? Why else do we buy lottery tickets, if we do not imagine ourselves winning?

Nonetheless, as people mature, the self changes and begins to reflect greater concern about the reactions of others. Parents, friends, co-workers, coaches, and teachers are often among those who play a major role in shaping a person's self. The term **significant others** is used to refer to those individuals who are most important in the development of the self. Many young people, for example, find themselves drawn to the same kind of work their parents engage in (H. Sullivan [1953] 1968).

In some instances, studies of significant others have generated controversy among researchers. For example, some researchers have contended that Black adolescents are more "peer-oriented" than their White counterparts because of presumed weaknesses in Black families. However, investigations indicate that these hasty conclusions were based on limited studies focusing on less affluent Blacks. In fact, there appears to be little difference in who Blacks and Whites from similar economic backgrounds regard as their significant others (Giordano et al. 1993; Juhasz 1989).

use your sociological *imagination*

How do you view yourself as you interact with others around you? How do you think you formed this view of yourself?

Goffman: Presentation of the Self   How do we manage our "self"? How do we display to others who we are? Erving Goffman, a sociologist associated with the interactionist perspective, suggested that many of our daily activities involve attempts to convey impressions of who we are. His observations help us to understand the sometimes subtle yet critical ways in which we learn to present ourselves socially. They also offer concrete examples of this aspect of socialization.

Early in life, the individual learns to slant his or her presentation of the self in order to create distinctive appearances and satisfy particular audiences. Goffman (1959) referred to this altering of the presentation of the self as **impression management**. Box 4-1 describes an everyday example of this concept—the way students behave after receiving their exam grades.

In analyzing such everyday social interactions, Goffman makes so many explicit parallels to the theater that his view has been termed the **dramaturgical approach**. According to this perspective, people resemble performers in action. For example, a clerk may try to appear busier than he or she actually is if a supervisor happens to be watching. A customer in a singles' bar may try to look as if he or she is waiting for a particular person to arrive.

SOCIOLOGY ON CAMPUS

4-1 Impression Management by Students

When you and fellow classmates get an exam back, you probably react differently depending on the grades that you and they earned. This distinction is part of *impression management*. Researchers have found that students' reactions differ depending on the grades that others received, compared to their own. These encounters can be divided into three categories: those in which all students earned high grades (Ace–Ace encounters); those between Aces and students who received low or failing grades (Ace–Bomber encounters); and those between students who all got low grades (Bomber–Bomber encounters).

Ace–Ace encounters occur in a rather open atmosphere, because there is comfort in sharing a high mark with another high achiever. It is even acceptable to violate the norm of modesty and brag when among other Aces, since as one student admitted, "It's much easier to admit a high mark to someone who has done better than you, or at least as well."

Ace–Bomber encounters are often sensitive. Bombers generally attempt to avoid such exchanges, because "you . . . emerge looking like the dumb one" or "feel like you are lazy or unreliable." When forced into interactions with Aces, Bombers work to appear gracious and congratulatory. For their part, Aces offer sympathy and support to the dissatisfied Bombers and even rationalize their own "lucky" high scores. To help Bombers save face, Aces may

> *When forced into interactions with Aces, Bombers work to appear gracious and congratulatory.*

emphasize the difficulty and unfairness of the examination.

Bomber–Bomber encounters tend to be closed, reflecting the group effort to wall off the feared disdain of others. Yet within the safety of these encounters, Bombers openly share their disappointment and engage in expressions of mutual self-pity that they themselves call "pity parties." They devise face-saving excuses for their poor performance, such as "I wasn't feeling well all week" or "I had four exams and two papers due that week."

Of course, grade comparisons are not the only occasion when students engage in impression management. Another study has shown that students' perceptions of how often fellow students work out can also influence their social encounters. In athletic terms, a bomber would be someone who doesn't work out; an ace would be someone who works hard at physical fitness.

LET'S DISCUSS

1. How do you react to those who have received higher or lower grades than you? Do you engage in impression management? How would you like others to react to your grade?
2. What social norms govern students' impression management strategies?

Sources: Albas and Albas 1988, 1996; M. Mack 2003.

Goffman (1959) also drew attention to another aspect of the self, **face-work**. How often do you initiate some kind of face-saving behavior when you feel embarrassed or rejected? In response to a rejection at the singles' bar, a person may engage in face-work by saying, "There really isn't an interesting person in this entire crowd." We feel the need to maintain a proper image of the self if we are to continue social interaction.

Face-work is a necessity for those who are unemployed. In an economic downturn like the recent recession, unemployment affects people of all social classes, many of whom are unaccustomed to being jobless. A recent ethnographic study found the newly unemployed redefining what it means to be out of work. They were focusing more than in the past on what they were accomplishing, and had begun to value volunteer work more since they had become volunteers themselves. Participants in this study engaged in both impression management and face-work (Garrett-Peters 2009).

In some cultures, people engage in elaborate deceptions to avoid losing face. In Japan, for example, where lifetime employment has until recently been the norm, *company men* thrown out of work by a deep economic recession may feign employment, rising as usual in the morning, donning suit and tie, and heading for the business district. But instead of going to the office, they congregate at places such as Tokyo's Hibiya Library, where they pass the time by reading before returning home at the usual hour. Many of these men are trying to protect family members, who would be shamed if neighbors discovered the family breadwinner was unemployed. Others are deceiving their wives and families as well (French 2000).

Goffman's work on the self represents a logical progression of sociological studies begun by Cooley and Mead on how personality is acquired through socialization and how we manage the presentation of the self to others. Cooley stressed the process by which we create a self; Mead focused on how the self develops as we learn to interact with others; Goffman emphasized the ways in which we consciously create images of ourselves for others.

Psychological Approaches to the Self

Psychologists have shared the interest of Cooley, Mead, and other sociologists in the development of the self. Early work in psychology, such as that of Sigmund Freud (1856–1939),

People judge us by our appearance, attire, body language, demeanor, and mannerisms. Knowing that they do, most of us alter the way we present ourselves to others, a strategy that Goffman called impression management.

Scholar	Key Concepts and Contributions	Major Points of Theory
Charles Horton Cooley 1864–1929 sociologist (USA)	Looking-glass self	Stages of development not distinct; feelings toward ourselves developed through interaction with others
George Herbert Mead 1863–1931 sociologist (USA)	The self Generalized other	Three distinct stages of development; self develops as children grasp the roles of others in their lives
Erving Goffman 1922–1982 sociologist (USA)	Impression management Dramaturgical approach Face-work	Self developed through the impressions we convey to others and to groups
Sigmund Freud 1856–1939 psychotherapist (Austria)	Psychoanalysis	Self influenced by parents and by inborn drives, such as the drive for sexual gratification
Jean Piaget 1896–1980 child psychologist (Switzerland)	Cognitive theory of development	Four stages of cognitive development

stressed the role of inborn drives—among them the drive for sexual gratification—in channeling human behavior. More recently, psychologists such as Jean Piaget have emphasized the stages through which human beings progress as the self develops.

Like Charles Horton Cooley and George Herbert Mead, Freud believed that the self is a social product, and that aspects of one's personality are influenced by other people (especially one's parents). However, unlike Cooley and Mead, he suggested that the self has components that work in opposition to each other. According to Freud, our natural impulsive instincts are in constant conflict with societal constraints. Part of us seeks limitless pleasure, while another part favors rational behavior. By interacting with others, we learn the expectations of society and then select behavior most appropriate to our culture. (Of course, as Freud was well aware, we sometimes distort reality and behave irrationally.)

Research on newborn babies by the Swiss child psychologist Jean Piaget (1896–1980) has underscored the importance of social interactions in developing a sense of self. Piaget found that newborns have no self in the sense of a looking-glass image. Ironically, though, they are quite self-centered; they demand that all attention be directed toward them. Newborns have not yet separated themselves from the universe of which they are a part. For these babies, the phrase "you and me" has no meaning; they understand only "me." However, as they mature, children are gradually socialized into social relationships, even within their rather self-centered world.

In his well-known **cognitive theory of development**, Piaget (1954) identified four stages in the development of children's thought processes. In the first, or *sensorimotor,* stage, young children use their senses to make discoveries. For example, through touching they discover that their hands are actually a part of themselves. During the second, or *preoperational,* stage, children begin to use words and symbols to distinguish objects and ideas. The milestone in the third, or *concrete operational,* stage is that children engage in more logical thinking. They learn that even when a formless lump of clay is shaped into a snake, it is still the same clay. In the fourth, or *formal operational,* stage, adolescents become capable of sophisticated abstract thought and can deal with ideas and values in a logical manner.

According to Piaget, social interaction is the key to development. As children grow older, they pay increasing attention to how other people think and why they act in particular ways. In order to develop a distinct personality, each of us needs opportunities to interact with others. As we saw earlier, Isabelle was deprived of the chance for normal social interactions, and the consequences were severe (Kitchener 1991).

We have seen that a number of thinkers considered social interaction the key to the development of an individual's sense of self. As is generally true, we can best understand this topic by drawing on a variety of theory and research. Table 4-2 summarizes the rich literature, both sociological and psychological, on the development of the self.

thinking CRITICALLY

Use Erving Goffman's dramaturgical approach to describe impression management among members of one of the following groups: athletes, college instructors, parents, physicians, and politicians.

Agents of Socialization

As we have seen, the culture of the United States is defined by rather gradual movements from one stage of socialization to the next. The continuing and lifelong socialization process involves many different social forces that influence our lives and alter our self-images.

The family is the most important agent of socialization in the United States, especially for children. In this chapter, we'll also discuss six other agents of socialization: the school, the peer group, the mass media and technology, the workplace, religion, and the state. We'll explore the role of religion in socializing young people into society's norms and values more fully in Chapter 15.

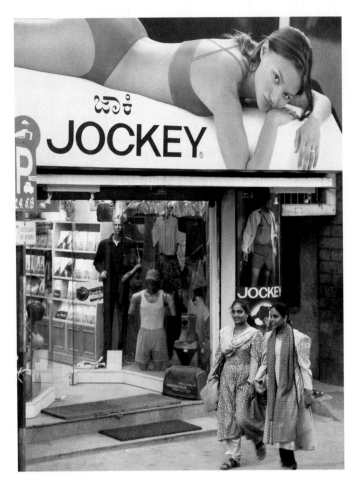

On a busy commercial street in Bangalore, India, pedestrians dressed in traditional garb stroll past a shop and billboard advertising Western fashions. Socialization comes from cultural influences as well as from family and friends. In today's globalized world, Western media expose children to cultural values that their parents and other authorities may not embrace.

Family

The lifelong process of learning begins shortly after birth. Since newborns can hear, see, smell, taste, and feel heat, cold, and pain, they are constantly orienting themselves to the surrounding world. Human beings, especially family members, constitute an important part of their social environment. People minister to the baby's needs by feeding, cleaning, carrying, and comforting the baby.

All families engage in socialization, but the way that Amish families encourage their children to accept their community's subculture is particularly striking. Box 4-2 describes their tolerance for the period of rebellion known as *rum springa,* during which Amish children flirt with the adolescent subculture of mainstream American society.

In the United States, social development also includes exposure to cultural assumptions regarding gender and race. Black parents, for example, have learned that children as young as age two can absorb negative messages about Blacks in children's books, toys, and television shows—all of which are designed primarily for White consumers. At the same time, Black children are exposed more often than others to the inner-city youth gang culture. Because most Blacks, even those who are middle class, live near very poor neighborhoods, children such as Charisse (see the chapter-opening excerpt) are susceptible to these influences,

despite their parents' strong family values (Linn and Poussaint 1999; Pattillo-McCoy 1999).

The term **gender role** refers to expectations regarding the proper behavior, attitudes, and activities of males and females. For example, we traditionally think of "toughness" as masculine—and desirable only in men—while we view "tenderness" as feminine. As we will see in Chapter 12, other cultures do not necessarily assign these qualities to each gender in the way that our culture does. The existence of gender roles does not imply that inevitably, males and females will assume certain roles, nor does it imply that those roles are quite distinct from one another. Rather, gender roles emphasize the fact that males and females are not genetically predetermined to occupy certain roles.

As the primary agents of childhood socialization, parents play a critical role in guiding children into those gender roles deemed appropriate in a society. Other adults, older siblings, the mass media, and religious and educational institutions also have a noticeable impact on a child's socialization into feminine and masculine norms. A culture or subculture may require that one sex or the other take primary responsibility for the socialization of children, economic support of the family, or religious or intellectual leadership. In some societies, girls are socialized mainly by their mothers and boys by their fathers—an arrangement that may prevent girls from learning critical survival skills. In

A young girl in Michigan displays Razanne, a modestly dressed doll made especially for Muslim children. Because girls learn about themselves and their social roles by playing with dolls, having a doll that represents their own heritage is important to them.

RESEARCH TODY

4-2 *Rum Springa*: Raising Children Amish Style

All families face challenges raising their children, but what if your parents expected you not to dance, listen to music, watch television, or access the Internet? This is the challenge faced by Amish teens and their parents, who embrace a lifestyle of the mid-1800s. Amish youths—boys in particular—often rebel against their parents' strict morals by getting drunk, behaving disrespectfully, and indulging in "worldly" activities, such as buying a car. At times even the girls may become involved, to their families' dismay. As one scholar puts it, "The rowdiness of Amish youth is an embarrassment to church leaders and a stigma in the larger community" (Kraybill 2001:138).

Yet the strong pull of mainstream American culture has led Amish parents to routinize, almost to accept, some of their children's

All families face challenges raising their children, but what if your parents expected you not to dance, listen to music, watch television, or access the Internet?

worldly activities. They expect adolescents to test their subculture's boundaries during a period of discovery called *rum springa*, a German term meaning "running around." A common occurrence during which young people attend barn dances and break social norms that forbid drinking, smoking, and driving cars, *rum springa* is definitely not supported by the Amish religion.

Parents often react to these escapades by looking the other way, sometimes literally. If they hear radio music coming from the barn, or a motorcycle driving onto their property in the middle of the night, they don't retaliate by punishing their offspring. Instead, they pretend not to notice, secure in the knowledge that Amish

children almost always return to the community's traditional values. Indeed, despite the flirtation with popular culture and modern technology that is common during the *rum springa*, the vast majority of Amish youths do return to the Amish community and become baptized. Scholars report that 85 to 90 percent of Amish children accept the faith as young adults.

To mainstream Americans, this little known and understood subculture became a source of entertainment when in 2004, UPN aired a 10-week reality program called *Amish in the City*. In the series, five Amish youths allegedly on *rum springa* moved in with six worldly wise young adults in Los Angeles. On behalf of the Amish community, some critics called the series exploitative, a sign of how vulnerable the Amish are. No similar series would be developed on the rebellion of Muslim or Orthodox Jewish youths, they charged.

LET'S DISCUSS

1. Do you or anyone you know come from a subculture that rejects mainstream American culture? If so, describe the community's norms and values. How do they resemble and how do they differ from Amish norms and values?

2. Why do you think so many Amish youths return to their families' way of life after rebelling against it?

Sources: Kraybill 2001; Shachtman 2006; Stevick 2007; Weinraub 2004.

South Asia, fathers teach their sons to swim to prepare them for a life as fishermen; girls typically do not learn to swim. When a deadly tsunami hit the coast of South Asia in 2004, many more men survived than women.

School

Like the family, schools have an explicit mandate to socialize people in the United States—especially children—into the norms and values of our culture.

As conflict theorists Samuel Bowles and Herbert Gintis (1976) have observed, schools in this country foster competition through built-in systems of reward and punishment, such as grades and evaluations by teachers. Consequently, a child who is experiencing difficulty trying to learn a new skill can sometimes come to feel stupid and unsuccessful. However, as the self matures, children become capable of increasingly realistic assessments of their intellectual, physical, and social abilities.

Functionalists point out that schools, as agents of socialization, fulfill the function of teaching children the values and customs of the larger society. Conflict theorists agree, but add that schools can reinforce the divisive aspects of society, especially those of social class. For example, higher education in

the United States is costly despite the existence of financial aid programs. Students from affluent backgrounds therefore have an advantage in gaining access to universities and professional training. At the same time, less affluent young people may never receive the preparation that would qualify them for the best-paying and most prestigious jobs. The contrast between the functionalist and conflict views of education will be discussed in more detail in Chapter 16.

In other cultures as well, schools serve socialization functions. Until the overthrow of Saddam Hussein in 2003, the sixth-grade textbooks used in Iraqi schools concentrated almost entirely on the military and its values of loyalty, honor, and sacrifice. Children were taught that their enemies were Iran, the United States, Israel and its supporters, and NATO, the European military alliance. Within months of the regime's fall, the curriculum had been rewritten to remove indoctrination on behalf of Hussein, his army, and his Baath Socialist Party (Marr 2003).

Peer Group

As a child grows older, the family becomes somewhat less important in social development. Instead, peer groups increasingly assume the role of Mead's significant others. Within the peer group, young

TAKING SOCIOLOGY TO WORK

Rakefet Avramovitz, **Program Administrator, Child Care Law Center**

Rakefet Avramovitz has been working at the Child Care Center in San Francisco since 2003. The center uses legal tools to foster the development of quality, affordable child care, with the goal of expanding child care options, particularly for low-income families. As a support person for the center's attorneys, she manages grants, oversees the center's publications, and sets up conferences and training sessions.

Avramovitz graduated from Dickinson College in 2000. She first became interested in sociology when she took a social analysis course. Though she enjoyed her qualitative courses most, she found her quantitative courses fun, "in that we got to do surveys of people on campus. I've always enjoyed fieldwork," she notes. Avramovitz's most memorable course was one that gave her the opportunity to interact with migrant farmworkers for an entire semester. "I learned ethnography and how to work with people of different cultures. It changed my life," she says.

Avramovitz finds that the skills she learned in her sociology courses are a great help to her on the job. "Sociology taught me how to work with people . . . and how to think critically. It taught me how to listen and find

the stories that people are telling," she explains. Before joining the Child Care Law Center, Avramovitz worked as a counselor for women who were facing difficult issues. "My background in ethnography helped me to talk to these women and listen effectively," she notes. "I was able to help many women by understanding and being able to express their needs to the attorneys we worked with."

Avramovitz is enthusiastic about her work and her ability to make a difference in other people's lives. Maybe that is why she looks forward to summer at the center, when the staff welcomes several law students as interns. "It is really neat to see people learn and get jazzed about child care issues," she says.

LET'S DISCUSS

1. What might be some of the broad, long-term effects of the center's work to expand child care options? Explain.
2. Besides the law, what other professions might benefit from the skills a sociology major has to offer?

---

people associate with others who are approximately their age, and who often enjoy a similar social status (Giordano 2003).

We can see how important peer groups are to young people when their social lives are strained by war or disaster. In Baghdad, the overthrow of Saddam Hussein has profoundly changed teenagers' worlds, casting doubt on their future. Some young people have lost relatives or friends; others have become involved with fundamentalist groups or fled with their families to safer countries. Those youths who are left behind can suffer intense loneliness and boredom. Confined to their homes by crime and terrorism, those fortunate enough to have computers turn to Internet chat rooms or immerse themselves in their studies. Through e-mail, they struggle to maintain old friendships interrupted by wartime dislocation (Sanders 2004).

Gender differences are noteworthy among adolescents. Boys and girls are socialized by their parents, peers, and the media to identify many of the same paths to popularity, but to different

degrees. Table 4-3 compares male and female college students' reports of how girls and boys they knew became popular in high school. The two groups named many of the same paths to popularity but gave them a different order of importance. While neither men nor women named sexual activity, drug use, or alcohol use as one of the top five paths, college men were much more likely than women to mention those behaviors as a means to becoming popular, for both boys and girls.

Mass Media and Technology

In the past 80 years, media innovations—radio, motion pictures, recorded music, television, and the Internet—have become important agents of socialization. Television, and increasingly the Internet, are critical forces in the socialization of children in the United States. One national survey indicates that 68 percent of U.S. children have a television in their bedroom, and nearly 50 percent of all youths ages 8 to 18 use the Internet every day (Figure 4-2).

TABLE **4-3** HIGH SCHOOL POPULARITY

What makes high school girls popular?		What makes high school boys popular?	
According to college men:	According to college women:	According to college men:	According to college women:
1. Physical attractiveness	1. Grades/intelligence	1. Participation in sports	1. Participation in sports
2. Grades/intelligence	2. Participation in sports	2. Grades/intelligence	2. Grades/intelligence
3. Participation in sports	3. General sociability	3. Popularity with girls	3. General sociability
4. General sociability	4. Physical attractiveness	4. General sociability	4. Physical attractiveness
5. Popularity with boys	5. Clothes	5. Car	5. School clubs/government

Note: Students at the following universities were asked in which ways adolescents in their high schools had gained prestige with their peers: Cornell University, Louisiana State University, Southeastern Louisiana University, State University of New York at Albany, State University of New York at Stony Brook, University of Georgia, and University of New Hampshire.

Source: Suitor et al. 2001:445.

These media, however, are not always a negative socializing influence. Television programs and even commercials can introduce young people to unfamiliar lifestyles and cultures. Not only do children in the United States learn about life in "faraway lands," but inner-city children learn about the lives of farm children, and vice versa. The same thing happens in other countries.

Sociologists and other social scientists have begun to consider the impact of technology on socialization. They are particularly interested in the online friendship networks, like Facebook. Does this way of communicating resemble face-to-face interaction, or does it represent a new form of social interaction? Box 4-3 explores the significance of this social phenomenon.

Not just in industrial nations, but in Africa and other developing areas, people have been socialized into relying on new communications technologies. Not long ago, if Zadhe Iyombe wanted to talk to his mother, he had to make an eight-day trip from the capital city of Kinshasa up the Congo River by boat to the rural town where he was born. Now both he and his mother have access to a cell phone, and they send text messages to each other daily. Iyombe and his mother are not atypical. Although cell phones aren't cheap, 1.4 billion owners in developing countries have come to consider them a necessity. Today, there are more cell phones in developing nations than in industrial nations—the first time in history that developing nations have outpaced the developed world in the adoption of a telecommunications technology (K. Sullivan 2006).

Workplace

Learning to behave appropriately in an occupation is a fundamental aspect of human socialization. It used to be that going to work began with the end of our formal schooling, but that is no longer the case, at least not in the United States. More and more young people work today, and not just for a parent or relative. Adolescents generally seek jobs in order to make spending money; 80 percent of high school seniors say that little or none of what they earn goes to family expenses. These teens rarely

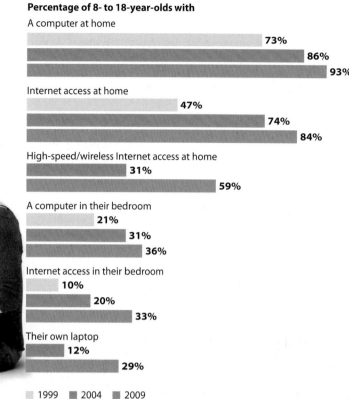

FIGURE **4-2** THE NEW NORMAL: INTERNET AT HOME

Percentage of 8- to 18-year-olds with

A computer at home
- 73%
- 86%
- 93%

Internet access at home
- 47%
- 74%
- 84%

High-speed/wireless Internet access at home
- 31%
- 59%

A computer in their bedroom
- 21%
- 31%
- 36%

Internet access in their bedroom
- 10%
- 20%
- 33%

Their own laptop
- 12%
- 29%

■ 1999   ■ 2004   ■ 2009

Source: Rideout et al. 2010.

look on their employment as a means of exploring vocational interests or getting on-the-job training.

Some observers feel that the increasing number of teenagers who are working earlier in life and for longer hours are finding the workplace almost as important an agent of socialization as school. In fact, a number of educators complain that student time at work is adversely affecting schoolwork. The level of teenage employment in the United States is the highest among industrial countries, which may provide one explanation for why U.S. high school students lag behind those in other countries on international achievement tests.

Socialization in the workplace changes when it involves a more permanent shift from an after-school job to full-time employment. Occupational socialization can be most intense during the transition from school to job, but it continues throughout one's work history. Technological advances may alter the requirements of the position and necessitate some degree of resocialization. Today, men and women change occupations, employers, or places of work many times during their adult years. For example, the typical worker spends about four years with an employer. Occupational socialization continues, then, throughout a person's years in the labor market (Bialik 2010).

College students today recognize that occupational socialization is not socialization into one lifetime occupation. They anticipate going through a number of jobs. The Bureau of Labor Statistics (2008a) has found that from ages 18 to 42, the typical person has held 11 jobs. This high rate of turnover in employment applies to both men and women, and to those with a college degree as well as those with a high school diploma.

RESEARCH TODAY

4-3 Online Socializing: A New Agent of Socialization

Membership in the online social networks Facebook, Friendster, and MySpace has grown exponentially in recent years. At first, young adults monopolized these social networks. Indeed, Facebook was created in 2004 as a way for students on a single campus to become acquainted with one another before actually meeting.

Even in the brief history of online networking, sociologists can see social trends. For example, older people are now creating profiles on these sites. As the accompanying figure shows, there is still a clear correlation between age and online profiles: in a national survey of community college students, younger people were much more likely than older people to be online. However, the fastest-growing age groups are now those over 30, including those who are much older. As a result, online socializing is becoming much less age-specific—more like socializing in the real world. Moreover, this new agent of socialization can continue to influence people throughout the life course. Twitter is largely the exception to this trend; it is still a very age-specific method of social interaction.

Online networks—especially those that indicate how many "friends" an individual has—can also be seen in terms of social capital. In fact, "friending" is one, if not *the,* main activity on some online sites. Often the number of friends a person socializes with becomes the subject of boasting. By extension, individuals may use these sites to search for "friends" who may prove helpful to them in future endeavors. Becoming aware of new opportunities, either social or economic, through friends is a significant benefit of social capital.

Researchers have looked at the relationship between the display of friends online and the number of real-world friends people socialize with, and have proposed two competing hypotheses. According to the social enhancement hypothesis ("the rich get richer"), those who are popular offline further increase their popularity through online networking sites. According to the social compensation hypothesis ("the poor get richer"), however, social network users try to increase their popularity online to compensate for inadequate popularity offline. The social compensation hypothesis, if correct, would be an example of impression management. Research supports elements of both hypotheses; neither hypothesis fully defines the participants in online networking sites.

Online networks—especially those that indicate how many "friends" an individual has—can also be seen in terms of social capital.

Viewed from a societal perspective, socializing online can have both positive and negative functions. For members of some marginalized populations, it is a way to socialize with like-minded people. For example, Muslims in Great Britain connect with friends online to learn how to navigate through a society in which they form a distinct minority. For other people, such as members of the Nazis in Germany and the Mafia in Italy, online networking is a way to proclaim allegiance to socially objectionable organizations. Governments frown on such online organizing, seeing it as dysfunctional, and periodically monitor these sites to see whether any laws have been violated.

LET'S DISCUSS

1. Do you list your "friends" on an online social networking site? If so, what is your motivation for doing so? How much social capital do you think your list represents?

2. Do you think the advantages of online social networking outweigh the disadvantages?

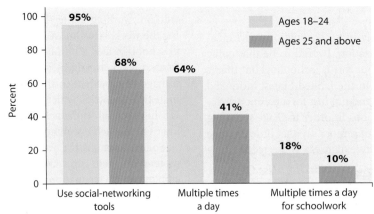

STAYING CONNECTED: COMMUNITY COLLEGE STUDENTS

Legend: Ages 18–24, Ages 25 and above

- Use social-networking tools: 95% (18–24), 68% (25 and above)
- Multiple times a day: 64% (18–24), 41% (25 and above)
- Multiple times a day for schoolwork: 18% (18–24), 10% (25 and above)

Note: Question asked was "How often do you use social networking tools, such as instant messaging, text messaging, MySpace and/or Facebook, Twitter, etc., for any purpose? (This does not include e-mail.)"
Source: Center for Community College Student Engagement 2009:8.

Sources: Donadio 2009; N. Ellison et al. 2007; Facebook 2011; Gentile 2009; Hundley and Ramirez 2008; Lenhart 2009; Miyata and Kobayashi 2008; Zywica and Danowski 2008.

Religion and the State

Increasingly, social scientists are recognizing the importance of both religion and government ("the state") as agents of socialization, because of their impact on the life course. Traditionally, family members have served as the primary caregivers in our culture, but in the 20th century, the family's protective function was steadily transferred to outside agencies such as hospitals, mental health clinics, and child care centers. Many of these agencies are run by groups affiliated with certain religions or by the state.

Both organized religion and government have impacted the life course by reinstituting some of the rites of passage once observed in agricultural communities and early industrial societies. For example, religious organizations stipulate certain traditional rites that may bring together all the members of an extended family, even if they never meet for any other reason. And government regulations stipulate the ages at which a person may drive a car, drink alcohol, vote in elections, marry without parental permission, work overtime, and retire. These regulations do not constitute strict rites of passage: most 18-year-olds choose not to vote, and most people choose their age of retirement without reference to government dictates.

In the Social Policy section at the end of this chapter, we will see that government is under pressure to become a provider of child care, which would give it a new and direct role in the socialization of infants and young children.

thinking CRITICALLY

How would functionalist and conflict theorists differ in their analysis of socialization by the mass media?

Socialization throughout the Life Course

The Life Course

Among the Kota people of the Congo in Africa, adolescents paint themselves blue. Mexican American girls go on a daylong religious retreat before dancing the night away. Egyptian mothers step over their newborn infants seven times, and graduating students at the Naval Academy throw their hats in the air. These are all ways of celebrating **rites of passage**, a means of dramatizing and validating changes in a person's status. Rites of passage can mark a separation, as in a graduation ceremony, or an incorporation, as in an initiation into an organization (Van Gennep [1909] 1960).

Rites of passage are a worldwide social phenomenon. The Kota rite marks the passage to adulthood. The color blue, viewed as the color of death, symbolizes the death of childhood. Hispanic girls celebrate reaching womanhood with a *quinceañera* ceremony at age 15. In the Cuban American community of Miami, the popularity of the *quinceañera* supports a network of party planners, caterers, dress designers, and the Miss Quinceañera Latina pageant. For thousands of years, Egyptian mothers have welcomed their newborns to the world in the Soboa ceremony by stepping over the seven-day-old infant seven times.

These specific ceremonies mark stages of development in the life course. They indicate that the process of socialization continues through all stages of the life cycle. In fact, some researchers have chosen to concentrate on socialization as a lifelong process. Sociologists and other social scientists who take such a **life course approach** look closely at the social factors that influence people throughout their lives, from birth to death, including gender and income. They recognize that biological changes mold but do not dictate human behavior.

Several life events mark the passage to adulthood. Of course, these turning points vary from one society and even one generation to the next. In the United States, the key event seems to be the completion of formal schooling (Table 4-4). On average,

Americans expect this milestone to occur by a person's 23rd birthday. Other major events in the life course, such as getting married or becoming a parent, are expected to follow three or four years later. Interestingly, comparatively few survey respondents identified marriage and parenthood as important milestones (S. Furstenberg et al. 2004).

One result of these staggered steps to independence is that in the United States, unlike some other societies, there is no clear dividing line between adolescence and adulthood. Nowadays, few young people finish school, get married, and leave home at about the same age, clearly establishing their transition to adulthood. The terms *youthhood, emerging adulthood,* and *not quite adult* have been coined to describe the prolonged ambiguous status that young people in their 20s experience (Côté 2000; Settersten and Ray 2011; Christian Smith 2007).

Anticipatory Socialization and Resocialization

The development of a social self is literally a lifelong transformation that begins in the crib and continues as one prepares for death. Two types of socialization occur at many points throughout the life course: anticipatory socialization and resocialization.

Anticipatory socialization refers to processes of socialization in which a person rehearses for future positions, occupations, and social relationships. A culture can function more efficiently and smoothly if members become acquainted with the norms, values, and behavior associated with a social position before actually assuming that status. Preparation for many aspects of adult life begins with anticipatory socialization during childhood and adolescence, and continues throughout our lives as we prepare for new responsibilities.

You can see the process of anticipatory socialization take place when high school students start to consider what colleges they may attend. Traditionally, this task meant looking at publications received in the mail or making campus visits. However, with new technology, more and more students are using the web to begin their college experience. Colleges are investing more time and money in developing attractive websites through which students

A young Apache woman undergoes a mudding ceremony traditionally used in rites of passage, such as puberty and in some cases weddings.

TABLE **4-4** MILESTONES IN THE TRANSITION TO ADULTHOOD

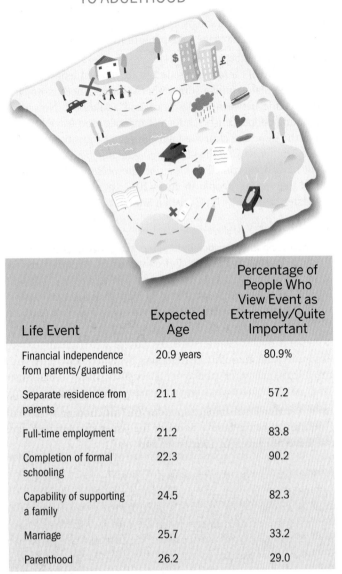

Life Event	Expected Age	Percentage of People Who View Event as Extremely/Quite Important
Financial independence from parents/guardians	20.9 years	80.9%
Separate residence from parents	21.1	57.2
Full-time employment	21.2	83.8
Completion of formal schooling	22.3	90.2
Capability of supporting a family	24.5	82.3
Marriage	25.7	33.2
Parenthood	26.2	29.0

Note: Based on the 2002 General Social Survey of 1,398 people.
Source: T. Smith 2003.

Think about It

Why did so few respondents consider marriage and parenthood to be important milestones? Which milestones do you think are most important?

can take virtual campus tours and hear audio clips of everything from the college anthem to a sample zoology lecture.

Occasionally, assuming a new social or occupational position requires us to *unlearn* an established orientation. **Resocialization** refers to the process of discarding former behavior patterns and accepting new ones as part of a transition in one's life. Often resocialization occurs during an explicit effort to transform an individual, as happens in reform schools, therapy groups, prisons, religious conversion settings, and political indoctrination camps. The process of resocialization typically involves considerable stress

Prisons are centers of resocialization, where people are placed under pressure to discard old behavior patterns and accept new ones. These prisoners are learning to use weights to release tension and exert their strength—a socially acceptable method of handling antisocial impulses.

for the individual—much more so than socialization in general, or even anticipatory socialization (Gecas 2004).

Resocialization is particularly effective when it occurs within a total institution. Erving Goffman (1961) coined the term **total institution** to refer to an institution that regulates all aspects of a person's life under a single authority, such as a prison, the military, a mental hospital, or a convent. Because the total institution is generally cut off from the rest of society, it provides for all the needs of its members. Quite literally, the crew of a merchant vessel at sea becomes part of a total institution. So elaborate are its requirements, so all-encompassing its activities, a total institution often represents a miniature society.

Goffman (1961) identified four common traits of total institutions:

- All aspects of life are conducted in the same place under the control of a single authority.

- Any activities within the institution are conducted in the company of others in the same circumstances—for example, army recruits or novices in a convent.

- The authorities devise rules and schedule activities without consulting the participants.

- All aspects of life within a total institution are designed to fulfill the purpose of the organization. Thus, all activities in a monastery might be centered on prayer and communion with God. (C. Davies 1989; P. Rose et al. 1979)

People often lose their individuality within total institutions. For example, a person entering prison may experience the humiliation of a **degradation ceremony** as he or she is stripped of clothing, jewelry, and other personal possessions. From this point on, scheduled daily routines allow for little or no personal initiative. The individual becomes secondary and rather invisible in the overbearing social environment (Garfinkel 1956).

Child care programs are not just babysitting services; they have an enormous influence on the development of young children—an influence that has been growing with the movement of more and more women into the paid labor force. The rise in single-parent families, increased job opportunities for women, and the need for additional family income have all propelled mothers of young children into the working world. Who should care for the children of working mothers during working hours?

Looking at the Issue

Preschoolers typically are not cared for by their parents. Seventy-three percent of employed mothers depend on others to care for their children, and 30 percent of mothers who aren't employed have regular care arrangements. In fact, children under age five are more likely to be cared for on a daily basis by their grandparents than by their parents. Over a third of them are cared for by nonrelatives in nursery schools, Head Start programs, day care centers, family day care, and other arrangements (Bureau of the Census 2008c).

Researchers have found that high-quality child care centers do not adversely affect the socialization of children; in fact, good day care benefits children. The value of preschool programs was documented in a series of studies conducted in the United States. Researchers found no significant differences in infants who had received extensive nonmaternal care compared with those who had been cared for solely by their mothers. They also reported that more and more infants in the United States are being placed in child care outside the home, and that, overall, the

Children play at the Communicare day care center in Perth, Australia. The Australian government subsidizes children's attendance at day care and after-school programs from birth to age 12.

quality of those arrangements is better than has been found in previous studies. It is difficult, however, to generalize about child care, since there is so much variability among day care providers, and even among government policies from one state to another (Loeb et al. 2004; Ludwig and Sawhill 2007; NICHD 2007).

Few people in the United States or elsewhere can afford the luxury of having a parent stay at home, or of paying for high-quality live-in child care. For millions of mothers and fathers, finding the right kind of child care is a challenge both to parenting and to the pocketbook. At present, the federal government supports child care through subsidized programs, which target low-income families, and income tax credits, which benefit families with moderate incomes. The annual expenditure to assist low-income parents is about $12 billion; the expenditure to support parents with moderate incomes is $58 billion (Cushing-Daniels and Zedlewski 2008).

Applying Sociology

Studies that assess the quality of child care outside the home reflect the micro level of analysis and the interest of interactionists in the impact of face-to-face interaction. These studies also explore macro-level implications for the functioning of social institutions like the family. Some of the issues surrounding day care have also been of interest to those who take the conflict perspective.

In the United States, high-quality day care is not equally available to all families. Parents in affluent communities have an easier time finding day care than those in poor or working-class communities. Finding *affordable* child care is also a problem. Viewed from a conflict perspective, child care costs are an especially serious burden for lower-class families. The poorest families spend 25 percent of their income for preschool child care, whereas families who are *not* poor pay only 6 percent or less of their income.

Feminist theorists echo the concern of conflict theorists that high-quality child care receives little government support because it is regarded as "merely a way to let women work." Nearly all child care workers (97 percent) are women; many find themselves in low-status, minimum-wage jobs. Typically, food servers, messengers, and gas station attendants make more money than the 1.2 million child care workers in the United States, who averaged $9.43 per hour in 2008. Not surprisingly, turnover among employees in child care centers runs at 25 to 40 percent per year (Bureau of the Census 2010a; NACCRRA 2010).

Initiating Policy

Policies regarding child care outside the home vary throughout the world. Most developing nations do not have the economic base to provide subsidized child care. Thus, working mothers rely largely on relatives or take their children to work. In the comparatively wealthy industrialized countries of western Europe, government provides child care as a basic service, at little or no expense to parents. But even those countries with tax-subsidized programs occasionally fall short of the need for high-quality child care.

When policymakers decide that child care is desirable, they must determine the degree to which taxpayers should subsidize it. In Sweden and Denmark, one-half to two-thirds of preschoolers were in government-subsidized child care full-time in 2003. In the United States, annual fees for full-time child care of a four-year-old range from an average of $3,900 in Mississippi to an average of $11,678 in Massachusetts (Immervoll and Barber 2005; NACCRRA 2010).

We have a long way to go in making high-quality child care more affordable and accessible, not just in the United States but throughout the world as well. In an attempt to reduce government spending, France is considering cutting back the budgets of subsidized nurseries, even though waiting lists exist and the French public heartily disapproves of cutbacks. In Germany, reunification has reduced the options previously open to East German mothers, who had become accustomed to government-supported child care. Experts in child development view such reports as a vivid reminder of the need for greater government and private-sector support for child care (Hank 2001; L. King 1998).

Take the Issue with You

1. Were you ever in a day care program? If so, do you recall the experience as good or bad? In general, do you think it is desirable to expose young children to the socializing influence of day care?

2. In the view of conflict theorists, child care receives little government support because it is "merely a way to let women work." Can you think of other explanations?

3. Should the costs of day care programs be paid by government, by the private sector, or entirely by parents?

MASTERING THIS CHAPTER

Summary

Socialization is the process through which people learn the attitudes, values, and actions appropriate for members of a particular culture. This chapter examines the role of socialization in human development; the way in which people develop perceptions, feelings, and beliefs about themselves; important agents of socialization; and the lifelong nature of the socialization process.

1. **Socialization** affects the overall cultural practices of a society; it also shapes the images that we hold of ourselves.

2. Heredity and environmental factors interact in influencing the socialization process.

3. In the early 1900s, Charles Horton Cooley advanced the belief that we learn who we are by interacting with others, a phenomenon he called the **looking-glass self.**

4. George Herbert Mead, best known for his theory of the **self,** proposed that as people mature, their selves begin to reflect their concern about reactions from others—both **generalized others** and **significant others.**

5. Erving Goffman has shown that in many of our daily activities, we try to convey distinct impressions of who we are, a process he called **impression management.**

6. As the primary agents of socialization, parents play a critical role in guiding children into those **gender roles** deemed appropriate in a society.

7. Like the family, schools in the United States have an explicit mandate to socialize people—especially children—into the norms and values of our culture.

8. Peer groups and the mass media, especially television and the Internet, are important agents of socialization for adolescents.

9. Socialization in the workplace begins with part-time employment while we are in school and continues as we work full-time and change jobs throughout our lives.

10. Religion and the state shape the socialization process by regulating the life course and influencing our views of appropriate behavior at particular ages.

11. Socialization proceeds throughout the life course. Some societies mark stages of development with formal **rites of passage.** In the culture of the United States, significant events such as marriage and parenthood serve to change a person's status.

12. As more and more mothers of young children have entered the labor market, the demand for child care has increased dramatically, posing policy questions for many nations around the world.

Key Terms

Anticipatory socialization Processes of socialization in which a person rehearses for future positions, occupations, and social relationships. (page 89)

Cognitive theory of development The theory that children's thought progresses through four stages of development. (83)

Degradation ceremony An aspect of the socialization process within some total institutions, in which people are subjected to humiliating rituals. (90)

Dramaturgical approach A view of social interaction in which people are seen as theatrical performers. (81)

Face-work The efforts people make to maintain the proper image and avoid public embarrassment. (82)

Gender role Expectations regarding the proper behavior, attitudes, and activities of males and females. (84)

Generalized other The attitudes, viewpoints, and expectations of society as a whole that a child takes into account in his or her behavior. (81)

Impression management The altering of the presentation of the self in order to create distinctive appearances and satisfy particular audiences. (81)

Life course approach A research orientation in which sociologists and other social scientists look closely at the social factors that influence people throughout their lives, from birth to death. (89)

Looking-glass self A concept that emphasizes the self as the product of our social interactions. (80)

Personality A person's typical patterns of attitudes, needs, characteristics, and behavior. (77)

Resocialization The process of discarding former behavior patterns and accepting new ones as part of a transition in one's life. (90)

Rite of passage A ritual marking the symbolic transition from one social position to another. (89)

Role taking The process of mentally assuming the perspective of another and responding from that imagined viewpoint. (80)

Self A distinct identity that sets us apart from others. (80)

Significant other An individual who is most important in the development of the self, such as a parent, friend, or teacher. (81)

Socialization The lifelong process in which people learn the attitudes, values, and behaviors appropriate for members of a particular culture. (76)

Total institution An institution that regulates all aspects of a person's life under a single authority, such as a prison, the military, a mental hospital, or a convent. (90)

TAKING SOCIOLOGY with you

1. Examine your looking-glass self. What was it like in high school? How did it change when you entered college, and who were the people who caused you to see yourself differently?

2. For two days, keep a record of your use of the mass media—television, the Internet, and so on—including what you watched, read, or communicated and your reasons for doing so. Then take the role of a sociologist and ask how you might have been socialized by the media you used. What norms and values were you exposed to, and how did they affect you?

3. Interview a person who has recently changed jobs. Ask about the process of resocialization required by the new job. Was the job change voluntary or involuntary, and how did it affect the person's adjustment? Which of the concepts you learned in this chapter seem relevant to the experience?

Self-Quiz

Read each question carefully and then select the best answer.

1. Which of the following social scientists used the phrase *looking-glass self* to emphasize that the self is the product of our social interactions with other people?
   - **a.** George Herbert Mead
   - **b.** Charles Horton Cooley
   - **c.** Erving Goffman
   - **d.** Jean Piaget

2. In what he called the *play stage* of socialization, George Herbert Mead asserted that people mentally assume the perspectives of others, thereby enabling them to respond from that imagined viewpoint. This process is referred to as
   - **a.** role taking.
   - **b.** the generalized other.
   - **c.** the significant other.
   - **d.** impression management.

3. George Herbert Mead is best known for his theory of what?
   - **a.** presentation of the self
   - **b.** cognitive development
   - **c.** the self
   - **d.** impression management

4. Suppose a clerk tries to appear busier than he or she actually is when a supervisor happens to be watching. Erving Goffman would study this behavior from what approach?
   - **a.** functionalist
   - **b.** conflict
   - **c.** psychological
   - **d.** interactionist

5. According to child psychologist Jean Piaget's cognitive theory of development, children begin to use words and symbols to distinguish objects and ideas during which stage in the development of the thought process?
   - **a.** the sensorimotor stage
   - **b.** the preoperational stage
   - **c.** the concrete operational stage
   - **d.** the formal operational stage

6. On the first day of basic training in the army, a recruit has his civilian clothes replaced by army "greens," has his hair shaved off, loses his privacy, and finds that he must use a communal bathroom. All these humiliating activities are part of
   - **a.** becoming a significant other.
   - **b.** impression management.
   - **c.** a degradation ceremony.
   - **d.** face-work.

7. Which social institution is considered to be the most important agent of socialization in the United States, especially for children?
   - **a.** the family
   - **b.** the school
   - **c.** the peer group
   - **d.** the mass media

8. The term *gender role* refers to
   - **a.** the biological fact that we are male or female.
   - **b.** a role that is given to us by a teacher.
   - **c.** a role that is given to us in a play.
   - **d.** expectations regarding the proper behavior, attitudes, and activities of males and females.

9. Which sociological perspective emphasizes that schools in the United States foster competition through built-in systems of reward and punishment?

    a. the functionalist perspective

    b. the conflict perspective

    c. the interactionist perspective

    d. the psychological perspective

10. Which of the following statements about teenagers in Baghdad is true?

    a. They have lost much of their peer group due to death and relocation.

    b. They have lost peers who have joined fundamentalist groups.

    c. If they own a computer, they use it in an attempt to stay in contact with their pre-war peer group.

    d. all of the above

11. _____ is the term used by sociologists in referring to the lifelong process whereby people learn the attitudes, values, and behaviors appropriate for members of a particular culture.

12. In everyday speech, the term _____ is used to refer to a person's typical patterns of attitudes, needs, characteristics, and behavior.

13. Studies of twins raised apart suggest that both _____ and _____ influence human development.

14. A _____ _____ is an individual such as a parent, friend, or teacher who is most important in the development of the self.

15. Early work in _____, such as that by Sigmund Freud, stressed the role of inborn drives—among them the drive for sexual gratification—in channeling human behavior.

16. The Swiss psychologist Jean Piaget developed the _____ theory of development.

17. Preparation for many aspects of adult life begins with _____ socialization during childhood and adolescence and continues throughout our lives as we prepare for new responsibilities.

18. Resocialization is particularly effective when it occurs within a(n) _____ institution.

19. The _____ perspective emphasizes the role of schools in teaching the values and customs of the larger society.

20. As children grow older, the family becomes less important in social development, while _____ groups become more important.

_____
18 total; 19 functionalist; 20 peer

Answers
1 (b); 2 (a); 3 (c); 4 (d); 5 (b); 6 (c); 7 (a); 8 (d); 9 (b); 10 (d); 11 Socialization; 12 personality; 13 heredity, environment; 14 significant other; 15 psychology; 16 cognitive; 17 anticipatory;

THINKING ABOUT MOVIES

The Blind Side

Through football and the help of significant others, a young man's self-identity changes.

Grown Ups

Five childhood friends reunite and come to terms with the aging process.

The Town

A man from Boston struggles against his socialization within a subculture of bank robbers.

A rowing team practices for
a race in Samoa. Around the
world, much of people's social
activity takes place in groups.

96

Social Interaction and Social Structure **5**

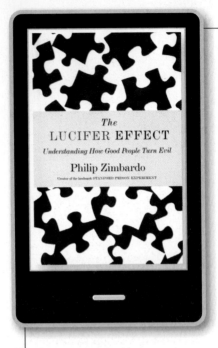

> As each of the blindfolded prisoners is escorted down the flight of steps in front of Jordan Hall into our little jail, our guards order them to strip and remain standing naked with their arms outstretched against the wall and legs spread apart. They hold that uncomfortable position for a long time as the guards ignore them because they are busy with last-minute chores, like packing away the prisoners' belongings for safekeeping, fixing up their guards quarters, and arranging beds in the three cells. Before being given his uniform, each prisoner is sprayed with powder, alleged to be a delouser, to rid him of lice that might be brought in to contaminate our jail. . . . The humiliation of being a prisoner has begun, much as it does in many institutions from military boot camps to prisons, hospitals, and low-level jobs. . . .
>
> The morning shift comes on in the middle of the night, 2 a.m. . . .
>
> The prisoners are sound asleep. Some are snoring in their dark, cramped cells. Suddenly the silence is shattered. Loud whistles shriek, voices yell, "Up and at 'em." "Wake up and get out here for the count!" "Okay, you sleeping beauties, it's time to see if you learned how to count." Dazed prisoners line up against the wall and count off mindlessly as the three guards alternate in coming up with new variations on count themes. The count and its attendant push-ups and jumping jacks for failures continue on and on for nearly a weary hour. Finally, the prisoners are ordered back to sleep—until reveille a few hours later. . . .
>
> [By Tuesday] our prisoners are looking raggedy and bleary-eyed, and our little prison is beginning to smell like a men's toilet in a New York subway station. Seems that some guards have made toilet visits a privilege to be awarded infrequently and never after lights out. During the night, prisoners have to urinate and defecate in buckets in their cells, and some guards refuse to allow them to be emptied till morning. Complaints are coming fast and furiously from many of the prisoners. . . .
>
> After less than three days into this bizarre situation, some of the students role-playing prison guards have moved far beyond mere play-acting. They have internalized the hostility, negative affect, and mindset characteristic of some real prison guards, as is evident from their shift reports, retrospective diaries, and personal reflections. . . .
>
> The depersonalization of the prisoners and the spreading extent of dehumanization are beginning to affect [one of the guards], too: "As I got angrier and angrier, I didn't question this behavior as much. I couldn't let it affect me, so I started hiding myself deeper behind my role. It was the only way of not hurting yourself. I was really lost on what was happening but didn't even think about quitting."
>
> Blaming the victims for their sorry condition—created by our failure to provide adequate shower and sanitation facilities—became common among the staff. We see this victim blame in operation as [the guard] complains, "I got tired of seeing the prisoners in rags, smelling bad, and the prison stink. "

After less than three days into this bizarre situation, some of the students role-playing prison guards have moved far beyond mere playacting. They have internalized the hostility, negative affect, and mind-set characteristic of some real prison guards.

(Zimbardo 2007b:40, 41, 52, 53, 80, 86) Additional information about this excerpt can be found on the Online Learning Center at www.mhhe.com/schaefer13e.

In this study, directed and described by social psychologist Philip Zimbardo, college students adopted the patterns of social interaction expected of guards and prisoners when they were placed in a mock prison. Sociologists use the term **social interaction** to refer to the ways in which people respond to one another, whether face-to-face or over the telephone or on the computer. In the mock prison, social interactions between guards and prisoners were highly impersonal. The guards addressed the prisoners by number rather than name, and they wore reflective sunglasses that made eye contact impossible.

As in many real-life prisons, the simulated prison at Stanford University had a social structure in which guards held virtually total control over prisoners. The term **social structure** refers to the way in which a society is organized into predictable relationships. The social structure of Zimbardo's mock prison influenced how the guards and prisoners interacted. Zimbardo and his colleagues (2009:516) note that it was a real prison "in the minds of the jailers and their captives." His simulated prison experiment, first conducted more than 30 years ago, has subsequently been repeated (with similar findings) both in the United States and in other countries.

Zimbardo's experiment took on new relevance in 2004, in the wake of shocking revelations of prisoner abuse at the U.S.-run Abu Ghraib military facility in Iraq. Graphic "trophy photos" showed U.S. soldiers humiliating naked Iraqi prisoners and threatening to attack them with police dogs. The structure of the wartime prison, coupled with intense pressure on military intelligence officers to secure information regarding terrorist plots, contributed to the breakdown in the guards' behavior. But Zimbardo himself noted that the guards' depraved conduct could have been predicted simply on the basis of his research. So strong was public reaction to the Abu Ghraib scandal that in 2009, during his first week in office, President Barack Obama declared that henceforth interrogators will use only noncoercive methods for questioning suspected terrorists (Zimbardo 2007a).

The two concepts of social interaction and social structure are central to sociological study. They are closely related to socialization (see Chapter 4), the process through which people learn the attitudes, values, and behaviors appropriate to their culture. When the students in Zimbardo's experiment entered the mock prison, they began a process of resocialization. In that process, they adjusted to a new social structure and learned new rules for social interaction.

In this chapter we will study social structure and its effect on our social interactions. What determines a person's status in society? How do our social roles affect our social interactions? What is the place of social institutions such as the family, religion, and government in our social structure? How can we better understand and manage large

In Zimbardo's mock prison experiment, a guard orders prisoners to line up against the wall. The social interactions fostered by the prison's social structure quickly led to a breakdown in the guards' and prisoners' behavior.

organizations such as multinational corporations? We'll begin by considering how social interactions shape the way we view the world around us. Next, we'll focus on the five basic elements of social structure: statuses, social roles, groups, social networks, and social institutions such as the family, religion, government and the mass media. We'll see that functionalists, conflict theorists, and interactionists approach social institutions quite differently. We'll also touch on a new element of social structure, *virtual worlds.* In a special case study, we'll examine the Second Life virtual world. Finally, we'll compare our modern social structure with simpler forms, using typologies developed by Émile Durkheim, Ferdinand Tönnies, and Gerhard Lenski. The Social Policy section at the end of the chapter focuses on the recent concentration of the mass media in the hands of a few large corporations.

Social Interaction and Reality

When someone in a crowd shoves you, do you automatically push back? Or do you consider the circumstances of the incident and the attitude of the instigator before you react? Chances are you do the latter. According to sociologist Herbert Blumer (1969:79), the distinctive characteristic of social interaction among people is that "human beings interpret or 'define' each other's actions instead of merely reacting to each other's actions." In other words, our response to someone's behavior is based on the *meaning* we attach to his or her actions. Reality is shaped by our perceptions, evaluations, and definitions.

These meanings typically reflect the norms and values of the dominant culture and our socialization experiences within that culture. As interactionists emphasize, the meanings that we attach to people's behavior are shaped by our interactions with them and with the larger society. Social reality is literally constructed from our social interactions (Berger and Luckmann 1966).

How do we define our social reality? Consider something as simple as how we regard tattoos. At one time, most of us in the United States considered tattoos weird or kooky. We associated them with fringe countercultural groups, such as punk rockers, biker gangs, and skinheads. Among many people, a tattoo elicited an automatic negative response. Now, however, so many people have tattoos—including society's trendsetters and major sports figures—and the ritual of getting a tattoo has become so legitimized, that mainstream culture regards tattoos differently.

At this point, as a result of increased social interaction with tattooed people, tattoos look perfectly at home to us in a number of settings.

The nature of social interaction and what constitutes reality varies across cultures. In Western societies, with their emphasis on romantic love, couples see marriage as a relationship as well as a social status. From Valentine's Day flowers to more informal, everyday gestures, professions of love are an expected part of marriage. In Japan, however, marriage is considered more a social status than a relationship. Although many or most Japanese couples undoubtedly do love each other, saying "I love you" does not come easily to them, especially not to husbands. Nor do most husbands call their wives by name (they prefer "Mother") or look them in the eyes. In 2006, in an effort to change these restrictive customs, some Japanese men formed the Devoted Husband Organization, which has been sponsoring a new holiday, Beloved Wives Day. In 2008, this group organized an event called Shout Your Love from the Middle of a Cabbage Patch Day. Dozens of men stood in a cabbage patch north of Tokyo and shouted, "I love you!" to their wives, some of whom had never heard their husbands say those words (Kambayashi 2008).

The ability to define social reality reflects a group's power within a society. In fact, one of the most crucial aspects of the relationship between dominant and subordinate groups is the ability of the dominant or majority group to define a society's values. Sociologist William I. Thomas (1923), an early critic of theories of racial and gender differences, recognized that the "definition of the situation" could mold the thinking and personality of the individual. Writing from an interactionist

perspective, Thomas observed that people respond not only to the objective features of a person or situation but also to the *meaning* that person or situation has for them. For example, in Philip Zimbardo's mock prison experiment, student "guards" and "prisoners" accepted the definition of the situation (including the traditional roles and behavior associated with being a guard or prisoner) and acted accordingly.

As we have seen throughout the past 60 years—first in the civil rights movement of the 1950s and 1960s and since then among such groups as women, the elderly, gays and lesbians, and people with disabilities—an important aspect of the process of social change involves redefining or reconstructing social reality. Members of subordinate groups challenge traditional definitions and begin to perceive and experience reality in a new way.

thinking CRITICALLY

Think back over the events of the past few days. Identify two occasions on which different people defined the same social reality differently.

Elements of Social Structure

All social interaction takes place within a social structure, including those interactions that redefine social reality. For purposes of study, we can break down any social structure into five elements: statuses, social roles, groups, social networks, and social institutions. These elements make up social structure just as a foundation, walls, and ceilings make up a building's structure. The elements of social structure are developed through the lifelong process of socialization described in Chapter 4.

Statuses

We normally think of a person's *status* as having to do with influence, wealth, and fame. However, sociologists use the term **status** to refer to any of the full range of socially defined positions within a large group or society, from the lowest to the highest. Within our society, a person can occupy the status of president of the United States, fruit picker, son or daughter, violinist, teenager, resident of Minneapolis, dental technician, or neighbor. A person can hold a number of statuses at the same time.

Ascribed and Achieved Status Sociologists view some statuses as *ascribed* and others as *achieved* (Figure 5-1). An **ascribed status** is assigned to a person by society without regard for the person's unique talents or characteristics. Generally, the assignment takes place at birth; thus, a person's racial background, gender, and age are all considered ascribed statuses. Though these characteristics are biological in origin, they are significant mainly because of the *social* meanings they have in our culture. Conflict theorists are especially interested in ascribed statuses, since they often confer privileges or reflect a person's membership in a subordinate group. The social meanings of race, ethnicity, and gender will be analyzed more fully in Chapters 11 and 12.

In most cases, we can do little to change an ascribed status, but we can attempt to change the traditional constraints associated with it. For example, the Gray Panthers—an activist political

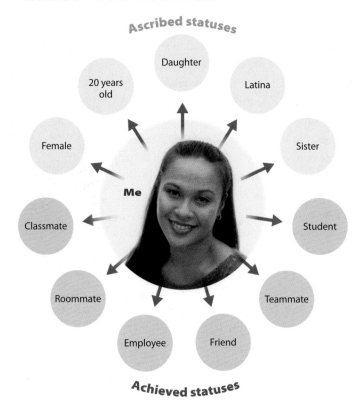

FIGURE **5-1** SOCIAL STATUSES

Ascribed statuses

Daughter · 20 years old · Latina · Female · Sister · Me · Classmate · Student · Roommate · Teammate · Employee · Friend

Achieved statuses

Think about It
The young woman in this figure—"me"—occupies many positions in society, each of which involves distinct statuses. How would you define your statuses? Which have the most influence in your life?

group founded in 1971 to work for the rights of older people—have tried to modify society's negative and confining stereotypes of the elderly. As a result of their work and that of other groups supporting older citizens, the ascribed status of "senior citizen" is no longer as difficult for millions of older people.

An ascribed status does not necessarily have the same social meaning in every society. In a cross-cultural study, sociologist Gary Huang (1988) confirmed the long-held view that respect for the elderly is an important cultural norm in China. In many cases, the prefix "old" is used respectfully: calling someone "old teacher" or "old person" is like calling a judge in the United States "your honor." Huang points out that positive age-seniority language distinctions are uncommon in the United States; consequently, we view the term *old man* as more of an insult than a celebration of seniority and wisdom.

Unlike ascribed statuses, an **achieved status** comes to us largely through our own efforts. Both "computer programmer" and "prison guard" are achieved statuses, as are "lawyer," "pianist," "sorority member," "convict," and "social worker." We must do something to acquire an achieved status—go to school, learn a skill, establish a friendship, invent a new product. But as we will see in the next section, our ascribed status heavily influences our achieved status. Being male, for example, would decrease the likelihood that we would consider child care as a career.

Master Status Each person holds many different and sometimes conflicting statuses; some may connote higher social position and some, lower position. How, then, do others view one's overall social position? According to sociologist Everett Hughes (1945), societies deal with inconsistencies by agreeing that certain statuses are more important than others. A **master status** is a status that dominates others and thereby determines a person's general position in society. For example, Arthur Ashe, who died of AIDS in 1993, had a remarkable career as a tennis star, but at the end of his life, his status as a well-known personality with AIDS may have outweighed his statuses as a retired athlete, author, and political activist. Throughout the world, many people with disabilities find that their status as disabled receives undue weight, overshadowing their actual ability to perform successfully in meaningful employment (Box 5-1).

Our society gives such importance to race and gender that they often dominate our lives. These ascribed statuses frequently influence our achieved status. The Black activist Malcolm X (1925–1965), an eloquent and controversial advocate of Black power and Black pride during the early 1960s, recalled that his feelings and perspectives changed dramatically while in eighth grade. When his English teacher, a White man, advised him that his goal of becoming a lawyer was "no realistic goal for a nigger" and encouraged him instead to become a carpenter, Malcolm X ([1964] 1999:37) found that his being a Black man (ascribed status) was an obstacle to his dream of becoming a lawyer (achieved status). In the United States, the ascribed statuses of race and gender can function as master statuses that have an important impact on one's potential to achieve a desired professional and social status.

Ascribed status may intersect with a person's achieved status. As this doorman greets a resident, the worker's achieved status as a low-wage worker combines with his ethnic status as an African American, an identity that many in this society consider to be lower than that of Whites.

thinking CRITICALLY

Describe a specific master status and explain how it was established. Is it a negative status? If so, how would a person overcome it?

Social Roles

What Are Social Roles? Throughout our lives, we acquire what sociologists call social roles. A **social role** is a set of expectations for people who occupy a given social position or status. Thus, in the United States, we expect that cab drivers will know how to get around a city, that receptionists will be reliable in handling phone messages, and that police officers will take action if they see a citizen being threatened. With each distinctive social status—whether ascribed or achieved—come particular role expectations. However, actual performance varies from individual to individual. One secretary may assume extensive administrative responsibilities, while another may focus on clerical duties. Similarly, in Philip Zimbardo's mock prison experiment, some students were brutal and sadistic guards; others were not.

Roles are a significant component of social structure. Viewed from a functionalist perspective, roles contribute to a society's stability by enabling members to anticipate the behavior of others and to pattern their actions accordingly. Yet social roles can also be dysfunctional if they restrict people's interactions and relationships. If we view a person *only* as a "police officer" or "supervisor," it will be difficult to relate to him or her as a friend or neighbor.

Role Conflict Imagine the delicate situation of a woman who has worked for a decade on an assembly line in an electrical plant, and has recently been named supervisor of her unit. How is this woman expected to relate to her longtime friends and co-workers? Should she still go out to lunch with them, as she has done almost daily for years? Is it her responsibility to recommend the firing of an old friend who cannot keep up with the demands of the assembly line?

Role conflict occurs when incompatible expectations arise from two or more social positions held by the same person. Fulfillment of the roles associated with one status may directly violate the roles linked to a second status. In the example just given, the newly promoted supervisor will most likely experience a sharp conflict between her social and occupational roles. Such role conflicts call for important ethical choices. The new supervisor will have to make a difficult decision about how much allegiance she owes her friend and how much she owes her employers, who have given her supervisory responsibilities.

Another type of role conflict occurs when individuals move into occupations that are not common among people with their ascribed status. Male preschool teachers and female police officers experience this type of role conflict. In the latter case, female officers must strive to reconcile their workplace role in law enforcement with the societal view of a woman's role, which does not embrace many skills needed in police work. And while female police officers encounter sexual harassment, as women do throughout the labor force, they must also deal with the "code of silence," an informal norm that precludes their implicating fellow officers in wrongdoing (Fletcher 1995; S. Martin 1994).

RESEARCH TODAY

5-1 Disability as a Master Status

Throughout history and around the world, people with disabilities have been subjected to cruel and inhuman treatment. For example, in the 20th century, the disabled were frequently viewed as subhuman creatures who were a menace to society. In Japan more than 16,000 women with disabilities were involuntarily sterilized with government approval from 1945 to 1995. Sweden apologized for the same action taken against 62,000 of its citizens in the 1970s.

Such blatantly hostile treatment of people with disabilities has given way to a *medical model,* in which the disabled are viewed as chronic patients. Increasingly, however, people concerned with the rights of the disabled have criticized this model as well. In their view, it is the unnecessary and discriminatory barriers present in the environment—both physical and attitudinal—that stand in the way of people with disabilities, more than any biological limitations. Applying a *civil rights model,* activists emphasize that those with disabilities face widespread prejudice, discrimination, and segregation. For example, most voting places are inaccessible to wheelchair users and fail to provide ballots that can be used by those unable to read print.

Drawing on the earlier work of Erving Goffman, contemporary sociologists have suggested that society attaches a stigma to many forms of disability, a stigma that leads to prejudicial treatment. People with disabilities frequently observe that the nondisabled see them only as blind, wheelchair users, and so forth, rather than as complex human beings with individual

> *In Japan more than 16,000 women with disabilities were involuntarily sterilized with government approval from 1945 to 1995.*

strengths and weaknesses, whose blindness or use of a wheelchair is merely one aspect of their lives.

Although discrimination against the disabled occurs around the world, attitudes are changing. The African nation of Botswana has plans to assist its disabled, most of whom live in rural areas and need special services for mobility and economic development. In many countries, disability rights activists are targeting issues essential to overcoming this master status and becoming a full citizen, including

employment, housing, education, and access to public buildings.

LET'S DISCUSS

1. Does your campus present barriers to disabled students? If so, what kinds of barriers—physical, attitudinal, or both? Describe some of them.
2. Why do you think nondisabled people see disability as the most important characteristic of a disabled person? What can be done to help people see beyond the wheelchair and the Seeing Eye dog?

Sources: Albrecht 2004; Goffman 1963; D. Murphy 1997; *Newsday* 1997; Schaefer 2012; Joseph Shapiro 1993.

---

use your sociological *imagination*

If you were a male nurse, what aspects of role conflict might you experience? Now imagine you are a professional boxer and a woman. What conflicting role expectations might that involve? In both cases, how well do you think you would handle role conflict?

Role Strain Role conflict describes the situation of a person dealing with the challenge of occupying two social positions simultaneously. However, even a single position can cause problems. Sociologists use the term **role strain** to describe the difficulty that arises when the same social position imposes conflicting demands and expectations.

People who belong to minority cultures may experience role strain while working in the mainstream culture. Criminologist Larry Gould (2002) interviewed officers of the Navajo Nation Police Department about their relations with conventional law enforcement officials, such as sheriffs and FBI agents. Besides enforcing the law, Navajo Nation officers practice an alternative form of justice known as Peacemaking, in which they seek reconciliation between the parties to a crime. The officers expressed great confidence in Peacemaking, but worried that if they did not make arrests, other law enforcement officials would think they were too soft, or "just taking care of their own." Regardless of the strength of their ties to traditional Navajo ways, all felt the strain of being considered "too Navajo" or "not Navajo enough."

Role Exit Often, when we think of assuming a social role, we focus on the preparation and anticipatory socialization a person undergoes for that role. Such is true if a person is about to become an attorney, a chef, a spouse, or a parent. Yet until recently, social scientists have given little attention to the adjustments involved in *leaving* social roles.

Sociologist Helen Rose Fuchs Ebaugh (1988) developed the term **role exit** to describe the process of disengagement from a role that is central to one's self-identity in order to establish a new role and identity. Drawing on interviews with 185 people—among them ex-convicts, divorced men and women, recovering alcoholics, ex-nuns, former doctors, retirees, and transexuals—Ebaugh (herself an ex-nun) studied the process of voluntarily exiting from significant social roles.

Ebaugh has offered a four-stage model of role exit. The first stage begins with *doubt.* The person experiences frustration, burnout, or simply unhappiness with an accustomed status and the roles associated with the social position. The second stage involves a *search for alternatives.* A person who is unhappy with his or her career may take a leave of absence; an unhappily married couple may begin what they see as a temporary separation.

TAKING SOCIOLOGY TO WORK

Danielle Taylor, **Account Manager, Cash Cycle Solutions**

When Danielle Taylor entered Clemson University, she was planning to study medicine, but then she discovered that sociology was "ten times more interesting." Today she is an account manager with a company in Charlotte, North Carolina, that provides transaction processing services.

Taylor began her business career as a restaurant manager, a job that involved a good deal of interaction with the public. Sociology prepared her for a diverse work environment, she says, and helped her to handle customer complaints, allowing her to "defuse these often delicate situations more easily and with much less struggle" than managers without her background.

Taylor was managing a corporate restaurant when she made the connection that led to her present position as an account manager. "I was privy to meeting many people with lots of connections in other fields," she explains. "Networking is never as formal as it sounds and just simply conversing with my customers led to me finding a much better suited career."

Taylor thinks she is a more open and understanding person thanks to her sociological training. "I tend to judge less and analyze more," she says. She also sees the big picture that other people might miss. "Managing a restaurant with a degree in sociology was an eye-opening experience," she concludes.

LET'S DISCUSS

1. Before you read this box, would you have thought that a sociology major could be successful as a business manager? Why or why not?
2. Take the skills that Danielle Taylor gained from studying sociology and apply them to the job you hope to get when you graduate. Do they apply just as well to your chosen field?

According to sociologist Helen Rose Fuchs Ebaugh, role exit is a four-stage process. Is this transexual in the first or the fourth stage of changing genders?

The third stage of role exit is the *action stage* or *departure.* Ebaugh found that the vast majority of her respondents could identify a clear turning point that made them feel it was essential to take final action and leave their jobs, end their marriages, or engage in another type of role exit. Twenty percent of respondents saw their role exit as a gradual, evolutionary process that had no single turning point.

The fourth stage of role exit involves the *creation of a new identity.* Many of you participated in a role exit when you made the transition from high school to college. You left behind the role of offspring living at home and took on the role of a somewhat independent college student living with peers in a dorm. Sociologist Ira Silver (1996) has studied the central role that material objects play in this transition. The objects students choose to leave at home (like stuffed animals and dolls) are associated with their prior identities. They may remain deeply attached to those objects, but do not want them to be seen as part of their new identities at college. The objects they bring with them symbolize how they now see themselves and how they wish to be perceived. iPods and wall posters, for example, are calculated to say, "This is me."

Groups

In sociological terms, a **group** is any number of people with similar norms, values, and expectations who interact with one another on a regular basis. The members of a women's basketball team, a hospital's business office, a synagogue, or a symphony orchestra constitute a group. However, the residents of a suburb would not be considered a group, since they rarely interact with one another at one time.

Groups play a vital part in a society's social structure. Much of our social interaction takes place within groups and is influenced by their norms and sanctions. Being a teenager or a retired person takes on special meanings when we interact within groups designed for people with that particular status. The expectations associated with many social roles, including those accompanying the statuses of brother, sister, and student, become more clearly defined in the context of a group. We will examine groups more closely in Chapter 6.

Social Institutions

The mass media, the government, the economy, the family, and the health care system are all examples of social institutions found in our society. **Social institutions** are organized patterns of beliefs and behavior centered on basic social needs, such as replacing personnel (the family) and preserving order (the government).

103

Chapter 5

A close look at social institutions gives sociologists insight into the structure of a society. Consider religion, for example. The institution of religion adapts to the segment of society that it serves. Church work has very different meanings for ministers who serve a skid row area and those who serve a suburban middle-class community. Religious leaders assigned to a skid row mission will focus on tending to the ill and providing food and shelter. In contrast, clergy in affluent suburbs will be occupied with counseling those considering marriage and divorce, arranging youth activities, and overseeing cultural events (R. Schaefer 2008b).

Functionalist View One way to understand social institutions is to see how they fulfill essential functions. Anthropologists and sociologists have identified five major tasks, or functional prerequisites, that a society or relatively permanent group must accomplish if it is to survive:

1. *Replacing personnel.* Any group or society must replace personnel when they die, leave, or become incapacitated. This task is accomplished through such means as immigration, annexation of neighboring groups, acquisition of slaves, or sexual reproduction. The Shakers, a religious sect that came to the United States in 1774, are a conspicuous example of a group that has *failed* to replace personnel. Their religious beliefs commit the Shakers to celibacy; to survive, the group must recruit new members. At first, the Shakers proved quite successful in attracting members, reaching a peak of about 6,000 members in the United States during the 1840s. As of 2011, however, the only Shaker community left in this country was a farm in Maine with three members—one man and two women (R. Schaefer and Zellner 2011).

2. *Teaching new recruits.* No group or society can survive if many of its members reject the group's established behavior and responsibilities. Thus, finding or producing new members is not sufficient; the group or society must also encourage recruits to learn and accept its values and customs. Such learning can take place formally, within schools (where learning is a manifest function), or informally, through interaction in peer groups (where learning is a latent function).

3. *Producing and distributing goods and services.* Any relatively permanent group or society must provide and distribute desired goods and services to its members. Each society establishes a set of rules for the allocation of financial and other resources. The group must satisfy the needs of most members to some extent, or it will risk the possibility of discontent and ultimately disorder.

4. *Preserving order.* Throughout the world, indigenous and aboriginal peoples have struggled to protect themselves from outside invaders, with varying degrees of success. Failure to preserve order and defend against conquest leads to the death not only of a people, but of a culture as well.

5. *Providing and maintaining a sense of purpose.* People must feel motivated to continue as members of a group or society in order to fulfill the first four requirements. On January 20, 2009, in the midst of what would prove the worst economic crisis since the Great Depression, some 2 million Americans crowded the National Mall to witness the inauguration of President Barack Obama, the first African American to be elected to the nation's highest office. The celebration, an expression of

Waving flags and dressed in red, white, and blue, nearly 2 million Americans came together to celebrate the inauguration of President Barack Obama, the nation's first African American president, in January 2009. In the midst of a deepening economic and financial crisis, at that time Obama's election brought hope to Americans of all races, helping them to maintain a sense of purpose in the face of adversity.

both patriotism and Black pride, convinced people of all races that change was possible and better times lay ahead. Faced with huge layoffs and massive home foreclosures, Americans heard the new president's call to serve their nation. Patriotism and racial pride, then, can help people to develop and maintain a sense of purpose. For others, tribal identities, religious values, or personal moral codes are especially meaningful. Whatever the motivator, in any society there remains one common and critical reality: if an individual does not have a sense of purpose, he or she has little reason to contribute to a society's survival.

This list of functional prerequisites does not specify *how* a society and its corresponding social institutions will perform each task. For example, one society may protect itself from external attack by amassing a frightening arsenal of weaponry, while another may make determined efforts to remain neutral in world politics and to promote cooperative relationships with its neighbors. No matter what its particular strategy, any society or relatively permanent group must attempt to satisfy all these functional prerequisites for survival. If it fails on even one condition, the society runs the risk of extinction (Aberle et al. 1950; R. Mack and Bradford 1979).

Perspective	Role of Social Institutions	Focus
Functionalist	Meeting basic social needs	Essential functions
Conflict	Meeting basic social needs	Maintenance of privileges and inequality
Interactionist	Fostering everyday behavior	Influence of the roles and statuses we accept

Conflict View Conflict theorists do not agree with the functionalist approach to social institutions. Although proponents of both perspectives agree that social institutions are organized to meet basic social needs, conflict theorists object to the idea that the outcome is necessarily efficient and desirable.

From a conflict perspective, the present organization of social institutions is no accident. Major institutions, such as education, help to maintain the privileges of the most powerful individuals and groups within a society, while contributing to the powerlessness of others. To give one example, public schools in the United States are financed largely through property taxes. This arrangement allows more affluent areas to provide their children with better-equipped schools and better-paid teachers than low-income areas can afford. As a result, children from prosperous communities are better prepared to compete academically than children from impoverished communities. The structure of the nation's educational system permits and even promotes such unequal treatment of schoolchildren.

Conflict theorists argue that social institutions such as education have an inherently conservative nature. Without question, it has been difficult to implement educational reforms that promote equal opportunity—whether bilingual education, school desegregation, or mainstreaming of students with disabilities. From a functionalist perspective, social change can be dysfunctional, since it often leads to instability. However, from a conflict view, why should we preserve the existing social structure if it is unfair and discriminatory?

Social institutions also operate in gendered and racist environments, as conflict theorists, as well as feminists and interactionists, have pointed out. In schools, offices, and government institutions, assumptions about what people can do reflect the sexism and racism of the larger society. For instance, many people assume that women cannot make tough decisions—even those in the top echelons of corporate management. Others assume that all Black students at elite colleges represent affirmative action admissions. Inequality based on gender, economic status, race, and ethnicity thrives in such an environment—to which we might add discrimination based on age, physical disability, and sexual orientation. The truth of this assertion can be seen in routine decisions by employers on how to advertise jobs, as well as whether to provide fringe benefits such as child care and parental leave.

Interactionist View Social institutions affect our everyday behavior, whether we are driving down the street or waiting in a long shopping line. Sociologist Mitchell Duneier (1994a, 1994b) studied the social behavior of the word processors, all women, who work in the service center of a large Chicago law firm. Duneier was interested in the informal social norms that emerged in this work environment and the rich social network these female employees created.

The Network Center, as it is called, is a single, windowless room in a large office building where the law firm occupies seven floors. The center is staffed by two shifts of word processors, who work either from 4:00 p.m. to midnight or from midnight to 8:00 a.m. Each word processor works in a cubicle with just enough room for her keyboard, terminal, printer, and telephone. Work assignments for the word processors are placed in a central basket and then completed according to precise procedures.

At first glance, we might think that these women labor with little social contact, apart from limited breaks and occasional conversations with their supervisor. However, drawing on the interactionist perspective, Duneier learned that despite working in a large office, these women find private moments to talk (often in the halls or outside the washroom) and share a critical view of the law firm's attorneys and day-shift secretaries. Indeed, the word processors routinely suggest that their assignments represent work that the "lazy" secretaries should have completed during the normal workday. Duneier (1994b) tells of one word processor who resented the lawyers' superior attitude and pointedly refused to recognize or speak with any attorney who would not address her by name.

Interactionist theorists emphasize that our social behavior is conditioned by the roles and statuses we accept, the groups to which we belong, and the institutions within which we function. For example, the social roles associated with being a judge occur within the larger context of the criminal justice system. The status of judge stands in relation to other statuses, such as attorney, plaintiff, defendant, and witness, as well as to the social institution of government. Although courts and jails have great symbolic importance, the judicial system derives its continued significance from the roles people carry out in social interactions (Berger and Luckmann 1966).

Table 5-1 summarizes the three major sociological perspectives on social institutions.

Social Networks

Groups do not merely serve to define other elements of the social structure, such as roles and statuses; they also link the individual with the larger society. We all belong to a number of different groups, and through our acquaintances make connections with people in different social circles. These connections are known as a **social network**—a series of social relationships that links a person directly to others, and through them indirectly to still more people. Social networks are one of the five basic elements of social structure.

Social networks can center on virtually any activity, from sharing job information to exchanging news and gossip, or even sharing sex. In the mid-1990s, sociologists studied romantic relationships at a high school with about 1,000 students. They found that about 61 percent of the girls had been sexually active over

RESEARCH TODAY

Over the past two generations, obesity has become a public health problem in the United States. To explain the trend toward excess weight, researchers have focused on Americans' nutritional practices, as well as on their genetic tendencies. Another variable that contributes to obesity, less obvious than diet and heredity, is social networking.

Researchers identified this last variable in the course of a long-term heart health survey, during which they tracked the weight of 12,067 respondents. At the same time, they mapped the social networks that respondents belonged to (see the accompanying figure). Over the three decades since the survey began, they have

> *Weight gain in one person is often associated with weight gain in his or her friends, siblings, spouse, and neighbors.*

noted that weight gain in one person is often associated with weight gain in his or her friends, siblings, spouse, and neighbors. In fact, a person's chances of becoming obese increased by 57 percent if a friend became overweight during the same period. This association, they found, was attributable solely to selectivity in the choice of friends—that is, to people of a certain weight seeking out others of roughly the same weight.

This study shows that social networks do influence the way people behave. More important, the results suggest that networking could be exploited to spread positive health behaviors—for example, by recruiting friends to participate in a person's weight-loss plan. Through a similar approach, health practitioners

A NETWORK OF THE OBESE

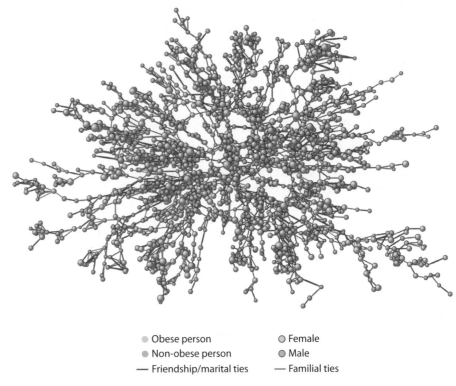

- ● Obese person
- ● Non-obese person
- ○ Female
- ● Male
- — Friendship/marital ties
- — Familial ties

Larger circles represent heavier people.

could include social networking in efforts to control smoking, drinking, and drug abuse.

LET'S DISCUSS

1. Have you ever tried to lose weight, and if so, did your cluster of friends and family help or hinder you? In your experience, do people who are overweight tend to cluster in separate groups from those of normal weight?

2. Besides public health campaigns, what applications can you think of for research on social networking?

Sources: Christakis and Fowler 2007, 2009; Haas et al. 2010.

TREND SPOTTING

The Growth of Online Societies

Sociologists and other scholars who study social structure are turning their attention to online societies. Why? These virtual societies have been growing exponentially. India and China, whose roots go back for thousands of years, both have well over a billion people—an enormous population compared to most other countries. By 2011, however, over 600 million people per month were active in Facebook, an online society that has existed for less than a decade. Facebook's competitor, MySpace, had over 300 million members worldwide that year—a number comparable to the population of the United States. Twitter had 190 million users, more than the population of Pakistan.

the past 18 months. Among the sexually active respondents, the researchers counted only 63 steady couples, or pairs with no other partners. A much larger group of 288 students—almost a third of the sample—was involved in a free-flowing network of relationships (Bearman et al. 2004).

This research on high schoolers' sexual activity, an example of applied sociology, has clear implications for public health. Box 5-2 describes a similar but longer-term study in which public health officials used network analysis to curb obesity.

Involvement in social networks—commonly known as *networking*—is especially valuable in finding employment.

Albert Einstein was successful in finding a job only when a classmate's father put him in touch with his future employer. These kinds of contacts—even those that are weak and distant—can be crucial in establishing social networks and facilitating the transmission of information.

During the recent economic downturn, electronic social networks have served a new purpose, encouraging the jobless. Websites and chat rooms that cannot locate jobs for those who have been thrown out of work concentrate instead on helping them to stick together, support one another, and maintain a positive attitude. For the unemployed, online conversations with friends or even strangers in the same predicament can be an invaluable morale booster (Scherer 2010b).

Virtual Worlds

Today, with recent advances in technology, people can maintain their social networks electronically; they don't need face-to-face contacts. Whether through text-messaging, handheld devices, or social networking sites like Facebook, a significant amount of networking occurs online. Adolescents can now interact freely with distant friends, even under close scrutiny by parents or teachers. Without leaving their cubicles, employees with a taste for adventure can escape their work environments. In Box 4-3 (page 88), we considered the impact of online social networks on the process of socialization.

Virtual networks also can help to preserve real-world networks interrupted by war and other dislocations. The recent deployment of U.S. troops in the Middle East and Afghanistan increased many people's reliance on e-mail. Today, digital photos

and sound files accompany e-mail messages between soldiers and their families and friends. GIs can even view siblings' graduations or children's birthday parties live, via webcams. And U.S. soldiers and Iraqi citizens have been posting their opinions of the war in Iraq in online journals called web logs, or blogs. Though critics are skeptical of the identity of some of the authors, these postings have become yet another source of news about the war (Faith 2005; O'Connor 2004; Sisson 2007).

Case Study The Second Life Virtual World

E-mail, webcams, and blogs are only the first stage in the creation of alternative forms of social reality. Recently a whole new society, the Second Life® world, has sprung up in virtual space. web-based and three-dimensional, the Second Life virtual world included about 18 million networked "players" as of November 2010. In this game, players assume avatars that may represent looking-glass selves very different from their actual identities. Once equipped with an avatar, they go about their lives in the

virtual world, establishing businesses, even buying and decorating homes.

Just like real worlds, virtual worlds have become politicized and commercialized. In 2007, Sweden became the first real-world country to place an "embassy" in the Second Life world. Elsewhere in this virtual world, virtual protesters have paraded on behalf of a far-right French group in a confrontation with anti-Nazi protesters. The Second Life virtual world is now open

Virtual worlds have just begun to test our imaginations. On the left, a group of avatars interacts in the Second Life® world. On the right, in the blockbuster film *Avatar,* the Na'vi people interact in the screen-based virtual world of Pandora.

to real-world corporations that want to "build" their stores in it. Some corporations have even purchased "islands" to use for training sessions or employee conferences. Employees who attend these exclusive functions may show up in their finest avatar attire. The commercialization of these spaces has been met with a good deal of antagonism: Reebok has weathered a virtual nuclear bomb attack, and "customers" have been "shot" outside the American Apparel store.

A more positive side of the Second Life virtual world is evident in Al-Andalus, a democratically run nonprofit community dedicated to interfaith understanding. Begun after 9/11, Al-Andalus has equal numbers of Jewish, Muslim, Christian, and atheist avatars. It even boasts a library to provide objective information on religion, run by an avatar who in real life is a librarian at the Smithsonian Institution (Boellstorff 2008; Borrelli 2010; Castells 2010a, 2010b, 2010c; Gilsdorf 2010; Malaby 2009).

Sociologist Manuel Castells views these emerging electronic social networks as fundamental to new organizations, and to the growth of existing businesses and associations. With other scholars, sociologists are now scrambling to understand these environments and their social processes. The Second Life world went public in 2003—a millennium ago in the world of cyberspace. Scholars worry that after the current period of transition, given the absence of a historical record, reconstructing these worlds as they existed when they were populated by only a hundred avatars, much less tens of thousands, will be impossible.

use your sociological *imagination*

What features of the Second Life world would you like to investigate, and why? How would you go about doing so?

Social Structure in Global Perspective

Modern societies are complex, especially compared to earlier social arrangements. Sociologists Émile Durkheim, Ferdinand Tönnies, and Gerhard Lenski developed ways to contrast modern societies with simpler forms of social structure.

Durkheim's Mechanical and Organic Solidarity

In his *Division of Labor* ([1893] 1933), Durkheim argued that social structure depends on the division of labor in a society—in other words, on the manner in which tasks are performed. Thus, a task such as providing food can be carried out almost totally by one individual, or it can be divided among many people. The latter pattern is typical of modern societies, in which the cultivation, processing, distribution, and retailing of a single food item are performed by literally hundreds of people.

In societies in which there is minimal division of labor, a collective consciousness develops that emphasizes group solidarity. Durkheim termed this collective frame of mind **mechanical solidarity**, implying that all individuals perform the same tasks. In this type of society, no one needs to ask, "What do your parents do?" since all are engaged in similar work. Each person prepares food, hunts, makes clothing, builds homes, and so forth. Because people have few options regarding what to do with their lives, there is little concern for individual needs. Instead, the group is the dominating force in society. Both social interaction and negotiation are based on close, intimate, face-to-face social contacts. Since there is little specialization, there are few social roles.

As societies become more advanced technologically, they rely on greater division of labor, so that no individual can go it alone. Dependence on others becomes essential for group survival. In Durkheim's terms, mechanical solidarity is replaced by **organic**

solidarity, a collective consciousness resting on the need a society's members have for one another. Durkheim chose the term *organic solidarity* because in his view, individuals become interdependent in much the same way as organs of the human body.

Tönnies's *Gemeinschaft* and *Gesellschaft*

Ferdinand Tönnies (1855–1936) was appalled by the rise of an industrial city in his native Germany during the late 1800s. In his view, the city marked a dramatic change from the ideal of a close-knit community, which Tönnies termed a *Gemeinschaft*, to that of an impersonal mass society, known as a *Gesellschaft* (Tönnies [1887] 1988).

The ***Gemeinschaft*** (pronounced guh-MINE-shoft) is typical of rural life. It is a small community in which people have similar backgrounds and life experiences. Virtually everyone knows one another, and social interactions are intimate and familiar, almost as among kinfolk. In this community there is a commitment to the larger social group and a sense of togetherness among members. People relate to others in a personal way, not just as "clerk" or "manager." With this personal interaction comes little privacy, however: we know too much about everyone.

Social control in the *Gemeinschaft* is maintained through informal means such as moral persuasion, gossip, and even

"I'd like to think of you as a person, David, but it's my job to think of you as personnel."

In a *Gesellschaft*, people are likely to relate to one another in terms of their roles rather than their relationships.

Gemeinschaft	Gesellschaft
Rural life typifies this form.	Urban life typifies this form.
People share a feeling of community that results from their similar backgrounds and life experiences.	People have little sense of commonality. Their differences appear more striking than their similarities.
Social interactions are intimate and familiar.	Social interactions are likely to be impersonal and task-specific.
People maintain a spirit of cooperation and unity of will.	Self-interest dominates.
Tasks and personal relationships cannot be separated.	The task being performed is paramount; relationships are subordinate.
People place little emphasis on individual privacy.	Privacy is valued.
Informal social control predominates.	Formal social control is evident.
People are not very tolerant of deviance.	People are more tolerant of deviance.
Emphasis is on ascribed statuses.	Emphasis is on achieved statuses.
Social change is relatively limited.	Social change is very evident, even within a generation.

Think about It

How would you classify the communities with which you are familiar? Are they more *Gemeinschaft* or more *Gesellschaft*?

gestures. These techniques work effectively because people genuinely care how others feel about them. Social change is relatively limited in the *Gemeinschaft;* the lives of members of one generation may be quite similar to those of their grandparents.

In contrast, the ***Gesellschaft*** (pronounced guh-ZELL-shoft) is an ideal community that is characteristic of modern urban life. In this community most people are strangers who feel little in common with other residents. Relationships are governed by social roles that grow out of immediate tasks, such as purchasing a product or arranging a business meeting. Self-interest dominates, and there is little consensus concerning values or commitment to the group. As a result, social control must rest on more formal techniques, such as laws and legally defined punishments. Social change is an important aspect of life in the *Gesellschaft;* it can be strikingly evident even within a single generation.

Table 5-2 summarizes the differences between the *Gemeinschaft* and the *Gesellschaft.* Sociologists have used these terms to compare social structures that stress close relationships with those that emphasize less personal ties. It is easy to view the *Gemeinschaft* with nostalgia, as a far better way of life than the rat race of contemporary existence. However, the more intimate relationships of the *Gemeinschaft* come at a price. The prejudice and discrimination found there can be quite confining; ascribed statuses such as family background often outweigh a person's unique talents and achievements. In addition, the *Gemeinschaft* tends to distrust individuals who seek to be creative or just to be different.

Lenski's Sociocultural Evolution Approach

Sociologist Gerhard Lenski takes a very different view of society and social structure. Rather than distinguishing between two opposite types of society, as Tönnies did, Lenski sees human societies as undergoing a process of change characterized by a dominant pattern known as **sociocultural evolution**. This term refers to long-term trends in societies resulting from the interplay of continuity, innovation, and selection (Nolan and Lenski 2009:361).

In Lenski's view, a society's level of technology is critical to the way it is organized. Lenski defines **technology** as "cultural information about the ways in which the material resources of the environment may be used to satisfy human needs and desires" (Nolan and Lenski 2009:357). The available technology does not completely define the form that a particular society and its social structure take. Nevertheless, a low level of technology may limit the degree to which a society can depend on such things as irrigation or complex machinery. As technology advances, Lenski writes, a community evolves from a preindustrial to an industrial and finally a postindustrial society.

Preindustrial Societies How does a preindustrial society organize its economy? If we know that, we can categorize the society. The first type of preindustrial society to emerge in human history was the **hunting-and-gathering society**, in which people simply rely on whatever foods and fibers are readily available. Technology in such societies is minimal. Organized into groups, people move constantly in search of food. There is little division of labor into specialized tasks.

Hunting-and-gathering societies are composed of small, widely dispersed groups. Each group consists almost entirely of people who are related to one another. As a result, kinship ties are the source of authority and influence, and the social institution of the family takes on a particularly important role. Tönnies would certainly view such societies as examples of the *Gemeinschaft.*

Social differentiation within the hunting-and-gathering society is based on ascribed statuses such as gender, age, and family background. Since resources are scarce, there is relatively little inequality in terms of material goods. By the close of the 20th century, hunting-and-gathering societies had virtually disappeared (Nolan and Lenski 2009).

Chapter 5

Societal Type	First Appearance	Characteristics
Hunting-and-gathering	Beginning of human life	Nomadic; reliance on readily available food and fibers
Horticultural	About 12,000 years ago	More settled; development of agriculture and limited technology
Agrarian	About 5,000 years ago	Larger, more stable settlements; improved technology and increased crop yields
Industrial	1760–1850	Reliance on mechanical power and new sources of energy; centralized workplaces; economic interdependence; formal education
Postindustrial	1960s	Reliance on services, especially the processing and control of information; expanded middle class
Postmodern	Latter 1970s	High technology; mass consumption of consumer goods and media images; cross-cultural integration

Horticultural societies, in which people plant seeds and crops rather than merely subsist on available foods, emerged about 12,000 years ago. Members of horticultural societies are much less nomadic than hunters and gatherers. They place greater emphasis on the production of tools and household objects. Yet technology remains rather limited in these societies, whose members cultivate crops with the aid of digging sticks or hoes (Wilford 1997).

The last stage of preindustrial development is the **agrarian society**, which emerged about 5,000 years ago. As in horticultural societies, members of agrarian societies engage primarily in the production of food. However, technological innovations such as the plow allow farmers to dramatically increase their crop yields. They can cultivate the same fields over generations, allowing the emergence of larger settlements.

The agrarian society continues to rely on the physical power of humans and animals (as opposed to mechanical power). Nevertheless, its social structure has more carefully defined roles than that of horticultural societies. Individuals focus on specialized tasks, such as the repair of fishing nets or blacksmithing. As human settlements become more established and stable, social institutions become more elaborate and property rights more important. The comparative permanence and greater

Preindustrial societies still exist in some remote areas. These indigenous people are from the Envira region of the Amazon rain forest, in Brazil.

surpluses of an agrarian society allow members to create artifacts such as statues, public monuments, and art objects and to pass them on from one generation to the next.

Table 5-3 summarizes Lenski's three stages of sociocultural evolution, as well as the stages that follow, described next.

Industrial Societies Although the Industrial Revolution did not topple monarchs, it produced changes every bit as significant as those resulting from political revolutions. The Industrial Revolution, which took place largely in England during the period 1760 to 1830, was a scientific revolution focused on the application of nonanimal (mechanical) sources of power to labor tasks. An **industrial society** is a society that depends on mechanization to produce its goods and services. Industrial societies rely on new inventions that facilitate agricultural and industrial production, and on new sources of energy, such as steam.

As the Industrial Revolution proceeded, a new form of social structure emerged. Many societies underwent an irrevocable shift from an agrarian-oriented economy to an industrial base. No longer did an individual or a family typically make an entire product. Instead, specialization of tasks and manufacturing of goods became increasingly common. Workers, generally men but also women and even children, left their family homesteads to work in central locations such as factories.

Postindustrial and Postmodern Societies When Lenski first proposed the sociocultural evolutionary approach in the 1960s, he paid relatively little attention to how maturing industrialized societies may change with the emergence of even more advanced forms of technology. More recently, he and other sociologists have studied the significant changes in the occupational structure of industrial societies as they shift from manufacturing to service economies. In the 1970s, sociologist Daniel Bell wrote about the technologically advanced **postindustrial society**, whose economic system is engaged primarily in the processing and control of information. The main output of a postindustrial society is services rather than manufactured goods. Large numbers of people become involved in occupations devoted to the teaching, generation, or dissemination of ideas. Jobs in fields such as advertising, public relations, human

Believe it or not, this photograph was taken in Japan, at Universal Studios theme park in Osaka. In a postmodern society, people consume goods, information, and media images en masse. Universal's park is popularizing U.S. media images abroad, illustrating another characteristic of postmodern societies, globalization.

interaction. Within sociology, the postmodern view offers support for integrating the insights of various theoretical perspectives—functionalism, conflict theory, feminist theory, and interactionism—while incorporating other contemporary approaches. Feminist sociologists argue optimistically that with its indifference to hierarchies and distinctions, the postmodern society will discard traditional values of male dominance in favor of gender equality. Yet, others contend that despite new technologies, postindustrial and postmodern societies can be expected to display the same problems of inequality that plague industrial societies (Denzin 2004; Smart 1990; B. Turner 1990; van Vucht Tijssen 1990).

Durkheim, Tönnies, and Lenski present three visions of society's social structure. While they differ, each is useful, and this textbook will draw on all three. The sociocultural evolutionary approach emphasizes a historical perspective. It does not picture different types of social structure coexisting within the same society. Consequently, one would not expect a single society to include hunters and gatherers along with a postmodern culture. In contrast, Durkheim's and Tönnies's theories allow for the existence of different types of community—such as a *Gemeinschaft* and a *Gesellschaft*—in the same society. Thus, a rural New Hampshire community located 100 miles from Boston can be linked to the city by modern information technology. The main difference between these two theories is a matter of emphasis. While Tönnies emphasized the overriding concern in each type of community—one's own self-interest or the well-being of the larger society—Durkheim emphasized the division (or lack of division) of labor.

The work of these three thinkers reminds us that a major focus of sociology has been to identify changes in social structure and the consequences for human behavior. At the macro level, we see society shifting to more advanced forms of technology. The social structure becomes increasingly complex, and new social institutions emerge to assume some functions that once were performed by the family. On the micro level, these changes affect the nature of social interactions. Each individual takes on multiple social roles, and people come to rely more on social networks and less on kinship ties. As the social structure becomes more complex, people's relationships become more impersonal, transient, and fragmented.

resources, and computer information systems would be typical of a postindustrial society (D. Bell 1999).

Bell views the transition from industrial to postindustrial society as a positive development. He sees a general decline in organized working-class groups and a rise in interest groups concerned with national issues such as health, education, and the environment. Bell's outlook is functionalist, because he portrays the postindustrial society as basically consensual. As organizations and interest groups engage in an open and competitive process of decision making, Bell believes, the level of conflict between diverse groups will diminish, strengthening social stability.

Conflict theorists take issue with Bell's functionalist analysis of the postindustrial society. For example, Michael Harrington (1980), who alerted the nation to the problems of the poor in his book *The Other America,* questioned the significance that Bell attached to the growing class of white-collar workers. Harrington conceded that scientists, engineers, and economists are involved in important political and economic decisions, but he disagreed with Bell's claim that they have a free hand in decision making, independent of the interests of the rich. Harrington followed in the tradition of Marx by arguing that conflict between social classes will continue in the postindustrial society.

Sociologists have gone beyond discussion of the postindustrial society to the ideal of the postmodern society. A **postmodern society** is a technologically sophisticated society that is preoccupied with consumer goods and media images (Brannigan 1992). Such societies consume goods and information on a mass scale. Postmodern theorists take a global perspective, noting the ways that culture crosses national boundaries. For example, residents of the United States may listen to reggae music from Jamaica, eat sushi and other Japanese foods, and wear clogs from Sweden. And online social networks know no national boundaries.

The emphasis of postmodern theorists is on observing and describing newly emerging cultural forms and patterns of social

thinking CRITICALLY

Describe any personal experiences you have had with a nonindustrial, or developing, society. If you have not had that kind of experience, how do you think you would prepare for it?

Media Concentration

One of the most pervasive social institutions in our society, the mass media encompass information outlets ranging from printed leaflets to online virtual worlds. Perhaps more than any other institution, they exemplify our postmodern society. According to Lenski's theory of sociocultural evolution, all societies undergo continual change, whether rapid or slow. In today's postmodern world, one of the more noticeable changes—and a potentially undesirable one—is the trend toward control of the media by fewer and fewer corporations.

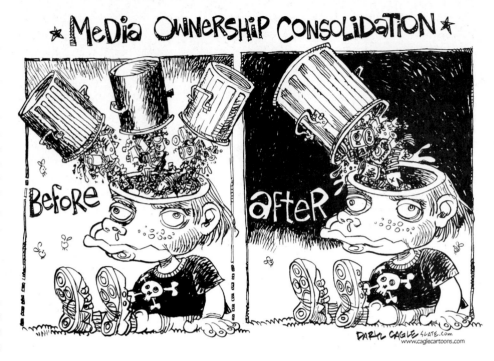

Looking at the Issue

Who owns the media production and distribution process? Increasingly, the answer is a small number of very large corporations. The social consequences of this trend toward the concentration of media ownership are a reduction in the number of information outlets.

True, the United States still has thousands of independent media outlets—small-town newspapers, radio stations, and television broadcasters—but the clear trend in the media industry is toward the consolidation of ownership. The fact is, a few multinational corporations dominate the publishing, broadcasting, and film industries, although their influence may be hard to identify, since global conglomerates manage many different product names. Consider Time Warner (HBO, CNN, AOL, *Time* and *People* magazines); Rupert Murdoch's News Corporation, founded in Australia (Fox Network Television, several book publishers, numerous newspapers and magazines, MySpace.com, Second Life virtual world, and 20th Century Fox); Sony of Japan (Columbia Pictures, IMAX, CBS Records, and Columbia Records); and Viacom/CBS (Paramount, DreamWorks SKG, MTV, and Black Entertainment Television), and the extent of their power becomes clear.

Similar concerns have been raised about the situation in countries such as China, Cuba, Iraq, and North Korea, where the ruling party owns and controls the media. The difference, which is considerable, is that in the United States the gatekeeping process lies in the hands of private individuals, whose main desire is to maximize profits. In totalitarian countries, the gatekeeping process belongs to political leaders, whose desire is to maintain control of the government.

We should note one significant exception to the centralization and concentration of the media: the Internet. Today, more and more people receive their media content through the Internet. The World Wide Web is now accessible to millions of producers of media content, through independent outlets. Obviously, the producer must be technologically proficient and must have access to a computer, but compared to other media outlets, the Internet is much more readily available. Media conglomerates, well aware of the Internet's potential, are already delivering their material via the web. But for now, the Internet is the only medium that allows the average individual to become a media entrepreneur with a potential audience of millions. Some media scholars warn, however, that it is only a matter of time before corporate giants like AT&T and Comcast begin to dominate the Internet (Noam 2009; Wu 2010).

Applying Sociology

Concentration of ownership is not unique to the media (think about aircraft and automobile manufacturers). However, the media deserve special attention given the way they filter our view of reality. New media technologies also form the basis for group membership and networking, making them a powerful influence on today's society.

Functionalists see media concentration—or the consolidation of any business—as a step toward greater economic efficiency. In their view, consolidation reduces the cost of operations, freeing capital for the development of new creative outlets. Furthermore, they believe that global trade in the media facilitates the free exchange of intellectual property, which is often hampered by arbitrary local restrictions (Croteau and Hoynes 2006).

Conflict theorists believe that media concentration stifles opportunities for minority ownership. According to the most recent FCC data, less than 4 percent of television stations in the United States are owned by racial and ethnic minorities; less than 5 percent are owned by women. Minority owners are underrepresented even in markets where minorities make up the majority of the audience (S. Turner and Cooper 2006).

Interactionists see a change in the way people get their news, although not in their interest in it. In the past people may have met or called one another to discuss the latest episode of *Survivor;* now they share the latest Internet news via e-mail or buddy list. Why wait for the evening news when online sources are at your fingertips? Because savvy media users can seek out the media they consume, interactionists suggest that warnings about media concentration may be overdone (Bielby and Harrington 2008).

Initiating Policy

Any discussion of media regulation must begin with the Telecommunications Act of 1996, which marked the first overhaul of media policy since the early 1930s. The act, which covers everything from cable service to social issues such as obscenity and violence, made a significant distinction between information services, such as the Internet, and promoters of telecommunications service—that is, traditional telephone and wireless phone companies, as well as cable companies that offer phone service. Nevertheless, rapid technological development has rendered the act obsolete in many people's minds. With the convergence of telephone service, videocasting, and the Internet, not to mention the delivery of motion pictures online, such distinctions became archaic only a decade after the act was passed.

Significantly, the act eliminated most restrictions on media ownership; those that remain appear to be on their way out, as well. In 2007 the Federal Communications Commission went even further by allowing the consolidation of newspaper and television ownership in cities with only one local newspaper and one local television station. Critics worried that once the transition to digital television was completed in 2009, a single local media outlet could transmit a dozen signals *and* deliver the daily newspaper (Rice 2008).

The lack of governmental restraint of media concentration—indeed, the move toward deregulation of the media under several recent administrations—has been ascribed to the unique relationship politicians have with the media industry, compared to other industries. Elected leaders fear the impact that the media may have on their careers, given the control the media exercise over the flow of information to voters. Although they often complain about bias in the media, they shrink from attacking the corporate and commercial interests that lie behind the media (McChesney 2008).

Take the Issue with You

1. Are you aware of who owns or manages the media you watch or listen to? If not, find out.

2. Do concerns about media concentration differ from concerns over the monopoly of certain products or services? Explain.

3. Does the trend toward media concentration affect traditional media outlets (print, radio, and broadcast television) differently from the Internet? Why or why not?

MASTERING THIS CHAPTER

Summary

Social interaction refers to the ways in which people respond to one another. **Social structure** refers to the way in which a society is organized into predictable relationships. This chapter examines the five basic elements of social structure: **statuses, social roles, groups, social networks,** and **social institutions.**

1. People shape their social reality based on what they learn through their **social interactions**. Social change comes from redefining or reconstructing social reality.

2. An **ascribed status** is generally assigned to a person at birth, whereas an **achieved status** is largely attained through one's own effort. Some ascribed statuses, such as race and gender, can function as **master statuses** that affect one's potential to achieve a certain professional or social status.

3. With each distinctive status—whether ascribed or achieved—comes a particular **social role**, the set of expectations for people who occupy that status.

4. Much of our social behavior takes place in **groups**, which are often linked to **social networks** and their vast resources.

5. **Social institutions** fulfill essential functions, such as replacing personnel, training new recruits, and preserving order. The mass media, the government, the economy, the family, and the health care system are all examples of social institutions.

6. Conflict theorists charge that social institutions help to maintain the privileges of the powerful while contributing to the powerlessness of others.

7. Interactionist theorists stress that our social behavior is conditioned by the roles and statuses we accept, the groups to which we belong, and the institutions within which we function.

8. Recent advances in technology have created virtual worlds in which people can socialize electronically, without face-to-face contacts. Sociologist Manual Castells sees these emerging social networks as fundamental to new organizations and the growth of existing businesses and associations.

9. Émile Durkheim thought that social structure depends on the division of labor in a society. According to Durkheim, societies with minimal division of labor have a collective consciousness called **mechanical solidarity**; those with greater division of labor show an interdependence called **organic solidarity**.

10. Ferdinand Tönnies distinguished the close-knit community of *Gemeinschaft* from the impersonal mass society known as *Gesellschaft*.

11. Gerhard Lenski thinks that a society's social structure changes as its culture and technology become more sophisticated, a process he calls **sociocultural evolution**.

12. The Internet is the one significant exception to the trend toward media concentration, allowing millions of people to produce their own media content.

Key Terms

Achieved status A social position that a person attains largely through his or her own efforts. (page 100)

Agrarian society The most technologically advanced form of preindustrial society. Members engage primarily in the production of food, but increase their crop yields through technological innovations such as the plow. (110)

Ascribed status A social position assigned to a person by society without regard for the person's unique talents or characteristics. (100)

Gemeinschaft A close-knit community, often found in rural areas, in which strong personal bonds unite members. (108)

Gesellschaft A community, often urban, that is large and impersonal, with little commitment to the group or consensus on values. (109)

Group Any number of people with similar norms, values, and expectations who interact with one another on a regular basis. (103)

Horticultural society A preindustrial society in which people plant seeds and crops rather than merely subsist on available foods. (110)

Hunting-and-gathering society A preindustrial society in which people rely on whatever foods and fibers are readily available in order to survive. (109)

Industrial society A society that depends on mechanization to produce its goods and services. (110)

Master status A status that dominates others and thereby determines a person's general position in society. (101)

Mechanical solidarity A collective consciousness that emphasizes group solidarity, characteristic of societies with minimal division of labor. (108)

Organic solidarity A collective consciousness that rests on mutual interdependence, characteristic of societies with a complex division of labor. (108)

Postindustrial society A society whose economic system is engaged primarily in the processing and control of information. (110)

Postmodern society A technologically sophisticated society that is preoccupied with consumer goods and media images. (111)

Role conflict The situation that occurs when incompatible expectations arise from two or more social positions held by the same person. (101)

Role exit The process of disengagement from a role that is central to one's self-identity in order to establish a new role and identity. (102)

Role strain The difficulty that arises when the same social position imposes conflicting demands and expectations. (102)

Social institution An organized pattern of beliefs and behavior centered on basic social needs. (103)

Social interaction The ways in which people respond to one another. (98)

Social network A series of social relationships that links a person directly to others, and through them indirectly to still more people. (105)

Social role A set of expectations for people who occupy a given social position or status. (101)

Social structure The way in which a society is organized into predictable relationships. (98)

Sociocultural evolution Long-term trends in societies resulting from the interplay of continuity, innovation, and selection. (109)

Status A term used by sociologists to refer to any of the full range of socially defined positions within a large group or society. (100)

Technology Cultural information about the ways in which the material resources of the environment may be used to satisfy human needs and desires. (109)

TAKING SOCIOLOGY with you

1. For one day, categorize every media message you receive in terms of its function: Does it socialize, enforce a social norm, confer status, or promote consumption? Keep a record and tally the results. Which function was the most common? What can you conclude from the results?

2. People in certain professions seem particularly susceptible to role conflict. For example, journalists commonly experience role conflict during disasters, crimes, and other distressing situations. Should they offer assistance to the needy or cover breaking news? Select two occupations you may wish to enter and discuss the role conflicts people in them might experience.

3. The functionalist, conflict, and interactionist perspectives can all be used in analyzing social institutions. What are the strengths and weaknesses in each perspective's analysis of those institutions?

Self-Quiz

Read each question carefully and then select the best answer.

1. In the United States, we expect that cab drivers will know how to get around a city. This expectation is an example of which of the following?
   a. role conflict
   b. role strain
   c. social role
   d. master status

2. What occurs when incompatible expectations arise from two or more social positions held by the same person?
   a. role conflict
   b. role strain
   c. role exit
   d. both a and b

3. In sociological terms, what do we call any number of people with similar norms, values, and expectations who interact with one another on a regular basis?
   a. a category
   b. a group
   c. an aggregate
   d. a society

4. Which sociological perspective argues that the present organization of social institutions is no accident?
   a. the functionalist perspective
   b. the conflict perspective
   c. the interactionist perspective
   d. the global perspective

5. The Shakers, a religious sect that came to the United States in 1774, has seen its group membership diminish significantly due to its inability to
   a. teach new recruits.
   b. preserve order.
   c. replace personnel.
   d. provide and maintain a sense of purpose.

6. Which sociologist saw that the "definition of the situation" could mold the thinking and personality of the individual?
   a. Philip Zimbardo
   b. Herbert Blumer
   c. William I. Thomas
   d. Erving Goffman

7. In Zimbardo's mock prison experiment at Stanford University,
   a. the social interactions between the prisoners and the guards influenced the social structure of the prison.
   b. the social structure of the prison influenced the social interactions between the prisoners and the guards.
   c. there was no relationship between social interaction and social structure.
   d. Zimbardo believed that social structure and social interaction influence each other.

8. Social control in what Ferdinand Tönnies termed a *Gemeinschaft* community is maintained through all but which of the following means?
   a. moral persuasion
   b. gossip
   c. legally defined punishment
   d. gestures

9. Sociologist Daniel Bell uses which of the following terms to refer to a society whose economic system is engaged primarily in the processing and control of information?
   a. postmodern
   b. horticultural
   c. industrial
   d. postindustrial

10. A key challenge for sociologists who study virtual social networks is that
    a. people using online social networking often lie about themselves.
    b. technology changes too rapidly.
    c. due to their rapid growth and lack of historical record, reconstructing these virtual worlds as they existed when they were first populated will be impossible.
    d. it's expensive to join a virtual social network.

11. The term _____ _____ refers to the way in which a society is organized into predictable relationships.

12. The Black activist Malcolm X wrote in his autobiography that his position as a Black man, a(n) _____ status, was an obstacle to his dream of becoming a lawyer, a(n) _____ status.

13. Sociologist Helen Rose Fuchs Ebaugh developed the term _____ _____ to describe the process of disengagement from a role that is central to one's self-identity in order to establish a new role and identity.

14. The mass media, the government, the economy, the family, and the health care system are all examples of _____ _____ found in the United States.

15. According to Herbert Blumer, our response to someone's behavior is based on the _____ we attach to his or her actions.

16. In studying the social behavior of word processors in a Chicago law firm, sociologist Mitchell Duneier drew on the _____ perspective.

17. Public health researchers have studied the relationship between social networks and _____.

18. According to Émile Durkheim, societies with a minimal division of labor are characterized by _____ solidarity, while societies with a complex division of labor are characterized by _____ solidarity.

19. In Gerhard Lenski's theory of sociocultural evolution, a society's level of _____ is critical to the way it is organized.

20. A(n) _____ society is a technologically sophisticated society that is preoccupied with consumer goods and media images.

The answers appear upside down

Answers

1 (c); 2 (a); 3 (b); 4 (b); 5 (c); 6 (c); 7 (b); 8 (c); 9 (d); 10 (c); 11 social structure; 12 ascribed; achieved; 13 role exit; 14 social institutions; 15 meaning; 16 interactionist; 17 obesity; 18 mechanical; organic; 19 technology; 20 postmodern

THINKING ABOUT **MOVIES**

Invictus

In post-apartheid South Africa, a rugby team helps Nelson Mandela to build national unity.

The Social Network

This dramatization of the rise of Facebook illustrates the way people connect to one another in the 21st century.

Wendy and Lucy

A young woman wanders through life disconnected from social institutions.

The women's rugby team of
Brown University struggles for
victory. Groups help individuals
to navigate through the larger
social world, including complex
social organizations like
educational institutions.

Ray Kroc (1902–1984), the genius behind the franchising of McDonald's restaurants, was a man with big ideas and grand ambitions. But even Kroc could not have anticipated the astounding impact of his creation. McDonald's is the basis of one of the most influential developments in contemporary society. Its reverberations extend far beyond its point of origin in the United States and in the fast-food business. It has influenced a wide range of undertakings, indeed the way of life, of a significant portion of the world. And having rebounded from some well-publicized economic difficulties, that impact is likely to expand at an accelerating rate in the early 21st century.

. . . I devote all this attention to McDonald's . . . because it serves here as the major example of, and the paradigm for, a wide-ranging process I call McDonaldization. . . . McDonaldization has shown every sign of being an inexorable process, sweeping through seemingly impervious institutions (e.g., religion) and regions (European nations such as France) of the world.

Other types of business are increasingly adapting the principles of the fast-food industry to their needs. Said the vice chairman of Toys "R" Us, "We want to be thought of as a sort of McDonald's of toys." . . . Other chains with similar ambitions include Gap, Jiffy Lube, AAMCO Transmissions, Midas Muffler & Brake Shops, Great Clips, H&R Block, Pearle Vision, Bally's. . . .

Other nations have developed their own variants on the McDonald's chain. . . . Paris, a city whose love for fine cuisine might lead you to think it would prove immune to fast food, has a large number of fast-food croissanteries; the revered French bread has also been McDonaldized. India has a chain of fast-food restaurants, Nirula's, that sells mutton burgers (about 80% of Indians are Hindus, who eat no beef) as well as local Indian cuisine. Mos Burger is a Japanese chain with 1,373 restaurants that, in addition to the usual fare, sell Teriyaki chicken burgers, rice burgers, and "Oshiruko with brown rice cake." . . .

McDonald's is such a powerful model that many businesses have acquired nicknames beginning with Mc. Examples include "McDentists" and "McDoctors," meaning drive-in clinics designed to deal quickly and efficiently with minor dental and medical problems; "McChild" care centers, meaning child care centers such as KinderCare; "McStables," designating the nationwide race horse–training operation of D. Wayne Lucas; and "McPaper," describing the newspaper *USA TODAY.*

> *Ray Kroc (1902–1984), the genius behind the franchising of McDonald's restaurants, was a man with big ideas and grand ambitions.*

(Ritzer 2011:1, 3, 5, 12) Additional information about this excerpt can be found on the Online Learning Center at www.mhhe.com/schaefer13e.

In this excerpt from *The McDonaldization of Society*, sociologist George Ritzer contemplates the enormous influence of a well-known fast-food organization on modern-day culture and social life. Ritzer defines **McDonaldization** as "the process by which the principles of the fast-food restaurant are coming to dominate more and more sectors of American society as well as of the rest of the world" (Ritzer 2011:1). In his book, he shows how the business principles on which the fast-food industry is founded—efficiency, calculability, predictability, and control—have changed not only the way Americans do business and run their organizations, but the way they live their lives. Today, busy families rely on the takeout meals served up by fast-food establishments, and McDonald's has become a regular meeting place for social groups from adolescents to senior citizens.

Despite the runaway success of McDonald's and its imitators, and the advantages these enterprises bring to millions of people around the world (see Box 6-2, page 127), Ritzer is critical of their effect on society. The waste and environmental degradation created by billions of disposable containers and the dehumanized work routines of fast-food crews are two of the disadvantages he cites in his critique. Would the modern world be a better one, Ritzer asks, if it were less McDonaldized?

This chapter considers the impact of groups and organizations on social interaction. Do we behave differently in large groups than in small ones? How do we make large organizations manageable? What effect are current social changes having on the structure of groups? We'll begin by noting the distinctions between various types of groups, with particular attention to the dynamics of small groups. We'll examine how and why formal organizations came into existence and describe Max Weber's model of the modern bureaucracy. Finally, we'll look at recent changes in the workplace, some of which are designed to counteract the failures of bureaucracies. The Social Policy section at the end of the chapter focuses on the status of organized labor today.

Understanding Groups

Most of us use the term *group* loosely to describe any collection of individuals, whether three strangers sharing an elevator or hundreds attending a rock concert. However, in sociological terms a **group** is any number of people with similar norms, values, and expectations who interact with one another on a regular basis. College sororities and fraternities, dance companies, tenants' associations, and chess clubs are all considered groups. The important point is that members of a group share some sense of belonging. This characteristic distinguishes groups from mere *aggregates* of people, such as passengers who happen to be together on an airplane flight, or from *categories* of people, such as those who share a common feature (such as being retired) but otherwise do not act together.

Consider the case of a college singing group. It has agreed-on values and social norms. All members want to improve their singing skills and schedule lots of performances. In addition, like many groups, the singing ensemble has both a formal and an informal structure. The members meet regularly to rehearse; they choose leaders to run the rehearsals and manage their affairs. At the same time, some group members may take on unofficial leadership roles by coaching new members in singing techniques and performing skills.

The study of groups has become an important part of sociological investigation because they play such a key role in the transmission of culture. As we interact with others, we pass on our ways of thinking and acting—from language and values to ways of dressing and leisure activities.

Types of Groups

Sociologists have made a number of useful distinctions between types of groups—primary and secondary groups, in-groups and out-groups, and reference groups.

Primary and Secondary Groups Charles Horton Cooley (1902) coined the term **primary group** to refer to a small group characterized by intimate, face-to-face association and cooperation. The members of a street gang constitute a primary group; so do members of a family living in the same household, as do a group of "sisters" in a college sorority.

Primary groups play a pivotal role both in the socialization process (see Chapter 4) and in the development of roles and statuses. Indeed, primary groups can be instrumental in a person's day-to-day existence. When we find ourselves identifying closely with a group, it is probably a primary group.

We also participate in many groups that are not characterized by close bonds of friendship, such as large college classes and business associations. The term **secondary group** refers to a formal, impersonal group in which there is little social intimacy or mutual understanding (Table 6-1). Secondary groups often emerge in the workplace among those who share special understandings about their occupation. The distinction between primary and secondary groups is not always clear-cut, however. Some social clubs may become so large and impersonal that they no longer function as primary groups.

A pizza delivery crew is an example of a *secondary group*—a formal, impersonal group in which there is little social intimacy or mutual understanding. While waiting for the next delivery, members of this crew will become well enough acquainted to distinguish those who see the job as temporary from those who view it as permanent. They will learn who looks forward to deliveries in perceived high-risk areas and who does not. They may even spend time together after work, joking or boasting about their exploits on the job, but their friendships typically will not develop beyond that point.

A significant amount of sociological research has been done on people's behavior in groups. Box 6-1 on page 122 describes the findings on one well-known but short-lived group, the jury.

TABLE **6-1** COMPARISON OF PRIMARY AND SECONDARY GROUPS

Primary Group	Secondary Group
Generally small	Usually large
Relatively long period of interaction	Relatively short duration, often temporary
Intimate, face-to-face association	Little social intimacy or mutual understanding
Some emotional depth to relationships	Relationships generally superficial
Cooperative, friendly	More formal and impersonal

summingup

In-Groups and Out-Groups A group can hold special meaning for members because of its relationship to other groups. For example, people in one group sometimes feel antagonistic toward or threatened by another group, especially if that group is perceived as being different, either culturally or racially. To identify these "we" and "they" feelings, sociologists use two terms first employed by William Graham Sumner (1906): *in-group* and *out-group*.

An **in-group** can be defined as any group or category to which people feel they belong. Simply put, it comprises everyone who is regarded as "we" or "us." The in-group may be as narrow as a teenage clique or as broad as an entire society. The very existence of an in-group implies that there is an out-group that is viewed as "they" or "them." An **out-group** is a group or category to which people feel they do *not* belong.

In-group members typically feel distinct and superior, seeing themselves as better than people in the out-group. Proper behavior for the in-group is simultaneously viewed as unacceptable behavior for the out-group. This double standard enhances the sense of superiority. Sociologist Robert Merton (1968) described this process as the conversion of "in-group virtues" into "out-group vices." We can see this differential standard operating in worldwide discussions of terrorism. When a group or a nation takes aggressive actions, it usually justifies them as necessary, even if civilians are hurt or killed. Opponents are quick to label such actions with the emotion-laden term of *terrorist* and appeal to the world community for condemnation. Yet these same people may themselves retaliate with actions that hurt civilians, which the first group will then condemn.

"So long, Bill. This is my club. You can't come in."

An exclusive social club is an in-group whose members consider themselves superior to others.

use your sociological *imagination*

Try putting yourself in the shoes of an out-group member. What does your in-group look like from that perspective?

Conflict between in-groups and out-groups can turn violent on a personal as well as a political level. In 1999 two disaffected students at Columbine High School in Littleton, Colorado, launched an attack on the school that left 15 students and teachers dead, including themselves. The gunmen, members of an out-group that other students referred to as the Trenchcoat Mafia, apparently resented taunting by an in-group referred to as the Jocks. Similar episodes have occurred in schools across the nation, where rejected adolescents, overwhelmed by personal and family problems, peer group pressure, academic responsibilities, or media images of violence, have struck out against more popular classmates.

Reference Groups Both primary groups and in-groups can dramatically influence the way an individual thinks and behaves. Sociologists call any group that individuals use as a standard for evaluating themselves and their own behavior a **reference group.** For example, a high school student who aspires to join a social circle of hip-hop music devotees will pattern his or her behavior after that of the group. The student will begin dressing like these peers, listening to the same downloads and DVDs, and hanging out at the same stores and clubs.

Reference groups have two basic purposes. They serve a normative function by setting and enforcing standards of conduct

At a powwow, a drum circle breathes spirit into an ancient tribal tradition. These accomplished ceremonial musicians may serve as a reference group for onlookers who want to know more about drumming.

and belief. The high school student who wants the approval of the hip-hop crowd will have to follow the group's dictates, at least to some extent. Reference groups also perform a comparison function by serving as a standard against which people can measure themselves and others. An actor will evaluate himself or herself against a reference group composed of others in the acting profession (Merton and Kitt 1950).

Reference groups may help the process of anticipatory socialization. For example, a college student majoring in finance may read the *Wall Street Journal,* study the annual reports of corporations, and listen to midday stock market news on the radio. Such a student is using financial experts as a reference group to which he or she aspires.

Often, two or more reference groups influence us at the same time. Our family members, neighbors, and co-workers all shape different aspects of our self-evaluation. In addition, reference group attachments change during the life cycle. A corporate executive who quits the rat race at age 45 to become a social worker will find new reference groups to use as standards for evaluation. We shift reference groups as we take on different statuses during our lives.

Coalitions As groups grow larger, coalitions begin to develop. A **coalition** is a temporary or permanent alliance geared toward a common goal. Coalitions can be broad-based or narrow and can take on many different objectives. Sociologist William Julius Wilson (1999) has described community-based organizations in Texas that include Whites and Latinos, working class and affluent, who have banded together to work for improved sidewalks, better drainage systems, and comprehensive street paving. Out of this type of coalition building, Wilson hopes, will emerge better interracial understanding.

Some coalitions are intentionally short-lived. For example, short-term coalition building is a key to success in popular TV programs like *Survivor.* In the program's first season, *Survivor: Borneo,* broadcast in 2000, the four members of the "Tagi alliance" banded together to vote fellow castaways off the island. The political world is also the scene of many temporary coalitions. For example, in 1997 big tobacco companies joined with anti-smoking groups to draw up a settlement for reimbursing states for tobacco-related medical costs. Soon after the settlement was announced the coalition members returned to their decades-long fight against each other (Pear 1997).

Studying Small Groups

Sociological research done on the micro level and research done from the interactionist perspective usually focus on the study of small groups. Box 6-1, for example, describes microsociological research on juries. The term **small group** refers to a group small enough for all members to interact simultaneously—that is, to talk with one another or at least be well acquainted.

In 2010, when 33 Chilean miners were trapped together far beneath the earth's surface, their plight created a highly unusual opportunity for scholars to study their small group. Researchers were especially interested in how the 33 men would form coalitions or subgroups. The miners first divided into work groups, to move rocks and debris and prepare for their eventual rescue. There were some rifts in their social structure. Five men who worked for a different subcontractor chose to live apart from the others and to collaborate on their own escape strategy. And friction developed when the overstressed miners sent their first videos up to the surface, and some men felt that others were showing off. As the details of the escape plan being developed aboveground became clear, however, the group united around their shared goal of survival and escape (R. Carroll and Franklin 2010).

Throughout the 70-day ordeal, the miners remained aware of the attention their story was drawing in the international news media. To prepare themselves to speak to the press when they surfaced, they studied a manual called *Tactics for Public Speaking.* As their rescue drew closer, the anticipatory socialization intensified. Via closed-circuit TV, the men received training on how to remain poised during interviews and on how to indicate politely that they preferred not to answer a question (Jonathan Franklin 2010, 2011; Kluger 2010).

Size of a Group At what point does a collection of people become too large to be called a small group? That is not clear. In a group with more than 20 members, it is difficult for individuals to interact regularly in a direct and intimate manner. But even within a range of 2 to 20 people, group size can substantially alter the quality of social relationships. For example, as the number of group participants increases, the most active communicators become even more active relative to others. Therefore, a person who dominates a group of 3 or 4 members will be relatively more dominant in a 15-person group.

Can you outwit, outplay, outlast your competition? Maybe a coalition can help. In *Survivor: Redemption Island,* coalition building continued to be one of the keys to success in the long-running television series, now in its 22nd season.

121

RESEARCH TODAY

6-1 The Drinking Rape Victim: Jury Decision Making

She was heavily intoxicated. He had drunk a few beers. They had sex. She said she was raped. He said it was consensual. The jury deliberated, and the verdict was. . . .

This is not an actual case, but an experiment in group decision making. Few small groups have received as much attention from sociologists over the past decade and a half as juries. Scholars have used several research methods to investigate juries' decision making: interviews with jury members after they have reached a verdict; observation of jurors as they sit through and react to courtroom events; observation of actual jury deliberations, which presiding judges have permitted in a few instances; and experiments involving mock juries. The findings indicate that jurors do not always make decisions the way they are supposed to.

How do jurors form impressions in rape cases, especially those that involve intoxication?

To find out, legal scholars Emily Finch and Vanessa Munro simulated a rape trial in which intoxication was an issue. The two researchers varied the story to see what the effect might be on the verdict. In one version the alleged victim was drunk; in another

> *Finch and Munro found that male or female, the mock jurors in their study followed a double standard.*

she was drugged by a third person; in another she was drugged by the defendant.

Finch and Munro found that male or female, the mock jurors in their study followed a double standard. The more intoxicated the *defendant* was said to have been, the less likely jurors were to regard him as culpable. They were far more likely to regard a *victim* who had drunk too much as having contributed to her rape. This finding applied even in cases in which the victim's drink had been

spiked. In short, before jurors could summon up much sympathy for the victim, the defendant had to engage in a great deal of bad behavior.

Today, research on juries is expanding to deal with generational changes in the experience of being a juror. Some jurors arrive at court expecting to see the kind of sophisticated DNA analysis or investigative methods featured on televised crime shows, such as *CSI*. Improved methods of documenting crime scenes, including the use of computer-generated re-creations, mean that today's jurors are more likely than past jurors to be exposed to images of graphic violence and gore.

LET'S DISCUSS

1. Have you ever served on a jury? If so, were you aware of jurors who made up their minds early in the trial, despite the judge's instructions? Did you experience stress from being exposed to graphic images of violence and bloodshed?
2. Is a jury a typical group? Why or why not?

Sources: S. Diamond and Rose 2005; Finch and Munro 2005, 2007, 2008; McGlynn and Munro 2010.

Group size also has noticeable social implications for members who do not assume leadership roles. In a larger group, each member has less time to speak, more points of view to absorb, and a more elaborate structure to function in. At the same time, an individual has greater freedom to ignore certain members or viewpoints than he or she would in a smaller group. It is harder to disregard someone in a 4-person workforce than someone in an office with 30 employees, harder to disregard someone in a string quartet than someone in a college band with 50 members.

The German sociologist Georg Simmel (1858–1918) is credited as the first sociologist to emphasize the importance of interactive processes within groups and to note how they change as the group's size changes. The simplest of all social groups or relationships is the **dyad,** or two-member group. A wife and husband constitute a dyad, as does a business partnership or a singing duo. The dyad offers a special level of intimacy that cannot be duplicated in larger groups. However, as Simmel ([1917] 1950) noted, a dyad, unlike any other group, can be destroyed by the loss of a single member. Therefore, the threat of termination hangs over a dyadic relationship perhaps more than over any other.

Obviously, the introduction of one additional person to a dyad dramatically transforms the character of the small group. The dyad becomes a three-member group, or **triad.** The third member has many ways of interacting with and influencing the dynamics of the group. The new person may play a *unifying* role in the triad. When a married couple has their first child, the baby may serve to bind the group closer together. A newcomer also may play a *mediating* role

Miners trapped underground in Chile raise a flag, putting a brave face on their plight in a video made for their friends and families. Their extended stay together gave scholars a rare opportunity to study a small group under stress.

in a three-person group. If two roommates are perpetually sniping at each other, the third roommate may attempt to remain on good terms with both and to arrange compromise solutions to problems. Finally, a member of a triad can choose to employ a *divide-and-rule* strategy. Such is the case, for example, with a coach who tries to gain greater control over two assistants by making them rivals (Lawler et al. 2008; H. Nixon 1979).

Groupthink Can mere membership in a group cause those who belong to reach faulty decisions? William H. Whyte Jr. (1952) thought so. To describe the uncritical acceptance of or conformity to the prevailing viewpoint—a phenomenon that too often characterizes group decision making—Whyte coined the term **groupthink.** Simply put, group members experience a collective pressure to conform to the predominant line of thought. This social pressure effectively discourages the open expression of dissent.

In Whyte's opinion, high-level government leaders and their advisers are particularly prone to groupthink. These people confer regularly with one another, often in closed meetings in which they hear no one else's viewpoint. When decision makers are isolated from others in this way, they are liable to adopt unpopular or even disastrous policies. Of course, groupthink is not limited to the upper echelons of government. It occurs in jury rooms, corporate boardrooms, and even among high school students selecting a theme for their senior prom.

There are ways to avoid the illusion of unanimity created by groupthink. Small-group studies have shown the value of having outside facilitators lead groups. Dividing an established group into smaller units also encourages the expression of new perspectives (Janis 1967; Street 1997).

The effects of group size and groupthink on group dynamics are but two of the many aspects of the small group that sociologists have studied. Another aspect, conformity and deviance, is examined in Chapter 8. Although it is clear that small-group encounters have considerable influence on our lives, we are also deeply affected by much larger groups of people, as we'll see in the next section.

Focus Groups Sociological study of small groups led to the development of the *focus group,* a research tool commonly used in marketing and politics. A **focus group** is a carefully selected discussion group led by a trained moderator. Typically composed of 8 to 10 participants, focus groups are used to collect qualitative data on people's opinions, feelings, and ideas. Often, they are used to gauge the attractiveness of a new consumer product, such as a car, or to evaluate a 30-second TV ad for a political candidate.

Focus groups were developed by the sociologist Robert Merton during World War II. Merton was doing government-funded research to determine how military and civilian morale could be improved during wartime. The groups allowed researchers to gather data quickly, by interviewing several people at once rather than individually. They also allowed researchers to observe how people make decisions in groups rather than as individuals. Today, the techniques for selecting groups, moderating discussions, and interpreting participants' comments have evolved to the point that many researchers specialize in

Researchers watch members of a focus group through a one-way mirror. The idea of observing or monitoring a group's discussion of an idea or product was conceived by the sociologist Robert Merton.

the creation of focus groups. In fact, focus groups are one of the most widespread, if often unheralded practical applications not only of the study of groups, but of the entire discipline of sociology (R. Lee 2010; Merton and Kendall 1946).

Focus groups reflect Merton's belief in the integration of macrosociology and microsociology (see Chapter 1). Although the observation of focus groups is an application of microsociology, it has implications for society as a whole. For example, in the jury study described in this chapter (see Box 6-1), focus groups served as mock juries, allowing researchers to observe how jurors make decisions. The researchers then used this microsociological data to generalize about how the judicial system as a whole handles rape cases involving drinking or illegal drugs.

Understanding Organizations

Formal Organizations and Bureaucracies

As contemporary societies have shifted to more advanced forms of technology and their social structures have become more complex, our lives have become increasingly dominated by large secondary groups referred to as *formal organizations.* A **formal organization** is a group designed for a special purpose and structured for maximum efficiency. The U.S. Postal Service, McDonald's, and the Boston Pops orchestra are examples of formal organizations. Though organizations vary in their size, specificity of goals, and degree of efficiency, they are all structured to facilitate the management of large-scale operations. They also have a bureaucratic form of organization, described in the next section.

In our society, formal organizations fulfill an enormous variety of personal and societal needs, shaping the lives of every one of us. In fact, formal organizations have become such a dominant force that we must create organizations to supervise other organizations, such as the Securities and Exchange Commission (SEC) to regulate brokerage companies. Although it sounds more exciting to say that we live in the "computer age" than to say that we live in the "age of formal organization," the latter is probably a more accurate description (Azumi and Hage 1972; Etzioni 1964).

Ascribed statuses such as gender, race, and ethnicity can influence how we see ourselves within formal organizations. For example, a study of female lawyers in the nation's largest law firms found significant differences in the women's self-images, depending on the relative presence or absence of women in positions of power. In firms in which less than 15 percent of partners were women, the female lawyers were likely to believe that "feminine" traits were strongly devalued and that "masculine" traits were equated with success. As one female attorney put it, "Let's face it: this is a man's environment, and it's sort of Jock City, especially at my firm." Women in firms where female lawyers were better represented in positions of power had a stronger desire for and higher expectations of promotion (Ely 1995:619).

Characteristics of a Bureaucracy

A **bureaucracy** is a component of formal organization that uses rules and hierarchical ranking to achieve efficiency. Rows of desks staffed by seemingly faceless people, endless lines and forms, impossibly complex language, and frustrating encounters with red tape—all these unpleasant images have combined to make *bureaucracy* a dirty word and an easy target in political campaigns. As a result, few people want to identify their occupation as "bureaucrat," despite the fact that all of us perform various bureaucratic tasks. In an industrial society, elements of bureaucracy enter into almost every occupation.

Max Weber ([1913–1922] 1947) first directed researchers to the significance of bureaucratic structure. In an important sociological advance, Weber emphasized the basic similarity of structure and process found in the otherwise dissimilar enterprises of religion, government, education, and business. Weber saw bureaucracy as a form of organization quite different from the family-run business. For analytical purposes, he developed an ideal type of bureaucracy that would reflect the most characteristic aspects of all human organizations. By **ideal type** Weber meant a construct or model for evaluating specific cases. In actuality, perfect bureaucracies do not exist; no real-world organization corresponds exactly to Weber's ideal type.

Weber proposed that whether the purpose is to run a church, a corporation, or an army, the ideal bureaucracy displays five basic characteristics. A discussion of those characteristics, as well as the dysfunctions of a bureaucracy, follows.

1. **Division of labor.** Specialized experts perform specific tasks. In your college bureaucracy, the admissions officer does not do the job of registrar; the guidance counselor does not see to the maintenance of buildings. By working at a specific task, people are likely to become highly skilled and carry out a job with maximum efficiency. This emphasis on specialization is so basic a part of our lives that we may not realize it is a fairly recent development in Western culture.

The downside of division of labor is that the fragmentation of work into smaller and smaller tasks can divide workers and remove any connection they might feel to the overall objective of the bureaucracy. In *The Communist Manifesto* (written in 1848), Karl Marx and Friedrich Engels charged that the capitalist system reduces workers to a mere

Being an accountant in a large corporation may be a relatively high-paying occupation. In Marxist terms, however, accountants are vulnerable to alienation, since they are far removed from the product or service that the corporation creates.

"appendage of the machine" (Tucker 1978). Such a work arrangement, they wrote, produces extreme **alienation**—a condition of estrangement or dissociation from the surrounding society. According to both Marx and conflict theorists, restricting workers to very small tasks also weakens their job security, since new employees can easily be trained to replace them.

Although division of labor has certainly enhanced the performance of many complex bureaucracies, in some cases it can lead to **trained incapacity;** that is, workers become so specialized that they develop blind spots and fail to notice obvious problems. Even worse, they may not care about what is happening in the next department. Some observers believe that such developments have caused workers in the United States to become less productive on the job.

In some cases, the bureaucratic division of labor can have tragic results. In the wake of the coordinated attacks on the World Trade Center and the Pentagon on September 11, 2001, Americans wondered aloud how the FBI and CIA could have failed to detect the terrorists' elaborately planned operation. The problem, in part, turned out to be the division of labor between the FBI, which focuses on domestic matters, and the CIA, which operates overseas. Officials at these intelligence-gathering organizations, both of which are huge bureaucracies, are well known for jealously guarding information from one another. Subsequent investigations revealed that they knew about Osama bin Laden and his Al-Qaeda terrorist network in the early 1990s. Unfortunately, five federal agencies—the CIA, FBI, National Security Agency, Defense Intelligence Agency, and National Reconnaissance Office—failed to share their leads on the network. Although the hijacking of the four commercial airliners used in the massive attacks may not have been preventable, the bureaucratic division of labor definitely hindered efforts to defend against terrorism, undermining U.S. national security.

2. **Hierarchy of authority.** Bureaucracies follow the principle of hierarchy; that is, each position is under the supervision of a higher authority. A president heads a college bureaucracy; he or she selects members of the administration, who in turn hire their own staff. In the Roman Catholic Church, the pope is the supreme authority; under him are cardinals, bishops, and so forth.

3. **Written rules and regulations.** What if your sociology professor gave your classmate an A for having such a friendly smile? You might think that wasn't fair, that it was against the rules. Through written rules and regulations, bureaucracies generally offer employees clear standards for an adequate (or exceptional) performance. In addition, procedures provide a valuable sense of continuity in a bureaucracy. Individual workers will come and go, but the structure and past records of the organization give it a life of its own that outlives the services of any one bureaucrat.

Of course, rules and regulations can overshadow the larger goals of an organization to the point that they become dysfunctional. What if a hospital emergency room physician failed to treat a seriously injured person because he or she had no valid proof of U.S. citizenship? If blindly applied, rules no longer serve as a means to achieving an objective, but instead become important (and perhaps too important) in their own right. Robert Merton (1968) used the term **goal displacement** to refer to overzealous conformity to official regulations.

4. **Impersonality.** Max Weber wrote that in a bureaucracy, work is carried out *sine ira et studio*, "without hatred or passion." Bureaucratic norms dictate that officials perform their duties without giving personal consideration to people as individuals. Although this norm is intended to guarantee equal treatment for each person, it also contributes to the often cold and uncaring feeling associated with modern organizations. We typically think of big government and big business when we think of impersonal bureaucracies. In some cases, the impersonality that is associated with a bureaucracy can have tragic results. More frequently, bureaucratic impersonality produces frustration and disaffection. Today, even small firms filter callers with electronic menus.

5. **Employment based on technical qualifications.** Within the ideal bureaucracy, hiring is based on technical qualifications rather than on favoritism, and performance is measured against specific standards. Written personnel policies dictate who gets promoted, and people often have a right to appeal if they believe that particular rules have been violated. Such procedures protect bureaucrats against arbitrary dismissal, provide a measure of security, and encourage loyalty to the organization.

Although ideally, any bureaucracy will value technical and professional competence, personnel decisions do not always follow that ideal pattern. Dysfunctions within bureaucracy have become well publicized, particularly because of the work of Laurence J. Peter. According to the **Peter principle,** every employee within a hierarchy tends to rise to his or her level of incompetence (Peter and Hull 1969). This hypothesis, which has not been directly or systematically tested, reflects a possible dysfunctional outcome of advancement on the basis of merit. Talented people receive promotion after promotion, until sadly, some of them finally achieve positions that they cannot handle with their usual competence.

Table 6-2 summarizes the five characteristics of bureaucracy. These characteristics, developed by Max Weber more than 80 years ago, describe an ideal type rather than an actual bureaucracy. Not every formal organization will possess all five of Weber's characteristics. In fact, wide variation exists among actual bureaucratic organizations.

Bureaucracy pervades modern life; through McDonaldization, it has reached new heights. As Box 6-2 on page 127 shows, the McDonald's organization provides an excellent illustration of Weber's concept of bureaucracy (Ritzer 2011).

---

use your sociological *imagination*

Your school or workplace suddenly ceases to exhibit one of the five characteristics of bureaucracy. Which characteristic is it, and what are the consequences?

Bureaucratization as a Process Have you ever had to speak to 10 or 12 individuals in a corporation or government agency just to find out which official has jurisdiction over a particular problem? Ever been transferred from one department to another until you finally hung up in disgust? Sociologists have used the term **bureaucratization** to refer to the process by which a group, organization, or social movement becomes increasingly bureaucratic.

Normally, we think of bureaucratization in terms of large organizations. But bureaucratization also takes place within small-group settings. Sociologist Jennifer Bickman Mendez (1998)

TREND
SPOTTING

Joining Up: Voluntary Associations in the United States

One alternative to the formal, bureaucratic organization is the *voluntary association*, a collection of people with a common interest whose members volunteer or even pay to join. Voluntary associations have always been popular in the United States. By 2011, more than 25,000 such nonprofit associations existed, from the Girl Scouts of America to the American Association of Aardvark Aficionados.

What accounts for the popularity of the voluntary association? Some scholars see Americans as individualists who prefer to pursue their own interests on their own terms. Others see the United States as a nation of joiners. Data tend to support the second explanation. Since 1974, fully 70 percent of adults in the United States have belonged to at least one voluntary association; more than 25 percent belong to three or more. This proportion has not changed over time. In other countries, the willingness to join is not as great as in the United States, largely because of lower participation in religious groups.

Characteristic	Positive Consequence	Negative Consequence	
		For the Individual	For the Organization
Division of labor	Produces efficiency in a large-scale corporation	Produces trained incapacity	Produces a narrow perspective
Hierarchy of authority	Clarifies who is in command	Deprives employees of a voice in decision making	Permits concealment of mistakes
Written rules and regulations	Let workers know what is expected of them	Stifle initiative and imagination	Lead to goal displacement
Impersonality	Reduces bias	Contributes to feelings of alienation	Discourages loyalty to company
Employment based on technical qualifications	Discourages favoritism and reduces petty rivalries	Discourages ambition to improve oneself elsewhere	Fosters Peter principle

studied domestic houseworkers employed in central California by a nationwide franchise. She found that housekeeping tasks were minutely defined, to the point that employees had to follow 22 written steps for cleaning a bathroom. Complaints and special requests went not to the workers, but to an office-based manager.

Oligarchy: Rule by a Few Conflict theorists have examined the bureaucratization of social movements. The German sociologist Robert Michels (1915) studied socialist parties and labor unions in Europe before World War I and found that such organizations were becoming increasingly bureaucratic. The emerging leaders of the organizations—even some of the most radical—had a vested interest in clinging to power. If they lost their leadership posts, they would have to return to full-time work as manual laborers. (For a discussion of the status of labor unions today, see the Social Policy section at the end of this chapter.)

Through his research, Michels originated the idea of the **iron law of oligarchy,** which describes how even a democratic organization will eventually develop into a bureaucracy ruled by a few, called an oligarchy. Why do oligarchies emerge? People who achieve leadership roles usually have the skills, knowledge, or charismatic appeal (as Weber noted) to direct, if not control, others. Michels argued that the rank and file of a movement or organization look to leaders for direction and thereby reinforce the process of rule by a few. In addition, members of an oligarchy are strongly motivated to maintain their leadership roles, privileges, and power.

Bureaucracy and Organizational Culture

How does bureaucratization affect the average individual who works in an organization? The early theorists of formal organizations tended to neglect this question. Max Weber, for example, focused on the management personnel in bureaucracies, but had little to say about workers in industry or clerks in government agencies.

According to the **classical theory,** or **scientific management approach,** of formal organizations, workers are motivated almost entirely by economic rewards. This theory stresses that only the physical constraints on workers limit their productivity. Therefore, workers may be treated as a resource, much like the machines that began to replace them in the 20th century. Under the scientific management approach, management attempts to achieve maximum work efficiency through scientific planning, established performance standards, and careful supervision of workers and production. Planning involves efficiency studies but not studies of workers' attitudes or job satisfaction.

SOCIOLOGY IN THE GLOBAL COMMUNITY

6-2 McDonald's and the Worldwide Bureaucratization of Society

In his book *The McDonaldization of Society,* sociologist George Ritzer notes the enormous influence of a well-known fast-food organization on modern-day culture and social life.

Not surprisingly, Max Weber's five characteristics of bureaucracy are apparent in McDonald's restaurants, as well as in the global corporation behind them. Food preparation and order-taking reflect a painstaking *division of labor,* implemented by a *hierarchy of authority* that stretches from the food workers up to the store operator, and ultimately to the corporate board of directors. Store operators learn McDonald's *written rules and regulations,* which govern even the amount of ketchup or mustard placed on a hamburger, at McDonald's Hamburger University. Little bonding occurs between servers and customers, creating a pervasive sense of *impersonality.* Finally, employees are expected to have specific *technical qualifications,* although most of the skills they need to perform routine tasks can be learned in a brief training period.

The real significance of McDonaldization is that it is not confined to the food-service industry or to coffee shops like Starbucks. Worldwide, McDonald's brand of predictability, efficiency, and dependence on nonhuman technology have become customary in a number of services, ranging from medical care to wedding planning to education. Even sporting events reflect the influence of bureaucratization. Around the world, stadiums are becoming increasingly similar, both physically and in the way they present the sport to spectators. All seats offer spectators an unrestricted view, and a big screen guarantees them access to instant replays. Scores, player statistics, and attendance figures are updated automatically by computer and displayed on an automated scoreboard or fed to people's smartphones. Spectator enthusiasm is manufactured through digital displays urging

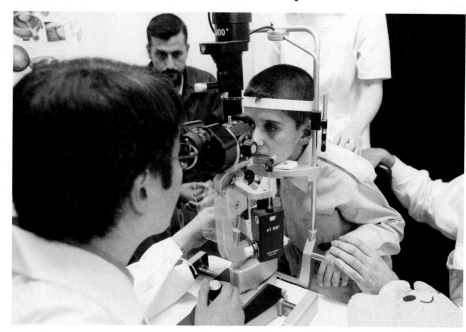

The worldwide success of highly efficient fast-food operations has led to the bureaucratization of many other services, including eye care and other forms of medical treatment.

applause or rhythmic chanting. And of course, the merchandising of teams' and even players' names and images is highly controlled.

> *Worldwide, McDonald's brand of predictability, efficiency, and dependence on nonhuman technology have become customary in a number of services, ranging from medical care to wedding planning to education.*

McDonald's reliance on the five characteristics of bureaucracy is not revolutionary.

What is new is the bureaucratization of services and life events that once were highly individualized, at times even spontaneous. More and more, society itself is undergoing McDonaldization.

LET'S DISCUSS

1. What features of fast-food restaurants do you appreciate? Do you have any complaints about them?
2. Analyze life at your college using Weber's model of bureaucracy. What elements of McDonaldization do you see? Do you wish life were less McDonaldized?

Sources: Ormond 2005; Ritzer 2008, 2011.

Not until workers organized unions—and forced management to recognize that they were not objects—did theorists of formal organizations begin to revise the classical approach. Social scientists became aware that along with management and administrators, informal groups of workers have an important impact on organizations. An alternative way of considering bureaucratic dynamics, the **human relations approach,** emphasizes the role of people, communication, and participation in a bureaucracy. This type of analysis reflects the interest of interactionist theorists in small-group behavior. Unlike planning under the scientific management approach, planning based on the human relations approach focuses on

workers' feelings, frustrations, and emotional need for job satisfaction.

The gradual move away from a sole focus on the physical aspects of getting the job done—and toward the concerns and needs of workers—led advocates of the human relations approach to stress the less formal aspects of bureaucratic structure. Informal groups and social networks within organizations develop partly as a result of people's ability to create more direct forms of communication than under the formal structure. Charles Page (1946) used the term *bureaucracy's other face* to refer to the unofficial activities and interactions that are such a basic part of daily organizational life.

Today, research on formal organizations is following new avenues. Among them are

- the recent arrival of a small number of women and minority group members in high-level management;
- in large corporations, the decision-making role of groups that lie outside the top ranks of leadership;
- the loss of fixed boundaries in organizations that have outsourced key functions; and
- the role of the Internet and virtual worlds in influencing business and consumer preferences.

Though research on organizations still embraces Max Weber's insights, then, it has gone well beyond them (Hamm 2007; Kleiner 2003; W. Scott and Davis 2007).

thinking CRITICALLY

Select an organization that is familiar to you—for example, your college, workplace, religious institution, or civic association—and apply Weber's five characteristics of bureaucracy to it. To what degree does it correspond to Weber's ideal type of bureaucracy?

The Changing Workplace

Weber's work on bureaucracy and Michels's thinking on oligarchy are still applicable to the organizational structure and culture of the workplace. However, today's factories and offices are undergoing rapid, profound changes unanticipated a century or more ago. Besides the far-reaching impact of technological advances such as computerization, workers must cope with organizational restructuring. This section will detail the dramatic changes evident in today's workplace.

Organizational Restructuring

To some extent, individual businesses, community organizations, and government agencies are always changing, if only because of personnel turnover. Since the late 20th century, however, formal organizations have been experimenting with new ways of getting the job done, some of which have significantly altered the workplace.

Collective decision making, or the active involvement of employee problem-solving groups in corporate management, first became popular in the United States in the 1980s. Management gurus had noted the dazzling success of Japanese automobile and consumer products manufacturers. In studying these companies, they found that problem-solving groups and an emphasis on continuous improvement were two keys to success. However, even the most successful Japanese corporations must constantly retool. Over the last few years, a series of embarrassing recalls at Toyota has forced the world's largest automobile company to restructure. Now, even a single consumer complaint receives quick attention, and problems with a product in one country are communicated worldwide (Maynard 2010).

Another innovation in the workplace, called *minimal hierarchy,* replaces the traditional bureaucratic hierarchy of authority with a flatter organizational structure. Minimal hierarchy offers workers

Work teams are a part of formal organizations.

greater access to those in authority, giving them an opportunity to voice concerns that might not be heard in a traditional bureaucracy. This new organizational structure is thought to minimize the potential for costly and dangerous bureaucratic oversights.

Finally, organizational *work teams* have become increasingly common, even in smaller organizations. There are two types of work team. *Project teams* address ongoing issues, such as safety or compliance with the Americans with Disabilities Act. *Task forces* pursue nonrecurring issues, such as a major building renovation. In both cases, team members are released to some degree from their regular duties in order to contribute to the organizationwide effort (W. Scott and Davis 2007; Huff 2007).

The common purpose of work teams, minimal hierarchy, and collective decision making is to empower workers. For that reason, these new organizational structures can be exciting for the employees who participate in them. But these innovations rarely touch the vast numbers of workers who perform routine jobs in factories and office buildings. The 1.7 million who are paid by the hour and who earn the minimum wage or lower know little about organizational restructuring (Bureau of Labor Statistics 2009).

Together with organizational restructuring, societal changes well in place at the beginning of the 21st century have weakened the impact of bureaucratization on the workplace. As a result of globalization, today's formal organizations are less likely than those of the past to be self-contained. New information technologies have both increased employers' reliance on outside providers and facilitated direct communication between those at the very top and the very bottom of corporate hierarchies.

The Postmodern Job

As we saw in Chapter 5, today many societies have moved into a postmodern stage of sociocultural development, one that is dominated by high technology. For workers, this transition has manifested itself in a greater reliance on electronic communication—even if the co-workers involved are separated only by a cubicle wall. The transition to postmodern society has also fostered telecommuting, or *homeshoring,* as it has come to be called in a play on the term *offshoring* (see Chapter 18). **Telecommuters** are employees who work

TAKING SOCIOLOGY TO WORK

Sarah Levy, **Owner, Sarah's Pastries & Candies**

Sarah Levy didn't know anything about sociology when she entered Northwestern University, but she knew that someday she wanted to start a bakery. After graduating from Northwestern with a major in sociology, she enrolled in Chicago's French Pastry School and spent some time interning at local bakeries and restaurants. A year later she started her own bakery in her mother's kitchen. Today Sarah owns and manages two locations in downtown Chicago, one on Oak Street and a second in Macy's, on State Street. Sarah's Pastries & Candies makes fine pastries and chocolates from scratch, along with custom-made wedding cakes and gift baskets.

Like many small business owners, Sarah does anything and everything in a typical workweek, from consulting with brides to helping in the kitchen. She manages 20 employees and provides her own marketing and public relations services. A gifted publicist, Sarah has welcomed Martha Stewart to her store and participated in a Food Network challenge that involved baking a three-foot animated dinosaur cake. Sarah's Pastries & Candies

gives back to the community by contributing to several charities, including Meals on Wheels, Common Threads, and For the Love of Chocolate Foundation.

Sarah saw the connection between business and sociology in her introductory sociology course, in which she used this textbook. Learning about how people interact, she says, has broadened her horizons and taught her how to step back and analyze a situation from a sociological perspective. "In my job, I am constantly interacting with people—employees, customers, vendors," she explains. "I think one of my greatest strengths is my ability to get along with people from all sorts of backgrounds, and make everyone get along with each other and work together towards the same goal."

LET'S DISCUSS

1. Have you ever thought of starting your own business? If so, what do you think the key to your success would be?
2. Would business have been a more practical major for Sarah? Why or why not?

---

full-time or part-time at home rather than in an outside office, and who are linked to their supervisors and colleagues through phone lines, Wi-Fi, the Internet, and smartphones. Not surprisingly, the number of telecommuters increased from 8.5 million in 1995 to 40 million in 2008 and an estimated 63 million by 2011 (Schadler 2009).

What are the social implications of this shift toward the virtual office? Table 6-3 summarizes the pros and cons. From an interactionist perspective, the workplace is a major source of friendships; restricting face-to-face social opportunities could destroy the trust that is created by "handshake agreements." Thus, telecommuting may move society further along the continuum from *Gemeinschaft* to *Gesellschaft*. And like it or not, when employees work at home, they tend to become available 24/7. On a more positive note, telecommuting may be the first social change that pulls fathers and mothers back into the home rather than pushing them out. The trend, if it continues, should also increase autonomy and job satisfaction for many employees (Castells 2001; DiMaggio et al. 2001).

Electronic communication in the workplace has generated some heat lately. On the one hand, e-mailing is a convenient way to push messages around, especially with the copy button. It's democratic, too: lower-status employees are more likely to participate in e-mail discussions than in face-to-face communications, giving organizations the benefit of their experience and views. But e-mail doesn't convey body language, which in face-to-face communication can soften insensitive phrasing and make unpleasant messages (such as a reprimand) easier to take. It also leaves a permanent record, which can be a problem if messages are written thoughtlessly (DiMaggio et al. 2001).

Electronic communication has contributed significantly to the fragmentation of work. Today, work is frequently interrupted by e-mail, pagers, and pop-up windows, as well as face-to-face interruptions. In one observation study of office workers, researchers found that employees spent an average of only 11 minutes on any given project before being interrupted.

Typically, 25 minutes passed before they returned to their original tasks. While multitasking may increase a person's efficiency in some situations, it has become an integral and not necessarily helpful feature of work for many employees (Mark et al. 2005; C. Thompson 2005).

---

use your sociological *imagination*

If your first full-time job after college involved telecommuting, what do you think would be the advantages and disadvantages of working out of a home office? Do you think you would be satisfied as a telecommuter? Why or why not?

TABLE **6-3** TELECOMMUTING: PROS AND CONS

Pros	Cons
Flexible schedule	Disconnectedness from fellow employees
Freedom to work anywhere	"At home" means still at work
Reduced expense and stress from commuting	For promotions, out of sight may mean out of mind
Environmental benefits of reduced commuting	Requires excellent Internet connectivity
Facilitates caregiving for children and aged parents	Loss of managerial control
Reduces terrorist targets	Downgraded security of electronic information
	Scams that masquerade as telecommuting opportunities

summingup

How many people do you know who belong to a labor union? Chances are you can name a lot fewer people than someone could 50 years ago. In 1954 unions represented 39 percent of workers in the private sector of the U.S. economy; in 2010 they represented only 11.9 percent—the lowest share in more than 70 years. As Figure 6-1 shows, the decline in unionization is common to virtually all industrial nations. What has happened to diminish the importance of organized labor? Have unions outlived their usefulness in a rapidly changing global economy that is dominated by the service sector?

Looking at the Issue

Labor unions consist of organized workers who share either the same skill (as in electronics) or the same employer (as in the case of postal employees). Unions began to emerge during the Industrial Revolution in England, in the 1700s. Groups of workers banded together to extract concessions from employers (for example, safer working conditions, a shorter workweek), as well as to protect their positions.

Historically, labor unions have engaged in restrictive practices that are regarded today as discriminatory. They frequently tried to protect their jobs by limiting entry to their occupation based on

gender, race, ethnicity, citizenship, age, and sometimes rather arbitrary measures of skill levels. Today we see less of this protection of special interests, but individual labor unions are still the target of charges of discrimination, as are employers (J. Rosenfeld 2010).

The power of labor unions varies widely from country to country. In some countries, such as Britain and Mexico, unions play a key role in the foundation of governments. In others, such as Japan and Korea, their role in politics is very limited, and even their ability to influence the private sector is relatively weak. In the United States, unions can sometimes have a significant influence on employers and elected officials, but their effect varies dramatically by type of industry and even region of the country (S. Zimmerman 2008c).

Few people today would dispute the fact that union membership is declining. Among the reasons for the decline are the following:

1. **Changes in the type of industry.** Manufacturing jobs, the traditional heart of the labor union, have declined, giving way to postindustrial service jobs.

2. **Growth in part-time jobs.** Between 1982 and 1998 the number of temporary jobs in the United States rose 577 percent, while total employment increased only 41 percent. Only in 2000 did laws governing collective bargaining allow temporary workers to join a union.

3. **The legal system.** The United States has not made it particularly easy for unions to organize and bargain, and some government measures have made it more difficult. A dramatic example was President Ronald Reagan's firing of 11,000 air traffic controllers in 1981, when their union threatened they would walk off the job while seeking a new contract.

4. **Globalization.** The threat of jobs leaving the country has undercut the ability of union leaders to organize workers at home. Some say that labor union demands for wage increases and additional benefits have themselves spurred the exodus of jobs to developing nations, where wages are significantly lower and unions are virtually nonexistent.

5. **Employer offensives.** Increasingly hostile employers have taken court action to block unions' efforts to represent their members.

6. **Union rigidity and bureaucratization.** In the past, labor has been slow to embrace women, minorities, and immigrants. Furthermore, in some unions the election of leaders seems to dominate the organization's activity.

Around the world, the economic downturn that began in 2008 has had special consequences for labor unions. Like nonunion workers, many union members lost their jobs in the recession; others saw their contracts renegotiated. As part of the $17.4 billion auto bailout legislation passed by the U.S. Congress, the United Auto Workers (UAW) accepted a nearly 20 percent pay cut. This and other rollbacks of benefits were largely accepted by U.S. unions, but in Europe, thousands of workers turned out in protest. In a few highly publicized cases, unions took the company bosses hostage.

FIGURE **6-1**   LABOR UNION MEMBERSHIP WORLDWIDE

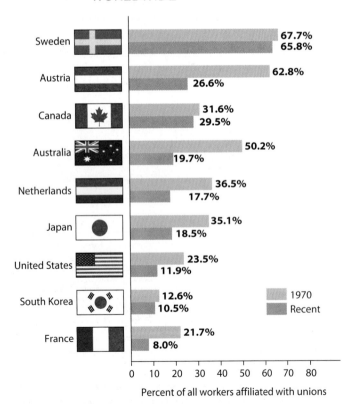

Country	1970	Recent
Sweden	67.7%	65.8%
Austria	62.8%	26.6%
Canada	31.6%	29.5%
Australia	50.2%	19.7%
Netherlands	36.5%	17.7%
Japan	35.1%	18.5%
United States	23.5%	11.9%
South Korea	12.6%	10.5%
France	21.7%	8.0%

Percent of all workers affiliated with unions

Note: Recent data from 2008–2010, except for Sweden and the Netherlands (2007).
Sources: Bureau of Labor Statistics 2011; New Unionism Network 2011; Visser 2006:45.

Although some union leaders in the United States expect the hardship caused by the economic slowdown to raise union membership, how well unions will be able to represent their members through tough times remains to be seen (Greenhouse 2008a, 2009).

Applying Sociology

Both Marxists and functionalists would view unions as a logical response to the emergence of impersonal, large-scale, formal, and often alienating organizations. This view certainly characterized the growth of unions in major manufacturing industries with a sharp division of labor. However, as manufacturing has declined, unions have had to look elsewhere for growth.

Worldwide, today's labor unions bear little resemblance to those early unions organized spontaneously by exploited workers. In line with Robert Michels's iron law of oligarchy (see page 126), unions have become increasingly bureaucratized under a self-serving leadership. Conflict theorists would point out that the longer union leaders are in office, the less responsive they are to the needs and demands of the rank and file, and the more concerned with maintaining their own positions and power. Yet research shows that under certain circumstances, union leadership can change significantly. Smaller unions are vulnerable to changes in leadership, as are unions whose membership shifts in composition from predominantly White to African American or Latino.

Initiating Policy

U.S. law grants workers the right to self-organize via unions. However, the United States is unique among industrial democracies in allowing employers to actively oppose their employees' decision to organize. The recent economic recession has compounded employers' opposition to unions and is even threatening workers' rights in established unions. Today, state and local governments across the United States are facing significant budget deficits. In an effort to cut costs, many elected officials are moving to shrink the pensions that government workers gained through collective bargaining. In some states, officials want not only to reduce retirees' benefits, but also to curtail union workers' collective bargaining rights.

In Europe, labor unions tend to play a major role in political elections. The ruling party in Great Britain, in fact, is called the Labour Party. Unions play a lesser role in U.S. politics, although they have recently been attacked for their large financial contributions to political campaigns. In addition to the role of unions in national politics, international trade unions sometimes speak out on common issues. In 2009 one of them condemned "corporate grand theft"—a reference to corporate executives who spend lavishly on themselves while laying off workers. Despite efforts dating back to Karl Marx and Friedrich Engels's call for the workers of all countries to unite (1847), no global union has emerged (International Trade Union Confederation 2009).

Though unions are a global force, their form and substance varies from country to country. In China, where there is only one political party, the government ordered Walmart's 31,000 workers to unionize, over the corporation's objections. Chinese unions are controlled by the Communist Party, whose membership has declined as the party's pervasive control has weakened. Nevertheless, these unions are more likely to listen to the government than independent unions, which listen to the workers who are their members (Zhang 2009).

Take the Issue with You

1. What unions are represented on your college campus? Have you been aware of union activity? Has there been any opposition to the unions on the part of the administration?

2. Do you think nurses should be allowed to strike? Why or why not? What about teachers or police officers?

3. Should state and local officials be allowed to reduce government workers' retirement benefits and take away their right to collective bargaining?

MASTERING THIS CHAPTER

Summary

Social interaction among human beings is necessary to the transmission of culture and the survival of every society. This chapter examines the social behavior of **groups and formal organizations.**

1. When we find ourselves identifying closely with a group, it is probably a **primary group.** A **secondary group** is more formal and impersonal.

2. People tend to see the world in terms of **in-groups** and **out-groups,** a perception often fostered by the very groups to which they belong.

3. **Reference groups** set and enforce standards of conduct and serve as a source of comparison for people's evaluations of themselves and others.

4. Interactionist researchers have noted distinct and predictable processes in the functioning of **small groups.** The simplest group is a **dyad,** composed of two members. **Triads** and larger groups increase the ways of interacting and allow for **coalitions** to form.

5. The **focus group,** developed by sociologist Robert Merton to collect qualitative data on people's opinions, feelings, and ideas, also allows researchers to observe how people make decisions in small groups.

6. As societies have become more complex, large **formal organizations** have become more powerful and pervasive.

7. Max Weber argued that in its ideal form, every **bureaucracy** has five basic characteristics: division of labor, hierarchical authority, written rules and regulations, impersonality, and employment based on technical qualifications.

8. Bureaucracy can be understood both as a process and as a matter of degree. Thus, an organization may be more or less bureaucratic than other organizations.

9. When leaders of an organization build up their power, the result can be *oligarchy* (rule by a few).

10. The informal structure of an organization can undermine and redefine official bureaucratic policies.

11. Organizational restructuring and new technologies have transformed the workplace through innovations such as *collective decision making* and *telecommuting*.

12. **Labor unions** are on the decline because of major shifts in the economy.

Key Terms

Alienation A condition of estrangement or dissociation from the surrounding society. (page 124)

Bureaucracy A component of formal organization that uses rules and hierarchical ranking to achieve efficiency. (124)

Bureaucratization The process by which a group, organization, or social movement becomes increasingly bureaucratic. (125)

Classical theory An approach to the study of formal organizations that views workers as being motivated almost entirely by economic rewards. (126)

Coalition A temporary or permanent alliance geared toward a common goal. (121)

Dyad A two-member group. (122)

Focus group A carefully selected discussion group led by a trained moderator. (123)

Formal organization A group designed for a special purpose and structured for maximum efficiency. (123)

Goal displacement Overzealous conformity to official regulations of a bureaucracy. (125)

Group Any number of people with similar norms, values, and expectations who interact with one another on a regular basis. (119)

Groupthink Uncritical acceptance of or conformity to the prevailing viewpoint. (123)

Human relations approach An approach to the study of formal organizations that emphasizes the role of people, communication, and participation in a bureaucracy and tends to focus on the informal structure of the organization. (127)

Ideal type A construct or model for evaluating specific cases. (124)

In-group Any group or category to which people feel they belong. (120)

Iron law of oligarchy A principle of organizational life under which even a democratic organization will eventually develop into a bureaucracy ruled by a few individuals. (126)

Labor union Organized workers who share either the same skill or the same employer. (130)

McDonaldization The process by which the principles of the fast-food restaurant are coming to dominate more and more sectors of American society as well as of the rest of the world. (118)

Out-group A group or category to which people feel they do not belong. (120)

Peter principle A principle of organizational life according to which every employee within a hierarchy tends to rise to his or her level of incompetence. (125)

Primary group A small group characterized by intimate, face-to-face association and cooperation. (119)

Reference group Any group that individuals use as a standard for evaluating themselves and their own behavior. (120)

Scientific management approach Another name for the classical theory of formal organizations. (126)

Secondary group A formal, impersonal group in which there is little social intimacy or mutual understanding. (119)

Small group A group small enough for all members to interact simultaneously—that is, to talk with one another or at least be well acquainted. (121)

Telecommuter An employee who works full-time or part-time at home rather than in an outside office, and who is linked to supervisor and colleagues through phone lines, Wi-Fi, the Internet, and smartphones. (128)

Trained incapacity The tendency of workers in a bureaucracy to become so specialized that they develop blind spots and fail to notice obvious problems. (124)

Triad A three-member group. (122)

TAKING SOCIOLOGY with you

1. Are primary groups, secondary groups, in-groups, out-groups, and reference groups likely to be found within a formal organization? What functions do these groups serve for a formal organization? What dysfunctions might occur as a result of their presence?

2. Max Weber identified five basic characteristics of bureaucracy. Select an actual organization familiar to you (for example, your college, a workplace, or a religious institution or civic association you belong to) and apply Weber's five characteristics to that organization. To what degree does it correspond to Weber's ideal type of bureaucracy?

3. Talk with two or three business students or businesspeople about the bureaucratization of business. On balance, do they see bureaucratization as a positive or negative trend? What bureaucratic dysfunctions are common in business, and how do managers attempt to counteract them?

Self-Quiz

Read each question carefully and then select the best answer.

1. George Ritzer's belief that business principles of the fast-food industry have greatly influenced how we live and do business has been coined
   a. Fast Food Nation.
   b. Drive-Through Life.
   c. McDonaldization.
   d. Burger USA.

2. _____ groups often emerge in the workplace among those who share special understandings about their occupation.
   a. Primary
   b. Secondary
   c. Out-
   d. Formal

3. The purpose of a reference group is to serve a(n)
   a. normative function by enforcing standards of conduct and belief.
   b. comparison function by setting a standard against which people can measure themselves and others.
   c. elimination function by dissolving groups that no longer have a social purpose.
   d. both a and b

4. The president of the United States need not be a good typist, and a surgeon need not be able to fill a cavity, because of the bureaucratic characteristic of
   a. division of labor.
   b. impersonality.
   c. employment based on technical qualifications.
   d. written rules and regulations.

5. Which pioneer of sociology first directed researchers to the significance of bureaucratic structure?
   a. Émile Durkheim
   b. Max Weber
   c. Karl Marx
   d. Ferdinand Tönnies

6. Minimal hierarchy involves a(n)
   a. traditional bureaucracy.
   b. lack of rules in the workplace.
   c. flatter organizational structure.
   d. absence of traditional job titles.

7. The U.S. Postal Service, the Boston Pops orchestra, and the college or university in which you are currently enrolled as a student are all examples of
   a. primary groups.
   b. reference groups.
   c. formal organizations.
   d. triads.

8. One positive consequence of bureaucracy is that it reduces bias. Reduction of bias results from which characteristic of a bureaucracy?
   a. impersonality
   b. hierarchy of authority
   c. written rules and regulations
   d. employment based on technical qualifications

9. According to the Peter principle,
   a. all bureaucracies are notoriously inefficient.
   b. if something *can* go wrong, it *will*.
   c. every employee within a hierarchy tends to rise to his or her level of incompetence.
   d. all line workers get burned in the end.

10. What are the social implications of a shift toward the virtual office as a result of the increasing number of telecommuters?
    a. Supervisors will find that performance goals must be defined more clearly, which may lead to further bureaucratization.
    b. It should increase autonomy and job satisfaction for many employees.
    c. It will lead to greater worker privacy and job security.
    d. both a and b

11. William Graham Sumner distinguished between _____ and _____.

12. Formal organizations have a(n) _____ form of organization.

13. Sociologist Robert Merton devised the often-used methodology of monitoring a discussion that is called a _____ _____.

14. _____ groups often emerge in the workplace among those who share special understandings about their occupation.

15. In many cases, people model their behavior after groups to which they may not belong. These groups are called _____ groups.

16. Trained incapacity, goal displacement, and the Peter principle are all examples of bureaucratic _____.

17. The iron law of oligarchy was developed by German sociologist _____ _____.

18. People who happen to be in the same place at the same time, such as members of a Broadway theater audience, are a(n) _____.

19. When we find ourselves identifying closely with a group, it is probably a(n) _____ group.

20. Max Weber developed a(n) _____ _____ of bureaucracy, which reflects the most characteristic aspects of all human organizations.

THINKING ABOUT MOVIES

Bread and Roses

Poorly paid janitors in Los Angeles struggle to unionize.

Restrepo

This documentary shows a U.S. military platoon serving in a dangerous part of Afghanistan.

Toy Story 3

Rejected toys band together to improve their social circumstances.

The mass media are an
integral part of modern
culture. In Alaska, an Inuit
man checks his laptop.

134

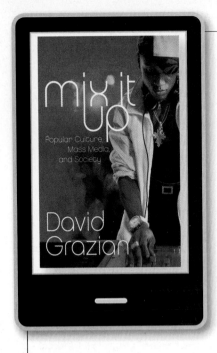

"Over forty years ago communications theorist Marshall McLuhan (1967) developed a pathbreaking idea—media not only pass along messages from sender to receiver but actively reshape how we process information, knowledge, and text. . . .

. . . For instance, about $60 billion is illegally gambled in Internet poker games each year, a pursuit that draws in an estimated 1.6 million U.S. college students. . . . In 2005 Lehigh University sophomore class president Greg Hogan, Jr., lost $7,500 playing online poker, and out of desperation, in December of that year he held up a Wachovia bank for $2,871 in cash. With no casino dealers, card shuffling, or friendly table partners to distract him, Hogan found the seamless, fast-paced action of digital poker "paralyzing" and "narcotic," a familiar sensation among addicts, men and women alike. According to M. Schwartz (2006), "Many, like Lauren Patrizi, a 21-year-old senior at Loyola University in Chicago, have had weeks when they're playing poker during most of their waking hours. Rarely leaving their rooms, they take their laptops with them to bed, fall asleep each night in the middle of a hand and think, talk and dream nothing but poker."

According to cultural anthropologist Natasha Dow Schull (2005, p. 73), digital technologies succeed in creating what consumers call the *zone,* a dissociated subjective state marked by a suspension of normative parameters—monetary, bodily, temporal, and spatial. Gambling sites rely on cashless transactions (performed with credit and debit card numbers) in which financial stakes are transformed into pixilated "chips" that no longer seem like real money. Unlike dorm-lounge poker games in which classmates eventually get tired, punch-drunk, or else lose their shirts, online casinos never close, but consistently and relentlessly maintain a steady rhythm of play that keeps addicts glued to their screens alone for hours, nights, and weeks on end. With only computer keys to depress, players never drop their cards;

With no casino dealers, card shuffling, or friendly table partners to distract him, Hogan found the seamless, fast-paced action of digital poker "paralyzing" and "narcotic," a familiar sensation among addicts, men and women alike.

moreover, gambling software allows gamers to bet multiple hands simultaneously, further increasing the hypnotic speed and tempo with which one gains and (more often) loses.

How else do goings-on within the virtual world impact our everyday lives offline? Certainly, the ease with which information flows online among otherwise discrete interpersonal networks has obvious consequences for how we maintain control over our reputations and identities. . . . Since anyone with an Internet connection can post intimate photographs, juicy gossip, or vicious rumors on the Web for a potential worldwide audience of billions, personal reputations can easily be maligned within hours. In 2003 Kelley D. Parker, a partner at the elite New York law firm of Paul, Weiss, Rifkind, Wharton and Garrison, allegedly ordered a paralegal to conduct research on nearby sushi restaurants after eating some bad takeout. The underling wrote up a three-page memo replete with interview quotes, footnotes, and exhibitions, and the scanned document later appeared on the Web site Gawker for her colleagues to mock. . . . While it was never determined whether the infamous "sushi memo" was a hoax or a prank, it presumably hardly matters to Ms. Parker, whose reputation has been forever marred by the online posting.

Of course, rumors of bad behavior among celebrities likely travel faster online than any other kind of hearsay. Web sites like Gawker, The Smoking Gun, TMZ, and YouTube are veritable clearinghouses for such gossip, as actor Christian Bale learned after he cursed out the director of photography on the movie set of *Terminator: Salvation* in 2008 for nearly four minutes, and a full-length audio recording of his tantrum resurfaced on YouTube the following year. (Bale has since apologized for the outburst, but notably did so only after its public airing.) The Web site Bitter Waitress provides an ongoing list of celebrity (as well as civilian) diners who have stingily tipped less than 15 percent of their check: famous cheapskates shamed by the site include actresses Lindsay Lohan and Helena Bonham Carter, former Miami Dolphins quarterback Dan Marino, rock singer David Lee Roth, and reality TV figure Dog the Bounty Hunter. In March 2009, People for the Ethical Treatment of Animals (or PETA) published an online list of celebrities who unabashedly wear fur, including Madonna, Maggie Gyllenhaal, Kanye West, Elizabeth Hurley, Kate Moss, Demi Moore, Ashton Kutcher, Mary J. Blige, and Mary-Kate and Ashley Olsen."

(Grazian 2010:197, 200, 203; see also Glater 2003; Schull 2005; M. Schwartz 2006) Additional information about this excerpt can be found on the Online Learning Center at www.mhhe.com/schaeferbrief13e.

In this excerpt from *Mix It Up: Popular Culture, Mass Media, and Society,* sociologist David Grazian describes how today's mass media are actively reshaping the way we process information, as Marshall McLuhan predicted they would in 1967. Playing poker and video games online, Grazian writes, is a qualitatively different experience from playing them in person. He also discusses the social consequences of the instant dissemination of information through the mass media, from the embarrassment of an attorney who assigned a paralegal to research a lunch locale to the humiliation of an actor whose four-minute tantrum went viral on YouTube. In this age, thanks to digital recording, anyone can become a global personality for any reason, at any time.

We have come a long way from the 1950s, when rabbit-ear antennas sat atop black-and-white television sets. Both television and the Net are forms of **mass media,** a term that refers to the print and electronic means of communication that carry messages to widespread audiences. Print media include newspapers, magazines, and books; electronic media include radio, satellite radio, television, motion pictures, and the Internet. Advertising, which falls into both categories, is also a form of mass media.

The social impact of the mass media is obvious. Consider a few examples. TV dinners were invented to accommodate the millions of couch potatoes who can't bear to miss their favorite television programs. Today, *screen time* encompasses not just television viewing but playing video games and surfing the Internet as well. Candidates for political office rely on their media consultants to project a winning image both in print and in the electronic media. World leaders use all forms of media for political advantage, whether to gain territory or to bid on hosting the Olympics. In parts of Africa and Asia, AIDS education projects owe much of their success to media campaigns. And during the 2003 war in Iraq, both the British and U.S. governments allowed journalists to be embedded with frontline troops as a means of "telling their story."

Few aspects of society are as central as the mass media. Through the media we expand our understanding of people and events beyond what we experience in person. The media inform us about different cultures and lifestyles and about the latest forms of technology. For sociologists, the key questions are how the mass media affect our social institutions and how they influence our social behavior.

The social impact of the mass media has become so huge, in fact, that scholars have begun to speak of *cultural convergence*. The term **cultural convergence** refers to the flow of content across multiple media, and the accompanying migration of media audiences. As you watch a television program, for example, you wonder what the star of the show is doing at the moment, and turn to the Internet. Later, while texting your best friend, you tell her what you learned, accompanied by a Google Earth map showing the celebrity's location. Using Photoshop, you may even include the star's image next to your own, post the photo on your Facebook page, and then tweet your friends (send them a mini-blog) to create a caption. Media convergence is not orchestrated by the media, sophisticated though they may be. You initiate it, using techniques you likely learned by interacting with others, either face-to-face or through the media (H. Jenkins 2006).

Why are the media so influential? Who benefits from media influence and why? How do we maintain cultural and ethical standards in the face of negative media images? In this chapter we will consider the ways sociology helps us to answer these questions. First we will look at how proponents of the various sociological perspectives view the media. Then we will examine just who makes up the media's audience, not just at home but around the world. The chapter closes with a Social Policy section on the right to privacy in a digital age.

Sociological Perspectives on the Media

Over the past decade, new technologies have made new forms of mass media available to U.S. households. These new technologies have changed people's viewing and listening habits. People spend a lot of time with the media, more and more of it on the Internet. Media consumers have moved away from television and toward digital images downloaded to their computers and portable devices. Increasingly, they learn not just about the famous but about ordinary people by viewing their Facebook or MySpace pages or by keeping in touch with their friends via Twitter.

In studying the impact of the mass media on socialization, sociologists must consider the wide variety of contact people have with communication outlets, from immersion in all types of media to relative isolation, especially from recent innovations. In 2007 the Pew Research Center released a report that sorted U.S. residents into 10 categories based on their use of information and communications technologies (ICTs; Table 7-1). According to the report, about 32 percent of the adult population falls into the top four categories, from the "Omnivores," who use these devices as a means of self-expression, to the "Productivity Enhancers," who use them to get the job done. Middle-of-the-road users, who represent about 19 percent of the population, take advantage of new technologies but aren't as excited about them. They range from the "Mobile Centrics," who are strongly attached to their cell phones, to the "Connected but Hassled."

Close to half the people in the nation have few if any technology devices, or if they do, they are not wedded to them. Typically, younger people embrace technological change more than older people, who tend either to be indifferent toward new technologies or to find them annoying.

How do people's viewing and listening habits affect their social behavior? In the following sections we'll use the four major sociological perspectives to examine the impact of the mass media and changes in their usage patterns (Nelson 2004).

Functionalist View

One obvious function of the mass media is to entertain. Except for clearly identified news or educational programming, we often think the explicit purpose of the mass media is to occupy our leisure time—from newspaper comics and crossword puzzles to the latest music releases on the Internet. While that is true, the media have other important functions. They also socialize us, enforce social norms, confer status, and promote consumption. An important dysfunction of the mass media is that they may act as a narcotic, desensitizing us to distressing events (Lazarsfeld and Merton 1948; C. Wright 1986).

Agent of Socialization The media increase social cohesion by presenting a common, more or less standardized view of culture through mass communication. Sociologist Robert Park (1922) studied how newspapers helped immigrants to the United States adjust to their environment by changing their customary habits

Omnivores: 8% of American adults constitute the most active participants in the information society, consuming information goods and services at a high rate and using them as a platform for participation and self-expression.

The Connectors: 7% of the adult population surround themselves with technology and use it to connect with people and digital content. They get a lot out of their mobile devices and participate actively in online life.

Lackluster Veterans: 8% of American adults make up a group who are not at all passionate about their abundance of modern ICTs. Few like the intrusiveness their gadgets add to their lives and not many see ICTs adding to their personal productivity.

Productivity Enhancers: 9% of American adults happily get a lot of things done with information technology, both at home and at work.

Mobile Centrics: 10% of the general population are strongly attached to their cell phones and take advantage of a range of mobile applications.

Connected but Hassled: 9% of American adults fit into this group. They have invested in a lot of technology, but the connectivity is a hassle for them.

Inexperienced Experimenters: 8% of adults have less ICT on hand than others. They feel competent in dealing with technology, and might do more with it if they had more.

Light but Satisfied: 15% of adults have the basics of information technology but use it infrequently, so it does not register as an important part of their lives.

Indifferents: 11% of adults have a fair amount of technology on hand, but it does not play a central role in their daily lives.

Off the Net: 15% of the population, mainly older Americans, is off the modern information network.

Note: From a Pew Internet and American Life Project survey conducted in April 2006.
Source: Horrigan 2007:vii.

Think about It
What category would you place yourself in?

and teaching them the opinions of people in their new home country. Unquestionably, the mass media play a significant role in providing a collective experience for members of society. Think about how the mass media bring together members of a community or even a nation by broadcasting important events and ceremonies (such as inaugurations, press conferences, parades, state funerals, and the Olympics) and by covering disasters.

Which media outlets did people turn to in the aftermath of the September 11, 2001, tragedy? Television, radio, and the telephone were the primary means by which people in the United States bonded. But the Internet also played a prominent role. About half of all Internet users—more than 5 million people—received some kind of news about the attacks online (D. Miller and Darlington 2002).

Today, the news media have moved further online. Afghans of all political persuasions now connect with the Muslim community overseas to gain both social and financial support. In the realm of popular culture, a spontaneous global sharing of reactions to Michael Jackson's sudden death in 2009 crashed the websites for Google, the *Los Angeles Times,* TMZ celebrity news, Perez Hilton's blog, and Twitter (Rawlinson and Hunt 2009; Shane 2010).

Some are concerned about the media's socialization function, however. For instance, many people worry about the effect of using television as a babysitter and the impact of violent programming on viewer behavior. Some people adopt a blame-the-media mentality, holding the media accountable for anything that goes wrong, especially with young people. Yet the media also have positive effects on young people. For young and even not-so-young adults, for example, a new sort of tribalism is emerging online, in which communities develop around common interests or shared identities (Adams and Smith 2008).

Enforcer of Social Norms The media often reaffirm proper behavior by showing what happens to people who act in a way that violates societal expectations. These messages are conveyed when the bad guy gets clobbered in cartoons or is thrown in jail on *CSI.* Yet the media also sometimes glorify disapproved behavior, whether it is physical violence, disrespect to a teacher, or drug use.

The media play a critical role in human sexuality. Many people object to the widespread availability of pornography on the web; others are concerned about the way sexual predators use chat rooms to take advantage of children. Yet innovative uses of new media may also have positive consequences. On Valentine's Day 2007, New York City introduced the official "NYC Condom" on Facebook, in an attempt to make safer sex a social norm. Not only has New York's Department of Health and Mental Hygiene given away millions of condoms, but thousands of *e-condoms,* as they are called, have been distributed to Facebook users.

Programs have also been created to persuade teens not to send nude images of themselves to selected friends. Such images often go viral (that is, spread across the Internet) and may be used to harass teens and their parents. To define normative behavior regarding these images, one organization has launched a "That's not cool" campaign, complete with stalker messages that can be e-mailed to those who misuse such images. The widespread dissemination of compromising images that were meant to be shared only among close friends is just one aspect of the new social phenomenon called *cyberbullying* (Chan 2009; Clifford 2009a; Gentile 2009).

Conferral of Status The mass media confer status on people, organizations, and public issues. Whether it is an issue like the homeless or a celebrity like Cameron Diaz, they single out one from thousands of other similarly placed issues or people to become significant. Table 7-2 shows how often certain public figures are prominently featured on weekly magazine covers.

TABLE **7-2** STATUS CONFERRED BY MAGAZINES

Rank/Person/Times on Cover of *Time*	Rank/Person/Times on Cover of *People*	Rank/Person/Times on Cover of *Ebony*	Rank/Person/Times on Cover of *Rolling Stone*
1. Richard Nixon (55)	1. Princess Diana (54)	1. Janet Jackson (18)	1. Paul McCartney (27)
2. Ronald Reagan (37)	2. Jennifer Aniston (37)	2. Michael Jackson (17)	2. John Lennon (26)
3. Bill Clinton (34)	3. Julia Roberts (35)	3. Muhammad Ali (16)	3. Bono (22)
4. George W. Bush (31)	4. Brad Pitt (28)	3. Halle Berry (16)	3. Bob Dylan (22)
5. Hillary Clinton (30)	5. Prince William (18)	3. Whitney Houston (16)	5. Mick Jagger (21)
6. Barack Obama (26)	5. Britney Spears (18)	6. Diahann Carroll (11)	5. Bruce Springsteen (21)
7. George H. W. Bush (25)	7. Michael Jackson (17)	6. Lena Horne (11)	7. Madonna (19)
8. Dwight Eisenhower (22)	8. Angelina Jolie (16)	6. Sidney Poitier (11)	8. Keith Richards (18)
8. Lyndon Johnson (22)	9. Nicole Kidman (15)	9. Denzel Washington (10)	9. George Harrison (17)
8. Gerald Ford (22)	9. Elizabeth Taylor (15)	9. Bill Cosby (10)	10. Jimi Hendrix (16)

Source: Author's content analysis of primary cover subject for full run of the periodicals beginning with *Time,* March 3, 1923; *People,* March 4, 1974; *Ebony,* November 1945; and *Rolling Stone,* September 1967 through January 1, 2011. When a periodical runs multiple covers, each version is counted. In case of ties, the more recent cover person is listed first.

Think about It

How do these magazines differ in the types of people they feature on their covers? Which type do you think enjoys the most status? Why?

Obviously, *People* magazine alone was not responsible for making Princess Diana into a worldwide figure, but collectively, all the media outlets created a notoriety that Princess Victoria of Sweden, for one, did not enjoy.

Another way the media confer celebrity status on individuals is by publishing information about the frequency of Internet searches. Some newspapers and websites carry regularly updated lists of the most heavily researched individuals and topics of the week. The means may have changed since the first issue of *Time* magazine hit the stands in 1923, but the media still confer status—often electronically.

use your sociological *imagination*

You are browsing at a newsstand. Are you more likely than not to pick up a magazine because of the person on the cover? What kind of cover shot would attract you?

Promotion of Consumption Twenty thousand commercials a year—that is the number the average child in the United States watches on television, according to the American Academy of Pediatrics. Young people cannot escape commercial messages. They show up on high school scoreboards, at rock concerts, and as banners on web pages. They also surface in the form of *product placement*—for example, the Coca-Cola glasses that sit in front of the judges on *American Idol.* Product placement is nothing new. In 1951 *The African Queen* prominently displayed Gordon's Gin aboard the boat carrying Katharine Hepburn and Humphrey Bogart. However, commercial promotion has become far more common today: *American Idol* alone features over 4,600 product appearances each season. Moreover, advertisers are attempting to develop brand or logo loyalty at younger and younger ages (Buckingham 2007; Rodman 2011:395).

Using advertising to develop a brand name with global appeal is an especially powerful way to encourage consumption. U.S. corporations have been particularly successful in creating global brands. An analysis of the 100 most successful brands worldwide, each of which derives at least a third of its earnings outside the

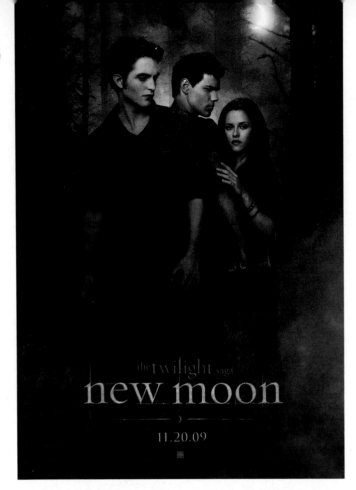

Product placement ("brand casting") is an increasingly important source of revenue for motion picture studios. The movie *New Moon* (2009), which was geared toward teens, featured many brands, including Coca-Cola and Apple. But the real winner was Burger King, which integrated its entire marketing strategy with the film's release (Brandchannel.com 2010).

home country, shows that 51 of them originated in the United States; 49 others come from 12 different countries (Figure 7-1).

Media advertising has several clear functions: it supports the economy, provides information about products, and underwrites the cost of media. In some cases, advertising becomes part of the entertainment. A national survey showed that one-half of viewers watch the Super Bowl primarily for the commercials, and one-third of online conversations about the Super Bowl the day of and the day after the event are driven by Super Bowl advertising. Yet advertising's functions are related to dysfunctions. Media advertising contributes to a consumer culture that creates needs and raises unrealistic expectations of what is required to be happy or satisfied. Moreover, because the media depend heavily on advertising revenue, advertisers can influence media content (Carey and Gelles 2010; Nielsen Company 2009).

use your sociological *imagination*

You are a news junkie. Where do you gather your facts or information—from newspapers, tabloids, magazines, TV newscasts, blogs, or the Internet? Why did you choose that medium?

Dysfunction: The Narcotizing Effect In addition to the functions just noted, the media perform a *dysfunction*. Sociologists Paul Lazarsfeld and Robert Merton (1948) created the term **narcotizing dysfunction** to refer to the phenomenon in which the media provide such massive amounts of coverage that the audience becomes numb and fails to act on the information, regardless of how compelling the issue. Interested citizens may take in the information but make no decision or take no action.

Consider how often the media initiate a great outpouring of philanthropic support in response to natural disasters or family crises. But then what happens? Research shows that as time passes, viewer fatigue sets in. The mass media audience becomes numb, desensitized to the suffering, and may even conclude that a solution to the crisis has been found (Moeller 1999).

The media's narcotizing dysfunction was identified 70 years ago, when just a few homes had television—well before the advent of electronic media. At that time, the dysfunction went largely unnoticed, but today commentators often point out the ill effects of addiction to television or the Internet, especially among young people. Street crime, explicit sex, war, and HIV/AIDS apparently are such overwhelming topics that some in the audience may feel they have acted—or at the very least learned all they need to know—simply by watching the news.

Conflict View

Conflict theorists emphasize that the media reflect and even exacerbate many of the divisions in our society and world, including those based on gender, race, ethnicity, and social class. They point in particular to the media's ability to decide what is transmitted, through a process called *gatekeeping*. Conflict theorists also stress the way interest groups monitor media content; the way powerful groups transmit society's dominant ideology through the mass media; and the technological gap between the haves and have-nots, which limits people's access to the Internet.

Gatekeeping What story appears on page 1 of the morning newspaper? What motion picture plays on three screens rather than one at the local cineplex? What picture isn't released at all? Behind these decisions are powerful figures—publishers, editors, and other media moguls.

The mass media constitute a form of big business in which profits are generally more important than the quality of the programming. Within the mass media, a relatively small number of people control what eventually reaches the audience through **gatekeeping.** This term describes how material must travel through a series of gates (or checkpoints) before reaching the public. Thus, a select few decide what images to bring to a broad audience. In many countries the government plays a gatekeeping role. A study done for the World Bank found that in 97 countries, 60 percent of the top five TV stations and 72 percent of the largest radio stations are government-owned (World Bank 2001:183).

Gatekeeping, which prevails in all kinds of media, is not a new concept. The term was coined by a journalism scholar in the 1940s to refer to the way that small-town newspaper editors control which events receive public attention. As sociologist C. Wright Mills ([1956] 2000b) observed, the real power of the media is that they can control what is being presented. In the recording industry, gatekeepers may reject a popular local band because it competes with a group already on their label. Even if

MAPPING LIFE WORLDWIDE
FIGURE **7-1** BRANDING THE GLOBE

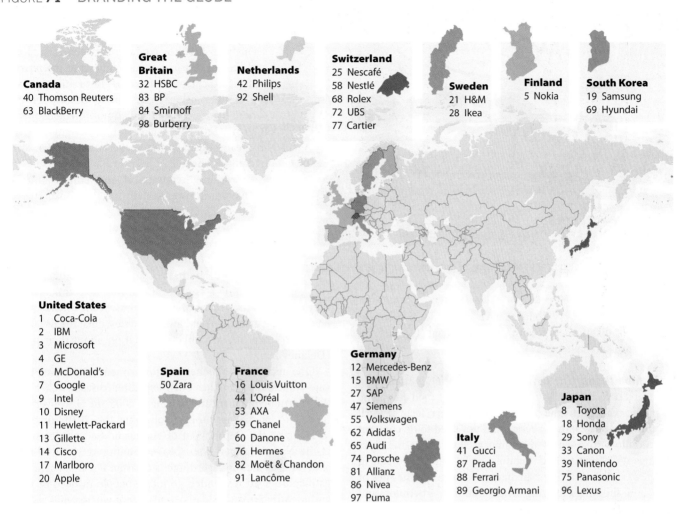

Canada
40 Thomson Reuters
63 BlackBerry

Great Britain
32 HSBC
83 BP
84 Smirnoff
98 Burberry

Netherlands
42 Philips
92 Shell

Switzerland
25 Nescafé
58 Nestlé
68 Rolex
72 UBS
77 Cartier

Sweden
21 H&M
28 Ikea

Finland
5 Nokia

South Korea
19 Samsung
69 Hyundai

United States
1 Coca-Cola
2 IBM
3 Microsoft
4 GE
6 McDonald's
7 Google
9 Intel
10 Disney
11 Hewlett-Packard
13 Gillette
14 Cisco
17 Marlboro
20 Apple

Spain
50 Zara

France
16 Louis Vuitton
44 L'Oréal
53 AXA
59 Chanel
60 Danone
76 Hermes
82 Moët & Chandon
91 Lancôme

Germany
12 Mercedes-Benz
15 BMW
27 SAP
47 Siemens
55 Volkswagen
62 Adidas
65 Audi
74 Porsche
81 Allianz
86 Nivea
97 Puma

Italy
41 Gucci
87 Prada
88 Ferrari
89 Georgio Armani

Japan
8 Toyota
18 Honda
29 Sony
33 Canon
39 Nintendo
75 Panasonic
96 Lexus

Note: Map shows the top 100 brands in the world by country of ownership, except for the United States, for which only brands in the top 20 are shown.
Source: Based on Interbrand 2010.

Based on revenue and name recognition, these are the brands that dominate the global marketplace. Just 13 nations account for all the top 100 brands.

Think about It
How many of these brands do you recognize?

---

the band is recorded, radio programmers may reject the music because it does not fit the station's sound. Television programmers may keep a pilot for a new TV series off the air because they believe it does not appeal to the target audience (which is sometimes determined by advertising sponsors). Similar decisions are made by gatekeepers in the publishing industry (Hanson 2005; White 1950).

Gatekeeping is not as dominant in at least one form of mass media, the Internet. You can send virtually any message to an electronic bulletin board, and create a web page or web log (blog) to advance any argument, including one that insists the earth is flat. The Internet is a means of quickly disseminating information (or misinformation) without going through any significant gatekeeping process.

Nevertheless, the Internet is not totally without restrictions. In many nations, laws regulate content on issues such as gambling, pornography, and even politics. And popular Internet service providers will terminate accounts for offensive behavior. After the terrorist attacks in 2001, eBay did not allow people to sell parts of the World Trade Center via its online auction. Despite such interference, growing numbers of people are actively involved in online communities. These **netizens** are committed to the free flow of information, with few outside controls.

Today, many countries try to control political dissent by restricting citizens' access to online comments unfavorable to the government. In 2011, online criticism fueled dissent in Arab countries like Egypt, Tunisia, Libya, and Bahrain. Using social media, activists in these countries encouraged their followers to demonstrate against the government at predetermined locales. To further encourage the opposition, they posted cell phone videos of the protests on the Internet. Even in China, where the government limits or even bans access to Google, Facebook,

Social media have facilitated both public criticism of government and government attempts to monitor dissent.

and Twitter, media-savvy Chinese have created local networks to share their dissatisfaction with the government (C. MacLeod 2010; Preston and Stelter 2011).

Media Monitoring The term *media monitoring* is used most often to refer to interest groups' monitoring of media content. The public reaction to the shootings at Virginia Tech in April 2007 provides one example. People did not need to be constant news monitors to learn of the rampage. Ever since the mass shootings at Columbine High School near Littleton, Colorado, in 1999, news outlets of every type have descended on the sites of such school shootings, offering insight into the perpetrators and their families, covering the mass expressions of grief, and following the communities' efforts to recover. Once again, though media outlets provided valuable information and quickly reassured viewers, listeners, and readers that the shooters posed no further danger, many people criticized the reality that they constructed through their coverage.

Reactions ran the gamut. Some observers, including groups representing Asian Americans, questioned the recurring racial identifier used to describe the shooter at Virginia Tech. Indeed, when the news began to leak out that the shooter was "foreign" or "Asian," many people of color commented that they hoped he would not turn out to be one of their own, since people of color appear so rarely, if at all, in news coverage. Other observers objected to another form of stigmatization, the detailed disclosure of the shooter's history of mental illness, which seemed to some to vilify anyone who has ever had a mental health problem. Others objected to what they saw as the media's heavily antigun posture, which damned those who work to preserve the right to own firearms. In such emotional circumstances, the media's construction of reality certainly is not to everyone's liking and rarely satisfies anyone completely (Asian American Journalists Association 2007; Groening 2007; Stanley 2007).

The term *media monitoring* can also be applied to government monitoring of individuals' phone calls without their

knowledge. For example, the federal government has been criticized for authorizing wiretaps of U.S. citizens' telephone conversations without judicial approval. Government officials argue that the wiretaps were undertaken in the interest of national security, to monitor contacts between U.S. citizens and known terrorist groups following the terrorist attacks of September 11, 2001. But critics who take the conflict perspective, among others, are concerned by the apparent invasion of people's privacy (Gertner 2005). We will examine the right to privacy in greater detail in the Social Policy section at the end of this chapter.

What are the practical and ethical limits of media monitoring? In daily life, parents often oversee their children's online activities and scan the blogs they read—which are, of course, available for anyone to see. Most parents see such monitoring of children's media use and communications as an appropriate part of adult supervision. Yet their snooping sets an example for their children, who may use the technique for their own ends. Some media analysts have noted a growing trend among adolescents: the use of new media to learn not-so-public information about their parents (Delaney 2005).

One unanticipated benefit of government monitoring of private communications has been expedited disaster relief. As in the aftermath of Hurricane Katrina in 2005, the U.S. government turned to media monitoring following the 2010 earthquake in Haiti. At the Department of Homeland Security, employees at the National Operations Center monitored 31 social media sites for information regarding the disaster. The intelligence they gathered helped responders to locate people in need of rescue and identify areas outside Port-au-Prince where relief was necessary (Department of Homeland Security 2010).

Government media monitoring isn't always sinister. In the days following the 2010 earthquake in Haiti, the Department of Homeland Security monitored social media sites to identify potential locations for rescue missions and supply deliveries.

Dominant Ideology: Constructing Reality Conflict theorists argue that the mass media maintain the privileges of certain groups. Moreover, powerful groups may limit the media's representation of others to protect their own interests. The term **dominant ideology** describes a set of cultural beliefs and practices that helps to maintain powerful social, economic, and political interests. The media transmit messages that essentially define what we regard as the real world, even though those images frequently vary from the ones that the larger society experiences.

Mass media decision makers are overwhelmingly White, male, and wealthy. It may come as no surprise, then, that the media tend to ignore the lives and ambitions of subordinate groups, among them working-class people, African Americans, Hispanics, gays and lesbians, people with disabilities, overweight people, and older people. Worse yet, media content may create false images or stereotypes of these groups that then become accepted as accurate portrayals of reality. **Stereotypes** are unreliable generalizations about all members of a group that do not recognize individual differences within the group. Some broadcasters use stereotypes deliberately in a desperate bid for attention, with the winking approval of media executives. Shock radio host Don Imus may have been banned from the airwaves for his stereotyped description of Black female athletes, but within 10 months he was back on the air, earning a seven-figure income.

Television content is another example of this tendency to ignore reality. How many overweight TV characters can you name? Even though in real life 1 out of every 4 women is obese (30 or more pounds over a healthy body weight), only 3 out of 100 TV characters are portrayed as obese. Heavyset television characters have fewer romances, talk less about sex, eat more often, and are more often the object of ridicule than their thin counterparts (Hellmich 2001).

On the other hand, television news and other media outlets do alert people to the health implications of obesity. As with constructions of reality, whether some of this coverage is truly educational is debatable. Increasingly, the media have framed the problem not merely as an individual or personal one, but as a broad structural problem involving, for example, the manner in which food is processed and sold (Saguy and Almeling 2008).

As of 2011, 45 percent of all youths in the United States were children of color, yet few of the faces they saw on television reflected their race or cultural heritage. Using content analysis, sociologists have found that only 2 of the nearly 60 prime-time series aired in recent years—*Ugly Betty* and *George Lopez*—focused on minority performers. What is more, programs that are shown earlier in the evening, when young people are most likely to watch television, are the least diverse. Researchers have noted one positive trend, however. Today, television is dominated by reality shows, which are particularly popular among younger viewers. Box 7-1 shows how the diverse audience for these shows is reflected in the programs themselves.

Another concern about the media, from the conflict perspective, is that television distorts the political process. Until the U.S. campaign finance system is truly reformed, the candidates with the most money (often backed by powerful lobbying groups) will be able to buy exposure to voters and saturate the air with commercials attacking their opponents.

Dominant Ideology: Whose Culture? In the United States, on the popular television contest *The Apprentice,* the dreaded dismissal line is "You're fired." In Finland, on *Dilli (The Deal),* it's *"Olet vapautettu"* ("You're free to leave"); in Germany, on *Big Boss,* it's *"Sie haben frei"* ("You're off"). Although people throughout the world decry U.S. exports, from films to language to Bart Simpson, the U.S. media are still widely imitated. Sociologist Todd Gitlin describes American popular culture as something that "people love, and love to hate" (2002:177; Wentz and Atkinson 2005).

We risk being ethnocentric if we overstress U.S. dominance, however. For example, *Survivor, Who Wants to Be a Millionaire, Big Brother,* and *Iron Chef*—immensely popular TV programs in the United States—came from Sweden, Britain, the Netherlands, and Japan, respectively. Even *American Idol* originated in Britain as *Pop Idol,* featuring Simon Cowell. And the steamy telenovelas of Mexico and other Spanish-speaking countries owe very little of their origin to the soap operas on U.S. television. Unlike motion pictures, television is gradually moving away from U.S. domination and is now more likely to be locally produced. By 2003, all the top 50 British TV shows were locally produced. *Medium* may appear on television in London, but it is shown late at night. Even U.S.-owned TV ventures such as Disney, MTV, and CNN had dramatically increased their locally produced programming overseas. Still, *CSI: NY* was on top in

Despite the popularity of Hollywood entertainment, media that are produced abroad for local consumption also do well. The animated series *Freej* features Muslim grandmothers who stumble on a cursed book while tackling their culture's wedding traditions. Produced in Dubai, the United Arab Emirates, for adult viewers, the series was launched in 2006.

7-1 Diversity in Reality Television

The underrepresentation of racial and ethnic minorities in the television industry is well documented. Not only are minorities less likely than Whites to play recurring roles; they are also underrepresented among key decision makers, such as directors, producers, and casting agents.

The new media phenomenon of reality TV may be an exception to this rule. Reality, or unscripted, television dominated prime-time television during the first decade of the 21st century. Popular with consumers and relatively inexpensive to produce, it soon became a staple on both broadcast and cable networks. Shows featured ordinary people or C-list celebrities confronting various challenges.

Although these series have been criticized on artistic grounds, they do present a diverse cast of characters. Content analysis shows that as a group, reality programs accurately represent the diversity of the general population. As such, they offer a new and significant exception to television programming that is otherwise dominated by White actors and actresses. One show, *America's Got Talent,* even has a minority host, African American Nick Cannon.

Reality shows do not necessarily promote racial and ethnic enlightenment. Instead, the broad collection of players often seems to fuel friction and build racial, social class, or sexual tension, based on either explicit or implicit issues. Far from being a multicultural paradise, reality TV is a low-wage segment of the industry in which the stars, unlike the actors in scripted dramas, receive little to no compensation. Perhaps not much has changed after all.

The color line remains in place in one segment of the reality genre, shows that promote romantic partnerships. For the first 17 seasons (through 2009), *The Bachelor* and *The Bachelorette* featured an all-White dating gallery. Like

A rare sight on prime-time television: people of color playing leading roles. Reality shows such as *America's Next Top Model* are one of the few categories in network TV that Whites do not dominate.

> *Far from being a multicultural paradise, reality TV is a low-wage segment of the industry in which the stars, unlike the actors in scripted dramas, receive little to no compensation.*

scripted TV, these shows are likely to remain White-only. Of the nearly 70 scripted pilot projects under development by the four major networks in 2009, just 4 featured a minority person in a starring role.

LET'S DISCUSS

1. Do you watch reality TV? If so, what do you like about the shows? Have you noted any tension or conflict based on race, social class, or sex? What about friendship and support that cross those lines—have you seen it?
2. What does the popularity of reality TV shows tell us about our culture and society?

Sources: Belton 2009; Braxton 2009; Grazian 2010:129; NAACP 2008; Wyatt 2009.

France, where only sports programs had a higher rating (Bielby and Harrington 2008; Colucci 2008; *The Economist* 2003).

Nations that feel a loss of identity may try to defend against the cultural invasion from foreign countries, especially the economically dominant United States. Yet as sociologists know, audiences are not necessarily passive recipients of foreign cultural messages, either in developing nations or in industrial nations. Thus, research on consumers of cultural products like television, music, and film must be placed in social context. Although people may watch and even enjoy media content, that does not mean that they will accept values that are alien to their own (Bielby and Harrington 2008).

Many developing nations have long argued for a greatly improved two-way flow of news and information between industrial nations and developing nations. They complain that news from the Third World is scant, and what news there is reflects unfavorably on the developing nations. For example, what do you know about South America? Most people in the United States will mention the two topics that dominate the news from countries south of the border: revolution and drugs. Most know little else about the continent.

To remedy this imbalance, a resolution to monitor the news and content that cross the borders of developing nations was passed by the United Nations Educational, Scientific, and Cultural Organization (UNESCO) in the 1980s. The United States disagreed with the proposal, which became one factor in the U.S. decision to withdraw from UNESCO in the mid-1980s. In 2005, the United States opposed another UNESCO plan, meant

SOCIOLOGY IN THE GLOBAL COMMUNITY

7-2 The Global Disconnect

Bogdan Ghirda, a Romanian, is paid 50 cents an hour to participate in multiplayer Internet games like City of Heroes and Star Wars. He is sitting in for someone in an industrialized country who does not want to spend days ascending to the highest levels of competition in order to compete with players who are already "well armed." This arrangement is not unusual. U.S.-based services can earn hundreds of dollars for recruiting someone in a less developed country, like Ghirda, to represent a single player in an affluent industrial country.

Meanwhile, villagers in Arumugam, India, are beginning to benefit from their new Knowledge Centre. The facility, funded by a nonprofit organization, contains five computers that offer Internet access—an amenity unknown until now to thousands of villagers.

These two situations illustrate the technological disconnect between the developing and industrial nations. Around the world, developing nations lag far behind industrial nations in their access to and use of new technologies. The World Economic Forum's Networked Readiness Index (NRI), a ranking of 139 nations, shows the relative preparedness of individuals, businesses, and governments to benefit from information technologies. As the accompanying table shows, the haves of the world—countries like Singapore, the United States, and Denmark—are network ready; the have-nots—countries like Zimbabwe, Chad, and Nepal—are not.

For developing nations, the consequences of the global disconnect are far more serious than an inability to surf the Net. Thanks to the Internet, multinational organizations can now function as a single global unit, responding instantly in real time, 24 hours a day. This new capability has fostered the emergence of what sociologist Manuel Castells calls a "global economy." But if large numbers of people—indeed, entire

> *For developing nations, the consequences of the global disconnect are far more serious than an inability to surf the Net.*

nations—are disconnected from the new global economy, their economic growth will remain slow and the well-being of their people will remain retarded. Those citizens who are educated and skilled will immigrate to other labor markets, deepening the impoverishment of nations on the periphery.

LET'S DISCUSS

1. For nations on the periphery, what are some of the social and economic consequences of the global disconnect?

NETWORKED READINESS INDEX

Top 10 Countries	Bottom 10 Countries
1. Switzerland	130. Nepal
2. Sweden	131. Mozambique
3. Singapore	132. Mali
4. United States	133. Timor-Leste
5. Germany	134. Burkina Faso
6. Japan	135. Mauritania
7. Finland	136. Zimbabwe
8. Netherlands	137. Burundi
9. Denmark	138. Angola
10. Canada	139. Chad

2. What factors might complicate efforts to remedy the global disconnect in developing nations?

Sources: Castells 2010a; Dutta and Mia 2010; *The Economist* 2005c; Lim 2007; Tony Thompson 2005; World Economic Forum 2010.

---

to reduce the diminishment of cultural differences. Hailed as an important step toward protecting threatened cultures, particularly the media markets in developing nations, the measure passed the UN's General Assembly by a vote of 148–2. The United States, one of the two dissenters, objected officially to the measure's vague wording, but the real concern was clearly the measure's potential impact on a major U.S. export (Dominick 2009; Riding 2005).

The Digital Divide Finally, as numerous studies have shown, advances in communications technology are not evenly distributed. Worldwide, low-income groups, racial and ethnic minorities, rural residents, and the citizens of developing countries have far less access than others to the latest technologies—a gap that is called the **digital divide.** People in low-income households and developing countries, for example, are less likely than others to have Internet access. When marginalized people do gain Internet access, they are still likely to trail the privileged. They may have dial-up service instead of broadband, or broadband instead of wireless Internet.

The implications of the digital divide go well beyond an inability to check sports results or celebrity comings and goings. The Internet and other new media are becoming essential to economic progress, whether it is finding a job or accessing information needed to improve one's skills.

The digital divide is most evident in developing countries. In Africa, 4 percent of the population has Internet access. These fortunate few typically pay the highest rates in the world—$250 to $300 a month—for the slowest connection speeds. Box 7-2 examines the global disconnect between the haves and have-nots of the information age (Robinson and Crenshaw 2010; P. Schaefer 2008).

use your sociological *imagination*

How do your favorite media reflect U.S. culture? How do they reflect the cultures of the rest of the world?

Feminist View

Feminists share the view of conflict theorists that the mass media stereotype and misrepresent social reality. According to

145

FIGURE **7-2** NETWORK COVERAGE OF WOMEN'S VERSUS MEN'S SPORTS

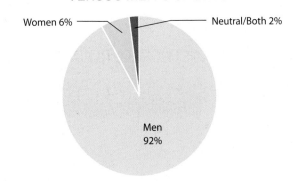

Note: Based on a content analysis of 2004 televised sports news and highlights shows.
Source: Messner et al. 2006:35.

this view, the media powerfully influence how we look at men and women, communicating unrealistic, stereotypical, and limiting images of the sexes.

Educators and social scientists have long noted the stereotypical portrayal of women and men in the mass media. Women are often shown as being shallow and obsessed with beauty. They are more likely than men to be presented unclothed, in danger, or even physically victimized. When women achieve newsworthy feats in fields traditionally dominated by men, such as professional sports, the media are often slow to recognize their accomplishments. As Figure 7-2 shows, only about 6 percent of network sports coverage is devoted to women. The situation is even worse on ESPN's *SportsCenter*, where content analysis shows that only 2 percent of airtime is devoted to women's sports.

Even when they are covered by the press, female athletes are not treated equally by television commentators. Communications researchers conducted a content analysis of over 200 hours of nationally televised coverage of professional golf events. The study showed that when female golfers are successful, they are more likely than male golfers to be called strong and intelligent. When they are not successful, they are more likely than men to be described as lacking in athletic ability. In contrast, male golfers receive more comments on their concentration and commitment. These findings suggest a subtle sexism, with women being portrayed as innately talented and men being portrayed as superior in mental or emotional makeup (T. Jacobs 2009).

Another aim of feminist research is to determine whether the media have a different impact on women than on men. Recently, researchers found that adolescent boys are almost three times as likely as adolescent girls to participate in online gaming. Young females who do participate are more likely than boy gamers to get into serious fights and report obesity. Clearly, this topic deserves further study (R. Desai et al. 2010).

A continuing, troubling issue for feminists and society as a whole is pornography. Feminists tend to be very supportive of freedom of expression and self-determination, rights that are denied to women more often than to men. Yet pornography presents women as sex objects and seems to make viewing women that way acceptable. Nor are concerns about

pornography limited to this type of objectification and imagery, as well as their implicit endorsement of violence against women. The industry that creates risqué adult images for videos, DVDs, and the Internet is largely unregulated, even putting its performers at risk.

Feminist scholars are cautiously optimistic about new media. Although women are represented among bloggers, by some measures they are responsible for only about 10 percent of the most popular blogs. Still, in conservative cultures like Saudi Arabia, online media offer women the opportunity to explore lifestyles that traditional media outlets largely ignore (Jesella 2008; Worth 2008).

As in other areas of sociology, feminist researchers caution against assuming that what holds true for men's media use is true for everyone. Researchers, for example, have studied the different ways that women and men approach the Internet. Though men are only slightly more likely than women ever to have used the Internet, they are much more likely to use it daily. Yet according to a 2009 study, more women than men use the Internet. Not surprisingly, men account for 91 percent of the players in online sports fantasy leagues. Perhaps more socially significant, however, is the finding that women are more likely than men to maintain friendship networks through e-mail (Boase et al. 2006; Fallows 2006; Pew Internet Project 2009; Rainie 2005).

Interactionist View

Interactionists are especially interested in shared understandings of everyday behavior. These scholars examine the media on the micro level to see how they shape day-to-day social behavior. Increasingly, researchers point to the mass media as the source of major daily activity; some argue that television serves essentially as a primary group for many individuals who share TV viewing. Other mass-media participation is not necessarily face-to-face. For example, we usually listen to the radio or read the newspaper as a solitary activity, although it is possible to share either with others (Cerulo et al. 1992; Waite 2000).

Online social networks, in fact, have become a new way of promoting consumption. As Figure 7-3 shows, advertisers have traditionally marketed products and services through spot ads, mass mailings, or billboards, whether they are promoting flat-screen televisions or public service messages like "Don't drink and drive." Now, using social networks (see Box 4-3, page 88), they can find consumers online and attempt to develop a relationship with them there. Through Facebook, for example, Burger King awarded a free Whopper to anyone who would delete 10 friends. Facebook's staff was not happy with Burger King's promotion, which notified 239,906 Facebook users that they had been dropped for a burger—an action that violated the network's policy. Nevertheless, Burger King created a vast network of consumers who enjoy Whoppers. Similarly, Kraft Foods encouraged people to post images of the Wiener-mobile on the photo site Flickr (Bacon Lovers' Talk 2009; Burger King 2009; Gaudin 2009).

Interactionists note, too, that friendship networks can emerge from shared viewing habits or from recollection of a cherished television series from the past. Family members and friends often gather for parties centered on the broadcasting of popular events such as the Super Bowl or the Academy Awards. And as

FIGURE **7-3** MARKETING ONLINE THROUGH SOCIAL NETWORKS

Traditional Marketing

Online Marketing

Advertiser

Advertiser

Traditional forms of advertising (left) allow only one-way communication, from the advertiser to the consumer. Online social networks (right) offer two-way communication, allowing advertisers to develop a relationship with consumers.

we've seen, television often serves as a babysitter or playmate for children and even infants.

The rise of the Internet has also facilitated new forms of communication and social interaction. Grandparents can now keep up with their grandchildren via e-mail, or even watch them on their laptops via Skype. Gay and lesbian teens have online resources for support and information. People can even find their lifetime partners through computer dating services.

Some troubling issues have been raised about day-to-day life on the Internet, however. What, if anything, should be done about terrorists and other extremist groups who use the Internet to exchange messages of hatred and even bomb-making recipes? What, if anything, should be done about the issue of sexual expression on the Internet? How can children be protected from it? Should "hot chat" and X-rated film clips be censored? Or should expression be completely free?

Though the Internet has created a new platform for extremists, hate groups, and pornographers, it has also given people greater control over what they see and hear. That is, the Internet allows people to manage their media exposure so as to avoid sounds, images, and ideas they do not enjoy or approve of. The legal scholar Cass Sunstein (2002) has referred to this personalized approach to news information gathering as *egocasting*. One social consequence of this trend may

be a less tolerant society. If we read, see, and hear only what we know and agree with, we may be much less prepared to meet people from different backgrounds or converse with those who express new viewpoints.

Furthermore, while many people in the United States embrace the Internet, we should note that information is not evenly distributed throughout the population. The same people, by and large, who experience poor health and have few job opportunities have been left off the information highway. Figure 7-4 breaks down Internet usage by gender, age, race, income, education, and community type. Note the large disparities in usage between those with high and low incomes, and between those with more and less education. The data also show a significant racial disparity. Though educators and politicians have touted the potential benefits to the disadvantaged, Internet usage may be reinforcing existing social-class and racial barriers.

The interactionist perspective helps us to understand one important aspect of the entire mass media system—the audience. How do we actively participate in media events? How do we construct with others the meaning of media messages? We will explore these questions in the section that follows. (Table 7-3 on page 149 summarizes the various sociological perspectives on the media.)

thinking CRITICALLY

What do you think is the most important function of the mass media in our society? Why? Which of the problems associated with the media troubles you most, and why?

TREND SPOTTING

Internet Dropouts

Although more and more people are surfing the Internet, the number of people who are going offline has also been rising. In 2009, one out of five nonusers had once surfed the Net and even used e-mail. For some of these people, the cost or lack of reliable access to the Internet was the reason for dropping offline. A significant number, however, simply lost interest. The overwhelming majority of these dropouts—89 percent—had no desire ever to go online again.

Surprisingly, almost one out of three people under age 30 take this attitude toward the Net. Some have a spouse or other relative who goes online for them, but others have deliberately distanced themselves from the online world. Their reasons vary from embarrassment over their lack of skill with computers to fear of being victimized by online crime and bad experiences online in the past. The Internet may be popular, but it is not for everyone.

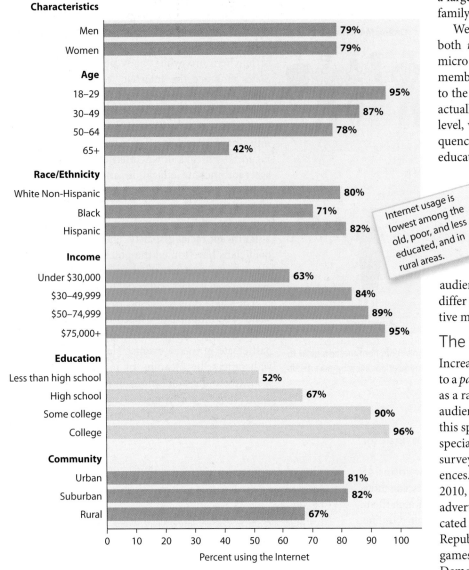

Characteristics

Note: Based on a national survey taken April–May 2010. Hispanic data limited to English-speaking respondents.
Source: Pew Internet Project 2010.

Internet usage is lowest among the old, poor, and less educated, and in rural areas.

audience may be a secondary group gathered in a large auditorium or a primary group, such as a family watching the latest Disney video at home.

We can look at the audience from the level of both *microsociology* and *macrosociology*. At the micro level, we might consider how audience members, interacting among themselves, respond to the media, or in the case of live performances, actually influence the performers. At the macro level, we might examine broader societal consequences of the media, such as the early childhood education delivered through programming like *Sesame Street*.

Even if an audience is spread out over a wide geographic area and members don't know one another, it is still distinctive in terms of age, gender, income, political party, formal schooling, race, and ethnicity. The audience for a ballet, for example, would likely differ substantially from the audience for alternative music.

The Segmented Audience

Increasingly, the media are marketing themselves to a *particular* audience. Once a media outlet, such as a radio station or a magazine, has identified its audience, it targets that group. To some degree, this specialization is driven by advertising. Media specialists have sharpened their ability, through survey research, to identify particular target audiences. Thus, during the midterm elections in 2010, the two major political parties placed TV advertisements in markets where surveys indicated they would find support. For example, the Republican Party placed ads on college football games and *America's Funniest Home Videos*. The Democratic Party bought time on *Brothers & Sisters* and *Dr. Phil* (Ashley Parker 2010).

The Audience

Ever feel like text-messaging everyone you know, to encourage them to vote for your favorite performer on a certain reality program? Ever looked over someone's shoulder as he watched last week's episode of *American Idol* on his iPhone—and been tempted to reveal the ending to him? Ever come across an old CD and tried to remember the last time you or a friend listened to one, or heard the songs in the order in which they were recorded? In this and many other ways, we are reminded that we are all part of a larger audience.

Who Is in the Audience?

The mass media are distinguished from other social institutions by the necessary presence of an audience. It can be an identifiable, finite group, such as an audience at a jazz club or a Broadway musical, or a much larger and undefined group, such as VH-1 viewers or readers of the same issue of *USA Today*. The

The specialized targeting of audiences has led some scholars to question the "mass" in mass media. For example, the British social psychologist Sonia Livingstone (2004) has written that the media have become so segmented, they have taken on the appearance almost of individualization. Are viewing audiences so segmented that large collective audiences are a thing of the past? That is not yet clear. Even though we seem to be living

TABLE 7-3 SOCIOLOGICAL PERSPECTIVES ON THE MASS MEDIA

Theoretical Perspective	Emphasis
Functionalist	Socialization
	Enforcement of social norms
	Conferral of status
	Promotion of consumption
	Narcotizing effect (dysfunction)
Conflict	Gatekeeping
	Media monitoring
	Construction of reality
	Digital divide
Feminist	Misrepresentation of women
	Differential impact on women
Interactionist	Impact on social behavior
	Source of friendship networks

Where's the President? The media target audience interests, so in 2009 *Us Weekly* featured the new family in the White House on its cover, but blocked out President Barack Obama with photos of the supposedly overweight Jessica Simpson and a single Jennifer Anniston. If you look closely, you can see the President's white-shirted arm behind First Lady Michelle Obama.

in an age of *personal* computers and *personal* digital assistants (PDAs), large formal organizations still do transmit public messages that reach a sizable, heterogeneous, and scattered audience.

use your sociological *imagination*

How might you use the concept of audience segmentation in your future occupation?

Audience Behavior

Sociologists have long researched how audiences interact with one another and how they share information after a media event. The role of audience members as opinion leaders particularly intrigues social researchers. An **opinion leader** is someone who influences the opinions and decisions of others through day-to-day personal contact and communication. For example, a movie or theater critic functions as an opinion leader. Sociologist Paul Lazarsfeld and his colleagues (1948) pioneered the study of opinion leaders in their research on voting behavior in the 1940s. They found that opinion leaders encourage their relatives, friends, and co-workers to think positively about a particular candidate, perhaps pushing them to listen to the politician's speeches or read the campaign literature.

Despite the role of opinion leaders, members of an audience do not all interpret media in the same way. Often their response is influenced by their social characteristics, such as occupation,

race, education, and income. Take the example of the televised news coverage of the riots in Los Angeles in 1992. The riots were an angry response to the acquittal of two White police officers accused of severely beating a Black motorist. Sociologist Darnell Hunt (1997) wondered how the social composition of audience members would affect the way they interpreted the news coverage. Hunt gathered 15 groups from the Los Angeles area, whose members were equally divided among Whites, Blacks, and Latinos. He showed each group a 17-minute clip from the televised coverage of the riots and asked members to discuss how they would describe what they had just seen to a 12-year-old. In analyzing the discussions, Hunt found that although gender and class did not cause respondents to vary their answers much, race did.

Hunt went beyond noting simple racial differences in perceptions; he analyzed how the differences were manifested. For example, Black viewers were much more likely than Latinos or Whites to refer to the events in terms of "us" versus "them." Another difference was that Black and Latino viewers were more animated and critical than White viewers as they watched the film clip. White viewers tended to sit quietly, still and unquestioning, suggesting that they were more comfortable with the news coverage than the Blacks or Latinos.

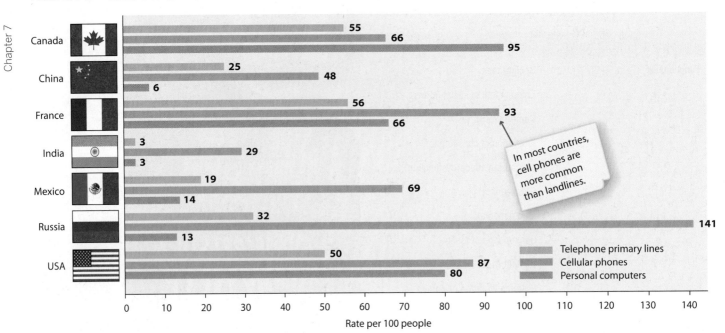

FIGURE 7-5 MEDIA PENETRATION IN SELECTED COUNTRIES

In most countries, cell phones are more common than landlines.

Telephone primary lines
Cellular phones
Personal computers

Rate per 100 people

Note: Personal computer data for 2006, released in 2009; for 2008, released in 2011.
Sources: Bureau of the Census 2009a:Table 1345; 2010a:Table 1392.

Think about It
What is the economic and political significance of media penetration?

thinking CRITICALLY

What kind of audience is targeted by the producers of televised professional wrestling? By the creators of an animated film? By a rap group? What factors determine who makes up a particular audience?

The Media's Global Reach

Has the rise of the electronic media created a *global village*? Canadian media theorist Marshall McLuhan predicted it would nearly 50 years ago. Today, physical distance is no longer a barrier, and instant messaging is possible across the world. The mass media have indeed created a global village. Not all countries are equally connected, as Figure 7-5 shows, but the progress has

In 2010, hip-hop artist UnK's "2 Step" was one of the most frequently downloaded cell phone ringtones. Because today's media provide multiple services, music fans can use the Internet to access recorded music and listen to it on their cell phones.

SOCIOLOGY IN THE GLOBAL COMMUNITY

7-3 Al Jazeera Is on the Air

A 24-hour-a-day televised news network with short bulletins every hour, followed by a fast-paced montage of news clips—all broadcast globally by satellite-linked cable stations. This could be CNN, but it's Al Jazeera, the Arabic-language television news network founded in 1996 and based in the small Persian Gulf state of Qatar. The name Al Jazeera means "island" or "peninsula," in reference to the network's home country.

Most people in the United States had never heard of Al Jazeera until October 7, 2001. That was when the channel aired the first of several videotaped messages from Osama bin Laden, the mastermind of the Al-Qaeda terrorist network. U.S. news outlets also televised the messages, but stopped after the government objected to the airing of bin Laden's calls for violence against U.S. citizens.

Though many media observers see Al Jazeera as biased, many viewers around the world might see CNN, ABC, and Fox News as biased. According to Kenton Keith, a former

In 2006, Al Jazeera expanded its programming to include an all-English channel; since then its following has grown. Israel's top cable company, for example, dropped CNN and added AJE to its lineup.

> "You have to be a supporter of Al Jazeera, even if you have to hold your nose sometimes."

U.S. ambassador to Qatar, Al Jazeera has a slant, but no more than other news organizations. It just happens to be a slant that most Americans aren't comfortable with.

Al Jazeera does offer diverse views. On its popular talk show *The Opposing View*, two women hotly debated polygamy among Muslim men. On another popular program, *Shari'a [Islamic Law] and Life*, the speaker dared to reassure Muslim women that the Koran does not force them to marry suitors designated by their parents. Ambassador Keith believes that "for the long-range importance of press freedom in the Middle East and the advantages that will ultimately have for the West, you have to be a supporter of Al Jazeera, even if you have to hold your nose sometimes" (Barr 2002:7).

LET'S DISCUSS

1. Do you find news outlets in the United States biased? How would you judge?
2. What do you think of the Al Jazeera network? Could the news coverage it provides and the editorial perspectives it takes be useful to the U.S. government? Explain.

Sources: Al Jazeera 2010; Barr 2002; Daniszewski 2003; S. MacLeod and Walt 2005; H. Rosenberg 2003; Urbina 2002.

---

been staggering, considering that voice transmission was just beginning 100 years ago (McLuhan 1964, 1967).

Sociologist Todd Gitlin considers *global torrent* a more apt metaphor for the media's reach than *global village*. The media permeate all aspects of everyday life. Take advertising, for example. Consumer goods are marketed vigorously worldwide, from advertisements on airport baggage carriers to imprints on sandy beaches. Little wonder that people around the world develop loyalty to a brand and are as likely to sport a Nike, Coca-Cola, or Harley-Davidson logo as they are their favorite soccer or baseball insignia (Gitlin 2002; Klein 1999).

A highly visible part of the media, whether it be print or electronic, is news. In the past, most people in the United States had little familiarity with news outlets outside their own country, with the possible exception of the British-based Reuters and BBC News.

Like so many other things, however, that changed after September 11, 2001, when an Arab news network took center stage (Box 7-3).

The Internet has facilitated all forms of communication. Reference materials and data banks can now be made accessible across national boundaries. Information related to international finance, marketing, trade, and manufacturing is literally just a keystroke away. We have seen the emergence of true world news outlets and the promotion of a world music that is not clearly identifiable with any single culture. Even the most future-oriented thinker would find the growth in the reach of the mass media in postindustrial and postmodern societies remarkable (Castells 2001, 2010b; Croteau and Hoynes 2003, 2006).

Although in the United States we may take television for granted, even thinking of it as an old-fashioned medium, worldwide that is not necessarily the case. In India, half of all households

New technologies can create new social norms. In Gurupá, Brazil, television watching became a community social activity when three new TV owners agreed to share their sets with the community of 3,000.

do not have television; in Nigeria and Bangladesh, more than 70 percent of households go without. Two technological advances are likely to change this pattern, however. First, advances in battery power now allow viewers to watch television even in areas where there is no electricity. Second, digital signal transmission permits television reception via cable or satellite.

In some developing countries, people manage to watch television even though they don't own one. Consider the town of Gurupá, in the remote Amazon area of Brazil. In 1982, the wealthiest three households in this community bought televisions. To please the rest of the town, they agreed to place their TVs near the window so that their neighbors could watch them as well. As the TV owners proudly displayed their new status symbol, TV watching became a community social activity. The introduction of a new technology had created a new social norm (Kenny 2009; Pace 1993, 1998).

Around the world, people rely increasingly on digital media, from cell phones to the Internet. This trend toward online communication has raised new concerns about the right to privacy. The Social Policy section that follows examines the social implications of digital media, from censorship to criminal activity.

thinking CRITICALLY

Use the functionalist, conflict, and interactionist perspectives to assess the effects of global TV programming on developing countries.

social**policy** and the Mass Media

The Right to Privacy

In 2010, humans added 1.2 zettabytes of digital information to the world's already huge data library. A zettabyte equals 1 trillion gigabytes—a quantity which, if placed on DVDs, would require a stack of disks stretching to the moon and back. By 2020, the size of this imaginary DVD tower will triple, quadruple, or even quintuple (Acohido 2010).

Within this mound of data lies personal information about people's finances, health, and individual tastes. In the postmodern digital age, do people have a right to keep that kind of information private? If so, can they expect others to respect that right?

Looking at the Issue

Although much of the sweeping change that accompanied the transition to digital media has benefited society, scholars have noted some negative effects. In particular, recent advances in computer technology have made it increasingly easy for business firms, government agencies, and even criminals to retrieve and store information about private individuals. In public places, at work, and on the Internet, surveillance devices track our every move, whether it is a keystroke or an ATM withdrawal. The

information they accumulate includes everything from our buying habits to our web-surfing patterns.

As these technologies increase the power to monitor our behavior, they raise fears of their misuse for criminal or even undemocratic purposes. In short, they threaten not just our privacy, but our freedom from crime and censorship as well. Some obvious violations of privacy, such as identity theft—the misuse of credit card and Social Security numbers to masquerade as another person—have been well documented. Other violations involve online surveillance of dissident political groups by authoritarian regimes and the unauthorized release of classified government documents. In 2010, WikiLeaks released thousands of classified U.S. foreign policy documents on its website, causing some people to condemn the action as treasonous and others to praise it as a blow against government censorship (O'Harrow Jr. 2005).

Other privacy violations are subtler, and not strictly illegal. For example, many commercial websites use "cookies" and tracking technology to monitor visitors' websurfing. Using that information, marketers can estimate a visitor's age, gender, and zip code, and from that data, the person's income. They can then

Our society's growing dependence on electronic transactions has greatly increased concerns about our privacy.

select advertisements that will appeal specifically to that person. So depending on who we are, or at least appear to be, one of us might see ads about weight-loss products and another, ads about travel to exotic locations.

Is this approach to online marketing just effective advertising, or is it an invasion of privacy? Because the information that marketers gather in this way can be tied to other devices a person uses, such as a cell phone or computer, some critics see online tracking as a form of fingerprinting (Angwin 2010; Angwin and Valentino-DeVries 2010a).

Applying Sociology

From a sociological point of view, the complex issues of privacy and censorship can be considered illustrations of culture lag. As usual, the material culture (technology) is changing faster than the nonmaterial culture (norms for controlling the use of technology). Too often, the result is an anything-goes approach to the use of new technologies.

Sociologists' views on the use and abuse of new technologies differ depending on their theoretical perspective. Functionalists take a generally positive view of the Internet, pointing to its manifest function of facilitating communication. From their perspective, the Internet performs the latent function of empowering people with few resources—from hate groups to special-interest organizations—to communicate with the masses.

In contrast, conflict theorists stress the danger that the most powerful groups in a society will use technology to violate the privacy of the less powerful.

Initiating Policy

Legislation regarding the surveillance of electronic communications has not always upheld citizens' right to privacy. In 1986, the federal government passed the Electronic Communications Privacy Act, which outlawed the surveillance of telephone calls except

with the permission of both the U.S. attorney general and a federal judge. Telegrams, faxes, and e-mails did not receive the same degree of protection, however. In 2001, one month after the terrorist attacks of September 11, Congress passed the Patriot Act, which relaxed existing legal checks on surveillance by law enforcement officers. Federal agencies are now freer to gather data electronically, including people's credit card receipts and banking records (Gertner 2005).

Today, most other types of online monitoring have yet to be tested in court, including the use of tracking technologies and the compilation and sale of personal profiles. Consistent with the concept of culture lag, privacy advocates complain that the law hasn't kept pace with advancing technology. In 2010, Congress began to draft federal legislation to inform cell phone and computer owners that their devices are being "fingerprinted," and to allow them to opt out of being monitored. The next year, seeking to head off the measure, some tracking organizations began voluntarily to allow people to edit the information collected in their online profiles. At the same time, the Federal Trade Commission issued a report that faulted the industry for not doing enough to protect consumers' privacy online (Angwin and Valentino-DeVries 2010b; Federal Trade Commission 2010; Steel 2010; *The Week* 2010b).

If anything, however, people seem to be less vigilant about maintaining their privacy today than they were before the information age. Young people who have grown up browsing the Internet seem to accept the existence of the "cookies" and "spyware" they may pick up while surfing. They have become accustomed to adult surveillance of their conversation in electronic chat rooms. And many see no risk in providing personal information about themselves to strangers they meet online. Little wonder that college professors find their students do not appreciate the political significance of their right to privacy (Turkle 2004, 2011).

Compared to online tracking, most people seem more worried about government surveillance and crimes like identity theft. Although online piracy is a real threat, in the long run, online tracking and other questionable forms of surveillance may pose a greater threat to society. As Nicholas Carr (2010:W2), former editor of the *Harvard Business Review,* has noted, "The continuing erosion of personal privacy . . . may lead us as a society to devalue the concept of privacy, to see it as outdated and unimportant . . . merely as a barrier to efficient shopping and socializing." From the point of view of many technology companies, however, abandoning the right to privacy is only realistic. As Sun Microsystems CEO Scott McNealy remarked in 1999, "You have no privacy. Get over it" (Carr 2010:W2).

Take the Issue with You

1. How would you react if you discovered that the government was monitoring your use of the mass media?

2. If your safety were in jeopardy, would you be willing to sacrifice your privacy?

3. Which do you consider the greatest threat to society: government censorship, cybercrime, or Internet surveillance? Explain. **153**

MASTERING THIS CHAPTER

Summary

The **mass media** are print and electronic instruments of communication that carry messages to often widespread audiences. They pervade all social institutions, from entertainment to education to politics. This chapter examines how the mass media affect those institutions and influence our social behavior.

1. From the functionalist perspective, the media entertain, socialize, enforce social norms, confer status, and promote consumption. They can be dysfunctional to the extent that they desensitize us to serious events and issues, a phenomenon called the **narcotizing dysfunction.**

2. Conflict theorists think the media reflect and even deepen the divisions in society through **gatekeeping,** or control over which material reaches the public; media monitoring, the covert observation of people's media usage and choices; and support of the **dominant ideology,** which defines reality, overwhelming local cultures.

3. Feminist theorists point out that media images of the sexes communicate unrealistic, stereotypical, limiting, and sometimes violent perceptions of women.

4. Interactionists examine the media on the micro level to see how they shape day-to-day social behavior. Interactionists have studied shared TV viewing and intergenerational e-mail.

5. The mass media require the presence of an audience, whether it is small and well defined or large and amorphous. With increasing numbers of media outlets has come more and more targeting of segmented (or specialized) audiences.

6. Social researchers have studied the role of **opinion leaders** in influencing audiences.

7. The media have a global reach thanks to new communications technologies, especially the Internet. Some people are concerned that this global reach will spread unhealthy influences to other cultures.

8. In the postmodern digital age, new technologies that facilitate the collection and sharing of personal information are threatening people's right to privacy.

Key Terms

Cultural convergence The flow of content across multiple media, and the accompanying migration of media audiences. (page 137)

Digital divide The relative lack of access to the latest technologies among low-income groups, racial and ethnic minorities, rural residents, and the citizens of developing countries. (145)

Dominant ideology A set of cultural beliefs and practices that helps to maintain powerful social, economic, and political interests. (143)

Gatekeeping The process by which a relatively small number of people in the media industry control what material eventually reaches the audience. (140)

Mass media Print and electronic means of communication that carry messages to widespread audiences. (136)

Narcotizing dysfunction The phenomenon in which the media provide such massive amounts of coverage that the audience becomes numb and fails to act on the information, regardless of how compelling the issue. (140)

Netizen A person who is actively involved in online communities and is committed to the free flow of information, with few outside controls. (141)

Opinion leader Someone who influences the opinions and decisions of others through day-to-day personal contact and communication. (149)

Stereotype An unreliable generalization about all members of a group that does not recognize individual differences within the group. (143)

TAKING SOCIOLOGY with you

1. For one day, categorize every media message you receive in terms of its function: Does it socialize, enforce a social norm, confer status, or promote consumption? Keep a record and tally the results. Which function was the most common? What can you conclude from the results?

2. Pick a specific audience—residents of your dorm, for example—and track their media preferences over the next day or two. Which mass media are they watching, reading, or listening to? Which media are the most popular and which the least popular? How segmented is this particular mass media audience?

3. Pick a foreign film, television program, or Internet site and study it from the point of view of a sociologist. What does it tell you about the culture that produced it?

Self-Quiz

Read each question carefully and then select the best answer.

1. From the functionalist perspective, the media can be dysfunctional in what way?
   a. They enforce social norms.
   b. They confer status.
   c. They desensitize us to events.
   d. They are agents of socialization.

2. Sociologist Robert Park studied how newspapers helped immigrants to the United States adjust to their environment by changing their customary habits and by teaching them the opinions held by people in their new home country. His study was conducted from which sociological perspective?
   a. the functionalist perspective
   b. the conflict perspective
   c. the interactionist perspective
   d. the dramaturgical perspective

3. There are problems inherent in the socialization function of the mass media. For example, many people worry about
   a. the effect of using the television as a babysitter.
   b. the impact of violent programming on viewer behavior.
   c. the unequal ability of all individuals to purchase televisions.
   d. both a and b.

4. Media advertising has several clear functions, but it also has dysfunctions. Sociologists are concerned that
   a. it creates unrealistic expectations of what is required to be happy.
   b. it creates new consumer needs.
   c. advertisers are able to influence media content.
   d. all of the above

5. Gatekeeping, the process by which a relatively small number of people control what material reaches an audience, is largely dominant in all but which of the following media?
   a. television
   b. the Internet
   c. publishing
   d. music

6. Which sociological perspective is especially concerned with the media's ability to decide what gets transmitted through gatekeeping?
   a. the functionalist perspective
   b. the conflict perspective
   c. the interactionist perspective
   d. the dramaturgical perspective

7. Which of the following is *not* a problem feminist theorists see with media coverage?
   a. Women are underrepresented, suggesting that men are the cultural standard and that women are insignificant.
   b. Men and women are portrayed in ways that reflect and perpetuate stereotypical views of gender.
   c. Female athletes are treated differently from male athletes in television commentary.
   d. The increasing frequency of single moms in the media is providing a negative role model for women.

8. Which of the following is *not* true concerning how men and women use the Internet?
   a. Men are more likely to use the Internet daily.
   b. Women are more likely to use e-mail to maintain friendships.
   c. Men account for 100 percent of players in online sports fantasy leagues.
   d. Men are slightly more likely to have ever used the Internet than women are.

9. Sociologist Paul Lazarsfeld and his colleagues pioneered the study of
   a. the audience.
   b. opinion leaders.
   c. the media's global reach.
   d. media violence.

10. In his study of how the social composition of audience members affected how they interpreted the news coverage of riots in Los Angeles in 1992, sociologist Darnell Hunt found what kind of differences in perception?
    a. racial
    b. gender
    c. class
    d. religious

11. The mass media increase social cohesion by presenting a more or less standardized, common view of culture through mass communication. This statement reflects the _____ perspective.

12. Paul Lazarsfeld and Robert Merton created the term _____ _____ to refer to the phenomenon in which the media provide such massive amounts of information that the audience becomes numb and generally fails to act on the information, regardless of how compelling the issue.

13. _____ is the term used to describe the set of cultural beliefs and practices that helps to maintain powerful social, economic, and political interests.

14. Sociologists blame the mass media for the creation and perpetuation of _____, or generalizations about all members of a group that do not recognize individual differences within the group.

15. The _____ perspective contends that television distorts the political process.

16. We risk being _____ if we overstress U.S. dominance and assume that other nations do not play a role in media cultural exports.

17. Both _____ and _____ theorists are troubled that the victims depicted in violent imagery are often those who are given less respect in real life: women, children, the poor, racial minorities, citizens of foreign countries, and even the physically disabled.

18. The _____ perspective examines the media on the micro level to see how they shape day-to-day social behavior.

19. From a sociological point of view, the current controversy over privacy and media censorship illustrates the concept of _____ _____.

20. Nearly 50 years ago, Canadian media theorist _____ _____ predicted that the rise of the electronic media would create a "global village."

THINKING ABOUT MOVIES

Pirate Radio

In the 1960s, an independent English radio station broadcasts from international waters, threatening the British Broadcasting Corporation's monopoly.

Talk to Me

In Washington, D.C., an R&B station struggles to keep its radio audience during the massive social change that followed the civil rights movement.

We Live in Public

This documentary traces the rise and fall of an Internet entrepreneur.

A potential shopper examines
a marijuana plant at the
Cannabis Crown competition
for medical marijuana growers
in Aspen, Colorado. Although
deviant behavior violates the
standards of conduct of a group
or society, it is not necessarily
criminal behavior.

COP IN THE HOOD

My Year Policing Baltimore's Eastern District

PETER MOSKOS

66 Living in Baltimore City, I was required to carry my gun both on and off duty. I never fired a shot outside of training. Only rarely was my service weapon—a charged semi-automatic nine-millimeter Glock-17 with no safety and a seventeen-round clip—pointed at somebody. But in my police duties, my gun was very routinely removed from its holster, probably every other shift. I did occasionally chase people down alleys and wrestled a few suspects. I maced one person, but did not hit anybody. As a police officer, I tried to speak softly and carry a big stick. The department issued a twenty-nine-inch straight wooden baton just for this purpose. I brought it along to all my calls.

In any account of police work, inevitably the noncriminal public, the routine, and the working folks all get short shrift. Police don't deal with a random cross-section of society, even within the areas they work. And this book reflects that. The ghetto transcends stereotypes. Families try to make it against the odds. Old women sweep the streets. People rise before dawn to go to work. On Sundays, ladies go to church wearing beautiful hats and preachers preach to the choir. But if you're looking for stereotypes, they're there. Between the vacant and abandoned buildings you'll find liquor stores, fast food, Korean corner stores, and a Jewish pawn shop.

Living conditions are worse than third-world shanty towns: children in filthy apartments without plumbing or electricity, entire homes put out on eviction day, forty-five-year-old great-grand parents, junkies not raising their kids, drug dealers, and everywhere signs of violence and despair.

As a middle-class white man policing the ghetto, I should address the charge of "exoticism," that I use poor residents for my own advantage. I plead no-contest. If you're not from the ghetto, and though it may not be politically correct to say so, the ghetto *is* exotic. One field-training officer accused me of being "*fascinated* by the ghetto." I am. There are very few aspects of urban life that don't fascinate me. But it is not my intent to sensationalize the ghetto. This is a book about police.

If you want to read about the ghetto, good books are out there. Ghettos are diverse and encompass many cultures and classes. Some object to the very term ghetto. I use the word because it is the vernacular of police officers and many (though by no means all) of the residents. If you really want to learn about the ghetto, go there. There's probably one near you. Visit a church; walk down the street; buy something from the corner store; have a beer; eat. But most importantly, talk to people. That's how you learn. When the subject turns to drugs and crime, you'll hear a common refrain: "It just don't make sense."

Twenty months in Baltimore wasn't very long, but it was long enough to see five police officers killed in the line of duty. And there were other cops, friends of mine, who were hurt, shot, and lucky to live. A year after I quit the force, my friend and academy classmate became the first Baltimore police woman killed in the line of duty, dying in a car crash on the way to back up another police officer. 99

Twenty months in Baltimore wasn't very long, but it was long enough to see five police officers killed in the line of duty.

(Moskos 2008:15–17) Additional information about this excerpt can be found on the Online Learning Center at www.mhhe.com/schaefer13e.

Peter Moskos's route to becoming a sworn police officer was a bit unusual, considering that becoming one was never his goal. None of his friends were on the force, nor did he come from a family of police officers: his father was a well-known and respected sociologist. During his graduate studies, however, Moskos decided that he wanted to learn more about law enforcement. So he persuaded Baltimore's police commissioner to let him attend the police academy, as both a student and a sociologist.

On the second day of class, the commissioner was suddenly and unexpectedly ousted from office, to be replaced by a new commissioner who questioned Moskos's motives. "Why don't you want to be a cop for real?" he challenged Moskos. That was the beginning of Moskos's 20-month tour of duty with the Baltimore Police Department, during which he responded to crimes that included disorderly conduct, domestic abuse, and a 12-person shooting.

In this excerpt from his book *Cop in the Hood: My Year Policing Baltimore's Eastern District,* Moskos describes his beat as seen through the eyes of a sociologist doing an ethnographic study. Looking beyond the stereotypes, he found a diverse and vibrant community, one he would get to know by mingling with its residents. Moskos took the same approach in his study of police work, taking sociology with him to the academy, the station house, and the street.

Moskos notes that the residents he served simply could not fathom the crime that plagued their inner-city neighborhood. What does explain it? Although drug dealing, prostitution, and the sale of stolen goods are illegal activities, they provide a certain level of stability to those who live on the edge, including the homeless, drug addicts, and frightened, neglected youths. Only a thin line separates their *deviant behavior*—behavior that violates social norms, such as dropping out of school or sleeping on the street—from their illegal activities. Crime is functional in their subculture, even if it is socially unacceptable to the rest of the neighborhood.

Another example of a behavior that can be seen as either socially acceptable or socially unacceptable depending on your reference group is binge drinking. On the one hand, we can view binge drinking as *deviant,* as violating a school's standards of conduct and endangering a person's health. On the other hand, we can see it as *conforming,* or complying with peer culture. In the United States, people are socialized to have mixed feelings about both conforming and nonconforming behavior. The term *conformity* can conjure up images of mindless imitation of a peer group—whether a circle of teenagers wearing "phat pants" or a group of business executives all dressed in gray suits. Yet the same term can also suggest that an individual is cooperative, or a "team player." What about those who do not conform? They may be respected as individualists, leaders, or creative thinkers who break new ground. Or they may be labeled as "troublemakers" and "weirdos."

This chapter examines the relationships among deviance and conformity, crime and social control. What is deviance, and what are its consequences? What causes crime? How does society control people's behavior, convincing us to conform to both unwritten rules and formal laws? We will begin by defining deviance

and describing the stigma that is associated with it. Then we will distinguish between conformity and obedience, and examine a surprising experiment on obedience to authority. We will study the mechanisms societies use, both formal and informal, to encourage conformity and discourage deviance, paying particular attention to the law and how it reflects our social values.

Next, we will focus on theoretical explanations for deviance, including the functionalist approach employed by Émile Durkheim and Robert Merton; interactionist-based theories; labeling theory, which draws on both the interactionist and the conflict perspectives; and conflict theory. In the last part of the chapter we will focus on crime, a specific type of deviant behavior. As a form of deviance that is subject to official, written norms, crime has been a special concern of both policymakers and the public in general. We will look at various types of crime found in the United States, the ways crime is measured, and international crime rates. Finally, the Social Policy section considers the controversial topic of the death penalty.

What Is Deviance?

For sociologists, the term *deviance* does not mean perversion or depravity. **Deviance** is behavior that violates the standards of conduct or expectations of a group or society. In the United States, alcoholics, compulsive gamblers, and the mentally ill would all be classified as deviants. Being late for class is categorized as a deviant act; the same is true of wearing jeans to a formal wedding. On the basis of the sociological definition, we are all deviant from time to time. Each of us violates common social norms in certain situations (Best 2004).

Is being overweight an example of deviance? In the United States and many other cultures, unrealistic standards of appearance

In 2009, baseball fans were shocked by the revelation that, like several other baseball greats, superstar Alex Rodriguez had used banned substances and lied about it.

Think about It

If your friends or teammates violate a social norm, is their behavior still deviant?

and body image place a huge strain on people—especially women and girls—based on how they look. Journalist Naomi Wolf (1992) has used the term *beauty myth* to refer to an exaggerated ideal of beauty, beyond the reach of all but a few females, which has unfortunate consequences. In order to shed their "deviant" image and conform to unrealistic societal norms, many women and girls become consumed with adjusting their appearances. Yet what is deviant in one culture may be celebrated in another.

Deviance involves the violation of group norms, which may or may not be formalized into law. It is a comprehensive concept that includes not only criminal behavior but also many actions that are not subject to prosecution. The public official who takes a bribe has defied social norms, but so has the high school student who refuses to sit in an assigned seat or cuts class. Of course, deviation from norms is not always negative, let alone criminal. A member of an exclusive social club who speaks out against a traditional policy of not admitting women, Blacks, and Jews is deviating from the club's norms. So is a police officer who blows the whistle on corruption or brutality within the department.

From a sociological perspective, deviance is hardly objective or set in stone. Rather, it is subject to social definition within a particular society and at a particular time. For that reason, what is considered deviant can shift from one social era to another. In most instances, those individuals and groups with the greatest status and power define what is acceptable and what is deviant. For example, despite serious medical warnings against the dangers of tobacco, made since 1964, cigarette smoking continued to be accepted for decades—in good part because of the power of tobacco farmers and cigarette manufacturers. Only after a long campaign led by public health and anticancer activists did cigarette smoking become more of a deviant activity. Today, many state and local laws limit where people can smoke.

Deviance and Social Stigma

A person can acquire a deviant identity in many ways. Because of physical or behavioral characteristics, some people are unwillingly

Deviant or normal? Television personality and recording artist Heidi Montag shocked fans in 2010 by revealing that she had undergone 10 plastic surgery procedures in a single day. Montag had already undergone breast augmentation, collagen lip injections, and rhinoplasty. Would you consider her behavior deviant?

cast in negative social roles. Once assigned a deviant role, they have trouble presenting a positive image to others and may even experience lowered self-esteem. Whole groups of people—for instance, "short people" or "redheads"—may be labeled in this way. The interactionist Erving Goffman coined the term **stigma** to describe the labels society uses to devalue members of certain social groups (Goffman 1963; Heckert and Best 1997).

Prevailing expectations about beauty and body shape may prevent people who are regarded as ugly or obese from advancing as rapidly as their abilities permit. Both overweight and anorexic people are assumed to be weak in character, slaves to their appetites or to media images. Because they do not conform to the beauty myth, they may be viewed as "disfigured" or "strange" in appearance, bearers of what Goffman calls a "spoiled identity." However, what constitutes disfigurement is a matter of interpretation. Of the 17 million cosmetic procedures done every year in the United States alone, many are performed on women who would be defined objectively as having a normal appearance. And while feminist sociologists have accurately noted that the beauty myth makes many women feel uncomfortable with themselves, men too lack confidence in their appearance. The number of males who choose to undergo cosmetic procedures has risen sharply in recent years (American Academy of Cosmetic Surgery 2010).

Often people are stigmatized for deviant behaviors they may no longer engage in. The labels "compulsive gambler," "ex-convict," "recovering alcoholic," and "ex–mental patient" can stick to a person for life. Goffman draws a useful distinction between a

prestige symbol that draws attention to a positive aspect of one's identity, such as a wedding band or a badge, and a stigma symbol that discredits or debases one's identity, such as a conviction for child molestation. While stigma symbols may not always be obvious, they can become a matter of public knowledge. Starting in 1994, many states required convicted sex offenders to register with local police departments. Some communities publish the names and addresses, and in some instances even the pictures, of convicted sex offenders on the web.

While some types of deviance will stigmatize a person, other types do not carry a significant penalty. Examples of socially tolerated forms of deviance can be found in the world of high technology.

Deviance and Technology

Technological innovations such as pagers and voice mail can redefine social interactions and the standards of behavior related to them. When the Internet was first made available to the general public, no norms or regulations governed its use. Because online communication offers a high degree of anonymity, uncivil behavior—speaking harshly of others or monopolizing chat room space—quickly became common. Online bulletin boards designed to carry items of community interest became littered with commercial advertisements. Such deviant acts are beginning to provoke calls for the establishment of formal rules for online behavior. For example, policymakers have debated whether to regulate the content of websites featuring hate speech and pornography.

Some deviant uses of technology are criminal, though not all participants see it that way. The pirating of software, motion pictures, and music has become a big business. At conventions and swap meets, pirated copies of DVDs are sold openly. Some of the products are obviously counterfeit, but many come in sophisticated packaging, complete with warranty cards. The vendors say they merely want to be compensated for their time and the cost of materials, or that the software they have copied is in the public domain.

Similarly, the downloading of music from the Internet, which is typically protected by copyright, is widely accepted. But file sharing, like the pirating of DVDs, has grown to the point that it is threatening the profits of copyright owners. Napster, the renegade website that allowed thousands of people to download from a wide selection of music files for free, has been shut down, the victim of a court challenge by the music industry. Nevertheless, its fleeting success has encouraged imitators, many of them college students who run file-sharing programs from their dorm rooms. The music industry is fighting back by urging law enforcement agents to track the pirates down and prosecute them.

Though most of these black market activities are clearly illegal, many consumers and small-time pirates are proud of their behavior. They may even think themselves smart for figuring out a way to avoid the "unfair" prices charged by "big corporations." Few people see the pirating of a new software program or a first-run movie as a threat to the public good, as they would see embezzling from a bank. Similarly, most businesspeople who "borrow" software from another department, even though they lack a site license, do not think they are doing anything wrong. No social stigma attaches to their illegal behavior.

Deviance, then, is a complex concept. Sometimes it is trivial, sometimes profoundly harmful. Sometimes it is accepted by society and sometimes soundly rejected.

Social Control

As we saw in Chapter 3, each culture, subculture, and group has distinctive norms governing appropriate behavior. Laws, dress codes, organizational bylaws, course requirements, and the rules of sports and games all express social norms.

How does a society bring about acceptance of basic norms? The term **social control** refers to the techniques and strategies for preventing deviant human behavior in any society. Social control occurs on all levels of society. In the family, we are socialized to obey our parents simply because they are our parents. Peer groups introduce us to informal norms, such as dress codes, that govern the behavior of their members. Colleges establish standards they expect of students. In bureaucratic organizations, workers encounter a formal system of rules and regulations. Finally, the government of every society legislates and enforces social norms.

Most of us respect and accept basic social norms and assume that others will do the same. Even without thinking, we obey the instructions of police officers, follow the day-to-day rules at our jobs, and move to the rear of elevators when people enter. Such behavior reflects an effective process of socialization to the dominant standards of a culture. At the same time, we are well aware that individuals, groups, and institutions *expect* us to act "properly." This expectation carries with it **sanctions,** or penalties and rewards for conduct concerning a social norm. If we fail to live up to the norm, we may face punishment through informal sanctions such as fear and ridicule or formal sanctions such as jail sentences or fines.

The challenge to effective social control is that people often receive competing messages about how to behave. While the state or government may clearly define acceptable behavior, friends or fellow employees may encourage quite different behavior patterns. Historically, legal measures aimed at blocking discrimination based on race, religion, gender, age, and sexual orientation have been difficult to implement, because many people tacitly encourage the violation of such measures.

Functionalists maintain that people must respect social norms if any group or society is to survive. In their view, societies literally could not function if massive numbers of people defied standards of appropriate conduct. In contrast, conflict theorists contend that the successful functioning of a society will consistently benefit the powerful and work to the disadvantage of other groups. They point out that in the United States, widespread resistance to social norms was necessary to win our independence from England, to overturn the institution of slavery, to allow women to vote, to secure civil rights, and to force an end to the war in Vietnam.

Conformity and Obedience

Techniques for social control operate on both the group level and the societal level. People we think of as peers or equals influence us to act in particular ways; the same is true of people who hold authority over us or occupy awe-inspiring positions. Social psychologist Stanley Milgram (1975) made a useful distinction between these two levels of social control.

The Milgram Experiment Milgram used the term **conformity** to mean going along with peers—individuals of our own status who have no special right to direct our behavior. In contrast, **obedience** is compliance with higher authorities in a hierarchical structure. Thus, a recruit entering military service will typically *conform* to the habits and language of other recruits and *obey* the orders of superior officers. Students will *conform* to the drinking behavior of their peers and *obey* the requests of campus security officers.

If ordered to do so, would you comply with an experimenter's instruction to administer increasingly painful electric shocks to a subject? Most people would say no; yet Milgram's research

In Finland (left), a young man relaxes in his prison cell, which resembles a college dorm room. In the United States (right), prisoners at a super-maximum-security prison watch television in cages that prevent them from making physical contact with guards or other prisoners. The rate of imprisonment in Finland is less than one-half that of England and one-fourth that of the United States.

(1963, 1975) suggests that most of us *would* obey such orders. In his words (1975:xi), "Behavior that is unthinkable in an individual . . . acting on his own may be executed without hesitation when carried out under orders."

Milgram placed advertisements in New Haven, Connecticut, newspapers to recruit subjects for a learning experiment at Yale University. Participants included postal clerks, engineers, high school teachers, and laborers. They were told that the purpose of the research was to investigate the effects of punishment on learning. The experimenter, dressed in a gray technician's coat, explained that in each test, one subject would be randomly selected as the "learner," while another would function as the "teacher." However, the experiment was rigged so that the real subject would always be the teacher, while an associate of Milgram's served as the learner.

At this point, the learner's hand was strapped to an electric apparatus. The teacher was taken to an electronic "shock generator" with 30 levered switches labeled from 15 to 450 volts. Before beginning the experiment, all subjects received sample shocks of 45 volts, to convince them of the authenticity of the experiment. The experimenter then instructed the teacher to apply shocks of increasing voltage each time the learner gave an incorrect answer on a memory test. Teachers were told that "although the shocks can be extremely painful, they cause no permanent tissue damage." In reality, the learner did not receive any shocks.

In a prearranged script, the learner deliberately gave incorrect answers and expressed pain when "shocked." For example, at 150 volts, the learner would cry out, "Get me out of here!" At 270 volts, the learner would scream in agony. When the shock reached 350 volts, the learner would fall silent. If the teacher wanted to stop the experiment, the experimenter would insist that the teacher continue, using such statements as "The experiment requires that you continue" and "You have no other choice; you *must* go on" (Milgram 1975:19–23).

Reflecting on the Milgram Experiment The results of this unusual experiment stunned and dismayed Milgram and other social scientists. A sample of psychiatrists had predicted that virtually all subjects would refuse to shock innocent victims. In their view, only a "pathological fringe" of less than 2 percent would continue administering shocks up to the maximum level. Yet almost *two-thirds* of participants fell into the category of "obedient subjects."

Why did these subjects obey? Why were they willing to inflict seemingly painful shocks on innocent victims who had never done them any harm? There is no evidence that these subjects were unusually sadistic; few seemed to enjoy administering the shocks. Instead, in Milgram's view, the key to obedience was the experimenter's social role as a "scientist" and "seeker of knowledge."

Milgram pointed out that in the modern industrial world, we are accustomed to submitting to impersonal authority figures whose status is indicated by a title (professor, lieutenant, doctor) or by a uniform (the technician's coat). Because we view the authority as larger and more important than the individual, we shift responsibility for our behavior to the authority figure. Milgram's subjects frequently stated, "If it were up to me, I would not have administered shocks." They saw themselves as merely doing their duty (Milgram 1975).

From a conflict perspective, our obedience may be affected by the value we place on those whom our behavior affects. While Milgram's experiment shows that in general, people are willing

In one of Stanley Milgram's experiments, the learner supposedly received an electric shock from a shock plate when he answered a question incorrectly. At the 150-volt level, the learner would demand to be released and would refuse to place his hand on the shock plate. The experimenter would then order the actual subject, the teacher, to force the hand onto the plate, as shown in the photo. Though 40 percent of the true subjects stopped complying with Milgram at this point, 30 percent did force the learner's hand onto the shock plate, despite his pretended agony.

to obey authority figures, other studies show that they are even more willing to obey if they feel the "victim" is deserving of punishment. Sociologist Gary Schulman (1974) re-created Milgram's experiment and found that White students were significantly more likely to shock Black learners than White learners. By a margin of 70 percent to 48 percent, they imposed more shocks on the Black learners than on the White learners.

From an interactionist perspective, one important aspect of Milgram's findings is the fact that subjects in follow-up studies were less likely to inflict the supposed shocks as they were moved physically closer to their victims. Moreover, interactionists emphasize the effect of *incrementally* administering additional dosages of 15 volts. In effect, the experimenter negotiated with the teacher and convinced the teacher to continue inflicting higher levels of punishment. It is doubtful that anywhere near the two-thirds rate of obedience would have been reached had the experimenter told the teachers to administer 450 volts immediately (B. Allen 1978; Katovich 1987).

Milgram launched his experimental study of obedience to better understand the involvement of Germans in the annihilation of 6 million Jews and millions of other people during World War II. In an interview conducted long after the publication of his study, he suggested that "if a system of death camps were set up in the United States of the sort we had seen in Nazi Germany, one would be able to find sufficient personnel for those camps in any medium-sized American town." Though many people questioned his remark, the revealing photos taken at Iraq's Abu Ghraib prison in 2004, showing U.S. military guards humiliating if not torturing Iraqi prisoners, recalled the experiment Milgram had done two generations earlier. Under conducive circumstances, otherwise normal people can and often do treat one another inhumanely (CBS News 1979:7–8; Hayden 2004; Zimbardo 2007a).

How willing would participants in this experiment be to shock learners today? Although many people may be skeptical of the high levels of conformity Milgram found, recent replications of his experiment confirm his findings. In 2006, using additional safeguards to protect participants' welfare, psychologist Jerry Burger (2009) repeated part of Milgram's experiment with college undergraduates. To avoid biasing the participants, Burger was careful to screen out students who had heard of Milgram's study. The results of the replication were startlingly similar to Milgram's: participants showed a high level of willingness to shock the learner, just as the participants in Milgram's experiment had almost half a century earlier. At the most comparable point in the two studies, Burger measured a rate of 70 percent full obedience—lower, but not significantly so, than the rate of 82.5 percent measured two generations earlier.

use your sociological *imagination*

If you were a participant in Milgram's research on conformity, how far do you think you would go in carrying out orders? Do you see any ethical problem with the experimenter's manipulation of the subjects?

Informal and Formal Social Control

The sanctions that are used to encourage conformity and obedience—and to discourage violation of social norms—are carried out through both informal and formal social control. As the term implies, people use **informal social control** casually to enforce norms. Examples include smiles, laughter, a raised eyebrow, and ridicule.

In the United States and many other cultures, adults often view spanking, slapping, or kicking children as a proper and necessary means of informal social control. Child development specialists counter that such corporal punishment is inappropriate because it teaches children to solve problems through violence. They warn that slapping and spanking can escalate into more serious forms of abuse. Yet, despite a 1998 policy statement by the American Academy of Pediatrics that corporal punishment is not effective and can indeed be harmful, 59 percent of pediatricians support the use of corporal punishment, at least in certain situations. Our culture widely accepts this form of informal social control (Chung et al. 2009).

Formal social control is carried out by authorized agents, such as police officers, judges, school administrators, employers, military officers, and managers of movie theaters. It can serve as a last resort when socialization and informal sanctions do not bring about desired behavior. Sometimes, informal social control can actually undermine formal social control, encouraging people to violate social norms. Box 8-1 examines binge drinking among college students, who receive conflicting messages about the acceptability of the behavior from sources of social control.

An increasingly significant means of formal social control in the United States is to imprison people. During the course of a year, over 7 million adults undergo some form of

correctional supervision—jail, prison, probation, or parole. Put another way, almost 1 out of every 30 adult Americans is subject to this very formal type of social control every year (Sabol et al. 2009).

In 2007, in the wake of the mass shootings at Virginia Tech, many college officials reviewed security measures on their campuses. Administrators were reluctant to end or even limit the relative freedom of movement students on their campuses enjoyed. Instead, they concentrated on improving emergency communications between campus police and students, faculty, and staff. Reflecting a reliance on technology to maintain social control, college leaders called for replacement of the "old" technology of e-mail with instant alerts that could be sent to people's cell phones via instant messaging.

Six years earlier, in the aftermath of September 11, 2001, new measures of social control became the norm in the United States. Some of them, such as stepped-up security at airports and high-rise buildings, were highly visible to the public. The federal government has also publicly urged citizens to engage in informal social control by watching for and reporting people whose actions seem suspicious.

Many people think this kind of social control goes too far. Civil rights advocates worry that the government's request for information on suspicious activities may encourage negative stereotyping of

Though formal social control usually involves fines, probation, or incarceration, some judges have used public humiliation as a sanction.

SOCIOLOGY ON CAMPUS

8-1 Binge Drinking

About 1,700 college students die each year of unintentional alcohol-related injuries. According to a study published by the Harvard School of Public Health, 44 percent of college students indulge in binge drinking (defined as at least five drinks in a row for men and four in a row for women). These numbers represent an increase from 1990s data, despite efforts on many campuses across the nation to educate students about the risks of binge drinking.

The problem is not confined to the United States—Britain, Russia, and South Africa all report regular "drink till you drop" alcoholic consumption among young people. According to a study that compared data from 22 countries, however, college students in the United States have the highest rate of drinking and driving. Nor does binge drinking begin in college. A national study found that over a 30-day period, 29 percent of high school students engaged in binge drinking.

Binge drinking on campus presents a difficult social problem. On the one hand, it can be regarded as *deviant,* violating the standards of conduct expected of those in an academic setting. In fact, Harvard researchers consider binge drinking the most serious public health hazard facing colleges. On the other hand, binge drinking represents *conformity* to the peer culture, especially in fraternities and sororities, which serve as social centers on many campuses. Most students seem to take an "everybody does it—no big deal" attitude toward the behavior.

Some colleges and universities are taking steps to make binge drinking a bit less "normal" by means of *social control*—banning kegs, closing fraternities and sororities, encouraging liquor retailers not to sell in high volume to students, and expelling students

44 percent of college students indulge in binge drinking.

after three alcohol-related infractions. Despite privacy laws, many schools are notifying parents whenever their underage children are caught drinking. Even with these measures, however, curbing underage drinking is a challenge.

Sources: E. Bernstein 2007; Centers for Disease Control and Prevention 2010; J. Miller et al. 2007; National Center on Addiction and Substance Abuse at Columbia University 2007; Outside the Classroom 2009; Wechsler et al. 2002, 2004.

LET'S DISCUSS

1. Why do you think most college students regard binge drinking as a normal rather than a deviant behavior?
2. Which do you think would be more effective in stopping binge drinking on your campus, informal or formal social control?

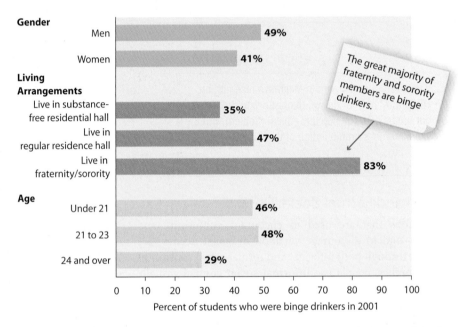

The great majority of fraternity and sorority members are binge drinkers.

Note: Based on a 2001 national survey of more than 10,000 college students. Binge drinking was defined as one drinking session of at least five drinks for men or four drinks for women during the two weeks prior to the self-administered questionnaire.
Source: Wechsler et al. 2002:208.

Muslims and Arab Americans. Clearly, there is a trade-off between the benefits of surveillance and the right to privacy.

thinking CRITICALLY

Think about a job you once held. How did your employer exercise social control over the employees? How did you, as an employee, use social control in relating to those around you?

Law and Society

Some norms are so important to a society that they are formalized into laws regarding people's behavior. **Law** may be defined as governmental social control (Black 1995). Some laws, such as the prohibition against murder, are directed at all members of society. Others, such as fishing and hunting regulations, affect particular categories of people. Still others govern the behavior of social institutions (for instance, corporate law and laws regarding the taxing of nonprofit enterprises).

Sociologists see the creation of laws as a social process. Because laws are passed in response to a perceived need for formal social control, sociologists have sought to explain how and why such a perception arises. In their view, law is not merely a static body of rules handed down from generation to generation. Rather, it reflects continually changing standards of what is right and wrong, of how violations are to be determined, and of what sanctions are to be applied (Schur 1968).

Sociologists representing varying theoretical perspectives agree that the legal order reflects the values of those in a position to exercise authority. Therefore, the creation of civil and criminal law can be a most controversial matter. Should it be against the law to employ illegal immigrants, to have an abortion (see Chapter 12), to allow prayer in public schools, or to smoke on an airplane? Such issues have been bitterly debated, because they require a choice among competing values. Not surprisingly, laws that are unpopular—such as the one-time prohibition of alcohol under the Eighteenth Amendment and the widespread establishment of a 55-mile-per-hour speed limit on highways—become difficult to enforce when there is no consensus supporting the norms.

One current and controversial debate over laws governing behavior is whether people should be allowed to use marijuana legally, for medical purposes. Although the majority of adults polled in national surveys support such a use, the federal government continues to regard all uses of marijuana as illegal. In 2005 the Supreme Court upheld the federal government's position. Nevertheless, 15 states and the District of Columbia have granted citizens the right to use marijuana for medical purposes—even if that privilege rests on dubious legal grounds (Figure 8-1).

In Singapore, a custodian removes a bit of litter from an otherwise spotless floor. Strict social controls prevail in the city-state, where the careless disposal of a cigarette butt or candy wrapper carries a $200 fine.

thinking CRITICALLY

Should some illegal drugs be decriminalized? Why or why not?

Socialization is the primary source of conforming and obedient behavior, including obedience to law. Generally, it is not external pressure from a peer group or authority figure that makes us go along with social norms. Rather, we have internalized such norms as valid and desirable and are committed to observing them. In a profound sense, we want to see ourselves (and to be seen) as loyal, cooperative, responsible, and respectful of others. In the United States and other societies around the world, people are socialized both to want to belong and to fear being viewed as different or deviant.

Control theory suggests that our connection to members of society leads us to systematically conform to society's norms. According to sociologist Travis Hirschi and other control theorists, our bonds to family members, friends, and peers induce us to follow the mores and folkways of our society. We give little conscious thought to whether we will be sanctioned if we fail to conform. Socialization develops our self-control so well that we don't need further pressure to obey social norms. Although control theory does not effectively explain the rationale for every conforming act, it nevertheless reminds us that while the media may focus on crime and disorder, most members of most societies conform to and obey basic norms (Brewis et al. 2011; Gottfredson and Hirschi 1990; Hirschi 1969).

TREND SPOTTING

Incarceration Nation

Since 1980, through prosperity and recession, war and peace, the United States has been sending more and more people to prison. Today, about 1.6 million people reside in federal or state institutions. That number is higher than the population of the fifth largest U.S. city, Phoenix.

Both the number of prisoners and the rate of incarceration have grown steadily. From 1980 through the end of 2008, the prison population increased from just over 1 in 1,000 to 1 in 198. If only adults are counted, the current proportion is 1 in every 100. The trend becomes even more disturbing when we consider the growing reliance on early-release programs. If cash-strapped states were not using electronic monitoring devices, like ankle bracelets, to lower their prison populations, the statistics would be even more dismal.

Internationally, the United States' incarceration rate stands out as one of the highest in the world—more than three times as high as that of Mexico or Canada. Even China with its huge population does not have as many people behind bars as the United States.

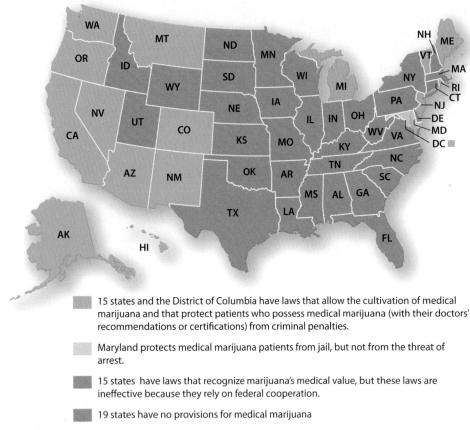

15 states and the District of Columbia have laws that allow the cultivation of medical marijuana and that protect patients who possess medical marijuana (with their doctors' recommendations or certifications) from criminal penalties.

Maryland protects medical marijuana patients from jail, but not from the threat of arrest.

15 states have laws that recognize marijuana's medical value, but these laws are ineffective because they rely on federal cooperation.

19 states have no provisions for medical marijuana

Source: NORML 2010.

The actions some states have taken to legalize marijuana are largely symbolic. Federal law still prohibits doctors from writing prescriptions for marijuana, and pharmacies from distributing the substance. Although patients can still be prosecuted by the federal government for possessing or using marijuana, the Obama administration has decided not to prosecute medical marijuana users who comply with state laws.

The contemporary study of the possible biological roots of criminality is but one aspect of the larger debate over sociobiology. In general, sociologists reject any emphasis on the genetic roots of crime and deviance. The limitations of current knowledge, the possibility of reinforcing racist and sexist assumptions, and the disturbing implications for the rehabilitation of criminals have led sociologists to draw largely on other approaches to explain deviance (Sagarin and Sanchez 1988).

Functionalist Perspective

According to functionalists, deviance is a common part of human existence, with positive as well as negative consequences for social stability. Deviance helps to define the limits of proper behavior. Children who see one parent scold the other for belching at the dinner table learn about approved conduct. The same is true of the driver who receives a speeding ticket, the department store cashier who is fired for yelling at a customer, and the college student who is penalized for handing in papers weeks overdue.

Sociological Perspectives on Deviance

Why do people violate social norms? We have seen that deviant acts are subject to both informal and formal social control. The nonconforming or disobedient person may face disapproval, loss of friends, fines, or even imprisonment. Why, then, does deviance occur?

Early explanations for behavior that deviated from societal expectations blamed supernatural causes or genetic factors (such as "bad blood" or evolutionary throwbacks to primitive ancestors). By the 1800s, substantial research efforts were being made to identify biological factors that lead to deviance, and especially to criminal activity. Though such research was discredited in the 20th century, contemporary studies, primarily by biochemists, have sought to isolate genetic factors that suggest a likelihood of certain personality traits. Although criminality (much less deviance) is hardly a personality characteristic, researchers have focused on traits that might lead to crime, such as aggression. Of course, aggression can also lead to success in the corporate world, in professional sports, or in other walks of life.

Durkheim's Legacy Émile Durkheim ([1895] 1964) focused his sociological investigations mainly on criminal acts, yet his conclusions have implications for all types of deviant behavior. In Durkheim's view, the punishments established within a culture (including both formal and informal mechanisms of social control) help to define acceptable behavior and thus contribute to stability. If improper acts were not sanctioned, people might stretch their standards of what constitutes appropriate conduct.

Sociologist Kai Erikson (1966) illustrated the boundary-maintenance function of deviance in his study of the Puritans of 17th-century New England. By today's standards, the Puritans placed tremendous emphasis on conventional morals. Their persecution and execution of women as witches represented a continuing attempt to define and redefine the boundaries of their community. In effect, their changing social norms created crime waves, as people whose behavior was previously acceptable suddenly faced punishment for being deviant (R. Schaefer and Zellner 2011).

Durkheim ([1897] 1951) introduced the term **anomie** into sociological literature to describe the loss of direction felt in a society when social control of individual behavior has become ineffective. Anomie is a state of normlessness that typically occurs during a period of profound social change and disorder, such as a time of economic collapse. People become more aggressive or depressed, which results in higher rates of violent crime and suicide. Since there is much less agreement on what constitutes proper behavior during times of revolution, sudden prosperity, or economic depression, conformity and obedience become less significant as social forces. It also becomes much more difficult to state exactly what constitutes deviance.

Merton's Theory of Deviance What do a mugger and a teacher have in common? Each is "working" to obtain money that can then be exchanged for desired goods. As this example illustrates, behavior that violates accepted norms (such as mugging) may be performed with the same basic objectives in mind as those of people who pursue more conventional lifestyles.

On the basis of this kind of analysis, sociologist Robert Merton (1968) adapted Durkheim's notion of anomie to explain why people accept or reject the goals of a society, the socially approved means of fulfilling their aspirations, or both. Merton maintained that one important cultural goal in the United States is success, measured largely in terms of money. In addition to providing this goal for people, our society offers specific instructions on how to pursue success—go to school, work hard, do not quit, take advantage of opportunities, and so forth.

What happens to individuals in a society with a heavy emphasis on wealth as a basic symbol of success? Merton reasoned that people adapt in certain ways, either by conforming to or by deviating from such cultural expectations. His **anomie theory of deviance** posits five basic forms of adaptation (Table 8-1).

Conformity to social norms, the most common adaptation in Merton's typology, is the opposite of deviance. It involves acceptance of both the overall societal goal ("become affluent") and the approved means ("work hard"). In Merton's view, there must be some consensus regarding accepted cultural goals and the legitimate means for attaining them. Without such a consensus, societies could exist only as collectives of people rather than as unified cultures, and might experience continual chaos.

The other four types of behavior represented in Table 8-1 all involve some departure from conformity. The "innovator" accepts the goals of society but pursues them with means that are regarded as improper. For instance, a safecracker may steal money to buy consumer goods and expensive vacations.

In Merton's typology, the "ritualist" has abandoned the goal of material success and become compulsively committed to the institutional means. Work becomes simply a way of life rather than a means to the goal of success. An example would be the bureaucratic official who blindly applies rules and regulations without remembering the larger goals of the organization. Certainly that would be true of a welfare caseworker who refuses to assist a homeless family because their last apartment was in another district.

The "retreatist," as described by Merton, has basically retreated (or withdrawn) from both the goals and the means of society. In the United States, drug addicts and vagrants are typically portrayed as retreatists. Concern has been growing that adolescents who are addicted to alcohol will become retreatists at an early age.

TABLE **8-1** MODES OF INDIVIDUAL ADAPTATION

Mode	Institutionalized Means (hard work)	Societal Goal (acquisition of wealth)
Nondeviant		
Conformity	Accept	Accept
Deviant		
Innovation	Reject	Accept
Ritualism	Accept	Reject
Retreatism	Reject	Reject
Rebellion	Replace with new means	Replace with new goals

Source: Adapted from Merton 1968:194.

The final adaptation identified by Merton reflects people's attempts to create a *new* social structure. The "rebel" feels alienated from the dominant means and goals and may seek a dramatically different social order. Members of a revolutionary political organization, such as a militia group, can be categorized as rebels according to Merton's model.

Merton made a key contribution to the sociological understanding of deviance by pointing out that deviants such as innovators and ritualists share a great deal with conforming people. The convicted felon may hold many of the same aspirations as people with no criminal background. The theory helps us to understand deviance as a socially created behavior rather than as the result of momentary pathological impulses. However, this theory of deviance has not been applied systematically to real-world crime. Box 8-2 examines scholars' efforts to confirm the theory's validity.

thinking CRITICALLY

Using examples drawn from work or college life, illustrate each of Merton's five modes of individual adaption.

Interactionist Perspective

The functionalist approach to deviance explains why rule violations continue to happen despite pressure to conform and obey. However, functionalists do not indicate how a given person comes to commit a deviant act or why on some occasions crimes do or do not occur. The emphasis on everyday behavior that is the focus of the interactionist perspective offers two explanations of crime: cultural transmission and routine activities theory.

Cultural Transmission In the course of studying graffiti writing by gangs in Los Angeles, sociologist Susan A. Phillips (1999) discovered that the writers learned from one another. In fact, Phillips was surprised by how stable their focus was over time. She also noted how other ethnic groups built on the models of the African American and Chicano gangs, superimposing Cambodian, Chinese, or Vietnamese symbols.

Humans *learn* how to behave in social situations, whether properly or improperly. There is no natural, innate manner in which people interact with one another. These simple ideas are not disputed today, but such was not the case when sociologist

RESEARCH TODAY

8-2 Does Crime Pay?

A driver violates the speed limit to get to a job interview on time. A financially strapped parent shoplifts goods that her family needs. These people may feel justified in violating the law because they do so to meet a reasonable objective. In Robert Merton's terms, they are *innovators*—people who violate social norms to achieve a commonly shared societal goal. Although their actions are criminal and potentially hurtful to others, from their own short-term perspective, their actions are functional.

Carried to its logical conclusion, innovation can and does become a career for some people. Yet from a purely economic point of view, even considering the fact that crime may pay is controversial, because doing so may seem to tolerate or encourage rule violation. Nothing is more controversial than the suggestion that gang-run drug deals are profitable and produce "good jobs." Although some people may see drug dealers as a cross between MBA-educated professionals and streetwise entrepreneurs, society in general does not admire these innovators.

Sociologist Sudhir Venkatesh collected detailed data on the illegal drug trade during his observation research on a Chicago street gang.

Working with economist Steven Levitt, coauthor of the best seller *Freakonomics,* to analyze the business of selling crack cocaine, he found that less than 5 percent of even the gang leaders earned $100,000 per year. The rest of the leaders and virtually all the rank and file earned less than the minimum wage. In fact, most were unpaid workers seeking to move up in the gang hierarchy. (Thus the title of a chapter in Levitt's book, "Why Do Drug Dealers Still Live with Their Moms?") As Levitt notes, the drug gang is like most corporations: the top 2 percent of workers take home most of the money.

Less than 5 percent of even the gang leaders earned $100,000 per year. The rest of the leaders and virtually all the rank and file earned less than the minimum wage.

Why, from a sociological *and* an economic perspective, do these nonprofitable practices persist, especially considering that one in every four members of drug-oriented street gangs is eventually killed? One reason, of course, is the public's almost insatiable demand for illegal drugs. And from the drug peddler's perspective, few legitimate jobs are available to young adults in poverty-stricken areas, urban or rural. Functionally, these youths are contributing to their household incomes by dealing drugs.

Scholars see a need for further research on Merton's concept of innovation. Why, for example, do some disadvantaged groups have lower rates of reported crime than others? Why do many people who are caught in adverse circumstances reject criminal activity as a viable alternative? Merton's theory of deviance does not easily answer such questions.

LET'S DISCUSS

1. Do you know anyone who has stolen out of need? If so, did the person feel justified in stealing, or did he or she feel guilty? How long did the theft continue?
2. Economically, profit is the difference between revenues and costs. What are the costs of the illegal drug trade, both economic and social? Is this economic activity profitable for society?

Sources: Clinard and Miller 1998; Kingsbury 2008; S. Levitt and Dubner 2006; S. Levitt and Venkatesh 2000; Rosen and Venkatesh 2008; Venkatesh 2008.

Edwin Sutherland (1883–1950) first advanced the idea that an individual undergoes the same basic socialization process in learning conforming and deviant acts.

Sutherland's ideas have been the dominating force in criminology. He drew on the **cultural transmission** school, which emphasizes that one learns criminal behavior by interacting with others. Such learning includes not only the techniques of lawbreaking (for example, how to break into a car quickly and quietly) but also the motives, drives, and rationalizations of the criminal. The cultural transmission approach can also be used to explain the behavior of those who habitually abuse alcohol or drugs.

Sutherland maintained that through interactions with a primary group and significant others, people acquire definitions of proper and improper behavior. He used the term **differential association** to describe the process through which exposure to attitudes *favorable* to criminal acts leads to the violation of rules. Research suggests that this view of differential association also applies to noncriminal deviant acts, such as smoking, truancy, and early sexual behavior.

Sutherland offers the example of a boy who is sociable, outgoing, and athletic and who lives in an area with a high rate of delinquency. The youth is very likely to come into contact with peers who commit acts of vandalism, fail to attend school, and so forth,

Under cover of darkness, drag racers await the start signal on a deserted Los Angeles street. Sutherland's concepts of differential association and cultural transmission would both apply to the practice of drag racing on city streets.

and may come to adopt such behavior. However, an introverted boy who lives in the same neighborhood may stay away from his peers and avoid delinquency. In another community, an outgoing and athletic boy may join a Little League baseball team or a scout troop because of his interactions with peers. Thus, Sutherland views improper behavior as the result of the types of groups to which one belongs and the kinds of friendships one has.

According to critics, the cultural transmission approach may explain the deviant behavior of juvenile delinquents or graffiti artists, but it fails to explain the conduct of the first-time impulsive shoplifter or the impoverished person who steals out of necessity. While it is not a precise statement of the process through which one becomes a criminal, differential association theory does direct our attention to the paramount role of social interaction in increasing a person's motivation to engage in deviant behavior (Harding 2009; Sutherland et al. 1992).

Social Disorganization Theory The social relationships that exist in a community or neighborhood affect people's behavior. Philip Zimbardo (2007a:24–25), author of the mock prison experiment described in Chapter 5, once did an experiment that demonstrated the power of communal relationships. He abandoned a car in each of two different neighborhoods, leaving its hood up and removing its hub caps. In one neighborhood, people started to strip the car for parts before Zimbardo had finished setting up a remote video camera to record their behavior. In the other neighborhood, weeks passed without the car being touched, except for a pedestrian who stopped to close the hood during a rainstorm.

What accounts for the strikingly different outcomes of Zimbardo's experiment in the two communities? According to **social disorganization theory,** increases in crime and deviance can be attributed to the absence or breakdown of communal relationships and social institutions, such as the family, school, church, and local government. This theory was developed at the University of Chicago in the early 1900s to describe the apparent disorganization that occurred as cities expanded with rapid immigration and migration from rural areas. Using the latest survey techniques, Clifford Shaw and Henry McKay literally mapped the distribution of social problems in Chicago. They found high rates of social problems in neighborhoods where buildings had deteriorated and the population had declined. Interestingly, the patterns persisted over time, despite changes in the neighborhoods' ethnic and racial composition.

This theory is not without its critics. To some, social disorganization theory seems to "blame the victim," leaving larger societal forces, such as the lack of jobs or high-quality schools, unaccountable. Critics also argue that even troubled neighborhoods have viable, healthy organizations, which persist despite the problems that surround them.

More recently, social disorganization theorists have taken to emphasizing the effect of social networks on communal bonds. These researchers acknowledge that communities are not isolated islands. Residents' bonds may be enhanced or weakened by their ties to groups outside the immediate community (Jensen 2005; Sampson and Graves 1989; Shaw and McKay 1942).

Labeling Theory

The Saints and the Roughnecks were groups of high school males who were continually engaged in excessive drinking, reckless driving, truancy, petty theft, and vandalism. There the similarity ended. None of the Saints was ever arrested, but every Roughneck was frequently in trouble with police and townspeople. Why the disparity in their treatment? On the basis of observation research in their high school, sociologist William Chambliss (1973) concluded that social class played an important role in the varying fortunes of the two groups.

The Saints hid behind a facade of respectability. They came from "good families," were active in school organizations, planned on attending college, and received good grades. People generally viewed their delinquent acts as a few isolated cases of sowing wild oats. The Roughnecks had no such aura of respectability. They drove around town in beat-up cars, were generally unsuccessful in school, and aroused suspicion no matter what they did.

We can understand such discrepancies by using an approach to deviance known as **labeling theory.** Unlike Sutherland's work, labeling theory does not focus on why some individuals come to commit deviant acts. Instead, it attempts to explain why certain people (such as the Roughnecks) are *viewed* as deviants, delinquents, bad kids, losers, and criminals, whereas others whose behavior is similar (such as the Saints) are not seen in such harsh terms. Reflecting the contribution of interactionist theorists, labeling theory emphasizes how a person comes to be labeled as deviant or to accept that label. Sociologist Howard Becker (1963:9; 1964), who popularized this approach, summed it up with this statement: "Deviant behavior is behavior that people so label."

Labeling theory is also called the **societal-reaction approach,** reminding us that it is the *response* to an act, not the behavior itself, that determines deviance. For example, studies have shown that some school personnel and therapists expand educational programs designed for learning-disabled students to include those with behavioral problems. Consequently, a "troublemaker" can be improperly labeled as "learning-disabled," and vice versa.

Labeling and Agents of Social Control Traditionally, research on deviance has focused on people who violate social norms. In contrast, labeling theory focuses on police, probation officers, psychiatrists, judges, teachers, employers, school officials, and other regulators of social control. These agents, it is argued, play a significant role in creating the deviant identity by designating certain people (and not others) as deviant. An important aspect of labeling theory is the recognition that some individuals or groups have the power to *define* labels and *apply* them to others. This view ties into the conflict perspective's emphasis on the social significance of power.

In recent years the practice of *racial profiling,* in which people are identified as criminal suspects purely on the basis of their race, has come under public scrutiny. Studies confirm the public's suspicions that in some jurisdictions, police officers are much more likely to stop Black males than White males for routine traffic violations, in the expectation of finding drugs or guns in their cars. Civil rights activists refer to these cases sarcastically as DWB (Driving While Black) violations. Beginning in 2001, profiling took a new turn as people who appeared to be Arab or Muslim came under special scrutiny. (Racial profiling will be examined in more detail in Chapter 11).

The popularity of labeling theory is reflected in the emergence of a related perspective, called social constructionism.

According to the **social constructionist perspective,** deviance is the product of the culture we live in. Social constructionists focus specifically on the decision-making process that creates the deviant identity. They point out that "child abductors," "deadbeat dads," "spree killers," and "date rapists" have always been with us, but at times have become *the* major social concern of policymakers because of intensive media coverage (Liska and Messner 1999; E. R. Wright et al. 2000).

How do certain behaviors come to be viewed as a problem? Cigarette smoking, which was once regarded as a polite, gentlemanly activity, is now considered a serious health hazard, not only to the smoker but also to others nearby who don't smoke. Recently, people have become concerned about the danger, especially to children, posed by *thirdhand smoke*—smoke-related chemicals that cling to clothes and linger in rooms, cars, even elevators (Winickoff et al. 2009).

Labeling and Sexual Deviance Labels have been applied to many types of deviance. Certainly one of the most visible examples has to do with human sexuality and gender. What is deviant sexual behavior? What is criminal sexual behavior? Labeling theory focuses on the process through which these behaviors come to be considered deviant.

The definition of deviant sexual behavior has varied significantly both over time and from culture to culture. Until 1973, the American Psychiatric Association considered homosexuality a "sociopathic personality disorder," which in effect meant that homosexuals should seek therapy. Two years later, however, the association removed homosexuality from its list of mental illnesses. Today, the organization publicly proclaims that "being gay is just as healthy as being straight." To use Goffman's term (see page 160), mental health professionals have removed the stigma from this form of sexual expression. As a result, in the United States and many other countries, consensual sex between same-sex adults is no longer a crime (American Psychological Association 2008; International Gay and Lesbian Human Rights Commission 2010).

Despite the change in health professionals' attitudes, the social stigma of homosexuality lingers. As a result, many people prefer the more positive terms *gay* and *lesbian.* Others, in defiance of the stigma, have proudly adopted the pejorative term *queer* in a deliberate reaction to the ridicule they have borne because of their sexual orientation. Still others maintain that constructing one's sexual orientation as either homosexual or heterosexual is too limiting. Indeed, such either/or language ignores those who are *bisexual,* or sexually attracted to both sexes.

Another group whose sexual orientation does not fit into the usual categories is *transgendered persons,* or those people whose current gender identity does not match their physical identity at birth. Some transgendered persons see themselves as both male and female. Others, called *transexuals,* may take hormones or undergo surgery in an effort to draw physically closer to their chosen gender identity. Transgendered persons are sometimes confused with *transvestites,* or cross-dressers who wear the clothing of the opposite sex. Transvestites are typically men, either gay or heterosexual, who choose to wear women's clothing.

The use of all these terms even in a positive or nonjudgmental way is problematic, since they imply that human sexuality can be confined in neat, mutually exclusive categories. Moreover, the destigmatization of these labels tends to reflect the influence

The true story of Brandon Teena, presented in the 1999 motion picture *Boys Don't Cry,* illustrates the complexity of human sexuality. The transgendered teen from Nebraska, played by Hilary Swank (right), was born female but preferred life as a male.

of the socially privileged—that is, the affluent—who have the resources to overcome the stigma. In contrast, the traditional Native American concept of the *two spirit,* a personality that blends the masculine and the feminine, has been largely ridiculed or ignored (Gilley 2006; Wentling et al. 2008).

What does constitute sexual deviance, then? The answer to this question seems to change with each generation. Today, U.S. laws allow married women to accuse their husbands of rape, when a generation ago such an offense was not recognized. Similarly, *pedophilia*—an adult having sex with a minor—is generally regarded with disgust today, even when it is consensual. Yet in many countries, fringe groups now speak positively of "intergenerational sex," arguing that "childhood" is not a biological given (Hendershott 2002).

Though this and some other aspects of sexual expression are still against the law, the meaning of the labels is beginning to blur. Similarly, child pornography is both illegal and abhorrent to most people, yet many fashion advertisements in mainstream magazines seem to verge on it. And while sex work and sex trafficking seem wrong to most of us, society tolerates and even regulates many aspects of those activities (Barton 2006).

use your sociological *imagination*

You are a teacher. What labels, freely used in education, might you attach to your students?

Conflict Theory

Conflict theorists point out that people with power protect their interests and define deviance to suit their needs. Sociologist Richard Quinney (1974, 1979, 1980) is a leading exponent of the

In the 1930s, the Federal Bureau of Narcotics launched a campaign to portray marijuana as a dangerous drug rather than a pleasure-inducing substance. From a conflict perspective, those in power often use such tactics to coerce others into adopting a different point of view.

view that the criminal justice system serves the interests of the powerful. Crime, according to Quinney (1970), is a definition of conduct created by authorized agents of social control—such as legislators and law enforcement officers—in a politically organized society. He and other conflict theorists argue that lawmaking is often an attempt by the powerful to coerce others into their morality (see also Spitzer 1975).

This theory helps to explain why our society has laws against gambling, drug use, and prostitution, many of which are violated on a massive scale. (We will examine these "victimless crimes" later in the chapter.) According to conflict theorists, criminal law does not represent a consistent application of societal values, but instead reflects competing values and interests. Thus, the U.S. criminal code outlaws marijuana because of its alleged harm to users, yet cigarettes and alcohol—both of which can be harmful to users—are sold legally almost everywhere.

In fact, conflict theorists contend that the entire criminal justice system in the United States treats suspects differently based on their racial, ethnic, or social-class background. In many cases, officials in the system use their own discretion to make biased decisions about whether to press charges or drop them, whether to set bail and how much, whether to offer parole or deny it. Researchers have found that this kind of **differential justice**— differences in the way social control is exercised over different

groups—puts African Americans and Latinos at a disadvantage in the justice system, both as juveniles and as adults. On average, White offenders receive shorter sentences than comparable Latino and African American offenders, even when prior arrest records and the relative severity of the crime are taken into consideration (R. Brewer and Heitzeg 2008; Quinney 1974; Sandefur 2008; Schlesinger 2011).

The perspective advanced by conflict and labeling theorists forms quite a contrast to the functionalist approach to deviance. Functionalists see standards of deviant behavior as merely reflecting cultural norms; conflict and labeling theorists point out that the most powerful groups in a society can shape laws and standards and determine who is (or is not) prosecuted as a criminal. These groups would be unlikely to apply the label "deviant" to the corporate executive whose decisions lead to large-scale environmental pollution. In the opinion of conflict theorists, agents of social control and other powerful groups can impose their own self-serving definitions of deviance on the general public.

Feminist Perspective

Feminist criminologists such as Freda Adler and Meda Chesney-Lind have suggested that many of the existing approaches to deviance and crime were developed with only men in mind. For example, in the United States, for many years any husband who forced his wife to have sexual intercourse—without her consent and against her will—was not legally considered to have committed rape. The law defined rape as pertaining only to sexual relations between people who were not married to each other, reflecting the overwhelmingly male composition of state legislatures at the time.

It took repeated protests by feminist organizations to get changes in the criminal law defining rape. Beginning in 1993, husbands in all 50 states could be prosecuted under most circumstances for the rape of their wives. There remain alarming exceptions in no fewer than 30 states, however. For example, the husband is exempt when he does not need to use force because his wife is asleep, unconscious, or mentally or physically impaired. These interpretations still rest on the notion that the marriage contract entitles a husband to sex (Bergen 2006).

In the future, feminist scholarship can be expected to grow dramatically. Particularly on topics such as white-collar crime, drinking behavior, drug abuse, and differential sentencing rates between the genders, as well as on the fundamental question of how to define deviance, feminist scholars will have much to say.

We have seen that over the past century, sociologists have taken many different approaches in studying deviance, arousing some controversy in the process. Table 8-2 summarizes the various theoretical approaches to this topic.

Crime

Crime is a violation of criminal law for which some governmental authority applies formal penalties. It represents a deviation from formal social norms administered by the state. Laws divide crimes into various categories, depending on the severity of the offense, the age of the offender, the potential punishment, and the court that holds jurisdiction over the case.

Crime is on everyone's mind. Until recently, college campuses were viewed as havens from crime. But as Box 8-3 on page 173

Approach	Theoretical Perspective	Proponents	Emphasis
Anomie	Functionalist	Émile Durkheim Robert Merton	Adaptation to societal norms
Cultural transmission/ Differential association	Interactionist	Edwin Sutherland	Patterns learned through others
Social disorganization	Interactionist	Clifford Shaw Henry McKay	Communal relationships
Labeling/Social constructionist	Interactionist	Howard Becker	Societal response to acts
Conflict	Conflict	Richard Quinney	Dominance by authorized agents Discretionary justice
Feminist	Conflict/Feminist	Freda Adler Meda Chesney-Lind	Role of gender Women as victims and perpetrators

shows, at today's colleges and universities, crime goes well beyond cheating and senior class pranks.

The term **index crimes** refers to the eight types of crime that are tabulated each year by the Federal Bureau of Investigation (FBI). This category of criminal behavior generally consists of those serious offenses that people think of when they express concern about the nation's crime problem. Index crimes include murder, rape, robbery, and assault—all of which are violent crimes committed against people—as well as the property crimes of burglary, theft, motor vehicle theft, and arson.

Types of Crime

Rather than relying solely on legal categories, sociologists classify crimes in terms of how they are committed and how society views the offenses. In this section we will examine five types of crime differentiated by sociologists: victimless crimes, professional crime, organized crime, white-collar and technology-based crime, and transnational crime.

Victimless Crimes   When we think of crime, we tend to think of acts that endanger people's economic or personal well-being against their will (or without their direct knowledge). In contrast, sociologists use the term **victimless crime** to describe the willing exchange among adults of widely desired but illegal goods and services, such as prostitution (Schur 1965, 1985).

Some activists are working to decriminalize many of these illegal practices. Supporters of decriminalization are troubled by the attempt to legislate a moral code for adults. In their view, prostitution, drug abuse, gambling, and other victimless crimes are impossible to prevent. The already overburdened criminal justice system should instead devote its resources to street crimes and other offenses with obvious victims.

Despite widespread use of the term *victimless crime,* however, many people object to the notion that there is no victim other than the offender in such crimes. Excessive drinking, compulsive gambling, and illegal drug use contribute to an enormous amount of personal and property damage. A person with a drinking problem may become abusive to a spouse or children; a compulsive gambler or drug user may steal to pursue his or her obsession. And feminist sociologists contend that prostitution, as well as the more disturbing aspects of pornography, reinforce the misconception that women are "toys" who can be treated as objects rather than people. According to critics of decriminalization, society must not give tacit approval to conduct that has such harmful consequences (Melissa Farley and Malarek 2008).

The controversy over decriminalization reminds us of the important insights of labeling and conflict theorists presented earlier. Underlying this debate are two questions: Who has the power to label gambling, prostitution, and public drunkenness as "crimes"? and Who has the power to label such behaviors as "victimless"? The answer is generally the state legislatures, and in some cases, the police and the courts.

Professional Crime   Although the adage "Crime doesn't pay" is familiar, many people do make a career of illegal activities. A **professional criminal,** or *career criminal,* is a person who pursues crime as a day-to-day occupation, developing skilled techniques and enjoying a certain degree of status among other criminals. Some professional criminals specialize in burglary, safecracking, hijacking of cargo, pickpocketing, and shoplifting. Such people have acquired skills that reduce the likelihood of arrest, conviction, and imprisonment. As a result, they may have long careers in their chosen professions.

Edwin Sutherland (1937) offered pioneering insights into the behavior of professional criminals by publishing an annotated account written by a professional thief. Unlike the person who engages in crime only once or twice, professional thieves make a business of stealing. They devote their entire working time to planning and executing crimes, and sometimes travel across the nation to pursue their "professional duties." Like

SOCIOLOGY ON CAMPUS

8-3 Campus Crime

According to a national survey released in 2008, 72 percent of college students consider campus safety "very important" in selecting a college. A generation earlier, would campus crime have been uppermost in the minds of prospective students?

Research on crime in college has focused on interpersonal violence ("date rape," as it is sometimes trivialized) and the way in which colleges handle such incidents. In 2007, two very different events brought campus crime to national attention. First, there was the April 16, 2007, rampage at Virginia Tech. In its aftermath, observers questioned whether campus officials should have notified students and employees of the first shootings, at a dormitory, during the two hours that passed before the gunman's second attack in a classroom building. The federal law known as the Clery Act, passed in 1990, requires timely warnings of campus crime, but how they should be delivered and how specific they should be (for example, whether the names of alleged assailants should be revealed) is unclear.

The second incident, the death of a girl in her dormitory room at Eastern Michigan University, led to the resignation of the university's president. For two months, officials had assured

The federal law known as the Clery Act, passed in 1990, requires timely warnings of campus crime, but how they should be delivered and how specific they should be is unclear.

her parents that she died a natural death. Later, her family learned that she had been raped and murdered, and that her body had been missing for three days.

These and other less publicized incidents have prompted colleges to become more forthcoming about campus crime and to provide better security. However, the growing trend toward living (and partying) off campus poses a challenge to their efforts. Student safety at internship sites and study-abroad programs is even more difficult to ensure.

Making judgments about campus crime based on the reports mandated by the Clery Act is difficult. Because these documents include only reported incidents, they may or may not be accurate. The latest data from the University of California, which has over 20,000 students, for example, show that the total number of forcible sex offenses per year ranges from 2 to more than 62.

LET'S DISCUSS

1. Do some research on campus crime. What is the crime rate on your college campus,

and how does it compare to crime rates at other schools? Relate what you have learned to sociological theory.

2. What have officials at your college done to discourage campus crime?

Sources: Department of Justice 2009; Interface Group Report (Virginia Tech) 2007; Lipka 2009; National Institute of Justice 2005; New York Times 2007, 2008; Security on Campus 2008.

---

people in regular occupations, professional thieves consult with their colleagues concerning the demands of work, becoming part of a subculture of similarly occupied individuals. They exchange information on places to burglarize, on outlets for unloading stolen goods, and on ways of securing bail bonds if arrested.

Organized Crime A 1976 government report devotes three pages to defining the term *organized crime.* For our purposes, we will consider **organized crime** to be the work of a group that regulates relations among criminal enterprises involved in illegal activities, including prostitution, gambling, and the smuggling and sale of illegal drugs. Organized crime dominates the world of illegal business just as large corporations dominate the conventional business world. It allocates territory, sets prices for goods and services, and acts as an arbitrator in internal disputes. A secret, conspiratorial activity, it generally evades law enforcement. It takes over legitimate businesses, gains influence over labor unions, corrupts public officials, intimidates witnesses in criminal trials, and even "taxes" merchants in exchange for "protection" (National Advisory Commission on Criminal Justice 1976).

Organized crime serves as a means of upward mobility for groups of people struggling to escape poverty. Sociologist Daniel Bell (1953) used the term *ethnic succession* to describe the sequential passage of leadership from Irish Americans in the early part of the 20th century to Jewish Americans in the 1920s and then to Italian Americans in the early 1930s. Ethnic succession has become more complex, reflecting the diversity of the nation's latest immigrants. Colombian, Mexican, Russian, Chinese, Pakistani, and Nigerian immigrants are among those who have begun to play a significant role in organized crime activities (Chin 1996; Kleinknecht 1996).

White-Collar and Technology-Based Crime Income tax evasion, stock manipulation, consumer fraud, bribery and extraction of kickbacks, embezzlement, and misrepresentation in advertising—these are all examples of **white-collar crime,** illegal acts committed in the course of business activities, often by affluent, "respectable" people. Edwin Sutherland (1949, 1983) likened these crimes to organized crime because they are often perpetrated through occupational roles.

"KICKBACKS, EMBEZZLEMENT, PRICE-FIXING, BRIBERY... THIS IS AN EXTREMELY HIGH-CRIME AREA."

A new type of white-collar crime has emerged in recent decades: computer crime. The use of high technology allows criminals to carry out embezzlement or electronic fraud, often leaving few traces, or to gain access to a company's inventory without leaving home. According to a study by the FBI and the National White Collar Crime Center, over 270,000 Internet crimes are reported every year, ranging from scams on online auction sites to identity theft (Internet Crime Complaint Center 2009).

When Charles Horton Cooley spoke of the self and Erving Goffman of impression management, surely neither scholar could have envisioned the insidious crime of identity theft. Each year about 14 percent of all adults find that their personal information has been misused for criminal purposes. Unfortunately, with our society's growing reliance on electronic financial transactions, assuming someone else's identity has become increasingly easy (Vamosi et al. 2010).

Identity theft does not necessarily require technology. A criminal can obtain someone's personal information by pickpocketing or by intercepting mail. However, the widespread exchange of information online has allowed criminals to access large amounts of personal information. Public awareness of the potential harm from identity theft took a giant leap in the aftermath of September 11, 2001, when investigations revealed that several hijackers had used fraudulent IDs to open bank accounts, rent apartments, and board planes. A law enacted in 2004 makes identity theft punishable by a mandatory prison sentence if it is linked to other crimes. Still, unauthorized disclosures of information, even if accidental, persist (Brubaker 2008).

Sutherland (1940) coined the term *white-collar crime* in 1939 to refer to acts by individuals, but the term has been broadened

more recently to include offenses by businesses and corporations as well. *Corporate crime,* or any act by a corporation that is punishable by the government, takes many forms and includes individuals, organizations, and institutions among its victims. Corporations may engage in anticompetitive behavior, environmental pollution, medical fraud, tax fraud, stock fraud and manipulation, accounting fraud, the production of unsafe goods, bribery and corruption, and health and safety violations (J. Coleman 2006).

For many years, corporate wrongdoers got off lightly in court by documenting their long history of charitable contributions and agreeing to help law enforcement officials find other white-collar criminals. Unfortunately, that is still the case. The highly visible jailing of multimedia personality Martha Stewart in 2004, as well as recent disclosures of "Wall Street greed," may lead the casual observer to think that government is cracking down on white-collar crime. However, an independent analysis found that from 2000 through 2009, the number of white-collar crimes that were prosecuted increased only modestly (Transactional Records Access Clearinghouse 2009).

Even when a person is convicted of corporate crime, the verdict generally does not harm his or her reputation and career aspirations nearly so much as conviction for street crime would. Apparently, the label "white-collar criminal" does not carry the stigma of the label "felon convicted of a violent crime." Conflict theorists don't find such differential treatment surprising. They argue that the criminal justice system largely disregards the crimes of the affluent, focusing on crimes committed by the poor. Generally, if an offender holds a position of status and influence, his or her crime is treated as less serious, and the sanction is much more lenient.

Hate Crime In contrast to other crimes, hate crimes are defined not only by the perpetrators' actions, but by the purpose of their conduct. The government considers an ordinary crime to be a **hate crime** when the offender is motivated to choose a victim based on race, ethnicity, religion, or some other personal characteristic, and when evidence shows that hatred prompted the offender to commit the crime. Hate crimes are sometimes referred to as *bias crimes* (Department of Justice 2008).

In 1990, Congress passed the Hate Crimes Statistics Act, which created a national mandate to identify crimes based on race, religion, ethnic group, and national origin. (Before that time, only 12 states had monitored such crimes.) Since then the act has been broadened to include disabilities, both physical and mental, and sexual orientation. In addition, some jurisdictions impose harsher sanctions (jail time or fines) for hate crimes than for other crimes. For example, if the penalty for assault is a year in jail, the penalty for an assault identified as a hate crime might be two years.

In 2010, law enforcement agencies in 91 percent of the United States submitted data on hate crimes to the federal government. The statistics included official reports of more than 8,300 hate crimes and bias-motivated incidents. As Figure 8-2 shows, race was the apparent motivation in approximately 48 percent of the reports. Religion, sexual orientation, and ethnicity accounted for another 51 percent. Although vandalism and intimidation were

FIGURE **8-2** CATEGORIZATION OF REPORTED HATE CRIMES

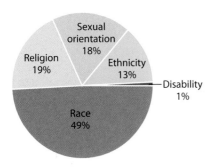

Source: Incidents reported for 2009 in 2010. Department of Justice 2010.

TABLE **8-3** TYPES OF TRANSNATIONAL CRIME

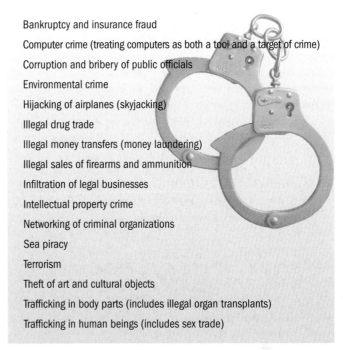

Bankruptcy and insurance fraud

Computer crime (treating computers as both a tool and a target of crime)

Corruption and bribery of public officials

Environmental crime

Hijacking of airplanes (skyjacking)

Illegal drug trade

Illegal money transfers (money laundering)

Illegal sales of firearms and ammunition

Infiltration of legal businesses

Intellectual property crime

Networking of criminal organizations

Sea piracy

Terrorism

Theft of art and cultural objects

Trafficking in body parts (includes illegal organ transplants)

Trafficking in human beings (includes sex trade)

Source: Compiled and updated by the author based on Mueller 2001 and United Nations Office on Drugs and Crime 2005.

the most common crimes, 33 percent of the incidents involved assault, rape, or murder.

The vast majority of hate crimes, although not all of them, are committed by members of the dominant group against those who are relatively powerless. One in every six racially based hate crimes is an anti-White incident. Except for the most horrific hate crimes, these offenses receive little media attention; anti-White incidents probably receive even less. Clearly, hostility based on race knows no boundaries (Department of Justice 2010).

Transnational Crime More and more, scholars and police officials are turning their attention to **transnational crime,** or crime that occurs across multiple national borders. In the past, international crime was often limited to the clandestine shipment of goods across the border between two countries. But increasingly, crime is no more restricted by such borders than is legal commerce. Rather than concentrating on specific countries, international crime now spans the globe.

Historically, probably the most dreadful example of transnational crime has been slavery. At first, governments did not regard slavery as a crime, but merely regulated it as they would the trade in goods. In the 20th century, transnational crime grew to embrace trafficking in endangered species, drugs, and stolen art and antiquities.

Transnational crime is not exclusive of some of the other types of crime we have discussed. For example, organized criminal networks are increasingly global. Technology definitely facilitates their illegal activities, such as trafficking in child pornography. Beginning in the 1990s, the United Nations began to categorize transnational crimes; Table 8-3 lists some of the more common types.

Bilateral cooperation in the pursuit of border criminals such as smugglers has been common for many years. The first global effort to control international crime was the International Criminal Police Organization (Interpol), a cooperative network of European police forces founded to stem the movement of political revolutionaries across borders. While such efforts to fight transnational crime may seem lofty—an activity with which any government should cooperate—they are complicated by sensitive legal and security issues. Most nations that have signed protocols issued by the United Nations, including the United States, have expressed concern over potential encroachments on their national judicial systems, as well as concern over their national

security. Thus, they have been reluctant to share certain types of intelligence data. The terrorist attacks of September 11, 2001, increased both the interest in combating transnational crime and sensitivity to the risks of sharing intelligence data (Deflem 2005; Felson and Kalaitzidis 2005).

use your sociological *imagination*

As the editor of an online news service, how might you treat stories on corporate or white-collar crime differently from those on violent crime?

Crime Statistics

Crime statistics are not as accurate as social scientists would like, especially since they deal with an issue of grave concern to the people of the United States. Unfortunately, they are frequently cited as if they were completely reliable. Such data do serve as an indicator of police activity, as well as an approximate indication of the level of certain crimes. Yet it would be a mistake to interpret these data as an exact representation of the incidence of crime.

Understanding Crime Statistics Because reported crime is very high in the United States, the public regards crime as a major social problem. However, there has been a significant decline in violent crime nationwide following many years of increases. In fact, reported rates in the United States are the

Crime Index Offenses in 2008	Number Reported	Rate per 100,000 Inhabitants	Percentage Change in Rate Since 1999
Violent crime			
Murder	16,272	5	−6
Forcible rape	89,000	29	−11
Robbery	444,855	145	−3
Aggravated assault	834,885	275	−8
Total	1,382,012	455	−13
Property crime			
Burglary	2,222,196	731	−5
Larceny-theft	6,558,873	2,167	−15
Motor vehicle theft	956,846	315	−26
Total	9,767,915	3,213	−14

Notes: Arson was designated an index offense beginning in 1979; data on arson were still incomplete as of 2008. Because of rounding, the offenses may not add to totals.

Source: Department of Justice 2009:Tables 1, 1a.

lowest in about 40 years. Several explanations have been offered, including these:

- Community-oriented policing and crime prevention programs
- New gun control laws
- A massive increase in the prison population, which at least prevents inmates from committing crimes outside prison

It remains to be seen whether this pattern of decline will continue. Even with current declines, however, reported crimes remain well above those of other nations.

Feminist scholars draw our attention to one significant countertrend: the proportion of major crimes committed by women has increased. Nevertheless, violent crimes by women, which have never been common, have actually declined. Despite the "mean girls" headlines in the tabloid magazines, every reliable measure shows that among women, fights, weapons possession, assaults, and violent injuries have plunged over the last decade (Males and Lind 2010).

Typically, the crime data used in the United States are based on the index crimes described earlier. The crime index, published annually by the FBI as part of the *Uniform Crime Reports,* includes statistics on murder, rape, robbery, assault, burglary, larceny-theft, motor vehicle theft, and arson (Table 8-4). Obviously, many serious offenses, such as white-collar crimes, are not included in this index (although they are recorded elsewhere). In addition, the crime index is disproportionately devoted to property crimes, whereas most citizens are more worried about violent crimes. Thus, a significant decrease in the number of rapes and robberies could be overshadowed by a slightly larger increase in the number of automobiles stolen, leading to the mistaken impression that *personal* safety is more at risk than before.

The most serious limitation of official crime statistics is that they include only those crimes actually *reported* to law enforcement agencies. Because members of racial and ethnic minority groups often distrust law enforcement agencies, they may not contact the police. Feminist sociologists and others have noted that many women do not report rape or spousal abuse out of fear they will be blamed for the crime.

Partly because of these deficiencies in official statistics, the National Crime Victimization Survey was initiated in 1972. The Bureau of Justice Statistics, in compiling this annual report, seeks information from law enforcement agencies, but also interviews households across the nation and asks if they were victims of a specific set of crimes during the preceding year. In general, those who administer **victimization surveys** question ordinary people, not police officers, to determine whether they have been victims of crime.

Unfortunately, like other crime data, victimization surveys have particular limitations. They require that victims understand what has happened to them and are willing to disclose such information to interviewers. Fraud, income tax evasion, and blackmail are examples of crimes that are unlikely to be reported in victimization studies. As Figure 8-3 shows, data from these surveys reveal a fluctuating crime rate, with significant declines in the 1980s and relatively low rates well into the 21st century. In 2009, reported crime continued to drop nationwide, declining 5.5 percent compared to the previous year. In the first quarter of 2010, most large cities continued to report declines.

What explains these declines? No single explanation suffices, but improvements in community-oriented policing, surveillance technologies, and the allocation of limited resources have helped to hold down crime rates, along with massive use of imprisonment and probation. Another contributing factor has been the job loss that millions of people suffered in recent years: more people have been home during the day to thwart attempted

TAKING SOCIOLOGY TO WORK

Stephanie Vezzani, **Special Agent, U.S. Secret Service**

Stephanie Vezzani wasn't sure what she wanted to major in when she entered the University of Akron, but she did know what she wanted to do with her life: she wanted a career as a crime fighter. Vezzani began as an accounting major, but switched to sociology when she discovered the department offered a special concentration in law enforcement.

Vezzani is now an agent with the U.S. Secret Service, whose twofold mission is to protect high-ranking officials and their families and to investigate financial crimes, including counterfeiting, identity theft, and computer-based attacks on the financial, banking, and telecommunications industries. She has tackled both aspects of the job. For her, a typical week would include working on a criminal investigation in a field office or traveling around the country with a government official in need of protection.

Vezzani finds that travel is one of the most exciting aspects of her job. Over the past six years she has visited Russia, Turkey, Jordan, Vietnam, and South Korea. She also attended the 2002 Winter Olympics in Salt Lake City, where she provided protection for the athletes living in the Olympic Village. Vezzani relishes meeting people from

different cultures, and of course she loves the sights she gets to see. "The architecture in St. Petersburg, Russia, was amazing," she says.

Vezzani uses her training in sociology on a daily basis, as she interviews suspects, witnesses, and victims of crime. "It is critical in the field of law enforcement to have an understanding of people's relationships and the beliefs and value systems that contribute to their decision making," she explains. "Sociology has provided me the knowledge to speak to and listen to people with different values and cultures in order to complete my job at the highest level possible."

LET'S DISCUSS

1. Besides an awareness of different beliefs, values, and cultures, what else might sociology offer to those who serve in law enforcement?
2. Law enforcement is a relatively new career option for women. What special strengths do you think a woman might bring to police work?

---

burglaries (Blumstein and Wallman 2006; *The Economist* 2009b; Perez 2010; *The Week* 2010a).

International Crime Rates If developing reliable crime data is difficult in the United States, making useful cross-national comparisons is even more difficult. Nevertheless, with some care, we can offer preliminary conclusions about how crime rates differ around the world.

During the 1980s and 1990s, violent crimes were much more common in the United States than in western Europe. Murders, rapes, and robberies were reported to the police at much higher rates in the United States. Yet the incidence of certain other types of crime appears to be higher elsewhere. For example, England, Italy, Australia, and New Zealand all have higher rates of car theft than the United States. Developing nations have significant rates of reported homicide due to civil unrest and political con-

flict among civilians (International Crime Victim Survey 2004; World Bank 2003).

A particularly worrisome development has been the rapid escalation in homicide rates in developing countries that supply drugs to industrialized countries, especially the United States. The huge profits generated by cocaine exports to North America and Europe have allowed drug gangs to arm themselves to the point of becoming illegal armies. Homicide rates in Mexico are now about twice as high as those in the United States. Honduras, Guatemala, Venezuela, and El Salvador's homicide rates are 3 to 5 times those of Mexico (*The Economist* 2010c).

Why are rates of violent crime generally so much higher in the United States than in western Europe? Sociologist Elliot Currie (1985, 1998) has suggested that our society places greater emphasis on individual economic achievement than other societies. At the same time, many observers have noted that the culture of the United States has long tolerated, if not condoned, many forms of violence. Coupled with sharp disparities between poor and affluent citizens, significant unemployment, and substantial alcohol and drug abuse, these factors combine to produce a climate conducive to crime.

In the United States, high rates of violent crime, especially in the cities, have long fueled calls for greater use of the death penalty. We will take a close look at the controversy over the ultimate penalty in the Social Policy section that follows.

FIGURE **8-3** VICTIMIZATION RATES, 1973–2009

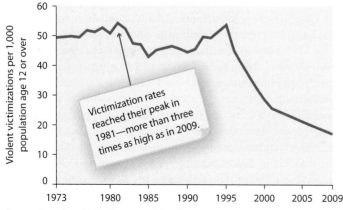

Sources: Rennison 2002; Truman and Rand 2010.

thinking CRITICALLY

Why is it useful to sociologists to have victimization surveys in addition to reported crime data?

On June 11, 2001, Timothy McVeigh—the man who killed hundreds of innocent people when he bombed the federal building in Oklahoma City in 1995—was executed by the U.S. government. McVeigh was the first federal prisoner to be put to death in nearly four decades. His execution, and that of others who received the death penalty for their crimes, has raised many questions, both from supporters and from critics of capital punishment. How can the government prevent the execution of innocent men and women? Is it right to resort to a punishment that imitates the crime it seeks to condemn? Is life in prison enough of a punishment for a truly heinous crime?

Looking at the Issue

Historically, execution has been a significant form of punishment, both for deviance from social norms and for criminal behavior. In North America, the death penalty has been used for centuries to punish murder, alleged witchcraft, and a few other crimes. Yet for most of that time, little thought was given to its justification; capital punishment was simply assumed to be morally and religiously right. Today, the death penalty is still on the books in most states, where it is used to a greater or lesser extent (Figure 8-4).

In other parts of the world, serious thought has been given to the ethical implications of the ultimate penalty. As of late 2010, 95 nations had renounced capital punishment, and many more use it only sparingly, if at all (Figure 8-5).

Applying Sociology

Traditionally, the debate over the death penalty has focused on its appropriateness as a form of punishment and its value in deterring crime. Viewed from Émile Durkheim's functionalist perspective, sanctions against deviant acts help to reinforce society's standards of proper behavior. Supporters of capital punishment insist that fear of execution will prevent at least some criminals from committing serious offenses. Moreover, even if it does not serve as a deterrent, they still see the death penalty as justified, because they believe the worst criminals deserve to die for their crimes.

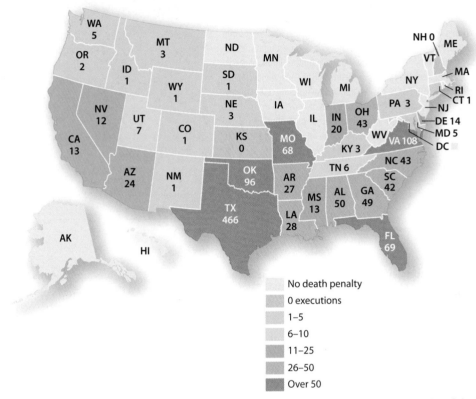

MAPPING LIFE NATIONWIDE

FIGURE **8-4**   EXECUTIONS BY STATE SINCE 1976

- No death penalty
- 0 executions
- 1–5
- 6–10
- 11–25
- 26–50
- Over 50

Note: Number of executions carried out from January 17, 1977, to January 2, 2008, as of March 10, 2011. Three federal executions not included.
Source: Death Penalty Information Center 2011.

The death penalty also creates some dysfunctions, however. Although many citizens are concerned that the alternative to execution, life in prison, is unnecessarily expensive, sentencing a person to death is not cheap. According to a recent analysis, imprisoning a person for life costs $1.1 million, but a reasonable estimate of prosecution costs is $10 million. The legal costs of jury-selection consultants and subsequent appeals account for the tremendous costs (Roman et al. 2008; Dwyer 2011).

Conflict theorists counter that the persistence of social inequality in today's society puts poor people at a disadvantage in the criminal justice system. Simply put, the poor cannot afford to hire the best lawyers, but must rely instead on court-appointed attorneys, who typically are overworked and underpaid. This unequal access to legal resources may mean the difference between life and death for poor defendants. Indeed, the American Bar Association (1997) has repeatedly expressed concern about the limited defense most defendants who face the death penalty receive. As of late 2010, DNA analysis and other new technologies had exonerated 17 death row inmates.

FIGURE **8-5** DEATH PENALTY STATUS BY COUNTRY

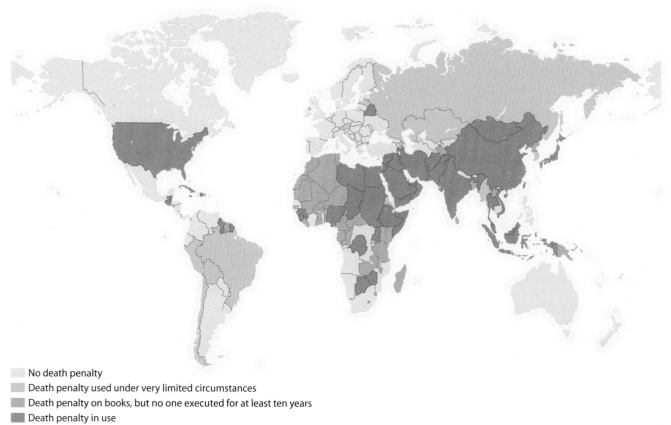

- No death penalty
- Death penalty used under very limited circumstances
- Death penalty on books, but no one executed for at least ten years
- Death penalty in use

Source: Amnesty International 2009.

Another issue of crucial concern to conflict theorists and researchers is the possibility of racial discrimination. Numerous studies show that defendants are more likely to be sentenced to death if their victims were White rather than Black. About 79 percent of the victims in death penalty cases are White, even though only 50 percent of all murder victims are White. And there is some evidence that Black defendants, who constituted 42 percent of all death row inmates in 2010, are more likely to face execution than Whites in the same legal circumstance. About 70 percent of those who have been exonerated by DNA testing are members of minority groups. Evidence exists, too, that capital defendants receive poor legal services because of the racist attitudes of their own defense counsel. While racism is never acceptable, it is particularly devastating in the criminal justice system, where the legal process can result in an execution (Innocence Project 2010).

Initiating Policy

Many people hesitate to endorse the death penalty, yet when confronted with a horrendous crime, they feel the death penalty should be available, at least in some cases. In most people's minds, for example, Timothy McVeigh's sentence would be an appropriate use of the death penalty, although opinion on this point has fluctuated. In 2010, support for the death penalty was 67 percent—about the same level as when the question was first posed in 1936, in a national survey (Newport 2010a).

Recently, policy initiatives have moved in two different directions. In several death penalty states, legislators are considering broadening the range of offenses for which convicted criminals may be sentenced to execution. In these states, child molesters who did not murder their victims could become eligible for the death penalty, along with certain repeat offenders. The countertrend, a movement away from the death penalty, is based on doubts about whether an execution can be carried out humanely.

Legal action has been taken on behalf of those convicted to die, especially by lethal injection, which is used in virtually all death penalty jurisdictions. Concerns about lethal injection range from medical ethics (the injection must be administered by a medical technician) to the effectiveness of the technique, which sometimes takes a long time to cause death. In 2008, the Supreme Court ruled that Kentucky's procedures were constitutional, but specified protocols for the use of chemicals, personnel training, medical supervision, and error risk that apply in all 35 states that use lethal injection (L. Greenhouse 2008).

Surprisingly, only about 110 death sentences are handed out for the more than 17,000 reported murders that occur every year. Courts continue to address the question of how this ultimate penalty can be administered in a judicially fair manner. Policymakers, however, do not seem concerned with such questions. In recent years, federal and state legislatures have declared additional crimes to be punishable by death, curtailed appeals by death row inmates, and reimbursed far fewer lawyers for their defense of condemned criminals.

Internationally, attention has focused on those nations where executions are relatively common, such as China and Iran. Foes of the death penalty see these nations as violators of human rights. In the United States, which usually regards itself as a champion of human rights, pressure to abolish capital punishment has grown both at home and abroad.

Take the Issue with You

1. Does the death penalty deter crime? If so, why are crime rates in the United States high compared to those in other nations?

2. What is your position on the death penalty—should it be legal or should it be abolished? Explain your reasoning.

3. Should youths who have been convicted of violent crimes be subject to the death penalty? Why or why not?

MASTERING THIS CHAPTER

Summary

Conformity and **deviance** are two ways in which people respond to real or imagined pressure from others. In this chapter we examined the relationships among deviance and conformity, **crime** and **social control.** We studied the mechanisms societies use, both formal and informal, to encourage conformity and discourage deviance, paying particular attention to the law and how it reflects our social values.

1. Deviant behavior violates social norms. Some forms of **deviance** carry a negative social **stigma,** while other forms are more or less accepted.

2. A society uses **social control** to encourage the acceptance of basic norms.

3. Stanley Milgram defined **conformity** as going along with one's peers; **obedience** is defined as compliance with higher authorities in a hierarchical structure.

4. Some norms are so important to a society, they are formalized into **laws.** Socialization is a primary source of conforming and obedient behavior, including obedience to law.

5. From a functionalist point of view, deviance and its consequences help to define the limits of proper behavior.

6. Some interactionists maintain that people learn criminal behavior by interacting with others **(cultural transmission).** To them, deviance results from exposure to attitudes that are favorable to criminal acts **(differential association).**

7. Other interactionists attribute increases in crime and deviance to the absence or breakdown of communal relationships and social

institutions, such as the family, school, church, and local government **(social disorganization theory).**

8. An important aspect of **labeling theory** is the recognition that some people are viewed as deviant, while others who engage in the same behavior are not.

9. From the conflict perspective, laws and punishments are a reflection of the interests of the powerful.

10. The feminist perspective emphasizes that cultural attitudes and differential economic relationships help to explain gender differences in deviance and crime.

11. **Crime** represents a deviation from formal social norms administered by the state.

12. Sociologists differentiate among **victimless crimes** (such as drug use and prostitution), *professional crime,* **organized crime, white-collar crime, hate crime,** and **transnational crime.**

13. Crime statistics are among the least reliable social data, partly because so many crimes are not reported to law enforcement agencies. Rates of violent crime are higher in the United States than in other Western societies, although they have been dropping.

14. The death penalty is the ultimate sanction, one that functionalists believe deters serious crime. However, it is applied disproportionately to the economically disadvantaged and to racial minorities. Worldwide, many countries have renounced the death penalty.

Key Terms

Anomie Durkheim's term for the loss of direction felt in a society when social control of individual behavior has become ineffective. (page 166)

Anomie theory of deviance Robert Merton's theory of deviance as an adaptation of socially prescribed goals or of the means governing their attainment, or both. (167)

Conformity Going along with peers—individuals of our own status who have no special right to direct our behavior. (161)

Control theory A view of conformity and deviance that suggests that our connection to members of society leads us to systematically conform to society's norms. (165)

Crime A violation of criminal law for which some governmental authority applies formal penalties. (171)

Cultural transmission A school of criminology that argues that criminal behavior is learned through social interactions. (168)

Deviance Behavior that violates the standards of conduct or expectations of a group or society. (159)

Differential association A theory of deviance that holds that violation of rules results from exposure to attitudes favorable to criminal acts. (168)

Differential justice Differences in the way social control is exercised over different groups. (171)

Formal social control Social control that is carried out by authorized agents, such as police officers, judges, school administrators, and employers. (163)

Hate crime A criminal offense committed because of the offender's bias against a race, religion, ethnic group, national origin, or sexual orientation. Also referred to as *bias crime*. (174)

Index crimes The eight types of crime reported annually by the FBI in the *Uniform Crime Reports:* murder, rape, robbery, assault, burglary, theft, motor vehicle theft, and arson. (172)

Informal social control Social control that is carried out casually by ordinary people through such means as laughter, smiles, and ridicule. (163)

Labeling theory An approach to deviance that attempts to explain why certain people are viewed as deviants while others engaged in the same behavior are not. (169)

Law Governmental social control. (164)

Obedience Compliance with higher authorities in a hierarchical structure. (161)

Organized crime The work of a group that regulates relations among criminal enterprises involved in illegal activities, including prostitution, gambling, and the smuggling and sale of illegal drugs. (173)

Professional criminal A person who pursues crime as a day-to-day occupation, developing skilled techniques and enjoying a certain degree of status among other criminals. (172)

Sanction A penalty or reward for conduct concerning a social norm. (161)

Social constructionist perspective An approach to deviance that emphasizes the role of culture in the creation of the deviant identity. (170)

Social control The techniques and strategies for preventing deviant human behavior in any society. (161)

Social disorganization theory The theory that crime and deviance are caused by the absence or breakdown of communal relationships and social institutions. (169)

Societal-reaction approach Another name for *labeling theory*. (169)

Stigma A label used to devalue members of certain social groups. (160)

Transnational crime Crime that occurs across multiple national borders. (175)

Victimization survey A questionnaire or interview given to a sample of the population to determine whether people have been victims of crime. (176)

Victimless crime A term used by sociologists to describe the willing exchange among adults of widely desired but illegal goods and services. (172)

White-collar crime Illegal acts committed by affluent, "respectable" individuals in the course of business activities. (173)

TAKING SOCIOLOGY with you

1. Describe the mechanisms of social control, both formal and informal, on your campus. Which is more effective, formal or informal control?

2. Explain the presence of both criminals and law-abiding citizens in an inner-city neighborhood in terms of the interactionist perspective.

3. Pay a visit to your local courthouse and observe a trial by jury from the point of view of a sociologist. Then describe what you saw and heard using sociological concepts.

Self-Quiz

Read each question carefully and then select the best answer.

1. Society brings about acceptance of basic norms through techniques and strategies for preventing deviant human behavior. This process is termed
   a. stigmatization.
   b. labeling.
   c. law.
   d. social control.

2. Which sociological perspective argues that people must respect social norms if any group or society is to survive?
   a. the conflict perspective
   b. the interactionist perspective
   c. the functionalist perspective
   d. the feminist perspective

3. Stanley Milgram used the word *conformity* to mean
   a. going along with peers.
   b. compliance with higher authorities in a hierarchical structure.
   c. techniques and strategies for preventing deviant human behavior in any society.
   d. penalties and rewards for conduct concerning a social norm.

4. Which sociological theory suggests that our connection to members of society leads us to conform systematically to society's norms?
   a. feminist theory
   b. control theory

   c. interactionist theory
   d. functionalist theory

5. Which of the following statements is true of deviance?
   a. Deviance is always criminal behavior.
   b. Deviance is behavior that violates the standards of conduct or expectations of a group or society.
   c. Deviance is perverse behavior.
   d. Deviance is inappropriate behavior that cuts across all cultures and social orders.

6. Which sociologist illustrated the boundary-maintenance function of deviance in his study of Puritans in 17th-century New England?
   a. Kai Erikson
   b. Émile Durkheim
   c. Robert Merton
   d. Edwin Sutherland

7. Which of the following is *not* one of the basic forms of adaptation specified in Robert Merton's anomie theory of deviance?
   a. conformity
   b. innovation
   c. ritualism
   d. hostility

8. Which sociologist first advanced the idea that an individual undergoes the same basic socialization process whether learning conforming or deviant acts?
   a. Robert Merton
   b. Edwin Sutherland
   c. Travis Hirschi
   d. William Chambliss

9. Which of the following theories contends that criminal victimization increases when communal relationships and social institutions break down?
   a. labeling theory
   b. conflict theory
   c. social disorganization theory
   d. differential association theory

10. Which of the following conducted observation research on two groups of high school males (the Saints and the Roughnecks) and concluded that social class played an important role in the varying fortunes of the two groups?
    a. Richard Quinney
    b. Edwin Sutherland
    c. Émile Durkheim
    d. William Chambliss

11. If we fail to respect and obey social norms, we may face punishment through informal or formal _____.

12. Police officers, judges, administrators, employers, military officers, and managers of movie theaters are all instruments of _____ social control.

13. Some norms are considered so important by a society that they are formalized into _____ controlling people's behavior.

14. It is important to underscore the fact that _____ is the primary source of conformity and obedience, including obedience to law.

15. _____ is a state of normlessness that typically occurs during a period of profound social change and disorder, such as a time of economic collapse.

16. Labeling theory is also called the _____ _____ approach.

17. _____ theorists view standards of deviant behavior as merely reflecting cultural norms, whereas _____ and _____ theorists point out that the most powerful groups in a society can shape laws and standards and determine who is (or is not) prosecuted as a criminal.

18. Feminists contend that prostitution and some forms of pornography are not _____ crimes.

19. Daniel Bell used the term _____ _____ to describe the process during which leadership of organized crime was transferred from Irish Americans to Jewish Americans and later to Italian Americans and others.

20. Consumer fraud, bribery, and income tax evasion are considered _____ _____ crimes.

THINKING ABOUT **MOVIES**

American Gypsy

This documentary sheds light on the Romani, a minority group whose members are often stereotyped as criminals.

Hurt Locker

During the Iraq War, a U.S. Army sergeant who uses unorthodox methods assumes command of a bomb squad.

Temple Grandin

An autistic woman fights for animal rights.

Pedestrians pass by a man panhandling for change in Las Vegas. The United States is a society of contrasts among great wealth, modest means, and deep poverty.

It's too bad so many people are falling into poverty at a time when it's almost illegal to be poor. You won't be arrested for shopping in a Dollar Store, but if you are truly, deeply, in-the-streets poor, you're well advised not to engage in any of the biological necessities of life—like sitting, sleeping, lying down or loitering. City officials boast that there is nothing discriminatory about the ordinances that afflict the destitute, most of which go back to the dawn of gentrification in the '80s and '90s. "If you're lying on a sidewalk, whether you're homeless or a millionaire, you're in violation of the ordinance," a city attorney in St. Petersburg, Fla., said in June, echoing Anatole France's immortal observation that "the law, in its majestic equality, forbids the rich as well as the poor to sleep under bridges."

In defiance of all reason and compassion, the criminalization of poverty has actually been intensifying as the recession generates ever more poverty. So concludes a new study from the National Law Center on Homelessness and Poverty, which found that the number of ordinances against the publicly poor has been rising since 2006, along with ticketing and arrests for more "neutral" infractions like jaywalking, littering or carrying an open container of alcohol.

The report lists America's 10 "meanest" cities—the largest of which are Honolulu, Los Angeles and San Francisco—but new contestants are springing up every day. The City Council in Grand Junction, Colo., has been considering a ban on begging, and at the end of June, Tempe, Ariz., carried out a four-day crackdown on the indigent. How do you know when someone is indigent? As a Las Vegas statute puts it, "An indigent person is a person whom a reasonable ordinary person would believe to be entitled to apply for or receive" public assistance.

That could be me before the blow-drying and eyeliner, and it's definitely Al Szekely at any time of day. A grizzled 62-year-old, he inhabits a wheelchair and is often found on G Street in Washington—the city that is ultimately responsible for the bullet he took in the spine in Fu Bai, Vietnam, in 1972. He had been enjoying the luxury of an indoor bed until last December, when the police swept through the shelter in the middle of the night looking for men with outstanding warrants.

It turned out that Mr. Szekely, who is an ordained minister and does not drink, do drugs or curse in front of ladies, did indeed have a warrant—for not appearing in court to face a charge of "criminal trespassing" (for sleeping on a sidewalk in a Washington suburb). So he was dragged out of the shelter and put in jail. "Can you imagine?" asked Eric Sheptock, the homeless advocate (himself a shelter resident) who introduced me to Mr. Szekely. "They arrested a homeless man in a shelter for being homeless."

By far the most reliable way to be criminalized by poverty is to have the wrong-color skin. Indignation runs high when a celebrity professor encounters racial profiling, but for decades whole communities have been effectively "profiled" for the suspicious combination of being both dark-skinned and poor, thanks to the "broken windows" or "zero tolerance" theory of policing popularized by Rudy Giuliani, when he was mayor of New York City, and his police chief William Bratton.

Flick a cigarette in a heavily patrolled community of color and you're littering; wear the wrong color T-shirt and you're displaying gang allegiance. Just strolling around in a dodgy neighborhood can mark you as a potential suspect, according to "Let's Get Free: A Hip-Hop Theory of Justice," an eye-opening new book by Paul Butler, a former federal prosecutor in Washington. If you seem at all evasive, which I suppose is like looking "overly anxious" in an airport, Mr. Butler writes, the police "can force you to stop just to investigate why you don't want to talk to them." And don't get grumpy about it or you could be "resisting arrest." ❞

In defiance of all reason and compassion, the criminalization of poverty has actually been intensifying as the recession generates ever more poverty.

(Ehrenreich 2009:1–2, 2–3, 4) Additional information about this excerpt can be found on the Online Learning Center at www.mhhe.com/schaefer13e.

Being down and out is a miserable experience; being homeless is worse. Yet recently, public patience with the homeless has begun to wear thin. In this excerpt from her article "Is It Now a Crime to Be Poor?" journalist Barbara Ehrenreich laments the fact that in some cities, homelessness is becoming not just a deviant social status, but a criminal offense as well. In a period when real estate values have declined precipitously, the presence of homeless people on the city streets sends much the same signal as boarded-up, foreclosed properties. These signs of decay are deeply disturbing to the middle class and to those who inhabit newly gentrified neighborhoods. Paradoxically, just as those who can no longer pay the rent or the mortgage are swelling the ranks of the homeless, cities are taking steps to remove them from view, to ban them from public places.

Ever since people first began to speculate about the nature of human society, their attention has been drawn to the differences between individuals and groups within society. The term **social inequality** describes a condition in which members of society have differing amounts of wealth, prestige, or power. Some degree of social inequality characterizes every society.

When a system of social inequality is based on a hierarchy of groups, sociologists refer to it as **stratification:** a structured ranking of entire groups of people that perpetuates unequal economic rewards and power in a society. These unequal rewards are evident, not only in the distribution of wealth and income, but even in the distressing mortality rates of impoverished communities. Stratification involves the ways in which one generation passes on social inequalities to the next, producing groups of people arranged in rank order, from low to high.

Stratification is a crucial subject of sociological investigation because of its pervasive influence on human interactions and institutions. It results inevitably in social inequality, because certain groups of people stand higher in social rankings, control scarce resources, wield power, and receive special treatment. As we will see in this chapter, the consequences of stratification are evident in the unequal distribution of both income and wealth in industrial societies. The term **income** refers to salaries and wages. In contrast, **wealth** is an inclusive term encompassing all a person's material assets, including land, stocks, and other types of property.

Is social inequality an inescapable part of society? How does government policy affect the life chances of the working poor? Is this country still a place where a hardworking person can move up the social ladder? This chapter focuses on the unequal distribution of socially valued rewards and its consequences. We will begin by examining four general systems of stratification, including the one most familiar to us, the social class system. We will examine three sociological perspectives on stratification, paying particular attention to the theories of Karl Marx and Max Weber. We'll also ask whether stratification is universal and see what sociologists, including functionalist and conflict theorists, have to say about that question. We will see how sociologists define social class and examine the consequences of stratification for people's wealth and income, safety, and educational opportunities. Then we will take a close look at poverty, particularly the question of who belongs to the underclass and why. And we will confront the question of social mobility, both upward and downward. Finally, in the Social Policy section, we will examine the issue of executive compensation—the huge salaries and bonuses that corporate executives earn even when their companies are losing money and employees are losing their jobs.

Systems of Stratification

Sociologists consider stratification on many levels, ranging from its impact on the individual to worldwide patterns of inequality. No matter where we look, however, disparities in wealth and income are substantial. Take income and poverty patterns in the United States, for example. As the top part of Figure 9-1 shows, in many states the median household income is 25 percent higher than that in other states. And as the bottom part of the figure shows, the poverty rate in many states is 200 percent that of other states. Later in this chapter we will address the meaning of such statistics. We'll begin our discussion here with an overview of the four basic systems of stratification. Then we'll see what sociologists have had to say on the subject of social inequality.

Look at the four general systems of stratification examined here—slavery, castes, estates, and social classes—as ideal types useful for purposes of analysis. Any stratification system may include elements of more than one type. For example, prior to the Civil War, you could find in the southern states of the United States both social classes dividing Whites from Whites and the institutionalized enslavement of Blacks.

To understand these systems better, it may be helpful to review the distinction between *achieved status* and *ascribed status*, explained in Chapter 5. **Ascribed status** is a social position assigned to a person by society without regard for the person's unique talents or characteristics. In contrast, **achieved status** is a social position that a person attains largely through his or her efforts. The two are closely linked. The nation's most affluent families generally inherit wealth and status, while many members of racial and ethnic minorities inherit disadvantaged status. Age and gender, as well, are ascribed statuses that influence a person's wealth and social position.

Slavery

The most extreme form of legalized social inequality for both individuals and groups is **slavery.** What distinguishes this oppressive system of stratification is that enslaved individuals are *owned* by other people, who treat these human beings as property, just as if they were household pets or appliances.

Slavery has varied in the way it has been practiced. In ancient Greece, the main source of slaves was piracy and captives of war. Although succeeding generations could inherit slave status, it was not necessarily permanent. A person's status might change, depending on which city-state happened to triumph in a military conflict. In effect, all citizens had the potential of becoming slaves or of receiving freedom, depending on the circumstances of history. In contrast, in the United States and Latin America, where slavery was an ascribed status, racial and legal barriers prevented the freeing of slaves.

Today, the Universal Declaration of Human Rights, which is binding on all members of the United Nations, prohibits slavery in all its forms. Yet more people are enslaved today than at any point in world history. In many developing countries, bonded laborers are imprisoned in virtual lifetime employment; in some countries, human beings are owned outright. But a form of slavery also exists in Europe and the United States, where guest workers and illegal immigrants have been forced to labor for years under terrible conditions, either to pay off debts or to avoid being turned over to immigration authorities.

Both these situations are likely to involve the transnational crime of trafficking in humans. Each year an estimated 600,000 to 800,000 men, women, and children are transported across international borders for slavery or sexual exploitation. In 2000, the U.S. Congress passed the Trafficking Victims Protection Act, which established minimum standards for the elimination of human trafficking. The act requires the State Department to monitor other countries' efforts to vigorously investigate, prosecute, and convict individuals who participate in trafficking—including government officials. Each year, the department reports its findings, some of which are shown in Table 9-1 on page 189. Tier 1 and Tier 2 countries are thought to be largely in compliance with the act. Tier 2 Watch countries are making efforts to comply, though trafficking remains a significant

MAPPING LIFE NATIONWIDE

FIGURE 9-1   THE 50 STATES: CONTRASTS IN INCOME AND POVERTY LEVELS

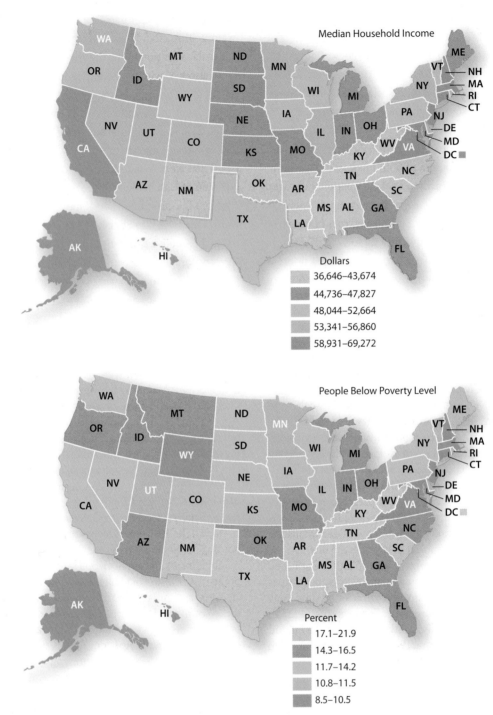

Median Household Income

Dollars
	36,646–43,674
	44,736–47,827
	48,044–52,664
	53,341–56,860
	58,931–69,272

People Below Poverty Level

Percent
	17.1–21.9
	14.3–16.5
	11.7–14.2
	10.8–11.5
	8.5–10.5

Note: National median household income was $51,168; national poverty rate, 14.3 percent.
Source: 2009 census data presented in American Community Survey 2010:Tables R1701, R1901.

concern. Tier 3 countries are not compliant and are not making significant efforts to comply (Bernat and Zhilina 2011).

Castes

Castes are hereditary ranks that are usually religiously dictated and that tend to be fixed and immobile. Caste membership is an ascribed status (at birth, children automatically assume the same position as their parents). Each caste is quite sharply defined, and members are expected to marry within that caste.

The caste system is generally associated with Hinduism in India and other countries. In India there are four major castes, called *varnas.* A fifth category of outcastes, referred to as the *untouchables,* represents 16 percent of the population; its members are considered so lowly and unclean as to have no place within this stratification system. In an effort to avoid perpetuating the historical stigma these people bear, the government now refers to the untouchables as *scheduled castes.* The untouchables themselves prefer *Dalit* ("the repressed"), a term

TABLE **9-1** *HUMAN TRAFFICKING REPORT* 189

Tier 1 Full Compliance	Tier 2 Significant Effort	Tier 2 Watch List Some Effort, But Trafficking Remains a Concern	Tier 3 Noncompliant, No Effort
Australia	Bolivia	Afghanistan	Burma
Canada	Brazil	China	Congo (Dem. Rep.)
Colombia	Cambodia	Fiji	Cuba
Denmark	Chile	Guatemala	Dominican Republic
France	Greece	India	Iran
Germany	Israel	Malaysia	Mauritania
Great Britain	Japan	Philippines	North Korea
Norway	Mexico	Russia	Papua New Guinea
Poland	Romania	Syria	Saudi Arabia
South Korea	South Africa	Ukraine	Sudan
Spain	Turkey	Vietnam	Zimbabwe

Note: Table is incomplete; each tier lists only a sample of all nations classified. Since the *Human Trafficking Report* is created by the State Department, the level of compliance by the United States is considered to be "full compliance."
Source: Department of State 2010b.

that communicates their desire to overcome their disadvantaged status (P. Smith 2008).

In 1950, after gaining independence from Great Britain, India adopted a new constitution that formally outlawed the caste system. Over the past decade or two, however, urbanization and technological advances have brought more change to India's caste system than the government or politics has in more than half a century. The anonymity of city life tends to blur caste boundaries, allowing the *Dalit* to pass unrecognized in temples, schools, and places of employment. And the globalization of high technology has opened up India's social order, bringing new opportunities to those who possess the skills and ability to capitalize on them.

The term *caste* can also be applied in recent historical contexts outside India. For example, the system of stratification that characterized the southern United States from the end of the Civil War through the 1960s resembled a caste system. So did the rigid system of segregation that prevailed in the Republic of South Africa under apartheid, from 1948 through the 1990s. In both cases, race was the defining factor that placed a person in the social hierarchy.

Estates

A third type of stratification system, called *estates,* was associated with feudal societies during the Middle Ages. The **estate system,** or *feudalism,* required peasants to work land leased to them by nobles in exchange for military protection and other services. The basis for the system was the nobles' ownership of land, which was critical to their superior and privileged status. As in systems based on slavery and caste, inheritance of one's position largely defined the estate system. The nobles inherited their titles and property; the peasants were born into a subservient position within an agrarian society.

As the estate system developed, it became more differentiated. Nobles began to achieve varying degrees of authority. By

the 12th century, a priesthood had emerged in most of Europe, along with classes of merchants and artisans. For the first time there were groups of people whose wealth did not depend on land ownership or agriculture. This economic change had profound social consequences as the estate system ended and a class system of stratification came into existence.

Social Classes

A **class system** is a social ranking based primarily on economic position in which achieved characteristics can influence social mobility. In contrast to slavery and caste systems, the boundaries between classes are imprecisely defined, and one can move from one stratum, or level, of society to another. Even so, class systems maintain stable stratification hierarchies and patterns of class divisions, and they, too, are marked by unequal distribution of wealth and power. Class standing, although it is achieved, is heavily dependent on family and ascribed factors, such as race and ethnicity.

Sociologist Daniel Rossides (1997) uses a five-class model to describe the class system of the United States: the upper class, the upper-middle class, the lower-middle class, the working class, and the lower class. Although the lines separating social classes in his model are not so sharp as the divisions between castes, members of the five classes differ significantly in ways other than just income level.

Upper and Lower Classes Rossides characterizes about 1 to 2 percent of the people of the United States as *upper class.* This group is limited to the very wealthy, who associate in exclusive clubs and social circles. In contrast, the *lower class,* consisting of approximately 20 to 25 percent of the population, disproportionately consists of Blacks, Hispanics, single mothers with dependent children, and people who cannot find regular work or must make do with low-paying work. This class lacks both wealth and income and is too weak politically to exercise significant power.

TAKING SOCIOLOGY TO WORK

Jessica Houston Su, **Research Assistant, Joblessness and Urban Poverty Research Program**

Jessica Houston Su chose sociology as her major "because it was the first class that appealed to my desire to understand the roots of inequality." It also helped her to make sense of what was going on around her at Dartmouth College. "I grew up in a rural, working-class community," she explains; "it was quite a culture shock to attend an affluent, Ivy League college." Learning about social structures and institutions helped Su to navigate through a new environment filled with people from many different backgrounds.

Su went through several potential majors before taking a sociology course and realizing that she was interested in almost every course the department offered. When she was hired for a work-study job in the department, she "soon realized that I was spending a lot of time reading all of the articles I was supposed to be photocopying," she jokes. "It became very obvious to me that I had found my major."

Su works with Harvard University's John F. Kennedy School of Government on a research program directed by the well-known sociologist William Julius Wilson. She is currently assigned to a large-scale longitudinal study of welfare reform in Boston, Chicago, and San Antonio. Her primary responsibility is to analyze the qualitative data from the study, gathered through ethnographic interviews with families who are affected by welfare reform, by searching for themes that might help to explain the study's quantitative data. She finds it exciting to be able to follow the same families over a long period. "I feel like I almost know some of the people," she explains.

Of all the things she learned as a sociology major, Su thinks one of the most important was the concept of social construction. "We consider many things to simply be facts of life," she explains, "but upon further investigation it is clear that most things have been socially constructed in some way." The concept of social construction has helped her to look more carefully at the world around her: "My worldview is much more nuanced and I've gained a much better understanding of how society works, both the good and the bad."

Su uses the research methods she learned in her sociology courses all the time. "I love going to work each day," she says. "I am challenged academically and I feel fulfilled knowing that I am working on something that will benefit society and perhaps influence future policy."

LET'S DISCUSS

1. Did you experience a sense of culture shock when you entered college and were exposed to students from different social classes? If so, has studying sociology helped you to adjust to the diversity in students' backgrounds?
2. Have you begun to see the world differently since you learned about the social construction of reality? If so, what in particular do you see in a different light?

Both these classes, at opposite ends of the nation's social hierarchy, reflect the importance of ascribed status and achieved status. Ascribed statuses such as race clearly influence a person's wealth and social position. And as sociologist Richard Jenkins (1991) has shown, the ascribed status of being disabled marginalizes a person in the U.S. labor market. People with disabilities are particularly vulnerable to unemployment, are often poorly paid, and tend to occupy the lower rungs of the occupational ladder. Regardless of their actual performance on the job, the disabled are stigmatized as not earning their keep. Such are the effects of ascribed status. We will look again at the plight of the lower class when we consider poverty and welfare policies.

The economist John Kenneth Galbraith (1977:44) observed that "of all classes the rich are the most noticed and the least studied." The poor receive a good deal of attention from reporters, social activists, and policymakers seeking to alleviate their poverty, but the very affluent, who live apart from the rest of the population, are largely a mystery. Since Galbraith's comment, moreover, the residential separation of the rich has grown. The newspaper's society page may give us a peek at members of this class, but we know very little about their everyday lives. Statistically, over 2 million households in the United States are worth more than $10 million each. Less than 10 percent of these people inherited their money, and very few of them are celebrities (Massey 2007).

Middle Class Sandwiched between the upper and lower classes in this model are the upper-middle class, the lower-middle class, and the working class. The *upper-middle class,* about 10 to 15 percent of the population, includes professionals such as doctors, lawyers, and architects. They participate extensively in politics and

Supersized homes like this one typically belong to upper-middle-class families, who may also enjoy vacation retreats and luxury condos in the city. These conspicuous homes mark their owners as members of a privileged 10 to 15 percent of the population—just shy of the truly wealthy 1 or 2 percent who constitute the upper class.

Today, the once broadly based middle class is on the defensive and is slowly being squeezed by two growing groups, the rich and the poor.

• *The rise of new growth industries and nonunion workplaces, like fast-food restaurants.* Industries may have added employment opportunities, but they are at the lower end of the wage scale.

Middle-class families want comfortable homes, college degrees for their children, occasional family vacations, affordable health care—the cost of which has been growing faster than inflation—and retirement security. The answer, for many people, is either to go without or to work longer hours at multiple jobs (Billitteri 2009; Blank 2010; Massey 2007; Thurow 1984).

Working Class Rossides describes the *working class*—about 40 to 45 percent of the population—as people who hold regular manual or blue-collar jobs. Certain members of this class, such as electricians, may have higher incomes than people in the lower-middle class. Yet even if they have achieved some degree of economic security, they tend to identify with manual workers and their long history of involvement in the labor movement of the United States. Of the five classes, the working class is declining noticeably in size. In the economy of the United States, service and technical jobs are replacing those involved in the actual manufacturing or transportation of goods.

Social class is one of the independent or explanatory variables most frequently used by social scientists to shed light on social issues. In later chapters, we will analyze the relationships between social class and child rearing (Chapter 14), religious affiliation (Chapter 15), and formal schooling (Chapter 16), as well as other relationships in which social class is a variable.

take leadership roles in voluntary associations. The *lower-middle class,* about 30 to 35 percent of the population, includes less affluent professionals (such as elementary school teachers and nurses), owners of small businesses, and a sizable number of clerical workers. While not all members of the middle class hold degrees from a college, they share the goal of sending their children there.

The middle class is currently under a great deal of economic pressure. Close analysis indicates that of those who lost their middle-class standing during the latter 20th century, about half rose to a higher ranking in the social class system, while half dropped to a lower position. These data mean that the United States is moving toward a "bipolar income distribution." That is, a broadly based middle class is slowly being replaced by two growing groups of rich and poor.

Sociologists and other scholars have identified several factors that have contributed to the shrinking size of the middle class:

• *Disappearing opportunities for those with little education.* Today, most jobs require formal schooling, yet less than a third of adults between ages 35 and 44 have prepared themselves with a college degree.

• *Global competition and rapid advances in technology.* These two trends, which began several decades ago, mean that workers are more easily replaced now than they were in the past. Increasingly, globalization and technological advances are affecting the more complex jobs that were once the bread and butter of middle-class workers.

• *Growing dependence on the temporary workforce.* For those workers who have no other job, temporary positions are tenuous at best, because they rarely offer health care coverage or retirement benefits.

thinking CRITICALLY

What are the differences between slavery and caste systems? What are the similarities?

Sociological Perspectives on Stratification

Sociologists have hotly debated stratification and social inequality and have reached varying conclusions. No theorist stressed the significance of class for society—and for social change—more strongly than Karl Marx. Marx viewed class differentiation as the crucial determinant of social, economic, and political inequality. In contrast, Max Weber questioned Marx's emphasis on the overriding importance of the economic sector, arguing that stratification should be viewed as having many dimensions.

Karl Marx's View of Class Differentiation

Karl Marx has been aptly described as both a revolutionary and a social scientist. Marx was concerned with stratification in all types of human society, beginning with primitive agricultural tribes and continuing into feudalism. But his main focus was on the effects of economic inequality on all aspects of 19th-century Europe. The plight of the working class made him feel that it was imperative to strive for changes in the class structure of society.

In Marx's view, social relations during any period of history depend on who controls the primary mode of economic production, such as land or factories. Differential access to scarce resources shapes the relationship between groups. Thus, under the feudal estate system, most production was agricultural, and the land was owned by the nobility. Peasants had little choice but to work according to terms dictated by those who owned the land.

Using this type of analysis, Marx examined social relations within **capitalism**—an economic system in which the means of production are held largely in private hands and the main incentive for economic activity is the accumulation of profits. Marx focused on the two classes that began to emerge as the feudal estate system declined, the bourgeoisie and the proletariat. The **bourgeoisie,** or capitalist class, owns the means of production, such as factories and machinery; the **proletariat** is the working class. In capitalist societies, the members of the bourgeoisie maximize profit in competition with other firms. In the process, they exploit workers, who must exchange their labor for subsistence wages. In Marx's view, members of each class share a distinctive culture. Marx was most interested in the culture of the proletariat, but he also examined the ideology of the bourgeoisie, through which that class justifies its dominance over workers.

According to Marx, exploitation of the proletariat will inevitably lead to the destruction of the capitalist system, because the workers will revolt. But first, the working class must develop **class consciousness**—a subjective awareness of common vested interests and the need for collective political action to bring about social change. Often, workers must overcome what Marx termed **false consciousness,** or an attitude held by members of a class that does not accurately reflect their objective position. A worker with false consciousness may adopt an individualistic viewpoint toward capitalist exploitation ("*I* am being exploited by *my* boss"). In contrast, the class-conscious worker realizes that all workers are being exploited by the bourgeoisie and have a common stake in revolution.

For Marx, class consciousness was part of a collective process in which the proletariat comes to identify the bourgeoisie as the source of its oppression. Revolutionary leaders will guide the working class in its struggle. Ultimately, the proletariat will overthrow the rule of both the bourgeoisie and the government (which Marx saw as representing the interests of capitalists) and will eliminate private ownership of the means of production. In Marx's rather utopian view, classes and oppression will cease to exist in the postrevolutionary workers' state.

How accurate were Marx's predictions? He failed to anticipate the emergence of labor unions, whose power in collective bargaining weakens the stranglehold that capitalists maintain over workers. Moreover, as contemporary conflict theorists note, he did not foresee the extent to which political liberties and relative prosperity could contribute to false consciousness. Many workers have come to view themselves as individuals striving for improvement within free societies that offer substantial mobility, rather than as downtrodden members of a social class who face a collective fate. Finally, Marx did not predict that Communist Party rule would be established and later overthrown in the former Soviet Union and throughout Eastern Europe. Still, the Marxist approach to the study of class is useful in stressing the importance of stratification as a determinant of social behavior and the fundamental separation in many societies between two distinct groups, the rich and the poor.

A miner peers into the dark at the Logan Orion coal mine in West Virginia's Logan County. Karl Marx would identify coal miners as members of the proletariat, or working class. Even today, miners are poorly compensated for the considerable dangers they face. Such exploitation of the working class is a core principle of Marxist theory.

use your sociological *imagination*

Have you ever been unaware of your true position in society—that is, have you experienced false consciousness? Explain.

Max Weber's View of Stratification

Unlike Karl Marx, Max Weber ([1913–1922] 1947) insisted that no single characteristic (such as class) totally defines a person's position within the stratification system. Instead, writing in 1916, he identified three distinct components of stratification: class, status, and power.

Weber used the term **class** to refer to a group of people who have a similar level of wealth and income. For example, certain workers in the United States try to support their families through minimum-wage jobs. According to Weber's definition, these wage earners constitute a class because they share the same economic position and fate. Although Weber agreed with Marx on the importance of this economic dimension of stratification, he argued that the actions of individuals and groups cannot be understood *solely* in economic terms.

Weber used the term **status group** to refer to people who have the same prestige or lifestyle. An individual gains status through membership in a desirable group, such as the medical profession. But status is not the same as economic class standing. In our culture, a successful pickpocket may belong to the same income class as a college professor. Yet the thief is widely regarded as holding low status, whereas the professor holds high status.

For Weber, the third major component of stratification has a political dimension. **Power** is the ability to exercise one's will over others. In the United States, power stems from membership in particularly influential groups, such as corporate boards of directors, government bodies, and interest groups. Conflict theorists generally agree that two major sources of power—big business and government—are closely interrelated. For instance, many of the heads of major corporations also hold powerful positions in the government or military. The Social Policy section at the end of this chapter examines the executive compensation that the powerful heads of corporations in the United States enjoy.

To summarize, in Weber's view, each of us has not one rank in society but three. Our position in a stratification system reflects some combination of class, status, and power. Each factor influences the other two, and in fact the rankings on these three dimensions often tend to coincide. John F. Kennedy came from an extremely wealthy family, attended exclusive preparatory schools, graduated from Harvard University, and went on to become president of the United States. Like Kennedy, many people from affluent backgrounds achieve impressive status and power.

Interactionist View

Both Karl Marx and Max Weber looked at inequality primarily from a macrosociological perspective, considering the entire society or even the global economy. Marx did suggest the importance of a more microsociological analysis, however, when he stressed the ways in which individuals develop a true class consciousness.

Interactionists, as well as economists, have long been interested in the importance of social class in shaping a person's lifestyle. The theorist

Thorstein Veblen (1857–1929) noted that those at the top of the social hierarchy typically convert part of their wealth into **conspicuous consumption**—that is, they purchase goods not to survive but to flaunt their superior wealth and social standing. For example, they may purchase more automobiles than they can reasonably use, or build homes with more rooms than they can possibly occupy. In an element of conspicuous consumption called *conspicuous leisure,* they may jet to a remote destination, staying just long enough to have dinner or view a sunset over some historic locale (Veblen [1899] 1964).

At the other end of the spectrum, behavior that is judged to be typical of the lower class is subject not only to ridicule but even to legal action. Communities have, from time to time, banned trailers from people's front yards and sofas from their front porches. In some communities, it is illegal to leave a pickup truck in front of the house overnight.

---

thinking CRITICALLY

Give some examples of conspicuous consumption among your fellow college students. Which are obvious and which more subtle?

Is Stratification Universal?

Must some members of society receive greater rewards than others? Do people need to feel socially and economically superior to others? Can social life be organized without structured inequality? These questions have been debated for centuries, especially among political activists. Utopian socialists, religious minorities,

With Mt. Everest in the background, a wealthy golfer plays a shot in a remote location, which he reached by helicopter. Traveling to exotic places to indulge in sports that most people play at home is an example of Thorstein Veblen's concept of conspicuous consumption, a spending pattern common to those at the very top of the social ladder.

and members of recent countercultures have all attempted to establish communities that to some extent or other would abolish inequality in social relationships.

Social scientists have found that inequality exists in all societies—even the simplest. For example, when anthropologist Gunnar Landtman ([1938] 1968) studied the Kiwai Papuans of New Guinea, at first he noticed little differentiation among them. Every man in the village did the same work and lived in similar housing. However, on closer inspection, Landtman observed that certain Papuans—men who were warriors, harpooners, and sorcerers—were described as "a little more high" than others. In contrast, villagers who were female, unemployed, or unmarried were considered "down a little bit" and were barred from owning land.

Stratification is universal in that all societies maintain some form of social inequality among members. Depending on its values, a society may assign people to distinctive ranks based on their religious knowledge, skill in hunting, physical attractiveness, trading expertise, or ability to provide health care. But why has such inequality developed in human societies? And how much differentiation among people, if any, is actually essential?

Functionalist and conflict sociologists offer contrasting explanations for the existence and necessity of social stratification. Functionalists maintain that a differential system of rewards and punishments is necessary for the efficient operation of society. Conflict theorists argue that competition for scarce resources results in significant political, economic, and social inequality.

Functionalist View

Would people go to school for many years to become physicians if they could make as much money and gain as much respect working as street cleaners? Functionalists say no, which is partly why they believe that a stratified society is universal.

In the view of Kingsley Davis and Wilbert Moore (1945), society must distribute its members among a variety of social positions. It must not only make sure that these positions are filled but also see that they are filled by people with the appropriate talents and abilities. Rewards, including money and prestige, are based on the importance of a position and the relative scarcity of qualified personnel. Yet this assessment often devalues work performed by certain segments of society, such as women's work in the home or in occupations traditionally filled by women, or low-status work in fast-food outlets.

Davis and Moore argue that stratification is universal and that social inequality is necessary so that people will be motivated to fill functionally important positions. But critics say that unequal rewards are not the only means of encouraging people to fill critical positions and occupations. Personal pleasure, intrinsic satisfaction, and value orientations also motivate people to enter particular careers. Functionalists agree, but they note that society must use some type of reward to motivate people to enter unpleasant or dangerous jobs and professions that require a long training period. This response does not address stratification systems in which status is largely inherited, such as slave or caste societies. Moreover, even if stratification is inevitable, the functionalist explanation for differential rewards does not explain the wide disparity between the rich and the poor (R. Collins 1975; Kerbo 2009).

As the reality television series *Ice Road Truckers* suggests, long-haul truck drivers take pride in their low-prestige job. According to the conflict perspective, the cultural beliefs that form a society's dominant ideology, such as the popular image of the truck driver as hero, help the wealthy to maintain their power and control at the expense of the lower classes.

Conflict View

The writings of Karl Marx lie at the heart of conflict theory. Marx viewed history as a continuous struggle between the oppressors and the oppressed, which ultimately would culminate in an egalitarian, classless society. In terms of stratification, he argued that under capitalism, the dominant class—the bourgeoisie—manipulates the economic and political systems in order to maintain control over the exploited proletariat. Marx did not believe that stratification was inevitable, but he did see inequality and oppression as inherent in capitalism (E. O. Wright et al. 1982).

Like Marx, contemporary conflict theorists believe that human beings are prone to conflict over scarce resources such as wealth, status, and power. However, Marx focused primarily on class conflict; more recent theorists have extended the analysis to include conflicts based on gender, race, age, and other dimensions. British sociologist Ralf Dahrendorf (1929–2009) is one of the most influential contributors to the conflict approach.

Dahrendorf (1959) has modified Marx's analysis of capitalist society to apply to modern capitalist societies. For Dahrendorf, social classes are groups of people who share common interests resulting from their authority relationships. In identifying the most powerful groups in society, he includes not only the bourgeoisie—the owners of the means of production—but also the managers of industry, legislators, the judiciary, heads of the government bureaucracy, and others. In that respect, Dahrendorf has merged Marx's emphasis on class conflict with Weber's recognition that power is an important element of stratification (Cuff et al. 1990).

Conflict theorists, including Dahrendorf, contend that the powerful of today, like the bourgeoisie of Marx's time, want society to run smoothly so that they can enjoy their privileged positions. Because the status quo suits those with wealth, status, and power, they have a clear interest in preventing, minimizing, or controlling societal conflict.

One way for the powerful to maintain the status quo is to define and disseminate the society's dominant ideology. The term **dominant ideology** describes a set of cultural beliefs and practices that helps to maintain powerful social, economic, and political interests. For Marx, the dominant ideology in a capitalist society served the interests of the ruling class. From a conflict perspective, the social significance of the dominant ideology is that not only do a society's most powerful groups and institutions control wealth and property; even more important, they control the means of producing beliefs about reality through religion, education, and the media (Abercrombie et al. 1980, 1990; Robertson 1988).

The powerful, such as leaders of government, also use limited social reforms to buy off the oppressed and reduce the danger of challenges to their dominance. For example, minimum-wage laws and unemployment compensation unquestionably give some valuable assistance to needy men and women. Yet these reforms also serve to pacify those who might otherwise rebel. Of course, in the view of conflict theorists, such maneuvers can never entirely eliminate conflict, since workers will continue to demand equality, and the powerful will not give up their control of society.

Conflict theorists see stratification as a major source of societal tension and conflict. They do not agree with Davis and Moore that stratification is functional for a society or that it serves as a source of stability. Rather, conflict sociologists argue that stratification will inevitably lead to instability and social change (R. Collins 1975; L. Coser 1977).

Table 9-2 summarizes and compares the three major perspectives on social stratification.

Lenski's Viewpoint

Let's return to the question posed earlier—Is stratification universal?—and consider the sociological response. Some form of differentiation is found in every culture, from the most primitive to the most advanced industrial societies of our time. Sociologist Gerhard Lenski, in his sociocultural evolution approach, described how economic systems change as their level of technology becomes more complex, beginning with hunting and gathering and culminating eventually with industrial society.

In subsistence-based hunting-and-gathering societies, people focus on survival. While some inequality and differentiation are evident, a stratification system based on social class does not emerge because there is no real wealth to be claimed. As a society advances technologically, it becomes capable of producing a considerable surplus of goods. The emergence of surplus resources greatly expands the possibilities for inequality in status, influence, and power, allowing a well-defined, rigid social class system to develop. To minimize strikes, slowdowns, and industrial sabotage, the elites may share a portion of the economic surplus with the lower classes, but not enough to reduce their own power and privilege.

As Lenski argued, the allocation of surplus goods and services controlled by those with wealth, status, and power reinforces the social inequality that accompanies stratification systems. While this reward system may once have served the overall purposes of society, as functionalists contend, the same cannot be said for the large disparities separating the haves from the have-nots in current societies. In contemporary industrial society, the degree of social and economic inequality far exceeds what is needed to provide for goods and services (Lenski 1966; Nolan and Lenski 2009).

thinking CRITICALLY

In your view, is the extent of social inequality in the United States helpful or harmful to society as a whole? Explain.

Stratification by Social Class

We continually assess how wealthy people are by looking at the cars they drive, the houses they live in, the clothes they wear, and so on. Yet it is not so easy to locate an individual within our social hierarchies as it would be in slavery or caste systems of stratification. To determine someone's class position, sociologists generally rely on the objective method.

Objective Method of Measuring Social Class

In the **objective method** of measuring social class, class is viewed largely as a statistical category. Researchers assign individuals to social classes on the basis of criteria such as occupation, education, income, and place of residence. The key to the objective method is that the *researcher*, rather than the person being classified, identifies an individual's class position.

TABLE **9-2** SOCIOLOGICAL PERSPECTIVES ON SOCIAL STRATIFICATION   summing**up**

	Functionalist	Conflict	Interactionist
Purpose of social stratification	Facilitates filling of social positions	Facilitates exploitation	Influences people's lifestyles
Attitude toward social inequality	Necessary to some extent	Excessive and growing	Influences intergroup relations
Analysis of the wealthy	Talented and skilled, creating opportunities for others	Use the dominant ideology to further their own interests	Exhibit conspicuous consumption and conspicuous leisure

The first step in using this method is to decide what indicators or causal factors will be measured objectively, whether wealth, income, education, or occupation. The prestige ranking of occupations has proved to be a useful indicator of a person's class position. For one thing, it is much easier to determine accurately than income or wealth. The term **prestige** refers to the respect and admiration that an occupation holds in a society. "My daughter, the physicist" connotes something very different from "my daughter, the waitress." Prestige is independent of the particular individual who occupies a job, a characteristic that distinguishes it from esteem. **Esteem** refers to the reputation that a specific person has earned within an occupation. Therefore, one can say that the position of president of the United States has high prestige, even though it has been occupied by people with varying degrees of esteem. A hairdresser may have the esteem of his clients, but he lacks the prestige of a corporate executive.

Table 9-3 ranks the prestige of a number of well-known occupations. In a series of national surveys, sociologists assigned prestige rankings to about 500 occupations, ranging from surgeon to panhandler. The highest possible prestige score was 100; the lowest was 0. Surgeon, physician, lawyer, dentist, and college professor were the most highly regarded occupations. Sociologists have used such data to assign prestige rankings to virtually all jobs and have found a stability in rankings from 1925 to the present. Similar studies in other countries have also developed useful prestige rankings of occupations (Nakao and Treas 1994).

Gender and Occupational Prestige

For many years, studies of social class tended to neglect the occupations and incomes of *women* as determinants of social rank. With more than half of all married women now working outside the home (see Chapter 12), this approach seems outmoded. How should we judge class or status in dual-career families—by the occupation regarded as having greater prestige, the average, or some other combination of the two? Sociologists—in particular, feminist sociologists in Great Britain—are drawing on new approaches to assess women's social class standing. One approach is to focus on the individual (rather than the family or household) as the basis for categorizing a woman's class position. Thus, a woman would be classified according to her own occupational status rather than that of her spouse (O'Donnell 1992).

Another feminist effort to measure the contribution of women to the economy reflects a more clearly political agenda. International Women Count Network, a global grassroots feminist organization, has sought to give a monetary value to women's unpaid work. Besides providing symbolic recognition of women's role in labor, this value would also be

TABLE 9-3 PRESTIGE RANKINGS OF OCCUPATIONS

Occupation	Score	Occupation	Score
Surgeon	87	Farm manager	48
Physician	86	Mail carrier	47
Lawyer	75	Secretary	46
Dentist	74	Insurance agent	45
College professor	74	Bank teller	43
Architect	73	Nurse's aide	42
Psychiatrist	72	Farmer	40
Clergy	69	Correctional officer	40
Pharmacist	68	Receptionist	39
Registered nurse	66	Carpenter	39
High school teacher	66	Barber	36
Accountant	65	Child care worker	35
Optician	65	Hotel clerk	32
Elementary school teacher	64	Bus driver	32
Banker	63	Auto body repairer	31
Veterinarian	62	Truck driver	30
Legislator	61	Salesworker (shoes)	28
Airline pilot	60	Garbage collector	28
Police officer or detective	60	Waiter and waitress	28
Prekindergarten teacher	55	Cook in a pizza shop	27
Librarian	54	Bartender	25
Firefighter	53	Farmworker	23
Social worker	52	Janitor	22
Dental hygienist	52	Newspaper vendor	19
Electrician	51	Prostitute	14
Funeral director	49	Panhandler	11

Note: 100 is the highest and 0 the lowest possible prestige score.
Source: J. Davis et al. 2009. See also Nakao and Treas 1994.

Think about It

Can you name what you think are two more high-prestige occupations? Two more low-prestige occupations?

used to calculate pension and other benefits that are usually based on wages received. The United Nations has placed an $11 trillion price tag on unpaid labor by women, largely in child care, housework, and agriculture. Whatever the figure, the continued undercounting of many workers' contributions to a family and to an entire economy means that virtually all measures of stratification are in need of reform (United Nations Development Programme 1995; United Nations Economic and Social Council 2010; Wages for Housework Campaign 1999).

Multiple Measures

Another complication in measuring social class is that advances in statistical methods and computer technology have multiplied the factors used to define class under the objective method. No longer are sociologists limited to annual income and education in evaluating a person's class position. Today, studies use as criteria the value of homes, sources of income, assets, years in present occupations, neighborhoods, and considerations regarding dual careers. Adding these variables will not necessarily paint a different picture of class differentiation in the United States, but it does allow sociologists to measure class in a more complex and multidimensional way. When researchers use multiple measures, they typically speak of **socioeconomic status (SES),** a measure of social class that is based on income, education, and occupation. To determine the socioeconomic status of a young person, such as a college student under age 25, they use *parental* income, education, and occupation.

Whatever the technique used to measure class, the sociologist is interested in real and often dramatic differences in power, privilege, and opportunity in a society. The study of stratification is a study of inequality. Nowhere is the truth of that statement more evident than in the distribution of income and wealth.

thinking CRITICALLY

To what degree are students motivated by the prestige of their future occupations?

Income and Wealth

By all measures, income in the United States is distributed unevenly. Nobel Prize–winning economist Paul Samuelson has described the situation in the following words: "If we made an income pyramid out of building blocks, with each layer portraying $500 of income, the peak would be far higher than Mount Everest, but most people would be within a few feet of the ground" (Samuelson and Nordhaus 2010:324).

Recent data support Samuelson's analogy. In 2009, the median household income in the United States was $49,777. In other words, half of all households had higher incomes that year and half had lower incomes. However, this fact does not fully convey the income disparities in our society. We can get some sense of income inequality by contrasting this median (middle) income with the mean arithmetic average, which in 2009 was $67,976. The mean is so much higher than the median because some people make a lot more money than others, which draws the mean up. Thus, the mean is a less useful statistic than the median for describing the average, or typical, income (DeNavas-Walt et al. 2010:33).

We can gain additional insight into income inequality in the United States by looking at the relative placement of households within the income distribution. One of the most common ways of doing so is to line up all income-earning households from low to high and then break them into quintiles, or fifths. Because there are approximately 118 million households in the United States, each quintile includes an equal number of about 23.4 million households. This method gives us a sense of the average income within each quintile, along with the percentage of the nation's total income earned in each quintile.

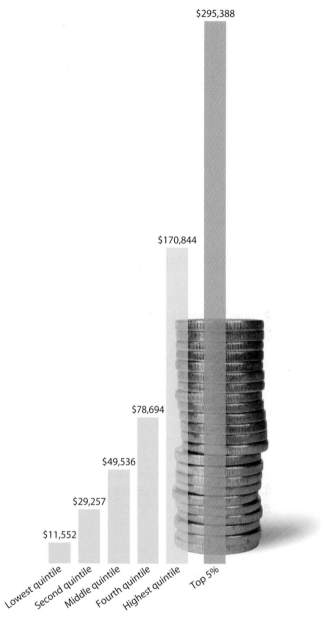

Source: Data for 2009 in DeNavas-Walt et al. 2010:40; Bureau of the Census 2010d: Table H-3.

As Figure 9-2 shows, looking at the population in this way reveals a significant degree of income inequality. The mean income for households in the lowest quintile is $11,552; in the top quintile, it is $170,844. Those households in the top 5 percent—the ones most responsible for bringing up the arithmetic mean—average a staggering $295,388 in annual income. If we were to move up even higher in the income distribution, we would find that the top 0.01 percent of taxpayers—about 15,000 households—make incomes of at least $11.5 million a year. Collectively, they control 6 percent of the nation's total income (Sloan 2009:27).

There has been a modest redistribution of income in the United States over the past 80 years, but not always to the benefit of the poor or even the middle class. From 1929 through 1970, the government's economic and tax policies shifted some income to the poor. However, in the past four decades—especially in the 1980s and in the decade from 2001 through 2010—federal tax policies favored the affluent. Moreover, while the salaries of highly skilled workers and professionals have continued to rise, the wages of less skilled workers have *decreased* when controlled for inflation.

Just how dramatic has this growth in inequality been? Consider the period between 1984 and 2008. In just 25 years, the following changes occurred in real household income (adjusted for inflation):

- For the lowest 20 percent of the population, income rose 9 percent.

- For the next lowest 20 percent of the population, income rose 10 percent.

- For the middle 20 percent of the population, income rose 13 percent.

- For the next highest 20 percent of the population, income rose 20 percent.

- For the top 20 percent of the population, income rose a whopping 40 percent.

The pattern is clear. Though income has increased for all segments of the population, by far the biggest winners have been the affluent.

Has the recent economic slowdown reduced income inequality? Not really. A comparison of household incomes in 1999 (the peak before the 2001 recession) with the most recent data for 2009 shows that lower-income households' earnings have declined, while higher-income households' earnings have held steady. By one measure, inequality between the top 10th and the bottom 10th of the income distribution has increased 9 percent (DeNavas-Walt et al. 2009:38–39).

Careful economic analysis has shown that over the past 30 years, federal and state tax policies have tended to accentuate this trend toward income inequality. During one 25-year period, the top 1 percent of income earners *after taxes* saw their incomes rise 228 percent, compared to only 21 percent for households in the middle quintile. Little wonder that the middle class is shrinking (Billitteri 2009; Sherman 2007).

Finally, the impact of the recent recession is unlikely to be shared evenly among racial and ethnic groups. During the recession of 1999–2001, the median household wealth of Hispanic and Black Americans fell 27 percent. At the same time, White households' wealth grew 2 percent (Hamilton and Darity 2009).

Globalization is often blamed for this growing inequality, because it has forced less skilled workers to compete with lower-paid foreign-born workers. While that is true, research suggests that the number of displaced workers who are reemployed at similarly paid or even higher-paid jobs roughly equals the number of workers whose earnings drop (S. Zimmerman 2008a).

Wealth is distributed much more unevenly than income in the United States. A 2009 Federal Reserve Bank study showed that half the population controls 2.5 percent of the nation's wealth; the other half controls over 97 percent (Figure 9-3). Put another way, the wealth of the top 1 percent exceeds the collective wealth of the bottom 90 percent.

Researchers have also found a dramatic disparity in the wealth of African Americans and Hispanics compared to that of Whites. This disparity is evident even when educational backgrounds are held constant. The households of college-educated Whites have about three times as much wealth as the households of college-educated Blacks (Conley 2010; Kennickell 2009; Kent 2010; Oliver and Shapiro 2006; Shapiro et al. 2010).

thinking CRITICALLY

What does the pattern of income distribution in the United States tell you about your future income? How much can you expect it to grow over the years?

TREND SPOTTING

Women as Wage Earners

In 2010, for the first time, women outnumbered men in the U.S. workforce. The historic reversal was caused by long-term changes in women's roles that began four decades ago. In the 2008 recession, massive job losses among men tipped the balance.

This change in the trend reflects the growing importance of women as wage earners, although on average, women still work fewer hours than men. They also hold more part-time jobs than men, and they earn only 77 percent of what men make. And of course, men still dominate the higher-paying executive levels of the workforce.

Women's share of the once heavily male labor force has been growing for nearly a century. Big expansions occurred during the Great Depression, when payrolls were limited, and World War II, when millions of men left their jobs to join the service. In 2008, the boost to women's employment came from a severe economic slowdown that hit hard at male-dominated occupations, such as construction and manufacturing.

Although women's outnumbering of men in the labor force may be temporary—an artifact of the recent recession—their transformation of the U.S. workplace is permanent. There are no signs of a countertrend to their participation in the workforce.

Poverty

Approximately one out of every nine people in the United States lives below the poverty line established by the federal government. In 2007, no fewer than 37.2 million people were living in poverty. The economic boom of the 1990s passed these people by. A Bureau of the Census report shows that one in five households has trouble meeting basic needs, from paying the utility bills to buying dinner (Bauman 1999; DeNavas-Walt et al. 2009).

One contributor to the United States' high poverty rate has been the large number of workers employed at minimum wage. The federal government has raised the minimum wage over the past half century from 75 cents in 1950 to $6.55 in 2008 and $7.25 in 2009. But in terms of

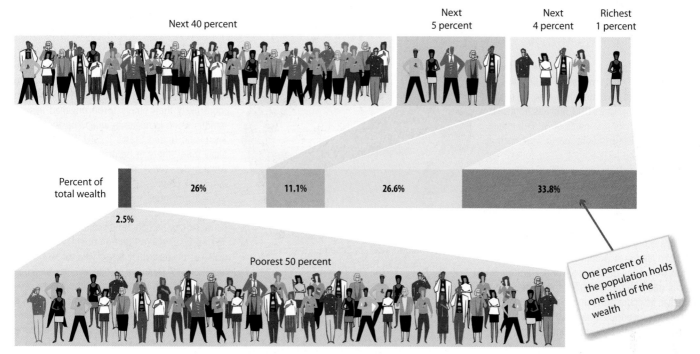

Source: Data for 2007, as reported in a 2009 Federal Reserve Bank study. See Kennickell 2009:35.

its real value adjusted for inflation, the minimum wage has frequently failed to keep pace with the cost of living.

Moreover, raising the minimum wage does not remedy other difficulties that low-wage workers encounter. A 2009 survey of workers in various low-wage occupations, such as apparel manufacturing, child care (see Chapter 4), and discount retailing, showed that these workers lose about 15 percent of the pay that is due them through employers' wage violations. Typically, employers limit workers' wages by pressuring them not to file for workers' compensation after on-the-job injuries, requiring them to work off the clock, and paying the straight hourly wage rate for overtime hours. Women are far more likely than men to be cheated in this way (Bernhardt et al. 2009).

Sociologists have long had an interest in the impact of substandard work on society, beginning with the writings of Karl Marx, Émile Durkheim, and Max Weber. Their interest increased with the global economic decline that began in 2008, which trapped many people in jobs they did not want or left them unemployed. Box 9-1 considers recent sociological work on *precarious work.*

In this section, we'll consider just how social scientists define *poverty.* We'll also take a closer look at the people who fall into that category—including the working poor.

Studying Poverty

The efforts of sociologists and other social scientists to better understand poverty are complicated by the difficulty of defining it. This problem is evident even in government programs that conceive of poverty in either absolute or relative terms. **Absolute poverty** refers to a minimum level of subsistence that no family should be expected to live below.

One commonly used measure of absolute poverty is the federal government's *poverty line,* a money income figure that is adjusted annually to reflect the consumption requirements of families based on their size and composition. The poverty line serves as an official definition of which people are poor. In 2008, for example, any family of four (two adults and two children) with a combined income of $21,834 or less fell below the poverty line. This definition determines which individuals and families will be eligible for certain government benefits (DeNavas-Walt et al. 2009:43).

Although by absolute standards, poverty has declined in the United States, it remains higher than in many other industrial nations. As Figure 9-4 on page 201 shows, a comparatively high proportion of U.S. households is poor, meaning that they are unable to purchase basic consumer goods. If anything, this cross-national comparison understates the extent of poverty in the United States, since U.S. residents are likely to pay more for housing, health care, child care, and education than residents of other countries, where such expenses are often subsidized (Smeeding 2008).

In contrast, **relative poverty** is a floating standard of deprivation by which people at the bottom of a society, whatever their lifestyles, are judged to be disadvantaged *in comparison with the nation as a whole.* Therefore, even if the poor of 2005 are better off in absolute terms than the poor of the 1930s or 1960s, they are still seen as deserving of special assistance.

Debate has been growing over the accuracy of the federal government's measure of poverty, which has remained largely unchanged since 1963. If noncash benefits such as Medicare, Medicaid, tax credits, food stamps, public housing, and health care and other employer-provided fringe benefits were included, the reported poverty rate would be lower. On the other hand, if out-of-pocket medical expenses and mandatory work expenses for transportation and child care were included, the poverty rate would be higher. Although the current poverty measure does consider family size, it does not consider a household's location,

RESEARCH TODAY

9-1 Precarious Work

In 2008 Jim Marshall, age 39, lost his job in Detroit's faltering auto industry. Figuring that job prospects had to be better elsewhere, he moved to Florida. But by May 2009 Jim was homeless, living in a tent city just north of St. Petersburg. "My parents always taught me to work hard in school, graduate high school, go to college, get a degree and you'll do fine. You'll do better than your parents' generation," Marshall says. "I did all those things. . . . For a while, I did have that good life, but nowadays that's not the reality" (Bazar 2009:A2).

Jim's story is all too common. He is one of the millions of Americans who have been reduced to doing **precarious work**—employment that is poorly paid, and from the worker's perspective, insecure and unprotected. People who engage in precarious work often cannot support a household, and they are vulnerable to falling into poverty.

Even before economists recognized the economic downturn in 2009, there was ample statistical evidence that precarious work was increasing, despite the fact that the unemployment rate remained steady. In his presidential address to the ASA, Arne L. Kalleberg offered the following five social indicators:

1. *A decline in the average length of time workers remain with an employer.* This trend has been especially noticeable among older White men, who in the past were protected by employers.
2. *An increase in long-term unemployment.* The proportion of workers who remained unemployed after six months rose in the 2000s, when the number of manufacturing jobs shrank and fewer new jobs were created.
3. *A decrease in job security.* Given the increase in long-term unemployment and

the decrease in average time spent with an employer, workers became increasingly insecure about their ability to replace a lost job.
4. *An increase in outsourcing and temporary work.* To meet cyclical fluctuations in supply and demand, employers have turned more and more to nontraditional labor sources. Today, virtually any job can be outsourced, including accounting, legal, and military services.

To meet cyclical fluctuations in supply and demand, employers have turned more and more to nontraditional labor sources. Today, virtually any job can be outsourced, including accounting, legal, and military services.

5. *A shift in risk from employers to employees.* Few companies offer traditional pensions anymore. Employees are being asked to shoulder at least part of the cost and risk not only of their retirement investments, but of their health insurance plans as well.

Although precarious work is becoming more common, people differ in their vulnerability to it. Members of racial and ethnic minorities are more likely than others to be engaged in precarious work. Immigrants, including those who are in the United States legally, are also more likely than others to be precariously employed. Around the world—in the United States, other industrial countries, and developing nations—women are much more likely than men to do precarious work.

What can be done to revitalize labor markets so that fewer workers end up doing substandard work—or at least, that those who do will suffer less from it? Denmark is one country that has tried to deal with the problem. Although the government there cannot make jobs more secure, it does provide significant assistance to the unemployed. Help finding a job, significant income compensation (90 percent of a worker's previous wage for one year, without conditions), and subsidized education and training are all available to Danish workers who have lost their jobs.

LET'S DISCUSS

1. Has the trend toward increasing reliance on precarious work touched your family or friends? Has anyone you know been unemployed longer than six months? If so, did that person or persons belong to one or more of the groups that are particularly vulnerable to precarious work?
2. Looking forward to your own career, can you think of a strategy for avoiding precarious work, frequent job loss, and long-term unemployment?

Sources: Bazar 2009; European Metalworkers' Federation 2010; Fudge and Owens 2006; Kalleberg 2009; McDowell et al. 2009; Somavia 2008; Westergaard-Nielsen 2008.

---

whether in a relatively expensive city like New York or in a less expensive rural area. Nor does it consider whether a householder pays rent or a mortgage installment, lives at home or with someone else. To address some of these shortcomings, in 2010 the federal government launched a second statistic called the Supplemental Poverty Measure (SPM), which will be used to estimate economic hardship. The SPM is a relative poverty measure that is based on a broad range of changing household resources and expenses. It will be calculated beginning in late 2011, but will not replace the poverty line in determining a household's eligibility for benefits (Department of Commerce 2010; D. Johnson 2010).

Who Are the Poor?

Not only does the category of the poor defy any simple definition; it counters the common stereotypes about "poor people." For example, many people in the United States believe that the vast majority of the poor are able to work but will not. Yet many poor adults do work outside the home, although only a small portion of them work full-time throughout the year. In 2009, about 36 percent of all poor working adults worked full-time, compared to 65 percent of all adults. Of those poor adults who do not work, most are ill or disabled, or are occupied in maintaining a home (DeNavas-Walt et al. 2010:15).

FIGURE **9-4** POVERTY IN SELECTED COUNTRIES

201

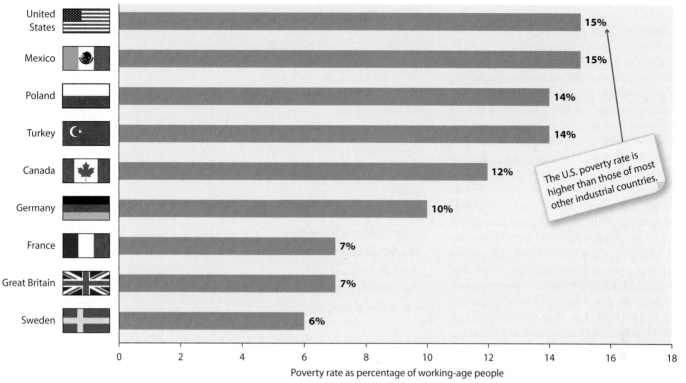

The U.S. poverty rate is higher than those of most other industrial countries.

Poverty rate as percentage of working-age people

Note: Data are averages for mid-2000s, as reported in 2009. Poverty threshold is 50 percent of a nation's median household income.
Source: Organisation for Economic Co-operation and Development 2009a.

Though many of the poor live in urban slums, a majority live outside those poverty-stricken areas. Poverty is no stranger in rural areas, from Appalachia to hard-hit farming regions to Native American reservations. Table 9-4 provides additional statistical information regarding low-income people in the United States.

Feminization of Poverty

Since World War II, an increasing proportion of the poor people of the United States have been women, many of whom are divorced or never-married mothers. In 1959, female householders accounted for 26 percent of the nation's poor; by 2009, that figure had risen to 51 percent (see Table 9-4). This alarming trend, known as the **feminization of poverty,** is evident not just in the United States but around the world.

About half of all women living in poverty in the United States are in transition, coping with an economic crisis caused by the departure, disability, or death of a husband. The other half tend to be economically dependent either on the welfare system or on friends and relatives living nearby. A major factor in the feminization of poverty has been the increase in families with women as single heads of the household (see Chapter 14). Conflict theorists and other observers trace the higher rates of poverty among women to three distinct factors: the difficulty in finding affordable

Even if this single parent works her way up the chain of command, supporting her family will still be difficult.

child care, sexual harassment, and sex discrimination in the labor market (Burns 2010).

The Underclass

In 2009, 43 percent of poor people in the United States were living in central cities. These highly visible urban residents are the focus of most government efforts to alleviate poverty. Yet according to many observers, the plight of the urban poor is growing worse, owing to the devastating interplay of inadequate education and limited employment prospects. Traditional employment opportunities in the industrial sector are largely closed to the unskilled poor. Past and present discrimination heightens these problems for those low-income urban residents who are Black or Hispanic.

Along with other social scientists, sociologist William Julius Wilson (1980, 1987, 1996) and his colleagues (2004) have used the term **underclass** to describe the long-term poor who lack training and skills. According to an analysis of Census 2000 data, 7.9 million people live in high-poverty neighborhoods. About 30 percent of the population in these neighborhoods is Black, 29 percent Hispanic, and 24 percent White. In central cities, about 49 percent of the underclass is Black, 29 percent Hispanic, 17 percent White, and 5 percent "other" (Jargowsky and Yang 2006; O'Hare and Curry-White 1992).

Those statistics may sound high, but they could climb higher. Some scholars are predicting that the recent economic downturn may swell the ranks of the underclass, increasing the proportion of the U.S. population that they represent. Indeed, the recession seems to have accelerated the demise of less efficient, less profitable firms. When the downturn is over, jobs will not return to declining industries (Rampell 2010).

Analyses of the poor in general reveal that they are not a static social class. The overall composition of the poor changes continually, because some individuals and families near the top edge of poverty move above the poverty level after a year or two, while others slip below it. Still, hundreds of thousands of people remain in poverty for many years at a time. Blacks and Latinos are more likely than Whites to be persistently poor. Both Latinos and Blacks are less likely than Whites to leave the welfare rolls as a result of welfare reform (Jäntti 2009).

Explaining Poverty

Why is it that poverty pervades a nation of such vast wealth? Sociologist Herbert Gans (1995), who has applied functionalist analysis to the existence of poverty, argues that various segments of society actually *benefit* from the existence of the poor. Gans has identified a number of social, economic, and political functions that the poor perform for society:

- The presence of poor people means that society's dirty work—physically dirty or dangerous, dead-end and underpaid, undignified and menial jobs—will be performed at low cost.

- Poverty creates jobs for occupations and professions that serve the poor. It creates both legal employment (public health experts, welfare caseworkers) and illegal jobs (drug dealers, numbers runners).

- The identification and punishment of the poor as deviants upholds the legitimacy of conventional social norms and mainstream values regarding hard work, thrift, and honesty.

- Within a relatively hierarchical society, the existence of poor people guarantees the higher status of the rich. As psychologist William Ryan (1976) noted, affluent people may justify inequality (and gain a measure of satisfaction) by *blaming the victims* of poverty for their disadvantaged condition.

- Because of their lack of political power, the poor often absorb the costs of social change. Under the policy of deinstitutionalization, mental patients released from long-term hospitals have been transferred primarily to low-income communities and neighborhoods. Similarly, halfway houses for rehabilitated drug abusers, rejected by more affluent communities, often end up in poorer neighborhoods.

In Gans's view, then, poverty and the poor actually satisfy positive functions for many nonpoor groups in the United States.

TABLE **9-4**   WHO ARE THE POOR IN THE UNITED STATES?

Group	Percentage of the Population of the United States	Percentage of the Poor of the United States
Age		
Under 18 years old	25%	35%
18 to 64 years old	62	57
65 years and older	13	8
Race-Ethnicity		
Whites (non-Hispanic)	65	43
Blacks	13	23
Hispanics	16	28
Asians and Pacific Islanders	4	4
Family Composition		
Married couples with male householders	75	39
Female householders	18	51

Source: Data for 2009, as reported by the Bureau of the Census; DeNavas-Walt et al. 2010:15.

thinking CRITICALLY

How do you identify areas of poverty in your community or one nearby? Do you consider residents' achieved or ascribed characteristics?

Life Chances

Max Weber saw class as being closely related to people's **life chances**—that is, their opportunities to provide themselves with material goods, positive living conditions, and favorable life experiences (Gerth and Mills 1958). Life chances are reflected in measures such as housing, education, and health. Occupying a higher social class in a society improves your life chances and brings greater access to social rewards. In contrast, people in the lower social classes are forced to devote a larger proportion of their limited resources to the necessities of life.

In times of danger, the affluent and powerful have a better chance of surviving than people of ordinary means. When the supposedly unsinkable British ocean liner *Titanic* hit an iceberg in 1912, it was not carrying enough lifeboats to accommodate all passengers. Plans had been made to evacuate only first- and second-class passengers. About 62 percent of the first-class passengers survived the disaster. Despite a rule that women and children would go first, about a third of those passengers were male. In contrast, only 25 percent of the third-class passengers survived. The first attempt to alert them to the need to abandon ship came well after other passengers had been notified (Butler 1998; Crouse 1999; Riding 1998).

Class position also affects people's vulnerability to natural disasters. When Hurricane Katrina hit the Gulf Coast of the

Class position affects people's vulnerability to natural disasters. Today, years after Hurricane Katrina forced the evacuation of New Orleans, many of the city's poor still have not returned home.

United States in 2005, affluent and poor people alike became its victims. However, poor people who did not own automobiles (100,000 of them in New Orleans alone) were less able than others to evacuate in advance of the storm. The poor who survived its fury had no nest egg to draw on, and thus were more likely than others to accept relocation wherever social service agencies could place them—sometimes hundreds or thousands of miles from home. Those who were able to return are still dealing with the toxic debris left behind (Bullard and Wright 2009).

Wealth, status, and power may not ensure happiness, but they certainly provide additional ways of coping with problems and disappointments. For this reason, the opportunity for advancement—for social mobility—is of special significance to those on the bottom of society. Most people want the rewards and privileges that are granted to high-ranking members of a culture. What can society do to increase their social mobility? One strategy is to offer financial aid to college students from low-income families, on the theory that education lifts people out of poverty. Yet such programs are not having as great an effect as their authors once hoped (Box 9-2).

use your sociological *imagination*

Imagine a society in which there are no social classes—no differences in people's wealth, income, and life chances. What would such a society be like? Would it be stable, or would its social structure change over time?

thinking CRITICALLY

How do people's life chances affect society as a whole?

Social Mobility

In the movie *Maid in Manhattan,* Jennifer Lopez plays the lead in a modern-day Cinderella story, rising from the lowly status of chambermaid in a big-city hotel to a company supervisor and the girlfriend of a well-to-do politician. The ascent of a person from a poor background to a position of prestige, power, or financial reward is an example of social mobility. Formally defined, the term **social mobility** refers to the movement of individuals or groups from one position in a society's stratification system to another. But how significant—how frequent, how dramatic—is mobility in a class society such as the United States?

Open versus Closed Stratification Systems

Sociologists use the terms *open stratification system* and *closed stratification system* to indicate the degree of social mobility in a society. An **open system** implies that the position of each individual is influenced by his or her *achieved* status. Such a system encourages competition among members of society. The United States is moving toward this ideal type as the government attempts to reduce the barriers faced by women, racial and ethnic minorities, and people born in lower social classes. Even in the midst of the economic downturn of 2008–2009, nearly 80 percent of people in the United States felt they could get ahead (Economic Mobility Project 2009).

At the other extreme of social mobility is the **closed system,** which allows little or no possibility of individual social mobility. The slavery and caste systems of stratification are examples of closed systems. In such societies, social placement is based on *ascribed* statuses, such as race or family background, which cannot be changed.

Types of Social Mobility

An airline pilot who becomes a police officer moves from one social position to another of the same rank. Each occupation has the same prestige ranking: 60 on a scale ranging from a low of 0 to a high of 100 (see Table 9-3 on page 196). Sociologists call this kind of movement **horizontal mobility.** However, if the pilot were to become a lawyer (prestige ranking of 75), he or she would experience **vertical mobility,** the movement of an individual from one social position to another of a different rank. Vertical mobility can also involve moving *downward* in a society's stratification system, as would be the case if the airline pilot became a bank teller (ranking of 43). Pitirim Sorokin ([1927] 1959) was the first sociologist to distinguish between horizontal and vertical mobility. Most sociological analysis, however, focuses on vertical rather than horizontal mobility.

One way of examining vertical social mobility is to contrast its two types, intergenerational and intragenerational mobility. **Intergenerational mobility** involves changes in the social position of children relative to their parents. Thus, a plumber whose father was a physician provides an example of downward intergenerational mobility. A film star whose parents were both factory workers illustrates upward intergenerational mobility. Because education contributes significantly to upward mobility, any barrier to the pursuit of advanced degrees can definitely limit intergenerational mobility (see Box 9-2; Isaacs 2007a; Isaacs et al. 2008; Sawhill and Morton 2007).

9-2 Social Class and Financial Aid

Today's young people have been dubbed Generation Y, but a more appropriate name for them could be Generation Debt. Every year, millions of prospective college students and their parents struggle through the intricate and time-consuming process of applying for financial aid. Originally, financial aid programs were intended to level the playing field—to allow qualified students from all walks of life to attend college, regardless of the cost. But have these programs fulfilled their promise?

> *Statistics that show the educational level in the United States rising overall obscure the widening gap between the advantaged and the less advantaged.*

In 2004, 40 percent of first-year students at major state universities came from families with incomes of more than $100,000 a year. In other words, close to half of all students came from high-income families. This statistic should not be surprising, given the high cost of tuition, room, and board at state universities. For students from families with the lowest incomes, the cost can be prohibitive. Only 11 percent of children from the poorest families in the United States have earned college degrees, compared to 53 percent of children from families in the top fifth of the population. Those moderate-income students who do graduate, and even those who fail to complete their degrees, are often saddled with heavy postgraduate debt.

Community colleges, with their low tuition, are often regarded as a hedge against the high costs of higher education. Although these two-year commuter colleges may be cheaper than four-year residential schools, they are not inexpensive. In the academic year 2009–2010, the annual cost of attending community college was more than $14,000. For students at these schools, a greater proportion of their expenses goes to transportation and child care than for students who live on campus at four-year schools.

Besides the spiraling cost of an education, the widespread difficulty in paying for college stems from three trends. First, over the past few decades, colleges and universities have been moving away from making outright grants, such as scholarships, to deserving students, and toward low-interest student loans. Second, much of the assistance schools offer in the form of loans is not based strictly on need. Third, interest rates on federally guaranteed loans have risen steadily, increasing the burden of repayment.

These trends in financial aid for higher education are closely tied to trends in social inequality. As noted earlier in this chapter, over the past half century, rather than declining, inequality in income and wealth has actually increased. According to one analysis of U.S. economic trends over the past 30 years, this increase in wealth and income inequality has contributed to a modest increase in educational inequality, as measured by the number of years of formal schooling students achieve. In a variation on the truism that the rich tend to get richer while the poor get poorer, the rich are getting better educations and the poor are

getting poorer educations. Statistics that show the educational level in the United States rising overall obscure the widening gap between the advantaged and the less advantaged.

LET'S DISCUSS

1. How important is financial aid (grants, loans, work-study income) to you and your friends? Without these types of aid, would you be able to cover your college expenses?

2. Aside from a reduction in individual social mobility, what might be the long-term effects of the shortage of need-based financial aid? Relate your answer to the trend toward globalization.

Sources: Boushey 2005; M. Campbell et al. 2005; College Board 2009; Isaacs et al. 2008; Kamenetz 2006; Leonhardt 2004; Michals 2003; Trumbull 2006.

Figure 9-5 shows intergenerational mobility based on income. In 1978–1980, a national survey looked at the family income of 6,000 young people. Two decades later, in 1997–2003, researchers followed up on those young adults and their income. The results showed a strong stickiness in both the bottom and top quintiles, or fifths, of the income distribution. Just over 33 percent of those whose parents were in the bottom quintile and 37 percent of those who were in the top quintile remained in the same quintile as adults. Yet the study also showed mobility: almost 66 percent of those in the bottom quintile moved up, and over 60 percent of those at the top experienced downward mobility.

Among men born in the 1960s, this consistent intergenerational mobility resulted largely from economic growth. On average, these men earned more than their fathers did at the same age; their family incomes improved as well. However, the trend did not continue into the next generation. Currently, young men are earning less than their fathers did at the same age—about 12 percent less. Family incomes are slightly higher than in the last generation, but only because women have moved into the paid labor force to supplement their husbands' earnings. With so few women left to join the labor force, most families will need to increase their wages to raise their incomes further (Sawhill and Haskins 2009).

Intragenerational mobility involves changes in social position within a person's adult life. A woman who begins work as a teacher's aide and eventually becomes superintendent of the school district experiences upward intragenerational mobility. A man who becomes a taxicab driver after his accounting firm goes bankrupt undergoes downward intragenerational mobility.

FIGURE **9-5** INTERGENERATIONAL INCOME MOBILITY

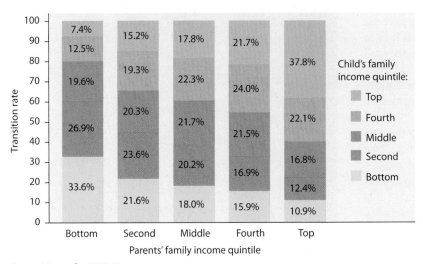

Source: Mazumder 2008:10.

Over a 25-year period, adult children often end up in the same income bracket as their parents. About 7 percent of those who begin in the bottom quintile reach the top quintile as adults; their story is one of rags to riches. About 11 percent of those who start in the top quintile fall to the bottom.

Social Mobility in the United States

The belief in upward mobility is an important value in our society. Does that mean that the United States is indeed the land of opportunity? Not unless such ascriptive characteristics as race, gender, and family background have ceased to be significant in determining one's future prospects. We can see the impact of these factors in the occupational structure.

Occupational Mobility Two sociological studies conducted a decade apart offer insight into the degree of mobility in the nation's occupational structure (Blau and Duncan 1967; Featherman and Hauser 1978). Taken together, these investigations lead to several noteworthy conclusions. First, occupational mobility (both intergenerational and intragenerational) has been common among males. Approximately 60 to 70 percent of sons are employed in higher-ranked occupations than their fathers.

Second, although there is a great deal of mobility in the United States, much of it is minor. That is, people who reach an occupational level above or below that of their parents usually advance or fall back only one or two out of a possible eight occupational levels. Thus, the child of a laborer may become an artisan or a technician, but he or she is less likely to become a manager or professional. The odds against reaching the top are extremely high unless one begins from a relatively privileged position.

The Impact of Education Another conclusion of both studies is that education plays a critical role in social mobility. The impact of formal schooling on adult status is even greater than that of family background (although as we have seen, family background influences the likelihood that one will receive higher education). Furthermore, education represents an important

means of intergenerational mobility. A person who was born into a poor family but who graduates from college has a one in five chance of entering the top fifth of all income earners as an adult (Isaacs et al. 2008).

The impact of education on mobility has diminished somewhat in the past decade, however. An undergraduate degree—a BA or a BS— serves less as a guarantee of upward mobility now than it did in the past, simply because more and more entrants into the job market hold such a degree. Moreover, intergenerational mobility is declining, since there is no longer such a stark difference between generations. In earlier decades, many high school–educated parents successfully sent their children to college, but today's college students are increasingly likely to have college-educated parents (Sawhill and Morton 2007).

The Impact of Race and Ethnicity Sociologists have long documented the fact that the class system is more rigid for African Americans than it is for members of other racial groups. African American men who have good jobs, for example, are less likely than White men to see their adult children attain the same status. The cumulative disadvantage of discrimination plays a significant role in the disparity between the two groups' experiences. Compared to White households, the relatively modest wealth of African American households means that adult African American children are less likely than adult White children to receive financial support from their parents. Indeed, young African American couples are much more likely than young White couples to be assisting their parents— a sacrifice that hampers their social mobility (Favreault 2008).

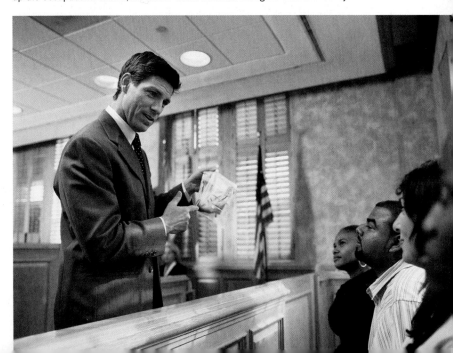

If this lawyer were the son of a car mechanic, his rise to the upper-middle class would illustrate intergenerational mobility. If he had begun as a paralegal and worked his way up the occupational ladder, his career would illustrate intragenerational mobility.

Not surprisingly, African Americans are more likely than Whites to experience downward intergenerational mobility, and less likely to move up the social ladder. A study of the income data for people born between 1955 and 1970 shows that four in five Black children who began in the top quintile experienced downward mobility, compared to just two in five White children. Similarly, three in five White children who began in the bottom two quintiles experienced upward social mobility, compared to one in four Black children (Sharkey 2009).

The African American middle class has grown over the past few decades, due to economic expansion and the benefits of the civil rights movement of the 1960s. Yet many of these middle-class households have little savings, a fact that puts them in danger during times of crisis. We noted earlier that recession hits Black and Latino households harder than White households. Studies have consistently shown that downward mobility is significantly higher for Blacks than it is for Whites (Conley 2010; Oliver and Shapiro 2006; Sernau 2001; W. Wilson 1996).

The Latino population is not doing much better. The typical Hispanic has less than 10 percent of the wealth that a White person has. A 2008 study suggests that in recent years, Latinos have even lost ground. Their continuing immigration accounts for part of the disparity: most of the new arrivals are destitute. But even the wealthiest 5 percent of Latino households have only a third as much net worth as the top 5 percent of White households (Kochhar 2008).

The Impact of Gender Studies of mobility, even more than those of class, have traditionally ignored the significance of gender, but some research findings are now available that explore the relationship between gender and mobility.

Women's employment opportunities are much more limited than men's (as Chapter 12 will show). Moreover, according to recent research, women whose skills far exceed the jobs offered them are more likely than men to withdraw entirely from the paid labor force. Their withdrawal violates an assumption common to traditional mobility studies: that most people will aspire to upward mobility and seek to make the most of their opportunities.

In contrast to men, women have a rather large range of clerical occupations open to them. But the modest salary ranges and few prospects for advancement in many of these positions limit the possibility of upward mobility. Self-employment as shopkeepers, entrepreneurs, independent professionals, and the like—an important road to upward mobility for men—is more difficult for women, who find it harder to secure the necessary financing. Although sons commonly follow in the footsteps of their fathers, women are unlikely to move into their fathers' positions. Consequently, gender remains an important factor in shaping social mobility. Women in the United States (and in other parts of the world) are especially likely to be trapped in poverty, unable to rise out of their low-income status (Beller 2009; Heilman 2001).

On the positive side, though today's women lag behind men in employment, their earnings have increased faster than their

Andrea Jung, chairman and chief executive officer of Avon Corporation since 1999, is one of the few women in the United States who have risen to the top of the corporate hierarchy. In 2008, Jung was elected to Apple's board of directors. Despite the passage of equal opportunity laws, occupational barriers still limit most women's social mobility.

mothers' did at a comparable age so that their incomes are substantially higher. The one glaring exception to this trend is the daughters of low-income parents. Because these women typically care for children—many as single parents—and sometimes for other relatives as well, their mobility is severely restricted (Isaacs 2007b).

thinking CRITICALLY

Which factor—occupation, education, race and ethnicity, or gender—do you expect will have the greatest effect on your own social mobility? Explain.

Executive Compensation

Few topics in the news today have led to such public outrage as the compensation received by top executives in the private sector. In the wake of recent corporate meltdowns, such as those involving several huge mortgage lending institutions, executive salaries and bonuses that run into the millions of dollars have begun to strike people as inappropriate. Is multi-million-dollar compensation really necessary, much less desirable, to attract talented corporate leaders?

In 2011, as the U.S. economy began to pull out of a deep, long-lasting recession, corporate executives were still earning huge salaries and bonuses—despite the fact that many workers remained jobless.

Looking at the Issue

Over the period from 2000 to 2010, Barry Diller, CEO of Expedia, received a staggering $1.14 billion in compensation—despite the fact that the company's shares *lost* 22 percent of their value. Over an eight-year period, United Health's top executive, William McGuire, took home $453 million, even though the company's stockholders lost 99 percent of their investment. In defense, spokesmen for the two men claimed that their compensation reflected the stocks' solid performance during earlier periods (Thurm 2010).

Although executive pay has always been high in the United States, in recent years it has grown dramatically. The corporate executives who head private companies now earn the highest incomes in the nation. In fact, the gap between their salaries and those of average workers has widened significantly over time. In 1965, top executives earned only 24 times the average worker's pay. By 1980 the gap had widened to 40 times the average paycheck and, by 2009, to 300 times the average (Herman 2009; Mackey 2009).

Applying Sociology

From a functionalist perspective, such generous compensation seems reasonable given the potential for gain that a talented executive brings to a corporation. Today, even a small increase in a multi-billion-dollar company's performance can add hundreds of millions of dollars to its bottom line. Not surprisingly, then, competition to attract top-performing executives to a company is fierce. Not all these executives are successful all the time, however; sometimes their leadership reduces profits. Critics point out that 7 of the top 25 highly paid executives presided over companies that lost money during the last decade (Frank 2010; Thurm 2010).

Conflict theorists question not only the relatively high levels of executive compensation, but also the process through which executives' pay is determined. The board of directors, which holds the responsibility for determining executives' pay, has an incentive to go along with arrangements that are favorable to top executives. Board members themselves earned an average of about $228,000

in 2009, so they have a natural desire to avoid conflict over high salaries (Bebchuk and Fried 2010; Strauss 2011).

Taking an almost interactionist approach, sociologist Thomas DiPrete and his colleagues have observed that today, corporations must report executives' compensation relative to their peer group's compensation—that is, to the compensation received by leaders of similar businesses of similar size. Although members of such peer groups do not interact in the way that members of a primary group or even a secondary group would, they do form a social network. Thus, public comparisons of executive compensation within particular industries may influence board members' decisions, prompting them to tie executives' compensation more directly to their performance (DiPrete et al. 2010).

Initiating Policy

Although policymakers have long been concerned about executive compensation, until recently hard data have been difficult to obtain. Before 1992, corporations were required to disclose executives' pay, but not in a uniform manner. Many companies disguised the dollar amounts by literally spelling the words out in the midst of long, densely written documents. Today, the law mandates that companies publish "summary compensation tables." In 2006, reporting requirements were expanded to include retirement packages, including the "golden parachute" clauses that protect executives who bail out of failing companies (Bebchuk and Fried 2010).

During the economic downturn that began in 2008, the value of the stock that top executives received as part of their compensation packages did decline. Yet overall, CEOs' salaries in the

207

500 largest corporations still rose 3 percent in 2009. In response, the White House appointed a Treasury Department official, whom reporters quickly dubbed the "pay czar," to look into executive compensation. Given the deferred stock payments, expense accounts, and other perquisites executives typically receive, the assignment was a difficult one (D. Jones and Hansen 2009).

In the short time the pay czar has been in office, results have been mixed. Critics complain the office hasn't made significant progress in curbing executive pay, while companies claim that the government is hampering their ability to compete. Although the czar has managed to change some compensation practices, critics worry that companies may develop new ways to inflate executives' pay (Congressional Oversight Panel 2011; Edmans and Gabaix 2010; Grusky and Wimer 2010; Reuters 2010).

Take the Issue with You

1. Should corporate executives earn high salaries even when their companies are losing money? Explain. How do you think functionalists would defend such a practice?

2. What do you think of the "golden parachute" clauses that allow executives to bail out of failing companies unharmed? What might be the effect of such clauses on executives' performance? On shareholders and on lower-level employees?

3. Relate the increases in executive compensation over the past half century to changes in U.S. social structure during that time. How have those changes affected you and your family?

MASTERING THIS CHAPTER

Summary

Stratification is the structured ranking of entire groups of people that perpetuates unequal economic rewards and **power** in a society. In this chapter we examine four general systems of stratification, the explanations offered by functionalist and conflict theorists for the existence of **social inequality,** and the relationship between stratification and **social mobility.**

1. Some degree of **social inequality** characterizes all cultures.

2. Systems of social **stratification** include **slavery, castes,** the **estate system,** and social classes.

3. Karl Marx saw that differences in access to the means of production created social, economic, and political inequality, as well as two distinct classes, owners and laborers.

4. Max Weber identified three analytically distinct components of stratification: **class, status group,** and **power.**

5. Functionalists argue that stratification is necessary to motivate people to fill society's important positions. Conflict theorists see stratification as a major source of societal tension and conflict. Interactionists stress the importance of social class in determining a person's lifestyle.

6. One consequence of social class in the United States is that both **income** and **wealth** are distributed unevenly.

7. Many of those who live in poverty are full-time workers who struggle to support their families at minimum-wage jobs. The long-term poor—those who lack the training and skills to lift themselves out of poverty—form an **underclass.**

8. Functionalists find that the poor satisfy positive functions for many of the nonpoor in the United States.

9. One's **life chances**—opportunities for obtaining material goods, positive living conditions, and favorable life experiences—are related to one's social class. Occupying a high social position improves a person's life chances.

10. **Social mobility** is more likely to be found in an **open system** that emphasizes **achieved status** than in a **closed system** that emphasizes **ascribed status.** Race, gender, and family background are important factors in social mobility.

11. During the past half century, the gap between executive compensation and the average worker's pay has increased almost 300 times. Although corporations claim that talented leaders enhance their performance, making executive pay packages well worth the money, they have gone to some trouble to disguise the expense from public scrutiny.

Key Terms

Absolute poverty A minimum level of subsistence that no family should be expected to live below. (page 199)

Achieved status A social position that a person attains largely through his or her own efforts. (187)

Ascribed status A social position assigned to a person by society without regard for the person's unique talents or characteristics. (187)

Bourgeoisie Karl Marx's term for the capitalist class, comprising the owners of the means of production. (192)

Capitalism An economic system in which the means of production are held largely in private hands and the main incentive for economic activity is the accumulation of profits. (192)

Caste A hereditary rank, usually religiously dictated, that tends to be fixed and immobile. (185)

Class A group of people who have a similar level of wealth and income. (193)

Class consciousness In Karl Marx's view, a subjective awareness held by members of a class regarding their common vested interests and the need for collective political action to bring about social change. (192)

Class system A social ranking based primarily on economic position in which achieved characteristics can influence social mobility. (189)

Closed system A social system in which there is little or no possibility of individual social mobility. (203)

Conspicuous consumption Purchasing and using goods not to survive but to flaunt one's superior wealth and social standing. (193)

Dominant ideology A set of cultural beliefs and practices that helps to maintain powerful social, economic, and political interests. (195)

Estate system A system of stratification under which peasants were required to work land leased to them by nobles in exchange for military protection and other services. Also known as *feudalism*. (189)

Esteem The reputation that a specific person has earned within an occupation. (196)

False consciousness A term used by Karl Marx to describe an attitude held by members of a class that does not accurately reflect their objective position. (192)

Feminization of poverty A trend in which women constitute an increasing proportion of the poor people of the United States. (201)

Horizontal mobility The movement of an individual from one social position to another of the same rank. (203)

Income Salaries and wages. (187)

Intergenerational mobility Changes in the social position of children relative to their parents. (203)

Intragenerational mobility Changes in social position within a person's adult life. (204)

Life chances The opportunities people have to provide themselves with material goods, positive living conditions, and favorable life experiences. (202)

Objective method A technique for measuring social class that assigns individuals to classes on the basis of criteria such as occupation, education, income, and place of residence. (195)

Open system A social system in which the position of each individual is influenced by his or her achieved status. (203)

Power The ability to exercise one's will over others. (193)

Precarious work Employment that is poorly paid, and from the worker's perspective, insecure and unprotected. (200)

Prestige The respect and admiration that an occupation holds in a society. (196)

Proletariat Karl Marx's term for the working class in a capitalist society. (192)

Relative poverty A floating standard of deprivation by which people at the bottom of a society, whatever their lifestyles, are judged to be disadvantaged *in comparison with the nation as a whole.* (199)

Slavery A system of enforced servitude in which some people are owned by other people. (187)

Social inequality A condition in which members of society have differing amounts of wealth, prestige, or power. (186)

Social mobility Movement of individuals or groups from one position in a society's stratification system to another. (203)

Socioeconomic status (SES) A measure of social class that is based on income, education, and occupation. (197)

Status group People who have the same prestige or lifestyle, independent of their class positions. (193)

Stratification A structured ranking of entire groups of people that perpetuates unequal economic rewards and power in a society. (186)

Underclass The long-term poor who lack training and skills. (201)

Vertical mobility The movement of an individual from one social position to another of a different rank. (203)

Wealth An inclusive term encompassing all a person's material assets, including land, stocks, and other types of property. (187)

TAKING SOCIOLOGY with you

1. Do some research on the educational and occupational levels in the city or town where you live. Based on what you have learned, describe the social-class stratification of your community.

2. Use census data to create a map showing the median income levels and/or property values in the geographic areas surrounding your home. What patterns does it show?

3. Talk with a parent or grandparent about your family's history. What can you learn about your forebears' life chances? About their social mobility? How do you hope to fit into the story?

Self-Quiz

Read each question carefully and then select the best answer.

1. Which of the following describes a condition in which members of a society have different amounts of wealth, prestige, or power?
   a. stratification
   b. status inconsistency
   c. slavery
   d. social inequality

2. In Karl Marx's view, the destruction of the capitalist system will occur only if the working class first develops
   a. bourgeois consciousness.
   b. false consciousness.
   c. class consciousness.
   d. caste consciousness.

3. Which of the following were viewed by Max Weber as analytically distinct components of stratification?
   a. conformity, deviance, and social control
   b. class, status, and power
   c. class, caste, and age
   d. class, prestige, and esteem

4. Which sociological perspective argues that stratification is universal and that social inequality is necessary so that people will be motivated to fill socially important positions?
   a. the functionalist perspective
   b. the conflict perspective
   c. the interactionist perspective
   d. the labeling perspective

5. British sociologist Ralf Dahrendorf views social classes as groups of people who share common interests resulting from their authority relationships. Dahrendorf's ideology aligns best with which theoretical perspective?

    a. the functionalist perspective

    b. the conflict perspective

    c. the interactionist perspective

    d. sociocultural evolution

6. The respect or admiration that an occupation holds in a society is referred to as

    a. status.

    b. esteem.

    c. prestige.

    d. ranking.

7. Approximately how many out of every nine people in the United States live(s) below the poverty line established by the federal government?

    a. one

    b. two

    c. three

    d. four

8. Which sociologist has applied functionalist analysis to the existence of poverty and argues that various segments of society actually benefit from the existence of the poor?

    a. Émile Durkheim

    b. Max Weber

    c. Karl Marx

    d. Herbert Gans

9. A measure of social class that is based on income, education, and occupation is known as

    a. the objective method.

    b. stratification.

    c. socioeconomic status.

    d. the open system.

10. A plumber whose father was a physician is an example of

    a. downward intergenerational mobility.

    b. upward intergenerational mobility.

    c. downward intragenerational mobility.

    d. upward intragenerational mobility.

11. _____ is the most extreme form of legalized social inequality for individuals or groups.

12. In the _____ system of stratification, or feudalism, peasants were required to work land leased to them by nobles in exchange for military protection and other services.

13. Karl Marx viewed _____ differentiation as the crucial determinant of social, economic, and political inequality.

14. _____ _____ is the term Thorstein Veblen used to describe the extravagant spending patterns of those at the top of the class hierarchy.

15. _____ poverty is the minimum level of subsistence that no family should be expected to live below.

16. _____ poverty is a floating standard of deprivation by which people at the bottom of a society, whatever their lifestyles, are judged to be disadvantaged in comparison with the nation as a whole.

17. Sociologist William Julius Wilson and other social scientists have used the term _____ to describe the long-term poor who lack training and skills.

18. Max Weber used the term _____ _____ to refer to people's opportunities to provide themselves with material goods, positive living conditions, and favorable life experiences.

19. An open class system implies that the position of each individual is influenced by the person's _____ status.

20. _____ mobility involves changes in social position within a person's adult life.

THINKING ABOUT MOVIES

The Fighter

Two working-class brothers strive for upward mobility in the world of professional boxing.

Pursuit of Happyness

A homeless man struggles to climb out of the underclass and make a life for his son.

Titanic

Social class pervades this story of two lovers on the ill-fated luxury liner.

In Trinidad, Bolivia, open drains threaten children's health. Bolivia is a highly stratified society in which a significant portion of the population lives in poverty.

Global Inequality

THE BOTTOM BILLION

Why the Poorest Countries Are Failing
and What Can Be Done About It

"Set to become a classic." —*The Economist*

PAUL COLLIER

66 The third world has shrunk. For forty years the development challenge has been a rich world of one billion people facing a poor world of five billion people.... By 2015, however, it will be apparent that this way of conceptualizing development has become outdated. Most of the five billion, about 80 percent, live in countries that are indeed developing, often at amazing speed. The real challenge of development is that there is a group of countries at the bottom that are falling behind, and often falling apart.

The countries at the bottom coexist with the twenty-first century, but their reality is the fourteenth century: civil war, plague, ignorance. They are concentrated in Africa and Central Asia, with a scattering elsewhere. Even during the 1990s, in retrospect the golden decade between the end of the Cold War and 9/11, incomes in this group declined by 5 percent. We must learn to turn the familiar numbers upside down: a total of five billion people who are already prosperous, or at least are on track to be so, and one billion who are stuck at the bottom.

This problem matters, and not just to the billion people who are living and dying in fourteenth-century conditions. It matters to us.

The twenty-first-century world of material comfort, global travel, and economic interdependence will become increasingly vulnerable to these large islands of chaos. And it matters now. As the bottom billion diverges from an increasingly sophisticated world economy, integration will become harder, not easier.

And yet it is a problem denied, both by development *biz* and by development *buzz*. Development biz is run by the aid agencies and the companies that get the contracts for their projects. They will fight this thesis with the tenacity of bureaucracies endangered, because they like things the way they are. A definition of development that encompasses five billion people gives them license to be everywhere, or more honestly, everywhere but the bottom billion. At the bottom, conditions are rather rough. Every development agency has difficulty getting its staff to serve in Chad and Laos; the glamour postings are for countries such as Brazil and China. The World Bank has large offices in every major middle-income country but not a single person resident in the Central African Republic. . . .

What of the governments of the countries at the bottom? The prevailing conditions bring out extremes. Leaders are sometimes psychopaths who have shot their way to power, sometimes crooks who have bought it, and sometimes brave people who, against the odds, are trying to build a better future. Even the appearance of modern government in these states is sometimes a façade, . . . the government of Somalia continued to be officially "represented" in the international arena for years after Somalia ceased to have a functioning government in the country itself. So don't expect the governments of the bottom billion to unite in formulating a practical agenda. 99

The real challenge of development is that there is a group of countries at the bottom that are falling behind, and often falling apart.

(Collier 2007:3–5) Additional information about this excerpt can be found on the Online Learning Center at www.mhhe.com/schaefer13e.

How should we help the poor—not just a poor household or a poor neighborhood, but hundreds of millions of the world's poorest people? For most of his adult life, Paul Collier, an economist at Oxford University, has pondered this question. In this excerpt from his book *The Bottom Billion: Why the Poorest Countries Are Failing and What Can Be Done About It*, Collier outlines the magnitude of the challenge. He thinks that the answer lies in avoiding the traps that developing countries often fall into: wasteful depletion of their natural resources, ineffective government, prolonged internal conflict, protracted wars, and insufficient economic development.

In this chapter we will consider social inequality both *between* developing and developed nations and *within* them. Inequality exists within all countries, not just in the United States. Even in the poorest countries, Collier writes, the very wealthy rub shoulders with the very poor.

What economic and political conditions explain the divide between rich nations and poor? Within developing nations, how are wealth and income distributed, and how much opportunity does the average worker have to move up the social ladder? How do race and gender affect social mobility in these countries? In this chapter we will focus on global inequality, beginning with the global divide. We will consider the impact of colonialism and neocolonialism, globalization, the rise of multinational corporations, and the trend toward modernization. Then we will focus on stratification within nations, in terms of the distribution of wealth and income as well as social mobility. In a special case study, we will look closely at social stratification in Mexico, including the social impact of race and gender and the economic effects of industrialization. The chapter closes with a Social Policy section on welfare reform in Europe and North America.

The Global Divide

FIGURE **10-1** FUNDAMENTAL GLOBAL INEQUALITY 215

Global Inequality

In some parts of the world, the people who have dedicated their lives to fighting starvation refer to what they call "coping mechanisms"—ways in which the desperately poor attempt to control their hunger. Eritrean women will strap flat stones to their stomachs to lessen their hunger pangs. In Mozambique, people eat the grasshoppers that have destroyed their crops, calling them "flying shrimp." Though dirt eating is considered a pathological condition (called *pica*) among the well-fed, the world's poor eat dirt to add minerals to their diet. And in many countries, mothers have been known to boil stones in water, to convince their hungry children that supper is almost ready. As they hover over the pot, these women hope that their malnourished children will fall asleep (McNeil 2004).

Around the world, inequality is a significant determinant of human behavior, opening doors of opportunity to some and closing them to others. Indeed, disparities in life chances are so extreme that in some places, the poorest of the poor may not be aware of them. Western media images may have circled the globe, but in extremely depressed rural areas, those at the bottom of society are not likely to see them.

A few centuries ago, such vast divides in global wealth did not exist. Except for a very few rulers and landowners, everyone in the world was poor. In much of Europe, life was as difficult as it was in Asia or South America. This was true until the Industrial Revolution and rising agricultural productivity produced explosive economic growth. The resulting rise in living standards was not evenly distributed across the world.

Figure 10-1 compares the industrialized nations of the world to the developing nations. Using total population as a yardstick, we see that the developing countries have more than their fair share of rural population, as well as of total births, disease, and childhood deaths. At the same time, the industrialized nations of the world, with a much smaller share of total population, have much more income and exports than the developing nations. Industrialized nations also spend more on health and the military than other nations, and they emit more carbon dioxide (CO_2; Sachs 2005; Sutcliffe 2002).

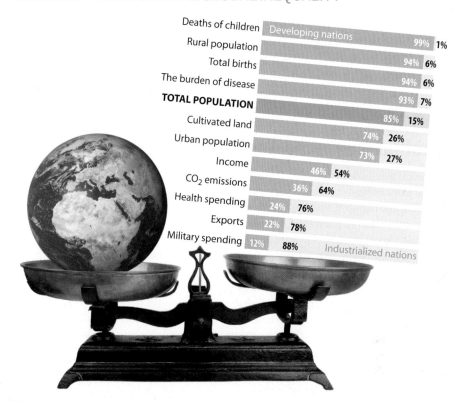

Note: In this comparison, industrialized nations include the United States and Canada, Japan, western Europe, and Australasia. Developing nations include Africa, Asia (except for Japan), Latin America, eastern Europe, the Caribbean, and the Pacific.
Source: Adapted from Sutcliffe 2002:18.

Think about It

What is the relationship between health spending, disease, and deaths of children? Between CO_2 emissions, income, and exports?

What do we stand in line for? People's needs and desires differ dramatically depending on where they live. On the left, eager customers line up outside a store in New York City to purchase the newly released version of X-Box 360. On the right, residents of Ethiopia line up to receive water.

Stratification in the World System

Although the divide between industrialized and developing nations is sharp, sociologists recognize a continuum of nations, from the richest of the rich to the poorest of the poor. For example, in 2008, the average value of goods and services produced per citizen (or per capita gross national income) in the industrialized countries of the United States, the Netherlands, Switzerland, France, and Norway was more than $47,000. In at least 39 poorer countries, the value was just $1,000 or less. However, most countries fell somewhere between those extremes, as Figure 10-2 shows.

Still, the contrasts are stark. Three forces discussed here are particularly responsible for the domination of the world marketplace by a few nations: the legacy of colonialism, the advent of multinational corporations, and modernization.

The Legacy of Colonialism

Colonialism occurs when a foreign power maintains political, social, economic, and cultural domination over a people for an extended period. In simple terms, it is rule by outsiders. The long reign of the British Empire over much of North America, parts of Africa, and India was an example of colonial domination. The same can be said of French rule over Algeria, Tunisia, and other parts of North Africa. Relations between the colonial nation and colonized people are similar to those between the dominant capitalist class and the proletariat, as described by Karl Marx.

By the 1980s, colonialism had largely disappeared. Most of the nations that were colonies before World War I had achieved political independence and established their own governments. However, for many of those countries, the transition to genuine self-rule was not yet complete. Colonial domination had established patterns of economic exploitation that continued even after nationhood was achieved—in part because former colonies were unable to develop their own industry and technology. Their dependence on more industrialized nations, including their former colonial masters, for managerial and technical expertise, investment capital, and manufactured goods kept former colonies in a subservient position. Such continuing dependence and foreign domination are referred to as **neocolonialism.**

The economic and political consequences of colonialism and neocolonialism are readily apparent. Drawing on the conflict perspective, sociologist Immanuel Wallerstein (1974, 1979a, 2000) views the global economic system as being divided between nations that control wealth and nations from which resources are taken. Through his **world systems analysis,** Wallerstein has described the unequal economic and political relationships in which certain industrialized nations (among them the United States, Japan, and Germany) and their global corporations dominate the *core* of this system (Figure 10-3, page 218). At the *semiperiphery* of the system are countries with marginal economic status, such as Israel, Ireland, and South Korea. Wallerstein suggests that the poor developing countries of Asia, Africa, and Latin America are on the *periphery* of the world economic system. The key to Wallerstein's macro-level analysis is the exploitative relationship of *core* nations toward *noncore* nations. Core nations and their corporations control and exploit noncore nations' economies. Unlike other nations, they are relatively independent of outside control (Chase-Dunn and Grimes 1995).

The division between core and periphery nations is significant and remarkably stable. A study by the International Monetary Fund (2000) found little change over the course of the *past 100 years* for the 42 economies that were studied. The only changes were Japan's movement up into the group of core nations and China's movement down toward the margins of the semiperiphery nations. Yet Immanuel Wallerstein (2000) speculates that the world system as we currently understand it may soon undergo unpredictable changes. The world is becoming increasingly urbanized, a trend that is gradually eliminating the large pools of low-cost workers in rural areas. In the future, core nations will have to find other ways to reduce their labor costs. Exhaustion of land and water resources through clear-cutting and pollution is also driving up the costs of production.

Wallerstein's world systems analysis is the most widely used version of **dependency theory.** According to this macro-level theory, even as developing countries make economic advances, they remain weak and subservient to core nations and corporations in an increasingly intertwined global

Feeding the World

As we saw in the last chapter, life chances are the opportunities (or lack of them) individuals have to improve their quality of life. One of the most basic life chances—and a growing concern around the world—is the opportunity to eat an adequate amount of food. For years, food prices have been rising, a trend that is expected to continue. Bad weather, poor crop yields, and the high cost of fuel have always affected the price of food. Now, production of biofuels like ethanol is reducing the supply of grain that is available for human consumption. Moreover, as incomes have risen in developing countries like China and India, people's dietary preferences have begun to shift from the relatively inexpensive cereals to pricier meat and vegetables. These environmental and economic pressures have reduced the amount of food available for distribution to the malnourished and starving.

Although worldwide, population growth is slowing, the outlook is far from rosy. Farmers may be able to feed the world for the foreseeable future, but charities and government organizations are falling behind in their efforts to distribute food fairly and to eliminate waste. Today, as the world's population passes the seven-billion mark, finding adequate food is becoming more—not less—of a challenge for more and more people.

MAPPING LIFE WORLDWIDE

FIGURE 10-2   GROSS NATIONAL INCOME PER CAPITA

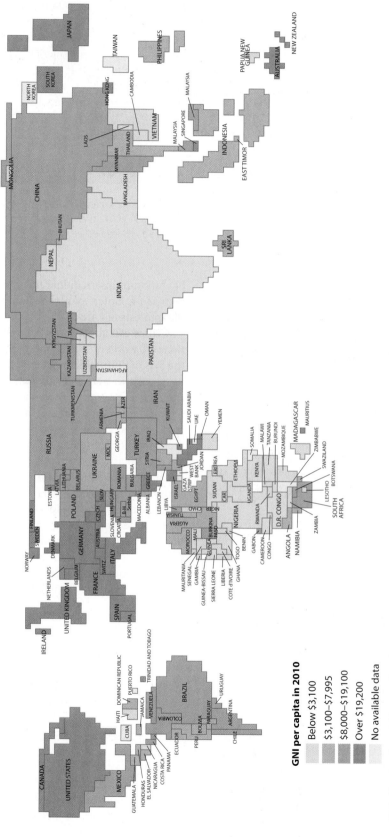

GNI per capita in 2010

- Below $3,100
- $3,100–$7,995
- $8,000–$19,100
- Over $19,200
- No available data

Note: Country sizes and incomes based on 2010 estimates. Includes only those countries with 3 million or more people.
Sources: Haub 2010; Weeks 2012.

This stylized map reflects the relative population sizes of the world's nations. The color for each country shows the gross national income (the total value of goods and services produced by the nation in a given year) per capita.

218 economy. This interdependency allows industrialized nations to continue to exploit developing countries. In a sense, dependency theory applies the conflict perspective on a global scale.

In the view of world systems analysts and dependency theorists, a growing share of the human and natural resources of developing countries is being redistributed to the core industrialized nations. This redistribution happens in part because developing countries owe huge sums of money to industrialized nations as a result of foreign aid, loans, and trade deficits. The global debt crisis has intensified the Third World dependency begun under colonialism, neocolonialism, and multinational investment. International financial institutions are pressuring indebted countries to take severe measures to meet their interest payments. The result is that developing nations may be forced to devalue their currencies, freeze workers' wages, increase the privatization of industry, and reduce government services and employment.

Closely related to these problems is **globalization,** the worldwide integration of government policies, cultures, social movements, and financial markets through trade and the exchange of ideas. Because world financial markets transcend governance by conventional nation-states, international organizations such as the World Bank and the International Monetary Fund have emerged as major players in the global economy. The function of these institutions, which are heavily funded and influenced by core nations, is to encourage economic trade and development and to ensure the smooth

In a factory in China, workers assemble toys for export to the United States. The pitfalls of globalization were brought home—literally—to U.S. consumers in 2007, when U.S. companies were forced to recall toys manufactured in China because they were finished with lead-based paint.

operation of international financial markets. As such, they are seen as promoters of globalization and defenders primarily of the interests of core nations.

Critics call attention to a variety of issues, including violations of workers' rights, the destruction of the environment, the loss of cultural identity, and discrimination against minority groups in periphery nations. The impact of globalization appears to be most problematic for developing countries in Latin America and Africa. In Asia, developing nations seem to do better. Foreign investment there involves the high-tech sector, which produces more sustainable economic growth (Kerbo 2006). Even there, however, globalization definitely has not reduced income disparities, either between nations or within countries (Box 10-1).

Some observers see globalization and its effects as the natural result of advances in communications technology, particularly the Internet and worldwide transmission of the mass media. Others view it more critically, as a process that allows multinational corporations to expand unchecked, as we will see in the next section (Chase-Dunn et al. 2000).

FIGURE **10-3** WORLD SYSTEMS ANALYSIS

Core	Semiperiphery	Periphery
Canada	China	Afghanistan
France	India	Bolivia
Germany	Ireland	Chad
Japan	Mexico	Dominican Republic
United Kingdom	Pakistan	Egypt
United States	Panama	Haiti
		Philippines
		Vietnam

Note: Figure shows only a partial listing of countries, selected by the author.

use your sociological *imagination*

You are traveling through a developing country. What evidence do you see of neocolonialism and globalization?

Multinational Corporations

Worldwide, corporate giants play a key role in neocolonialism. The term **multinational corporations** refers to commercial organizations that are headquartered in one country but do business throughout the world. Such private trade and lending relationships are not new; merchants have conducted business abroad for hundreds of years, trading gems, spices, garments, and other goods. However, today's multinational giants are not

SOCIOLOGY IN THE GLOBAL COMMUNITY

10-1 Income Inequality: A Global Perspective

Just how do incomes compare across the globe? Within nations? Sociologists Roberto Korzeniewicz and Timothy Moran faced these questions head-on and obtained some dramatic answers.

To simplify the task of comparing incomes across billions of people, the two researchers divided residents of each country into 10 deciles, or groups of 10 percent, based on per capita incomes. Then they ranked each set of deciles from the highest (Decile 10) to the lowest (Decile 1). Finally, they did the same for the world as a whole, dividing the world's population into deciles based on income.

Korzeniewicz and Moran found that in Norway and Switzerland, members of Decile 10 made slightly more income than members of the same decile in Denmark, Canada, and Germany. Outside Europe and North America, however, inequality became more apparent, both between and within nations. In the United States, members of Decile 4—that is, those people with incomes in the bottom 31 to 40 percent—fell within the top decile for the world as a whole. In the United States (or Germany or France, for that matter), members of Decile 4 were better off than members of Decile 10 in Brazil, Malaysia, Poland, and Russia.

You might think you would rather be in the richest decile in Poland than the seventh richest decile in the United States. However, in Poland an engineer or doctor may earn a salary equivalent to a factory worker's salary in the United States. Although the Polish professor may enjoy a relatively high status, he or she may not be able to afford to own a home or to go away on vacation. Similarly, the average income of a food service worker in Decile 2 in the United States

> *The American Pet Products Manufacturers Association estimates the average annual expenditure on a dog in the United States at around $1,400—a figure comparable to human incomes in nations like Paraguay and Egypt.*

may exceed the earnings of a middle-class worker in China, Romania, or Mexico. From the perspective of a U.S. resident, income inequality within the nation may be sharp, but from a global perspective it is not nearly as dramatic as income inequality in a world where hundreds of millions of people struggle just to survive.

The degree of global inequality becomes even more apparent if we compare the resources consumed by dogs in the United States to the incomes of people around the world. The American Pet Products Manufacturers Association estimates the average annual expenditure on a dog in the United States at around $1,400—a figure comparable to human incomes in nations like Paraguay and Egypt. U.S. dogs, in fact, are better off than 40 percent of the world's people. Their health care expenditures alone exceed those of 80 percent of the world's humans.

LET'S DISCUSS

1. Does your family have a pet? If so, how much money do you think you spend on your pet every year? How does that figure compare to the average annual income in China or India?
2. By itself, do you think Korzeniewicz and Moran's income-based measure is a sufficient indicator of global inequality? If not, what other kinds of information would you want to consider?

Sources: Korzeniewicz and Moran 2009; Therborn 2010.

---

merely buying and selling overseas; they are also *producing* goods all over the world (Wallerstein 1974).

Moreover, today's "global factories" (factories throughout the developing world that are run by multinational corporations) may soon have the "global office" sitting alongside them. Multinationals based in core countries are beginning to establish reservation services and centers for processing data and insurance claims in periphery nations. As service industries become a more important part of the international marketplace, many companies are concluding that the low costs of overseas operations more than offset the expense of transmitting information around the world.

Do not underestimate the size of these global corporations. As Figure 10-4 shows, the total revenues of multinational businesses are on a par with the total value of goods and services exchanged in *entire nations*. Foreign sales represent an important source of profit for multinational corporations, which are constantly seeking to expand into other countries (in many cases, developing nations). The economy of the United States depends heavily on foreign commerce, much of which is conducted by multinationals. Over 10 percent of all goods and

services produced in the United States relates to the export of goods to foreign countries, which accounts for 20 percent of the nation's annual growth (U.S. Trade Representative 2007).

Functionalist View Functionalists believe that multinational corporations can actually help the developing nations of the world. They bring jobs and industry to areas where subsistence agriculture once served as the only means of survival. Multinationals also promote rapid development through the diffusion of inventions and innovations from industrialized nations. Viewed from a functionalist perspective, the combination of skilled technology and management provided by multinationals and the relatively cheap labor available in developing nations is ideal for a global enterprise. Multinationals can take maximum advantage of technology while reducing costs and boosting profits.

Through their international ties, multinational corporations also make the nations of the world more interdependent. These ties may prevent certain disputes from reaching the point of serious conflict. A country cannot afford to sever diplomatic relations or engage in warfare with a nation that is the headquarters for its main business suppliers or a key outlet for its exports.

219

FIGURE **10-4** MULTINATIONAL CORPORATIONS COMPARED TO NATIONS

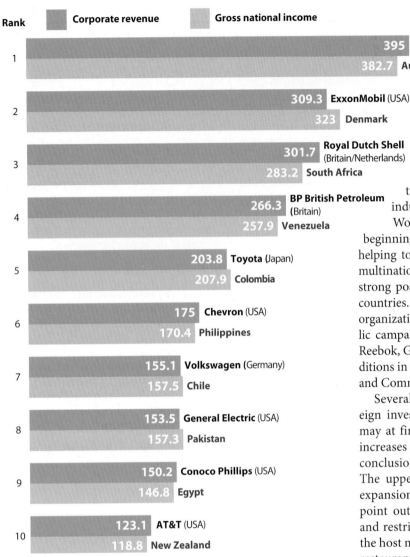

Rank		
	■ **Corporate revenue**	■ **Gross national income**

1 — 395 **Walmart** (USA) / 382.7 **Austria**
2 — 309.3 **ExxonMobil** (USA) / 323 **Denmark**
3 — 301.7 **Royal Dutch Shell** (Britain/Netherlands) / 283.2 **South Africa**
4 — 266.3 **BP British Petroleum** (Britain) / 257.9 **Venezuela**
5 — 203.8 **Toyota** (Japan) / 207.9 **Colombia**
6 — 175 **Chevron** (USA) / 170.4 **Philippines**
7 — 155.1 **Volkswagen** (Germany) / 157.5 **Chile**
8 — 153.5 **General Electric** (USA) / 157.3 **Pakistan**
9 — 150.2 **Conoco Phillips** (USA) / 146.8 **Egypt**
10 — 123.1 **AT&T** (USA) / 118.8 **New Zealand**

Sources: Ranking prepared by author. Revenue from corporate quarterly report statements (Q2 2009 through Q2 2010). GNI from World Bank 2010a:32–34.

Think about It
What happens to society when corporations grow richer than countries and spill across international borders?

conditions, but governments seeking to attract or keep multinationals may develop a "climate for investment" that includes repressive antilabor laws which restrict union activity and collective bargaining. If labor's demands become too threatening, the multinational firm will simply move its plant elsewhere, leaving a trail of unemployment behind. Nike, for example, moved its factories from the United States to Korea to Indonesia to Vietnam in search of the lowest labor costs. Conflict theorists conclude that on the whole, multinational corporations have a negative social impact on workers in *both* industrialized and developing nations.

Workers in the United States and other core countries are beginning to recognize that their own interests are served by helping to organize workers in developing nations. As long as multinationals can exploit cheap labor abroad, they will be in a strong position to reduce wages and benefits in industrialized countries. With this in mind, in the 1990s, labor unions, religious organizations, campus groups, and other activists mounted public campaigns to pressure companies such as Nike, Starbucks, Reebok, Gap, and Walmart to improve wages and working conditions in their overseas operations (Global Alliance for Workers and Communities 2003; Gonzalez 2003).

Several sociologists who have surveyed the effects of foreign investment by multinationals conclude that although it may at first contribute to a host nation's wealth, it eventually increases economic inequality within developing nations. This conclusion holds true for both income and land ownership. The upper and middle classes benefit most from economic expansion; the lower classes benefit least. As conflict theorists point out, multinationals invest in limited economic sectors and restricted regions of a nation. Although certain sectors of the host nation's economy expand, such as hotels and expensive restaurants, their very expansion appears to retard growth in agriculture and other economic sectors. Moreover, multinational corporations often buy out or force out local entrepreneurs and companies, thereby increasing economic and cultural dependence (Chase-Dunn and Grimes 1995; Kerbo 2009; Wallerstein 1979b).

Conflict View Conflict theorists challenge this favorable evaluation of the impact of multinational corporations. They emphasize that multinationals exploit local workers to maximize profits. Starbucks—the international coffee retailer based in Seattle—gets some of its coffee from farms in Guatemala. But to earn enough money to buy a pound of Starbucks coffee, a Guatemalan farmworker would have to pick 500 pounds of beans, representing five days of work: see Box 1-2, page 20 (Entine and Nichols 1996).

The pool of cheap labor in the developing world prompts multinationals to move factories out of core countries. An added bonus for the multinationals is that the developing world discourages strong trade unions. In industrialized countries, organized labor insists on decent wages and humane working

use your sociological *imagination*

Think of something you bought recently that was made by a multinational corporation. How do you know the maker was a multinational?

Worldwide Poverty

In developing countries, any deterioration of the economic well-being of those who are least well off threatens their very survival. By U.S. standards, even the wealthy in the developing world are poor. Those who are poor in developing countries are truly destitute.

FIGURE **10-5** POVERTY WORLDWIDE

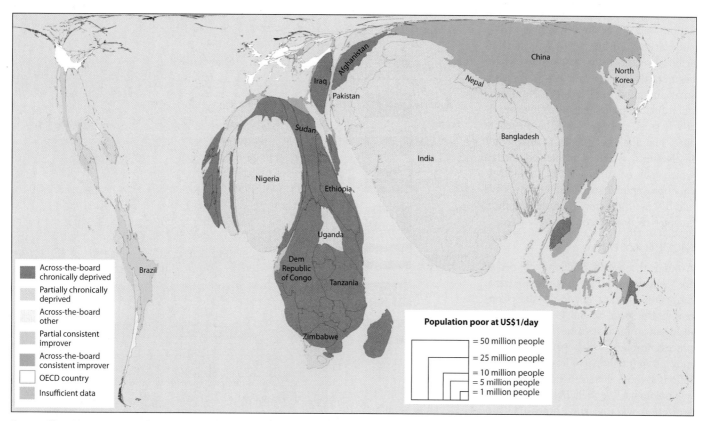

Sources: Chronic Poverty Research Centre 2009.

The scale of this map is based on the number of people in each region who are chronically poor. The colors represent the income levels of those who are poorest. In OECD countries—those that belong to the Organisation for Economic Co-Operation and Development (white)—chronic poverty is not a nationwide issue.

Think about It
To what degree does this map minimize those countries you have studied or might want to visit?
To what degree does it emphasize parts of the world about which you know very little?

What would a map of the world look like if we drew it to a scale that reflects the number of *poor* people in each country instead of the number of people, as in Figure 10-2 (page 217)? As Figure 10-5 shows, when we focus on the poverty level rather than the population, the world looks quite different. Note the huge areas of poverty in Africa and Asia, and the comparatively small areas of affluence in industrialized North America and Europe. Poverty is a worldwide problem that blights the lives of billions of people.

How do social scientists measure global poverty? As we saw in Chapter 9, there is significant disagreement over where to draw the poverty line in the United States. Adding the rest of the world to the equation further complicates the task. Individually, many developing nations define poverty based on the minimum income a person needs to survive—an amount that typically ranges from a low of $1 a day to a high of $2 a day. Zambia defines poverty in terms of the inability to afford specific foods in a subsistence diet (Oxford Poverty and Human Development Initiative 2011).

In 2000 the United Nations launched the Millennium Project, whose objective is to eliminate extreme poverty worldwide by the year 2015. Although 15 years may seem a long time, the challenge is great. Today, almost 3 billion people subsist on $2 a

day or less. To reach the project's goal, planners estimated that industrialized nations must set aside 0.51 percent of their *gross national income*—that is, the total value of a nation's goods and services (GNP), plus or minus income received from and sent to other nations—to aid developing countries (Landler and Sanger 2009; Sachs 2005; United Nations 2005).

At the time the Millennium Project was launched, only five countries were giving at that target rate: Denmark, Luxembourg, the Netherlands, Norway, and Sweden. As of 2010, the United States would need to multiply its present aid level by 150 percent to match the Millennium target of 0.51 percent of gross national income. Although in dollar terms the U.S. government delivers far more aid to foreign countries and multinational organizations than any other nation, the amount is not impressive considering the nation's tremendous wealth relative to other countries. In terms of the percentage of gross national income, the United States' contribution is among the lowest of the 22 most advanced industrialized countries, on a par with Japan's (Figure 10-6).

Direct government-to-government foreign aid is only one way of alleviating poverty, however. Although per capita aid from the U.S. government may not be strong, private spending by U.S. residents is. Individual charitable giving is much higher in the United States than in other industrialized nations.

Privileged people in industrialized nations tend to assume that the world's poor lack significant assets. Yet again and again, observers from these countries have been startled to discover how far even a small amount of capital can go. Numerous microfinance programs, which involve relatively small grants or loans, have encouraged marginalized people to invest not in livestock, which may die, or jewelry, which may be stolen, but in technological improvements such as small stoves. We will discuss this topic in greater depth in Chapter 18, on the economy.

Modernization

Around the world, millions of people are witnessing a revolutionary transformation of their day-to-day life. Contemporary social scientists use the term **modernization** to describe the far-reaching process through which periphery nations move from traditional or less developed institutions to those characteristic of more developed societies.

Sociologist Wendell Bell (1981), whose definition of modernization we are using, notes that modern societies tend to be urban, literate, and industrial. These societies have sophisticated transportation and media systems. Their families tend to be organized within the nuclear family model rather than the extended-family model (see Chapter 14). Thus, members of societies that undergo modernization must shift their allegiance from traditional authorities, such as parents and priests, to newer authorities, such as government officials.

Many sociologists are quick to note that terms such as *modernization* and even *development* contain an ethnocentric bias. The unstated assumption behind these terms is that "they" (people living in developing nations) are struggling to become more like "us" (people in core industrialized nations). Viewed from a conflict perspective, these terms perpetuate the dominant ideology of capitalist societies.

The term *modernization* also suggests positive change. Yet change, if it comes, often comes slowly, and when it does it tends to serve the affluent segments of industrialized nations. This truism seems to apply to the spread of the latest electronic technologies to the developing world (see Box 7-2 on page 145).

A similar criticism has been made of **modernization theory,** a functionalist approach that proposes that modernization and development will gradually improve the lives of people in developing nations. According to this theory, even though nations develop at uneven rates, the development of peripheral nations will be assisted by innovations transferred from the industrialized world. Critics of modernization theory, including dependency theorists, counter that any such technology transfer only increases the dominance of core nations over developing nations and facilitates further exploitation.

When we see all the Coca-Cola and IBM signs going up in developing nations, it is easy to assume that globalization and

FIGURE 10-6 FOREIGN AID PER CAPITA IN NINE COUNTRIES

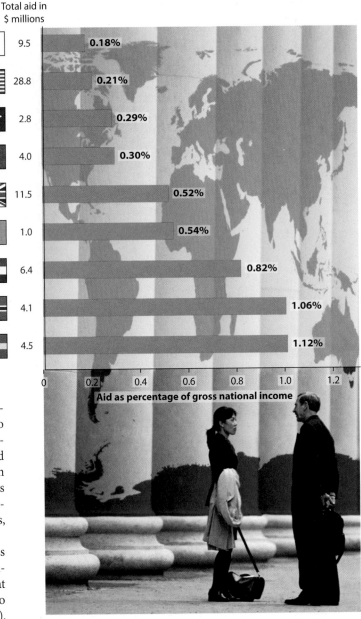

	Total aid in $ millions	
Japan	9.5	0.18%
USA	28.8	0.21%
Australia	2.8	0.29%
Canada	4.0	0.30%
Great Britain	11.5	0.52%
Ireland	1.0	0.54%
Netherlands	6.4	0.82%
Norway	4.1	1.06%
Sweden	4.5	1.12%

Aid as percentage of gross national income (0 – 1.2)

Note: Actual net development assistance in 2009.
Source: Organisation for Economic Co-operation and Development 2011:2.

economic change are effecting cultural change. But that is not always the case, researchers note. Distinctive cultural traditions, such as a particular religious orientation or a nationalistic identity, often persist and can soften the impact of modernization on a developing nation. Some contemporary sociologists emphasize that both industrialized and developing countries are "modern." Increasingly, researchers gauge modernization using a series of social indicators—among them degree of urbanization, energy use, literacy, political democracy, and use of birth control. Clearly, some of these are subjective indicators; even in industrialized nations, not everyone would agree that wider use of birth control is an example of progress (Armer and Katsillis 1992; Hedley 1992; Inglehart and Baker 2000).

Current modernization studies generally take a convergence perspective. Using the indicators just noted, researchers focus

TABLE 10-1 SOCIOLOGICAL PERSPECTIVES ON GLOBAL INEQUALITY

summing up

Approach	Sociological Perspective	Explanation
World systems analysis	Functionalist and conflict	Unequal economic and political relationships maintain sharp divisions between nations.
Dependency theory	Conflict	Industrialized nations exploit developing nations through colonialism and multinational corporations.
Modernization theory	Functionalist	Developing nations move away from traditional cultures and toward the cultures of industrialized nations.

on how societies are moving closer together, despite traditional differences. From a conflict perspective, the modernization of developing nations often perpetuates their dependence on and continued exploitation by industrialized nations. Conflict theorists view such continuing dependence on foreign powers as an example of contemporary neocolonialism.

Table 10-1 summarizes the three major approaches to global inequality.

thinking CRITICALLY

Relate modernization theory to dependency theory. Do you agree with critics that modernization will increase the dominance of core nations? Why or why not?

Where am I wearing? This UNICEF poster reminds affluent Western consumers that the brand-name jeans they wear may be produced by exploited workers in developing countries. In sweatshops throughout the developing world, non-union garment workers—some of them children—labor long hours for what we would consider extremely low wages—even if for the workers in those semiperiphery countries, those wages are relatively high.

Stratification within Nations: A Comparative Perspective

At the same time that the gap between rich and poor nations is widening, so too is the gap between rich and poor citizens *within* nations. As discussed earlier, stratification in developing nations is closely related to their relatively weak and dependent position in the global economy. Local elites work hand in hand with multinational corporations and prosper from such alliances. At the same time, the economic system creates and perpetuates the exploitation of industrial and agricultural workers. That is why foreign investment in developing countries tends to increase economic inequality. As Box 10-2 makes clear, inequality within a society is evident in Latin America's most populous nation, Brazil.

Distribution of Wealth and Income

Global inequality is staggering. Worldwide, the richest 2 percent of adults own more than 50 percent of the world's household wealth. In at least 24 nations around the world, the most affluent 10 percent of the population receives at least 40 percent of all income. The list includes the African nation of Namibia (the leader, at 65 percent of all income), as well as Colombia, Nigeria, and South Africa. Figure 10-7 on page 225 compares the distribution of income in selected industrialized and developing nations (World Bank 2010a:94–96).

use your sociological *imagination*

Imagine that the United States borders a country with a much higher standard of living. In this neighboring country, the salaries of workers with a college degree start at $120,000 a year. What is life in the United States like?

Social Mobility

Mobility in Industrial Nations Studies of intergenerational mobility in industrialized nations have found the following patterns:

1. Substantial similarities exist in the ways that parents' positions in the stratification system are transmitted to their children.

2. As in the United States, mobility opportunities in other nations have been influenced by structural factors, such as labor market changes that lead to the rise or decline of an occupational group within the social hierarchy.

3. Immigration continues to be a significant factor in shaping a society's level of intergenerational mobility.

Cross-cultural studies suggest that intergenerational mobility has been increasing over the past 50 years in most but not all countries. In particular, researchers have noted a common pattern of movement away from agriculture-based occupations. However, they are quick to point out that growth in mobility does not necessarily bring growth in equality. Indeed, despite the evidence of steady upward mobility, their studies show that

SOCIOLOGY IN THE GLOBAL COMMUNITY

10-2 Stratification in Brazil

Brazil conjures up exotic images: dazzling beaches, tropical foliage, colorful *Carnival* in Rio de Janeiro. Deep, grinding poverty and persistent inequality may not spring to mind, yet they are as much a part of South America's largest nation and economy as the expensive tourist resorts. Brazil has been described as three nations in one: a rich country with a population the size of Canada's; a poor country with a population equal to Mexico's; and a third nation of indigents—totally impoverished people with no income at all—whose population equals Argentina's.

> *As in the United States, Brazil's social inequality is compounded by racial distinctions that originated in slavery.*

Not until 1988 did Brazil's government begin to consider a redistribution of wealth or land to remedy these inequities. The resulting program did not get under way until 2003. Since then, the gap between rich and poor has narrowed only a bit.

As in the United States, Brazil's social inequality is compounded by racial distinctions that originated in slavery. However, race is not socially constructed as it is in the United States. In Brazil, unlike the United States, dark skin color has never been a measure of innate inferiority.

Still, Brazil is no racial paradise. Rather, it is a multitiered racist society, one whose government has acknowledged the existence of racism. A country that once prided itself on its freedom

INCOME BY RACE, BRAZIL AND THE UNITED STATES

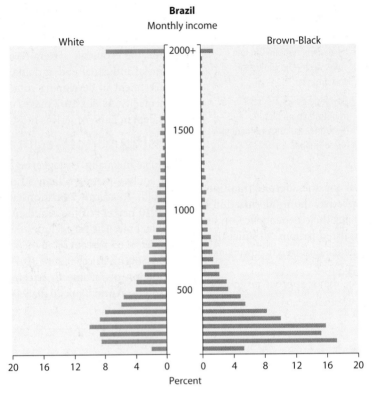

Brazil
Monthly income

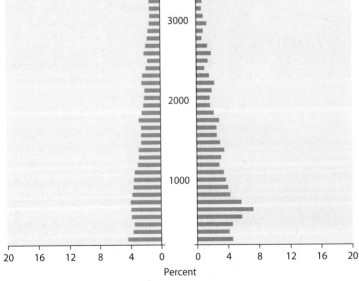

United States
Monthly income

Source: Government agencies, as reported in Telles 2004:108.

from racial intolerance, Brazil has now outlawed discrimination against people of color. Opinion is divided over the effectiveness of the legislation.

Today, the Brazilian economy shows a significant degree of racially related income disparity. As the accompanying figure shows, people of color are clustered disproportionately on the lowest levels of the income pyramid. To remedy this entrenched inequality, Brazil's government has instituted a quota-based affirmative action program that ensures access to higher education for people of color. Because of the lack of clear-cut racial categories in Brazil—Brazilians recognize many different color gradients—charges of reverse racism and complaints about inexplicable classifications have been common. As in the United States, finding solutions to the twin problems of racism and inequality is a challenge.

LET'S DISCUSS

1. Look at the bottom of each of the accompanying graphs. Which income distribution, Brazil's or the United States', appears to be more unequal? Now look at the top of each graph. Which income distribution appears to be more unequal? What aspect of these graphs do you find most striking?

2. Race-based college admissions quotas have been the subject of hot debate in the United States. Why do you think they have been accepted as law in Brazilian society?

Sources: Ash 2007; Daniel 2006; Dzidzienyo 1987; Fiola 2008; Margolis 2009; Santos 2006; SustainAbility 2006; Telles 2004.

FIGURE **10-7** DISTRIBUTION OF INCOME IN NINE NATIONS

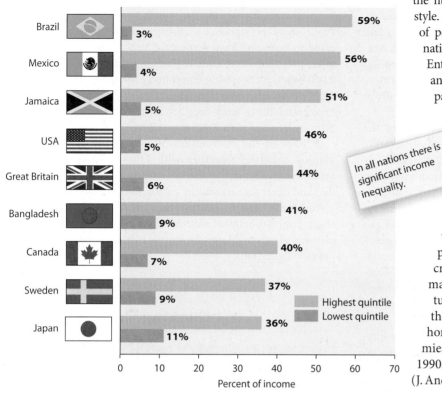

Note: Data are considered comparable although based on statistics covering 1993 to 2008.
Source: World Bank 2010a:94–96.

around the world, they have also noted some growth in the number of people who enjoy a middle-class life-style. At the beginning of the 21st century, millions of people entered the middle class in the populous nations of China, India, Russia, Brazil, and Mexico. Entrepreneurship, microfinancing, merchandising, and in some countries, a growing, relatively well-paid government sector have fostered this increase in upward social mobility (R. Adler 2008; *The Economist* 2009a).

Gender Differences in Mobility Women in developing countries find life espe-cially difficult. Karuna Chanana Ahmed, an anthropologist from India who has studied women in developing nations, calls women the most exploited of oppressed peo-ple. Beginning at birth women face sex dis-crimination. They are commonly fed less than male children, are denied educational oppor-tunities, and are often hospitalized only when they are critically ill. Inside or outside the home, women's work is devalued. When econo-mies fail, as they did in Asian countries in the late 1990s, women are the first to be laid off from work (J. Anderson and Moore 1993; Kristof 1998).

the gap between the rich and the poor has grown. Over the past 20 years, poverty levels in the 30 largest industrial economies have remained relatively constant (Organisation for Economic Co-operation and Development 2008).

Mobility in Developing Nations Mobility patterns in indus-trialized countries are usually associated with both intergenera-tional and intragenerational mobility. However, in developing nations, macro-level social and economic changes often over-shadow micro-level movement from one occupation to another. For example, there is typically a substantial wage differential between rural and urban areas, which leads to high levels of migration to the cities. Yet the urban industrial sectors of devel-oping countries generally cannot provide sufficient employment for all those seeking work.

In large developing nations, the most socially significant mobility is the movement out of poverty. This type of mobil-ity is difficult to measure and confirm, however, because eco-nomic trends can differ from one area of a country to another. For instance, China's rapid income growth has been accompa-nied by a growing disparity in income between urban and rural areas and among different regions. Similarly, in India during the 1990s, poverty declined in urban areas but may have remained static at best in rural areas. Around the world, downward social mobility is also dramatically influenced by catastrophes such as crop failure and warfare.

Despite the continuing struggles of massive numbers of peo-ple, the global economic situation is not entirely bleak. Although economists have documented the stubborn persistence of poverty

In developing countries, people who hope to rise out of poverty often move from the country to the city, where employment prospects are better. The jobs available in industrialized urban areas offer perhaps the best means of upward mobility. This woman works in an electronics factory in Kuala Lumpur, Malaysia.

Surveys show a significant degree of *female infanticide* (the killing of baby girls) in China and rural areas of India. Only one-third of Pakistan's sexually segregated schools are for women, and one-third of those schools have no buildings. In Kenya and Tanzania, it is illegal for a woman to own a house. In Saudi Arabia, women are prohibited from driving, walking alone in public, and socializing with men outside their families. We will explore women's second-class status throughout the world more fully in Chapter 12.

Only recently have researchers begun to investigate the impact of gender on the mobility patterns of developing nations. Many aspects of the development process—especially modernization in rural areas and the rural-to-urban migration just described—may result in the modification or abandonment of traditional cultural practices and even marital systems. The effects on women's social standing and mobility are not necessarily positive. As a country develops and modernizes, women's vital role in food production deteriorates, jeopardizing both their autonomy and their material well-being. Moreover, the movement of families to the cities weakens women's ties to relatives who can provide food, financial assistance, and social support (Lawson 2008).

In the Philippines, however, women have moved to the forefront of the indigenous peoples' struggle to protect their ancestral land from exploitation by outsiders. Having established their right to its rich minerals and forests, members of indigenous groups had begun to feud among themselves over the way in which the land's resources should be developed. Aided by the United Nations Partners in Development Programme, women volunteers established the Pan-Cordillera Women's Network for Peace and Development, a coalition of women's groups dedicated to resolving local disputes. The women mapped boundaries, prepared development plans, and negotiated more than 2,000 peace pacts among community members. They have also run in elections, campaigned against social problems, and organized residents to work together for the common good (United Nations Development Programme 2000:87).

Studies of the distribution of wealth and income within various countries, together with cross-cultural research on mobility, consistently reveal stratification based on class, gender, and other factors within a wide range of societies. Clearly, a worldwide view of stratification must include not only the sharp contrast *between* wealthy and impoverished nations but also the layers of hierarchy *within* industrialized nations and developing nations.

thinking CRITICALLY

Contrast social mobility in developing and industrialized nations. Do you think the differences will eventually disappear? Why or why not?

casestudy Stratification in Mexico

In the period since 1994, when the United States began beefing up patrols along the 2,000-mile border with Mexico, more than 6,000 Mexicans—about 1 every 24 hours—died attempting to cross the border illegally (Jimenez 2009). Why do Mexicans risk their lives crossing the dangerous desert that lies between the two countries? The answer to this question can be found in the income disparity between the two nations—one an industrial giant and the other a partially developed country still recovering from a history of colonialism and neocolonialism. In this section we will look in some detail at the dynamics of stratification in Mexico, a country of 108 million people. Since the early 20th century there has been a close cultural, economic, and political relationship between Mexico and the United States, one in which the United States is the dominant party. According to Immanuel Wallerstein's analysis, the United States is at the core while neighboring Mexico is still on the semiperiphery of the world economic system.

Mexico's Economy

Although the faltering U.S. economy is no longer a magnet for foreigners seeking work, Mexico's economy has faltered even more. Many out-of-work Mexicans have begun to return home from the United States, increasing the ranks of the unemployed in Mexico. Those who remain in the United States are less likely than they once were to send money back to their families in Mexico (Jordan 2009).

Although Mexico is unquestionably a poor country, the gap between its richest and poorest citizens is one of the widest in the world (refer back to Figure 10-7 on page 225). The World Bank reports that in 2008, 8.2 percent of Mexico's population survived on $2 per day. At the same time, the wealthiest 10 percent of Mexico's people accounted for 41 percent of the entire nation's income. According to *Forbes* magazine's 2010 portrait of the world's wealthiest individuals, that year Mexico was home to the wealthiest person in the world, telecom tycoon Carlos Slim Helu, worth $53.5 billion. *Forbes'* story also mentioned many other Mexicans who had become wealthy through banking, mining, and retail merchandising ventures (Kroll and Miller 2010; World Bank 2010a:90, 95).

Political scientist Jorge Castañeda (1995:71) calls Mexico a "polarized society with enormous gaps between rich and poor, town and country, north and south, white and brown (or *criollos* and *mestizos*)." He adds that the country is also divided along lines of class, race, religion, gender, and age. We will examine stratification within Mexico by focusing on race relations and the plight of Mexican Indians; the status of Mexican women; and emigration to the United States and its impact on the U.S.–Mexican borderlands.

A gardener tends the grounds at the opulent Hacienda Temozon hotel in Yucatán State, near Mérida, Mexico. Although international tourism is a major industry in Mexico, most Mexicans have not benefited much from it. Hotel workers earn low wages, and their jobs are jeopardized by the travel industry's frequent boom and bust cycles.

The Status of Women in Mexico

In 1975, Mexico City hosted the first international conference on the status of women, convened by the United Nations. Much of the discussion concerned the status of women in developing countries; in that regard, the situation is mixed. Women now constitute 46 percent of the labor force—an increase from 34 percent in 1980, but still less than in industrialized countries. Unfortunately, Mexican women are even more mired in the lowest-paying jobs than their counterparts in industrialized nations (Bureau of the Census 2009a).

Feminist sociologists emphasize that even when Mexican women work outside the home, they often are not recognized as active and productive household members, whereas men are typically viewed as heads of the household. As one consequence, women find it difficult to obtain credit and technical assistance in many parts of the country, and to inherit land in rural areas. Within manufacturing and service industries, women generally receive little training and tend to work in the least-automated and least-skilled jobs—in good part because there is little expectation that women will pursue career advancement, organize for better working conditions, or become active in labor unions.

In recent decades, Mexican women have begun to organize to address an array of economic, political, and health issues. Since women continue to serve as the household managers for their families, even when they work outside the home, they are well aware of the consequences of the inadequate public services in lower-income urban neighborhoods. In Mexico's cities, they have organized to improve the quality of water service. And because women are often victimized by criminals on public transport, they have pioneered "pink taxis," women-only buses, and women-only spaces in the subway (Bennett et al. 2005; Llana 2009).

The Borderlands

Growing recognition of the borderlands reflects the increasingly close and complex relationship between Mexico and the United States. The term **borderlands** refers to the area of common culture along the border between these two countries. Legal and illegal emigration from Mexico to the United States, day laborers crossing the border regularly to go to jobs in the United States, the implementation of the North American Free Trade Agreement (NAFTA), and the exchange of media across the border all make the notion of separate Mexican and U.S. cultures obsolete in the borderlands.

The economic position of the borderlands is rather complicated, as we can see in the emergence of *maquiladoras* on the Mexican side (Figure 10-8). These are foreign-owned factories established just across the border in Mexico, where the companies that own them do not have to pay taxes or provide insurance and benefits to workers. The *maquiladoras* have attracted manufacturing jobs from other parts of North America to Mexico. However, they are now experiencing the same challenge from global trade as U.S. manufacturing plants. Beginning in 2001, some companies

Race Relations in Mexico: The Color Hierarchy

Mexico's indigenous Indians account for an estimated 14 percent of the nation's population. More than 90 percent of them live in houses without sewers, compared with 21 percent of the population as a whole. And whereas just 10 percent of Mexican adults are illiterate, the proportion for Mexican Indians is 44 percent (Boudreaux 2002; *The Economist* 2004; G. Thompson 2001).

The subordinate status of Mexico's Indians is but one reflection of the nation's color hierarchy, which links social class to the appearance of racial purity. At the top of this hierarchy are the *criollos*, the 10 percent of the population who are typically White, well-educated members of the business and intellectual elites, with familial roots in Spain. In the middle is the large, impoverished *mestizo* majority, most of whom have brown skin and a mixed racial lineage as a result of intermarriage. At the bottom of the color hierarchy are the destitute, full-blooded Mexican Indian minority and a small number of Blacks, some descended from 200,000 African slaves brought to Mexico. This color hierarchy is an important part of day-to-day life—enough so that some Mexicans in the cities use hair dyes, skin lighteners, and blue or green contact lenses to appear White and European. Ironically, however, nearly all Mexicans are considered part Indian because of centuries of intermarriage (Castañeda 1995; Stahler-Sholk 2008).

Many observers take note of widespread denial of prejudice and discrimination against people of color in Mexico. Schoolchildren are taught that the election of Benito Juárez, a Zapotec Indian, as president of Mexico in the 19th century proves that all Mexicans are equal. Yet there has been a marked growth in the past decade of formal organizations and voluntary associations representing indigenous Indians (Escárcega 2008; Muñoz 2008).

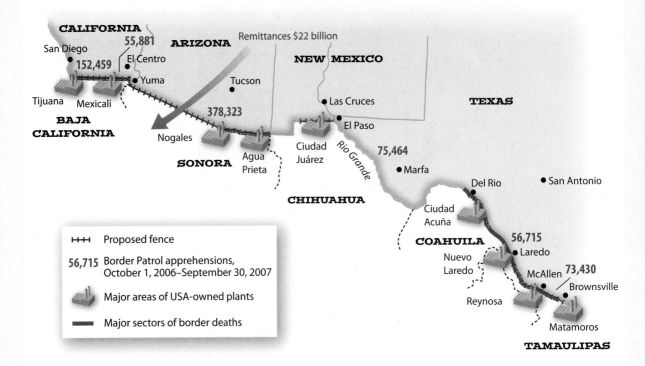

Source: Prepared by the author based on Archibold and Preston 2008; Department of Homeland Security 2008; Marosi 2007; and Ratha et al. 2010.

Maquiladoras located just south of the U.S.–Mexican border employ Mexican workers at wages far lower than those earned by U.S. workers. In search of higher wages, undocumented Mexicans often attempt to cross the border illegally, risking their lives in the process. Mexicans who do reach the United States send large amounts of money, called remittances, back to family in Mexican communities.

Think about It
Do U.S. consumers benefit from the buildup of factories along the U.S.–Mexican border? How or how not?

began shifting their operations to China. While Mexican labor costs (wages plus benefits) are just $3 an hour, Chinese labor costs are even lower—72 cents an hour. Of the 700,000 new *maquiladora* jobs created by NAFTA, 43 percent were eliminated between 2000 and 2003 (Cañas et al. 2007).

The social impact of emigration to the United States is felt throughout Mexico. According to sociological research, the earliest emigrants were typically married men of working age who came from the middle of the stratification system. They had enough financial resources to afford the costs and risks of emigration, yet were experiencing enough financial strain that entering the United States was attractive to them. Over time, kinship ties to migrants multiplied and emigration became less class-selective, with entire families making the trek to the United States. More recently, the occupational backgrounds of Mexican emigrants have widened further, reflecting not only changes in U.S. immigration policy but the continuing crisis in the Mexican economy as well (Massey 1998, 2008).

Many Mexicans who have come to the United States send some part of their earnings back across the border to family members still in Mexico. This substantial flow of money, sometimes referred to as **remittances** or *migradollars,* is estimated at a minimum of $22 billion a year and is surpassed only by oil as a source of income. If these funds went solely into the purchase of consumer goods, they would underscore the view of dependency theory, that Mexico's economy is little more than an extension of the economy of the United States. In fact, however, some of these migradollars are used by Mexicans to establish and maintain small business enterprises, such as handicraft workshops and farms. Consequently, the transfer of migradollars does stimulate the local and national economies of Mexico (Ratha et al. 2010).

We have seen that inequality is a problem not just in Mexico, but throughout the world. We turn now to a comparison of the welfare systems that countries have established to help those at the bottom of the social ladder.

thinking CRITICALLY

How do the borderlands increase social mobility within Mexico? How do they hinder it?

Rethinking Welfare in Europe and North America

In Pasadena, Denise Sims-Bowles, who has been out of work for more than two years, has sent 273 résumés to prospective employers. A victim of the deep economic recession that followed the stock market crash of 2008, she has more than two decades of experience as a white-collar worker, yet she cannot find an opening. She is not alone. At the end of 2009, about 40 percent of the nation's unemployed had been out of work for half a year or more.

In a suburb in Spain not far from Madrid, Mari Cruz, who used to dine out each week with her husband, eats at a soup kitchen to save money for her children's meals. Both Mari, who once worked for a catering firm, and her husband, Antonio, a construction worker, are unemployed. Once prosperous enough to buy a home, cars, and designer clothes, the couple is now on the verge of poverty, unable to pay the mortgage on their home with their only income, Antonio's unemployment compensation. Hundreds of thousands of families in Spain are in the same predicament, thrown out of work by the global recession.

In Middlebury, Indiana, Scott and Kelly Nichols confront a hard reality. Scott, once a well-paid blue-collar worker, and Kelly, an office clerk, have been out of work since the recreational vehicle industry collapsed, hit by high gas prices and tight credit. Now, nine months later, the Nichols can no longer afford the rent. They will move in with Kelly's mother, in her basement (Hay 2009; Scherer 2010a; Schwartzman 2009).

These are the faces of people living on the edge—including women with children who are seeking to make a go of it amid changing social policies. Governments in all parts of the world are searching for the right solution to welfare: How much subsidy should they provide? How much responsibility should fall on the shoulders of the poor?

Looking at the Issue

In the 1990s, an intense debate took place in the United States over the issue of welfare. Welfare programs were costly, and concern was widespread (however unfounded) that welfare payments discouraged recipients from seeking jobs. Both Democrats and Republicans vowed to "end welfare as we know it."

In late 1996, in a historic shift in federal policy, Congress passed the Personal Responsibility and Work Opportunity Reconciliation Act, ending the long-standing federal guarantee of assistance to every poor family that meets eligibility requirements. The law set a lifetime limit of five years of welfare benefits, and required all able-bodied adults to work after receiving two years of benefits (although hardship exceptions were allowed). The federal government would give block grants to the states to use as they wished in assisting poor and needy residents, and it would permit states to experiment with ways to move people off welfare (Seccombe 2011).

In the United States, the government safety net now falls far short of that in Europe, even after recent cutbacks there. Available data indicate that in Great Britain and Sweden, 82 percent of health expenditures are paid for by the government; in Canada, 70 percent; but in the United States, only 46 percent. In fact, most industrialized nations devote higher proportions of their expenditures to housing, social security, welfare, health care, and unemployment compensation than the United States does. As U.S. economist Dean Baker declared recently, "The increase in social spending is still relatively modest given the severity of the downturn. We're not France" (Cauchon 2009; World Bank 2010a:120–122).

Applying Sociology

Many sociologists tend to view the debate over welfare reform in industrialized nations from a conflict perspective: the "haves" in positions of policymaking listen to the interests of other "haves," while the cries of the "have-nots" are drowned out. Critics of welfare reform believe that the nation's economic problems are unfairly blamed on welfare spending and

In northern and western Europe, following the deep worldwide recession that began in 2008, countries with strong social safety nets were forced to cut back benefits. These civil servants in Granada, Spain, are protesting salary cutbacks.

the poor. From a conflict perspective, this backlash against welfare recipients reflects deep fears and hostility toward the nation's urban, predominantly African American and Hispanic underclass.

Those who are critical of the backlash note that "welfare scapegoating" conveniently ignores the lucrative federal handouts that go to *affluent* individuals and families. For example, while federal housing aid to the poor was cut drastically in the 1980s, tax deductions for mortgage interest and property taxes more than doubled.

Conflict theorists have noted an oft-ignored aspect of the welfare system, administrative sanctions. The law allows administrators to end welfare payments if clients fail to complete job-readiness classes, community work, or job searches. A great deal of discretion is used in applying sanctions. According to one study, Black clients are more likely to be sanctioned than White clients (Schram et al. 2009).

Those who take a conflict perspective also urge policymakers and the general public to look closely at **corporate welfare**—the tax breaks, bailouts, direct payments, and grants that the government gives to corporations—rather than looking closely at the comparatively small allowances being given to mothers and their children. Yet any suggestion to curtail such corporate welfare brings a strong response from special-interest groups that are much more powerful than any coalition on behalf of the poor. One example of corporate welfare is the huge federal bailouts of distressed financial institutions in fall 2008 and of bankrupt automobile companies in 2009. Although the outlay of hundreds of billions of dollars was vital to the nation's economic recovery, the measure received relatively little scrutiny from Congress. Just a few months later, however, when legislation was proposed to extend the safety net for laid-off workers—unemployment compensation, food stamps, subsidized child care, assistance to the homeless, disability support, and infant nutrition—it met with loud demands for the monitoring of expenditures (DeParle 2009; Piven and Cloward 1996).

Initiating Policy

The government likes to highlight welfare-reform success stories. Though many people who once depended on tax dollars are now working and paying taxes themselves, it is much too soon to see if "workfare" will be successful. The new jobs that were generated by the booming economy of the late 1990s were an unrealistic test of the system. Prospects have faded for the hard-core jobless—people who are difficult to train or are encumbered by drug or alcohol abuse, physical disabilities, or child care needs—since the boom passed and the economy moved into recession.

True, fewer people remain on the rolls since welfare reform was enacted in August 1996. By September 2010 just under 1.9 million families were still on the rolls, down 65 percent from a high of 5.1 million in 1994. But while those families that have left the rolls are modestly better off now, most of their breadwinners continue to hold low-paying, unskilled jobs. For them, the economic downturn that was well in place by 2009 made finding work tougher than ever. Of those adults who remain on welfare, nearly 60 percent are not in school or in welfare-to-work programs, as the law requires them to be. This group tends to face the greatest challenges—substance abuse, mental illness, or a criminal record (Bitler and Hoynes 2010; Danziger 2010; Department of Health and Human Services 2011a).

European governments have encountered many of the same citizen demands as in North America: keep our taxes low, even if it means reducing services to the poor. However, nations in eastern and central Europe have faced a special challenge since the end of communism. Though governments in those nations traditionally provided an impressive array of social services, they differed from capitalist systems in several important respects. First, the communist system was premised on full employment, so there was no need to provide unemployment insurance; social services focused on the old and the disabled. Second, subsidies for housing and even utilities played an important role. With new competition from the West and tight budgets, some of these countries are beginning to realize that universal coverage is no longer affordable and must be replaced with targeted programs.

The reduction in state assistance to the unemployed is not limited to the former Soviet bloc. Even Sweden, despite its long history of social welfare programs, is feeling the pinch. Welfare payments have been reduced there over the past two years, and the number of sick days and other employment benefits trimmed. Yet by any standard, the European safety net is still significantly stronger than that of the United States (*The Economist* 2010d; Petrášová 2006; Walker and Thurow 2009).

Both in North America and in Europe, people are beginning to turn to private means to support themselves. For instance, they are investing money for their later years rather than depending on government social security programs. That solution works only if you have a job and can save money, however. Increasingly, people are seeing the gap between themselves and the affluent grow, with fewer government programs available to assist them. Solutions are frequently left to the private sector, while government policy initiatives at the national level all but disappear.

Take the Issue with You

1. Do you personally know anyone who has had to depend on public assistance, such as food stamps? If so, what were the circumstances? Would you yourself need government assistance under such circumstances?

2. Do you think welfare recipients should be required to work? If so, what kind of support should they receive? Should any exceptions be granted to the work requirement?

3. Why do you think western and northern European countries have more generous welfare programs than the United States?

Summary

Worldwide, stratification can be seen both in the gap between rich and poor nations and in the inequality within countries. This chapter examines the global divide and stratification within the world economic system; the impact of **globalization, modernization,** and **multinational corporations** on developing countries; and the distribution of wealth and income in various nations.

1. Developing nations account for most of the world's population and most of its births, but they also bear the burden of most of its poverty, disease, and childhood deaths.

2. Former colonized nations are kept in a subservient position, subject to foreign domination, through the process of **neocolonialism.**

3. Drawing on the conflict perspective, sociologist Immanuel Wallerstein's **world systems analysis** views the global economic system as one divided between nations that control wealth (core nations) and those from which capital is taken (periphery nations).

4. According to **dependency theory,** even as developing countries make economic advances, they remain weak and subservient to core nations and corporations in an increasingly integrated global economy.

5. **Globalization,** or the worldwide integration of government policies, cultures, social movements, and financial markets through trade and the exchange of ideas, is a controversial trend that critics blame for contributing to the cultural domination of periphery nations by core nations.

6. **Multinational corporations** bring jobs and industry to developing nations, but they also tend to exploit workers in order to maximize profits.

7. Poverty is a worldwide problem that blights the lives of billions of people. In 2000 the United Nations launched the Millennium Project, whose goal is to eliminate extreme poverty worldwide by the year 2015.

8. Many sociologists are quick to note that terms such as **modernization** and even *development* contain an ethnocentric bias.

9. According to **modernization theory,** the development of periphery countries will be assisted by innovations transferred from the industrialized world.

10. Although Mexico is unquestionably a poor country, the gap between its richest and poorest citizens is one of the widest in the world.

11. The subordinate status of Mexico's Indians is but one reflection of the nation's color hierarchy, which links social class to the appearance of racial purity.

12. Growing recognition of the **borderlands** reflects the increasingly close and complex relationship between Mexico and the United States.

13. In Europe and North America, countries have been forced to cut back welfare programs after a deep recession drained their treasuries. Even Sweden, known worldwide for its social safety net, has had to cut benefits.

Key Terms

Borderlands The area of common culture along the border between Mexico and the United States. (page 227)

Colonialism The maintenance of political, social, economic, and cultural domination over a people by a foreign power for an extended period. (216)

Corporate welfare Tax breaks, bailouts, direct payments, and grants that the government gives to corporations. (230)

Dependency theory An approach that contends that industrialized nations continue to exploit developing countries for their own gain. (216)

Globalization The worldwide integration of government policies, cultures, social movements, and financial markets through trade and the exchange of ideas. (218)

Modernization The far-reaching process through which periphery nations move from traditional or less developed institutions to those characteristic of more developed societies. (222)

Modernization theory A functionalist approach that proposes that modernization and development will gradually improve the lives of people in developing nations. (222)

Multinational corporation A commercial organization that is headquartered in one country but does business throughout the world. (218)

Neocolonialism Continuing dependence of former colonies on foreign countries. (216)

Remittances The monies that immigrants return to their families of origin. Also called *migradollars.* (228)

World systems analysis A view of the global economic system as one divided between certain industrialized nations that control wealth and developing countries that are controlled and exploited. (216)

TAKING SOCIOLOGY with you

1. Pick a multinational corporation whose products you are familiar with and look up its financial statements. In which countries does the corporation produce products and in which does it sell products? In which country does the corporation pay taxes? To which country do its profits flow? Why should the answers to these questions matter to you?

2. Choose a foreign country that you are interested in and do some research on social stratification in that country. How equally or unequally are wealth and income distributed there, in comparison to the United States? How extensive is social mobility? Explain the reasons for any differences in stratification.

3. Choose a European country and a developing country and do some research on their welfare systems. How do the two systems differ? How does each reflect the culture and society it serves?

Self-Quiz

Read each question carefully and then select the best answer.

1. The maintenance of political, social, economic, and cultural domination over a people by a foreign power for an extended period is referred to as
   a. neocolonialism.
   b. government-imposed stratification.
   c. colonialism.
   d. dependency.

2. In viewing the global economic system as divided between nations that control wealth and those that are controlled and exploited, sociologist Immanuel Wallerstein draws on the
   a. functionalist perspective.
   b. conflict perspective.
   c. interactionist perspective.
   d. dramaturgical approach.

3. Which of the following nations would Immanuel Wallerstein classify as a *core* country within the world economic system?
   a. Germany
   b. South Korea
   c. Ireland
   d. Mexico

4. Which sociological perspective argues that multinational corporations can actually help the developing nations of the world?
   a. the interactionist perspective
   b. the feminist perspective
   c. the functionalist perspective
   d. the conflict perspective

5. Which of the following terms is used by contemporary social scientists to describe the far-reaching process by which peripheral nations move from traditional or less developed institutions to those characteristic of more developed societies?
   a. dependency
   b. globalization
   c. industrialization
   d. modernization

6. In at least 24 nations around the world, the most affluent 10 percent receives at least what percentage of all income?
   a. 20 percent
   b. 30 percent
   c. 40 percent
   d. 50 percent

7. Karuna Chanana Ahmed, an anthropologist from India who has studied developing nations, calls which group the most exploited of oppressed people?
   a. children
   b. women
   c. the elderly
   d. the poor

8. Which of the following terms is used to refer to Mexico's large, impoverished majority, most of whom have brown skin and a mixed racial lineage due to intermarriage?
   a. *criollo*
   b. *indio*
   c. *mestizo*
   d. *zapatista*

9. In Mexico, women now constitute what percentage of the labor force?
   a. 15 percent
   b. 23 percent
   c. 34 percent
   d. 46 percent

10. Which of the following terms refers to the foreign-owned factories established just across the border in Mexico, where the companies that own them don't have to pay taxes or provide insurance or benefits for their workers?
    a. *maquiladoras*
    b. *hombres*
    c. *mujeres*
    d. *toreadors*

11. Colonial domination established patterns of economic exploitation leading to former colonies remaining dependent on more industrialized nations. Such continuing dependence and foreign domination are referred to as _____.

12. According to Immanuel Wallerstein's analysis, the United States is at the _____ while neighboring Mexico is on the _____ of the world economic system.

13. Wallerstein's world systems analysis is the most widely used version of _____ theory.

14. _____ factories are factories found throughout the developing world that are run by multinational corporations.

15. As _____ industries become a more important part of the international marketplace, many companies have concluded that the low costs of overseas operations more than offset the expense of transmitting information around the world.

16. Viewed from a(n) _____ perspective, the combination of skilled technology and management provided by multinationals and the relatively cheap labor available in developing nations is ideal for a global enterprise.

17. In 2000 the United Nations launched the _____ _____; its objective is to eliminate extreme poverty worldwide by the year 2015.

18. Modernization theory reflects the _____ perspective.

19. At the top of the color hierarchy in Mexico are the _____, the 10 percent of the population who are typically White, well-educated members of the business and intellectual elites, and who have familial roots in Spain.

20. The term _____ refers to the area of a common culture along the border between Mexico and the United States.

Answers
1 (c); 2 (b); 3(a); 4 (c); 5 (d); 6 (c); 7 (b); 8 (c); 9 (d); 10 (a); 11 neocolonialism; 12 core, semiperiphery; 13 dependency; 14 Global; 15 service; 16 functionalist 17 Millennium Project; 18 functionalist; 19 *criollos*; 20 borderlands

232

THINKING ABOUT **MOVIES**

The End of Poverty?

This documentary asks whether we can close the gap between rich and poor nations by redistributing the world's wealth.

Hotel Rwanda

A hotel becomes a safe haven from the Rwandan genocide.

Slumdog Millionaire

Authorities question a young man's victory on India's version of Who Wants to Be a Millionaire? because of his low socioeconomic status.

▶ INSIDE

In Boise, Idaho, proud new citizens take the oath of allegiance during their naturalization ceremony. U.S. society is becoming increasingly diverse as immigrants from around the world bring their skills, languages, and cultures with them to their new home.

Racial and Ethnic Inequality

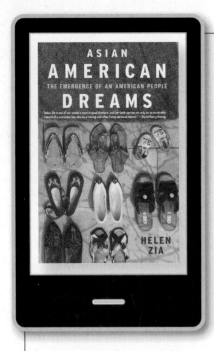

> Ah so. No tickee, no washee. So sorry, so sollee. Chinkee, Chink. Jap, Nip, zero, kamikaze. Dothead, flat face, flat nose, slant eye, slope. Slit, mamasan, dragon lady. Gook, VC, Flip, Hindoo.
>
> By the time I was ten, I'd heard such words so many times I could feel them coming before they parted lips. I knew they were meant in the unkindest way. Still, we didn't talk about these incidents at home, we just accepted them as part of being in America, something to learn to rise above.

The most common taunting didn't even utilize words but a string of unintelligible gobbledygook that kids—and adults—would spew as they pretended to speak Chinese or some other Asian language. It was a mockery of how they imagined my parents talked to me.

Truth was that Mom and Dad rarely spoke to us in Chinese, except to scold or call us to dinner. Worried that we might develop an accent, my father insisted that we speak English at home. This, he explained, would lessen the hardships we might encounter and make us more acceptable as Americans.

Truth was that Mom and Dad rarely spoke to us in Chinese, except to scold or call us to dinner. Worried that we might develop an accent, my father insisted that we speak English at home.

I'll never know if my father's language decision was right. On the one hand, I, like most Asian Americans, have been complimented countless times on my spoken English by people who assumed I was a foreigner. "My, you speak such good English," they'd cluck. "No kidding, I ought to," I would think to myself, then wonder: should I thank them for assuming that English isn't my native language? Or should I correct them on the proper usage of "well" and "good"?

More often than feeling grateful for my American accent, I've wished that I could jump into a heated exchange of rapid-fire Chinese, volume high and spit flying. But with a vocabulary limited to *"Ni hao?"* (How are you?) and *"Ting bu dong"* (I hear but don't understand), meaningful exchanges are woefully impossible. I find myself smiling and nodding like a dashboard ornament. I'm envious of the many people I know who grew up speaking an Asian language yet converse in English beautifully.

Armed with standard English and my flat New Jersey "a," I still couldn't escape the name-calling. I became all too familiar with other names and faces that supposedly matched mine—Fu Manchu, Suzie Wong, Hop Sing, Madame Butterfly, Charlie Chan, Ming the Merciless—the "Asians" produced for mass consumption. Their faces filled me with shame whenever I saw them on TV or in the movies. They defined my face to the rest of the world: a sinister Fu, Suzie the whore, subservient Hop Sing, pathetic Butterfly, cunning Chan, and warlike Ming. Inscrutable Orientals all, real Americans none.

(Zia 2000:109–110) Additional information about this excerpt can be found on the Online Learning Center at www.mhhe.com/schaeferbrief13e.

Helen Zia, the successful journalist and community activist who wrote this reminiscence from her childhood, is the daughter of Chinese immigrants to the United States. As her story shows, Zia experienced blatant prejudice against Chinese Americans, even though she spoke flawless English. In fact, all new immigrants and their families have faced stereotyping and hostility, whether they were White or non-White, Asian, African, or East European. In this multicultural society, those who are different from the dominant social group have never been welcome.

Today, millions of African Americans, Asian Americans, Hispanic Americans, and many other racial and ethnic minorities continue to experience the often bitter contrast between the "American dream" and the grim realities of poverty, prejudice, and discrimination. Like class, the social definitions of race and ethnicity still affect people's place and status in a stratification system, not only in this country, but throughout the world. High incomes,

a good command of English, and hard-earned professional credentials do not always override racial and ethnic stereotypes or protect those who fit them from the sting of racism.

What is prejudice, and how is it institutionalized in the form of discrimination? In what ways have race and ethnicity affected the experience of immigrants from other countries? What are the fastest-growing minority groups in the United States today? In this chapter we will focus on the meaning of race and ethnicity. We will begin by identifying the basic characteristics of a minority group and distinguishing between racial and ethnic groups. Then we will examine the dynamics of prejudice and discrimination. After considering four sociological perspectives on race and ethnicity, we'll take a look at common patterns of intergroup relations. The following section will describe the major racial and ethnic groups in the United States. Finally, in the Social Policy section we will explore the issue of global immigration.

Minority, Racial, and Ethnic Groups

Sociologists frequently distinguish between racial and ethnic groups. The term **racial group** describes a group that is set apart from others because of physical differences that have taken on social significance. Whites, African Americans, and Asian Americans are all considered racial groups in the United States. While race does turn on physical differences, it is the culture of a particular society that constructs and attaches social significance to those differences, as we will see later. Unlike racial groups, an **ethnic group** is set apart from others primarily because of its national origin or distinctive cultural patterns. In the United States, Puerto Ricans, Jews, and Polish Americans are all categorized as ethnic groups (Table 11-1).

Minority Groups

A numerical minority is any group that makes up less than half of some larger population. The population of the United States includes thousands of numerical minorities, including television actors, green-eyed people, tax lawyers, and descendants of the Pilgrims who arrived on the *Mayflower*. However, these numerical minorities are not considered to be minorities in the sociological sense; in fact, the number of people in a group does not necessarily determine its status as a social minority (or a dominant group). When sociologists define a minority group, they are concerned primarily with the economic and political power, or powerlessness, of that group. A **minority group** is a subordinate group whose members have significantly less control or power over their lives than the members of a dominant or majority group have over theirs.

Sociologists have identified five basic properties of a minority group: unequal treatment, physical or cultural traits, ascribed status, solidarity, and in-group marriage (Wagley and Harris 1958):

1. Members of a minority group experience unequal treatment compared to members of a dominant group. For example, the management of an apartment complex may refuse to rent to African Americans, Hispanics, or Jews. Social inequality may be created or maintained by prejudice, discrimination, segregation, or even extermination.

2. Members of a minority group share physical or cultural characteristics that distinguish them from the dominant group. Each society arbitrarily decides which characteristics are most important in defining groups.

3. Membership in a minority (or dominant) group is not voluntary; people are born into the group. Thus, race and ethnicity are considered *ascribed* statuses.

4. Minority group members have a strong sense of group solidarity. William Graham Sumner, writing in 1906, noted that people make distinctions between members of their own group (the *in-group*) and everyone else (the *out-group*). When a group is the object of long-term prejudice and discrimination, the feeling of "us versus them" can and often does become extremely intense.

5. Members of a minority group generally marry others from the same group. A member of a dominant group is often unwilling to marry into a supposedly inferior minority group. In addition, the minority group's sense of solidarity encourages marriage within the group and discourages marriage to outsiders.

TABLE **11-1** RACIAL AND ETHNIC GROUPS IN THE UNITED STATES

Classification	Number in Thousands	Percentage of Total Population
Racial Groups		
Whites (non-Hispanic)	194,553	63.0%
Blacks/African Americans	34,658	11.2
Native Americans, Alaskan Natives	2,476	0.8
Asian Americans	14,229	4.6
Chinese	3,106	1.0
Asian Indians	2,602	0.8
Filipinos	2,476	0.8
Vietnamese	1,482	0.5
Koreans	1,336	0.4
Japanese	767	0.2
Pacific Islanders and other	2,460	0.8
Ethnic Groups		
White ancestry (single or mixed, non-Hispanic)		
Germans	50,708	16.5
Irish	36,915	12.0
English	27,658	9.0
Italians	18,085	5.9
Poles	10,091	3.3
Scottish and Scotch-Irish	9,417	3.1
French	9,412	3.1
Jews	6,452	2.1
Hispanics (or Latinos)	50,478	16.3
Mexican Americans	31,798	10.3
Puerto Ricans	4,624	1.5
Cubans	1,785	0.6
Salvadorans	1,648	0.5
Dominicans	1,415	0.5
Other Hispanics	8,164	2.6
TOTAL (all groups)	**308,746**	

Note: All data for 2009 except three racial groups listed at top, Hispanic total and subgroups, and total population figure, which are for 2010. Percentages do not total 100 percent, and subheads do not add up to totals in major categories because of overlap between groups (e.g., Polish American Jews or people of mixed ancestry such as Irish and Italian).
Source: 2009 data from American Community Survey 2010:Tables B02006, B03001, C04006; 2010 data from Davidson and Pyle 2011:117; Ennis et al. 2011; Humes et al. 2011.

Race

Many people think of race as a series of biological classifications. However, research shows that is not a meaningful way of differentiating people. Genetically, there are no systematic differences between the races that affect people's social behavior and abilities. Instead, sociologists use the term *racial group* to refer to those minorities (and the corresponding dominant groups) who are set apart from others by obvious physical differences. But what is an "obvious" physical difference? Each society labels those differences that people consider important, while ignoring other characteristics that could serve as a basis for social differentiation.

Social Construction of Race Because race is a social construction, the process of defining races typically benefits those who have more power and privilege than others. In the United States, we see differences in both skin color and hair color. Yet people learn informally that differences in skin color have a dramatic social and political meaning, whereas differences in hair color do not.

When observing skin color, many people in the United States tend to lump others rather casually into the traditional categories of "Black," "White," and "Asian." Subtle differences in skin color often go unnoticed. In many nations of Central America and South America, in contrast, people recognize color gradients on a continuum from light to dark skin color. Brazil has approximately 40 color groupings, while in other countries people may be described as "Mestizo Hondurans," "Mulatto Colombians," or "African Panamanians." What we see as "obvious" differences, then, are subject to each society's social definitions.

The largest racial minorities in the United States are African Americans (or Blacks), Native Americans (or American Indians), and Asian Americans (Japanese Americans, Chinese Americans, and other Asian peoples). Figure 11-1 provides information about the population of racial and ethnic groups in the United States over the past five centuries.

Given current population patterns, it is clear that the nation's diversity will continue to increase. In 2011, for the first time ever, census data revealed that the majority of all children ages three and under are now either Hispanic or non-White. This turning point marks the beginning of a pattern in which the nation's minority population will slowly become the majority. By 2050, if not sooner, the majority of all school-age children in the United States will belong to racial or ethnic minority groups (Frey 2011).

Racial definitions are crystallized through what Michael Omi and Howard Winant (1994) have called **racial formation,** a sociohistorical process in which racial categories are created, inhabited, transformed, and destroyed. In this process, those who have power define groups of people according to a racist social structure. The creation of a reservation system for Native Americans in the late 1800s is one example of racial formation. Federal officials combined what were distinctive tribes into a single racial group, which we refer to today as Native Americans. The extent and frequency with which peoples are subject to racial formation is such that no one escapes it.

Another example of racial formation from the 1800s was known as the "one-drop rule." If a person had even a single drop of "Black blood," that person was defined and viewed as Black, even if he or she *appeared* to be White. Clearly, race had social significance, enough so that White legislators established official standards about who was "Black" and who was "White."

The one-drop rule was a vivid example of the *social construction of race*—the process by which people come to define a group as a race based in part on physical characteristics, but also on historical, cultural, and economic factors. For example, in the 1800s,

FIGURE **11-1** RACIAL AND ETHNIC GROUPS IN THE UNITED STATES, 1500–2100 (PROJECTED)

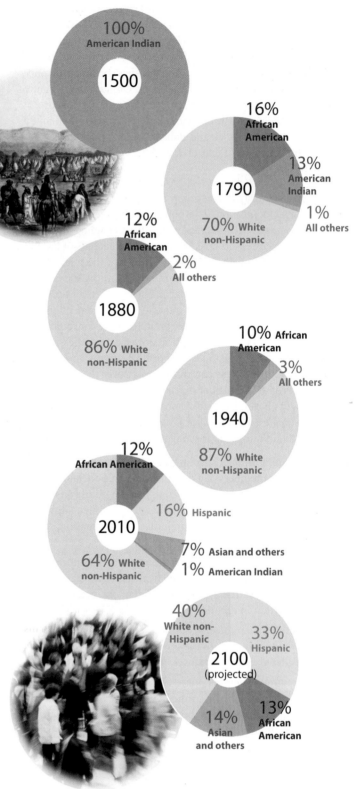

Sources: Author's estimate; Bureau of the Census 2004a; Humes et al. 2011. Data for 2010 and 2100, African American and Asian and others, are for non-Hispanics.

The racial and ethnic composition of what is today the United States has been undergoing change not just for the past 50 years, but for the past 500. Five centuries ago the land was populated only by indigenous Native Americans.

immigrant groups such as Italian and Irish Americans were not at first seen as being "White," but as foreigners who were not necessarily trustworthy. The social construction of race is an ongoing process that is subject to debate, especially in a diverse society such as the United States, where each year increasing numbers of children are born to parents of different racial backgrounds.

Recognition of Multiple Identities In 1900, in an address to the Anti-Slavery Union in London, scholar W. E. B. DuBois predicted that "the color line" would become the foremost problem of the 20th century. DuBois, born a free Black man in 1868, had witnessed prejudice and discrimination throughout the United States. His comment was prophetic. Today, over a century later, race and ethnicity still carry enormous weight in the United States (DuBois [1900] 1969).

The color line has blurred significantly since 1900, however. Interracial marriage is no longer forbidden by law and custom. Thus, Geetha Lakshmi-narayanan, a native of Ann Arbor, Michigan, is both White and Asian Indian. Often mistaken for a Filipina or Latina, she has grown accustomed to the blunt question "What are you?" (Navarro 2005).

In the late 20th century, with immigration from Latin America rising, the fluid nature of racial formation became evident. Suddenly, people were speaking about the "Latin Americanization" of the United States, or about a biracial, Black/White society being replaced by a triracial one. In the 2010 Census, over 9 million people in the United States (or about 2.9 percent of the population) reported that they were of two or more races. Half the people classified as multiracial were under age 18, suggesting that this segment of the population will grow in the years to come. People who claimed both White and American Indian ancestry were the largest group of multiracial residents (Bonilla-Silva 2004; Humes et al. 2011).

This statistical finding of millions of multiracial people obscures how individuals are often asked to handle their identity. For example, the enrollment forms for government programs typically include only a few broad racial-ethnic categories. This approach to racial categorization is part of a long history that dictates single-race identities. Still, many individuals, especially young adults, struggle against social pressure to choose a single identity and, instead, openly embrace multiple heritages. Public figures, rather than hide their mixed ancestry, now flaunt it. Singer Mariah Carey celebrates her Irish American background, and President Barack Obama speaks of being born in Hawaii to a Kenyan father and a White mother from Kansas. Tiger Woods, the world's best-known professional golfer, considers himself both Asian and African American.

A dominant or majority group has the power not only to define itself legally but to define a society's values as well. The interactionist William I. Thomas, observing how we assign social meanings, saw that the "definition of the situation" could mold the individual personality. To put it another way, people respond not only to the objective features of a situation or person but also to the *meaning* that situation or person has for them. Thus, we can create false images or stereotypes that become real in their consequences. **Stereotypes** are unreliable generalizations about all members of a group that do not recognize individual differences within the group.

Today, some children of mixed-race families identify themselves as biracial or multiracial, rejecting efforts to place them in a single racial category.

use your sociological *imagination*

Using a TV remote control, how quickly do you think you could find a television show in which all the characters share your racial or ethnic background? What about a show in which all the characters share a different background from yours—how quickly could you find one?

An ethnic group, unlike a racial group, is set apart from others because of its national origin or distinctive cultural patterns. Among the ethnic groups in the United States are peoples with a Spanish-speaking background, referred to collectively as *Latinos* or *Hispanics,* such as Puerto Ricans, Mexican Americans, Cuban Americans, and other Latin Americans. Other ethnic groups in this country include Jewish, Irish, Italian, and Norwegian Americans. Although these groupings are convenient, they serve to obscure differences *within* ethnic categories (as in the case of Hispanics), as well as to overlook the mixed ancestry of so many people in the United States.

The distinction between racial and ethnic minorities is not always clear-cut. Some members of racial minorities, such as Asian Americans, may have significant cultural differences from other racial groups. At the same time, certain ethnic minorities, such as Latinos, may have obvious physical differences that set them apart from other ethnic groups in the United States.

Despite categorization problems, sociologists continue to feel that the distinction between racial groups and ethnic groups is socially significant. In most societies, including the United States, socially constructed physical differences tend to be more visible than ethnic differences. Partly as a result of this fact, stratification along racial lines is more resistant to change than stratification along ethnic lines. Over time, members of an ethnic minority can sometimes become indistinguishable from the majority—although the process may take generations and may never include all members of the group. In contrast, members of a racial minority find it much more difficult to blend in with the larger society and gain acceptance from the majority.

The inauguration of President Barack Obama in 2009 was clearly historic. To put its significance in perspective, however, Obama's Senate seat was the only one held by a Black man when he left it to become president. More than half of White voters in the 2008 presidential election—57 percent—cast their ballots for candidates other than Obama.

thinking CRITICALLY

Why does the social construction of race defy the traditional notion of race as a biological category?

Prejudice and Discrimination

Looking at the United States in the 21st century, some people wonder aloud if race and ethnicity are still relevant to social stratification. After all, African Americans have served as secretary of state, secretary of defense, and chairman of the Joint Chiefs of Staff; the office of attorney general has been held by both an African American and a Hispanic. Most notably, an African American now serves as president. As historic as these leaders' achievements have been, however, in every case their elevation meant that they left behind a virtually all-White government department or assembly.

At the same time, college campuses across the United States have been the scene of bias-related incidents. Student-run newspapers and radio stations have ridiculed racial and ethnic minorities; threatening literature has been stuffed under the doors of minority students; graffiti endorsing the views of White supremacist organizations such as the Ku Klux Klan have been scrawled on university walls. In some cases, there have even been violent clashes between groups of White and Black students (Southern Poverty Law Center 2010). What causes such ugly incidents?

Prejudice

Prejudice is a negative attitude toward an entire category of people, often an ethnic or racial minority. If you resent your roommate because he or she is sloppy, you are not necessarily guilty of prejudice. However, if you immediately stereotype your roommate on the basis of such characteristics as race, ethnicity, or religion, that is a form of prejudice. Prejudice tends to perpetuate false definitions of individuals and groups.

Sometimes prejudice results from **ethnocentrism**—the tendency to assume that one's culture and way of life represent the norm or are superior to all others. Ethnocentric people judge other cultures by the standards of their group, which leads quite easily to prejudice against cultures they view as inferior.

One important and widespread ideology that reinforces prejudice is **racism,** the belief that one race is supreme and all others are innately inferior. When racism prevails in a society, members of subordinate groups generally experience prejudice, discrimination, and exploitation. In 1990, as concern mounted about racist attacks in the United States, Congress passed the Hate Crimes Statistics Act. As a result, hate crimes are now beginning to be reported and investigated in much the same way as conventional crimes against property and people (see Chapter 8).

Color-Blind Racism

Over the past three generations, nationwide surveys have consistently shown growing support among Whites for integration, interracial dating, and the election of minority group members to public office—including the presidency of the United States. How can this trend be explained, given the persistence

of residential segregation and the commission of thousands of hate crimes every year? The answer, to some extent, is that prejudice and discriminatory attitudes are no longer expressed as freely as they once were. Often, they are couched in terms of equal opportunity.

Color-blind racism is the use of the principle of race neutrality to defend a racially unequal status quo. Proponents of race neutrality claim they believe that everyone should be treated equally. However, the way they apply the principle to government policy is anything but neutral. Proponents of this approach oppose affirmative action (see page 244), public welfare assistance, and to a large extent, government-funded health insurance, all of which they see largely as favors to minority groups. Yet they do not object to practices that privilege Whites, such as college admissions criteria that give preference to the relatives of alumni. Nor do they oppose tax breaks for homeowners, most of whom are White, or government financial aid to college students, who are also disproportionately White. Though race neutrality is not based on theories of racial superiority or inferiority, then, the idea that society should be color-blind only perpetuates racial inequality.

Color-blind racism has also been referred to as "covert racism." Although its proponents rarely speak of racism, other indicators of social status, such as social class or citizenship, tend to become proxies for race. Thus, many White people can convince themselves that they are not racist—nor do they know anyone who is—and yet remain prejudiced against "welfare mothers" and "immigrants." They can conclude, mistakenly, that racial tolerance, or even racial and ethnic equality, has been achieved.

Researchers who have surveyed White attitudes toward African Americans over the past several decades have reached two inescapable conclusions. First, people's attitudes do change. In periods of social upheaval, dramatic attitudinal shifts can occur within a single generation. Second, less racial progress was made in the late 20th and early 21st centuries than in the relatively brief period of the 1950s and 1960s. Today, economically disadvantaged groups such as African Americans and Latinos have become so closely associated with urban decay, homelessness, welfare, and crime that those problems are now viewed as racial issues, even if they are not labeled as such. The tendency to *blame the victims* of these social ills complicates their resolution (see the Social Policy section in Chapter 10), especially at a time when government's ability to address social problems is limited by recession, antitax initiatives, and concern over terrorism. In short, the color line is still in place, even if more and more people refuse to acknowledge its existence (Ansell 2008; Bonilla-Silva 2006; Coates 2008; M. King 2007:3–4; Quillian 2006; Winant 1994:106–108).

Discriminatory Behavior

Prejudice often leads to **discrimination,** the denial of opportunities and equal rights to individuals and groups because of prejudice or other arbitrary reasons. Say that a White corporate president with a prejudice against Asian Americans has to fill an executive position. The most qualified candidate for the job is a Vietnamese American. If the president refuses to hire this candidate and instead selects an inferior White candidate, he or she is engaging in an act of racial discrimination.

A government public assistance office does brisk business. People who oppose government welfare programs but support other forms of government assistance, such as financial aid to college students, may be exhibiting color-blind racism.

Prejudiced *attitudes* should not be equated with discriminatory *behavior*. Although the two are generally related, they are not identical; either condition can be present without the other. A prejudiced person does not always act on his or her biases. The White corporate president, for example, might choose—despite his or her stereotypes—to hire the Vietnamese American. That would be prejudice without discrimination. On the other hand, a White corporate president with a completely respectful view of Vietnamese Americans might refuse to hire them for executive posts out of fear that biased clients would take their business elsewhere. In that case, the president's action would constitute discrimination without prejudice.

A field experiment by sociologist Devah Pager, then a doctoral candidate at the University of Wisconsin–Madison, documented racial discrimination in hiring. Pager sent four polite, well-dressed young men out to look for an entry-level job in Milwaukee, Wisconsin. All were 23-year-old college students, but they presented themselves as high school graduates with similar job histories. Two of the men were Black and two were White. One Black applicant and one White applicant claimed to have served 18 months in jail for a felony conviction—possession of cocaine with intent to distribute.

As one might expect, the four men's experiences with 350 potential employers were vastly different. Predictably, the White applicant with a purported prison record received only half as many callbacks as the other White applicant—17 percent compared to 34 percent. But as dramatic as the effect of his criminal record was, the effect of his race was more significant. Despite his prison record, he received slightly more callbacks than the Black applicant *with no criminal record* (17 percent compared to 14 percent). Race, it seems, was more of a concern to potential employers than a criminal background.

The implications of this research are not limited to any one city, such as Milwaukee. Similar studies have confirmed discriminatory handling of job applications in Chicago; New York City; Long Island, New York; San Diego; and Washington, D.C.

FIGURE **11-2** U.S. MEDIAN INCOME BY RACE, ETHNICITY, AND GENDER

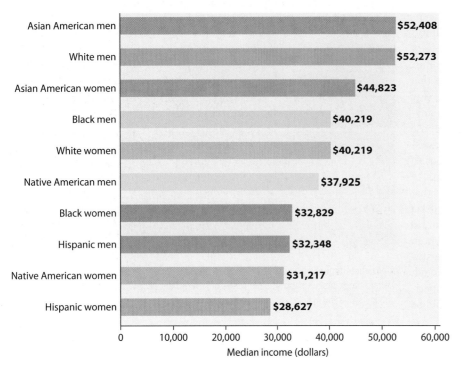

Group	Median income
Asian American men	$52,408
White men	$52,273
Asian American women	$44,823
Black men	$40,219
White women	$40,219
Native American men	$37,925
Black women	$32,829
Hispanic men	$32,348
Native American women	$31,217
Hispanic women	$28,627

Median income (dollars)

Note: Data released in 2010 for income earned in 2009. Median income is from all sources and is limited to year-round, full-time workers at least 25 years old. Data for White men and women are for non-Hispanics.
Sources: DeNavas-Walt et al. 2010:PINC-03; for Native Americans, author's estimate based on American Community Survey 2010:Tables B20017C, B20017H, and B20017I.

Over time, the cumulative effect of such differential behavior by employers contributes to significant differences in income. Figure 11-2 vividly illustrates the income inequality between White men and almost everyone else (Pager 2007; Pager et al. 2009).

If race serves as a barrier, why do Asian American men earn slightly more income than White men (see Figure 11-2)? Not all Asian American men earn high incomes; indeed, some Asian American groups, such as Laotians and Vietnamese, have high levels of poverty. Nevertheless, a significant number of Asian Americans have advanced degrees that qualify them for highly paid jobs, and which raise the median income for the group as a whole. Although these highly educated Asian Americans earn a lot of money, they do not earn quite as much as their White counterparts, however. With a doctorate holder in the family, the typical Asian American household earns an estimated $130,000, compared to $140,000 for a White household.

Sometimes racial and ethnic discrimination is overt. Internet forums like Craigslist.org or Roommate.com feature classified ads that state "African Americans and Arabians tend to clash with me" or "Clean, Godly Christian men only." While anti-discrimination laws prevent such notices from being published in the newspapers, existing law has not caught up with online bigotry in hiring and renting (Liptak 2006).

Discrimination persists even for the most educated and qualified minority group members from the best family backgrounds. Despite their talents and experiences, they sometimes encounter attitudinal or organizational bias that prevents them from reaching their full potential. The term **glass ceiling** refers to an invisible barrier that blocks the promotion of a qualified individual in a work environment because of the individual's gender, race, or ethnicity (R. Schaefer 2011; Yamagata et al. 1997).

In early 1995, the federal Glass Ceiling Commission issued the first comprehensive study of barriers to promotion in the United States. The commission found that glass ceilings continue to block women and minority group men from top management positions in the nation's industries. While White men constitute 45 percent of the paid labor force, they hold down a much higher proportion of top positions. Even in *Fortune* magazine's 2002 listing of the most diversified corporations, White men held more than 80 percent of both the board of directors seats and the top 50 paid positions in the firms. The existence of this glass ceiling results principally from the fears and prejudices of many middle- and upper-level White male managers, who believe that the inclusion of women and minority group men in management circles will threaten their own prospects for advancement (Department of Labor 1995a, 1995b; Hickman 2002).

use your sociological *imagination*

How might online social networking maintain prejudice and discrimination?

The Privileges of the Dominant

One aspect of discrimination that is often overlooked is the privileges that dominant groups enjoy at the expense of others. For instance, we tend to focus more on the difficulty women have getting ahead at work and getting a hand at home than on the ease with which men manage to make their way in the world and avoid household chores. Similarly, we concentrate more on discrimination against racial and ethnic minorities than on the advantages members of the White majority enjoy. Indeed, most White people rarely think about their "Whiteness," taking their status for granted.

Sociologists and other social scientists are becoming increasingly interested in what it means to be "White," for White privilege is the other side of the proverbial coin of racial discrimination. In this context, **White privilege** refers to rights or immunities granted to people as a particular benefit or favor simply because they are White (Ferber and Kimmel 2008). This view of whiteness as a privilege echoes an observation by W. E. B. DuBois, that rather than wanting fair working conditions for all laborers, White workers had accepted the "public and psychological wage" of whiteness ([1935] 1962:700).

The feminist scholar Peggy McIntosh (1988) became interested in White privilege after noticing that most men would not acknowledge that there were privileges attached to being male—even if they would agree that being female had its disadvantages. Did White people suffer from a similar blind spot regarding their racial privilege? she wondered. Intrigued, McIntosh began to list all the ways in which she benefited from her Whiteness. She soon realized that the list of unspoken advantages was long and significant.

McIntosh found that as a White person, she rarely needed to step out of her comfort zone, no matter where she went. If she wished to, she could spend most of her time with people of her race. She could find a good place to live in a pleasant neighborhood, buy the foods she liked to eat from almost any grocery store, and get her hair styled in almost any salon. She could attend a public meeting without feeling that she did not belong, that she was different from everyone else.

McIntosh discovered, too, that her skin color opened doors for her. She could cash checks and use credit cards without suspicion, browse through stores without being shadowed by security guards. She could be seated without difficulty in a restaurant. If she asked to see the manager,

she could assume he or she would be of her race. If she needed help from a doctor or a lawyer, she could get it.

McIntosh also realized that her Whiteness made the job of parenting easier. She did not need to worry about protecting her children from people who didn't like them. She could be sure that their schoolbooks would show pictures of people who looked like them, and that their history texts would describe White people's achievements. She knew that the television programs they watched would include White characters.

Finally, McIntosh had to admit that others did not constantly evaluate her in racial terms. When she appeared in public, she didn't need to worry that her clothing or behavior might reflect poorly on White people. If she was recognized for an achievement, it was seen as her achievement, not that of an entire race. And no one ever assumed that the personal opinions she voiced should be those of all White people. Because McIntosh blended in with the people around her, she wasn't always onstage.

These are not all the privileges White people take for granted as a result of their membership in the dominant racial group in the United States. As Devah Pager's study showed (see page 241), White job seekers enjoy a tremendous advantage over equally well-qualified—even better-qualified—Blacks. Whiteness *does* carry privileges—to a much greater extent than most White people realize (Fitzgerald 2008; Picca and Feagin 2007).

use your sociological *imagination*

How often do you think people are privileged because of their race or ethnicity? How about yourself—how often are you privileged?

White people are accustomed to seeing other White people in professional positions and jobs with authority and prestige. Whiteness *does* have its privileges.

TAKING SOCIOLOGY TO WORK

Prudence Hannis, **Liaison Officer, National Institute of Science Research, University of Québec**

Prudence Hannis is a First Nations (Native American) woman who serves as an official liaison between her people and Canadian researchers. In her position, she interacts with sociologists, anthropologists, political scientists, legal scholars, and researchers in health and medicine at several Canadian universities, all of whom wish to work with First Nations communities.

Hannis is enthusiastic about her job, which gives her an opportunity to educate and sensitize would-be researchers who "never set foot in First Nations communities." In 10 years of work on behalf of the native peoples of Canada, Hannis has seen a dramatic change in their representation in Canadian research and policy. "We are everywhere in research efforts and policy consultation, but whether we are listened to is another matter," she notes.

Before taking her current position, Hannis served as a researcher and community activist with Québec Native Women. There she oversaw the women's health portfolio, organized seminars on sexual abuse for local communities, and produced a resource booklet on the subject. "The purpose of my job was to defend First Nations' women's concerns, to be their spokesperson when needed, to analyze critical situations for our sisters, and mostly, to determine ways in which women can empower themselves, their families, and their communities," she says.

Hannis has also worked for the Centre of Excellence on Women's Health, Consortium Université de Montréal, where she focused on First Nations women's health issues. A member of the Abenaki tribe, Hannis received her BA in sociology from the University of Québec at Montréal. She has found her background in the discipline to be invaluable. "Sociology is now, more than it has ever been, a part of my job," she says.

LET'S DISCUSS

1. What may be some of the challenges to improving the health of Native Americans in Canada?
2. In speaking of empowering First Nations women, what sociological perspective do you think Hannis is drawing on?

Institutional Discrimination

Discrimination is practiced not only by individuals in one-to-one encounters but also by institutions in their daily operations. Social scientists are particularly concerned with the ways in which structural factors such as employment, housing, health care, and government operations maintain the social significance of race and ethnicity. **Institutional discrimination** refers to the denial of opportunities and equal rights to individuals and groups that results from the normal operations of a society. This kind of discrimination consistently affects certain racial and ethnic groups more than others.

The Commission on Civil Rights (1981:9–10) has identified various forms of institutional discrimination:

- Rules requiring that only English be spoken at a place of work, even when it is not a business necessity to restrict the use of other languages.
- Preferences shown by law and medical schools in the admission of children of wealthy and influential alumni, nearly all of whom are White.
- Restrictive employment-leave policies, coupled with prohibitions on part-time work, that make it difficult for the heads of single-parent families (most of whom are women) to obtain and keep jobs.

Institutional discrimination occurred in the wake of the September 11, 2001, terrorist attacks on the United States. In the heat of demands to prevent terrorist takeovers of commercial airplanes, Congress passed the Aviation and Transportation Security Act, which was intended to strengthen airport screening procedures. The law stipulated that all airport screeners must be U.S. citizens. Nationally, 28 percent of all airport screeners were legal residents but not citizens of the United States; as a group, they were disproportionately Latino, Black, and Asian. Many observers noted that other airport and airline workers, including pilots, cabin attendants, and even armed National Guardsmen stationed at airports, need not be citizens. Efforts are being made to test the constitutionality of the act. At the least, the debate over its fairness shows that even well-meant legal measures can have disastrous consequences for racial and ethnic minorities (H. Weinstein 2002).

In some cases, even seemingly neutral institutional standards can have discriminatory effects. African American students at a midwestern state university protested a policy under which fraternities and sororities that wished to use campus facilities for a dance were required to pay a $150 security deposit to cover possible damages. African American students complained that the policy had a discriminatory impact on minority student organizations. Campus police countered that the university's policy applied to all student groups interested in using the facilities. However, since the overwhelmingly White fraternities and sororities at the school had their own houses, which they used for dances, the policy indeed affected only the African American and other minority organizations.

Attempts have been made to eradicate or compensate for discrimination in the United States. The 1960s saw the passage of many pioneering civil rights laws, including the landmark 1964 Civil Rights Act (which prohibits discrimination in public accommodations and publicly owned facilities on the basis of race, color, creed, national origin, and gender).

For more than 40 years, affirmative action programs have been instituted to overcome past discrimination. **Affirmative action** refers to positive efforts to recruit minority group members or women for jobs, promotions, and educational opportunities. Many people resent these programs, arguing that advancing one group's cause merely shifts the discrimination to another group. By giving priority to African Americans in admissions, for example, schools may overlook more qualified White candidates. In many parts of the country and many sectors of the economy, affirmative action is being rolled back, even though it

Before passage of the Civil Rights Act (1964), segregation of public accommodations was the norm throughout the South. Whites used the most up-to-date bathrooms, waiting rooms, and even drinking fountains, while Blacks ("Colored") were directed to older facilities in inferior condition. Such separate but unequal arrangements are a blatant example of discrimination.

was never fully implemented. We will discuss affirmative action in more detail in Chapter 18.

Discriminatory practices continue to pervade nearly all areas of life in the United States today. In part, that is because various individuals and groups actually *benefit* from racial and ethnic discrimination in terms of money, status, and influence. Discrimination permits members of the majority to enhance their wealth, power, and prestige at the expense of others. Less qualified people get jobs and promotions simply because they are members of the dominant group. Such individuals and groups will not surrender these advantages easily. We'll turn now to a closer look at this functionalist analysis, as well as the conflict, labeling, and interactionist perspectives on race and ethnicity.

thinking CRITICALLY

Which would be more socially significant, the elimination of prejudice or the elimination of discrimination?

Sociological Perspectives on Race and Ethnicity

Relations among racial and ethnic groups lend themselves to analysis from four major sociological perspectives. Viewing race from the macro level, functionalists observe that racial prejudice and discrimination serve positive functions for dominant groups. Conflict theorists see the economic structure as a central factor in the exploitation of minorities. Labeling theorists note the way in which minorities are singled out for differential treatment by law enforcement officers. On the micro level, interactionist researchers stress the manner in which everyday contact between people from different racial and ethnic backgrounds contributes to tolerance or hostility.

Functionalist Perspective

What possible use could racial bigotry have? Functionalist theorists, while agreeing that racial hostility is hardly to be admired, point out that it serves positive functions for those who practice discrimination.

Anthropologist Manning Nash (1962) has identified three functions of racially prejudiced beliefs for the dominant group:

1. Racist views provide a moral justification for maintaining an unequal society that routinely deprives a minority group of its rights and privileges. Southern Whites justified slavery by believing that Africans were physically and spiritually subhuman and devoid of souls.

2. Racist beliefs discourage the subordinate minority from attempting to question its lowly status, which would be to question the very foundations of society.

3. Racial myths suggest that any major societal change (such as an end to discrimination) would only bring greater poverty to the minority and lower the majority's standard of living. As a result, racial prejudice grows when a society's value system (one underlying a colonial empire or slavery, for example) is threatened.

Although racial prejudice and discrimination may serve the powerful, such unequal treatment can also be dysfunctional for a society, and even for the dominant group. Sociologist Arnold Rose (1951) has outlined four dysfunctions that are associated with racism:

1. A society that practices discrimination fails to use the resources of all individuals. Discrimination limits the search for talent and leadership to the dominant group.

2. Discrimination aggravates social problems such as poverty, delinquency, and crime, and places the financial burden of alleviating those problems on the dominant group.

3. Society must invest a good deal of time and money to defend its barriers to the full participation of all members.

4. Racial prejudice and discrimination often undercut goodwill and friendly diplomatic relations between nations.

Conflict Perspective

Conflict theorists would certainly agree with Arnold Rose that racial prejudice and discrimination have many harmful consequences for society. Sociologists such as Oliver Cox (1948), Robert Blauner (1972), and Herbert M. Hunter (2000) have used the **exploitation theory** (or *Marxist class theory*) to explain the basis of racial subordination in the United States. As we saw in Chapter 9, Karl Marx viewed the exploitation of the lower class as a basic part of the capitalist economic system. From a Marxist point of view, racism keeps minorities in low-paying jobs, thereby supplying the capitalist ruling class with a pool of cheap labor. Moreover, by forcing racial minorities to accept low wages, capitalists can restrict the wages of *all* members of the proletariat. Workers from the dominant group who demand higher wages can always be replaced by minorities who have no choice but to accept low-paying jobs.

The conflict view of race relations seems persuasive in a number of instances. Japanese Americans were the object of little prejudice until they began to enter jobs that brought them into competition with Whites. The movement to keep Chinese immigrants out of the United States became most fervent during the latter half of the 19th century, when Chinese and Whites fought over dwindling work opportunities. Both the enslavement of Blacks and the extermination and removal westward of Native Americans were economically motivated.

However, the exploitation theory is too limited to explain prejudice in its many forms. Not all minority groups have been exploited to the same extent. In addition, many groups (such as the Quakers and the Mormons) have been victimized by prejudice for other than economic reasons. Still, as Gordon Allport (1979:210) concludes, the exploitation theory correctly "points a sure finger at one of the factors involved in prejudice, . . . rationalized self-interest of the upper classes."

Labeling Perspective

One practice that fits both the conflict perspective and labeling theory is racial profiling. **Racial profiling** is any arbitrary action initiated by an authority based on race, ethnicity, or national origin rather than on a person's behavior. Generally, racial profiling occurs when law enforcement officers, including customs officials, airport security, and police, assume that people who fit a certain description are likely to be engaged in illegal activities. Beginning in the 1980s with the emergence of the crack cocaine market, skin color became a key characteristic in racial profiling. This practice is often based on very explicit stereotypes. For example, one federal antidrug initiative encouraged officers to look specifically for people with dreadlocks and for Latino men traveling together.

Today, authorities continue to rely on racial profiling, despite overwhelming evidence that it is misleading. A recent study showed that Blacks are still more likely than Whites to be frisked and handled with force when they are stopped. Yet Whites are

more likely than Blacks to possess weapons, illegal drugs, or stolen property (A. Farrell and McDevitt 2010).

Research on the ineffectiveness of racial profiling, coupled with calls by minority communities to end the stigmatization, has led to growing demands to end the practice. But these efforts came to an abrupt halt after the September 11, 2001, terrorist attacks on the United States, when suspicions arose about Muslim and Arab immigrants. Foreign students from Arab countries were summoned for special questioning by authorities. Legal immigrants who were identified as Arab or Muslim were scrutinized for possible illegal activity and prosecuted for violations that authorities routinely ignored among immigrants of other ethnicities and faiths. National surveys have found little change since 2001 in public support for profiling of Arab Americans at airports. In 2010, 53 percent of Americans favored "ethnic and religious profiling" of air travelers—even those who are U.S. citizens—together with more intensive security checks of passengers who fit certain profiles (Zogby 2010).

Interactionist Perspective

A Hispanic woman is transferred from a job on an assembly line to a similar position working next to a White man. At first, the White man is patronizing, assuming that she must be incompetent. She is cold and resentful; even when she needs assistance, she refuses to admit it. After a week, the growing tension between the two leads to a bitter quarrel. Yet over time, each slowly comes to appreciate the other's strengths and talents. A year after they begin working together, these two workers become respectful friends. This story is an example of what interactionists call the *contact hypothesis* in action.

The **contact hypothesis** states that in cooperative circumstances, interracial contact between people of equal status will cause them to become less prejudiced and to abandon old stereotypes. People begin to see one another as individuals and discard the broad generalizations characteristic of stereotyping. Note the phrases *equal status* and *cooperative circumstances*. In the story just told, if the two workers had been competing for one vacancy as a supervisor, the racial hostility between them might have worsened (Allport 1979; Fine 2008).

As Latinos and other minorities slowly gain access to better-paying and more responsible jobs, the contact hypothesis may take on even greater significance. The trend in our society is toward increasing contact between individuals from dominant and subordinate groups. That may be one way of eliminating—or at least reducing—racial and ethnic stereotyping and prejudice. Another may be the establishment of interracial coalitions, an idea suggested by sociologist William Julius Wilson (1999). To work, such coalitions would obviously need to be built on an equal role for all members.

Table 11-2 summarizes the four major sociological perspectives on race. No matter what the explanation for racial and ethnic distinctions—functionalist, conflict, labeling, or interactionist—these socially constructed inequalities can have powerful consequences in the form of prejudice and discrimination. In the next section, we will see how inequality based on the ascribed characteristics of race and ethnicity can poison people's interpersonal relations, depriving whole groups of opportunities others take for granted.

In U.S. retail stores, Black customers have different experiences from White customers. They are more likely than Whites to have their checks or credit cards refused and more likely to be profiled by security personnel.

TABLE 11-2 SOCIOLOGICAL PERSPECTIVES ON RACE AND ETHNICITY

Perspective	Emphasis
Functionalist	The dominant majority benefits from the subordination of racial minorities.
Conflict	Vested interests perpetuate racial inequality through economic exploitation.
Labeling	People are profiled and stereotyped based on their racial and ethnic identity.
Interactionist	Cooperative interracial contacts can reduce hostility.

summing**up**

French police remove a member of the Roma minority who is resisting deportation to his home country. The expulsion of certain racial or ethnic groups is an extreme result of prejudice.

thinking CRITICALLY

Describe an example of labeling that you are personally familiar with.

Spectrum of Intergroup Relations

Racial and ethnic groups can relate to one another in a wide variety of ways, ranging from friendships and intermarriages to hostility, from behaviors that require mutual approval to behaviors imposed by the dominant group.

One devastating pattern of intergroup relations is **genocide**—the deliberate, systematic killing of an entire people or nation. This term describes the killing of 1 million Armenians by Turkey beginning in 1915. It is most commonly applied to Nazi Germany's extermination of 6 million European Jews, as well as gays, lesbians, and the Roma ("Gypsies"), during World War II. The term *genocide* is also appropriate in describing the United States' policies toward Native Americans in the 19th century. In 1800, the Native American (or American Indian) population of the United States was about 600,000; by 1850, it had been reduced to 250,000 through warfare with the U.S. cavalry, disease, and forced relocation to inhospitable environments.

The *expulsion* of a people is another extreme means of acting out racial or ethnic prejudice. In 1979, for example, the government

of Vietnam expelled nearly 1 million ethnic Chinese from the country. The action resulted partly from centuries of hostility between Vietnam and neighboring China.

More recently (beginning in 2009), France expelled over 10,000 ethnic Roma (or Gypsies) who had immigrated from their home countries of Bulgaria and Romania. The action appeared to violate the European Union's ban against targeting ethnic groups, as well as its policy of "freedom of movement" throughout the EU. In 2011, the EU withdrew the threat of legal action when the French government modified its policy to apply only to those Roma who lived in "illegal camps." However, many observers saw the concession as a thinly veiled attempt to circumvent the EU's long-standing human rights policies.

In a variation of expulsion, called *secession*, failure to resolve an ethnic or racial conflict results in the drawing of formal boundaries between the groups. In 1947, India was partitioned into two separate countries in an attempt to end violent conflict between Hindus and Muslims. The predominantly Muslim areas in the north became the new country of Pakistan; the rest of India became predominantly Hindu.

Secession, expulsion, and genocide are extreme behaviors, clustered on the negative end of what is called the Spectrum of Intergroup Relations (Figure 11-3). More typical intergroup relations follow four identifiable patterns: (1) segregation, (2) amalgamation, (3) assimilation, and (4) pluralism. Each pattern

FIGURE 11-3 SPECTRUM OF INTERGROUP RELATIONS

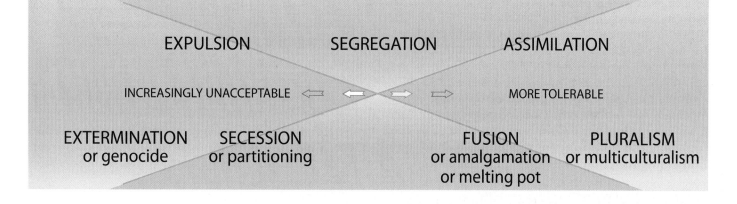

defines the dominant group's actions and the minority group's responses. Intergroup relations are rarely restricted to only one of the four patterns, although invariably one does tend to dominate. Think of these patterns primarily as ideal types.

Segregation

Separate schools, separate seating on buses and in restaurants, separate washrooms, even separate drinking fountains—these were all part of the lives of African Americans in the South when segregation ruled early in the 20th century. **Segregation** refers to the physical separation of two groups of people in terms of residence, workplace, and social events. Generally, a dominant group imposes this pattern on a minority group. Segregation is rarely complete, however. Intergroup contact inevitably occurs, even in the most segregated societies.

From 1948 (when it received its independence) to 1990, the Republic of South Africa severely restricted the movement of Blacks and other non-Whites by means of a wide-ranging system of segregation known as **apartheid.** Apartheid even included the creation of separate homelands where Blacks were expected to live. However, decades of local resistance to apartheid, combined with international pressure, led to marked political changes in the 1990s. In 1994, a prominent Black activist, Nelson Mandela, was elected South Africa's president in the first election in which Blacks (the majority of the nation's population) were allowed to vote. Mandela had spent almost 28 years in South African prisons for his anti-apartheid activities. His election was widely viewed as the final blow to South Africa's oppressive policy of segregation.

In contrast to the enforced segregation in South Africa, the United States exemplifies an unmandated but nevertheless persistent separation of the races. In their book *American Apartheid,* sociologists Douglas Massey and Nancy Denton (1993) described segregation in U.S. cities using 1990 census data. As the book's title suggests, the racial makeup of U.S. neighborhoods resembles the rigid government-imposed segregation that prevailed for so long in South Africa.

Analysis of more recent census data shows the continuing segregation of U.S. cities, despite the nation's growing racial and ethnic diversity. To measure the degree of separation, scholars use a segregation index ranging from 0 (complete integration) to 100 (complete segregation). Values in between the two extremes indicate the percentage of the minority group that would need to move to another neighborhood for the two groups to be distributed exactly alike. A Black–White segregation index of 60, for example, means that 60 percent of African Americans would need to move to be distributed as Whites are. Census data for the five years from 2005 through 2009 show that the Black–White segregation index was highest in Milwaukee (81), Detroit (80), New York City (79), and Chicago (78). The Hispanic–White index was highest in Springfield, Massachusetts (64), New York City (63), Los Angeles (63), and Providence, Rhode Island (62). And the Asian–White index was highest in Pittsburgh (60), Youngstown, Ohio (59), Buffalo (59), and Birmingham, Alabama (59).

Across the board, the residential segregation of African Americans has declined only modestly since 2000; for Asian Americans and Latinos it has increased. Even allowing for social class, these patterns of segregation persist (Bureau of the Census 2010b; Farley 2004; Frey 2011; Wilkes and Iceland 2004).

Amalgamation

Amalgamation happens when a majority group and a minority group combine to form a new group. Through intermarriage over several generations, various groups in society combine to form a new group. This pattern can be expressed as $A + B + C \rightarrow D$, where A, B, and C represent different groups in a society, and D signifies the end result, a unique cultural-racial group unlike any of the initial groups (Newman 1973).

The belief in the United States as a "melting pot" became compelling in the first part of the 20th century, particularly since that image suggested that the nation had an almost divine mission to amalgamate various groups into one people. However, in actuality, many residents were not willing to include Native Americans, Jews, African Americans, Asian Americans, and Irish Roman Catholics in the melting pot. Therefore, this pattern does not adequately describe dominant–subordinate relations in the United States.

Assimilation

In India, many Hindus complain about Indian citizens who copy the traditions and customs of the British. In France, people of Arab and African origin, many of them Muslim, complain they are treated as second-class citizens—a charge that provoked riots in 2005. In Australia, Aborigines who have become part of the dominant society refuse to acknowledge their darker-skinned grandparents on the street. And in the United States, some Italian Americans, Polish Americans, Hispanics, and Jews have changed their ethnic-sounding family names to names that are typically found among White Protestant families.

Assimilation is the process through which a person forsakes his or her cultural tradition to become part of a different culture. Generally, it is practiced by a minority group member who wants to conform to the standards of the dominant group. Assimilation can be described as a pattern in which $A + B + C \rightarrow A$. The majority, A, dominates in such a way that members of minorities B and C imitate it and attempt to become indistinguishable from it (Newman 1973).

Assimilation is no guarantee of social acceptance. A Chinese American such as Helen Zia (see the chapter-opening excerpt) may speak English fluently, achieve high educational standards, and become a well-respected professional or businessperson and *still* be seen as different. Other Americans may reject her as a business associate, neighbor, or marriage partner.

use your sociological *imagination*

You have immigrated to another country with a very different culture. What steps might you take to assimilate?

Pluralism

In a pluralistic society, a subordinate group does not have to forsake its lifestyle and traditions to avoid prejudice or discrimination. **Pluralism** is based on mutual respect for one another's cultures among the various groups in a society. This pattern allows a minority group to express its own culture and still participate without prejudice in the larger society. Earlier, we described amalgamation as A + B + C → D, and assimilation as A + B + C → A. Using this same approach, we can conceive of pluralism as A + B + C → A + B + C. All the groups coexist in the same society (Newman 1973).

In the United States, pluralism is more of an ideal than a reality. There are distinct instances of pluralism—the ethnic neighborhoods in major cities, such as Koreatown, Little Tokyo, Andersonville (Swedish Americans), and Spanish Harlem—yet there are also limits to cultural freedom. To survive, a society must promote a certain consensus among its members regarding basic ideals, values, and beliefs. Thus, if a Romanian immigrant to the United States wants to move up the occupational ladder, he or she cannot avoid learning the English language.

Switzerland exemplifies the modern pluralistic state. There, the absence of both a national language and a dominant religious faith leads to a tolerance for cultural diversity. In addition, various political devices safeguard the interests of ethnic groups in a way that has no parallel in the United States. In contrast, Great Britain has had difficulty achieving cultural pluralism in a multiracial society. East Indians, Pakistanis, and Blacks from the Caribbean and Africa experience prejudice and discrimination within the dominant White society there. Some British advocate cutting off all Asian and Black immigration, and a few even call for expulsion of those non-Whites currently living in Britain.

thinking CRITICALLY

Give examples of amalgamation, assimilation, segregation, and pluralism that you have seen on your campus or in your workplace.

Race and Ethnicity in the United States

Few societies have a more diverse population than the United States; the nation is truly a multiracial, multiethnic society. Of course, that has not always been the case. The population of what is now the United States has changed dramatically since the arrival of European settlers in the 1600s, as Figure 11-1 (see page 238) shows. Immigration, colonialism, and in the case of Blacks, slavery determined the racial and ethnic makeup of our present-day society.

Today, the largest racial minorities in the United States are African Americans, Native Americans, and Asian Americans. The largest ethnic groups are Latinos, Jews, and the various White ethnic groups. Figure 11-4 shows where the major racial and ethnic minorities are concentrated.

African Americans

"I am an invisible man," wrote Black author Ralph Ellison in his novel *Invisible Man* (1952:3). "I am a man of substance, of flesh and bone, fiber and liquids—and I might even be said to possess a mind. I am invisible, understand, simply because people refuse to see me."

Over five decades later, many African Americans still feel invisible. Despite their large numbers, they have long been treated as second-class citizens. Currently, by the standards of the federal government, more than 1 out of every 4 African Americans—as opposed to 1 out of every 11 White non-Hispanics—is poor (DeNavas-Walt et al. 2010:15).

Contemporary institutional discrimination and individual prejudice against African Americans are rooted in the history of slavery in the United States. Many other subordinate groups had little wealth and income, but as sociologist W. E. B. DuBois ([1909] 1970) and others have noted, enslaved African Americans were in an even more oppressive situation, because by law they could not own property and could not pass on the benefits of their labor to their children. Today, increasing numbers of African Americans and sympathetic Whites are calling for *slave reparations* to compensate for the injustices of forced servitude. Reparations could include official expressions of apology from governments such as the United States, ambitious programs to improve African Americans' economic status, or even direct payments to descendants of slaves (D. Williams and Collins 2004).

The end of the Civil War did not bring genuine freedom and equality for Blacks. The Southern states passed Jim Crow laws to enforce official segregation, and the Supreme Court upheld them as constitutional in 1896. In addition, Blacks faced the danger of lynching campaigns, often led by the Ku Klux Klan, during the late 1800s and early 1900s. From a conflict perspective, Whites maintained their dominance formally through legalized segregation and informally by means of vigilante terror and violence (Franklin and Higginbotham 2011).

During the 1960s, a vast civil rights movement emerged, with many competing factions and strategies for change. The Southern Christian Leadership Conference (SCLC), founded by Dr. Martin Luther King Jr., used nonviolent civil disobedience to oppose segregation. The National Association for the Advancement of Colored People (NAACP) favored use of the courts to press for equality for African Americans. But many younger Black leaders, most notably Malcolm X, turned toward an ideology of Black power. Proponents of **Black power** rejected the goal of assimilation into White middle-class society. They defended the beauty and dignity of Black and African cultures and supported the creation of Black-controlled political and economic institutions (Ture and Hamilton 1992).

Despite numerous courageous actions to achieve Black civil rights, Black and White citizens are still separate, still unequal. From birth to death, Blacks suffer in terms of their life chances. Life remains difficult for millions of poor Blacks, who must attempt to survive in ghetto areas shattered by high unemployment and abandoned housing. Today the

FIGURE **11-4** THE UNITED STATES: THE IMAGE OF DIVERSITY

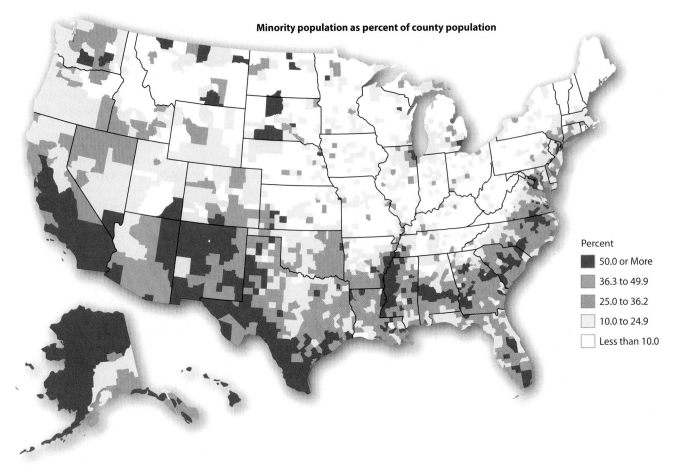

Minority population as percent of county population

Percent

- 50.0 or More
- 36.3 to 49.9
- 25.0 to 36.2
- 10.0 to 24.9
- Less than 10.0

Source: Humes et al. 2011:21.

Overall, 36.3 percent of the U.S. population belonged to a minority group in 2010. In four states (California, Hawaii, New Mexico, and Texas) and the District of Columbia, as well as in about a tenth of all counties, minorities constitute the numerical majority. The 2010 Census also showed that 11 percent of the nation's counties already have become "majority minority"—less than 50 percent non-Hispanic white. And another 7 percent of the nation's counties have reached the "tipping point" toward becoming majority minority sometime in the next decade.

Think about It
The United States is a diverse nation. Why, in many parts of the country, can't people see that diversity in their towns?

median household income of Blacks is still 60 percent that of Whites, and the unemployment rate among Blacks is more than twice that of Whites.

Some African Americans—especially middle-class men and women—have made economic gains over the past 50 years. For example, data show that the number of African Americans in management increased nationally from 2.4 percent of the total in 1958 to 6.2 percent in 2009. Yet Blacks still represent only 7 percent or less of all physicians, engineers, scientists, lawyers, judges, and marketing managers (Bureau of the Census 2010a:Table 615).

Native Americans

Today, about 2.5 million Native Americans represent a diverse array of cultures distinguishable by language, family organization, religion, and livelihood. The outsiders who came to the United States—European settlers—and their descendants came to know these native peoples' forefathers as "American Indians." By the time the Bureau of Indian Affairs (BIA) was organized as part of the War Department in 1824, Indian–White relations had already included more than two centuries of hostile actions that had led to the virtual elimination of native peoples (see Figure 11-1, page 238). During the 19th century, many bloody wars wiped out a significant part of the Indian population. By the end of the century, schools for Indians—operated by the BIA or by church missions—prohibited the practice of Native American cultures. Yet at the same time, such schools did little to make the children effective members of White society.

Today, life remains difficult for members of the 554 tribal groups in the United States, whether they live in cities or on reservations. For example, one Native American teenager in

SOCIOLOGY IN THE GLOBAL COMMUNITY

11-1 The Aboriginal People of Australia

The indigenous, or Aboriginal, people of Australia have inhabited their home continent continuously for at least 50,000 years. Today they make up about 2.4 percent of Australia's total population. Although their numbers are small, they are highly visible in Australian society.

The cultural practices of the Aboriginal people are quite diverse, given their many clans, language groups, and communities. Except for occasional connections between kin or trading partners, these groups have little social contact. When Europeans first arrived in Australia, the diversity of Aborigines was even greater: an estimated 600 to 700 different groups spoke 200 to 250 languages as distinct from each other as French is from German. The existence of many dialects, or variants of languages that were more or less understandable to others, increased the complexity.

Like the American Indians, Australia's Aboriginal population declined dramatically following European settlement. New diseases, some of which were not life-threatening to Europeans, had a devastating effect on Aboriginal communities, which lacked immunity to them. Mistreatment under the British colonial regime, dispossession of their land, and the disruption and disintegration of their culture also overwhelmed the Aboriginal people. Decades of protests and legal efforts regarding their land rights have brought little change.

Historically, the Aboriginal people received little legal recognition from Europeans. Only in 1967 did the government of Australia extend citizenship and voting rights to the Aboriginals, along with access to welfare and unemployment benefits. Yet it would be misleading to view the Aboriginal people as passive victims, either in colonial days or in more recent times. They have worked actively to secure their rights.

As in the United States, Whites' low regard for the Aboriginal people became the basis for an effort to stamp out their culture. From 1910 to 1970, thousands of Aboriginal children were forcibly removed from their families so they could be raised by

> *From 1910 to 1970, thousands of Aboriginal children were forcibly removed from their families so they could be raised by Whites and impressed into the dominant culture.*

Whites and impressed into the dominant culture. Between 10 to 30 percent of all Aboriginal children were affected by this program. Not until 2008 did the Australian government finally apologize to Aboriginals for "the Stolen Generations." The government has expressed its intention to improve the Aboriginal people's living conditions and their prospects for the future.

LET'S DISCUSS

1. Try to think of a situation in your culture in which the government might forcibly remove a child from his or her family. Do you know anyone who has had such an experience? If so, what were the repercussions?

2. What kind of reasoning do you think lay behind the Australian government's forced removal of Aboriginal children from their families? In sociological terms, what actually happened?

Sources: W. Anderson 2003; Attwood 2003; Australia 1997, 2008; R. Schaefer 2012.

six has attempted suicide—a rate four times higher than the rate for other teenagers. Traditionally, some Native Americans have chosen to assimilate and abandon all vestiges of their tribal cultures to escape certain forms of prejudice. However, by the 1990s, an increasing number of people in the United States were openly claiming a Native American identity. Since 1960, the federal government's count of Native Americans has tripled.

Native Americans have made some progress in redressing their past mistreatment. In 2009, the federal government settled a 13-year-old lawsuit for the recovery of lease payments due on tribal lands used by the government for oil and gas exploration and grazing. Although the $3.4 billion settlement was large, it was long overdue—some of the government's debts dated back to 1887—and from the perspective of tribal leaders, it was too little, too late. The United States is not the only country that has tried to redress the government's past actions toward indigenous peoples (Box 11-1).

Native American artists often break new ground to represent their life experiences. Dunne-Za member Brian Jungen used Nike shoes to make this three-dimensional piece, which suggests both his Pacific Northwest culture and his family's practice of stretching their modest means by reusing everything.

The introduction of gambling on Indian reservations has transformed the lives of some Native Americans. Native Americans got into the gaming industry in 1988, when Congress passed the Indian Gambling Regulatory Act. The law stipulates that states must negotiate agreements with tribes interested in commercial gaming; they cannot prevent tribes from engaging in gambling operations, even if state law prohibits such ventures. The income from these lucrative operations is not evenly distributed, however. About two-thirds of recognized Indian tribes are not involved in gambling ventures. Those tribes that earn substantial revenues from gambling constitute a small fraction of Native Americans (Conner and Taggart 2009).

Like Native Americans, many native peoples living in the United States have successfully established their autonomy, gaining control over their resources and business enterprises. In Chapter 17, we will consider Native Hawaiians' continuing struggle for recognition of their rights.

use your sociological *imagination*

You are a Native American whose tribe is about to open a reservation-based casino. Will the casino further the assimilation of your people into mainstream society or encourage pluralism?

Asian Americans

Asian Americans are a diverse group, one of the fastest-growing segments of the U.S. population (up 43 percent between 2000 and 2010). Among the many groups of Americans of Asian descent are Vietnamese Americans, Chinese Americans, Japanese Americans, and Korean Americans (Figure 11-5).

Asian Americans are also economically diverse. There are rich and poor Japanese Americans, rich and poor Filipino Americans, and so forth. In fact, Southeast Asians living in the United States have the highest rate of welfare dependency of any racial or ethnic group. Though Asian Americans have substantially more schooling than other ethnic groups, their median income is only slightly higher than Whites' income, and their poverty rate is higher. In 2008, for every Asian American household with an annual income of $100,000 or more, there was another earning less than $35,000 a year (DeNavas-Walt et al. 2010).

The fact that as a group, Asian Americans work in the same occupations as Whites suggests that they have been successful—and many have. However, there are some differences between the two groups. Asian immigrants, like other minorities and immigrants before them, are found disproportionately in low-paying service occupations. At the same time, better-educated Asian Americans are concentrated near the top in professional and managerial positions, although they rarely reach the pinnacle. Instead, they hit the glass ceiling, or try to "climb a broken ladder," as some put it.

Ironically, Asian Americans are often held up as a **model minority,** or **ideal minority,** supposedly because they have succeeded economically, socially, and educationally despite past prejudice and discrimination, and without resorting to confrontations with Whites. To some Whites, the existence of a model

FIGURE **11-5** ASIAN AMERICAN AND PACIFIC ISLANDER POPULATION BY ORIGIN

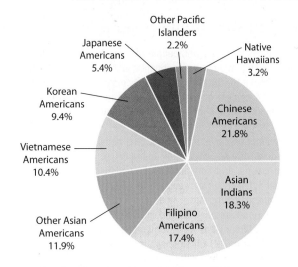

Source: 2009 data from American Community Survey 2010: Tables B02006, B02007.

Think about It
Do Asian Americans really have a common identity?

minority seems to reaffirm the notion that anyone can get ahead in the United States through talent and hard work. The implication is that those minorities that do not succeed are somehow responsible for their failure. Viewed from a conflict perspective, this attitude is yet another instance of *blaming the victims.* Moreover, the stereotype on which it is based is a false one (Bascara 2008; Choi and Lahey 2006).

Chinese Americans Unlike African slaves and Native Americans, the Chinese were initially encouraged to immigrate to the United States. From 1850 to 1880, thousands of Chinese immigrated to this country, lured by job opportunities created by the discovery of gold. However, as employment possibilities decreased and competition for mining jobs grew, the Chinese became the target of a bitter campaign to limit their numbers and restrict their rights. Chinese laborers were exploited, then discarded.

In 1882, Congress enacted the Chinese Exclusion Act, which prevented Chinese immigration and even forbade Chinese in the United States to send for their families. As a result, the Chinese population declined steadily until after World War II. More recently, the descendants of the 19th-century immigrants have been joined by a new influx from Hong Kong and Taiwan. These groups may contrast sharply in their degree of assimilation, desire to live in Chinatowns, and feelings about this country's relations with the People's Republic of China.

Currently, over 3 million Chinese Americans live in the United States. Some Chinese Americans have entered lucrative occupations, yet many immigrants struggle to survive under living and working conditions that belie the model-minority stereotype. New York City's Chinatown district is filled with illegal sweatshops in which recent immigrants—many of them Chinese women—work for minimal wages. Outside of Chinatown, 23 percent of Asian

Americans fall into the low-income category. At the other end of the income distribution, barely 5 percent of Chinatown's residents earn more than $100,000 a year, compared to 25 percent of Asian Americans who live elsewhere in New York City (Logan et al. 2002; Wong 2006).

Asian Indians After Chinese Americans, the second-largest Asian American group, immigrants from India and their descendants, numbers over 2.6 million. It is difficult to generalize about Asian Indian Americans because Asian Indians are such a diverse population. India, a country of more than 1.2 billion people that is fast becoming the most populous nation in the world, is multiethnic. Perhaps because Asian Indian immigrants feel threatened by mainstream U.S. culture, religious orthodoxy is often stronger among first-generation immigrants to the United States than it is in India. New immigrants try to practice their religion just as they did in India rather than join congregations already established by other immigrant groups.

Maintaining family traditions is a major challenge for Asian Indian immigrants to the United States. Family ties remain strong despite their immigration—so much so that many Asian Indians feel more connected to their relatives in India than Americans do to relatives nearby. These *Desi* (pronounced DAY-see, colloquial for people who trace their ancestry to South Asia, especially India) are particularly concerned about the erosion of traditional family authority. Indian American children dress like their peers, go to fast-food restaurants, and even eat hamburgers, rejecting the vegetarian diet typical of both Hindus and many Asian Indian Muslims. Sons do not feel the extent of responsibility to the family that tradition dictates. Daughters, whose occupations and marriage partners the family could control in India, assert their right to choose their careers, and even their husbands (Rangaswamy 2005).

Filipino Americans Filipinos are the third-largest Asian American group in the United States, with nearly 2.5 million people. For geographic reasons, social scientists consider them to be of Asian extraction, but physically and culturally this group also reflects centuries of Spanish and U.S. colonial rule, as well as the more recent U.S. military occupation.

Filipinos began immigrating to the United States as American nationals when the U.S. government gained possession of the Philippine Islands at the end of the Spanish–American War (1899). When the Philippines gained their independence in 1948, Filipinos lost their unrestricted immigration rights, although farmworkers were welcome to work in Hawai'i's pineapple groves. Aside from this exception, immigration was restricted to 50 to 100 Filipinos a year until 1965, when the Immigration Act lifted the strict quotas.

Today, a significant percentage of Filipino immigrants are well-educated professionals who work in the field of health care. Although they are a valuable human resource in the United States, their immigration has long drained the medical establishment in the Philippines. When the U.S. Immigration and Naturalization Service stopped giving preference to physicians, Filipino doctors began entering the country as nurses—a dramatic illustration of the incredible income differences between the two countries. Like other immigrant groups,

Asian Americans rarely head the casts of motion pictures, unless those films feature the martial arts. Two exceptions to the rule are John Cho (left) and Kal Penn, who co-star in the successful Harold & Kumar movies. Penn is the stage name used by Kalpen Modi, the son of Asian Indian immigrants to the United States. In 2009, President Obama appointed Modi associate director of the Office of Public Engagement, where he serves as a liaison to the Asian American and Pacific Islander communities.

Filipino Americans save much of their income and send a significant amount of money, called *remittances*, back to their extended families (Zarembo 2004b).

For several reasons, Filipino Americans have not coalesced in a single formal social organization, despite their numbers. Their strong loyalty to the family (*sa pamilya*) and to the church—particularly Roman Catholicism—reduces their need for a separate organization. Moreover, their diversity complicates the task of uniting the Filipino American community, which reflects the same regional, religious, and linguistic distinctions that divide their homeland. Thus, the many groups that Filipino Americans have organized tend to be club-like or fraternal in nature. Because those groups do not represent the general population of Filipino Americans, they remain largely invisible to Anglos. Although Filipinos remain interested in events in their homeland, they also seek to become involved in broader, non-Filipino organizations and to avoid exclusive activities (Bonus 2000; Kang 1996; Lau 2006; Padilla 2008).

Vietnamese Americans Vietnamese Americans came to the United States primarily during and after the Vietnam War—especially after U.S. withdrawal from the conflict in 1975. Refugees from the communist government in Vietnam, assisted by local agencies, settled throughout the United States, tens of thousands of them in small towns. But over time, Vietnamese Americans have gravitated toward the larger urban areas, establishing Vietnamese restaurants and grocery stores in their ethnic enclaves there.

In 1995, the United States resumed normal diplomatic relations with Vietnam. Gradually, the *Viet Kieu,* or Vietnamese living abroad, began to return to their old country to visit, but usually not to take up permanent residence. Today, more than

35 years after the end of the Vietnam War, sharp differences of opinion remain among Vietnamese Americans, especially the older ones, concerning the war and the present government of Vietnam (Pfeifer 2008).

Korean Americans At over 1.3 million, the population of Korean Americans now exceeds that of Japanese Americans. Yet Korean Americans are often overshadowed by other groups from Asia.

Today's Korean American community is the result of three waves of immigration. The initial wave arrived between 1903 and 1910, when Korean laborers migrated to Hawai'i. The second wave followed the end of the Korean War in 1953; most of those immigrants were wives of U.S. servicemen and war orphans. The third wave, continuing to the present, has reflected the admissions priorities set up in the 1965 Immigration Act. These well-educated immigrants arrive in the United States with professional skills. Yet because of language difficulties and discrimination, many must settle at least initially for positions of lower responsibility than those they held in Korea and must suffer through a period of disenchantment. Stress, loneliness, and family strife may accompany the pain of adjustment.

In the early 1990s, the apparent friction between Korean Americans and another subordinate racial group, African Americans, attracted nationwide attention. Conflict between the two groups was dramatized in Spike Lee's 1989 movie *Do the Right Thing.* The situation stemmed from Korean Americans' position as the latest immigrant group to cater to the needs of inner-city populations abandoned by those who have moved up the economic ladder. This type of friction is not new; generations of Jewish, Italian, and Arab merchants have encountered similar hostility from what to outsiders seems an unlikely source— another oppressed minority (Kim 1999).

Japanese Americans Approximately 100,000 Japanese Americans live in the United States. As a people, they are relatively recent arrivals. In 1880, only 148 Japanese lived in the United States, but by 1920 there were more than 110,000. Japanese immigrants— called the *Issei* (pronounced EE-say), or first generation—were usually males seeking employment opportunities. Many Whites saw them (along with Chinese immigrants) as a "yellow peril" and subjected them to prejudice and discrimination.

In 1941, the attack on Hawai'i's Pearl Harbor by Japan had severe repercussions for Japanese Americans. The federal government decreed that all Japanese Americans on the West Coast must leave their homes and report to "evacuation camps." In effect, Japanese Americans became scapegoats for the anger that other people in the United States felt concerning Japan's role in World War II. By August 1943, in an unprecedented application of guilt by virtue of ancestry, 113,000 Japanese Americans had been forced into hastily built camps. In striking contrast, only a few German Americans and Italian Americans were sent to evacuation camps (Hosokawa 1969).

In 1983, a federal commission recommended government payments to all surviving Japanese Americans who had been held in detention camps. The commission reported that the detention was motivated by "race prejudice, war hysteria, and a failure of political leadership." It added that "no documented acts of espionage, sabotage, or fifth-column activity were shown to have been committed" by Japanese Americans. In 1988, President Ronald Reagan signed the Civil Liberties Act, which required the federal government to issue individual apologies for all violations of Japanese Americans' constitutional rights, and established a $1.25 billion trust fund to pay reparations to the approximately 77,500 surviving Japanese Americans who had been interned (Department of Justice 2000).

Arab Americans

Arab Americans are immigrants, and their descendants, from the 22 nations of the Arab world. As defined by the League of Arab States, these are the nations of North Africa and what is popularly known as the Middle East, including Lebanon, Syria, Palestine, Morocco, Iraq, Saudi Arabia, and Somalia. Not all residents of those countries are Arab; for example, the Kurds, who live in northern Iraq, are not Arab. And some Arab Americans may have immigrated to the United States from non-Arab countries such as Great Britain or France, where their families have lived for generations.

The Arabic language is the single most unifying force among Arabs, although not all Arabs, and certainly not all Arab Americans, can read and speak Arabic. Moreover, the language has evolved over the centuries so that people in different parts of the Arab world speak different dialects. Still, the fact that the Koran (or Qur'an) was originally written in Arabic gives the language special importance to Muslims, just as the Torah's composition in Hebrew gives that language special significance to Jews.

In Chicago, a young Muslim woman sports an "I Love New York" T-shirt. Across the United States, racial and ethnic diversity has increased dramatically.

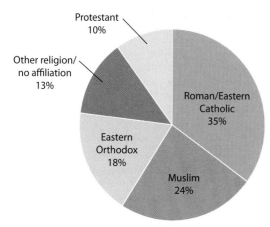

Protestant
10%

Other religion/
no affiliation
13%

Roman/Eastern
Catholic
35%

Eastern
Orthodox
18%

Muslim
24%

Notes: Roman/Eastern Catholic includes Roman Catholic, Maronite, and Melkite (Greek Catholic); Eastern Orthodox includes Antiochian, Syrian, Greek, and Coptic; Muslim includes Sunni, Shi'a, and Druze.
Source: Arab American Institute 2010, based on 2002 Zogby International Survey.

Unlike Arabs in other parts of the world, most Arab Americans are Christian.

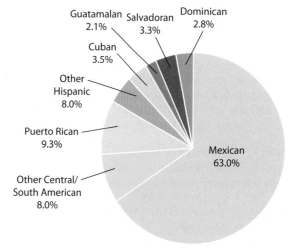

Guatamalan
2.1%

Salvadoran
3.3%

Dominican
2.8%

Cuban
3.5%

Other
Hispanic
8.0%

Puerto Rican
9.3%

Other Central/
South American
8.0%

Mexican
63.0%

Note: "Other Hispanic" includes Spanish Americans and Latinos identified as mixed ancestry as well as other Central and South Americans not otherwise indicated by specific country.
Source: 2010 census data in Ennis et al. 2011:33.

Think about It
Do Hispanic Americans really have a common identity?

Estimates of the size of the Arab American community differ widely. By some estimates, up to 3 million people of Arab ancestry reside in the United States. Among those who identify themselves as Arab Americans, the most common country of origin is Lebanon, followed by Syria, Egypt, and Palestine. In 2000, these four countries of origin accounted for two-thirds of all Arab Americans. Their rising numbers have led to the development of Arab retail centers in several cities, including Dearborn and Detroit, Michigan; Los Angeles; Chicago; New York City; and Washington, D.C.

As a group, Arab Americans are extremely diverse. Many families have lived in the United States for several generations; others are foreign born. Their points of origin range from the metropolis of Cairo, Egypt, to the rural villages of Morocco. Despite the stereotype, most Arab Americans are *not* Muslim (Figure 11-6). Nor can Arab Americans be characterized as having a specific family type, gender role, or occupational pattern (David 2004, 2008).

Despite this great diversity, profiling of potential terrorists at airports has put Arab and Muslim Americans under special surveillance. For years, a number of airlines and law enforcement authorities have used appearance and ethnic-sounding names to identify and take aside Arab Americans and search their belongings. After the terrorist attacks of September 2001, criticism of this practice declined as concern for the public's safety mounted.

Latinos

Together, the various groups included under the general category *Latinos* represent the largest minority in the United States. There are more than 50 million Hispanics in this country, including 30 million Mexican Americans, more than 4 million Puerto

Ricans, and smaller numbers of Cuban Americans and people of Central and South American origin (Figure 11-7). The latter group represents the fastest-growing and most diverse segment of the Hispanic community.

According to Census Bureau data, the Latino population now outnumbers the African American population in 6 of the 10 largest cities of the United States: Los Angeles, Houston, Phoenix, San Diego, Dallas, and San Antonio. Hispanics are now the majority of residents in cities such as Miami, Florida; El Paso, Texas; and Santa Ana, California. The rise in the Hispanic population of the United States—fueled by comparatively high birthrates and levels of immigration—has intensified debates over public policy issues such as bilingualism and immigration. Coincidentally, these discussions are taking place just as Latinos are beginning to flex their muscles as voters (Box 11-2).

The various Latino groups share a heritage of Spanish language and culture, which can cause serious problems in their assimilation. An intelligent student whose first language is Spanish may be presumed slow or even unruly by English-speaking schoolchildren, and frequently by English-speaking teachers as well. The labeling of Latino children as underachievers, as learning disabled, or as emotionally disturbed can act as a self-fulfilling prophecy for some children. Bilingual education aims at easing the educational difficulties experienced by Hispanic children and others whose first language is not English.

The educational difficulties of Latino students certainly contribute to Hispanics' generally low economic status. In 2008, about 17 percent of all Hispanic households earned

RESEARCH TODAY

11-2 Latinos in the Voting Booth

Over the past 40 years, the two major political parties have slowly acknowledged Latinos as a force at the ballot box. The rapid growth of the Hispanic population, together with policies that facilitate voting by non-English speakers, underlie this shift.

In 1975, Congress moved to recognize the multilingual background of the U.S. population. Federal law now requires bilingual or even multilingual ballots in voting districts where at least 10,000 people or 5 percent of the voting-age population do not speak English.

These voting reforms have not had the impact many advocates hoped, however, and turnout remains poor. Hispanics are interested in voting, but many are ineligible because they are not citizens. Thus, in the 2008 presidential election, Hispanics accounted for 15.4 percent of the total U.S. population but only 9.5 percent of the eligible electorate.

Apathy is another hurdle to voter participation. Like African Americans, many Latinos resent the fact that political movers and shakers seem to recognize their existence only once every four years. Between major elections, they hear little except from Latino elected officials.

Like African Americans, many Latinos resent the fact that political movers and shakers seem to recognize their existence only once every four years.

Although national surveys show that Latino policy concerns mirror those of the general electorate—the economy, education, health care, national security, the environment, and energy—there is one exception. Immigration policy usually ranks among Latinos' top five or six concerns. Latinos want less restrictive immigration laws that will speed up the immigration and naturalization process. Non-Hispanics tend to see immigration as either an economic threat or a national security concern.

The potential for a stronger Latino political presence is great. In anticipation of a larger turnout, both political parties are now nominating more Hispanic candidates. As a rule, Democrats have been more successful than Republicans in attracting the Hispanic vote. In the 2010 congressional elections, 60 percent of Latino voters backed Democratic candidates, compared to 37 percent of Whites.

LET'S DISCUSS

1. Do you vote in a community where polling places offer multilingual ballots? If so, do the names on the ballot mirror the community's multiethnic background?
2. If you were a campaign worker, how would you go about appealing to the Latino vote?

Sources: Connelly 2008; Lopez 2010.

---

less than $15,000, compared to 11 percent of White non-Hispanic households; and the poverty rate was 25.3 percent for Hispanics, compared to 9.4 percent for White non-Hispanics. Overall, Latinos are not as affluent as White non-Hispanics, but a middle class is beginning to emerge (DeNavas-Walt et al. 2010:15, 35, 38).

Mexican Americans The largest Latino population is Mexican Americans, who can be further subdivided into those descended from residents of the territories annexed after the Mexican American War of 1848 and those who have immigrated from Mexico to the United States. The opportunity for a Mexican to earn in one hour what it would take an entire day to earn in Mexico has pushed millions of legal and illegal immigrants north.

Aside from the family, the most important social organization in the Mexican American (or Chicano) community is the church, specifically the Roman Catholic Church. This strong identification with the Catholic faith has reinforced the already formidable barriers between Mexican Americans and their predominantly White and Protestant neighbors in the Southwest. At the same time, the Catholic Church helps many immigrants to develop a sense of identity and assists their assimilation into the norms and values of the dominant culture of the United States. The complexity of the Mexican American community is underscored by the fact that Protestant churches—especially those that endorse expressive, open worship—have attracted increasing numbers of Mexican Americans.

Puerto Ricans The second-largest segment of Latinos in the United States is Puerto Ricans. Since 1917, residents of Puerto Rico have held the status of American citizens; many have migrated to New York and other eastern cities. Unfortunately, Puerto Ricans have experienced serious poverty both in the United States and on the island. Those who live in the continental United States earn barely half the family income of Whites. As a result, a reverse migration began in the 1970s, when more Puerto Ricans were leaving for the island than were coming to the mainland (Torres 2008).

Politically, Puerto Ricans in the United States have not been as successful as Mexican Americans in organizing for their rights. For many mainland Puerto Ricans—as for many residents of the island—the paramount political issue is the destiny of Puerto Rico itself: should it continue in its present commonwealth status, petition for admission to the United States as the 51st state, or attempt to become an independent nation? This question has divided Puerto Rico for decades and remains a central issue in Puerto Rican elections. In a 1998 referendum, voters supported a "none of the above" option, effectively favoring continuation of the commonwealth status over statehood or independence.

Cuban Americans Cuban immigration to the United States dates back as far as 1831, but it began in earnest following Fidel Castro's assumption of power in the Cuban revolution (1959). The first wave of 200,000 Cubans included many professionals with relatively high levels of schooling; these men and women were largely welcomed as refugees from communist tyranny. However, more recent waves of immigrants have aroused growing concern, partly because they were less likely to be skilled professionals. Throughout these waves of immigration, Cuban Americans have been encouraged to locate around the United States. Nevertheless, many continue to settle in (or return to) metropolitan Miami, Florida, with its warm climate and proximity to Cuba.

The Cuban experience in the United States has been mixed. Some detractors worry about the vehement anticommunism of Cuban Americans and the apparent growth of an organized crime syndicate that engages in the drug trade and ganglike violence. Recently, Cuban Americans in Miami have expressed concern over what they view as the indifference of the city's Roman Catholic hierarchy. Like other Hispanics, Cuban Americans are underrepresented in leadership positions within the church. Also—despite many individual success stories—as a group, Cuban Americans in Miami remain behind Whites in income, rate of employment, and proportion of professionals (Masud-Piloto 2008).

Central and South Americans Immigrants from Central and South America are a diverse population that has not been closely studied. Indeed, most government statistics treat members of this group collectively as "other," rarely differentiating among them by nationality. Yet people from Chile and Costa Rica have little in common other than their hemisphere of origin and the Spanish language—if that. The fact is, not all Central and South Americans speak Spanish. Immigrants from Brazil, for example, speak Portuguese; immigrants from French Guyana speak French; and immigrants from Suriname speak Dutch.

Racially, many of the nations of Central and South America follow a complex classification system that recognizes a multitude of color gradients. Experience with this multiracial system does not prepare immigrants to the United States for the stark Black–White racial divide that characterizes U.S. society. Beyond their diversity in color and language, immigrants from Central and South America are differentiated by social class distinctions, religious differences, urban or rural upbringings, and dialects. Some of them may come from indigenous populations, especially in Guatemala and Belize. If so, their social identity would be separate from any national allegiance.

In short, social relations among Central and South Americans, who collectively number nearly 7 million people, defy generalization. The same can be said about their relations with other Latinos and with non-Latinos. Central and South Americans do not form, nor should they be expected to form, a cohesive group. Nor do they easily form coalitions with Cuban Americans, Mexican Americans, or Puerto Ricans.

Jewish Americans

Jews constitute about 2 percent of the population of the United States. They play a prominent role in the worldwide Jewish community, because the United States has the world's largest concentration of Jews. Like the Japanese, many Jewish immigrants came to this country and became white-collar professionals in spite of prejudice and discrimination.

Anti-Semitism—that is, anti-Jewish prejudice—has often been vicious in the United States, although rarely so widespread and never so formalized as in Europe. In many cases, Jews have been used as scapegoats for other people's failures. Not surprisingly, Jews have not achieved equality in the United States. Despite high levels of education and professional training, they

For practicing Jews, the Hebrew language is an important part of religious instruction. This teacher is showing flashcards of Hebrew alphabetic characters to deaf students.

are still conspicuously absent from the top management of large corporations (except for the few firms founded by Jews). Nonetheless, a national survey in 2009 showed that one out of four people in the United States blames "the Jews" for the financial crisis. In addition, private social clubs and fraternal groups frequently continue to limit membership to Gentiles (non-Jews), a practice upheld by the Supreme Court in the 1964 case *Bell v. Maryland* (Malhotra and Margalit 2009).

The Anti-Defamation League (ADL) of B'nai B'rith coordinates an annual tally of reported anti-Semitic incidents. Although the number has fluctuated, in 2009 the tabulation of the total reported incidents of harassment, threats, vandalism, and assaults came to 1,211. Some incidents were inspired and carried out by neo-Nazi skinheads—groups of young people who champion racist and anti-Semitic ideologies. Such threatening behavior only intensifies the fears of many Jewish Americans, who remember the Holocaust—the extermination of 6 million Jews by the Nazi Third Reich during World War II (Anti-Defamation League 2010).

As is true for other minorities discussed in this chapter, Jewish Americans face the choice of maintaining ties to their long religious and cultural heritage or becoming as indistinguishable as possible from Gentiles. Many Jews have tended to assimilate, as is evident from the rise in marriages between Jews and Christians. In marriages that occurred in the 1970s, more than 70 percent of Jews married Jews or people who converted to Judaism. In marriages since 1996, that proportion has dropped to 53 percent. This trend means that today, American Jews are almost as likely to marry a Gentile as a Jew. For many, religion is a nonissue—neither parent practices religious rituals. Two-thirds of the children of these Jewish–Gentile marriages are not raised as Jews. Finally, in 2005, two-thirds of Jews felt that the biggest threat to Jewish life was anti-Semitism; only one-third named intermarriage as the biggest threat (American Jewish Committee 2005; Sanua 2007).

White Ethnics

A significant segment of the population of the United States is made up of White ethnics whose ancestors arrived from Europe within the past century. The nation's White ethnic population includes about 50 million people who claim at least partial German ancestry, 36 million Irish Americans, 18 million Italian Americans, and 10 million Polish Americans, as well as immigrants from other European nations. Some of these people continue to live in close-knit ethnic neighborhoods, whereas others have largely assimilated and left the "old ways" behind.

Many White ethnics today identify only sporadically with their heritage. **Symbolic ethnicity** refers to an emphasis on concerns such as ethnic food or political issues rather than on deeper ties to one's ethnic heritage. It is reflected in the occasional family trip to an ethnic bakery, the celebration of a ceremonial event such as St. Joseph's Day among Italian Americans, or concern about the future of Northern Ireland among Irish Americans. Such practices are another example of the social construction of race and ethnicity. Except in cases in which new immigration reinforces old traditions, symbolic ethnicity tends to decline with each passing generation (Alba 1990; Winter 2008).

Although the White ethnic identity may be a point of pride to those who share it, they do not necessarily celebrate it at the expense of disadvantaged minorities. It is all too easy to assume that race relations are a zero-sum game in which one group gains at the expense of the other. Rather, the histories of several White ethnic groups, such as the Irish and the Italians, show that once marginalized people can rise to positions of prestige and influence (Alba 2009).

That is not to say that White ethnics and racial minorities have not been antagonistic toward one another because of economic competition—an interpretation that agrees with the conflict approach to sociology. As Blacks, Latinos, and Native Americans emerge from the lower class, they must compete with working-class Whites for jobs, housing, and educational opportunities. In times of high unemployment or inflation, any such competition can easily generate intense intergroup conflict.

In many respects, the plight of White ethnics raises the same basic issues as that of other subordinate people in the United States. How ethnic can people be—how much can they deviate from an essentially White, Anglo-Saxon, Protestant norm—before society punishes them for their willingness to be

White Americans often express their ethnicity with special celebrations, such as this Scandinavian Festival parade in Junction City, Oregon. Participants proudly display the flag of Denmark.

different? Our society does seem to reward people for assimilating, yet as we have seen, assimilation is no easy process. In the years to come, more and more people will face the challenge of fitting in, not only in the United States but around the world, as the flow of immigrants from one country to another continues to increase. In the Social Policy section that follows, we focus on global immigration and its implications for the future.

thinking CRITICALLY

Summarize the major differences (a) among Asian Indian, Vietnamese, Chinese, Japanese, and Korean Americans, or (b) among Mexican Americans, Puerto Ricans, Cuban Americans, and Central and South Americans.

social**policy** and Racial and Ethnic Inequality

Global Immigration

Worldwide, immigration is at an all-time high. Each year, about 191 million people move from one country to another—a number that is roughly the equivalent of the total populations of Russia and Italy. A million of these immigrants enter the United States legally, to join the 13 percent of the U.S. population who are foreign born. Perhaps more significantly, one-fourth of the U.S. labor force is foreign born—the largest proportion in at least 120 years (Passel and Cohn 2011).

Globally, these mass migrations have had a tremendous social impact. The constantly increasing numbers of immigrants and the pressure they put on job opportunities and welfare capabilities in the countries they enter raise troubling questions for many of the world's economic powers. Who should be allowed

in? At what point should immigration be curtailed (United Nations 2009)?

Looking at the Issue

The migration of people is not uniform across time or space. At certain times, war or famine may precipitate large movements of people, either temporarily or permanently. Temporary dislocations occur when people wait until it is safe to return to their home areas. However, more and more migrants who cannot make an adequate living in their home nations are making permanent moves to developed nations. The major migration streams flow into North America, the oil-rich areas of the Middle East, and the industrial economies of western Europe and Asia. Currently, seven of the world's wealthiest nations (including Germany, France, the United Kingdom, and the United States) shelter about one-third of the world's migrant population, but less than one-fifth of the world's total population. As long as disparities in job opportunities exist among countries, there is little reason to expect this international trend to reverse.

One consequence of global immigration is the emergence of **transnationals**—immigrants who sustain multiple social relationships that link their societies of origin with the society of settlement. The industrial tycoons of the early 20th century, whose power outmatched that of many nation-states, were among the world's first transnationals. Today, millions of people, many of very modest means, move back and forth between countries much as commuters do between city and suburbs. More and more of these people have dual citizenship. Rather than being shaped by allegiance to one country, their identity is rooted in their struggle to survive—and in some instances prosper—by transcending international borders (Croucher 2004; Sassen 2005). We will take a closer look at these citizens of the world in the Social Policy section of Chapter 22.

Countries that have long been a destination for immigrants, such as the United States, usually have policies regarding who has preference to enter. Often, clear racial and ethnic biases are built into these policies. In the 1920s, U.S. policy gave preference to people from western Europe, while making it difficult for residents of southern and eastern Europe, Asia, and Africa to enter the country. During the late 1930s and early 1940s, the federal government refused to lift or loosen restrictive immigration quotas in order to allow Jewish refugees to escape the terror of the Nazi regime. In line with this policy, the SS *St. Louis,* with more than 900 Jewish refugees on board, was denied permission to land in the United States in 1939. The ship was forced to sail back to Europe, where it is estimated that at least a few hundred of its passengers later died at the hands of the Nazis (Morse 1967; G. Thomas and Witts 1974).

Since the 1960s, U.S. policy has encouraged the immigration of relatives of U.S. residents as well as of people who have desirable skills. This change has significantly altered the pattern of sending nations. Previously, Europeans dominated, but for the past 40 years, immigrants have come primarily from Latin America and Asia. Thus, an ever-growing proportion of the U.S. population will be Asian or Hispanic (Figure 11-8). To a large degree, fear and resentment of growing racial and ethnic diversity is a key factor in opposition to immigration. In many nations, people are concerned that the new arrivals do not reflect their own cultural and racial heritage.

Applying Sociology

Research suggests that immigrants adapt well to life in the United States, becoming an asset to the nation's economy. In some areas, heavy immigration may drain a local community's resources, but in other areas it revitalizes the local economy.

FIGURE **11-8**   LEGAL MIGRATION TO THE UNITED STATES, 1820–2010

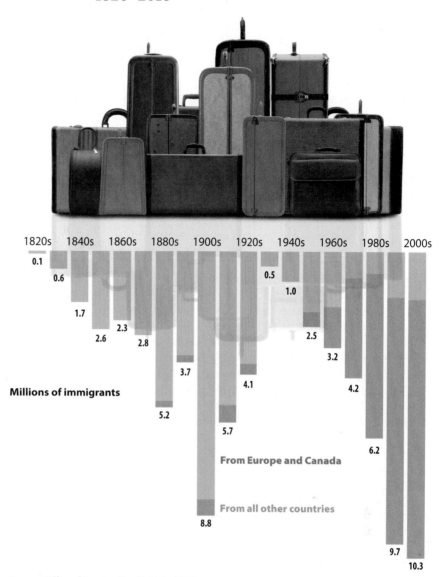

Millions of immigrants

1820s 0.1
1840s 0.6
1860s 1.7
1880s 2.6 / 2.3
1900s 2.8
1920s 3.7
1940s 0.5
1960s 1.0
1980s 2.5
2000s 3.2
4.1
5.2
5.7
6.2
8.8
9.7
10.3

From Europe and Canada

From all other countries

Sources: Office of Immigration Statistics 2011.

Despite people's fears, immigration performs many valuable functions. For the receiving society, it alleviates labor shortages, as it does in health care and technology in the United States. For the sending nation, migration can relieve an economy unable to support large numbers of people. Often overlooked is the large amount of money *(remittances),* that immigrants send *back* to their home nations.

Immigration can be dysfunctional as well. Although studies generally show that it has a positive impact on the receiving nation's economy, areas that accept high concentrations of immigrants may find it difficult to meet short-term social service needs. And when migrants with skills or educational potential leave developing countries, their departure can be dysfunctional for those nations. No amount of payments sent back home can make up for the loss of valuable human resources from poor nations (Borjas et al. 2006; Kochhar 2006; Sum et al. 2006).

Conflict theorists note how much of the debate over immigration is phrased in economic terms. But the debate intensifies when the arrivals are of a different racial and ethnic background from

U.S. employers' demand for low-paid labor fuels illegal immigration.

the host population. For example, Europeans often refer to "foreigners," but the term does not necessarily mean one of foreign birth. In Germany, "foreigners" refers to people of non-German ancestry, even if they were *born* in Germany; it does not refer to people of German ancestry born in another country, who may choose to return to their mother country. Fear and dislike of "new" ethnic groups divides countries throughout the world.

The feminist perspective pays special attention to the role that women play in global immigration. Immigrant women face all the challenges that immigrant men do, and some additional ones. Typically, they bear the responsibility for obtaining services for their families, particularly their children. Because the men are likely to be consumed with work, the women are left to navigate through the bureaucratic tangle of schools, city services, and medical facilities, as well as the unfamiliar stores and markets they must visit to feed their families. Women who need special medical services or are victims of domestic violence are often reluctant to seek outside help. Yet they are more likely than the men to serve as the liaison between their households and community and religious associations. Also, because many new immigrants view the United States as a dangerous place to raise a family, women must be especially watchful over their children's lives (Hondagneu-Sotelo 2003).

Initiating Policy

The long border with Mexico provides ample opportunity for illegal immigration into the United States. Throughout the 1980s, the public perception that the United States had lost control of its borders grew. Feeling pressure for immigration control, Congress ended a decade of debate by approving the Immigration Reform and Control Act of 1986. The act marked a historic change in the nation's immigration policy. For the first time, the hiring of illegal aliens was outlawed, and employers caught violating the law became subject to fines and even prison sentences. Just as significant a change was the extension of amnesty and legal status to many illegal immigrants already living in the United States. More than 20 years later, however, the act appears to have had mixed results. Substantial numbers of illegal immigrants continue to enter the country each year, with an estimated 11 million or more present at any given time—a marked increase since 2000, when their number was estimated at close to 8 million (Passel and Cohn 2011).

In 2010, frustrated by the continuing flow of illegal immigrants across the Mexican border, Arizona enacted a law empowering police to detain without authorization people whom they reasonably suspect of being illegal immigrants and to verify their immigration status. Immediately, opponents charged that the new law would lead to racial profiling. Legal experts questioned whether state enforcement of immigration law was constitutional. Although implementation of the law has been problematic, it has highlighted the resolve of those seeking to tighten control of the nation's borders. It has also galvanized those seeking to reform the nation's immigration law.

Recently, immigrants have staged massive marches to pressure Congress to speed the naturalization process and develop ways for illegal immigrants to gain legal residency. Counterdemonstrations by those who oppose illegal immigration have called for more resources with which to detect and deport illegal immigrants and to strengthen the U.S.–Mexican border. Despite this widespread public dissatisfaction with the nation's immigration policy, little progress has been made. Congress has had difficulty reaching a bipartisan compromise that pleases both sides: both supporters of strict social control and those who would allow illegal immigrants to remain in the country legally, under some circumstances.

The entire world feels the overwhelming impact of globalization on immigration patterns. The European Union agreement of 1997 gave the governing commission authority to propose a Europe-wide policy on immigration. An EU policy that allows residents of one EU country to live and work in another EU country is expected to complicate efforts by sending nations, such as Turkey, to become members of the EU. Immigrants from Turkey's predominantly Muslim population are not welcome in many EU countries (Denny 2004).

In the wake of the attacks of September 11, 2001, on the World Trade Center and the Pentagon, immigration procedures were complicated by the need to detect potential terrorists. Illegal immigrants especially, but even legal immigrants, have felt increased scrutiny by government officials around the world. For would-be immigrants to many nations, the wait to receive the right to enter a country—even to join relatives—has increased substantially, as immigration officials scrutinize more closely what were once routine applications.

The intense debate over immigration reflects deep value conflicts in the cultures of many nations. One strand of our culture, for example, has traditionally emphasized egalitarian principles and a desire to help people in time of need. At the same time, hostility to potential immigrants and refugees—whether the Chinese in the 1880s, European Jews in the 1930s and 1940s, or Mexicans, Haitians, and Arabs today—reflects not only racial, ethnic, and religious prejudice, but a desire to maintain the dominant culture of the in-group by keeping out those viewed as outsiders.

Take the Issue with You

1. Did you or your parents or grandparents immigrate to the United States from another nation? If so, when and where did your family come from, and why?

2. On balance, do the functions of immigration to the United States outweigh the dysfunctions?

3. Do you live, work, or study with recent immigrants to the United States? If so, are they well accepted in your community, or do they face prejudice and discrimination?

Summary

The social dimensions of race and ethnicity are important factors in shaping people's lives, both in the United States and in other countries. In this chapter, we examine the meaning of race and ethnicity and study the major **racial** and **ethnic groups** of the United States.

1. A **racial group** is set apart from others by physical differences; an **ethnic group** is set apart primarily by national origin or cultural patterns.

2. When sociologists define a **minority group,** they are concerned primarily with the economic and political power, or powerlessness, of the group.

3. The meaning people attach to the physical differences between races gives social significance to race, producing **stereotypes.**

4. **Prejudice** often but not always leads to **discrimination.** Sometimes, through **color-blind racism,** prejudiced people try to use the principle of racial neutrality to defend a racially unequal status quo.

5. **Institutional discrimination** results from the normal operations of a society.

6. Functionalists point out that discrimination is both functional and dysfunctional for a society. Conflict theorists explain racial subordination

through **exploitation theory.** Interactionists pose the **contact hypothesis** as a means of reducing prejudice and discrimination.

7. **Racial profiling** is any arbitrary action initiated by an authority based on race, ethnicity, or national origin rather than on a person's behavior. Based on false stereotypes of certain racial and ethnic groups, the practice is not an effective way to fight crime.

8. Four patterns describe typical intergroup relations in North America and elsewhere: **segregation, amalgamation, assimilation,** and **pluralism.** Pluralism remains more of an ideal than a reality.

9. Contemporary prejudice and discrimination against African Americans are rooted in the history of slavery in the United States.

10. Asian Americans are commonly viewed as a **model** or **ideal minority,** a false stereotype that is not necessarily beneficial to members of that group.

11. The various groups included under the general term *Latinos* represent the largest ethnic minority in the United States.

12. Worldwide, immigration is at an all-time high, fueling controversy not only in the United States but in the European Union as well. A new kind of immigrant, the **transnational,** moves back and forth across international borders in search of a better job or an education.

Key Terms

Affirmative action Positive efforts to recruit minority group members or women for jobs, promotions, and educational opportunities. (page 244)

Amalgamation The process through which a majority group and a minority group combine to form a new group. (248)

Anti-Semitism Anti-Jewish prejudice. (257)

Apartheid A former policy of the South African government, designed to maintain the separation of Blacks and other non-Whites from the dominant Whites. (248)

Assimilation The process through which a person forsakes his or her cultural tradition to become part of a different culture. (248)

Black power A political philosophy, promoted by many younger Blacks in the 1960s, that supported the creation of Black-controlled political and economic institutions. (249)

Color-blind racism The use of the principle of race neutrality to defend a racially unequal status quo. (241)

Contact hypothesis An interactionist perspective which states that in cooperative circumstances, interracial contact between people of equal status will reduce prejudice. (246)

Discrimination The denial of opportunities and equal rights to individuals and groups because of prejudice or other arbitrary reasons. (241)

Ethnic group A group that is set apart from others primarily because of its national origin or distinctive cultural patterns. (237)

Ethnocentrism The tendency to assume that one's own culture and way of life represent the norm or are superior to all others. (240)

Exploitation theory A Marxist theory that views racial subordination in the United States as a manifestation of the class system inherent in capitalism. (245)

Genocide The deliberate, systematic killing of an entire people or nation. (247)

Glass ceiling An invisible barrier that blocks the promotion of a qualified individual in a work environment because of the individual's gender, race, or ethnicity. (242)

Institutional discrimination The denial of opportunities and equal rights to individuals and groups that results from the normal operations of a society. (244)

Minority group A subordinate group whose members have significantly less control or power over their lives than the members of a dominant or majority group have over theirs. (237)

Model, or ideal, minority A subordinate group whose members supposedly have succeeded economically, socially, and educationally despite past prejudice and discrimination, and without resorting to confrontations with Whites. (252)

Pluralism Mutual respect for one another's cultures among the various groups in a society, which allows minorities to express their cultures without experiencing prejudice. (248)

Prejudice A negative attitude toward an entire category of people, often an ethnic or racial minority. (240)

Racial formation A sociohistorical process in which racial categories are created, inhabited, transformed, and destroyed. (238)

Racial group A group that is set apart from others because of physical differences that have taken on social significance. (237)

Racial profiling Any arbitrary action initiated by an authority based on race, ethnicity, or national origin rather than on a person's behavior. (246)

Racism The belief that one race is supreme and all others are innately inferior. (240)

Segregation The physical separation of two groups of people in terms of residence, workplace, and social events; often imposed on a minority group by a dominant group. (248)

Stereotype An unreliable generalization about all members of a group that does not recognize individual differences within the group. (239)

Symbolic ethnicity An ethnic identity that emphasizes concerns such as ethnic food or political issues rather than deeper ties to one's ethnic heritage. (258)

Transnational An immigrant who sustains multiple social relationships that link his or her society of origin with the society of settlement. (259)

White privilege Rights or immunities granted to people as a particular benefit or favor simply because they are White. (243)

TAKING SOCIOLOGY with you

1. Consider one or more jobs you have had, or an occupation you aspire to. How diverse is the staff you worked or would work with? What about your clients or customers? Do you expect racial and ethnic diversity to play an important role in your future career?

2. Talk with an older relative about your family's past. Did your ancestors experience prejudice or discrimination because of their race or ethnicity, and if so, in what way? Did they ever use racial or ethnic slurs to refer to people of other races or ethnicities? Have your family's attitudes toward members of other groups changed over the years, and if so, why?

3. Look up the census statistics on the racial and ethnic composition of your community. What are the predominant racial and ethnic groups? How many other groups are represented? How many members of your community are immigrants, and where do they come from?

Self-Quiz

Read each question carefully and then select the best answer.

1. Sociologists have identified five basic properties of a minority group. Which of the following is *not* one of those properties?
   a. unequal treatment
   b. physical traits
   c. ascribed status
   d. cultural bias

2. The largest racial minority group in the United States is
   a. Asian Americans.
   b. African Americans.
   c. Native Americans.
   d. Jewish Americans.

3. Racism is a form of which of the following?
   a. ethnocentrism
   b. discrimination
   c. prejudice
   d. both b and c

4. Suppose that a White employer refuses to hire a qualified Vietnamese American but hires an inferior White applicant. This decision is an act of
   a. prejudice.
   b. ethnocentrism.
   c. discrimination.
   d. stigmatization.

5. Suppose that a workplace requires that only English be spoken, even when it is not a business necessity to restrict the use of other languages. This requirement would be an example of
   a. prejudice.
   b. scapegoating.
   c. a self-fulfilling prophecy.
   d. institutional discrimination.

6. Working together as computer programmers for an electronics firm, a Hispanic woman and a Jewish man overcome their initial prejudices and come to appreciate each other's strengths and talents. This scenario is an example of
   a. the contact hypothesis.
   b. a self-fulfilling prophecy.
   c. amalgamation.
   d. reverse discrimination.

7. Intermarriage over several generations, resulting in various groups combining to form a new group, would be an example of
   a. amalgamation.
   b. assimilation.
   c. segregation.
   d. pluralism.

8. Alphonso D'Abruzzo changed his name to Alan Alda. His action is an example of
   a. amalgamation.
   b. assimilation.
   c. segregation.
   d. pluralism.

9. In which of the following racial or ethnic groups has one teenager in every six attempted suicide?
   a. African Americans
   b. Asian Americans
   c. Native Americans
   d. Latinos

10. Advocates of *Marxist class theory* argue that the basis for racial subordination in the United States lies within the capitalist economic system. Another representation of this point of view is reflected in which of the following theories?
    a. exploitation
    b. functionalist
    c. interactionist
    d. contact

11. Sociologists consider race and ethnicity to be _____ statuses, since people are born into racial and ethnic groups.

12. The one-drop rule was a vivid example of the social _____ of race—the process by which people come to define a group as a race based in part on physical characteristics, but also on historical, cultural, and economic factors.

13. _____ are unreliable generalizations about all members of a group that do not recognize individual differences within the group.

14. Sociologists use the term _____ to refer to a negative attitude toward an entire category of people, often an ethnic or racial minority.

15. When White Americans can use credit cards without suspicion and browse through stores without being shadowed by security guards, they are enjoying

_____ _____.

16. _____ _____ refers to positive efforts to recruit minority group members or women for jobs, promotions, and educational

opportunities.

17. After the Civil War, the Southern states passed "_____ _____" laws to enforce official segregation, and the Supreme Court upheld

them as constitutional in 1896.

18. In the 1960s, proponents of _____ _____ rejected the goal of assimilation into White, middle-class society. They defended the

beauty and dignity of Black and African cultures and supported the creation of Black-controlled political and economic institutions.

19. Asian Americans are held up as a(n) _____ or _____ minority group, supposedly because despite past suffering from prejudice and

discrimination, they have succeeded economically, socially, and educationally without resorting to confrontations with Whites.

20. Together, the various groups included under the general category _____ represent the largest minority group in the United States.

_____

THINKING ABOUT MOVIES

Amreeka

A Palestinian family that has immigrated to the United States struggles with judgments against their ethnicity.

Crash

The lives of multiple characters collide, revealing layers of prejudice directed at a wide range of races and ethnicities.

Pride

In the 1970s, an African American swim team battles racial prejudice in the United States.

Around the world, most occupations are dominated by either men or women. Men still predominate in military organizations, although women occupy many roles. Pictured here is Kirsty Moore, a female pilot with the RAF acrobatic display team the Red Arrows of Great Britain.

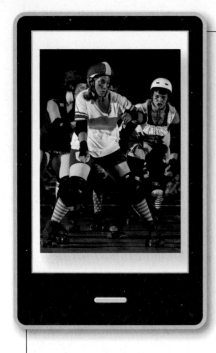

66 Her hair is in child-like pigtails, her tattoos glare through strategically placed holes in fishnet stockings, and a short skirt reveals the pink panties that match the tight T-shirt altered to provide the most potent view of breast cleavage. The image portrays the outlandish, extravagant conventions of sexuality associated with the tawdriness of "pin-up girls." And yet the salience of knee pads, shin pads, elbow pads, and helmets resist simple assessments of sexualized femininity, as do facial scowls and the brutish postures through which she powers her way around the skating rink. This roller derby girl is ready to "kick ass," and she's going to do it in a sports environment that is described as "women's space" despite large numbers of burly roaring male fans.

The recent emergence of women's roller derby onto the popular scene provides an opportunity to explore the dynamics through which alternative femininities are constructed and reinforced within a social context. . . . At a derby bout, skaters . . . make conscious efforts to disassociate their sport from ones that are "feminized softer" sports where one does not play too rough. As one skater describes it, "We are tough girls fighting their way through it. Not like other sports." Another boasts, "This is not synchronized swimming. It feels good to hit a girl and you're still standing; that's the evil part." Taunting danger and injury is normative in derby. When designated emergency rescue teams, who are present at all the bouts due to the large number of injuries, carry off skaters, skaters complain that "I just want to get back in there and skate." Derby Web sites often contain pictures of bruises presented as works of art in an Internet gallery. Skaters wear injuries like badges of honor. A young skater who is usually serene off the rink explains, "We're mean. You have a flame inside you. I think the fans know it. I think they're scared of us." Ferocious intimidation is part of the performance; skulls and crossbones adorn clothing and are embedded in logos.

Yet their skulls and crossbones have pink bows. Skaters are not striving for the image of the "gender neutral" tough athlete; this image is intentionally feminized. The bruises have fishnet patterns made from sliding across a rink floor with hosiery on one's legs. "Rink rash is sexy," says the poster. Uniforms are complemented by gold panties, Catholic schoolgirl skirts, and heavy makeup; there are pink shoelaces in their black skates. The quintessential posturing of the derby girl juxtaposes caricatured expressions of physical strength with teasing exposure of cleavage and clothes that mock conventional feminine modesty but that also serve as markers of femininity. As one skater sees it, "It wouldn't be the same to me if I were wearing pants".

. . .

One salient humorous pattern in derby is also one of the most bountiful areas for the juxtaposition of gender resistance and accommodation—the selection of a skater name. Everyone must select a skater name, such as "Harm School Teacher," "Maria Von Slap," "Calamity Jam," "Lola Fellonya," "Naturally Blood," and "Bomb Bastic," that mocks violence, sexuality, and convention while simultaneously claiming them. Names often blur the boundaries between masculine and feminine or reclaim pariah labels used to control women who are contaminating the gender order—"Wicked Wonder" or "Bitch Barbie." For some the name and character they use to skate becomes an alternate identity they can take off and put on with their skater garb. One skater said, "It definitely feels like being someone else; outfits and all." Several skaters said that they felt like a celebrity when they were in persona; several called it feeling like a "superhero" or "rock star." More than one mentioned that their persona made them feel "sexier than I ever have before." It is in sharp contrast to their daily lives, but as one confided, "I'm more like my derby self than people knew. **99**

(Finley 2010:359–360, 371–372, 377) Additional information about this excerpt can be found on the Online Learning Center at www.mhhe.com/schaefer13e.

> *"This is not synchronized swimming. It feels good to hit a girl and you're still standing; that's the evil part."*

For two years sociologist Nancy Finley attended women's flat-track roller-derby games, practices, fund-raisers, and public appearances. A fan of the sport, Finley was fascinated by the roller skaters' seemingly contradictory gender images. Through her fieldwork, which included in-depth interviews with skaters, referees, and volunteers, she learned how the women manage to observe conventional definitions of femininity while mocking them. In this excerpt from her journal article "Skating Femininity," Finley explains how "derby girls" manipulate gender meanings, embracing heightened feminism even as they exhibit the masculine values traditionally associated with violent team sports (Finley 2010; Women's Flat Track Derby Association 2011).

Obviously, women with skater names like Wicked Wonder or Bomb Bastic don't fit the conventional gender roles played by female athletes, much less by women in general. What are the accepted gender roles in today's society? Have men's and women's positions in society changed? How do gender roles differ from one culture or subculture to another? In this chapter we will study these and other questions by looking first at how various cultures, including our own, assign women and men to particular social roles. Then we will consider sociological explanations for gender stratification. We will see that around the world, women constitute an oppressed majority of the population. We'll learn that only recently have women begun to develop a collective consciousness of their oppression and the way in which their gender combines with other factors to create social inequality. Finally, we will close the chapter with a Social Policy section on the controversy over a woman's right to abortion.

Social Construction of Gender

How many airline passengers do you think are startled on hearing a female captain's voice from the cockpit? What do we make of a father who announces that he will be late for work because his son has a routine medical checkup? Consciously or unconsciously, we are likely to assume that flying a commercial plane is a *man's* job and that most parental duties are, in fact, a *woman's*. Gender is such a routine part of our everyday activities that we typically take notice only when someone deviates from conventional behavior and expectations.

Although a few people begin life with an unclear sexual identity, the overwhelming majority begin with a definite sex and quickly receive societal messages about how to behave. In fact, virtually all societies have established social distinctions between females and males that do not inevitably result from biological differences between the sexes (such as women's reproductive capabilities).

In studying gender, sociologists are interested in the gender-role socialization that leads females and males to behave differently. In Chapter 4, **gender roles** were defined as expectations regarding the proper behavior, attitudes, and activities of males and females. The application of dominant gender roles leads to many forms of differentiation between women and men. Both sexes are capable of learning to cook and sew, yet most Western societies determine that women should perform those tasks. Both men and women are capable of learning to weld and to fly airplanes, but those functions are generally assigned to men.

As we will see throughout this chapter, however, social behavior does not mirror the mutual exclusivity suggested by these gender roles. Nor are gender roles independent: in real life, the way men behave influences women's behavior, and the way women behave affects men's behavior. Thus, most people do not display strictly "masculine" or "feminine" qualities all the time. Indeed, such standards can be ambiguous. For instance, though men are supposed to be unemotional, they are allowed to become emotional when their favorite athletic team wins or loses a critical game. Yet our society still focuses on "masculine" and "feminine" qualities as if men and women must be evaluated in those terms. Despite recent inroads by women into male-dominated occupations, our construction of gender continues to define significantly different expectations for females and males (J. Howard and Hollander 1997; West and Zimmerman 1987).

Gender roles are evident not only in our work and behavior but also in how we react to others. We are constantly "doing gender" without realizing it. If the father mentioned earlier sits in the doctor's office with his son in the middle of a workday, he will probably receive approving glances from the receptionist and from other patients. "Isn't he a wonderful father?" runs through their minds. But if the boy's mother leaves *her* job and sits with the son in the doctor's office, she will not receive such silent applause.

We socially construct our behavior so as to create or exaggerate male/female differences. For example, men and women come in a variety of heights, sizes, and ages. Yet traditional norms regarding marriage and even casual dating tell us that in heterosexual couples, the man should be older, taller, and wiser than the woman. As we will see throughout this chapter, such social norms help to reinforce and legitimize patterns of male dominance.

Gender Roles in the United States

Gender-Role Socialization Male babies get blue blankets; females get pink ones. Boys are expected to play with trucks, blocks, and toy soldiers; girls receive dolls and kitchen goods. Boys must be masculine—active, aggressive, tough, daring, and dominant—but girls must be feminine—soft, emotional, sweet, and submissive. These traditional gender-role patterns have been influential in the socialization of children in the United States.

An important element in traditional views of proper "masculine" and "feminine" behavior is **homophobia,** fear of and prejudice against homosexuality. Homophobia contributes significantly to rigid gender-role socialization, since many people stereotypically associate male homosexuality with femininity and lesbianism with masculinity. Consequently, men and women who deviate from traditional expectations about gender roles are often presumed to be gay. Despite the advances made by the gay liberation movement, the continuing stigma attached to homosexuality in our culture places pressure on all males (whether gay or not) to exhibit only narrow masculine behavior and on all females (whether lesbian or not) to exhibit only narrow feminine behavior (Seidman 1994; see also Lehne 1995).

It is *adults,* of course, who play a critical role in guiding children into those gender roles deemed appropriate in a society. Parents are normally the first and most crucial agents of socialization. But other adults, older siblings, the mass media, and religious and educational institutions also exert an important influence on gender-role socialization, in the United States and elsewhere.

It is not hard to test how rigid gender-role socialization can be. Just try transgressing some gender norm—say, by smoking a cigar in public if you are female, or by carrying a purse if you are male. That was exactly the assignment given to sociology students at the University of Colorado and Luther College in Iowa. Professors asked students to behave in ways that they thought violated the norms of how a man or woman should act. The students had no trouble coming up with gender-norm transgressions (Table 12-1), and they kept careful notes on others' reactions to their behavior, ranging from amusement to disgust (Nielsen et al. 2000).

Women's Gender Roles How does a girl come to develop a feminine self-image, while a boy develops one that is masculine? In part, they do so by identifying with females and males in their families and neighborhoods and in the media. If a young girl regularly sees female television characters of all ages and body types, she is likely to grow up with a normal body image. And it will not hurt if the women she knows—her mother, sister, parents' friends, and neighbors—are comfortable with their body types, rather than constantly obsessed with their weight. In contrast, if this young girl sees only wafer-thin actresses and models on television, her self-image will be quite different. Even if she grows up to become a well-educated professional, she may secretly regret falling short of the media stereotype—a thin, sexy young woman in a bathing suit.

Television is far from alone in stereotyping women. Studies of children's books published in the United States in the 1940s, 1950s, and 1960s found that females were significantly underrepresented in central roles and illustrations. Virtually all female characters were portrayed as helpless, passive, incompetent, and

TABLE 12-1 AN EXPERIMENT IN GENDER NORM VIOLATION BY COLLEGE STUDENTS

Norm If by Women	Norm If by Men
Send men flowers	Wear fingernail polish
Spit in public	Do needlepoint in public
Use men's bathroom	Throw Tupperware party
Buy jock strap	Cry in public
Buy/chew tobacco	Have pedicure
Talk knowledgeably about cars	Apply to babysit
Open doors for men	Shave body hair

Source: Nielsen et al. 2000:287.

In an experiment testing gender-role stereotypes, sociology students were asked to behave in ways that might be regarded as violations of gender norms, and to keep notes on how others reacted. This is a sample of their choices of behavior over a seven-year period. Do you agree that these actions test the boundaries of conventional gender behavior?

In our society, men and women receive different messages about the ideal body image. For women, the Miss America pageant promotes a very slim, statuesque physique. For men, "action figures" like the G.I. Joe doll promote an exaggerated muscularity typical of professional wrestlers (Angier 1998; Byrd-Bredbenner and Murray 2003).

in need of a strong male caretaker. Studies of picture books published from the 1970s through the present have found some improvement, but males still dominate the central roles. While males are portrayed as a variety of characters, females tend to be shown mostly in traditional roles, such as mother, grandmother, or volunteer, even if they also hold nontraditional roles, such as working professional (Etaugh 2003). The pervasiveness of these traditional gender roles extends even to education.

Traditional gender roles have restricted females more severely than males. This chapter shows how women have been confined to subordinate roles in the political and economic institutions of the United States. Yet it is also true that gender roles have restricted males.

Men's Gender Roles Stay-at-home fathers? Until recent decades such an idea was unthinkable. Yet in a nationwide survey, 69 percent of respondents said that if one parent stays home with the children, it makes no difference whether that parent is the mother or the father. Only 30 percent thought that the mother should be the one to stay home. But while people's conceptions of gender roles are obviously changing, the fact is that men who stay home to care for their children are still an unusual phenomenon. For every stay-at-home dad there are 38 stay-at-home moms (Jason Fields 2004:11–12; Robison 2002).

While attitudes toward parenting may be changing, studies show little change in the traditional male gender role. Men's roles are socially constructed in much the same way as women's are. Family, peers, and the media all influence how a boy or man comes to view his appropriate role in society. The male gender role, besides being antifeminine (no "sissy stuff"), includes proving one's masculinity at work and sports—often by using force in dealing with others—as well as initiating and controlling all sexual relations.

Males who do not conform to the socially constructed gender role face constant criticism and even humiliation, both from children when they are boys and from adults as men. It can be agonizing to be treated as a "chicken" or a "sissy" as a youth—particularly if such remarks come from one's father or brothers. And grown men who pursue nontraditional occupations, such as preschool teaching or nursing, must constantly deal with others' misgivings and strange looks. In one study, interviewers found that such men frequently had to alter their behavior in order to minimize others' negative reactions. One 35-year-old nurse reported that he had to claim he was "a carpenter or something like that" when he "went clubbing," because women weren't interested in getting to know a male

Gender roles serve to discourage men from entering certain low-paying female-dominated occupations, such as child care. Only 5 percent of day care workers are male.

In the past 40 years, inspired in good part by the contemporary feminist movement (examined later in the chapter), increasing numbers of men in the United States have criticized the restrictive aspects of the traditional male gender role. Some men have taken strong public positions in support of women's struggle for full equality and have even organized voluntary associations for the purpose. However, their actions have been countered by other men who feel they are unfairly penalized by laws related to alimony, child support and custody, family violence, and affirmative action (Kimmel 2008; National Organization for Men Against Sexism 2011).

Recent research on gender roles has shown that in fact there is no single, simple characterization of the male gender role. Australian sociologist R. W. Connell (1987, 2002, 2005) has spoken of **multiple masculinities,** meaning that men play a variety of gender roles, including a nurturing-caring role and an effeminate-gay role, in addition to their traditional gender role of dominating women. Nevertheless, society reinforces their traditional, dominating role more than any other role (McCormack 2010).

nurse. The subjects made similar accommodations in casual exchanges with other men (Cross and Bagilhole 2002:215).

At the same time, boys who successfully adapt to cultural standards of masculinity may grow up to be inexpressive men who cannot share their feelings with others. They remain forceful and tough, but as a result they are also closed and isolated. In fact, a small but growing body of scholarship suggests that for men as well as women, traditional gender roles may be disadvantageous. In many communities across the nation, girls seem to outdo boys in high school, grabbing a disproportionate share of the leadership positions, from valedictorian to class president to yearbook editor—everything, in short, except captain of the boys' athletic teams. Their advantage continues after high school. In the 1980s, girls in the United States became more likely than boys to go to college. By 2008, women accounted for over 57 percent of college students nationwide. And in 2002, for the first time, more women than men in the United States earned doctoral degrees (Bureau of the Census 2010a:Table 275).

Aside from these disadvantages, many men find that traditional masculinity does not serve them well in the job market. The growth of a service economy over the past two generations has created a demand for skills, attitudes, and behaviors that are the antithesis of traditional masculinity. Increasingly, this sector is the place where low-skilled men must look for jobs. As a British study showed, many out-of-work men are reluctant to engage in the kind of sensitive, deferential behavior required by service sector jobs (Nixon 2009).

Gender and Human Sexuality As we saw in Chapter 8, society uses labels to condone or sanction specific sexual behaviors. Traditionally, those labels have derived from very definite gender-role distinctions, which are independent and do not overlap. Separating gender from sex is of course impossible. Yet it would be incorrect simply to equate males with stereotypically masculine expressions of sexuality, or females with stereotypically feminine expressions of sexuality.

Over time, social norms regarding sexual behavior have changed as gender roles have changed, becoming more ambiguous. Today, popularly coined words like *metrosexual* and *bromance* suggest that men should feel comfortable embracing traditionally feminine tastes or developing deep friendships with other men. Similarly, society is beginning to accept not only same-sex couples, but individuals whose gender and identity do not fit a simple either/or pattern, such as bisexuals and transgendered people.

Conventional notions of femininity, masculinity, and gender roles do not begin to address the complexities of contemporary society. Consider transgendered persons, whose current gender identity no longer matches their physical identity at birth.

use your sociological *imagination*

What evidence can you see of women's changing roles over the past few generations?

Cross-Cultural Perspective

To what extent do actual biological differences between the sexes contribute to the cultural differences associated with gender? This question brings us back to the debate over "nature versus nurture." In assessing the alleged and real differences between men and women, it is useful to examine cross-cultural data.

Around the world, anthropologists have documented highly diverse constructions of gender that do not always conform to our ideals of masculinity and femininity. Beginning with the path-breaking work of Margaret Mead ([1935] 2001) and continuing through contemporary fieldwork, these scholars have shown that gender roles can vary greatly from one physical environment, economy, and political system to the next. Peggy Reeves Sanday's (2002, 2008) work in West Sumatra, Indonesia, for example, describes the 4-million-member Minangkabau society as one in which men and women are not competitors, but partners for the common good. This society is based on a nurturing approach to the environment, blended with Islamic religious ethics. Women control the land through inheritance; in the event of a divorce, the ex-husband leaves with only his clothes. The larger community may be governed by men, women, or both men and women working together. Sanday's findings, together with Mead's, confirm the influential role of culture and socialization in gender-role differentiation. There appear to be no innate or biologically determined gender roles for men and women.

In any society, gender stratification requires not only individual socialization into traditional gender roles within the family, but also the promotion and support of those traditional roles by other social institutions, such as religion and education. Moreover, even with all major institutions socializing the young into conventional gender roles, every society has women and men who resist and successfully oppose the stereotypes: strong women who become leaders or professionals, gentle men who care for children, and so forth. It seems clear that differences between the sexes are not dictated by biology. Indeed, the maintenance of traditional gender roles requires constant social controls—and those controls are not always effective.

We can see the social construction of gender roles in process in societies strained by war and social upheaval. By summer 2004, a year after the war in Iraq began, young girls in Baghdad seldom ventured out to the park or swimming pool. When they did, their parents made sure they were dressed conservatively, in loose clothing and perhaps a head scarf. The overthrow of Saddam Hussein's secular regime had emboldened Islamic fundamentalists, who had begun visiting schools, urging young women to wear long sleeves and cover their heads. Though school officials resisted, many girls dropped out, some out of fear for their safety and others because of financial hardship. In the atmosphere of violence and lawlessness that followed the 2003 occupation, young women wondered what the future would hold for them, and whether they would ever have the opportunity to become educated professionals, as their mothers had (Sengupta 2004).

thinking CRITICALLY

Compare the social construction of gender with the social construction of race.

Gender differences are visible around the world, albeit in different ways. In some cities in Mexico, "pink taxis"—cabs driven by women for female passengers only—provide a safe alternative for women afraid to travel alone on public transportation.

Sociological Perspectives on Gender

Cross-cultural studies indicate that societies dominated by men are much more common than those in which women play the decisive role. Sociologists have turned to all the major theoretical perspectives to understand how and why these social distinctions are established. Each approach focuses on culture rather than biology as the primary determinant of gender differences. Yet in other respects, advocates of these sociological perspectives disagree widely.

Functionalist View

Functionalists maintain that gender differentiation has contributed to overall social stability. Sociologists Talcott Parsons and Robert Bales (1955) argued that to function most effectively, the family requires adults who specialize in particular roles. They viewed the traditional gender roles as arising out of the need to establish a division of labor between marital partners.

Parsons and Bales contended that women take the expressive, emotionally supportive role and men the instrumental, practical role, with the two complementing each other. **Expressiveness** denotes concern for the maintenance of harmony and the internal emotional affairs of the family. **Instrumentality** refers to an emphasis on tasks, a focus on more distant goals, and a concern for the external relationship between one's family and other social institutions. According to this theory, women's interest in expressive goals frees men for instrumental tasks, and vice versa. Women become anchored in the family as wives, mothers, and household managers; men become anchored in the occupational world outside the home. Of course, Parsons and Bales offered this framework in the 1950s, when many more women were full-time homemakers than is true today. These theorists did not explicitly endorse traditional gender roles, but they implied that dividing tasks between spouses was functional for the family as a unit.

Given the typical socialization of women and men in the United States, the functionalist view is initially persuasive. However, it would lead us to expect girls and women who have no interest in children to become babysitters and mothers. Similarly, males who love spending time with children might be programmed into careers in the business world. Such differentiation might harm the individual who does not fit into prescribed roles, as well as deprive society of the contributions of many talented people who feel confined by gender stereotyping. Moreover, the functionalist approach does not convincingly explain why men should be assigned categorically to the instrumental role and women to the expressive role.

Conflict Response

Viewed from a conflict perspective, the functionalist approach masks the underlying power relations between men and women. Parsons and Bales never explicitly presented the expressive and instrumental roles as being of unequal value to society, yet their inequality is quite evident. Although social institutions may pay lip service to women's expressive skills, men's instrumental skills are more highly rewarded, whether in terms of money or prestige. Consequently, according to feminists and conflict theorists, any division of labor by gender into instrumental and expressive tasks is far from neutral in its impact on women.

Conflict theorists contend that the relationship between females and males has traditionally been one of unequal power, with men in a dominant position over women. Men may originally have become powerful in preindustrial times because their size, physical strength, and freedom from childbearing duties allowed them to dominate women physically. In contemporary societies, such considerations are not so important, yet cultural beliefs about the sexes are long established, as anthropologist Margaret Mead and feminist sociologist Helen Mayer Hacker (1951, 1974) both stressed. Such beliefs support a social structure that places males in controlling positions.

Conflict theorists, then, see gender differences as a reflection of the subjugation of one group (women) by another group (men). If we use an analogy to Marx's analysis of class conflict, we can say that males are like the bourgeoisie, or capitalists; they control most of the society's wealth, prestige, and power. Females are like the proletariat, or workers; they can acquire valuable resources only by following the dictates of their bosses. Men's

Conflict theorists emphasize that men's work is uniformly valued, whereas women's work (whether unpaid labor in the home or wage labor) is devalued. This woman is assembling computer parts in a factory in Austin, Texas.

work is uniformly valued; women's work (whether unpaid labor in the home or wage labor) is devalued.

thinking CRITICALLY

Which aspects of the functionalist and conflict perspectives on gender make the most sense to you? Explain.

Feminist Perspective

A significant component of the conflict approach to gender stratification draws on feminist theory. Although use of the term *feminist theory* is comparatively recent, the critique of women's position in society and culture goes back to some of the earliest works that have influenced sociology. Among the most important are Mary Wollstonecraft's *A Vindication of the Rights of Women* (originally published in 1792), John Stuart Mill's *The Subjection of Women* (originally published in 1869), and Friedrich Engels's *The Origin of the Family, Private Property, and the State* (originally published in 1884).

Engels, a close associate of Karl Marx, argued that women's subjugation coincided with the rise of private property during industrialization. Only when people moved beyond an agrarian economy could males enjoy the luxury of leisure and withhold rewards and privileges from women. Drawing on the work of Marx and Engels, many contemporary feminist theorists view women's subordination as part of the overall exploitation and injustice that they see as inherent in capitalist societies. Some radical feminist theorists, however, view the oppression of women as inevitable in *all* male-dominated societies, whether they are labeled capitalist, socialist, or communist (Feuer 1989; Tuchman 1992; Tucker 1978:734–759).

Feminist sociologists would find little to disagree with in the conflict theorists' perspective, but are more likely to embrace a political agenda. Feminists would also argue that until the 1970s, the very discussion of women and society, however well meant, was distorted by the exclusion of women from academic thought, including sociology. We have noted the many accomplishments

271

of Jane Addams and Ida Wells-Barnett, but they generally worked outside the discipline, focusing on what we would now call applied sociology and social work. At the time, their efforts, while valued as humanitarian, were seen as unrelated to the research and conclusions being reached in academic circles, which of course were male academic circles (Andersen 2007; J. Howard 1999).

Intersections with Race, Class, and Other Social Factors

Contemporary feminists recognize the differential treatment of some women not only because of their gender, but also because of the intersection of their race, ethnicity, and socioeconomic status. Simply put, Whites dominate these poor, non-White women because they are non-White; men dominate them because they are women; and the affluent dominate them because they are poor. The African American feminist theorist Patricia Hill Collins (2000) has termed the convergence of social forces that contributes to the subordinate status of these low-status women the **matrix of domination** (Figure 12-1).

Gender, race, and social class are not the only sources of oppression in the United States, though they profoundly affect women and people of color. Other forms of categorization and stigmatization that might be included in the matrix are sexual orientation, religion, disability, and age. If we apply the matrix to the world as a whole, we might add citizenship status or perceived colonial or neocolonial status to the list (Winant 2006).

Though feminists have addressed themselves to the needs of minority women, these women are oppressed much more by their race and ethnicity than by their gender. The question for Latinas (Hispanic women), African American women, Asian American women, and Native American women appears to be whether they should unite with their brothers against racism or challenge them for their sexism. The answer is that our society must eradicate both sexism and racism (Beisel and Kay 2004; Breines 2007; Epstein 1999).

The discussion of gender roles among African Americans has always provoked controversy. Advocates of Black nationalism contend that feminism only distracts women from participating fully in the African American struggle. The existence of feminist groups among Blacks, in their view, simply divides the Black community, thereby serving the dominant White majority. In contrast, Black feminists such as bell hooks (1994) argue that little is to be gained by accepting the gender-role divisions of the dominant society, which place women in a separate, subservient position. Though the media commonly portray Black women in a negative light—as illiterates, welfare queens, or prostitutes—Black feminists emphasize that it is not solely Whites and the White-dominated media who focus on such negative images. Black men (most recently, Black male rap artists) have also portrayed Black women in a negative way (Raybon 1989; Threadcraft 2008).

Historically, Native Americans stand out as an exception to the patriarchal tradition in North America. At the time of the European settlers' arrival, Native American gender roles varied greatly from tribe to tribe. Southern tribes, for reasons unclear to today's scholars, were usually matriarchal and traced their descent through the mother. European missionaries, who sought to make

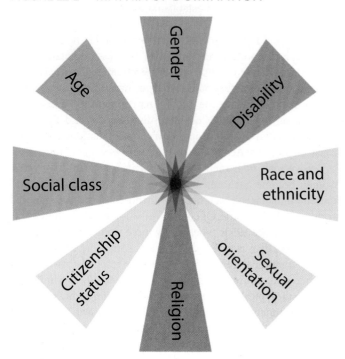

FIGURE **12-1**   MATRIX OF DOMINATION

Gender

Age

Disability

Social class

Race and ethnicity

Citizenship status

Religion

Sexual orientation

Source: Developed by author.

The matrix of domination illustrates how several social factors, including gender, social class, and race and ethnicity, can converge to create a cumulative impact on a person's social standing.

the native peoples more like Europeans, set out to transform this arrangement, which was not entirely universal. Like members of other groups, some Native American women have resisted gender stereotypes (Marubbio 2006).

Latinas are usually considered as part of either the Hispanic or feminist movements, and their distinctive experience ignored. In the past, they have been excluded from decision making in the two social institutions that most affect their daily lives: the family and the church. Particularly in the lower class, the Hispanic family suffers from the pervasive tradition of male domination. And the Catholic Church relegates women to supportive roles, while reserving the leadership positions for men (Browne 2001; De Anda 2004).

Prior to this chapter, much of our discussion has focused on the social effects of race and ethnicity, coupled with poverty, low incomes, and meager wealth. The matrix of domination highlights the confluence of these factors with gender discrimination, which we must include to fully understand the plight of women of color.

use your sociological *imagination*

Which elements of the matrix of domination privilege you? Which place you at a disadvantage?

TABLE 12-2 SOCIOLOGICAL PERSPECTIVES ON GENDER

summing up

Theoretical Perspective	Emphasis
Functionalist	Gender differentiation contributes to social stability
Conflict	Gender inequality is rooted in the female–male power relationship
Feminist	Women's subjugation is integral to society and social structure
Interactionist	Gender distinctions and "doing gender" are reflected in people's everyday behavior

Interactionist Approach

While functionalists and conflict theorists who study gender stratification typically focus on macro-level social forces and institutions, interactionist researchers tend to examine gender stratification on the micro level of everyday behavior. The key to this approach is the way gender is socially constructed in everyday interactions. We "do gender" by reinforcing traditionally masculine and feminine actions. For example, a man "does masculinity" by opening a door for his girlfriend; she "does femininity" by consenting to his assistance. Obviously, the social construction of gender goes beyond these relatively trivial rituals. Interactionists recognize, too, that people can challenge traditional gender roles. A female golfer who uses the men's tees and a man who actively arranges a birthday luncheon at work are redoing gender (Deutsch 2007; West and Zimmerman 1987).

One continuing subject of investigation is the role of gender in cross-sex conversations (sometimes referred to as "cross-talk"), specifically the idea that men interrupt women more than women interrupt men. Interestingly, empirical research does not clearly support this assertion. True, people in positions of authority or status—who are much more likely to be male than female—dominate interpersonal conversations. That does not necessarily mean that women per se cannot be heard, however. Future research results may deemphasize the clichéd advice that women must speak up and focus instead on the situational structures that cast men in dominant positions (Cameron 2007; Hyde 2005; Tannen 1990).

Table 12-2 summarizes the major sociological perspectives on gender.

Women: The Oppressed Majority

Many people, both male and female, find it difficult to conceive of women as a subordinate and oppressed group. Yet take a look at the political structure of the United States: women remain noticeably underrepresented. As of mid-2011, for example, only 6 of the nation's 50 states had a female governor (Arizona, New Mexico, North Carolina, Oklahoma, South Carolina, and Washington).

Women have made slow but steady progress in certain political arenas. In 1981, out of 535 members of Congress, there were only 21 women: 19 in the House of Representatives and 2 in the Senate. In contrast, the Congress that held office in mid-2011 had 88 women: 71 in the House and 17 in the Senate. Yet the membership and leadership of Congress remain overwhelmingly male.

In October 1981, Sandra Day O'Connor was sworn in as the nation's first female Supreme Court justice. Still, no woman has ever served as president of the United States, vice president, or chief justice of the Supreme Court.

Sexism and Sex Discrimination

Just as African Americans are victimized by racism, women in our society are victimized by sexism. **Sexism** is the ideology that one sex is superior to the other. The term is generally used to refer to male prejudice and discrimination against women. In Chapter 11, we noted that Blacks can suffer from both individual acts of racism and institutional discrimination. **Institutional discrimination** was defined as the denial of opportunities and equal rights to individuals and groups that results from the normal operations of a society. In the same sense, women suffer from both individual acts of sexism (such as sexist remarks and acts of violence) and institutional sexism.

It is not simply that particular men in the United States are biased in their treatment of women. All the major institutions of our society—including the government, armed forces, large corporations, the media, universities, and the medical establishment—are controlled by men. These institutions, in their normal, day-to-day operations, often discriminate against women and perpetuate sexism. For example, if the central office of a nationwide bank sets a policy that single women are a bad risk for loans—regardless of their incomes and investments—that bank will discriminate against women in state after state. It will do so even at branches where loan officers hold no personal biases toward women, but are merely "following orders."

Our society is run by male-dominated institutions, yet with the power that flows to men come responsibility and stress. Men have higher reported rates of certain types of mental illness than women, and a greater likelihood of death due to heart attack or stroke. The pressure on men to succeed, and then to remain on top in the competitive world of work, can be especially intense. That is not to suggest that gender stratification is as damaging to men as it is to women. But it is clear that the power and privilege men enjoy are no guarantee of personal well-being.

use your sociological *imagination*

Think of organizations or institutions you belong to whose leadership positions are customarily held by men. What would those organizations be like if they were led by women?

The Status of Women Worldwide

A detailed overview of the status of the world's women, issued by the United Nations, noted that women and men live in two

SOCIOLOGY IN THE GLOBAL COMMUNITY

12-1 The Head Scarf and the Veil: Complex Symbols

The wearing of a veil or head scarf by women is common to many but not all Middle Eastern societies. All Muslims, men and women alike, are expected to cover themselves and avoid revealing clothes designed to accentuate the body's contours or emphasize its physical beauty. The Koran does permit Muslims to wear revealing garments in private, with their families or with members of the same sex.

The Prophet Muhammad recommended that women cover all of their bodies except for the face, hands, and feet. The Koran adds that a woman's headcovering should fall over the neck and upper chest. A variety of women's outergarments comply with these guidelines for modest attire; collectively, they are referred to as the *hijab*. Face veils are dictated by cultural tradition, however—not by Islam.

In effect, the veil represents a rejection of the beauty myth (see Chapter 8), which is so prevalent in Western societies. By covering themselves almost completely, Muslim women assure themselves and their families that their physical appearance will not play a role in their contacts outside the family. Rather, these women will be known only for their faith, their intellect, and their personalities.

The veil was politicized by modernization movements that pitted Western cultural values against traditional Islamic values. In Turkey, for instance, in the early 20th century, government officials attempted to subordinate traditional ethnic and religious influences to their nationalistic goals. Though women weren't forbidden to wear the veil, they were not allowed to veil themselves in public places like schools. Many Muslims resented these forced social changes.

In the United States today, Muslim women select from an array of traditional garments, including a long, loose tailored coat and a loose black overgarment that is worn with a scarf or perhaps a face veil. However, they are just as apt to wear an overblouse and a long skirt or loose pants, which they can buy at local clothing stores.

Researchers have identified three perspectives on the *hijab* among Muslim women in the United States and other non-Islamic countries.

> *In effect, the veil represents a rejection of the beauty myth, which is so prevalent in Western societies.*

Younger, better-educated women who support wearing the *hijab* in public draw on Western ideas of individual rights, arguing in favor of veiling as a form of personal expression. In contrast, older, less-well-educated women who support the *hijab* do so without referring to Western ideology; they cannot see why veiling should be an issue. A third group of women, of all ages and educational backgrounds, opposes the *hijab*.

In some non-Muslim countries, notably France, officials have come under fire for banning the *hijab,* or the head scarf, in public schools, as well as a full-body, face-covering robe anywhere in public. The custom of covering generally has not been an issue in the United States, though one 11-year-old had to go to federal court to establish her right to wear a head scarf at school in Muskogee, Oklahoma. Interestingly, the U.S. Department of Justice supported her lawsuit.

The head scarf—an expression of modesty, a woman's right as an individual, or a sign of oppression?

LET'S DISCUSS

1. Consider life in a society in which women wear veils. Can you see any advantages, from the woman's point of view? From the man's?
2. Do you find the Western emphasis on physical beauty oppressive? If so, in what ways?

Sources: Al-Jadda 2006; Gauthier-Billars and Forelle 2010; Gurbuz and Gurbuz-Kucuksari 2009; Haq 2009; Killian 2003; Murphy 2009; Selod 2008b.

---

different worlds. In too many nations women are denied equal pay, sexually harassed at work, or dismissed from their jobs because they are pregnant. These abuses happen even in places where such treatment is prohibited by law. Women who assert their rights are routinely ignored or even punished for their protests. To achieve gender equality, the report concludes, society must hold the powerful accountable to women (United Nations Development Fund for Women 2009).

This critique applies to Western as well as non-Western countries. Although Westerners tend to view some societies—for example, Muslim countries—as being particularly harsh toward women, that perception is actually an overgeneralization. Muslim countries are exceedingly varied and complex and do not often fit the stereotypes created by the Western media. For a detailed discussion of the status of Muslim women today, see Box 12-1.

Regardless of culture, however, women everywhere suffer from second-class status. It is estimated that women grow half the world's food, but they rarely own land. They constitute one-third of the world's paid labor force, but are generally found in the lowest-paying jobs. Single-parent households headed by women, which appear to be on the rise in many nations, are typically found in the poorest sections of the population. The feminization of poverty has become a global phenomenon. As in the United States, women around the world are underrepresented politically.

Despite these challenges, women are not responding passively. They are mobilizing, individually and collectively. Given the significant underrepresentation of women in government offices and national legislatures, however, the task is difficult, as we shall see in Chapter 17.

Not surprisingly, there is a link between the wealth of industrialized nations and the poverty of women in developing countries. Viewed from a conflict perspective or through the lens of Immanuel Wallerstein's world systems analysis, the economies of developing nations are controlled and exploited by industrialized countries and multinational corporations based in those countries. Much of the exploited labor

FIGURE **12-2**   GENDER INEQUALITY IN HOUSEWORK

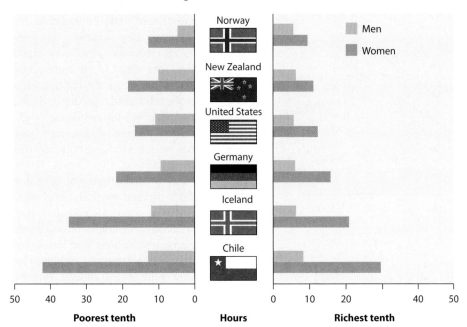

Note: Housework includes laundry, grocery shopping, dinner preparation, and care for sick family members.
Source: Adapted from Heisig 2011:84.

Around the world, rich or poor, women do much more housework than men.

in developing nations, especially in the nonindustrial sector, is performed by women. Women workers typically toil long hours for low pay, but contribute significantly to their families' incomes (Chubb et al. 2008).

In industrialized countries, women's unequal status can be seen in the division of housework, as well as in the jobs they hold and the pay they earn. Sociologist Jan Paul Heisig analyzed gender inequality among the rich (the top decile in income) and the poor (the bottom decile) in 33 industrialized countries. Typically, poor men did more housework than rich men, but as Figure 12-2 shows, rich or poor, men did much less housework than women.

thinking CRITICALLY

What are the challenges to comparing the status of women across different nations?

Women in the Workforce of the United States

More than 30 years ago, the U.S. Commission on Civil Rights (1976:1) concluded that the passage in the Declaration of Independence proclaiming that "all men are created equal" has been taken too literally for too long—especially with respect to women's opportunities for employment. In this section we will see how gender bias has limited women's opportunities for employment outside the home, at the same time that it forces them to carry a disproportionate burden inside the home.

Labor Force Participation

Women's participation in the paid labor force of the United States increased steadily throughout the 20th century and into the 21st century (Figure 12-3). Today, millions of women—married or single, with or without children, pregnant or recently having given birth—are in the labor force.

Overall, 59 percent of adult women in the United States were in the labor force in 2009, compared to 41 percent in 1970. For men, the data were 72 percent in 2009, compared to 76 percent in 1970 (Bureau of the Census 2010a:Table 585).

Still, women entering the job market find their options restricted in important ways. Women are *underrepresented* in occupations historically defined as "men's jobs," which often carry much greater financial rewards and prestige than women's jobs. For example, in 2008, women accounted for approximately 46 percent of the paid labor force of the United States, yet they constituted only 9 percent of civil engineers, 27 percent of computer systems analysts, and 32 percent of physicians (Table 12-3).

Such occupational segregation is not unique to the United States but typical of industrial countries. In Great Britain, for example, only 29 percent of computer analysts are women, while 81 percent of cashiers and 90 percent of nurses are women (Cross and Bagilhole 2002).

Women from all groups and men from minority groups sometimes encounter attitudinal or organizational bias that prevents them from reaching their full potential. As we saw in Chapter 11, the term **glass ceiling** refers to an invisible barrier that blocks the promotion of a qualified individual in a work environment because of the individual's gender, race, or ethnicity. A study of the *Fortune* 500 largest corporations in the United States showed that in 2009, barely 15 percent of the seats on their boards of directors were held by women. Furthermore, only 12 CEOs were female (Lang 2010; Lublin 2010).

When women do gain entry to corporate boards of directors, the response in the financial world is not entirely positive. Despite objective tests that show strong financial performance under gender-diverse leadership, some investors tend to balk. Research by Frank Dobbin and Jiwook Jung (2010) shows that small investors often sell their shares when women become corporate leaders, apparently falling for the stereotype that associates males with success. This sell pattern is not characteristic of larger investors, who have long argued that gender-diverse leadership is good for business.

This type of inequality is not unique to the United States. Worldwide, women hold less than 1 percent of corporate managerial positions. In recognition of the underrepresentation of women on boards of directors, the Norwegian legislature established minimum quotas for the number of female board members. As the architects of the plan put it, "instead of assuming what people *can't* do at work, provide opportunities for

FIGURE **12-3** TRENDS IN U.S. WOMEN'S PARTICIPATION IN THE PAID LABOR FORCE, 1890–2009

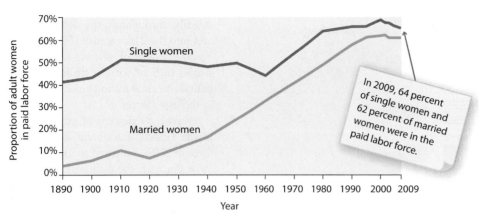

In 2009, 64 percent of single women and 62 percent of married women were in the paid labor force.

Sources: Bureau of the Census 1975, 2010a:Table 598.

employees to prove what they can do." The goal was not complete equity for women, but 40 percent representation by 2008. By 2010 the percentage stood at 10 percent (Crumley 2010).

Compensation

He works. She works. Both are physicians—a high-status occupation with considerable financial rewards. He makes $140,000. She makes $88,000.

These median annual earnings for physicians in the United States were released by the Census Bureau. They are typical of the results of the bureau's detailed study of occupations and income. Take air traffic controllers. He makes $67,000; she makes $56,000. Or housekeepers: he makes $19,000; she makes $15,000. What about teachers' assistants? He makes $20,000; she makes $15,000. Statisticians at the

bureau looked at the median annual earnings for no fewer than 821 occupations ranging from dishwasher to chief executive. After adjusting for workers' ages, education, and work experience, they came to an unmistakable conclusion: across the board, there is a substantial gender gap in the median earnings of full-time workers.

Men do not always earn more than women for doing the same work. Researchers at the Census Bureau found 2 occupations out of 821 in which women typically earn about 1 percent more income than men: hazardous materials recovery and telecommunications line installation. These two occupations employed less than 1 out of every 1,000 workers the bureau studied. Forecasting analyses show no convincing evidence that the wage gap is narrowing.

What accounts for these yawning wage gaps between men and women in the same occupation? Scholars at the Census Bureau studied the following characteristics of men and women in the same occupation:

- Age and degree of formal education
- Marital status and the presence of children at home
- Specialization within the occupation (for example, family practice versus surgical practice)
- Years of work experience
- Hours worked per year

TABLE **12-3** U.S. WOMEN IN SELECTED OCCUPATIONS: WOMEN AS A PERCENTAGE OF ALL WORKERS IN THE OCCUPATION

Underrepresented		Overrepresented	
Aircraft pilots	1%	High school teachers	55%
Firefighters	3	Cashiers	74
Civil engineers	9	Social workers	81
Police officers	16	Elementary teachers	82
Clergy	17	File clerks	82
Chefs and head cooks	21	Librarians	82
Computer systems analysts	27	Tellers	87
Dentists	30	Registered nurses	92
Coaches and umpires	32	Receptionists	92
Lawyers	32	Word processors and typists	92
Physicians	32	Child care workers	95
Mail carriers	35	Dental assistants	98

Note: Women constitute 47 percent of the entire labor force.
Source: Data for 2009 reported in Bureau of the Census 2010a:Table 615.

Taking all these factors into consideration reduced the pay gap between men and women by only 3 cents. Women still earned 80 cents for every dollar earned by men. In sum, the disparity in pay between men and women cannot be explained by pointing to women's career choices (Government Accountability Office 2003; Weinberg 2004, 2007).

Legally, sex discrimination in wage payments is difficult to prove. Witness the case of former Goodyear worker Lilly Ledbetter, who learned 19 years after she was hired that she was being paid less than men doing the same job. Ledbetter sued and was awarded damages, only to have the Supreme Court overturn the decision on the grounds that she made her claim more than six months after the first discriminatory paycheck was issued. Congress relaxed this restriction in 2009 (Pear 2009).

Not all the obstacles women face in the workplace originate with management. Unfortunately, many workers, both male and female, would prefer not to work for a woman (Box 12-2).

While women are at a disadvantage in male-dominated occupations, the same is not true for men in female-dominated occupations. Sociologist Michelle Budig (2002) examined a national

RESEARCH TODAY

12-2 Give Me a Male Boss, Please

As women increased their presence in the managerial ranks from 19.7 percent in 1972 to 51.4 percent in 2009, the desirability of having a male supervisor became a topic of casual conversation. Numerous studies suggest that compared to all the other social factors present in the workplace, the boss's gender has little effect on the nature and quality of the manager–employee relationship. However, that fact does not prevent potential workers—male or female—from preferring a male boss. National opinion polls consistently show that in general—that is, without reference to particular people—workers prefer to take orders from a man by a two-to-one margin. If anything, women are more likely than men to prefer a male supervisor.

> *National opinion polls consistently show that in general, workers prefer to take orders from a man by a two-to-one margin.*

This preference is so strong that many people are willing to accept less pay to get a male boss. Researchers at the University of Chicago's business school asked college students who were about to graduate to consider hypothetical job opportunities at consulting firms. The positions varied in terms of their starting salary, location, paid holidays, and the boss's sex. The results showed that students' choices matched their stated preferences for salary, location, and holidays. Surprisingly, the boss's sex turned out to be a far more important variable than the other three, whether students were male or female. In a variety of scenarios describing both salary and the boss's characteristics, students chose to take a 22 percent reduction in starting salary to get a male boss.

LET'S DISCUSS

1. Have you ever worked for a female boss? If so, were you comfortable taking orders from her? Did you notice any differences in the way your boss was treated, compared to men on her level?

2. What might explain the strong preference for a male boss? Do you expect this preference to remain stable or disappear over time? Explain.

Sources: Bureau of the Census 2010a:Table 615; Bureau of Labor Statistics 2003; Caruso et al. 2009; N. Gibbs 2009:31; Powell 2010; Whittaker 2006.

---

database containing career information on more than 12,000 men, collected over the course of 15 years. She found that men were uniformly advantaged in female occupations. Though male nurses, grade school teachers, and librarians may experience some scorn in the larger society, they are much more likely than women to be encouraged to become administrators. Observers of the labor force have termed this advantage for men in female-dominated occupations the *glass escalator*—quite a contrast to the glass ceiling (J. Jacobs 2003; C. L. Williams 1992, 1995).

Social Consequences of Women's Employment

Today, many women face the challenge of trying to juggle work and family. Their situation has many social consequences. For one thing, it puts pressure on child care facilities, public financing of day care, and even the fast-food industry, which provides many of the meals women used to prepare themselves. For another, it raises questions about what responsibility male wage earners have in the household.

Who does the housework when women become productive wage earners? Studies indicate that there is a clear gender gap in the performance of housework, although it has been narrowing (see Figure 12-2, page 275). Women do more housework and spend more time on child care than men do, whether on a workday or a nonworkday. Taken together, then, a woman's workday on and off the job is much longer than a man's (Sayer et al. 2004).

Sociologist Arlie Hochschild (1989, 1990, 2005) has used the phrase **second shift** to describe the double burden—work outside the home followed by child care and housework—that many women face and few men share equitably. Unfortunately, today's workplace is becoming a 24/7 virtual office thanks to the advent of mobile information technologies. As these devices take over what little personal time employees have left, the physical toll on women becomes even more burdensome.

What is life like for these women? On the basis of interviews with and observations of 52 couples over an eight-year period, Hochschild reports that the wives (and not their husbands) drive home from the office while planning domestic schedules and play dates for children—and then begin their second shift. Drawing on national studies, she concludes that women spend 15 fewer hours each week in leisure activities than their husbands. In a year, these women work an extra month of 24-hour days because of the second shift; over a dozen years, they work an extra year of 24-hour days. Hochschild found that the married couples she studied were fraying at the edges, and so were their careers and their marriages. With such reports in mind, many feminists have advocated greater governmental and corporate support for child care, more flexible family leave policies, and other reforms designed to ease the burden on the nation's families (Eby et al. 2010).

The greater amounts of time women put into caring for their children, and to a lesser degree into housework, take a special toll on women who are pursuing careers. In a survey published in the *Harvard Business Review,* about 40 percent of women indicated that they had voluntarily left work for months or years, compared to only 24 percent of men. As Figure 12-4 shows, women were much more likely than men to take time off for family reasons.

FIGURE **12-4**   WHY LEAVE WORK?

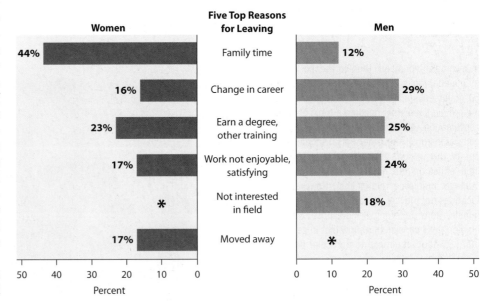

✱ Not one of top 5 reasons

Note: Based on a representative Harris Interactive survey of "highly qualified" workers, defined as those with a graduate degree, a professional degree, or a high honors undergraduate degree.
Source: Figure adapted from Sylvia Ann Hewlett and Carolyn Burk Luce, 2005. "Off-Ramps and On-Ramps: Keeping Talented Women on the Road to Success," *Harvard Business Review,* March 2005. Copyright © 2005 by the Harvard Business School Publishing Corporation, all rights reserved. Reprinted by permission of *Harvard Business Review.*

thinking CRITICALLY

How would you argue that women have come either very far or not far enough in their labor force participation?

TREND SPOTTING

Working Mothers

Women in the labor force, either working or seeking employment, is an established fact in the United States. So too is the participation of women with young children. Such was not always the case, however. Forty years ago only 30 percent of married mothers with children under age 6 were working outside the home. By 1995—just 25 years later—that proportion had more than doubled. For married mothers, work outside the home has been the norm ever since.

This rising trend has also affected single mothers, whose labor force participation has always been high. In 1970 the proportion of single mothers of preschoolers who worked outside the home was 52 percent—22 percent higher than for married mothers of young children. Today the proportion has climbed to 72 percent.

Another way to look at these statistics is to note the narrowing gap between the two groups' labor force participation rates. Today, a married woman with at least one child under age 6 is *more likely to be working* than a single mother was in 1970.

Emergence of a Collective Consciousness

Feminism is the belief in social, economic, and political equality for women. The feminist movement of the United States was born in upstate New York, in a town called Seneca Falls, in the summer of 1848. On July 19, the first women's rights convention began, attended by Elizabeth Cady Stanton, Lucretia Mott, and other pioneers in the struggle for women's rights. This first wave of *feminists,* as they are currently known, battled ridicule and scorn as they fought for legal and political equality for women. They were not afraid to risk controversy on behalf of their cause; in 1872, Susan B. Anthony was arrested for attempting to vote in that year's presidential election.

Ultimately, the early feminists won many victories, among them the passage and ratification of the Nineteenth Amendment to the Constitution, which granted women the right to vote in national elections beginning in 1920. But suffrage did not lead to other reforms in women's social and economic position, and in the early and middle 20th century the women's movement became a much less powerful force for social change.

TAKING SOCIOLOGY TO WORK

Abigail E. Drevs, **Former Program and Volunteer Coordinator, Y-ME Illinois**

For two and a half years, Abigail Drevs served as the program and volunteer coordinator for the Illinois affiliate of Y-ME National Breast Cancer Organization. Y-ME's mission is to provide support and educational outreach through workshops and peer-led support groups, to ensure that no one faces breast cancer alone.

As the coordinator, Drevs was responsible for recruiting, training, and retaining the volunteers who staff the organization's support groups. She also presented workshops about breast cancer and how to detect it early. To make sure that services were available to all and that funding was being managed effectively, she met with community leaders and organizations, corporate partners, and medical institutions. "A typical workweek, in one word, was juggling," she says. "In a small nonprofit, few people do the work of many."

Occasionally, Drevs traveled to conferences to network with other organizations dedicated to working with certain populations of breast cancer survivors, including young women. These organizations have banded together to develop a pilot program that will address young women's concerns with intimacy and infertility after breast cancer.

In Chicago, Drevs strove to raise the awareness of breast cancer among African American women from all walks of life. "As a middle-class white woman, the issue of race had been a very academic one in my experience," she says. "I read Studs Terkel and took racial disparities curricula, but never truly understood the issues until I became immersed in the community." Drevs's experience with Y-ME helped her to understand the position of thousands of

underinsured African American women in that city: "limited access to health care, distrust of the system, and the importance of their community and social networks."

Asked what insights she has drawn from her training in sociology, Drevs replies, "It reaffirmed my belief that no one perspective is the only perspective. From fundamental social theory to social conflict to developing nations, there are many ways to explain something, and oftentimes, there is something that can be gained from each perspective."

Drevs is now working for her alma mater, Dartmouth College, as the program manager for young alumni, students, and diversity at the Office of Alumni Relations. Her advice to current students of sociology: "Even if you don't major in this, make sure to take it with you wherever you go. Many of the world's problems can be traced to not communicating properly and not understanding another group's perspective. A good basis in sociology can serve you well, no matter what you do."

LET'S DISCUSS

1. Do some research on breast cancer. Does the survival rate differ among different racial and ethnic groups? What about different social classes? Why are education and early detection important?
2. Relate what you have learned about breast cancer to what you have learned about gender. What social patterns does your research illustrate?

The second wave of feminism in the United States emerged in the 1960s and came into full force in the 1970s. In part, the movement was inspired by three pioneering books arguing for women's rights: Simone de Beauvoir's *The Second Sex*, Betty Friedan's *The Feminine Mystique*, and Kate Millett's *Sexual Politics*. In addition, the general political activism of the 1960s led women—many of whom were working for Black civil rights or against the war in Vietnam—to reexamine their own powerlessness. The sexism often found within even allegedly progressive and radical political circles convinced many women that they needed to establish a movement for women's liberation (Breines 2007; Freeman 1973, 1975).

As more and more women became aware of sexist attitudes and practices, including attitudes they themselves had accepted through socialization into traditional gender roles, they began to challenge male dominance. A sense of sisterhood, much like the class consciousness that Marx hoped would emerge in the proletariat, became evident. Individual women identified their interests with those of the collectivity *women*. No longer were women happy in submissive, subordinate roles ("false consciousness" in Marxist terms).

National surveys done today, however, show that while women generally endorse feminist positions, they do not necessarily accept the label *feminist*. Some 57 percent of women considered themselves feminists in 1987; the proportion had dropped to about 25 percent in 2001. Feminism as a unified political cause, requiring one to accept a similar stance on everything from abortion to sexual harassment to pornography to

welfare, has fallen out of favor. Both women and men prefer to express their views on these complex issues individually, rather than under a convenient umbrella like feminism. Still, feminism is very much alive in the growing acceptance of women in nontraditional roles, and even the basic acknowledgment that a married mother not only can work outside the home but perhaps *belongs* in the labor force. A majority of women say that given the choice, they would prefer to work outside the home rather than stay home and take care of a house and family, and about one-quarter of women prefer *Ms.* to *Miss* or *Mrs.* (Feminist Majority Foundation 2007; Robison 2002).

The women's movement has undertaken public protests on a wide range of issues. Feminists have endorsed passage of the equal rights amendment, government subsidies for child care (see Chapter 4), affirmative action for women and minorities (see Chapter 18), federal legislation outlawing sex discrimination in education (see Chapter 16), greater representation of women in government (see Chapter 17), and the right to a legal abortion (discussed in the Social Policy section of this chapter).

thinking CRITICALLY

Today, is feminism more likely to produce social change or to respond to social change? Explain.

The Battle over Abortion from a Global Perspective

Few issues seem to stir as much intense conflict as abortion. A critical victory in the struggle for legalized abortion in the United States came in 1973, when the Supreme Court granted women the right to terminate pregnancies. This ruling, known as *Roe v. Wade*, was based on a woman's right to privacy. The Court's decision was generally applauded by pro-choice groups, which believe women should have the right to make their own decisions about their bodies and should have access to safe and legal abortions. It was bitterly condemned by those opposed to abortion. For these pro-life groups, abortion is a moral and often a religious issue. In their view, human life begins at the moment of conception, so that its termination through abortion is essentially an act of murder.

Looking at the Issue

The debate that has followed *Roe v. Wade* revolves around prohibiting abortion altogether, or at the very least, limiting it. In 1979, for example, Missouri required parental consent for minors wishing to obtain an abortion, and the Supreme Court upheld the law. Parental notification and consent have become especially sensitive issues in the debate. Pro-life activists argue that the parents of teenagers should have the right to be notified about—and to permit or prohibit—abortions. In their view, parental authority deserves full support at a time when the traditional nuclear family is embattled. However, pro-choice activists counter that many pregnant teenagers come from troubled families where they have been abused. These young women may have good reason to avoid discussing such explosive issues with their parents.

In the United States, people support a woman's right to a legal abortion, but with reservations. According to a 2009 national survey, 46 percent say that abortion should be legal in most or all cases; 44 percent say it should be illegal in most or all cases. There is no gender difference in opinion on this issue: women are just as likely as men to embrace a right-to-life orientation (Pew Research Center 2009).

The United States is not alone in debating abortion. Latin American countries typically have the strictest measures against the practice, but occasionally changes occur. In 2007, Mexico loosened decade-old restrictions to permit legal abortions during the first three months of a pregnancy, for any reason (M. Davis 2010).

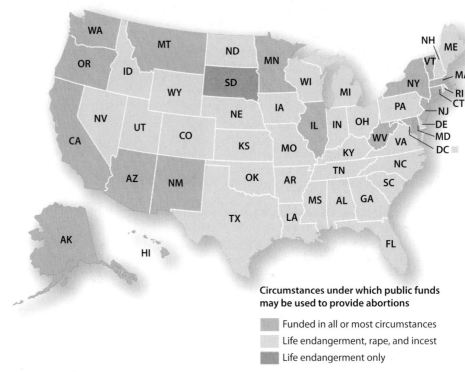

MAPPING LIFE NATIONWIDE
FIGURE **12-5**   RESTRICTIONS ON PUBLIC FUNDING FOR ABORTION

Circumstances under which public funds may be used to provide abortions

- Funded in all or most circumstances
- Life endangerment, rape, and incest
- Life endangerment only

Note: As of March 17, 2011.
Source: NARAL Pro-Choice America 2011.

Applying Sociology

Sociologists see gender and social class as the defining issues surrounding abortion. That is, the intense conflict over abortion reflects broader differences over women's position in society. Feminists involved in defending abortion rights typically believe that men and women are essentially similar. They support women's full participation in work outside the home and oppose all forms of sex discrimination. Feminists also claim that pregnancy and childbirth have been socially constructed by male-centered health care systems and patriarchal religious traditions. In contrast, most antiabortion activists believe that men and women are fundamentally different. In their view, men are best suited to the public world of work, while women are best suited to the demanding and crucial task of rearing children. These activists are troubled by women's growing participation in work outside the home, which they view as destructive to the family, and ultimately to society (Lorber 2005).

In regard to social class, the first major restriction on the legal right to terminate a pregnancy affected poor people. In 1976, Congress passed the Hyde Amendment, which banned the use of Medicaid and other federal funds for abortions. The Supreme Court upheld this legislation in 1980. State laws also restrict the use of public funds for abortions (Figure 12-5).

FIGURE **12-6**   THE GLOBAL DIVIDE ON ABORTION

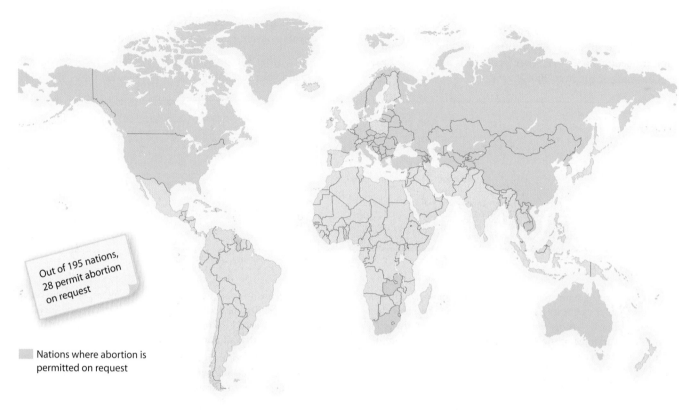

Out of 195 nations, 28 permit abortion on request

█ Nations where abortion is permitted on request

Note: Data current as of November 2007.
Source: Developed by the author based on United Nations Population Division 2007.

Another obstacle facing the poor is access to abortion providers. In the face of vocal pro-life sentiment, fewer and fewer hospitals throughout the world are allowing physicians to perform abortions, except in extreme cases. Moreover, some doctors who work in clinics, intimidated by death threats and murders, have stopped performing abortions. For poor people in rural areas, this reduction in service makes it more difficult to locate and travel to a facility that will accommodate their wishes. Viewed from a conflict perspective, this is one more financial burden that falls especially heavily on low-income women.

Finally, some antiabortion activists have charged that family-planning agencies and health care professionals are targeting young African American women for abortions. These pro-life proponents use the emotion-laden phrase "womb lynchings" to call attention to the issue. Abortion rights advocates counter that the campaign falsely portrays young Black women as naive and not in control of their own decisions (Dewan 2010).

Initiating Policy

In 1973 the Supreme Court supported the general right to terminate a pregnancy by a narrow 5–4 majority. Although pro-life activists continue to hope for an overruling of *Roe v. Wade,* they have focused in the interim on weakening the decision through tactics such as limiting the use of fetal tissue in medical experiments and prohibiting certain late-term abortions, which they term "partial-birth" abortions. The Supreme Court continues to hear cases involving such restrictions.

What is the policy in other countries? As in the United States, many European nations responded to public opinion and liberalized abortion laws beginning in the 1970s. However, many of those nations limit the procedure to the first 12 weeks of a pregnancy. (The United States, in contrast, allows abortions up to about the 24th week and beyond.) Inspired by the strong antiabortion movement in the United States, antiabortion activists in Europe have become more outspoken, especially in Great Britain, France, Portugal, Spain, Italy, and Germany.

The policies of the United States are intertwined with those of developing nations. From the 1980s through January 2009, members of Congress who opposed abortion successfully blocked foreign aid to countries that might use the funds to encourage abortion. Yet developing nations generally have the most restrictive abortion laws. As Figure 12-6 shows, it is primarily in Africa, Latin America, and parts of Asia that women are not allowed to terminate a pregnancy on request. As might be expected, illegal abortions are most common in those nations. An estimated quarter of the world's women live in countries where abortion is illegal or is permitted only if a woman's life is in jeopardy. Indeed, the rate of abortions in countries with legal restrictions on the procedure matches the rate in countries that permit it. Hence, 40 percent of abortions worldwide—about 16 million procedures each year—are performed illegally (P. Baker 2009; Guttmacher Institute 2008).

Take the Issue with You

1. How easy do you think it is for a young adult woman to obtain an abortion? What do you think should be the first step she takes in considering one?

2. Do you think teenage girls should be required to get their parents' consent before having an abortion? Why or why not?

3. Under what circumstances should abortions be allowed? Explain your reasoning.

MASTERING THIS CHAPTER

Summary

Gender is an ascribed status that provides a basis for social differentiation. This chapter examines the social construction of gender, theories of stratification by gender, women as an oppressed majority group, women in the workforce of the United States, and the emergence of a collective consciousness.

1. In the United States, the social construction of gender continues to define significantly different expectations for females and males.

2. **Gender roles** show up in our work and behavior and in how we react to others. Throughout history, these roles have restricted women much more than they have men.

3. Though men may exhibit a variety of different gender roles, called **multiple masculinities,** society reinforces their traditional role of dominating women.

4. Anthropological research points to the importance of cultural conditioning in defining the social roles of males and females.

5. Functionalists maintain that sex differentiation contributes to overall social stability, but conflict theorists charge that the relationship between females and males is one of unequal power, with men dominating women. This dominance shows up in people's everyday interactions.

6. Many women experience differential treatment, not only because of their gender but because of their race, ethnicity, and social class as well. Patricia Hill Collins has termed this convergence of social forces the **matrix of domination.**

7. As one example of their micro-level approach to the study of gender stratification, interactionists have analyzed men's verbal dominance over women through conversational interruptions.

8. Women around the world live and work with pervasive **sexism** and **institutional discrimination.**

9. In the United States today, almost as many women as men participate in the paid labor force, but women are underrepresented in managerial positions and underpaid compared to men in the same jobs.

10. As women have taken on more and more hours of paid employment outside the home, they have been only partially successful in getting their husbands to take on more homemaking duties, including child care.

11. Many women agree with the positions of the feminist movement but reject the label *feminist.*

12. The issue of abortion has bitterly divided the United States (as well as other nations), pitting pro-choice activists against pro-life activists.

Key Terms

Expressiveness Concern for the maintenance of harmony and the internal emotional affairs of the family. (page 271)

Feminism The belief in social, economic, and political equality for women. (278)

Gender role Expectations regarding the proper behavior, attitudes, and activities of males and females. (267)

Glass ceiling An invisible barrier that blocks the promotion of a qualified individual in a work environment because of the individual's gender, race, or ethnicity. (275)

Homophobia Fear of and prejudice against homosexuality. (267)

Institutional discrimination The denial of opportunities and equal rights to individuals and groups that results from the normal operations of a society. (273)

Instrumentality An emphasis on tasks, a focus on more distant goals, and a concern for the external relationship between one's family and other social institutions. (271)

Matrix of domination The cumulative impact of oppression because of race and ethnicity, gender, and social class, as well as religion, sexual orientation, disability, age, and citizenship status. (272)

Multiple masculinities A variety of male gender roles, including nurturing-caring and effeminate-gay roles, that men may play along with their more pervasive traditional role of dominating women. (269)

Second shift The double burden—work outside the home followed by child care and housework—that many women face and few men share equitably. (277)

Sexism The ideology that one sex is superior to the other. (273)

1. For a day or two, watch for examples of people "doing gender" on your campus. Record your sightings in a journal and compare them with those of your classmates.

2. Find out what percentage of the faculty members at your college are women. What percentage of the women has tenure, compared to the men? What percentage holds full professorships? Do the percentages vary much from one department to another, and if so, why?

3. Use your school's alumni network to get in touch with graduates who have entered the workforce. Are mothers of young children having difficulty balancing work and parenting? Do both men and women feel they have a chance to get ahead? Are both men and women well compensated?

Self-Quiz

Read each question carefully and then select the best answer.

1. Both males and females are physically capable of learning to cook and sew, yet most Western societies determine that women should perform these tasks. This illustrates the operation of
   a. gender roles.
   b. sociobiology.
   c. homophobia.
   d. comparable worth.

2. An important element in traditional views of proper "masculine" and "feminine" behavior is fear of homosexuality. This fear, along with accompanying prejudice, is referred to as
   a. lesbianism.
   b. femme fatalism.
   c. homophobia.
   d. claustrophobia.

3. The most crucial agents of socialization in teaching gender roles in the United States are
   a. peers.
   b. teachers.
   c. media personalities.
   d. parents.

4. Research by anthropologists Margaret Mead and Peggy Reeves Sanday has shown that
   a. biology is the most important factor in determining the social roles of males and females.
   b. cultural conditioning is the most important factor in determining the social roles of males and females.
   c. biology and cultural conditioning have an equal impact in determining the social roles of males and females.
   d. biology and cultural conditioning have a negligible impact in determining the social roles of males and females.

5. Which sociological perspective acknowledges that it is not possible to change gender roles drastically without dramatic revisions in a culture's social structure?
   a. functionalist perspective
   b. conflict perspective
   c. interactionist perspective
   d. both a and b

6. The term *sexism* is generally used to refer to
   a. female prejudice and discrimination against men.
   b. male prejudice and discrimination against women.
   c. female discrimination against men and male discrimination against women equally.
   d. discrimination between members of the same sex.

7. Which of these statements is true?
   a. More boys than girls take AP exams.
   b. Women in the United States are more likely than men to attend college.
   c. Women in the United States are less likely than men to obtain doctoral degrees.
   d. all of the above

8. Which sociological perspective distinguishes between instrumental and expressive roles?
   a. functionalist perspective
   b. conflict perspective
   c. interactionist perspective
   d. labeling theory

9. Contemporary feminists recognize the differential treatment of some women not only because of their gender, but also because of their
   a. race.
   b. ethnicity.
   c. socioeconomic status.
   d. all of the above

10. The sense of sisterhood that became evident during the rise of the contemporary feminist movement resembled the Marxist concept of
    a. alienation.
    b. dialectics.
    c. class consciousness.
    d. false consciousness.

11. Talcott Parsons and Robert Bales contend that women take the _____, emotionally supportive role in the family and that men take the _____, practical role, with the two complementing each other.

12. A significant component of the _____ approach to gender stratification draws on feminist theory.

13. It is not simply that particular men in the United States are biased in their treatment of women. All the major institutions of our society—including the government, the armed forces, large corporations, the media, the universities, and the medical establishment—are controlled by men. This situation is symptomatic of institutional _____.

14. Women from all groups and men from minority groups sometimes encounter attitudinal or organizational bias that prevents them from reaching their full potential. This is known as the _____ _____.

15. Sociologist Arlie Hochschild has used the phrase _____ _____ to describe the double burden that many women face and few men share equitably: work outside the home followed by child care and housework.

16. Within the general framework of their theory, _____ sociologists maintain that gender differentiation has contributed to overall social stability.

17. Through the rise of contemporary _____, women are developing a greater sense of group solidarity.

18. _____ contributes significantly to rigid gender-role socialization, since many people stereotypically associate male homosexuality with femininity and lesbianism with masculinity.

19. The term _____ _____ _____ was coined by feminist theorist Patricia Hill Collins to describe the convergence of social forces that contributes to the subordinate status of poor, non-White women.

20. The author of the pioneering argument for women's rights, *The Feminine Mystique*, was _____ _____.

THINKING ABOUT **MOVIES**

Easy A

A high school student is accused of being sexually promiscuous.

La Mission

A man redefines his masculinity after he learns that his son is gay.

North Country

A woman who works in an iron mine fights against sexual harassment.

Several generations enjoy
rafting on the Penobscot River in
Maine. Age serves as a basis for
social stratification, sometimes
separating the old from the
young more than is necessary
or desirable. To a great extent,
older people's quality of life,
including their livelihoods, their
social relationships, and their
leisure pursuits, depends on
society's view of aging.

Stratification by Age

TED C. FISHMAN

New York Times bestselling author of China, Inc.

SHOCK
OF GRAY

The aging of the world's
population and how it pits
young against old, child
against parent, worker against
boss, company against rival,
and nation against nation

66 Now in her eighties, my mother still dances at her grandsons' Led Zeppelin tribute concerts, swims Lake Michigan when the water is brisk, hikes among penguins in Patagonia, and dons cross-country skis as soon as the snow is deep enough. My late father, in contrast, was at the peak of his professional and creative success in his early sixties, but a barrage of ailments hit him hard at sixty-three. He began a cruel fifteen-year decline that left him blind, immobile, slow of speech, and utterly dependent. That he never lost his wit or kindness or his ability to hold on to the joys of life was, to me, heroic.

My parents' different experiences neatly represent what is happening to millions of Americans and to vast portions of the globe's population. The world is going gray. Getting not just older but *old.* Sometime after sixty, it seems to happen to everyone: life-altering events cascade one after another. In some combination, family nests are emptied; jobs end or change; spouses, friends, and kin grow gravely ill or die; bodies and minds decline; one's status and power in the family and in social circles inverts; money draws down; and, as remaining years grow fewer, relationships with time and eternity shift.

And yet new worlds can open up, too. Time can expand, social circles grow bigger, new passions take root. Freed from the relentless demands of family and work, older people may experience a sweet rejuvenation. People whom one might expect to be decrepit and infirm are, well, dancing at Led Zeppelin tribute concerts; Or even performing in them.

> *The aging of the globe is having profound economic, political, cultural, and familial effects that are only going to intensify.*

Meanwhile, although the world well understands how young people shape social life and business, it is just now beginning to see how the arrival of a historically enormous older population will affect all of us. Many old people, like my mother, will be healthy and vibrant, but many others, like my father, will need extraordinary resources to make it from one day to the next. The aging of the globe is having profound economic, political, cultural, and familial effects that are only going to intensify. Some of these changes will be welcome and others will not. Certain people will benefit and others will be harmed. Money and power are at stake, of course, as well as the well-being of millions of older people who have worked and loved and given themselves to all that life offers. But the well-being of the globe's young is also at stake, because it is they who need resources also required by the old, and because in the end, it is largely the young who, as family members, friends, and citizens traveling the continuum of an aging world, will eventually care for the old. And in time their older selves.

The signs of the shift, large and small, are everywhere, if we only will see them. Consider:

In a room full of telephones and flat-panel displays, where staff is on hand twenty-four hours a day, calls begin to pick up around 9:00 a.m. That's when the more than 6 million elderly customers of Philips Lifeline tend to begin their daily routines. The service allows its clients to alert the company if anything threatens them. The morning is rife with dangers. The average age of a customer is eighty-two, but thousands of centenarians use the service, too. The large majority are women, a predictable reality in an older group. The mornings see millions of Lifeline clients head to the showers, step out on slippery tiles, and then make their way to the kitchen, where fire, knives, tall cabinets, area rugs, and wood flooring are mortal threats. If customers slip and fall, or a sleeve catches fire, or if they are overcome with anxiety and fear as the day begins, devices around their necks or on their wrists let them send signals, sometimes automatically, to the Lifeline call center. By mid-morning on a beautiful fall day, Lifeline has handled nearly seven hundred thousand *calls.* 99

(Fishman 2010a:1–2) Additional information about this excerpt can be found on the Online Learning Center at www.mhhe.com/schaefer13e.

Journalist Ted C. Fishman, author of this opening excerpt, is known for his reporting on global trade and finance. During the course of his work, he became aware of a powerful demographic trend, the aging of the world's population. In his book *Shock of Gray,* Fishman confronts the consequences of the rise in the proportion of elderly, not only for elders themselves and their families, but for entire societies and economies. He predicts a growing conflict between young and old, developed and developing nations, over limited resources.

As Fishman notes, not all older people are frail and dependent, in need of support; many, like his mother, are healthy, energetic, and engaged. Unfortunately, younger people tend to stereotype the aged. Like race or gender, age is socially constructed, an ascribed status that dominates people's perceptions of others, obscuring individual differences. Rather than suggesting that a particular elderly person is no longer competent to drive, for instance, we may condemn the entire age group: "Those old codgers shouldn't be allowed on the road." Unless people can begin to look at the life course as a continuum, rather than as a series of finite stages with predictable consequences, such stereotypical attitudes toward age and aging are not likely to change.

How do people's roles change as they age? What are the social implications of the growing number of elderly in the United States? How does ageism affect an older person's employment opportunities? In this chapter we will look at the process of aging throughout the life course. We will examine aging around the world, focusing primarily on the United States. After exploring various theories of the impact of aging, both on the individual and on society, we will discuss the role transitions typical of the major stages in the life course. In the process we will consider the challenges facing the "sandwich generation," middle-aged people who care for both their children and their aging parents. We will pay particular attention to the effects of prejudice and discrimination on older people, and to the rise of a political consciousness among the elderly. Finally, in the Social Policy section we will discuss the controversial issue of the right to die.

Aging and Society

The Sherpas—a Tibetan-speaking Buddhist people in Nepal—live in a culture that idealizes old age. Almost all elderly members of the Sherpa culture own their homes, and most are in relatively good physical condition. Typically, older Sherpas value their independence and prefer not to live with their children. Among the Fulani of Africa, however, older men and women move to the edge of the family homestead. Since that is where people are buried, the elderly sleep over their own graves, for they are viewed socially as already dead. Like gender stratification, age stratification varies from culture to culture. One society may treat older people with great reverence, while another sees them as unproductive and "difficult" (M. Goldstein and Beall 1981; Stenning 1958; Tonkinson 1978).

It is understandable that all societies have some system of age stratification that associates certain social roles with distinct periods in life. Some of this age differentiation seems inevitable; it would make little sense to send young children off to war, or to expect most older citizens to handle physically demanding tasks, such as loading freight at shipyards. However, as is the case with stratification by gender, in the United States age stratification goes far beyond the physical constraints on human beings at different ages.

"Being old" is a master status that commonly overshadows all others in the United States. Thus, the insights of labeling theory can help us in analyzing the consequences of aging. Once people have been labeled "old," the designation has a major impact on how others perceive them, and even on how they view themselves. Negative stereotypes of the elderly contribute to their position as a minority group subject to discrimination, as we will see later in the chapter.

The model of five basic properties of a minority or subordinate group (introduced in Chapter 11) can be applied to older people in the United States to clarify their subordinate status:

1. Older people experience unequal treatment in employment and may face prejudice and discrimination.

2. Older people share physical characteristics that distinguish them from younger people. In addition, their cultural preferences and leisure-time activities often differ from those of the rest of society.

3. Membership in this disadvantaged group is involuntary.

4. Older people have a strong sense of group solidarity, as is reflected in the growth of senior citizens' centers, retirement communities, and advocacy organizations.

5. Older people generally are married to others of comparable age.

There is one crucial difference between older people and other subordinate groups, such as racial and ethnic minorities or women: *all* of us who live long enough will eventually assume the ascribed status of an older person (Barron 1953; Levin and Levin 1980; Wagley and Harris 1958).

Sociological Perspectives on Aging

Aging is one important aspect of socialization—the lifelong process through which an individual learns the cultural norms and values of a particular society. There are no clear-cut definitions for different periods of the aging cycle in the United States. *Old age* has typically been regarded as beginning at 65, which corresponds to the retirement age for many workers, but not everyone in the United States accepts that definition. With the increase in life expectancy, writers are beginning to refer to people in their 60s as the "young old," to distinguish them from those in their 80s and beyond (the "old old").

The particular problems of the elderly have become the focus of a specialized field of research and inquiry known as gerontology. **Gerontology** is the scientific study of the sociological and psychological aspects of aging and the problems of the aged. It

Extended family arrangements are important to Americans, especially Latinos. Thirty-one percent of Hispanic women age 65 and older live with their relatives, compared to 13 percent of White non-Hispanic women. Among men of the same age, the rate is 15 percent for Hispanics, compared to 6 percent for White non-Hispanics (Jacobsen et al. 2011).

TAKING SOCIOLOGY TO WORK

A. David Roberts, **Social Worker**

Dave Roberts admits to being a "people person," a trait that sociology courses fostered by showing how "everybody has differences; there are little bits of different cultures in all of us." He also had the benefit of "a lot of great teachers" at Florida State University, including Dr. Jill Quadagno in a course on aging. It was this class that sparked his interest in aging issues, which led to a certificate in gerontology in addition to a sociology degree in 1998. He realized that there was a good job market in working with the aging baby boom generation.

Volunteer work with the Meals on Wheels program steered him toward working with the elderly. Today Roberts is a social worker in a nursing home, where he is responsible for patients' care plans. In the course of his work, he meets regularly with patients, family members, and medical residents. Roberts finds that the concept of teamwork he learned in group projects in college has helped him in his job. Also, the projects he had to do in school taught him to work on a schedule. Perhaps most important, sociology has helped him "to grow as a person, to explore different angles, different theories. . . . I'm a better person."

His advice to sociology students: "Just give it a chance; they throw everything into an intro course. Don't get overwhelmed; take it as it comes."

LET'S DISCUSS

1. What other types of employment might be open to a college graduate with a certificate in gerontology?
2. What might be the special rewards of working with elderly people?

---

originated in the 1930s, as an increasing number of social scientists became aware of the plight of the elderly.

Gerontologists rely heavily on sociological principles and theories to explain the impact of aging on the individual and society. They also draw on psychology, anthropology, physical education, counseling, and medicine in their study of the aging process. Two influential views of aging—disengagement theory and activity theory—can best be understood in terms of the sociological perspectives of functionalism and interactionism, respectively. The conflict perspective also contributes to our sociological understanding of aging.

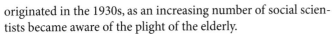

use your sociological *imagination*

Time has passed, and you are now in your 70s or 80s. How does old age in your generation compare with your parents' or grandparents' experience of old age?

Functionalist Approach: Disengagement Theory

After studying elderly people in good health and relatively comfortable economic circumstances, Elaine Cumming and William Henry (1961) introduced their **disengagement theory,** which implicitly suggests that society and the aging individual mutually sever many of their relationships. In keeping with the functionalist perspective, disengagement theory emphasizes that passing social roles on from one generation to another ensures social stability.

According to this theory, the approach of death forces people to drop most of their social roles—including those of worker, volunteer, spouse, hobby enthusiast, and even reader. Younger members of society then take on these functions. The aging person, it is held, withdraws into an increasing state of inactivity while preparing for death.

Since it was first outlined five decades ago, disengagement theory has generated considerable controversy. Today, gerontologists and sociologists are more likely to see the elderly in terms of social connectedness, postretirement employment, and volunteerism. For their part, producers and retailers of electronic products are likely to see the older set as e-savvy consumers. Since 2008, they note, growth in computer and digital camera sales has been greatest in that market segment. And retirement homes have had to make room for residents who want to bowl or play tennis on Nintendo's Wii system (Cornwell et al. 2008; NPD Group 2008).

Interactionist Approach: Activity Theory

How important is it for older people to stay actively involved, whether at a job or in other pursuits? A tragic disaster in Chicago in 1995 showed that it can be a matter of life and death. An intense heat wave lasting more than a week—with a heat index exceeding 115 degrees on two consecutive days—resulted in 733 heat-related deaths. About three-fourths of the deceased were 65 and older. Subsequent analysis showed that older people who lived alone had the highest risk of dying, suggesting that support networks for the elderly literally help to save lives. Older Hispanics and Asian Americans had lower death rates from the heat wave than other racial and ethnic groups. Their stronger social networks probably resulted in more regular contact with family members and friends (Klinenberg 2002; R. Schaefer 1998).

Often seen as an opposing approach to disengagement theory, **activity theory** suggests that those elderly people who remain active and socially involved will be best adjusted. Proponents of this perspective acknowledge that a person age 70 may not have the ability or desire to perform various social roles that he or she had at age 40. Yet they contend that old people have essentially the same need for social interaction as any other group.

The improved health of older people—sometimes overlooked by social scientists—has strengthened the arguments of activity theorists. Illness and chronic disease are no longer quite the scourge of the elderly that they once were. The recent emphasis on fitness, the availability of better medical care, greater control of infectious diseases, and the reduction of fatal strokes and heart attacks have combined to mitigate the traumas of growing old.

These "silver surfers" in California still enjoy life to the fullest, just as they did when they were young. According to activity theory, staying active and involved is healthy for the older population.

Understandably, many people would prefer to be considered old later rather than sooner. Those who advocate for the elderly would prefer a broader definition. For example, the AARP (see pages 298–299) offers membership to anyone age 50 or older. It argues that people should begin planning for old age in their 50s, but clearly, encouraging the "young old" to join gives them strength in numbers.

The labeling of old age also differs from one culture to the next, due in part to differences in physical health and life opportunities. In relatively prosperous cultures like the United States, 70 is the new 60. But in countries whose health and social support systems have been significantly weakened over the past 20 years—Russia, for example—50 is the new 60 (Sanderson and Scherbov 2008).

Accumulating medical research also points to the importance of remaining socially involved. Among those who decline in their mental capacities later in life, deterioration is most rapid in those who withdraw from social relationships and activities. Fortunately, older people are finding new ways to remain socially engaged, as evidenced by their increasing use of the Internet, especially to keep in touch with family and friends (Clifford 2009b).

Admittedly, many activities open to older adults involve unpaid labor, for which younger adults may receive salaries. Unpaid elderly workers include hospital volunteers (versus aides and orderlies), drivers for charities such as the Red Cross (versus chauffeurs), tutors (as opposed to teachers), and craftspeople for charity bazaars (as opposed to carpenters and dressmakers). However, some companies have recently begun programs to hire retirees for full-time or part-time work.

Though disengagement theory suggested that older people find satisfaction in withdrawal from society, conveniently receding into the background and allowing the next generation to take over, proponents of activity theory view such withdrawal as harmful to both the elderly and society. Activity theorists focus on the potential contributions of older people to the maintenance of society. In their opinion, aging citizens will feel satisfied only when they can be useful and productive in society's terms—primarily by working for wages (Charles and Carstensen 2009; Quadagno 2011).

Labeling Theory

Just who are "the elderly"? Labeling theorists, who study the way reality is constructed through our culture and social interactions, have noted that recently, our society has begun to reconsider what makes a person old.

As early as 1975, social scientists were suggesting that old age should be defined not in terms of how old one is, but in terms of how long one can be expected to live. As life expectancy lengthens, then, the age at which one is labeled old rises. Some have suggested that the threshold of old age should begin in the last 10 or 15 years of a person's expected life. Using that definition, old age would begin at about age 70 or 75, at least for those of us who live in the United States.

Is this new definition of old age likely to be accepted? From the labeling perspective, it all depends on who you are.

thinking CRITICALLY

Is labeling the same as stereotyping? Why or why not?

Conflict Approach

Conflict theorists have criticized both disengagement theorists and activity theorists for failing to consider the impact of social structure on aging patterns. Neither approach, they say, questions why social interaction must change or decrease in old age. In addition, they often ignore the impact of social class on the lives of elderly people.

The privileged upper class generally enjoys better health and vigor and less likelihood of dependency in old age. Affluence cannot forestall aging indefinitely, but it can soften the economic hardships people face in later years. Although pension plans, retirement packages, and insurance benefits may be developed to assist older people, those whose wealth allows them access to investment funds can generate the greatest income for their later years.

In contrast, the working class often faces greater health hazards and a greater risk of disability; aging is particularly difficult for those who suffer job-related injuries or illnesses. Working-class people also depend more heavily on Social Security benefits and private pension programs. During inflationary times, their relatively fixed incomes from these sources barely keep pace with the escalating costs of food, housing, utilities, and other necessities (Atchley and Barusch 2004).

According to the conflict approach, the treatment of older people in the United States reflects the many divisions in our society. The low status of older people is seen in prejudice and discrimination against them, in age segregation, and in unfair job practices—none of which are directly addressed by either disengagement or activity theory.

Conflict theorists have noted, too, that in the developing world, the transition from agricultural economies to industrialization and capitalism has not always been beneficial to the elderly. As a society's production methods change, the traditionally valued role of older people tends to erode. Their wisdom is no longer relevant in the new economy.

In sum, the four perspectives considered here take different views of the elderly. Functionalists portray older people as socially isolated, with reduced social roles; interactionists see them as involved in new networks and changing social roles. Labeling theorists see old age as a life stage that is defined by society. Conflict theorists see it as a time when people are victimized and their social roles devalued. Table 13-1 summarizes these perspectives.

use your sociological *imagination*

Have you noticed signs of second-class treatment of older people? If so, in what ways?

Aging Worldwide

Today the world's population is evenly divided between those people who are under age 28 and those who are over age 28. By the middle of the 21st century, the median age will have risen to 40. Even though the United Nations held the first world assembly on aging in 1982, few people gave much thought to this prospect of whole populations—that is, nations—growing older until the 1990s. By 2010, the world had more than 551 million people age 65 and over. Together they constituted about 8 percent of the world's population. By 2045, nearly twice that proportion, or 15.2 percent of the world's people, will be over 65.

In an important sense, this trend toward the aging of the world's population represents a major success story, one that unfolded during the latter years of the 20th century. Through the efforts of national governments and international agencies, many societies have drastically reduced their incidence of disease, and with it their rate of death. As a result, these nations—particularly the industrialized countries of Europe and North America—have a high and steadily rising proportion of older members (Figure 13-1); (Fishman 2010b; Haub 2010).

Overall, Europe's population is older than that of any other continent. Though many European countries have long prided themselves on their generous pension programs, as the proportion of older people continues to rise, government officials have reluctantly begun to reduce pension benefits and raise the age at which workers can receive them. Japan, too, has a relatively old population; the Japanese enjoy a life expectancy of 83 years, compared to 78 in the United States.

In most developing countries, people over 60 are likely to be in poorer health than their counterparts in industrialized nations. Yet few of those countries are in a position to offer extensive financial

TABLE **13-1** SOCIOLOGICAL PERSPECTIVES ON AGING

Sociological Perspective	View of Aging	Social Roles	Portrayal of Elderly
Functionalist	Disengagement	Reduced	Socially isolated
Interactionist	Activity	Changed	Involved in new networks
Labeling	Socially constructed	Changing	Varies by audience
Conflict	Competition	Relatively unchanged	Victimized, organized to confront their victimization

Summing up

support to the elderly. Ironically, though the modernization of the developing world has brought many social and economic advances, it has undercut the traditionally high status of the elderly. In many cultures, the earning power of younger adults now exceeds that of their older relatives (Beck 2009).

Role Transitions throughout the Life Course

Socialization is a lifelong process. We simply do not experience things the same way at different points in the life course. For example, one study found that even falling in love differs according to where we are in the life course. Young unmarried adults tend to treat love as a noncommittal game or an obsession characterized by possessiveness and dependency. People over age 50 are much more likely to see love as involving commitment, and they tend to take a practical approach to finding a partner who meets a set of rational criteria. That does not mean that romance is dead among the older

FIGURE **13-1** WORLD'S "OLDEST" COUNTRIES VERSUS THE UNITED STATES

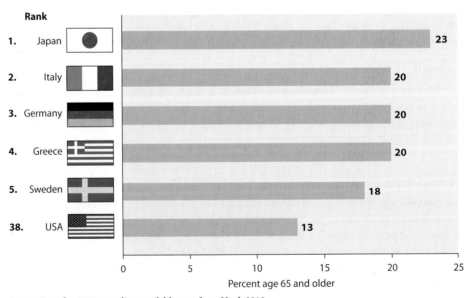

Rank		
1.	Japan	23
2.	Italy	20
3.	Germany	20
4.	Greece	20
5.	Sweden	18
38.	USA	13

Percent age 65 and older

Source: Data for 2009 or earliest available year from Haub 2010.

This sandwich-generation mom cares for both her aging parent and her children. Increasingly, members of the baby boom generation find themselves caring for two generations at once.

generation, however. Among those age 65 and over, 39 percent are "head over heels in love," compared to only 25 percent of those ages 18 to 34. The life course, then, affects the manner in which we relate to one another (G. Anderson 2009; Montgomery and Sorell 1997).

How we move through the life course varies dramatically, depending on our personal preferences and circumstances. Some of us marry early, others late; some have children and some don't. These individual patterns are influenced by social factors such as class, race, and gender. Only in the most general terms, then, can we speak of stages or periods in the life course.

One transitional stage, identified by psychologist Daniel Levinson, begins at the time at which an individual gradually enters the adult world, perhaps by moving out of the parental home, beginning a career, or entering a marriage. The next transitional period, the midlife transition, typically begins at about age 40. Men and women often experience a stressful period of self-evaluation, commonly known as the **midlife crisis,** in which they realize that they have not achieved basic goals and ambitions and have little time left to do so. Thus, Levinson (1978, 1996) found that most adults surveyed experienced tumultuous midlife conflicts within the self and with the external world.

Not all the challenges at this time of life come from career or one's partner. In the next section we will examine a special challenge faced by a growing number of middle-aged adults: caring for two generations at once.

The Sandwich Generation

During the late 1990s social scientists focused on the **sandwich generation**—adults who simultaneously try to meet the competing needs of their parents and their children. That is, caregiving goes in two directions: (1) to children, who even as young adults may still require significant direction, and (2) to aging parents, whose health and economic problems may demand intervention by their adult children. By 2010, 13 million Americans were caring for both their children *and* their parents.

Like the role of caring for children, the role of caring for aging parents falls disproportionately on women. Overall, women provide 66 percent of the care their parents receive, and even more as the demands of the role grow more intense and time-consuming. Increasingly, middle-aged women and younger are finding themselves on the "daughter track," as their time and attention are diverted by the needs of their aging mothers and fathers. So significant have the challenges of caring for two generations become that in his 2010 State of the Union message, President Obama called for tax credits for families who care for both children and parents (National Alliance for Caregiving 2009).

The last major transition identified by Levinson occurs after age 60—sometimes well after that age, given advances in health care, greater longevity, and gradual acceptance within society of older people. Nonetheless, there is a point at which people transition to a different lifestyle. As we will see, this is a time of dramatic changes in people's everyday lives.

Adjusting to Retirement

Retirement is a rite of passage that marks a critical transition from one phase of a person's life to another. Typically, symbolic events are associated with this rite of passage, such as retirement gifts, a retirement party, and special moments on the last day on the job. The preretirement period itself can be emotionally charged, especially if the retiree is expected to train his or her successor (Atchley 1976).

From 1950 to the mid-1990s, the average age at retirement in the United States declined, but over the past few years it has reversed direction. By 2011, 5 percent of women and 10 percent of men over 75 were still working. A variety of factors explains this reversal: changes in Social Security benefits, the recent economic recession, and workers' concern with maintaining their health insurance and pension benefits. At the same time, longevity has increased, and the quality of people's health has improved (Department of Labor 2011).

Phases of Retirement Gerontologist Robert Atchley (1976) has identified several phases of the retirement experience:

- *Preretirement,* a period of anticipatory socialization as the person prepares for retirement
- *The near phase,* when the person establishes a specific departure date from his or her job
- *The honeymoon phase,* an often euphoric period in which the person pursues activities that he or she never had time for before
- *The disenchantment phase,* in which retirees feel a sense of letdown or even depression as they cope with their new lives, which may include illness or poverty
- *The reorientation phase,* which involves the development of a more realistic view of retirement alternatives
- *The stability phase,* a period in which the person has learned to deal with life after retirement in a reasonable and comfortable fashion

• *The termination phase,* which begins when the person can no longer engage in basic, day-to-day activities such as self-care and housework

Retirement is not a single transition, then, but rather a series of adjustments that varies from one person to another. The length and timing of each phase will differ for each individual, depending on such factors as financial status and health. A particular person will not necessarily go through all the phases identified by Atchley (Reitzes and Mutran 2006).

Some factors, such as being forced into retirement or being burdened with financial difficulties, can further complicate the retirement process. People who enter retirement involuntarily or without the necessary means may never experience the honeymoon phase. In the United States, many retirees continue in the paid labor force, often taking part-time jobs to supplement their pensions. Although most younger workers expect to retire—in a 2009 national survey, only 6 percent of respondents ages 18 to 29 said they would never retire—16 percent of those ages 50 to 64 do not expect to retire (Morin 2009; Figure 13-2).

Like other aspects of life in the United States, the experience of retirement varies according to gender, race, and ethnicity. White males are most likely to benefit from retirement wages, as well as to have participated in a formal retirement preparation program. As a result, anticipatory socialization for retirement is most complete for White men. In contrast, members of racial and ethnic minority groups—especially African Americans—are more likely to exit the paid labor force through disability than through retirement. Because of their comparatively lower incomes and smaller savings, men and women from racial and ethnic minority groups work intermittently after retirement more often than older Whites (National Institute on Aging 1999; Quadagno 2011).

Naturally Occurring Retirement Communities (NORCs)
With recent improvements in health care, older Americans have gained new choices in where to live. Today, rather than residing in nursing homes or planned retirement communities, many of them congregate in areas that have gradually become informal centers for senior citizens. Social scientists have dubbed such areas **naturally occurring retirement communities (NORCs).**

"*Have you given much thought to what kind of job you want after you retire?*"

thinking CRITICALLY

Today, many young adults continue to live with their parents after finishing their schooling. Contrast their situation with that of the elderly who live with their children. Does society treat dependent adult children in the same way as dependent parents? Why or why not?

use your sociological *imagination*

How have people close to you, such as relatives, personally handled their retirement from the labor force?

FIGURE **13-2**   EXPECTED RETIREMENT AGE

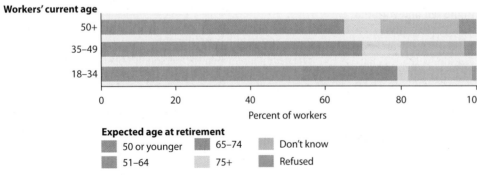

Workers' current age

Expected age at retirement
- 50 or younger
- 51–64
- 65–74
- 75+
- Don't know
- Refused

Note: Survey of 1,053 workers 18 and over conducted in July 2006.
Source: S. K. Brown 2006.

Using observation research, census data, and interviews, sociologists have developed some interesting conclusions about NORCs in the United States, which numbered approximately 300 in 2009. These communities can be as small as a single apartment building or as large as a neighborhood in a big city. Often, they emerge as singles and young couples move out and older people move in. Sometimes couples simply remain where they are; as they grow older, the community becomes noticeably grayer. In time, business establishments that cater to

Think about It
At what age do you expect to retire completely, without working for pay at all?

the elderly—pharmacies, medical supply outlets, small restaurants—relocate to NORCs, making them even more attractive to older citizens.

Unfortunately, residents of some of these communities are threatened by gentrification, or the takeover of low-income neighborhoods by higher-income residents. In Chicago, a high-rise building known as Ontario Place is converting to a condominium, at prices that current residents cannot afford. About half the building's occupants are Russian immigrants; most of the others are elderly or disabled people living on fixed incomes. These people are distressed not just because they will need to move, but because their community is being destroyed (Lansprey 1995; P. Moeller 2009; P. Morrison and Bryan 2010; Sheehan 2005).

Coffins in Ghana sometimes reflect the way the dead lived their lives. This Methodist burial service honors a woman who died at age 85, leaving behind 11 children, 82 grandchildren, and 60 great-grandchildren. Her coffin, designed to resemble a mother hen, features 11 chicks nestling beneath the wings (Secretan 1995).

Death and Dying

Among the role transitions that typically (but not always) come later in life is death. Until recently, death was viewed as a taboo topic in the United States. However, psychologist Elisabeth Kübler-Ross (1969), through her pioneering book *On Death and Dying,* greatly encouraged open discussion of the process of dying. Drawing on her work with 200 cancer patients, Kübler-Ross identified five stages of the experience: denial, anger, bargaining, depression, and finally acceptance.

Despite its popular appeal, the five-stage theory of dying has been challenged. Observers often cannot substantiate these stages. Moreover, research suggests that each person declines in his or her own way. Thus, one should not expect—much less counsel—a person to approach death in any particular way. Cross-culturally, the variation in approaches is even more marked. Box 13-1 describes some of the ways in which different Native American tribes acknowledge death (R. Epstein 2005; Fitchett 1980).

Functionalist analysis brings to mind the cherished yet controversial concept of a "good death." One researcher described a good death among the Kaliai, a people of the South Pacific. In that culture, the dying person calls together all his relatives, settles his debts, disposes of his possessions, and then announces that it is time for him to die (Counts 1977).

The Kaliai concept of a good death has a parallel in Western societies, where people may speak of a "natural death," an "appropriate death," or "death with dignity." The practice of **hospice care,** introduced in London, England, in 1967, is founded on this concept. Hospice workers seek to improve the quality of a dying person's last days by offering comfort and by helping the person to remain at home, or in a homelike setting at a hospital or other special facility, until the end. Currently, more than 3,200

hospice programs serve over 960,000 people a year in the United States through federal programs such as Medicare and Medicaid (Hospice Association of America 2008).

Although the Western ideal of the good death makes the experience of dying as positive as possible, some critics fear that acceptance of the concept of a good death may direct both individual efforts and social resources away from attempts to extend life. Still others argue that fatally ill older people should not just passively accept death, but should forgo further treatment in order to reduce public health care expenditures. Such issues are at the heart of current debates over the right to die and physician-assisted suicide.

Today, in many varied ways, people have broken through the historic taboos about death and are attempting to arrange certain aspects of the idealized good death. For example, bereavement practices—once highly structured—are becoming increasingly varied and therapeutic. More and more people are actively addressing the inevitability of death by making wills, leaving "living wills" (health care proxies that explain their feelings about the use of life-support equipment), donating organs, and providing instructions for family members about funerals, cremations, and burials. Given medical and technological advances and a breakthrough in open discussion and negotiation regarding death and dying, it is possible that good deaths may become a social norm in the United States.

Age Stratification in the United States

The "Graying of America"

When Lenore Schaefer, a ballroom dancer, tried to get on the *Tonight Show,* she was told she was "too young": she was in her early 90s. When she turned 101, she made it. But even at that age, Lenore is no longer

RESEARCH TODAY

13.1 Native Americans and Death

The native peoples of North America include hundreds of distinctive cultures, as different from one another as English culture is from Turkish culture. Their practices with respect to death and dying reflect this cultural diversity. Sociologist Gerry Cox conducted ethnographic fieldwork and interviews with tribal peoples on 42 reservations throughout the United States and Canada. He found that among the Creek and some other tribes, those closest to the deceased accompany the body in the days before the burial. In other tribes, such as the Navajo, Apache, and Hopi, relatives spend little time with the body.

In many cases, these practices evolved after contact with European Americans. Religious proselytizing, intermarriage, and the enforcement of colonial regulations all had an impact on cultural traditions. Among the first to experience Hispanic contact in the 16th century were the Zuni and other Pueblo peoples of present-day Arizona and New Mexico. In those cultures, burials that had once been done quickly, with little ceremony, moved onto church grounds or to graveyards consecrated by Christian ritual. At the same time, Native Americans continued their traditional burial practices, in secret when necessary.

Family members smudge the body with ashes immediately after death, then go with it to a funeral home for embalming.

Among the Flathead of Montana, who converted to Roman Catholicism a century ago, traditional practices persist. Family members smudge the body with ashes immediately

after death, then go with it to a funeral home for embalming. Before the body is placed in a coffin, they wash it in rose water. The Catholic funeral mass that precedes the burial includes native songs and ceremonial drums.

Today, Native Americans have won some concessions from hospitals that care for the dying. Lakota patients are allowed to have more relatives in the room than other patients. They may ask to use smoke for ceremonial purposes, even though smoking is strictly forbidden. Apaches, in contrast, prefer to die alone. Navajos may want to hold a "sing."

Native American rituals demonstrate reverence and respect for life as well as death. Despite the great diversity in their values, beliefs, and normative behavior regarding death, one broad belief unites Native Americans: death is

a natural and accepted part of the life cycle. Native Americans also share the belief that their dear ones continue to love, care for, and protect families and friends after death.

LET'S DISCUSS

1. Does your own family observe traditional cultural practices regarding death and dying, independent of formal religious ritual? If so, explain their meaning and importance to your family.
2. Apply the concepts you learned in Chapter 3 to Native American burial practices. Which of them do you find most useful in understanding these practices?

Sources: G. Cox 2010; Sharon Kaufman and Morgan 2005; A. Walker and Balk 2007.

---

unusual in our society. Today, people over 100 constitute, proportionately, the country's fastest-growing age group. They are part of the increasing proportion of the population of the United States that is composed of older people (Himes 2001; Rimer 1998).

As Figure 13-3 shows, in the future, an increasing proportion of the U.S. population will be composed of older people. This trend is expected to continue well into the 21st century, as the mortality rate declines and members of the postwar baby boom age. At the same time, the "oldest old"—that is, the segment of the population representing those who are age 85 or older—will grow at an even faster rate.

Compared with the rest of the population, the elderly are more likely to be female than male. Men tend to have higher death rates than women at every age. By old age, women outnumber

men by a ratio of 3 to 2. The gap widens with advancing age, so that among the oldest old, the ratio is 5 to 2.

The elderly are also more likely than others to be White: about 80 percent of the elderly are White and non-Hispanic. Although this segment of the population is becoming more racially and ethnically diverse, the higher death rates of racial and ethnic minorities, together with the continuing immigration of younger Latinos and Asians, is likely to keep it more White than the nation as a whole. Yet the overall pattern of an increasingly diversified population will show up among older Americans. As the projections in Figure 13-4 show, as the 21st century advances, non-Whites and Latinos will make up an increasing proportion of those who are 65 and over.

Finally, the elderly are more likely than the rest of the population to live in certain states. The highest proportions of

FIGURE **13-3** PERCENTAGE OF U.S. POPULATION IN SELECTED AGE GROUPS, 1970–2050

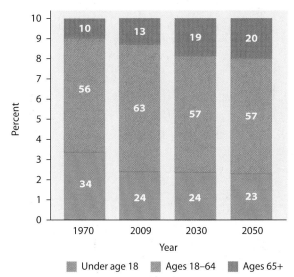

Source: Population Reference Bureau analysis of Bureau of the Census data, in Jacobsen et al. 2011:3.

FIGURE **13-4** MINORITY POPULATION AGE 65 AND OLDER, 2010–2050

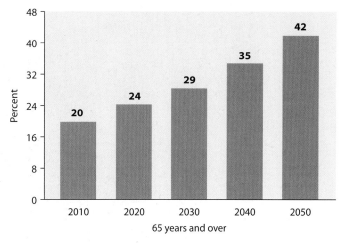

Source: Bureau of the Census in Vincent and Velkoff 2010.

older people are found in Florida, Pennsylvania, Rhode Island, Iowa, West Virginia, and Arkansas. However, that will soon change. In 2000, Florida was the state most populated by the elderly, with 17.6 percent of the population over age 65. Yet as Figure 13-5 shows, in less than 20 years, more than half the states will have an even greater proportion of elderly people than Florida does now.

The graying of the United States is a phenomenon that can no longer be ignored, either by social scientists or by government policymakers. Advocates for the elderly have spoken out on a wide range of issues. Politicians court the votes of older people, since they are the age group most likely to register and vote. In fact, in the 2008 presidential election, despite the upsurge in the youth vote, people over 60 made up 23 percent of those who voted, compared to 18 percent for those under 30 (Connelly 2008).

Wealth and Income

There is significant variation in wealth and poverty among the nation's older people. Some individuals and couples find themselves poor in part because of fixed pensions and skyrocketing health care costs (see Chapter 19). Nevertheless, as a group, older people in the United States are neither homogeneous nor poor. The typical elderly person enjoys a standard of living that is much higher now than at any point in the nation's past. Class differences among the elderly remain evident, but tend to narrow somewhat: those older people who enjoyed middle-class incomes while younger tend to remain better off after retirement, but less so than before (Denise Smith and Tillipman 2000).

To some extent, older people owe their overall improved standard of living to a greater accumulation of wealth—in the form of home ownership, private pensions, and other financial assets. But much of the improvement is due to more generous Social Security benefits. While modest when compared with

other countries' pension programs, Social Security nevertheless provides 39 percent of all income received by older people in the United States. Still, about 9 percent of the nation's elderly population lives below the federal government's poverty line. At the extremes of poverty are those groups who were more likely to be poor at earlier points in the life cycle: female-headed households and racial and ethnic minorities (He et al. 2005).

Viewed from a conflict perspective, it is not surprising that older women experience a double burden; the same is true of elderly members of racial and ethnic minorities. For example, in 2009 the proportion of older Latinos with incomes below the poverty level (18.3 percent) was almost three times as large as the proportion of older White non-Hispanics (6.6 percent). Moreover, 18.9 percent of older African Americans fell below the federal government's poverty line (Issa and Zedlewski 2011).

Ageism

Physician Robert Butler (1990) became concerned 49 years ago when he learned that a housing development near his home in metropolitan Washington, D.C., barred the elderly. Butler coined the term **ageism** to refer to prejudice and discrimination based on a person's age. Research shows that in the United States, a large majority of people over age 60—84 percent—have experienced ageism, from insulting jokes to outright disrespect (Roscigno 2010:7).

Ageism is especially difficult for the old, because at least youthful recipients of prejudice know that in time they will be "old enough." For many, old age symbolizes disease. With ageism all too common in the United States, it is hardly surprising that older people are barely visible on television. In 2002, the Senate Special Committee on Aging convened a panel on the media's portrayal of older people and sharply criticized media and marketing executives for bombarding audiences with negative images of the aged. The social consequences of such images

MAPPING LIFE NATIONWIDE

FIGURE **13-5** TWENTY-EIGHT FLORIDAS BY 2030

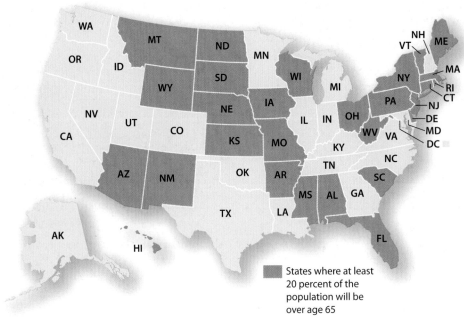

States where at least 20 percent of the population will be over age 65

Source: Bureau of the Census 2005a.

are significant. Research shows that older people who have positive perceptions of aging live an average of 7.5 years longer than those who have negative perceptions (M. Gardner 2003; Levy et al. 2002; Ramirez 2002).

Competition in the Labor Force

Although paid employment is not typical after age 65, since the 1980s it has become increasingly common. Concerned over their pension benefits, more and more people who are healthy enough to continue working have decided to postpone their retirement. Their decision has further eroded job opportunities for younger workers, already handicapped by the highest unemployment rates in a generation. Unfortunately, some people view older workers as "job stealers"—a biased judgment similar to that directed against illegal immigrants—instead of as experienced contributors to the labor force. Moreover, unemployed workers in their 50s find that potential employers rarely give them serious consideration. These difficulties not only intensify age conflict but lead to age discrimination as well (Jacobsen et al. 2011).

The federal Age Discrimination in Employment Act (ADEA), which went into effect in 1968, was passed to protect workers who are age 40 and older from being fired because of their age and replaced with younger workers, who would presumably receive lower salaries. The Supreme Court strengthened federal protection against age discrimination in 1996, ruling unanimously that such lawsuits can be successful even if an older worker is replaced by someone who is older than 40. Consequently, firing a 65-year-old employee to make way for a 45-year-old can be construed as age discrimination.

While firing people simply because they are old violates federal law, courts have upheld the right to lay off older workers for economic reasons. Critics contend that later, the same firms hire young, cheaper workers to replace experienced older workers. When economic growth began to slow in 2008 and companies cut back on their workforces, complaints of age bias grew sharply as older workers began to suspect they were bearing a disproportionate share of the layoffs (Roscigno 2010).

Given recent legislative and legal advances, has the climate changed significantly for older workers? Box 13-2 on page 300 presents several studies that have attempted to assess the extent of ageism, both in everyday life and in hiring.

---

use your sociological *imagination*

It is September and you are channel-surfing through the new fall TV series. How likely are you to watch a television show that is based on older characters who spend a lot of time together?

The Elderly: Emergence of a Collective Consciousness

During the 1960s, students at colleges and universities across the country, advocating "student power," collectively demanded a role in the governance of educational institutions. In the following decade, many older people became aware that *they* were being treated as second-class citizens and turned to collective action.

The AARP is a major voice for the elderly. By featuring Bruce Springsteen (born in 1949) on the cover of its widely distributed magazine, the organization is signaling a desire to represent the younger members of the older generation, as well as to portray the active lives many older people lead.

voters in the United States. The AARP has endorsed voter registration campaigns, nursing home reforms, and pension reforms. In acknowledgment of its difficulties recruiting members of racial and ethnic minority groups, the AARP recently began a Minority Affairs Initiative. The spokeswoman for the initiative, Margaret Dixon, became the AARP's first African American president in 1996 (Birnbaum 2005).

People grow old in many different ways. Not all elderly people face the same challenges or enjoy the same resources. While the AARP lobbies to protect the elderly in general, other groups work in more specific ways. For example, the National Committee to Preserve Social Security and Medicare, founded in 1982, has successfully lobbied Congress to keep Medicare benefits for the ailing poor elderly. Other large special interest groups represent retired federal employees, retired teachers, and retired union workers (Quadagno 2011).

Still another manifestation of the new awareness of older people is the formation of organizations for elderly homosexuals. One such group, Senior Action in a Gay Environment (SAGE), was established in New York City in 1977 and now oversees a nationwide network of community groups, as well as affiliates in Canada and Germany. Like traditional senior citizens' groups, SAGE sponsors workshops, classes, dances, and food deliveries to the homebound. At the same time, the group must deal with special concerns, such as informing gay people of their rights, supporting gay people with Alzheimer's, and advocating for gays who face eviction (Senior Action in a Gay Environment 2010).

The elderly in the United States are better off today both financially and physically than ever before. Many of them have strong financial assets and medical care packages that will meet almost any health need. But as we have seen, a significant segment is impoverished, faced with the prospect of declining health and mounting medical bills. And some older people must now add being aged to a lifetime of disadvantage. Like people in all other stages of the life course, the aged constitute a diverse group in the United States and around the world.

The largest organization representing the nation's elderly is the AARP, founded in 1958 by a retired school principal who was having difficulty getting insurance because of age prejudice. Many of the AARP's services involve discounts and insurance for its 40 million members (43 percent of Americans age 50 and older), but the organization is also a powerful lobbying group. Recognizing that many elderly people are still gainfully employed, it has dropped its full name, American Association of *Retired* Persons (Donnelly 2007; Eggen 2009).

The potential power of the AARP is enormous. It is the third-largest voluntary association in the United States (behind only the Roman Catholic Church and the American Automobile Association), representing one out of every four registered

Job Wanted—Over 65

From the 1940s through the early 1990s, the proportion of people over age 65 who were working declined steadily, and the rate dropped faster for men than for women. Since the 1990s this pattern has reversed for both men and women. In little more than a decade, the percentage of older people who are working doubled.

Even more remarkable is the shift of older workers to full-time employment. In 2002, for the first time, more older people were working full-time than part-time. This trend has continued through the recession that began in 2008. Older workers face high unemployment rates, but more and more have continued to seek work, perhaps to offset losses to their retirement savings.

As the baby boom generation ages, the share of workers in the 55-years-and-older age group is expected to increase dramatically, at least through 2018. Despite this trend, the participation rates of older workers are not expected to reach the working levels of those in their 40s.

RESEARCH TODAY

"Who did you used to be?" This comment reveals an unflattering assumption about what happens to people when they grow old. Unfortunately, such remarks are far too frequent. In fact, condescending language is so often directed at elderly people that gerontologists have come to call it *elderspeak.*

According to scholars who have done observation research in nursing homes and retirement facilities, staff in these institutions tend to relate to the elderly residents in a manner befitting infants, calling them "dear," "good girl," and "sweetie." Medical professionals may patronize elderly patients, asking "Did you understand what I said?" or cajole them with "You don't want to upset your family, do you?" Although the people who make these remarks do not regard them as derogatory, older people find the unintended insults demoralizing.

Many older people experience ageism long before they retire. They may find that past a certain age, they will not be hired or even interviewed for a job. Yet research has shown that older workers can be an asset to employers. In response to such findings, some U.S. corporations, including Home Depot, are actively recruiting retired people.

Still, many older people have difficulty finding work, often as the result of ageism. Economist Johanna Lahey sent similar résumés for fictitious women of different ages to employers in Boston and St. Petersburg, Florida. The results were striking. In Boston, a younger worker was 42 percent more likely than an older worker to be offered an interview for an entry-level job, such as a clerical

position. In St. Petersburg, the difference was 46 percent.

To determine why the older applicants had more difficulty getting an interview, Lahey tried making them look more desirable.

To prevent a 62-year-old applicant from being seen as inflexible, undependable, or out of touch, she added a certificate of completion of a recent computer course to the person's application, along with an indication of health insurance coverage. However, these "extras" had no effect on the call-back rate.

> *Many older people experience ageism long before they retire. They may find that past a certain age, they will not be hired or even interviewed for a job.*

This study mirrored the results of one done two decades earlier, which showed that younger applicants are significantly more welcome in the job market than older applicants. Although

About 30 percent of older workers choose to remain on the job past the usual retirement age. Research shows they can be retrained in new technologies and are more dependable than younger workers.

further research might be done, the pattern seems clear: ageism is entrenched in our society.

LET'S DISCUSS

1. Have you ever worked alongside an older person? If so, did that person's age affect the way he or she did the job? In what ways?
2. Are older people the only ones who experience ageism? What signs of ageism might those who are not old experience?

Sources: Bendick et al. 1993; Charness and Villeval 2009; Freudenheim 2005; Lahey 2006; Leland 2008; Lohr 2008; Roscigno 2010; K. Williams et al. 2009.

social policy and Age Stratification

The Right to Die Worldwide

On August 4, 1993, Dr. Jack Kevorkian, a retired pathologist, helped a 30-year-old Michigan man with Lou Gehrig's disease to commit suicide in a van. The patient died after inhaling carbon monoxide through a mask designed by Dr. Kevorkian; in doing so, he became the 17th person to commit suicide with Kevorkian's assistance. Kevorkian was openly challenging a Michigan law (aimed at him) that makes it a felony—punishable by up to four years in jail—to assist in a suicide. Since then Kevorkian has assisted in numerous other suicides, but not until he did it on television in 1998 did the charges brought against him result in his imprisonment for second-degree murder. Kevorkian completed his sentence in 2007 and died of circulatory problems in 2011.

Looking at the Issue

The issue of physician-assisted suicide is but one aspect of the larger debate in the United States and other countries over the ethics of suicide and euthanasia. The term **euthanasia** has been defined as the "act of bringing about the death of a hopelessly ill and suffering person in a relatively quick and painless way for reasons of mercy" (Council on Ethical and Judicial Affairs, American Medical Association 1992:229). This type of mercy killing reminds us of the ideal of the "good death" discussed earlier in the chapter. The debate over euthanasia and assisted suicide often focuses on cases involving older people, although it can involve younger adults with terminal and degenerative diseases, or even children.

National surveys show that public opinion on this controversial practice is divided. In 2007, 71 percent of respondents said that a physician should be legally permitted to end a patient's life if both the patient and the patient's family make such a request. However, an earlier survey found that only half of respondents could even imagine a situation in which they themselves would request physician-assisted suicide (J. Carroll 2007; Jost 2005).

Currently, public policy in the United States does not permit *active euthanasia* (such as a deliberate injection of lethal drugs into a terminally ill patient) or physician-assisted suicide. Although suicide itself is no longer a crime, assisting suicide is illegal in at least 29 states. There is greater legal tolerance for *passive euthanasia* (such as disconnecting life-support equipment from a comatose patient).

Applying Sociology

Many societies are known to have practiced *senilicide*—"killing of the aged"—because of extreme difficulties in providing basic necessities such as food and shelter. In a study of the treatment of elderly people in 41 nonindustrialized societies, Anthony Glascock (1990) found some form of "death-hastening" behavior in 21 of them. Killing of elderly people was evident in 14 of the societies; abandoning them was evident in 8. Typically, death hastening occurs when older people become decrepit and are viewed as already dead. In these nonindustrialized cultures it is open and socially approved. Family members generally make the decisions, often after open consultation with those who are about to die.

Although formal norms against euthanasia are still strict, informal norms seem to permit mercy killings. According to an estimate by the American Hospital Association, as many as 70 percent of all deaths in the United States are quietly negotiated, with patients, family members, and physicians agreeing not to use life-support technology. In an informal poll of internists, one in five reported that he or she had assisted or helped cause the death of a patient. In a period in which AIDS-related deaths are common, an AIDS underground is known to share information and assistance regarding suicide (N. Gibbs 1993; Martinez 1993).

Conflict theorists ask questions about the values raised by such decisions. By endorsing physician-assisted suicide, are we devaluing the disabled through an acceptance of their premature death? Critics note that we are all only temporarily able-bodied; disease or a speeding automobile can place any one of us among the disabled. By establishing a precedent for ending the lives of selected disabled people, we may unwittingly contribute to negative social views and labeling of all disabled people. Further reflecting the conflict perspective, gerontologist Elizabeth Markson (1992:6) argues that the "powerless, poor or undesirable are at special risk of being 'encouraged' to choose assisted death."

Despite these concerns, research to date shows little bias. In studies of physician-assisted suicide in Oregon and the Netherlands, researchers looked at how implementation of the controversial policy might affect people who were vulnerable because of their disability, age, mental health, or race and ethnicity. People with AIDS proved to be the only vulnerable group with a heightened use of physician-assisted suicide. Overall, those people who died with a doctor's help were more likely to be socially, economically, and educationally privileged than to be particularly vulnerable (Battin et al. 2007).

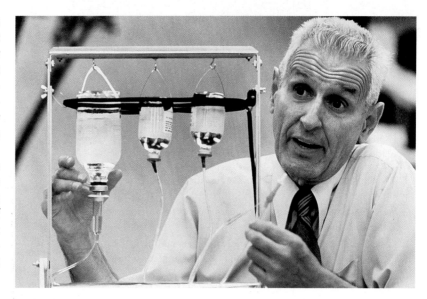

Dr. Jack Kevorkian with the apparatus that administered a lethal injection to those who wanted assistance in committing suicide.

Initiating Policy

In the industrialized world, euthanasia is legal and widely accepted in only three countries: the Netherlands, where about 3,800 such procedures are carried out legally each year; Belgium, which records about 350 procedures a year; and Switzerland, which records 200 a year. Unlike the Netherlands and Belgium, Switzerland allows foreigners to be euthanized; about 55 foreign nationals are euthanized there every year. While physician-assisted suicide is accepted by the public in all three countries, the "suicide tourism" that occurs in Switzerland is controversial (*The Economist* 2005a).

In the United States, the first state to allow assisted suicide was Oregon, where the Death with Dignity Act became law in 1997. By mid-2009, more than 400 terminally ill Oregonians had taken their lives with the assistance of a physician. President George W. Bush's administration had made an unsuccessful attempt to stop the prescription of lethal drugs to terminally ill patients in Oregon. In 2006, the Supreme Court ruled 6–3 that the federal government had overstepped its authority in punishing doctors in Oregon who had helped terminally ill patients to end their lives. Two years later, voters in Washington State passed a law similar to Oregon's, which took effect in 2009. Some local courts and state legislatures are also moving to legalize the practice, despite strong opposition (Fausset 2009; *The Week* 2009; W. Yardley 2009).

Advances in technology now allow us to prolong life in ways that were unimaginable decades ago. But should people be forced or expected to prolong lives that are unbearably painful, or that are in effect "lifeless"? Unfortunately, medical and technological advances cannot provide answers to these complex ethical, legal, and political questions.

Take the Issue with You

1. Why do you think "death-hastening" behavior is common in nonindustrialized countries?

2. In what ways are conflict theory and disengagement theory relevant to the debate over the "right to die"?

3. Do you think someone should be allowed to choose to die? Why or why not?

Summary

Age, like gender and race, is an ascribed status that serves as a basis for social differentiation. This chapter examines sociological perspectives on aging, role transitions in the life course, age stratification in the United States, the growing political activism of the nation's elderly population, and the controversy surrounding the right to die.

1. Like other forms of stratification, age stratification varies from culture to culture.

2. In the United States, being old is a master status that seems to overshadow all others.

3. The particular problems of the aged have become the focus for a specialized area of research and inquiry known as **gerontology.**

4. **Disengagement theory** implicitly suggests that society should help older people to withdraw from their accustomed social roles. In contrast, **activity theory** suggests that the elderly person who remains active and socially involved will be better adjusted.

5. Labeling theorists note that people of the same age are labeled differently in different societies, based largely on differences in physical health, life opportunities, and life expectancy in those societies.

6. From a conflict perspective, the low status of older people is reflected in prejudice and discrimination against them and in unfair job practices.

7. About 40 percent of those who look after their elderly relatives still have children to care for; these people have been dubbed the **sandwich generation.**

8. As we age, we go through role transitions, including adjustment to retirement and preparation for death.

9. An increasing proportion of the population of the United States is composed of older people.

10. **Ageism** reflects a deep uneasiness about growing old on the part of younger people.

11. The AARP is a powerful lobbying group that backs legislation to benefit senior citizens.

12. The "right to die" often entails physician-assisted suicide, a controversial issue worldwide.

Key Terms

Activity theory An interactionist theory of aging that suggests that those elderly people who remain active and socially involved will be best adjusted. (page 290)

Ageism Prejudice and discrimination based on a person's age. (297)

Disengagement theory A functionalist theory of aging that suggests that society and the aging individual mutually sever many of their relationships. (290)

Euthanasia The act of bringing about the death of a hopelessly ill and suffering person in a relatively quick and painless way for reasons of mercy. (300)

Gerontology The scientific study of the sociological and psychological aspects of aging and the problems of the aged. (289)

Hospice care Treatment of the terminally ill in their own homes, or in special hospital units or other facilities, with the goal of helping them to die easily, without pain. (295)

Midlife crisis A stressful period of self-evaluation that begins at about age 40. (293)

Naturally occurring retirement community (NORC) An area that has gradually become an informal center for senior citizens. (294)

Sandwich generation The generation of adults who simultaneously try to meet the competing needs of their parents and their children. (293)

TAKING SOCIOLOGY with you

1. Think about your grandparents: Would you describe them as active or disengaged? Do you think their social class has had an impact on the way they have aged? Explain. How well have they adjusted to retirement?

2. What public agency or organization—the senior center, council on aging—is responsible for serving seniors in your community? Visit the site and learn about the programs offered there. Then relate your findings to what you learned in this chapter.

3. Find out the percentage of people age 65 and over who live in your community. How does that percentage compare to your state or to the United States as a whole? If you can, determine whether residents in this age bracket are clustered in particular areas. Are you aware of any naturally occurring retirement communities (NORCs) where you live?

Self-Quiz

Read each question carefully and then select the best answer.

1. Activity theory is associated with the
   a. functionalist perspective.
   b. conflict perspective.
   c. interactionist perspective.
   d. labeling perspective.

2. What is the one crucial difference between older people and other subordinate groups, such as racial and ethnic minorities or women?
   a. Older people do not experience unequal treatment in employment.
   b. Older people have a strong sense of group solidarity and other groups do not.

   c. All of us who live long enough will eventually assume the ascribed status of being an older person.
   d. Older people are generally married to others of comparable age and other minorities do not marry within their group.

3. Which field of study was originally developed in the 1930s as an increasing number of social scientists became aware of the plight of the elderly?
   a. sociology
   b. gerontology
   c. gerontocracy
   d. senilicide

4. Which sociological perspective is most likely to emphasize the important role of social networks in providing life satisfaction for elderly people?
   a. functionalist perspective
   b. conflict perspective
   c. interactionist perspective
   d. labeling theory

5. Elaine Cumming and William Henry introduced an explanation of the impact of aging known as
   a. disengagement theory.
   b. activity theory.
   c. labeling theory.
   d. the contact hypothesis.

6. According to psychologist Elisabeth Kübler-Ross, the first stage of the experience of dying that a person may undergo is
   a. denial.
   b. anger.
   c. depression.
   d. bargaining.

7. Which of the following statements about the elderly is correct?
   a. Being old is a master status.
   b. Once people are labeled as "old," the designation has a major impact on how others perceive them, and even on how they view themselves.
   c. Negative stereotypes of the elderly contribute to their position as a minority group subject to discrimination.
   d. all of the above

8. The text points out that the model of five basic properties of a minority or subordinate group can be applied to older people in the United States. Which of the following is *not* one of those basic properties?
   a. Older people experience unequal treatment in employment and may face prejudice and discrimination.
   b. Statistically, the elderly represent a majority.
   c. Membership in this group is involuntary.
   d. Older people have a strong sense of group solidarity.

9. Which of the following theories argues that elderly people have essentially the same need for social interaction as any other group and that those who remain active and socially involved will be best adjusted?
   a. conflict theory
   b. functionalist theory
   c. activity theory
   d. disengagement theory

10. According to your text, which of the following statements is true?
   a. Functionalists portray the elderly as being socially isolated, with reduced social roles.
   b. Interactionists see older people as being involved in new networks of people and in changing social roles.
   c. Conflict theorists regard older people as being victimized by social structure, with their social roles relatively unchanged but devalued.
   d. all of the above

11. The elderly are _____ regarded in the traditional Sherpa (Tibet) culture.

12. In keeping with the _____ perspective of sociology, disengagement theory emphasizes that a society's stability is ensured when social roles are passed on from one generation to another.

13. The final phase of retirement, according to Robert Atchley, is the _____ phase, which begins when the person can no longer engage in basic, day-to-day activities such as self-care and housework.

14. _____ theorists argue that both the disengagement and the activity perspectives often ignore the impact of social class in the lives of elderly people.

15. The fastest-growing age group in the United States is people over age _____.

16. _____ is the scientific study of the sociological and psychological aspects of aging and the problems of the aged. It originated in the 1930s as an increasing number of social scientists became aware of the plight of elderly people.

17. Based on a study of elderly people in good health and relatively comfortable economic circumstances, _____ theory suggests that society and the aging individual mutually sever many of their relationships.

18. During the late 1990s, social scientists focused on the _____ _____—adults who simultaneously try to meet the competing needs of their parents and their children.

19. In 2000, _____ was the state most populated by the elderly, with 17.6 percent of the population over age 65.

20. Physician Robert Butler coined the term _____ to refer to prejudice and discrimination based on a person's age.

THINKING ABOUT MOVIES

Gran Torino

A retired automotive worker overcomes his racism and learns to accept his immigrant neighbors.

Joan Rivers: A Piece of Work

This documentary shows a popular comedian trying to maintain her success as she ages.

Please Give

Characters from different stages in the life course grow together.

In Ann Arbor, Michigan, several generations of Dulins celebrate their 18th family reunion. Despite marital strains and geographical separation, countless families come together every year to reaffirm the importance of this social institution.

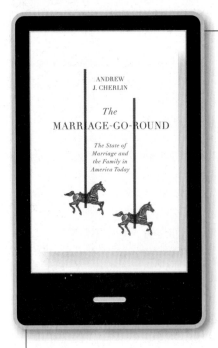

ANDREW
J. CHERLIN

The
MARRIAGE-GO-ROUND

The State of
Marriage and
the Family in
America Today

66 Although I have been writing about American families for three decades, I began to develop the idea for this book only in the past few years. It seemed to me that family life was different in the United States than in the other Western countries—Western Europe and the non-European English-speaking nations of Canada, Australia, and New Zealand—in a way no one really understood. I noticed, first of all, that in none of the other countries has marriage become a social and political battlefield. Nowhere else is the government spending money to promote marriage. In no other Western country would a person walking down the street see the advertisement I have seen on the sides of buses in Baltimore: a smiling couple proclaiming, "Marriage works." Moreover, nowhere else is the debate about same-sex marriage so fierce.

These observations imply that what's different about the United States is the strength of marriage as a cultural ideal. Although that's true, other signs suggested to me that the promarriage ideal is only part of the American difference. I know that in no other Western country is the waiting period for a no-fault divorce so short. I was stunned to read, buried in a footnote in an academic journal, that children living with two married parents in the United States have a higher risk of experiencing a family breakup than do children living with two unmarried parents in Sweden.

Moreover, I reflected on what happened when, in 1997, the Louisiana legislature passed the first law in the United States allowing "covenant marriage" as an option for couples applying for marriage licenses. In a covenant marriage, both spouses agree to restrictions on how quickly and easily they can obtain a divorce. . . . I was skeptical that most people would agree to lock the exit door so tightly. I guessed that maybe a

In no other Western country would a person walking down the street see the advertisement I have seen on the sides of buses in Baltimore: a smiling couple proclaiming, "Marriage works."

third of all couples would choose covenant marriage. Several years later, it became clear that my guess was wildly high; almost no one had chosen covenant marriage. Less than 2 percent had opted for it in Louisiana and in Arkansas, which introduced it in 2001.

Why did so many newlyweds turn down the opportunity to restrict their ability to divorce? The answer lies in the competing cultural models that Americans hold. Just as the word "marriage" taps a reservoir of positive sentiment in America, so does the phrase "individual freedom." The United States is unique among nations in its strong support for marriage, on one hand, and its postmodern penchant for self-expression and personal growth, on the other hand. . . . Consequently, Americans are conflicted about lifelong marriage: they value the stability and security of marriage, but they tend to believe that individuals who are unhappy with their marriages should be allowed to end them. What Americans want, in other words, is for everyone else to have a covenant marriage.

In fact, the United States has one of the highest levels of both marriage and divorce of any Western nation, and these rates appear to have been higher than in most other Western countries since the early days of the nation. The percentage of people who are projected to marry—close to 90 percent—is higher than elsewhere. Yet the United States has the highest divorce rate in the Western world, higher even than vanguard countries such as Sweden. At current rates, nearly half of all American marriages would end in divorce. In addition, Americans' cohabiting (living-together) relationships end more quickly—either with a breakup or with a marriage—than in other countries.

So while some observers focus on marriage, others on divorce, and others on unmarried parents, I believe that what truly makes American families different is the sum total of these differences—frequent marriage, frequent divorce, more short-term cohabiting relationships. Together these factors create a great turbulence in American family life, a family flux, a coming and going of partners on a scale seen nowhere else. . . . Americans step on and off the carousel of intimate partnerships (by which I mean marriages and cohabiting relationships) more often. 99

(Cherlin 2009:3–5) Additional information about this excerpt can be found on the Online Learning Center at www.mhhe.com/schaefer13e.

In this excerpt from *The Marriage-Go-Round: The State of Marriage and the Family in America Today,* sociologist Andrew J. Cherlin describes the peculiarly American approach to the universal institution of marriage. Only in the United States, Cherlin notes, has marriage become a battleground between two conflicting ideals. In other Western societies, couples do not struggle to reconcile individualism with their commitment to marriage. In countries that strongly value individualism, such as Sweden, couples may choose to cohabit rather than marry, but their relationships are remarkably stable. In countries that strongly support marriage, such as Italy, couples not only marry but stay

married longer than U.S. couples. The United States, Cherlin writes, is the only Western country where people ride a perpetually turning marriage-go-round, changing partners to fulfill their individualism even as they pay lip service to the sanctity of marriage.

As Cherlin's analysis suggests, the institution of marriage reflects the culture in which it is expressed. Just like other social institutions, it changes as the culture changes. The family of today is not what it was a century ago, or even a generation ago. New roles, new gender distinctions, new child-rearing patterns have all combined to create new forms of family life. Today, for example, more and more women are taking the breadwinner's role, whether married or as a single parent. Blended families—the result of divorce and remarriage—are almost the norm. And many people are seeking intimate relationships without being married, whether in gay partnerships or in cohabiting arrangements.

This chapter addresses family and intimate relationships in the United States as well as other parts of the world. As we will see, family patterns differ from one culture to another and even within the same culture. Despite the differences, however, the family is universal—found in every culture. A **family** can be defined as a set of people related by blood, marriage or some other agreed-on relationship, or adoption, who share the primary responsibility for reproduction and caring for members of society.

What are families in different parts of the world like? How do people select their mates? When a marriage fails, how does the divorce affect the children? What are the alternatives to the nuclear family, and how prevalent are they? In this chapter we will look at the family and intimate relationships from the functionalist, conflict, interactionist, and feminist points of view. We'll examine variations in marital patterns and family life, including child rearing, paying particular attention to the increasing numbers of people in dual-income and single-parent families. We'll examine divorce in the United States and consider diverse lifestyles such as cohabitation, lesbian and gay relationships, and marriage without children. In the Social Policy section we will confront the controversial issue of gay marriage.

Global View of the Family

Among Tibetans, a woman may be married simultaneously to more than one man, usually brothers. This system allows sons to share the limited amount of good land. Among the Betsileo of Madagascar, a man has multiple wives, each one living in a different village where he cultivates rice. Wherever he has the best rice field, that wife is considered his first or senior wife. Among the Yanomami of Brazil and Venezuela, it is considered proper to have sexual relations with your opposite-sex cousins if they are the children of your mother's brother or your father's sister. But if your opposite-sex cousins are the children of your mother's sister or your father's brother, the same practice is considered to be incest (Haviland et al. 2008; Kottak 2011).

As these examples illustrate, there are many variations in the family from culture to culture. Yet the family as a social institution exists in all cultures. Moreover, certain general principles concerning its composition, kinship patterns, and authority patterns are universal.

Composition: What Is the Family?

If we were to take our information on what a family is from what we see on television, we might come up with some very strange scenarios. The media do not always present a realistic view of the family. Moreover, many people still think of the family in very narrow terms—as a married couple and their unmarried children living together, like the family in the old *Cosby Show*. However, this is but one type of family, what sociologists refer to as a **nuclear family.** The term *nuclear family* is well chosen, since this type of family serves as the nucleus, or core, on which larger family groups are built.

Most people in the United States see the nuclear family as the preferred family arrangement. Yet by 2000, only about a third of the nation's family households fit this model. The proportion of households in the United States that is composed of married couples with children at home has decreased steadily over the past 40 years and is expected to continue shrinking. At the same time, the number of single-parent households has increased (Figure 14-1).

A family in which relatives—such as grandparents, aunts, or uncles—live in the same home as parents and their children is known as an **extended family.** Although not common, such living arrangements do exist in the United States. The structure of the extended family offers certain advantages over that of the nuclear family. Crises such as death, divorce, and illness put less strain on family members, since more people can provide assistance and emotional support. In addition, the extended family constitutes a larger economic unit than the nuclear family. If the family is engaged in a common enterprise—a farm or a small business—the additional family members may represent the difference between prosperity and failure.

In considering these different family types, we have limited ourselves to the form of marriage that is characteristic of the United States—monogamy. The term **monogamy** describes a form of marriage in which one woman and one man are married only to each other. Some observers, noting the high rate of divorce in the United States, have suggested that "serial monogamy" is a more accurate description of the form marriage takes in this country. In **serial monogamy,** a person may have several spouses in his or her lifetime, but only one spouse at a time.

Some cultures allow an individual to have several husbands or wives simultaneously. This form of marriage is known as **polygamy.** In fact, most societies throughout the world, past and present, have preferred polygamy to monogamy. Anthropologist George Murdock (1949, 1957) sampled 565 societies and found that in more than 80 percent, some type of polygamy was the preferred form. While polygamy declined steadily through most of the 20th century, in at least five countries in Africa 20 percent of men still have polygamous marriages (Population Reference Bureau 1996).

There are two basic types of polygamy. According to Murdock, the most common—endorsed by the majority of cultures he sampled—is *polygyny.* **Polygyny** refers to the marriage of a man to more than one woman at the same time. The wives are often sisters, who are expected to hold similar values and have already had experience sharing a household. In polygynous societies, relatively few men actually have multiple spouses. Most individuals live in monogamous families; having multiple wives is viewed as a mark of status.

The other principal variation of polygamy is **polyandry,** in which a woman may have more than one husband at the same time. Such is the case in the culture of the Nyinba, described in

FIGURE **14-1** U.S. HOUSEHOLDS BY FAMILY TYPE, 1940–2010

1940

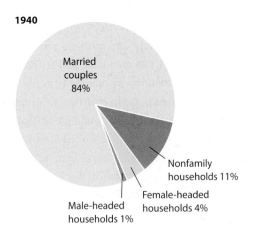

Married couples 84%

Nonfamily households 11%

Female-headed households 4%

Male-headed households 1%

1980

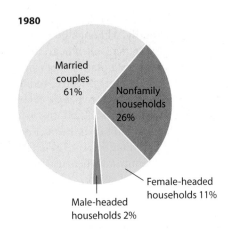

Married couples 61%

Nonfamily households 26%

Female-headed households 11%

Male-headed households 2%

2010

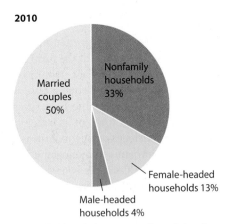

Nonfamily households 33%

Married couples 50%

Female-headed households 13%

Male-headed households 4%

Note: Nonfamily households include women and men living alone or exclusively with people to whom they are not related, as in a college dormitory, homeless shelter, or military base.
Source: Bureau of the Census 2010b:Table HH1.

Box 14-1. Polyandry, however, is exceedingly rare today, though it is accepted in some extremely poor societies. Like many other societies, polyandrous cultures devalue the social worth of women (Zeitzen 2008).

Kinship Patterns: To Whom Are We Related?

Many of us can trace our roots by looking at a family tree or by listening to elderly family members talk about their lives—and about the lives of ancestors who died long before we were born. Yet a person's lineage is more than simply a personal history; it

also reflects societal patterns that govern descent. In every culture, children encounter relatives to whom they are expected to show an emotional attachment. The state of being related to others is called **kinship.** Kinship is culturally learned, however, and is not totally determined by biological or marital ties. For example, adoption creates a kinship tie that is legally acknowledged and socially accepted.

The family and the kin group are not necessarily one and the same. Whereas the family is a household unit, kin do not always live together or function as a collective body on a daily basis. Kin groups include aunts, uncles, cousins, in-laws, and so forth. In a society such as the United States, the kinship group may come together only rarely, for a wedding or funeral. However, kinship ties frequently create obligations and responsibilities. We may feel compelled to assist our kin, and we may feel free to call on them for many types of aid, including loans and babysitting.

How do we identify kinship groups? The principle of descent assigns people to kinship groups according to their relationship to a mother or father. There are three primary ways of determining descent. The United States follows the system of **bilateral descent,** which means that both sides of a person's family are regarded as equally important. For example, no higher value is given to the brothers of one's father than to the brothers of one's mother.

Most societies—according to George Murdock, 64 percent—give preference to one side of the family or the other in tracing descent. In **patrilineal** (from the Latin *pater,* "father") **descent,** only the father's relatives are significant in terms of property, inheritance, and emotional ties. Conversely, in societies that favor **matrilineal** (from the Latin *mater,* "mother") **descent,** only the mother's relatives are significant.

New forms of reproductive technology will necessitate a new way of looking at kinship. Today, a combination of biological and social processes can "create" a family member, requiring that more distinctions be made about who is related to whom.

---

use your sociological *imagination*

In your family, which relatives do you have a significant relationship with? Which do you hardly ever see?

Authority Patterns: Who Rules?

Imagine that you have recently married and must begin to make decisions about the future of your new family. You and your spouse face many questions. Where will you live? How will you furnish your home? Who will do the cooking, the shopping, the cleaning? Whose friends will be invited to dinner? Each time a decision must be made, an issue is raised: Who has the power to make the decision? In simple terms, who rules the family? Conflict theorists examine these questions in the context of traditional gender stratification, under which men have held a dominant position over women.

Societies vary in the way power is distributed within the family. A society that expects males to dominate in all family decision

14-1 One Wife, Many Husbands: The Nyinba

The Nyinba culture of Nepal and Tibet is an agrarian society located in the remote valleys of the Himalaya Mountains, more than 9,000 feet above sea level. Despite the Nyinba's isolation, they have been closely studied. Scholars from around the world have traveled to the Himalayas to observe this people, one of the few remaining cultures on earth to practice polyandry.

In the physically challenging environment of the Himalayas, polyandry seems to work well. Because the land and climate make it difficult

Favoritism toward a particular husband is frowned on by the Nyinba. Thus, it is the wife's responsibility to see that each husband shares time with her in a rotational fashion.

to sustain crops, farming is labor-intensive: many Nyinba laborers must work the fields to support a single family. Thus, a typical marriage involving three brothers and one wife provides the necessary adult male laborers, yet minimizes the number of offspring—a necessity in a place where the food supply is limited.

While an outsider might suppose that Nyinba women dominate their families, in fact authority and inheritance rest on the husband or son. The birth of a son is celebrated; the birth of a daughter, regardless of who might be the father, brings disappointment. Paternity appears to be a nonissue in this culture, since households are shared by brothers from the same family. The literal head of the household is the oldest brother, who typically chooses a wife from outside his extended family.

Favoritism toward a particular husband is frowned on by the Nyinba. Thus, it is the wife's

A Nyinba family threshing buckwheat in the field. At left is the wife; in the center, one of her five husbands (with raised mallet); at right, her mother-in-law.

responsibility to see that each husband shares time with her in a rotational fashion. Often, over the morning meal, she will indicate which husband will sleep with her that night. To avoid any confusion, the chosen husband will place his shoes outside her bedroom door.

As in any society (for example, the United States), not all Nyinba households conform to the social norm. If a family has only one son, he must of necessity marry monogamously—an unfortunate outcome in this society. If a wife is unable to have children, a second wife, typically her sister or cousin, may be welcomed into the marriage.

LET'S DISCUSS

1. Why would a monogamous marriage be considered an unfortunate one in the Nyinba culture?
2. What might be some other ways for a society to handle the physical constraints of life in a mountainous terrain?

Sources: N. Levine 1988; Stockard 2002; Zeitzen 2008.

---

making is termed a **patriarchy.** In patriarchal societies, such as Iran, the eldest male often wields the greatest power, although wives are expected to be treated with respect and kindness. An Iranian woman's status is typically defined by her relationship to a male relative, usually as a wife or daughter. In many patriarchal societies, women find it more difficult to obtain a divorce than a man does. In contrast, in a **matriarchy,** women have greater authority than men. Matriarchies, which are very uncommon, emerged among Native American tribal societies and in nations in which men were absent for long periods because of warfare or food-gathering expeditions (Farr 1999).

In a third type of authority pattern, the **egalitarian family,** spouses are regarded as equals. That does not mean, however, that all decisions are shared in such families. Wives may hold authority in some spheres, husbands in others. Many sociologists believe the egalitarian family has begun to replace the patriarchal family as the social norm in the United States.

thinking CRITICALLY

From a woman's point of view, what are the economic advantages and disadvantages of monogamous, polygamous, and polyandrous families? What are the advantages and disadvantages of each of these family situations for men?

Although spouses in an egalitarian family may not share all their decisions, they regard themselves as equals. This pattern of authority is becoming more common in the United States.

Sociological Perspectives on the Family

Do we really need the family? Over a century ago, Friedrich Engels ([1884] 1959), a colleague of Karl Marx, described the family as the ultimate source of social inequality because of its role in the transfer of power, property, and privilege. More recently, conflict theorists have argued that the family contributes to societal injustice, denies women opportunities that are extended to men, and limits freedom in sexual expression and mate selection. In contrast, the functionalist view focuses on the ways in which the family gratifies the needs of its members and contributes to social stability. The interactionist view considers the intimate, face-to-face relationships that occur in the family. And the feminist approach examines the role of the wife and mother, especially in the absence of an adult male.

Functionalist View

The family performs six paramount functions, first outlined nearly 80 years ago by sociologist William F. Ogburn (Ogburn and Tibbits 1934):

1. **Reproduction.** For a society to maintain itself, it must replace dying members. In this sense, the family contributes to human survival through its function of reproduction.

2. **Protection.** In all cultures, the family assumes the ultimate responsibility for the protection and upbringing of children.

3. **Socialization.** Parents and other kin monitor a child's behavior and transmit the norms, values, and language of their culture to the child.

4. **Regulation of sexual behavior.** Sexual norms are subject to change both over time (for instance, in the customs for dating) and across cultures (compare strict Saudi Arabia to the more permissive Denmark). However, whatever the time period or cultural values of a society, standards of sexual behavior are most clearly defined within the family circle.

5. **Affection and companionship.** Ideally, the family provides members with warm and intimate relationships, helping them to feel satisfied and secure. Of course, a family member may find such rewards outside the family—from peers, in school, at work—and may even perceive the home as an unpleasant or abusive setting. Nevertheless, we expect our relatives to understand us, to care for us, and to be there for us when we need them.

6. **Provision of social status.** We inherit a social position because of the family background and reputation of our parents and siblings. The family presents the newborn child with an ascribed status based on race and ethnicity that helps to determine his or her place within society's stratification system. Moreover, family resources affect children's ability to pursue certain opportunities, such as higher education.

Traditionally, the family has fulfilled a number of other functions, such as providing religious training, education, and recreational outlets. But Ogburn argued that other social institutions have gradually assumed many of those functions. Education once took place at the family fireside; now it is the responsibility of professionals working in schools and colleges. Even the family's traditional recreational function has been transferred to outside groups such as Little Leagues, athletic clubs, and Twitter.

Conflict View

Conflict theorists view the family not as a contributor to social stability, but as a reflection of the inequality in wealth and power that is found within the larger society. Feminist and conflict theorists note that the family has traditionally legitimized and perpetuated male dominance. Throughout most of human history—and in a wide range of societies—husbands have exercised overwhelming power and authority within the family. Not until the first wave of contemporary feminism in the United States, in the mid-1800s, was there a substantial challenge to the historic status of wives and children as the legal property of husbands.

While the egalitarian family has become a more common pattern in the United States in recent decades—owing in good part to the activism of feminists beginning in the late 1960s and early 1970s—male dominance over the family has hardly disappeared.

Sociologists have found that while married men are increasing their involvement in child care, their wives still perform a disproportionate amount of it. Furthermore, for every stay-at-home dad there are 38 stay-at-home moms. And unfortunately, many husbands reinforce their power and control over wives and children through acts of domestic violence (Jason Fields 2004: 11–12; Garcia-Moreno et al. 2005; Sayer et al. 2004).

Conflict theorists also view the family as an economic unit that contributes to societal injustice. The family is the basis for transferring power, property, and privilege from one generation to the next. Although the United States is widely viewed as a land of opportunity, social mobility is restricted in important ways. Children inherit the privileged or less-than-privileged social and economic status of their parents (and in some cases, of earlier generations as well). The social class of parents significantly influences children's socialization experiences and the degree of protection they receive. Thus, the socioeconomic status of a child's family will have a marked influence on his or her nutrition, health care, housing, educational opportunities, and in many respects, life chances as an adult. For this reason, conflict theorists argue that the family helps to maintain inequality.

Interactionist View

Interactionists focus on the micro level of family and other intimate relationships. They are interested in how individuals interact with one another, whether they are cohabiting partners or longtime married couples. For example, in a study of both Black and White two-parent households, researchers found that when fathers are more involved with their children (reading to them, helping them with homework, or restricting their television viewing), the children have fewer behavior problems, get along better with others, and are more responsible (Mosley and Thomson 1995).

Another interactionist study might examine the role of the stepparent. The increased number of single parents who remarry has sparked an interest in those who are helping to raise other people's children. Studies have found that stepmothers are

Interactionists are particularly interested in the ways in which parents relate to each other and to their children. The close and loving relationship illustrated here is one of the foundations of a strong family.

more likely than stepfathers to accept the blame for bad relations with their stepchildren. Interactionists theorize that stepfathers (like most fathers) may simply be unaccustomed to interacting directly with children when the mother isn't there (Bray and Kelly 1999; F. Furstenberg and Cherlin 1991).

Feminist View

Because "women's work" has traditionally focused on family life, feminist sociologists have taken a strong interest in the family as a social institution. As we saw in Chapter 12, research on gender roles in child care and household chores has been extensive. Sociologists have looked particularly closely at how women's work outside the home impacts their child care and housework—duties Arlie Hochschild (1989, 1990, 2005) has referred to as the "second shift." Today, researchers recognize that for many women, the second shift includes the care of aging parents as well.

Feminist theorists have urged social scientists and social agencies to rethink the notion that families in which no adult male is present are automatically a cause for concern, or even dysfunctional. They have also contributed to research on single women, single-parent households, and lesbian couples. In the case of single mothers, researchers have focused on the resiliency of many such households, despite economic stress. According to Velma McBride Murray and her colleagues (2001) at the University of Georgia, such studies show that among African Americans, single mothers draw heavily on kinfolk for material resources, parenting advice, and social support. Considering feminist research on the family as a whole, one researcher concluded that the family is the "source of women's strength" (V. Taylor et al. 2009).

Finally, feminists who take the interactionist perspective stress the need to investigate neglected topics in family studies. For instance, in a growing number of dual-income households, the wife earns a higher income than the husband. In 2005, a study of 58 married couples revealed that 26 percent of the wives earned more than their husbands. In 1981, the proportion was just 16 percent. Yet beyond individual case studies, little research has been done on how these families may differ from those in which the husband is the major breadwinner (Wills and Risman 2006).

Table 14-1 summarizes the four major theoretical perspectives on the family.

TABLE 14-1 SOCIOLOGICAL PERSPECTIVES ON THE FAMILY

Theoretical Perspective	Emphasis
Functionalist	The family as a contributor to social stability Roles of family members
Conflict	The family as a perpetuator of inequality Transmission of poverty or wealth across generations
Interactionist	Relationships among family members
Feminist	The family as a perpetuator of gender roles Female-headed households

summingup

thinking CRITICALLY

How would functionalist, conflict, interactionist, and feminist theorists explain a polygamous family structure?

Marriage and Family

Currently, over 95 percent of all men and women in the United States marry at least once during their lifetimes. Historically, the most consistent aspect of family life in this country has been the high rate of marriage. In fact, despite the high rate of divorce, there are some indications of a miniboom in marriages of late.

In this part of the chapter, we will examine various aspects of love, marriage, and parenthood in the United States and contrast them with cross-cultural examples. Though we're used to thinking of romance and mate selection as strictly a matter of individual preference, sociological analysis tells us that social institutions and distinctive cultural norms and values also play an important role.

Courtship and Mate Selection

In the past, most couples met their partners through family, friends, or their neighborhood or workplace. Today, however, many couples meet on the Internet. According to a national survey done in 2010, the Internet is second only to friends as a source of romantic partners—ahead of family, workplace, and neighborhood. Significantly, online networking is just as important to mate-seekers in their 40s and 50s as to those under age 30. It is especially important to gays and lesbians, given the limited number of meeting places available to them: 61 percent of same-sex couples meet online, compared to 23 percent of heterosexual couples (Rosenfeld 2010).

Internet romance is only the latest courtship practice. In the central Asian nation of Uzbekistan and many other traditional cultures, courtship is defined largely through the interaction of two sets of parents, who arrange marriages for their children. Typically, a young Uzbekistani woman will be socialized to eagerly anticipate her marriage to a man whom she has met only once, when he is presented to her family at the time of the final inspection of her dowry. In the United States, in contrast, courtship is conducted primarily by individuals who have a romantic interest in each other. In our culture, courtship often requires these individuals to rely heavily on intricate games, gestures, and signals. Despite such differences, courtship—whether in the United States, Uzbekistan, or elsewhere—is influenced by the norms and values of the larger society (Carol J. Williams 1995).

One unmistakable trend in mate selection is that the process appears to be taking longer today than in the past. A variety of factors, including concerns about financial security and personal independence, has contributed to this delay in marriage. Most people are now well into their 20s before they marry, both in the United States and in other countries (Figure 14-2).

Aspects of Mate Selection Many societies have explicit or unstated rules that define potential mates as acceptable or unacceptable. These norms can be distinguished in terms of endogamy and exogamy. **Endogamy** (from the Greek *endon,* "within") specifies the groups within which a spouse must be found and prohibits marriage with others. For example, in the United States, many people are expected to marry within their racial, ethnic, or religious group, and are strongly discouraged or even prohibited from marrying outside the group. Endogamy is intended to reinforce the cohesiveness of the group by suggesting to the young that they should marry someone "of their own kind." Although interracial and interethnic marriages are still the exception, about one in every seven new marriages in the United States is either interracial or an interethnic union between Hispanics and non-Hispanics. About one-fourth of Latinos and one-third of Asian Americans now marry outside their group (Pew Research Center 2010).

In contrast, **exogamy** (from the Greek *exo,* "outside") requires mate selection outside certain groups, usually one's family or certain kinfolk. The **incest taboo,** a social norm common to virtually all societies, prohibits sexual relationships between certain culturally specified relatives. For those of us in the United States, this taboo means

Cougars on the Rise

Typically, people choose someone of the same age as a romantic partner. In the most common deviation from this pattern, the husband is older than the wife. Yet today, the number of marriages that involve a much older woman—at least 10 years older—is growing. In fact, there is at least one online dating service that is dedicated to matching older women, dubbed "cougars," with younger men. According to sociologist Andrew Beveridge, although this type of couple represents only 1.3 percent of all marriages, that percentage is double that of 1960.

A similar trend can be seen among dating couples. According to an AARP survey, 20 percent of single women ages 40 to 69 said they were dating or had recently dated a man who was at least five years younger. And an informal tally by one dating service, published in the *New York Times,* indicates a rapid increase in the percentage of women over 40 who want to date men much younger than they are.

Professor Sandra L. Caron of the University of Maine has studied the reasons for this new trend. She notes that unlike many younger women, mature women are self-sufficient and don't need to look for an older, better educated man to support them. She finds that in general, women who marry much younger men have happy marriages, although they may be insecure about their ages. That insecurity is probably misplaced. University of Washington sociologist Pepper Schwartz says she thinks young men are attracted to older women who are sexually free and don't make the demands that younger women do. As men become more accustomed to the idea of women earning more money than they do, the social barriers between young men and older women begin to melt away.

FIGURE 14-2 MEDIAN AGE AT FIRST MARRIAGE IN EIGHT COUNTRIES

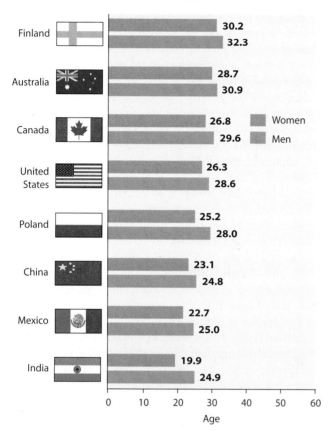

Country	Women	Men
Finland	30.2	32.3
Australia	28.7	30.9
Canada	26.8	29.6
United States	26.3	28.6
Poland	25.2	28.0
China	23.1	24.8
Mexico	22.7	25.0
India	19.9	24.9

Source: United Nations Statistics Division 2008.

Think about It
Why do people marry earlier in India than in Finland?

Although most interracial couples are not as visible as Seal and Heidi Klum, such unions are becoming increasingly common and accepted. They are also blurring the definitions of race. Will the children of these couples be considered Black or White? Why do you think so?

that we must marry outside the nuclear family. We cannot marry our siblings, and in most states we cannot marry our first cousins.

Another factor that influences the selection of a marriage partner is **homogamy,** the conscious or unconscious tendency to select a mate with personal characteristics similar to one's own. The "like marries like" rule can be seen in couples with similar personalities and cultural interests. However, mate selection is unpredictable. Though some people may follow the homogamous pattern, others observe the "opposites attract" rule: one person is dependent and submissive—almost childishly so—while the other is dominant and controlling.

Recently, the concept of homogamy has been incorporated into the process of seeking a date or marital partner online. The Internet dating site eHarmony, which claims to be the first to use a "scientific approach" to matching people based on a variety of abilities and interests, says that it "facilitates" 46 marriages a day. Sociologist Pepper Schwartz, a consultant for the competing site PerfectMatch.com, has developed a 48-question survey that covers everything from prospective mates' decision-making style to their degree of impulsivity (Gottlieb 2006; Kalmijn 1998).

The Love Relationship Today's generation of college students seems more likely to hook up or cruise in large packs than to

engage in the romantic dating relationships of their parents and grandparents. Still, at some point in their adult lives, the great majority of today's students will meet someone they love and enter into a long-term relationship that focuses on creating a family.

Parents in the United States tend to value love highly as a rationale for marriage, so they encourage their children to develop intimate relationships based on love and affection. Songs, films, books, magazines, television shows, and even cartoons and comic books reinforce the theme of love. At the same time, our society expects parents and peers to help a person confine his or her search for a mate to "socially acceptable" members of the opposite sex.

Though most people in the United States take the importance of falling in love for granted, the coupling of love and marriage is by no means a cultural universal. Many of the world's cultures give priority in mate selection to factors other than romantic feelings. In societies with *arranged marriages* engineered by parents or religious authorities, economic considerations play a significant role. The newly married couple is expected to develop a feeling of love *after* the legal union is formalized, if at all.

Throughout the world, even where marital arrangements differ from our own, new media technologies are changing the mating game. In a rural Turkish village, where a small minority of the population still practices polygyny, the search for a second wife has moved from neighboring Syria to an Internet café where local men can contact prospective brides in faraway Morocco. Moroccan women watch Turkish soap operas on television and tend to see Turkish men as more romantic than others. They have become familiar with Turkey's culture and religion, politics and economy through the international news media. With a weak economy at home, many of these women must look elsewhere for marriage, so they turn to the Arabic website Habibti.com ("Mydear.com") to find a traditional marriage in an untraditional way (Schleifer 2009).

use your sociological *imagination*

Your parents and/or a matchmaker are going to arrange a marriage for you. What kind of mate will they select? Will your chances of having a successful marriage be better or worse than if you selected your own mate?

Variations in Family Life and Intimate Relationships

Within the United States, social class, race, and ethnicity create variations in family life. Studying these variations will give us a more sophisticated understanding of contemporary family styles in our country.

Social Class Differences Various studies have documented the differences in family organization among social classes in the United States. In the upper class, the emphasis is on lineage and maintenance of family position. If you are in the upper class, you are not simply a member of a nuclear family, but rather a member of a larger family tradition (think of the Rockefellers or the Kennedys). As a result, upper-class families are quite concerned about what they see as proper training for children.

Lower-class families do not often have the luxury of worrying about the "family name"; they must first struggle to pay their bills and survive the crises often associated with a life of poverty. Such families are more likely to have only one parent at home, which creates special challenges in child care and financial management. Children from lower-class families typically assume adult responsibilities—including marriage and parenthood—at an earlier age than children from affluent homes. In part, that is because they may lack the money needed to remain in school.

Social class differences in family life are less striking today than they once were. In the past, family specialists agreed that the contrasts in child-rearing practices were pronounced. Lower-class families were found to be more authoritarian in rearing children and more inclined to use physical punishment. Middle-class families were more permissive and more restrained in punishing their children. And compared to lower-class families, middle-class families tended to schedule more of their children's time, or even to overstructure it. However, these differences may have narrowed as more and more families from all social classes turned to the same books, magazines, and even television talk shows for advice on rearing children (Kronstadt and Favreault 2008; Luster et al. 1989).

Among the poor, women often play a significant role in the economic support of the family. Men may earn low wages, may be unemployed, or may be entirely absent from the family. In 2009, 30 percent of all families headed by women with no husband present fell below the federal government's poverty line. In comparison, the poverty rate for married couples was only 5.5 percent. The disproportionate representation of female-headed households among the poor is a persistent and growing trend, referred to by sociologists as the *feminization of poverty* (see Chapter 9; DeNavas-Walt et al. 2010:15).

Many racial and ethnic groups appear to have distinctive family characteristics. However, racial and class factors are often closely related. In examining family life among racial and ethnic minorities, keep in mind that certain patterns may result from class as well as cultural factors.

Racial and Ethnic Differences The subordinate status of racial and ethnic minorities in the United States profoundly affects their family lives. For example, the lower incomes of African Americans, Native Americans, most Hispanic groups, and selected Asian American groups make creating and maintaining successful marital unions a difficult task. The economic restructuring of the past 60 years, described by sociologist William Julius Wilson (1996, 2009) and others, has especially affected people living in inner cities and desolate rural areas, such as reservations. Furthermore, the immigration policy of the United States has complicated the successful relocation of intact families from Asia and Latin America.

The African American family suffers from many negative and inaccurate stereotypes. It is true that in a significantly higher proportion of Black than White families, no husband is present in the home (Figure 14-3). Yet Black single mothers often belong to stable, functioning kin networks, which mitigate the pressures of sexism and racism. Members of these networks—predominantly female kin such as mothers, grandmothers, and aunts—ease financial strains by sharing goods and services. In addition to these strong kinship bonds, Black family life has emphasized deep religious commitment and high aspirations for achievement (DuBois [1909] 1970; F. Furstenberg 2007).

Like African Americans, Native Americans draw on family ties to cushion many of the hardships they face. On the Navajo reservation, for example, teenage parenthood is not regarded as the crisis that it is elsewhere in the United States. The Navajo trace their descent matrilineally. Traditionally, couples reside with the wife's family after marriage, allowing the grandparents to help with the child rearing. While the Navajo do not approve of teenage parenthood, the deep emotional commitment of their extended families provides a warm home environment for children, even when no father is present or involved (Dalla and Gamble 2001).

Sociologists also have taken note of differences in family patterns among other racial and ethnic groups. For example, Mexican American men have been described as exhibiting a sense of virility, personal worth, and pride in their maleness that is called **machismo.** Mexican Americans are also described as

FIGURE 14-3 RISE OF SINGLE-PARENT FAMILIES IN THE UNITED STATES, 1970–2010

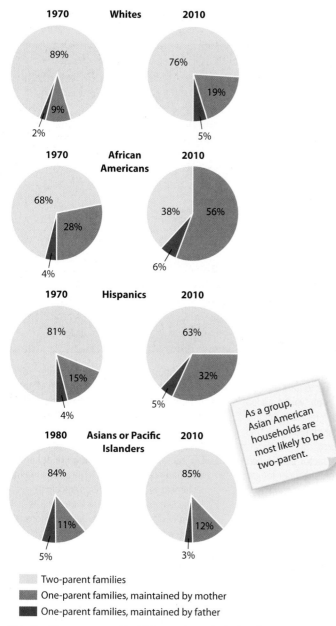

Whites

1970: 89%, 9%, 2%
2010: 76%, 19%, 5%

African Americans

1970: 68%, 28%, 4%
2010: 38%, 56%, 6%

Hispanics

1970: 81%, 15%, 4%
2010: 63%, 32%, 5%

Asians or Pacific Islanders

1980: 84%, 11%, 5%
2010: 85%, 12%, 3%

As a group, Asian American households are most likely to be two-parent.

- Two-parent families
- One-parent families, maintained by mother
- One-parent families, maintained by father

Note: Families are groups with children under 18. Early data for Asian Americans are for 1980. Hispanics can be of any race. Not included are unrelated people living together with no children present. All data exclude the 11 percent of children in nonparental households.
Sources: Bureau of the Census 2008a:56, 2010c:Table FG10.

being more familistic than many other subcultures. **Familism** refers to pride in the extended family, expressed through the maintenance of close ties and strong obligations to kinfolk outside the immediate family. Traditionally, Mexican Americans have placed proximity to their extended families above other needs and desires.

Although familism is often seen as a positive cultural attribute, it may also have negative consequences. Sociologists who have studied the relatively low college application rates of Hispanic students have found they have a strong desire to stay at home. Even the children of college-educated parents express this preference, which diminishes the likelihood of their getting a four-year degree and dramatically reduces the possibility that they will apply to a selective college (Desmond and Turley 2009).

These family patterns are changing, however, in response to changes in Latinos' social class standing, educational achievements, and occupations. Like other Americans, career-oriented Latinos in search of a mate but short on spare time are turning to Internet sites. As Latinos and other groups assimilate into the dominant culture of the United States, their family lives take on both the positive and negative characteristics associated with White households (Landale and Oropesa 2007).

Child-Rearing Patterns

The Nayars of southern India acknowledge the biological role of fathers, but the mother's eldest brother is responsible for her children. In contrast, uncles play only a peripheral role in child care in the United States. Caring for children is a universal function of the family, yet the ways in which different societies assign this function to family members can vary significantly. Even within the United States, child-rearing patterns are varied. We'll take a look here at parenthood and grandparenthood, adoption, dual-income families, single-parent families, and stepfamilies.

Parenthood and Grandparenthood The socialization of children is essential to the maintenance of any culture. Consequently, parenthood is one of the most important (and most demanding) social roles in the United States. Sociologist Alice Rossi (1968, 1984) has identified four factors that complicate the transition to parenthood and the role of socialization. First, there is little anticipatory socialization for the social role of caregiver. The normal school curriculum gives scant attention to the subjects most relevant to successful family life, such as child care and home maintenance. Second, only limited learning occurs during the period of pregnancy itself. Third, the transition to parenthood is quite abrupt. Unlike adolescence, it is not prolonged; unlike the transition to work, the duties of caregiving cannot be taken on gradually. Finally, in Rossi's view, our society lacks clear and helpful guidelines for successful parenthood. There is little consensus on how parents can produce happy and well-adjusted offspring—or even on what it means to be well adjusted. For these reasons, socialization for parenthood involves difficult challenges for most men and women in the United States.

One recent development in family life in the United States has been the extension of parenthood, as single adult children continue to live at home or return home after college. In 2009, 33 percent of men and 22 percent of women in their 20s lived with their parents. Some of these adult children were still pursuing an education, but in many instances, financial difficulties lay at the heart of these living arrangements. For younger job seekers, employment is often short-term or low paying. (This problem, along with the trend toward adult children living with their parents, is not unique to the United States; see Box 14-2.) Moreover, with many marriages now ending in divorce—most commonly in the first seven years of marriage— divorced sons and daughters often return to live with their parents, sometimes with their own children (Bureau of the Census 2010b:Table A2).

14-2 Family Life, Italian Style: Thirty-Something and Living with Mom

Bamboccioni—adult children who live with their parents—are no longer socially unacceptable in Italy. In fact, they're not even unusual. In December 2009, the Italian government released new data showing that 40 percent of Italian men between ages 30 and 34 live with their parents. So do 20 percent of Italian women in this age bracket. Among those a little older, ages 35 to 39, 17.5 percent of men and 9.3 percent of women live with their parents.

> *About 40 percent of* bamboccioni *live with their parents not because of financial need, but because they enjoy the company.*

This state of affairs is not a recent phenomenon. What is new is that 80 percent of these adult children say they cannot afford to leave their parents' homes. Salaries in Italy are low but rents are high, so these not-so-young adults linger on with mama and papa. As one of them, a 30-year-old biologist, put it, "We are the €1,000-per-month generation—who can afford spending more than €800 for an apartment?"

About 40 percent of *bamboccioni* live with their parents not because of financial need, but because they enjoy the company. Others feel responsible for their aging parents. Among the women ages 35 to 40, more than half feel it is a duty. Sociologist Giampiero dalla Zuanna says their commitment to the family means the elderly in Italy are much more likely to remain in their own homes than those in northern Europe, many of whom must move to retirement communities.

The pattern of adult children staying home with their parents is not unique to Italy. In North America and throughout Europe, young people are feeling the impact of the recent economic downturn. Many are delaying childbearing until their job prospects improve.

One relatively unnoticed factor that is contributing to the trend is parents' greater longevity. Today, more parents survive long enough for their children to become adults, and remain healthy enough to maintain a home for them.

What happens when adult children finally do leave the nest? So close are the ties between parent and child in Italy that services have emerged to support their relationship through the separation in living arrangements. For a small fee, special couriers will pick up Mother's fresh homemade pasta and even homegrown greens and deliver them to her adult children.

LET'S DISCUSS

1. Do you or someone you know live at home with parents? If so, do you see the situation as similar to that of the *bamboccioni*?
2. In the United States, what other factors might contribute to adult children choosing to live with their parents?

Sources: Meichtry 2011; Momigliana 2010; S. Roberts 2010.

Is this living arrangement a positive development for family members? Social scientists have just begun to examine the phenomenon, sometimes called the "boomerang generation" or the "full-nest syndrome" in the popular press. One survey in Virginia seemed to show that neither the parents nor their adult children were happy about continuing to live together. The children often felt resentful and isolated, but the parents suffered too: learning to live without children in the home is an essential stage of adult life and may even be a significant turning point for a marriage (*Berkeley Wellness Letter* 1990; Mogelonsky 1996).

In some homes, the full nest holds grandchildren. In 2009, 7 million children, or 9 percent of all children in the United States, lived in a household with a grandparent. In about a third of these homes, no parent was present to assume responsibility for the youngsters. Special difficulties are inherent in such relationships, including legal custodial concerns, financial issues,

and emotional problems for adults and youths alike. It is not surprising that support groups such as Grandparents as Parents have emerged to provide assistance (Bureau of the Census 2010b:Table C4).

thinking CRITICALLY

How do both cultural and socioeconomic factors contribute to the "boomerang generation"?

Adoption In a legal sense, **adoption** is a "process that allows for the transfer of the legal rights, responsibilities, and privileges of parenthood" to a new legal parent or parents (E. Cole 1985:638).

When nine-year-old Blake Brunson shows up for a basketball game, so do his *eight* grandparents—the result of his parents' remarriages. Blended families can be very supportive to children, but what message do they send to them on the permanency of marriage?

In many cases, these rights are transferred from a biological parent or parents (often called birth parents) to an adoptive parent or parents. At any given time, about 2 million adults in the United States are raising adopted children (Jo Jones 2009).

Viewed from a functionalist perspective, government has a strong interest in encouraging adoption. Policymakers, in fact, have both a humanitarian and a financial stake in the process. In theory, adoption offers a stable family environment for children who otherwise might not receive satisfactory care. Moreover, government data show that unwed mothers who keep their babies tend to be of lower socioeconomic status and often require public assistance to support their children. The government can lower its social welfare expenses, then, if children are transferred to economically self-sufficient families. From an interactionist perspective, however, adoption may require a child to adjust to a very different family environment and parental approach to child rearing.

About 4 percent of all people in the United States are adopted, about half of whom were adopted by persons not related to them at birth. There are two legal methods of adopting an unrelated person: the adoption may be arranged through a licensed agency, or in some states it may be arranged through a private agreement sanctioned by the courts. Adopted children may come from the United States or from abroad. In 2009, over 12,700 children entered the United States as the adopted children of U.S. citizens. International adoptions began to decline in 2004 after a long and steady increase. Recently China, the source for about one-fourth

of overseas adoptions, tightened the rules for foreign adoptions, effectively reducing their number. Applicants for adoption who are single, obese, or older than 50 are now automatically disqualified (Department of State 2010a).

The 2010 earthquake in Haiti drew attention to the foreign perspective on international adoptions, which is not always positive. When well-meaning people from the United States arrived in Haiti to rescue alleged orphans and arrange for their adoption in other countries, government officials objected. Some of the children, it turned out, were not orphans; their parents were simply too poor to care for them. For the governments of overstressed developing nations, adoption can be both a solution and a problem.

Adoption is controversial not only abroad but at home as well. In some cases, those who adopt children are not married. In 1995, an important court decision in New York held that a couple does not need to be married to adopt a child. Under this ruling, unmarried heterosexual couples, lesbian couples, and gay couples can all adopt children in New York. Today, most states permit gay and lesbian couples to adopt. Florida is the only state that explicitly forbids it; five others (Arkansas, Michigan, Mississippi, Nebraska, and Utah) prohibit couples who are not legally married from adopting (National Gay and Lesbian Task Force 2008).

For every child who is adopted, many more remain the wards of state-sponsored child protective services. At any given time, around half a million children in the United States are living in foster care. Every year, about 57,000 of them are adopted; another 103,000 are eligible and waiting to be adopted (Department of Health and Human Services 2011b).

Dual-Income Families The idea of a family consisting of a wage-earning husband and a wife who stays at home has largely given way to the dual-income household. Among married people between ages 25 and 34, 96 percent of the men and 69 percent of the women were in the labor force in 2007 (Bureau of the Census 2008a:375).

Why has there been such a rise in the number of dual-income couples? A major factor is economic need, coupled with a desire by both men *and* women to pursue their careers. Evidence of this trend can be found in the rise in the number of married couples living apart for reasons other than marital discord. The 3.6 million couples who now live apart represent 1 out of every 33 marriages. More than half of them live farther than 100 miles apart, and half of those live 1,000 or more miles apart. Of course, couples living apart are nothing new; men have worked at transient jobs for generations as soldiers, truck drivers, or traveling salesmen. Now, however, the woman's job is often the one that creates the separation. The existence of such household arrangements reflects an acceptance of the egalitarian family type (Higgins et al. 2010; Holmes 2009; Silverman 2009).

Miles Harvey reads to his children via Skype. Harvey, who is happily married, lives 900 miles from his family in Chicago. He accepted a job in New Orleans for economic reasons.

use your sociological *imagination*

What personal experience do you have with child rearing by grandparents, adoptive parents, or dual-income families? Describe what you observed using sociological concepts.

Single-Parent Families The 2004 *American Idol* winner Fantasia Barrino's song "Baby Mama" offers a tribute to young single mothers—a subject she knows about. Barrino was 17 when she became pregnant with her daughter. Though critics charged that the song sends the wrong message to teenage girls, Barrino says it is not about encouraging teens to have sex. Rather, she sees the song as an anthem for young mothers courageously trying to raise their children alone (Cherlin 2006).

In recent decades, the stigma attached to unwed mothers and other single parents has significantly diminished. **Single-parent families,** in which only one parent is present to care for the children, can hardly be viewed as a rarity in the United States. In 2010, a single parent headed about 24 percent of White families with children under 18, 37 percent of Hispanic families with children, and 62 percent of African American families with children (see Figure 14-3 on page 315).

The lives of single parents and their children are not inevitably more difficult than life in a traditional nuclear family. It is as inaccurate to assume that a single-parent family is necessarily deprived as it is to assume that a two-parent family is always secure and happy. Nevertheless, life in a single-parent family can be extremely stressful, in both economic and emotional terms. A family headed by a single mother faces especially difficult problems when the mother is a teenager.

Why might low-income teenage women wish to have children and face the obvious financial difficulties of motherhood? Viewed from an interactionist perspective, these women tend to have low self-esteem and limited options; a child may provide a sense of motivation and purpose for a teenager whose economic

worth in our society is limited at best. Given the barriers that many young women face because of their gender, race, ethnicity, and class, many teenagers may believe they have little to lose and much to gain by having a child.

According to a widely held stereotype, "unwed mothers" and "babies having babies" in the United States are predominantly African American. However, this view is not entirely accurate. African Americans account for a disproportionate share of births to unmarried women and teenagers, but the majority of all babies born to unmarried teenage mothers are born to White adolescents. Moreover, since 1980, birthrates among Black teenagers have generally declined (J. Martin et al. 2009).

Although 84 percent of single parents in the United States are mothers, the number of households headed by single fathers more than quadrupled from 1987 to 2010. Though single mothers often develop social networks, single fathers are typically more isolated. In addition, they must deal with schools and social service agencies that are more accustomed to women as custodial parents (Bureau of the Census 1994, 2010b).

Stepfamilies Approximately 45 percent of all people in the United States will marry, divorce, and then remarry. The rising rates of divorce and remarriage have led to a noticeable increase in stepfamily relationships.

The exact nature of blended families has social significance for adults and children alike. Certainly resocialization is required when an adult becomes a stepparent or a child becomes a stepchild and stepsibling. Moreover, an important distinction must be made between first-time stepfamilies and households where there have been repeated divorces, breakups, or changes in custodial arrangements.

In evaluating the rise of stepfamilies, some observers have assumed that children would benefit from remarriage because they would be gaining a second custodial parent, and would potentially enjoy greater economic security. However, after reviewing many studies of stepfamilies, sociologist Andrew J. Cherlin (2009:5) concluded that "children whose parents have remarried do not have higher levels of well-being than children in lone-parent families."

Stepparents can play valuable and unique roles in their stepchildren's lives, but their involvement does not guarantee an improvement in family life. In fact, standards may decline. Studies suggest that children raised in families with stepmothers are likely to have less health care, education, and money spent on their food than children raised by biological mothers. The measures are also negative for children raised by stepfathers, but only half as negative as in the case of stepmothers. These results don't mean that stepmothers are "evil"—it may be that the stepmother holds back out of concern for seeming too intrusive, or relies mistakenly on the biological father to carry out parental duties (Schmeeckle 2007; Schmeeckle et al. 2006).

Divorce

In the United States, the pattern of family life includes commitments both to marriage and to self-expression and personal growth. Needless to say, the tension between those competing commitments can undermine a marriage, working against the establishment of a lasting relationship. This approach to family life is distinctive to the United States. In some nations, such as Italy, the culture strongly supports marriage and discourages divorce. In others, such as Sweden, people treat marriage the same way as cohabitation, and both arrangements are just as lasting (Cherlin 2009).

Statistical Trends in Divorce

Just how common is divorce? Surprisingly, this is not a simple question; divorce statistics are difficult to interpret. The media frequently report that one out of every two marriages ends in divorce, but that figure is misleading. It is based on a comparison of all divorces that occur in a single year (regardless of when the couples were married) with the number of new marriages in the same year.

In many countries, divorce began to increase in the late 1960s but then leveled off; since the late 1980s, it has declined by 30 percent. (Figure 14-4 shows the pattern in the United States.) This trend is due partly to the aging of the baby boomer population and the corresponding decline in the proportion of people of marriageable age. But it also indicates an increase in marital stability in recent years (Coontz 2006).

Getting divorced obviously does not sour people on marriage. About 63 percent of all divorced people in the United States have remarried. Women are less likely than men to remarry because many retain custody of their children after a divorce, which complicates a new adult relationship (Bianchi and Spain 1996; Saad 2004).

Most households in the United States do not consist of two parents living with their unmarried children.

Some people regard the nation's high rate of remarriage as an endorsement of the institution of marriage, but it does lead to the new challenges of a kin network composed of both current and prior marital relationships. Such networks can be particularly complex if children are involved or if an ex-spouse remarries.

Factors Associated with Divorce

Perhaps the most important factor in the increase in divorce over the past hundred years has been the greater social *acceptance* of divorce. It is no longer considered necessary to endure an unhappy marriage. More important, various religious denominations have relaxed their negative attitudes toward divorce, so that most religious leaders no longer treat it as a sin.

The growing acceptance of divorce is a worldwide phenomenon. A decade ago, Sunoo, South Korea's foremost matchmaking service, had no divorced clients. Few Koreans divorced; those who did felt social pressure to resign themselves to the single life. But in one recent seven-year period, South Korea's divorce rate doubled. Today, 15 percent of Sunoo's membership are divorced (Onishi 2003; United Nations Statistics Division 2009:Table 23).

In the United States, several factors have contributed to the growing social acceptance of divorce:

- Most states have adopted more liberal divorce laws in the past three decades. No-fault divorce laws, which allow a couple to end their marriage without fault on either side (by specifying adultery, for instance), accounted for an initial surge in the divorce rate after they were introduced in the 1970s, but appear to have had little effect beyond that.

- Divorce has become a more practical option in newly formed families, since families tend to have fewer children now than in the past.

- A general increase in family incomes, coupled with the availability of free legal aid to some poor people, has meant that more couples can afford costly divorce proceedings.

FIGURE **14-4**   TRENDS IN MARRIAGE AND DIVORCE IN THE UNITED STATES, 1920–2009

The divorce rate has generally risen since 1920, while the marriage rate has declined.

Sources: Bureau of the Census 1975:64; *National Vital Statistics Reports* 2010.

RESEARCH TODAY

14-3   Divorce and Military Deployment

Whenever soldiers talk about the hardships of foreign deployment, separation from their families and the toll on their marital relationships are the main topic. Too often, military couples marry just before a deployment, following a brief romance. Then, when they are suddenly separated, the relationship begins to fall apart. To keep wives from worrying or to reduce their own homesickness, many soldiers avoid calling home. Those couples who do communicate by phone, letter, or e-mail often argue; some talk about divorce. Impulsively, a soldier may throw his wedding ring away. A wife struggling to manage on her own may empty the family's bank account.

Yet many couples make heroic efforts to hold together despite the hardship. Those who are left home continue to care for their families, coping with life as a single parent and

23 percent of soldiers stationed in Iraq in 2009 say they plan to divorce or separate after returning home.

Welcome home! Military families reunite after a long, anxious separation.

comforting children who miss their father or mother. They will themselves to overcome loneliness and anxiety. For these couples, every new deployment is a challenge; being apart doesn't get easier as they get older.

On balance, does overseas deployment affect the divorce rate among military couples? Current research delivers a mixed message. One long-term study published recently indicates that the longer the deployment, the lower the risk of divorce. Studies of soldiers who served in the Vietnam War and the 1991 Persian Gulf War came to the same conclusion. Yet 2009 data show that the current divorce rate among those in the military is 3.6 percent a year—slightly higher than the national rate of 3.4 percent. Furthermore, 23 percent of soldiers stationed in Iraq in 2009 say they plan to divorce or separate after returning home, compared to 12 percent in 2003.

There were other negative findings of the study. Female service members were found to be twice as likely as male service members to end their marriages. Moreover, enlisted service

members were more likely than officers to end their marriages. This second disparity may be due to the fact that officers tend to be older than enlisted personnel, and older couples are less likely than younger couples to divorce.

Studies of the impact of overseas deployment on couples' children have not been reassuring. In 2007, an Army-funded study found that the rate of child neglect among military families was almost four times higher when husbands were deployed than when they were home. Physical abuse of children in those cases was nearly twice as high when husbands were away. Given these findings, one can only hope that support programs for families separated by war will be strengthened.

There is a need for further research on this topic. The information that researchers have covers only the short term and pertains only to those soldiers who remained in the military. Could the long-term impact on military couples

be more telling? Could the outcome be different for those who leave the military soon after a war? And might soldiers consider marriage more carefully than the average person, knowing that their futures are uncertain? As with even the most detailed research, this study's conclusions raise new questions for scientific investigation.

LET'S DISCUSS

1. Do you know any married couples who have been separated by military deployment overseas? If so, how did they cope? What was the effect on their children?
2. Can you think of some other reasons why military marriages might survive the strain of war as well as they do?

Sources: Block 2009; Bowman 2009; D. Gibbs et al. 2007; Karney and Crown 2007; Krauss 1993; Perry 2007; Priest 2008; RAND 2007; Stone and Bello 2009; Wheller 2009; Zoroya 2009.

- As society provides greater opportunities for women, more and more wives are becoming less dependent on their husbands, both economically and emotionally. They may feel more able to leave a marriage if it seems hopeless.

What about the stress of separation caused by military duty? Forced transfer overseas, the tension of war, new duties at home, and anxiety over a spouse's return might seem a recipe for marital

failure. Box 14-3 considers military marriages' vulnerability while the husband or wife is away at war.

Impact of Divorce on Children

Divorce is traumatic for all involved, but it has special meaning for the more than 1 million children whose parents divorce each year. Of course, for some of these children, divorce signals the welcome end to a very dysfunctional relationship. Perhaps that

MAPPING LIFE NATIONWIDE

FIGURE **14-5** UNMARRIED-COUPLE HOUSEHOLDS BY STATE

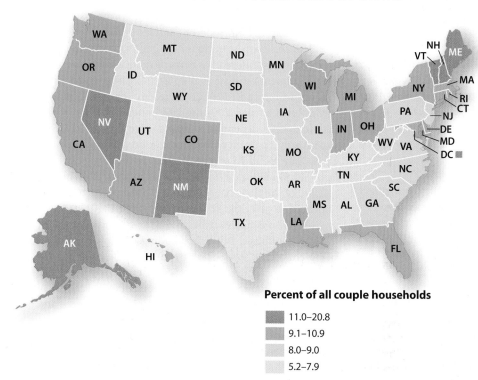

Percent of all couple households

- 11.0–20.8
- 9.1–10.9
- 8.0–9.0
- 5.2–7.9

Note: Data are for 2000 and include both opposite-sex and same-sex partners. U.S. average is 9.1 percent.
Source: Simmons and O'Connell 2003:4.

Cohabitation

In the United States, testing the marital waters by living together before making a commitment is a common practice among marriage-wary 20- and 30-somethings. The tremendous increase in the number of male–female couples who choose to live together without marrying, a practice called **cohabitation,** is one of the most dramatic trends of recent years.

About half of all *currently* married couples in the United States say that they lived together before marriage. This percentage is likely to increase. The number of households in the United States that are headed by unmarried opposite-sex couples has been rising steadily; in 2010 it was 6.7 million. Figure 14-5 shows regional variations in the rate of cohabitation (Kreider 2010).

In much of Europe, cohabitation is so common that the general sentiment seems to be "Love, yes; marriage, maybe." In Iceland, 62 percent of all children are born to single mothers; in France, Great Britain, and Norway, about 40 percent. Government policies in these countries make few legal distinctions between married and unmarried couples or households. Perhaps as a result, partnerships between cohabiting adults are not necessarily brief or lacking in commitment. Children born to a cohabiting couple in Sweden, for example, are less likely than children born to a cohabiting couple in the United States to see their parents break up (Cherlin 2009; Lyall 2002; M. Moore 2006).

People commonly associate cohabitation with younger couples. But according to a study done in Los Angeles, working couples are almost twice as likely to cohabit as college students. And census data show that in 2003, 45 percent of unmarried couples had one or more children present in the household. These cohabitants are more like spouses than dating partners. Moreover, in contrast to the common perception that people who cohabit have never been married, researchers report that about half of all people involved in cohabitation in the United States have been previously married. Cohabitation serves as a temporary or permanent alternative to matrimony for many men and women who have experienced their own or their parents' divorces (Jason Fields 2004; Popenoe and Whitehead 1999).

Periodically, legislators attempt to bolster the desirability of a lifelong commitment to marriage. In 2002, President George W. Bush backed funding for an initiative to promote marriage among those who receive public assistance. Under the Healthy Marriage Initiative, the federal government created a resource center that promoted marriage-related programs. Critics charged

---

is why a national study that tracked 6,332 children both before and after their parents' divorce found that their behavior did not suffer from the marital breakups. Other studies have shown greater unhappiness among children who live amid parental conflict than among children whose parents are divorced. Still, it would be simplistic to assume that children are automatically better off following the breakup of their parents' marriage. The interests of the parents do not necessarily serve children well (Zi 2007).

thinking CRITICALLY

In a society that maximizes the welfare of all family members, how easy should it be for couples to divorce? How easy should it be to get married?

Diverse Lifestyles

Marriage is no longer the presumed route from adolescence to adulthood. Instead, it is treated as just one of several paths to maturity. As a result, the marriage ceremony has lost much of its social significance as a rite of passage. The nation's marriage rate has declined since 1960 because people are postponing marriage until later in life, and because more couples, including same-sex couples, are deciding to form partnerships without marriage (Haq 2011).

that the effort was underfunded or an inappropriate mission for the federal government. Still, the Obama administration has indicated a desire to continue the initiative, although the fragile economy may jeopardize its funding (Jayson 2009).

Remaining Single

Looking at TV programs today, you would be justified in thinking that most households are composed of singles. Although that is not the case, it is true that more and more people in the United States are postponing entry into a first marriage. Over one out of three households with children in the United States is a single-parent household. Even so, less than 4 percent of women and men in the United States are likely to remain single throughout their lives (Bureau of the Census 2008a).

The trend toward maintaining a single lifestyle for a longer period is related to the growing economic independence of young people. This trend is especially significant for women. Freed from financial needs, women don't necessarily need to marry to enjoy a satisfying life. Divorce, late marriage, and longevity also figure into this trend.

There are many reasons why a person may choose not to marry. Some singles do not want to limit their sexual intimacy to one lifetime partner. Some men and women do not want to become highly dependent on any one person—and do not want anyone depending heavily on them. In a society that values individuality and self-fulfillment, the single lifestyle can offer certain freedoms that married couples may not enjoy. Even divorced parents may not feel the need to remarry. Andrew J. Cherlin (2009) contends that a single parent who connects with other adults, such as grandparents, to form a solid, supportive relationship for child rearing should not feel compelled to re-partner.

Nevertheless, remaining single represents a clear departure from societal expectations; indeed, it has been likened to "being single on Noah's Ark." A single adult must confront the inaccurate view that he or she is always lonely, is a workaholic, or is immature. These stereotypes help to support the traditional assumption in the United States and most other societies that to be truly happy and fulfilled, a person must get married and raise a family. To counter these societal expectations, singles have formed numerous support groups (Hertz 2006; Lundquist 2006).

Marriage without Children

There has been a modest increase in childlessness in the United States. According to census data, about 16 to 17 percent of women will now complete their childbearing years without having borne any children, compared to 10 percent in 1980. As many as 20 percent of women in their 30s expect to remain childless (Biddlecom and Martin 2006).

Childlessness within marriage has generally been viewed as a problem that can be solved through such means as adoption and artificial insemination. More and more couples today, however, choose not to have children and regard themselves as child-free rather than childless. They do not believe that having children automatically follows from marriage, nor do they feel that reproduction is the duty of all married couples. Childless couples have formed support groups (with names like No Kidding) and set up websites.

Economic considerations have contributed to this shift in attitudes; having children has become quite expensive. According to a government estimate made for 2012, the average middle-class family will spend $229,320 to feed, clothe, and shelter a child from birth to age 18. If the child attends college, that amount could double, depending on the college chosen. In 1960, parents spent only 2 percent of their income on child care and education; now they spend 16 percent, reflecting the rising dependence on nonfamily child care (see the Social Policy section in Chapter 4). Aware of the financial pressures, some couples are weighing the advantages of a child-free marriage (Lino 2010).

Childless couples are beginning to question current practices in the workplace. While applauding employers' efforts to provide child care and flexible work schedules, some nevertheless express concern about tolerance of employees who leave early to take children to doctors, ball games, or after-school classes. As more dual-career couples enter the paid labor force and struggle to balance career and familial responsibilities, conflicts with employees who have no children may increase (Biddlecom and Martin 2006).

use your sociological *imagination*

What would happen to our society if many more married couples suddenly decided not to have children? How would society change if cohabitation and/or singlehood became the norm?

Lesbian and Gay Relationships

Twenty-one-year-old Parke, a junior in college, grew up in a stable, loving family. A self-described fiscal conservative, he credits his parents with instilling in him a strong work ethic. Sound like an average child of an average family? The only break with traditional expectations in this case is that Parke is the son of a lesbian couple (P. Brown 2004).

The lifestyles of lesbians and gay men are varied. Some live in long-term, monogamous relationships; others live alone or with roommates. Some remain in "empty-shell" heterosexual marriages and do not publicly acknowledge their homosexuality. Others live with children from a former marriage or with adopted children. Based on election exit polls, researchers for the National Health and Social Life Survey and the Voter News Service estimate that 2 to 5 percent of the adult population identify themselves as either gay or lesbian. An analysis of the 2000 Census shows a minimum of at least 600,000 gay households, and a gay and lesbian adult population approaching 10 million (Laumann et al. 1994b:293; David M. Smith and Gates 2001).

Gay and lesbian couples face discrimination on both a personal and a legal level. Their inability to marry denies them many rights that married couples take for granted, from the ability to make decisions for an incapacitated partner to the right to receive government benefits to dependents, such as Social Security payments. Though gay couples consider themselves families just like the straight couples who live down the street, they are often treated as if they are not.

Precisely because of such inequities, many gay and lesbian couples are now demanding the right to marry. In the Social Policy section that follows, we will examine the highly controversial issue of gay marriage.

thinking CRITICALLY

How is romantic cohabitation similar to marriage? How is it different? Could gay and lesbian couples achieve all the benefits of marriage without actually marrying?

social**policy** and the Family

Gay Marriage

In the United States, attitudes toward marriage are complex. As always, society and popular culture suggest that a young man or woman should find the perfect mate, settle down and marry, have children, and live happily ever after. But young people are also bombarded by messages implying the frequency of adultery and the acceptability of divorce. In this atmosphere, the idea of same-sex marriage strikes some people as only the latest of many attacks on traditional marriage. To others, it seems an overdue acknowledgment of the formal relationships that faithful, monogamous gay couples have long maintained.

Looking at the Issue

What has made gay marriage the focus of national attention? Events in two states brought the issue to the forefront. In 1999, Vermont gave gay couples the legal benefits of marriage through civil union, but stopped short of calling the arrangement a marriage. Then, in 2003, the Massachusetts Supreme Court ruled 4–3 that under the state's constitution, gay couples have the right to marry—a ruling the U.S. Supreme Court has refused to review. Now, with gay married couples in this state passing their 5th anniversaries and approaching their 10th, scholars are beginning to study their experiences compared to those of opposite-sex couples.

Recently, national surveys of attitudes toward gay marriage in the United States have shown an almost even split among the public. A 2009 survey showed that 53 percent oppose allowing gay men and lesbians to marry. However, 57 percent favor allowing them to enter legal unions—arrangements that give gay couples many of the same rights as marriage (Kelley and Bazar 2010).

Applying Sociology

Functionalists have traditionally seen marriage as a social institution that is closely tied to human reproduction. Same-sex marriage would at first appear not to fit that arrangement. But many same-sex couples are entrusted with the socialization of young children, whether or not their relationship is recognized by the state. Functionalists also wonder whether religious views toward marriage can be ignored. The courts have focused on civil marriage, but religious views are hardly irrelevant, even in a country like the United States, which observes a separation between religion and the state. Indeed, religious teachings have led even some staunch supporters of gay rights to oppose same-sex marriage on spiritual grounds.

Conflict theorists have charged that denial of the right to marry reinforces the second-class status of gays and lesbians. Some have compared the ban

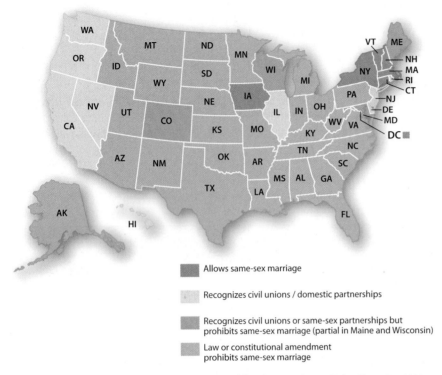

Allows same-sex marriage

Recognizes civil unions / domestic partnerships

Recognizes civil unions or same-sex partnerships but prohibits same-sex marriage (partial in Maine and Wisconsin)

Law or constitutional amendment prohibits same-sex marriage

Sources: As of May 2011, author based on news reports; Clabaugh 2010; Human Rights Campaign 2011; National Conference of State Legislatures 2011.

and have extended employee benefits to those relationships. Under such policies, a **domestic partnership** may be defined as two unrelated adults who share a mutually caring relationship, reside together, and agree to be jointly responsible for their dependents, basic living expenses, and other common necessities. Domestic partnership benefits can apply to couples' inheritance, parenting, pensions, taxation, housing, immigration, workplace fringe benefits such as life insurance, and health care. Even though the most passionate support for domestic partnership legislation has come from lesbian and gay activists, the majority of those eligible for such benefits would be cohabiting heterosexual couples.

In the United States, marriage has traditionally been under the jurisdiction of state lawmakers. But recently, pressure has been mounting for national legislation. The Defense of Marriage Act, passed in 1996, provided that no state is obliged to recognize same-sex marriages performed in another state. However, some legal scholars doubt that the law could withstand a constitutional challenge, since it violates a provision in the Constitution that requires states to recognize one another's laws.

Within the United States, state courts in California, Iowa, and Massachusetts have ruled that there is no state law that precludes same-sex marriage. In California, 18,000 same-sex couples were married before voters amended the state constitution to prohibit such marriages in the future. In August 2010, a federal court weighed in for the first time on gay marriage, ruling that California's ban on same-sex marriage was unconstitutional. Ultimately, the Supreme Court will consider the issue. As of mid-2011, the District of Columbia and six states (Connecticut, Iowa, Massachusetts, New Hampshire, New York, and Vermont) were issuing marriage licenses to same-sex couples. Gay rights activists claim their movement is gathering momentum, but opponents argue that their high-profile actions have galvanized conservatives who wish to define marriage as the union of one man and one woman.

against gay marriage to past policies that until 1967 banned interracial marriage in 32 states. Figure 14-6 illustrates the different ways same-sex partnerships are treated today in different states.

Interactionists generally avoid the policy question and focus instead on the nature of same-sex households. They ask many of the same questions about gay partner relations and child rearing that they ask about conventional couples. Of course, much less research has been done on same-sex households than on other families, but the studies published to date raise the same issues as those that apply to conventional married couples, plus a few more. For gay couples, the support or opposition of family, co-workers, and friends looms large (Dundas and Kaufman 2000; Dunne 2000; B. Powell et al. 2010).

Initiating Policy

The United States is not the first nation to consider this issue. Recognition of same-sex partnerships is common in Europe, and same-sex marriage is recognized in Argentina, Belgium, the Netherlands, Norway, Portugal, Spain, and Sweden. Today, as many as 8 percent of all marriages in the Netherlands are same-sex. The trend is toward recognition in North America as well, since gay couples can marry legally in Canada.

In the United States, many local jurisdictions have passed legislation allowing for the registration of domestic partnerships,

Take the Issue with You

1. If marriage is good for heterosexual couples and their families, why isn't it good for homosexual couples and their families?

2. How can interactionist studies of gay couples and their families inform policymakers who are dealing with the issue of gay marriage? Give a specific example.

3. Who are the stakeholders in the debate over gay marriage, and what do they stand to gain or lose? Whose interest do you think is most important?

Summary

The **family**, in its many varying forms, is present in all human cultures. This chapter examines the state of marriage, the family, and other intimate relationships in the United States and considers alternatives to the traditional **nuclear family.**

1. **Families** vary from culture to culture and even within the same culture.

2. The structure of the **extended family** can offer certain advantages over that of the **nuclear family.**

3. Societies determine **kinship** by descent from both parents (**bilateral descent**), from the father only (**patrilineal descent**), or from the mother only (**matrilineal descent**).

4. Sociologists do not agree on whether the **egalitarian family** has replaced the patriarchal family as the social norm in the United States.

5. William F. Ogburn outlined six basic functions of the family: reproduction, protection, socialization, regulation of sexual behavior, companionship, and the provision of social status.

6. Conflict theorists argue that male dominance of the family contributes to societal injustice and denies women opportunities that are extended to men.

7. Interactionists focus on how individuals interact in the family and in other intimate relationships.

8. Feminists stress the need to broaden research on the family. Like conflict theorists, they see the family's role in socializing children as the primary source of sexism.

9. People select mates in a variety of ways. Some marriages are arranged; in other societies, people choose their own mates. Some societies require mates to be chosen within a certain group (**endogamy**) or outside certain groups (**exogamy**). And consciously or unconsciously, many people look for a mate with similar personal characteristics (**homogamy).**

10. In the United States, family life varies with social class, race, and ethnicity.

11. Currently, in the majority of all married couples in the United States, both husband and wife work outside the home.

12. **Single-parent families** account for an increasing proportion of U.S. families.

13. Among the factors that contribute to the rising divorce rate in the United States are greater social acceptance of divorce and the liberalization of divorce laws in many states.

14. More and more people are living together without marrying, a practice known as **cohabitation.** People are also staying single longer, and some married couples are deciding not to have children.

15. The gay marriage movement, which would confer equal rights on gay and lesbian couples and their dependents, is strongly opposed by conservative religious and political groups.

Key Terms

Adoption In a legal sense, a process that allows for the transfer of the legal rights, responsibilities, and privileges of parenthood to a new legal parent or parents. (page 316)

Bilateral descent A kinship system in which both sides of a person's family are regarded as equally important. (308)

Cohabitation The practice of living together as a male–female couple without marrying. (321)

Domestic partnership Two unrelated adults who share a mutually caring relationship, reside together, and agree to be jointly responsible for their dependents, basic living expenses, and other common necessities. (324)

Egalitarian family An authority pattern in which spouses are regarded as equals. (309)

Endogamy The restriction of mate selection to people within the same group. (312)

Exogamy The requirement that people select a mate outside certain groups. (312)

Extended family A family in which relatives—such as grandparents, aunts, or uncles—live in the same home as parents and their children. (307)

Familism Pride in the extended family, expressed through the maintenance of close ties and strong obligations to kinfolk outside the immediate family. (315)

Family A set of people related by blood, marriage or some other agreed-on relationship, or adoption, who share the primary responsibility for reproduction and caring for members of society. (307)

Homogamy The conscious or unconscious tendency to select a mate with personal characteristics similar to one's own. (313)

Incest taboo The prohibition of sexual relationships between certain culturally specified relatives. (312)

Kinship The state of being related to others. (308)

Machismo A sense of virility, personal worth, and pride in one's maleness. (314)

Matriarchy A society in which women dominate in family decision making. (309)

Matrilineal descent A kinship system in which only the mother's relatives are significant. (308)

Monogamy A form of marriage in which one woman and one man are married only to each other. (307)

Nuclear family A married couple and their unmarried children living together. (307)

Patriarchy A society in which men dominate in family decision making. (309)

Patrilineal descent A kinship system in which only the father's relatives are significant. (308)

Polyandry A form of polygamy in which a woman may have more than one husband at the same time. (307)

Polygamy A form of marriage in which an individual may have several husbands or wives simultaneously. (307)

Polygyny A form of polygamy in which a man may have more than one wife at the same time. (307)

Serial monogamy A form of marriage in which a person may have several spouses in his or her lifetime, but only one spouse at a time. (307)

Single-parent family A family in which only one parent is present to care for the children. (318)

1. Go online and try tracing your family roots using one of the genealogical search sites. How far back can you go? Why might certain ancestral paths be more difficult to trace than others?

2. Do some research on the divorce law in your state. Has the law changed much over the past few decades, and if so, how? From a sociological perspective, why would the law change? Explain.

3. Talk to a marriage and family counselor or a professor of family law about the benefits of marriage versus cohabitation, or read what practical advice you can find on the Internet or in the library. What advantages does marriage offer that cohabitation does not? How important do those advantages seem to you?

Self-Quiz

Read each question carefully and then select the best answer.

1. Alice, age seven, lives in a private home with her parents, her grandmother, and her aunt. Alice's family is an example of a(n)
   a. nuclear family.
   b. dysfunctional family.
   c. extended family.
   d. polygynous family.

2. In which form of marriage may a person have several spouses in his or her lifetime, but only one spouse at a time?
   a. serial monogamy
   b. monogamy
   c. polygamy
   d. polyandry

3. The marriage of a woman to more than one man at the same time is referred to as
   a. polygyny.
   b. monogamy.
   c. serial monogamy.
   d. polyandry.

4. Which system of descent is followed in the United States?
   a. matrilineal
   b. patrilineal
   c. bilateral
   d. unilateral

5. According to the functionalist perspective, which of the following is *not* one of the paramount functions performed by the family?
   a. mediation
   b. reproduction
   c. regulation of sexual behavior
   d. affection and companionship

6. Which norm requires mate selection outside certain groups, usually one's own family or certain kinfolk?
   a. exogamy
   b. endogamy

   c. matriarchy
   d. patriarchy

7. According to the discussion of social class differences in family life and intimate relationships, which of the following statements is true?
   a. Social class differences in family life are more striking than they once were.
   b. The upper class emphasizes lineage and maintenance of family position.
   c. Among the poor, women usually play an insignificant role in the economic support of the family.
   d. In examining family life among racial and ethnic minorities, most patterns result from cultural, but *not* class, factors.

8. One recent development in family life in the United States has been the extension of parenthood as adult children continue to live at home or return home after college. The reason for this is
   a. the rising divorce rate.
   b. skyrocketing rent and real estate prices.
   c. financial difficulties.
   d. all of the above

9. In the United States, the *majority* of all babies born to unmarried teenage mothers are born to whom?
   a. African American adolescents
   b. White adolescents
   c. Latina adolescents
   d. Asian American adolescents

10. Which of the following factors is associated with the high divorce rate in the United States?
    a. the liberalization of divorce laws
    b. the fact that contemporary families have fewer children than earlier families did
    c. the general increase in family incomes
    d. all of the above

11. The principle of _____ assigns people to kinship groups according to their relationship to an individual's mother or father.

12. _____ emerged among Native American tribal societies, and in nations in which men were absent for long periods because of warfare or food-gathering expeditions.

13. In the view of many sociologists, the _____ family has begun to replace the patriarchal family as the social norm in the United States.

14. As _____ theorists point out, the social class of couples and their children significantly influences the socialization experiences to which the children are exposed and the protection they receive.

15. _____ focus on the micro level of family and other intimate relationships; for example, they are interested in whether people are cohabiting partners or are longtime married couples.

16. The rule of _____ specifies the groups within which a spouse must be found and prohibits marriage with others.

17. Social class differences in family life are less striking today than they once were; however, in the past, _____-class families were found to be more authoritarian in rearing children and more inclined to use physical punishment.

18. Caring for children is a(n) _____ function of the family, yet the ways in which different societies assign this function to family members can vary significantly.

19. Viewed from the _____ perspective, the government has a strong interest in encouraging adoption.

20. The rising rates of divorce and remarriage have led to a noticeable increase in _____ relationships.

_____

THINKING ABOUT MOVIES

Blue Valentine

A marriage unravels under personal and social pressure.

Goodbye Solo

In this moving drama about the role of family in people's lives, two quite different men form an unlikely pair.

The Kids Are Alright

A family copes when the children's birth father, a sperm donor, tries to become part of their lives.

▶ INSIDE

Religion is expressed in a variety of social settings. At this Christian rock festival in New Hampshire, fans pray in response to the music.

In the key case of *Engle v. Vitale,* the Supreme Court ruled in 1962 that the use of nondenominational prayer in New York schools was "wholly inconsistent" with the First Amendment's prohibition against government establishment of religion. In finding that organized school prayer violated the Constitution—even when no student was required to participate—the Court argued, in effect, that promoting religious observance was not a legitimate function of government or education. Subsequent Court decisions have allowed *voluntary* school prayer by students, but forbid school officials to *sponsor* any prayer or religious observance at school events. Despite these rulings, many public schools still regularly lead their students in prayer recitations or Bible readings. Other states have enacted "moments of silence" during the public school day, which many see as prayer in disguise (Robelon 2007).

As with school prayer, the teaching of creationism has significant support among the general public. Unlike Europeans, many people in the United States seem highly skeptical of evolutionary theory, which is taught as a matter of course in science classes. In 2009, a national survey showed that 39 percent of adults believe that God created humans in their present form. Almost as many believe that humans developed their present form with divine guidance (Gallup 2009a; Newport 2009).

The controversy over whether the biblical account of creation should be presented in school curricula recalls the famous "monkey trial" of 1925. In that trial, high school biology teacher John T. Scopes was convicted of violating a Tennessee law making it a crime to teach the scientific theory of evolution in public schools. Today, creationists have gone beyond espousing fundamentalist religious doctrine; they are attempting to reinforce their position regarding the origins of humanity and the universe with quasi-scientific data.

In 1987, the Supreme Court ruled that states could not compel the teaching of creationism in public schools if the primary purpose was to promote a religious viewpoint. In response, those who believe in the divine origin of life have recently advanced a concept called **intelligent design (ID),** the idea that life is so complex that it could only have been created by intelligent design. Though this concept is not based explicitly on the biblical account of creation, fundamentalists feel comfortable with it. Supporters of intelligent design consider it a more accurate account of the origin of life than Darwinism and hold that at the very least, ID should be taught as an alternative to the theory of evolution. But in 2005, in *Kitzmiller v. Dove Area School District,* a federal judge ended a Pennsylvania school district's plans to require teachers to present the concept in class. In essence, the judge found ID to be "a religious belief," a subtler but similar approach to creationism in that both find God's fingerprints in nature. The issue continues to be hotly debated and is expected to be the subject of future court cases (Clemmitt 2005; W. Tierney and Holley 2008).

Applying Sociology

Supporters of school prayer and of creationism feel that strict Court rulings have forced too great a separation between what Émile Durkheim called the *sacred* and the *profane.* They insist that the use of nondenominational prayer can in no way lead to the establishment of an ecclesia in the United States. Moreover, they believe that school prayer—and the teaching of creationism—can provide the spiritual guidance and socialization that many children today do not receive from parents or regular church attendance.

People on both sides of the debate between science and creationism invoke the name of Albert Einstein. Evolutionists emphasize the need for verifiable scientific data, like that which confirmed Einstein's groundbreaking scientific theories. Advocates of intelligent design quote the Nobel Prize-winning physicist's assertion that religion and science should coexist.

Many communities also believe that schools should transmit the dominant culture of the United States by encouraging prayer.

Opponents of school prayer and creationism argue that a religious majority in a community might impose viewpoints specific to its faith at the expense of religious minorities. These critics question whether school prayer can remain truly voluntary. Drawing on the interactionist perspective and small-group research, they suggest that children will face enormous social pressure to conform to the beliefs and practices of the majority.

Initiating Policy

Public school education is fundamentally a local issue, so most initiatives and lobbying have taken place at the local or state level. Federal courts have taken a hard line on religion in the schools. In a decision that the Supreme Court reversed in 2004, a federal appeals court ruled that reciting the phrase "under God" during the Pledge of Allegiance that opens each school day violates the U.S. Constitution (Religion News Service 2003).

Religion–school debates show no sign of ending. The activism of religious fundamentalists in the public school system raises the question "Whose ideas and values deserve a hearing in classrooms?" Critics see this campaign as one step toward sectarian religious control of public education. They worry that at some point in the future, teachers may not be able to use books or make statements that conflict with fundamentalist interpretations of the Bible. For advocates of a liberal education and of intellectual (and religious) diversity, this is a genuinely frightening prospect (Wilgoren 2005).

Take the Issue with You

1. Was there organized prayer in any school you attended? Was creationism part of the curriculum?

2. Do you think that promoting religious observance is a legitimate function of education?

3. How might a conflict theorist view the issue of organized school prayer?

66 There are many types of religious toys: stuffed torahs; Moses, David, and Jesus and the Tomb action figures; Noah's ark collections; and Resurrection Eggs, which supplement a young child's Easter book. "Lead your kids on a fun, faith-filled Easter egg hunt this year—one that teaches them about Jesus' death and resurrection! Each egg carton is filled with a dozen colorful plastic eggs. Pop them open and find miniature symbols of the Easter story inside." One of the dozen plastic eggs contains a crown of thorns, another is empty, representing the disappearance of the body of Jesus from the tomb, and pointing to his resurrection. Muslim toys include a mosque building set, mosque jewelry cases, and a prayer practice chart. Jewish toys include dreidels, wooden Shabbat sets, toy *sukkahs*, and a Plush Plagues Bag that includes "all 10 Plagues!"

Religious dolls are part of this wonderland of sacred fun. There are plush and plastic talking Bible dolls, pumped-up Christian action figures, dolls designed to support a Jewish girl's religious identity and conform to religious requirements, Goddess dolls designed for affluent young feminists, talking Muslim dolls that teach Arabic phrases, and "anti-Barbies"—Muslim dolls deliberately designed to compete with Barbie for the hearts and minds of young girls. There are plush Buddha and Siva dolls, and cuddly Jesus and Esther dolls as well.

Numerous card games and puzzles teach a variety of languages, including Hebrew, Arabic, and Punjabi. The Christian Book Distributors Web site not only offers religiously themed educational materials, they also offer nonreligious toys that appeal to parents with religious consciences who may be looking for nonviolent toys, such as a food groups toy with hand-painted pieces in four wooden crates, a pizza party game with different toppings, and a car towing game.

Not all religious toys are meant for the edification of the young. Many religious games and toys are satirical or simply products meant to be amusing enough to sell in an era where we are oversatiated with things, and any cultural phenomenon is fair game for marketing purposes. These items amuse or appall us, depending on how clever or offensive the item is, and for whom it is intended. . . .

Games and toys not only transmit cultural values but reflect them as well. . . . Games and religion have a long and complex history—they were used for divination and gambling, for this-worldly satire, and in the afterlife. Games were objects and methods used to interpret divine powers and influence supernatural forces. These religious and magical functions reflect the presence and movement of the sacred in the material world, indicators of a complex whole rather than a dualism where sacred and ordinary occupy separate realms.

Contemporary religious games have their roots in ancient practices, but their flavor—their style and substance—as well as their commercial focus reveal a specifically twenty-first century American form of religiosity. 99

Contemporary religious games have their roots in ancient practices, but their flavor—their style and substance—as well as their commercial focus reveal a specifically twenty-first century American form of religiosity.

(Bado-Fralick and Norris 2010:7–8, 29–30) Additional information about this excerpt can be found on the Online Learning Center at www.mhhe.com/schaefer13e.

In this excerpt from *Toying with God: The World of Religious Games and Dolls*, religious studies scholars Nikki Bado-Fralick and Rebecca Sachs Norris consider how religiously themed toys and games reflect both popular and religious culture. Depending on their purpose and design, the authors note, as well as on the social context in which they are used, these dolls and board games can either reinforce or undermine organized religion. Their impact on the children who play with them parallels the broader influence of religion on society. Despite the much-publicized decline of organized religion over the past century, even a casual observer can see that religion still permeates our social environment. As a result, nonbelievers are influenced by believers, whether they want to be or not. Similarly, believers are influenced by nonbelievers and by those of different faiths, despite any attempts they may make to screen out other points of view.

Indeed, religion plays a major role in people's lives, and religious practices of some sort are evident in every society. That makes religion a cultural universal, along with other common practices or beliefs found in every culture, such as dancing, food preparation, the family, and personal names. At present, an estimated 4 billion people belong to the world's many religious faiths.

When religion's influence on other social institutions in a society diminishes, the process of **secularization** is said to be under way. During this process, religion will survive in the private sphere of individual and family life (as in the case of many Native American families); it may even thrive on a personal level. But at the same time, other social institutions—such as the economy, politics, and education—maintain their own sets of norms, independent of religious guidance. Even so, religion is enormously resilient. Although specific faiths or organizations may change, their transformation does not signal the demise of religious faith. Rather, it contributes to the diversity of religious expression and organization (Christian Smith 2008; Stark 2004).

Like religion, education is a cultural universal. As such it is an important aspect of socialization—the lifelong process of learning the attitudes, values, and behavior considered appropriate to members of a particular culture. As we saw in Chapter 4, socialization can occur in the classroom or at home, through interactions with parents, teachers, friends, and even strangers. Exposure to books, toys and games, and other forms of communication also promotes socialization.

What social purposes does religion serve? Does it help to hold society together or foster social change? What happens when religion mixes with politics? Does religion belong in the public schools? In this chapter we will study the formal systems of religion that characterize modern industrial societies. We will begin with a brief description of the sociological perspectives on religion, followed by an overview of the world's major religions. Next, we will explore religion's role in societal integration, social support, social change, and social control. We'll examine three important components of religious behavior—belief, ritual, and experience—as well as the basic forms of religious organization, including new religious movements. In a case study, we'll take a fascinating look at religion in India. The chapter will close with a Social Policy section on religion in the schools.

Durkheim and the Sociological Approach to Religion

If a group believes that it is being directed by a "vision from God," sociologists do not attempt to prove or disprove the revelation. Instead, they assess the effects of the religious experience on the group. What sociologists are interested in is the social impact of religion on individuals and institutions.

Émile Durkheim was perhaps the first sociologist to recognize the critical importance of religion in human societies. He saw its appeal for the individual, but more important, he stressed the *social* impact of religion. In Durkheim's view, religion is a collective act that includes many forms of behavior in which people interact with others. As in his work on suicide, Durkheim was not so interested in the personalities of religious believers as he was in understanding religious behavior within a social context.

Durkheim defined **religion** as a "unified system of beliefs and practices relative to sacred things." In his view, religion involves a set of beliefs and practices that are uniquely the property of religion, as opposed to other social institutions and ways of thinking. Durkheim ([1893] 1933; [1912] 2001) argued that religious faiths distinguish between certain transcending

events and the everyday world. He referred to those realms as the *sacred* and the *profane.*

The **sacred** encompasses elements beyond everyday life that inspire awe, respect, and even fear. People become part of the sacred realm only by completing some ritual, such as prayer or sacrifice. Because believers have faith in the sacred, they accept what they cannot understand. In contrast, the **profane** includes the ordinary and commonplace. This concept can be confusing, however, because the same object can be either sacred or profane, depending on how it is viewed. A normal dining room table is profane, but it becomes sacred to some Christians if it bears the elements of a communion. A candelabra becomes sacred to Jews if it is a menorah. For Confucians and Taoists, incense sticks are not mere decorative items, but highly valued offerings to the gods in religious ceremonies that mark the new and full moons.

Following the direction established by Durkheim a century ago, contemporary sociologists view religion in two different ways. First, they study the norms and values of religious faiths by examining their substantive beliefs. For example, it is possible to compare the degree to which Christian faiths interpret the Bible literally, or Muslim groups follow the Qur'an (or Koran), the sacred book of Islam. At the same time, sociologists examine religion in terms of the social functions it fulfills, such as providing social support or reinforcing social norms. By exploring both the beliefs and the functions of religion, we can better understand its impact on the individual, on groups, and on society as a whole.

thinking CRITICALLY

What objects that you regard as profane might others consider to be sacred?

World Religions

Worldwide, tremendous diversity exists in religious beliefs and practices. Overall, about 89 percent of the world's population adheres to some religion; thus, only about 10 percent is nonreligious. This level of adherence changes over time and also varies by country and age group. In the United States today, those who are nonreligious account for about 16 percent of the population; in 1900, they accounted for a mere 1.3 percent of all Americans.

Faith	Current Following, in Millions (and Percentage of World Population)	Primary Location of Followers Today	Founder (and Approximate Birth Date)	Important Texts (and Holy Sites)
Buddhism	463 (6.7%)	Southeast Asia, Mongolia, Tibet	Gautama Siddhartha (563 B.C.)	Triptaka (areas in Nepal)
Christianity	2,281 (33.0%)	Europe, North America, South America	Jesus (6 B.C.)	Bible (Jerusalem, Rome)
Hinduism	935 (13.7%)	India, Indian communities overseas	No specific founder (1500 B.C.)	Sruti and Smrti texts (seven sacred cities, including Vavansi)
Islam	1,553 (22.5%)	Middle East, Central Asia, North Africa, Indonesia	Mohammad (A.D. 570)	Qur'an, or Koran (Mecca, Medina, Jerusalem)
Judaism	15 (0.2%)	Israel, United States, France, Russia	Abraham (2000 B.C.)	Torah, Talmud (Jerusalem)

Source: Author, based on Britannica Online 2011; Swatos 1998.

And in 2010, 23 percent of incoming U.S. college students had no religious preference, compared to 11 percent of their mothers (Newport 2010b; Pryor et al. 2010).

Christianity is the largest single faith in the world; the second largest is Islam (Table 15-1). Although global news events often suggest an inherent conflict between Christians and Muslims, the two faiths are similar in many ways. Both are monotheistic (based on a single deity); both include a belief in prophets, an afterlife, and a judgment day. In fact, Islam recognizes Jesus as a prophet, though not as the son of God. Both faiths impose a moral code on believers, which varies from fairly rigid proscriptions for fundamentalists to relatively relaxed guidelines for liberals.

The followers of Islam, called *Muslims,* believe that Islam's holy scriptures were received from Allah (God) by the prophet Mohammad nearly 1,400 years ago. They see Mohammad as the last in a long line of prophets, preceded by Adam, Abraham, Moses, and Jesus. Islam is more communal in its expression than Christianity, particularly the more individualistic Protestant denominations. Consequently, in countries that are predominantly Muslim, the separation of religion and the state is not considered necessary or even desirable. In fact, Muslim governments often reinforce Islamic practices through their laws. Muslims do vary sharply in their interpretation of several traditions, some of which—such as the wearing of veils by women—are more cultural than religious in origin.

Like Christianity and Islam, Judaism is monotheistic. Jews believe that God's true nature is revealed in the Torah, which Christians know as the first five books of the Old Testament. According to these scriptures, God formed a covenant, or pact, with Abraham and Sarah, the ancestors of the tribes of Israel. Even today, Jews believe, this covenant holds them accountable to God's will. If they follow both the letter and spirit of the Torah, a long-awaited Messiah will one day bring paradise to earth. Although Judaism has a relatively small following compared to other major faiths, it forms the historical foundation for both Christianity and Islam. That is why Jews revere many of the same sacred Middle Eastern sites as Christians and Muslims.

Two other major faiths developed in a different part of the world, India. The earliest, Hinduism, originated around 1500 B.C. Hinduism differs from Judaism, Christianity, and Islam in that it embraces a number of gods and minor gods, although most worshippers are devoted primarily to a single deity, such as Shiva or Vishnu. Hinduism is also distinguished by a belief in reincarnation, or the perpetual rebirth of the soul after death. Unlike Judaism, Christianity, and Islam, which are

SPOTTING

TREND

None of the Above: The Nonreligious

Many people noted and were dismayed by a statement in President Obama's inaugural address, "We are a nation of Christians and Muslims, Jews and Hindus, and nonbelievers." Yet the President was merely acknowledging a long-noted pattern, the gradual growth in the proportion of U.S. residents who indicate they have no religion.

National surveys reveal that between 1990 and 2008, the number of Americans who identify themselves as having no religion doubled. Moreover, the proportion of people who give no answer to questions about religion suggests that currently, about 20 percent of the adult population—well over 60 million people—has no overt religious identity.

The growth of the "none of the above" category does not mean that those respondents do not believe in God, however. A third of them say that they pray weekly or daily, and less than 1 percent call themselves atheists. Nevertheless, while the phrase "In God We Trust" still seems to apply, more and more people are choosing not to affiliate themselves with organized religion.

FIGURE **15-1** TEST YOUR RELIGIOUS KNOWLEDGE

333

Religion

Compare your knowledge of religion with that of the U.S. population as a whole. In a 2010 national survey, the average respondent answered seven or eight questions correctly.

Religious Knowledge Quiz

1 Which Bible figure is most closely associated with leading the exodus from Egypt?

- ○ Job
- ○ Elijah
- ○ Moses
- ○ Abraham

2 What was Mother Teresa's religion?

- ○ Catholic
- ○ Jewish
- ○ Buddhist
- ○ Mormon
- ○ Hindu

3. Which of the following is NOT one of the Ten Commandments?

- ○ Do not commit adultery
- ○ Do unto others as you would have them do unto you
- ○ Do not steal
- ○ Keep the Sabbath holy

4 When does the Jewish Sabbath begin?

- ○ Friday
- ○ Saturday
- ○ Sunday

5 Is Ramadan...?

- ○ The Hindu festival of lights
- ○ A Jewish day of atonement
- ○ The Islamic holy month

6 Which of the following best describes the Catholic teaching about the bread and wine used for Communion?

- ○ The bread and wine actually <u>become</u> the body and blood of Jesus Christ.
- ○ The bread and wine are <u>symbols</u> of the body and blood of Jesus Christ.

7 In which religion are Vishnu and Shiva central figures?

- ○ Islam
- ○ Hinduism
- ○ Taoism

8 Which Bible figure is most closely associated with remaining obedient to God despite suffering?

- ○ Job
- ○ Elijah
- ○ Moses
- ○ Abraham

9 What was Joseph Smith's religion?

- ○ Catholic
- ○ Jewish
- ○ Buddhist
- ○ Mormon
- ○ Hindu

10 According to rulings by the U.S. Supreme Court, is a public school teacher permitted to lead a class in prayer, or not?

- ○ Yes, permitted
- ○ No, not permitted

11 According to rulings by the U.S. Supreme Court, is a public school teacher permitted to read from the Bible as an example of literature, or not?

- ○ Yes, permitted
- ○ No, not permitted

12 What religion do <u>most</u> people in Pakistan consider themselves?

- ○ Buddhist
- ○ Hindu
- ○ Muslim
- ○ Christian

13 What was the name of the person whose writings and actions inspired the Protestant Reformation?

- ○ Martin Luther
- ○ Thomas Aquinas
- ○ John Wesley

14 Which of these religions aims at nirvana, the state of being free from suffering?

- ○ Islam
- ○ Buddhism
- ○ Hinduism

15 Which of these preachers participated in the period of religious activity known as the First Great Awakening?

- ○ Jonathan Edwards
- ○ Charles Finney
- ○ Billy Graham

ANSWERS: 1. Moses 2. Catholic 3. Do unto others as you would have them do unto you 4. Friday 5. The Islamic holy month 6. The bread and wine actually become the body and blood of Jesus Christ. 7. Hinduism 8. Job 9. Mormon 10. No, not permitted 11. Yes, permitted 12. Muslim 13. Martin Luther 14. Buddhism 15. Jonathan Edwards

Sources: Pew Forum on Religion and Public Life 2010a, 2010b.

based largely on sacred texts, Hindu beliefs have been preserved mostly through oral tradition.

A second religion, Buddhism, developed in the sixth century B.C. as a reaction against Hinduism. This faith is founded on the teachings of Siddhartha (later called Buddha, or "the enlightened one"). Through meditation, followers of Buddhism strive to overcome selfish cravings for physical or material pleasures, with the goal of reaching a state of enlightenment, or nirvana. Buddhists created the first monastic orders, which are thought to be the models for monastic orders in other religions, including

Christianity. Though Buddhism emerged in India, its followers were eventually driven out of that country by the Hindus. It is now found primarily in other parts of Asia. (Contemporary adherents of Buddhism in India are relatively recent converts.)

use your sociological *imagination*

What evidence do you see of different religions in the area surrounding your college or university? What about on campus?

Although the differences among religions are striking, they are exceeded by variations within faiths. Consider the variations within Christianity, from relatively liberal denominations such as Presbyterians or the United Church of Christ to the more conservative Mormons and Greek Orthodox Catholics. Similar variations exist within Hinduism, Islam, and other world religions (Barrett et al. 2008; Swatos 1998).

In 2010, the Pew Forum on Religion and Public Life conducted a national survey to determine how much Americans know about world religions. Figure 15-1 reproduces some of the questions from the survey. Try testing your own knowledge.

Sociological Perspectives on Religion

Since religion is a cultural universal, it is not surprising that it plays a basic role in human societies. In sociological terms, it performs both manifest and latent functions. Among its *manifest* (open and stated) functions, religion defines the spiritual world and gives meaning to the divine. It provides an explanation for events that seem difficult to understand, such as what lies beyond the grave. The *latent* functions of religion are unintended, covert, or hidden. Even though the manifest function of a church service is to offer a forum for religious worship, it might at the same time fulfill a latent social function as a meeting ground for unmarried members.

Functionalists and conflict theorists both evaluate religion's impact on human societies. We'll consider a functionalist view of religion's role in integrating society, providing social support, and promoting social change, and then look at religion from the conflict and feminist perspectives, as a means of social control. Note that for the most part, religion's impact is best understood from a macro-level viewpoint that is oriented toward the larger society. Its social support function is an exception: it is best understood on the micro, or individual, level.

The Integrative Function of Religion

Émile Durkheim viewed religion as an integrative force in human society—a perspective that is reflected in functionalist thought today. Durkheim sought to answer a perplexing question: "How can human societies be held together when they are generally composed of individuals and social groups with diverse interests and aspirations?" In his view, religious bonds often transcend these personal and divisive forces. Durkheim acknowledged that religion is not the only integrative force; nationalism or patriotism may serve the same end.

In 2010 Jose H. Gomez (at the podium) became archbishop of Los Angeles, the largest Roman Catholic archdiocese in the United States. Born in Mexico, Gomez became a U.S. citizen while serving as a priest in Texas. His elevation reflects the growth of the Hispanic faithful among Roman Catholics in the United States.

How does religion provide this "societal glue"? Religion, whether it be Buddhism, Islam, Christianity, or Judaism, gives meaning and purpose to people's lives. It offers certain ultimate values and ends to hold in common. Although they are subjective and not always fully accepted, these values and ends help society to function as an integrated social system. For example, funerals, weddings, bar and bat mitzvahs, and confirmations serve to integrate people into larger communities by providing shared beliefs and values about the ultimate questions of life.

Religion also holds society together by socializing young children. Many of the dolls, games, and toys that Bado-Fralick and Norris (2010) described in the chapter-opening excerpt fulfill the socialization function even as they entertain. Within the context of play, they not only socialize but educate and proselytize young people.

The integrative power of religion can be seen, too, in the role that churches, synagogues, and mosques have traditionally played and continue to play for immigrant groups in the United States. For example, Roman Catholic immigrants may settle near a parish church that offers services in their native language, such as Polish or Spanish. Similarly, Korean immigrants may join a Presbyterian church that has many Korean American members and follows religious practices like those of churches in Korea. Like other religious organizations, these Roman Catholic and Presbyterian churches help to integrate immigrants into their new homeland.

In recent years, the most talked about immigrant religious group has been Muslims. Throughout the world, including the United States, Muslims are divided into a variety of sects, including Sunni and Shia (or Shiite). However, inside and outside these sects, people express their Islamic faith in many different ways. To speak of Muslims as being either Sunni or Shia would be like speaking of Christians as either Roman Catholic or Baptist.

Depending on the circumstances, Islam in the United States can be integrative by faith, ethnicity, or both. The great majority of Muslims in the United States are Sunni Muslims—literally, those who follow the *Sunnah,* or way of the Prophet. Compared to other Muslims, Sunnis tend to be more moderate in their religious orthodoxy. The Shia, who come primarily from Iraq and Iran, are the second-largest group. Shia Muslims are more attentive to guidance from accepted Islamic scholars than are Sunnis. In sufficient numbers, these two Muslim groups will choose to worship separately, even if they must cross ethnic or linguistic lines to do so (Selod 2008a).

In some instances, religious loyalties are *dysfunctional;* that is, they contribute to tension and even conflict between groups or nations. During the Second World War, the German Nazis attempted to exterminate the Jewish people; approximately 6 million European Jews were killed. In modern times, nations such as Lebanon (Muslims versus Christians), Israel (Jews versus Muslims, as well as Orthodox versus secular Jews), Northern Ireland (Roman Catholics versus Protestants), and India (Hindus versus Muslims, and more recently, Sikhs) have been torn by clashes that are in large part based on religion. (See the case study on page 342 for a more detailed discussion of religious conflict in India.)

In the United States, Muslim Americans must focus strongly on their faith to survive within the permissive mainstream culture. This Islamic school allows Muslim girls to play basketball without compromising their modesty.

Religion and Social Support

Most of us find it difficult to accept the stressful events of life—the death of a loved one, serious injury, bankruptcy, divorce, and so forth—especially when something "senseless" happens. How can family and friends come to terms with the death of a talented college student, not even 20 years old?

Through its emphasis on the divine and the supernatural, religion allows us to "do something" about the calamities we face. In some faiths, adherents can offer sacrifices or pray to a deity in the belief that such acts will change their earthly condition. On a more basic level, religion encourages us to view our personal misfortunes as relatively unimportant in the broader perspective of human history—or even as part of an undisclosed divine purpose. Friends and relatives of the deceased college student may see his death as being "God's will," or as having some ultimate benefit that we cannot understand now. This perspective may be much more comforting than the terrifying feeling that any of us can die senselessly at any moment—and that there is no divine answer to why one person lives a long and full life, while another dies tragically at a relatively early age.

Faith-based community organizations have taken on more and more responsibilities in the area of social assistance. In fact, President George W. Bush created the Office of Faith-Based and Community Initiatives to give socially active religious groups access to government funding. Renamed the

Office of Faith-Based and Neighborhood Partnerships under the Obama administration, the agency has acquired three new tasks: encouraging pro-life and pro-choice advocates to cooperate in reducing abortions; dealing with the special problems of children raised in fatherless homes; and fostering interfaith dialogue with religious leaders around the world. There is some evidence of such groups' effectiveness in helping others. Sociologist William Julius Wilson (1999) has singled out faith-based organizations in 40 communities from California to Massachusetts as models of social reform. These organizations identify experienced leaders and assemble them into nonsectarian coalitions that are devoted to community development (White House 2011).

Religion and Social Change

The Weberian Thesis When someone seems driven to work and succeed, we often attribute the Protestant work ethic to that person. The term comes from the writings of Max Weber, who carefully examined the connection between religious allegiance and capitalist development. Weber's findings appeared in his pioneering work *The Protestant Ethic and the Spirit of Capitalism* ([1904] 2011).

Weber noted that in European nations with both Protestant and Catholic citizens, an overwhelming number of business leaders, owners of capital, and skilled workers were Protestant. In his view, this fact was no mere coincidence. Weber pointed out that the followers of John Calvin (1509–1564), a leader of the Protestant Reformation, emphasized a disciplined work ethic, this-worldly concerns, and a rational orientation to life that have become known as the **Protestant ethic.** One byproduct of the Protestant ethic was a drive to accumulate savings that could be used for future investment. This "spirit of capitalism," to use Weber's phrase, contrasted with the moderate work hours, leisurely work habits, and lack of ambition that Weber saw as typical of the times.

A Protestant congregation worships at Sunday service. Although Weber traced the "spirit of capitalism" to Protestant teachings, in the United States today Protestants and Catholics share the same work ethic.

Few books on the sociology of religion have aroused as much commentary and criticism as Weber's work. It has been hailed as one of the most important theoretical works in the field and an excellent example of macro-level analysis. Like Durkheim, Weber demonstrated that religion is not solely a matter of intimate personal beliefs. He stressed that the collective nature of religion has consequences for society as a whole.

Weber provided a convincing description of the origins of European capitalism. But this economic system has now been adopted by non-Calvinists in many parts of the world. Studies done in the United States today show little or no difference in achievement orientation between Roman Catholics and Protestants. Apparently, the "spirit of capitalism" has emerged as a generalized cultural trait rather than a specific religious tenet (Greeley 1989).

Conflict theorists caution that Weber's theory—even if it is accepted—should not be regarded as an analysis of mature capitalism, as reflected in the rise of multinational corporations. Marxists would disagree with Weber not on the origins of capitalism, but on its future. Unlike Marx, Weber believed that capitalism could endure indefinitely as an economic system. He added, however, that the decline of religion as an overriding force in society opened the way for workers to express their discontent more vocally (R. Collins 1980).

Liberation Theology Sometimes the clergy can be found in the forefront of social change. Many religious activists, especially in the Roman Catholic Church in Latin America, support **liberation theology**—the use of a church in a political effort to eliminate poverty, discrimination, and other forms of injustice from a secular society. Advocates of this religious movement sometimes sympathize with Marxism. Many believe that radical change, rather than economic development in itself, is the only acceptable solution to the desperation of the masses in impoverished developing countries. Activists associated with liberation theology believe that organized religion has a moral responsibility to take a strong public stand against the oppression of the poor, racial and ethnic minorities, and women (Christian Smith 1991).

The term *liberation theology* dates back to the publication in 1973 of the English translation of *A Theology of Liberation*. The book was written by a Peruvian priest, Gustavo Gutiérrez, who

lived in a slum area of Lima during the early 1960s. After years of exposure to the vast poverty around him, Gutiérrez concluded that "in order to serve the poor, one had to move into political action." Eventually, politically committed Latin American theologians came under the influence of social scientists who viewed the domination of capitalism and multinational corporations as central to the hemisphere's problems. One result was a new approach to theology that built on the cultural and religious traditions of Latin America rather than on models developed in Europe and the United States (R. M. Brown 1980:23; G. Gutiérrez 1990).

Liberation theology may be dysfunctional, however. Some Roman Catholic worshippers have come to believe that by focusing on political and governmental injustice, the clergy are no longer addressing their personal and spiritual needs. Partly as a result of such disenchantment, some Catholics in Latin America are converting to mainstream Protestant faiths or to Mormonism.

---

use your sociological *imagination*

The social support that religious groups provide is suddenly withdrawn from your community. How will your life or the lives of others change? What will happen if religious groups stop pushing for social change?

Religion and Social Control: A Conflict View

Liberation theology is a relatively recent phenomenon that marks a break with the traditional role of churches. It was this traditional role that Karl Marx ([1844] 1964) opposed. In his view, religion *impeded* social change by encouraging oppressed people to focus on otherworldly concerns rather than on their immediate poverty or exploitation. Marx described religion as an opiate that was particularly harmful to oppressed peoples. He felt that religion often drugged the masses into submission by offering a consolation for their harsh lives on earth: the hope of salvation in an ideal afterlife. For example, during the period of slavery in the United States, White masters forbade Blacks to practice native African religions, while encouraging them to adopt Christianity, which taught them that obedience would lead to salvation and eternal happiness in the hereafter. Viewed from a conflict perspective, Christianity may have pacified certain slaves and blunted the rage that often fuels rebellion.

Today, however, people around the world see religion more as a source of support through adversity than a source of oppression. In a combination of public opinion polls taken across 114 nations, 95 percent of those living in the poorest nations felt that religion was important in daily life, compared to only 47 percent of those in the wealthiest countries (Crabtree 2010).

Theoretical Perspective	Emphasis
Functionalist	Religion as a source of social integration and unification
	Religion as a source of social support for individuals
Conflict	Religion as a potential obstacle to structural social change
	Religion as a potential source of structural social change (through liberation theology)
Feminist	Religion as an instrument of women's subordination, except for their role in religious socialization
Interactionist	Individual religious expression through belief, ritual, and experience

Religion does play an important role in propping up the existing social structure. The values of religion, as already noted, tend to reinforce other social institutions and the social order as a whole. From Marx's perspective, however, religion's promotion of social stability only helps to perpetuate patterns of social inequality. According to Marx, the dominant religion reinforces the interests of those in power.

For example, contemporary Christianity reinforces traditional patterns of behavior that call for the subordination of the less powerful. The role of women in the church is an example of this uneven distribution of power. Assumptions about gender roles leave women in a subservient position both within Christian churches and at home. In fact, women find it as difficult to achieve leadership positions in many churches as they do in large corporations. A "stained glass ceiling" tends to stunt clergywomen's career development, even in the most liberal denominations.

Like Marx, conflict theorists argue that to whatever extent religion actually does influence social behavior, it reinforces existing patterns of dominance and inequality. From a Marxist perspective, religion keeps people from seeing their lives and societal conditions in political terms—for example, by obscuring the overriding significance of conflicting economic interests. Marxists suggest that by inducing a "false consciousness" among the disadvantaged, religion lessens the possibility of collective political action that could end capitalist oppression and transform society.

Feminist Perspective

Drawing on the feminist approach, researchers and theorists have stressed the fundamental role women play in religious socialization. Most people develop their allegiance to a particular faith in their childhood, with their mothers playing a critical role in the process. Significantly, nonworshipping mothers tend to influence their children to be highly skeptical of organized religion.

However, women generally take a subordinate role in religious governance. Indeed, most faiths have a long tradition of exclusively male spiritual leadership. Furthermore, because most religions are patriarchal, they tend to reinforce men's dominance in secular as well as spiritual matters. Women do play a vital role as volunteers, staff, and religious educators, but even today, religious decision making and leadership typically fall to the men. Exceptions to this rule, such as the Shakers and Christian Scientists, as well as Hinduism with its long goddess heritage, are rare (R. Schaefer and Zellner 2011).

In the United States, women are much more likely than men to be affiliated with religion, to pray, to believe in God, to claim that religion is important in their lives, and to attend weekly worship services. Yet organized religion typically does not give them leadership roles. Nationally, women compose 17 percent of U.S. clergy, though they account for 34 percent of students enrolled in theological institutions. Women clerics typically have shorter careers than men, often in related fields that do not involve congregational leadership, such as counseling. In faiths that restrict leadership positions to men, women serve unofficially. For example, about 4 percent of Roman Catholic congregations are led by women who hold nonordained pastoral positions—a necessity in a church facing a shortage of male priests (Association of Theological Schools 2011; Bureau of the Census 2010a:Table 615).

Table 15-2 summarizes the four major sociological perspectives on religion.

thinking CRITICALLY

Explain how the Weberian thesis and liberation theology promote social change.

Components of Religion

All religions have certain elements in common, yet those elements are expressed in the distinctive manner of each faith. These patterns of religious behavior, like other patterns of social behavior, are of great interest to sociologists—especially interactionists—because they underscore the relationship between religion and society.

Although the number of women clergy has increased, only about 1 in 6 spiritual leaders is a woman, and in many faiths women are still banned from serving.

Religious beliefs, religious rituals, and religious experience all help to define what is sacred and to differentiate the sacred from the profane. Let's examine these three components of religion, as seen through the eyes of interactionists.

Belief

Some people believe in life after death, in supreme beings with unlimited powers, or in supernatural forces. **Religious beliefs** are statements to which members of a particular religion adhere. These views can vary dramatically from religion to religion.

In the late 1960s, something rather remarkable took place in the expression of religious beliefs in the United States. Denominations that held to relatively liberal interpretations of religious scripture (such as the Presbyterians, Methodists, and Lutherans) declined in membership, while those that held to more conservative interpretations grew in numbers. Furthermore, in most faiths, those members who held strict views of scripture became more outspoken, questioning those who remained open to a variety of newer interpretations.

This trend toward *fundamentalism* ran counter to the secularization that was evident in the wider society. **Fundamentalism** may be defined as an emphasis on doctrinal conformity and the literal interpretation of sacred texts. The phrase "religious fundamentalism" was first applied to Protestant believers in the United States who took a literal interpretation of the Bible, but fundamentalism is found worldwide among all major religious groups, including Roman Catholicism, Islam, and Judaism. Even in relatively new faiths, some adherents contend that too much has changed. For followers of many religions, fundamentalists can be as challenging to accommodate as secularists.

Fundamentalists vary immensely in their behavior. Some stress the need to be strict in their own personal faith but take little interest in broad social issues. Others are watchful of societal actions, such as government policies, that they see as conflicting with fundamentalist doctrine.

The Adam and Eve account of creation found in Genesis, the first book of the Old Testament, is an example of a religious belief. Many people in the United States strongly adhere to this biblical explanation of creation and even insist that it be taught in public schools. These people, known as *creationists,* are worried by the secularization of society, and oppose teaching that directly or indirectly questions biblical scripture. The Social Policy section at the end of this chapter examines the issue of religion in the schools in depth.

In general, spirituality is not as strong in industrialized nations as in developing nations. The United States is an exception to the trend toward secularization, in part because the government encourages religious expression (without explicitly supporting it) by allowing religious groups to claim charitable status, and even to receive federal aid for activities such as educational services. And although belief in God is relatively weak in formerly communist states such as Russia, surveys show a growth in spirituality in those countries over the past 10 years (Norris and Inglehart 2004).

Ritual

Religious rituals are practices required or expected of members of a faith. Rituals usually honor the divine power (or powers) worshiped by believers; they also remind adherents of their religious duties and responsibilities. Rituals and beliefs can be interdependent; rituals generally affirm beliefs, as in a public or private statement confessing a sin. Like any social institution, religion develops distinctive norms to structure people's behavior. Moreover, sanctions are attached to religious rituals, whether rewards (bar mitzvah gifts) or penalties (expulsion from a religious institution for violation of norms).

In the United States, rituals may be quite simple, such as saying grace at a meal or observing a moment of silence to commemorate someone's death. Yet certain rituals, such as the process of canonizing a saint, are quite elaborate. Most religious rituals in our culture focus on services conducted at houses of worship. Attendance at a service, silent and spoken prayers, communion, and singing of spiritual hymns and chants are common forms of ritual behavior that generally take place in group settings. From an interactionist perspective, these rituals serve as important face-to-face encounters in which people reinforce their religious beliefs and their commitment to their faith.

For Muslims, a very important ritual is the *hajj,* a pilgrimage to the Grand Mosque in Mecca, Saudi Arabia. Every Muslim who is physically and financially able is expected to make this trip at least once. Each year 3 million pilgrims go to Mecca during the one-week period indicated by the Islamic lunar calendar. Muslims from all over the world make the *hajj,* including those in the United States, where many tours are arranged to facilitate the trip.

In recent decades, participation in religious rituals has tended to hold steady or decline in most countries. Figure 15-2 on page 340 shows religious participation in selected countries.

Experience

In the sociological study of religion, the term **religious experience** refers to the feeling or perception of being in direct contact with the ultimate reality, such as a divine being, or of being overcome with religious emotion. A religious experience may be rather slight, such as the feeling of exaltation a person receives from hearing a choir sing Handel's "Hallelujah Chorus." But many religious experiences are more profound, such as a Muslim's experience on a *hajj.* In his autobiography, the late African American activist Malcolm X ([1964] 1999:338) wrote of his *hajj* and how deeply moved he was by the way that Muslims in Mecca came together across race and color lines. For Malcolm X, the color blindness of the Muslim world "proved to me the power of the One God."

Another profound religious experience, for many Christians, is being *born again*—that is, at a turning point in one's life, making a personal commitment to Jesus. According to a 2010 national survey, 42 percent of people in the United States claim they have had a born-again Christian experience at some time in their lives. An earlier survey found that Southern Baptists (75 percent) were the most likely to report such experiences; in contrast, only 21 percent of Catholics and 24 percent of Episcopalians stated that they had been born again. The collective nature of religion, as emphasized by Durkheim, is evident in these statistics. The beliefs and rituals of a particular faith can create an atmosphere either friendly or indifferent to this type of religious experience. Thus, a Baptist would be encouraged to come forward and share such experiences with others, whereas an Episcopalian

Pilgrims on *hajj* to the Grand Mosque in Mecca, Saudi Arabia. Islam requires all Muslims who are able to undertake this religious ritual at least once in a lifetime.

Arabia and Buddhism in Thailand. However, significant differences exist within this category. In Saudi Arabia's Islamic regime, leaders of the ecclesia hold vast power over actions of the state. In contrast, the Lutheran Church in contemporary Sweden holds no such power over the Riksdag (parliament) or the prime minister.

Generally, ecclesiae are conservative, in that they do not challenge the leaders of a secular government. In a society with an ecclesia, the political and religious institutions often act in harmony and reinforce each other's power in their relative spheres of influence. In the modern world, ecclesiae are declining in power.

Denominations

A **denomination** is a large, organized religion that is not officially linked to the state or government. Like an ecclesia, it tends to have an explicit set of beliefs, a defined system of authority, and a generally respected position in society. Denominations claim as members large segments of a population. Generally, children accept the denomination of their parents and give little thought to membership in other faiths. Denominations also resemble ecclesiae in that they make few demands on members. However, there is a critical difference between these two forms of religious organization. Although the denomination is considered respectable and is not viewed as a challenge to the secular government, it lacks the official recognition and power held by an ecclesia (Doress and Porter 1977).

The United States is home to a large number of denominations. In good measure, this diversity is a result of our nation's immigrant heritage. Many settlers brought with them the religious commitments native to their homelands. Some Christian denominations in the United States, such as the Roman Catholics, Episcopalians, and Lutherans, are the outgrowth of ecclesiae established in Europe. New Christian denominations also emerged, including the Mormons and Christian Scientists. Within the past generation, immigrants have increased the number of Muslims, Hindus, and Buddhists living in the United States.

Although by far the largest denomination in the United States is Roman Catholicism, at least 22 other Christian faiths have 1 million or more members. Protestants collectively accounted for about 45 percent of the nation's adult population in 2010, compared to 21 percent for Roman Catholics and 2 percent for Jews. There are also 5 million Muslims in the United States, and large numbers of people adhere to Eastern faiths such as Buddhism (3 million) and Hinduism (1 million) (Britannica Online 2011; Gallup 2011a; Lindner 2011).

Sects

A **sect** can be defined as a relatively small religious group that has broken away from some other religious organization to renew what it considers the original vision of the faith. Many sects, such

---

who claims to have been born again would receive much less interest (Gallup 2011a; Gallup Opinion Index 1978).

Table 15-3 summarizes the three components of religion.

thinking CRITICALLY

Which component of religion is easiest to measure? Which is hardest to measure? Explain.

Religious Organization

The collective nature of religion has led to many forms of religious association. In modern societies, religion has become increasingly formalized. Specific structures such as churches and synagogues have been constructed for religious worship; individuals have been trained for occupational roles within various fields. These developments make it possible to distinguish clearly between the sacred and secular parts of one's life—a distinction that could not be made easily in earlier times, when religion was largely a family activity carried out in the home.

Sociologists find it useful to distinguish between four basic forms of organization: the ecclesia, the denomination, the sect, and the new religious movement, or cult. We can see differences among these four forms of organization in their size, power, degree of commitment that is expected from members, and historical ties to other faiths.

Ecclesiae

An **ecclesia** (plural, *ecclesiae*) is a religious organization that claims to include most or all members of a society and is recognized as the national or official religion. Since virtually everyone belongs to the faith, membership is by birth rather than conscious decision. Examples of ecclesiae include Islam in Saudi

FIGURE 15-2 RELIGIOUS PARTICIPATION IN SELECTED COUNTRIES

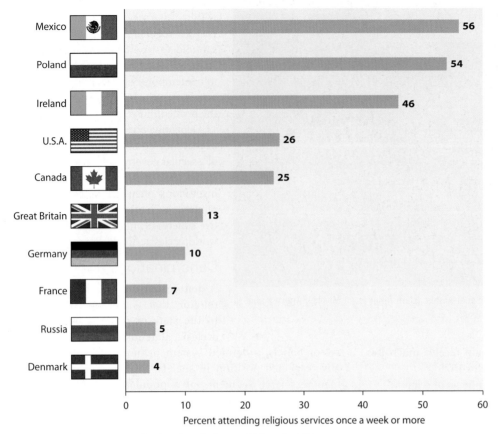

Percent attending religious services once a week or more

Note: Data are for 2006, except for Canada and Mexico, which are for 2004.
Source: Tom W. Smith 2009:28, 60, 72.

Think about It
Are you surprised by the variation in religious participation from one nation to another? Why or why not?

and Bainbridge 1985). Max Weber ([1916] 1958:114) termed the sect a "believer's church," because affiliation is based on conscious acceptance of a specific religious dogma.

Sects are fundamentally at odds with society and do not seek to become established national religions. Unlike ecclesiae and denominations, they require intensive commitments and demonstrations of belief by members. Partly owing to their outsider status, sects frequently exhibit a higher degree of religious fervor and loyalty than more established religious groups. Recruitment focuses mainly on adults, and acceptance comes through conversion.

Sects are often short-lived. Those that survive may become less antagonistic to society over time and begin to resemble denominations. In a few instances, sects have endured over several generations while remaining fairly separate from society. Sociologist J. Milton Yinger (1970:226–273) uses the term **established sect** to describe a religious group that is the outgrowth of a sect, yet remains isolated from society. Hutterites, Jehovah's Witnesses, Seventh-Day Adventists, and Amish are contemporary examples of established sects in the United States.

TABLE 15-3 COMPONENTS OF RELIGION

summing up

Element	Definition	Examples
Belief	Statement to which members of a particular religion adhere	Creation account Sacred characters or people
Ritual	Practice required or expected of members of a faith	Worship Prayer Singing or chanting
Experience	Feeling or perception of being in direct contact with the ultimate reality (such as a divine being) or of being overcome with religious emotion	Born-again experience Communion with holy spirit

Use Your Sociological *Imagination*

Choose a religious tradition other than your own. How would your religious beliefs, rituals, and experience differ if you had been raised in that tradition?

New Religious Movements or Cults

In 1997, 38 members of the Heaven's Gate cult were found dead in Southern California after a mass suicide timed to occur with the appearance of the Hale-Bopp comet. They believed the comet hid a spaceship on which they could catch a ride once they had broken free of their "bodily containers."

Partly as a result of the notoriety generated by such groups, the popular media have stigmatized the word *cult,* associating it with the occult and the use of intense and forceful conversion techniques. The stereotyping of cults as uniformly bizarre and unethical has led sociologists to abandon the term and refer instead to a *new religious movement (NRM).* While some NRMs exhibit

as that led by Martin Luther during the Reformation, claim to be the "true church," because they seek to cleanse the established faith of what they regard as extraneous beliefs and rituals (Stark

Characteristic	Ecclesia	Denomination	Sect	New Religious Movement (or Cult)
Size	Very large	Large	Small	Small
Wealth	Extensive	Extensive	Limited	Variable
Religious services	Formal, little participation	Formal, little participation	Informal, emotional	Variable
Doctrines	Specific, but interpretation may be tolerated	Specific, but interpretation may be tolerated	Specific, purity of doctrine emphasized	Innovative, pathbreaking
Clergy	Well-trained, full-time	Well-trained, full-time	Trained to some degree	Unspecialized
Membership	By virtue of being a member of society	By acceptance of doctrine	By acceptance of doctrine	By an emotional commitment
Relationship to the state	Recognized, closely aligned	Tolerated	Not encouraged	Ignored or challenged

Source: Adapted from Vernon 1962; see also Chalfant et al. 1994.

strange behavior, many do not. They attract new members just like any other religion, and often follow teachings similar to those of established Christian denominations, though with less ritual.

Sects are difficult to distinguish from cults. A **new religious movement (NRM)** or **cult** is generally a small, secretive religious group that represents either a new religion or a major innovation of an existing faith. NRMs are similar to sects in that they tend to be small and are often viewed as less respectable than more established faiths. Unlike sects, however, NRMs normally do not result from schisms or breaks with established ecclesiae or denominations. Some cults, such as those focused on UFO sightings, may be totally unrelated to existing faiths. Even when a cult does accept certain fundamental tenets of a dominant faith—such as a belief in Jesus as divine or in Mohammad as a messenger of God—it will offer new revelations or insights to justify its claim to being a more advanced religion (Stark and Bainbridge 1979, 1985).

Like sects, NRMs may be transformed over time into other types of religious organization. An example is the Christian Science Church, which began as a new religious movement under the leadership of Mary Baker Eddy. Today, this church exhibits the characteristics of a denomination. In fact, most major religions, including Christianity, began as cults. NRMs may be in the early stages of developing into a denomination or new religion, or they may just as easily fade away through the loss of members or weak leadership (R. Schaefer and Zellner 2011).

Comparing Forms of Religious Organization

How can we determine whether a particular religious group falls into the sociological category of ecclesia, denomination, sect, or NRM? As we have seen, these types of religious organization have somewhat different relationships to society. Ecclesiae are recognized as national churches; denominations, although not officially approved by the state, are generally widely respected. In contrast, sects and NRMs are much more likely to be at odds with the larger culture.

Still, ecclesiae, denominations, and sects are best viewed as types along a continuum rather than as mutually exclusive categories. Table 15-4 summarizes some of the primary characteristics of the ideal types. Since the United States has no ecclesiae, sociologists studying this country's religions have focused on the denomination

and the sect. These religious forms have been pictured on either end of a continuum, with denominations accommodating to the secular world and sects protesting against established religions. Although NRMs also are included in the table, they lie outside the continuum, because they generally define themselves in terms of a new view of life rather than in terms of existing religious faiths. In fact, one of the most controversial NRMs, Wicca, may not fully qualify as a religion (Box 15-1).

Sociologists look at religion from an organizational perspective, which tends to stress the stability of religious adherence, but there are other ways to view religion. From an individual perspective, religion and spirituality are remarkably fluid. People often change their places of worship or move from one denomination to another. In many countries, including the United States, churches, temples, and mosques operate in a highly competitive market (Pew Forum on Religion and Public Life 2008; Wolfe 2008).

One sign of this fluidity is the rapid rise of still another form of religious organization, the electronic church. Facilitated by cable television and satellite transmission, *televangelists* (as they are called) direct their messages to more people—especially in the United States—than are served by all but the largest denominations. While some televangelists are affiliated with religious denominations, most give viewers the impression that they are dissociated from established faiths.

At the close of the 1990s, the electronic church began to take on another dimension: the Internet. Today, rather than going to a service in person, many people shop online for a church or faith. Surfers can go to GodTube.com, a video-sharing and social-networking website, for spiritually oriented content. Even the Second Life virtual world (described in Chapter 5) has a rich spiritual landscape, with functioning congregations of Buddhist, Jewish, Muslim, and Christian avatars (Kiper 2008; MacDonald 2007; Simon 2007).

thinking CRITICALLY

In sociological terms, what attracts people to new religious movements?

RESEARCH TODAY

15-1 Wicca: Religion or Quasi-Religion?

"I'm not a Witch," Christine O'Donnell famously declared in her 2010 campaign for the U.S. Senate. Eleven years earlier, she admitted, she had dabbled in Witchcraft. To most voters, the idea was beyond the pale. Yet today, thousands of people, both men and women, do view themselves as Witches; they practice a little-known religion called Wicca (which should not be confused with Satanism—there is no place in the Craft for devil worship).

Wicca (Anglo-Saxon for *witch* and *wizard*) is a modern form of Witchcraft, practiced for the last hundred years. The Englishman Gerald Gardner, born in 1884, drew on past rituals to found the Craft. Gardner stressed the importance of worshipping *skyclad*, or "clothed by the sky"—that is, naked. Being skyclad, he believed, helped a person to gain insight.

Not all Wiccans follow in Gardner's tradition. Today, Wiccan ritual takes on a dizzying variety of forms, ranging from the elementary to the highly detailed and sophisticated. A Wiccan circle or meeting can include a single heartfelt prayer or a highly complex and time-consuming ritual. Like members of more accepted religions, Wiccans observe several rituals associated with the life cycle. Parents name their children at a *Wiccaning*, which includes a dedication to the Goddess and the God. Contemporary Wiccans also celebrate a wedding-like ceremony called a *handfasting*, which is typically performed by a High Priest and/or Priestess.

> *Some Witches practice alone, as a* solitaire; *others practice in a group of similarly minded Witches, called a* coven.

Just as Wiccans' worship varies, so does their organization. Some Witches practice alone, as a *solitaire;* others practice in a group of similarly minded Witches, called a *coven.* A coven may include just three or four Witches, male and/or female, or as many as thirty; members tend to come and go just as they do in a church or temple. In a mixed coven, the assembly is often governed by a High Priest or Priestess, or by both.

Revealing one's membership in any extraordinary group is always difficult, but perhaps especially so for Wiccans, who refer to the experience as "coming out of the broom closet." Many Wiccans are young, and so must come out to their parents. Parental reactions range from cutting off contact with the Witch to wanting to learn more about the Craft. Many parents treat the religion as a "phase" in their child's spiritual journey.

Most scholars treat Wicca as a **quasi-religion**, a category that includes organizations that may see themselves as religious, but are seen by others as "sort of religious." National surveys that allow respondents to self-identify showed 8,000 Wiccans in 1990; 134,000 in 2001; and 342,000 in 2008. These estimates suggest either an increase in willingness to identify as Wiccan or an absolute growth in the faithful—probably both.

LET'S DISCUSS

1. Do you know anyone who practices Wicca? If so, describe the person's practices.
2. Do you think that Wicca should be considered a religion? Why or why not?

Sources: Chase 2010; M. Howard 2009; Kosmin and Keysar 2009; Rabikovitch and Lewis 2004; R. Schaefer and Zellner 2011:347–377.

casestudy Religion in India

From a sociological point of view, the nation of India is large and complex enough that it might be considered a world of its own. Four hundred languages are spoken in India, 16 of which are officially recognized by the government. Besides the two major religions that originated there—Hinduism and Buddhism—several other faiths animate this society. Demographically the nation is huge, with over a billion residents. This teeming country is expected to overtake China as the most populous nation in the world in about three decades (Third World Institute 2007).

The Religious Tapestry in India

Hinduism and Islam, the two most important religions in India, were described on page 332. Islam arrived in India in A.D. 1000, with the first of many Muslim invasions. It flowered there during the Mogul empire (1526–1857), the period when the Taj Mahal was built. Today, Muslims account for 12 percent of India's population; Hindus make up 83 percent.

The presence of one dominant faith influences how a society views a variety of issues, even secular ones. For example, India has emerged as a leader in biotechnology, due at least partly to the Hindu faith's tolerance of stem cell research and cloning—techniques that have been questioned in nations where Christianity dominates. Hinduism is open to the latest biomedical techniques, as long as no evil is intended. The only legal prohibition is that fetuses cannot be terminated for the purpose of providing stem cells. Because of its respect for life in all forms, Hinduism has no major conflict with engineered life-forms of any kind, such as clones (Religion Watch 2006; Sengupta 2006).

Another religion, the Sikh faith, originated in the 15th century with a Hindu named Nanak, the first of a series of gurus (prophets). Sikhism shows the influence of Islam in India, in that it is monotheistic (based on a belief in one god rather than many). It resembles Buddhism in its emphasis on meditation and spiritual transcendence of the everyday world. *Sikhs* (learners) pursue their goal of spiritual enlightenment through meditation with the help of a guru.

Sikh men have a characteristic mode of dress, which in the United States often causes them to be mistaken—and discriminated against—as Muslims. They are highly patriotic. Although the 20 million Sikhs in India make up just 2 percent of the country's population, they account for 25 percent of India's army. In 2004 Manmohan Singh, a Sikh, became Prime Minister of India—an event that is almost comparable to a Black man becoming President of the United States. He is now serving his second term (Fausset 2003; Watson 2005).

Another group that forms a small segment of the faithful, Christians, also plays a disproportionate role in the country's social safety net. Christian schools, hospitals, and other social service organizations serve non-Christians as well as Christians. Interestingly, hundreds of priests who were trained at churches in India have since immigrated to the United States to ease the shortage of priests there. Together with Jains and Buddhists, Christians make up 3 percent of India's population (Embree 2003; Goodstein 2008).

Religion and the State in India

Religion was influential in India's drive to overturn British colonialism. The great Mohandas K. Gandhi (1869–1948) led the long struggle to regain India's sovereignty, which culminated in its independence in 1947. A proponent of nonviolent resistance, Gandhi persuaded Hindus and Muslims, ancient enemies, to join in defying British domination. But his influence as a peacemaker could not override the Muslims' demand for a separate state of their own. Immediately after independence was granted, India was partitioned into two states, Pakistan for the Muslims and India for the Hindus. The new arrangement caused large-scale migrations of Indians, especially Muslims, from one nation to the other, and sparked boundary disputes that continue to this day. In many areas, Muslims were forced to abandon places they considered sacred. In the chaotic months that followed, centuries of animosity between the two groups boiled over into riots, ending in Gandhi's assassination in January 1948.

Today, India is a secular state that is dominated by Hindus. Though the government is officially tolerant of the Muslim minority, tensions between Hindus and Muslims remain high in some states. Conflict also exists among various Hindu groups, from fundamentalists to more secular and ecumenical adherents (Embree 2003).

Many observers see religion as the moving force in Indian society. As in so many other parts of the world, religion is being redefined in India. To the dismay of Sikh spiritual leaders, increasing numbers of young Sikh men are trimming their long hair and abandoning the traditional turban. To show that the 300-year-old tradition is still cool in the 21st century, Sikh leaders now offer a CD-ROM called "Smart Turban 1.0" (Gentleman 2007).

Adherents of the Hindu religion participate in fire worship at a celebration in Kerala, India. The Hindu faith is enormously influential in India, the country where most Hindus live.

social**policy** and **Religion**

Religion in the Schools

Should public schools be allowed to sponsor organized prayer in the classroom? How about Bible reading, or just a collective moment of silence? Can athletes at public schools offer up a group prayer in a team huddle? Should students be able to initiate voluntary prayers at school events? Each of these situations has been an object of great dissension among those who see a role for prayer in the schools and those who want to maintain strict separation of church and state.

Another controversy concerns the teaching of theories about the origin of humans and the universe. Mainstream scientific thinking holds that humans evolved over billions of years from one-celled organisms, and that the universe came into being 15 billion years ago as a result of a huge cosmic explosion (the big bang theory). These theories are challenged by people who hold to the biblical account of the creation of humans and the universe some 10,000 years ago—a viewpoint known as **creationism**. Creationists, many of whom are Christian fundamentalists, want their belief taught in the schools as the only one—or at the very least, as an alternative to the theory of evolution.

Looking at the Issue

The issues just described go to the heart of the First Amendment's provisions regarding religious freedom. On the one hand, the government must protect the right to practice one's religion; on the other, it cannot take any measures that would seem to establish one religion over another (separation of church and state).

In the key case of *Engle v. Vitale,* the Supreme Court ruled in 1962 that the use of nondenominational prayer in New York schools was "wholly inconsistent" with the First Amendment's prohibition against government establishment of religion. In finding that organized school prayer violated the Constitution—even when no student was required to participate—the Court argued, in effect, that promoting religious observance was not a legitimate function of government or education. Subsequent Court decisions have allowed *voluntary* school prayer by students, but forbid school officials to *sponsor* any prayer or religious observance at school events. Despite these rulings, many public schools still regularly lead their students in prayer recitations or Bible readings. Other states have enacted "moments of silence" during the public school day, which many see as prayer in disguise (Robelon 2007).

As with school prayer, the teaching of creationism has significant support among the general public. Unlike Europeans, many people in the United States seem highly skeptical of evolutionary theory, which is taught as a matter of course in science classes. In 2009, a national survey showed that 39 percent of adults believe that God created humans in their present form. Almost as many believe that humans developed their present form with divine guidance (Gallup 2009a; Newport 2009).

The controversy over whether the biblical account of creation should be presented in school curricula recalls the famous "monkey trial" of 1925. In that trial, high school biology teacher John T. Scopes was convicted of violating a Tennessee law making it a crime to teach the scientific theory of evolution in public schools. Today, creationists have gone beyond espousing fundamentalist religious doctrine; they are attempting to reinforce their position regarding the origins of humanity and the universe with quasi-scientific data.

In 1987, the Supreme Court ruled that states could not compel the teaching of creationism in public schools if the primary purpose was to promote a religious viewpoint. In response, those who believe in the divine origin of life have recently advanced a concept called **intelligent design (ID),** the idea that life is so complex that it could only have been created by intelligent design. Though this concept is not based explicitly on the biblical account of creation, fundamentalists feel comfortable with it. Supporters of intelligent design consider it a more accurate account of the origin of life than Darwinism and hold that at the very least, ID should be taught as an alternative to the theory of evolution. But in 2005, in *Kitzmiller v. Dove Area School District,* a federal judge ended a Pennsylvania school district's plans to require teachers to present the concept in class. In essence, the judge found ID to be "a religious belief," a subtler but similar approach to creationism in that both find God's fingerprints in nature. The issue continues to be hotly debated and is expected to be the subject of future court cases (Clemmitt 2005; W. Tierney and Holley 2008).

Applying Sociology

Supporters of school prayer and of creationism feel that strict Court rulings have forced too great a separation between what Émile Durkheim called the *sacred* and the *profane.* They insist that the use of nondenominational prayer can in no way lead to the establishment of an ecclesia in the United States. Moreover, they believe that school prayer—and the teaching of creationism—can provide the spiritual guidance and socialization that many children today do not receive from parents or regular church attendance.

People on both sides of the debate between science and creationism invoke the name of Albert Einstein. Evolutionists emphasize the need for verifiable scientific data, like that which confirmed Einstein's groundbreaking scientific theories. Advocates of intelligent design quote the Nobel Prize–winning physicist's assertion that religion and science should coexist.

Many communities also believe that schools should transmit the dominant culture of the United States by encouraging prayer.

Opponents of school prayer and creationism argue that a religious majority in a community might impose viewpoints specific to its faith at the expense of religious minorities. These critics question whether school prayer can remain truly voluntary. Drawing on the interactionist perspective and small-group research, they suggest that children will face enormous social pressure to conform to the beliefs and practices of the majority.

Initiating Policy

Public school education is fundamentally a local issue, so most initiatives and lobbying have taken place at the local or state level. Federal courts have taken a hard line on religion in the schools. In a decision that the Supreme Court reversed in 2004, a federal appeals court ruled that reciting the phrase "under God" during the Pledge of Allegiance that opens each school day violates the U.S. Constitution (Religion News Service 2003).

Religion–school debates show no sign of ending. The activism of religious fundamentalists in the public school system raises the question "Whose ideas and values deserve a hearing in classrooms?" Critics see this campaign as one step toward sectarian religious control of public education. They worry that at some point in the future, teachers may not be able to use books or make statements that conflict with fundamentalist interpretations of the Bible. For advocates of a liberal education and of intellectual (and religious) diversity, this is a genuinely frightening prospect (Wilgoren 2005).

Take the Issue with You

1. Was there organized prayer in any school you attended? Was creationism part of the curriculum?

2. Do you think that promoting religious observance is a legitimate function of education?

3. How might a conflict theorist view the issue of organized school prayer?

Summary

Religion is a **cultural universal** found throughout the world in various forms. This chapter examines the major world religions, the functions and dimensions of religion, and the four basic types of religious organization.

1. Émile Durkheim stressed the social impact of religion in attempting to understand individual religious behavior within the context of the larger society.

2. Eighty-five percent of the world's population adheres to some form of **religion.** Tremendous diversity exists in religious beliefs and practices, which may be heavily influenced by culture.

3. Religion helps to integrate a diverse society and provides social support in time of need.

4. Max Weber saw a connection between religious allegiance and capitalistic behavior in a religious orientation he termed the **Protestant ethic.**

5. In **liberation theology,** the teachings of Christianity become the basis for political efforts to alleviate poverty and social injustice.

6. From a Marxist point of view, religion serves to reinforce the social control of those in power. It discourages collective political action, which could end capitalist oppression and transform society.

7. Religious behavior is expressed through **religious beliefs, rituals,** and **experience.**

8. Sociologists have identified four basic types of religious organization: the **ecclesia,** the **denomination,** the **sect,** and the **new religious movement (NRM),** or **cult.**

9. Advances in communications have led to a new type of church organization, the electronic church. Televangelists now preach to more people than belong to many denominations, and every day millions of people use the Internet for religious purposes.

10. India is a secular state that is dominated by a religious majority, the Hindus. The creation of a separate nation, Pakistan, for the Muslim minority following India's independence in 1947 did not end the centuries-old strife between the two groups, which has worsened with their political polarization.

11. Today, the question of how much religion, if any, should be permitted in the U.S. public schools is a matter of intense debate.

Key Terms

Creationism A literal interpretation of the Bible regarding the creation of humanity and the universe, used to argue that evolution should not be presented as established scientific fact. (page 343)

Denomination A large, organized religion that is not officially linked to the state or government. (339)

Ecclesia A religious organization that claims to include most or all members of a society and is recognized as the national or official religion. (339)

Established sect A religious group that is the outgrowth of a sect, yet remains isolated from society. (340)

Fundamentalism An emphasis on doctrinal conformity and the literal interpretation of sacred texts. (338)

Intelligent design (ID) The idea that life is so complex that it could only have been created by intelligent design. (344)

Liberation theology Use of a church, primarily Roman Catholic, in a political effort to eliminate poverty, discrimination, and other forms of injustice from a secular society. (336)

New religious movement (NRM) or **cult** A small, secretive religious group that represents either a new religion or a major innovation of an existing faith. (341)

Profane The ordinary and commonplace elements of life, as distinguished from the sacred. (331)

Protestant ethic Max Weber's term for the disciplined work ethic, this-worldly concerns, and rational orientation to life emphasized by John Calvin and his followers. (335)

Quasi-religion A scholarly category that includes organizations that may see themselves as religious but are seen by others as "sort of religious." (342)

Religion A unified system of beliefs and practices relative to sacred things. (331)

Religious belief A statement to which members of a particular religion adhere. (338)

Religious experience The feeling or perception of being in direct contact with the ultimate reality, such as a divine being, or of being overcome with religious emotion. (338)

Religious ritual A practice required or expected of members of a faith. (338)

Sacred Elements beyond everyday life that inspire awe, respect, and even fear. (331)

Sect A relatively small religious group that has broken away from some other religious organization to renew what it considers the original vision of the faith. (339)

Secularization The process through which religion's influence on other social institutions diminishes. (330)

TAKING SOCIOLOGY with you

1. Describe any experience you have had with, or observed in, what might be termed quasi-religion.

2. Interview someone who does not adhere to any religion. Was the person brought up in a religious tradition? What reasons does he or she give for not believing? Does this person participate in any secular rituals?

3. If your school or community has an interfaith organization, attend a meeting. What issues are the members currently dealing with? What sociological concepts are relevant to those issues?

Self-Quiz

Read each question carefully and then select the best answer.

1. Which of the following sociologists stressed the social impact of religion and was perhaps the first to recognize the critical importance of religion in human societies?
   a. Max Weber
   b. Karl Marx
   c. Émile Durkheim
   d. Talcott Parsons

2. A Roman Catholic parish church offers services in the native language of an immigrant community. This is an example of
   a. the integrative function of religion.
   b. the social support function of religion.
   c. the social control function of religion.
   d. none of the above.

3. Sociologist Max Weber pointed out that the followers of John Calvin emphasized a disciplined work ethic, this-worldly concerns, and a rational orientation to life. Collectively, this point of view has been referred to as
   a. capitalism.
   b. the Protestant ethic.
   c. the sacred.
   d. the profane.

4. The use of a church, primarily Roman Catholic, in a political effort to eliminate poverty, discrimination, and other forms of injustice evident in a secular society is referred to as
   a. creationism.
   b. ritualism.
   c. religious experience.
   d. liberation theology.

5. Many people in the United States strongly adhere to the biblical explanation of the beginning of the universe. Adherents of this point of view are known as
   a. liberationists.
   b. creationists.

   c. ritualists.
   d. experimentalists.

6. The Adam and Eve account of creation found in Genesis, the first book of the Old Testament, is an example of a religious
   a. ritual.
   b. experience.
   c. custom.
   d. belief.

7. Which of the following is *not* an example of an ecclesia?
   a. the Lutheran church in Sweden
   b. Islam in Saudi Arabia
   c. Buddhism in Thailand
   d. the Episcopal church in the United States

8. Religion defines the spiritual world and gives meaning to the divine. These are _____ functions of religion.
   a. manifest
   b. latent
   c. positive
   d. negative

9. Which sociological perspective emphasizes the integrative power of religion in human society?
   a. functionalist perspective
   b. conflict perspective
   c. interactionist perspective
   d. all of the above

10. John Calvin, a leader of the Protestant Reformation, emphasized
    a. disciplined work ethic.
    b. this-worldly concerns.
    c. a rational orientation to life.
    d. all of the above.

11. The _____ encompasses elements beyond everyday life that inspire awe, respect, and even fear, as compared to the _____, which includes the ordinary and the commonplace.

12. Wicca is an example of a(n) _____.

13. _____ is the largest single faith in the world; the second largest is _____.

14. _____ _____ are statements to which members of a particular religion adhere.

15. A(n) _____ is a religious organization that claims to include most or all members of a society and is recognized as the national or official religion.

16. Because they are _____, most religions tend to reinforce men's dominance in secular as well as spiritual matters.

17. The single largest denomination in the United States is _____ _____.

18. The big bang theory is challenged by _____, who hold to the biblical account of creation of humans and the universe.

19. Unlike ecclesiae and denominations, _____ require intensive commitments and demonstrations of belief by members.

20. A possible dysfunction of _____ _____ would be the belief that when Roman Catholics focus on political and governmental injustice, the clergy are no longer addressing people's personal and spiritual needs.

THINKING ABOUT **MOVIES**

Monsieur Ibrahim

In this film, which draws comparisons between Islam and Judaism, a Muslim grocer befriends a Jewish boy.

Saved!

A young woman tries to find her own voice in a Christian high school.

Trembling Before G-D

This documentary explores the tension between religious belief and sexual orientation.

Prospective students and their parents tour the campus of the University of Washington, Seattle. From informal learning in the family to formal study at an institution of higher learning, education is a cultural universal.

Education

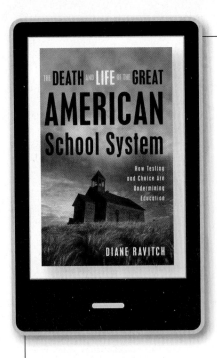

66 My favorite teacher was Mrs. Ruby Ratliff. She is the teacher I remember best, the one who influenced me most, who taught me to love literature and to write with careful attention to grammar and syntax. More than fifty years ago, she was my homeroom teacher at San Jacinto High School in Houston, and I was lucky enough to get into her English class as a senior.

Mrs. Ratliff was gruff and demanding. She did not tolerate foolishness or disruptions. She had a great reputation among students. . . . What I remember most about her was what she taught us. We studied the greatest writers of the English language. . . . We read Shakespeare, Keats, Shelley, Wordsworth, Milton, and other major English writers. Now, many years later, in times of stress or sadness, I still turn to poems that I first read in Mrs. Ratliff's class.

Mrs. Ratliff did nothing for our self-esteem. She challenged us to meet her exacting standards. I think she imagined herself bringing enlightenment to the barbarians (that was us). When you wrote something for her class, which happened with frequency, you paid close attention to proper English. Accuracy mattered. She had a red pen and she used it freely. Still, she was always sure to make a comment that encouraged us to do a better job. Clearly she had multiple goals for her students, beyond teaching literature and grammar. She was also teaching about character and personal responsibility. These are not the sorts of things that appear on any standardized test.

She loved her subject, and she enjoyed the respect the students showed her, especially since this was a large high school where students did not easily give respect to their teachers. Despite the passage of years, I still recall a class discussion of Shelley's "Ozymandias," and the close attention that thirty usually rowdy adolescents paid to a poem about a time and a place we could barely imagine. I wonder if Mrs. Ratliff has her counterparts today, teachers who love literature and love to teach it, or whether schools favor teachers who have been trained to elicit mechanical responses from their students about "text-to-self connections," "inferencing," "visualizing," and the other formalistic behaviors so beloved by au courant pedagogues. If Mrs. Ratliff were planning to teach these days, I expect that her education professors and supervisors would warn her to get rid of that red pen, to abandon her insistence on accuracy, and to stop being so judgmental. And they would surely demand that she replace those dated poems and essays with young adult literature that teaches adolescents about the lives of other adolescents just like themselves. . . .

I think of Mrs. Ratliff when I hear the latest proposals to improve the teaching force. Almost every day, I come across a statement by a journalist, superintendent, or economist who says we could solve all our problems in American education if we could just recruit a sufficient number of "great" teachers. I believe Mrs. Ratliff was a great teacher, but I don't think she would have been considered "great" if she had been judged by the kind of hard data that is used now. The policy experts who insist that teachers should be judged by their students' scores on standardized tests would have been frustrated by Mrs. Ratliff. Her classes never produced hard data. They didn't even produce test scores. How would the experts have measured what we learned? We never took a multiple-choice test. We wrote essays and took written tests, in which we had to explain our answers, not check a box or fill in a bubble. If she had been evaluated by the grades she gave, she would have been in deep trouble, because she did not award many A grades. An observer might have concluded that she was a very ineffective teacher who had no measurable gains to show for her work. 99

Clearly she had multiple goals for her students, beyond teaching literature and grammar. She was also teaching about character and personal responsibility. These are not the kinds of things that appear on any standardized test.

(Ravitch 2010: 169, 170, 171) Additional information about this excerpt can be found on the Online Learning Center at www.mhhe.com/schaefer13e.

In her book *The Death and Life of the Great American School System*, education historian Diane Ravitch laments our failure to improve the quality of education in the United States. In recalling her favorite teacher, Ravitch questions what she sees as the current tendency to reduce the art of teaching to cramming students' minds for standardized tests. She is asking the same questions that sociologists ask about education: what are its goals, and what is it supposed to accomplish, for individuals and for society as a whole? After considering how sociologists answer these questions, we will return to the issue of measuring school performance in the Social Policy section on charter schools.

Education, like the family and religion, is a cultural universal. As such it is an important aspect of socialization, the lifelong process of learning the attitudes, values, and behavior considered appropriate to members of a particular culture. As we saw in Chapter 4, socialization can occur in the classroom or at home, through interactions with parents, teachers, friends, and even strangers. Exposure to books, films, television, and other forms of communication also promotes socialization. When learning is explicit and formalized—when some people consciously teach, while others adopt the role of learner—the process of socialization is called **education.** But students learn far more about their society at school than what is included in the curriculum.

This chapter focuses in particular on the formal systems of education that characterize modern industrial societies. Do public schools offer everyone a way up the socioeconomic ladder, or do they reinforce existing divisions among social classes? What is the "hidden curriculum" in U.S. schools? And what have sociologists learned about the latest trends in education, such as competency testing? We will begin with a discussion of four theoretical perspectives on education: functionalist, conflict, feminist, and interactionist. An examination of schools as formal organizations—as bureaucracies and subcultures of teachers and students—follows. One contemporary educational trend, homeschooling, merits special mention. The chapter closes with a Social Policy section on charter schools.

Sociological Perspectives on Education

Besides being a major industry in the United States, education is the social institution that formally socializes members of our society. In the past few decades, increasing proportions of people have obtained high school diplomas, college degrees, and advanced professional degrees. Figure 16-1 shows the proportion of the college-educated population in selected countries.

Throughout the world, education has become a vast and complex social institution that prepares citizens for the roles demanded by other social institutions, such as the family, government, and the economy. The functionalist, conflict, feminist, and interactionist perspectives offer distinctive views of education as a social institution.

Functionalist View

Like other social institutions, education has both manifest (open, stated) and latent (hidden) functions. The most basic *manifest* function of education is the transmission of knowledge. Schools teach students how to read, speak foreign languages, and repair automobiles. Another important manifest function is the bestowal of status. Because many believe this function is performed inequitably, we will consider it later, in the section on the conflict view of education.

In addition to these manifest functions, schools perform a number of *latent* functions: transmitting culture, promoting social and political integration, maintaining social control, and serving as an agent of change.

Transmitting Culture As a social institution, education performs a rather conservative function—transmitting the dominant culture. Schooling exposes each generation of young people to the existing beliefs, norms, and values of their culture. In our society, we learn respect for social control and reverence for established institutions, such as religion, the family, and the presidency. Of course, this statement is true of many other cultures as well. While schoolchildren in the United States are hearing about the accomplishments of George Washington and Abraham Lincoln, British children are hearing about the distinctive contributions of Queen Elizabeth I and Winston Churchill.

In Great Britain, the transmission of the dominant culture through schools goes far beyond learning about monarchs and prime ministers. In 1996, the government's chief curriculum adviser—noting the need to fill a void left by the diminishing authority of the Church of England—proposed that British schools should socialize students into a set of core values. The list included honesty, respect for others, politeness, a sense of fair play, forgiveness, punctuality, nonviolent behavior, patience, faithfulness, and self-discipline (Charter and Sherman 1996).

Sometimes nations reassess the ways in which they transmit culture to students. In the last decade, the Chinese government revised the nation's history curriculum. Students are now taught that the Chinese Communist Party, not the United States, played a central role in defeating Japan in World War II. No mention is made of the estimated 30 million Chinese who died from famine because of party founder Mao Zedong's disastrous Great Leap Forward (1958–1962), a failed effort to transform China's

FIGURE **16-1**   CURRENT HIGHER EDUCATION GRADUATION RATES (BA/BS), SELECTED COUNTRIES

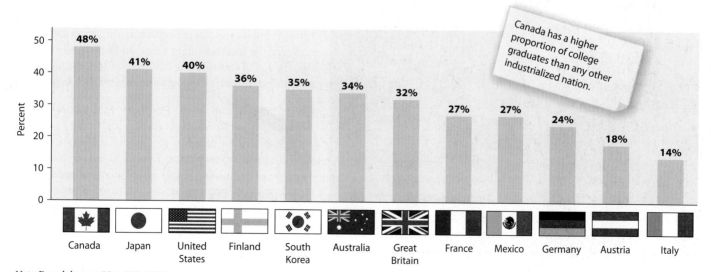

Note: For adults ages 25 to 64 in 2007.
Sources: Bureau of the Census 2010a:Table 1371.

SOCIOLOGY ON CAMPUS

16-1 Google University

From comic books, television, and fast-paced video games to educational films and online college courses, technological innovations in communication have been seen as both a threat to culture and a boon to education. Like these new media, the search engine called Google has been greeted with both praise and scorn. Founded by two students at Stanford University in 1998, Google handled some 65 percent of all Internet searches in the United States in early 2011. Its familiar multicolored logo stands for one of the most trusted brands in the world (see Figure 7-1, page 141).

Using Google or some other search engine, a researcher can now retrieve facts, viewpoints, images, and sounds within minutes. Just a few years ago, that task would have taken days. As Nicholas Carr (2008b:56), former editor of the *Harvard Business Review*, notes, "Once I was a scuba diver in the sea of words. Now I zip along the surface like a guy on a Jet Ski." Yet some critics of search engines charge that placing more and more of the world's knowledge just a mouse click away has made students lazy. Quick access to information, they point out, does not necessarily encourage concentration, let alone contemplation.

The availability of information online may also be changing the way people read. Educators worry that habitual skimming of the computer screen may carry over to students' print reading. Some have found that younger readers, faced with anything of length online, such as a short PDF file, simply ignore it. In response, researchers have begun to study whether those who read online in preference to books and other printed media still read sentence by sentence, as they were taught to do in school.

Other scholars are not disturbed by potential changes in what and how people read. They note that true literacy is not merely the ability

> *Like the invention of the printing press, Google's advent is changing not just the university, but the universe of learning.*

to read to the end of an article or book, but to find the information you need amid a flood of sources—not all of them trustworthy—and use it correctly and responsibly. In other words, literacy includes critical thinking.

Ultimately, education is more than just collecting, organizing, and comprehending information. Accessing information and arguments regarding political and social issues is a form of civic engagement. Thus, the search feature on a web page becomes a portal to a virtual town square. Perhaps that is why today's students are not only spending more time online than yesterday's students, but also doing more volunteer work.

Well before the advent of the Internet, much less Google, sociologist Daniel Bell (1973) wrote that *intellectual technologies* tend to institutionalize new approaches to the gathering and dissemination of information. Like the invention of the printing press, Google's advent is changing not just the university, but the universe of learning.

LET'S DISCUSS

1. Do you prefer to do your reading online or in a magazine, newspaper, or book? Has the availability of online information changed the way that you read the written word?

2. Have you participated in any social or political causes or volunteered your time while on campus? If so, did you use the Internet to organize or disseminate information about your activities?

Sources: Mark Bauerlein 2008; Brabazon 2007; Carr 2008a, 2008b; Maestretti 2009; Search Engine Watch 2011; Vaidhyanathan 2008; Workman 2008.

---

agrarian economy into an industrial powerhouse. In the urban, Western-oriented areas of Shanghai, textbooks acknowledge the technological advances made in Western industrialized countries but avoid any criticism of past policies of the Chinese government (French 2004; Kahn 2006).

Culture has been transmitted to students in schools, through books and the spoken word, for centuries. Today, however, the Internet offers a new and potentially revolutionary way of transmitting culture. Box 16-1 discusses the educational impact of Google and other search engines.

Promoting Social and Political Integration Many institutions require students in their first year or two of college to live on campus, to foster a sense of community among diverse groups. Education serves the latent function of promoting social and political integration by transforming a population composed of diverse racial, ethnic, and religious groups into a society whose members share—to some extent—a common identity. Historically, schools in the United States have played an important role in socializing the children of immigrants into the norms, values, and beliefs of the dominant culture. From a functionalist perspective, the common identity and social

Although the school Harry Potter attends in the film *Harry Potter and the Deathly Hallows: Part 2* is fictitious, like real schools, it transmits a socially sanctioned culture to students.

integration fostered by education contribute to societal stability and consensus (Touraine 1974).

In the past, the integrative function of education was most obvious in its emphasis on promoting a common language. Immigrant children were expected to learn English. In some instances, they were even forbidden to speak their native language on school grounds. More recently, bilingualism has been defended both for its educational value and as a means of encouraging cultural diversity. However, critics argue that bilingualism undermines the social and political integration that education has traditionally promoted.

In response to a high pregnancy rate among adolescent girls, many schools now offer sex education courses that promote abstinence as well as safe sex. When schools attempt to remedy negative social trends, they are serving as an agent of social change.

Maintaining Social Control In performing the manifest function of transmitting knowledge, schools go far beyond teaching skills like reading, writing, and mathematics. Like other social institutions, such as the family and religion, education prepares young people to lead productive and orderly lives as adults by introducing them to the norms, values, and sanctions of the larger society.

Through the exercise of social control, schools teach students various skills and values essential to their future positions in the labor force. They learn punctuality, discipline, scheduling, and responsible work habits, as well as how to negotiate the complexities of a bureaucratic organization. As a social institution, education reflects the interests of both the family and another social institution, the economy. Students are trained for what is ahead, whether it be the assembly line or a physician's office. In effect, then, schools serve as a transitional agent of social control, bridging the gap between parents and employers in the life cycle of most individuals (Bowles and Gintis 1976; M. Cole 1988).

Schools direct and even restrict students' aspirations in a manner that reflects societal values and prejudices. School administrators may allocate ample funds for athletic programs but give much less support to music, art, and dance. Teachers and guidance counselors may encourage male students to pursue careers in the sciences but steer female students into careers as early childhood teachers. Such socialization into traditional gender roles can be viewed as a form of social control.

thinking CRITICALLY

How do the functions of integration and social control reinforce each other? How do they work against each other?

Serving as an Agent of Change So far, we have focused on the conservative functions of education—on its role in transmitting the existing culture, promoting social and political integration, and maintaining social control. Yet education can also stimulate or bring about desired social change. Sex education classes were

introduced to public schools in response to the soaring pregnancy rate among teenagers. Affirmative action in admissions—giving priority to females or minorities—has been endorsed as a means of countering racial and sexual discrimination. And Project Head Start, an early childhood program that serves more than 904,000 children annually, has sought to compensate for the disadvantages in school readiness experienced by children from low-income families (Bureau of the Census 2010a:Table 572).

These educational programs can and have transformed people's lives. For example, continued formal education has had a positive effect on the income people earn; median earnings rise significantly with each step up the educational ladder (Figure 16-2). Consider the difference that these substantial annual increases can make when they are multiplied by the number of years a person works.

Education also promotes social change by serving as a meeting ground where people can share distinctive beliefs and traditions. In 2009–2010, U.S. campuses hosted over 690,000 international students. That number, an all-time high, followed a temporary decline in foreign enrollments after September 11, 2001. Figure 16-3 on page 355 shows the major sending nations of foreign students in the United States (left) and the primary destinations of U.S. students seeking to enrich their college experience abroad (right).

Numerous sociological studies have revealed that additional years of formal schooling are associated with openness to new ideas and liberal social and political viewpoints. Sociologist Robin Williams points out that better-educated people tend to have greater access to factual information, to hold more diverse opinions, and to possess the ability to make subtle distinctions in analysis. Formal education stresses both the importance of qualifying statements (in place of broad generalizations) and the need at least to question (rather than simply accept) established truths and practices. The scientific method, which relies on *testing* hypotheses, reflects the questioning spirit that characterizes modern education (Robin Williams et al. 1964).

Conflict View

The functionalist perspective portrays contemporary education as a basically benign institution. For example, it argues that schools

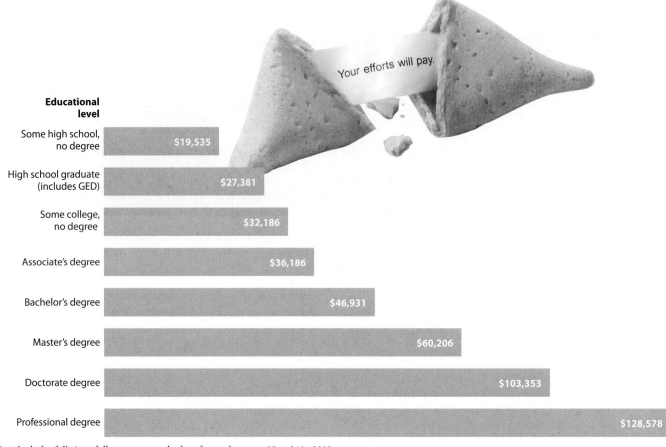

Educational level

Educational level	Annual median earnings
Some high school, no degree	$19,535
High school graduate (includes GED)	$27,381
Some college, no degree	$32,186
Associate's degree	$36,186
Bachelor's degree	$46,931
Master's degree	$60,206
Doctorate degree	$103,353
Professional degree	$128,578

Note: Includes full-time, full-year wage and salary for workers ages 25 to 34 in 2008.
Source: DeNavas-Walt et al. 2010:PINC-03.

rationally sort and select students for future high-status positions, thereby meeting society's need for talented and expert personnel. In contrast, the conflict perspective views education as an instrument of elite domination. Conflict theorists point out the sharp inequalities that exist in the educational opportunities available to different racial and ethnic groups. In 2004, the nation marked the 50th anniversary of the Supreme Court's landmark decision *Brown v. Board of Education,* which declared unconstitutional the segregation of public schools. Yet today, our schools are still characterized by racial isolation. Nationwide, White students are the most isolated: only 23 percent of their classmates came from minority groups in the 2005–2006 school year. In comparison, Black and Latino students have more classmates from different racial and ethnic backgrounds, although those classmates typically do not include Whites (Orfield and Lee 2007).

Conflict theorists also argue that the educational system socializes students into values dictated by the powerful, that schools stifle individualism and creativity in the name of maintaining order, and that the level of change they promote is relatively insignificant. From a conflict perspective, the inhibiting effects of education are particularly apparent in the "hidden curriculum" and the differential way in which status is bestowed.

The Hidden Curriculum Schools are highly bureaucratic organizations, as we will see later. Many teachers rely on rules and regulations to maintain order. Unfortunately, the need for control and discipline can take precedence over the learning process. Teachers may focus on obedience to the rules as an end in itself, in which case students and teachers alike become victims of what Philip Jackson (1968) has called the *hidden curriculum.*

The term **hidden curriculum** refers to standards of behavior that are deemed proper by society and are taught subtly in schools.

Studies conducted since 1987 suggest that the funding inequities between richer and poorer school districts have widened in recent years.

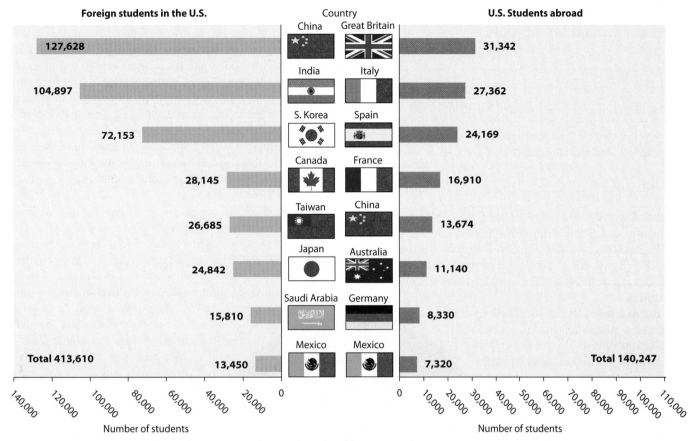

Foreign students in the U.S.   Country   **U.S. Students abroad**

Note: Foreign students in the United States for 2009–2010 and U.S. students abroad for 2008–2009.
Source: Institute of International Education 2010.

Think about It
How can we explain the differences between the countries that send students to the United States (left) and those that receive students from the United States (right)?

According to this curriculum, children must not speak until the teacher calls on them and must regulate their activities according to the clock or bells. In addition, they are expected to concentrate on their own work rather than to assist other students who learn more slowly. A hidden curriculum is evident in schools around the world. For example, Japanese schools offer guidance sessions that seek to improve the classroom experience and develop healthy living skills. In effect, these sessions instill values and encourage behavior that is useful in the Japanese business world, such as self-discipline and openness to group problem solving and decision making (Okano and Tsuchiya 1999).

In a classroom that is overly focused on obedience, value is placed on pleasing

Trend spotting

Rising College Enrollment among Racial and Ethnic Minorities, Women

The past 30 years have brought a consistent increase in college enrollment among all racial and ethnic groups in the United States. The typical measure that researchers use to track college enrollments is the college participation rate, or the percentage of all 18- to 24-year-olds enrolled in 2-year and 4-year colleges or universities. For Whites, the participation rate increased from 28 percent to 44 percent between 1978 and 2008. For African Americans, the rate climbed from 20 percent to 32 percent; for Latinos, from 16 percent to 26 percent.

Across the board, growth has been greater among females than among males. In 1980, more men than women were in college, whether among Whites, Blacks and Hispanics, or Asian Americans. By 1995 that pattern had reversed, and women outnumbered men. Only among Native Americans have women historically outnumbered men on college campuses.

the teacher and remaining quiet rather than on creative thought and academic learning. Habitual obedience to authority may result in the type of distressing behavior documented by Stanley Milgram in his classic obedience studies.

use your sociological *imagination*

In what ways did the high school you attended convey the hidden curriculum of education?

Credentialism Sixty years ago, a high school diploma was the minimum requirement for entry into the paid labor force of the United States. Today, a college diploma is virtually the bare minimum. This change reflects the process of **credentialism**—a term used to describe an increase in the lowest level of education needed to enter a field.

In recent decades, the number of occupations that are viewed as professions has risen. Credentialism is one symptom of this trend. Employers and occupational associations typically contend that such changes are a logical response to the increasing complexity of many jobs. However, in many cases, employers raise the degree requirements for a position simply because all applicants have achieved the existing minimum credential (David K. Brown 2001; Hurn 1985).

Conflict theorists observe that credentialism may reinforce social inequality. Applicants from poor and minority backgrounds are especially likely to suffer from the escalation of qualifications, since they lack the financial resources needed to obtain degree after degree. In addition, upgrading of credentials serves the self-interest of the two groups most responsible for this trend. Educational institutions profit from prolonging the investment of time and money that people make by staying in school. Moreover, as C. J. Hurn (1985) has suggested, current jobholders have a stake in raising occupational requirements, since credentialism can increase the status of an occupation and lead to demands for higher pay. Max Weber anticipated this possibility as early as 1916, concluding that the "universal clamor for the creation of educational certificates in all fields makes for the formation of a privileged stratum in businesses and in offices" (Gerth and Mills 1958:240–241).

use your sociological *imagination*

How would you react if the job you have or plan to pursue suddenly required a higher-level degree? If suddenly the requirements were lowered?

Bestowal of Status Sociologists have long recognized that schooling is central to social stratification. Both functionalist and conflict theorists agree that education performs the important function of bestowing status. As noted earlier, an increasing proportion of people in the United States are obtaining high school diplomas, college degrees, and advanced professional degrees. From a functionalist perspective, this widening bestowal of status is beneficial not only to particular recipients but to society as a whole. According to Kingsley Davis and Wilbert E. Moore (1945), society must distribute its members among a variety of social positions. Education can contribute to this process by sorting people into appropriate levels and courses of study that will prepare them for positions in the labor force.

Conflict theorists are far more critical of the *differential* way in which education bestows status. They stress that schools sort pupils according to their social class backgrounds. Although the educational system helps certain poor children to move into middle-class professional positions, it denies most disadvantaged children the same educational opportunities afforded to children of the affluent. In this way, schools tend to preserve social class inequalities in each new generation. Higher education in particular acts more like a sieve that sorts people out of the educated classes than a social ladder that helps all with ambition to rise (Alon 2009; Giroux 1988; Sacks 2007).

The status that comes with advanced training is not cheap and has been getting progressively more expensive for several decades. Over the past 30 years, average tuition and fees at community colleges have risen at a relatively modest pace that matches the inflation rate (Figure 16-4). The increases have been greater at four-year institutions. At the same time as tuition has been increasing, financial aid has become more difficult to obtain (see Chapter 9).

Even a single school can reinforce class differences by putting students in tracks. The term **tracking** refers to the practice of placing students in specific curriculum groups on the basis of their test scores and other criteria. Tracking begins very early, often in reading groups during first grade. The practice can reinforce the disadvantages that children from less affluent families may face if they haven't been exposed to reading materials, computers, and other forms of educational stimulation during their early childhood years. To ignore this connection between tracking and students' race and social class is to fundamentally misunderstand how schools perpetuate the existing social structure.

Not surprisingly, most recent research on tracking raises questions about its effectiveness, especially for low-ability students. In one study of low-income schools in California, researchers discovered a staggering difference between students who were tracked and those who were not. At one school, all interested students were allowed to enroll in advanced placement (AP) courses, not just those who were selected by the

FIGURE **16-4** TUITION COSTS, 1976–2009

Feminist View

357

Education

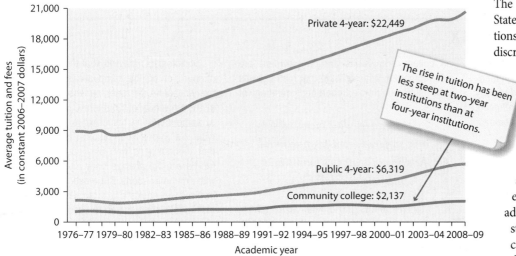

FIGURE 16-4 TUITION COSTS, 1976–2009

Private 4-year: $22,449

The rise in tuition has been less steep at two-year institutions than at four-year institutions.

Public 4-year: $6,319

Community college: $2,137

Note: Data cover the entire academic year and represent the average total charges, including tuition and fees, for full-time attendance.
Sources: National Center for Education Statistics 2011; Provasnik and Planty 2008:7.

administration. Half the open enrollment students scored high enough to qualify for college credit—a much higher proportion than in selective programs, in which only 17 percent of students qualified for college credit. Tracking programs do not necessarily identify those students with the potential to succeed (B. Ellison 2008; Sacks 2007).

Conflict theorists hold that the educational inequalities produced by tracking are designed to meet the needs of modern capitalist societies. Samuel Bowles and Herbert Gintis (1976) have argued that capitalism requires a skilled, disciplined labor force, and that the educational system of the United States is structured with that objective in mind. Citing numerous studies, they offer support for what they call the **correspondence principle.** According to this approach, schools promote the values expected of individuals in each social class and perpetuate social class divisions from one generation to the next. Thus, working-class children, assumed to be destined for subordinate positions, are likely to be placed in high school vocational and general tracks, which emphasize close supervision and compliance with authority. In contrast, young people from more affluent families are likely to be directed to college preparatory tracks, which stress leadership and decision making—the skills they are expected to need as adults (McLanahan and Percheski 2008).

Thinking CRITICALLY

What are the functions and dysfunctions of tracking in schools? In what ways might tracking have a positive impact on the self-concepts of various students? In what ways might it have a negative impact?

Feminist View

The educational system of the United States, like many other social institutions, has long been characterized by discriminatory treatment of women. In 1833, Oberlin College became the first institution of higher learning to admit female students—some 200 years after the first men's college was established. But Oberlin believed that women should aspire to become wives and mothers, not lawyers and intellectuals. In addition to attending classes, female students washed men's clothing, cared for their rooms, and served them at meals. In the 1840s, Lucy Stone, then an Oberlin undergraduate and later one of the nation's most outspoken feminist leaders, refused to write a commencement address because it would have been read to the audience by a male student.

In the 20th century, sexism in education showed up in many ways—in textbooks with negative stereotypes of women, counselors' pressure on female students to prepare for "women's work," and unequal funding for women's and men's athletic programs. But perhaps nowhere was educational discrimination more evident than in the employment of teachers. The positions of university professor and college administrator, which hold relatively high status in the United States, were generally filled by men. Public school teachers, who earn much lower salaries, were largely female.

Women have made great strides in one area: the proportion of women who continue their schooling. As recently as 1969, twice as many men as women received college degrees; today, women outnumber men at college commencements. Moreover, women's access to graduate education and to medical, dental, and law schools has increased dramatically in the past few decades as a result of the Education Act of 1972. Box 16-2 examines the far-reaching effects of Title IX, the part of the act that concerns discrimination against women in education.

Much has been made of the superior academic achievement of girls and women. Today, researchers are beginning to examine the reasons for their comparatively strong performance in school—or to put it another way, for men's lackluster performance. Some studies suggest that men's aggressiveness, together with the fact that they do better in the workplace than women, even with less schooling, predisposes them to undervalue higher education. While the "absence of men" on many college campuses has captured headlines, it has also created a false crisis in public discourse. Few students realize their potential exclusively through formal education; other factors, such as ambition and personal talent, contribute to their success. And many students, including

SOCIOLOGY ON CAMPUS

16-2 The Debate over Title IX

Few federal policies have had such a visible effect on education as Title IX, which mandates gender equity in education in federally funded schools. Congressional amendments to the Education Act of 1972 have brought significant changes for both men and women at all levels of schooling. Title IX eliminated sex-segregated classes, prohibited sex discrimination in admissions and financial aid, and mandated that girls receive more opportunities to play sports, in proportion to their enrollment and interest.

Under this landmark legislation, to receive federal funds, a school or college must pass one of three tests. First, the numbers of male and female athletes must be proportional to the numbers of men and women enrolled at the school. Second, lacking that, the school must show a continuing history of expanding opportunities for female athletes. Or third, the school must demonstrate that the level of female participation in sports meets female students' level of interest or ability.

Today, Title IX is still one of the more controversial attempts ever made by the federal government to promote equality for all citizens. Its consequences for the funding of college athletics programs are hotly debated, while its real and lasting effects on college admissions and employment are often forgotten. Critics charge that men's teams have suffered from proportional funding of

Critics charge that men's teams have suffered from proportional funding of women's teams and athletic scholarships.

women's teams and athletic scholarships, since schools with tight athletic budgets can expand women's sports only at the expense of men's sports.

To a certain extent, non-revenue-producing men's sports such as wrestling and golf do appear to have suffered as women's teams have been added. But the high expense of some men's sports, particularly football, would be beyond many schools' means even without Title IX expenditures. And the gains for women have more than made up for the losses to men. Since Title IX was enacted, female participation in high school athletics has increased by 904 percent; female participation in collegiate athletics has increased by 456 percent. Still, as of 2011, women were afforded just 43 percent of the opportunities to play college sports.

Sociologists note, too, that the social effects of sports on college campuses are not all positive. Michael A. Messner, professor of sociology at the University of Southern California, points to some troubling results of a survey by the Women's Sports Foundation. The study shows that teenage girls who play sports simply for fun have more positive body images than girls who don't play sports. But those who are "highly involved" in sports are more likely than other girls to take steroids and to become risk takers. "Everyone has tacitly agreed, it seems, to view men's sports as the standard to which women should strive to have equal access," Messner writes. He is skeptical of a system that propels a lucky few college athletes to stardom each year while leaving the majority, many of them African American, without a career or an education. Certainly that was not the kind of equal opportunity legislators envisioned when they wrote Title IX.

LET'S DISCUSS

1. Has Title IX had an effect on you personally? If so, explain. On balance, do you think the increase in women's participation in sports has been good for society as a whole?
2. How might Title IX affect the way students and the public view gender roles?

Sources: Brady 2010; Messner 2002; Pennington 2008; Spencer 2008; Tigay 2011; Women's Sports Foundation 2011.

---

low-income and immigrant children, face much greater challenges than the so-called gender gap in education (Buchmann et al. 2008; Corbett et al. 2008; Kimmel 2006).

In cultures in which traditional gender roles remain the social norm, women's education suffers appreciably. Since September 11, 2001, the growing awareness of the Taliban's repression of Afghan women has dramatized the gender disparities in education in developing nations. Research has demonstrated that women are critical to economic development and good governance, and that education is instrumental in preparing them for those roles. Educating women, especially young girls, yields high social returns by lowering birthrates and improving agricultural productivity through better management (I. Coleman 2004).

Interactionist View

High school students know who they are—the kids who qualify for a free lunch. So stigmatized are they that in some schools, these students will buy a bit of food in the cash line or simply go without eating to avoid being labeled a "poor kid." School officials in San Francisco are so concerned about their plight that they are moving to cashless cafeterias, in which everyone, rich or poor, uses a debit card (Pogash 2008).

As we saw in Chapter 8, the labeling approach suggests that if we treat people in particular ways, they may fulfill our expectations. Children who are labeled as "troublemakers" may come to view themselves as delinquents. Similarly, a dominant group's stereotyping of racial minorities may limit their opportunities to break away from expected roles.

Can the labeling process operate in the classroom? Because interactionist researchers focus on micro-level classroom dynamics, they have been particularly interested in this question. Sociologist Howard S. Becker (1952) studied public schools in low-income and affluent areas of Chicago. He noticed that administrators expected less of students from poor neighborhoods, and wondered if teachers accepted their view. A decade later, in *Pygmalion in the Classroom,* psychologist Robert Rosenthal and school principal Lenore Jacobson (1968, 1992) documented what they referred to as a **teacher-expectancy**

In Tokyo, a mother escorts her daughter to an admissions interview at a highly competitive private cram school. Some Japanese families enroll children as young as 2 in cram schools to better prepare them for such exams.

TABLE **16-1**   SOCIOLOGICAL PERSPECTIVES ON EDUCATION

summingup

Theoretical Perspective	Emphasis
Functionalist	Transmission of the dominant culture
	Integration of society
	Promotion of social norms, values, and sanctions
	Promotion of desirable social change
Conflict	Domination by the elite through unequal access to schooling
	Hidden curriculum
	Credentialism
	Bestowal of status
Interactionist	Teacher-expectancy effect
Feminist	Treatment of female students
	Role of women's education in economic development

effect—the impact that a teacher's expectations about a student's performance may have on the student's actual achievements. This effect is especially evident in the lower grades (through grade three).

Studies in the United States have revealed that teachers wait longer for an answer from a student they believe to be a high achiever and are more likely to give such children a second chance. In one experiment, teachers' expectations were even shown to have an impact on students' athletic achievements. Teachers obtained better athletic performance—as measured in the number of sit-ups or push-ups performed—from those students of whom they *expected* higher numbers. Despite the controversial nature of these findings, researchers continue to document the existence of the teacher-expectancy effect. Interactionists emphasize that ability alone may be less predictive of academic success than one might think (Babad and Taylor 1992; Brint 1998; R. Rosenthal and Jacobson 1992:247–262).

Table 16-1 summarizes the four major theoretical perspectives on education.

Schools as Formal Organizations

Nineteenth-century educators would be amazed at the scale of schools in the United States in the 21st century. For example, California's public school system, the largest in the nation, currently enrolls as many children as there were in secondary schools in the entire country in 1950 (Bureau of the Census 1975:368; 2010a).

In many respects, today's schools, when viewed as an example of a formal organization, are similar to factories, hospitals, and business firms. Like those organizations, schools do not operate autonomously; they are influenced by the market of potential students. This statement is especially true of private schools, but could have broader impact if acceptance of voucher plans and other school choice programs increases. The parallels between schools and other types of formal organizations will become more apparent as we examine the bureaucratic nature of schools, teaching as an occupation, and the student subculture (K. Dougherty and Hammack 1992).

Bureaucratization of Schools

It simply is not possible for a single teacher to transmit culture and skills to children of varying ages who will enter many diverse occupations. The growing number of students being served by school systems and the greater degree of specialization required within a technologically complex society have combined to bureaucratize schools.

Max Weber noted five basic characteristics of bureaucracy, all of which are evident in the vast majority of schools, whether at the elementary, secondary, or even college level:

1. **Division of labor.** Specialized experts teach particular age levels and specific subjects. Public elementary and secondary schools now employ instructors whose sole responsibility is to work with children with learning disabilities or physical impairments.

2. **Hierarchy of authority.** Each employee of a school system is responsible to a higher authority. Teachers must report to principals and assistant principals and may also be supervised by department heads. Principals are answerable to a superintendent of schools, and the superintendent is hired and fired by a board of education.

3. **Written rules and regulations.** Teachers and administrators must conform to numerous rules and regulations in

TAKING SOCIOLOGY TO WORK

Diane Belcher, Assistant Director of Volunteer Services, New River Community College

Not until Diane Belcher enrolled at New River Community College in Dublin, Virginia, did she realize that social work had always been part of her daily life. To this mother of two teenagers, helping people in need was something she just did, without even thinking about it.

Today, as assistant director of Volunteer Services at New River, Belcher assists Partners for Success, a mentoring program that matches struggling students with people in the community who have the time and energy to help them. With the director, she recruits and trains a "talent bank" of mentors, matches the mentors with student partners, and develops support programs for students experiencing problems with child care, transportation, and other necessities. The program's goal is to develop confident and successful learners who can take charge of their own studies.

Before she moved to Volunteer Services, Belcher was an administrative assistant in Workforce Development at New River, where she helped youths who lack direction and workers laid off from local factories to develop more marketable skills. In that job, she facilitated new students' transition to college, helping them to register and apply for financial aid and connecting them with professors in their fields of interest. Belcher also worked directly with the administration to develop a special fast-track program for laid-off workers.

As in all human services jobs, people skills, particularly sensitivity and compassion, are of paramount importance in Belcher's work. An understanding of the social and economic forces that affect the larger society is also essential. Belcher credits her sociology courses with helping her to "engage where needed." "Sociology exposed me to other people's situations and the role of society in creating them," she explains. "It helped me look beyond the individual level to understand societal impacts and solutions."

Asked what advice she might give to current sociology majors, Belcher says, "Drink it up, try and take it all in, relate it to the real world. Take notice of current cultural and economic conditions, understanding that when you attempt to 'fix' one part of society you must also be aware of how that will affect other parts of society."

LET'S DISCUSS

1. Have you, like Diane Belcher, realized through education that something you were doing without thinking about it has helped to prepare you for employment? Explain.
2. Do some research on Dublin, Virginia, and the surrounding area. What kind of economy does this community have? Relate the layoffs the community has been experiencing to larger societal forces.

---

the performance of their duties. This bureaucratic trait can become dysfunctional; the time invested in completing required forms could instead be spent in preparing lessons or conferring with students.

4. **Impersonality.** As class sizes have swelled at schools and universities, it has become more difficult for teachers to give personal attention to each student. In fact, bureaucratic norms may actually encourage teachers to treat all students in the same way, despite the fact that students have distinctive personalities and learning needs.

5. **Employment based on technical qualifications.** At least in theory, the hiring of instructors is based on professional competence and expertise. Promotions are normally dictated by written personnel policies; people who excel may be granted lifelong job security through tenure.

Functionalists take a generally positive view of the bureaucratization of education. Teachers can master the skills needed to work with a specialized clientele, since they no longer are expected to cover a broad range of instruction. The chain of command within schools is clear. Students are presumably treated in an unbiased fashion because of uniformly applied rules. Finally, security of position protects teachers from unjustified dismissal. In general, then, functionalists stress that the bureaucratization of education increases the likelihood that students, teachers, and administrators will be dealt with fairly—that is, on the basis of rational and equitable criteria.

In contrast, conflict theorists argue that the trend toward more centralized education has harmful consequences for disadvantaged people. The standardization of educational curricula, including textbooks, will generally reflect the values, interests, and lifestyles of the most powerful groups in our society, and may ignore those of racial and ethnic minorities. In addition, the disadvantaged, more so than the affluent, will find it difficult to sort through complex educational bureaucracies and to organize effective lobbying groups. Therefore, in the view of conflict theorists, low-income and minority parents will

Despite efforts to establish positive relationships among students and between teachers and students, many young people view their schools as impersonal institutions.

have even less influence over citywide and statewide educational administrators than they have over local school officials (Bowles and Gintis 1976; Katz 1971).

Sometimes schools can seem overwhelmingly bureaucratic, with the effect of stifling rather than nourishing intellectual curiosity in students. This concern has led many parents and policymakers to push for school choice programs—allowing parents to choose the school that suits their children's needs, and forcing schools to compete for their "customers."

In the United States, another significant countertrend to the bureaucratization of schools is the availability of education over the Internet. Increasingly, colleges and universities are reaching out via the web, offering entire courses and even majors to students in the comfort of their homes. Online curricula provide flexibility for working students and others who may have difficulty attending conventional classes because of distance or disability. Research on this type of learning is just beginning, so the question of whether teacher–student contact can thrive online remains to be settled. Computer-mediated instruction may also have an impact on instructors' status as employees, which we will discuss next, as well as on alternative forms of education like homeschooling.

---

use your sociological *imagination*

How would you make your school less bureaucratic? What would it be like?

Teachers: Employees and Instructors

Whether they serve as instructors of preschoolers or of graduate students, teachers are employees of formal organizations with bureaucratic structures. There is an inherent conflict in serving as a professional in a bureaucracy. The organization follows the principles of hierarchy and expects adherence to its rules, but professionalism demands the individual responsibility of the practitioner. This conflict is very real for teachers, who experience all the positive and negative consequences of working in bureaucracies (see Table 6-2, page 126).

A teacher undergoes many perplexing stresses every day. While teachers' academic assignments have become more specialized, the demands on their time remain diverse and contradictory. Conflicts arise from serving as an instructor, a disciplinarian, and an employee of a school district at the same time. In too many schools, discipline means dealing with violence. Burnout is one result of these stresses: between a quarter and a third of new teachers quit within their first three years, and as many as half leave poor urban schools in their first five years (Wallis 2008).

Given these difficulties, does teaching remain an attractive profession in the United States? In 2010, 3.6 percent of first-year college students indicated that they were interested in becoming elementary school teachers, and 3.9 percent, high school teachers. These figures are dramatically lower than the 11 percent of first-year male students and 37 percent of first-year female students who held those occupational aspirations in 1966 (Pryor et al. 2007:122, 76; 2010:28).

Undoubtedly, economic considerations enter into students' feelings about the attractiveness of teaching. In 2010, the average salary for all public elementary and secondary school teachers in the United States was reported at $55,350, placing teachers somewhere near the average of all the nation's wage earners. In most other industrial countries, teachers' salaries are higher in relation to the general standard of living. Of course, teachers' salaries vary considerably from state to state (Figure 16-5), and even more from one school district to another. Nevertheless, the economic reward for teaching is miniscule compared to some career options: the CEO of a major corporation makes more money in a day than the average teacher makes in a year.

The status of any job reflects several factors, including the level of education required, financial compensation, and the respect given the occupation by society. The teaching profession (see Table 9-3, page 196) is feeling pressure in all three of these areas. First, the level of formal schooling required for teaching remains high, and the public has begun to call for new competency examinations. Second, the statistics just cited demonstrate that teachers' salaries are significantly lower than those of many professionals and skilled workers. Third, the overall prestige of the teaching profession has declined in the past decade. Many teachers have become disappointed and frustrated and have left the educational world for careers in other professions.

Student Subcultures

An important latent function of education relates directly to student life: schools provide for students' social and recreational needs. Education helps toddlers and young children to develop interpersonal skills that are essential during adolescence and adulthood. In their high school and college years, students may meet future husbands and wives and establish lifelong friendships.

When people observe high schools, community colleges, or universities from the outside, students appear to constitute a cohesive, uniform group. However, the student subculture is actually quite complex and diverse. High school cliques and social groups may crop up according to race, social class, physical attractiveness, placement in courses, athletic ability, and leadership roles in the school and community. In his classic community study of "Elmtown," August B. Hollingshead (1975) found some 259 distinct cliques in a single high school. The cliques, whose average size was five, were centered on the school itself, on recreational activities, and on religious and community groups.

Amid these close-knit and often rigidly segregated cliques, gay and lesbian students are particularly vulnerable. Peer group pressure to conform is intense at this age. Although coming to terms with one's sexuality is difficult for all adolescents, it can be downright dangerous for those whose sexual orientation does not conform to societal expectations.

Teachers and administrators are becoming more sensitized to these issues. Perhaps more important, some schools are creating gay–straight alliances (GSAs), school-sponsored support groups that bring gay teens together with sympathetic straight peers. Begun in Los Angeles in 1984, these programs numbered nearly 3,000 nationwide in 2005; most were founded after the murder of Matthew Shepard, a gay college student, in 1998. In some districts parents have objected to these organizations, but the same court rulings that protect the right of conservative Bible groups to meet on school grounds also protect GSAs. In 2003, the gay–straight movement reached a milestone when the New York City public schools moved an in-school program for gays, bisexuals, and transgendered students to a separate school. The Harvey Milk High School was named in memory of San Francisco's first openly gay city supervisor, who was assassinated in 1978 (Gay, Lesbian and Straight Education Network 2010).

We can find a similar diversity of student groups at the college level. Burton Clark and Martin Trow (1966) and, more recently, Helen Lefkowitz Horowitz (1987) have identified four distinctive subcultures among college students:

1. The *collegiate* subculture focuses on having fun and socializing. These students define what constitutes a "reasonable" amount of academic work (and what amount of work is "excessive" and leads to being labeled as a "grind"). Members of the collegiate subculture have little commitment to academic pursuits. Athletes often fit into this subculture.

2. The *academic* subculture identifies with the intellectual concerns of the faculty and values knowledge for its own sake.

3. The *vocational* subculture is interested primarily in career prospects and views college as a means of obtaining degrees that are essential for advancement.

4. Finally, the *nonconformist* subculture is hostile to the college environment and seeks ideas that may or may not relate to academic studies. This group may find outlets through campus publications or issue-oriented groups.

Each college student is eventually exposed to these competing subcultures and must determine which (if any) seems most in line with his or her feelings and interests.

The typology used by the researchers reminds us that school is a complex social organization—almost like a community with different neighborhoods. Of course, these four subcultures are not the only ones evident on college campuses in the United

MAPPING LIFE NATIONWIDE
FIGURE **16-5** AVERAGE SALARY FOR TEACHERS

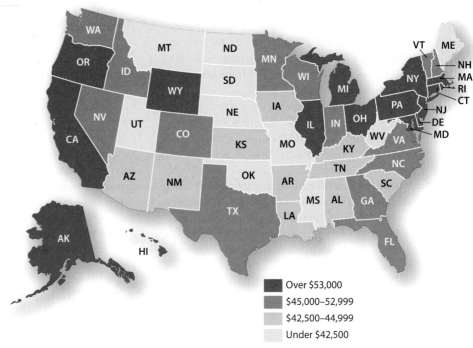

Legend:
- Over $53,000
- $45,000–52,999
- $42,500–44,999
- Under $42,500

Note: Data released in 2009 for 2009–2010.
Source: National Education Association 2009.

State averages for teacher salaries range from a low of $35,136 in South Dakota to a high of $68,000 in Massachusetts.

States. For example, one might find subcultures of Vietnam veterans or former full-time homemakers at community colleges and four-year commuter institutions. And as more and more students from minority groups decide to continue their formal education beyond high school, subcultures based on race and ethnicity will become more evident. As Figure 16-6 shows, college campuses are becoming increasingly diverse.

Sociologist Joe R. Feagin has studied a distinctive collegiate subculture: Black students at predominantly White universities. These students must function academically and socially within universities where there are few Black faculty members or administrators,

Student subcultures are more diverse today than in the past. Many adults are returning to college to obtain further education, advance their careers, or change their line of work.

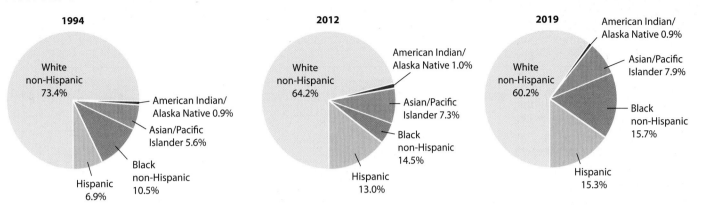

Note: Percentages do not add to 100 due to rounding error. Nonresident aliens whose race/ethnicity is unknown excluded.
Source: Hussar and Bailey 2011:Table 29.

where harassment of Blacks by campus police is common, and where curricula place little emphasis on Black contributions. Feagin (1989:11) suggests that "for minority students life at a predominantly White college or university means long-term encounters with pervasive whiteness." In Feagin's view, Black students at such institutions experience both blatant and subtle racial discrimination, which has a cumulative impact that can seriously damage the students' confidence (see also Feagin et al. 1996).

use your sociological *imagination*

What distinctive subcultures can you identify at your college?

Homeschooling

When most people think of school, they think of bricks and mortar and the teachers, administrators, and other employees who staff school buildings. But for an increasing number of students in the United States, home is the classroom and the teacher is a parent. About 1.5 million students are now being educated at home. That is about 3 percent of the K–12 school population. For these students, the issues of bureaucratization and social structure are less significant than they are for public school students (Grady et al. 2010).

In the 1800s, after the establishment of public schools, families that taught their children at home lived in isolated environments or held strict religious views that were at odds with the secular environment of public schools. But today, homeschooling is attracting a broader range of families not necessarily tied to organized religion. Poor academic quality, peer pressure, and school violence are motivating many parents to teach their children at home. In addition, some immigrants choose homeschooling as a way to ease their children's transition to a new society. For example, the growing Arab American population recently joined the movement toward homeschooling (MacFarquhar 2008; National Center for Education Statistics 2009).

While supporters of homeschooling believe children can do just as well or better in homeschools as in public schools, critics counter that because homeschooled children are isolated from the larger community, they lose an important chance to improve their socialization skills. But proponents of homeschooling claim their children benefit from contact with others besides their own age group. They also see homeschools as a good alternative for children who suffer from attention-deficit/hyperactivity disorder (ADHD) and learning disorders (LDs). Such children often do better in smaller classes, which present fewer distractions to disturb their concentration.

Quality control is an issue in homeschooling. While homeschooling is legal in all 50 states, 10 states require no notification that a child will be homeschooled, and another 14 require notification only. Other states may require parents to submit their children's curricula or test scores for professional evaluation. Despite the lack of uniform standards, a research review by the Home School Legal Defense Association (2005) reports that homeschooled students score higher than others on standardized tests, in every subject and every grade.

Who are the people who are running homeschools? In general, they tend to have higher-than-average incomes and educational levels. Most are two-parent families, and their children watch less television than average—both factors that are likely to support superior educational performance. The same students, with the same support from their parents, would probably do just as well in the public schools. As research has repeatedly shown, small classes are better than big classes, and strong parental and community involvement is key (R. Cox 2003:28).

Whatever the controversy over homeschooling in the United States, it is much less serious than in some other nations. In 2010, the U.S. Immigration and Naturalization Service began granting political asylum to German families who homeschool their children, in violation of their country's constitution. German parents can be fined and imprisoned for homeschooling their children (Francis 2010).

thinking CRITICALLY

Select two functions of education and suggest how they could be fulfilled through homeschooling.

socialpolicy and Education

Charter Schools

Discontent with public schools stretches back for decades. In the 1970s, "classrooms without walls" were supposed to open up the curriculum to students' creativity. In 2002, the No Child Left Behind initiative was supposed to guarantee that all students would learn the basics. Although test scores inched up a bit in response, critics complained that schools were becoming too test-oriented, and scores on interactive science and math tests sank compared to those in other nations (K. Clark 2010).

Meanwhile, the charter school movement had been gathering strength. **Charter schools** are experimental schools that are developed and managed by individuals, groups of parents, or educational management organizations. Although these schools are typically considered to be public schools, they are administered outside the official public school system. Their charters (legal contracts) permit them to establish their own rules, curricula, and admissions and professional standards. Within their communities, however, charter schools must still abide by prevailing standards for health, public safety, and equal opportunity (Renzulli and Roscigno 2007).

Looking at the Issue

Charter schools first opened in Minnesota in 1992; by 2011, nearly 5,000 of them had been established in 40 different states (Figure 16-7). Advocates of charter schools claim that they offer parents accountability for their children's education. In effect, charter schools compete with public schools, offering an alternative that was once available only to the wealthy (National Alliance for Public Charter Schools 2011).

Applying Sociology

Functionalists argue that charter schools meet society's need for education while serving a diverse student body. Despite criticism that charter schools are elitist institutions that serve the children of privileged White families, data show that 55 percent of the students enrolled in these schools are African American or Latino. More than a third of them qualify for free or reduced-price lunches (Gabriel 2010).

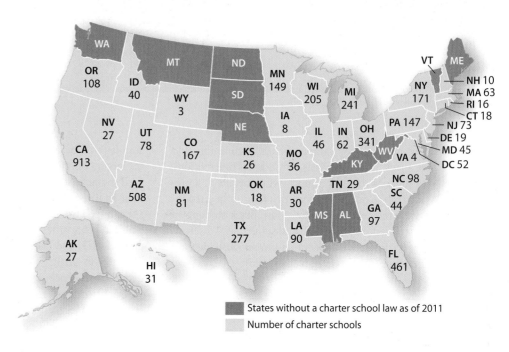

MAPPING LIFE NATIONWIDE

FIGURE **16-7** CHARTER SCHOOLS

States without a charter school law as of 2011

Number of charter schools

Source: National Alliance for Public Charter Schools. (2011). The Public Charter Schools Dashboard. Washington, DC: NAPCS.

Think about It

How does your state compare to others as far as being a part of the charter school movement?

Although charter schools are publicly financed, most are not unionized. From a conflict perspective, charter schools do not represent teachers' interests well and are contributing to the decline of labor unions (see Chapter 6). Partly in response to this concern, public school districts in Denver, Detroit, Milwaukee, Boston, and Minnesota have empowered teachers to create their own charter schools (Dillon 2009; Hu 2010).

Because the charter school movement is a comparatively recent one, we do not have much research on the long-term impact of charter versus non-charter schools. Of course, there is great variation among both within the same city much less the same state. News stories about individual charter schools and high-profile advocates like the Bill and Melinda Gates Foundation suggest that these schools' outcomes are quite positive. However, the diversity in purpose, funding, organization, and curriculum that characterizes charter schools makes generalizing from one school or community to another very difficult.

As an example of the different conclusions that can be seen, many top school lists disproportionately identify charter schools as outperforming non-charter schools, yet a Stanford University study showed that 37 percent of charter schools studied in 16 states produce test results that are worse than public schools (Center for Research on Education Outcomes 2009; Thomas and Wingert 2010)

Initiating Policy

In the United States, unlike virtually all other industrial nations, school policy is driven at the local level. Although the federal government may encourage certain policies through public funding, and may dictate certain standards like nondiscrimination, school policy is created largely at the community level following state-wide standards. Thus, in 2010, when the Department of Education began to expend $4.3 billion as part of a general educational stimulus program, it left the structure and organization of schools to local communities. Programs such as Race to the Top stressed only improvements in academic achievement (K. Clark 2010).

Today, the charter school movement is not the only approach to educational reform; other school choice programs are available to families. Homeschooling, described earlier in this chapter, could be viewed as the most complete alternative to public schools. In addition, some cities offer parents vouchers that allow them, in effect, to send their children to any local school, public, private, or religious, at taxpayers' expense. Yet as Karl Alexander (1997:17) eloquently noted in his presidential address to the Southern Sociological

Society, "The charter school movement, with its 'let 1,000 flowers bloom' philosophy, is certain to yield an occasional prize-winning rose. But is . . . [this approach to school choice] likely to prove a reliable guide for broad-based, systematic reform—the kind of reform that will carry the great mass of our children closer to where we want them to be? I hardly think so." Indeed, with such diversity in learning environments found among thousands of charter schools, the jury is still out on their effectiveness. As with most educational institutions, one cannot assume quality just based on a certain structure, size, affiliation, or funding source.

Take the Issue with You

1. Do you have any experience with educational reform, either as a student yourself or as a parent? If so, describe the changes that you witnessed. Were they successful in improving educational outcomes?

2. Which type of school choice program, if any, would you favor—homeschooling, charter schools, or school vouchers? Explain your choice.

3. Are you concerned about educational standards in the United States? If so, do you think schools should be reformed at the local level? Should the federal government become more involved in school reform?

MASTERING THIS CHAPTER

Summary

Education is a cultural universal found throughout the world, although in varied forms. This chapter examines sociological views of education and analyzes schools as an example of formal organizations.

1. The transmission of knowledge and bestowal of status are manifest functions of education. Among the latent functions are transmitting culture, promoting social and political integration, maintaining social control, and serving as an agent of social change.

2. In the view of conflict theorists, education serves as an instrument of elite domination by creating standards for entry into occupations, bestowing status unequally, and subordinating the role of women.

3. Teacher expectations about a student's performance can sometimes have an impact on the student's actual achievements.

4. Today, most schools in the United States are organized in a bureaucratic fashion. Weber's five basic characteristics of bureaucracy are all evident in schools.

5. Homeschooling has become a viable alternative to traditional public and private schools. An estimated 1.5 million or more American children are now educated at home.

6. **Charter schools**—experimental schools that are developed and managed by individuals, groups of parents, or educational management organizations—are one of several recent attempts to reform the public school system in the United States. Although charter schools are popular with parents, not enough research has been done to evaluate their effectiveness in improving educational outcomes.

Key Terms

Charter school An experimental school that is developed and managed by individuals, groups of parents, or educational management organizations. (364)

Correspondence principle The tendency of schools to promote the values expected of individuals in each social class and perpetuate social class divisions from one generation to the next. (357)

Credentialism An increase in the lowest level of education needed to enter a field. (356)

Education A formal process of learning in which some people consciously teach while others adopt the social role of learner. (350)

Hidden curriculum Standards of behavior that are deemed proper by society and are taught subtly in schools. (354)

Teacher-expectancy effect The impact that a teacher's expectations about a student's performance may have on the student's actual achievements. (358)

Tracking The practice of placing students in specific curriculum groups on the basis of their test scores and other criteria. (356)

TAKING SOCIOLOGY with You

1. Attend a meeting of a local Parent Teacher Association (PTA). What issues are parents talking about? Describe their concerns using one or more sociological perspectives.

2. Make a list of the student subcultures on your campus, then describe them using the concepts you learned in Chapter 3. Do any of these subcultures serve as out-groups for other subcultures?

3. Does your school have a gay–straight alliance? If so, speak with one of the officers. What are members doing to reduce prejudice and foster better relations among gay and straight students? Explain their approach using sociological theory.

Self-Quiz

Read each question carefully and then select the best answer.

1. Which sociological perspective emphasizes that the common identity and social integration fostered by education contribute to overall societal stability and consensus?
   a. the functionalist perspective
   b. the conflict perspective
   c. the interactionist perspective
   d. labeling theory

2. Which one of the following was introduced into school systems to promote social change?
   a. sex education classes
   b. affirmative action programs
   c. Project Head Start
   d. all of the above

3. The correspondence principle was developed by
   a. Max Weber.
   b. Karl Marx and Friedrich Engels.
   c. Samuel Bowles and Herbert Gintis.
   d. James Thurber.

4. The student subculture that is hostile to the college environment and seeks out ideas that may or may not relate to studies is called the
   a. collegiate subculture.
   b. academic subculture.
   c. vocational subculture.
   d. nonconformist subculture.

5. Most recent research on ability grouping raises questions about its
   a. effectiveness, especially for lower-achieving students.
   b. failure to improve the prospects of higher-achieving students.
   c. ability to improve the prospects of lower- and higher-achieving students.
   d. both a and b

6. The most basic *manifest* function of education is
   a. transmitting knowledge.
   b. transmitting culture.

   c. maintaining social control.
   d. serving as an agent of change.

7. Sixty years ago, a high school diploma was the minimum requirement for entry into the paid labor force of the United States. Today, a college diploma is virtually the bare minimum. This change reflects the process of
   a. tracking.
   b. credentialism.
   c. the hidden curriculum.
   d. the correspondence principle.

8. Samuel Bowles and Herbert Gintis have argued that capitalism requires a skilled, disciplined labor force and that the educational system of the United States is structured with that objective in mind. Citing numerous studies, they offer support for what they call
   a. tracking.
   b. credentialism.
   c. the correspondence principle.
   d. the teacher-expectancy effect.

9. The teacher-expectancy effect is most closely associated with
   a. the functionalist perspective.
   b. the conflict perspective.
   c. the interactionist perspective.
   d. anomie theory.

10. Sociologist Max Weber noted five basic characteristics of bureaucracy, all of which are evident in the vast majority of schools, whether at the elementary, secondary, or even college level. Which of the following is *not* one of them?
    a. division of labor
    b. written rules and regulations
    c. impersonality
    d. shared decision making

11. The _____ perspective stresses the importance of education in transmitting culture, maintaining social control, and promoting social change.

12. In the past, the integrative function of education was most obvious through its emphasis on promoting a common _____.

13. The _____ subculture identifies with the intellectual concerns of the faculty and values knowledge for its own sake.

14. A _____ _____ is an experimental school that is developed and managed outside the public school system.

15. Women's education tends to suffer in those cultures with traditional _____ _____.

16. Schools perform a variety of _____ functions, such as transmitting culture, promoting social and political integration, and maintaining social control.

17. Sociologist _____ _____ points out that better-educated people tend to have greater access to information, to hold more diverse opinions, and to possess the ability to make subtle distinctions in analysis.

18. The term _____ _____ refers to standards of behavior that are deemed proper by society and are taught subtly in schools. For example, children must not speak until the teacher calls on them and must regulate their activities according to the clock or the bell.

19. _____ is the practice of placing students in specific curriculum groups on the basis of their test scores and other criteria.

20. Of the four distinctive subcultures among college students discussed in the text, the _____ subculture is interested primarily in career prospects, and views college as a means of obtaining degrees that are essential for advancement.

THINKING ABOUT **MOVIES**

Freedom Writers

A teacher attempts to defuse conflict among her students.

Nursery University

This documentary, set in New York City, shows how early childhood education is becoming formalized.

Waiting for Superman

This film documents failures in the American educational system and their personal consequences.

Government affects society at all levels. In 2010, Microsoft founder Bill Gates and former President Bill Clinton testified before the U.S. Senate's Foreign Relations Committee on approaches to global health problems.

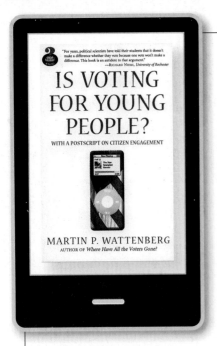

IS VOTING FOR YOUNG PEOPLE?

WITH A POSTSCRIPT ON CITIZEN ENGAGEMENT

MARTIN P. WATTENBERG

AUTHOR OF *Where Have All the Voters Gone?*

"For years, political scientists have told their students that it doesn't make a difference whether they vote because one vote won't make a difference. This book is an antidote to that argument."
—RICHARD NIEMI, *University of Rochester*

❝ Voting is for Old People," proclaimed a T-shirt printed and distributed in 2004 by Urban Outfitters, a popular American clothing company. At Harvard's Kennedy School of Government, the perceived message of the shirt hit a raw nerve. Its director issued a public statement criticizing the slogan, saying that it could not be further from the truth—that voting is for everyone. In response, Urban Outfitters said they never intended to discourage anyone from voting. Rather, they asserted that their goal was to draw attention to the relative lack of participation of young adults in politics, a problem that many analysts and politicians acknowledge but few seem to be genuinely concerned about. . . .

Over the last three decades, politics and voting have indeed become more and more the province of the elderly, which will be shown to be the case not only in the United States but also *throughout the world's advanced industrialized democracies.* There is in fact a rift between politicians and young adults, although not one of mutual contempt but rather of mutual neglect. Many young people don't vote simply because they don't follow politics. Moreover, because so many young people don't follow politics and don't vote, parties and politicians frequently don't

All too often, low turnout rates among the young are considered to be a natural part of political life, and hence not worth fretting about.

bother with young people, thereby further widening the age bias in electoral participation.

All too often, low turnout rates among the young are considered to be a natural part of political life, and hence not worth fretting about. Scholars often write of a life cycle pattern in which people become more aware of the political world as they age, and hence are more likely to vote. As such, it is often thought that today's young nonvoters will eventually show up at the polls and have their voices heard. If such a life cycle truly exists, it ought to be consistently found in: (1) different eras; and (2) across a wide range of democracies. The data . . . from a number of countries in the 1970s contradict the life cycle hypothesis. . . .

Communications technology is one . . . aspect of political life that has undergone transformation throughout the world's advanced industrialized societies . . . in recent years. . . . Changes in media habits from generation to generation have led to a new situation in which young people are far less likely to be exposed to news about public affairs than their elders. Young adults have not consciously decided to avoid political news in recent years; rather, having been socialized in a markedly different communications environment, they just have not picked up the same media habits that their parents and grandparents did. These media habits, which older people developed long ago in a different world, continue to serve them well in today's political environment—making them substantially more likely to follow politics and become familiar with the issues of the day. And the more one learns about public affairs and follows current events, the more one is likely to realize the stakes involved at the polls. ❞

(*Wattenberg 2008:1–2, 3*) Additional information about this excerpt can be found on the Online Learning Center at www.mhhe.com/schaefer13e.

In this excerpt from *Is Voting for Young People?* Martin P. Wattenberg, a professor of political science at the University of California at Irvine, confronts the generation gap in politics, not only in the United States but in industrialized countries around the world. Wattenberg thinks that the absence of young people from the voting booth reflects a generational difference in the way that citizens use the mass media. Few young people nowadays read the newspapers, so few know much about politics or think that it has any relevance to them. Most spend their time surfing the Internet, downloading music to their iPods and MP3s, text-messaging and snapping photos using their cell phones. Only in countries where these technological marvels are not available to the average youth is apathy among young people not a noteworthy phenomenon.

Those who vote (or who choose not to) operate within the framework of the existing political system, be it local, state, national, or international. By **political system,** sociologists mean the social institution that is founded on a recognized set of procedures for implementing and achieving society's goals, such as the allocation of valued resources. Like religion and the family, the political system is a cultural universal: it is found in every society. In the United States, the political system holds the ultimate responsibility for addressing the social policy issues examined in this textbook: child care, immigration, welfare reform, and so forth.

Are young people more interested in what's playing on their portable media players than in the political issues confronting their nation? How does government maintain its power, and how do political parties and public interest groups attempt to exert theirs? Does our campaign finance system put some groups at a disadvantage? In this chapter we will analyze the impact of government on people's lives from a sociological point of view. We will begin with a macro-level analysis of the sources of political power and authority, and the four major types of government in which that power and authority is exerted. We will see how politics works, with particular attention to citizens' participation and the changing role of women and minority groups. We'll look at two models of power in the United States, the elite and the pluralist models. Then we'll touch briefly on war, peace, and terrorism, and see how political activists have begun using the Internet to promote their causes. Finally, the Social Policy section will explore the controversy over campaign financing, an issue that vividly illustrates the close relationship between government and the moneyed elite who seek to influence the political process.

Power and Authority

In any society, someone or some group—whether it be a tribal chief, a dictator, or a parliament—makes important decisions about how to use resources and how to allocate goods. One cultural universal, then, is the exercise of power and authority. Inevitably, the struggle for power and authority involves **politics,** which political scientist Harold Lasswell (1936) tersely defined as "who gets what, when, and how." In their study of politics and government, sociologists are concerned with social interactions among individuals and groups and their impact on the larger political and economic order.

Power

Power lies at the heart of a political system. According to Max Weber, **power** is the ability to exercise one's will over others. To put it another way, whoever can overcome the resistance of others and control their behavior is exercising power. Power relations can involve large organizations, small groups, or even people in an intimate association.

Because Weber developed his conceptualization of power in the early 1900s, he focused primarily on the nation-state and its sphere of influence. Today scholars recognize that the trend toward globalization has brought new opportunities, and with them new concentrations of power. Power is now exercised on a global as well as a national stage, as countries and multinational corporations vie to control access to resources and manage the distribution of capital (R. Schaefer 2008b; Sernau 2001).

There are three basic sources of power within any political system: force, influence, and authority. **Force** is the actual or threatened use of coercion to impose one's will on others. When leaders imprison or even execute political dissidents, they are applying force; so, too, are terrorists when they seize or bomb an embassy or assassinate a political leader.

In the 21st century, force has taken on new meaning as nations clamp down on use of the Internet to oppose the central government or assert freedom of expression, human rights, and minority or religious views. When a military coup overthrew the democratically elected government of Thailand in September 2006, for example, citizens lost access to websites that criticized the takeover. As of 2008, 16 nations maintained selective to pervasive political controls on Internet content (Figure 17-1). Censorship of online content is just as much a use of force as closing down a newspaper or arresting dissidents (Deibert et al. 2008; OpenNet Initiative 2011; Zittrain and Palfrey 2008).

Influence, on the other hand, refers to the exercise of power through a process of persuasion. A citizen may change his or her view of a Supreme Court nominee because of a newspaper editorial, the expert testimony of a law school dean before the Senate Judiciary Committee, or a stirring speech by a political activist at a rally. In each case, sociologists would view such efforts to persuade people as examples of influence. Now let's take a look at the third source of power, *authority*.

Types of Authority

The term **authority** refers to institutionalized power that is recognized by the people over whom it is exercised. Sociologists commonly use the term in connection with those who hold legitimate power through elected or publicly acknowledged positions. A person's authority is often limited. Thus, a referee has the authority to decide whether a penalty should be called during a football game, but has no authority over the price of tickets to the game.

Max Weber ([1913] 1947) developed a classification system for authority that has become one of the most useful and frequently cited contributions of early sociology. He identified three ideal types of authority: traditional, rational-legal, and charismatic. Weber did not insist that only one type applies to a given society or organization. All can be present, but their relative importance will vary. Sociologists have found Weber's typology valuable in understanding different manifestations of legitimate power within a society.

Traditional Authority Until the middle of the past century, Japan was ruled by a revered emperor whose absolute power was passed down from generation to generation. In a political system based on **traditional authority,** legitimate power is conferred by custom and accepted practice. A king or queen is accepted as ruler of a nation simply by virtue of inheriting the crown; a tribal chief rules because that is the accepted practice. The ruler may be loved or hated, competent or destructive; in terms of legitimacy, that does not matter. For the traditional leader, authority rests in custom, not in personal characteristics, technical competence, or even written law. People accept the ruler's authority because that is how things have always been done. Traditional authority is absolute when the ruler has the ability to determine laws and policies.

Rational-Legal Authority The U.S. Constitution gives Congress and our president the authority to make and enforce laws and policies. Power made legitimate by law is known as **rational-legal authority.** Leaders derive their rational-legal authority from the written rules and regulations of political systems, such as a constitution. Generally, in societies based on rational-legal authority, leaders are thought to have specific areas

MAPPING LIFE WORLDWIDE

FIGURE **17-1** FILTERING INFORMATION: POLITICAL CONTENT

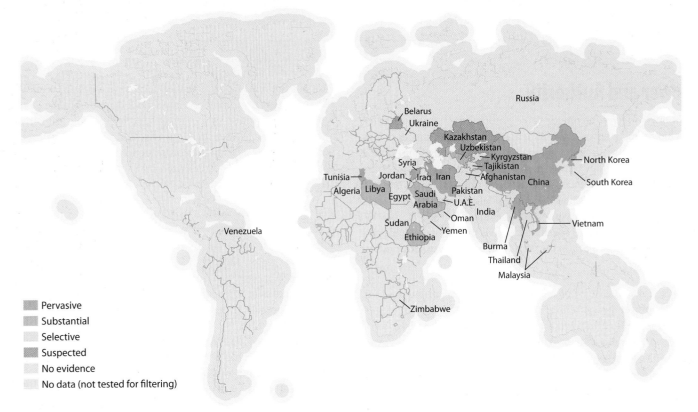

Pervasive

Substantial

Selective

Suspected

No evidence

No data (not tested for filtering)

Note: "No data" (see the gray portions of the map) does not necessarily indicate an absence of filtering.
Sources: OpenNet Initiative 2011; see also Deibert et al. 2008; Faris and Villeneuve 2008.

This map highlights nations that filter or restrict content that opposes the current government's views, or that is related to human rights, freedom of expression, minority rights, and religious movements.

of competence and authority but are not thought to be endowed with divine inspiration, as in certain societies with traditional forms of authority.

Charismatic Authority Joan of Arc was a simple peasant girl in medieval France, yet she was able to rally the French people and lead them into major battles against English invaders. How was this possible? As Weber observed, power can be legitimized by the *charisma* of an individual. The term **charismatic authority** refers to power made legitimate by a leader's exceptional personal or emotional appeal to his or her followers.

Charisma lets a person lead or inspire without relying on set rules or traditions. In fact, charismatic authority is derived more from the beliefs of followers than from the actual qualities of leaders. So long as people perceive a charismatic leader such as Jesus, Joan of Arc, Gandhi, Malcolm X, or Martin Luther King Jr. as having qualities that set him or her apart from ordinary citizens, that leader's authority will remain secure and often unquestioned.

Observing charismatic authority from an interactionist perspective, sociologist Carl Couch (1996) points out that the growth of the electronic media has facilitated the development of charismatic authority. During the 1930s and 1940s, the heads of state of the United States, Great Britain, and Germany all used radio to issue direct appeals to citizens. Now, television and the Internet allow leaders to "visit" people's homes and communicate

with them. In both Taiwan and South Korea in 1996, troubled political leaders facing reelection campaigns spoke frequently to national audiences and exaggerated military threats from neighboring China and North Korea, respectively.

As we noted earlier, Weber used traditional, rational-legal, and charismatic authority as ideal types. In reality, particular leaders and political systems combine elements of two or more of these forms. Presidents Franklin D. Roosevelt, John F. Kennedy, and Ronald Reagan wielded power largely through the rational-legal basis of their authority. At the same time, they were unusually charismatic leaders who commanded the personal loyalty of large numbers of citizens.

thinking CRITICALLY

On your campus, what are some examples of the three types of authority?

Types of Government

Each society establishes a political system through which it is governed. In modern industrialized nations, these formal systems of government make a significant number of critical political decisions. We will survey five basic types of government here: monarchy, oligarchy, dictatorship, totalitarianism, and democracy.

Monarchy

A **monarchy** is a form of government headed by a single member of a royal family, usually a king, queen, or some other hereditary ruler. In earlier times, many monarchs claimed that God had granted them a divine right to rule. Typically, they governed on the basis of traditional forms of authority, sometimes accompanied by the use of force. By the beginning of the 21st century, however, monarchs held genuine governmental power in only a few nations, such as Monaco. Most monarchs now have little practical power; they serve primarily ceremonial purposes.

Oligarchy

An **oligarchy** is a form of government in which a few individuals rule. A rather old method of governing that flourished in ancient Greece and Egypt, oligarchy now often takes the form of military rule. In developing nations in Africa, Asia, and Latin America, small factions of military officers will forcibly seize power, either from legally elected regimes or from other military cliques.

Strictly speaking, the term *oligarchy* is reserved for governments that are run by a few selected individuals. However, the People's Republic of China can be classified as an oligarchy if we stretch the meaning of the term. In China, power rests in the hands of a large but exclusive ruling *group,* the Communist Party. In a similar vein, drawing on conflict theory, one might argue that many industrialized nations of the West should be considered oligarchies (rather than democracies), since only a powerful few—leaders of big business, government, and the military—actually rule. Later in this chapter, we will examine the *elite model* of the U.S. political system in greater detail.

Dictatorship and Totalitarianism

A **dictatorship** is a government in which one person has nearly total power to make and enforce laws. Dictators rule primarily through the use of coercion, which often includes torture and executions. Typically, they *seize* power rather than being freely elected (as in a democracy) or inheriting power (as in a monarchy). Some dictators are quite charismatic and manage to achieve a certain popularity, though their supporters' enthusiasm is almost certainly tinged with fear. Other dictators are bitterly hated by the people over whom they rule.

Frequently, dictators develop such overwhelming control over people's lives that their governments are called *totalitarian.* (Monarchies and oligarchies may also achieve this type of dominance.) **Totalitarianism** involves virtually complete government control and surveillance over all aspects of a society's social and political life. Germany during Hitler's reign, the Soviet Union in the 1930s, and North Korea today are classified as totalitarian states.

North Korea has a totalitarian government whose leadership attempts to control all aspects of people's lives. This billboard, a blatant example of government propaganda, portrays the country's ruthless leader as a benevolent father figure.

Democracy

In a literal sense, **democracy** means government by the people. The word *democracy* originated in two Greek roots— *demos,* meaning "the populace" or "the common people," and *kratia,* meaning "rule." Of course, in large, populous nations such as the United States, government by the people is impractical at the national level. Americans cannot vote on every important issue that comes before Congress. Consequently, popular rule is generally maintained through **representative democracy,** a form of government in which certain individuals are selected to speak for the people.

The United States is commonly classified as a representative democracy, since the elected members of Congress and state legislatures make our laws. However, critics have questioned whether our democracy really is representative. Even today, not everyone in the United States feels included. Conspicuous among those who view themselves as excluded are Native Hawaiians (Box 17-1).

Do Congress and the state legislatures genuinely represent the masses, including minorities? Are the people of the United States legitimately self-governing, or has our government become a forum for powerful elites? We will explore these issues in the remainder of the chapter.

thinking CRITICALLY

Contrast the use of power as defined by Max Weber in a dictatorship in a democracy.

Political Behavior in the United States

Citizens of the United States take for granted many aspects of their political system. They are accustomed to living in a nation with a Bill of Rights, two major political parties, voting by secret ballot, an elected president, state and local governments distinct from the national government, and so forth. Yet each society has its own ways of governing itself and making decisions. U.S. residents expect Democratic and Republican candidates to compete for public office; residents of Cuba and the People's Republic of China are accustomed to one-party rule by the Communist Party. In this section, we will examine several aspects of political behavior within the United States.

Participation and Apathy

In theory, a representative democracy will function most effectively and fairly if an informed and active electorate communicates its views to government leaders. Unfortunately, that is hardly the case in the United States. Virtually all citizens are familiar with the basics of the political process, and most tend to identify to some extent with a political party. In 2011, about 29 percent of registered voters in the United States saw themselves as Democrats and 29 percent as Republicans; an impressive 39 percent were independent. However, only a small minority of citizens, often members of the higher social classes, actually participate in political organizations on a local or national level. Studies reveal that only 8 percent of Americans belong to a political club or organization. Not more than 20 percent have ever contacted an official of national, state, or local government about a political issue or problem (Gallup 2011b; Orum and Dale 2009).

By the 1980s, it had become clear that many people in the United States were beginning to be turned off by political parties, politicians, and big government. The most dramatic indication of this growing alienation came from voting statistics. Today, voters of all ages and races appear to be less enthusiastic than ever about elections, even presidential contests. For example, in the presidential election of 1896, almost 80 percent of eligible voters in the United States went to the polls. Yet by the 2008 election, despite its drama and historic nature, turnout was only 62 percent of all eligible voters—well below the levels of the 1960s. Obviously, even modestly higher voter turnout could dramatically change an election outcome, as the razor-thin margin in the 2000 presidential election demonstrated (McDonald 2008, 2009a).

Although a few nations still command high voter turnout, increasingly, national leaders of other countries also complain of voter apathy. Even so, among the 140 countries that held parliamentary elections between 1945 and 1998, the United States ranked 114th in voter turnout. No other industrialized nation has recorded a lower average turnout (Figure 17-2, page 376).

Despite poor voter turnout, participation in politics may be increasing, especially on the Internet. In terms of both antigovernment activities and financial contributions to political parties, online participation rivals the political rallies and doorbell-ringing efforts of yesteryear. Fifty-five percent of the entire adult population of the United States went online in 2008 to get news and information about the presidential election. One in every five of those online participants went so far as to post comments for others to read (A. Smith 2009).

In the end, political participation makes government accountable to the voters. If participation declines, government operates with less of a sense of accountability to society. This issue

SPOTTING TREND

Democracy on the Rise?

The breakup of the Soviet Union in 1991 launched several new countries in Eastern Europe, whose citizens were eager to escape foreign domination. In parts of Europe and Asia, democracy seemed to bloom where it never had grown before. What has happened since then?

Applying our own standards of democracy to nations in other parts of the world can be difficult. If a country holds free elections that are open to all citizens, is that enough to qualify it as a democracy? What if the government bans certain political parties? What if the media cannot criticize the government or report on opposition parties?

Freedom House, founded in 1941, is an international organization that advocates for democracy. Although it receives significant funding from the U.S. government, its annual review of democratic trends is generally regarded as a reasonable barometer of the spread (or lack thereof) of democracy. According to Freedom House, in 1989, only 41 percent of the world's countries could be considered democracies. The percentage rose dramatically after the collapse of the Soviet Union, reaching 60 percent in 1995. Since then, however, little has changed; the percentage of democracies has fluctuated between 59 and 64 percent.

Although recently, citizen-led revolts in countries like Egypt have offered some optimism, the overall trend is not encouraging. The industrialized democracies of North America and Europe often shrink from pressuring developing countries to reform their governments. Furthermore, in some areas of the world, violence and organized crime make democratic reform difficult. On the other hand, although the recent worldwide recession might easily have unsettled some fragile democracies, that fortunately has not happened.

SOCIOLOGY IN THE GLOBAL COMMUNITY

17-1 Sovereignty in the Aloha State

The people of Hawai'i are definitely multiracial. Twenty-three percent of the population is White; 38 percent, Asian American; 9 percent, Hawaiian or other Pacific Islander; 9 percent, Hispanic; and 2 percent, African American. Another 19 percent of the population, including Hawai'i-born Barack Obama, declare themselves to be of two or more races. Yet Hawai'i is not a racial paradise: certain occupations and even social classes tend to be dominated by Whites, Chinese, or Japanese Americans. Nor is Hawai'i immune to intolerance, although compared to the mainland and much of the rest of the world, race relations there are more harmonious than discordant.

For one group in particular, Native Hawaiians, access to any kind of power has been severely limited for generations. Now, through the **sovereignty movement,** the indigenous people of Hawai'i are hoping to win self-government, as well as restoration of—or compensation for—1.2 million acres of ancestral lands they have lost over the last century. Their movement is comparable to efforts made by American Indian tribes in the continental United States, both in its roots and in its significance.

The sovereignty movement began in 1996, when Native Hawaiians held a referendum on the question "Shall the Hawaiian people elect delegates to propose a Native Hawaiian government?" The results indicated that 73 percent of those who voted favored such an effort. Since then, the state Office of Hawaiian Affairs has sought to create a registry of the estimated 200,000 people of significant Hawaiian descent on the islands. Officials are about halfway to reaching their goal of

convincing all Native Hawaiians to come forward and register.

In Washington, D.C., Hawai'i's congressional delegation is seeking passage of the Native Hawaiian Government Reorganization Act, also referred to as the Akaka Bill, after U.S. Senator Daniel Akaka. The act would give people of Hawaiian ancestry more say over the use of local resources, including land and fresh water; provide them with affordable housing; take steps to preserve their culture; and create ways for them to better express their grievances. If the act passes, Native Hawaiians will become the last remaining indigenous group in the United States to be allowed to establish their own government—a right already extended to Alaskan Natives and 564 Native American tribes. As of mid-2011, the measure had passed the U.S. House of

Representatives, but had not yet been discussed on the floor of the Senate.

Meanwhile, Native Hawaiians do what they can to create political pressure for their cause. On occasion, they form alliances with environmental groups that want to halt commercial development on the islands. And in 2008, a Native Hawaiian independence group seized the royal palace in Honolulu to protest the U.S.-backed overthrow of the Hawaiian monarchy in

If the act passes, Native Hawaiians will become the last remaining indigenous group in the United States to be allowed to establish their own government.

1893. Although the occupation lasted barely a day, the political discontent it revealed persists. Little wonder that in 2009, the 50th anniversary of Hawai'i's statehood passed without a single government-sponsored celebration. Instead, Native Hawaiians concentrated their attention on Washington, D.C., and pushed for passage of the Akaka Bill.

LET'S DISCUSS

1. From a mainstream point of view, what might be the advantages and disadvantages of extending sovereignty to an indigenous group? Discuss using sociological concepts.
2. Do some research on the legal basis for tribal sovereignty. How did American Indian tribes gain the status of separate nations?

Sources: Halvalani 2002; Niesse 2008, 2011; Staton 2004; Toensing 2009; Welch 2011.

---

is most serious for the least powerful individuals and groups in the United States. Voter turnout has been particularly low among members of racial and ethnic minorities. In postelection surveys, fewer African Americans and Hispanics than Whites report that they actually voted. Many more potential voters fail to register to vote. The poor—whose focus understandably is on survival—are traditionally underrepresented among voters as well. The low turnout found among these groups is explained at least in part by their common feeling of powerlessness. Yet these low statistics encourage political power brokers to continue to ignore the interests of the less affluent and the nation's minorities. The segment of the voting population that has shown the most voter apathy is the young, as discussed in Box 17-2 on page 377 (File and Crissey 2010).

use your sociological *imagination*

Were you brought up to consider political involvement an important civic duty? If so, do you take that duty seriously by informing yourself about the issues and voting?

Race and Gender in Politics

Because politics is synonymous with power and authority, we should not be surprised that political strength is lacking in marginalized groups, such as women and racial and ethnic minorities. Nationally, women did not get the vote until 1920. Most Chinese Americans

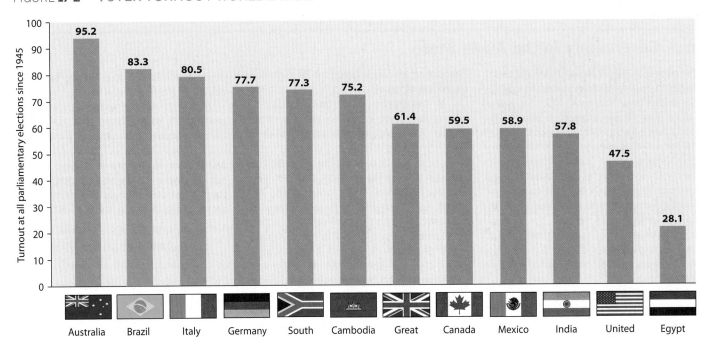

Note: Based on turnout in recent elections for seats in national congress or parliament. Data are for 2008 except for Australia (2007), Brazil, Cambodia, and Mexico (2006), Egypt, Germany, and Great Britain (2005), India (2004), and South Africa (2009).
Source: International Institute for Democracy and Electoral Assistance 2011.

were turned away from the polls until 1926. And African Americans were disenfranchised until 1965, when national voting rights legislation was passed. Predictably, it has taken these groups some time to develop their political power and begin to exercise it effectively.

Progress toward the inclusion of minority groups in government has been slow. As of mid-2011, 17 out of 100 U.S. senators

Minnesota Democrat Keith Ellison created quite a stir in 2007 when he became the first person to take the congressional oath of office on a Qur'an. The newly elected member of the House of Representatives, who is Muslim, thought the Qur'an would make his oath more meaningful than a Bible. Speaker of the House Nancy Pelosi (left) borrowed Thomas Jefferson's two-volume Qur'an for the occasion—a reminder that acknowledging diversity is nothing new in U.S. politics.

were women; 2 were Latino and 2 were Asian Americans, leaving 79 White non-Hispanic men. Among the 435 members of the U.S. House of Representatives, 310 were White non-Hispanic men; 71 were women, 42 were African Americans (including 13 women), 29 were Latinos (including 7 Latinas), and 7 were Asian Americans (including 4 women). These numbers, although low, represent a high-water mark for most of these groups.

Today, with record-high numbers of Blacks and Latinos holding elective office, many critics still decry what has been termed *fiesta politics.* White power brokers tend to visit racial and ethnic minority communities only when they need electoral support, making a quick appearance on a national or ethnic holiday to get their pictures taken and then vanishing. When the election is over, they too often forget to consult the residents who supported them about community needs and concerns.

Female politicians may be enjoying more electoral success now than in the past, but there is some evidence that the media cover them differently from male politicians. A content analysis of newspaper coverage of recent gubernatorial races showed that reporters wrote more often about a female candidate's personal life, appearance, or personality than a male candidate's, and less often about her political positions and voting record. Furthermore, when political issues were raised in newspaper articles, reporters were more likely to illustrate them with statements made by male candidates than by female candidates (Devitt 1999; Jost 2008).

RESEARCH TODAY

17-2　Why Don't More Young People Vote?

All through the 1960s, young people in the United States participated actively in a range of political issues, from pushing civil rights to protesting the Vietnam War. They were especially disturbed by the fact that young men were barred from voting but were being drafted to serve in the military and were dying for their country. In response to these concerns, the Twenty-Sixth Amendment to the Constitution was ratified in 1971, lowering the voting age from 21 to 18.

Now, more than 40 years later, we can consider the available research and see what happened. Frankly, what is remarkable is what did *not* happen. First, young voters (those between ages 18 and 21) have not united in any particular political sentiment. We can see in the way the young vote the same divisions of race, ethnicity, and gender that are apparent among older age groups.

Second, while the momentum for lowering the voting age came from college campuses, the majority of young voters are not students. Third, and particularly troubling, is their relatively low turnout. The 2008 presidential election, held against a background of war in Iraq, the historic candidacy of Barack Obama, and a global economic decline, did pique the interest of young voters. In that election, 51.4 percent of eligible voters under age 30 turned out, compared to 49 percent in 2004.

What lies behind voter apathy among the young? The popular explanation is that people—especially young people—are alienated from the political system, turned off by the shallowness and negativity of candidates and campaigns. However, young people do vote as they age.

While the momentum for lowering the voting age came from college campuses, the majority of young voters are not students at all.

Other explanations for the lower turnout among the young seem more plausible. First, the United States is virtually alone in requiring citizens to vote twice, in effect. They must first *register* to vote, often at a time when issues are not on the front burner and candidates haven't even declared. Second, though citizens in the United States tend to be more active in politics at the community level than those in other countries, young people often feel unmoved by local issues such as public school financing.

One way in which youths *are* impacting elections is through their reliance on the Internet for information. Today, every political campaign maintains a presence on the Web, not only through an official website, but on social networking sites. During the 2008 presidential election, two-thirds of young adults with online profiles took part in some form of political activity on those sites. Time will tell whether the Internet will ultimately reduce political apathy among younger citizens.

LET'S DISCUSS

1. How often do you vote? If you do not vote, what accounts for your apathy? Are you too busy to register? Are community issues uninteresting to you?
2. Do you think voter apathy is a serious social problem? What might be done to increase voter participation in your age group and community?

Sources: Alwin 2002; Clymer 2000; Higher Education Research Institute 2004; McDonald 2009b; Niemi and Hanmer 2010; Patterson 2005; A. Smith 2009; Vargas 2007; Wattenberg 2008.

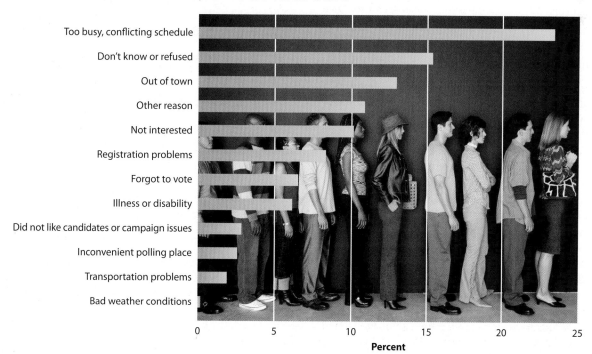

REASONS FOR NOT VOTING, 18- TO 24-YEAR-OLDS

Too busy, conflicting schedule
Don't know or refused
Out of town
Other reason
Not interested
Registration problems
Forgot to vote
Illness or disability
Did not like candidates or campaign issues
Inconvenient polling place
Transportation problems
Bad weather conditions

0　5　10　15　20　25
Percent

Source: Holder 2006:13.

Figure 17-3 shows the representation of women in selected national legislatures. While the proportion of women in national legislatures has increased in the United States and many other nations, in all but one country women still do not account for half the members of the national legislature. The African Republic of Rwanda, the exception, ranks the highest, with 56.3 percent of its legislative seats held by women. Overall, the United States ranked 89th among 186 nations in the proportion of women serving as national legislators in 2011.

To remedy this situation, many countries have adopted quotas for female representatives. In some, the government sets aside a certain percentage of seats for women, usually from 14 to 30 percent. In others, political parties have decided that 20 to 40 percent of their candidates should be women. Thirty-two countries now have some kind of female quota system (Rubin and Dagher 2009; Vasagar 2005).

thinking CRITICALLY

In the United States, which plays a more significant role in political behavior, gender or race? Explain.

Models of Power Structure in the United States

Who really holds power in the United States? Do "we the people" genuinely run the country through our elected representatives? Or is it true that behind the scenes, a small elite controls both the government and the economic system? It is difficult to determine the location of power in a society as complex as the United States. In exploring this critical question, social scientists have developed two basic views of our nation's power structure: the power elite and the pluralist models.

Power Elite Models

Karl Marx believed that 19th-century representative democracy was essentially a sham. He argued that industrialized societies were dominated by relatively small numbers of people who owned factories and controlled natural resources. In Marx's view, government officials and military leaders were essentially servants of this capitalist class and followed their wishes. Therefore, any key decisions made by politicians inevitably reflected the interests of the dominant bourgeoisie. Like others who share an **elite model** of power relations, Marx believed that society is ruled by a small group of individuals who share a common set of political and economic interests.

Mills's Model Sociologist C. Wright Mills took this model a step further in his pioneering work *The Power Elite* ([1956] 2000b). Mills described a small group of military, industrial, and government leaders who controlled the fate of the United States—the **power elite.** Power rested in the hands of a few, both inside and outside government.

A pyramid illustrates the power structure of the United States in Mills's model (Figure 17-4a). At the top are the corporate rich,

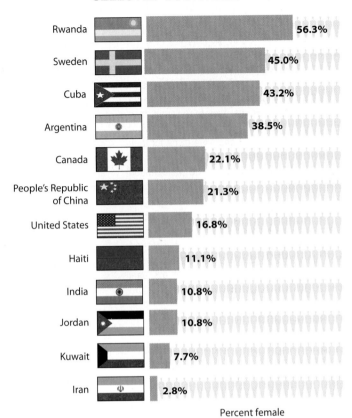

FIGURE **17-3** WOMEN IN NATIONAL LEGISLATURES, SELECTED COUNTRIES

Country	Percent female
Rwanda	56.3%
Sweden	45.0%
Cuba	43.2%
Argentina	38.5%
Canada	22.1%
People's Republic of China	21.3%
United States	16.8%
Haiti	11.1%
India	10.8%
Jordan	10.8%
Kuwait	7.7%
Iran	2.8%

Percent female

Notes: Data are for lower legislative houses only, as of March 31, 2011; data on upper houses, such as the U.S. Senate, are not included. In 2005, the all-male Kuwaiti Parliament granted women the right to vote and serve in elected offices, which allowed women to run for office in 2007.
Source: Inter-Parliamentary Union 2011.

Think about It
Why do you think being elected to Congress is so difficult for women?

leaders of the executive branch of government, and heads of the military (whom Mills called the "warlords"). Directly below are local opinion leaders, members of the legislative branch of government, and leaders of special-interest groups. Mills contended that these individuals and groups would basically follow the wishes of the dominant power elite. At the bottom of the pyramid are the unorganized, exploited masses.

The power elite model is in many respects similar to the work of Karl Marx. The most striking difference is that Mills believed that the economically powerful coordinate their maneuvers with the military and political establishments to serve their common interests. He rejected Marx's belief that by itself, the economic structure of capitalism could create a ruling class. Still, the powerless masses at the bottom of Mills's power elite model certainly bring to mind Marx's portrait of the oppressed workers of the world, who have "nothing to lose but their chains."

A fundamental element in Mills's thesis is that the power elite not only includes relatively few members but also operates as a self-conscious, cohesive unit. Although not necessarily

FIGURE **17-4** POWER ELITE MODELS

379

Government and Politics

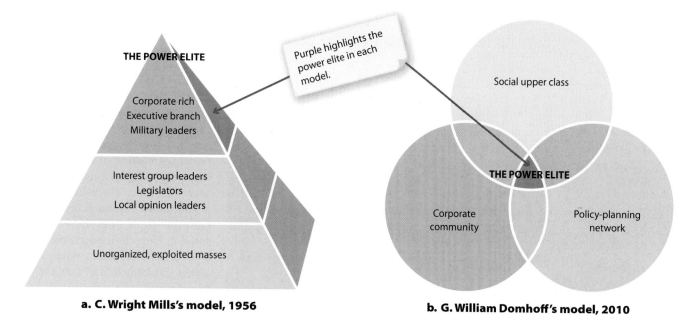

a. C. Wright Mills's model, 1956

b. G. William Domhoff's model, 2010

Source: Left, author based on Mills [1956] 2000b; right, Domhoff 2010:116.

diabolical or ruthless, the elite comprises similar types of people who interact regularly with one another and have essentially the same political and economic interests. Mills's power elite is not a conspiracy, but rather a community of interest and sentiment among a small number of influential people (A. Hacker 1964).

Admittedly, Mills failed to clarify when the elite opposes protests and when it tolerates them; he also failed to provide detailed case studies that would substantiate the interrelationships among members of the power elite. Nevertheless, his challenging theories forced scholars to look more critically at the democratic political system of the United States.

In commenting on the scandals that have rocked major corporations such as Enron and AIG over the past 15 years, observers have noted that members of the business elite *are* closely interrelated. In a study of the members of the boards of directors of *Fortune* 1000 corporations, researchers found that each director can reach *every* other board of directors in just 3.7 steps. That is, by consulting acquaintances of acquaintances, each director can quickly reach someone who sits on each of the other 999 boards. Furthermore, the face-to-face contact directors regularly have in their board meetings makes them a highly cohesive elite. Finally, the corporate elite is not only wealthy, powerful, and cohesive; it is also overwhelmingly White and male (G. Davis 2003, 2004; Kentor and Jang 2004; Mizruchi 1996; R. Schaefer 2008b; Strauss 2002).

One outgrowth of Mills's power elite model is current research on the presence of a *global* power elite—that is, those business, political, and former military leaders who exercise influence across national borders. Because this avenue of scholarship is relatively new, there is some disagreement on the definition of the term. Must the members of the global power elite demonstrate as much consensus as the members of Mills's power elite? Or can the global power elite include such diverse voices as publisher Rupert Murdoch, illegal arms dealer Viktor Bout, and

former President Bill Clinton, in his role as head of the Clinton Global Initiative (L. Miller 2008; Rothkopf 2008)?

Domhoff's Model Over the past three decades, sociologist G. William Domhoff (2010) has agreed with Mills that a powerful elite runs the United States. He finds that it is still largely White, male, and upper class, as he wrote in his book with Richard L. Zweigenhaft (2006). But Domhoff stresses the role played both by elites of the corporate community and by leaders of organizations in the policy-planning network, such as chambers of commerce and labor unions. Many of the people in both groups are also members of the social upper class. And he notes the presence of a small number of women and minority men in key positions—groups that were excluded from Mills's top echelon and are still underrepresented today.

Though the three groups in Domhoff's power elite model overlap, as Figure 17-4b shows, they do not necessarily agree on specific policies. Domhoff notes that in the electoral arena, two coalitions have exercised influence. A *corporate-conservative coalition* has played a large role in both political parties, generating support for particular candidates through direct-mail appeals. A *liberal-labor coalition* is based in unions, local environmental organizations, a segment of the minority group community, liberal churches, and the university and arts communities (Zweigenhaft and Domhoff 2006).

Pluralist Model

Several social scientists insist that power in the United States is shared more widely than the elite models indicate. In their view, a pluralist model more accurately describes the nation's political system. According to the **pluralist model,** many competing groups within the community have access to government, so that no single group is dominant.

The pluralist model suggests that a variety of groups play a significant role in decision making. Typically, pluralists make use of intensive case studies or community studies based on

At the 2011 summit in Paris, world leaders addressed the crisis in Libya.

observation research. One of the most famous—an investigation of decision making in New Haven, Connecticut—was reported by Robert Dahl (1961). Dahl found that although the number of people involved in any important decision was rather small, community power was nonetheless diffuse. Few political actors exercised decision-making power on all issues. One individual or group might be influential in a battle over urban renewal, but have little impact on educational policy.

The pluralist model, however, has not escaped serious questioning. Domhoff (1978, 2010) reexamined Dahl's study of decision making in New Haven and argued that Dahl and other pluralists had failed to trace how local elites who were prominent in decision making belonged to a larger national ruling class. In addition, studies of community power, such as Dahl's work in New Haven, can examine decision making only on issues that

become part of the political agenda. They fail to address the potential power of elites to keep certain matters entirely out of the realm of government debate.

Dianne Pinderhughes (1987) has criticized the pluralist model for failing to account for the exclusion of African Americans from the political process. Drawing on her studies of Chicago politics, Pinderhughes points out that the residential and occupational segregation of Blacks and their long political disenfranchisement violates the logic of pluralism—which would hold that such a substantial minority should always have been influential in community decision making. This critique applies to many cities across the United States, where other large racial and ethnic minorities, among them Asian Americans, Puerto Ricans, and Mexican Americans, are relatively powerless.

Historically, pluralists have stressed ways in which large numbers of people can participate in or influence governmental decision making. New communications technologies like the Internet are increasing the opportunity to be heard, not just in countries such as the United States, but in developing countries the world over. One common point of the elite and pluralist perspectives stands out, however: in the political system of the United States, power is unequally distributed. All citizens may be equal in theory, yet those who are high in the nation's power structure are "more equal." New communications technology may or may not change that distribution of power (A. McFarland 2007).

Perhaps the ultimate test of power, no matter what a nation's power structure, is the decision to go to war. Because the rank and file of any army is generally drawn from the lower classes—the least powerful groups in society—such a decision has life-and-death consequences for people far removed from the center of power. In the long run, if the general population is not convinced that war is necessary, military action is unlikely to succeed. Thus, war is a risky way in which to address conflict between nations. In the following section we will contrast war and peace as ways of addressing societal conflict, and more recently, the threat of terrorism.

thinking CRITICALLY

Which is a better model of the power structure in the United States, the power elite model or the pluralist model? Justify your answer.

Pluralism can be seen in action in the activity of lobbying groups attempting to influence public policy. The highly publicized battle over stem cell research is one example; it has pitted conservative religious groups against health advocacy groups, dividing political leaders in the process. Though legislation to support the controversial research technique had the backing of several prominent Republican lawmakers, including Senator Orrin Hatch (R-Utah), shown here with actor and activist Michael J. Fox, it fell victim to a presidential veto in 2006.

War and Peace

Conflict is a central aspect of social relations. Too often it becomes ongoing and violent, engulfing innocent bystanders as well as intentional participants. Sociologists Theodore

TAKING SOCIOLOGY TO WORK

Joseph W. Drummond, Management Analyst, U.S. Army Space and Missile Defense Command

When Joseph Drummond entered Morehouse College, he was planning to major in political science. But after taking an introductory sociology course, he felt that sociology gave him a clearer picture of the complexity and interconnectedness of society. "The career track that I had in mind was to enter the field of sociology as a researcher/policy maker," he explains. However, he soon ran into "a disconnect between academia and policy making," and an apparent lack of representation of sociologists at the policymaking level.

Drummond credits one of his sociology professors for steering him toward quantitative courses. "If you ever plan on having a job," the professor suggested, "make sure you have a lot of classes with quantitative analysis—for example, statistics and data analysis. These classes tell whatever company you want to work for that you have practical skills." Later, when Drummond asked his current employer why he had gotten the job he now holds, he was told that his data analysis and social statistics courses had made him competitive.

Today, Drummond works at the U.S. Army's Space and Missile Defense Command (SMDC), near Huntsville, Alabama. He began there as an intern, after responding to an email from Morehouse College's career office. Drummond is now a junior analyst with a team that formulates and develops doctrine, organization, and material requirements for Army units assigned to space and missile defense. In a typical workweek, he reviews military force structure—units, battalions, and so on—and helps to implement directives from Department of the Army headquarters. "A lot of what we do is attempting to translate very high-level guidance to something that's practical," he explains.

Drummond values the support and professional development he has received from the Army, including classes on program management, data analysis, national security, and force management. An Army-sponsored Technology and Government in Your Future event emphasized the need for interns to pursue graduate studies in math and science to land the best jobs. Drummond says the real-world experience he got as an intern at SMDC not only brought classroom theory to life; it also made him more attractive to future employers.

Asked how he uses sociology in his work, Drummond replies that his academic training has helped him to look critically at problems and to think about the second- and third-order effects of a decision. Seeing society from a macro-level view is also invaluable to him. "When U.S. leadership began to realize that a 'hearts and mind' campaign means that we need to understand the social-historical context of the people whose country we're occupying, that changed the way that we did business and also impacted the way U.S. military force structure was managed," he explains. "A lot of people had problems making the connection." Finally, sociology has taught Drummond not to take things at face value. "Most problems/issues that we come across very seldom have easy fixes," he notes. "Sociology taught me that thorough analysis means leaving no stone unturned."

LET'S DISCUSS

1. Have you ever considered a career in national defense? Do you know anyone with a college degree who works in the field?
2. Why do you think quantitative analysis is such an important skill to employers? How might you use it in your career?

Caplow and Louis Hicks (2002:3) have defined **war** as conflict between organizations that possess trained combat forces equipped with deadly weapons. This meaning is broader than the legal definition, which typically requires a formal declaration of hostilities.

War

Sociologists approach war in three different ways. Those who take a *global view* study how and why two or more nations become engaged in military conflict. Those who take a *nation-state view* stress the interaction of internal political, socioeconomic, and cultural forces. And those who take a *micro view* focus on the social impact of war on individuals and the groups they belong to (Kiser 1992).

From the nation-state perspective, there is little to be said for the supposed socioeconomic benefits of war. Although armed conflicts increase government expenditures on troops and weapons, which tends to stimulate the economy, they also divert workers from civilian health and medical services. Thus, they have a negative effect on civilians' life chances, causing higher levels of civilian mortality. It is exceedingly difficult for a society to engage in armed conflict while maintaining citizens' well-being at home (Carlton-Ford 2010).

Although the decision to go to war is made by government leaders, public opinion plays a significant role in its execution. By 1971, the number of U.S. soldiers killed in Vietnam had surpassed 50,000, and antiwar sentiment was strong. Surveys done at that time showed the public was split roughly equally on the question of whether war was an appropriate way to settle differences between nations (Figure 17-5). This division in public opinion continued until the United States became involved in the Gulf War following Iraq's invasion of Kuwait in 1990. Since then, U.S. sentiment has been more supportive of war as a means of resolving disputes.

A major change in the composition of the U.S. military is the growing presence of women. Over 197,000 women, or about 14 percent of active U.S. military forces, are now in uniform, serving not just as support personnel but as an integral part of combat units. The first casualty of the war in Iraq, in fact, was Private First Class Lori Piestewa, a member of the Hopi tribe and a descendant of Mexican settlers in the Southwest (Bureau of the Census 2008a:328).

From a micro view, war can bring out the worst as well as the best in people. In 2004, graphic images of the abuse of Iraqi prisoners by U.S. soldiers at Iraq's Abu Ghraib prison shocked the world. For social scientists, the deterioration of the guards' behavior brought to mind Philip Zimbardo's mock prison experiment, done in 1971. Although the results of the experiment, highlighted in Chapter 5, have been applied primarily to civilian correctional facilities, Zimbardo's study was actually funded by the Office of Naval Research. In July 2004, the U.S. military began using a documentary film about the experiment to train military interrogators to avoid mistreatment of prisoners (Zarembo 2004; Zimbardo 2004).

FIGURE **17-5** U.S. PUBLIC OPINION ON THE NECESSITY OF WAR, 1971–2007

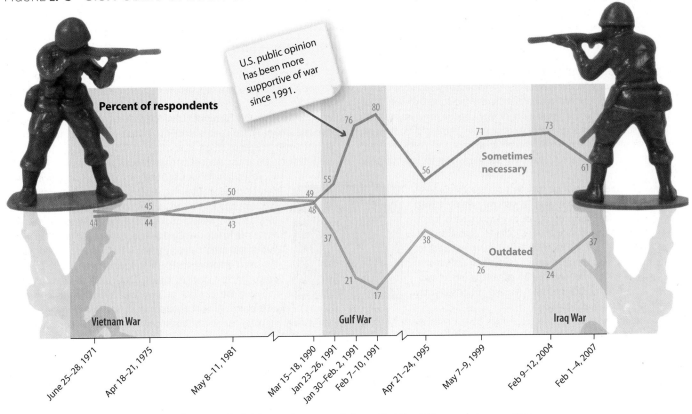

Percent of respondents

U.S. public opinion has been more supportive of war since 1991.

80
76
73
71
55   56   **Sometimes necessary**   61
50
45   49
44   44   48   43
37   38   **Outdated**   37
21   26   24
17

Vietnam War   Gulf War   Iraq War

June 25–28, 1971
Apr 18–21, 1975
May 8–11, 1981
Mar 15–18, 1990
Jan 23–26, 1991
Jan 30–Feb. 2, 1991
Feb 7–10, 1991
Apr 21–24, 1995
May 7–9, 1999
Feb 9–12, 2004
Feb 1–4, 2007

Note: Respondents replied to the question "Some people feel that war is an outmoded way of settling differences between nations. Others feel that wars are sometimes necessary to settle differences. With which point of view do you agree?"
Source: Gallup 2009b.

Peace

Sociologists have considered **peace** both as the absence of war and as a proactive effort to develop cooperative relations among nations. While we will focus here on international relations, we should note that in the 1990s, 90 percent of the world's armed conflicts occurred *within* rather than between states. Often, outside powers became involved in these internal conflicts, either as supporters of particular factions or in an attempt to broker a peace accord. In at least 28 countries where such conflicts occurred—none of which would be considered core nations in world systems analysis—at least 10,000 people died (Kriesberg 1992; Dan Smith 1999).

Another way of picturing the relative peacefulness of nations around the world is the Global Peace Index (Figure 17-6). This index is based on 24 indicators, including organized internal conflict, violent crime, political instability, the potential for terrorist acts, and a nation's level of military expenditures compared to its neighbors'. Currently, New Zealand is at the top of the index (very peaceful);

Somalia, Afghanistan, and Iraq are at the bottom. The United States ranks 83 on this list of 144 nations, between Ukraine and Kazakhstan.

A representative of the International Red Crescent Society delivers an aid parcel in the southern Iraqi town of Safwan. The Red Crescent provides emergency aid to victims of war and disaster in Muslim communities. Such nongovernmental organizations (NGOs) help to bind countries together, promoting peaceful relations.

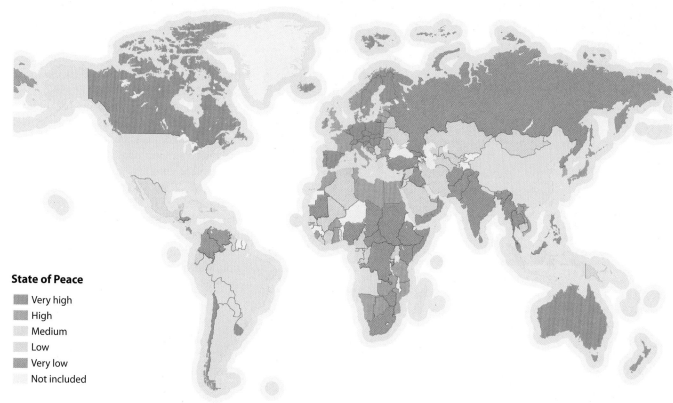

State of Peace

- Very high
- High
- Medium
- Low
- Very low
- Not included

Source: Institute for Economics and Peace 2010.

Sociologists and other social scientists who draw on sociological theory and research have tried to identify conditions that deter war. One of their findings is that international trade may act as a deterrent to armed conflict. As countries exchange goods, people, and then cultures, they become more integrated and less likely to threaten each other's security. Viewed from this perspective, not just trade but immigration and foreign exchange programs have a beneficial effect on international relations.

Another means of fostering peace is the activity of international charities and activist groups called nongovernmental organizations (NGOs). The Red Cross and Red Crescent, Doctors Without Borders, and Amnesty International donate their services wherever they are needed, without regard to nationality. In the past decade or more, these global organizations have been expanding in number, size, and scope. By sharing news of local conditions and clarifying local issues, they often prevent conflicts from escalating into violence and war. Some NGOs have initiated cease-fires, reached settlements, and even ended warfare between former adversaries.

Finally, many analysts stress that nations cannot maintain their security by threatening violence. Peace, they contend, can best be maintained by developing strong mutual security agreements between potential adversaries (Etzioni 1965; Shostak 2002).

In recent years, the United States has begun to recognize that its security can be threatened not just by nation-states, but by political groups that operate outside the bounds of legitimate authority. Indeed, terrorism is now considered the foremost threat to U.S. security—one the U.S. military is unaccustomed to fighting.

use your sociological *imagination*

Do you hear much discussion of how to promote worldwide peace, or do the conversations you hear focus more on ending a particular conflict?

Terrorism

Acts of terror, whether perpetrated by a few or by many people, can be a powerful political force. Formally defined, **terrorism** is the use or threat of violence against random or symbolic targets in pursuit of political aims. For terrorists, the end justifies the means. They believe the status quo is oppressive and that desperate measures are essential to end the suffering of the deprived. Convinced that working through the formal political process will not effect the desired political change, terrorists insist that illegal actions—often directed against innocent people—are needed. Ultimately, they hope to intimidate society and thereby bring about a new political order.

Global terrorism is just that—global in scope and impact. In March 2010, two female suicide bombers from the Caucasus region took 40 lives on the Moscow subway to call attention to their homeland's struggle for political independence from Russia.

about the heightened anxiety created by the vague alerts issued by the federal government from time to time. Worldwide, immigration and the processing of refugees have slowed to a crawl, separating families and preventing employers from filling job openings. As these efforts to combat political violence illustrate, the term *terrorism* is an apt one (R. Howard and Sawyer 2003; Lee 1983; R. Miller 1988).

Increasingly, governments are becoming concerned about another form of political violence, the potential for malicious cyberattacks. In an age in which computer viruses can spread worldwide through the Internet, this kind of attack could render a nation's computer systems useless, or even shut down its power plants. A few years ago, such a scenario would have been considered pulp fiction, but it is now the subject of contingency planning throughout the world. In the next section, we will consider some other ways that the Internet has affected government (Clayton 2011).

An essential aspect of contemporary terrorism involves use of the media. Terrorists may wish to keep secret their individual identities, but they want their political messages and goals to receive as much publicity as possible. Drawing on Erving Goffman's dramaturgical approach, sociologist Alfred McClung Lee has likened terrorism to the theater, where certain scenes are played out in predictable fashion. Whether through calls to the media, anonymous manifestos, or other means, terrorists typically admit responsibility for and defend their violent acts.

Sociologists and others have studied the role of different factors in the development of terrorism. They find that both democratic and repressive regimes can facilitate terrorism, although in different ways. The likelihood of violence is higher in youthful populations and among alienated groups, especially expatriate (overseas) communities (P. Davis and Cragin 2009).

Since September 11, 2001, governments worldwide have renewed their efforts to fight terrorism. Although the public generally regards increased surveillance and social control as a necessary evil, these measures have nonetheless raised governance issues. For example, some citizens in the United States and elsewhere have questioned whether measures such as the USA Patriot Act of 2001 threaten civil liberties. Citizens have also complained

thinking CRITICALLY

What is the greatest threat to world peace, and how would you counter it?

Political Activism on the Internet

By any measure, the Internet has become a force to be reckoned with in politics. Although television and newspapers still serve as sources of political news, 73 percent of adult

Tibetan monks in exile check the news from Tibet at a technological center in Dharamsala, India. Once a military network, the Internet has become a hotbed of political activism.

Internet users in the United States, or 54 percent of all adults, went online to get news about the 2010 election. Surfers are less likely to visit candidates' official websites than to check the chatter on Twitter. By 2010, 22 percent of online adults were using the social media site, which was created in 2006, for political purposes (A. Howard 2011). These developments have turned political campaigning into a 24/7 activity, especially in the United States. President Barack Obama, now a candidate for reelection, has maintained his 13-million-name e-mail list not only to inform and persuade citizens but also to seek campaign donations (M. Scherer/Owings 2010).

On the Internet, political activity is not limited to traditional party politics, and certainly not to domestic politics. In far-flung places including Egypt, Indonesia, Kosovo, and Malaysia, citizens are making themselves heard through *cyberactivism* or Net activism—the use of the Internet for political purposes. In China, 10,000 members of the fast-growing Falun Gong religious sect surprised government officials with a mass rally organized on the web and through YouTube videos. In Kosovo, the staff of Koha Ditore, a dissident newspaper, took to the web after Serbian soldiers closed their office. And in Mexico, the revolutionary Zapatista movement gained support from an online campaign for self-rule in the state of Chiapas.

As these incidents illustrate, organizers find the web especially useful in circumventing the restrictive controls of authoritarian regimes. In fact, groups branded as terrorists in a variety of states have used the web to their advantage. Websites can be established outside a country's borders, beyond the control of government officials yet still accessible to the country's citizens.

The use of online technology by political activists has not been lost on traditional sources of authority, be they charismatic, legal-rational, or traditional. From Queen Elizabeth II to Prime Minister Manmohan Singh of India, legitimate authority figures have mounted a major effort to create an online presence, sometimes called *e-government*. The competition is on, both online and offline (Lucas 2008).

Also growing in importance are borderless organizations that unite people of like mind—from peace activists to terrorists—around the world. These are very tightly knit communities, notes Professor Juan Enriquez of Harvard University. Labor groups and environmental organizations such as Greenpeace have become particularly adept at using e-mail to mobilize activists quickly, wherever they are needed. The result: a completely new kind of power structure, compared to the more familiar face-to-face approach of Washington lobbyists. "The new people with power are those with credibility and an e-mail list," says political consultant Jennifer Laszlo. "You have no idea who they are, where they are, what color they are" (Engardio 1999:145).

---

use your sociological *imagination*

Imagine a future in which everyone in the United States has access to the Internet, and the Internet is the foremost political medium. How would government in that society differ from government today?

---

social**policy** and Politics

Campaign Financing

How much does it cost to become president of the United States? All told, Barack Obama's 2008 campaign raised $745 million; John McCain's, $768 million. If we include all presidential and congressional candidates in 2008, win or lose, the price tag was over $5.2 billion.

Is the enormous cost of modern political campaigns a big issue with voters? The answer is yes and no. Surveys show that 61 percent of voters favor limits on campaign spending. Yet 38 percent feel that a candidate—maybe their candidate?—should be allowed to spend whatever he or she wants. What is more, over 60 percent of both Republicans and Democrats agree that campaign contributions are free speech, and as such are protected by the First Amendment to the Constitution (Center for Responsive Politics 2010a, 2010b; Saad 2010a).

Looking at the Issue

Regulation of campaign contributions has a long history, beginning with efforts to bar the requirement that government employees contribute to their bosses' campaign funds. More recently, the focus on both the state and national levels has been on remedying the shortcomings of the Federal Campaign Act of 1974, which placed restrictions on so-called *hard money,* or donations made to specific candidates for national office. Hard money is now limited to $10,000 per organization or $2,000 per individual donor per election cycle (the primary and election being separate cycles). These limits were intended to keep national candidates or elected officials from being bought by the wealthy or the powerful.

However, soon after passage of the act, contributors and potential recipients—that is, politicians—found loopholes in the new law. In 2002, Congress passed the Bipartisan Campaign Reform Act (BCRA), also referred to as the McCain-Feingold Act, to address some of those shortcomings. For the first time, limitations were placed on contributions of *soft money*—donations to the major political parties, leadership committees, and political action committees by corporations and special-interest groups. Soft money was not permitted in federal elections, and its use in state and local elections was limited.

Perhaps the weakest link in campaign finance regulations is the fact that most of them do not apply to candidates who refuse public funding. In the 2004 presidential primary, both George W. Bush and John Kerry declined to accept federal campaign financing. More dramatic was Barack Obama's decision to forgo public funding in the 2008 general election, which allowed him great latitude in receiving private funds. Although Obama argued that his fund-raising was transparent, the sky was, in effect, the limit (Luo 2008).

Applying Sociology

Functionalists would say that political contributions keep the public involved in the democratic process and connected to the candidates. Issue advocacy money also offers voters a way to express their views on issues directly, rather than through the candidates. But conflict theorists would counter that since money brings influence, this use of material wealth allows donors to influence government policymakers in ways that tend to preserve their own wealth. In increasing numbers of cases, candidates like the multimillionaires Ross Perot and Steve Forbes have used their own private fortunes to finance their campaigns—an approach that allows them to sidestep public disclosure requirements.

Interactionists would point out the symbolic significance of the public perception that big money drives elections in the United States. Accurate or not, this impression encourages voter apathy, which is reflected in low turnout at the polls. What good does participating in politics do, voters may wonder, when special interests can spend millions to counteract their efforts?

Initiating Policy

On the national level, traditional reform groups—Common Cause, the League of Women Voters, and Ralph Nader's organization Public Citizen—continue to call for tighter limits on contributions by both individuals and organizations. To these groups and others seeking to curb campaign spending, the Supreme Court's 2010 decision in *Citizens United v. Federal Election Commission,* which ended restrictions on organizational contributions (that is, soft money) was a step in the wrong direction. The Court's decision allowed businesses, labor unions, and other groups, from Planned Parenthood to the National Rifle Association, to spend their own money on campaign materials, and in doing so to effectively circumvent the BCRA.

The impact of the Supreme Court's decision on future elections probably will not be as great as the storm over the decision would indicate. Candidates and their bankers, whatever their party, have become skilled at mobilizing big money and generating grassroots passion for particular individuals or issues (Hasen 2010).

Take the Issue with You

1. Did you vote in the most recent election? Does your vote count, or do special-interest groups wield more power than voters like you?

2. Do you work for or contribute to political candidates? What about groups that promote special issues, like school prayer, gun control, and free trade? Which is more important to you, the candidate or the issue?

3. Would strict across-the-board spending limits on all candidates for public office help to make the political process more democratic? What about limits on political contributions of all kinds?

Summary

Every society must have a **political system** in order to allocate valued resources. This chapter examines the sources of **power** and **authority** in such systems; the four major types of government; political behavior, including voter apathy and women's representation in government; two basic models of power structure in the United States; **war** and **peace**; political activism on the Internet; and campaign finance reform.

1. There are three basic sources of **power** within any political system: **force, influence,** and **authority.**

2. Max Weber identified three ideal types of authority: **traditional, rational-legal,** and **charismatic.**

3. There are five basic types of government: **monarchy, oligarchy, dictatorship, totalitarianism,** and **democracy.**

4. Political participation makes government accountable to citizens, but voters display a great deal of apathy, both in the United States and in other countries.

5. Women are still underrepresented in politics, but are becoming more successful at winning election to public office.

6. Advocates of the **elite model** of the U.S. power structure see the nation as being ruled by a small group of individuals who share common political and economic interests (a **power elite**). Advocates of a **pluralist model** believe that power is shared more widely among conflicting groups.

7. **War** may be defined as conflict between organizations that possess trained combat forces equipped with deadly weapons—a definition that includes conflict with terrorist organizations.

8. Around the world, the Internet has become a potent political arena, one that dissident groups can use to oppose the power of authoritarian regimes.

9. Despite legislative efforts to reform campaign financing methods, wealthy donors and special-interest groups still wield enormous power in U.S. government through their contributions to candidates, political parties, and issue advocacy.

Key Terms

Authority Institutionalized power that is recognized by the people over whom it is exercised.   (page 371)

Charismatic authority Power made legitimate by a leader's exceptional personal or emotional appeal to his or her followers.   (372)

Democracy In a literal sense, government by the people.   (373)

Dictatorship A government in which one person has nearly total power to make and enforce laws.   (373)

Elite model A view of society as being ruled by a small group of individuals who share a common set of political and economic interests.   (378)

Force The actual or threatened use of coercion to impose one's will on others.   (371)

Influence The exercise of power through a process of persuasion.   (371)

Monarchy A form of government headed by a single member of a royal family, usually a king, queen, or some other hereditary ruler.   (373)

Oligarchy A form of government in which a few individuals rule.   (373)

Peace The absence of war, or more broadly, a proactive effort to develop cooperative relations among nations.   (382)

Pluralist model A view of society in which many competing groups within the community have access to government, so that no single group is dominant.   (379)

Political system The social institution that is founded on a recognized set of procedures for implementing and achieving society's goals.   (370)

Politics In Harold Lasswell's words, "who gets what, when, and how."   (371)

Power The ability to exercise one's will over others.   (371)

Power elite A small group of military, industrial, and government leaders who control the fate of the United States.   (378)

Rational-legal authority Power made legitimate by law.   (371)

Representative democracy A form of government in which certain individuals are selected to speak for the people.   (373)

Sovereignty movement The effort by the indigenous people of Hawai'i to win self-government, as well as the restoration of—or compensation for—their ancestral lands.   (375)

Terrorism The use or threat of violence against random or symbolic targets in pursuit of political aims.   (383)

Totalitarianism Virtually complete government control and surveillance over all aspects of a society's social and political life.   (373)

Traditional authority Legitimate power conferred by custom and accepted practice.   (371)

War Conflict between organizations that possess trained combat forces equipped with deadly weapons.   (381)

TAKING SOCIOLOGY with you

1. If your college has a club for young Republicans or Democrats, attend one of their meetings. What issues are members interested in, and why? How are they planning to put their beliefs into action? Are they concerned about voter apathy among young people?

2. Pick a nongovernmental organization with worldwide recognition, such as the Red Cross, Doctors Without Borders, or Amnesty International. Go online and find out how the organization works on behalf of peace. What specifically has this NGO done to prevent or stop war?

3. Federal campaign regulations require candidates to reveal the names of people and organizations that make large campaign donations. Go online and look up the names of groups that spent large amounts of money on a political campaign that interests you. Why do you think those groups supported that particular candidate? Was an economic interest at stake?

Self-Quiz

Read each question carefully and then select the best answer.

1. Which one of the following is a cultural universal?
   a. religion
   b. the political system
   c. family
   d. all of the above

2. A king or queen is accepted as ruler of a nation simply by virtue of inheriting the crown. This is an example of
   a. totalitarianism.
   b. charismatic authority.
   c. traditional authority.
   d. rational-legal authority.

3. Totalitarian states typically control which of the following institutions?
   a. family
   b. economy
   c. politics
   d. all of the above

4. G. William Domhoff's model is an example of
   a. an elite theory of power.
   b. a pluralist theory of power.
   c. a functionalist theory of power.
   d. an interactionist theory of power.

5. In terms of voter turnout, the United States typically ranks
   a. highest among all countries.
   b. highest among industrialized nations.
   c. lowest among industrialized nations.
   d. lowest among all countries.

6. Political scientist Harold Lasswell defined *politics* as
   a. the struggle for power and authority.
   b. the allocation of valued resources.
   c. who gets what, when, and how.
   d. a cultural universal.

7. What are the three basic sources of power within any political system?
   a. force, influence, and authority
   b. force, influence, and democracy
   c. force, legitimacy, and charisma
   d. influence, charisma, and bureaucracy

8. Which of the following is *not* part of the classification system of authority developed by Max Weber?
   a. traditional authority
   b. pluralist authority
   c. legal-rational authority
   d. charismatic authority

9. According to C. Wright Mills, power rests in the hands of the
   a. people.
   b. representative democracy.
   c. aristocracy.
   d. power elite.

10. The use or threat of violence against random or symbolic targets in pursuit of political aims is referred to as
    a. politics.
    b. power.
    c. authority.
    d. terrorism.

11. _____ is the actual or threatened use of coercion to impose one's will on others.

12. In most of today's _____, kings and queens have little practical power.

13. The elite model of political power implies that the U.S. has a(n) _____ as its form of government.

14. As of mid-2011, only _____ out of 100 United States senators were women.

15. Sexism has been the most serious barrier to women interested in holding public office. To remedy this situation, many countries have adopted _____ for female representatives.

16. _____ is the exercise of power through a process of persuasion.

17. Joan of Arc, Gandhi, Malcolm X, Adolf Hitler, and Martin Luther King Jr., all possessed _____ authority.

18. _____ involves virtually complete government control and surveillance over all aspects of a society's social and political life.

19. The United States is commonly classified as a(n)_____ _____, because the elected members of Congress and state legislatures make our laws.

20. Advocates of the _____ model suggest that competing groups within the community have access to government, so that no single group is dominant.

Answers
1 (d); 2 (c); 3 (d); 4 (a); 5 (c); 6 (c); 7 (a); 8 (b); 9 (d); 10 (d); 11 Force; 12 monarchies; 13 oligarchy; 14 17; 15 quotas; 16 Influence; 17 charismatic; 18 Totalitarianism; 19 representative democracy; 20 pluralist

THINKING ABOUT MOVIES

Countdown to Zero

This documentary explores the dangers of nuclear weapons in a global context.

The Last King of Scotland

This dramatization of Idi Amin's rise to power in Uganda in the 1970s illustrates the infamous dictator's charismatic authority.

The Visitor

Two men become friends, but their relationship is disrupted when one of them is deported by the U.S. government.

Fresh produce tempts shoppers
at an outdoor market in
Bend, Oregon. In any society,
the exchange of goods and
services depends on the
interaction of people.

> It is rare in life to have a moment of personal epiphany. Mine came in the millennium year when, at the Co-op, we had just introduced the UK's first own brand Fairtrade product: a chocolate bar with its key ingredient sourced from Ghana. We had supported the concept of fair trade right from the beginning but, although always empathetic to the ethical agenda, my interest was primarily commercial; the intention was to develop responsible retailing, a holistic approach to this agenda, as a modern day reflection of cooperative values and a vehicle for differentiating the business from its competitors. But in concert with the chocolate initiative a BBC crew visited Kuapa Kokoo in Ghana and their 14-minute film changed my view of the world. At the end of their report they unwrapped a chocolate bar, which was starting to melt in the heat, and gave some to a young woman and her daughter. As they tasted the product their eyes lit up and their faces were transformed into bright smiles and the young woman said 'oh, it's so sweet, so sweet'. This lady had spent her whole life toiling in the fields for a pittance and had never tasted the product of her own labours; she had no concept of what it was about chocolate that made it so important and appealing to the people living thousands of miles away in the northern hemisphere. In one sense the film captured a joyous experience but in another it was extraordinarily sad. I felt a catch in my throat and knew I was hooked for the rest of my life.
> . . .
>
> It has been estimated that fair trade may, currently, be benefiting more than 7 million people in the developing world. This is an impressive achievement but set in the context of the sheer scale of world poverty it still represents only a relatively small contribution towards addressing an enormous problem.
>
> It is estimated that 1.4 billion people, one fifth of the world's population, are trying to survive at or below the World Bank's official poverty line of just $1.25 a day. And 2.6 billion people, about 40 per cent of humanity, are living on less than $2 a day.
>
> These astonishing numbers are so large that it is difficult to fully comprehend them. They reflect the appalling collective failure of human society. And the scale of the failure becomes even more dramatic when we consider *disparities* in world income. The poorest 40 per cent account for just 5 per cent of global income whilst the richest 20 per cent take three quarters of the pot. The truth is that fair trade is still very much in its infancy. Those who are committed to making a real difference in the developing world will recognise that we are not at the end of a process, or anywhere near the end, but really only at the very beginning. If we strip away all of the commercial spin, and occasional wishful thinking, we might be left with the uncomfortable conclusion that, far from capitalising on a consumer movement, we have perhaps not yet recognised its full potential and have so far failed to put mechanisms into place to ensure that its momentum can be fully realised.
> . . .
>
> The United States of America is the largest consumer market on Earth. No other country on the planet could do more to address the climate problem and establish a fairer trading system. While fair trade has experienced strong growth in the States, which in absolute terms is the largest single market for fair trade products, overall market penetration is low. Yet, if we are to have a true revolution in trading practices it is difficult to see how it can be achieved without the US fully on board. This represents the greatest single challenge for fair trade campaigners. . . .

The United States of America is the largest consumer market on Earth. No other country on the planet could do more to address the climate problem and establish a fairer trading system.

(Bowes 2011:ix, 2–3, 231–232) Additional information about this excerpt can be found on the Online Learning Center at www.mhhe.com/schaefer13e.

John Bowes, editor of this excerpt from *The Fair Trade Revolution*, once served as a top executive in a British grocery chain. In the process, he became acutely aware of the low wages paid to those who harvest the food sold in grocery stores. To address their plight, he helped to originate a movement called **fair trade**, in which consumers in industrialized countries voluntarily pay above-market prices for certain foods so that the workers who plant, pick, and pack the crops can receive higher wages. Supporters of fair trade often seek to subsidize export crops grown in developing countries, such as coffee, bananas, and chocolate (A. Stark 2011).

While acknowledging Bowes's point of view, sociologists also try to see foreign agricultural laborers and farm owners from the perspective of their own cultures—an approach called **cultural relativism** (see Chapter 3). That is, besides comparing farm work in developing countries to similar work in industrial nations, sociologists would compare it to the other jobs available to foreign workers. For example, sweatshops certainly aren't the sort of places where people in industrial countries would want to work, but from the foreign worker's perspective, they may be preferable to a farm in an isolated rural area or a lower-paying job with a local employer. In sum, foreign workers and producers face a different *economic system* from the one in industrial nations, so their attitudes and the choices they make may differ from our own.

The term **economic system** refers to the social institution through which goods and services are produced, distributed, and consumed. As with social institutions such as the family, religion, and government, the economic system shapes other aspects of the social order and is in turn influenced by them.

Throughout this textbook, you have been reminded of the economy's impact on social behavior—for example, on individual and group behavior in factories and offices. You have studied the work of Karl Marx and Friedrich Engels, who emphasized that a society's economic system can promote social inequality. And you have learned that foreign investment in developing countries can intensify inequality among residents.

This chapter will present a sociological analysis of the impact of the economy on people's lives. What makes work satisfying? How has the trend toward deindustrialization changed the work people do? What will the workforce of the 21st century look like? We will begin to answer these questions with a macro-level analysis of two ideal types of economic system—capitalism and socialism—and the real-world institution known as the informal economy. A case study on China, a socialist society that has been moving toward capitalism, follows. Next, we will examine various aspects of work, including worker alienation and worker satisfaction. We will also look at the ways in which the U.S. economy is changing. Finally, in the Social Policy section we will explore the effects of a financial innovation called *microfinancing* on the lives of poor people in developing countries.

Economic Systems

The sociocultural evolution approach developed by Gerhard Lenski categorizes preindustrial society according to the way in which the economy is organized. The principal types of preindustrial society, as you recall, are hunting-and-gathering societies, horticultural societies, and agrarian societies.

As we noted in Chapter 5, the *Industrial Revolution*—which took place largely in England during the period 1760 to 1830—brought about changes in the social organization of the workplace. People left their homesteads and began working in central locations such as factories. As the Industrial Revolution proceeded, a new form of social structure emerged: the **industrial society**, a society that depends on mechanization to produce its goods and services.

Two basic types of economic system distinguish contemporary industrial societies: capitalism and socialism. As described in the following sections, capitalism and socialism serve as ideal types of economic system. No nation precisely fits either model. Instead, the economy of each individual state represents a mixture of capitalism and socialism, although one type or the other is generally more useful in describing a society's economic structure.

Capitalism

In preindustrial societies, land functioned as the source of virtually all wealth. The Industrial Revolution changed all that. It required that certain individuals and institutions be willing to take substantial risks in order to finance new inventions, machinery, and business enterprises. Eventually, bankers, industrialists, and other holders of large sums of money replaced landowners as the most powerful economic force. These people invested their funds in the hope of realizing even greater profits, and thereby became owners of property and business firms.

The transition to private ownership of business was accompanied by the emergence of the capitalist economic system. **Capitalism** is an economic system in which the means of production are held largely in private hands and the main incentive for economic activity is the accumulation of profits. In practice, capitalist systems vary in the degree to which the government regulates private ownership and economic activity (D. Rosenberg 1991).

Immediately following the Industrial Revolution, the prevailing form of capitalism was what is termed **laissez-faire** ("let them do"). Under the principle of laissez-faire, as expounded and endorsed by British economist Adam Smith (1723–1790), people could compete freely, with minimal government intervention in the economy. Business retained the right to regulate itself and operated essentially without fear of government interference (Smelser 1963).

Occupational Growth and Decline

One of the most closely watched trends in the U.S. economy is the growth or decline of particular occupations. In good economic times and bad, people want to know where the jobs of the future will be. As a result, the Bureau of Labor Statistics regularly projects job growth over the next 10 years.

In the United States today, most new job openings are expected to require little formal education, or at most on-the-job training. Construction laborers, groundskeepers, and food preparers are three occupations that are expected to see a large increase in employment. Skilled occupations such as nurses, accountants, and teachers from preschool through high school are also expected to see strong growth.

The fastest-growing occupations—those that show the highest growth proportionately—are almost all skilled occupations, most of them in health and medicine. They include biomedical engineers—expected to grow 72 percent over the next 10 years—health aides, physician assistants, and physical therapists. Skilled non-health-related occupations, such as financial examiners and computer software engineers, are also expected to grow.

Finally, there is the other side of the ledger—occupations that are declining in number. The steepest decline, down 33 percent, is expected to occur among sewing machine operators. Other occupations that are expected to see big job losses are farmers, postal workers, telemarketers, switchboard operators, and door-to-door sales workers.

For more than a century, the board game of Monopoly has entertained millions of people around the world. In the game, players strive to dominate the fictitious economy, gleefully bankrupting other players. Ironically, Monopoly was actually developed to demonstrate the weaknesses of capitalist economies, such as excessive rents and the tendency for money to accumulate in the hands of a few.

Two centuries later, capitalism has taken on a somewhat different form. Private ownership and maximization of profits still remain the most significant characteristics of capitalist economic systems. However, in contrast to the era of laissez-faire, capitalism today features government regulation of economic relations. Without restrictions, business firms can mislead consumers, endanger workers' safety, and even defraud the companies' investors—all in the pursuit of greater profits. That is why the government of a capitalist nation often monitors prices, sets safety and environmental standards for industries, protects the rights of consumers, and regulates collective bargaining between labor unions and management. Yet under capitalism as an ideal type, government rarely takes over ownership of an entire industry.

Contemporary capitalism also differs from laissez-faire in another important respect: capitalism tolerates monopolistic practices. A **monopoly** exists when a single business firm controls the market. Domination of an industry allows the firm to effectively control a commodity by dictating pricing, quality standards, and availability. Buyers have little choice but to yield to the firm's decisions; there is no other place to purchase the product or service. Monopolistic practices violate the ideal of free competition cherished by Adam Smith and other supporters of laissez-faire capitalism.

Some capitalistic nations, such as the United States, outlaw monopolies through antitrust legislation. Such laws prevent any business from taking over so much of the competition in an industry that it controls the market. The U.S. federal government allows monopolies to exist only in certain exceptional cases, such as the utility and transportation industries. Even then, regulatory agencies scrutinize these officially approved monopolies to protect the

public. The protracted legal battle between the Justice Department and Microsoft, owner of the dominant operating system for personal computers, illustrates the uneasy relationship between government and private monopolies in capitalistic countries.

Conflict theorists point out that although *pure* monopolies are not a basic element of the economy of the United States, competition is still much more restricted than one might expect in what is called a *free enterprise system*. In numerous industries, a few companies largely dominate the field and keep new enterprises from entering the marketplace.

During the severe economic downturn that began in 2008, the United States moved even further away from the laissez-faire ideal. To keep major financial institutions from going under, the federal government invested hundreds of millions of dollars in distressed banking, investment, and insurance companies. Then in 2009, the government bailed out the failing automobile industry, taking a 60 percent interest in General Motors. The Canadian government took another 12 percent.

As we have seen in earlier chapters, globalization and the rise of multinational corporations have spread the capitalistic pursuit of profits around the world. Especially in developing countries, governments are not always prepared to deal with the sudden influx of foreign capital and its effects on their economies. One particularly striking example of how unfettered capitalism can harm developing nations is found in the Democratic Republic of Congo (formerly Zaire). The Congo has significant deposits of the metal columbite-tantalite—coltan, for short—which is used in the production of electronic circuit boards. Until the market for cell phones, pagers, and laptop computers heated up recently, U.S. manufacturers got most of their coltan from Australia. But at the height of consumer demand, they turned to miners in the Congo to increase their supply.

Predictably, the escalating price of the metal—as much as $600 a kilogram at one point, or more than three times the average

A worker mines for coltan with sweat and a stick. The sudden increase in demand for the metal by U.S. computer manufacturers caused incursions into the Congo by neighboring countries hungry for capital to finance a war. Too often, globalization can have unintended consequences for a nation's economy and social welfare.

Congolese worker's yearly wages—attracted undesirable attention. Soon the neighboring countries of Rwanda, Uganda, and Burundi, at war with one another and desperate for resources to finance the conflict, were raiding the Congo's national parks, slashing and burning to expose the coltan beneath the forest floor. Indirectly, the sudden increase in the demand for coltan was financing war and the rape of the environment. U.S. manufacturers have since cut off their sources in the Congo in an effort to avoid abetting the destruction. But their action has only penalized legitimate miners in the impoverished country (Austin 2002; Friends of the Congo 2011).

use your sociological *imagination*

Which aspects of capitalism do you personally appreciate? Which do you find worrisome?

Socialism

Socialist theory was refined in the writings of Karl Marx and Friedrich Engels. These European radicals were disturbed by the exploitation of the working class that emerged during the Industrial Revolution. In their view, capitalism forced large numbers of people to exchange their labor for low wages. The owners of an industry profit from the labor of workers primarily because they pay workers less than the value of the goods produced.

As an ideal type, a socialist economic system attempts to eliminate such economic exploitation. Under **socialism**, the means of production and distribution in a society are collectively rather than privately owned. The basic objective of the economic system is to meet people's needs rather than to maximize profits. Socialists reject the laissez-faire philosophy that free competition benefits the general public. Instead, they believe that the central government, acting as the representative of the people, should make basic economic decisions. Therefore, government ownership of all major industries—including steel production, automobile manufacturing, and agriculture—is a primary feature of socialism as an ideal type.

In practice, socialist economic systems vary in the extent to which they tolerate private ownership. For example, in Great Britain, a nation with some aspects of both a socialist and a capitalist economy, passenger airline service is concentrated in the government-owned corporation British Airways. Yet private airlines are allowed to compete with it.

Socialist nations differ from capitalist nations in their commitment to social service programs. For example, the U.S. government provides health care and health insurance to the elderly and poor through the Medicare and Medicaid programs. But socialist countries typically offer government-financed medical care to *all* citizens. In theory, the wealth of the people as a collectivity is used to provide health care, housing, education, and other key services to each individual and family.

Marx believed that socialist societies would eventually "wither away" and evolve into *communist* societies. As an ideal type, **communism** refers to an economic system under which all property is communally owned and no social distinctions are made on the basis of people's ability to produce. In recent decades, the Soviet Union, the People's Republic of China, Vietnam, Cuba, and

TABLE 18-1 CHARACTERISTICS OF THE THREE MAJOR ECONOMIC SYSTEMS

Economic System	Characteristics	Contemporary Examples
Capitalism	Private ownership of the means of production. Accumulation of profits the main incentive	Canada Mexico United States
Socialism	Collective ownership of the means of production. Meeting people's needs the basic objective	Germany Russia Sweden
Communism	Communal ownership of all property. No social distinctions made on basis of people's ability to produce	Cuba North Korea Vietnam

Note: Countries listed in column 3 are typical of one of the three economic systems, but not perfectly so. In practice, the economies of most countries include a mix of elements from the three major systems.

nations in Eastern Europe were popularly thought of as examples of communist economic systems. However, this usage represents an incorrect application of a term with sensitive political connotations. All nations known as communist in the 20th century actually fell far short of the ideal type (Walder and Nguyen 2008).

By the early 1990s, Communist parties were no longer ruling the nations of Eastern Europe. As of 2010, however, China, Cuba, Laos, North Korea, and Vietnam remained socialist societies ruled by Communist parties. Yet even in those countries, capitalism had begun to make inroads. In Vietnam, for example, the Ho Chi Minh City Stock Exchange, which opened in 1990, now trades 600 stocks representing almost 40 percent of the country's gross domestic product (GDP) (K. Chu 2010).

As we have seen, capitalism and socialism serve as ideal types of economic systems. In reality, the economy of each industrial society—including the United States, the European Union, and Japan—includes certain elements of both capitalism and socialism (Table 18-1). Whatever the differences—whether a society more closely fits the ideal type of capitalism or socialism—all industrial societies rely chiefly on mechanization in the production of goods and services.

The Informal Economy

In many countries, one aspect of the economy defies description as either capitalist or socialist. In the **informal economy**, transfers of money, goods, or services take place but are not reported to the government. Examples of the informal economy include trading services with someone—say, a haircut for a computer lesson; selling goods on the street; and engaging in illegal transactions, such as gambling or drug deals. The informal economy also includes off-the-books work in landscaping, street vending, child care, and housecleaning. Participants in this type of economy avoid taxes and government regulations.

In the United States, the informal economy accounts for about 8 percent of total economic activity. In other industrialized nations it varies, from 11 percent in Great Britain to 20 percent in Spain

SOCIOLOGY IN THE GLOBAL COMMUNITY

18-1 Working Women in Nepal

Nepal, a small and mountainous Asian country of about 28 million people, has a per capita gross domestic product (GDP) of just $1,120 per year. (The comparable figure in the United States is $45,850.) However, gross domestic product seriously understates the true production level in Nepal, for several reasons. Among the most important is that many Nepalese women work in the informal economy, whose activities are not included in the GDP.

Because women's work is undervalued in this traditional society, it is also underreported and underestimated. Official figures state that women account for 27 percent of GDP and form 40 percent of the labor force. But Nepalese women are responsible for 60 percent of additional nonmarket production—that is, work done in the informal economy—and 93 percent of the housework (see the accompanying figure).

> *Because women's work is undervalued in this traditional society, it is also underreported and underestimated.*

Most female workers cultivate corn, rice, and wheat on the family farm, where they spend hours on labor-intensive tasks such as fetching water and feeding livestock. Because much of the food they raise is consumed at home, however, it is considered to be non-market production. At home, women concentrate on food processing and preparation, caregiving, and other household tasks, such as clothes making. Childbearing and rearing and elder care are particularly crucial activities. Yet none of these chores are considered part of GDP; instead, they are dismissed as "women's work," both by economists and by the women themselves.

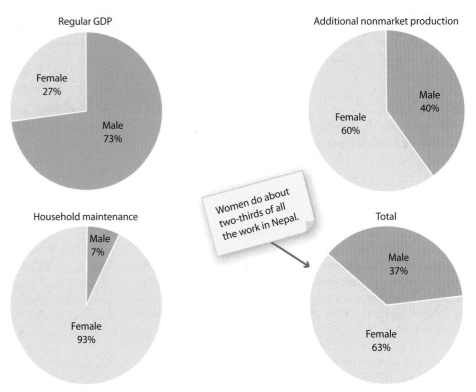

GENDER CONTRIBUTIONS TO GDP AND HOUSEHOLD MAINTENANCE IN NEPAL

Regular GDP: Female 27%, Male 73%

Additional nonmarket production: Male 40%, Female 60%

Household maintenance: Male 7%, Female 93%

Women do about two-thirds of all the work in Nepal.

Total: Male 37%, Female 63%

Source: Survey by M. Acharya as cited in Mahbub ul Haq Human Development Centre 2000:54.

The figures on housework and nonmarket production in Nepal come from an independent economic study. To compile them, researchers had to adapt the conventional accounting system by adding a special account dedicated to household maintenance activities. When they did so, women's "invisible work" suddenly became visible and valuable. Not just in Nepal, but in every country, economists need to expand their definitions of work and the labor force to account for the tremendous contributions women make to the world economy.

LET'S DISCUSS

1. In your family, is "women's work" taken for granted? Have you ever tried to figure out what it would cost your family to pay for all the unpaid work women do?

2. Why is recognizing women's work important? How might life for both men and women change if the true economic value of women's work were recognized?

Sources: Acharya 2000; Haub 2010; Mahbub ul Haq Human Development Centre 2000:54–57.

---

and Portugal and 25 percent in Greece. In developing nations, the informal economy represents a much larger (40 to 60 percent) and often unmeasured part of total economic activity. Yet because this sector of the economy depends to a large extent on the labor of women, work in the informal economy is undervalued or even unrecognized the world over. Box 18-1 explains how the informal economy operates in Nepal (T. Barnes 2009; Schneider 2010).

Functionalists contend that bureaucratic regulations sometimes contribute to the rise of an informal, underground, economy. In the developing world, governments often set up burdensome business regulations that overworked bureaucrats must administer. When requests for licenses and permits pile up, delaying business projects,

legitimate entrepreneurs find they need to go underground to get anything done. Despite its apparent efficiency, this type of informal economy is dysfunctional for a country's overall political and economic well-being. Since informal firms typically operate in remote locations to avoid detection, they cannot easily expand when they become profitable. And given the limited protection for their property and contractual rights, participants in the informal economy are less likely than others to save and invest their income.

Whatever the functions an informal economy may serve, it is in some respects dysfunctional for workers. Working conditions in these illegal businesses are often unsafe or dangerous, and the jobs rarely provide any benefits to those who become ill or cannot

casestudy Capitalism in China

Today's China is not the China of past generations; it is expected to become the world's largest economy by 2020. (Figure 18-1 shows the world's largest economies over the past 20 years.) In this country where the Communist Party once dominated people's lives, few now bother to follow party proceedings. Instead, after a decade of rapid economic growth, most Chinese are more interested in acquiring the latest consumer goods. Ironically, it was party officials' decision to transform China's economy by opening it up to capitalism that reduced the once-omnipotent institution's influence.

The Road to Capitalism

When the communists assumed leadership of China in 1949, they cast themselves as the champions of workers and peasants and the enemies of those who exploited workers, namely landlords and capitalists. Profit making was outlawed, and those who engaged in it were arrested. By the 1960s, China's economy was dominated by huge state-controlled enterprises, such as factories. Even private farms were transformed into community-owned organizations. Peasants essentially worked for the government, receiving payment in goods based on their contribution to the collective good. In addition, they could receive a small plot of land on which to produce food for their families or for exchange with others. But while the centralization of production for the benefit of all seemed to make sense ideologically, it did not work well economically.

In the 1980s, the government eased restrictions on private enterprise somewhat, permitting small businesses with no more than seven employees. But business owners could not hold policymaking positions in the party, at any level. Late in the decade, party leaders began to make market-oriented reforms, revising the nation's legal structure to promote private business. For the first time, private entrepreneurs were allowed to compete with some state-controlled businesses. By the mid-1990s, impressed with the results of the experiment, party officials had begun to hand some ailing state-controlled businesses over to private entrepreneurs, in hopes they could be turned around (D. Bell 2008).

The Chinese Economy Today

Today, the entrepreneurs who weathered government harassment during the Communist Party's early years are among the nation's wealthiest capitalists. Some even hold positions on government advisory boards. The growing free-market economy they spawned has brought significant inequality to Chinese workers, however, especially between urban and rural workers. Though the move toward market-driven development has been slowing, questions are still being raised about the accumulation of wealth by a few (Sicular et al. 2006).

Chinese capitalists have had to compete with multinational corporations, which can operate more easily in China now, thanks to government economic reforms. General Motors (GM) first became interested in China in 1992, hoping to use the nation's low-cost labor to manufacture cars for overseas markets. But more and more, foreign-owned enterprises like GM are selling to the Chinese market. By 2009 the Chinese were buying more automobiles than people were in the United States (Kahn 2003; Miles 2009).

FIGURE **18-1** WORLD'S LARGEST ECONOMIES

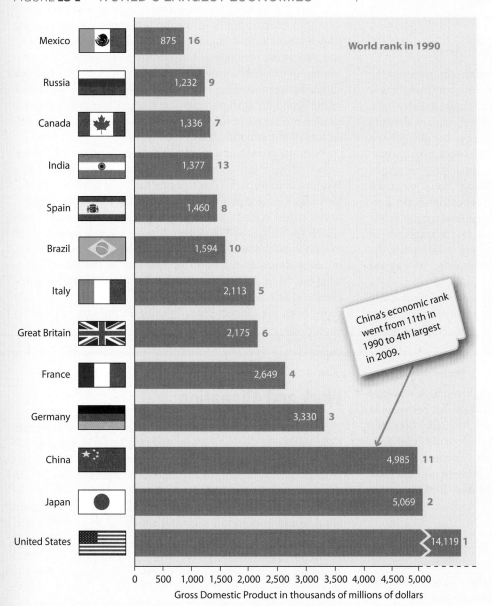

World rank in 1990

Country	GDP	World rank
Mexico	875	16
Russia	1,232	9
Canada	1,336	7
India	1,377	13
Spain	1,460	8
Brazil	1,594	10
Italy	2,113	5
Great Britain	2,175	6
France	2,649	4
Germany	3,330	3
China	4,985	11
Japan	5,069	2
United States	14,119	1

China's economic rank went from 11th in 1990 to 4th largest in 2009.

Gross Domestic Product in thousands of millions of dollars

Note: 2009 data standardized in terms of estimated purchasing power parity to eliminate differences in buying power.
Sources: World Bank 2007:194–196; 2011.

For better or worse, the expansion of capitalism in China has linked U.S. businesses to that expanding economy.

Chinese Workers in the New Economy

For Chinese workers, the loosening of state control over the economy has meant a rise in occupational mobility, which was severely limited in the early days of Communist Party rule. The new markets created by private entrepreneurs are allowing ambitious workers to advance their careers by changing jobs or even cities. On the other hand, many middle-aged urban workers have lost their jobs to rural migrants seeking higher wages. Moreover, the privately owned factories that churn out lawn chairs and power tools for multinational corporations offer limited opportunities and very long hours. Wages average just below $400 a month for a six-day workweek. As low as wages are in China, they are still double what workers earn in Indonesia, the Philippines, and Vietnam, where multinationals are now establishing factories (*The Economist* 2010b).

Serious social problems have accompanied China's massive economic growth. Because safety is not a priority in many businesses, workers suffer from high injury rates. Harsh working conditions contribute to rapid turnover in the labor force. There is no pension system in China, so retirees must struggle to find other ways to support themselves. Pollution is common in urban areas, and environmental problems are extraordinary (Barboza 2008; French 2008).

For the average worker, party membership is less important now than in the past. Instead, managerial skill and experience are much in demand. Hong Kong sociologist Xiaowei Zang (2002) surveyed 900 workers in a key industrial city and found that party members still had an advantage in government and state-owned companies, where they earned higher salaries than other workers. But in private businesses, seniority and either managerial or entrepreneurial experience were what counted. As might be expected, being male and well educated also helped.

Women have been slower to advance in the workplace than men. Traditionally, Chinese women have been relegated to subservient roles in the patriarchal family structure. Communist Party rule has allowed them to make significant gains in employment, income, and education, although not as quickly as promised. For rural women in China, the growth of a market economy has meant a choice between working in a factory or on a farm. Still, despite recent economic changes, emerging research shows that Chinese women receive lower wages than men who work in the same job sectors (Wang and Cai 2006).

With the growth of a middle class and increased education, many Chinese are seeking the same opportunities as their Western counterparts. The struggle has been particularly visible in the Chinese people's desire for open, unrestricted access to the World Wide Web. In most countries of the world, a web search for images of Tiananmen Square will call up photos of the 1989 crackdown on student protesters, in which soldiers in tanks attacked unarmed students. But on the other side of what has been dubbed the Great Firewall of China, the same search yields only photos of visiting diplomats—including those from the United States—posing in the square (Deibert et al. 2008).

continue to work. Perhaps more significant, the longer a worker remains in the informal economy, the less likely that person is to make the transition to the regular economy. No matter how efficient or productive a worker, employers expect to see experience in the formal economy on a job application. Experience as a successful street vendor or self-employed cleaning person does not carry much weight with interviewers (Venkatesh 2006).

thinking CRITICALLY

In the United States, what factors might encourage the growth of the informal economy? Are those factors related to the country's economic system?

Work and Alienation

"A moron could learn this job, it's so easy," says one Burger King worker in George Ritzer's study of the fast-food industry (2000:137). Doing repetitive tasks that take minimal skills can be demoralizing, leading to a sense of alienation and isolation in the workplace. Jeremy Rifkin took this concern a step further: as work becomes more and more automated, human skills become obsolete and workers lose their jobs altogether, or are forced into low-skills service jobs (Rifkin 1996).

All the pioneers of sociological thought were concerned about the negative impact on workers of the changes brought about by the Industrial Revolution. Émile Durkheim ([1893] 1933) argued that as labor becomes more and more differentiated, individuals experience *anomie,* or loss of direction. Workers can't feel as much fulfillment from performing one specialized

TAKING SOCIOLOGY TO WORK

Amy Wang, **Product Manager, Norman International Company**

When Amy Wang entered the University of Texas at Austin in 1999, she didn't know what subject she wanted to major in, but she soon became fascinated by sociology. "Sociology was intriguing in the sense that it combined everything in life," she explains. "I am a people person and I enjoy knowing and learning about all aspects of how people live and interact in society." Wang particularly enjoyed the criminology course she took, as well as another on the sociology of gender, which she found to be eye-opening.

Wang's employer, Norman International Company, is a manufacturer of fine, hand-crafted interior window furnishings. In launching a new product, Wang works closely with a research and development team based in China. Part of her job is to research the domestic market and suggest which options are likely to be popular with U.S. consumers—a task in which she puts her training in doing sociological research to good use. After the R&D team has finalized a new product's specifications, Wang outsources the production of samples to vendors in China. When the product is finally ready for sale, she coordinates the company's U.S.-based operations, including information systems, advertising, and shipping, to ensure a smooth introduction.

Wang, who was born in Taiwan, grew up in a suburb of Dallas, where she became assimilated to mainstream U.S. culture. When she began work with Norman International, the company sent her to southern China for a month and a half to meet the R&D team and work with them closely on a new product. "It was an exciting experience, because it was the first time I had been to China," she remembers. "I was absorbing all of the cultural differences and their way of life. It is very different than the U.S. and I really appreciated my life in the States afterwards."

Wang believes that her background in sociology helps her to adjust to different cultures when she travels on the job. She also thinks that a familiarity with the interactionist perspective fosters teamwork, which is essential to success in business. "Not only do you have to do your job well, but you have to get along with your co-workers so that projects can be finished efficiently," she emphasizes. In a global marketplace, that insight is especially important.

LET'S DISCUSS

1. Given what you have learned about globalization, how likely do you think it is that you will someday be working abroad, on either a temporary or a permanent basis? Do you feel ready for that challenge?
2. What kind of cultural differences might complicate business relations between employees in two different countries—for example, the United States and China?

---

task in a factory as they did when they were totally responsible for creating a product. Clearly, the impersonality of bureaucratic organizations can produce a cold and uncaring workplace. But the most penetrating analysis of the dehumanizing aspects of industrialization was offered by Karl Marx.

Marx's View

Marx believed that as the process of industrialization advanced, workers were robbed of any meaningful relationship to their work. The emphasis on the specialization of tasks, he believed, contributed to a growing sense of alienation among industrial workers. The term **alienation** refers to a condition of estrangement or dissociation from the surrounding society. Consider today's telemarketers, who make "cold calls" to sell people products and services. Do they feel a part of the financial institution that employs them? But it wasn't just the monotonous repetition of the same tasks that concerned Marx. In his view, an even deeper cause of alienation was the *powerlessness* of workers in a capitalist economic system. Workers had no control over their occupational tasks, the products of their labor, or the distribution of profits. Moreover, they were constantly producing property that was owned by others (the members of the capitalist class) (Erikson 1986).

The solution to the problem of workers' alienation, according to Marx, was to give workers greater control over the workplace and the products of their labor. Marx didn't focus on the limited reform of factory life; rather, he envisioned a revolutionary overthrow of capitalist oppression. After a transition to collective ownership of the means of production (socialism), the ideal of communism would eventually be achieved. Yet the trend in capitalist societies has been toward concentration of ownership by giant corporations. Through mergers and acquisitions, such corporations become even larger, and individual workers find themselves dwarfed by firms of overwhelming size and power.

When Marx wrote about work and alienation in 1844, the physical conditions of labor were much harsher than they are today. Yet his writings inspired research that persists today, even though the majority of workers now enjoy safer, more comfortable surroundings. Most studies of alienation have focused on how structural changes in the economy serve to increase or decrease worker satisfaction. In fact, the growth of the size of businesses, the emergence of huge franchise chains, and the dominance of multinational corporations have only increased the isolation of laborers. Large business organizations report an escalation in episodes of "desk rage," in which employees or angry ex-employees act out their frustrations, disrupting the workplace and often raising other workers' alienation in the process (Hodson and Sullivan 1995; Hymowitz and Silverman 2001).

Marx focused on alienation among the proletariat, whom he viewed as powerless to effect change in capitalist institutions. But by the 1980s, the term *burnout* was increasingly being used to describe the stress experienced by a wide range of workers, including professionals, self-employed persons, and even unpaid volunteers. The concept of work-related anxiety now covers alienation even among more affluent workers, who have a greater degree of control over their working conditions. From a conflict perspective, we have masked the fact that alienation falls most heavily on the lower and working classes by making it appear to be endemic, from the boardroom to the shop floor.

Worker Satisfaction

In general, people with greater responsibility for a finished product (such as white-collar professionals and managers) experience more satisfaction than those with less responsibility. For women

Working at the checkout counter may help to pay the bills, but it isn't likely to provide much job satisfaction—especially in a large supermarket where workers enjoy little responsibility or personal recognition.

and men working in blue-collar jobs, the repetitive nature of work can be particularly unsatisfying. Repeatedly assembling parts for a cell phone or laptop computer is monotonous work. Not surprisingly, sociologist Robert Blauner's (1964) classic research study revealed that printers—who often work in small shops and supervise apprentices—were more satisfied with their work than laborers who performed repetitive tasks on automobile assembly lines.

A number of general factors can reduce the level of dissatisfaction of contemporary industrial workers. Higher wages give workers a sense of accomplishment apart from the task before them. A shorter workweek is supposed to increase the amount of time people can devote to recreation and leisure, reducing some of the discontent of the workplace. But the number of hours Americans work actually *increased* in the 1990s, by the equivalent of about one workweek. Short staffing because of low unemployment rates may have accounted for part of the increase in hours worked; however, many Americans took a second job during this period, just to make ends meet (Gerson and Jacobs 2004).

Numerous studies have shown that positive relationships with co-workers can make a boring job tolerable or even enjoyable. In his often cited "banana time" study, sociologist Donald Roy (1959) examined worker satisfaction in a two-month participant observation of a small group of machine operators. Drawing on the interactionist perspective, Roy carefully recorded the social interactions among members of his work group, including many structured "times" and "themes" designed to break up long days of simple, repetitive work. For example, the workers divided their food breaks into coffee time, peach time, banana time, fish time, Coke time, and lunch time—each of which occurred daily and involved distinctive responsibilities, jokes, and insults. Roy (1959:166) concluded that his observations "seem to support the generally accepted notion that one key source of job satisfaction lies in the informal interaction shared by members of a work group." The patterned conversation and horseplay of these workers reduced the monotony of their workdays.

Sociologist George Ritzer (1977, 2000) has suggested that the relatively positive impression many workers present is misleading. In his view, manual workers are so deeply alienated that they come to expect little from their jobs. Their satisfaction comes from nonwork tasks, and any job-related gratification results from receiving wages. Ritzer's interpretation explains why

manual workers—although they say they are satisfied with their occupations—would not choose the same line of work if they could begin their lives over.

The Changing U.S. Economy

As advocates of the power elite model point out, the trend in capitalist societies has been toward concentration of ownership by giant corporations, especially multinational ones. In the following sections, we will examine three outgrowths of this trend in the United States: the changing face of the workforce, deindustrialization, and offshoring. As these trends show, any change in the economy has social and political implications.

The Changing Face of the Workforce

The workforce in the United States is constantly changing. During World War II, when men were mobilized to fight abroad, women entered the workforce in large numbers. And with the rise of the civil rights movement in the 1960s, minorities found numerous job opportunities opening to them. Box 18-2 takes a closer look at the active recruitment of women and minorities into the workplace, known as *affirmative action.*

Although predictions are not always reliable, sociologists and labor specialists foresee a workforce increasingly composed of women and racial and ethnic minorities. In 1960 there were twice as many men in the labor force as women. From 1988 to 2018, however, 52 percent of new workers are expected to be women. The dynamics for minority group workers are even more dramatic, as the number of Black, Latino, and Asian American workers continues to increase at a faster rate than the number of White workers (Toossi 2009).

More and more, then, the workforce reflects the diversity of the population, as ethnic minorities enter the labor force and immigrants and their children move from marginal jobs or employment in the informal economy to positions of greater visibility and responsibility. The impact of this changing labor force is not merely statistical. A more diverse workforce means that relationships between workers are more likely to cross gender, racial, and ethnic lines. Interactionists note that people will soon find themselves supervising and being supervised by people very different from themselves.

RESEARCH TODAY

18-2 Affirmative Action

Jessie Sherrod began picking cotton in the fields of Mississippi when she was eight years old, earning $1.67 for a 12-hour day. Today she is a Harvard-educated pediatrician who specializes in infectious diseases. But the road from the cotton fields to the medical profession was hardly an easy one. "You can't make up for 400 years of slavery and mistreatment and unequal opportunity in 20 years," she says angrily. "We had to ride the school bus for five miles . . . and pass by a white school to get to our black elementary school. Our books were used books. Our instructors were not as good. We didn't have the proper equipment. How do you make up for that?" (Stolberg 1995:A14). Some people think it should be done through affirmative action programs.

The term *affirmative action* first appeared in an executive order issued by President John F. Kennedy in 1961. That order called for contractors to "take affirmative action to ensure that applicants are employed, and that employees are treated during employment, without regard to their race, creed, color, or national origin." In 1967, the order was amended by President Lyndon Johnson to prohibit discrimination on the basis of sex as well, but affirmative action remained a vague concept. Currently, **affirmative action** refers to positive efforts to recruit minority group members or women for jobs, promotions, and educational opportunities.

> *Critics warn against hiring and admissions quotas, complaining that they constitute a kind of "reverse discrimination" against White males.*

Sociologists—especially conflict and feminist theorists—view affirmative action as a legislative attempt to reduce the inequality embedded in the social structure by increasing opportunities for groups who were deprived in the past, such as women and African Americans. Despite the clear disparity in earnings between White males and other groups, however, many people doubt that everything done in the name of affirmative action is desirable. Critics warn against hiring and admissions quotas, complaining that they constitute a kind of "reverse discrimination" against White males.

Affirmative action became a prominent issue in state and national political campaigns in 1996, when California's voters approved by a 54 to 46 percent margin the California Civil Rights Initiative. Better known as Proposition 209, this measure amends the state constitution to *prohibit* any program that gives preference to women and minorities in college admissions, hiring, promotion, or government contracts. In other words, it aims to abolish affirmative action programs. The courts have since upheld the measure. In 1998, voters in Washington State passed a similar anti–affirmative action measure.

In 2003, focusing specifically on college admissions in a pair of decisions involving policies at the University of Michigan, the Supreme Court ruled that colleges may consider race and ethnicity as one factor in their admissions decisions. However, they cannot assign a specific value to being a minority candidate in such a way that race becomes the overriding factor in a decision. The ruling allowed many colleges and universities to continue their existing affirmative action policies.

Increasingly, critics of affirmative action are calling for color-blind policies that would end affirmative action. Presumably, such policies would allow all applicants to be judged fairly. However, opponents warn against the danger of **color-blind racism**—the use of the principle of race neutrality to defend a racially unequal

The Supreme Court's many decisions on the constitutionality of affirmative action programs have made it difficult for organizations to encourage diversity without transgressing the law.

status quo (see Chapter 11). Will "color-blind" policies put an end to institutional practices that now favor Whites, they ask? According to the latest data, for example, Harvard University admits 40 percent of those applicants who are children of alumni—almost all of whom are White—compared to 11 percent of nonalumni children. Ironically, studies show that children of alumni are far more likely than either minority students or athletes to run into trouble academically.

LET'S DISCUSS

1. Is affirmative action part of the admissions policy at the college or university you attend? If so, do you think the policy has helped to level the playing field? Might it have excluded some qualified White applicants?
2. Take a poll of your classmates. What percentage of the class supports affirmative action in hiring and college admissions? How does that group break down in terms of gender, race, and ethnicity?

Sources: Massey and Mooney 2007; Pincus 2003, 2008; Stolberg 1995; University of Michigan 2003.

Deindustrialization

What happens when a company decides it is more profitable to move its operations out of a long-established community to another part of the country, or out of the country altogether? People lose jobs; stores lose customers; the local government's tax base declines and it cuts services. This devastating process has occurred again and again in the past decade or so.

The term **deindustrialization** refers to the systematic, widespread withdrawal of investment in basic aspects of productivity, such as factories and plants. Giant corporations that deindustrialize are not necessarily refusing to invest in new economic opportunities. Rather, the targets and locations of investment change, and the need for labor decreases as advances in technology continue to automate production. First, companies may

Gutted factories like this one in Boston, Massachusetts, contrast with the glamorous corporate campus of Google Corporation in Mountain View, California. Deindustrialization and the rise of high technology have shifted the U.S. labor market, displacing many workers in the process.

move their plants from the nation's central cities to the suburbs. The next step may be relocation from suburban areas of the Northeast and Midwest to the South, where labor laws place more restrictions on unions. Finally, a corporation may simply relocate *outside* the United States to a country with a lower rate of prevailing wages. General Motors, for example, decided to build a multi-billion-dollar plant in China rather than in Kansas City or even in Mexico (Lynn 2003).

Although deindustrialization often involves relocation, in some instances it takes the form of corporate restructuring, as companies seek to reduce costs in the face of growing worldwide competition. When such restructuring occurs, the impact on the bureaucratic hierarchy of formal organizations can be significant. A large corporation may choose to sell off or entirely abandon less productive divisions and to eliminate layers of management viewed as unnecessary. Wages and salaries may be frozen and benefits cut—all in the name of restructuring. Increasing reliance on automation also spells the end of work as we have known it.

The term **downsizing** was introduced in 1987 to refer to reductions taken in a company's workforce as part of deindustrialization. Viewed from a conflict perspective, the unprecedented attention given to downsizing in the mid-1990s reflected the continuing importance of social class in the United States. Conflict theorists note that job loss has long been a feature of deindustrialization among blue-collar workers. But when large numbers of middle-class managers and other white-collar employees with substantial incomes began to be laid off, suddenly the media began expressing great concern over downsizing.

The extended economic downturn that began in 2008 accelerated the processes of deindustrialization and downsizing. As the recession deepened, many plants shut down either temporarily or permanently, leaving more and more workers without jobs. With those jobs and shuttered plants went any hope of restoring or expanding heavy industry, including automobile manufacturing. The bankruptcy of Chrysler and General Motors hit the midwestern states particularly hard.

The social costs of deindustrialization and downsizing cannot be overemphasized. Plant closings lead to substantial unemployment in a community, which has a devastating impact on both the micro and macro levels. On the micro level, the unemployed person and his or her family must adjust to a loss of

spending power. Painting or re-siding the house, buying health insurance or saving for retirement, even thinking about having another child must be put aside. Both marital happiness and family cohesion may suffer as a result. Although many dismissed workers eventually reenter the paid labor force, they must often accept less desirable positions with lower salaries and fewer benefits. Unemployment and underemployment are tied to many of the social problems discussed throughout this textbook, among them the need for child care and the controversy over welfare.

thinking CRITICALLY

What evidence of deindustrialization or downsizing do you see, specifically, in your community? What broad economic shifts brought about those changes?

Offshoring

U.S. firms have been outsourcing certain types of work for generations. For example, moderate-sized businesses such as furniture stores and commercial laundries have long relied on outside trucking firms to make deliveries to their customers. The new trend toward **offshoring** carries this practice one step further, by transferring other types of work to foreign contractors. Now, even large companies are turning to overseas firms, many of them located in developing countries. Offshoring has become the latest tactic in the time-worn business strategy of raising profits by reducing costs.

Significantly, the transfer of work from one country to another is no longer limited to manufacturing. Office and professional jobs are being exported, too, thanks to advanced telecommunications. Table 18-2 lists those occupations most likely to be offshored.

Because offshoring, like outsourcing in general, tends to improve the efficiency of business operations, it can be viewed as functional to society. Offshoring also increases economic interdependence in the production of goods and services, both in enterprises located just across town and in those located around the globe. Still, conflict theorists charge that this aspect of globalization furthers social inequality. Although moving high-tech work to developing countries does help to lower a company's

TABLE 18-2 OCCUPATIONS MOST VULNERABLE TO OFFSHORING

Rank	Occupation
1	Computer programming
2	Data entry
3	Electrical and electronics drafting
4	Mechanical drafting
5	Computer and information science, research
6	Actuarial science
7	Mathematics
8	Statistics
9	Mathematical science (all other)
10	Film and video editing

Sources: Bureau of Labor Statistics data cited in Hira 2008; Moncarz et al. 2008.

costs, the impact on technical and service workers at home is clearly devastating. Certainly middle-class workers are alarmed by the trend. Because offshoring increases efficiency, economists oppose efforts to block the practice and instead recommend assistance to displaced workers.

There is a downside to offshoring for foreigners, as well. Although outsourcing is a significant source of employment for the upper-middle class in developing countries, hundreds of millions of other foreign workers have seen little to no positive impact from the trend. Thus the long-term impact of offshoring on developing nations is difficult to predict. Another practice, *microfinancing,* is having a more positive impact on the lower classes in developing nations: see the Social Policy section that follows (Goering 2008b; Waldman 2004a, 2004b, 2004c).

use your sociological *imagination*

Do you know anyone whose job has been transferred to a foreign country? If so, was the person able to find a comparable job in the same town, or did he or she have to relocate? How long was the person unemployed?

social**policy** and the Economy

Microfinancing

In India, a very small loan has made a big change in a young mother's life. Not many years ago Siyawati was dependent on what little income her husband could earn as a day laborer. Then a $212 microloan allowed her to buy a machine for making candles. Today, Siyawati's cottage venture has expanded into a factory with eight employees, and her monthly income has climbed from $42 to $425. Her increased earnings have allowed her to enroll her children in a good school—the dream of struggling parents in developing countries around the world (Glazer 2010:1).

Looking at the Issue

In some respects it offers a small solution to a big problem. **Microfinancing** is lending small sums of money to the poor so they can work their way out of poverty. Borrowers use the money to start small businesses in the informal economy—to buy yarn to weave into cloth, cows to produce milk, or tools, equipment, and bamboo to make stools. The products they produce are then sold in the local shops. Typically, microloans are less than $600, often as little as $20. The recipients are people who ordinarily would not be able to qualify for banking services.

Sometimes referred to as "banking the unbanked," microfinancing was the brainchild of Bangladeshi economist Muhammad Yunus (pronounced Iunus). In 1976, in the midst of a devastating famine in Bangladesh, Yunus founded the Grameen (meaning "Village") Bank, which he headed until 2011. The idea came to him when he reached into his pocket to lend money to a group of villagers who had asked him for help. Working through local halls or meeting places, the Grameen Bank has now extended credit to

In 2006 Muhammad Yunus, founder of the Grameen Bank, was awarded the Nobel Peace Prize for his work in championing the concept of microfinancing. The small loans his bank makes to the poor, many of them women, have improved the quality of life of countless families.

nearly 7 million people. The idea has spread, and has even been underwritten by over a thousand for-profit banks and multinational organizations. According to 2011 estimates, microfinancing is now reaching 91 million people in 100 countries (Microfinance Information Exchange 2011; Yunus 2010).

Although microfinancing has benefited many families, critics charge that some lenders are taking advantage of the poor.

Especially in India, the extension of microloans to financially questionable projects with little chance for success has left some borrowers in debt. At the other extreme, some lenders have reaped extraordinary profits, both for themselves and for the investment banks they have created.

In some countries, politicians resent microfinancing because it competes with the central government's path to self-sufficiency. In Nicaragua, President Daniel Ortega supports the *movimento no pago,* or no-pay movement, which encourages borrowers not to repay their debts. So successful has the movement been that one of that nation's leading microfinanciers has been driven out of business.

Applying Sociology

Researchers who draw on the interactionist approach have shown that there is more to microfinancing than money. A study done by microfinance expert Daryl Collins and his colleagues (2009) shows how even with modest assistance, poor people can significantly improve their circumstances through mutual support. Collins asked villagers and slum dwellers in Bangladesh, India, and South Africa to keep diaries of how they spent every penny they earned. He and his team found that most of the poor households they studied did not live hand to mouth, spending everything they earned as soon as they got it. Instead, they used financial tools that were linked to their extended families and informal social networks. They saved money, squeezed it out of creditors whenever possible, ran sophisticated savings clubs, and took advantage of microfinancing whenever it was available. Their tactics suggested new methods of fighting poverty and encouraged the development of broader microfinance programs.

Because an estimated 90 percent of the recipients of microcredit are women, feminist theorists are especially interested in the growth of microfinancing. Women's economic status has been found to be critical to the well-being of their children, and the key to a healthy household environment. In developing countries, where women often are not treated as well as men, being entrusted with credit is particularly empowering to them. Research indicates that women recipients are more likely than men to participate in networks and collective action groups, perhaps because they must overcome resistance to women as economic decision makers (Karides 2010; Sanyal 2009).

Drawing on world systems analysis (see Chapter 10), sociologist Marina Karides (2010) contrasts microfinancing with the Western model of economic development, in which multinational corporations based in core countries take advantage of the low wages and natural resources in periphery and semi-periphery countries. The low-wage workers employed by the multinationals rarely escape subsistence living, while the vast majority of people in core nations enjoy a comparatively high standard of living. Microfinanciers hope that in contrast, the cottage industries they help to establish will contribute to the local economies in developing countries, and ultimately to the well-being of those societies, rather than merely serve the economic interests of core nations.

Some critics complain that the creation of small home-based industries reduces the demand for formal employment opportunities. Supporters of microenterprise counter that much time has passed without a significant change in job growth. Microfinancing,

At a workshop in Mumbai, India, Sharda Bhandare cuts the pieces for a pair of gloves from a towel. Microloans make such small businesses possible, and help them to become self-sustaining.

they claim, is the best way to create sustainable market opportunities for the poor in developing nations, even if those opportunities are much less attractive than those available in core nations.

Initiating Policy

Even supporters of microfinancing acknowledge the need to reduce overlending and monitor the success of small loans in helping borrowers to escape poverty. Some indicators suggest that many borrowers do not achieve self-sufficiency. If that is true, lenders should increase their oversight and attempt to identify best practices—that is, those types of assistance that are most effective in helping the poor. Less than a decade ago, microfinancing was hailed as the single best solution to world poverty. With modifications, it should continue to reduce hardship and suffering among the poor (Bajaj 2011a, 2011b; Glazer 2011).

Lenders also need to work with political leaders, and vice versa, to ensure that they do not regard one another as competitors for political support from the poor. Some government leaders have gone so far as to charge lenders with profiteering at the expense of the poor, and to take extraordinary measures for the protection of borrowers. In 2010, officials of one state in India required all loans to be approved by the government, and their eventual repayment to be made in person before a public official. To the degree that profiteering is truly a problem, some type of remedy, whether through legislation or self-monitoring, may need to be introduced. Given the cultural, political, and legal differences among nations where microfinanciers operate, the development of this type of government policy will be a major undertaking.

Taking Sociology with You

1. Do you think microfinancing might be useful in the United States? If so, how and under what conditions?

2. Using sociological concepts, explain why some politicians might resent microfinancing programs.

3. What obstacles might prevent poor people, either in the United States or elsewhere, from improving their lives through microfinancing? Might the government have a role to play in removing those obstacles?

Summary

The **economic system** of a society has an important influence on social behavior and on other social institutions. This chapter examines the major economic systems, the rise of **capitalism** in China, work and **alienation** from work, the changing U.S. economy, and **microfinancing,** a strategy for helping the poor to lift themselves out of poverty.

1. With the Industrial Revolution, a new form of social structure emerged: the **industrial society.**

2. Systems of **capitalism** vary in the degree to which the government regulates private ownership and economic activity, but all emphasize the profit motive.

3. The basic objective of **socialism** is to eliminate economic exploitation and meet people's needs.

4. Marx believed that **communism** would evolve naturally out of socialism.

5. In developing nations, the **informal economy** represents a significant part of total economic activity. Yet because this sector depends largely on women's work, it is undervalued.

6. In the 1980s, the Chinese Communist Party began allowing Chinese entrepreneurs to experiment with capitalist ventures. Today, multinational corporations are capitalizing on China's huge workforce to produce goods and services for sale not just to those in industrialized nations, but to the people of China.

7. Industrial jobs can lead to a sense of **alienation** in the workplace. Karl Marx expected that powerless workers would eventually overthrow the capitalist system.

8. **Affirmative action** is intended to remedy the effects of discrimination against minority groups and women in education and the workplace. The concept is controversial, however, because some people see it as reverse discrimination against majority groups.

9. The U.S. economy is changing rapidly. Workers are coping with **deindustrialization** and **downsizing;** employers are training an increasingly diverse workforce. Many companies are turning to **offshoring,** or the outsourcing of work to foreign contractors, to lower their costs so they can compete in a global marketplace.

10. In developing countries, **microfinancing** ("banking the unbanked") is improving the lives of millions of poor people.

Key Terms

Affirmative action Positive efforts to recruit minority group members or women for jobs, promotions, and educational opportunities. (page 401)

Alienation A condition of estrangement or dissociation from the surrounding society. (399)

Capitalism An economic system in which the means of production are held largely in private hands and the main incentive for economic activity is the accumulation of profits. (393)

Color-blind racism The use of the principle of race neutrality to defend a racially unequal status quo. (402)

Communism As an ideal type, an economic system under which all property is communally owned and no social distinctions are made on the basis of people's ability to produce. (395)

Cultural relativism The viewing of people's behavior from the perspective of their own culture. (392)

Deindustrialization The systematic, widespread withdrawal of investment in basic aspects of productivity, such as factories and plants. (401)

Downsizing Reductions taken in a company's workforce as part of deindustrialization. (402)

Economic system The social institution through which goods and services are produced, distributed, and consumed. (392)

Fair trade A movement in which consumers in industrialized countries voluntarily pay above-market prices for certain foods so that the workers who plant, pick, and pack the crops can receive higher wages. (392)

Industrial society A society that depends on mechanization to produce its goods and services. (393)

Informal economy Transfers of money, goods, or services that are not reported to the government. (395)

Laissez-faire A form of capitalism under which people compete freely, with minimal government intervention in the economy. (393)

Microfinancing Lending small sums of money to the poor so they can work their way out of poverty. (403)

Monopoly Control of a market by a single business firm. (394)

Offshoring The transfer of work to foreign contractors. (402)

Socialism An economic system under which the means of production and distribution are collectively owned. (395)

TAKING SOCIOLOGY with you

1. Observe and/or interview some of the service workers in the college or university you attend. Do any of them show signs of alienation from the workplace?

2. Do some original research on the economy of the nearest city using a survey, experiment, or observation research. Then compare the results to what you can learn from existing sources, including this textbook. Did you learn anything new from your research?

3. If your college has a program for study abroad, find someone who has spent time in a developing country and interview him or her. What was the country's economy like? Was there a large informal sector, and if so, what goods or services were exchanged? Was microcredit available to small borrowers? How many people worked for multinational corporations? How many lived in poverty?

Self-Quiz

Read each question carefully and then select the best answer.

1. Which two basic types of economic system distinguish contemporary industrial societies?
   a. capitalism and communism
   b. capitalism and socialism
   c. socialism and communism
   d. capitalism and dictatorship

2. According to the discussion of capitalism in the text, which of the following statements is true?
   a. The means of production are held largely in private hands.
   b. The main incentive for economic activity is the accumulation of profits.
   c. The degree to which the government regulates private ownership and economic activity will vary.
   d. all of the above.

3. Which sociological perspective points out that while *pure* monopolies are not a basic element of the economy of the United States, competition is much more restricted than one might expect in what is called a *free enterprise system*?
   a. the functionalist perspective
   b. the conflict perspective
   c. the interactionist perspective
   d. labeling theory

4. Which of the following is *not* an example of the informal economy?
   a. trading a haircut for a computer lesson
   b. selling illegal drugs on the street
   c. working as a computer programmer for a major corporation
   d. providing child care out of a private home, without reporting the income to the IRS

5. The systematic, widespread withdrawal of investment in basic aspects of productivity such as factories and plants is called
   a. deindustrialization.
   b. downsizing.
   c. postindustrialization.
   d. gentrification.

6. Karl Marx is associated with which of the following concepts?
   a. anomie
   b. assimilation
   c. apartheid
   d. alienation

7. Sociologists and labor specialists foresee a workforce increasingly composed of
   a. women.
   b. racial minorities.
   c. ethnic minorities.
   d. all of the above.

8. Currently, _____ _____ refers to positive efforts to recruit minority group members or women for jobs, promotions, and educational opportunities.
   a. equal rights
   b. affirmative action
   c. work programs
   d. equal action

9. The principle of laissez-faire was expounded and endorsed by the British economist
   a. John Maynard Keynes.
   b. Adam Smith.
   c. Paul Samuelson.
   d. Arthur Scargill.

10. Which sociologist, using the interactionist perspective, noted that "one key source of job satisfaction lies in the informal interaction shared by members of a work group"?
    a. Robert Blauner
    b. Donald Roy
    c. George Ritzer
    d. Karl Marx

11. The term _____ _____ refers to the social institution through which goods and services are produced, distributed, and consumed.

12. The principle of _____ _____, as expounded and endorsed by the British economist Adam Smith, was the prevailing form of capitalism immediately following the Industrial Revolution.

13. Under _____, the means of production and distribution in a society are collectively rather than privately owned, and the basic objective of the economic system is to meet people's needs rather than to maximize profits.

14. _____ is an economic system under which all property is communally owned and no social distinctions are made based on people's ability to produce.

15. The term _____ was introduced in 1987 to refer to reductions taken in a company's workforce as part of deindustrialization.

16. A(n) _____ society depends on mechanization to produce its goods and services.

17. _____ theorists point out that while pure monopolies are not a basic element of the economy of the United States, competition is much more restricted than one might expect in what is called a free enterprise system.

18. Émile Durkheim argued that as labor becomes more and more differentiated, individuals experience _____, or loss of direction.

19. Most studies of _____ have focused on factors that serve to increase or decrease worker satisfaction.

20. Some capitalist nations, such as the United States, outlaw _____ through antitrust legislation.

Answers
1 (b); 2 (d); 3 (b); 4 (c); 5 (a); 6 (d); 7 (d); 8 (b); 9 (b); 10 (b); 11 economic system; 12 laissez-faire; 13 socialism; 14 Communism; 15 downsizing; 16 industrial; 17 Conflict; 18 anomie; 19 alienation; 20 monopolies

406

THINKING ABOUT MOVIES

The Company Men

Corporate downsizing forces a white-collar worker to enter a blue-collar profession.

Inside Job

This documentary explores the near collapse of the global financial industry in 2008.

Up in the Air

The tables are about to turn on a corporate downsizing expert who makes his living by laying people off.

The environment is a major influence on our health and well-being. By providing clean, sustainable energy, this wind farm in Dhule, India, helps to preserve our ecosystem. Since 1980, nations around the world have been turning to wind turbines as a source of electric power.

Health and the Environment 19

" Not that long ago, hardly a generation back, people did not worry about the food they ate. They did not worry about the water they drank or the air they breathed. It never occurred to them that eating, drinking water, satisfying basic, mundane bodily needs, might be dangerous things to do. Parents thought it was good for their kids to go outside, get some sun.

That is all changed now. People see danger everywhere. Food, water, air, sun. We cannot do without them. Sadly, we now also fear them. We suspect that the water that flows from the tap is contaminated with chemicals that can make us ill. We have learned that conventionally grown fruits and vegetables have pesticide residues and that when we eat meat from conventionally raised animals, we are probably getting a dose of antibiotics and hormones, too. Contaminants can be colorless, tasteless, and odorless, invisible to the senses, and that fact increases the feeling of vulnerability.

According to the Environmental Protection Agency (EPA), indoor air is more toxic than outdoor air. That is because many household cleaning products and many contemporary home furnishings—carpets, drapes, the fabrics that cover sofas and easy chairs, furniture made of particle board—outgas toxic volatile organic chemicals. OK, we will go outside . . . only to inhale diesel exhaust, particulates suspended in the air, molecules of toxic chemicals wafting from factory smokestacks.

Even sunshine is now considered by many a hazard. Expose yourself to too much sun and your skin will age prematurely. You risk getting skin cancer. The ozone layer has thinned, making exposure to sunlight even more dangerous. The incidence of melanoma, the deadliest form of skin cancer, is on the rise.

The response has been swift. Everywhere one looks, Americans are buying consumer products that promise to reduce their exposure to harmful substances.

In 1975, Americans were drinking, on average, one gallon of bottled water per person per year. By 2005, the latest year for which we have data, consumption had grown to twenty-six gallons per person per year, over seven and a half billion gallons of bottled water. Bottled water used to account for only a tiny fraction of beverage consumption, inconsequential when compared to soft drinks, coffee and tea, beer, milk, and juice. Today, after enjoying years of "enviable, unending growth," bottled water has become the "superstar [of] the beverage industry." In addition, nearly half of all households use some kind of water filter in the home.

A couple of decades back, organic foods had only a tiny share of the overall food market. Organically grown foods were sold, typically, in small "health food" stores. They were hard to find, even if you wanted them. Few people did. But now, after years of 20 percent annual growth, organic food is mainstream. There are not only organic fruits and vegetables but organic breads and cereals, organic meat, fish, and dairy, organic beer, organic snack food. One can find organic foods in large, attractive, upscale chain stores, such as Whole Foods, and also increasingly in mainstream supermarkets. Safeway and Wal-Mart both sell organic foods.

Those who can afford it buy "organic" or "natural" personal hygiene products, shampoo, soap, makeup; "nontoxic" home cleaning products; clothing made of natural fibers; furniture made of real wood; and rugs made of natural fiber. There is a new ritual in America (at least in middle-class America): applying 30 SPF sunscreen to our children's exposed skin every morning before they go to school, to summer camp, or to the beach. "

People see danger everywhere. Food, water, air, sun. We cannot do without them. Sadly, we now also fear them.

(A. Szasz 2007:1–2) Additional information about this excerpt can be found on the Online Learning Center at www.mhhe.com/schaefer13e.

In this excerpt from *Shopping Our Way to Safety: How We Changed from Protecting the Environment to Protecting Ourselves,* sociologist Andrew Szasz links the environmental consciousness that arose from the environmental movement to a new category of products and services. Today, he notes, many people fear the everyday environmental hazards present in their immediate environment, from the tap water to the air. Rather than work for the health of the environment as a whole, some try to quarantine themselves from these perceived threats by shopping for supposedly pure, uncontaminated food, clothing, furniture, and cleaning products.

There is little question that some people do try to shop their way to safety. However, as Szasz notes, unless their largely individual responses go beyond self-protection, they won't improve society's health. What are the many people who cannot afford to drink bottled water or move to a healthier environment supposed to do? Won't the environment eventually reach a state that will threaten everyone, no matter how much organic food they consume?

What defines a healthy environment? How does health care vary from one social class to another and from one nation to another? In this chapter, we present a sociological overview of health, illness, health care, and medicine as a social institution. We begin by examining how functionalists, conflict theorists, interactionists, and labeling theorists look at health-related issues. Then we study the distribution of diseases in a society by social class, race and ethnicity, gender, and age.

We'll look too at the evolution of the U.S. health care system. Sociologists are interested in the roles people play in the health care system and the organizations that deal with issues of health and sickness. Therefore, we will analyze the interactions among physicians, nurses, and patients; alternatives to traditional health care; and the role of government in providing health care services to the needy. We'll take a special look at mental illness and its treatment.

Later in the chapter, we examine the environmental problems facing the world in the 21st century, and we draw on the functionalist and conflict perspectives to better understand environmental issues. We'll see that it is important not to oversimplify the relationship between health and the environment. Finally, in the Social Policy section we explore the recently renewed interest in environmentalism.

Sociological Perspectives on Health and Illness

How can we define health? Imagine a continuum with health on one end and death on the other. In the preamble to its 1946 constitution, the World Health Organization defined **health** as a "state of complete physical, mental, and social well-being, and not merely the absence of disease and infirmity" (Leavell and Clark 1965:14). In this definition, the "healthy" end of the continuum represents an ideal rather than a precise condition.

Along the continuum, individuals define themselves as healthy or sick on the basis of criteria established by themselves and relatives, friends, co-workers, and medical practitioners. Health and illness, in other words, are socially constructed. They are rooted in culture and are defined by claims makers—people who describe themselves as healthy or ill—as well as by a broad range of interested parties, including health care providers, pharmaceutical firms, and even food providers (Conrad and Barker 2010).

Because health is socially constructed, we can consider how it varies in different situations or cultures. Why is it that you may consider yourself sick or well when others do not agree? Who controls definitions of health and illness in our society, and for what ends? What are the consequences of viewing yourself (or of being viewed) as ill or disabled? By drawing on four sociological perspectives—functionalism, conflict theory, interactionism, and labeling theory—we can gain greater insight into the social context that shapes definitions of health and the treatment of illness.

Functionalist Approach

Illness entails breaks in our social interactions, both at work and at home. From a functionalist perspective, being sick must therefore be controlled, so that not too many people are released from their societal responsibilities at any one time. Functionalists contend that an overly broad definition of illness would disrupt the workings of a society.

Sickness requires that one take on a social role, if only temporarily. The **sick role** refers to societal expectations about the attitudes and behavior of a person viewed as being ill. Sociologist Talcott Parsons (1951, 1975), well known for his contributions to functionalist theory, outlined the behavior required of people who are considered sick. They are exempted from their normal, day-to-day responsibilities and generally do not suffer blame for their condition. Yet they are obligated to try to get well, which includes seeking competent professional care. This

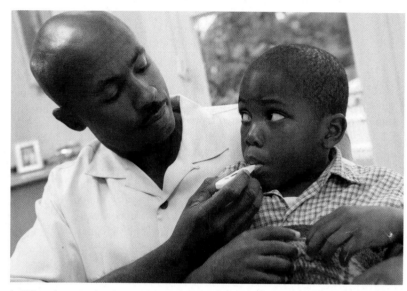

In U.S. society, people who are sick are supposed to stay home and rest until they feel better. Though different societies have different expectations of a person who is seen as being ill, all recognize the significance of the *sick role*.

obligation arises from the common view that illness is dysfunctional, because it can undermine social stability. Attempting to get well is particularly important in the world's developing countries. Modern automated industrial societies can absorb a greater degree of illness or disability than horticultural or agrarian societies, in which the availability of workers is far more critical (Conrad 2009b).

According to Parsons's theory, physicians function as *gatekeepers* for the sick role. They verify a patient's condition either as "illness" or as "recovered." The ill person becomes dependent on the physician, because the latter can control valued rewards (not only treatment of illness, but also excused absences from work and school). Parsons suggests that the physician–patient relationship is somewhat like that between parent and child. Like a parent, the physician helps the patient to enter society as a full and functioning adult (Weitz 2007).

The concept of the sick role is not without criticism. First, patients' judgments regarding their own state of health may be related to their gender, age, social class, and ethnic group. For example, younger people may fail to detect warning signs of a dangerous illness, while elderly people may focus too much on the slightest physical malady. Second, the sick role may be more applicable to people who are experiencing short-term illnesses than to those with recurring, long-term illnesses. Finally, even simple factors, such as whether a person is employed, seem to affect one's willingness to assume the sick role—as does the impact of socialization into a particular occupation or activity.

For example, beginning in childhood, athletes learn to define certain ailments as "sports injuries" and therefore do not regard themselves as "sick." Nonetheless, sociologists continue to rely on Parsons's model for functionalist analysis of the relationship between illness and societal expectations of the sick (Curry 1993).

> ## use your sociological *imagination*
>
> Describe some situations you have witnessed that illustrate different definitions of the "sick role."

Conflict Approach

Conflict theorists observe that the medical profession has assumed a preeminence that extends well beyond whether to excuse a student from school or an employee from work. Sociologist Eliot Freidson (1970:5) has likened the position of medicine today to that of state religions yesterday—it has an officially approved monopoly of the right to define health and illness and to treat illness. Conflict theorists use the term *medicalization of society* to refer to the growing role of medicine as a major institution of social control (Conrad 2009a; McKinlay and McKinlay 1977; Zola 1972, 1983).

The Medicalization of Society Social control involves techniques and strategies for regulating behavior in order to enforce the distinctive norms and values of a culture. Typically, we think of informal social control as occurring within families and peer groups, and formal social control as being carried out by authorized agents such as police officers, judges, school administrators, and employers. Viewed from a conflict perspective, however, medicine is not simply a "healing profession"; it is a regulating mechanism.

How does medicine manifest its social control? First, medicine has greatly expanded its domain of expertise in recent decades. Physicians now examine a wide range of issues, among them sexuality, old age, anxiety, obesity, child development, alcoholism, and drug addiction. We tolerate this expansion of the boundaries of medicine because we hope that these experts can bring new "miracle cures" to complex human problems, as they have to the control of certain infectious diseases.

The social significance of this expanding medicalization is that once a problem is viewed using a *medical model*—once medical experts become influential in proposing and assessing relevant public policies—it becomes more difficult for common people to join the discussion and exert influence on decision making. It also becomes more difficult to view these issues as being shaped by social, cultural, or psychological factors, rather than simply by physical or medical factors (Caplan 1989; Conrad 2009a).

Second, medicine serves as an agent of social control by retaining absolute jurisdiction over many health care procedures. It has even attempted to guard its jurisdiction by placing health care professionals such as chiropractors and nurse-midwives outside the realm of acceptable medicine. Despite the fact that midwives first brought professionalism to child delivery, they have been portrayed as having invaded the "legitimate" field of obstetrics, in both the United States and Mexico. Nurse-midwives have sought licensing as a way to achieve professional respectability, but physicians continue to exert power to ensure that midwifery remains a subordinate occupation (Scharnberg 2007).

Inequities in Health Care The medicalization of society is but one concern of conflict theorists as they assess the workings of health care institutions. As we have seen throughout this textbook, in analyzing any issue, conflict theorists seek to determine who benefits, who suffers, and who dominates at the expense of others. Viewed from a conflict perspective, glaring inequities exist in health care delivery in the United States. For example, poor areas tend to be underserved because medical services concentrate where people are wealthy.

Similarly, from a global perspective, obvious inequities exist in health care delivery. Today, the United States has about 27 physicians per 10,000 people, while African nations have fewer than 1 per 10,000. This situation is only worsened by the **brain drain**—the immigration to the United States and other industrialized nations of skilled workers, professionals, and technicians who are desperately needed in their home countries. As part of this brain drain, physicians, nurses, and other health care professionals have come to the United States from developing countries such as India, Pakistan, and various African states. Conflict theorists view their emigration out of the Third World as yet another way in which the world's core industrialized nations

The growing concern about obesity among the young has focused attention on their eating habits and their need for exercise. Concern about obesity is a sign of the medicalization of society.

enhance their quality of life at the expense of developing countries. One way the developing countries suffer is in lower life expectancy. In Africa and much of Latin America and Asia, life expectancy is far lower than in industrialized nations (Bureau of the Census 2010a; World Bank 2009).

Conflict theorists emphasize that inequities in health care have clear life-and-death consequences. From a conflict perspective, the dramatic differences in *infant mortality rates* around the world (Figure 19-1) reflect, at least in part, unequal distribution of health care resources based on the wealth or poverty of various nations. The **infant mortality rate** is the number of deaths of infants under 1 year old per 1,000 live births in a given year. This measure is an important indicator of a society's level of health care; it reflects prenatal nutrition, delivery procedures, and infant screening measures. Still, despite the wealth of the United States, at least 46 nations have *lower* infant mortality rates, among them Canada, Sweden, and Japan. Conflict theorists point out that unlike the United States, these countries offer some form of government-supported health care for all citizens, which typically leads to greater availability and use of prenatal care (Mathews and MacDorman 2009).

use your sociological *imagination*

From a sociological point of view, what might be the greatest challenge to reducing inequities in health care?

Interactionist Approach

From an interactionist point of view, patients are not passive; often, they actively seek the services of a health care practitioner. In examining health, illness, and medicine as a social institution, then, interactionists engage in micro-level study of the roles played by health care professionals and patients. Interactionists are particularly interested in how physicians learn to play their occupational role. According to Brenda L. Beagan (2001), the technical language students learn in medical school becomes the basis for the script they follow as novice physicians. The familiar white coat is their costume—one that helps them to appear confident and professional at the same time that it identifies them as doctors to patients and other staff members. Beagan found that many medical students struggle to project the appearance of competence that they think their role demands.

Sometimes patients play an active role in health care by *failing* to follow a physician's advice. For example, some patients stop taking medications long before they should. Some take an incorrect dosage on purpose, and others never even fill their prescriptions. Such noncompliance results in part from the prevalence of self-medication in our society; many people are accustomed to self-diagnosis and self-treatment. On the other hand, patients' active involvement in their health care can sometimes have very *positive*

consequences. Some patients read books about preventive health care techniques, attempt to maintain a healthful and nutritious diet, carefully monitor any side effects of medication, and adjust the dosage based on perceived side effects.

Labeling Approach

Labeling theory helps us to understand why certain people are *viewed* as deviants, "bad kids," or criminals, whereas others whose behavior is similar are not. Labeling theorists also suggest that the designation "healthy" or "ill" generally involves social definition by others. Just as police officers, judges, and other regulators of social control have the power to define certain

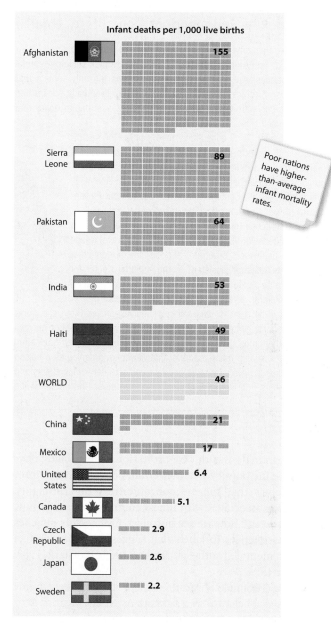

Poor nations have higher-than-average infant mortality rates.

Source: Haub 2010.

people as criminals, health care professionals (especially physicians) have the power to define certain people as sick. Moreover, like labels that suggest nonconformity or criminality, labels that are associated with illness commonly reshape how others treat us and how we see ourselves. Our society attaches serious consequences to labels that suggest less-than-perfect physical or mental health (H. Becker 1963; C. Clark 1983; H. Schwartz 1994).

A historical example illustrates perhaps the ultimate extreme in labeling social behavior as a sickness. As enslavement of Africans in the United States came under increasing attack in the 19th century, medical authorities provided new rationalizations for the oppressive practice. Noted physicians published articles stating that the skin color of Africans deviated from "healthy" white skin coloring because Africans suffered from congenital leprosy. Moreover, the continuing efforts of enslaved Africans to escape from their White masters were classified as an example of the "disease" of drapetomania (or "crazy runaways"). The prestigious *New Orleans Medical and Surgical Journal* suggested that the remedy for this "disease" was to treat slaves kindly, as one might treat children. Apparently, these medical authorities would not entertain the view that it was healthy and sane to flee slavery or join in a slave revolt (T. Szasz 2010).

According to labeling theorists, we can view a variety of life experiences as illnesses or not. Premenstrual syndrome, posttraumatic stress disorders, and hyperactivity have now been labeled medically recognized disorders. In addition, the medical community continues to disagree over whether chronic fatigue syndrome constitutes a medical illness.

Probably the most noteworthy medical example of labeling is the case of homosexuality. For years, psychiatrists classified being gay or lesbian not as a lifestyle but as a mental disorder subject to treatment. This official sanction became an early target of the growing gay and lesbian rights movement in the United States. In 1974, members of the American Psychiatric Association voted to drop homosexuality from the standard manual on mental disorders (Conrad 2009a).

Table 19-1 summarizes four major sociological perspectives on health and illness. Although they may seem quite different, two common themes unite them. First, any person's health or illness is more than an organic condition, since it is subject to the interpretation of others. The impact of culture, family and friends, and the medical profession means that health and illness are not purely biological occurrences, but sociological occurrences as well. Second, since members of a society (especially industrial societies) share the same health care delivery system, health is a group and societal concern. Although health may be defined as the complete well-being of an individual, it is also the result of one's social environment, as the next section will show (Cockerham 2009).

thinking CRITICALLY

Describe an occasion on which people you know disagreed about a socially applied medical label. What was the label, and why did people disagree?

	Functionalist	Conflict	Interactionist	Labeling
Major emphasis	Control of the number of people who are considered sick	Overmedicalization Gross inequities in health care	Doctor-patient relationship Interaction of medical staff	Definition of illness and health
Controlling factors	Physician as gatekeeper	Medical profession Social inequities	Medical profession	Medical profession
Proponents	Talcott Parsons	Paul Starr Thomas Szasz Irving Zola	Doug Maynard	Thomas Szasz

Social Epidemiology and Health

Social epidemiology is the study of the distribution of disease, impairment, and general health status across a population. Initially, epidemiologists concentrated on the scientific study of epidemics, focusing on how they started and spread. Contemporary social epidemiology is much broader in scope, concerned not only with epidemics but also with nonepidemic diseases, injuries, drug addiction and alcoholism, suicide, and mental illness. Epidemiologists have taken on the new role of tracking bioterrorism. In 2001, they mobilized to trace the anthrax outbreak and prepare for any terrorist use of smallpox or other lethal microbes. Epidemiologists draw on the work of a wide variety of scientists and researchers, among them physicians, sociologists, public health officials, biologists, veterinarians, demographers, anthropologists, psychologists, and meteorologists.

Researchers in social epidemiology commonly use two concepts: *incidence* and *prevalence*. **Incidence** refers to the number of new cases of a specific disorder that occur within a given population during a stated period, usually a year. For example, the incidence of AIDS in the United States in 2007 was 42,655 cases. In contrast, **prevalence** refers to the total number of cases of a specific disorder that exist at a given time. The prevalence of HIV/AIDS in the United States through 2010 was about 1 million cases.

Worldwide, an estimated 33 million people were infected with HIV at the end of 2009. Women account for a growing proportion of new cases of HIV/AIDS, especially among racial and ethnic minorities. Although the spread of AIDS is stabilizing, with only gradual increases in reported cases, the disease is not evenly distributed. Those areas that are least equipped to deal with it—the developing nations of sub-Saharan Africa—face the greatest challenge (Centers for Disease Control and Prevention 2011a; Figure 19-2).

When disease incidence figures are presented as rates, or as the number of reports per 100,000 people, they are called **morbidity rates**. The term **mortality rate** refers to the incidence of *death* in a given population. Sociologists find morbidity rates useful because they reveal that a specific disease occurs more frequently in one segment of a population than another. As we shall see, social class, race, ethnicity, gender, and age can all affect a population's morbidity rates.

Social Class

Social class is clearly associated with differences in morbidity and mortality rates. Studies in the United States and other countries have consistently shown that people in the lower classes have higher rates of mortality and disability than others.

Why is class linked to health? Crowded living conditions, substandard housing, poor diet, and stress all contribute to the ill health of many low-income people in the United States. In certain instances, poor education may lead to a lack of awareness of measures necessary to maintain good health. Financial strains are certainly a major factor in the health problems of less affluent people.

What is particularly troubling about social class differences is that they appear to be cumulative. Little or no health care in

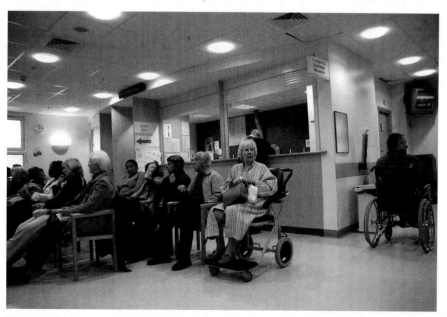

When people who do not have health insurance seek medical care, their condition is often more critical than it would be had they been receiving regular preventive care from a primary care provider. And the care they receive, especially in an emergency room, is much more expensive than the care in a doctor's office.

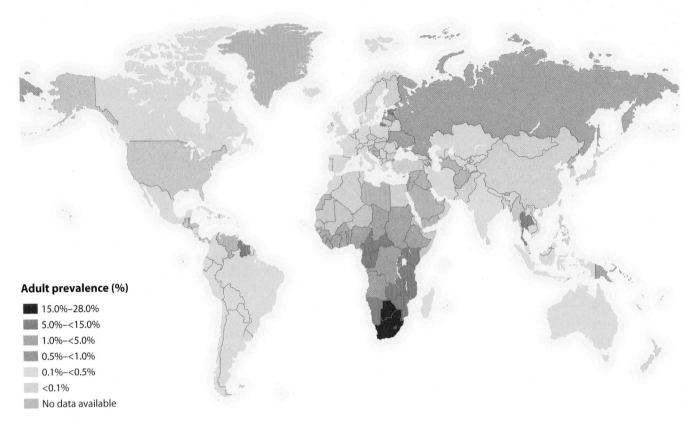

Adult prevalence (%)

- 15.0%–28.0%
- 5.0%–<15.0%
- 1.0%–<5.0%
- 0.5%–<1.0%
- 0.1%–<0.5%
- <0.1%
- No data available

Note: Data for the 33.3 million people (estimated range, 31.4–35.8 million) living with HIV at the end of 2009.
Source: UNAIDS 2010:23.

childhood or young adulthood is likely to mean more illness later in life. The longer that low income presents a barrier to adequate health care, the more chronic and difficult to treat illness becomes (Pampel et al. 2010; Phelan et al. 2010).

Another reason for the link between social class and health is that the poor—many of whom belong to racial and ethnic minorities—are less able than others to afford quality medical care. The affluent are more likely than others to have health insurance, either because they can afford it or because they have jobs that provide it. This situation has been deteriorating over time, as employer-provided coverage (the most common form of health insurance) declined steadily from 2000 through 2009. In 2008, 46.3 million people reported going without health care because they could not pay for it; in 2009, 50.7 million went without. And increasingly, pharmacists reported that people were purchasing only those medications they "needed the most," or were buying in small quantities, such as four pills at a time. Even for children, many of whom are eligible for government-subsidized health insurance, coverage varies widely, ranging from 98.5 percent in Massachusetts to 81.6 percent in Nevada (Figure 19-3).

In 2010, largely in response to the millions of people who do not have health insurance, Congress enacted the Patient Protection and Affordable Care Act. Beginning in 2014, this legislation—the most significant health care reform since passage of Medicare in 1965—will help people who are sick or have

lost a job to afford medical care. In the meantime, certain high-risk people will receive immediate coverage. By 2019, about 95 percent of citizens and legal residents who are not covered by Medicare should have health insurance. In the next few years, researchers will be busy assessing the effect of the legislation on health care inequities (Starr 2010).

Finally, in the view of Karl Marx and contemporary conflict theorists, capitalist societies such as the United States care more about maximizing profits than they do about the health and safety of industrial workers. As a result, government agencies do not take forceful action to regulate conditions in the workplace, and workers suffer many preventable job-related injuries and illnesses. As we will see later in this chapter, research also shows that the lower classes are more vulnerable to environmental pollution than are the affluent, not only where they work but where they live.

use your sociological *imagination*

Does the cost of health care affect the way you receive medical services?

FIGURE **19-3** PERCENTAGE OF CHILDREN WITHOUT HEALTH INSURANCE

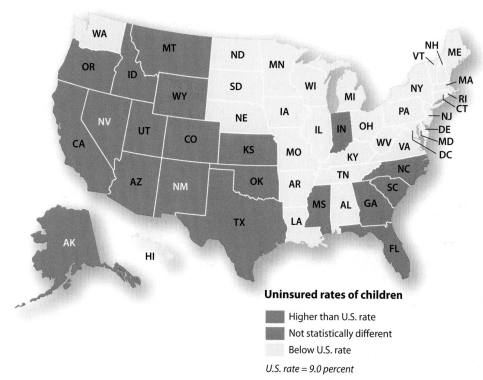

Uninsured rates of children

- Higher than U.S. rate
- Not statistically different
- Below U.S. rate

U.S. rate = 9.0 percent

Source: Mach and Blumenthal 2010:2.

Think about It

Do you know people whose children don't have health insurance? If so, how has the lack of insurance affected their decisions about their children's medical treatment?

Race and Ethnicity

The health profiles of many racial and ethnic minorities reflect the social inequality evident in the United States. The poor economic and environmental conditions of groups such as African Americans, Hispanics, and Native Americans are manifested in high morbidity and mortality rates for those groups. It is true that some diseases, such as sickle-cell anemia among Blacks, have a clear genetic basis. But in most instances, environmental factors contribute to the differential rates of disease and death.

As noted earlier, infant mortality is regarded as a primary indicator of health care. There is a significant gap in the United States between the infant mortality rates of African Americans and Whites. Generally, the rate of infant death is more than twice as high among Blacks (MacDorman and Mathews 2011).

The medical establishment is not exempt from racism. Unfortunately, the media often focus on obvious forms of racism, such as hate crimes, while overlooking more insidious forms in social institutions like the medical establishment. Minorities receive inferior medical care even when they are insured. Despite having access to care, Blacks, Latinos, and Native Americans are treated unequally as a result of racial prejudice and differences in the quality of various health care plans. Furthermore, national clinical studies have shown that even allowing for differences in income and insurance coverage, racial and ethnic minorities are less likely than other groups to receive both standard health care and life-saving treatment for conditions such as HIV infection (Centers for Disease Control and Prevention 2011b; Long and Masi 2009).

Drawing on the conflict perspective, sociologist Howard Waitzkin (1986) suggests that racial tensions also contribute to the medical problems of Blacks. In his view, the stress that results from racial prejudice and discrimination helps to explain the higher rates of hypertension found among African Americans (and Hispanics) compared to Whites. Hypertension—twice as common in Blacks as in Whites—is believed to be a critical factor in Blacks' high mortality rates from heart disease, kidney disease, and stroke (Centers for Disease Control and Prevention 2011b).

Some Mexican Americans and many other Latinos adhere to cultural beliefs that make them less likely to use the established medical system. They may interpret their illnesses according to *curanderismo*, or traditional Latino folk medicine—a form of holistic health care and healing. *Curanderismo* influences how one approaches health care and even how one defines illness. Most Hispanics probably use *curanderos*, or folk healers, infrequently, but perhaps 20 percent rely on home remedies. Some define such illnesses as *susto* (fright sickness) and *atague* (fighting attack) according to folk beliefs. Because these complaints often have biological bases, sensitive medical practitioners need to deal with them carefully in order to diagnose and treat illnesses accurately. Moreover, it would be a mistake to blame the poor health care that Latinos receive on cultural differences. Latinos are much more likely to seek treatment for pressing medical problems at clinics and emergency rooms than they are to receive regular preventive care through a family physician (Centers for Disease Control and Prevention 2011b; Durden and Hummer 2006; Trotter and Chavira 1997).

Gender

A large body of research indicates that compared with men, women experience a higher prevalence of many illnesses, although they tend to live longer. There are some variations—for example, men are more likely to have parasitic diseases, whereas women are more likely to become diabetic—but as a group, women appear to be in poorer health than men.

The apparent inconsistency between the ill health of women and their greater longevity deserves an explanation, and researchers have advanced a theory. Women's lower rate of cigarette smoking (reducing their risk of heart disease, lung cancer, and emphysema), lower consumption of alcohol (reducing the risk of auto accidents and cirrhosis of the liver), and lower rate of employment in dangerous occupations explain about one-third of their greater longevity than men. Moreover, some clinical studies suggest that the differences in morbidity may actually be less pronounced than the data show. Researchers argue that women are much more likely than men to seek treatment, to be diagnosed as having a disease, and thus to have their illnesses reflected in the data examined by epidemiologists.

From a conflict perspective, women have been particularly vulnerable to the medicalization of society, with everything from birth to beauty being treated in an increasingly medical context. Such medicalization may contribute to women's higher morbidity rates compared to those of men. Ironically, even though women have been especially affected by medicalization, medical researchers have often excluded them from clinical studies. Female physicians and researchers charge that sexism lies at the heart of such research practices, and insist there is a desperate need for studies of female subjects (Centers for Disease Control and Prevention 2011b; Rieker and Bird 2000).

thinking CRITICALLY

Which is a more important factor in the adequate delivery of health care, race or gender?

Age

Health is the overriding concern of the elderly. Most older people in the United States report having at least one chronic illness, but only some of those conditions are potentially life threatening or require medical care. At the same time, health problems can affect the quality of life of older people in important ways. Almost half of older people in the United States are troubled by arthritis, and many have visual or hearing impairments that can interfere with the performance of everyday tasks.

Older people are also especially vulnerable to certain mental health problems. Alzheimer's disease, the leading cause of dementia in the United States, afflicts an estimated 5.1 million people age 65 or over—that is, 13 percent of that segment of the population. While some individuals with Alzheimer's exhibit only mild symptoms, the risk of severe problems resulting

from the disease rises substantially with age (Alzheimer's Association 2010:10).

Not surprisingly, older people in the United States (age 75 and older) are five times more likely to use health services than younger people (ages 15–24). The disproportionate use of the U.S. health care system by older people is a critical factor in all discussions about the cost of health care and possible reforms of the health care system (Bureau of the Census 2010a).

In sum, to achieve greater access and reduce health disparities, federal health officials must overcome inequities that are rooted not just in age, but in social class, race and ethnicity, and gender. If that were not enough, they must also deal with a geographical disparity in health care resources.

Health Care in the United States

As the entire nation is well aware, the costs of health care have skyrocketed. In 1997, total expenditures for health care in the United States crossed the trillion-dollar threshold—more than four times the 1980 total (Figure 19-4). In 2000, the amount spent on health care equaled that spent on education, defense, prisons, farm subsidies, food stamps, and foreign aid combined. By the year 2019,

FIGURE **19-4** TOTAL HEALTH CARE EXPENDITURES IN THE UNITED STATES, 1970–2019 (PROJECTED)

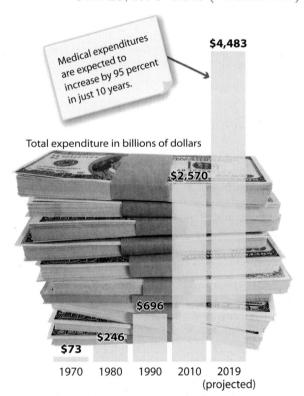

Medical expenditures are expected to increase by 95 percent in just 10 years.

$4,483

Total expenditure in billions of dollars

$2,570

$696

$246

$73

| 1970 | 1980 | 1990 | 2010 | 2019 (projected) |

Sources: Centers for Medicare and Medicaid Services 2010: Table 1 (2004–2019 data); Health Care Financing Administration 2001 (1970–1990 data).

Think about It
What social changes in the United States might account for the rise in health care costs from $73 billion in 1970 to almost 2.6 trillion in 2010?

"I'm going to hold up a number of outstanding medical bills. Tell me how many you see."

health care proceeded, the medical profession gained control over both the market for its services and the various organizational hierarchies that govern medical practice, financing, and policy-making. By the 1920s, physicians controlled hospital technology, the division of labor of health personnel, and indirectly, other professional practices such as nursing and pharmacy (R. Coser 1984).

Physicians, Nurses, and Patients

Traditionally, physicians have held a position of dominance in their dealings with both patients and nurses. The functionalist and interactionist perspectives offer a framework for understanding the professional socialization of physicians as it relates to patient care. Functionalists suggest that established physicians and medical school professors serve as mentors or role models who transmit knowledge, skills, and values to the passive learner—the medical student. Interactionists emphasize that students are molded by the medical school environment as they interact with their classmates.

Both approaches argue that the typical training of physicians in the United States leads to rather dehumanizing physician–patient encounters. As Dr. Lori Arviso Alvord, a Navajo physician, writes in *The Scalpel and the Silver Bear,* "I had been trained by a group of physicians who placed much more emphasis on their technical abilities and clinical skills than on their abilities to be caring and sensitive" (Alvord and Van Pelt 1999:13). Despite many efforts to formally introduce a humanistic approach to patient care into the medical school curriculum, patient overload and cost-cutting by hospitals have tended to undercut positive relations. Moreover, widespread publicity about malpractice suits and high medical costs has further strained the physician–patient relationship. Interactionists have closely examined compliance and negotiation between physician and patient. They concur with Talcott Parsons's view that the relationship is generally asymmetrical, with doctors holding a position of dominance and controlling rewards.

Just as physicians have maintained dominance in their interactions with patients, they have controlled interactions with nurses. Despite their training and professional status, nurses commonly take orders from physicians. Traditionally, the

total expenditures for health care in the United States are expected to exceed $4.4 trillion. The rising costs of medical care are especially burdensome in the event of catastrophic illnesses or confinement to a nursing home. Bills of tens of thousands of dollars are not unusual in the treatment of cancer, Alzheimer's disease, and other chronic illnesses requiring custodial care.

The health care system of the United States has moved far beyond the days when general practitioners living in a neighborhood or community typically made house calls and charged modest fees for their services. How did health care become a big business involving nationwide hospital chains and marketing campaigns? How have these changes reshaped the interactions between doctors, nurses, and patients? We will address these questions in the next section of the chapter.

A Historical View

Today, state licensing and medical degrees confer an authority on medical professionals that is maintained from one generation to the next. However, health care in the United States has not always followed this model. The "popular health movement" of the 1830s and 1840s emphasized preventive care and what is termed "self-help." Strong criticism was voiced of "doctoring" as a paid occupation. New medical philosophies or sects established their own medical schools and challenged the authority and methods of more traditional doctors. By the 1840s, most states had repealed medical licensing laws.

In response, through the leadership of the American Medical Association (AMA), founded in 1848, "regular" doctors attacked lay practitioners, sectarian doctors, and female physicians in general. Once they had institutionalized their authority through standardized programs of education and licensing, they conferred it on all who successfully completed their programs. The authority of the physician no longer depended on lay attitudes or on the person occupying the sick role; increasingly, it was built into the structure of the medical profession and the health care system. As the institutionalization of

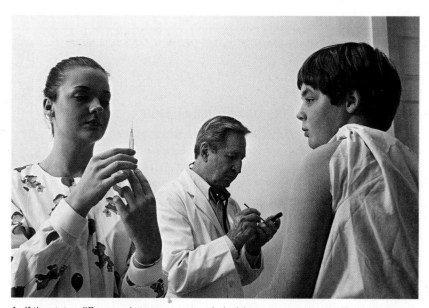

As if the status differences between nurses and physicians were not clear to all, the cheery uniform of nurses and the formal white doctor's coat reinforce the distinction.

relationship between doctors and nurses has paralleled the male dominance of the United States: most physicians have been male, while virtually all nurses have been female.

Like other women in subordinate roles, nurses have been expected to perform their duties without challenging the authority of men. Psychiatrist Leonard Stein (1967) refers to this process as the *doctor–nurse game.* According to the rules of this "game," the nurse must never openly disagree with the physician. When she has recommendations concerning a patient's care, she must communicate them indirectly, in a deferential tone. For example, if asked by a hospital's medical resident, "What sleeping medication has been helpful to Mrs. Brown in the past?" (an indirect request for a recommendation), the nurse will respond with a disguised recommendation, such as "Pentobarbital 100 mg was quite effective night before last." Her careful response allows the physician to authoritatively restate the same prescription as if it were *his* idea.

Like nurses, female physicians have traditionally found themselves in a subordinate position because of their gender, but that is slowly changing. In fall 2010, 49 percent of all new medical school students in the United States were female, along with 35 percent of all faculty members at medical schools. A study of male and female medical residents suggests that the increasing number of women physicians may alter the traditional doctor–patient relationship. Male residents were found to be more focused on the intellectual challenges of medicine and the prestige associated with certain medical specialties. In contrast, female residents were more likely to express a commitment to caring for patients and devoting time to them. In terms of the functionalist analysis of gender stratification offered by sociologists Talcott Parsons and Robert Bales, male residents took the *instrumental,* achievement-oriented role, while female residents took the *expressive,* interpersonal-oriented role. As women continue to enter and move higher in the hierarchies of the medical profession, sociological studies will surely be done to see whether these apparent gender differences persist (American Academy of Medical Colleges 2011:Tables 1, 3).

Patients have traditionally relied on medical personnel to inform them of health care issues, but increasingly they are turning to the media for health care information. Recognizing this change, pharmaceutical firms are advertising their prescription drugs directly to potential customers through television and magazines. The Internet is another growing source for patient information. Medical professionals are understandably suspicious of these new sources of information. Today, consumers get more than their health care information in new ways. Over the past decade, they have discovered a new way to access traditional medicine: going to the store (Box 19-1).

use your sociological *imagination*

If you were a patient, would you put yourself entirely in the physician's hands, or would you do some research on your own? If you were a doctor, would you want your patient checking medical information on the Internet? Explain your positions.

Alternatives to Traditional Health Care

In traditional forms of health care, people rely on physicians and hospitals for the treatment of illness. Yet at least one out of every three adults in the United States attempts to maintain good health or respond to illness through the use of alternative health care techniques. For example, in recent decades interest has been growing in *holistic* (also spelled *wholistic*) medical principles, first developed in China. **Holistic medicine** refers to therapies in which the health care practitioner considers the person's physical, mental, emotional, and spiritual characteristics. The individual is regarded as a totality rather than a collection of interrelated organ systems. Treatment methods include massage, chiropractic medicine, acupuncture (which involves the insertion of fine needles into surface points), respiratory exercises, and the use of herbs as remedies. Nutrition, exercise, and visualization may also be used to treat ailments that are generally treated through medication or hospitalization (Sharma and Bodeker 1998).

Practitioners of holistic medicine do not necessarily function totally outside the traditional health care system. Some have medical degrees and rely on X-rays and

SPOTTING

TREND

Medical Technology and Telemedicine

Technological advances touch all aspects of society, including medicine. To reverse paralysis, doctors have inserted microchips in patients' limbs. These space-age devices respond to the electrical impulses the brain sends out and initiate movement. Someday, microchips may even replace chemical medications.

Robotics is another up-and-coming medical technology. Already, voice-activated robotic instruments are being used in heart surgery. NASA is currently developing a robotic probe that can locate brain tumors.

Both these technologies raise the possibility of doing medicine from a distance. To activate microchips or robots, medical personnel do not need to be standing next to a patient. Soon, remote monitoring may supplement the familiar bedside monitor.

RESEARCH TODAY

19-1 Health Care, Retail Style

Greeting cards are in aisle 7; vaccinations, in aisle 4. Today, over 1,200 health clinics are located in retail stores throughout the United States, including Walgreens, CVS, and Walmart. Staffed by nurse-practitioners and nurses with advanced degrees, these in-store clinics treat a limited menu of complaints, including sore throats, ear infections, pinkeye, and noncomplicated respiratory conditions. And the nurses do write prescriptions.

What are the implications of these new clinics for traditional health care? Having a regular physician is becoming less and less common in the United States, given the many people who lack health insurance, as well as the frequent changes in corporate health plans. Like it or not, the physician you see this year simply may not be available to you next year. Under these circumstances, retail medical care may not pose much of a challenge to traditional medical practices.

For three acute conditions—sore throat, middle ear infection, and urinary tract infection—retail clinics delivered the same or better quality care than traditional medical settings.

What about the quality of care offered at in-store clinics? Recently, researchers compared the care delivered in retail clinics to the care available in doctors' offices, urgent care departments, and emergency rooms. For three acute conditions—sore throat, middle ear infection, and urinary tract infection—they found that retail clinics delivered the same or better-quality care

than traditional medical settings, including preventive care during or after the first visit. Costs were much lower, especially compared to those in emergency rooms.

In-store clinics are another example of **McDonaldization,** the process through which the principles of the fast-food restaurant are coming to dominate more and more sectors of society (see Chapter 6). McDonaldization offers the benefit of clearly stated services and prices, but the drawback of impersonality. Family doctors note that 40 percent of clinic patients have a family physician. Yet given the shortcomings of health care delivery in the United States, it

is difficult to argue against an innovative new method of providing health care.

LET'S DISCUSS

1. Have you ever been treated at an in-store clinic? If so, were you satisfied with the care you received? What about the price you paid—was it reasonable?
2. Evaluate the emergence of clinics from a functionalist and then a conflict perspective. On balance, do you think these clinics are a benefit to society?

Sources: Pickert 2009; RAND 2010; Ritzer 2011.

EKG machines for diagnostic assistance. Others who staff holistic clinics, often referred to as *wellness clinics,* reject the use of medical technology. The recent resurgence of holistic medicine comes amid widespread recognition of the value of nutrition and the dangers of overreliance on prescription drugs (especially those used to reduce stress, such as Valium).

The medical establishment—professional organizations, research hospitals, and medical schools—has generally served as a stern protector of traditionally accepted health care techniques. However, a major breakthrough occurred in 1992 when the federal government's National Institutes of Health—the nation's major funding source for biomedical research—opened an Office of Alternative Medicine, empowered to accept grant requests. NIH-sponsored national surveys conducted in 2002 and 2007 found that one in four adults in the United States had used some form of "complementary and alternative medicine" during the previous month or year. Examples included

acupuncture, folk medicine, meditation, yoga, homeopathic treatments, megavitamin therapy, and chiropractic treatment. When prayer was included as an alternative or complementary form of medicine, the proportion of adults who used alternative medicine rose to over 62 percent (Figure 19-5).

On the international level, the World Health Organization (WHO) has begun to monitor the use of alternative medicine around the world. According to WHO, 80 percent of people who live in the poorest countries in the world use some form of alternative medicine, from herbal treatments to the services of a faith healer. In most countries, these treatments are largely unregulated, even though some of them can be fatal. For example, kava kava, an herbal tea used in the Pacific Islands to relieve anxiety, can be toxic to the liver in concentrated form. However, other alternative treatments have been found to be effective in the treatment of serious diseases, such as malaria and sickle-cell anemia. WHO's goal is to compile a list of such

FIGURE 19-5 USE OF COMPLEMENTARY AND ALTERNATIVE MEDICINE

Diets	3.6 %
Yoga	6.1 %
Massage	8.3%
Chiropractic	8.6%
Meditation	9.4%
Prayer group	9.6%
Deep breathing	12.7%
Natural products	17.1%
Prayer/others	24.4%
Prayer/self	43.0%

Note: Data from 2007 survey, except for prayer data from 2002 survey.
Source: Barnes et al. 2004, 2008.

Tea Party members protest the passage of health care reform outside a congressional representative's office in Schaumburg, Illinois. Although the legislation would help millions of Americans who lack health insurance, opponents worry that the cost would be prohibitive.

practices, as well as to encourage the development of universal training programs and ethical standards for practitioners of alternative medicine. To date, the organization has published findings on about 100 of the 5,000 plants believed to be used as herbal remedies (McNeil 2002).

The Role of Government

Not until the 20th century did health care receive federal aid. The first significant involvement was the 1946 Hill-Burton Act, which provided subsidies for building and improving hospitals, especially in rural areas. A far more important change came with the enactment in 1965 of two wide-ranging government assistance programs: Medicare, which is essentially a compulsory health insurance plan for the elderly, and Medicaid, which is a noncontributory federal and state insurance plan for the poor. These programs greatly expanded federal involvement in health care financing for needy men, women, and children.

Given the high rates of illness and disability among elderly people, Medicare has had a huge impact on the health care system. Initially, Medicare simply reimbursed health care providers such as physicians and hospitals for the billed costs of their services. However, in 1983, as the overall costs of Medicare increased dramatically, the federal government introduced a price-control system. Under this system, private hospitals often transfer patients whose treatment may be unprofitable to public facilities. In fact, many private hospitals have begun to conduct "wallet biopsies"—that is, to investigate the financial status of potential patients. Those judged undesirable are then refused admission or dumped. Although a federal law passed in 1987 made it illegal for any hospital receiving Medicare funds to dump patients, the practice continues (E. Gould 2007; Light 2004).

The expansion of health insurance coverage enacted by Congress in 2010 raised the hope of improved health care. It also brought severe criticism from the Tea Party movement, whose members charged that legislators were spending money they did not have. The costs of the legislation, Tea party members warned, would lead inevitably to higher taxes.

thinking CRITICALLY

In the United States, a nation with a world-renowned medical system, why do so many people seek alternative forms of health care?

Mental Illness in the United States

Like other illnesses, mental disorders affect not just individuals and their families, but society as a whole. In industrial economies, mental disorders are a significant cause of disability. Thus, as a British medical journal declared in connection with the

Global Mental Health Summit, there can be "no health without mental health" (Prince et al. 2007).

Sadly, the words *mental illness* and *insanity* evoke dramatic and often inaccurate images of emotional problems. Though the media routinely emphasize the most violent behavior of those with emotional disturbances, mental health and mental illness can more appropriately be viewed as a continuum of behavior that we ourselves move along. Using this definition, we can consider a person to have a mental disorder "if he or she is so disturbed that coping with routine, everyday life is difficult or impossible." The term **mental illness** should be reserved for a disorder of the brain that disrupts a person's thinking, feeling, and ability to interact with others (J. Coleman and Cressey 1980:315; National Alliance on Mental Illness 2008).

Traditionally, people in the United States have maintained a negative and suspicious view of those with mental disorders. Holding the status of "mental patient" or even "former mental patient" can have unfortunate and undeserved consequences. Voting rights are denied in some instances, acceptance for jury duty is problematic, and past emotional problems are an issue in divorce and custody cases. Moreover, content analysis of network television programs and films shows that mentally ill characters are uniformly portrayed in a demeaning and derogatory fashion; many are labeled as "criminally insane," "wackos," or "psychos." From an interactionist perspective, a key social institution is shaping social behavior by manipulating symbols and intensifying people's fears about the mentally ill (Diefenbach and West 2007).

In 2011, actress Catherine Zeta-Jones announced that she was being treated for bipolar disorder, a condition she shares with an estimated 2 percent of the U.S. population. The stigma of mental illness is slowly diminishing as celebrities come forward to reveal they are being treated for various mental disorders.

Despite this stigmatization of mental illness, more people are seeking care and professional assistance than in the past. In the military services, the depression and post-traumatic stress that many veterans experience is receiving growing attention. And increasingly, legislators are recognizing the need to provide services for all who suffer from mental illness (Kessler 2006; Tanielian 2009).

Even so, the need for mental health care seems to outstrip the available resources. In 2009, for example, mental health professionals expressed concern for the well-being of children and adults who had been displaced by Hurricane Katrina. In the aftermath of the disaster, residents of New Orleans were displaying unusually high levels of depression, anxiety, suicide, drug and alcohol abuse, and other high-risk behaviors. The crisis called for new intervention strategies, but the city's health care system was already overwhelmed (Abramson et al. 2007; Guarino 2009; Waelde et al. 2008).

Theoretical Models of Mental Disorders

In studying mental illness, we can draw on both a medical model and a more sociological approach derived from labeling theory. Each model rests on distinctive assumptions regarding treatment of people with mental disorders.

According to the *medical model,* mental illness is rooted in biological causes that can be treated through medical intervention. Problems in brain structure or in the biochemical balance in the brain, sometimes due to injury and sometimes due to genetic inheritance, are thought to be at the bottom of these disorders. The U.S. Surgeon General (1999) released an exhaustive report on mental health in which he declared that the accumulated weight of scientific evidence leaves no doubt about the physical origins of mental illness.

That is not to say that social factors do not contribute to mental illness. Just as culture affects the incidence and prevalence of illness and its treatment, so too it can affect mental illness. In fact, the very definition of mental illness differs from one culture to the next. Mainstream U.S. culture, for instance, considers hallucinations highly abnormal. However, many traditional cultures view them as evidence of divine favor and confer a special status on those who experience them. As we have noted throughout this textbook, a given behavior may be viewed as normal in one society, disapproved of but tolerated in a second, and labeled as sick and heavily sanctioned in a third.

In contrast to the medical model, *labeling theory* suggests that some behaviors that are viewed as mental illnesses may not really be illnesses, since the individual's problems arise from living in society and not from physical maladies. For example, the U.S. Surgeon General's report (1999:5) notes that "bereavement symptoms" of less than two months' duration do not qualify as a mental disorder, but beyond that they may be redefined. Sociologists would see this approach to bereavement as labeling by those with the power to affix labels rather than as an acknowledgment of a biological condition.

Psychiatrist Thomas Szasz (2010), in his book *The Myth of Mental Illness,* which first appeared in 1960, advanced the view that numerous personality disorders are not diseases, but simply patterns of conduct labeled as disorders by significant others. The response to Szasz's challenging thesis was sharp: the commissioner of the New York State Department of Hygiene demanded his dismissal from his university position because Szasz did not "believe" in mental illness. But many sociologists

At a community mental health center, outpatients create a newsletter for their day program. In the 1980s, community-based mental health care replaced hospitalization as the typical form of treatment for people with serious mental illnesses.

embraced his model as a logical extension of examining individual behavior in a social context.

In sum, the medical model is persuasive because it pinpoints the causes of mental illness and offers treatment for disorders. Yet proponents of the labeling perspective maintain that mental illness is a distinctively social process, whatever other processes are involved. From a sociological perspective, the ideal approach to mental illness integrates the insights of labeling theory with those of the medical approach (Horwitz 2002).

Patterns of Care

For most of human history, those who suffered from mental disorders were deemed the responsibility of their families. Yet mental illness has been a matter of governmental concern much longer than physical illness has. That is because severe emotional disorders threaten stable social relationships and entail prolonged incapacitation. As early as the 1600s, European cities began to confine the insane in public facilities along with the poor and criminals. Prisoners, indignant at being forced to live with "lunatics," resisted this approach. The isolation of the mentally ill from others in the same facility and from the larger society soon made physicians the central and ultimate authority over their welfare.

A major policy development in caring for those with mental disorders came with the passage of the Community Mental Health Centers Act (1963). The CMHC program, as it is known, not only increased the federal government's involvement in the treatment of the mentally ill. It also established community-based mental health centers to treat clients on an *outpatient* basis, thereby allowing them to continue working and living at home. The program showed that outpatient treatment could be more effective than the institutionalized programs of state and county mental hospitals.

Expansion of the federally funded CMHC program decreased inpatient care. By the 1980s, community-based mental health care had replaced hospitalization as the typical form of treatment. Across the United States, deinstitutionalization of the mentally ill reached dramatic proportions. Deinstitutionalization had been conceived as a social reform that would effectively reintegrate the mentally ill into the outside world. However, the authentic humanitarian concern behind the approach proved to be a convenient front for politicians whose goal was simply to cut costs (Kelly 2009).

In a marked shift from public policy over the past three decades, several states have recently made it easier to commit mental patients to hospitals involuntarily. These changes have come in part because community groups and individual residents have voiced increasing fear and anger about the growing number of mentally ill homeless people living in their midst, many of them on the streets. All too often, the severely mentally ill end up in jail or prison after committing crimes that lead to their prosecution. Ironically, family members of these mentally ill men and women complain that they cannot get adequate treatment for their loved ones *until* they have committed violent acts. Nevertheless, civil liberties advocates and voluntary associations of mentally ill people worry about the risks of denying people their constitutional rights, and cite horror stories about the abuses people have experienced during institutionalization (Marquis and Morain 1999; Shogren 1994).

Finally, although mental health care is often considered to be qualitatively different from other types of health care, many of the observations that apply to traditional medicine also apply to mental health care. For example, African Americans, Latinos, and American Indians have higher prevalence rates for several mental disorders, but are much less likely than Whites to receive treatment. Documented prejudice by practitioners contributes to the disparity, along with inadequate insurance and geographic isolation. In both rural and inner-city areas, mental health care is difficult to access and often poor in quality, especially for members of minority groups (McGuire and Miranda 2008).

use your sociological *imagination*

How are your views of mental illness different from or similar to your views of physical illness?

Sociological Perspectives on the Environment

We have seen that the environment people live in has a noticeable effect on their health. Those who live in stressful, overcrowded places suffer more from disease than those who do not. Likewise, people have a noticeable effect on their environment. Around the world, increases in population, together with the economic development that accompanies them, have had serious environmental consequences. We can see signs of despoliation almost everywhere: our air, our water, and our land are being polluted, whether we live in St. Louis, Mexico City, or Lagos, Nigeria.

Though environmental problems may be easy to identify, devising socially and politically acceptable solutions to them is much more difficult. In this section we will see what sociologists have to say about the trade-off between economic growth and development and its effects on the environment. In the section that follows we will look more closely at specific environmental issues.

Human Ecology

Human ecology is an area of study that is concerned with the interrelationships between people and their environment. As the environmentalist Barry Commoner (1971:39) put it, "Everything is connected to everything else." Human ecologists focus on how the physical environment shapes people's lives and on how people influence the surrounding environment.

There is no shortage of illustrations of the interconnectedness of people and their environment. For example, scientific research has linked pollutants in the physical environment to people's health and behavior. The increasing prevalence of asthma, lead poisoning, and cancer have all been tied to human alterations to the environment. Similarly, the rise in melanoma (skin cancer) diagnoses has been linked to global warming. And ecological changes in our food and diet have been related to early obesity and diabetes.

With its view that "everything is connected to everything else," human ecology stresses the trade-offs inherent in every decision that alters the environment. In facing the environmental challenges of the 21st century, government policymakers and environmentalists must determine how they can fulfill humans' pressing needs for food, clothing, and shelter while preserving the environment.

Can you identify these slowly sinking replicas of world-famous landmarks? Greenpeace staged the publicity stunt to draw attention to global warming during climate talks in Cancún, Mexico, in 2010.

Conflict View of the Environment

In Chapter 10, we drew on world systems analysis to show how a growing share of the human and natural resources of developing countries is being redistributed to the core industrialized nations. This process only intensifies the destruction of natural resources in poorer regions of the world. From a conflict perspective, less affluent nations are being forced to exploit their mineral deposits, forests, and fisheries in order to meet their debt obligations. The poor turn to the only means of survival available to them: they plow mountain slopes, burn plots in tropical forests, and overgraze grasslands (World Bank 2010b).

Brazil exemplifies this interplay between economic troubles and environmental destruction. Each year more than 5.7 million acres of forest are cleared for crops and livestock. The elimination of the rain forest affects worldwide weather patterns, heightening the gradual warming of the earth. These socioeconomic patterns, with their harmful environmental consequences, are evident not only in Latin America but in many regions of Africa and Asia.

Conflict theorists are well aware of the environmental implications of land use policies in the Third World, but they contend that focusing on the developing countries is ethnocentric. Who, they ask, is more to blame for environmental deterioration: the poverty-stricken and "food-hungry" populations of the world or the "energy-hungry" industrialized nations? These theorists point out that the industrialized nations of North America and Europe account for only 12 percent of the world's population but are responsible for 60 percent of worldwide consumption. The money their residents spend on ocean cruises each year could provide clean drinking water for everyone on the planet. Ice cream expenditures in Europe alone could be used to immunize every child in the world. Thus, conflict theorists charge, the most serious threat to the environment comes from the global consumer class (Gardner et al. 2004; Shah 2009).

Allan Schnaiberg (1994) further refined this analysis by shifting the focus from affluent consumers to the capitalist system as the cause of environmental troubles. In his view, a capitalist system creates a "treadmill of production" because of its inherent need to build ever-expanding profits. This treadmill necessitates the creation of increasing demand for products, the purchase of natural resources at minimal cost, and the manufacturing of products as quickly and cheaply as possible—no matter what the long-term environmental consequences.

Ecological Modernization

Critics of the human ecological and conflict models argue that they are too rooted in the past. People who take these approaches, they charge, have become bogged down in addressing existing practices. Instead, proponents of **ecological modernization**, an approach that emerged in the 1980s, focus on the alignment of environmentally favorable practices with economic self-interest through constant adaptation and restructuring (Mol 2010; Mol and Sonnenfeld 2000; Mol et al. 2009).

Ecological modernization can occur on both the macro and micro levels. On a macro level, adaptation and restructuring can mean reintegrating industrial waste back into the production process. On a micro level, it can mean reshaping individual lifestyles, including the consumption patterns described at the start of this chapter (York et al. 2010). In a sense, those who practice ecological modernization seek to refute the oft-expressed notion that being environmentally conscious means "going back to nature" or "living off the grid." Even modest changes in production and consumption patterns, they believe, can increase environmental sustainability.

From the perspective of developing nations, many calls for the reduction of greenhouse gases unfairly target countries that are just beginning to industrialize.

Environmental Justice

In autumn 1982, nearly 500 African Americans participated in a six-week protest against a hazardous waste landfill in North Carolina. Their protests and legal actions against the dangerous cancer-causing chemicals continued until 2002, when decontamination of the site finally began. This 20-year battle could be seen as yet another "not in my backyard" (NIMBY) event. But today, the Warren County struggle is viewed as a transformative moment in contemporary environmentalism: the beginning of the *environmental justice* movement (Bullard 1993; McGurty 2000; North Carolina Department of Environmental and Natural Resources 2008).

Environmental justice is a legal strategy based on claims that racial minorities are subjected disproportionately to environmental hazards. Some observers have heralded environmental justice as the "new civil rights of the 21st century" (Kokmen 2008:42). Since the start of the environmental justice movement, activists and scholars have discovered other environmental disparities that break along racial and social class lines. In general, poor people and people of color are much more likely than others to be victimized by the everyday consequences of our built environment, including the air pollution from expressways and incinerators.

Sociologists Paul Mohai and Robin Saha (2007) examined over 600 identified hazardous waste treatment, storage, and disposal facilities in the United States. They found that non-Whites and Latinos make up 43 percent of the people who live within one mile of these dangerous sites. Skeptics often argue that minorities move near such sites because of low housing prices. However, two recent longitudinal (long-term) research studies, done over 30- and 50-year periods, found that toxic facilities tend to be located in minority communities (Mohai et al. 2009:413).

The environmental justice movement has become globalized, for several reasons. In many nations, activists have noticed similar patterns in the location of hazardous waste sites. These groups have begun to network across international borders, to share their tactics and remedies. Their unified approach is wise, because the offending corporations are often multinational entities (see Chapter 10); influencing their actions, much less prosecuting them, is difficult. As we have noted before, the global warming debate often focuses criticism on developing nations like China and India, rather than on established industrial giants with a long history of greenhouse gas emissions (Mohai et al. 2009; Shah 2009).

Sociologists, then, have emphasized both the interconnectedness of humans and the environment and the divisiveness of race and social class in their work on humans and their alteration of the environment. Scientists, too, have taken different approaches,

disagreeing sharply on the likely outcomes of environmental change. When these disagreements threaten to affect government policy and economic regulations, they become highly politicized. For some perspective on this struggle between environmental preservation and economic self-interest, let's revisit the Nacirema, introduced in the opening excerpt for Chapter 3. Box 19-2 presents this unusual culture through the eyes of environmentalists.

thinking CRITICALLY

How are the physical and human environments connected in your neighborhood or community?

Environmental Issues

Around the world, people are recognizing the need to address challenges to the environment. Yet in the United States, survey respondents do not see environmental issues as the most pressing of concerns, and they often balk at proposed solutions. Unfortunately, framing environmental issues as "problems" may prevent people from seeing environmental deterioration as the by-product of both institutional practices and their own behavior. Thus, in a 2010 national survey, nearly half the respondents said they were unsure about the scientific evidence of global warming, and 48 percent thought the seriousness of the climate trend was generally exaggerated. Only 10 percent of those surveyed expected that they would see the effects of global warming in their lifetime (Newport 2010c).

We will discuss the enormous challenge of global warming in this section, along with three broad areas of environmental concern. Two of them, air and water pollution, are thought to be contributors to global warming.

Air Pollution

Worldwide, more than 1 billion people are exposed to potentially health-damaging levels of air pollution. Unfortunately, in cities around the world, residents have come to accept smog and polluted air as normal. Urban air pollution is caused primarily by emissions from automobiles and secondarily by emissions from

SOCIOLOGY IN THE GLOBAL COMMUNITY

19-2 The Mysterious Fall of the Nacirema

Chapter 3 opened with anthropologist Horace Miner's description of the strange rituals practiced by the Nacirema (*American* spelled backward). Sixteen years after Miner first described the culture, American Studies scholar Neil B. Thompson wrote a follow-up article, "The Mysterious Fall of the Nacirema," that was in effect the culture's epitaph.

The Nacirema, Thompson wrote, were master engineers who had created extensive networks of "narrow ribbons, called streets," which covered the landscape. From the air, the ribbons around major population centers could be seen to be very elaborate. The purpose of these networks, Thompson speculated, might have been to promote the centralization of government or to separate "persons of lower caste" from others, in neighborhoods referred to as "ottehgs."

A special group of highly privileged priests, called the "ssenisub community," directed such massive projects. The priests lived in gated areas secured by electronic alarm systems. The ssenisub enjoyed complete freedom in creating their vast engineering marvels. "There is no evidence,"

Thompson wrote, "to suggest that any restraints—moral, sociological, or engineering—were placed on their self-determined enterprises."

Looking back over the past 300 "solar cycles" of the culture, Thompson noted that the Nacirema had devoted a great deal of time and attention to changing the color of the air and water. For the first 250 cycles they had little success, "but during the short period before the fall of the culture, they mastered their art magnificently,"

> *Looking back over the past 300 "solar cycles" of the culture, Thompson noted that the Nacirema had devoted a great deal of time and attention to changing the color of the air and water.*

changing the water from bluish-green to reddish-brown and the air from blue to grayish-yellow.

To accomplish this great engineering feat, the Nacirema built huge plants near large cities. "These plants constantly produced a variety of

reagents . . . which were then pumped into the rivers and lakes or released into the atmosphere in the form of hot gases." To solve the problem of what to do with the by-products of these processes, the Nacirema distributed them to people's homes, where they were kept for a short time before being sent to a landfill.

Thompson wrote his article in 1972. To date, archaeologists have not been able to explain the demise of this fascinating culture.

LET'S DISCUSS

1. Have you ever visited a foreign culture and been struck by something that seemed odd to you, but perfectly normal to everyone else? If so, did you discuss your reaction with others? Could they see your point of view?
2. If all of us could step back and take an objective look at what we are doing to the environment, would our society change for the better? Why or why not?

Sources: Miner 1956; N. Thompson 1972.

---

electric power plants and heavy industries. Smog not only limits visibility; it also can lead to health problems as uncomfortable as eye irritation and as deadly as lung cancer. Such problems are especially severe in developing countries.

Although people are capable of changing their behavior, they are unwilling to make such changes permanent. During the 1984 Olympics in Los Angeles, residents were asked to carpool and stagger their work hours to relieve traffic congestion and improve the quality of the air athletes would breathe. These changes resulted in a remarkable 12 percent drop in ozone levels. But when the Olympians left, people reverted to their normal behavior and the ozone levels climbed back up. Similarly, in the 2008 Olympics, China took drastic action to ensure that Beijing's high levels of air pollution did not mar the games. Construction work in the city ceased, polluting factories and power plants closed down, and roads were swept and sprayed with water several times a day. This temporary solution hardly solved China's ongoing problem, however (A. Jacobs 2010).

On an everyday basis—that is, when cities are not holding down their emissions because of global sports events—air pollution is still a serious issue in the United States. Today, 6 out of every 10 people in the United States live in communities with dangerously high levels of air pollution, either short-term or year-round. Solutions range from community efforts to clean up power plants and enforce or strengthen air quality standards to individual actions, like driving less often or using less electricity (American Lung Association 2009; *The Economist* 2008a).

Water Pollution

Throughout the United States, dumping of waste materials by industries and local governments has polluted streams, rivers,

and lakes. Consequently, many bodies of water have become unsafe for drinking, fishing, and swimming. Around the world, pollution of the oceans is an issue of growing concern. Such pollution results regularly from waste dumping and is made worse by fuel leaks from shipping and occasional oil spills. When the oil tanker *Exxon Valdez* ran aground in Prince William Sound, Alaska, in 1989, its cargo of more than 11 million gallons of crude oil spilled into the sound and washed onto the shore, contaminating 1,285 miles of shoreline. All together, about 11,000 people joined in a massive cleanup effort that cost over $2 billion. Globally, tanker oil spills occur regularly. Much more dramatic has been the oil spilled from BP's Deepwater Horizon oil platform in 2010, estimated at *sixteen times* or more than that of the *Exxon Valdez* (ITOPF 2006; Shapley 2010).

Less dramatic than large-scale accidents or disasters, but more common in many parts of the world, are problems with the basic water supply. Worldwide, over 1.1 billion people lack safe and adequate drinking water, and 2.5 billion have no acceptable means of sanitation—a problem that further threatens the quality of water supplies. The health costs of unsafe water are enormous.

Water scarcity in and of itself is another critical issue. For centuries, competition for limited supplies of water has led to conflict. Today, for example, the continuing war over the Darfur region of the Sudan is fueled by a growing population and a shrinking water supply. In many of the world's poorest regions, particularly in Africa, millions of people spend much of their day simply searching for water. Obviously, their time and labor could be better used in creating a self-sustaining environment (Pacific Institute 2010a, 2010b; Velasquez-Manoff 2009).

427

Global Warming

Based primarily on complex computer models, scientists have made hundreds of projections of global warming. The term *global warming* refers to the significant rise in the earth's surface temperatures that occurs when industrial gases like carbon dioxide turn the planet's atmosphere into a virtual greenhouse. These *greenhouse gas emissions,* which also include methane, nitrous oxide, and ozone, trap heat in the lower atmosphere. Even one additional degree of warmth in the globe's average surface temperature can increase the likelihood of wildfires, shrinkage of rivers and lakes, expansion of deserts, and torrential downpours, including typhoons and hurricanes. As Figure 19-6 shows, scientists now track and project carbon dioxide emissions around the world (Lynas 2008).

Although scientific concern over global warming has heated up, climate change remains low on policymakers' list of concerns. The problem seems abstract, and in many countries, officials think that the real impact of any action they may take depends on decisive action by other nations. The Kyoto Protocol (1997) was intended to reduce global emissions of heat-trapped gases, which can contribute to global warming and climate change. To date, 190 countries are party to the accord, but the United States has failed to ratify it. Opponents of the protocol argue that doing so would place the nation at a disadvantage in the global marketplace.

In writing about the global environment, activists often assert, "We're all in this together." Though we are all in this together, the reality is that globally, the most vulnerable countries tend to be the poorest. Developing nations are more likely than others to have economies that are built on limited resources or on a small number of crops that are vulnerable to drought, flood, and fluctuations in worldwide demand (Nordhaus and Shellenberger 2007; Revkin 2007).

We can view global warming from the point of view of world systems analysis. Historically, core nations have been the major emitters of greenhouse gases. Today, however, manufacturing has moved to semi-periphery and periphery nations, where greenhouse gas emissions are escalating. Ironically, many of the forces that are now calling for a reduction in the human activity that contributes to global warming are located in core nations, which have contributed disproportionately to the problem. We want our hamburgers, but we decry the destruction of

the rain forests to create grazing land for cattle. We want inexpensive clothes and toys, but we condemn developing countries for depending on coal-fired power plants, which are expected to increase 46 percent by 2030. The challenge of global warming, then, is closely tied to global inequality (M. Jenkins 2008; J. Roberts et al. 2003).

What are the causes of this global environmental crisis? Some observers, such as Paul Ehrlich and Anne Ehrlich, see the pressure of world population growth as the central factor in environmental deterioration. They argue that population control is essential in preventing widespread starvation and environmental decay.

Barry Commoner, a biologist, counters that the primary cause of environmental ills is the increasing use of technological innovations that are destructive to the environment—among them plastics, detergents, synthetic fibers, pesticides, herbicides, and chemical fertilizers. Conflict theorists see the despoliation of the environment through the lens of world systems analysis. And interactionists stress efforts by informed individuals and groups to reduce their carbon footprint—that is, their daily or even lifetime production of greenhouse gases—through careful selection of the goods they consume (Carbon Trust 2010; Commoner 1990, 2007; Ehrlich and Ellison 2002).

use your sociological *imagination*

As you think about all the issues facing our society, how often do you consider global warming? How often do your friends give it much thought?

"Two can live as carbon-neutral as one."

To combat global warming, increasing numbers of people are seeking to achieve net-zero carbon emissions, both by avoiding emissions when possible—for example, by walking rather than driving—and through offsets (such as planting trees).

The Impact of Globalization

Globalization can be both good and bad for the environment. On the negative side, it can create a race to the bottom, as polluting companies relocate to countries with less stringent environmental standards. Similarly, globalization allows multinationals to reap the resources of developing countries for short-term profit. From Mexico to China, the industrialization that often accompanies globalization has increased pollution of all types.

Yet globalization can have a positive impact, as well. As barriers to the international movement of goods, services, and people fall, multinational corporations have an incentive to carefully consider the cost of natural resources. Overusing or wasting resources makes little sense, especially when they are in danger of depletion (Gallagher 2009; Kwong 2005).

Vacation in an unspoiled paradise! Increasingly, people from developed countries are turning to ecotourism as an environmentally friendly way to see the world. The new trend bridges the interests of environmentalists and businesspeople, especially in developing countries. These bird-watchers are vacationing in Belize.

MAPPING LIFE WORLDWIDE

FIGURE **19-6**   INCREASE IN CARBON DIOXIDE EMISSIONS

2004   ▪ Each square equals 25 million metric tons of carbon dioxide (CO₂)

CANADA

UNITED STATES

About **one-third** of U.S. emissions come from transportation.

MEXICO

BRAZIL

CENTRAL AND SOUTH AMERICA

Mexico and Brazil account for **more than half** of all emissions from Central and South America.

OTHER FORMER SOVIET UNION/YUGOSLAVIA

RUSSIA

EUROPE

MIDDLE EAST

CHINA

SOUTH KOREA

JAPAN

INDIA

OTHER ASIA

AFRICA

In 2004, emissions from China and India made up **22 percent** of the world's total.

AUSTRALIA/ NEW ZEALAND

2030

By 2030, U.S. emissions could grow **34 percent** and account for **19 percent** of the world's total.

CANADA

UNITED STATES

MEXICO

CENTRAL AND SOUTH AMERICA

BRAZIL

OTHER FORMER SOVIET UNION/YUGOSLAVIA

RUSSIA

EUROPE

MIDDLE EAST

CHINA

SOUTH KOREA

JAPAN

INDIA

OTHER ASIA

AFRICA

Japan's emissions are set to grow **3 percent**, or **0.1 percent** a year.

Europe's emissions are expected to rise **7 percent**, or **0.3 percent** a year.

China's emissions are projected to grow **139 percent** by 2030 and make up **26 percent** of the world's total.

AUSTRALIA/ NEW ZEALAND

Source: Mufson 2007:6.

Throughout the world, carbon dioxide emissions are expected to increase over the coming generation. However, new global agreements may stem the projected increases.

One reflection of the interplay between globalization and the environment is the emergence of *environmental refugees*. Europe in particular is beginning to see an influx of such immigrants from developing nations. According to a European Union report, global warming can be viewed as a "threat multiplier" that exacerbates prolonged droughts and a shortage of arable land, and along with them, poverty, poor health, and poor living conditions. Viewed through the lens of world systems analysis, periphery countries may become overburdened by environmental problems, precipitating either migrations to industrial nations or conflicts that cause mass displacements of their populations. "Europe must expect substantially increased migratory pressure" from these environmental refugees, the report concludes (Traynor 2008).

Against these potentially negative effects of globalization we must note the potential for new jobs in what are called green industries. Installing solar panels, weatherizing homes, brewing biofuels, building hybrid cars, growing organic foods, manufacturing organic garments, and erecting giant wind turbines are all classified as *green-collar jobs*. However, skeptics question how many such jobs will be created, and to what degree they will offset job losses in pollution-prone industries like oil, gas, and coal mining (S. Greenhouse 2008b; R. Pinderhughes 2008).

thinking CRITICALLY

Which issue is more significant in your local community, air or water pollution? Why?

social policy and the Environment

Environmentalism

On April 22, 1970, in a dramatic manifestation of growing grassroots concern over preservation of the environment, an estimated 25 million people turned out to observe the nation's first Earth Day. Two thousand communities held planned celebrations, and more than 2,000 colleges and 10,000 schools hosted environmental teach-ins. In many parts of the United States, citizens marched on behalf of specific environmental causes. That same year, the activism of these early environmentalists convinced Congress to establish the Environmental Protection Agency. The Clean Air, Clean Water, and Endangered Species acts soon followed (Brulle and Jenkins 2008).

Looking at the Issue

Sociologist Manual Castells (2010a:72) has declared environmentalism "the most comprehensive, influential movement of our time." Several social trends helped to mobilize the environmental movement. First, the activist subculture of the 1960s and early 1970s encouraged people, especially young people, to engage in direct action regarding social issues. Second, the dissemination of scientific knowledge about serious environmental problems like oil spills and air pollution alarmed many Americans. And third, the growing popularity of outdoor recreation increased the number of people who were concerned about the environment. In this climate of broad-based interest in environmental issues, many organizations that had once focused narrowly on the conservation of natural resources evolved into full-fledged environmental groups (Dunlap and Mertig 1991).

Today, Earth Day has been enshrined on the calendars of city councils, zoos, and museums worldwide. Environmental issues have also moved up the agenda of mainstream political parties. Increasingly, efforts to publicize environmental concerns and create support for action have moved to the Internet. Although times have changed, two beliefs continue to galvanize environmentalists: the environment is in dire need of protection, and the government must take strong action in response. Although environmentalists recognize that they must "think locally" and monitor their own carbon footprints, they also see preservation of the environment as a global challenge. They note that while significant progress has been made toward environmental protection, government regulation of the environment has been curtailed in some ways (Brulle and Jenkins 2008; Rootes 2007; Sieber et al. 2006).

The general public has a mixed reaction to environmental issues. Many people question the scientific arguments behind the theory of global warming. And although the economic cost of environmental protection has always been an issue, the broad economic downturn that began in 2008 tipped the balance of public opinion in favor of economic growth. In 2009, for the first time, a majority of people gave economic growth priority over the environment (Figure 19-7). In times of economic stress, people tend to put off or ignore environmental concerns. Thus, there seems to be little public enthusiasm for the positive, forward-looking approach of ecological modernization. Not surprisingly, the political debate over the environmental movement grew more partisan between 2000 and 2010: Democrats became more sympathetic and Republicans more antagonistic (Dunlap 2010).

Today's college students also show less interest in the environment than students of past decades. In 2010, about 27 percent of first-year college students in the United States wanted to clean up the environment—down from 45.9 percent in 1972 (see Figure 3-2 on page 65). And as Figure 19-8 shows, U.S. high school students' interest in the issue does not compare favorably with that of teens in other major countries. In a 30-nation comparative study, 15-year-olds in the United States tied those in another country for 22nd place in their knowledge of environmental issues.

FIGURE 19-7 THE ENVIRONMENT VERSUS THE ECONOMY

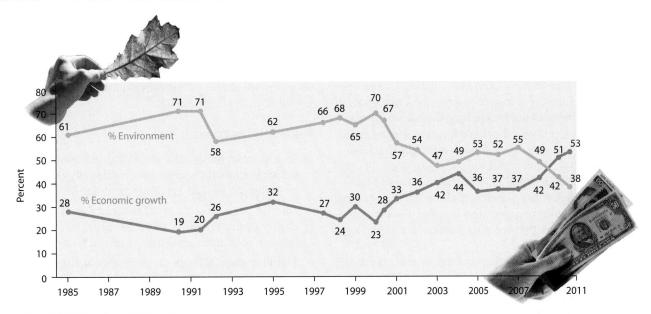

Source: Gallup Poll 2011, see Jones 2011 in references.

Applying Sociology

Even those who support environmentalists' goals are troubled by the fact that nationwide, the most powerful environmental organizations are predominantly White, male-dominated, and affluent. One study notes that while women are overrepresented in the environmental movement (particularly in grassroots environmental groups), men continue to hold most of the high-profile upper-management positions in mainstream national organizations. The perceived middle-class orientation of the movement is especially relevant given the class, racial, and ethnic factors associated with environmental hazards. As we saw earlier in the context of environmental justice, low-income communities and areas with significant minority populations are more likely than affluent White communities to be located near waste sites. Sociologists Liam Downey and Brian

Hawkins (2008) found that an average Black household with an income of $50,000 to $60,000 a year coped with higher levels of pollution than an average White household with an income of less than $10,000 a year.

Viewed from a conflict perspective, it is significant that some environmental organizations accept funding from oil companies, chemical giants, and other powerful corporations. Perhaps as a result, the environmental movement has often emphasized limited reform rather than profound structural change. Activists may recommend making cars more energy-efficient, for example, instead of drastically reducing the number of vehicles on the road (Navarro 2009; Sale 1996).

Like any social movement, the environmental movement has aroused resistance. Some opponents question the environmentalists' move to replace fossil fuels such as coal and oil with biofuels such as ethanol. They complain that diverting corn and other crops into fuel production will raise food prices, hampering efforts to reduce global hunger (Helvarg 1994; Pontin 2007).

Initiating Policy

The global economic downturn that began in 2008 has been a mixed blessing for environmentalists. As noted earlier, public opinion in the United States currently favors economic growth over environmental protection. Yet at the same time, the recession has sharply reduced the use of fossil fuels such as coal and oil. Moreover, the federal government's efforts to stimulate economic activity have emphasized the creation of green-collar jobs. By one estimate,

FIGURE 19-8 ARE U.S. TEENS GREEN ENOUGH?

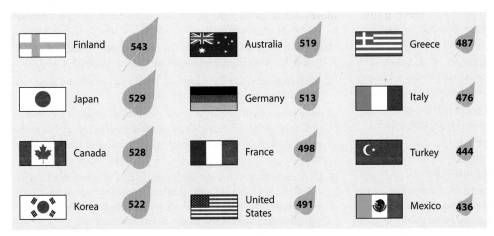

Note: Mean score for 15-year-old students' knowledge of environmental issues = 543.
Source: Organisation for Economic Co-operation and Development 2009b.

every $1 billion invested in well-conceived green programs generates over 30,000 jobs and $450 million in cost savings per year. More specific environmental measures, such as raising federal gas mileage standards for automobiles, face a tough battle in Congress (Houser et al. 2009).

Environmentalism has moved onto a much bigger stage than the one it occupied on the first Earth Day. In 2008, for the first time, the leaders of the G8 economic powers (the United States, Japan, Germany, Great Britain, France, Italy, Canada, and Russia) set an explicit long-term target for eliminating greenhouse gases, which scientists have long warned were warming the planet. "Long-term" may be an understatement: their target date for cutting greenhouse gases in half is 2050. Environmentalists sharply criticized the G8's failure to set specific goals for the nearer term. The challenge is significant, given the fact that G8 emissions *increased* 35 percent over the preceding 15 years (Longhofer and Schofer 2010; Stolberg 2008).

Conventional wisdom holds that concern for environmental quality is limited to wealthy industrialized nations. However, the results of a 47-nation survey show that around the world, people are increasingly reluctant to ignore environmental issues. Concern has risen sharply in Latin America and Europe, as well as in Japan and India. The survey also noted a general increase in the percentage of people who cite pollution and environmental problems as a top global threat. Many people in other countries blame the United States, and to a lesser extent China, for environmental problems, and look to Washington, D.C., for a solution. Time will tell whether policymakers in the United States or elsewhere will address their concern for the environment (Pew Global Attitudes Project 2007).

Take the Issue with You

1. In your community, how would you act locally to preserve the environment? Describe your community's environmental problems and explain how you would seek to solve them.

2. How do you see the trade-off between the economy and the environment? Which is more important? Is it possible to improve both at the same time? Explain.

3. Thinking globally about the environment, list what you consider the most pressing priorities. How important are world hunger and economic justice compared to global warming, clean air and water, and economic development? Are some of your priorities related? In what way?

MASTERING THIS CHAPTER

Summary

Both culture and the environment have a significant effect on our **health** and well-being. The concept of health is shaped by social definitions of behavior. This chapter considers sociological perspectives on health and the environment; the distribution of disease in a society; the evolution of the U.S. health care system; mental illness and its treatment; and the environmental issues facing our planet.

1. According to Talcott Parsons's functionalist perspective, physicians function as gatekeepers for the **sick role,** either verifying a person's condition as "illness" or designating the person as "recovered."

2. Conflict theorists use the term *medicalization of society* to refer to medicine's growing role as a major institution of social control.

3. Labeling theorists suggest that the designation of a person as "healthy" or "ill" generally involves social definition by others. These definitions affect how others see us and how we view ourselves.

4. Contemporary **social epidemiology** is concerned not only with epidemics but also with nonepidemic diseases, injuries, drug addiction and alcoholism, suicide, and mental illness.

5. Studies have consistently shown that people in the lower classes have higher rates of mortality and disability than others.

6. Racial and ethnic minorities have higher rates of morbidity and mortality than Whites. Women tend to be in poorer health than men but live longer. Older people are especially vulnerable to mental health problems, such as Alzheimer's disease.

7. The preeminent role of physicians in the U.S. health care system has given them a position of dominance in their dealings with nurses and patients.

8. Many people use alternative health care techniques, such as **holistic medicine** and self-help groups.

9. Mental disorders may be viewed from two different perspectives, the medical model and the sociological model, which is based on labeling theory. In the United States, society has traditionally taken a negative, suspicious attitude toward people with mental disorders.

10. The human ecological perspective stresses the interrelationships between people and their environment.

11. Conflict theorists charge that the most serious threat to the environment comes from Western industrialized nations.

12. **Environmental justice** addresses the disproportionate subjection of minorities to environmental hazards.

13. Four broad areas of environmental concern include air and water pollution, global warming, and globalization. Though globalization can contribute to environmental woes, it can also have beneficial effects.

14. Environmentalism is a social movement that is dominated by affluent White people from industrialized countries. Increasingly, however, people of all races, ethnicities, social classes, and nationalities are becoming concerned about global warming and the threat it poses to our planet's health.

Key Terms

Brain drain The immigration to the United States and other industrialized nations of skilled workers, professionals, and technicians who are desperately needed in their home countries. (page 412)

Curanderismo Latino folk medicine, a form of holistic health care and healing. (417)

Ecological modernization The alignment of environmentally favorable practices with economic self-interest through constant adaptation and restructuring. (425)

Environmental justice A legal strategy based on claims that racial minorities are subjected disproportionately to environmental hazards. (426)

Health As defined by the World Health Organization, a state of complete physical, mental, and social well-being, and not merely the absence of disease and infirmity. (411)

Holistic medicine Therapies in which the health care practitioner considers the person's physical, mental, emotional, and spiritual characteristics. (420)

Human ecology An area of study that is concerned with the interrelationships between people and their environment. (425)

Incidence The number of new cases of a specific disorder that occur within a given population during a stated period. (415)

Infant mortality rate The number of deaths of infants under one year old per 1,000 live births in a given year. (413)

McDonaldization The process by which the principles of the fast-food restaurant are coming to dominate more and more sectors of American society as well as of the rest of the world. (421)

Mental illness A disorder of the brain that disrupts a person's thinking, feeling, and ability to interact with others. (423)

Morbidity rate The incidence of disease in a given population. (415)

Mortality rate The incidence of death in a given population. (415)

Prevalence The total number of cases of a specific disorder that exist at a given time. (415)

Sick role Societal expectations about the attitudes and behavior of a person viewed as being ill. (411)

Social epidemiology The study of the distribution of disease, impairment, and general health status across a population. (415)

TAKING SOCIOLOGY with you

1. Do some research on the incidence and prevalence of HIV/AIDS in your city or state. Now look up the corresponding morbidity and mortality rates. How do those rates compare to the rates in other cities or states? What might account for any differences in the rates from one place to another?

2. Visit the emergency room of your local hospital and observe what is going on in the waiting room. How crowded is the waiting room?

How many people in the room appear to be severely ill or injured? How many do not seem to have an emergency? What else can you observe about the people who are gathered there, and how might that help to explain their presence?

3. Do an Internet search to locate the hazardous waste sites nearest your school or home. How many of them have been cleaned up, and at what cost? Who paid that cost? How many of these sites are still a problem?

Self-Quiz

Read each question carefully and then select the best answer.

1. Which sociologist developed the concept of the sick role?
   a. Émile Durkheim
   b. Talcott Parsons
   c. Wright Mills
   d. Erving Goffman

2. Regarding health care inequities, the conflict perspective would note that
   a. physicians serve as gatekeepers for the sick role, either verifying a patient's condition as "illness" or designating the patient as "recovered."
   b. patients play an active role in health care by failing to follow a physician's advice.
   c. emigration out of the Third World by physicians is yet another way that the world's core industrialized nations enhance their quality of life at the expense of developing countries.
   d. the designation "healthy" or "ill" generally involves social definition by others.

3. Which one of the following nations has the lowest infant mortality rate?
   a. the United States
   b. Mozambique

   c. Canada
   d. Sweden

4. Compared with Whites, Blacks have higher death rates from
   a. heart disease.
   b. diabetes.
   c. cancer.
   d. all of the above.

5. Which theorist notes that capitalist societies, such as the United States, care more about maximizing profits than they do about the health and safety of industrial workers?
   a. Thomas Szasz
   b. Talcott Parsons
   c. Erving Goffman
   d. Karl Marx

6. Which program is essentially a compulsory health insurance plan for the elderly?
   a. Medicare
   b. Medicaid

c. Blue Cross

d. Healthpac

7. Which of the following is a criticism of the sick role?

  a. Patients' judgments regarding their own state of health may be related to their gender, age, social class, and ethnic group.

  b. The sick role may be more applicable to people experiencing short-term illnesses than to those with recurring long-term illnesses.

  c. Even such simple factors as whether a person is employed or not seem to affect the person's willingness to assume the sick role.

  d. all of the above

8. Which of the following terms do conflict theorists use in referring to the growing role of medicine as a major institution of social control?

  a. the sick role

  b. the medicalization of society

c. medical labeling

d. epidemiology

9. Which of the following approaches stresses the alignment of environmentally favorable practices with economic self-interest?

  a. conflict theory

  b. human ecology

  c. ecological modernization

  d. environmental justice

10. Conflict theorists would contend that blaming developing countries for the world's environmental deterioration contains an element of

  a. ethnocentrism.

  b. xenocentrism.

  c. separatism.

  d. goal displacement.

11. A _____ _____ studies the effects of social class, race and ethnicity, gender, and age on the distribution of disease, impairment, and general health across a population.

12. From a(n) _____ perspective, "being sick" must be controlled so as to ensure that not too many people are released from their societal responsibilities at any one time.

13. The immigration to the United States and other industrialized nations of skilled workers, professionals, and technicians who are desperately needed by their home countries is known as the _____ _____.

14. Traditionally, the relationship between doctors and nurses has paralleled _____ dominance of the larger society.

15. Sociologists find it useful to consider _____ rates because they reveal that a specific disease occurs more frequently among one segment of a population compared with another.

16. The system of reimbursement used by Medicare has contributed to the controversial practice of "_____," under which patients whose treatment may be unprofitable are transferred by private hospitals to public facilities.

17. As defined by the World Health Organization, _____ is a "state of complete physical, mental, and social well-being, and not merely the absence of disease and infirmity."

18. The biologist _____ _____ blames environmental degradation primarily on technological innovations such as plastics and pesticides.

19. Regarding environmental problems, four broad areas of concern stand out: _____ pollution, _____ pollution, _____ _____, and _____.

20. _____ _____ is a legal strategy based on claims that racial minorities are subjected disproportionately to environmental hazards.

THINKING ABOUT MOVIES

The Cove

This documentary exposes a dark side of the dolphin industry and its health effects on humans.

Food, Inc.

As this film shows, dietary staples such as beef, poultry, and corn are often produced by multinational corporations using methods that maximize profit but dehumanize workers.

Gasland

This documentary shows some of the health consequences of increased drilling for natural gas.

▶ INSIDE

Merchants and shoppers, pedestrians and cars fill the street in Algiers, Algeria. Around the world, migration and rapid increases in population are swelling our cities, straining resources and the communities that depend on them.

436

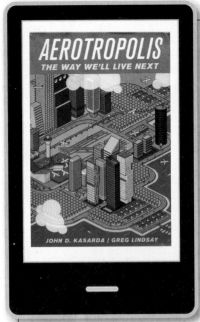

AEROTROPOLIS
THE WAY WE'LL LIVE NEXT

JOHN D. KASARDA | GREG LINDSAY

❝ An aerotropolis is basically an airport-integrated region, extending as far as sixty miles from the inner clusters of hotels, offices, distribution and logistics facilities.... All kinds of activities are served by and enhanced by the airport. Whether it's supply chains, whether it's enterprise networks, whether it's biosciences and pharmaceuticals and time-sensitive organic materials, the airport itself is really the nucleus of a range of "New Economy" functions, with the ultimate aim of bolstering the city's competitiveness, job creation, and quality of life. . . .

By the mid-1990s, we found ourselves operating in an environment defined by two words: "turbulence" and "uncertainty." How do you adapt to constantly changing and unpredictable environments? The companies that can do that—the communities and regions that can do that—gain competitive advantage. Individual companies no longer compete; their entire supply chains do. . . . Some links in those chains might be cut loose or switch sides; others might hopscotch from city to city or country to country, or even across continents, as the stakes of global rivalry wear down their margins. And more than a few are playing for every team.

As the distance between these far-flung links in the chain increased, so did the need to traverse that distance as fast as possible. Because even as the size of the playing field has grown, the pace has gotten faster, and the increments counted in a just-in-time system have shrunk from seconds to something less. . . .

This combination of the death of distance and the just-in-time world has changed not only how companies compete but how cities

> *With the right infrastructure, a hinterland can become a hub, toppling capitals. The fundamental laws of real estate—location, location, location—have been supplanted by three new ones:* access, access, access.

compete as well. In the Instant Age, cities and their hinterlands go head-to-head for the most lucrative links in the chains. Civic pride, national heritage, and executive prestige mean little or nothing when pitted against falling trade barriers, cross-border conglomerates, quicksilver liquidity, and the overweening need for speed. The only trump card a city can play is the last one. If it's *faster* than its rivals, it can win. With the right infrastructure, a hinterland can become a hub, toppling capitals. The fundamental laws of real estate—location, location, location—have been supplanted by three new ones: *access, access, access.*

[This] framework dovetails with what we already know about globalization. The world is a network. Cities now connect more easily to each other than to the towns and villages that lie just beyond their borders, or to the national capitals that supposedly call their shots. It's how the cities of the Pearl River Delta can become "the world's factory," and why their fate is bound up in the flat-screen TV you dragged home from Best Buy. It's how Las Vegas and Macau—an oasis and an island, separated by seven thousand miles—can duel to become the world's gambling mecca. And it's why the manicured lawns of the Infosys campus in Bangalore still abut urban squalor outside its gates: because the Microsoft of India has nothing in common with the countryside. We think local and act global.

How did this happen? The short answer is the Internet, if you allow it to stand in for the pervasive wiring of the world over the past forty years and all the changes it has wrought. First corporations, then cities rebuilt themselves according to the logic of networks, as hubs and nodes, and soon we will too, assuming we haven't already.

. . .

As the world has flattened, all kinds of commerce have moved around the globe. They have to remain connected, even more so than before. Aviation is the means; it is the physical Internet, and your airport is the node. What else is going to connect us?... Airports are no longer a piece of transportation infrastructure, and this is no longer a city airport, but a city itself. The airport city. ❞

(Kasarda and Lindsay 2011:174–176) Additional information about this excerpt can be found on the Online Learning Center at www.mhhe.com/schaefer13e.

In this excerpt from *Aerotropolis: The Way We'll Live Next*, sociologist John Kasarda joins with journalist Greg Lindsay to present a new view of community-building. Their thesis is that airports don't serve cities; they give birth to urban developments. In the past, they note, airports were built near existing cities, like London, Chicago, and New York. Now that the global economy has created a need for speed and connectedness, however, airports have begun to spur the growth of new urban centers, such as Dallas–Fort Worth, Beijing, and Dubai. To refer to these new urban communities—to the concentrations of hotels, office complexes, entertainment venues, and distribution facilities that are popping up around airports—Kasarda (2011) has popularized the term **aerotropolis**.

What makes a place a community? In sociological terms, a **community** may be defined as a spatial or political unit of social organization that gives people a sense of belonging. That sense of belonging can be based either on shared residence in a particular place or on a common identity, such as that of college students. Whatever the members have in common, communities give people the feeling that they are part of something larger than themselves (Dotson 1991; see also Hillery 1955).

Communities can be large or small, homogeneous or heterogeneous. They are directly affected by changes in population and by the growing trend toward urbanization—that is, the concentration of the world's population in cities. How does rapid population growth contribute to the movement of large groups of people? Why have large cities grown at the expense of small villages in many parts of the world? And why, even in nations like the United States, are many residents of large and prosperous communities homeless? In this chapter we will take a sociological overview of the world's population and its communities. We will begin with Thomas Robert Malthus's controversial analysis of population trends and Karl Marx's critical response to it. A brief overview of world population history follows. We'll pay particular attention to the current problem of overpopulation and to the prospects for and potential consequences of stable population growth in the United States. We'll see, too, how population growth fuels the migration of large numbers of people from one area of the world to another.

In the second half of the chapter we will trace the development of communities from their ancient origins to the birth of the modern city and its growth through technological change. In particular, we will examine the rapid and dramatic urbanization that occurred around the world during the 20th century. Then we will study two different sociological views of urbanization, one stressing its functions and the other its dysfunctions. We'll compare rural, suburban, and urban communities in the United States today. Finally, in the Social Policy section, we'll analyze the disturbing phenomenon of homelessness, an all-too-familiar feature of community life.

Demography: The Study of Population

The study of population issues engages the attention of both natural and social scientists. The biologist explores the nature of reproduction and casts light on factors that affect **fertility**, the level of reproduction in a society. The medical pathologist examines and analyzes trends in the causes of death. Geographers, historians, and psychologists also have distinctive contributions to make to our understanding of population. Sociologists, more than these other researchers, focus on the *social* factors that influence population rates and trends.

In their study of population issues, sociologists are aware that the norms, values, and social patterns of a society profoundly affect various elements of population, such as fertility, *mortality* (the death rate), and migration. Fertility is influenced by people's age of entry into sexual unions and by their use of contraception—both of which, in turn, reflect the social and religious values that guide a particular culture. Mortality is shaped by a nation's level of nutrition, acceptance of immunization, and provisions for sanitation, as well as its general commitment to health care and health education.

Migration from one country to another can depend on marital and kinship ties, the relative degree of racial and religious tolerance in various societies, and people's evaluation of their employment opportunities.

Demography is the scientific study of population. It draws on several components of population, including size, composition, and territorial distribution, to understand the social consequences of population change. Demographers study geographical variations and historical trends in their effort to develop population forecasts. They also analyze the structure of a population—the age, gender, race, and ethnicity of its members. A key figure in this analysis was Thomas Malthus.

Malthus's Thesis and Marx's Response

The Reverend Thomas Robert Malthus (1766–1834), who was educated at Cambridge University, spent his life teaching history and political economy. He strongly criticized two major institutions of his time—the church and slavery—yet his most significant legacy to contemporary scholars is his still-controversial *Essays on the Principle of Population,* published in 1798.

Essentially, Malthus held that the world's population was growing more rapidly than the available food supply. He argued that food supply increases in arithmetic progression (1, 2, 3, 4, and so on), whereas population expands by geometric progression (1, 2, 4, 8, and so on). According to his analysis, the gap between food supply and population will continue to grow over time. Even though the food supply will increase, it will not increase nearly enough to meet the needs of an expanding world population.

Malthus advocated population control to close the gap between rising population and the food supply, yet he explicitly denounced artificial means of birth control because they were not sanctioned by religion. For Malthus, one appropriate way to control population was to postpone marriage. He argued that couples must take responsibility for the number of children they choose to bear; without such restraint, the world would face widespread hunger, poverty, and misery (Malthus et al. [1824] 1960; W. Petersen 1979).

An immigration officer checks the passports of passengers arriving at Palermo Airport, on the Italian island of Sicily. Population growth is a dynamic process that is affected not just by birth and death rates, but by the migration of people from one place or country to another.

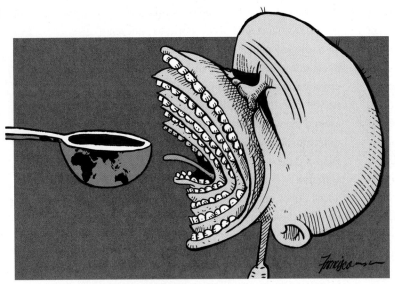

In this cartoon, Manny Francisco, based in the heavily populated Philippine Islands, takes a grim Malthusian view of world hunger.

Karl Marx strongly criticized Malthus's views on population. Marx pointed to the nature of economic relations in Europe's industrial societies as the central problem. He could not accept the Malthusian notion that rising world population, rather than capitalism, was the cause of social ills. In Marx's opinion, there was no special relationship between world population and the supply of resources (including food). If society were well ordered, increases in population would lead to greater wealth, not to hunger and misery.

Of course, Marx did not believe that capitalism operated under these ideal conditions. He maintained that capitalism devoted resources to the financing of buildings and tools rather than to the equitable distribution of food, housing, and other necessities of life. Marx's work is important to the study of population because he linked overpopulation to the unequal distribution of resources—a topic that will be taken up later in this chapter. His concern with the writings of Malthus also testifies to the importance of population in political and economic affairs.

The insights of Malthus and Marx regarding population issues have come together in what is termed the *neo-Malthusian view*, best exemplified by the work of Paul Ehrlich (1968; Ehrlich and Ehrlich 1990), author of *The Population Bomb*. Neo-Malthusians agree with Malthus that population growth is outstretching the world's natural resources. However, in contrast to the British theorist, they insist that birth control measures are needed to regulate population increases. Showing a Marxist bent, neo-Malthusians condemn the developed nations, which despite their low birthrates consume a disproportionately large share of world resources. While rather pessimistic about the future, these theorists stress that birth control and sensible use of resources are essential responses to rising world population (J. Tierney 1990; Weeks 2008).

Studying Population Today

The relative balance of births and deaths is no less important today than it was during the lifetime of Malthus and Marx. The suffering that Malthus spoke of is certainly a reality for many people of the world. Malnutrition remains the largest contributing factor to illness and death among children in developing countries. Almost 18 percent of these children will die before age five—a rate over 11 times higher than in developed nations. Warfare and large-scale migration intensify problems of population and food supply. For example, recent strife in Afghanistan, the Congo, and Iraq has caused maldistribution of food supplies, leading to regional health concerns. Combating world hunger may require reducing human births, dramatically increasing the world's food supply, or perhaps both. The study of population-related issues, then, seems to be essential.

In the United States and most other countries, the census is the primary mechanism for collecting population information. A **census** is an enumeration, or counting, of a population. The Constitution of the United States requires that a census be held every 10 years to determine congressional representation. This periodic investigation is supplemented by **vital statistics**, or records of births, deaths, marriages, and divorces that are gathered through a registration system maintained by governmental units. In addition, other government surveys provide up-to-date information on commercial developments, educational trends, industrial expansion, agricultural practices, and the status of groups such as children, the elderly, racial minorities, and single parents.

In administering a nationwide census and conducting other types of research, demographers employ many of the skills and techniques described in Chapter 2, including questionnaires, interviews, and sampling. The precision of population projections depends on the accuracy of a series of estimates demographers must make. First, they must determine past population trends and establish a current base population. Next, birthrates and death rates must be determined, along with estimates of future fluctuations. In projecting a nation's population trends for the future, demographers must consider migration as well, since a significant number of individuals may enter and leave a country.

Elements of Demography

Demographers communicate population facts with a language derived from the basic elements of human life—birth and death. The **birthrate** (or more specifically, the *crude birthrate*) is the number of live births per 1,000 population in a given year. In 2008, for example, there were 14 live births per 1,000 people in the United States. The birthrate provides information on the reproductive patterns of a society.

One way demographers can project future growth in a society is to make use of the **total fertility rate (TFR)**. The TFR is the average number of children born alive to any woman, assuming that she conforms to current fertility rates. The TFR reported for the United States in 2010 was 2.0 live births per woman, compared to over 7 births per woman in a developing country such as Niger.

Mortality, like fertility, is measured in several different ways. The **death rate** (also known as the *crude death rate*) is the number of deaths per 1,000 population in a given year. In 2010, the United States had a death rate of 8.0 per 1,000 population. The **infant mortality rate** is the number of deaths of infants under age 1 year per 1,000 live births in a given year. This particular measure serves as an important indicator of a society's level of health care (see Figure 19-1, page 413); it reflects prenatal nutrition, delivery procedures, and infant screening measures. The infant mortality rate

TAKING SOCIOLOGY TO WORK

Kelsie Lenor Wilson-Dorsett, **Deputy Director, Department of Statistics, Government of Bahamas**

Kelsie Wilson-Dorsett was born in the Bahamas, where she received her primary and secondary education. She graduated from McMaster University in Hamilton, Ontario, with a combined honors degree in sociology and political science. In studying for her master's degree in sociology at the University of Western Ontario in London, she specialized in demography.

Currently, Wilson-Dorsett holds the positions of Deputy Director, Department of Statistics and Head of the Social Statistics Division, Government of Bahamas, where she oversees the country's census, vital statistics, and other surveys. In this position, she is responsible for the execution of the Bahamas' first Living Conditions Survey (BLCS), which when completed will enable the government to establish a poverty line and to measure the incidence and extent of poverty in that country.

Wilson-Dorsett's study of sociology is directly related to her current job. She states, "The study of sociology has enabled me to put meaning to the figures which come into my office and has provided me with avenues to interpret these figures and determine the direction of future data collection. The analysis of census data, for instance, allows me to see where my country was several years ago, where it is now, and where it is likely to be in the years ahead."

LET'S DISCUSS

1. What challenges do you think Wilson-Dorsett might encounter as she oversees a national census in a country like the Bahamas?
2. What other areas of specialization in sociology would be helpful to someone interpreting the results of a project such as the Living Conditions Survey (BLCS)?

---

also functions as a useful indicator of future population growth, since those infants who survive to adulthood will contribute to further population increases.

A general measure of health used by demographers is **life expectancy**, the median number of years a person can be expected to live under current mortality conditions. Usually the figure is reported as life expectancy *at birth*. At present, Japan reports a life expectancy at birth of 83 years—slightly higher than the United States' figure of 78 years. In contrast, life expectancy at birth is as low as 41 in the African nation of Lesotho (Haub 2010).

The **growth rate** of a society is the difference between births and deaths, plus the difference between *immigrants* (those who enter a country to establish permanent residence) and *emigrants* (those who leave a country permanently) per 1,000 population. For the world as a whole, the growth rate is simply the difference between births and deaths per 1,000 population, since worldwide immigration and emigration must of necessity be equal. In 2010, the United States had a growth rate of 0.6 percent, compared to an estimated 1.2 percent for the entire world (Figure 20-1).

FIGURE **20-1** POPULATION GROWTH RATE IN SELECTED COUNTRIES

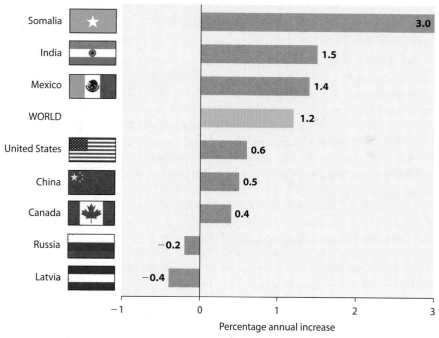

Source: Haub 2010.

World Population Patterns

One important aspect of demographic work involves a study of the history of population. But how is that possible? After all, official national censuses were relatively rare before 1850. Researchers interested in early population must turn to archaeological remains, burial sites, baptismal and tax records, and oral history sources. In the next section we will see what such detective work has told us about changes in population over time.

Demographic Transition

On October 13, 1999, in a maternity clinic in Sarajevo, Bosnia-Herzegovina, Helac Fatina gave birth to a son who has been designated the 6 billionth person on this planet. Until modern times, relatively few humans lived in the world. One estimate places the global population of a million years ago at only 125,000 people. As Table 20-1 on page 443 indicates, in the past 200 years the world's population has exploded (World Health Organization 2000:3).

The phenomenal growth of population in recent times can be accounted for by changing patterns in births and deaths. Beginning in the late 1700s—and continuing until the mid-1900s—death rates in northern and western Europe gradually decreased. People were beginning to live longer because of advances in food production, sanitation, nutrition, and public health care. But while death rates fell, birthrates remained high; as a result, this period of European history brought unprecedented population growth. By the late 1800s, however, the birthrates of many European countries had begun to decline, and the rate of population growth had also decreased.

The changes in birthrates and death rates that occurred in 19th-century Europe serve as an example of *demographic transition*. Demographers use the term **demographic transition** to describe changes in birthrates and death rates that occur during a nation's development, resulting in new patterns of vital statistics. In many nations today, we are seeing a demographic transition from high birthrates and death rates to low birthrates and death rates. As Figure 20-2 shows, this process typically takes place in three stages:

1. Pretransition stage: high birthrates and death rates with little population growth.

2. Transition stage: declining death rates—primarily the result of reductions in infant deaths—along with high to medium fertility, resulting in significant population growth.

3. Posttransition stage: low birthrates and death rates with little population growth.

The demographic transition should be regarded not as a "law of population growth," but rather as a generalization of the population history of industrial nations. This concept helps us to understand world population problems better. About two-thirds of the world's nations have yet to pass fully through the second stage of the demographic transition. Even if such nations make dramatic advances in fertility control, their populations will nevertheless increase greatly because of the large base of people already at prime childbearing age.

The pattern of demographic transition varies from nation to nation. One particularly useful distinction is the contrast between the rapid transition now occurring in developing nations—which include about two-thirds of the world's population—and that which occurred over the course of almost a century in more industrialized countries. In developing nations, the demographic transition has involved a rapid decline in death rates without adjustments in birthrates.

Specifically, in the post–World War II period, the death rates of developing nations began a sharp decline. This revolution in "death control" was triggered by antibiotics, immunization, insecticides (such as DDT, used to strike at malaria-bearing mosquitoes), and largely successful campaigns against such fatal diseases as smallpox. Substantial medical and public health technology was imported almost overnight from more developed nations. As a result, the drop in death rates that had taken a century in Europe was telescoped into two decades in many developing countries.

Birthrates had little time to adjust. Cultural beliefs about the proper size of families could not possibly change as quickly as the falling death rates. For centuries, couples had given birth to as many as eight or more children, knowing that perhaps only

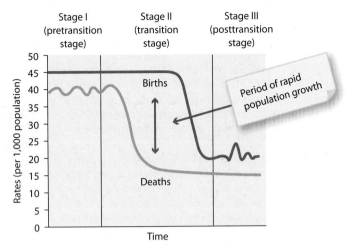

FIGURE **20-2**   DEMOGRAPHIC TRANSITION

Demographers use the concept of *demographic transition* to describe changes in birthrates and death rates that occur during a nation's development. This graph shows the pattern that took place in presently developed nations. In the first stage, both birthrates and death rates were high, so that there was little population growth. In the second stage, the birthrate remained high while the death rate declined sharply, which led to rapid population growth. By the last stage, which many developing countries have yet to enter, the birthrate had declined as well, reducing population growth.

two or three would survive to adulthood. Families were more willing to accept technological advances that prolonged life than to abandon fertility patterns that reflected time-honored tradition and religious training. The result was an astronomical population explosion that was well under way by the middle 1900s. By the middle 1970s, however, demographers had observed a slight decline in the growth rate of many developing nations, as family-planning efforts began to take hold (Kent and Haub 2005).

The Population Explosion

Often, rapid population growth is referred to in emotional terms as the "population bomb" or the "population explosion." Such striking language is not surprising, given the staggering increases in world population recorded during the 20th century (Table 20-1).

Beginning in the 1960s, governments in certain developing nations sponsored or supported campaigns to encourage family planning. In China, the government's strict one-child policy actually produced a negative growth rate in some urban areas (Box 20-1 on page 445). Yet even if family-planning efforts are successful in reducing fertility rates, the momentum toward a growing world population is well established. Developing nations face the prospect of continued population growth, since a substantial proportion of their population is approaching the childbearing years (see the population pyramid for Afghanistan at the top of Figure 20-3 on page 444).

A **population pyramid** is a special type of bar chart that shows the distribution of a population by gender and age; it is generally used to illustrate the population structure of a society. As Figure 20-3 shows, a substantial portion of the population of Afghanistan consists of children under age 15, whose childbearing years are still to come. Thus, the built-in momentum for population growth is much greater in Afghanistan (and in many other developing countries in other parts of the world) than in the United States and especially in many European nations (see the population pyramid for Italy in the middle of Figure 20-3).

Consider the population data for India, which in 2000 surpassed 1 billion residents. Sometime around 2025, India's population will exceed China's. The substantial momentum for growth that is built into India's age structure means that the nation will face a staggering increase in population in the coming decades, even if its birthrate declines sharply (Bureau of the Census 2011b).

Population growth is not a problem in all nations. Today, a handful of countries are even adopting policies that encourage growth. One such country is Japan, where the total fertility rate has fallen sharply. Nevertheless, a global perspective underscores the serious consequences that could result from continued population growth overall.

---

use your sociological *imagination*

You are living in a country that is so heavily populated, basic resources such as food, water, and living space are running short. What will you do? How will you respond to the crisis if you are a government social planner? A politician?

Fertility Patterns in the United States

Over the past six decades, the United States and other industrial nations have passed through two different patterns of population growth—the first marked by high fertility and rapid growth (stage II in the theory of demographic transition), the second marked by declining fertility and little growth (stage III). Sociologists are keenly aware of the social impact of these fertility patterns.

The Baby Boom

The most recent period of high fertility in the United States has often been referred to as the *baby boom*. During World War II, large numbers of military personnel were separated from their spouses. When they returned, the annual number of births began to rise dramatically. Still, the baby boom was not a return to the large families common in the 1800s. In fact, there was only a slight increase in the proportion of couples having three or more children. Instead, the boom was the result of a striking decrease in the number of childless marriages and one-child families. Although a peak was reached in 1957, the nation maintained a relatively high birthrate of over 20 live births per 1,000 population until 1964. By 2010 the birthrate had fallen to 14 live births per 1,000 population (Bureau of the Census 1975; Haub 2010).

It would be a mistake to attribute the baby boom solely to the return home of large numbers of soldiers. High wages and general prosperity during the postwar period encouraged many married couples to purchase homes and have children. In addition, several sociologists—as well as feminist author Betty Friedan (1963)—have noted the strong societal pressure on women during the 1950s to marry and become mothers and homemakers (Bouvier 1980).

Throughout the world, population patterns vary widely. As this scene in Warsaw, the capital of Poland, suggests, Eastern Europe has been losing population as the birthrate falls and young people emigrate to other countries. In Africa, in contrast, the population is growing. Over the next four decades, the country of Somalia is expected to double in population.

TABLE **20-1** ESTIMATED TIME FOR EACH SUCCESSIVE INCREASE OF 1 BILLION PEOPLE IN WORLD POPULATION

Population Level	Time Taken to Reach New Population Level	Year of Attainment
First billion	Human history before 1800	1804
Second billion	123 years	1927
Third billion	32 years	1959
Fourth billion	15 years	1974
Fifth billion	13 years	1987
Sixth billion	12 years	1999
Seventh billion	12 years	2011
Eighth billion	13 years	2024
Ninth billion	21 years	2045

Sources: Bureau of the Census 2011b; Kunzig 2011:40.

POPULATION STRUCTURE OF AFGHANISTAN, ITALY, AND THE UNITED STATES, 2014

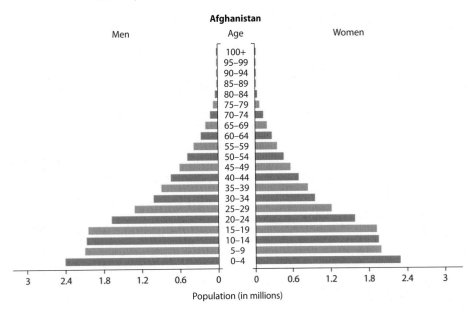

Afghanistan

Men | Age | Women

Population (in millions)

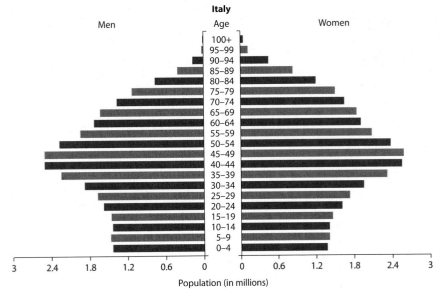

Italy

Men | Age | Women

Population (in millions)

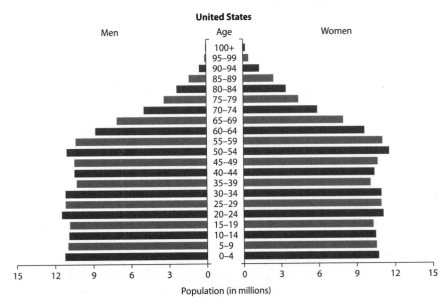

United States

Men | Age | Women

Population (in millions)

Source: Projections updated as of December 2010. Bureau of the Census 2011b.

Stable Population Growth

Although the total fertility rate of the United States has remained low over the past three decades, the nation continues to grow in size because of two factors: the momentum built into our age structure by the postwar population boom and continued high rates of immigration. Because of the upsurge of births beginning in the 1950s, there are now many more people in their child-bearing years than in older age groups (in which most deaths occur). This growth of the childbearing population represents a "demographic echo" of the baby boom generation. Consequently, the number of people born each year in the United States continues to exceed the number who die. In addition, the nation allows a large number of immigrants to enter each year; immigrants currently account for between one-fourth and one-third of annual growth.

Despite these trends, some analysts in the 1980s and early 1990s projected relatively low fertility levels and moderate net migration over the coming decades. As a result, it seemed possible that the United States might reach **zero population growth (ZPG)**. ZPG is the state of a population in which the number of births plus immigrants equals the number of deaths plus emigrants. In the recent past, although some nations have achieved ZPG, it has been relatively short-lived. Yet today, projections of population change between 2010 and 2050 indicate that 28 countries, including 20 in Europe, are showing a *decline* in population (Haub 2010).

What would a society with stable population growth be like? In demographic terms, it would be quite different from the United States of the 1990s. There would be relatively equal numbers of people in each age group, and the median age of the population might perhaps be as high as 38 (compared to 35 in 2000). As a result, the population pyramid of the United States (as shown in Figure 20-3) would look more like a rectangle.

There would also be a much larger proportion of older people, especially age 75 and over. These citizens would place a greater demand on the nation's social service programs and health care institutions. On a more positive note, the economy would be less volatile under ZPG, since the number of entrants into the paid labor force would remain stable. ZPG would also lead to changes in family life. With fertility rates

SOCIOLOGY IN THE GLOBAL COMMUNITY

20-1 Population Policy In China

In a residential district in Shanghai, a member of the local family-planning committee knocks on the door of a childless couple. Why, she inquires, have they not started a family?

Such a question would have been unthinkable in 1979, when family-planning officials, in an attempt to avoid a looming population explosion, began resorting to sterilization to enforce the government rule of one child per family. Since then, the government has granted some limited exceptions to the one-child policy. For example, in 2008 officials allowed parents who had lost a child in an earthquake to have another child.

Chinese families are beset, too, by the unforeseen results of their attempts to circumvent the one-child policy. In the past, in an effort to ensure that their one child would be a male capable of perpetuating the family line, many couples chose to abort female fetuses, or quietly allowed female infants to die of neglect. As a result, in 2011, among children ages one to four, China's sex ratio (the ratio of males to females) was about 120 to 100—well above the normal rate at birth of 105 to 100.

As a result of the rising sex ratio, Chinese officials have begun to worry about a future with too few women.

As a result of the rising sex ratio, Chinese officials have begun to worry about a future with too few women. In about 20 to 25 years, they expect, almost one-fifth of the baby boys now being born will be unable to find brides. In an attempt to reverse the situation, the government is paying the parents of daughters to speak with other parents and persuade them to raise girls.

This billboard, photographed in China, promotes the government's policy of allowing only one child per family. For several decades, the People's Republic of China has been struggling with a population explosion that threatens to outstrip the nation's ability to provide for all its citizens.

Another legacy of the one-child policy is a shortage of caretakers for the elderly. Coupled with improvements in longevity, the generation long decline in births has greatly increased the ratio of dependent elders to able-bodied children. The migration of young adults to other parts of China has further compromised the care of the elderly. To compound the crisis, barely one in four of China's elders receives any pension at all. No other country in the world faces the prospect of caring for such a large population of seniors with so little social support.

LET'S DISCUSS

1. Does any government, no matter how overpopulated a country is, have a right to sterilize people who do not voluntarily limit the size of their families? Why or why not?

2. What do you think has been the most dramatic consequence of the one-child policy?

Sources: *The Economist* 2011b; Greenhalgh 2008; J. Page 2011; F. Wang 2011; F. Wang and Yong 2011.

---

declining, women would devote fewer years to child rearing and to the social roles of motherhood; the proportion of married women entering the labor force would continue to rise (McFalls 2007; Weeks 2008).

Population and Migration

Along with births and deaths, migration is one of the three factors that affect population growth or decline. The term **migration** refers to the relatively permanent movement of people, with the purpose of changing their place of residence (Prehn 1991). Migration usually describes movement over a sizable distance, rather than from one side of a city to another.

As a social phenomenon, migration is fairly complex; it results from a variety of factors. The most important tend to be economic—financial failure in the "old country" and a perception of greater economic opportunity and prosperity in the new homeland. Other factors that contribute to migration include racial and religious bigotry, dislike for prevailing political regimes, and a desire to reunite one's family. All these forces combine to *push* some individuals out of their homelands and *pull* them to areas they believe to be more attractive.

International Migration

International migration—changes of residence across national boundaries—has been a significant force in redistributing the world's population during certain periods of history. For example, the composition of the United States has been significantly altered by immigrants who came here beginning in the 19th century and continuing through the present. Their entry was encouraged or restricted by various immigration policies.

Today, in the second decade of the 21st century, legal immigrants to the United States account for about 50 to 60 percent of the nation's growth. To some observers, this nation is already overpopulated. Recognizing that additional people place greater strain on our natural resources, members of a respected environmental organization, the Sierra Club, have debated taking an official position against the present immigration rate. Thus far, rather than enter the politically charged debate over immigration, the majority of the club's members have preferred to remain neutral (R. Schaefer 2012).

In the past decade, immigration has become a controversial issue throughout much of Europe. Western Europe in particular has become a desirable destination for individuals and families from former colonies or former communist-bloc countries who are fleeing the poverty, persecution, and warfare of their native lands. The number of immigrants and refugees has been increasing at a time of widespread unemployment and housing shortages, provoking a striking rise in antiforeign (and often openly racist) sentiment in Germany, France, the Netherlands, and other countries.

Developing countries in Asia and Africa are also encountering difficulties as thousands of displaced people seek assistance and asylum. At the end of 2009, an estimated 10.4 million people worldwide were refugees or asylum seekers. Needless to say, the political and economic problems of developing nations (see Chapter 10) are only intensified by such massive migration, begun under desperate conditions (UNHCR 2010).

Refugees at a camp in Turkey in 2011 flee the violent conflict in Syria. Catastrophic conflicts such as war and terrorism often trigger massive international migrations.

Internal Migration

Migratory movements within societies can vary in important ways. In traditional societies, migration often represents a way of life, as people move to accommodate the changing availability of fertile soil and wild game. In industrial societies, people may relocate because of job transfers or because they believe that a particular region offers better employment opportunities or a more desirable climate.

Although nations typically have laws and policies governing movement across their borders, the same is not true of internal movement. Generally, the residents of a country are legally free to move from one locality to another. Of course, that is not the case in all nations; historically, the Republic of South Africa restricted the movement of Blacks and other non-Whites through the system of segregation known as *apartheid* (see Chapter 11).

use your sociological *imagination*

What would happen if present patterns of migration, both internal and international, reversed themselves? How would your hometown change? What would be the effect on the nation's economy? Would your own life change?

How Have Communities Changed?

The nature of community has changed greatly over the course of history—from early hunting-and-gathering societies to highly modernized postindustrial cities. For most of human history, people used basic tools and knowledge to survive. They satisfied their need for an adequate food supply through hunting, foraging for fruits or vegetables, fishing, and herding. In comparison with later, industrial societies, then, early civilizations were much more dependent on the physical environment and much less able to alter that environment to their advantage. Even when they discovered how to cultivate food rather than forage for it, their use of tools and thus the amount of food they could produce were limited. Gradually, however, farming communities began to accumulate a surplus of food, which allowed some people to turn to the production of other goods and services. This economic breakthrough laid the foundation for social stratification and the eventual rise of preindustrial cities.

Preindustrial Cities

It is estimated that beginning about 10,000 B.C., permanent settlements that were free from dependence on crop cultivation emerged. By today's standards, these early communities would barely qualify as cities. The **preindustrial city**, as it is termed, generally had only a few thousand people living within its borders, and was characterized by a relatively closed class system and limited mobility. In these early cities, status was usually based on ascribed characteristics such as family background, and education was limited to members of the elite. All the residents relied on perhaps 100,000 farmers and their own part-time farming to provide the needed agricultural surplus. The Mesopotamian city of Ur had a population of about 10,000 and was limited to roughly 220 acres of land, including the canals, the temple, and the harbor.

Why were these early cities so small and relatively few in number? Several key factors restricted urbanization:

- **Reliance on animal power (both humans and beasts of burden) as a source of energy for economic production.** This factor limited the ability of humans to make use of and alter the physical environment.

- **Modest levels of surplus produced by the agricultural sector.** Between 50 and 90 farmers may have been required to support one city resident (K. Davis [1949] 1995).

- **Problems in transportation and the storage of food and other goods.** Even an excellent crop could easily be lost as a result of such difficulties.

- **Hardships of migration to the city.** For many peasants, migration was both physically and economically impossible. A few weeks of travel was out of the question without more sophisticated food storage techniques.

- **Dangers of city life.** Concentrating a society's population in a small area left it open to attack from outsiders, as well as more susceptible to extreme damage from plagues and fires.

A sophisticated social organization was also an essential precondition for urban existence. Specialized social roles brought people together in new ways through the exchange of goods and services. A well-developed social organization ensured that those relationships were clearly defined and generally acceptable to all parties.

Industrial and Postindustrial Cities

Advances in agricultural technology led to dramatic changes in community life, but so did the process of industrialization. The *Industrial Revolution,* which began in the middle of the 18th century, focused on the application of nonanimal sources of power to labor tasks. Imagine how harnessing the energy of air, water, and other natural resources could change a society. Industrialization had a wide range of effects on people's lifestyles, as well as on the structure of communities. Emerging urban settlements became centers not only of industry but of banking, finance, and industrial management as well.

The factory system that developed during the Industrial Revolution led to a much more refined division of labor than was evident in preindustrial cities. The many new occupations that were created produced a complex set of relationships among workers. Thus, the **industrial city** was not merely more populous than its predecessors; it was based on very different principles of social organization (see Table 20-2).

In comparison with preindustrial cities, industrial cities had a more open class system and more social mobility. After initiatives in industrial cities by women's rights groups, labor unions, and other political activists, formal education gradually became available to many children from poor and working-class families.

Over the centuries, communities of all sizes have undergone significant social change. Like the Canadian city of Toronto, many have become increasingly diverse in race and ethnicity.

While ascribed characteristics such as gender, race, and ethnicity remained important, a talented or skilled individual had greater opportunity to better his or her social position. In these and other respects, the industrial city was genuinely a different world from the preindustrial urban community.

In the latter part of the 20th century, a new type of urban community emerged. The **postindustrial city** is one in which global finance and the electronic flow of information dominate the economy. Production is decentralized and often takes place outside urban centers, but control is centralized in multinational corporations whose influence transcends urban and even national boundaries. Social change is a constant feature of the postindustrial city. Economic restructuring and spatial change seem to occur each decade, if not more frequently. In the postindustrial world, cities are forced into increasing competition for economic opportunities, which deepens the plight of the urban poor (E. Phillips 1996; D. A. Smith and Timberlake 1993).

Sociologist Louis Wirth (1928, 1938) argued that a relatively large and permanent settlement leads to distinctive patterns of behavior, which he called **urbanism.** He identified three critical factors that contribute to urbanism: the size of the population, population density, and the heterogeneity (variety) of the population. A frequent result of urbanism, according to Wirth, is that we become insensitive to events around us and restrict our attention to the primary groups to which we are emotionally attached.

Table 20-2 summarizes the differences among preindustrial, industrial, and postindustrial cities.

use your sociological *imagination*

What would the ideal city of the future look like? Describe its architecture, public transportation, neighborhoods, schools, and workplaces. What kinds of people would live and work there?

Preindustrial Cities (through 18th century)	Industrial Cities (18th through mid-20th century)	Postindustrial Cities (beginning late 20th century)
Closed class system—pervasive influence of social class at birth	Open class system—mobility based on achieved characteristics	Wealth based on ability to obtain and use information
Economic realm controlled by guilds and a few families	Relatively open competition	Corporate power dominates
Beginnings of division of labor in the creation of goods	Elaborate specialization in manufacturing of goods	Sense of place fades, transnational networks emerge
Pervasive influence of religion on social norms	Influence of religion limited as society becomes more secularized	Religion becomes more fragmented; greater openness to new religious faiths
Little standardization of prices, weights, and measures	Standardization enforced by custom and law	Conflicting views of prevailing standards
Population largely illiterate, communication by word of mouth	Emergence of communication through posters, bulletins, and newspapers	Emergence of extended electronic networks
Schools limited to elites and designed to perpetuate their privileged status	Formal schooling open to the masses and viewed as a means of advancing the social order	Professional, scientific, and technical personnel become increasingly important

Sources: Based on E. Phillips 1996:132–135; Sjoberg 1960:323–328.

Urbanization

Urbanization has become a central aspect of life in the United States, as well as of the rest of the world. In 1950, only two of the world's urban areas, New York and Tokyo, had populations of over 10 million. By 2010 there were 22 such areas; by 2025 there will be more than 30 (Bruinius 2010). Figure 20-4 shows the projected major urban areas in the year 2015. What explains this rapid concentration of people in a single place? In this section we will study two views of urbanization: urban ecology, a functionalist view, and new urban sociology, a conflict view.

Functionalist View: Urban Ecology

Human ecology is an area of study that is concerned with the interrelationships between people and their environment. Human ecologists have long been interested in how the physical environment shapes people's lives (for example, how rivers can serve as a barrier to residential expansion) and in how people influence the surrounding environment (for example, how air-conditioning has accelerated the growth of major metropolitan areas in the Southwest). **Urban ecology** focuses on such relationships as they emerge in urban areas. Although the urban ecological approach focuses on social change in cities, it is nevertheless functionalist in orientation because it emphasizes how different elements in urban areas contribute to social stability.

Early urban ecologists such as Robert Park (1916, 1936) and Ernest Burgess (1925) concentrated on city life but drew on the approaches used by ecologists who study plant and animal communities. With few exceptions, urban ecologists trace their work back to the **concentric-zone theory** devised in the 1920s by Burgess (Figure 20-5a). Using Chicago as an example, Burgess proposed a theory for describing land use in industrial cities. At the center, or nucleus, of such a city is the central business district. Large department stores, hotels, theaters, and financial institutions occupy this highly valued land. Surrounding this urban center are zones devoted to other types of land use, which illustrate the growth of the urban area over time.

Note that the creation of zones is a *social* process, not the result of nature alone. Families and business firms compete for the most valuable land; those who possess the most wealth and power are generally the winners. The concentric-zone theory proposed by Burgess represented a dynamic model of urban growth. As urban growth proceeded, each zone would move even farther from the central business district.

Because of its functionalist orientation and its emphasis on stability, the concentric-zone theory tended to understate or ignore certain tensions that were apparent in metropolitan areas. For example, the growing use by the affluent of land in a city's peripheral areas was uncritically approved, while the arrival of African Americans in White neighborhoods in the 1930s was described by some sociologists in terms such as *invasion* and *succession*. Moreover, the urban ecological perspective gave little thought to gender inequities, such as the establishment of men's softball and golf leagues in city parks, without any programs for women's sports. Consequently, the urban ecological approach has been criticized for its failure to address issues of gender, race, and class.

By the middle of the 20th century, urban populations had spilled beyond traditional city limits. No longer could urban ecologists focus exclusively on *growth* in the central city, for large numbers of urban residents were abandoning the cities to live in suburban areas. As a response to the emergence of more than one focal point in some metropolitan areas, Chauncy D. Harris and Edward Ullman (1945) presented the **multiple-nuclei theory** (Figure 20-5b). In their view, all urban growth does not radiate outward from a central business district. Instead, a metropolitan area may have many centers of development, each of which reflects a particular urban need or activity. Thus, a city may have a financial district, a manufacturing zone, a waterfront area, an entertainment center, and so forth. Certain types of

MAPPING LIFE WORLDWIDE
FIGURE **20-4** GLOBAL URBANIZATION 2015 (PROJECTED)

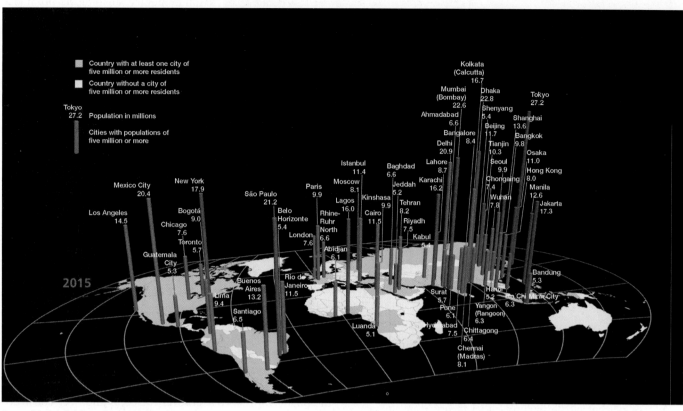

Source: *National Geographic* 2005:104–105.

FIGURE **20-5** COMPARISON OF ECOLOGICAL THEORIES OF URBAN GROWTH

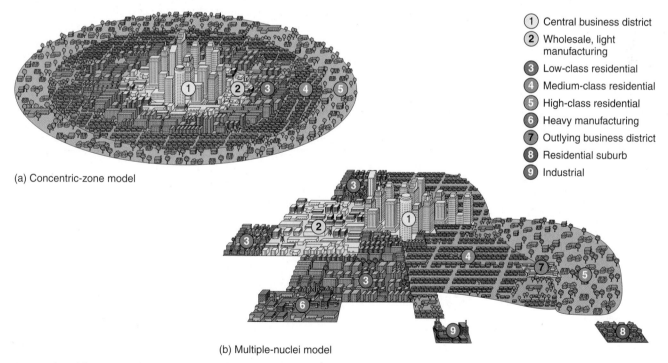

(a) Concentric-zone model

(b) Multiple-nuclei model

1. Central business district
2. Wholesale, light manufacturing
3. Low-class residential
4. Medium-class residential
5. High-class residential
6. Heavy manufacturing
7. Outlying business district
8. Residential suburb
9. Industrial

Source: Adapted from Harris and Ullmann 1945:13.

business firms and certain types of housing will naturally cluster around each distinctive nucleus (Squires 2002).

The rise of suburban shopping malls is a vivid example of the phenomenon of multiple nuclei within metropolitan areas. Initially, all major retailing in urban areas was located in the central business district. Each residential neighborhood had its own grocers, bakers, and butchers, but people traveled to the center of the city to make major purchases at department stores. However,

Between 2000 and 2010, metropolitan Las Vegas grew by more than 575,000 people, to a total population of over 1.9 million. Cities that are undergoing such rapid growth give rise to both multiple-nuclei and edge cities.

Conflict View: New Urban Sociology

Contemporary sociologists point out that metropolitan growth is not governed by waterways and rail lines, as a purely ecological interpretation might suggest. From a conflict perspective, communities are human creations that reflect people's needs, choices, and decisions—though some people have more influence over those decisions than others. Drawing on conflict theory, an approach called the **new urban sociology** considers the interplay of local, national, and worldwide forces and their effect on local space, with special emphasis on the impact of global economic activity (Gottdiener and Hutchison 2011).

New urban sociologists note that proponents of the ecological approaches have typically avoided examining the social forces, largely economic in nature, that have guided urban growth. For example, central business districts may be upgraded or abandoned, depending on whether urban policymakers grant substantial tax exemptions to developers. The suburban boom in the post–World War II era was fueled by highway construction and federal housing policies that channeled investment capital into the construction of single-family homes rather than affordable rental housing in the cities. Similarly, while some observers suggest that the growth of sun-belt cities is due to a "good business climate," new urban sociologists counter that the term is actually a euphemism for hefty state and local government subsidies and antilabor policies intended to draw manufacturers (Gottdiener and Feagin 1988; M. Smith 1988).

The new urban sociology draws on the conflict perspective, and more specifically, on sociologist Immanuel Wallerstein's **world systems analysis**. Wallerstein argues that certain industrialized nations (among them the United States, Japan, and Germany) hold a dominant position at the *core* of the global economic system. At the same time, the poor developing countries of Asia, Africa, and Latin America lie on the *periphery* of the global economy, controlled and exploited by core industrialized nations.

Using world systems analysis, new urban sociologists consider urbanization from a global perspective. They view cities not as independent and autonomous entities, but as the outcome of decision-making processes directed or influenced by a society's dominant classes and by core industrialized nations. New urban sociologists note that the rapidly growing cities of the world's developing countries were shaped first by colonialism and then by a global economy controlled by core nations and multinational corporations. The outcome has not been beneficial to the poorest citizens, as Box 20-2 shows. An unmistakable feature of many cities in developing countries is the existence of large

as metropolitan areas expanded and the suburbs became more populous, increasing numbers of people began to shop nearer their homes. Today, the suburban mall is a significant retailing and social center in communities across the United States.

In a refinement of the multiple-nuclei theory, contemporary urban ecologists have begun to study what journalist Joel Garreau (1991) has called "edge cities." These communities, which have grown up on the outskirts of major metropolitan areas, are economic and social centers with identities of their own. By any standard of measurement—height of buildings, amount of office space, presence of medical facilities, presence of leisure-time facilities, or of course, population—edge cities qualify as independent cities rather than large suburbs. The aerotropolis, discussed in this chapter's opening excerpt, is an edge city (Kasarda and Lindsay 2011:11).

Whether metropolitan areas include edge cities or multiple nuclei, more and more of them are characterized by spread-out development and unchecked growth. In recent years, Las Vegas has been the most dramatic example. By 2009 the city had grown to nine times its size in 1950, and its population had exploded from less than 25,000 to about 600,000. The social consequences of such rapid growth are equally dramatic, from a shortage of affordable housing and an inadequate number of food pantries to an overstretched water supply, poor health care delivery, and impossible traffic. Today's cities are very different from the preindustrial cities of a thousand years ago.

use your sociological *imagination*

Consider the spatial arrangements in your everyday life from the point of view of urban ecology. How do man-made constructions and barriers affect your travel patterns?

SOCIOLOGY IN THE GLOBAL COMMUNITY

20-2 Squatter Settlements

Bariadas, favelas, bustees, kampungs, and *bidonvilles:* The terms vary depending on the nation and language, but the meaning is the same—"squatter settlements." In **squatter settlements,** areas occupied by the very poor on the fringe of cities, housing is constructed by the settlers themselves from discarded material, including crates from loading docks and loose lumber from building projects. While the term *squatter settlement* has wide use, many observers prefer to use a less pejorative term, such as *autonomous settlements.*

This type of settlement is typical of cities in the world's developing nations. In such countries, new housing has not kept pace with the combined urban population growth resulting from births and migration from rural areas. Squatter settlements also swell when city dwellers are forced out of housing by astronomical jumps in rent. By definition, squatters living on vacant land are trespassers and can be legally evicted. However, given the large number of poor people who live in such settlements, governments generally look the other way.

Obviously, squatters live in substandard housing, yet that is only one of the many problems they face. Residents do not receive most public services, since their presence cannot be legally recognized. Police and fire protection, paved streets, and sanitary sewers are virtually nonexistent. In some countries, squatters may have trouble voting or enrolling their children in public schools.

Despite such conditions, squatter settlements are not always as bleak as they may appear from the outside. You can often find a well-developed social organization there, rather than a disorganized collection of people. Typically, a thriving "informal economy" develops: residents establish small, home-based businesses such as grocery stores, jewelry shops, and the like. Local churches, men's clubs, and women's clubs are often established in specific neighborhoods within settlements.

Even Mongolia has squatter communities. Nomadic herders created this shantytown near Mongolia's capital, Ulan Bator, home to one-quarter of the nation's population.

> *Squatter settlements are not always as bleak as they may appear from the outside.*

Squatter settlements remind us that theoretical models that were developed in the United States may not apply directly to other cultures. The various ecological models of urban growth, for example, would not explain a metropolitan expansion that locates the poorest people on the urban fringes. Furthermore, solutions that are logical in a highly industrialized nation may not be relevant to developing nations. In developing nations, rather than focusing on large-scale solutions to urban problems, planners must think in terms of providing basic amenities, such as water or electrical power for the ever-expanding squatter settlements.

LET'S DISCUSS

1. Do you know of any squatters in your community? If so, describe them and the place where they live.
2. Given the number of homeless people in the United States, why aren't there more squatters?

Sources: Perlman 2010; Neuwirth 2004; Yap 1998.

TABLE 20-3 SOCIOLOGICAL PERSPECTIVES ON URBANIZATION

	Urban Ecology	New Urban Sociology
Theoretical perspective	Functionalist	Conflict
Primary focus	Relationship of urban areas to their spatial setting and physical environment	Relationship of urban areas to global, national, and local forces
Key source of change	Technological innovations such as new methods of transportation	Economic competition and monopolization of power
Initiator of actions	Individuals, neighborhoods, communities	Real estate developers, banks and other financial institutions, multinational corporations
Allied disciplines	Geography, architecture	Political science, economics

squatter settlements just outside city limits (Gottdiener and Feagin 1988; D. A. Smith 1995).

As we have seen throughout this textbook in studying such varied issues as deviance, race and ethnicity, and aging, no single theoretical approach necessarily offers the only valuable perspective. As Table 20-3 shows, urban ecology and the new urban sociology offer significantly different ways of viewing urbanization, both of which enrich our understanding of this complex phenomenon.

Types of Communities

Communities vary substantially in the degree to which their members feel connected and share a common identity. Ferdinand Tönnies ([1887]1988) used the term *Gemeinschaft* to describe a close-knit community where social interaction among people is intimate and familiar. This is the kind of place where people in a coffee shop will stop talking whenever anyone enters, because they are sure to know whoever walks through the door. A shopper at the small grocery store in this town would expect to know every employee, and probably every other customer as well. In contrast, the ideal type of *Gesellschaft* describes modern urban life, in which people have little in common with others. Social relationships often result from interactions focused on immediate tasks, such as purchasing a product. In the United States, contemporary city life generally resembles a *Gesellschaft*.

In the following sections we will examine different types of communities found in the United States, focusing on the distinctive characteristics and problems of central cities, suburbs, and rural areas.

Central Cities

In terms of both land and population, the United States is the fourth-largest nation in the world. Yet three-quarters of the population is concentrated in a mere 1.5 percent of the nation's land area. In 2010 some 233 million people—or 83 percent of the nation's population—lived in metropolitan areas. Even those who live outside central cities, such as residents of suburban and rural communities, find that urban centers heavily influence their lifestyles (Mackun and Wilson 2011:4).

C stands for "congestion." In 2003, to alleviate gridlock, officials of the city of London began to charge vehicles about $16 a day to enter designated congestion zones. At least initially, significant traffic reductions resulted, leading cities such as Singapore, Stockholm, Oslo, and Rome to copy the idea. The revenue from the fees is used to pay for more buses, road improvements, and upgraded bicycle paths.

Urban Dwellers Many urban residents are the descendants of European immigrants—Irish, Italians, Jews, Poles, and others—who came to the United States in the 19th and early 20th centuries. The cities socialized these newcomers to the norms, values, and language of their new homeland and gave them an opportunity to work their way up the economic ladder. In addition, a substantial number of low-income African Americans and Whites came to the cities from rural areas in the period following World War II.

Even today, cities in the United States are the destinations of immigrants from around the world—including Mexico, Ireland, Cuba, Vietnam, and Haiti—as well as of migrants from the U.S. commonwealth of Puerto Rico. Yet unlike those who came to this country 100 years ago, current immigrants are arriving at a time of growing urban decay. Thus they have more difficulty finding employment and decent housing.

Urban life is noteworthy for its diversity, so it would be a serious mistake to see all city residents as being alike. Sociologist Herbert J. Gans (1991) has distinguished five types of people found in cities:

TREND SPOTTING

Urbanization and Its Costs

The 20th century brought rapid urbanization not just to the United States, but to countries around the world. Globally, the proportion of the population that lives in cities increased from 13 percent in 1900 to 29 percent in 1950. By 2005, according to the United Nations, the proportion had reached 49 percent.

In developing countries, this rush toward urbanization is complicating government efforts to improve people's living conditions. Providing adequate food and water is more difficult in cities than it is in rural areas, where wells, garden plots, and farm animals are often enough to sustain residents. In cities, food must be trucked in from the countryside, and water must be purified and piped from one location to the next.

Somehow, rapidly expanding cities must find the resources to expand their infrastructures—a challenge considering the poverty of many residents. Compared to industrialized countries, developing countries are urbanizing with a relatively lower per capita income. The United States did not reach 65 percent urbanization until 1950, when per capita income had risen to nearly $13,000 in today's dollars. In comparison, Nigeria, Pakistan, and the Philippines are approaching the same level of urbanization with just one-fifth of that per capita income. In these countries, the bright lights of the city—assuming that the power grid is working—may not herald such a bright future.

1. **Cosmopolites.** These residents remain in cities to take advantage of unique cultural and intellectual benefits. Writers, artists, and scholars fall into this category.

2. **Unmarried and childless people.** Such people choose to live in cities because of the active nightlife and varied recreational opportunities.

3. **Ethnic villagers.** These urban residents prefer to live in their own tight-knit communities. Typically, immigrant groups isolate themselves in such neighborhoods to avoid resentment from well-established urban dwellers.

4. **The deprived.** Very poor people and families have little choice but to live in low-rent and often run-down urban neighborhoods.

5. **The trapped.** Some city residents wish to leave urban centers but cannot because of their limited economic resources and prospects. Gans includes the "downward mobiles" in this category—people who once held higher social positions, but who are forced to live in less prestigious neighborhoods owing to loss of a job, death of a wage earner, or old age.

To this list we can add a sixth type, people who live in naturally occurring retirement communities (see Chapter 13, page 294). These varied categories remind us that the city represents a choice (even a dream) for certain people and a nightmare for others.

Issues Facing Cities Within any city in the United States, people and neighborhoods vary greatly. Yet all residents of a central city—regardless of social class, racial, and ethnic differences—face certain common problems. Crime, air pollution, noise, unemployment, overcrowded schools, inadequate public transportation—these unpleasant realities and many more are an increasingly common feature of contemporary urban life.

Perhaps the single most dramatic reflection of the nation's urban ills has been the apparent death of entire neighborhoods. In some urban districts, business activity seems virtually nonexistent. Visitors can walk for blocks and find little more than deteriorated, boarded-up, abandoned, and burned-out buildings. Vacant factories mark the sites of businesses that relocated a generation ago. Such urban devastation has contributed greatly to the growing problem of homelessness.

Residential segregation has also been a persistent problem in cities across the United States. Segregation has resulted from the policies of financial institutions, the business practices of real estate agents, the actions of home sellers, and even urban planning initiatives (for example, decisions about where to locate public housing). Sociologists Douglas Massey and Nancy Denton (1993) have used the term *American apartheid* to refer to such residential patterns. In their view, we no longer perceive segregation as a problem, but rather accept it as a feature of the urban landscape. For subordinate minority groups, segregation means not only limited housing opportunities but reduced access to employment, retail outlets, and medical services.

Another critical problem for the cities has been mass transportation. Since 1950, the number of cars in the United States has multiplied twice as fast as the number of people. Growing traffic congestion in metropolitan areas has led many cities to recognize the need for safe, efficient, and inexpensive mass transit systems. However, the federal government has traditionally given much more assistance to highway programs than to public transportation. Conflict theorists note that such a bias favors the relatively affluent (automobile owners) as well as corporations such as auto manufacturers, tire makers, and oil companies. Meanwhile, low-income residents of metropolitan areas, who are much less likely to own cars than members of the middle and upper classes, face higher fares on public transit along with deteriorating service (J. W. Mason 1998; Reschovsky 2004).

Suburbs

The term *suburb* derives from the Latin *sub urbe,* meaning "under the city." Until recent times, most suburbs were just that—tiny communities totally dependent on urban centers for jobs, recreation, and even water.

Today, the term **suburb** defies simple definition. The term generally refers to any community near a large city—or as the Census Bureau would say, any territory within a metropolitan area that is not included in the central city.

Three social factors differentiate suburbs from cities. First, suburbs are generally less dense than cities; in some suburbs, no more than two dwellings may occupy an acre of land. Second, the suburbs consist almost exclusively of private space. For the most part, private ornamental lawns replace common park areas. Third, suburbs have more exacting building design codes than cities, and those codes have become increasingly precise in the past decade. While the suburbs may be diverse in population, their design standards give the impression of uniformity.

Distinguishing between suburbs and rural areas can also be difficult. Certain criteria generally define suburbs: most people work at urban (as opposed to rural) jobs, and local governments provide services such as water supply, sewage disposal, and fire protection. In rural areas, those services are less common, and a greater proportion of residents is employed in farming and related activities.

Suburban Expansion Whatever the precise definition of a suburb, it is clear that suburbs have expanded. In fact, suburbanization was the most dramatic population trend in the United States throughout the 20th century. Suburban areas grew at first along railroad lines, then at the end of streetcar tracks, and by the 1950s along the nation's growing system of freeways and expressways. The suburban boom has been especially evident since World War II.

Proponents of the new urban sociology contend that initially, industries moved their factories from central cities to suburbs to reduce the power of labor unions. Subsequently, many suburban communities induced businesses to relocate there by offering them subsidies and tax incentives. These enticements created a job migration that was virtually unstoppable. As sociologist William Julius Wilson (1996) has observed, federal housing policies contributed to the suburban boom by withholding mortgage capital from inner-city neighborhoods, by offering favorable **453** mortgages to military veterans, and by assisting the rapid development of massive amounts of affordable tract housing in the suburbs. Moreover, federal highway and transportation policies provided substantial funding for expressway systems (which made commuting to the cities much easier), while undermining urban communities by building freeway networks through their heart (Scherer 2009; Sharp and Clark 2008).

All these factors contributed to the movement of the (predominantly White) middle class out of the central cities, and as we shall see, out of the suburbs as well. From the perspective of new urban sociology, suburban expansion is far from a natural ecological process; rather, it reflects the distinct priorities of powerful economic and political interests.

Suburban Diversity In terms of their residents' age, household type, educational level, and social class, suburbs and cities have similar levels of diversity. Race and ethnicity remain the most important factors that distinguish cities from suburbs. Nevertheless, the common assumption that suburbia includes only prosperous Whites is far from correct. The past 30 years have witnessed the diversification of suburbs in terms of race and ethnicity. According to a 2009 study, White non-Hispanic enrollments in suburban schools dropped from 72 percent in 1993 to 59 percent in 2007. Like the rest of the nation, members of racial and ethnic minorities are becoming suburban dwellers.

But are the suburban areas re-creating the racial segregation of the central cities? A definite pattern of clustering, if not outright segregation, is emerging. A study of suburban residential patterns in 11 metropolitan areas found that Asian Americans and Hispanics tend to reside in the same socioeconomic areas as Whites—that is, affluent Hispanics live alongside affluent Whites, poor Asians near poor Whites, and so on. Yet minority students are only modestly less segregated in the suburbs than they are in the central cities.

Again, in contrast to prevailing stereotypes, the suburbs include a significant number of low-income people from all ethnic backgrounds—White, Black, and Hispanic. Poverty is not conventionally associated with the suburbs, partly because the suburban poor tend to be scattered among more affluent people. In some instances, suburban communities intentionally hide social problems such as homelessness so they can maintain a "respectable image." Soaring housing costs have contributed to suburban poverty, which is rising at a faster rate than urban poverty (Guarino 2010; Matthew Hall and Lee 2011).

Rural Areas

As we have seen, the people of the United States live mainly in urban areas. Yet according to the 2010 census, 50 million Americans—17 percent of the nation's population—live outside a metropolitan area. Put another way, these rural residents do not live near any city with a population of at least 50,000. There

The growth of the Hispanic population in small towns and agricultural areas has been a welcome countertrend to the stagnation of most rural areas in the United States. This community in Beardstown, Illinois, is thriving.

are striking variations from state to state in the ratio of rural to urban residents. In California, less than 6 percent of residents live in rural areas; in Vermont, more than 60 percent do (Bureau of the Census 2006a; Mackun and Wilson 2011:4).

Rural Diversity

As with the suburbs, it would be a mistake to view rural communities as fitting one set image. Turkey farms, coal-mining towns, cattle ranches, and gas stations along interstate highways are all part of the rural landscape in the United States. And though globalization usually brings to mind the world's financial capitals, rural areas, including those in the United States, also play a fundamental role in the global economy. Like their urban counterparts, rural communities have adjusted to world competition. U.S. farmers now produce 38 percent of the world's supply of soybeans. In response to global concerns over oil shortages, they developed ethanol, a gasoline substitute produced from agricultural feed or grains like corn and wheat (American Soybean Association 2011; Flora and Flora with Fey 2004).

Competition is missing, however, in the very communities where farmers have accommodated themselves to global competition. Much of the rural United States, sociologist Cornelia Flora writes, has witnessed the *decoupling* of agriculture and the small rural communities where it is practiced. No longer do most farmers buy their cars, clothes, and farm equipment locally. Instead, they travel to metropolitan centers, where prices are more competitive and the selection of goods is broader (Belz 2011).

Recently, the catastrophic Hurricane Katrina, which devastated Gulf Coast cities and towns in 2005, has contributed to a rural resurgence in the Deep South. Faced with the slow reconstruction of New Orleans and other hard-hit cities, many displaced residents have relocated from the coast to rural areas farther inland. African Americans in particular have begun to gravitate toward communities that offer jobs in the fish farming industry. These small rural communities have become an economic and social magnet for displaced Gulf residents (Eaton 2007; Kandel 2005).

Population, Communities, and Urbanization

Percent change

- 50.0 or more
- 25.0 to 49.9
- 10.0 to 24.9
- 0.0 to 9.9
- −9.9 to −0.0
- Less than −9.9
- Comparable data not available

Source: 2010 Census in Mackun and Wilson 2011:7.

During the 10 years from 2000 to 2010, most urban areas in the United States experienced a growth in population. As the population of the coastal states expanded, however, much of the Great Plains was depopulated.

Think about It

What was the population trend where you lived?

Rural Challenges

Today, many rural areas are facing problems that were first associated with the central cities, and are now evident in the suburbs. Overdevelopment, gang warfare, drug trafficking, and poverty can be found on the policymaking agenda far outside major metropolitan areas. While the magnitude of the problems may not be as great as in the central cities, rural resources cannot begin to match those that city mayors can marshall in an attempt to address social ills.

The postindustrial revolution has been far from kind to the rural communities of the United States. As Figure 20-6 shows, population growth has been rare in rural counties. Instead, the rural Great Plains area, which stretches from northwestern Texas to the Canadian border, has been marked by population loss. The depopulation of farming areas has been especially hard on the youngest residents. It is not uncommon for rural children to travel 90 minutes each way to school, compared to a nationwide one-way commute of less than 26 minutes for urban workers.

While the press often notes the consolidation of rural school districts, rural educational problems are not limited to the elementary and secondary schools. From Washington State to rural West Virginia, college-age youths often have only limited access to two-year colleges. Although long-distance learning opportunities have expanded to meet their needs, college-bound residents of rural areas are more likely than their urban counterparts to face a patchwork of programs (Carr and Kefalas 2009; Dillon 2004; C. Dougherty 2011; Hebel 2006; Mackun and Wilson 2011).

The construction of large businesses can create its own problems, as small communities that have experienced the arrival of large discount stores, such as Walmart, Target, Home Depot, or Costco, have discovered. Although many residents welcome the new employment opportunities and the convenience of one-stop shopping, local merchants see their longtime family businesses endangered by formidable 200,000-square-foot competitors with a national reputation. Even when such discount stores provide a boost to a town's economy (and they do not always do so), they can undermine the town's sense of community and identity.

On a more positive note, advances in electronic communications have allowed some people in the United States to work wherever they wish. For those who are concerned about quality-of-life issues, working at home in a rural area that has access to the latest high-tech services is the perfect arrangement. As of 2011, however, 40 percent of rural households did not have access to broadband Internet service. No matter where people make their homes—whether in the city, the suburbs, or a country village—economic and technological change will have an impact on their quality of life (Department of Commerce 2011).

use your sociological *imagination*

Have you seen rural areas change? If so, in what ways? In your opinion, are the changes you have seen for the better or worse?

Seeking Shelter Worldwide

A chance meeting brought two old classmates together. In late 1997, Prince Charles encountered Clive Harold during a tour of the offices of a magazine sold by the homeless in London. But while Prince Charles can call several palaces home, Harold is homeless. This modern-day version of *The Prince and the Pauper* intrigued many people with its message that "it can happen to anyone." Harold had been a successful author and journalist until his marriage fell apart and alcohol turned his life inside out (*Chicago Tribune* 1997).

In the United States, the recent economic downturn has created another group of homeless people, former homeowners who can no longer pay their mortgages. This group includes not just the working poor, but middle-class families hit by layoffs and/or ill health. Many of those who can't find an affordable rental apartment move in with family or friends; others end up in homeless shelters or sleep in their cars.

Looking at the Issue

The issue of inadequate shelter manifests itself in many ways, for all housing problems can be considered relative. To a relatively affluent family in the United States, it may mean a somewhat smaller house than they need, because that is all they can afford. For a single working adult in Tokyo, it may mean having to commute two hours to a full-time job. For many people worldwide, however, the housing problem means finding shelter of any kind that they can afford, in a place where anyone would reasonably wish to live.

Homelessness is evident in both industrialized and developing countries. According to estimates, on any given night, the number of homeless persons in the United States is at least 650,000 (Figure 20-7), only about half of whom are sheltered. Over 1 million Americans stay at a homeless shelter at some time each year (Housing and Urban Development 2010; National Alliance to End Homelessness 2011).

In Third World countries, rapid population growth has outpaced the expansion of housing by a wide margin, leading to a rise in homelessness. For example, estimates of homelessness in Mexico City range from 10,000 to 100,000, and do not include the many people living in caves or squatter settlements (see Box 20-2, page 451) (M. Davis 2005; G. Goldstein 1998; Ross 1996; Stoner 2008).

Applying Sociology

Both in the United States and around the world, homelessness functions as a master status that largely defines a person's position in society. In this case, homelessness means that in many important respects, the individual is *outside* society. Without a home address and telephone, it is difficult to look for work or even apply for public assistance. Moreover, the master status of being homeless carries a serious stigma that can lead to prejudice and discrimination. Poor treatment of people suspected of being homeless is common in stores and restaurants, and many communities have reported acts of random violence against homeless people. In 2009, in response to such violence, Maryland became the first state to include homeless people in its hate crime legislation (National Law Center on Homelessness and Poverty 2009b).

The profile of homelessness has changed significantly over the past 40 years. In the past, most homeless people were older White males living as alcoholics in skid-row areas. Today's homeless population is comparatively younger. What is more, the proportion of Black Americans in shelters is now three times the proportion of Blacks in the population as a whole. The homeless population is growing faster than the increase in emergency food and shelter space (Housing and Urban Development 2010; B. Lee et al. 2010).

Changing economic and residential patterns account for much of this increase in homelessness. In recent decades, the process of urban renewal has included a noticeable boom in **gentrification**. This term refers to the resettlement of low-income city neighborhoods by prosperous families and business firms. In some instances, city governments have promoted gentrification by granting lucrative tax breaks to developers who convert low-cost rental units into luxury apartments and condominiums. Conflict theorists note that although the affluent may derive both financial and emotional benefits from gentrification and redevelopment, the poor often end up being thrown out on the street.

Initiating Policy

The major federal program intended to assist the homeless is the McKinney Homeless Assistance Act, passed in 1987. This act authorizes federal aid for emergency food, shelter, physical and mental health care, job training, and education for homeless children and adults. Thus far, most policymakers have been content to steer the homeless toward large, overcrowded, unhealthy shelters. Yet many neighborhoods and communities have resisted plans to open large shelters or even smaller residences for the homeless, often raising the familiar cry of "Not in my backyard!"

According to an analysis by the National Law Center on Homelessness and Poverty (2009a), the past 20 years have seen a growing trend toward the adoption of anti-homeless public policies and the "criminalization" of homeless people. Many cities have enacted curbs on panhandling, sitting on sidewalks, standing near automated teller machines, and other behavior sometimes evident among the homeless. At the same time, more and more policymakers—especially conservative officials—have advocated cutbacks in government funding for the homeless and argued that voluntary associations and religious organizations should assume a more important role in addressing the problem.

Public opinion polls show that homelessness is part of the national consciousness, though not an overriding concern. In a 2011 national survey, 41 percent of respondents called "hunger/homelessness" a concern. Respondents who professed concern over energy, the environment, crime, health care, and Social Security all outnumbered those who were concerned about homelessness (Saad 2011).

Developing nations have special problems. They have understandably given highest priority to economic productivity, as measured by jobs with living wages. Unfortunately, even the most ambitious economic and social programs may be overwhelmed by minor currency fluctuations, a drop in the value of a nation's major export, or an influx of refugees from a neighboring country. Some of the reforms implemented have included promoting private (as opposed to government-controlled) housing markets, allowing dwellings to be places of business as well, and loosening restrictions on building materials.

All three of those short-term solutions have shortcomings, however. Private housing markets invite exploitation; mixed residential/commercial use may only cause good housing to deteriorate faster; and the use of marginal building materials leaves low-income residential areas more vulnerable to calamities such as floods, fires, and earthquakes. Large-scale rental housing under government supervision, the typical solution in North America and Europe, has been successful only in economically advanced city-states such as Hong Kong and Singapore (Speak and Tipple 2006; Strassman 1998; Toro 2007).

In sum, though homeless people in the United States and abroad are not getting the shelter they need, they lack the political clout to gain policymakers' attention.

Take the Issue with You

1. Have you ever worked as a volunteer in a shelter or soup kitchen? If so, were you surprised by the type of people who lived or ate there? Has anyone you know ever had to move into a shelter?

2. Is gentrification of low-income housing a problem where you live? Have you ever had difficulty finding an affordable place to live?

MAPPING LIFE NATIONWIDE
FIGURE **20-7**   HOMELESS ESTIMATES BY STATE

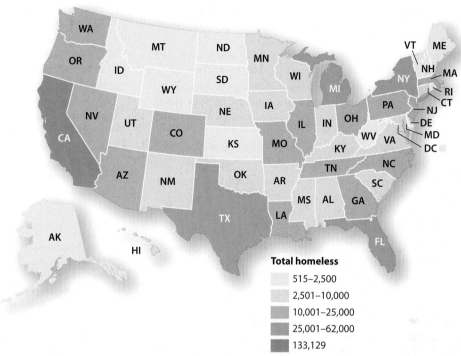

Total homeless
- 515–2,500
- 2,501–10,000
- 10,001–25,000
- 25,001–62,000
- 133,129

Source: Based on 2009 data reported by National Alliance to End Homelessness 2011:Table 1.1. Though homelessness tends to be concentrated in the more populous states, such as California, hundreds of homeless people can be found in every state.

3. What kind of assistance is available to homeless people in the community where you live? Does the help come from the government, from private charities, or both? What about housing assistance for people with low incomes, such as rent subsidies—is it available?

MASTERING THIS CHAPTER

Summary

A **community** is a spatial or political unit of social organization that gives people a sense of belonging. This chapter explains how population trends affect the world's communities. It covers the size, composition, and distribution of the population; various elements of population; the current problem of overpopulation; and the possibility of **zero population growth.** It also shows how communities have changed over time through urbanization and suburbanization.

1. Thomas Robert Malthus suggested that the world's population was growing more rapidly than the available food supply, and that the gap would increase over time. However, Karl Marx saw capitalism, rather than rising world population, as the real cause of social ills.

2. The primary mechanism for obtaining population information in the United States and most other countries is the **census.**

3. Roughly two-thirds of the world's nations have yet to pass fully through the second stage of **demographic transition.** Thus they continue to experience significant population growth.

4. Developing nations face the prospect of continued population growth because a substantial portion of their population is approaching childbearing age. Some developed nations have begun to stabilize their population growth, however.

5. The most important factors in **migration** tend to be economic— financial failure in the "old country" and a perception of greater economic opportunity elsewhere.

6. Stable **communities** began to develop when people stayed in one place to cultivate crops; eventually, surplus production enabled cities to emerge.

7. Over time, cities changed and developed with their economies. In the Industrial Revolution, the **preindustrial city** of agricultural societies gave way to the **industrial city;** the advent of electronic networking brought with it the **postindustrial city.**

8. Urbanization is evident not only in the United States but throughout the world. By 2010, 22 of the world's cities had populations of more than 10 million.

9. The **urban ecological** approach is functionalist because it emphasizes how different elements in urban areas contribute to social stability.

10. Drawing on conflict theory, **new urban sociology** emphasizes the interplay of a community's political and economic interests, as well as the impact of the global economy on communities in the United States and other countries.

11. Many urban residents are immigrants from other nations who tend to live together in ethnic neighborhoods.

12. In the past three decades, cities have confronted an overwhelming array of economic and social problems, including crime, unemployment, and the deterioration of schools and public transit systems.

13. Suburbanization was the most dramatic population trend in the United States throughout the 20th century. In recent decades, **suburbs** have become more racially and ethnically diverse.

14. Rural communities are economically, ethnically, and racially diverse. Though farming—once the mainstay of rural areas—has declined, new groups are moving in to take advantage of the opportunities rural areas offer.

15. Soaring housing costs, unemployment, cutbacks in public assistance, and rapid population growth have contributed to rising homelessness around the world. Most social policy is directed toward sending the homeless to large shelters.

Key Terms

Aerotropolis An urban community that is centered around an airport and the hotels, office complexes, entertainment venues, and distribution facilities it supports. (page 438)

Birthrate The number of live births per 1,000 population in a given year. Also known as the *crude birthrate*. (440)

Census An enumeration, or counting, of a population. (440)

Community A spatial or political unit of social organization that gives people a sense of belonging, based either on shared residence in a particular place or on a common identity. (438)

Concentric-zone theory A theory of urban growth devised by Ernest Burgess that sees growth in terms of a series of rings radiating from the central business district. (448)

Death rate The number of deaths per 1,000 population in a given year. Also known as the *crude death rate*. (440)

Demographic transition A term used to describe the change from high birthrates and death rates to low birthrates and death rates. (442)

Demography The scientific study of population. (439)

Fertility The level of reproduction in a society. (439)

Gentrification The resettlement of low-income city neighborhoods by prosperous families and business firms. (456)

Growth rate The difference between births and deaths, plus the difference between immigrants and emigrants, per 1,000 population. (441)

Human ecology An area of study that is concerned with the interrelationships between people and their environment. (448)

Industrial city A relatively large city characterized by open competition, an open class system, and elaborate specialization in the manufacturing of goods. (447)

Infant mortality rate The number of deaths of infants under age 1 year per 1,000 live births in a given year. (440)

Life expectancy The median number of years a person can be expected to live under current mortality conditions. (441)

Migration The relatively permanent movement of people, with the purpose of changing their place of residence. (445)

Multiple-nuclei theory A theory of urban growth developed by Harris and Ullman that views growth as emerging from many centers of development, each of which reflects a particular urban need or activity. (448)

New urban sociology An approach to urbanization that considers the interplay of local, national, and worldwide forces and their effect on local space, with special emphasis on the impact of global economic activity. (450)

Population pyramid A special type of bar chart that shows the distribution of a population by gender and age. (442)

Postindustrial city A city in which global finance and the electronic flow of information dominate the economy. (447)

Preindustrial city A city of only a few thousand people that is characterized by a relatively closed class system and limited mobility. (446)

Squatter settlement An area occupied by the very poor on the fringe of a city, in which housing is constructed by the settlers themselves from discarded material. (451)

Suburb According to the Census Bureau, any territory within a metropolitan area that is not included in the central city. (453)

Total fertility rate (TFR) The average number of children born alive to any woman, assuming that she conforms to current fertility rates. (440)

Urban ecology An area of study that focuses on the interrelationships between people and their environment in urban areas. (448)

Urbanism A term used by Louis Wirth to describe distinctive patterns of social behavior evident among city residents. (447)

Vital statistics Records of births, deaths, marriages, and divorces gathered through a registration system maintained by governmental units. (440)

World systems analysis Immanuel Wallerstein's view of the global economic system as one divided between certain industrialized nations that control wealth and developing countries that are controlled and exploited. (450)

Zero population growth (ZPG) The state of a population in which the number of births plus immigrants equals the number of deaths plus emigrants. (444)

TAKING SOCIOLOGY with you

1. Select a social policy issue that particularly interests you and analyze in detail how the size, composition, and distribution of the population of the United States might influence that issue.

2. Go online and look up the Bureau of the Census population statistics for your city, town, or county. Has the population been increasing, decreasing, or holding fairly steady? What accounts for the trend? What statistics can you cite to support your analysis?

3. Contact the mayor or other local official and ask what he or she considers the most pressing problems facing your community. Then examine those problems from the functionalist and conflict perspectives. What solutions do they suggest?

Self-Quiz

Read each question carefully and then select the best answer.

1. Which of the following argued that food supply increases in an arithmetic progression, whereas population expands by a geometric progression?
   a. Thomas Robert Malthus
   b. Karl Marx
   c. Émile Durkheim
   d. Max Weber

2. The final stage in demographic transition is marked by
   a. high birthrates and high death rates.
   b. high birthrates and low death rates.
   c. low birthrates and high death rates.
   d. low birthrates and low death rates.

3. The most recent period of high fertility in the United States, which began after the end of World War II, has often been referred to as the
   a. baby bust.
   b. baby boom.
   c. population bomb.
   d. age of Aquarius.

4. In studying population, which of the following would most interest a sociologist?
   a. the impact of natural disasters on population trends
   b. the relationship between climate and fertility
   c. availability of natural resources, such as oil and arable land, and how it influences mortality rates
   d. social factors that influence population rates and trends

5. Louis Wirth argued that a relatively large and permanent settlement leads to distinctive patterns of behavior, which he called
   a. squatting.
   b. linear development.
   c. urbanism.
   d. gentrification.

6. In comparison with industrial cities, preindustrial cities had
   a. relatively open class systems.
   b. extensive social mobility.
   c. a largely illiterate population.
   d. all of the above.

7. According to Herbert Gans, residents who remain in the city to take advantage of unique cultural and intellectual benefits of the city are called
   a. cosmopolites.
   b. ethnic villagers.
   c. urban villagers.
   d. the trapped.

8. The most dramatic population trend in the United States throughout the 20th century was
   a. urbanization.
   b. suburbanization.
   c. the move to the sun belt.
   d. the move to the "old homestead" in rural areas.

9. In which type of city is there a greater openness to new religious faiths?
   a. preindustrial city
   b. industrial city
   c. postindustrial city
   d. edge city

10. Which of these results from gentrification, according to conflict theorists?
    a. low-income families receive tax breaks
    b. locally owned businesses suffer
    c. poor people are displaced
    d. pollution increases

11. Drawing on several components, including size, composition, and territorial distribution, _____ is the scientific study of population.

12. _____ _____ are records of births, deaths, marriages, and divorces that are gathered through a registration system maintained by governmental units.

13. The _____ _____ is the number of live births per 1,000 population in a given year.

14. A general measure of health used by demographers is _____ _____.

15. Neo-Malthusians are _____ in their condemnation of developed nations, which despite their low birthrates, consume a disproportionately large share of world resources.

16. A less pejorative term for squatter settlements is _____ _____.

17. _____ _____ is concerned with the interrelationships between people and their environment.

18. According to the concentric-zone theory, at the core of the city is the _____ business district.

19. Ferdinand Tönnies used the term _____ to describe a close-knit community where social interaction among people is intimate and familiar.

20. While some observers suggest that the growth of sun-belt cities is due to a "good business climate," _____ theorists counter that this term is actually a euphemism for hefty government subsidies and antilabor policies.

Answers

1 (a); 2 (d); 3 (b); 4 (d); 5 (c); 6 (c); 7 (a); 8 (b); 9 (c); 10 (c); 11 demography; 12 Vital statistics; 13 crude birthrate; 14 life expectancy; 15 Marxist; 16 autonomous settlements; 17 Human ecology; 18 central; 19 Gemeinschaft; 20 conflict

THINKING ABOUT MOVIES

Dark Days

This documentary tells the story of a community of homeless people who live underground near a railroad station in New York City.

Holy Rollers

Two young men from a traditional Jewish community become involved in drug smuggling.

Winter's Bone

In an economically disadvantaged part of rural America, a young woman uses community ties to search for her father.

▶ INSIDE

Activists rally at Toys R Us in Times Square, New York, to voice concern over the presence of toxic chemicals in children's toys. Our health is inextricably linked to our environment, and the use of toxic chemicals in manufacturing imperils both.

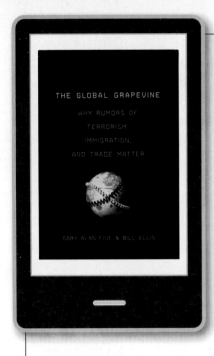

66 In a world so frighteningly diverse, we can conclude that anything is possible. What can we believe and by what standards do we judge? Were Israeli secret agents responsible for the carnage on September 11? Do border-jumping Mexicans deliberately spread deadly flu? Are children's toys manufactured in China maliciously poisoned with lead? Are Caribbean cabana boys waiting to spread AIDS? . . . The comforting and snug local communities that we once knew have been overwhelmed by a splintered and intimidating global community. Whereas in the past the American nation was a mighty fortress, many citizens feel that today its walls have been breached. Anywhere is everywhere, or so it seems.

. . . It is easy to take rumors and legends for granted: we hear and read variations on them on a daily basis. Because they are so much part of our commonplace life, we often minimize them as merely funny and peculiar claims. But that is precisely the point: because they are so much a part of our daily routine, they have real impact. What we think determines how we see the world around us and invisibly influences our political and personal choices. Rumors and legends affect how we live our lives.

Whether the concern is terrorism, immigration, or international trade, Americans—along with citizens of other advanced nations—see threats from abroad. . . . Nations that were proud of their accomplishments, history, patriotism, and personality find these sources of pride under threat from those who are defined as strangers. Unwashed masses seem to threaten our clean lives. Our comfort zones are continuously shrinking. So long as we can maintain our daily habits, we feel comfortable and secure, but when our familiar world changes, due to globalizing forces, we become disoriented. We first see new features of our lives as "strange" and "incomprehensible." It is tempting to perceive such perplexing factors as signs of a loss of control or a threat to our livelihood or our families. What begins as puzzlement and

annoyance can become a profound fear coupled with a readiness to accept accounts of conspiracy and moral decay. By bringing the unexpected close to home, the anxieties and uncertainties created by globalism become crystallized as rumors, legends, and subversion myths. These are claims that we are prepared to accept either with certainty or provisionally, but for which we have little concrete evidence.

Yet, in truth, was the United States ever the insular fortress many politicians invoke? Its original inhabitants, their land taken from them by stealth and force, their numbers decimated by epidemics caused by contact with the European newcomers, justifiably feel that their culture was destroyed by contact with foreigners. But the continued vitality of America has been based on its ability to absorb and accommodate wave after wave of immigrants from colonial times to the present. And it is not only America that is under siege, as other nations have had to cope with the impact of Americans and their culture for decades. While localities and regions have not entirely lost their unique flavor, the expansion of multinational companies, global franchises, rapid immigration, and travel opportunities increase the similarities among places and societies. What made places special threatens to melt into an international soup. As the world has become more tight-knit, both Americans and those influenced by our culture have become nervous about these changes.

The concern extends further because these changes affect Americans individually and collectively. . . . The fact that Americans spread so many rumors about this topic suggests that we doubt our own future. One consequence of the creation of a global social system is that Americans are more aware of once-distant others. Increasingly, we confront strangers in political, economic, or cultural arenas. Some of the information gleaned is accurate; some is wildly, fantastically inaccurate; and much is based on uncertain and imperfect sources. These claims may be amusing, frightening, or both, but the fact that many are accepted reveals how ready people are to believe and shape their actions based on what they have been told. As a result, rumors demand attention. Sometimes we share rumors about terrorist cells planning a new attack on a shopping mall; other times we mutter about illegal immigrants receiving special treatment; and on still other occasions we worry about the importation of illegal drugs or frightening new diseases spread from abroad. Through its ability to make audible the unspoken, rumor provides an opportunity for people and communities to explore how their nation is changing. 99

Through its ability to make audible the unspoken, rumor provides an opportunity for people and communities to explore how their nation is changing.

(Fine and Ellis 2011:1–3) Additional information about this excerpt can be found on the Online Learning Center at www.mhhe.com/schaefer13e.

In this excerpt from *The Global Grapevine: Why Rumors of Terrorism, Immigration, and Trade Matter,* sociologists Gary Fine and Bill Ellis analyze an informal aspect of global information sharing. They are concerned not with official government news releases or with bulletins from overseas financial exchanges, but with rumors—unconfirmed reports that may or may not be accurate, but which can nevertheless have powerful social effects.

Rumors are one form of *collective behavior.* Practically all behavior can be thought of as collective behavior, but sociologists

have given distinct meaning to the term. Neil Smelser (1981:431), a sociologist who specializes in this field of study, has defined **collective behavior** as the "relatively spontaneous and unstructured behavior of a group of people who are reacting to a common influence in an ambiguous situation." Rumors are a form of collective behavior; so is public opinion—people's reactions to shared events such as wars and elections.

What guides and governs collective behavior? Why do people participate in fads, and what causes mass panics? How do new social movements spread their message to others? In this chapter we will examine a number of sociological theories of collective behavior, including the emergent-norm, value-added, and assembling perspectives. We will give particular attention to certain types of collective behavior, among them crowd behavior, disaster behavior, fads and fashions, panics and crazes, rumors, public opinion, and social movements. We will also look at the role communications technology plays in globalizing collective behavior. Sociologists study collective behavior because it incorporates activities that we all engage in on a regular basis. Moreover, they acknowledge the crucial role that social movements can play in mobilizing discontented members of a society and initiating social change. In the Social Policy section, we will focus on the role that the social movement for disability rights plays in promoting change.

Theories of Collective Behavior

In 1979, 11 rock fans died of suffocation after a crowd outside Cincinnati's Riverfront Stadium pushed to gain entrance to a concert by The Who. In 2003, 100 people died after a pyrotechnics display by Great White ignited a fire at a nightclub in West Warwick, Rhode Island. Many had watched excitedly as flames engulfed the bandstand, thinking they were part of the act. And in 2008, a healthy 34-year-old security guard was crushed to death—still standing but unable to breathe—as excited shoppers at a Walmart store in Long Island, New York, surged through the doors in quest of Black Friday bargains.

Like these incidents, collective behavior is usually unstructured and spontaneous. Its fluidity makes it more difficult for sociologists to generalize about people's behavior in such situations. Nevertheless, sociologists have developed various theoretical perspectives that can help us to study—and deal with in a constructive manner—crowds, riots, fads, and other types of collective behavior.

Because collective behavior is often unstructured and spontaneous, it can prove deadly. So strong was the surge of shoppers when this Walmart store opened on the day after Thanksgiving, a security guard was asphyxiated.

Emergent-Norm Perspective

Early writings on collective behavior implied that crowds are basically ungovernable. However, that is not always the case. In many situations, crowds are effectively governed by norms and procedures, including queuing, or waiting in line. We routinely encounter queues when we await service in a fast-food restaurant or bank, or when we enter or exit a movie theater or football stadium. Normally, physical barriers, such as guardrails and checkout counters, help to regulate queuing. When massive crowds are involved, ushers or security personnel may be present to assist in the orderly movement of the crowd. Nevertheless, there are times when such measures prove inadequate, as the examples just given and the one that follows demonstrate.

In December 1991, more than 5,000 people showed up early for a heavily promoted celebrity basketball game at the City College gymnasium in New York City. Seeing the size of the crowd, many of them must have realized that they could not all fit into the gym, which would accommodate only 2,730 people. As frustrated patrons waited to see which of them would be allowed in, restlessness and discontent swept through the crowd, and sporadic fights broke out.

When the doors to the gym finally opened, only 50 people at a time were allowed to enter. They then had to descend two flights of stairs and enter the gym through a single unlocked entrance—a maddeningly slow process in the overcrowded passageway. Finally, well past the game's starting time and with the arena more than full, the doors to the gym were closed. As rumors spread outside the building that the game was beginning, more than 1,000 additional fans poured through the building's entrance and headed for the stairs. Trapped between the locked gymnasium doors and those pushing down the stairs behind them, 9 young men and women died and 29 were injured through the sheer pressure of bodies pressing against walls and doors (Mollen 1992).

Sociologists Ralph Turner and Lewis Killian (1987) have offered a view of collective behavior that is helpful in assessing a tragic event like this. It begins with the assumption that a large crowd, such as a group of rock or soccer fans, is governed by expectations of proper behavior just as much as four people playing doubles tennis. But during an episode of collective behavior, a definition of what behavior is appropriate or not emerges from the crowd. Turner and Killian call this view the **emergent-norm perspective**. Like other social norms, the emergent norm reflects shared convictions held by members of the group and is enforced through sanctions. The new norm of proper behavior may arise in what seems at first to be an ambiguous situation. There is latitude for a wide range of acts within a general framework established by the emergent norm (for a critique of this perspective, see McPhail 1991).

Using the emergent-norm perspective, we can see that fans outside the charity basketball game at City College found themselves in an ambiguous situation. Normal procedures of crowd control, such

as orderly queues, were rapidly dissolving. Simultaneously, a new norm was emerging: it is acceptable to push forward, even if the people in front protest. Some members of the crowd—especially those with valid tickets—may have felt that their push forward was justified as a way of ensuring that they would get to see the game. Others pushed forward simply to relieve the physical pressure of those pushing behind them. Even individuals who rejected the emergent norm may have felt afraid to oppose it, fearing ridicule or injury. Thus, conforming behavior, which we usually associate with highly structured situations, was evident in this rather chaotic crowd, as it had been at the concerts by The Who and Great White and at Walmart's Black Friday sale. However, it would be misleading to assume that these fans acted simply as a united, collective unit in creating a dangerous situation.

Value-Added Perspective

Neil Smelser (1962) proposed a different sociological explanation for collective behavior. He used the **value-added model** to explain how broad social conditions are transformed in a definite pattern into some form of collective behavior. This model outlines six important determinants of collective behavior: structural conduciveness, structural strain, a generalized belief, a precipitating factor, mobilization for action, and the exercise of social control.

In Smelser's view, certain elements must be present for an incident of collective behavior to take place. He used the term *structural conduciveness* to indicate that the organization of society can facilitate the emergence of conflicting interests. Structural conduciveness was evident in the former East Germany in 1989, just a year before the collapse of the ruling Communist Party and the reunification of Germany. The government of East Germany was extremely unpopular, and there was growing freedom to publicly express

and be exposed to new and challenging viewpoints. Such structural conduciveness makes collective behavior possible, though not inevitable.

The second determinant of collective behavior, *structural strain,* occurs when the conduciveness of the social structure to potential conflict gives way to a perception that conflicting interests do, in fact, exist. The intense desire of many East Germans to travel to or emigrate to western European countries placed great strain on the social control exercised by the Communist Party. Such structural strain contributes to what Smelser calls a *generalized belief*—a shared view of reality that redefines social action and serves to guide behavior. The overthrow of communist rule in East Germany and other Soviet-bloc nations occurred in part as a result of a generalized belief that the communist regimes were oppressive and that popular resistance *could* lead to social change.

Smelser suggests that a specific event or incident, known as a *precipitating factor,* triggers collective behavior. The event may grow out of the social structure, but whatever its origins, it contributes to the strains and beliefs shared by a group or community. For example, studies of race riots have found that interracial fights or arrests and searches of minority individuals by police officers often precede disturbances. The 1992 riots in South Central Los Angeles, which claimed 58 lives, were sparked by the acquittal of four White police officers charged after the videotaped beating of Rodney King, a Black construction worker.

According to Smelser, the four determinants just identified are necessary for collective behavior to occur. In addition to these factors, the group must be *mobilized for action.* An extended thundershower or severe snowstorm may preclude such mobilization. People are more likely to come together on weekends than on weekdays, and in the evening rather than during the day.

The *manner in which social control is exercised*—both formally and informally—can be significant in determining whether the preceding factors will end in collective behavior. Stated simply, social control may prevent, delay, or interrupt a collective outburst. In some instances, those using social control may be guilty of misjudgments that intensify the severity of an outbreak. Many observers believe that the Los Angeles

police did not respond fast enough when the rioting began in 1992, which allowed the level of violence to escalate.

Sociologists have questioned the validity of both the emergent-norm and value-added perspectives because of their imprecise definitions and the difficulty of testing them empirically. For example, some have criticized the emergent-norm perspective for being too vague in defining what constitutes a norm; others have challenged the value-added model for lack of specificity in defining generalized belief and structural strain. Of these two theories, the emergent-norm perspective appears to offer a more useful explanation of society-wide episodes of collective behavior, such as crazes and fashions, than the value-added approach (M. Brown and Goldin 1973; Quarantelli and Hundley 1975; K. Tierney 1980).

Smelser's value-added model, however, represents an advance over earlier theories that treated crowd behavior as being dominated by irrational, extreme impulses. The value-added approach firmly relates episodes of collective behavior to the overall social structure of a society (for a critique, see McPhail 1991, 1994).

Assembling Perspective

A series of football victory celebrations at the University of Texas that had spilled over into the main streets of Austin came under the scrutiny of sociologists (Snow et al. 1981). Some participants had actively tried to recruit passersby for the celebrations by thrusting out open palms "to get five," or by yelling at drivers to honk their horns. In fact, encouraging further assembling became a preoccupation of the celebrators. Whenever passersby were absent, participants were relatively quiet. As we have seen, a key determinant of collective behavior is mobilization for action. How do people come together to undertake collective action?

Clark McPhail, perhaps the most prolific researcher of collective behavior in the past four decades, sees people and organizations consciously responding to one another's actions. Building on the interactionist approach, McPhail and Miller (1973) introduced the concept of the assembling process. In their **assembling perspective**, they sought to examine how and why people move from different points in space to a common location. Before the advent of new technologies, the process of assembling for collective action was slower and more deliberate than it is today, but McPhail's approach still applies.

A basic distinction has been made between two types of assemblies. **Periodic assemblies** include recurring, relatively routine gatherings of people such as work groups, college classes, and season-ticket holders in an athletic series. These assemblies are characterized by advance scheduling and recurring attendance of the majority of participants. For example, members of an introductory sociology class may gather for lectures every Monday, Wednesday, and Friday morning at 10 a.m. In contrast, **nonperiodic assemblies** include demonstrations, parades, and gatherings at the scene of fires, accidents, and arrests. Such assemblies, which often result from word-of-mouth information, are generally less formal than periodic assemblies. One example would be an organized rally held at Gallaudet University in 1988 to back a deaf person for president of the school for

Antiwar protesters in front of the White House rally against their nation's participation in the military intervention in Libya in 2011. According to the assembling perspective, nonperiodic assemblies like this one are relatively spontaneous, loosely organized reactions to galvanizing events.

deaf students—see the photo of the campaign leaflet on page 472 (McPhail 2006, 2008; D. L. Miller 2000).

These three approaches to collective behavior give us deeper insight into relatively spontaneous and unstructured situations. Although episodes of collective behavior may seem irrational to outsiders, norms emerge among the participants, and organized efforts are made to assemble at a certain time and place.

use your sociological *imagination*

Think about the practice of assembling to attend class or to study in the library. On a daily basis, how is this practice affected by the direct or indirect actions of your fellow students, co-workers, relatives, or teammates?

Forms of Collective Behavior

Do you remember the Ninja Turtles? Did you collect Beanie Babies when you were young? Any grunge clothes or tube tops lurking in your closet? These are all fads and fashions that depend on collective behavior. Using the emergent-norm, value-added, and assembling perspectives along with other aspects of sociological study, sociologists have investigated many forms of collective behavior—not only fads and fashions but also crowds, disaster behavior, panics and crazes, rumors, and public opinion. In this section we will study all these forms of collective behavior. The section that follows will be devoted to the most significant form of collective behavior, social movements.

A **crowd** is a temporary gathering of people in close proximity who share a common focus or interest. Spectators at a baseball game, participants at a pep rally, and rioters are all examples of a crowd. Sociologists have been interested in the characteristics that are common to crowds. Of course, it can be difficult to generalize, since the nature of crowds varies dramatically. Think about how hostages on a hijacked airplane might feel, as opposed to participants in a religious revival.

Like other forms of collective behavior, crowds are not totally lacking in structure. Even during riots, participants are governed by identifiable social norms and exhibit definite patterns of behavior. In fact, crowds are no more emotional, suggestible, or destructive than any other social gathering. Sociologists Richard Berk and Howard Aldrich (1972) analyzed patterns of vandalism in 15 cities in the United States during the riots of the 1960s. They found that the stores of merchants who were perceived as exploitative were more likely to be attacked, while private homes and public agencies with positive reputations were more likely to be spared. Apparently, looters had reached a collective agreement as to what constituted a "proper" or "improper" target for destruction. Today, this type of information can be shared instantly via text-messaging.

The emergent-norm perspective suggests that during urban rioting, a new social norm that basically condones looting is accepted, at least temporarily. The norms of respect for private property—as well as norms involving obedience to the law—are replaced by a concept of all goods being community property. All desirable items, including those behind locked doors, can be used for the "general welfare." In effect, the emergent norm allows looters to take what they regard as properly theirs—a scenario that was played out in Baghdad after the collapse of Saddam Hussein's regime in 2003. Yet not everyone participates in the free-for-all. Typically, most community residents reject the new norm, and either stand by passively or attempt to stop the wholesale theft (Couch 1968; Quarantelli and Dynes 1970; see also McPhail 1991, 2006, 2008).

Crowds have taken on new meaning in the Internet age. The term *crowdsourcing* has been coined to describe the online practice of asking Internet surfers for ideas or participation in an activity or movement. The compilation of Wikipedia, an online encyclopedia that is written and edited entirely by unrelated users, is the best-known example of crowdsourcing. Online crowds have also helped astronomers to map the galaxy, political activists to track politicians' travels, and marketers to spread the word about a new product (*The Economist* 2008b:10).

Disaster Behavior

Newspapers, television reports, and even rumors bring word of many disasters around the world. The term **disaster** refers to a sudden or disruptive event or set of events that overtaxes a community's resources, so that outside aid is necessary. Traditionally, disasters have been catastrophes related to nature, such as earthquakes, floods, and fires. Yet in an industrial age, natural disasters have been joined by such "technological disasters" as airplane crashes, industrial explosions, nuclear power plant meltdowns, and massive chemical poisonings. However, there is no real distinction between the two types of disaster. As environmentalists have observed, human practices either contribute to or trigger natural disasters. Building in floodplains, engineering natural waterways, clear-cutting forests, and erecting rigid structures in

When a terrorist attack destroyed New York City's emergency command center, officials quickly set up a new one to direct the search and recovery effort. Even in times of unimaginable disaster, people respond in predictable ways.

earthquake zones all create the potential for disaster (Marshall and Picou 2008).

Disaster Research Sociologists have made enormous strides in disaster research, despite the problems inherent in this type of investigation. The work of the Disaster Research Center at the University of Delaware has been especially important. The center has teams of trained researchers prepared to leave for the site of any disaster on four hours' notice. Their field kits include identification material, recording equipment, and interview guidelines for use in various types of disasters. En route to the scene, these researchers try to become informed about the conditions they may encounter. On arrival, they establish a communication post to coordinate fieldwork and maintain contact with the center's headquarters.

Since its founding in 1963, the Disaster Research Center has conducted more than 685 field studies of natural and technological disasters in the United States and other nations. Its research has been used to develop effective planning in the delivery of emergency health care, the establishment and operation of rumor-control centers, the coordination of mental health services after disasters, and the implementation of disaster-preparedness and emergency-response programs. The center has also provided training and field research for graduate students, who maintain a professional commitment to disaster research and often go on to work for disaster service organizations such as the Red Cross and civil defense agencies (Disaster Research Center 2011; K. Tierney 2007).

Case Studies: Collapse of the World Trade Center and Hurricane Katrina Two devastating but very different disasters have provided fascinating case studies for researchers to examine. One was the collapse of the World Trade Center following the terrorist attack of September 11, 2001, which caused nearly three thousand deaths and billions of dollars worth of property damage. The other was the unprecedented destruction caused by Hurricane Katrina in August 2005, which left hundreds of thousands of people homeless.

Sociologists who have studied such disasters have found some common patterns in people's response. Disasters are often followed by the creation of an emergency operations group, which coordinates both public services and some private-sector services, such as food distribution. Decision making becomes more centralized during these periods than it is in normal times. Such was the case on September 11, 2001. New York City's well-designed Emergency Management Center, located in the World Trade Center, was destroyed when the building collapsed and all power at nearby City Hall was cut off. Yet within hours, both an incident command post and a new emergency operations center had been established to direct the search and recovery effort at the 16-acre site. Shortly thereafter came a victims' center, information kiosks, and an office for issuing death certificates, staffed around the clock by counselors, as well as facilities for serving meals to rescue workers. To identify potential hazards to rescuers and survey what had become a gigantic crime scene, police and public safety officials turned to computer maps and aerial photographs. They also designated places where victims could be identified, human resource functions relocated, and charitable contributions collected (Wachtendorf 2002).

Hurricane Katrina was an entirely different kind of disaster. Although unlike September 11, the storm's arrival was expected, its path of destruction was much greater, covering 90,000 square miles—an enormous area compared to the World Trade Center. In the four years since September 11, 2001, all levels of government in the United States had worked to improve their response to disasters, whatever the origin. Yet while the destruction of low-lying coastal areas in the Southeast by a catastrophic hurricane could have been anticipated, days passed before authorities managed to mount a full-scale rescue effort in response to Katrina. With streets flooded and communications knocked out, stranded residents waited on their rooftops for food, water, or a helicopter lift, wondering where the rescue teams were.

What went wrong? A monumental lack of coordination stymied government authorities. Confusion reigned among the numerous agencies involved in the effort, including the Federal Emergency Management Agency (FEMA), which had been reorganized under the authority of the Department of Homeland Security less than two years earlier; the National Guard, with a different command structure in each state; the active-duty military; and literally thousands of city, county, and state governments, each with its own sphere of authority. Part of the problem was that when federal officials revised the nation's emergency response plan following September 11, they relied on local government to manage in the first few days after a disaster. However, Katrina overwhelmed both local police and National Guard units stationed near the Gulf. In this case, the centralization of decision making that typically follows a disaster occurred over a period of days, not hours. In reviewing what happened, federal officials revised their emergency-response plan and reexamined laws governing change-of-command authority to expedite federal and military aid when necessary.

The long-term recovery from Katrina was even more complicated than the rescue operation. In contrast to the World Trade Center's collapse, Hurricane Katrina had a disproportionately large effect on the poor, who possessed few if any resources to

A helicopter hovers over a flooded New Orleans neighborhood, searching for survivors on the rooftops. In the days that followed the storm, federal, state, and local authorities struggled to coordinate their rescue efforts, as thousands of stranded residents went without food or water.

draw on in the emergency. Lacking a nest egg, these families had little choice in where to relocate, and they faced much more difficulty than others in finding permanent shelter and employment.

Disaster research has shown that in the wake of calamity, maintaining and restoring communications is vital not just to directing relief efforts, but to reducing survivors' anxiety. On September 11, most cell phones in Manhattan were rendered useless by the destruction of communications towers and relay stations. To contact loved ones or to plan their escape from a city clogged with emergency vehicles, people stood in line at pay phones. In the days to follow, families seeking information about their loved ones posted fliers at makeshift information centers. Following Hurricane Katrina, survivors who had been dispersed to shelters across the nation—often without knowing whether family members were alive or dead—turned to special websites to find their kin, business associates, teachers, and even pets. In the aftermath of unimaginable disaster, people and organizations responded in predictable ways (Dreifus 2003, 2004; Hall 2005; P. Light 2005).

Fads and Fashions

An almost endless list of objects and behavior patterns seems temporarily to catch the fancy of adults and children. Think about Silly

Putty, Hula Hoops, the Rubik's Cube, break dancing, Sudoku puzzles, Nintendo video, and mosh pits. Fads and fashions are sudden movements toward the acceptance of some lifestyle or particular taste in clothing, music, or recreation (Aguirre et al. 1988; R. Johnson 1985).

Fads are temporary patterns of behavior involving large numbers of people; they spring up independently of preceding trends and do not give rise to successors. In contrast, **fashions** are pleasurable mass involvements that feature a certain amount of acceptance by society and have a line of historical continuity (J. Lofland 1981, 1985). Thus, punk haircuts would be considered a fashion, part of the constantly changing standards of hair length and style, whereas dancing the Macarena would be considered a fad of the mid-1990s.

Typically, when people think of *fashions,* they think of clothing, particularly women's clothing. In reality, fads and fashions enter every aspect of life in which choices are not dictated by sheer necessity—vehicles, sports, music, drama, beverages, art, and even the selection of pets. Any area of our lives that is subject to continuing change is open to fads and fashions. There is a clear commercial motive behind these norms of collective behavior. For example, in about seven months of 1955, retailers sold over $100 million of Davy Crockett items (worth over $700 million in 2002 dollars), including coonskin caps, toy rifles, knives, camping gear, cameras, and jigsaw puzzles. In 1999 Nintendo took in $5 billion from sales of Pokémon paraphernalia, ranging from virtual pets to compact discs (S. King 1999).

Fads and fashions allow people to identify with something different from the dominant institutions and symbols of a culture. Members of a subculture can break with tradition while remaining in with a significant reference group of peers. Fads are generally short-lived and tend to be viewed with amusement or lack of interest by most nonparticipants. Fashions, in contrast, often have wider implications, because they can reflect (or give the impression of) wealth and status.

In the new fad called *planking,* facilitated by the Internet, people pretend they are wooden planks and rest rigid—often precariously—on trees, police cars, basketball hoops, or just about anything else. Often, someone photographs the stunt and shares the image through social media. This photograph was taken in York, England.

use your sociological *imagination*

List some current fads and fashions. Now think back to when you were in elementary school. Can you name at least two fads from that time that seem to have faded away?

Panics and Crazes

Panics and crazes both represent responses to some generalized belief. A **craze** is an exciting mass involvement that lasts for a relatively long period (J. Lofland 1981, 1985). For example, in late 1973, a press release from a Wisconsin congressman described how the federal bureaucracy had failed to contract for enough toilet paper for government buildings. Then, on December 19, as part of his nightly monologue, *Tonight Show* host Johnny Carson suggested that it would not be strange if the entire nation experienced a shortage of toilet paper. Millions of people took his humorous comment seriously and immediately began stockpiling the item out of fear that it would soon be unavailable. Shortly thereafter, as a consequence of this craze, a shortage of toilet paper actually did occur. Its effects were felt into 1974 (Malcolm 1974; *Money* 1987).

In contrast, a **panic** is a fearful arousal or collective flight based on a generalized belief that may or may not be accurate. In a panic, people commonly think there is insufficient time or inadequate means to avoid injury. Panics often occur on battlefields, in overcrowded burning buildings, or during stock market crashes. The key distinction between panics and crazes is that panics are flights *from* something, whereas crazes are movements *toward* something.

One of the most famous cases of panic in the United States was touched off by a media event: the 1938 Halloween eve radio dramatization of H. G. Wells's science fiction novel *The War of the Worlds.* This broadcast told realistically of an invasion from Mars, with interplanetary visitors landing in northern New Jersey and taking over New York City 15 minutes later. The announcer indicated at the beginning of the broadcast that the account was fictional, but about 80 percent of the listeners tuned in late. Many became frightened by what they assumed to be a news report.

Some accounts have exaggerated the extent of people's reactions to *The War of the Worlds.* One report concluded that "people all over the United States were praying, crying, fleeing frantically to escape death from the Martians." In contrast, a CBS national survey of listeners found that only 20 percent were genuinely scared by the broadcast. Although perhaps a million people *reacted* to the program, many reacted by switching to other stations to see if the "news" was being carried elsewhere. This "invasion from outer space" set off a limited panic rather than mass hysteria (Roger Brown 1954; Cantril 1940; Houseman 1972).

It is often believed that people who are engaged in panics or crazes are unaware of their actions, but that is certainly not the case. As the emergent-norm perspective suggests, people take cues from one another about how to act during such forms of collective behavior. Even in the midst of an escape from a life-threatening situation, such as a fire in a crowded theater, people do not tend to run in a headlong stampede.

"Did you hear that?" Rumors are a common type of social interaction that underscores shared understandings—even if the information they convey is incorrect. Today more and more rumors, many of them personal and highly inflammatory, are spread through the Internet.

Rather, they adjust their behavior on the basis of the perceived circumstances and the conduct of others who are assembling in a given location. To outside observers studying the events, people's decisions may seem foolish (pushing against a locked door) or suicidal (jumping from a balcony). Yet for that individual at that moment, the action may genuinely seem appropriate—or the only desperate choice available (L. Clarke 2002; Quarantelli 1957).

Rumors

"Oscar Mayer doesn't support the troops in Iraq and Afghanistan." Although this accusation was a hoax, e-mail kept it circulating for years on the Internet. Oscar Mayer is certainly not the first corporation to become the target of baseless allegations. However, the Internet lends an air of authenticity to such rumors, allowing them to spread very quickly. Not surprisingly, businesses that have been victimized in this way turn back to the Internet to defend themselves. On its website, Oscar Mayer now publicizes its long history of providing hot dogs and deli meats to soldiers, sailors, airmen and women, and Marines (Kraft Foods 2009).

None of us is immune to hearing or starting such rumors. A **rumor** is a piece of information gathered informally that is used to interpret an ambiguous situation. Rumors serve a function by providing a group with a shared belief. As a group strives for consensus, members eliminate those rumors that are least useful or credible. Research reveals that in the workplace, rumors about what is or may be happening are usually highly accurate. Therefore, rumors can serve as a means of adapting to change. If a business is about to be taken over by another firm, rumors will usually abound as to the significance the move will have for personnel. Gradually, such rumors

are either verified or discarded, but the very exchange of rumors allows people to cope with changes over which they have little control. Scary rumors probably spread the fastest, because fear induces stress and stress is reduced by sharing the fear with others. Moreover, some people enjoy provoking fear in others (DiFonzo and Bordia 2007; D. E. Miller 2006; Shibutani 1966).

The attack on the Pentagon and the World Trade Center produced a flurry of rumors. According to one false account, a police officer "surfed" a steel beam down 86 floors as one of the towers collapsed. Given the role of the media in covering the event, many rumors centered on them. For example, one rumor suggested that a CNN film of Palestinians dancing in the streets after the attack was actually file footage photographed during the Gulf War. In Pakistan, rumors spread that the vivid photos of the hijacked planes crashing into the World Trade Center had actually been staged. Like these examples, rumors often reinforce people's ideologies and their suspicion of the mass media (Fine and Ellis 2011; Slackman 2008).

Publics and Public Opinion

The least organized and most individualized form of collective behavior is the public. The term **public** refers to a dispersed group of people, not necessarily in contact with one another, who share an interest in an issue. As the term is used in the study of collective behavior, the public does not include everyone. Rather, it is a collective of people who focus on some issue, engage in discussion, agree or disagree, and sometimes dissolve when the issue has been decided (Blumer 1955, 1969; R. Turner and Killian 1987).

The term **public opinion** refers to expressions of attitudes on matters of public policy that are communicated to decision makers. The last part of this definition is particularly important. Theorists of collective behavior see no public opinion without both a public and a decision maker. In studying public opinion,

TREND SPOTTING

Gun Control: The Public Speaks

Every year, poll takers survey public opinion on a wide variety of topics. Many of the questions they ask, such as voters' opinions of particular candidates for elective office, are time-specific. Other questions that have been asked for decades, such as "Should it be legal for a White person to marry a Black person?" have been rendered obsolete by changing social norms.

One question that has spanned the last two generations concerns handgun controls. Since 1959, national surveys have regularly included the question "Do you think there should or should not be a law that would ban the possession of handguns, except by the police and other authorized persons?" Despite several attempts on the lives of presidents, as well as the shooting of Congresswoman Gabrielle Giffords in Tucson, Arizona, in January 2011, the public generally opposes handgun controls. Over the decades, in fact, support for such controls has declined from 60 percent in 1959 to around 40 percent in the 1980s, and a low of 29 percent in 2010.

Measuring public opinion on a complex issue like firearms control can be difficult, because many people distinguish between different kinds of legislation. For example, some people who support private purchases of semi-automatic weapons may wish to restrict the right to carry a handgun as a concealed weapon. The man who shot Congresswoman Giffords bought his semi-automatic pistol legally and was carrying it as a concealed weapon—also legal in Arizona—when he approached the shopping center where he shot Giffords. Despite such complexities, a drop in approval from 60 percent to 29 percent is difficult to interpret as anything other than declining enthusiasm for handgun controls.

Form	Definition	Example
Crowd	Temporary gathering of people in close proximity who share a common focus or interest	Political or team rally
Disaster	Sudden or disruptive event or set of events that overtaxes a community's resources, so that outside aid is necessary	Response to a tornado, hurricane, or refinery fire
Fad	Temporary pattern of behavior that involves large numbers of people and is independent of preceding trends	Backpack zipper pulls (charms, cartoon characters, superheroes)
Fashion	Pleasurable mass involvement that has a line of historical continuity	Designer purses
Panic	Fearful arousal or collective flight based on a generalized belief that may or may not be accurate	Travel cancellations during an epidemic
Craze	Exciting mass involvement that lasts for a relatively long period	Traveling fans of a music group or sports team
Rumor	Piece of information gathered informally that is used to interpret an ambiguous situation	Fabrication of U.S. moon landings using special effects
Public	Dispersed group of people, not necessarily in contact with one another, who share an interest in an issue	Environmentalists
Public opinion	Expressions of attitudes on matters of public policy that are communicated to decision makers	Views on global warming
Social movement	Organized collective activity to bring about or resist fundamental change in an existing group or society	Gay rights movement

we are not concerned with the formation of an *individual's* attitudes on social and political issues. Instead, we focus on the ways in which a public's attitudes are communicated to decision makers, and on the ultimate outcome of the public's attempts to influence policymaking (R. Turner and Killian 1987).

Polls and surveys play a major role in assessing public opinion. Using the techniques for developing reliable questionnaire and interview schedules, survey specialists conduct studies of public opinion for business firms (market analyses), the government, the mass media (program ratings), and of course, politicians. Survey data have become extremely influential not only in preselecting the products we buy but in determining which political candidates are likely to win an election and even which potential Supreme Court nominees should be selected (Brower 1988).

Today's political polls are well-constructed surveys based on representative sampling techniques. As a result, their projections of presidential elections often fall within a few percentage points of the actual vote. In marked contrast to these polls, some surveys are downright misleading, such as those in which people are asked to text a certain number to register an opinion.

Table 21-1 summarizes the 10 forms of collective behavior that sociologists study, including social movements, the topic of the next section.

use your sociological *imagination*

Can you recall a time when you changed your view on some issue after hearing or reading about prevailing public opinion on that issue?

Social Movements

Although such factors as the physical environment, population, technology, and social inequality serve as sources of change, it is the *collective* effort of individuals organized in social movements that ultimately leads to change. Sociologists use the term **social movements** to refer to organized collective activities to bring about or resist fundamental change in an existing group or society (Benford 1992). Herbert Blumer (1955:19) recognized the special importance of social movements when he defined them as "collective enterprises to establish a new order of life."

In many nations, including the United States, social movements have had a dramatic impact on the course of history and the evolution of the social structure. Consider the actions of abolitionists, suffragists, civil rights workers, and activists opposed to the war in Vietnam. Members of each social movement stepped outside traditional channels for bringing about social change, yet each had a noticeable influence on public policy. In Eastern Europe, equally dramatic collective efforts helped to topple communist regimes in a largely peaceful manner, in nations that many observers had thought were "immune" to such social change (Ramet 1991).

Though social movements imply the existence of conflict, we can also analyze their activities from a functionalist perspective. Even when they are unsuccessful, social movements contribute to the formation of public opinion. Initially, people thought the ideas of Margaret Sanger and other early advocates of birth control were radical, yet contraceptives are now widely available in the United States.

Because social movements know no borders, even nationalistic movements are deeply influenced by global events. Increasingly, social movements are taking on an international dimension from the start. Global enterprises, in particular, lend themselves to targeting through international mobilization, whether they are corporations like McDonald's or governmental bodies like the World Trade Organization. Global activism is not new, however; it began with the writing of Karl Marx, who sought to mobilize oppressed peoples in other industrialized countries. Today, activist networking is facilitated by the Internet. Participation in transnational activism is much wider now than in the past, and passions are quicker to ignite.

How and why do social movements emerge? Obviously, people are often discontented with the way things are. But what causes them to organize at a particular moment in a collective effort to effect change? Sociologists rely on two explanations for why people mobilize: the relative deprivation and resource mobilization approaches.

use your sociological *imagination*

What social movements are most visible on your campus? In the community where you live?

Relative Deprivation Approach

Those members of a society who feel most frustrated and disgruntled by social and economic conditions are not necessarily the worst off in an objective sense. Social scientists have long recognized that what is most significant is the way in which people *perceive* their situation. As Karl Marx pointed out, although the misery of the workers was important to their perception of their oppressed state, so was their position *in relation to* the capitalist ruling class (Marx and Engels [1847] 1955).

The term **relative deprivation** is defined as the conscious feeling of a negative discrepancy between legitimate expectations and present actualities (J. Wilson 1973). In other words, things aren't as good as you hoped they would be. Such a state

In 2010, protesters in London disguised themselves as characters in the movie *Avatar* to draw attention to the plight of an indigenous tribe in India. The Dongria Kondh people's way of life, they charged, was threatened by a multinational corporation's plan to construct a mine on their land. The Indian government blocked the project, agreeing with protesters that it would have violated the tribe's rights.

may be characterized by scarcity rather than a complete lack of necessities (as we saw in the distinction between absolute and relative poverty in Chapter 9). A relatively deprived person is dissatisfied because he or she feels downtrodden relative to some appropriate reference group. Thus, blue-collar workers who live in two-family houses on small plots of land—though hardly at the bottom of the economic ladder—may nevertheless feel deprived in comparison to corporate managers and professionals who live in lavish homes in exclusive suburbs.

In addition to the feeling of relative deprivation, two other elements must be present before discontent will be channeled into a social movement. People must feel that they have a *right* to their goals, that they deserve better than what they have. At the same time, the disadvantaged group must perceive that its goals cannot be attained through conventional means. This belief may or may not be correct. Whichever is the case, the group will not mobilize into a social movement unless there is a shared perception that members can end their relative deprivation only through collective action (Morrison 1971).

Critics of this approach have noted that people don't need to feel deprived to be moved to act. In addition, this approach fails to explain why certain feelings of deprivation are transformed into social movements, whereas in similar situations, no collective effort is made to reshape society. Consequently, in recent

Two members of People for the Ethical Treatment of Animals (PETA) protest against the killing of animals for fur coats. Social movements like PETA seek public attention for the positions they espouse.

years, sociologists have paid increasing attention to the forces needed to bring about the emergence of social movements (Alain 1985; Finkel and Rule 1987; Orum and Dale 2009).

Resource Mobilization Approach

It takes more than desire to start a social movement. It helps to have money, political influence, access to the media, and personnel. The term **resource mobilization** refers to the ways in which a social movement utilizes such resources. The success of a movement for change will depend in good part on what resources it has and how effectively it mobilizes them. In other words, recruiting adherents and marshalling resources is critical to the growth and success of social movements (Gamson 1989; Tilly 1964, 2003; Walder 2009).

Sociologist Anthony Oberschall (1973:199) has argued that to sustain social protest or resistance, there must be an "organizational base and continuity of leadership." As people become part of a social movement, norms develop to guide their behavior. Members of the movement may be expected to attend regular meetings of organizations, pay dues, recruit new adherents, and boycott "enemy" products or speakers.

Leadership is a central factor in the mobilization of the discontented into social movements. Often, a movement will be led by a charismatic figure, such as Dr. Martin Luther King Jr. As Max Weber described it in 1904, *charisma* is that quality of an individual that sets him or her apart from ordinary people. Of course, charisma can fade abruptly, which helps to account for the fragility of certain social movements (Morris 2000).

Many social movements are mobilized by institutional insiders. During the nationwide debate of the Obama administration's plan for health care reform in 2009, for example, health insurance companies encouraged their employees to attend the forums arranged by the White House. Managers distributed "Town Hall Tips" that included a list of concerns employees could raise and suggestions on how to make their comments as personal as possible, by talking about their own health issues (E. Walker 2010).

Why do certain individuals join a social movement while others who are in similar situations do not? Some of them are recruited to join. Karl Marx recognized the importance of recruitment when he called on workers to become *aware* of their oppressed status and to develop a class consciousness. Like theorists of the resource mobilization approach, Marx held that a social movement (specifically, the revolt of the proletariat) would require leaders to sharpen the awareness of the oppressed. They would need to help workers to overcome feelings of **false consciousness**, or attitudes that do not reflect workers' objective position, in order to organize a revolutionary movement. Similarly, one of the challenges faced by women's liberation activists of the late 1960s and early 1970s was to convince women that they were being deprived of their rights and of socially valued resources.

Gender and Social Movements

Sociologists point out that gender is an important element in understanding social movements. In our male-dominated society, women find it more difficult than men to assume leadership positions in social movement organizations. Though women often serve disproportionately as volunteers in these movements, their work is not always recognized, nor are their voices as easily heard as men's. Gender bias causes the real extent of their influence to be overlooked. Indeed, traditional examination of the sociopolitical system tends to focus on such male-dominated corridors of power as legislatures and corporate

Gallaudet University in Washington, D.C., is the only four-year liberal arts college for deaf students in the United States. A leaflet (left) was distributed in 1988 as part of a successful effort by students, faculty, and alumni to force the appointment of the university's first deaf president. In 2007, after that president's retirement, students protested once again over the election process (right). The mobilization of resources is one key to the success of a social movement.

boardrooms, to the neglect of more female-dominated domains such as households, community-based groups, and faith-based networks. But efforts to influence family values, child rearing, relationships between parents and schools, and spiritual values are clearly significant to a culture and society (Ferree and Merrill 2000; Noonan 1995).

Scholars of social movements now realize that gender can affect even the way we view organized efforts to bring about or resist change. For example, an emphasis on using rationality and cold logic to achieve goals helps to obscure the importance of passion and emotion in successful social movements. It would be difficult to find any movement—from labor battles to voting rights to animal rights—in which passion was not part of the consensus-building force. Yet calls for a more serious study of the role of emotion are frequently seen as applying only to the women's movement, because emotion is traditionally thought of as being feminine (Ferree and Merrill 2000; V. Taylor 1999, 2004).

---

use your sociological *imagination*

Try to imagine a society without any social movements. Under what conditions could such a society exist? Would you want to live in it?

New Social Movements

Beginning in the late 1960s, European social scientists observed a change in both the composition and the targets of emerging social movements. Previously, traditional social movements had focused on economic issues, often led by labor unions or by people who shared the same occupation. However, many social movements that have become active in recent decades—including the contemporary women's movement, the peace movement, and the environmental movement—do not have the social class roots typical of the labor protests in the United States and Europe over the past century (Tilly 1993, 2004).

The term **new social movements** refers to organized collective activities that address values and social identities, as well as improvements in the quality of life. These movements may be involved in developing collective identities. Many have complex agendas that go beyond a single issue, and even cross national boundaries. Educated, middle-class people are significantly represented in some of these new social movements, such as the women's movement and the movement for lesbian and gay rights. Box 21-1 describes some new social movements in India.

New social movements generally do not view government as their ally in the struggle for a better society. While they typically do not seek to overthrow the government, they may criticize, protest, or harass public officials. Researchers have found that members of new social movements show little inclination to accept established authority, even scientific or technical authority. This characteristic is especially evident in the environmental and anti–nuclear power movements, whose activists present their own experts to counter those of government or big business (Garner 1996; Polletta and Jasper 2001; A. Scott 1990).

TABLE **21-2** CONTRIBUTIONS TO SOCIAL MOVEMENT THEORY

Approach	Emphasis
Relative deprivation approach	Social movements are especially likely to arise when expectations are frustrated.
Resource mobilization approach	The success of social movements depends on which resources are available and how effectively they are used.
New social movement theory	Social movements arise when people are motivated by value issues and social identity questions.

The environmental movement is one of many new movements with a worldwide focus (see the Social Policy section in Chapter 19). In their efforts to reduce air and water pollution, curtail global warming, and protect endangered animal species, environmental activists have realized that strong regulatory measures within a single country are not sufficient. Similarly, labor union leaders and human rights advocates cannot adequately address exploitative sweatshop conditions in a developing country if multinational corporations can simply move their factories to another country, where workers earn even less. Whereas traditional views of social movements tended to emphasize resource mobilization on a local level, new social movement theory offers a broader, global perspective on social and political activism.

Table 21-2 summarizes the sociological approaches that have contributed to social movement theory. Each has added to our understanding of the development of social movements.

---

thinking CRITICALLY

What aspects of traditional gender roles explain the roles that women and men typically play in social movements?

Communications and the Globalization of Social Movements

Today, through global text-messaging and the Internet, social activists can reach a large number of people around the world almost instantaneously, with relatively little effort and expense. The Internet's listservs and chat rooms—a form of social networking—allow organizers of social movements to enlist like-minded people without face-to-face contact, or even simultaneous interaction (Calhoun 1998; Kavada 2005).

Moreover, television and the Internet, as contrasted with books and newspapers, often convey a false sense of intimacy reinforced by immediacy. We seem to be personally affected by the latest celebrity news. Therefore, the latest technology brings us together to act and react in an electronic global village (Della Porta and Tarrow 2005; Garner 1999).

473

SOCIOLOGY IN THE GLOBAL COMMUNITY

21-1 Women and New Social Movements in India

In the more than 60 years since India gained its independence from Great Britain, a variety of new social movements has emerged. These grassroots efforts deal primarily with women's rights, discrimination against the *Dalits* (untouchables), environmental issues, and farming problems. Although they tend to be most visible in the media when their demonstrations occur in cities, most of these movements are based in India's vast rural areas, where about 71 percent of the nation's 1.2 billion people live.

Sociologists and other scholars have emphasized the central role that women play in starting these movements and creating social networks with activists in neighboring villages and adjacent states. Sometimes these movements connect to form nationwide networks through the assistance of the Women's Development Program (WDP). Founded by UNICEF in 1984, the WDP helps women to improve their quality of life, freeing them from dependence on slow and cumbersome government bureaucracies.

> *The initial goal of the movement was to provide drought relief for villagers, but the deeper goal was to empower rural areas.*

One notable social movement occurred in the Indian textile industry. In the mid-1980s, 5,000 striking textile workers came home from Mumbai to mobilize support in their rural villages and gather food for strikers in the city. As the strike wore on, some remained in their villages and sought employment on government drought-relief projects. However, there weren't enough jobs for rural residents, much less for these new migrants from Mumbai.

This experience became the origin of a new social movement in rural India. With unemployment threatening an expanded population in rural areas, activists formed what came to be called the *Shoshit, Shetkari, Kashtakari, Kamgar, Mukti Sangharsh (SSKKMS)*, which means "exploited peasants, toilers, workers liberation struggle." The initial goal of the movement was to provide drought relief for villagers, but the deeper goal was to empower rural areas.

The SSKKMS was unusual compared to other social movements in India: about half its participants and many of its leaders were women. This was no accident, for the movement also sought to address gender inequities. Some men have joined the women of the SSKKMS in their political activism, using direct-action tactics such as roadblocks.

Women have also marched on government offices to demand that at least a third of the seats in Parliament and the state assemblies be reserved for them. And they have begun to improve their families' lot through microfinance programs (see Chapter 18). Clearly, Indian women's traditional role of maintaining their households' health and nutrition is critical to their families' survival. Thus, their leadership in seeking improved living conditions is winning them new respect in India's patriarchal society. From the environment to the voting booth, from untouchables' rights to workers' rights, women's social movements are an increasingly common feature of Indian politics.

LET'S DISCUSS

1. Why do you think so many of India's women participate in new social movements? Describe their goals.
2. What would happen if "powerless" people in the United States formed a similar social movement? Would it succeed? Why or why not?

Sources: Bystydzienski and Sekhon 1999; Daley-Harris 2002; Desai 1996; Haub 2010; Ray 1999; Sengupta 2009; Subramaniam 2006; Working Women's Forum 2010.

This sense of online togetherness extends to social movements, which more and more are being mounted on the web. Through the instantaneous communication that is possible over the Internet, Mexican Zapatistas and other groups of indigenous peoples can transform their cause into an international lobbying effort, and Greenpeace organizers can link environmental activists throughout the world via video recorded on members' cell phones.

Sociologists have begun to refer to such electronic enhancement of established social movements as *computer-mediated communication (CMC)*. Electronic communication strengthens a group's solidarity, allowing fledgling social movements to grow and develop faster than they might otherwise. Thus the face-to-face contact that once was critical to a social movement is no longer necessary. As Box 21-2 suggests, however, the

RESEARCH TODEY

Organizing for Controversy on the Web

Concern about the spread of terrorism is not limited to border checks. Worldwide, government leaders worry about people using the Internet to incite terrorist acts. But where do you draw the line between legitimate political activity on behalf of respectable causes and criminal activity that seeks to create havoc among innocent civilians?

Thirty-one-year-old Babar Ahmad is a case in point. The British-born mechanical engineer was arrested in London in 2004 on the charge that his websites were a fund-raising front for Islamic extremists, including Chechen rebels, the Taliban militia, and Al-Qaeda affiliates. Freed a few days later amid charges of police brutality, he was rearrested on an extradition warrant from the United States on similar charges. Still

Where do you draw the line between legitimate political activity on behalf of respectable causes and criminal activity that seeks to create havoc among innocent civilians?

in prison in 2011, Ahmad was relying on supporters to publicize his struggle to be released from custody. He maintains that he is being persecuted not for promoting terrorism, but for speaking his mind. As one supporter declared, the war in Iraq is not an information war being fought on the Internet.

In truth, the Internet has become host to more and more Islamic extremist websites,

many of which are technologically advanced, and even more important, written in English. These websites have been garnering support for Islamic causes outside the Middle East. Such sites are not the only ones in cyberspace that tie extremist beliefs to religion. Ku Klux Klan websites have also been growing in number, complete with online "news shows" and streaming video.

Equally disturbing are sites that promote what many see as self-destructive behavior. The Internet allows people who are engaged in unusual activities, such as collecting parking

meters, to network and become a virtual group. More troubling still for many doctors and parents are the slick websites that encourage anorexia and bulimia (disorders characterized by little or no eating or by overeating and purging) and self-mutilation. Internet chat rooms that support those engaged in these life-threatening behaviors are flourishing. Participants are urged to "go public" and send in for a beaded bracelet that shows support for their behavior.

To counteract these sites, members of the medical community have established websites to promote recovery and safe behavior. Their actions illustrate the double-edged nature of free expression. On the street or on the Internet, social movements may be seen either as promoting desirable social change or as supporting negative behaviors that many people find objectionable.

LET'S DISCUSS

1. Have you ever been involved in a social or political movement whose legitimacy some people considered questionable? If so, what was the movement, and what were the objections to it? Did you consider the objections to be legitimate?
2. Can any social movement ever be totally free from controversy? Would you want to live in a society in which controversy is not tolerated?

Sources: FreeBabarAhmad 2011; Reuters 2009; Thomasrobb.com 2007; Tibbles 2007; Whitlock 2005.

In the 21st century, technology links people in even the remotest areas. In 2008, Mongolia's capital was rocked by protests over election fraud; two years later, by angry demands for better distribution of the nation's mining wealth. In both cases, the protests were swelled by people from rural areas, mobilized on the Internet.

legitimacy of such online movements is a matter of opinion (Castells 2010b; Niezen 2005).

The new global communications technology also helps to create enclaves of similarly minded people. Alex Steffen (2008), editor of the book *World Changing*, notes that the Internet is changing the way people relate to one another across vast distances, allowing small, focused audiences to become part of a global conversation. In doing so, they may find a common purpose. These social connections happen because of the Internet's technological structure. Websites are not autonomous and independent; they are connected by a global electronic network. One website generally lists a variety of other sites that serve as links. For example, seeking information on domestic partnerships may lead you to an electronic enclave that is supportive of cohabitation between men and women or to an enclave that is supportive of gay and lesbian couples. New developments in communications technology have clearly broadened the way we interact with one another (Calhoun 1998).

thinking CRITICALLY

What might be some drawbacks of global communications technology?

social policy and Social Movements

Disability Rights

In the early 1960s, Ed Roberts joined forces with some other young adults who wanted to attend the University of California at Berkeley. Members of the group had more than their educational aspirations in common: all had disabilities. The university, reluctant to admit them at first, finally agreed, and found living quarters for them in the infirmary. Dubbed the Rolling Quads, these students proved they could succeed in college despite the extraordinary challenges they faced. Berkeley's administrators, convinced they were there to stay, awarded them their own student center. Eventually, the group turned their attention to the surrounding community, establishing the Berkeley Center for Independent Living, which became a model for hundreds of other independent living centers. Their activism marked the beginning of advocacy for people with disabilities (Brannon 1995).

Since then, the effort to ensure not only the health but also the rights of people with disabilities has been growing steadily. Like members of other advocacy organizations, the women and men of the disability rights movement are working to challenge negative stereotypes of disabled people; to gain a greater voice in the agency and public policy decisions that affect them; and to reshape laws, institutions, and environments so that people with disabilities can be fully integrated into mainstream society.

One of the obstacles the disability rights movement faces is the invisibility of many disabilities. Most of us are unaware of how many people struggle, some silently, with unseen disabilities. Table 21-3 challenges you to match some famous people with their disabilities.

Looking at the Issue

According to disability rights activists, there is an important distinction between organizations *for* disabled people and organizations *of* disabled people. Because people with disabilities do not control the service providers, charitable associations, and parents' groups that work for their welfare, those organizations do not stress the goals of independence and self-help that are important to people with disabilities (Scotch 1989, 2001).

In 1990, working with a presidentially appointed council, organizations representing people with disabilities achieved passage of the Americans with Disabilities Act (ADA). In many respects the most sweeping antidiscrimination legislation since the Civil Rights Act (1964), the ADA took effect in 1992. The act defines a disability as a condition that substantially limits a major life activity, such as walking or seeing. It prohibits bias against people with disabilities in employment, transportation, public accommodations, and telecommunications. Businesses with more than 25 employees cannot refuse to hire a qualified applicant with a disability. Instead, they must make reasonable accommodations that will allow workers with disabilities to do their jobs. Nor can commercial establishments such as offices, buildings, hotels, theaters, supermarkets, and dry cleaners deny service to people with disabilities.

The responsibility for enforcing the ADA has been given to several federal agencies. For example, the Equal Employment Opportunity Commission oversees employment of people with disabilities; the Department of Transportation is responsible for enforcing transportation requirements (Burgdorf Jr. 2005).

Applying Sociology

From a labeling perspective, the ADA represents a significant framing of the issue of disability rights. Through its civil rights approach to disabilities, it seeks to humanize the way society sees and treats people with disabilities. In other nations, such as Great Britain, disability is seen as an entitlement issue: that is, people with disabilities can expect to receive certain benefits from the government. That is quite different from the perspective that the disabled must not be denied certain rights—rights that everyone should possess, whether disabled or not. As activist Mark Johnson has put it, "Black people fought for the right to ride in the front of the bus. We're fighting for the right to get on the bus" (Shapiro 1993:128; see also Albrecht 1995, 1997; Gooding 1994).

Conflict theorists see the mobilization of resources on behalf of people with disabilities as part of a 40-year-long civil rights movement, one that has also benefited racial and ethnic minorities, women, and gays and lesbians. Interactionists focus on the everyday relationships between people with and without disabilities. More and more, they point out, people with disabilities are being seen as *people* rather than as wheelchair occupants or guide-dog owners.

Initiating Policy

Today, policymakers and the courts are confronting issues that weren't even considered 30 years ago, when disability activists mobilized to pass the ADA. In the past, the courts have often ruled that citizens cannot sue the federal or state governments. Yet in 2004, in *Tennessee v. Lane and Jones,* the Supreme Court upheld the right of individuals with disabilities to gain physical access to the courts. Despite such victories, however, the groups who worked for the ADA's passage feel that federal agencies are still too cautious in enforcing the law (Burgdorf Jr. 2005; National Council on Disability 2004).

TABLE **21-3** CAN YOU MATCH THE PERSON WITH
THE DISABILITY?

All the famous people listed in this table have (or had) at least one
disability. Match each person with one or more disabilities; then check
your answers below.

Match the people in Column A with the disabilities in Column B

Column A	Column B
1. _____ Lance Armstrong	A. Attention Deficit Disorder
2. _____ Beethoven	B. Bipolar Disorder
3. _____ Ray Charles	C. Blindness
4. _____ Tom Cruise	D. Cancer
5. _____ Patrick Dempsey	E. Deafness
6. _____ Michael J. Fox	F. Dwarfism
7. _____ Magic Johnson	G. Epilepsy
8. _____ James Earl Jones	H. HIV/AIDS
9. _____ Frida Kahlo	I. Learning Disability
10. _____ Jay Leno	J. Multiple Sclerosis
11. _____ John Lennon	K. Quadriplegia
12. _____ John Mellencamp	L. Parkinson's Disease
13. _____ Verne "Mini-me" Troyer	M. Polio
14. _____ Napoleon	N. Spina Bifida
15. _____ Christopher Reeve	O. Stuttering
16. _____ Franklin Delano Roosevelt	
17. _____ Axl Rose	
18. _____ Charles Schwab	
19. _____ Steven Spielberg	
20. _____ Sting	
21. _____ Montel Williams	
22. _____ Robin Williams	
23. _____ Bruce Willis	
24. _____ Stevie Wonder	

Answers: 1. D, 2. E, 3. C, 4. I, 5. I, 6. L, 7. H, 8. O, 9. M, 10. I, 11. A, 12. N, 13. F,
14. G, 15. K, 16. M, 17. B, 18. I, 19. A, 20. B, 21. J, 22. B, 23. O, 24. C.

Source: Meyer 2011, revised and updated by author.

New on the agenda of disability rights activists is the concept of **visitability**, or the accessibility of private homes to
visitors with disabilities. In the mid-1990s, cities such as
Atlanta, Georgia, and Austin, Texas, as well as some cities in
Great Britain, passed construction ordinances that encouraged
the installation of accommodations such as no-step entrances,
wide doorways, and grab bars in the bathroom. The idea is that
all environments should be accessible to those with disabilities,
not just public places such as classrooms and courtrooms. Many
people consider such ordinances to be unnecessary interference
from the government, but others see them as a long-overdue
recognition that people with disabilities should be able to move
freely throughout the country (Buchholz 2003; Visitability 2009).

The passage of the ADA in the United States sparked similar actions in several other countries, including Great Britain.
The European Union has mandated that by the end of 2006,
all EU member countries must put in place laws that protect
people with disabilities against discrimination in employment
and training. As in the United States, disability rights activists
in Europe have raised concerns about the interpretation and lax
enforcement of the law (J. Cooper 2005; Ruebain 2005).

Disability rights activists are encouraged by the progress they
have made since the ADA's passage. Studies show that a little more
than 20 years later, people with disabilities feel empowered and
enjoy access to better employment opportunities. However, we must
remember that civil rights activists felt a measure of optimism after
passage of the Civil Rights Act almost 50 years ago—and the nation
still has a long way to go in enforcing that legislation (Albrecht 2005;
Meyer 2008).

Take the Issue with You

1. Think of someone you know who has a disability. Could that
person easily visit your home? If not, what are the barriers
that would make a visit difficult?

2. Why do you think the Supreme Court ruled as it did in *Tennessee v. Lane and Jones*? Do some research: What legal principle
or precedent did the Supreme Court consider more important
than the immunity of government from citizens' lawsuits?

3. Contrast the British approach to disabilities as entitlements
with the U.S. emphasis on disability rights. What might be the
benefits and the drawbacks of each approach?

MASTERING THIS CHAPTER

Summary

Collective behavior is the relatively spontaneous and unstructured
behavior of a group that is reacting to a common influence in an ambiguous situation. This chapter examines sociological theories used to
understand collective behavior and forms of collective behavior, with
particular attention to **social movements** and their important role in
promoting social change.

1. Turner and Killian's **emergent-norm perspective** suggests that
new forms of proper or improper behavior may emerge from a
crowd during an episode of collective behavior.

2. Smelser's **value-added model** of collective behavior outlines six
important determinants of such behavior: structural conduciveness,
structural strain, generalized belief, a precipitating factor, mobilization of participants for action, and the operation of social control.

3. The **assembling perspective** introduced by McPhail and Miller
examines how and why people move from different points in space
to a common location.

4. In **crowds**, people are in relatively close contact and interaction for
a period and are focused on something of common interest.

5. Researchers are interested in how groups interact in times of **disaster.**

6. **Fads** are temporary patterns of behavior involving large numbers of people; **fashions** have more historical continuity than fads.

7. The key distinction between a **panic** and a **craze** is that a panic is a flight *from* something, whereas a craze is a mass movement *toward* something.

8. A **rumor** is a piece of information used to interpret an ambiguous situation. It serves a social function by providing a group with a shared belief.

9. **Publics** represent the most individualized and least organized form of collective behavior. **Public opinion** is the expression of attitudes on public policy to decision makers.

10. **Social movements** are more structured than other forms of collective behavior and persist over longer periods.

11. A group will not mobilize into a social movement without a shared perception that its **relative deprivation** can be ended only through collective action.

12. The success of a social movement depends in good part on effective **resource mobilization.**

13. **New social movements** tend to focus on more than just economic issues, and often cross national boundaries.

14. Advances in communications technology—especially the Internet—have had a major impact on various forms of collective behavior.

15. The disability rights movement, which began at the University of California in Berkeley in the 1960s, achieved a major victory with passage of the Americans with Disabilities Act in 1990. The act, which prohibits discrimination against people with disabilities in employment, transportation, public accommodations, and telecommunications, has prompted significant changes in employment and public accommodations.

Key Terms

Assembling perspective A theory of collective behavior introduced by McPhail and Miller that seeks to examine how and why people move from different points in space to a common location. (page 465)

Collective behavior In the view of sociologist Neil Smelser, the relatively spontaneous and unstructured behavior of a group of people who are reacting to a common influence in an ambiguous situation. (462)

Craze An exciting mass involvement that lasts for a relatively long period. (468)

Crowd A temporary gathering of people in close proximity who share a common focus or interest. (466)

Disaster A sudden or disruptive event or set of events that overtaxes a community's resources, so that outside aid is necessary. (466)

Emergent-norm perspective A theory of collective behavior proposed by Turner and Killian that holds that a collective definition of appropriate or inappropriate behavior emerges during episodes of collective behavior. (463)

Fad A temporary pattern of behavior that involves large numbers of people and is independent of preceding trends. (468)

False consciousness A term used by Karl Marx to describe an attitude held by members of a class that does not accurately reflect their objective position. (472)

Fashion A pleasurable mass involvement that has a line of historical continuity. (468)

New social movement An organized collective activity that addresses values and social identities, as well as improvements in the quality of life. (473)

Nonperiodic assembly A nonrecurring gathering of people that often results from word-of-mouth information. (465)

Panic A fearful arousal or collective flight based on a generalized belief that may or may not be accurate. (468)

Periodic assembly A recurring, relatively routine gathering of people, such as a college class. (465)

Public A dispersed group of people, not necessarily in contact with one another, who share an interest in an issue. (469)

Public opinion Expressions of attitudes on matters of public policy that are communicated to decision makers. (469)

Relative deprivation The conscious feeling of a negative discrepancy between legitimate expectations and present actualities. (471)

Resource mobilization The ways in which a social movement utilizes such resources as money, political influence, access to the media, and personnel. (472)

Rumor A piece of information gathered informally that is used to interpret an ambiguous situation. (469)

Social movement An organized collective activity to bring about or resist fundamental change in an existing group or society. (470)

Value-added model A theory of collective behavior proposed by Neil Smelser to explain how broad social conditions are transformed in a definite pattern into some form of collective behavior. (464)

Visitability The accessibility of private homes to visitors with disabilities. (477)

1. Scour your memory for incidents of collective behavior on your campus. Find out as much as you can about them by tracking down and talking with students who participated. Then analyze what you have learned. Which theory of collective behavior—the emergent-norm, value-added, or assembling perspective—seems to fit each best? What form of collective behavior does each illustrate?

2. Check the back issues of your local or campus newspaper for stories about a nearby disaster. Describe the emergency response that followed. Did the collective response to this particular disaster illustrate the findings of disaster research?

3. Choose a social movement that you are interested in and do some research on it. If possible, visit with members of the movement in your local community. Which sociological theory fits this movement better, relative deprivation or resource mobilization? Would you describe the movement as a new social movement? What has been the role of communications in the movement?

Self-Quiz

Read each question carefully and then select the best answer.

1. The early writings on collective behavior imply that crowds are basically
   a. functional.
   b. value-added.
   c. structured.
   d. ungovernable.

2. The emergent-norm perspective has been criticized for being too vague in defining what constitutes a
   a. riot.
   b. crowd.
   c. belief.
   d. norm.

3. In sociological terms, which of the following constitute a crowd?
   a. spectators at a baseball game
   b. participants at a college pep rally
   c. urban rioters
   d. all of the above

4. The least organized and most individualized form of collective behavior is represented by
   a. rumors.
   b. publics.
   c. fashions.
   d. panics.

5. Which sociological perspective would be most likely to emphasize that rumors serve a function by providing a group with a shared belief?
   a. the functionalist perspective
   b. the conflict perspective
   c. the interactionist perspective
   d. labeling theory

6. From the point of view of theorists of collective behavior, there can be no public opinion unless there is both
   a. a public and mass media.
   b. a decision maker and mass media.
   c. a public and a decision maker.
   d. relative deprivation and resource mobilization.

7. The most all-encompassing type of collective behavior is
   a. public opinion.
   b. social movements.
   c. rumors.
   d. crowds.

8. From the point of view of social scientists, call-in telephone polls using 1-900 numbers are misleading because
   a. of the Hawthorne effect.
   b. the sample that emerges is hardly representative.
   c. they rely on improper resource mobilization.
   d. all of the above.

9. "Collective enterprises to establish a new order of life" refers to
   a. public opinion.
   b. social movements.
   c. rumors.
   d. crowds.

10. The resource mobilization perspective would be most interested in looking at the influence of _____ on social movements.
    a. tenacity
    b. desire
    c. emotion
    d. money

11. Like other social norms, the emergent norm reflects shared convictions held by members of a group, and is enforced through _____.

12. Building on the _____ perspective, Clark McPhail and David Miller introduced the concept of the assembling process.

13. The term _____ refers to a sudden or disruptive event or set of events that overtaxes a community's resources, so that outside aid is necessary.

14. Members of a(n) _____ may adopt a fad or fashion in order to break with tradition while remaining "in" with (accepted by) a significant reference group of peers.

15. In the wake of many natural and technological disasters, decision making becomes more _____ than in normal times.

16. The _____ perspective emphasizes that even when unsuccessful, social movements contribute to the formation of public opinion.

17. A relatively deprived person is dissatisfied because he or she feels deprived relative to some appropriate _____ group.

18. As Max Weber described it in 1904, _____ is the quality of an individual that sets him or her apart from ordinary people.

19. _____ _____ is the conscious feeling of a negative discrepancy between legitimate expectations and present actualities.

20. The SSKKMS movement was unusual when compared to other social movements in India in that about one-half of its participants, and many of its leaders, were _____.

_____

THINKING ABOUT **MOVIES**

Exit through the Gift Shop

In this documentary, graffiti artists achieve success in the art market.

Milk

This film tells the story of Harvey Milk, a politician and activist who worked to uphold the rights of gay and lesbian people.

Norma Rae

A woman fights to unionize mill workers in a small Alabama town.

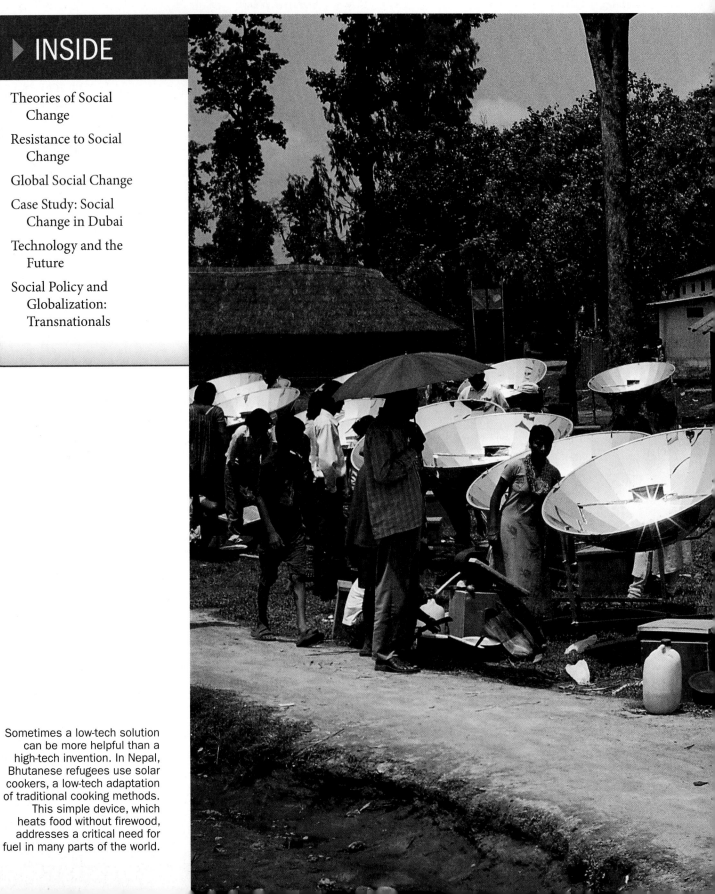

Sometimes a low-tech solution can be more helpful than a high-tech invention. In Nepal, Bhutanese refugees use solar cookers, a low-tech adaptation of traditional cooking methods. This simple device, which heats food without firewood, addresses a critical need for fuel in many parts of the world.

I live in
the future
&
here's how
it works

Why Your World, Work, and
Brain Are Being Creatively Disrupted

NICK BILTON

Lead Writer and Technology Reporter for the New York Times Bits Blog

"If you pull out your smart phone and click the button that says "locate me" on your Google or Yahoo! map application, you will see a small dot appear in the middle of your screen.

That's you!

If you start walking down the street in any direction, the whole screen will move right along with you, no matter where you go. This is a dramatic change from the print-on-paper world, where maps and locations are based around places and landmarks, not on you or your location. People don't go to the store and say, "Oh, excuse me, can I buy a map of me?" They go to the store and ask for a map of New York, or Amsterdam, or the subway system. You and I aren't anywhere to be seen on these maps. The maps are locations that we fit into.

But today's digital world has changed that. Kevin Slavin, a creator of location-based services and games and the cofounder of the gaming company Area/Code, put this succinctly at a technology conference last year: "We are always in the center of the map."

Though Slavin was talking about location-based games and Google maps, the center of the map, it turns out, is actually much bigger than a dot on the screen. It's a very powerful place to be.

Being in the center—instead of somewhere off to the side or off the page altogether—changes everything. It changes your conception of space, time, and location. It changes your sense of place and community. It changes the way you view the information, news, and data coming in over your computer and your phone. And it changes your role in a transaction, empowering you to decide quite specifically what content to buy and how to buy and use it rather than simply accepting the traditional material that companies have packaged on your behalf.

Now you are the starting point. Now the digital world follows you, not the other way around.

. . .

I got my own hard lesson in this new Me! Now! world when some friends stopped by our house with their teenage cousin Lauren. As I started making coffee for our guests, Lauren asked if she could use my laptop to "check the news." I handed it over.

I was curious about which news sites she was going to, so I asked her, expecting to hear something like CNN or NYTimes, or maybe TMZ, the Hollywood gossip site. With a sincere face she looked up at me and said, "Facebook." Then she turned back to the computer and continued reading.

"I thought you were going to read the news," I said.

"This is my news," she replied.

To Lauren and many in her age group, news is not defined by newspapers, or broadcast television stations, or even bloggers or renegades. Instead, news is what is relevant to the individual. . . . "

Being in the center—instead of somewhere off to the side or off the page altogether—changes everything. It changes your conception of space, time, and location. It changes your sense of place and community.

(Bilton 2011:161–162, 164–165) Additional information about this excerpt can be found on the Online Learning Center at www.mhhe.com/schaefer13e.

In this excerpt from *I Live in the Future and Here's How It Works: Why Your World, Work, and Brain Are Being Creatively Disrupted,* technology writer Nick Bilton suggests that increasingly, new communications technologies are allowing us to center our communities, as well as our news and entertainment, on ourselves. So besides the global community—a virtual community knit together by new information technologies—we are creating a multitude of personal communities, each revolving around a single individual. How will this self-centered approach to information gathering change what we know (or do not know) about our society and other societies? More important, will our society change? The answers to these questions rest with each of us.

Social change often does follow the introduction of a new technology, in this case the computer. **Social change** has been defined as significant alteration over time in behavior patterns and culture (W. Moore 1967). But what constitutes a "significant" alteration? Certainly the dramatic rise in formal education

documented in Chapter 16 represents a change that has had profound social consequences. Other social changes that have had long-term and important consequences include the emergence of slavery as a system of stratification (Chapter 9), the Industrial Revolution (Chapter 5), and the increased participation of women in the paid labor forces of the United States and Europe (Chapter 12).

How does social change happen? Is the process unpredictable, or can we make certain generalizations about it? Has globalization contributed to social change? We begin this chapter with three theories of social change: the evolutionary, functionalist, and conflict approaches. Then we discuss vested interests, which often attempt to block changes they see as threatening. And we recognize the influence of globalization in spreading social change around the world. In a case study, we note the rapid social change that has occurred over a matter of decades in the Middle Eastern city-state of Dubai. Finally, we turn to the unanticipated social change that occurs when innovations such as new technologies sweep through society. The chapter closes with a Social Policy section on a controversial aspect of global social change, the creation of *transnationals*—immigrants with an allegiance to more than one nation.   **485**

Social Change in the Global Community

Theories of Social Change

A new millennium provides the occasion to offer explanations of *social change*, which we have defined as significant alteration over time in behavior patterns and culture. Social change can occur so slowly as to be almost undetectable to those it affects, but it can also happen with breathtaking rapidity. As Table 22-1 shows, some changes that have occurred in U.S. society over the past century and a half have been relatively slow or slight; others have been rapid or striking in magnitude.

Explanations of social change are clearly a challenge in the diverse and complex world we inhabit today. Nevertheless, theorists from several disciplines have sought to analyze social change. In some instances, they have examined historical events to arrive at a better understanding of contemporary changes. We will review three theoretical approaches to change—evolutionary, functionalist, and conflict theory—and then take a look at resistance to social change.

Evolutionary Theory

The pioneering work of Charles Darwin (1809–1882) in biological evolution contributed to 19th-century theories of social change. Darwin's approach stresses a continuing progression of successive life-forms. For example, human beings came at a later stage of evolution than reptiles and represent a more complex form of life. Social theorists seeking an analogy to this biological model originated **evolutionary theory**, in which society is viewed as moving in a definite direction. Early evolutionary theorists generally agreed that society was progressing inevitably toward a higher state. As might be expected, they concluded in ethnocentric fashion that their behavior and culture were more advanced than those of earlier civilizations.

Auguste Comte (1798–1857), a founder of sociology, was an evolutionary theorist of change. He saw human societies as moving forward in their thinking, from mythology to the scientific method. Similarly, Émile Durkheim ([1893]1933) maintained that society progressed from simple to more complex forms of social organization.

Today, evolutionary theory influences sociologists in a variety of ways. For example, it has encouraged sociobiologists to investigate the behavioral links between humans and other animals. It has also influenced human ecology, the study of the interaction between communities and their environment (Maryanski 2004).

Functionalist Theory

Because functionalist sociologists focus on what *maintains* a system, not on what changes it, they might seem to offer little to the study of social change. Yet as the work of sociologist Talcott Parsons demonstrates, functionalists have made a distinctive contribution to this area of sociological investigation.

Parsons (1902–1979), a leading proponent of functionalist theory, viewed society as being in a natural state of equilibrium. By "equilibrium," he meant that society tends toward a state of stability or balance. Parsons would view even prolonged labor strikes or civilian riots as temporary disruptions in the status quo rather than as significant alterations in social structure. Therefore, according to his **equilibrium model**, as changes occur in one part of society, adjustments must be made in other parts. If not, society's equilibrium will be threatened and strains will occur.

TABLE **22-1** THE UNITED STATES: A CHANGING NATION

Population	1850	1940	1960	2011
Total in millions	23.2	132.1	180.7	313.2
Percentage under age 15	41%	25%	31%	20%
Education	**1850**	**1940**	**1960**	**2009**
Percentage not completing high school	88%	18%	13%	13%
Percentage ages 19-24 enrolled in higher education	Under 1%	8%	40%	40%
Labor Force Participation	**1850**	**1940**	**1960**	**2009**
Men working in their 20s	94%	88%	86%	83%
Women working in their 20s	22%	39%	74%	72%
Health	**1850**	**1940**	**1960**	**2010**
Physicians per 100,000 population	176	133	150	272
Life expectancy at birth, in years	38	63	70	78.3
Technology	**1870**	**1940**	**1960**	**2009**
Copyrights issued	5,600	176,997	243,926	381,300
Patents issued	12,127	42,238	47,170	191,900
Family	**1890**	**1940**	**1960**	**2008**
Median age at first marriage				
Men	26	24	23	28
Women	22	22	20	26
Number of children born per family	3.25	2.7	3.65	2.12

Note: Data are comparable, although definitions vary. Definition of the United States changes between 1850 and 1940 and between 1940 and 1960. Earliest date for children born per family is 1905.
Source: Author, based on federal data collected in Bureau of the Census 2010a:Tables 3, 83, 113, 219, 225, 585, 772, 774; Sutch and Carter 2006:1–28/29, 391, 401–402, 440, 541, 685, 697, 709, 2–441/442, and 3–424/425, 427/428.

Think about It
Which of the social changes shown in this table surprises you the most? Which category do you think will change the most in the next 20 years?

Reflecting the evolutionary approach, Parsons (1966) maintained that four processes of social change are inevitable. *Differentiation* refers to the increasing complexity of social organization. The transition from medicine man to physician, nurse, and pharmacist is an illustration of differentiation in the field of health. This process is accompanied by *adaptive upgrading,* in which social institutions become more specialized in their purposes. The division of physicians into obstetricians, internists, surgeons, and so forth is an example of adaptive upgrading.

The next process Parsons identified is the *inclusion* of groups that were previously excluded because of their gender, race, ethnicity, or social class. Medical schools have practiced inclusion by admitting increasing numbers of women and African Americans. Finally, Parsons contends that societies experience *value generalization,* the

On the outskirts of Buenos Aires, Argentina, a squatter settlement forms a stark contrast to the gleaming skyscrapers in the wealthy downtown area. Marxists and conflict theorists see social change as a way of overcoming the kind of social inequality evident in this photograph.

development of new values that tolerate and legitimate a greater range of activities. The acceptance of preventive and alternative medicine is an example of value generalization: society has broadened its view of health care. All four processes identified by Parsons stress consensus—societal agreement on the nature of social organization and values (B. Johnson 1975; Wallace and Wolf 1980).

Although Parsons's approach explicitly incorporates the evolutionary notion of continuing progress, the dominant theme in his model is stability. Society may change, but it remains stable through new forms of integration. For example, in place of the kinship ties that provided social cohesion in the past, people develop laws, judicial processes, and new values and belief systems.

Conflict Theory

Functionalist theory minimizes the importance of change. It emphasizes the persistence of social life and sees change as a means of maintaining society's equilibrium (or balance). In contrast, conflict theorists contend that social institutions and practices persist because powerful groups have the ability to maintain the status quo. Change has crucial significance, since it is needed to correct social injustices and inequalities.

Karl Marx accepted the evolutionary argument that societies develop along a particular path. However, unlike Comte and Spencer, he did not view each successive stage as an inevitable improvement over the previous one. History, according to Marx, proceeds through a series of stages, each of which exploits a class of people. Ancient society exploited slaves; the estate system of feudalism exploited serfs; modern capitalist society exploits the working class. Ultimately, through a socialist revolution led by the proletariat, human society will move toward the final stage of development: a classless communist society, or "community of free individuals," as

Marx described it in 1867 in *Das Kapital* (see Bottomore and Rubel 1956:250).

As we have seen, Marx had an important influence on the development of sociology. His thinking offered insights into such institutions as the economy, the family, religion, and government. The Marxist view of social change is appealing because it does not restrict people to a passive role in responding to inevitable cycles or changes in material culture. Rather, Marxist theory offers a tool for those who wish to seize control of the historical process and gain their freedom from injustice. In contrast to functionalists' emphasis on stability, Marx argues that conflict is a normal and desirable aspect of social change. In fact, change must be encouraged as a means of eliminating social inequality (Lauer 1982).

One conflict theorist, Ralf Dahrendorf (1958), has noted that the contrast between the functionalist perspective's emphasis on stability and the conflict perspective's focus on change reflects the contradictory nature of society. Human societies are stable and long-lasting, yet they also experience serious conflict. Dahrendorf found that the functionalist approach and the conflict approach were ultimately compatible, despite their many points of disagreement. Indeed, Parsons spoke of new functions that result from social change, and Marx recognized the need for change so that societies could function more equitably.

Table 22-2 summarizes the differences between the three major theories of social change.

thinking CRITICALLY

Which theory of social change do you find most convincing? Why?

summing up

TABLE 22-2 SOCIOLOGICAL PERSPECTIVES ON SOCIAL CHANGE

Evolutionary	Social change moves society in a definite direction, frequently from simple to more complex.
Functionalist	Social change must contribute to society's stability.
	Modest adjustments must be made to accommodate social change.
Conflict	Social change can correct social injustices and inequalities.

Resistance to Social Change

Efforts to promote social change are likely to meet with resistance. In the midst of rapid scientific and technological innovations, many people are frightened by the demands of an ever-changing society. Moreover, certain individuals and groups have a stake in maintaining the existing state of affairs.

Social economist Thorstein Veblen (1857–1929) coined the term **vested interests** to refer to those people or groups who will suffer in the event of social change. For example, in 2010 President Obama proposed scuttling NASA's Constellation project, whose primary goal was to return humans to the moon. Although many people expressed disappointment with the decision to abandon manned space flights, key opposition came from just 27 members of Congress. All represented districts in Alabama and Texas that were home to large suppliers to the project. Ironically, many of those representatives had gone on record as opponents of large federal spending projects. In general, those with a disproportionate share of society's wealth, status, and power, such as members of Congress and representatives of big business, have a vested interest in preserving the status quo (Friedman 2010; Veblen 1919).

Economic and Cultural Factors

Economic factors play an important role in resistance to social change. For example, it can be expensive for manufacturers to meet high standards for the safety of products and workers, and for the protection of the environment. Conflict theorists argue that in a capitalist economic system, many firms are not willing to pay the price of meeting strict safety and environmental standards. They may resist social change by cutting corners or by pressuring the government to ease regulations.

Communities, too, protect their vested interests, often in the name of "protecting property values." The abbreviation *NIMBY* stands for "not in my backyard," a cry often heard when people protest landfills, prisons, nuclear power facilities, and even bike trails and group homes for people with developmental disabilities. The targeted community may not challenge the need for the facility, but may simply insist that it be located elsewhere. The "not in my backyard" attitude has become so common that it is almost impossible for policymakers to find acceptable locations for facilities such as hazardous-waste dumps (Jasper 1997).

On the world stage, what amounts to a "not on planet Earth" campaign has emerged. Members of this movement stress many issues, from profiteering to nuclear proliferation, from labor

A Google Street View car drives through Broughton, England, photographing it for use with Google's online map service. Residents of the rural village see the technology that may encourage motorists and truckers to drive through their community as an invasion of their privacy, but many others appreciate the innovation.

rights to the eradication of poverty and disease. Essentially an antiglobalization movement, it manifests itself at international meetings of trade ministers and heads of state.

Like economic factors, cultural factors frequently shape resistance to change. William F. Ogburn (1922) distinguished between material and nonmaterial aspects of culture. *Material culture* includes inventions, artifacts, and technology; *nonmaterial culture* encompasses ideas, norms, communications, and social organization. Ogburn pointed out that one cannot devise methods for controlling and using new technology before the introduction of a technique. Thus, nonmaterial culture typically must respond to changes in material culture. Ogburn introduced the term **culture lag** to refer to the period of maladjustment when the nonmaterial culture is still struggling to adapt to new material conditions. One example is the Internet. Its rapid, uncontrolled growth raises questions about whether to regulate it, and if so, how much.

In certain cases, changes in material culture can strain the relationships between social institutions. For example, new means of birth control have been developed in recent decades. Large families are no longer economically necessary, nor are they commonly endorsed by social norms. However, certain religious faiths, among them Roman Catholicism, continue to extol large families and to disapprove methods of limiting family size, such as contraception and abortion. This issue represents a lag between aspects of material culture (technology) and nonmaterial culture (religious beliefs). Conflicts may also emerge between religion and other social institutions, such as government and the educational system, over the dissemination of birth control and family-planning information (Riley et al. 1994a, 1994b).

use your sociological *imagination*

What kind of change do you find the hardest to accept? The easiest?

Resistance to Technology

Technology is cultural information about the ways in which the material resources of the environment may be used to satisfy human needs and desires. Technological innovations are examples of changes in material culture that often provoke resistance. The *Industrial Revolution,* which took place largely in England during the period 1760 to 1830, was a scientific revolution focused on the application of non-animal sources of power to labor tasks. As this revolution proceeded, societies came to rely on new inventions that facilitated agricultural and industrial production and on new sources of energy such as steam. In some industries, the introduction of power-driven machinery reduced the need for factory workers and made it easier for factory owners to cut wages.

Strong resistance to the Industrial Revolution emerged in some countries. In England, beginning in 1811, masked craft workers took extreme measures: they mounted nighttime raids on factories and destroyed some of the new machinery. The government hunted these rebels, known as **Luddites**, and ultimately banished or hung them. In a similar effort in France, angry workers threw their *sabots* (wooden shoes) into factory machinery to destroy it, giving rise to the term *sabotage.* While the resistance of the Luddites and the French workers was short-lived and unsuccessful, they have come to symbolize resistance to technology.

Are we now in the midst of a second industrial revolution, with a contemporary group of Luddites engaged in resisting? Many sociologists believe that we are living in a *postindustrial society.* It is difficult to pinpoint exactly when this era began. Generally, it is viewed as having begun in the 1950s, when for the first time the majority of workers in industrial societies became involved in services rather than in the actual manufacture of goods (D. Bell 1999; Fiala 1992).

Just as the Luddites resisted the Industrial Revolution, people in many countries have resisted postindustrial technological changes. The term *neo-Luddites* refers to those who are wary of technological innovations and who question the incessant expansion of industrialization, the increasing destruction of the natural and agrarian world, and the "throw-it-away" mentality of contemporary capitalism, with its resulting pollution of the environment.

A new slang term, *urban amish,* refers specifically to those who resist technological devices that have become part of our daily lives, such as cell phones. Such people insist that whatever the presumed benefits of industrial and postindustrial technology, such technology has distinctive social costs and may represent a danger to both the future of the human species and our planet (Bauerlein 1996; Rifkin 1995; Sale 1996; Slack and Wise 2007; Snyder 1996; Urban Dictionary 2010).

Even today, many people will resist a new technology, either because they find it difficult to use or because they suspect that it will complicate their lives. Both these objections are especially true of new information and media technologies. Whether it is TiVo, the iPhone, or even the latest digital camera, many consumers are leery of these so-called must-have items.

thinking CRITICALLY

Which do you think play more of a role in resistance to social change, economic or cultural factors? Why?

TREND SPOTTING

Longer Life Spans, More Social Change

Improved public health—a significant social change in itself—brings longer life expectancy. Ironically, this particular social change means that people living in the 21st century will experience more social change than past generations, and more stress because of it.

On average, a person born in the United States in 1900 could anticipate living to the age of 47. By 1927, life expectancy in the United States had been extended to age 60; by 1964, to age 70. By 1994, the birth year of many first-year college students today, average life expectancy had risen to 75 years. Those born in 2020 are expected to live—and experience social change—for over 79 years.

Significant differences in life expectancy exist among subgroups of the population. Women live longer than men, and Whites live longer than Blacks. Among those born in 1994, for example, a White female can anticipate living to 79.6 years of age, while a Black male can anticipate a life span of 64.9 years—the expected age of White females born in 1935.

Global Social Change

We are at a truly dramatic time in history to consider global social change. Maureen Hallinan (1997), in her presidential address to the American Sociological Association, asked those present to consider just a few of the recent events: the collapse of communism; terrorism in various parts of the world, including the United States; major regime changes and severe economic disruptions in Africa, the Middle East, and Eastern Europe; the spread of AIDS; and the computer revolution. Just a few months after her remarks came the first verification of the cloning of a complex animal, Dolly the sheep.

In this era of massive social, political, and economic change, global in scale, is it possible to predict change? Some technological changes seem obvious, but the collapse of communist governments in the former Soviet Union and Eastern Europe in the early 1990s took people by surprise. Yet prior to the Soviet collapse, sociologist Randall Collins (1986, 1995), a conflict theorist, had observed a crucial sequence of events that most observers had missed.

In seminars as far back as 1980, and in a book published in 1986, Collins had argued that Soviet expansionism had resulted in an overextension of resources, including disproportionate spending on military forces. Such an overextension will strain a regime's stability. Moreover, geopolitical theory suggests that nations in the middle of a geographic region, such as the Soviet Union, tend to fragment into smaller units over time. Collins predicted that the coincidence of social crises on several frontiers would precipitate the collapse of the Soviet Union.

And that is just what happened. In 1979, the success of the Iranian revolution had led to an upsurge of Islamic fundamentalism in nearby Afghanistan, as well as in Soviet republics with substantial Muslim populations. At the same time, resistance to communist rule was growing both throughout Eastern Europe and within the Soviet Union itself. Collins had predicted that the rise of a dissident form of communism within the Soviet Union might facilitate the breakdown of the regime. Beginning in the late 1980s, Soviet leader Mikhail Gorbachev chose not to use military power and other types of repression to crush dissidents in Eastern Europe. Instead, he offered plans for democratization and social reform of Soviet society, and seemed willing to reshape the Soviet Union into a loose federation of somewhat autonomous states. But in 1991, six republics on the western periphery declared their independence, and within months the entire Soviet Union had formally disintegrated into Russia and a number of other independent nations.

In her address, Hallinan (1997) cautioned that we need to move beyond the restrictive models of social change—the linear view of evolutionary theory and the assumptions about equilibrium in functionalist theory. She and other sociologists have looked to the "chaos theory" advanced by mathematicians to understand erratic events as a part of change. Hallinan noted that upheavals and major chaotic shifts do occur, and that sociologists must learn to predict their occurrence, as Collins did with the Soviet Union. For example, imagine the dramatic non-linear social change that accompanies the transformation of a small, undeveloped principality into a major financial and communications hub: see the Case Study on Dubai that follows.

thinking CRITICALLY

Using chaos theory, what kind of global social change might you predict for the 21st century?

casestudy Social Change in Dubai

The story of Dubai, a Middle Eastern principality the size of Rhode Island, is a tale of two cities. When the Maktoum family took control of Dubai (pronounced Doo-Bye) in 1883, it was a pearl-fishing village on the Persian Gulf. But in 1966, the discovery of oil changed everything. When the state's oil reserves proved too limited to fund significant economic and social change, Dubai reinvented itself as a free-trade oasis. By 2000 it had become a tax-free information-technology hub of the world. In less than a single generation—barely a decade—Dubai had transformed itself into what *Forbes* magazine calls the richest city in the world. In many ways it is the prototype aerotropolis described in Chapter 20. This is a place that in the late 1950s had no electricity and no paved roads.

Wide-eyed journalists have described Dubai's air-conditioned indoor ski run, open year-round in a country where the daytime temperature averages 92 degrees. Then there is the 160-story Burj Khalifa, which opened in 2010; at a half-mile high, it is by far the world's tallest building. At one point, so much of the city was under construction that 10 percent of the world's construction cranes were located there.

A constitutional monarchy, Dubai is no democratic utopia—there are no contested elections, and there is little public opposition to the government. Socially, however, Dubai is relatively progressive for an Arab state. Women are encouraged to work, and there is little separation of the sexes, as is common in neighboring states. Alcohol is freely available, speech is relatively free, and the media are largely uncensored.

The citizens of Dubai share its affluence: they receive cheap electricity, free land and water, free health care and education (including graduate study abroad), as well as an average subsidy of $55,000 per year. They pay no income or property taxes. Ironically, the government handouts that citizens enjoy mean that most have little interest in competitive work, so high-skilled positions tend to go to foreigners. The social consequences of Dubai's wealth have been less than benign, however. Environmentally, the cost of its lavish lifestyle is exorbitant. Dubai ranks at the top of the list in terms of its greenhouse gas emissions, at twice the level of the United States and triple the global average.

Another significant social problem, hidden from the investment bankers and tourists who visit Dubai, is the treatment of immigrant laborers. About 95 percent of Dubaians are foreigners from India, Pakistan, the Philippines, Sri Lanka, North Korea, Bangladesh, China, and Yemen. A million of them—seven times the number of Dubai nationals—come from India alone. These migrant laborers sold everything they owned to come to Dubai and take jobs stacking bricks, watering lawns, and cleaning floors. The pay is good relative to their home countries—$275 a month for a skilled electrician—but very poor compared to what the lowest-paid citizen of Dubai earns. At best, an immigrant must work two years just to break even.

There is little government oversight of working or living conditions in Dubai, both of which are poor. For foreign workers seeking to escape the slums in distant deserts, one-bedroom apartments rent for $1,400 per month. In 2008, fire investigators found 500 laborers living in a house built for a single family. Little wonder that late in 2009, when Dubai's economic expansion ground to a halt, foreign workers were heading home at an estimated rate of 5,000 a day.

The area surrounding the Emirates Golf Club in Dubai changed dramatically from 1990 to 2008.

The global economic downturn that began in 2008 has been particularly savage to Dubai. Having borrowed heavily and invested not always wisely, both the government and major companies are groaning under a debt load that is heavier than even the United States' or Europe's. By 2010, however, Dubai's economy was back on the move, although a bit moderated. The state's story is hardly finished. At the beginning of the second decade of the 21st century, the well-to-do are still flying lobster in for extravagant parties. Overworked foreign laborers, although many fewer of them remain, are still earning wages well above those available in their home countries. Political analysts note that Dubai is the most stable country in the Arab world, with a measured tolerance for outside cultural influences and an intolerance for corruption (Alderman 2010; Ali 2010; Harman 2009; Krane 2009, 2010; McGirk 2009; Rogan 2009; Tatchell 2009).

thinking CRITICALLY

Could some of the problems Dubai faces have been anticipated?

Technology and the Future

Technological advances—the airplane, the automobile, the television, the atomic bomb, and more recently, the computer, digital media, and the cell phone—have brought striking changes to our cultures, our patterns of socialization, our social institutions, and our day-to-day social interactions. Technological innovations are, in fact, emerging and being accepted with remarkable speed.

In the past generation alone, industrial countries have seen a major shift in consumer technologies. No longer do we buy electronic devices to last for even 10 years. Increasingly, we buy them with the expectation that within as little as 3 years, we will need to upgrade to an entirely new technology, whether it be a handheld device or a home computer. Of course, there are those people who either reject the latest gadgets or become frustrated trying to adapt to them. And then there are the "tech-no's"—people who resist the worldwide movement toward electronic networking. Those who become tech-no's are finding that it is a life choice that sets them apart from their peers, much like deciding to be "child free" (Darlin 2006; Kornblum 2007).

In the following sections, we examine various aspects of our technological future and consider their impact on social change, including the social strain they will cause. We focus in particular on recent developments in computer technology, electronic censorship, and biotechnology.

Happy, sad, or confused? This "face robot" was developed at the Science University of Tokyo during research on machines that can show and respond to human emotional expressions. Nonverbal communication is the latest innovation in robotics.

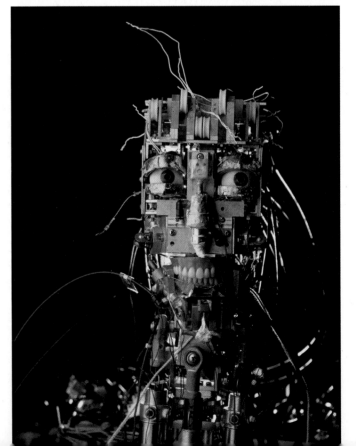

"We have to move - they're putting in a cell phone tower here."

Finding a place where you can't receive a text message is getting harder and harder.

Computer Technology

The past decade witnessed an explosion of computer technology in the United States and around the world. Its effects were particularly noteworthy with regard to the Internet, the world's largest computer network. In 2010 the Internet reached 1.8 billion users, compared to just 50 million in 1996. Box 22-1 sketches the worldwide access to and use of the Internet.

The Internet evolved from a computer system built in 1962 by the U.S. Defense Department to enable scholars and military researchers to continue their government work even if part of the nation's communications system were destroyed by a nuclear attack. Until a generation ago, it was difficult to gain access to the Internet without holding a position at a university or a government research laboratory. Today, however, virtually anyone can reach the Internet with a phone line, a computer, and a modem. People buy and sell cars, trade stocks, auction off items, research new medical remedies, vote, and track down long-lost friends online—to mention just a few of the thousands of possibilities. Earlier in this book we discussed the impact of the Internet on social interaction and the creation of new virtual worlds (see Chapter 5).

Unfortunately, not everyone can get onto the information highway, especially not the less affluent. Moreover, this pattern of inequality is global. The core nations that Immanuel Wallerstein described in his world systems analysis have a virtual monopoly on information technology; the peripheral nations of Asia, Africa, and Latin America depend on the core nations both for technology and for the information it provides. For example, North America, Europe, and a few industrialized nations in other regions possess almost all the world's *Internet hosts*—computers that are connected directly to the worldwide network.

What is the solution to this global disconnect between the haves and the have-nots? Some people have suggested giving everyone a computer—or at least, everyone who can't afford one.

use your sociological *imagination*

Have you ever learned about a social movement outside the United States via the Internet?

Privacy and Censorship in a Global Village

As we saw in the chapter-opening excerpt, new technologies like smartphones with mapping applications are bringing about sweeping social change. While much of that change is beneficial, there are some negative effects. Recent advances in computer technology have made it increasingly easy for business firms, government agencies, and even criminals to retrieve and store information about everything from our buying habits to our web-surfing patterns. In public places, at work, and on the Internet, surveillance devices now track our every move, be it a keystroke or an ATM withdrawal. At the same time that these innovations have increased others' power to monitor our behavior, they have raised fears that they might be misused for criminal or undemocratic purposes. In short, new technologies threaten not just our privacy, but our freedom from crime and censorship (O'Harrow Jr. 2005).

In recent years, concern about the criminal misuse of personal information has been underscored by the accidental loss of some huge databases. In 2006, for example, the theft of a laptop computer from the home of an employee of the Veterans' Administration compromised the names, Social Security numbers, and dates of birth of up to 26.5 million veterans. Unfortunately, technologies that facilitate the sharing of information have also created new types of crime.

From a sociological point of view, the complex issues of privacy and censorship can be considered illustrations of culture lag. As usual, the material culture (technology) is changing faster than the nonmaterial culture (norms for controlling the use of technology). Too often, the result is an anything-goes approach to the use of new technologies.

RESEARCH TODAY

22-1   The Internet's Global Profile

The old notion of an Internet accessed primarily in the United States and dominated by English-only content is passé. In fact, usage patterns are changing so fast, generalizing about global use of the Internet requires careful research and phrasing.

For example, Figure A, Internet Users by World Region, shows an Internet that is dominated by users in Asia and Europe, two relatively populous continents. However, Figure B, Internet Penetration by World Region, shows a dramatically different picture, one in which the *proportion* of people in each region who access the Internet is highest in North America and Australia. That is, numerically, most Internet users live in Asia and Europe, but the likelihood of a person being an Internet user is greatest in North America and Australia. Figure B shows dramatically low Internet use in Africa, where only 10.9 percent of residents access the global network.

> *The old notion of an Internet accessed primarily in the United States and dominated by English-only content is passé.*

Though English is still the primary language of Internet users, as Figure C shows, use of the Chinese language has become much more common. Chinese usage on the Internet increased 1,277 percent between 2000 and 2010, compared to 281 percent for English. Interestingly, 82 percent of all Japanese speakers use the Internet, compared to 42 percent of all English speakers, though in absolute terms, speakers of Japanese are a significantly smaller group.

LET'S DISCUSS

1. In surfing the web, how often do you encounter a website that is written in a language you do not read or speak? Do you think that experience will become increasingly common in the future?

2. Why do you think the use of Chinese on the Internet has increased so dramatically in just a decade? What kind of information would you expect to find in Chinese? Who would use it?

FIGURE **A**   INTERNET USERS BY WORLD REGION

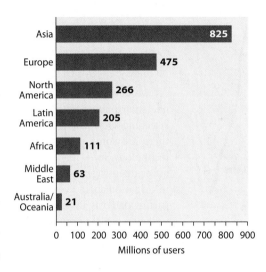

FIGURE **B**   INTERNET PENETRATION BY WORLD REGION

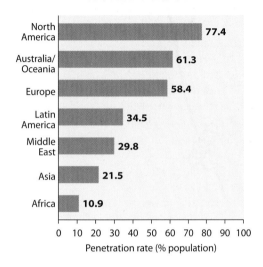

FIGURE **C**   INTERNET'S TOP 10 LANGUAGES

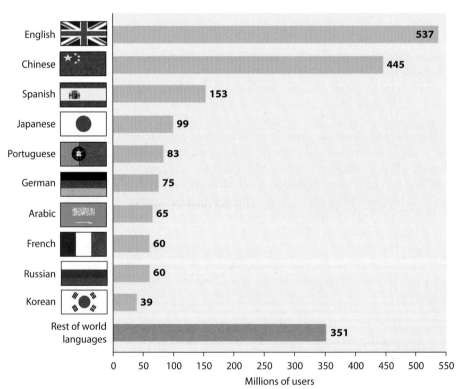

Source: All data taken from Internet World Stats 2011 as of April 25, 2011.

Legislation regarding the surveillance of electronic communications has not always upheld citizens' right to privacy. In 1986, the federal government passed the Electronic Communications Privacy Act, which outlawed the surveillance of telephone calls except with the permission of both the U.S. attorney general and a federal judge. Telegrams, faxes, and e-mail did not receive the same degree of protection, however. Then in 2001, one month after the terrorist attacks of September 11, Congress passed the USA Patriot Act, which relaxed existing legal checks on surveillance by law enforcement officers. As a result, federal agencies are now freer to gather electronic data, including credit-card receipts and banking records. In 2005, Americans learned that the National Security Agency was covertly monitoring phone calls with the cooperation of major U.S. telecommunications companies. Four years later, a federal court ruled that wiretapping without warrants is legal (Eckenwiler 1995; Lichtblau 2009; Vaidhyanathan 2008).

Sociologists' views on the use and abuse of new technologies differ depending on their theoretical perspective. Functionalists take a generally positive view of the Internet, pointing to its manifest function of facilitating communication. From their perspective, the Internet performs the latent function of empowering those with few resources—from hate groups to special-interest organizations—to communicate with the masses. Conflict theorists, in contrast, stress the danger that the most powerful groups in a society will use technology to violate the privacy of the less powerful. Indeed, officials in the People's Republic of China have attempted to censor online discussion groups and web postings that criticize the government. The same abuses can occur in the United States, civil liberties advocates remind us, if citizens are not vigilant in protecting their right to privacy (Magnier 2004).

Another source of controversy is the widespread use of GPS devices to track the location of cars or even people, not to mention the electronic tracking of handheld communications devices. Technology allows you to tweet your whereabouts to your friends, but should others, including the government, be able to home in on you? Put another way, is your location at any given moment covered by the Fourth Amendment to the U.S. Constitution, which protects your right to privacy? Both public opinion and court rulings on this question remain divided. The issue is yet another example of culture lag, or the time it takes for society to reconcile a new technology with traditional cultural values and behavior (Zipp 2009).

If anything, people seem to be less vigilant today about maintaining their privacy than they were before the information age. Young people who have grown up browsing the Internet seem to accept the existence of the cookies and spyware they may pick up while surfing. They have become accustomed to adult surveillance of their conversation in electronic chat rooms. Many see no risk in providing personal information about themselves to the strangers they meet online. Little wonder that college professors find their students do not appreciate the political significance of their right to privacy (Turkle 2004).

---

use your sociological *imagination*

Do you hold strong views regarding the privacy of your electronic communications? If your safety were in jeopardy, would you be willing to sacrifice your privacy?

Biotechnology and the Gene Pool

Another field in which technological advances have spurred global social change is biotechnology. Sex selection of fetuses, genetically engineered organisms, cloning of sheep, cows, and some small animals—these have been among the significant yet controversial scientific advances in the field of biotechnology. George Ritzer's concept of McDonaldization applies to the entire area of biotechnology. Just as the fast-food concept has permeated society, no phase of life now seems exempt from therapeutic or medical intervention. In fact, sociologists view many aspects of biotechnology as an extension of the recent trend toward the medicalization of society, discussed in Chapter 19. Through genetic manipulation, the medical profession is expanding its turf still further (Clarke et al. 2003; Human Genome Project 2010).

One notable success of biotechnology—an unintended consequence of modern warfare—has been progress in the treatment of traumatic injuries. In response to the massive numbers of soldiers who survived serious injury in Iraq and Afghanistan, military doctors and therapists have come up with electronically controlled prosthetic devices. Their innovations include artificial limbs that respond to thought-generated nerve impulses, allowing amputees to move legs, arms, and even individual fingers. These applications of computer science to the rehabilitation of the injured will no doubt be extended to civilians (J. Ellison 2008; Gailey 2007).

One startling biotechnological advance is the possibility of altering human behavior or physical traits through genetic engineering. Fish and plant genes have already been mixed to create frost-resistant potato and tomato crops. More recently, human genes have been implanted in pigs to provide humanlike kidneys for organ transplant. William F. Ogburn probably could not have anticipated such scientific developments when he wrote of culture lag over 80 years earlier. However, advances like these or even the successful cloning of sheep illustrate again how quickly material culture can change, and how nonmaterial culture moves more slowly in absorbing such changes.

Although today's biotechnology holds itself out as totally beneficial to human beings, it is in constant need of monitoring. Biotechnological advances have raised many difficult ethical and political questions, among them the desirability of tinkering with the gene pool, which could alter our environment in unexpected and unwanted ways. In particular, controversy has been growing concerning genetically modified (GM) food, an issue that arose in Europe but has since spread to other parts of the world, including the United States. The idea behind the technology is to increase food production and make agriculture more economical. But critics use the term *Frankenfood* (as in "Frankenstein") to refer to everything from breakfast cereals made from genetically engineered grains to fresh GM tomatoes. Members of the antibiotech movement object to tampering with nature, and are concerned about the possible health effects of GM food. Supporters of genetically modified food include not just biotech companies, but those who see the technology as a way to help feed the burgeoning populations of Africa and Asia (Petersen 2009; World Health Organization 2009).

In contrast, less expensive and controversial technologies can further agriculture where it is needed more, in the

RESEARCH TODAY

22-2　The Human Genome Project

Together with geneticists, pathologists, and microbiologists, sociologist Troy Duster of New York University has been grappling with the ethical, legal, and social issues raised by the Human Genome Project since 1989. An original member of the oversight committee appointed to deal with such matters, he does not expect that his work will be done anytime in the near future.

Duster, who is also past president of the American Sociological Association, has been asked to explain why his committee is taking so long to conclude its work. In reply, he lists the many issues raised by the massive project. First, he is concerned that the medical breakthroughs made possible by the project will not benefit all people equally. He notes that biotechnology firms have used the project's data to develop a test for cystic fibrosis in Whites, but not for the same syndrome in Zunis. Biotechnology companies are profit-making ventures, not humanitarian organizations. So while the scientists involved in the Human Genome Project hope to map the genes of all the world's peoples, not everyone may benefit from the project in practical ways.

A group's economic and political power helps to determine which diseases scientists study.

Duster's committee has also struggled with the question of informed consent—making sure that everyone who donates genes to the project will do so voluntarily, after being informed of the risks and benefits. In Western societies, scientists commonly obtain such consent from the individuals who participate in their research. But according to Duster, many non-Western societies do not acknowledge the individual's right to make such decisions. Instead, a leader makes the decision for the group as a whole. "When Western-trained researchers descend upon a village," Duster asks, "who should they turn to for consent?" (Duster 2002:69). And what if the answer is no?

Race, too, is a knotty problem for Duster's committee. DNA analysis shows conclusively that there is no genetic difference between the races. Given that analysis, many geneticists do not want to invest more time and effort in research on racial differences. As a sociologist, Duster knows that race is socially constructed. Yet he also knows that for millions of people around the world, race has a significant effect on their health and well-being. More to the point, he knows that a group's economic and political power helps to determine which diseases scientists study.

On the other hand, Duster worries that some researchers may be putting too much emphasis on biological differences between the races. He notes that those racial groups who are socially disadvantaged suffer much higher rates of disease than advantaged groups. In the United States, for example, Black men suffer from prostate cancer at twice the rate of White men. Yet in the Caribbean and sub-Saharan Africa, Black men have a much lower rate of prostate cancer than American men, White or Black. How can genes explain this disparity? Duster suspects that the explanation for Blacks' higher disease rates lies not in their genes, but in their stressful environment, where they are routinely subjected to racial profiling and other forms of institutional

Troy Duster, a sociologist at NYU, also teaches and directs the American Cultures Center at the University of California, Berkeley.

discrimination. "We may be 99.9 percent alike at the level of DNA," Duster writes, "but if that were the end of the story, we could all pack up and go home" (Duster 2002:70).

LET'S DISCUSS

1. What other criteria besides the power of a racial or ethnic group could be used to determine how much research is done on diseases that affect the group?
2. What should a researcher do if a tribal leader refuses to allow members of the tribe to participate in a research project?

Sources: Dreifus 2005; Duster 2002; Human Genome Project 2011.

A Ugandan farmer checks the price of coffee beans on his cell phone.

developing world. Consider cell phones. Unlike most new technologies, the majority of the world's cell phones are used in *less* developed countries. Relatively cheap and not as dependent as computers on expensive communications infrastructure, cell phones are common in the world's poorest areas. In Uganda, farmers use them to check weather forecasts and commodity prices. In South Africa, laborers use them to look for work. Researchers at the London Business School have found that in developing countries, a 10 percent increase in cell phone use is correlated with a 0.6 percent rise in GDP (Bures 2011).

Another form of biotechnology with a potentially wide-ranging impact is the Human Genome Project. This effort involves teams of scientists around the world in sequencing and mapping all 20,000 to 25,000 human genes in existence, collectively known as the *human genome.* Supporters say that the resulting knowledge could revolutionize doctors' ability to treat and even prevent disease. But sociologists worry about the ethical implications of such research. Box 22-2 provides an overview of the many issues the project has raised.

social**policy** and **Globalization**

Transnationals

Around the world, new communications technologies—cell phones, the World Wide Web—have definitely hastened the process of globalization. Yet without human capital, these innovations would not have spurred the huge increase in global trade and development that occurred over the last several decades. Who are the people behind the trend toward globalization? Often, they are people who see a business opportunity abroad and strike out on their own to take advantage of it. In the process, many of them become migrants.

To facilitate trade and investment with other countries, migrants often exploit their social connections and their familiarity with their home language and culture. In Southeast Asia, for example, Chinese migrants dominate the trade with China; in Africa, Indian migrants dominate. Some migrants invest directly in their home countries to get the manufactured goods they sell abroad. Opportunities abound, and those with capital and good business skills can become quite wealthy (Guest 2011).

The millions of migrant laborers who leave home in search of a better life also play a role in the global economy, filling jobs where there are shortages in the labor market. Although they do not become wealthy working as landscapers or short-order cooks, they consider themselves better off than they were in the old country. Unfortunately, citizens of the host countries often react negatively to the migrants' arrival, worrying that they will take jobs away from the native-born.

Looking at the Issue

As of 2011, 192 million people, or about 3 percent of the world's population, were international migrants. That is more than double the number in 1970. The rest of the world's population were "stayers"—that is, people who continued to live in the countries where they were born (International Organization for Migration 2011).

Figure 22-1 shows the worldwide movement of workers with and without the legal right to immigrate. Several areas, such as the European Union, have instituted international agreements that provide for the free movement of laborers. But in most other parts of the world, immigration restrictions give foreign workers only temporary status. Despite such legal restrictions, the labor market has become an increasingly global one. Just as globalization has integrated government policies, cultures, social movements, and financial markets, it has unified what were once discrete national labor markets. So today, for example, immigrants from at least eight different countries work in one small Middle Eastern state, Dubai.

Globalization has changed the immigrant experience as well as the labor market. In generations past, immigrants read foreign language newspapers to keep in touch with events in their home countries. Today, the Internet gives them immediate access to their countries and kinfolk. In this global framework, immigrants are less likely than they were in the past to think of themselves as residents of just one country. **Transnationals** are immigrants who sustain multiple social relationships that link their societies of origin with their societies of settlement (P. Levitt and Jaworsky 2007).

Applying Sociology

As with other issues, sociologists differ in their opinion of transnationals, depending on their theoretical perspective. Functionalists see the free flow of immigrants, even when it is legally restricted, as one way for economies to maximize their use of human labor. Given the law of supply and demand, they note, countries with too few workers will inevitably attract laborers, while those with too many will become unattractive to residents.

Conflict theorists charge that globalization and international migration have increased the economic gulf between developed and developing nations. Today, residents of North America, Europe, and Japan consume 32 times more resources than the billions of people who live in developing countries. Through tourism and the global reach of the mass media, people in the poorer countries have become aware of the affluent lifestyle common in developed nations—and of course, many of them now aspire to it (Diamond 2003).

Interactionists are interested in the day-to-day relationships transnationals have with the people around them, from those of their country of origin to those of the host country and fellow workers from other countries. These scholars are studying transnationals' involvement in local ethnic organizations, to see whether their membership facilitates or retards their integration into the host society. They have discovered that members of global social networks provide one another with mutual support and trust. Just as interesting is the question of how migrants see themselves—how they see their own identities as well as those of their children. In effect, transnationals negotiate their identities, depending on which social network they belong to at the moment. Some sociologists note that while being a transnational can be exhilarating, it can also isolate a person, even in a city of millions. Others worry that transnationals may become so cosmopolitan that they will lose touch with their national identities (Calhoun 2003; Evergeti and Zontini 2006; Plüss 2005; Portes et al. 2008; Rajan and Sharma 2006; Tilly 2007).

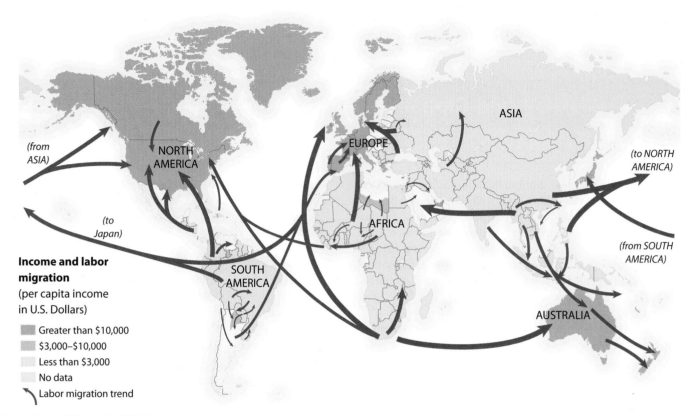

Income and labor migration
(per capita income in U.S. Dollars)

■ Greater than $10,000
■ $3,000–$10,000
■ Less than $3,000
■ No data
⟍ Labor migration trend

Source: National Geographic 2005:16.

Initiating Policy

Although connecting to two societies can be an enriching experience, transnationals face continuing adjustment problems in their new home countries. As we saw in the case study of Dubai, immigrant laborers often face difficult living and working conditions. Some sending countries, such as Indonesia and the Philippines, have created national agencies to ensure the protection of their workers abroad. Their objective is ambitious, given that funding for the agencies is limited, and diplomatic and legal challenges complicate their task (United Nations Development Programme 2009:102–104).

Another unresolved transnational issue is voter eligibility. Not all nations allow dual citizenship; even those countries that do may not allow absent nationals to vote. The United States and Great Britain are rather liberal in this regard, permitting dual citizenship and allowing émigrés to continue to vote. Mexico, in contrast, has been reluctant to allow citizens who have emigrated to vote. Mexican politicians worry that the large number of Mexicans who live abroad (especially those in the United States) might vote differently from local voters, causing different outcomes (P. Levitt and Jaworsky 2007; Sellers 2004).

Finally, the controversial issue of illegal immigration has yet to be settled, perhaps because of culture lag. That is, both public attitudes and government policies (nonmaterial culture) have not kept pace with, much less adjusted to, the increasing ease of migration around the globe (material culture). Though globalization has created a global labor market—one that many countries depend on, legal or illegal—the general public's attitude toward illegal immigrants remains hostile, especially in the United States.

Take the Issue with You

1. Suppose you live in an impoverished developing country and have the opportunity to earn a much higher income by immigrating to the United States. Will you do it, even if it means entering the country illegally and working long hours doing menial labor? If so, how will you justify your decision to those who condemn illegal immigration?

2. The U.S. economy depends on the cheap labor that immigrants provide. Should immigrants receive the same social services that U.S. citizens receive? What about their children who are born in the United States (and therefore are U.S. citizens)? Explain your reasoning.

3. Globalization has increased international trade and development at the same time that it has strained nations' social service systems, as migrant workers flow toward countries offering the most extensive social protection. On balance, do you think its overall effect has been beneficial or harmful? What might be done to alleviate the harmful effects of globalization?

Summary

Social change is significant alteration over time in behavior patterns and culture, including norms and values. **Technology** is cultural information about the ways in which the material resources of the environment may be used to satisfy human needs and desires. This chapter examines sociological theories of social change, resistance to change, global social change, and the impact of technology on society's future.

1. Early advocates of the **evolutionary theory** of social change believed that society was progressing inevitably toward a higher state.

2. Talcott Parsons, a leading advocate of functionalist theory, viewed society as being in a natural state of equilibrium or balance.

3. Conflict theorists see change as having crucial significance, since it is needed to correct social injustices and inequalities.

4. In general, those with a disproportionate share of society's wealth, status, and power, called **vested interests,** have a stake in preserving the status quo and will resist change.

5. The period of maladjustment when a nonmaterial culture is still struggling to adapt to new material conditions is known as **culture lag.**

6. We are living in a time of sweeping social, political, and economic change—change that occurs not just on a local or national basis, but on a global scale.

7. The core industrialized nations have a virtual monopoly on information technology, making the peripheral nations dependent on them both for technology and for the information it provides.

8. Computer technology has made it increasingly easy for any individual, business firm, or government agency to retrieve more and more information about any of us, thereby infringing on our privacy.

9. Advances in biotechnology have raised difficult ethical questions about genetic engineering and the sex selection of fetuses.

10. Globalization has increased the international migration of laborers, producing a new kind of immigrant. **Transnationals** are immigrants who sustain multiple social relationships that link their societies of origin with their societies of settlement.

Key Terms

Culture lag A period of maladjustment when the nonmaterial culture is still struggling to adapt to new material conditions. (page 487)

Equilibrium model The functionalist view that society tends toward a state of stability or balance. (485)

Evolutionary theory A theory of social change that holds that society is moving in a definite direction. (485)

Luddites Rebellious craft workers in 19th-century England who destroyed new factory machinery as part of their resistance to the Industrial Revolution. (488)

Social change Significant alteration over time in behavior patterns and culture, including norms and values. (484)

Technology Cultural information about the ways in which the material resources of the environment may be used to satisfy human needs and desires. (488)

Transnational An immigrant who sustains multiple social relationships that link his or her society of origin with the society of settlement. (495)

Vested interests Those people or groups who will suffer in the event of social change, and who have a stake in maintaining the status quo. (487)

TAKING SOCIOLOGY with you

1. Consider one of the technological advances discussed in the section on technology and the future. Analyze this new technology, focusing on whether it is likely to increase or reduce inequality in the coming decades. Address any related issues of gender, race, ethnicity, and class, as well as inequality between nations.

2. Think about social interaction in your college community. In what ways has it been affected by the technological advances examined in this chapter? Are particular subcultures more or less likely than others to employ new forms of electronic communication?

3. Choose a new technology that interests you and analyze it from a sociological point of view. What do you think this technology might contribute to society? What might be some negative effects of the technology? Have you noticed any resistance to it, and if so, on what grounds?

Self-Quiz

Read each question carefully and then select the best answer.

1. Nineteenth-century theories of social change reflect the pioneering work in biological evolution done by
   a. Albert Einstein.
   b. Charles Darwin.
   c. Harriet Martineau.
   d. Benjamin Franklin.

2. The writings of Auguste Comte and Émile Durkheim are examples of
   a. cyclical theory.
   b. evolutionary theory.
   c. interactionist theory.
   d. conflict theory.

3. The acceptance of preventive medicine is an example of the process that Parsons called
   a. differentiation.
   b. value generalization.
   c. inclusion.
   d. adaptive upgrading.

4. The term *vested interests* was coined by social economist
   a. William F. Ogburn.
   b. Talcott Parsons.
   c. Auguste Comte.
   d. Thorstein Veblen.

5. Which of the following theorists argued that conflict is a normal and desirable aspect of social change?
   a. Karl Marx
   b. Talcott Parsons
   c. Émile Durkheim
   d. all of the above

6. The abbreviation *NIMBY* stands for "not in my backyard," a cry often heard when people protest
   a. landfills.
   b. prisons.
   c. nuclear power facilities.
   d. all of the above.

7. Which sociologist introduced the concept of culture lag?
   a. William F. Ogburn
   b. Talcott Parsons
   c. Auguste Comte
   d. Thorstein Veblen

8. Which term refers to an immigrant who sustains multiple social relationships that link his or her society of origin with the society of settlement?
   a. transnational
   b. transglobal
   c. global citizen
   d. none of the above

9. Internationally, which language is most common on the Internet?
   a. English
   b. Russian
   c. German
   d. Japanese

10. Which sociological perspective sees transnationals as a way for economies to maximize their use of human labor?
    a. functionalist
    b. conflict
    c. interactionist
    d. feminist

11. Early evolutionary theorists concluded in a(n) _____ fashion that their own behavior and culture were more advanced than those of earlier civilizations.

12. Talcott Parsons used the term _____ to refer to the increasing complexity of social organization.

13. _____ argued that conflict is a normal and desirable aspect of social change.

14. _____ is cultural information about the ways in which the material resources of the environment may be used to satisfy human needs and desires.

15. The _____ is the world's largest computer network.

16. The term _____ refers to those who are wary of technological innovations, and who question the incessant expansion of industrialization, the increasing destruction of the natural and agrarian world, and the "throw-it-away" mentality of contemporary capitalism.

17. The usage of _____ on the Internet increased by more than 1,200 percent between the years 2000 and 2010.

18. In developing countries, _____ _____ are a less expensive way of furthering agriculture than biotechnology.

19. The _____ perspective would stress the danger that the most powerful groups in a society will use technology to violate the privacy of the less powerful.

20. Regarding privacy on the Internet, young people who have grown up browsing the Internet seem to accept the existence of the _____ and _____ they may pick up while surfing.

THINKING ABOUT MOVIES

Afghan Star

This documentary presents the Afghan version of *American Idol*.

Babies

This cross-cultural comparison explores the lives of several real-life babies from different parts of the world.

Up the Yangtze

A ship cruises the Yangtze River, revealing the dramatic changes occurring in China today.

glossary

Numbers following the definitions indicate pages where the terms were identified. Consult the index for further page references.

A

Absolute poverty A minimum level of subsistence that no family should be expected to live below. (199)

Achieved status A social position that a person attains largely through his or her own efforts. (100, 187)

Activity theory An interactionist theory of aging that suggests that those elderly people who remain active and socially involved will be best adjusted. (290)

Adoption In a legal sense, a process that allows for the transfer of the legal rights, responsibilities, and privileges of parenthood to a new legal parent or parents. (316)

Aerotropolis An urban community that is centered around an airport and the hotels, office complexes, entertainment venues, and distribution facilities it supports. (438)

Affirmative action Positive efforts to recruit minority group members or women for jobs, promotions, and educational opportunities. (244, 401)

Ageism Prejudice and discrimination based on a person's age. (297)

Agrarian society The most technologically advanced form of preindustrial society. Members engage primarily in the production of food, but increase their crop yields through technological innovations such as the plow. (110)

Alienation A condition of estrangement or dissociation from the surrounding society. (124, 399)

Amalgamation The process through which a majority group and a minority group combine to form a new group. (248)

Anomie Durkheim's term for the loss of direction felt in a society when social control of individual behavior has become ineffective. (10, 166)

Anomie theory of deviance Robert Merton's theory of deviance as an adaptation of socially prescribed goals or of the means governing their attainment, or both. (167)

Anticipatory socialization Processes of socialization in which a person rehearses for future positions, occupations, and social relationships. (89)

Anti-Semitism Anti-Jewish prejudice. (257)

Apartheid A former policy of the South African government, designed to maintain the separation of Blacks and other non-Whites from the dominant Whites. (248)

Applied sociology The use of the discipline of sociology with the specific intent of yielding practical applications for human behavior and organizations. (18)

Argot Specialized language used by members of a group or subculture. (59)

Ascribed status A social position assigned to a person by society without regard for the person's unique talents or characteristics. (100, 187)

Assembling perspective A theory of collective behavior introduced by McPhail and Miller that seeks to examine how and why people move from different points in space to a common location. (465)

Assimilation The process through which a person forsakes his or her cultural tradition to become part of a different culture. (248)

Authority Institutionalized power that is recognized by the people over whom it is exercised. (371)

B

Basic sociology Sociological inquiry conducted with the objective of gaining a more profound knowledge of the fundamental aspects of social phenomena. Also known as *pure sociology*. (19)

Bilateral descent A kinship system in which both sides of a person's family are regarded as equally important. (308)

Bilingualism The use of two languages in a particular setting, such as the workplace or schoolroom, treating each language as equally legitimate. (68)

Birthrate The number of live births per 1,000 population in a given year. Also known as the *crude birthrate*. (440)

Black power A political philosophy, promoted by many younger Blacks in the 1960s, that supported the creation of Black-controlled political and economic institutions. (249)

Borderlands The area of common culture along the border between Mexico and the United States. (227)

Bourgeoisie Karl Marx's term for the capitalist class, comprising the owners of the means of production. (192)

Brain drain The immigration to the United States and other industrialized nations of skilled workers, professionals, and technicians who are desperately needed in their home countries. (412)

Bureaucracy A component of formal organization that uses rules and hierarchical ranking to achieve efficiency. (124)

Bureaucratization The process by which a group, organization, or social movement becomes increasingly bureaucratic. (125)

C

Capitalism An economic system in which the means of production are held largely in private hands and the main incentive for economic activity is the accumulation of profits. (192, 393)

Caste A hereditary rank, usually religiously dictated, that tends to be fixed and immobile. (185)

Causal logic The relationship between a condition or variable and a particular consequence, with one leading to the other. (30)

Census An enumeration, or counting, of a population. (440)

Charismatic authority Max Weber's term for power made legitimate by a leader's exceptional personal or emotional appeal to his or her followers. (371)

Charter school An experimental school that is developed and managed by individuals, groups of parents, or educational management organizations. (364)

Class A group of people who have a similar level of wealth and income. (193)

Class consciousness In Karl Marx's view, a subjective awareness held by members of a class regarding their common vested interests and the need for collective political action to bring about social change. (192)

Class system A social ranking based primarily on economic position in which achieved characteristics can influence social mobility. (189)

Classical theory An approach to the study of formal organizations that views workers as being motivated almost entirely by economic rewards. (126)

Clinical sociology The use of the discipline of sociology with the specific intent of altering social relationships or restructuring social institutions. (19)

Closed system A social system in which there is little or no possibility of individual social mobility. (203)

Coalition A temporary or permanent alliance geared toward a common goal. (121)

Code of ethics The standards of acceptable behavior developed by and for members of a profession. (38)

Cognitive theory of development Jean Piaget's theory that children's thought progresses through four stages of development. (83)

Cohabitation The practice of living together as a male–female couple without marrying. (321)

Collective behavior In the view of sociologist Neil Smelser, the relatively spontaneous and unstructured behavior of a group of people who are reacting to a common influence in an ambiguous situation. (462)

Colonialism The maintenance of political, social, economic, and cultural domination over a people by a foreign power for an extended period. (216)

Color-blind racism The use of the principle of race neutrality to defend a racially unequal status quo. (241, 402)

Communism As an ideal type, an economic system under which all property is communally owned and no social distinctions are made on the basis of people's ability to produce. (395)

Community A spatial or political unit of social organization that gives people a sense of belonging, based either on shared residence in a particular place or on a common identity. (438)

Concentric-zone theory A theory of urban growth devised by Ernest Burgess that sees growth in terms of a series of rings radiating from the central business district. (448)

Conflict perspective A sociological approach that assumes that social behavior is best understood in terms of tension between groups over power or the allocation of resources, including housing, money, access to services, and political representation. (14)

Conformity Going along with peers—individuals of our own status who have no special right to direct our behavior. (161)

Conspicuous consumption Purchasing and using goods not to survive but to flaunt one's superior wealth and social standing. (193)

Contact hypothesis An interactionist perspective which states that in cooperative circumstances, interracial contact between people of equal status will reduce prejudice. (246)

Content analysis The systematic coding and objective recording of data, guided by some rationale. (38)

Control group The subjects in an experiment who are not introduced to the independent variable by the researcher. (37)

Control theory A view of conformity and deviance that suggests that our connection to members of society leads us to systematically conform to society's norms. (165)

Control variable A factor that is held constant to test the relative impact of an independent variable. (33)

Corporate welfare Tax breaks, bailouts, direct payments, and grants that the government gives to corporations. (230)

Correlation A relationship between two variables in which a change in one coincides with a change in the other. (30)

Correspondence principle A term used by Bowles and Gintis to refer to the tendency of schools to promote the values expected of individuals in each social class and perpetuate social class divisions from one generation to the next. (357)

Counterculture A subculture that deliberately opposes certain aspects of the larger culture. (60)

Craze An exciting mass involvement that lasts for a relatively long period. (468)

Creationism A literal interpretation of the Bible regarding the creation of humanity and the universe, used to argue that evolution should not be presented as established scientific fact. (343)

Credentialism An increase in the lowest level of education needed to enter a field. (356)

Crime A violation of criminal law for which some governmental authority applies formal penalties. (171)

Cross-tabulation A table or matrix that shows the relationship between two or more variables. (44)

Crowd A temporary gathering of people in close proximity who share a common focus or interest. (466)

Cultural capital Noneconomic goods, such as family background and education, which are reflected in a knowledge of language and the arts. (13)

Cultural convergence The flow of content across multiple media, and the accompanying migration of media audiences. (137)

Cultural genocide The systematic destruction of a group's culture. (55)

Cultural relativism The viewing of people's behavior from the perspective of their own culture. (54, 392)

Cultural transmission A school of criminology that argues that criminal behavior is learned through social interactions. (168)

Cultural universal A common practice or belief found in every culture. (54)

Culture The totality of learned, socially transmitted customs, knowledge, material objects, and behavior. (53)

Culture industry The worldwide media industry that standardizes the goods and services demanded by consumers. (54)

Culture lag A period of maladjustment when the nonmaterial culture is still struggling to adapt to new material conditions. (58, 487)

Culture shock The feeling of surprise and disorientation that people experience when they encounter cultural practices that are different from their own. (60)

Culture war The polarization of society over controversial cultural elements. (65)

Curanderismo Latino folk medicine, a form of holistic health care and healing. (417)

D

Death rate The number of deaths per 1,000 population in a given year. Also known as the *crude death rate*. (440)

Degradation ceremony An aspect of the socialization process within some total institutions, in which people are subjected to humiliating rituals. (90)

Deindustrialization The systematic, widespread withdrawal of investment in basic aspects of productivity, such as factories and plants. (401)

Democracy In a literal sense, government by the people. (373)

Demographic transition A term used to describe the change from high birthrates and death rates to low birthrates and death rates. (442)

Demography The scientific study of population. (439)

Denomination A large, organized religion that is not officially linked to the state or government. (339)

Dependency theory An approach that contends that industrialized nations continue to exploit developing countries for their own gain. (216)

Dependent variable The variable in a causal relationship that is subject to the influence of another variable. (30)

Deviance Behavior that violates the standards of conduct or expectations of a group or society. (159)

Dictatorship A government in which one person has nearly total power to make and enforce laws. (373)

Differential association A theory of deviance proposed by Edwin Sutherland that holds that violation of rules results from exposure to attitudes favorable to criminal acts. (168)

Differential justice Differences in the way social control is exercised over different groups. (171)

Diffusion The process by which a cultural item spreads from group to group or society to society. (57)

Digital divide The relative lack of access to the latest technologies among low-income groups, racial and ethnic minorities, rural residents, and the citizens of developing countries. (145)

Disaster A sudden or disruptive event or set of events that overtaxes a community's resources, so that outside aid is necessary. (466)

Discovery The process of making known or sharing the existence of an aspect of reality. (56)

Discrimination The denial of opportunities and equal rights to individuals and groups because of prejudice or other arbitrary reasons. (241)

Disengagement theory A functionalist theory of aging that suggests that society and the aging individual mutually sever many of their relationships. (290)

Domestic partnership Two unrelated adults who share a mutually caring relationship, reside together, and agree to be jointly responsible for their dependents, basic living expenses, and other common necessities. (324)

Dominant ideology A set of cultural beliefs and practices that helps to maintain powerful social, economic, and political interests. (67, 143, 195)

Double consciousness The division of an individual's identity into two or more social realities. (12)

Downsizing Reductions taken in a company's workforce as part of deindustrialization. (402)

Dramaturgical approach A view of social interaction, popularized by Erving Goffman, in which people are seen as theatrical performers. (16, 81)

Dyad A two-member group. (122)

Dysfunction An element or process of a society that may disrupt the social system or reduce its stability. (14)

E

Ecclesia A religious organization that claims to include most or all members of a society and is recognized as the national or official religion. (339)

Ecological modernization The alignment of environmentally favorable practices with economic self-interest through constant adaptation and restructuring. (425)

Economic system The social institution through which goods and services are produced, distributed, and consumed. (392)

Education A formal process of learning in which some people consciously teach while others adopt the social role of learner. (350)

Egalitarian family An authority pattern in which spouses are regarded as equals. (309)

Elite model A view of society as being ruled by a small group of individuals who share a common set of political and economic interests. (378)

Emergent-norm perspective A theory of collective behavior proposed by Turner and Killian that holds that a collective definition of appropriate or inappropriate behavior emerges during episodes of collective behavior. (463)

Endogamy The restriction of mate selection to people within the same group. (312)

Environmental justice A legal strategy based on claims that racial minorities are subjected disproportionately to environmental hazards. (426)

Equilibrium model Talcott Parsons's functionalist view that society tends toward a state of stability or balance. (485)

Established sect J. Milton Yinger's term for a religious group that is the outgrowth of a sect, yet remains isolated from society. (340)

Estate system A system of stratification under which peasants were required to work land leased to them by nobles in exchange for military protection and other services. Also known as *feudalism*. (189)

Esteem The reputation that a specific person has earned within an occupation. (196)

Ethnic group A group that is set apart from others primarily because of its national origin or distinctive cultural patterns. (237)

Ethnocentrism The tendency to assume that one's own culture and way of life represent the norm or are superior to all others. (54, 240)

Ethnography The study of an entire social setting through extended systematic fieldwork. (36)

Euthanasia The act of bringing about the death of a hopelessly ill and suffering person in a relatively quick and painless way for reasons of mercy. (300)

Evolutionary theory A theory of social change that holds that society is moving in a definite direction. (485)

Exogamy The requirement that people select a mate outside certain groups. (312)

Experiment An artificially created situation that allows a researcher to manipulate variables. (37)

Experimental group The subjects in an experiment who are exposed to an independent variable introduced by a researcher. (37)

Exploitation theory A Marxist theory that views racial subordination in the United States as a manifestation of the class system inherent in capitalism. (245)

Expressiveness Concern for the maintenance of harmony and the internal emotional affairs of the family. (271)

Extended family A family in which relatives—such as grandparents, aunts, or uncles—live in the same home as parents and their children. (307)

F

Face-work A term used by Erving Goffman to refer to the efforts people make to maintain the proper image and avoid public embarrassment. (82)

Fad A temporary pattern of behavior that involves large numbers of people and is independent of preceding trends. (468)

Fair trade A movement in which consumers in industrialized countries voluntarily pay above-market prices for certain foods so that the workers who plant, pick, and pack the crops can receive higher wages. (392)

False consciousness A term used by Karl Marx to describe an attitude held by members of a class that does not accurately reflect their objective position. (192, 472)

Familism Pride in the extended family, expressed through the maintenance of close ties and strong obligations to kinfolk outside the immediate family. (315)

Family A set of people related by blood, marriage or some other agreed-on relationship, or adoption, who share the primary responsibility for reproduction and caring for members of society. (307)

Fashion A pleasurable mass involvement that has a line of historical continuity. (468)

Feminism The belief in social, economic, and political equality for women. (278)

Feminist view A sociological approach that views inequity in gender as central to all behavior and organization. (14)

Feminization of poverty A trend in which women constitute an increasing proportion of the poor people of the United States. (201)

Fertility The level of reproduction in a society. (439)

Focus group A carefully selected discussion group led by a trained moderator. (123)

Folkway A norm governing everyday behavior whose violation raises comparatively little concern. (63)

Force The actual or threatened use of coercion to impose one's will on others. (371)

Formal norm A norm that has been written down and that specifies strict punishments for violators. (63)

Formal organization A group designed for a special purpose and structured for maximum efficiency. (123)

Formal social control Social control that is carried out by authorized agents, such as police officers, judges, school administrators, and employers. (163)

Functionalist perspective A sociological approach that emphasizes the way in which the parts of a society are structured to maintain its stability. (13)

Fundamentalism An emphasis on doctrinal conformity and the literal interpretation of sacred texts. (338)

G

Gatekeeping The process by which a relatively small number of people in the media industry control what material eventually reaches the audience. (140)

Gemeinschaft A term used by Ferdinand Tönnies to describe a close-knit community, often found in rural areas, in which strong personal bonds unite members. (108)

Gender role Expectations regarding the proper behavior, attitudes, and activities of males and females. (184, 267)

Generalized other A term used by George Herbert Mead to refer to the attitudes, viewpoints, and expectations of society as a whole that a child takes into account in his or her behavior. (81)

Genocide The deliberate, systematic killing of an entire people or nation. (55, 247)

Gentrification The resettlement of low-income city neighborhoods by prosperous families and business firms. (456)

Gerontology The scientific study of the sociological and psychological aspects of aging and the problems of the aged. (289)

Gesellschaft A term used by Ferdinand Tönnies to describe a community, often urban, that is large and impersonal, with little commitment to the group or consensus on values. (109)

Glass ceiling An invisible barrier that blocks the promotion of a qualified individual in a work environment because of the individual's gender, race, or ethnicity. (242, 275)

Globalization The worldwide integration of government policies, cultures, social movements, and financial markets through trade and the exchange of ideas. (19, 218)

Goal displacement Overzealous conformity to official regulations of a bureaucracy. (125)

Group Any number of people with similar norms, values, and expectations who interact with one another on a regular basis. (103, 119)

Groupthink Uncritical acceptance of or conformity to the prevailing viewpoint. (123)

Growth rate The difference between births and deaths, plus the difference between immigrants and emigrants, per 1,000 population. (441)

H

Hate crime A criminal offense committed because of the offender's bias against a race, religion, ethnic group, national origin, or sexual orientation. Also referred to as *bias crime*. (174)

Hawthorne effect The unintended influence that observers of experiments can have on their subjects. (37)

Health As defined by the World Health Organization, a state of complete physical, mental, and social well-being, and not merely the absence of disease and infirmity. (411)

Hidden curriculum Standards of behavior that are deemed proper by society and are taught subtly in schools. (354)

Holistic medicine Therapies in which the health care practitioner considers the person's physical, mental, emotional, and spiritual characteristics. (420)

Homogamy The conscious or unconscious tendency to select a mate with personal characteristics similar to one's own. (312)

Homophobia Fear of and prejudice against homosexuality. (267)

Horizontal mobility The movement of an individual from one social position to another of the same rank. (203)

Horticultural society A preindustrial society in which people plant seeds and crops rather than merely subsist on available foods. (110)

Hospice care Treatment of the terminally ill in their own homes, or in special hospital units or other facilities, with the goal of helping them to die easily, without pain. (295)

Human ecology An area of study that is concerned with the interrelationships between people and their environment. (425, 448)

Human relations approach An approach to the study of formal organizations that emphasizes the role of people, communication, and participation in a bureaucracy and tends to focus on the informal structure of the organization. (127)

Hunting-and-gathering society A preindustrial society in which people rely on whatever foods and fibers are readily available in order to survive. (109)

Hypothesis A speculative statement about the relationship between two or more variables. (30)

I

Ideal type A construct or model for evaluating specific cases. (10, 124)

Impression management A term used by Erving Goffman to refer to the altering of the presentation of the self in order to create distinctive appearances and satisfy particular audiences. (81)

Incest taboo The prohibition of sexual relationships between certain culturally specified relatives. (312)

Incidence The number of new cases of a specific disorder that occur within a given population during a stated period. (415)

Income Salaries and wages. (87)

Independent variable The variable in a causal relationship that causes or influences a change in a second variable. (30)

Index crimes The eight types of crime reported annually by the FBI in the *Uniform Crime Reports*: murder, rape, robbery, assault, burglary, theft, motor vehicle theft, and arson. (172)

Industrial city A relatively large city characterized by open competition, an open class system, and elaborate specialization in the manufacturing of goods. (447)

Industrial society A society that depends on mechanization to produce its goods and services. (110, 393)

Infant mortality rate The number of deaths of infants under one year old per 1,000 live births in a given year. (413, 440)

Influence The exercise of power through a process of persuasion. (371)

Informal economy Transfers of money, goods, or services that are not reported to the government. (395)

Informal norm A norm that is generally understood but not precisely recorded. (63)

Informal social control Social control that is carried out casually by ordinary people through such means as laughter, smiles, and ridicule. (163)

In-group Any group or category to which people feel they belong. (120)

Innovation The process of introducing a new idea or object to a culture through discovery or invention. (56)

Institutional discrimination The denial of opportunities and equal rights to individuals and groups that results from the normal operations of a society. (244, 273)

Instrumentality An emphasis on tasks, a focus on more distant goals, and a concern for the external relationship between one's family and other social institutions. (271)

Intelligent design (ID) The idea that life is so complex that it could only have been created by intelligent design. (344)

Interactionist perspective A sociological approach that generalizes about everyday forms of social interaction in order to explain society as a whole. (15)

Intergenerational mobility Changes in the social position of children relative to their parents. (203)

Interview A face-to-face, telephone, or online questioning of a respondent to obtain desired information. (34)

Intragenerational mobility Changes in social position within a person's adult life. (204)

Invention The combination of existing cultural items into a form that did not exist before. (56)

Iron law of oligarchy A principle of organizational life developed by Robert Michels, under which even a democratic organization will eventually develop into a bureaucracy ruled by a few individuals. (126)

K

Kinship The state of being related to others. (308)

L

Labeling theory An approach to deviance that attempts to explain why certain people are viewed as deviants while others engaged in the same behavior are not. (169)

Labor union Organized workers who share either the same skill or the same employer. (130)

Laissez-faire A form of capitalism under which people compete freely, with minimal government intervention in the economy. (393)

Language An abstract system of word meanings and symbols for all aspects of culture; includes gestures and other nonverbal communication. (61)

Latent function An unconscious or unintended function that may reflect hidden purposes. (14)

Law Governmental social control. (63, 164)

Liberation theology Use of a church, primarily Roman Catholicism, in a political effort to eliminate poverty, discrimination, and other forms of injustice from a secular society. (336)

Life chances Max Weber's term for the opportunities people have to provide themselves with material goods, positive living conditions, and favorable life experiences. (202)

Life course approach A research orientation in which sociologists and other social scientists look closely at the social factors that influence people throughout their lives, from birth to death. (89)

Life expectancy The median number of years a person can be expected to live under current mortality conditions. (441)

Looking-glass self A concept used by Charles Horton Cooley that emphasizes the self as the product of our social interactions. (80)

Luddites Rebellious craft workers in 19th-century England who destroyed new factory machinery as part of their resistance to the Industrial Revolution. (488)

M

Machismo A sense of virility, personal worth, and pride in one's maleness. (314)

Macrosociology Sociological investigation that concentrates on large-scale phenomena or entire civilizations. (13)

Manifest function An open, stated, and conscious function. (14)

Mass media Print and electronic means of communication that carry messages to widespread audiences. (136)

Master status A status that dominates others and thereby determines a person's general position in society. (101)

Material culture The physical or technological aspects of our daily lives. (58)

Matriarchy A society in which women dominate in family decision making. (309)

Matrilineal descent A kinship system in which only the mother's relatives are significant. (308)

Matrix of domination The cumulative impact of oppression because of race and ethnicity, gender, and social class, as well as religion, sexual orientation, disability, age, and citizenship status. (272)

McDonaldization The process by which the principles of the fast-food restaurant are coming to dominate more and more sectors of American society as well as the rest of the world. (118, 421)

Mean A number calculated by adding a series of values and then dividing by the number of values. (44)

Mechanical solidarity A collective consciousness that emphasizes group solidarity, characteristic of societies with minimal division of labor. (108)

Median The midpoint or number that divides a series of values into two groups of equal numbers of values. (44)

Mental illness A disorder of the brain that disrupts a person's thinking, feeling, and ability to interact with others. (423)

Microfinancing Lending small sums of money to the poor so they can work their way out of poverty. (403)

Microsociology Sociological investigation that stresses the study of small groups, often through experimental means. (13)

Midlife crisis A stressful period of self-evaluation that begins at about age 40. (293)

Migration The relatively permanent movement of people, with the purpose of changing their place of residence. (445)

Minority group A subordinate group whose members have significantly less control or power over their own lives than the members of a dominant or majority group have over theirs. (237)

Mode The single most common value in a series of scores. (44)

Model, or ideal, minority A subordinate group whose members supposedly have succeeded economically, socially, and educationally despite past prejudice and discrimination, and without resorting to confrontations with Whites. (252)

Modernization The far-reaching process through which periphery nations move from traditional or less developed institutions to those characteristic of more developed societies. (222)

Modernization theory A functionalist approach that proposes that modernization and development will gradually improve the lives of people in developing nations. (222)

Monarchy A form of government headed by a single member of a royal family, usually a king, queen, or some other hereditary ruler. (373)

Monogamy A form of marriage in which one woman and one man are married only to each other. (307)

Monopoly Control of a market by a single business firm. (394)

Morbidity rate The incidence of disease in a given population. (415)

Mores Norms deemed highly necessary to the welfare of a society. (65)

Mortality rate The incidence of death in a given population. (415)

Multinational corporation A commercial organization that is headquartered in one country but does business throughout the world. (218)

Multiple masculinities A variety of male gender roles, including nurturing-caring and effeminate-gay roles, that men may play along with their more pervasive traditional role of dominating women. (269)

Multiple-nuclei theory A theory of urban growth developed by Harris and Ullman that views growth as emerging from many centers of development, each of which reflects a particular urban need or activity. (448)

N

Narcotizing dysfunction The phenomenon in which the media provide such massive amounts of coverage that the audience becomes numb and fails to act on the information, regardless of how compelling the issue. (140)

Natural science The study of the physical features of nature and the ways in which they interact and change. (6)

Naturally occurring retirement community (NORC) An area that has gradually become an informal center for senior citizens. (294)

Neocolonialism Continuing dependence of former colonies on foreign countries. (216)

Netizen A person who is actively involved in online communities and is committed to the free flow of information, with few outside controls. (141)

New religious movement (NRM) or cult A small, secretive religious group that represents either a new religion or a major innovation of an existing faith. (341)

New social movement An organized collective activity that addresses values and social identities, as well as improvements in the quality of life. (473)

New urban sociology An approach to urbanization that considers the interplay of local, national, and worldwide forces and their effect on local space, with special emphasis on the impact of global economic activity. (450)

Nonmaterial culture Ways of using material objects, as well as customs, beliefs, philosophies, governments, and patterns of communication. (58)

Nonperiodic assembly A nonrecurring gathering of people that often results from word-of-mouth information. (465)

Nonverbal communication The sending of messages through the use of gestures, facial expressions, and postures. (16)

Norm An established standard of behavior maintained by a society. (62)

Nuclear family A married couple and their unmarried children living together. (307)

O

Obedience Compliance with higher authorities in a hierarchical structure. (161)

Objective method A technique for measuring social class that assigns individuals to classes on the basis of criteria such as occupation, education, income, and place of residence. (195)

Observation A research technique in which an investigator collects information through direct participation by closely watching a group or community. (36)

Offshoring The transfer of work to foreign contractors. (402)

Oligarchy A form of government in which a few individuals rule. (373)

Open system A social system in which the position of each individual is influenced by his or her achieved status. (203)

Operational definition An explanation of an abstract concept that is specific enough to allow a researcher to assess the concept. (29)

Opinion leader Someone who influences the opinions and decisions of others through day-to-day personal contact and communication. (149)

Organic solidarity A collective consciousness that rests on mutual interdependence, characteristic of societies with a complex division of labor. (108)

Organized crime The work of a group that regulates relations between criminal enterprises involved in illegal activities, including prostitution, gambling, and the smuggling and sale of illegal drugs. (173)

Out-group A group or category to which people feel they do not belong. (120)

P

Panic A fearful arousal or collective flight based on a generalized belief that may or may not be accurate. (468)

Patriarchy A society in which men dominate in family decision making. (309)

Patrilineal descent A kinship system in which only the father's relatives are significant. (308)

Peace The absence of war or, more broadly, a proactive effort to develop cooperative relations among nations. (382)

Percentage A portion of 100. (29)

Periodic assembly A recurring, relatively routine gathering of people, such as a college class. (465)

Personality A person's typical patterns of attitudes, needs, characteristics, and behavior. (77)

Peter principle A principle of organizational life, originated by Laurence J. Peter, according to which every employee within a hierarchy tends to rise to his or her level of incompetence. (125)

Pluralism Mutual respect for one another's cultures among the various groups in a society, which allows minorities to express their cultures without experiencing prejudice. (248)

Pluralist model A view of society in which many competing groups within the community have access to government, so that no single group is dominant. (379)

Political system The social institution that is founded on a recognized set of procedures for implementing and achieving society's goals. (370)

Politics In Harold Lasswell's words, "who gets what, when, and how." (371)

Polyandry A form of polygamy in which a woman may have more than one husband at the same time. (307)

Polygamy A form of marriage in which an individual may have several husbands or wives simultaneously. (307)

Polygyny A form of polygamy in which a man may have more than one wife at the same time. (307)

Population pyramid A special type of bar chart that shows the distribution of a population by gender and age. (442)

Postindustrial city A city in which global finance and the electronic flow of information dominate the economy. (447)

Postindustrial society A society whose economic system is engaged primarily in the processing and control of information. (110)

Postmodern society A technologically sophisticated society that is preoccupied with consumer goods and media images. (111)

Power The ability to exercise one's will over others. (193, 371)

Power elite A term used by C. Wright Mills to refer to a small group of military, industrial, and government leaders who control the fate of the United States. (378)

Precarious work Employment that is poorly paid, and from the worker's perspective, insecure and unprotected. (200)

Preindustrial city A city of only a few thousand people that is characterized by a relatively closed class system and limited mobility. (446)

Prejudice A negative attitude toward an entire category of people, often an ethnic or racial minority. (240)

Prestige The respect and admiration that an occupation holds in a society. (196)

Prevalence The total number of cases of a specific disorder that exist at a given time. (415)

Primary group A small group characterized by intimate, face-to-face association and cooperation. (119)

Profane The ordinary and commonplace elements of life, as distinguished from the sacred. (331)

Professional criminal A person who pursues crime as a day-to-day occupation, developing skilled techniques and enjoying a certain degree of status among other criminals. (172)

Proletariat Karl Marx's term for the working class in a capitalist society. (192)

Protestant ethic Max Weber's term for the disciplined work ethic, this-worldly concerns, and rational orientation to life emphasized by John Calvin and his followers. (335)

Public A dispersed group of people, not necessarily in contact with one another, who share an interest in an issue. (469)

Public opinion Expressions of attitudes on matters of public policy that are communicated to decision makers. (469)

Q

Qualitative research Research that relies on what is seen in field or naturalistic settings more than on statistical data. (36)

Quantitative research Research that collects and reports data primarily in numerical form. (36)

Quasi-religion A scholarly category that includes organizations that may see themselves as religious but are seen by others as "sort of religious." (342)

Questionnaire A printed or written form used to obtain information from a respondent. (34)

R

Racial formation A sociohistorical process in which racial categories are created, inhibited, transformed, and destroyed. (238)

Racial group A group that is set apart from others because of physical differences that have taken on social significance. (237)

Racial profiling Any arbitrary action initiated by an authority based on race, ethnicity, or national origin rather than on a person's behavior. (246)

Racism The belief that one race is supreme and all others are innately inferior. (240)

Random sample A sample for which every member of an entire population has the same chance of being selected. (32)

Rational-legal authority Power made legitimate by law. (371)

Reference group Any group that individuals use as a standard for evaluating themselves and their own behavior. (120)

Relative deprivation The conscious feeling of a negative discrepancy between legitimate expectations and present actualities. (471)

Relative poverty A floating standard of deprivation by which people at the bottom of a society, whatever their lifestyles, are judged to be disadvantaged *in comparison with the nation as a whole*. (199)

Reliability The extent to which a measure produces consistent results. (32)

Religion According to Émile Durkheim, a unified system of beliefs and practices relative to sacred things. (33)

Religious belief A statement to which members of a particular religion adhere. (338)

Religious experience The feeling or perception of being in direct contact with the ultimate reality, such as a divine being, or of being overcome with religious emotion. (338)

Religious ritual A practice required or expected of members of a faith. (338)

Remittances The monies that immigrants return to their families of origin. Also called *migradollars*. (228)

Representative democracy A form of government in which certain individuals are selected to speak for the people. (373)

Research design A detailed plan or method for obtaining data scientifically. (34)

Resocialization The process of discarding former behavior patterns and accepting new ones as part of a transition in one's life. (90)

Resource mobilization The ways in which a social movement utilizes such resources as money, political influence, access to the media, and personnel. (472)

Rite of passage A ritual marking the symbolic transition from one social position to another. (89)

Role conflict The situation that occurs when incompatible expectations arise from two or more social positions held by the same person. (101)

Role exit The process of disengagement from a role that is central to one's self-identity in order to establish a new role and identity. (102)

Role strain The difficulty that arises when the same social position imposes conflicting demands and expectations. (102)

Role taking The process of mentally assuming the perspective of another and responding from that imagined viewpoint. (80)

Rumor A piece of information gathered informally that is used to interpret an ambiguous situation. (469)

S

Sacred Elements beyond everyday life that inspire awe, respect, and even fear. (331)

Sample A selection from a larger population that is statistically representative of that population. (31)

Sanction A penalty or reward for conduct concerning a social norm. (64, 161)

Sandwich generation The generation of adults who simultaneously try to meet the competing needs of their parents and their children. (293)

Sapir-Whorf hypothesis A hypothesis concerning the role of language in shaping our interpretation of reality. It holds that language is culturally determined. (61)

Science The body of knowledge obtained by methods based on systematic observation. (5)

Scientific management approach Another name for the classical theory of formal organizations. (126)

Scientific method A systematic, organized series of steps that ensures maximum objectivity and consistency in researching a problem. (29)

Second shift The double burden—work outside the home followed by child care and housework—that many women face and few men share equitably. (277)

Secondary analysis A variety of research techniques that make use of previously collected and publicly accessible information and data. (37)

Secondary group A formal, impersonal group in which there is little social intimacy or mutual understanding. (119)

Sect A relatively small religious group that has broken away from some other religious organization to renew what it considers the original vision of the faith. (339)

Secularization The process through which religion's influence on other social institutions diminishes. (330)

Segregation The physical separation of two groups of people in terms of residence, workplace, and social events; often imposed on a minority group by a dominant group. (248)

Self According to George Herbert Mead, a distinct identity that sets us apart from others. (80)

Serial monogamy A form of marriage in which a person may have several spouses in his or her lifetime, but only one spouse at a time. (307)

Sexism The ideology that one sex is superior to the other. (273)

Sick role Societal expectations about the attitudes and behavior of a person viewed as being ill. (411)

Significant other A term used by George Herbert Mead to refer to an individual who is most important in the development of the self, such as a parent, friend, or teacher. (81)

Single-parent family A family in which only one parent is present to care for the children. (318)

Slavery A system of enforced servitude in which some people are owned by other people. (187)

Small group A group small enough for all members to interact simultaneously—that is, to talk with one another or at least be well acquainted. (121)

Social capital The collective benefit of social networks, which are built on reciprocal trust. (13)

Social change Significant alteration over time in behavior patterns and culture, including norms and values. (484)

Social constructionist perspective An approach to deviance that emphasizes the role of culture in the creation of the deviant identity. (170)

Social control The techniques and strategies for preventing deviant human behavior in any society. (161)

Social disorganization theory The theory that crime and deviance are caused by the absence or breakdown of communal relationships and social institutions. (169)

Social epidemiology The study of the distribution of disease, impairment, and general health status across a population. (415)

Social inequality A condition in which members of society have differing amounts of wealth, prestige, or power. (19, 186)

Social institution An organized pattern of beliefs and behavior centered on basic social needs. (103)

Social interaction The ways in which people respond to one another. (98)

Social mobility Movement of individuals or groups from one position in a society's stratification system to another. (203)

Social movement An organized collective activity to bring about or resist fundamental change in an existing group or society. (470)

Social network A series of social relationships that links a person directly to others, and through them indirectly to still more people. (105)

Social role A set of expectations for people who occupy a given social position or status. (101)

Social science The study of the social features of humans and the ways in which they interact and change. (6)

Social structure The way in which society is organized into predictable relationships. (98)

Socialism An economic system under which the means of production and distribution are collectively owned. (395)

Socialization The lifelong process in which people learn the attitudes, values, and behaviors appropriate for members of a particular culture. (76)

Societal-reaction approach Another name for *labeling theory*. (169)

Society A fairly large number of people who live in the same territory, are relatively independent of people outside their area, and participate in a common culture. (53)

Sociobiology The systematic study of how biology affects human social behavior. (54)

Sociocultural evolution Long-term trends in societies resulting from the interplay of continuity, innovation, and selection. (109)

Socioeconomic status (SES) A measure of social class that is based on income, education, and occupation. (197)

Sociological imagination An awareness of the relationship between an individual and the wider society, both today and in the past. (5)

Sociology The scientific study of social behavior and human groups. (5)

Sovereignty movement The effort by the indigenous people of Hawai'i to win self-government, as well as the restoration of—or compensation for—their ancestral lands. (375)

Squatter settlement An area occupied by the very poor on the fringe of a city, in which housing is constructed by the settlers themselves from discarded material. (451)

Status A term used by sociologists to refer to any of the full range of socially defined positions within a large group or society. (100)

Status group A term used by Max Weber to refer to people who have the same prestige or lifestyle, independent of their class positions. (193)

Stereotype An unreliable generalization about all members of a group that does not recognize individual differences within the group. (143, 239)

Stigma A label used to devalue members of certain social groups. (168)

Stratification A structured ranking of entire groups of people that perpetuates unequal economic rewards and power in a society. (186)

Subculture A segment of society that shares a distinctive pattern of customs, rules, and traditions that differs from the pattern of the larger society. (59)

Suburb According to the Census Bureau, any territory within a metropolitan area that is not included in the central city. (453)

Survey A study, generally in the form of an interview or questionnaire, that provides researchers with information about how people think and act. (34)

Symbol A gesture, object, or word that forms the basis of human communication. (62)

Symbolic ethnicity An ethnic identity that emphasizes concerns such as ethnic food or political issues rather than deeper ties to one's ethnic heritage. (258)

T

Teacher-expectancy effect The impact that a teacher's expectations about a student's performance may have on the student's actual achievements. (358)

Technology Cultural information about the ways in which the material resources of the environment may be used to satisfy human needs and desires. (58, 109)

Telecommuter An employee who works full-time or part-time at home rather than in an outside office, and who is linked to supervisor and colleagues through phone lines, Wi-Fi, the Internet, and smartphones. (128)

Terrorism The use or threat of violence against random or symbolic targets in pursuit of political aims. (383)

Theory In sociology, a set of statements that seeks to explain problems, actions, or behavior. (8)

Total fertility rate (TFR) The average number of children born alive to any woman, assuming that she conforms to current fertility rates. (440)

Total institution A term coined by Erving Goffman to refer to an institution that regulates all aspects of a person's life under a single authority, such as a prison, the military, a mental hospital, or a convent. (90)

Totalitarianism Virtually complete government control and surveillance over all aspects of a society's social and political life. (373)

Tracking The practice of placing students in specific curriculum groups on the basis of their test scores and other criteria. (356)

Traditional authority Legitimate power conferred by custom and accepted practice. (371)

Trained incapacity The tendency of workers in a bureaucracy to become so specialized that they develop blind spots and fail to notice obvious problems. (124)

Transnational An immigrant who sustains multiple social relationships that link his or her society of origin with the society of settlement. (259, 495)

Transnational crime Crime that occurs across multiple national borders. (175)

Triad A three-member group. (122)

U

Underclass The long-term poor who lack training and skills. (201)

Urban ecology An area of study that focuses on the interrelationships between people and their environment in urban areas. (448)

Urbanism A term used by Louis Wirth to describe distinctive patterns of social behavior evident among city residents. (447)

V

Validity The degree to which a measure or scale truly reflects the phenomenon under study. (31)

Value A collective conception of what is considered good, desirable, and proper—or bad, undesirable, and improper—in a culture. (64)

Value-added model A theory of collective behavior proposed by sociologist Neil Smelser to explain how broad social conditions are transformed in a definite pattern into some form of collective behavior. (464)

Value neutrality Max Weber's term for objectivity of sociologists in the interpretation of data. (40)

Variable A measurable trait or characteristic that is subject to change under different conditions. (30)

Verstehen The German word for "understanding" or "insight"; used by Max Weber to stress the need for sociologists to take into account the subjective meanings people attach to their actions. (10)

Vertical mobility The movement of an individual from one social position to another of a different rank. (203)

Vested interests Veblen's term for those people or groups who will suffer in the event of social change, and who have a stake in maintaining the status quo. (487)

Victimization survey A questionnaire or interview given to a sample of the population to determine whether people have been victims of crime. (176)

Victimless crime A term used by sociologists to describe the willing exchange among adults of widely desired but illegal goods and services. (172)

Visitability The accessibility of private homes to visitors with disabilities. (477)

Vital statistics Records of births, deaths, marriages, and divorces gathered through a registration system maintained by governmental units. (440)

W

War Conflict between organizations that possess trained combat forces equipped with deadly weapons. (381)

Wealth An inclusive term encompassing all a person's material assets, including land, stocks, and other types of property. (187)

White-collar crime Illegal acts committed by affluent, "respectable" individuals in the course of business activities. (173)

White privilege Rights or immunities granted to people as a particular benefit or favor simply because they are White. (243)

World systems analysis Immanuel Wallerstein's view of the global economic system as one divided between certain industrialized nations that control wealth and developing countries that are controlled and exploited. (216, 450)

Z

Zero population growth (ZPG) The state of a population in which the number of births plus immigrants equals the number of deaths plus emigrants. (444)

references

A

Abercrombie, Nicholas, Bryan S. Turner, and Stephen Hill, eds. 1990. *Dominant Ideologies.* Cambridge, MA: Unwin Hyman.

———, Stephen Hill, and Bryan S. Turner. 1980. *The Dominant Ideology Thesis.* London: Allen and Unwin.

Aberle, David F., A. K. Cohen, A. K. Davis, M. J. Leng, Jr., and F. N. Sutton. 1950. "The Functional Prerequisites of a Society." *Ethics* 60 (January):100–111.

Abramson, David, Irwin Redlener, Tasha Stehling-Ariza, and Elizabeth Fuller. 2007. *The Legacy of Katrina's Children: Estimating the Numbers of At-Risk Children in the Gulf Coast States of Louisiana and Mississippi.* New York: Columbia University Mailman School of Public Health.

Acharya, Meena. 2000. *Labor Market Developments and Poverty: With Focus on Economic Opportunities for Women.* Kathmandu, Nepal: Tanka Prasad Acharya Foundation/FES.

Acohido, Byron. 2010. "Tech-Savvy Put Explosion to Work." *USA Today,* November 17, pp. B1, B2.

Adams, Tyrene L., and Stephen A. Smith. 2008. *Electronic Tribes: The Virtual Worlds of Geeks, Gamas, Shamans, and Scammers.* Austin: University of Texas Press.

Adamy, Janet. 2008. "Starbucks Plans to License 150 Stores in Europe." *New York Times,* June 12, p. B3.

Addams, Jane. 1910. *Twenty Years at Hull-House.* New York: Macmillan.

———. 1930. *The Second Twenty Years at Hull-House.* New York: Macmillan.

Adler, Patricia A., and Peter Adler. 2007. "The Demedicalization of Self-Injury: From Psychopathology to Sociological Deviance." *Journal of Contemporary Ethnography* 36 (October):537–570.

———, ———, and John M. Johnson. 1992. "Street Corner Society Revisited." *Journal of Contemporary Ethnography* 21 (April):3–10.

Adler, Roy D. 2008. "Counting on the Middle-Class." *Miller-McCune* (November–December):20–23.

Adorno, Theodor. [1971] 1991. *The Culture Industry.* London: Routledge.

Aguirre, Benigno E., E. L. Quarantelli, and Jorge L. Mendoza. 1988. "The Collective Behavior of Fads: The Characteristics, Effects, and Career of Streaking." *American Sociological Review* 53 (August):569–584.

Alain, Michel. 1985. "An Empirical Validation of Relative Deprivation." *Human Relations* 38 (8):739–749.

Alba, Richard D. 2009. *Blurring the Color Line: The New Chance for a More Integrated America.* Cambridge, MA: Harvard University Press.

———. 1990. *Ethnic Identity: The Transformation of White America.* New Haven, CT: Yale University Press.

Albas, Cheryl, and Daniel Albas. 1996. "An Invitation to the Ethnographic Study of University Examination Behavior: Concepts, Methodology and Implications." *Canadian Journal of Higher Education* 26 (3):1–26.

Albas, Daniel, and Cheryl Albas. 1988. "Aces and Bombers: The Post-Exam Impression Management Strategies of Students." *Symbolic Interaction* 11 (Fall):289–302.

Albrecht, Gary L. 1995. "Review of Disability Laws, Enabling Acts: Disability Rights in Britain and America." *Contemporary Sociology* 24 (5):627–629.

———. 1997. "Disability Is Area Rich with Sociological Opportunity." *Footnotes* 25 (December):6.

———. 2004. "Disability: Sociological Perspectives." Pp. 3710–3713 in *International Encyclopedia of the Social and Behavioral Sciences,* edited by Neil J. Smelser and Paul B. Baltes. New York: Elsevier.

———, ed. 2005. *Encyclopedia of Disability.* Thousand Oaks, CA: Sage.

Alderman, Liz. 2010. "Dubai Rises from Ashes of Debt Crisis." *International Herald Tribune,* August 30, pp. 1, 20.

Alexander, Karl L. 1997. "Public Schools and the Public Good." *Social Forces* 70 (September):1–30.

Ali, Syed. 2010. "Permanent Impermanence." *Contexts* (Spring):26–31.

Al-Jadda, Souheila. 2006. "A Veil Doesn't Mean 'Oppressed.'" *USA Today,* June 22, p. A13.

Al Jazeera. 2010. Home Page. Accessed February 7 (http://english.aljazeera.net/HomePage).

Allen, Bem P. 1978. *Social Behavior: Fact and Falsehood.* Chicago: Nelson-Hall.

Alliance for Board Diversity. 2008. *Women and Minorities on* Fortune *100 Boards.* Washington, DC: Catalyst, Prout Group, Executive Leadership Council, and Hispanic Association on Corporate Responsibility.

Allport, Gordon W. 1979. *The Nature of Prejudice.* 25th anniversary ed. Reading, MA: Addison-Wesley.

Alon, Sigal. 2009. "The Evolution of Class Inequality in Higher Education: Competition, Exclusion, and Adaptation." *American Sociological Review* 74 (October):731–755.

Alvord, Lori Arviso, and Elizabeth Cohen Van Pelt. 1999. *The Scalpel and the Silver Bear.* New York: Bantam Books.

Alwin, Duane F. 2002. "Generations X, Y, and Z: Are They Changing America?" *Contexts* (Fall–Winter):42–51.

Alzheimer's Association. 2010. *2010 Alzheimer's Disease Facts and Figures.* Chicago: Alzheimer's Association.

American Academy of Cosmetic Surgery. 2010. "New Survey Indicates More than 17 Million Cosmetic Procedures Performed Last Year in U.S." Chicago: AACS.

American Bar Association. 1997. *Section of the Individual Rights and Responsibilities: Section of Litigation (Capital Punishment).* Chicago: Division for Policy Administration, ABA.

American Community Survey. 2010. "2008 American Community Survey." Accessed at http://factfinder.census.gov.

American Jewish Committee. 2005. *2005 Annual Survey of American Jewish Opinion.* New York: AJC.

American Lung Association. 2009. *State of the Air 2009.* Washington, DC: ALA.

American Psychological Association. 2008. "Being Gay Is Just as Healthy as Being Straight." Accessed February 25 (www.apa.org).

American Sociological Association. 1997. *Code of Ethics.* Washington, DC: American Sociological Association. Accessible at www.asanet.org/members/ecoderev.html.

———. 2005. "Need Today's Data Yesterday." Accessed December 17 (www.asanet.org).

———. 2009. *21st Century Careers with an Undergraduate Degree in Sociology.* Washington, DC: ASA.

———. 2010a. *2010 Guide to Graduate Departments of Sociology.* Washington, DC: ASA.

———. 2010b. "What Are Sections?" Accessed January 4 (www.asanet.org/cs/root/leftnav/sections/overview).

American Soybean Association. 2011. "World Soybean Production 2009." Accessed June 1 (www.soystats.com).

Amnesty International. 2009. *Death Sentences and Executions 2009.* London: Amnesty International. Accessible at http://www.amnesty.org/en/library/asset/ACT50/001/2010/en/17348b70-3fc7-40b2-a258-af92778c73e5/act500012010en.pdf.

Andersen, Margaret. 2007. *Thinking about Women: Sociological Perspectives on Sex and Gender.* 7th ed. New York: Allyn and Bacon.

Anderson, Elijah. 1990. *Streetwise: Race, Class, and Change in an Urban Community.* Chicago: University of Chicago Press.

Anderson, Gretchen. 2009. *Love, Actually: A National Survey of Adults 18+ on Love, Relationships, and Romance.* Washington, DC: AARP.

Anderson, John Ward, and Molly Moore. 1993. "The Burden of Womanhood." *Washington Post National Weekly Edition* 10 (March 22–28):6–7.

Anderson, Warwick. 2003. *The Cultivation of Whiteness: Science, Health and Racial Destiny in Australia.* New York: Perseus.

Angier, Natalie. 1998. "Drugs, Sports, Body Image and G.I. Joe." *New York Times,* December 22, pp. D1, D3.

Angwin, Julia. 2010. "The Web's New Gold Mine: Your Secrets." *Wall Street Journal,* July 31, pp. W1, W2.

———, and Jennifer Valentino-DeVries. 2010a. "Race Is On to 'Fingerprint' Phones, PCs." *Wall Street Journal,* December 1, pp. A1, A15.

———, and ———. 2010b. "Web Privacy 'Inadequate.'" *Wall Street Journal,* December 2, pp. B1, B2.

Ansell, Amy E. 2008. "Color Blindness." Pp. 320–321, vol. 1, in *Encyclopedia of Race, Ethnicity, and Society,* edited by Richard T. Schaefer. Thousand Oaks, CA: Sage.

Anti-Defamation League. 2010. "2009 Audit of Anti-Semitic Incidents: Summary of Findings." Accessed March 18, 2011 (www.adl.org/main_anti_semitism_domestic/2009_Audit.htm).

References

Arab American Institute. 2010. "Demographics." Accessed March 7 (www.aaiusa.org/arab-americans/22/demographics).

Archibold, Randal C., and Julia Preston. 2008. "Homeland Security Stands by Its Fence." *New York Times,* May 21.

Argetsinger, Amy, and Jonathan Krim. 2002. "Stopping the Music." *Washington Post National Weekly Edition* 20 (December 2):20.

Arias, Elizabeth. 2010. "United States Life Tables, 2006." *National Vital Statistics Reports* 58 (June 28).

Armer, J. Michael, and John Katsillis. 1992. "Modernization Theory." Pp. 1299–1304, vol. 4, in *Encyclopedia of Sociology,* edited by Edgar F. Borgatta and Marie L. Borgatta. New York: Macmillan.

Ash, Timothy Garton. 2007. "Welcome to a Mixed-Up World." *Globe and Mail* (Toronto), July 14, p. A19.

Asian American Journalists Association. 2007. "Media Advisory: Coverage on Virginia Tech Shooting Incident." Accessed May 16 (www.aaja.org).

Association of American Medical Colleges. 2011. "AAMC Faculty Roster, May 2009" and "AAMC Data Warehouse." Accessible at www.aamc.org.

Association of Theological Schools. 2011. "2010–2011 Annual Data Tables: Table 2-12A." Accessed March 28 (www.ats.edu/Resources/Publications/Documents/AnnualDataTables/2010-11Annual-DataTables.pdf).

Atchley, Robert C. 1976. *The Sociology of Retirement.* New York: Wiley.

———, and Amanda S. Barusch. 2004. *Social Forces and Agency: An Introduction to Social Gerontology.* 10th ed. Belmont, CA: Thomson.

Attwood, Bain. 2003. *Rights for Aborigines.* Crows Nest, Australia: Allen and Unwin.

Aud, Susan, Mary Ann Fox, and Angelina KewalRamani. 2010. *Status and Trends in the Education of Racial and Ethnic Groups.* Washington, DC: National Center for Education Statistics, U.S. Department of Education.

Austin, April. 2002. "Cellphones and Strife in Congo." *Christian Science Monitor,* December 5, p. 11.

Australia. 1997. "Bringing Them Home: Report of the National Inquiry into the Separation of Aboriginal and Torres Strait Islander Children from Their Families." Accessible at www.human-rights.gov.au.

———. 2008. "Apology to Australia's Indigenous Peoples, House of Representatives, Parliament House, Canberra." Accessed February 13 (www.pm.gov.au/media/speech/2008/speech_0073.cfm).

Azumi, Koya, and Jerald Hage. 1972. *Organizational Systems.* Lexington, MA: Heath.

B

Babad, Elisha Y., and P. J. Taylor. 1992. "Transparency of Teacher Expectancies across Language, Cultural Boundaries." *Journal of Educational Research* 86:120–125.

Baby Name Wizard. 2010. "Name Voyager." Accessed January 17 (www.babynamewizard.com).

Bacon Lovers' Talk. 2009. "Bacon Lovers' Talk." Accessed February 4 (www.bacontalk.com/).

Bado-Fralick, Nikki, and Rebecca Sachs Norris. 2010. *Toying with God: The World of Religious Games and Dolls.* Waco, TX: Baylor University Press.

Bajaj, Vikas. 2011a. "15 Years in Microcredit Has Suffered a Black Eye." *New York Times,* January 6, p. B3.

———. 2011b. "Luster Dims for a Public Microlender." *New York Times,* May 11, pp. 1, 4.

Baker, Joseph O., and Buster G. Smith. 2009. "The Names: Social Characteristics of the Religiously Unfaithful." *Social Forces* 87(March):1251–1263.

Baker, Peter. 2009. "Obama Reverses Rules on U.S. Abortion Aid." *New York Times,* January 24.

Baker, Therese L. 1999. *Doing Social Research.* 3rd ed. New York: McGraw-Hill.

Barbaro, Michael. 2008. "Wal-Mart Says Most Workers Have Health Plan." *New York Times,* January 22.

Barboza, David. 2008. "Reform Stalls in Chinese Factories." *New York Times,* January 5, pp. B1, B6.

Barnes, Patricia, Barbara Bloom, and Richard Nahin. 2008. "Complementary and Alternative Medicine Use among Adults and Children: United States, 2007." *National Health Statistics Reports,* December 10.

———, Eve Powell-Griner, Ken McFann, and Richard L. Nation. 2004. "Complementary and Alternative Medicine Use among Adults: United States, 2002." *Advance Data from Vital and Health Statistics,* No. 343. Hyattsville, MD: National Center for Health Statistics.

Barnes, Taylor. 2009. "Rise of the Shadow Economy." *Christian Science Monitor,* November 8, pp. 30–31.

Barr, Cameron W. 2002. "Top Arab TV Network to Hit US Market." *Christian Science Monitor,* December 26, pp. 1, 7.

Barrett, David B., Todd M. Johnson, and Peter F. Crossing. 2008. "The 2007 Annual Megacensus of Religions." Chicago: Encyclopaedia Britannica.

Barron, Milton L. 1953. "Minority Group Characteristics of the Aged in American Society." *Journal of Gerontology* 8:477–482.

Bartlett, Thomas. 2009. "How the International Essay Mill Has Changed Cheating." *Chronicle of Higher Education,* March 20, pp. A1, A22–A25.

Barton, Bernadette. 2006. *Stripped: Inside the Lives of Exotic Dancers.* New York: New York University Press.

Bascara, Victor. 2008. "Model Minority." Pp. 910–912, vol. 2, in *Encyclopedia of Race, Ethnicity, and Society,* edited by Richard T. Schaefer. Thousand Oaks, CA: Sage.

Battin, Margaret P., Agnes van der Heide, and Bregje D. Onwuleaka-Philipsen. 2007. "Legal Physician-Assisted Dying in Oregon and the Netherlands: Evidence Concerning the Impact on Patients in 'Vulnerable' Groups." *Journal of Medical Ethics* 33 (October):591–597.

Bauerlein, Mark. 2008. "Online Literacy Is a Lesser Kind." *Chronicle of Higher Education,* September 19, pp. B10–B11.

Bauerlein, Monika. 1996. "The Luddites Are Back." *Utne Reader* (March–April):24, 26.

Bauman, Kurt J. 1999. "Extended Measures of Well-Being: Meeting Basic Needs." *Current Population Reports,* ser. P-70, no. 67. Washington, DC: U.S. Government Printing Office.

Bazar, Emily. 2009. "Tent Cities Filling up with Casualties of the Economy." *USA Today,* May 5, pp. 1A–2A.

BBC News. 2005. "Indonesian Village Report: January 12, 2005." Accessed January 19 (www.theworld.org).

Beagan, Brenda L. 2001. "'Even If I Don't Know What I'm Doing I Can Make It Look Like I Know What I'm Doing': Becoming a Doctor in the 1990s." *Canadian Review of Sociology and Anthropology* 38:275–292.

Bearman, Peter S., James Moody, and Katherine Stovel. 2004. "Chains of Affection: The Structure of Adolescent Romantic and Sexual Networks." *American Journal of Sociology* 110 (July):44–91.

Bebchuk, Lucian A., and Jesse M. Fried. 2010. "Tackling the Managerial Power Problem." *Pathways* (Summer):9–12.

Beck, Barbara. 2009. "A Slow-Burning Fuse: A Special Report on Ageing Populations." *The Economist* (June 27).

Becker, Anne E. 2007. "Facets of Acculturation and Their Diverse Relations to Body Shape Concerns in Fiji." *International Journal of Eating Disorders* 40 (1):42–50.

Becker, Howard S. 1952. "Social Class Variations in the Teacher-Pupil Relationship." *Journal of Educational Sociology* 25 (April):451–465.

———. 1963. *The Outsiders: Studies in the Sociology of Deviance.* New York: Free Press.

Beisel, Nicola, and Tamara Kay. 2004. "Abortion, Race, and Gender in Nineteenth-Century America." *American Sociological Review* 69 (4):498–518.

Bell, Daniel. 1953. "Crime as an American Way of Life." *Antioch Review* 13 (Summer):131–154.

———. 1973. *The Coming of Post-Industrial Society.* New York: Basic Books.

———. 1999. *The Coming of Post-Industrial Society: A Venture in Social Forecasting.* With new foreword. New York: Basic Books.

———. 2008. *China's New Confucianism: Politics and Everyday Life in a Changing Society.* Princeton, NJ: Princeton University Press.

Bell, Wendell. 1981. "Modernization." Pp. 186–187 in *Encyclopedia of Sociology.* Guilford, CT: DPG Publishing.

Beller, Emily. 2009. "Bringing Intergenerational Social Mobility Research into the Twenty-first Century: Why Mothers Matter." *America Sociological Review* 74 (August):507–528.

Belton, Danielle C. 2009. "Blacks in Space." *American Prospect* (June):47–49.

Belz, Adam. 2011. "Farm Boom Leaves Main Street Wanting." *USA Today,* June 1, p. 6A.

Bendick, Marc, Jr., Charles W. Jackson, and J. Horacio Romero. 1993. *Employment Discrimination against Older Workers: An Experimental Study of Hiring Practices.* Washington, DC: Fair Employment Council of Greater Washington.

Benford, Robert D. 1992. "Social Movements." Pp. 1880–1887, vol. 4, in *Encyclopedia of Sociology,* edited by Edgar F. Borgatta and Marie Borgatta. New York: Macmillan.

Bennett, Vivienne, S. Dávila-Poblete, and M. N. Rico, eds. 2005. *Opposing Currents: The Politics of Water and Gender in Latin America.* Pittsburgh: University of Pittsburgh Press.

Bergen, Raquel Kennedy. 2006. *Marital Rape: New Research and Directions.* Harrisburg, PA: VAW Net.

Berger, Peter, and Thomas Luckmann. 1966. *The Social Construction of Reality.* New York: Doubleday.

Berk, Richard A., and Howard E. Aldrich. 1972. "Patterns of Vandalism during Civil Disorders as an Indicator of Selection of Targets." *American Sociological Review* 37 (October):533–547.

Berkeley Wellness Letter. 1990. "The Nest Refilled." 6 (February):1–2.

Berman, Paul. 2003. *Terror and Liberalism.* New York: Norton.

Bernat, Frances P., and Tatyana Zhilina. 2011. "Trafficking in Humans: The TIP Report." *Sociology Compass* 5 (June):452–462.

Bernhardt, Annette, et al. (10 additional co-anchors). 2009. *Broken Laws, Unprotected Workers.* New York: Ford, Joyce, Haynes, and Russell Sage Foundations.

Bernstein, Elizabeth. 2007. "Colleges Move Boldly on Student Drinking." *Wall Street Journal,* December 6, pp. D1, D2.

Best, Joel. 2004. *Deviance: Career of a Concept.* Belmont, CA: Wadsworth Thomson.

Bhagat, Chetan. 2007. *One Night at the Call Centre.* London: Black Swan.

Bialik, Carol. 2010. "Seven Careers in a Lifetime? Think Twice, Researchers Say." *Wall Street Journal,* September 4, p. A6.

Bianchi, Suzanne M., and Daphne Spain. 1996. "Women, Work, and Family in America." *Population Bulletin* 51 (December).

Biddlecom, Ann, and Steven Martin. 2006. "Childless in America." *Contexts* 5 (Fall):54.

Bielby, Denise D., and C. Lee Harrington. 2008. *Global TV: Exporting Television and Culture in the World Market.* New York: New York University Press.

Billitteri, Thomas, J. 2009. "Middle-Class Squeeze." *CQ Researcher* 19 (March 6):201–224.

Bilton, Nick. 2011. *I Live in the Future and Here's How It Works.* New York: Crown Business.

Birnbaum, Jeffrey H. 2005. "Listen to the Wallet." *Washington Post National Weekly Edition,* April 4, p. 11.

Bitler, Marianne, and Hilary W. Hoynes. 2010. "The State of the Safety Net in the Post-Welfare Reform Era". Paper prepared for Brooking Papers on Economic Activity, Washington, DC, September 16–20.

Black, Donald. 1995. "The Epistemology of Pure Sociology." *Law and Social Inquiry* 20 (Summer): 829–870.

Blank, Rebecca M. 2010. "Middle Class in America." *Focus* 27 (Summer):1–8.

Blau, Peter M., and Otis Dudley Duncan. 1967. *The American Occupational Structure.* New York: Wiley.

Blauner, Robert. 1964. *Alienation and Freedom.* Chicago: University of Chicago Press.

———. 1972. *Racial Oppression in America.* New York: Harper and Row.

Blumer, Herbert. 1955. "Collective Behavior." Pp. 165–198 in *Principles of Sociology,* 2nd ed., edited by Alfred McClung Lee. New York: Barnes and Noble.

———. 1969. *Symbolic Interactionism: Perspective and Method.* Englewood Cliffs, NJ: Prentice Hall.

———. 1972. *Racial Oppression in America.* New York: Harper and Row.

Block, Melissa. 2009. "Toll of War: Broken Hearts, Marriages for Marines." Accessed August 20 (http://npr.org/templates/transcript/transcript. php?storyly=111988038).

Blumberg, Stephen J., and Julian V. Luke. 2007. "Coverage Bias in Traditional Telephone Surveys of Low-Income and Young Adults." *Public Opinion Quarterly* 71 (5):734–749.

Blumer, Herbert. 1955. "Collective Behavior." Pp. 165–198 in *Principles of Sociology,* 2nd ed., edited by Alfred McClung Lee. New York: Barnes and Noble.

———. 1969. *Symbolic Interactionism: Perspective and Method.* Englewood Cliffs, NJ: Prentice Hall.

Blumstein, Alfred, and Joel Wallman. 2006. "The Crime Drops and Beyond." *Annual Review of Law and Society* 2:125–146.

Boase, Jeffery, John B. Horrigan, Barry Wellman, and Lee Rainie. 2006. *The Strength of Internet Ties.* Washington, DC: Pew Internet and American Life Project.

Boellstorff, Tom. 2008. *Coming of Age in Second Life: An Anthropologist Explores the Virtually Human.* Princeton, NJ: Princeton University Press.

Bonikowski, Bart, and Miller McPherson. 2006. "The Sociology of Voluntary Associations." In 21st Century Sociology (online version accessed February 6, 2010). Thousand Oaks, CA: Sage.

Bonilla-Silva, Eduardo. 2004. "From Bi-Racial to Tri-Racial: Towards a New System of Racial Stratification in the USA." *Ethics and Racial Studies* 27 (November):931–950.

———. 2006. *Racism without Racists.* Lanham, MD: Rowman and Littlefield.

Bonus, Rick. 2000. *Locating Filipino Americans: Ethnicity and the Cultural Politics of Space.* Philadelphia: Temple University Press.

Borjas, George S., Jeffrey Grogger, and Gordon H. Hanson. 2006. "Immigration and African-American Employment Opportunities: The Response of Wages, Employment, and Incarceration to Labor Supply Shocks." Working Paper 12518. Cambridge, MA: National Bureau of Economic Research.

Borrelli, Christopher. 2010. "*Second Life Talk Given Both Locally, Virtually.*" *Chicago Tribune,* November 8, sec. 3, p. 1.

Bottomore, Tom, and Maximilien Rubel, eds. 1956. *Karl Marx: Selected Writings in Sociology and Social Philosophy.* New York: McGraw-Hill.

Boudreaux, Richard. 2002. "Indian Rights Law Is Upheld in Mexico." *Los Angeles Times,* September 7, p. A3.

Bourdieu, Pierre, and Jean-Claude Passerson. 1990. *Reproduction in Education, Society and Culture.* 2nd ed. London. Sage. Originally published as *La reproduction.*

Boushey, Heather. 2005. *Student Debt: Bigger and Bigger.* Washington, DC: Center for Economic and Policy Research.

Bouvier, Leon F. 1980. "America's Baby Boom Generation: The Fateful Bulge." *Population Bulletin* 35 (April).

Bowes, John. 2011. *The Fair Trade Revolution.* London: Pluto Press.

Bowles, Samuel, and Herbert Gintis. 1976. *Schooling in Capitalistic America: Educational Reforms and the Contradictions of Economic Life.* New York: Basic Books.

Bowman, Tom. 2009. "Toll of War: Broken Hearts, Marriages for Marines." Accessed August 20 (http://npr.org/templates/transcript/transcript. php?storyly=111988038).

Brabazon, Tara. 2007. *The University of Google: Education in the (post) Information Age.* Burlingaton, VT: Ashgate.

Brady, Erik. 2010. "Title IX Model Survey Policy to Be Rescinded." *USA Today,* April 20, p. C1.

Brandchannel.com. 2010. "2009 Movie Lust." Accessed February 7 (www. brandchannel.com/brandcameo_films. asp?movie_year_az=2009#movie_list).

Brannigan, Augustine. 1992. "Postmodernism." Pp. 1522–1525 in *Encyclopedia of Sociology,* vol. 3, edited by Edgar F. Borgatta and Marie L. Borgatta. New York: Macmillan.

Brannon, Rush. 1995. "The Use of the Concept of Disability Culture: A Historian's View." *Disability Studies* 15 (Fall):3–15.

Braxton, Gregory. 2009. "'Reality Television' in More Ways than One." *Los Angeles Times,* February 17, pp. A1, A15.

Bray, James H., and John Kelly. 1999. *Stepfamilies: Love, Marriage, and Parenting in the First Decade.* New York: Broadway Books.

Brazier, Chris, and Amir Hamed, eds. 2007. *The World Guide.* 11th ed. Oxford, UK: New Internationalist.

Breines, Winifred. 2007. "Struggling to Connect: White and Black Feminism in the Movement Years." *Contexts* 6 (Winter):18–24.

Brewer, Rose M., and Nancy A. Heitzeg. 2008. "The Racialization of Criminal Punishment." *American Behavioral Scientist* 51 (January):625–644.

Brewis, Alexandra, Amber Wutich, Ashlan Falletta-Cowden, and Isa Rodriguez-Soto. 2011. "Body Norms and Fat Stigma in Global Perspective." *Current Anthropology* 52 (April):269–276.

Brint, Steven. 1998. *Schools and Societies.* Thousand Oaks, CA: Pine Forge Press.

Britannica Online. 2011. "Worldwide Adherents of All Religions by Six Continental Areas. Mid-2010." Accessed March 28.

Brower, Brock. 1988. "The Pernicious Power of the Polls." *Money,* March 17, pp. 144–163.

Brown, David. 2009. "Doing a Number on Surveys." *Washington Post National Weekly Edition* 26 (January 19):37.

Brown, David K. 2001. "The Social Sources of Educational Credentialism: Status Cultures, Labor Markets, and Organizations." *Sociology of Education* 74 (Extra issue):19–34.

Brown, Michael, and Amy Goldin. 1973. *Collective Behavior: A Review and Reinterpretation of the Literature.* Pacific Palisades, CA: Goodyear.

Brown, Patricia Leigh. 2004. "For Children of Gays, Marriage Brings Joy." *New York Times,* March 19, p. A13.

Brown, Robert McAfee. 1980. *Gustavo Gutierrez.* Atlanta: John Knox.

Brown, Roger W. 1954. "Mass Phenomena." Pp. 833–873, vol. 2, in *Handbook of Social Psychology,* edited by Gardner Lindzey. Reading, MA: Addison-Wesley.

Brown, S. Kathi. 2006. *Attitudes toward Work and Job Security.* Washington, DC: AARP.

Browne, Irene, ed. 2001. *Latinas and African American Women at Work: Race, Gender, and Economic Inequality.* New York: Russell Sage Foundation.

Brubaker, Bill. 2008. "Social Insecurity: Many People's Numbers Are Readily Available Online to Identity Thieves." *Washington Post National Weekly Edition,* January 14, p. 34.

Bruinius, Harry. 2010. "March of the Megacities." *Christian Science Monitor,* May 10, pp. 26–30.

Brulle, Robert, and J. Craig Jenkins. 2008. "Fixing the Bungled U.S. Environmental Movement." *Contexts* 7 (Spring):14–18.

References

Buchholz, Barbara Ballinger. 2003. "Expanded Access." *Chicago Tribune,* January 26, sec. 16, pp. 1R, 5R.

Buchmann, Claudia, Thomas A. DiPrete, and Anne McDaniel. 2008. "Gender Inequalities in Education." *Annual Review of Sociology* 34:319–337.

Buckingham, David. 2007. "Selling Childhood? Children and Consumer Culture." *Journal of Children and Media* 1 (1):15–24.

Budig, Michelle J. 2002. "Male Advantage and the Gender Composition of Jobs: Who Rides the Glass Escalator?" *Social Problems* 49 (2):258–277.

Bullard, Robert D. 1993. *Dumping in Dixie: Race, Class, and Environmental Quality.* 2nd ed. Boulder, CO: Westview Press.

——, and Beverly Wright. 2009. *Race, Place, and Environmental Justice after Hurricane Katrina.* Boulder, CO: Westview Press.

Burawoy, Michael. 2005. "For Public Sociology." *American Sociological Review* 70 (February):4–28.

Bureau of Justice Statistics. 2010. "Key Facts at a Glance." Accessible at http://bjs.ojp.usdoj.gov/content/glance/incrt.cfm.

Bureau of Labor Statistics. 2003. "Women at Work: A Visual Essay." *Monthly Labor Review* (October):45–50.

——. 2008a. "Economic News Release: Number of Jobs Held." Accessible at www.bls.gov/news.release/nlsoy.nr0.htm.

——. 2008b. "Spotlight on Statistics: Older Workers." Accessible at http://www.bls.gov/spotlight/2008/older_workers.

——. 2009. "Characteristics of Minimum Wage Workers: 2007." Accessed January 29 (www.bls.gov/cps/minwage2007.htm).

——. 2010. "Record Unemployment among Older Workers Does Not Keep Them Out of the Job Market." *Issues in Labor Statistics* (Summary 10-04, March 2010).

——. 2011. "Union Members—2010." News Release, January 21. Accessible at http://www.bls.gov/news.release/pdf/union2.pdf.

Bureau of the Census. 1975. *Historical Statistics of the United States, Colonial Times to 1970.* Washington, DC: U.S. Government Printing Office.

——. 1994. *Statistical Abstract of the United States, 1994.* Washington, DC: U.S. Government Printing Office.

——. 2003. *Meeting 21st Century Demographic Data Needs—Implementing the American Community Survey.* Washington, DC: U.S. Government Printing Office.

——. 2004a. *Statistical Abstract of the United States, 2004–2005.* Washington, DC: U.S. Government Printing Office.

——. 2004b. "Census 2000 Final Response Rates." Accessed January 16, 2010 (www.census.gov/dmd/www/response/2000response.html).

——. 2005a. *Florida, California and Texas Future Population Growth,* Census Bureau Reports, CB05-52. Washington, DC: U.S. Government Printing Office.

——. 2005b. "American Fact Finder: Places with United States." Accessed December 12 (http://factfinder.census.gov).

——. 2006a. *Statistical Abstract of the United States 2007.* Washington, DC: U.S. Government Printing Office.

——. 2008a. *Statistical Abstract of the United States, 2008.* Washington, DC: U.S. Government Printing Office.

——. 2008b. "Total Midyear Population for the World:1900–2050." (Data updated 3/27/2008.) Accessed April 9 (www.census.gov).

——. 2008c. "America's Families and Living Arrangements 2008." Accessed at www.census.gov/population/www/socdemo/hh-fam/cps2008.html.

——. 2009a. *Statistical Abstract of the United States 2010.* Washington, DC: U.S. Government Printing Office.

——. 2009b. Population Analysis. Accessed at www.census.gov.

——. 2009c. "Historical Tables on Income Inequality." Accessed February 20, 2010 (www.census.gov/hhes/www/income/incomestats.html#incomeineq).

——. 2010a. *Statistical Abstract of the United States 2011.* Washington, DC: U.S. Government Printing Office.

——. 2010b. "America's Families and Living Arrangements: 2010." Released January. Accessible at www.census.gov/population/www/socdemo/hh-fam/cps2010.html.

——. 2010c. "Total Midyear Population for the World: 1950–2050." Updated March 10. Accessed April 20 (www.census.gov/ipc/www/idb/worldpop.php).

——. 2010d. "Historical Income Tables." Accessed April 29, 2011 (http://www.census.gov/hhes/www/income/data/historical/index.html).

——. 2011a. *Statistical Abstract of the United States 2012.* Washington, DC: U.S. Government Printing Office.

——. 2011b. International Data Base (IDB). Accessible at http://www.census.gov/ipc/www/idb/informationGateway.php.

Bures, Frank. 2011. "Can You Hear Us Now?" *Utne Reader* (March–April):8–9, 11.

Burgdorf, Robert L., Jr. 2005. "Americans with Disabilities Act of 1990 (United States)." Pp. 93–101 in *Encyclopedia of Disability,* edited by Gary Albrecht. Thousand Oaks, CA: Sage.

Burger, Jerry M. 2009. "Replicating Milgram: Would People Still Obey Today?" *American Psychologist* 64 (January):1–11.

Burger King. 2009. "Whopper Sacrifice." Accessed February 4 (www.whoppersacrifice.com/).

Burgess, Ernest W. 1925. "The Growth of the City." Pp. 47–62 in *The City,* edited by Robert E. Park, Ernest W. Burgess, and Roderick D. McKenzie. Chicago: University of Chicago Press.

Burns, Melinda. 2010. "Workfare and the Low-Wage Woman." *Miller-McClune* (November–December):76–81.

Butler, Daniel Allen. 1998. *"Unsinkable": The Full Story.* Mechanicsburg, PA: Stackpole Books.

Butler, Robert N. 1990. "A Disease Called Ageism." *Journal of American Geriatrics Society* 38 (February):178–180.

Byrd-Bredbenner, Carol, and Jessica Murray. 2003. "Comparison of the Anthropometric Measurements of Idealized Female Body Images in Media Directed to Men, Women, and Mixed Gender Audiences." *Topics in Clinical Nutrition* 18 (2):117–129.

Bystydzienski, Jill M., and Joti Sekhon. 1999. *Democratization and Women's Grassroots Movements.* Bloomington: Indiana University Press.

C

Calhoun, Craig. 1998. "Community without Propinquity Revisited." *Sociological Inquiry* 68 (Summer):373–397.

——. 2003. "Belonging in the Cosmopolitan Imaginary." *Ethnicities* 3 (December):531–553.

Call, V. R., and Teachman, J. D. 1991. "Military Service and Stability in the Family Life Course." *Military Psychology* 3:233–250.

Cameron, Deborah. 2007. *The Myth of Mars and Venus.* Oxford: Oxford University Press.

Campbell, Mary, Robert Haveman, Gary Sandefur, and Barbara Wolte. 2005. "Economic Inequality and Educational Attainment across a Generation." *Focus* 23 (Spring):11–15.

Cañas, Jesus, Roberto Coronado, and Robert W. Gilman. 2007. "Southwest Economy." March/April. Accessed April 18 (http://dallasfed.org/research/swe/2007/swe0702b.cfm).

Cantril, Hadley. 1940. *The Invasion from Mars: A Study in the Psychology of Panic.* Princeton, NJ: Princeton University Press.

Cantzler, Julia Miller. 2008. "Indian, Child Welfare Act of 1978." Pp. 714–716, vol. 2, in *Encyclopedia of Race, Ethnicity, and Society,* edited by Richard T. Schaefer. Thousand Oaks, CA: Sage.

Caplan, Ronald L. 1989. "The Commodification of American Health Care." *Social Science and Medicine* 28 (11):1139–1148.

Caplow, Theodore, and Louis Hicks. 2002. *Systems of War and Peace.* 2nd ed. Lanham, MD: University Press of America.

Capriccioso, Rob. 2010. "Obama Mentions Tribes as Part of Oil Spill Restoration; Chief Testifies on Mess." *Indian Country Today,* June 23, pp. 1, 2.

Carbon Trust. 2010. "About the Carbon Trust." Accessed April 27 (www.carbontrust.co.uk/about-carbon-trust/pages/default.aspx).

Carey, Anne R., and Karl Gelles. 2010. "What Viewers Enjoy Most about Watching the Super Bowl on TV." *USA Today,* February 5, p. A1; *Gallup Poll* (May):3.

Carlton-Ford, Steve. 2010. "Major Armed Conflicts, Militarization, and Life Chances." *Armed Forces and Society* 36 (October):864–899.

Carr, Nicholas. 2008a. *The Big Switch: Rewiring the World: From Edison to Google.* New York: Norton.

——. 2008b. "Is Google Making Us Stoopid?" *Atlantic* (July/August):56–58, 60, 62–63.

——. 2010. "Tracking Is an Assault on Liberty, with Real Dangers." *Wall Street Journal,* August 7, pp. W1, W2.

Carr, Patrick J., and Maria J. Kefalas. 2009. "The Rural Brain Drain." *Chronicle of Higher Education* (September 25):B7–B9.

Carroll, Joseph. 2006. "Public National Anthem Should Be Sung in English." *Gallup Poll* (May):3.

——. 2007. "Public Divide Over Moral Acceptability of Doctor-Assisted Suicide." Accessed June 18, 2009 (www.galluppoll.com).

Carroll, Rory, and Jonathan Franklin. 2010. "Chile Miners: Rescued Foreman Luis Urzúa's First Interview." *The Guardian,* October 14.

Caruso, Eugene M., Dobromir A. Rahnev, and Mahzarin R. Banaji. 2009. "Using Conjoint Analysis to Detect Discrimination: Revealing Covert Preferences from Overt Choices." *Social Cognition* 27 (1):128–137.

Castañeda, Jorge G. 1995. "Ferocious Differences." *Atlantic Monthly* 276 (July):68–69, 71–76.

Castells, Manuel. 2001. *The Internet Galaxy: Reflections on the Internet, Business, and Society.* New York: Oxford University Press.

———. 2010a. *The Rise of the Network Society.* 2nd ed. With a new preface. Malden, MA: Wiley-Blackwell.

———. 2010b. *The Power of Identity.* 2nd ed. With a new preface. Malden, MA: Wiley-Blackwell.

———. 2010c. *End of Millennium.* 2nd ed. With a new preface. Malden, MA: Wiley-Blackwell.

Cauchon, Dennis. 2009. "Women Gain in Historic Job Shift." *USA Today,* September 3, p. A1.

CBS News. 1979. Transcript of *Sixty Minutes* segment, "I Was Only Following Orders." March 31, pp. 2–8.

Center for Academic Integrity. 2006. *CAI Research.* Accessed January 10 (www.academicintegrity.org).

Center for American Women and Politics. 2010. *Fact Sheet: Women in the U.S. Congress 2010 and Statewide Elective Women 2010.* Rutgers, NJ: CAWP.

Center for Community College Student Engagement. 2009. *Making Connections: Dimensions of Student Engagement* (2009 CCSS Findings). Austin: University of Texas at Austin, Community College Leadership Program. Accessible at www.ccsse.org/publications/national_report_2009/ccsse09_nationalreport.pdf.

Center for Research on Education Outcomes. 2009. *Multiple Choice: Charter School Performances in 16 States.* Palo Alto, CA: CREDO, Stanford University. Accessible at http://credo.stanford.edu.

Center for Responsive Politics. 2010a. "Banking on Becoming President." Accessed April 13 (www.opensecrets.org/pres08/index.php).

———. 2010b. "Banking on Becoming President" and "The Money Behind the Elections." Accessed April 13 (www.opensecrets.org).

Centers for Disease Control and Prevention. 2010. "Binge Drinking among High School Students and Adults—United States, 2009." Washington, DC: CDC. Accessible at http://www.cdc.gov/mmwr/preview/mmwrhtml/mm5939a4.htm?s_cid=mm5939a4_w.

———. 2011a. *HIV in the United States.* Accessed May 24 (www.cdc.gov).

———. 2011b. *Health Disparities and Inequalities Report—United States, 2011.*

Centers for Medicare and Medicaid Services. 2010. "NHE Projections 2009–2019." Accessed April 18 (www.cms.hhs.gov).

Cerulo, Karen A., Janet M. Ruane, and Mary Chagko. 1992. "Technological Ties That Bind: Media Generated Primary Groups." *Communication Research* 19:109–129.

Chalfant, H. Paul, Robert E. Beckley, and C. Eddie Palmer. 1994. *Religion in Contemporary Society.* 3rd ed. Itasca, IL: F. E. Peacock.

Chambliss, William. 1973. "The Saints and the Roughnecks." *Society* 11 (November–December): 24–31.

Chan, Sewell. 2009. "City Unveils Facebook Page to Encourage Condom Use." *New York Times,* February 12, p. A32.

Charles, Susan T., and Laura L. Carstensen. 2009. "Social and Emotional Aging." *Annual Review of Psychology* 61:383–409.

Charness, Gary, and Marie-Claire Villeval. 2009. "Cooperation and Competition in International Experiments in the Field and the Laboratory." *American Economic Review* 99 (3):956–978.

Charter, David, and Jill Sherman. 1996. "Schools Must Teach New Code of Values." *London Times,* January 15, p. 1.

Chase, Randall. 2010. "O'Donnell: 'I'm Not a Witch.'" *Washington Times,* October 4. Accessed March 23 (http://www.washingtontimes.com/news/2010/oct/4/odonnell-im-not-witch/?page=2).

Chase-Dunn, Christopher, and Peter Grimes. 1995. "World-Systems Analysis." Pp. 387–417 in *Annual Review of Sociology,* 1995, edited by John Hagan. Palo Alto, CA: Annual Reviews.

———, Yukio Kawano, and Benjamin D. Brewer. 2000. "Trade Globalization Since 1795: Waves of Integration in the World System." *American Sociological Review* 65 (February):77–95.

Cheng, Shu-Ju Ada. 2003. "Rethinking the Globalization of Domestic Service." *Gender and Society* 17 (2):166–186.

Cherlin, Andrew J. 2003. "Should the Government Promote Marriage?" *Contexts* 2 (Fall):22–29.

———. 2006. On Single Mothers "Doing" Family. *Journal of Marriage and Family* 68 (November):800–803.

———. 2009. *The Marriage-Go-Round: The State of Marriage and the Family in America Today.* New York: Knopf.

———. 2010. *Public and Private Families: An Introduction.* 6th ed. New York: McGraw-Hill.

Chicago Tribune. 1997. "In London, Prince Meets a Pauper, an Ex-Classmate." December 5, p. 19.

Chin, Kolin. 1996. *Chinatown Gangs: Extortion, Enterprise, and Ethnicity.* New York: Oxford University Press.

Choi, Yoonsun, and Benjamin B. Lahey. 2006. "Testing the Model Minority Stereotype: Youth Behaviors across Racial and Ethnic Groups." *Social Science Review* (September):419–452.

Christakis, Nicholas A., and James H. Fowler. 2007. "The Spread of Obesity in a Large Social Network over 32 Years." *New England Journal of Medicine* 357 (July 26):370–379.

———, and James Fowler. 2009. *Connected: The Amazing Power of Social Networks and How They Shape Our Lives.* New York: Harper.

Chronic Poverty Research Centre. 2009. *The Chronic Poverty Report 2008–09: Escaping Poverty Traps.* Geneva: Chronic Poverty Research Centre.

Chu, Henry. 2005. "Tractors Crush Heart of a Nation." *Los Angeles Times,* July 10, p. A9.

Chu, Kathy. 2010. "Vietnam's Market Grows Up." *USA Today,* August 23, p. B3.

Chubb, Catherine, Simone Melis, Louisa Potter, and Raymond Storry. 2008. *The Global Gender Pay Gap.* London: Incomes Data Services.

Chung, Esther K., Leny Mathew, Amy C. Rothkopt, Irma T. Elo, James C. Cayne, and Jennifer F. Culhane. 2009. "Parenting Attitudes and Infant Spanking: The Influence of Childhood Experiences." *Pediatrics* 124 (August):278–286.

Clabaugh, Riche. 2010. "Gay Marriage in the States." *Christian Science Monitor,* January 24, p. 19.

Clark, Burton, and Martin Trow. 1966. "The Organizational Context." Pp. 17–70 in *The Study of College Peer Groups,* edited by Theodore M. Newcomb and Everett K. Wilson. Chicago: Aldine.

Clark, Candace. 1983. "Sickness and Social Control." Pp. 346–365 in *Social Interaction: Readings in Sociology,* 2nd ed., edited by Howard Robboy and Candace Clark. New York: St. Martin's Press.

Clark, Kim. 2010. "Can School Reform Even Really Work?" *US News and World Report* (January):23–26, 30–31.

Clarke, Adele E., Janet K. Shim, Laura Maro, Jennifer Ruth Fusket, and Jennifer R. Fishman. 2003. "Bio Medicalization: Technoscientific Transformations of Health, Illness, and U.S. Biomedicine." *American Sociological Review* 68 (April):161–194.

Clarke, Lee. 2002. "Panic: Myth or Reality?" *Contexts* 1 (Fall):21–26.

Clayton, Mark. 2011. "The New Cyber Arms Race." *Christian Science Monitor,* March 7, pp. 26–71.

Clemmitt, Marcia. 2005. "Intelligent Design." *CQ Researcher* 15 (July 29):637–660.

Clifford, Stephanie. 2008. "Billboards That Look Back." *New York Times,* May 31.

———. 2009a. "Teaching Teenagers about Harassment." *New York Times,* January 27, p. B1.

———. 2009b. "Online 'A Reason to Keep On Going.'" *New York Times,* June 2, pp. D5–D6.

Clinard, Marshall B., and Robert F. Miller. 1998. *Sociology of Deviant Behavior.* 10th ed. Fort Worth, TX: Harcourt Brace.

Clymer, Adam. 2000. "College Students Not Drawn to Voting or Politics, Poll Shows." *New York Times,* January 2, p. A14.

Coates, Rodney. 2008. "Covert Racism in the USA and Globally." *Sociology Compass* 2:208–231.

Cockerham, William C. 2009. *Medical Sociology.* 11th ed. Upper Saddle River, NJ: Prentice Hall.

Cole, Elizabeth S. 1985. "Adoption, History, Policy, and Program." Pp. 638–666 in *A Handbook of Child Welfare,* edited by John Laird and Ann Hartman. New York: Free Press.

Cole, Mike. 1988. *Bowles and Gintis Revisited: Correspondence and Contradiction in Educational Theory.* Philadelphia: Falmer.

Coleman, Isobel. 2004. "The Payoff from Women's Rights." *Foreign Affairs* 83 (May–June):80–95.

Coleman, James William. 2006. *The Criminal Elite: Understanding White-Collar Crime.* 6th ed. New York: Worth.

———, and Donald R. Cressey. 1980. *Social Problems.* New York: Harper and Row.

College Board. 2009. *Trends in College Pricing.* New York: College Board.

Collier, Paul. 2007. *The Bottom Billion.* Oxford: Oxford University Press.

Collins, Daryl, Jonathan Morduch, Stuart Rutherford, and Orlanda Ruthgen. 2009. *Portfolios of the Poor: How the World's Poor Live on $2 a Day.* Princeton, NJ: Princeton University Press.

Collins, Patricia Hill. 2000. *Black Feminist Thought: Knowledge, Consciousness, and the Politics of Empowerment.* Revised 10th anniv. 2nd ed. New York: Routledge.

Collins, Randall. 1975. *Conflict Sociology: Toward an Explanatory Sociology.* New York: Academic Press.

———. 1980. "Weber's Last Theory of Capitalism: A Systematization." *American Sociological Review* 45 (December):925–942.

———. 1986. *Weberian Sociological Theory.* New York: Cambridge University Press.

———. 1995. "Prediction in Macrosociology: The Case of the Soviet Collapse." *American Journal of Sociology* 100 (May):1552–1593.

Colucci, Jim. 2008. "All the World's a Screen." *Watch!* (June):50–53.

Commission on Civil Rights. 1976. *A Guide to Federal Laws and Regulations Prohibiting Sex Discrimination.* Washington, DC: U.S. Government Printing Office.

———. 1981. *Affirmative Action in the 1980s: Dismantling the Process of Discrimination.* Washington, DC: U.S. Government Printing Office.

Commoner, Barry. 1971. *The Closing Circle.* New York: Knopf.

———. 1990. *Making Peace with the Planet.* New York: Pantheon.

———. 2007. "At 90, an Environmentalist from the 70's Still Has Hope." *New York Times,* June 19, p. D2.

Congressional Oversight Panel. 2011. "February Oversight Report: Executive Compensation Restrictions in the Troubled Asset Relief Program." Washington, DC: COP.

Conley, Dalton. 2010. *Being Black, Living in the Red.* 10th anniversary edition. Berkeley: University of California Press.

Connell, R. W. 1987. *Gendered Power: Society, the Person, and Sexual Politics.* Stanford, CA: Stanford University Press.

———. 2002. *Gender.* Cambridge, UK: Polity Press.

———. 2005. *Masculinities.* 2nd ed. Berkeley: University of California Press.

Connelly, Marjorie. 2008. "Dissecting the Changing Electorate." *New York Times,* November 8, sec. WK.

Conner, Thaddieus, and William A. Taggart. 2009. "The Impact of Gaming on the Indian Nations in New Mexico." *Social Science Quarterly* 90 (March):52–70.

Conrad, Peter, ed. 2009a. *The Medicalization of Society: On the Transformation of Human Conditions into Treatable Disorders.* 11th ed. Baltimore, MD: Johns Hopkins University.

———. 2009b. *The Sociology of Health and Illness: Cultural Perspectives.* 8th ed. New York: Worth.

Conrad, Peter, and Kristin K. Barker. 2010. "The Social Construction of Illness: Key Insights and Policy Implications." *Journal of Health and Social Behavior* 51 (5):567–579.

Cooley, Charles. H. 1902. *Human Nature and the Social Order.* New York: Scribner.

Coontz, Stephanie. 2006. "A Pop Quiz on Marriage." *New York Times,* February 19, p. 12.

Cooper, Jeremy. 2005. "Disability Law: Europe." Pp. 444–449 in *Encyclopedia of Disability,* edited by Gary Albrecht. Thousand Oaks, CA: Sage.

Cooper, K., S. Day, A. Green, and H. Ward. 2007. "Maids, Migrants and Occupational Health in the London Sex Industry. *Anthropology and Medicine* 14 (April):41–53.

Corbett, Christianne, Catherine Hill, and Andresse St. Rose. 2008. *Where the Girls Are: The Facts about Gender Equity in Education.* Washington, DC: American Association of University Women.

Cornwell, Benjamin, Edward O. Laumann, and L. Phip Schumm. 2008. "The Social Connectedness of Older Adults: A National Profile." *American Sociological Review* 73 (April):185–203.

Coser, Lewis A. 1977. *Masters of Sociological Thought: Ideas in Historical and Social Context.* 2nd ed. New York: Harcourt, Brace and Jovanovich.

Coser, Rose Laub. 1984. "American Medicine's Ambiguous Progress." *Contemporary Sociology* 13 (January):9–13.

Côté, James E. 2000. *Arrested Adulthood: The Changing Nature of Identity and Maturity in the Late World.* New York: New York University.

Couch, Carl J. 1968. "Collective Behavior: An Examination of Some Stereotypes." *Social Problems* 15:310–322.

——— 1996. *Information Technologies and Social Orders.* Edited with an introduction by David R. Maines and Shing-Ling Chien. New York: Aldine de Gruyter.

Council on Ethical and Judicial Affairs, American Medical Association. 1992. "Decisions Near the End of Life." *Journal of the American Medical Association* 267 (April 22–29):2229–2333.

Counts, D. A. 1977. "The Good Death in Kaliai: Preparation for Death in Western New Britain." *Omega* 7:367–372.

Cox, Gerry R. 2010. *Death and the American Indian.* Omaha, NE: Grief Illustrated Press.

Cox, Oliver C. 1948. *Caste, Class, and Race: A Study in Social Dynamics.* Detroit: Wayne State University Press.

Cox, Rachel S. 2003. "Home Schooling Debate." *CQ Researcher* 13 (January 17):25–48.

Crabtree, Steve. 2010. *Religiosity Highest in World's Poorest Nations.* August 31. Accessible at www.gallup.com.

Cross, Simon, and Barbara Bagilhole. 2002. "Girls' Jobs for the Boys? Men, Masculinity and Non-Traditional Occupations." *Gender, Work, and Organization* 9 (April):204–226.

Croteau, David, and William Hoynes. 2003. *Media/Society: Industries, Images, and Audiences.* 3rd ed. Thousand Oaks, CA: Pine Forge Press.

———, and ———. 2006. *The Business of the Media: Corporate Media and the Public Interest.* 2nd ed. Thousand Oaks, CA: Pine Forge Press.

Croucher, Sheila L. 2004. *Globalization and Belonging: The Politics of Identity in a Changing World.* Lanham, MD: Rowman and Littlefield.

Crouse, Kelly. 1999. "Sociology of the *Titanic.*" *Teaching Sociology Listserv.* May 24.

Crowe, Jerry, and Valli Herman. 2005. "NBA Lists Fashion Do's and Don'ts." *Los Angeles Times,* October 19, pp. A1, A23.

Crumley, Bruce. 2010. "Boardroom Revolution." *Time,* April 26, Global section, pp. 1–2.

Cuff, E. C., W. W. Sharrock, and D. W. Francis, eds. 1990. *Perspectives in Sociology.* 3rd ed. Boston: Unwin Hyman.

Cumming, Elaine, and William E. Henry. 1961. *Growing Old: The Process of Disengagement.* New York: Basic Books.

Currie, Elliot. 1985. *Confronting Crime: An American Challenge.* New York: Pantheon.

———. 1998. *Crime and Punishment in America.* New York: Metropolis Books.

Curry, Timothy Jon. 1993. "A Little Pain Never Hurt Anyone: Athletic Career Socialization and the Normalization of Sports Injury." *Symbolic Interaction* 26 (Fall):273–290.

Curtiss, Susan. 1977. *Genie: A Psycholinguistic Study of a Modern Day "Wild Child."* New York: Academic Press.

———. 1985. "The Development of Human Cerebral Lateralization." Pp. 97–116 in *The Dual Brain,* edited by D. Frank Benson and Eran Zaidel. New York: Guilford Press.

Cushing-Daniels, Brenda, and Sheila R. Zedlewski. 2008. "Tax and Spending Policy and Economic Mobility." Washington, DC: Economic Mobility Project. Also accessible at www.economic-mobility.org/reports_and_research/literature_reviews?id=0004.

D

Dahl, Robert A. 1961. *Who Governs?* New Haven, CT: Yale University Press.

Dahrendorf, Ralf. 1958. "Toward a Theory of Social Conflict." *Journal of Conflict Resolution* 2 (June):170–183.

———. 1959. *Class and Class Conflict in Industrial Sociology.* Stanford, CA: Stanford University Press.

Daley-Harris, Sam, ed. 2002. *Pathways out of Poverty: Innovations in Microfinance for the Poorest Families.* Bloomfield, CT: Komarian Press.

Dalla, Rochelle L., and Wendy C. Gamble. 2001. "Teenage Mothering and the Navajo Reservation: An Examination of Intergovernmental Perceptions and Beliefs." *American Indian Culture and Research Journal* 25 (1):1–19.

Daniel, G. Reginald. 2006. *Race and Multiraciality in Brazil and the United States: Converging Paths?* University Park: Pennsylvania State University Press.

Daniszewski, John. 2003. "Al-Jazeera TV Draws Flak Outside—and Inside—the Arab World." *Los Angeles Times,* January 5, pp. A1, A5.

Danziger, Sandra K. 2010. "The Decline of Cash Welfare and Implications for Social Policy and Poverty." *Annual Review of Sociology* 36:523–545.

Darlin, Damon. 2006. "It's O.K to Fall Behind the Technology Curve." *New York Times,* December 30, p. B6.

Darwin, Charles. 1859. *On the Origin of Species.* London: John Murray.

David, Gary. 2004. "Scholarship on Arab Americans Distorted Past 9/11." *Al Jadid* (Winter–Spring):26–27.

———. 2008. "Arab Americans." Pp. 84–87, vol. 1, in *Encyclopedia of Race, Ethnicity, and Society,* edited by Richard T. Schaefer. Thousand Oaks, CA: Sage.

Davidson, James D., and Ralph E. Pyle. 2011. *Ranking Faiths: Religious Stratification in America.* Lanham, MD: Rowman and Littlefield.

Davies, Christie. 1989. "Goffman's Concept of the Total Institution: Criticisms and Revisions." *Human Studies* 12 (June):77–95.

Davies, Lizzy. 2010. "Sarkozy Admits Rwanda Genocide 'Flaws.'" *Guardian Weekly,* May 3, p. 12.

Davis, Darren W., and Brian D. Silver. 2003. "Stereotype Threat and Race of Interviewer Knowledge." *American Journal of Political Science* 47 (January):33–45.

Davis, Gerald. 2003. *America's Corporate Banks Are Separated by Just Four Handshakes.* Accessed March 7 (www.bus.umich.edu/research/davis.html).

———. 2004. "American Cronyism: How Executive Networks Inflated the Corporate Bubble." *Contexts* (Summer):34–40.

Davis, James A., Tom W. Smith, and Peter V. Marsden. 2009. *General Social Surveys, 1972–2008:*

Cumulative Codebook. Chicago: National Opinion Research Center.

Davis, Kingsley. 1940. "Extreme Social Isolation of a Child." *American Journal of Sociology* 45 (January):554–565.

———. 1947. "A Final Note on a Case of Extreme Isolation." *American Journal of Sociology* 52 (March):432–437.

———. [1949] 1995. *Human Society.* Reprint. New York: Macmillan.

———, and Wilbert E. Moore. 1945. "Some Principles of Stratification." *American Sociological Review* 10 (April):242–249.

Davis, Martha F. 2010. "Abortion Access in the Global Marketplace." *North Carolina Law Review* 88:1657–1685.

Davis, Mike. 2005. *Planet of Slums.* London: Verso.

Davis, Paul K., and Kim Cragin, eds. 2009. *Social Science for Counterterrorism: Putting the Pieces Together.* Santa Monica, CA: RAND.

De Anda, Roberto M. 2004. *Chicanas and Chicanos in Contemporary Society.* 2nd ed. Lanham, MD: Rowman and Littlefield.

Death Penalty Information Center. 2011. "Facts about the Death Penalty." Accessible at www. deathpenaltyinfo.org.

Deegan, Mary Jo, ed. 1991. *Women in Sociology: A Bio-Biographical Sourcebook.* Westport, CT: Greenwood.

———. 2003. "Textbooks, the History of Sociology, and the Sociological Stock of Knowledge." *Sociological Theory* 21 (November):298–305.

Deflem, Mathieu. 2005. "'Wild Beasts without Nationality': The Uncertain Origins of Interpol, 1898–1910." Pp. 275–285 in *Handbook of Transnational Crime and Justice,* edited by Philip Rerchel. Thousand Oaks, CA: Sage.

Deibert, Ronald J., John Palfrey, Rafal Rohozinski, and Jonathan Zittrain. 2008. *Access Denied: The Practice and Policy of Global Internet Filtering.* Cambridge, MA: MIT Press.

Delaney, Kevin J. 2005. "Big Mother Is Watching." *Wall Street Journal,* November 26, pp. A1, A6.

Della Porta, Donatella, and Sidney Tarrow, eds. 2005. *Transnational Protest and Global Activism.* Lanham, MD: Rowman and Littlefield.

DeNavas-Walt, Carmen, Bernadette D. Proctor, and Jessica C. Smith. 2010. "Income, Poverty, and Health Insurance Coverage in the United States: 2009." P60-238 in *Current Population Survey.* Washington, DC: U.S. Government Printing Office.

Denny, Charlotte. 2004. "Migration Myths Hold No Fears." *Guardian Weekly,* February 26, p. 12.

Denzin, Norman K. 2004. "Postmodernism." Pp. 581–583 in *Encyclopedia of Social Theory,* edited by George Ritzer. Thousand Oaks, CA: Sage.

DeParle, Jason. 2009. "The 'W' Word, Re-Engaged." *New York Times,* February 8, Week in Review, p. 1.

Department of Commerce. 2010. "Observations from the Interagency Technical Working Group on Developing a Supplemental Poverty Measure." Accessible at www.census.gov/hhes/www/povmeas/SPM_TWGobservations.pdf.

———. 2011. *NTIA Launches National Broadband Map.* Washington, DC: Department of Commerce.

Department of Education. 2006. *Integrated Postsecondary Education Data Systems, Completions, 1995–2004.* Washington, DC: NCES.

Department of Health and Human Services. 2011a. "TANF: Total Number of Families." As of 1/3/2011. Accessible at www.acf.hhs.gov/programs/ofa/data-reports/caseload/2010/2010_family_tan.htm.

———. 2011b. "AFCARS, Report." Accessed April 6 (www.acf.hhs.gov/programs/cb/stats_research/afcars/tar/report17.htm).

Department of Homeland Security. 2008. "Immigration Enforcement Actions: 2007." In *Annual Report December 2008.* Washington, DC: Department of Homeland Security.

———. 2010. *Haiti Social Media: Disaster Monitoring Initiative.* January 21. Washington, DC: U.S. Department of Homeland Security.

Department of Justice. 2000. *The Civil Liberties Act of 1988: Redress for Japanese Americans.* Accessed June 29 (www.usdoj.gov/crt/ora/main.html).

———. 2008. "Hate Crime Statistics, 2007." Accessible at www.Fbi.gov/ucr/ucr.htm.

———. 2009. *2008 Crime in the United States.* (Uniform Crime Report). Accessible at http://www.fbi.gov/ucr/cius2008/index.html.

———. 2010. "Hate Crime Statistics." Accessed November 28 (http://www2.fbi.gov/ucr/hc2009/data/table_01.html).

Department of Labor. 1995a. *Good for Business: Making Full Use of the Nation's Capital.* Washington, DC: U.S. Government Printing Office.

———. 1995b. *A Solid Investment: Making Full Use of the Nation's Human Capital.* Washington, DC: U.S. Government Printing Office.

———. 2011. "Labor Force Statistics: Table 3." Accessed March 21, 2011 (www.bls.gov/cps/tables.htm).

Department of State. 2010a. "Total Adoptions to the United States." Accessed March 31 (http://adoption.state.gov/news/total_chart.html?css=print).

———. 2010b. "Trafficking in Persons: Tier Placements." Accessed March 5, 2011 (http://www.state.gov/g/tip/rls/tiprpt/2010/142755/htm).

Desai, Manisha. 1996. "If Peasants Build Their Own Dams, What Would the State Have Left to Do?" Pp. 209–224, vol. 19, in *Research in Social Movements, Conflicts and Change,* edited by Michael Dobkowski and Isidor Wallimann. Greenwich, CT: JAI Press.

Desai, Rani A., Suchitra Krishnan-Sarin, Dana Cavallo, and Marc N. Potenza. 2010. "Video-Gaming among High School Students: Health Correlates, Gender Differences, and Problematic Gaming." *Pediatrics* 126 (November 15):1414–1424.

Deutsch, Francine M. 2007. "Undoing Gender." *Gender and Society* 21 (February):106–127.

Devitt, James. 1999. *Framing Gender on the Campaign Trail: Women's Executive Leadership and the Press.* New York: Women's Leadership Conference.

Dewan, Shaila. 2010. "To Court Blacks, Foes of Abortion Make Racial Case." *New York Times,* February 27, pp. A1, A13.

Diamond, Jared. 2003. "Globalization, Then." *Los Angeles Times,* September 14, pp. M1, M3.

Diamond, Shari Seidman, and Mary R. Rose. 2005. "Real Juries." Pp. 255–284 in *Annual Review of Law and Social Science 2005.* Palo Alto, CA: Annual Reviews.

Diefenbach, Donald L., and Mark D. West. 2007. "Television and Attitudes toward Mental Health Issues: Cultivation Analysis and the Third Person Effect." *Journal of Community Psychology* 35 (2):181–195.

Diehl, William C., and Esther Prins. 2008. "Unintentional Outcomes in Second Life: Intercultural Literacy and Cultural Identity in a Virtual World." *Language and Intercultural Communication* 8(2):101–116.

DiFonzo, Nicholas, and Prashant Bordia. 2007. *Rumor Psychology: Social and Organizational Approaches.* Washington, DC: American Psychological Association.

Dillon, Sam. 2004. "Education Can Be Long, Hard Haul for Nation's Rural Kids." *Chicago Tribune,* May 28, p. 13.

———. 2009. "As More Charter Schools Unionize, Educators Debate the Effect." *New York Times,* July 27, pp. A1, A14.

DiMaggio, Paul, Eszter Hargittai, W. Russell Neuman, and John P. Robinson. 2001. "Social Implications of the Internet." Pp. 307–336 in *Annual Review of Sociology, 2001,* edited by Karen S. Cook and John Hogan. Palo Alto, CA: Annual Reviews.

DiPrete, Thomas A., Gregory M. Eirich, and Matthew Pittinsky. 2010. "Compensation Benchmarking, Leapfrogs, and the Surge in Executive Pay." *American Journal of Sociology* 115 (May):1671–1712.

Disaster Research Center. 2011. "About the DRC." Accessed April 25 (www.udel.edu/DRC/aboutus/about.html).

Dobbin, Frank, and Jiwook Jung. 2010. "Corporate Board Gender Diversity and Stock Performance: The Competence Gap on Institutional Investor Bias?" *North Carolina Law Review* 89.

Dodds, Klaus. 2000. *Geopolitics in a Changing World.* Harlow, UK: Pearson Education.

Domhoff, G. William. 1978. *Who Really Rules? New Haven and Community Power Reexamined.* New Brunswick, NJ: Transaction.

———. 2010. *Who Rules America?* 6th ed. New York: McGraw-Hill.

Dominick, Joseph R. 2009. *The Dynamics of Mass Communication: Media in the Digital Age.* 10th ed. New York: McGraw-Hill.

Donadio, Rachel. 2009. "Facebook 'Fans' of the Mafia May Be More, Authorities Say." *New York Times,* January 20, pp. A1, A8.

Donnelly, Sally B. 2007. "Growing Younger." *Time* (January bonus section):A13–A14.

Doress, Irwin, and Jack Nusan Porter. 1977. *Kids in Cults: Why They Join, Why They Stay, Why They Leave.* Brookline, MA: Reconciliation Associates.

Dotson, Floyd. 1991. "Community." P. 55 in *Encyclopedic Dictionary of Sociology.* 4th ed. Guilford, CT: Dushkin.

Dougherty, Conor. 2011. "Population Leaves Heartland Behind." *Wall Street Journal,* April 11, p. A6.

Dougherty, Kevin, and Floyd M. Hammack. 1992. "Education Organization." Pp. 535–541 in *Encyclopedia of Sociology,* vol. 2, edited by Edgar F. Borgatta and Marie L. Borgatta. New York: Macmillan.

Downey, Liam, and Brian Hawkins. 2008. "Race, Income, and Environmental Inequality in the United States." *Sociological Perspectives* 50 (4):759–781.

Dreifus, Claudia. 2003. "A Conversation with Lee Clarke." *New York Times,* May 20, Science Times section, p. 2.

———. 2004. "A Sociologist with an Advanced Degree in Calamity." *New York Times,* September 7, p. D2.

———. 2005. "A Sociologist Confronts 'the Messy Stuff' of Race, Genes and Disease." *New York Times,* October 18.

DuBois, W. E. B. [1899] 1995. *The Philadelphia Negro: A Social Study.* Philadelphia: University of Pennsylvania Press.

———. [1900] 1969. "To the Nations of the World." Pp. 19–23 in *An ABC of Color,* edited by W. E. B. DuBois. New York: International Publishers.

———. [1903] 1961. *The Souls of Black Folks: Essays and Sketches.* New York: Fawcett.

———. [1903] 2003. *The Negro Church.* Walnut Creek, CA: AltaMira Press.

———. [1909] 1970. *The Negro American Family.* Atlanta University. Reprinted 1970. Cambridge, MA: MIT Press.

———. [1935] 1962. *Black Reconstruction in America 1860–1880.* New York: Athenaeum.

———. [1940] 1968. *Dusk of Dawn.* New York: Harcourt, Brace. Reprint. New York: Schocken Books.

Dukić, Vanja, Hedibert F. Lopes, and Nicholas G. Polson. 2011. "Tracking Flu Epidemics Using Google Flu Trends and Particle Learning." Accessible at http://faculty.chicagobooth.edu/nicholas.polson/research/papers/Track.pdf.

Dundas, Susan, and Miriam Kaufman. 2000. "The Toronto Lesbian Family Study." *Journal of Homosexuality* 40 (20):65–79.

Duneier, Mitchell. 1994a. "On the Job, but Behind the Scenes." *Chicago Tribune,* December 26, pp. 1, 24.

———. 1994b. "Battling for Control." *Chicago Tribune,* December 28, pp. 1, 8.

Dunlap, Riley E. 2010. "At 40, Environmental Movement Endures with Less Consensus." April 22. Accessed April 27 (www.gallup.com/poll/127487/Environmental-Movement-Endures-Less-Consensus.aspx?version=print).

———, and Angela G. Mertig. 1991. "The Evolution of the U.S. Environmental Movement from 1970 to 1990: An Overview." *Society of National Resources* 4 (July–September):209–218.

Dunne, Gillian A. 2000. "Opting into Motherhood: Lesbians Blurring the Boundaries and Transforming the Meaning of Parenthood and Kinship." *Gender and Society* 14 (February):11–35.

Durden, T. Elizabeth, and Robert A. Hummer. 2006. "Access to Healthcare among Working-Aged Hispanic Adults in the United States." *Social Science Quarterly* 87 (December):1319–1343.

Durex. 2007. "The Face of Global Sex 2007—First Sex: An Opportunity of a Lifetime." Accessible at http://www.durexnetwork.org/SiteCollectionDocuments/Research%20%20Face%20of%20Global%20Sex%202007.pdf.

Durkheim, Émile. [1893] 1933. *Division of Labor in Society.* Translated by George Simpson. Reprint. New York: Free Press.

———. [1895] 1964. *The Rules of Sociological Method.* Translated by Sarah A. Solovay and John H. Mueller. Reprint. New York: Free Press.

———. [1897] 1951. *Suicide.* Translated by John A. Spaulding and George Simpson. Reprint. New York: Free Press.

———. [1912] 2001. *The Elementary Forms of Religious Life.* A new translation by Carol Cosman. New York: Oxford University Press.

Duster, Troy. 2002. "Sociological Stranger in the Land of the Human Genome Project." *Contexts* 1 (Fall):69–70.

Dutta, Soumitra, and Irene Mia. 2009. *The Global Information Technology Report 2008–2009.* New York: Palgrave Macmillan.

———, and ———. 2010. *The Global Information Technology Report 2009–2010.* Geneva: World Economic Forum and INSEAD. Accessible at http://networkedreadiness.com/gitr/main/fullreport/index.html.

Dwyer, Jim. 2011. "Dizzying Price for Seeking Death Penalty." *New York Times,* June 3, p. A15.

Dzidzienyo, Anani. 1987. "Brazil." In *International Handbook on Race and Race Relations,* edited by Jay A. Sigler. New York: Greenwood Press.

E

Eaton, Leslie. 2007. "Urban to Care, Storm Evacuees Give Farm a Try." *New York Times,* April 28, pp. A1, A9.

Ebaugh, Helen Rose Fuchs. 1988. *Becoming an Ex: The Process of Role Exit.* Chicago: University of Chicago Press.

Eby, Lillian T., Charleen P. Maher, and Marcus M. Butts. 2010. "The Intersection of Work and Family Life: The Role of Affect." *Annual Review of Psychology* 61:599–622.

Eckenwiler, Mark. 1995. "In the Eyes of the Law." *Internet World* (August):74, 76–77.

Economic Mobility Project. 2009. *Findings from a National Survey and Focus Groups on Economic Mobility.* Washington, DC: Pew Charitable Trusts.

The Economist. 2003. "The One Where Pooh Goes to Sweden." (April 5):59.

———. 2004. "Battle on the Home Front." (February 21):8–10.

———. 2005a. "The Policeman's Dilemma." 377 (October 15):58–59.

———. 2005b. "We Are Tous Québécois." (January 8):39.

———. 2005c. "Behind the Digital Divide." (March 2):22–25.

———. 2008a. "A Ravenous Dragon: A Special Report on China's Quest for Resources." (March 15):1–22.

———. 2008b. "Following the Crowd." (September 6):10–11.

———. 2009a. "Burgeoning Bourgeoisie." (February 14):1–22.

———. 2009b. "Serener Streets." (August 29):28–29.

———. 2010a. "The Future Is Another Country." (July 24).

———. 2010b. "Plus One Country." (September 4):46.

———. 2010c. "The Dark Side." (September 11):15.

———. 2010d. "The Strange Death of Social-Democratic Sweden." (September 18):16–17.

———. 2011a. "The 9-Billion-People Question." (February 26):1–16.

———. 2011b. "China's Population: The Most Surprising Demographic Crisis." (May 7):43–44.

Edmans, Alex, and Xavier Gabaix. 2010. "What's Right, What's Wrong, and What's Fixable." *Pathways* (Summer):13–16.

Eggen, Dan. 2009. "AARP's Dual Role." *Washington Post National Weekly Edition* 27 (November 2):11.

Ehrenreich, Barbara. 2001. *Nickel and Dimed: On (Not)Getting By in America.* New York: Metropolitan.

———. 2009. "Is It Now a Crime to Be Poor?" *New York Times,* August 2.

Ehrlich, Paul R. 1968. *The Population Bomb.* New York: Ballantine.

———, and Anne H. Ehrlich. 1990. *The Population Explosion.* New York: Simon and Schuster.

——— and Katherine Ellison. 2002. "A Looming Threat We Won't Face." *Los Angeles Times,* January 20, p. M6.

Ellison, Brandy. 2008. "Tracking." Pp. 301–304, vol. 2, in *Encyclopedia of Race, Ethnicity, and Society,* edited by Richard T. Schaefer. Thousand Oaks, CA: Sage.

Ellison, Jesse. 2008. "A New Grip on Life." *Newsweek* 152 (December 15):64.

Ellison, Nicole, Charles Stein Field, and Cliff Lampe. 2007. "The Benefits of Facebook 'Friends': Exploring the Relationship between College Students' Use of Online Social Networks and Social Capital." *Journal of Computer-Mediated Communication* 12 (4):1143–1168.

Ellison, Ralph. 1952. *Invisible Man.* New York: Random House.

El Nasser, Haya, and Paul Overberg. 2009. "U.S. Making Sure Census Isn't Overcounted." *USA Today,* January 16.

Ely, Robin J. 1995. "The Power of Demography: Women's Social Construction of Gender Identity at Work." *Academy of Management Journal* 38 (3):589–634.

Embree, Ainslie. 2003. "Religion." Pp. 101–220 in *Understanding Contemporary India,* edited by Sumit Ganguly and Neil DeVotta. Boulder, CO: Lynne Rienner.

Engardio, Pete. 1999. "Activists without Borders." *BusinessWeek,* October 4, pp. 144–145, 148, 150.

Engels, Friedrich [1884] 1959. "The Origin of the Family, Private Property, and the State." Pp. 392–394, excerpted in *Marx and Engels: Basic Writings on Politics and Philosophy,* edited by Lewis Feuer. Garden City, NY: Anchor Books.

Ennis, Sharon R., Merarys Rios-Vargas, and Nora G. Albert. 2011. *The Hispanic Population: 2010.* 2010 Census Brief BR-04. Washington, DC: U.S. Government Printing Office.

Entine, Jon, and Martha Nichols. 1996. "Blowing the Whistle on Meaningless 'Good Intentions.'" *Chicago Tribune,* June 20, sec. 1, p. 21.

Epstein, Cynthia Fuchs. 1999. "The Major Myth of the Women's Movement." *Dissent* (Fall):83–111.

Epstein, Robert. 2005. "Psychology's Top 10 Misguided Ideas." *Psychology Today* 38 (January–February):55–58, 60.

Erikson, Kai. 1966. *Wayward Puritans: A Study in the Sociology of Deviance.* New York: Wiley.

———. 1986. "On Work and Alienation." *American Sociological Review* 51 (February):1–8.

Esbenshade, Jill. 2008. "Giving Up Against the Global Economy: New Developments in the Anti-Sweatshops Movement." *Critical Sociology* 34 (3):453–470.

Escárcega, Sylvia. 2008. "Mexico." Pp. 898–902, vol. 2, in *Encyclopedia of Race, Ethnicity, and Society,* edited by Richard T. Schaefer. Thousand Oaks, CA: Sage.

Etaugh, Claire. 2003. "Witches, Mothers and Others: Females in Children's Books." *Hilltopics* (Winter):10–13.

Etzioni, Amitai. 1964. *Modern Organization.* Englewood Cliffs, NJ: Prentice Hall.

———. 1965. *Political Unification.* New York: Holt, Rinehart and Winston.

European Metalworkers' Federation. 2010. "What Is Precious Work?" Accessed March 1, 2011 (www.emf-fem.org).

Evergeti, Venetia, and Elisabetta Zontini. 2006. "Introduction: Some Critical Reflections on Social Capital, Migration and Transnational Families." *Ethnic and Racial Studies* 29 (November):1025–1039.

Facebook. 2011. Statistics. Accessed January 21 (www.facebook.com/press/info.php?statistics).

Fairtrade Foundation. 2010. "Retail Products." Accessed Jan. 5 (www.fairtrade.org.uk/products/retail_products/default.aspx).

Faith, Nazila. 2005. "Iranian Cleric Turns Blogger in Campaign for Reform." *New York Times,* January 16, p. 4.

Fallows, Deborah. 2006. *Pew Internet Project Data.* Washington, DC: Pew Internet and American Life Project.

Faris, Robert, and Nart Villeneuve. 2008. "Measuring Global Internet Filtering." Pp. 5–56 in *Access Denied: The Practice and Policy of Global Internet Filtering,* edited by Ronald Deibert, John Palfrey, Rafal Rohozinski, and Jonathan Zittrain. Cambridge, MA: MIT Press.

Farley, Maggie. 2004. "U.N. Gay Policy Is Assailed." *Los Angeles Times,* April 9, p. A3.

Farley, Melissa, and Victor Malarek. 2008. "The Myth of the Victimless Crime." *New York Times,* March 12, p. A27.

Farr, Grant M. 1999. *Modern Iran.* New York: McGraw-Hill.

Farrell, Amy, and Jack McDevitt. 2010. "Identifying and Measuring Racial Profiling by the Police." *Sociology Compass* 4:77–88.

Farrell, Dan, and James C. Petersen. 2010. "The Growth of Internet Research Methods and the Reluctant Sociologist." *Alpha Kappa Delta* 80 (February):114–125.

Fausset, Richard. 2003. "Sikhs Mark New Year, Fight Post-September 11 Bias." *Los Angeles Times,* April 14, pp. B1, B7.

———. 2009. "Assisted-Suicide Debate Heats Up." *Los Angeles Times,* February 27, pp. A1, A20.

Favreault, Melissa. 2008. "Discrimination and Economic Mobility." Washington, DC: Economic Mobility Project. Also accessible at www.economicmobility.org/reports_and_research/literature_reviews?id=0004.

Feagin, Joe R. 1989. *Minority Group Issues in Higher Education: Learning from Qualitative Research.* Norman: Center for Research on Minority Education, University of Oklahoma.

———, Harnán Vera, and Nikitah Imani. 1996. *The Agony of Education: Black Students at White Colleges and Universities.* New York: Routledge.

Featherman, David L., and Robert M. Hauser. 1978. *Opportunity and Change.* New York: Aeodus.

Federal Trade Commission. 2010. "Protecting Consumer Privacy in an Era of Rapid Change: A Proposed Framework for Businesses and Policymakers." Accessible at http://www.ftc.gov/os/2010/12/101201privacyreport.pdf.

Felson, David, and Akis Kalaitzidis. 2005. "A Historical Overview of Transnational Crime."

Pp. 3–19 in *Handbook of Transnational Crime and Justice,* edited by Philip Reichel. Thousand Oaks, CA: Sage.

Feminist Majority Foundation. 2007. "Feminists Are the Majority." Accessed February 25 (www.feminist.org).

Ferber, Abby L., and Michael S. Kimmel. 2008. "The Gendered Face of Terrorism." *Sociology Compass* 2:870–887.

Ferree, Myra Marx, and David A. Merrill. 2000. "Hot Movements, Cold Cognition: Thinking about Social Movements in Gendered Frames." *Contemporary Society* 29 (May):454–462.

Feuer, Lewis S. 1989. *Marx and Engels: Basic Writings on Politics and Philosophy.* New York: Anchor Books.

Fiala, Robert. 1992. "Postindustrial Society." Pp. 1512–1522 in *Encyclopedia of Sociology,* vol. 3, edited by Edgar F. Borgatta and Marie L. Borgatta. New York: Macmillan.

Field, John. 2008. *Social Capital.* 2nd ed. London: Routledge.

Fields, Jason. 2004. "America's Families and Living Arrangements: 2003." *Current Population Reports,* ser. P-20, no. 553. Washington, DC: U.S. Government Printing Office.

Fieser, Ezra. 2009. "What Price for Good Coffee?" *Time,* October 5, pp. 61–62.

Fiji TV. 2010. Home Page. Accessed January 17 (www.fijitv.com.fj).

File, Thom, and Sarah Crissey. 2010. "Voting and Registration in the Election of November 2008." *Current Population Reports,* ser. P-20, no. 562.

Finch, Emily, and Vanessa E. Munro. 2005. "Juror Stereotypes and Blame Attribution in Rape Cases Involving Intoxicants." *British Journal of Criminology* 45 (June):25–38.

———, and ———. 2007. "The Demon Drink and the Demonized Woman: Socio-Sexual Stereotypes and Responsibility Attribution in Rape Trials Involving Intoxicants." 16 (4):591–614.

———, and ———. 2008. "Lifting the Veil: The Use of Focus Groups and Trial Simulations in Legal Research." *Journal of Law and Society* 35:30–51.

Fine, Gary Alan, and Bill Ellis. 2011. *The Global Grapevine: Why Rumors of Terrorism, Immigration, and Trade Matter.* New York: Oxford University Press.

Fine, Gary C. 2008. " Robbers Cave." Pp. 1163–1164, vol. 3, in *Encyclopedia of Race, Ethnicity, and Society,* edited by Richard T. Schaefer. Thousand Oaks, CA: Sage.

Finkel, Steven E., and James B. Rule. 1987. "Relative Deprivation and Related Psychological Theories of Civil Violence: A Critical Review." *Research in Social Movements* 9:47–69.

Finley, Nancy J. 2010. "Skating Femininity: Gender Maneuvering in Women's Roller Derby." *Journal of Contemporary Ethnography* 39 (4):359–387.

Fiola, Jan. 2008. "Brazil." Pp. 200–204, vol. 2, in *Encyclopedia of Race, Ethnicity, and Society,* edited by Richard T. Schaefer. Thousand Oaks, CA: Sage.

Fishman, Ted C. 2010a. *Shock of Gray.* New York: Scribner.

———. 2010b. "The Old World." *New York Times Magazine* (October 17):48–53.

Fiss, Peer C., and Paul M. Hirsch. 2005. "The Discourse of Globalization: Framing of an Emerging Concept." *American Sociological Review* (February):29–52.

Fitchett, George. 1980. "It's Time to Bury the Stage Theory of Death and Dying." *Oncology Nurse Exchange II* (Fall).

Fitzgerald, Kathleen J. 2008. "White Privilege." Pp. 1403–1405, vol. 3, in *Encyclopedia of Race, Ethnicity, and Society,* edited by Richard T. Schaefer. Thousand Oaks, CA: Sage.

Fitzpatrick, Maureen J., and Barbara J. McPherson. 2010. "Coloring within the Lines: Gender Stereotypes in Contemporary Coloring Books." *Sex Roles* 62:127–137.

Flacks, Richard. 1971. *Youth and Social Change.* Chicago: Markham.

Fletcher, Connie. 1995. "On the Line: Women Cops Speak Out." *Chicago Tribune Magazine,* February 19, pp. 14–19.

Flora, Cornelia Butter, and Jan L. Flora, with Susan Fey. 2004. *Rural Communities: Legacy and Change.* 2nd ed. Boulder, CO: Westview Press.

Flynn, Laurie J. 2008. "MySpace Mind-Set Finally Shows Up at the Office." *New York Times,* April 9, p. H7.

Fonseca, Felicia. 2008. "Dine College on Quest to Rename Navajo Cancer Terms." *News from Indian Country* 22 (January 7):11.

Francis, David. 2010. "Homeschoolers Seek Asylum in US." *Christian Science Monitor,* March 8, p. 12.

Frank, Robert H. 2010. "A Remedy Worse than the Disease." *Pathways* (Summer):17–21.

Franke, Richard Herbert, and James D. Kaul. 1978. "The Hawthorne Experiments: First Statistical Interpretation." *American Sociological Review* 43 (October):623–643.

Franklin, John Hope, and Evelyn Brooks Higginbotham. 2011. *From Slavery to Freedom.* 9th ed. New York: McGraw-Hill.

Franklin, Jonathan. 2010. "Chilean Miners Get Media Training to Prepare for Life above Ground." *The Guardian,* September 22.

———. 2011. *33 Men: Inside the Miraculous Survival and Dramatic Rescue of the Chilean Miners.* New York: Putnam Adult.

FreeBabarAhmad. 2011. "Home page." Accessed April 22 (www.freebabarahmad.com).

Freedom House. 2011. *Freedom in the World 2011.* Washington, DC: Freedom House.

Freeman, Jo. 1973. "The Origins of the Women's Liberation Movement." *American Journal of Sociology* 78 (January):792–811.

———. 1975. *The Politics of Women's Liberation.* New York: McKay.

Freese, Jeremy. 2008. "Genetics and the Social Science Explanation of Individual Outcomes." *American Journal of Sociology* 114 (Suppl.):51–535.

Freidson, Eliot. 1970. *Profession of Medicine.* New York: Dodd, Mead.

French, Howard W. 2000. "The Pretenders." *New York Times Magazine,* December 3, pp. 86–88.

———. 2004. "China's Textbooks Twist and Omit History." *New York Times,* December 6, p. A10.

———. 2008. "Lines of Grinding Poverty, Untouched by China's Boom." *New York Times,* January 13, p. 4.

Freudenburg, William, and Robert Gramling. 2010. *Blowout in the Gulf: The BP Oil Spill Disaster and the Future of Energy in America.* Cambridge: MIT Press.

Freudenburg, William R. 2005. "Seeing Science, Courting Conclusions: Reexamining the Intersection of Science, Corporate Cash, and the Law." *Sociological Forum* 20 (March):3–33.

References

Freudenheim, Milt. 2005. "Help Wanted: Oldest Workers Please Apply." *New York Times,* March 23, pp. A1, C3.

Frey, William H. 2011. *A Demographic Tipping Point among America's Three-Year-Olds.* February 7. Accessible at http://www.brookings.edu/opinions/2011/0207_population_frey.aspx?p=1.

Fridlund, Alan J., Paul Erkman, and Harriet Oster. 1987. "Facial Expressions of Emotion; Review of Literature 1970–1983." Pp. 143–224 in *Nonverbal Behavior and Communication,* 2nd ed., edited by Aron W. Seigman and Stanley Feldstein. Hillsdale, NJ: Erlbaum.

Friedan, Betty. 1963. *The Feminine Mystique.* New York: Dell.

Friedman, Louis. 2010. "NASA's Down-to-Earth Problems." *Star-Telegram* (Fort Worth), March 28. Accessible at http://www.star-telegram.com/2010/03/28/2072608/friedman-nasas-down-to-earth-problem.html.

Friends of the Congo. 2011. "Coltan: What You Should Know." Accessed May 21 (www.friendsofthecongo.org/new/coltan.php).

Fudge, Judy, and Rosemary Owens, eds. 2006. *Precarious Work, Women, and the New Economy: The Challenge to Legal Norms.* Oxford, UK: Hart.

Furstenberg, Frank F. 2007. "The Making of the Black Family: Race and Class in Qualitative Studies in the Twentieth Century." *Annual Review of Sociology* 33:429–448.

———, and Andrew Cherlin. 1991. *Divided Families: What Happens to Children When Parents Part.* Cambridge, MA: Harvard University Press.

Furstenberg, Sheela Kennedy, Jr., Vonnie C. McCloyd, Rubén G. Rumbaut, and Richard A. Setterstein, Jr. 2004. "Growing Up Is Harder to Do." *Contexts* 3:33–41.

G

Gabriel, Trip. 2010. "Despite Push, Success at Charter Schools Is Mixed." *New York Times,* May 1, pp. A1, A24–A25.

Gailey, Robert. 2007. "As History Repeats Itself, Unexpected Developments Move Us Forward." *Journal of Rehabilitation Research and Development* 44 (4):vii–xiv.

Galbraith, John Kenneth. 1977. *The Age of Uncertainty.* Boston: Houghton Mifflin.

Gale Encyclopedia of Associations: National Organizations of the U.S. 2010. Farmington Hills, MI: Gale.

Gallagher, Kevin P. 2009. "Economic Globalization and the Environment." *Annual Review of Environmental Resources* 34:279–304.

Gallup. 2009a. "Religion." Accessed April 9 (www.gallup.com).

———. 2009b. "Military and National Defense." Accessed April 17 (www.gallup.com/poll/1666/military-national-defense-aspx).

———. 2011a. *Religion.* Accessed March 27 (www.gallup.com).

———. 2011b. *Party Affiliations: 2004–2011.* Accessed April 11 (www.gallup.com/poll/15370/Party-Affiliation.aspx?version=print).

Gallup Opinion Index. 1978. "Religion in America, 1977–1978." 145 (January).

Gamson, Joshua. 1989. "Silence, Death, and the Invisible Enemy: AIDS Activism and Social Movement 'Newness.'" *Social Problems* 36 (October):351–367.

Gans, Herbert J. 1991. *People, Plans, and Policies: Essays on Poverty, Racism, and Other National Urban Problems.* New York: Columbia University Press and Russell Sage Foundation.

———.1995. *The War against the Poor: The Underclass and Antipoverty Policy.* New York: Basic Books.

Garcia-Moreno, Claudia, Henrica A. F. M. Jansen, Mary Ellsberg, Lori Heise, and Charlotte Watts. 2005. *WHO Multi-Country Study on Women's Health and Domestic Violence against Women.* Geneva, Switzerland: WHO.

Gardner, Gary, Erik Assadourian, and Radhika Sarin. 2004. "The State of Consumption Today." Pp. 3–21 in *State of the World 2004,* edited by Brian Halweil and Lisa Mastny. New York: Norton.

Gardner, Marilyn. 2003. "This View of Seniors Just Doesn't 'Ad' Up." *Christian Science Monitor,* January 15, p. 15.

Garfinkel, Harold. 1956. "Conditions of Successful Degradation Ceremonies." *American Journal of Sociology* 61 (March):420–424.

Garner, Roberta. 1996. *Contemporary Movements and Ideologies.* New York: McGraw-Hill.

———. 1999. "Virtual Social Movements." Presented at Zaldfest: A conference in honor of Mayer Zald. September 17, Ann Arbor, MI.

Garreau, Joel. 1991. *Edge City: Life on the New Frontier.* New York: Doubleday.

Garrett-Peters, Raymond. 2009. "'If I Don't Have to Work Anymore, Who Am I?': Job Loss and Collaborative Self-Concept Repair." *Journal of Contemporary Ethnography* 38 (5):547–583.

Gaudin, Sharon. 2009. "Facebook Has Whopper of a Problem with Burger King Campaign." *Computerworld,* January 15.

Gauthier-Billars, David, and Charles Forelle. 2010. "Burqa Is Banned in France." *Wall Street Journal,* September 15, pp. A1, A12.

Gay, Lesbian and Straight Education Network. 2010. "About GLSEN." Accessed April 11 (www.glsen.org).

Gecas, Viktor. 2004. "Socialization, Sociology of." Pp. 14525–14530 in *International Encyclopedia of the Social and Behavioral Sciences,* edited by Neil J. Smelser and Paul B. Baltes. Cambridge, MA: Elsevier.

Gentile, Carmen. 2009. "Student Fights Record of 'Cyberbullying.'" *New York Times,* February 8, p. 20.

Gentleman, Amelia. 2006. "Bollywood Captivated by the Call Centre Culture." *Guardian Weekly,* June 2, p. 17.

———. 2007. "Young Sikh Men Get Haircuts, Annoying Their Elders." *New York Times,* March 29, p. A3.

Gerson, Kathleen, and Jerry A. Jacobs. 2004. "The Work-Home Crunch." *Contexts* 3 (Fall):29–37.

Gerth, H. H., and C. Wright Mills. 1958. *From Max Weber: Essays in Sociology.* New York: Galaxy.

Gertner, Jon. 2005. "Our Ratings, Ourselves." *New York Times Magazine,* April 10, pp. 34–41, 56, 58, 64–65.

Gibbs, Deborah A., Sandra L. Mortin, Lawrence L. Kupper, and Ruby E. Johnson. 2007. "Child Maltreatment in Enlisted Soldiers' Families during Combat-Related Deployments." *Journal of the American Medical Association* 298 (5):528–535.

Gibbs, Nancy. 1993. "Rx for Death." *Time,* May 31, pp. 34–39.

——— 2009. "What Women Want Now." *Time* 174 (16):24–33.

Giddens, Anthony. 1991. *Modernity and Self-Identity: Self and Society in the Late Modern Age.* Cambridge, UK: Polity.

Giddings, Paul J. 2008. *Ida: A Sword among Lions.* New York: Amistad.

Gilley, Brian Joseph. 2006. *Becoming Two-Spirit: Gay Identity and Social Acceptance in Indian Country.* Lincoln: University of Nebraska Press.

Gilsdorf, Ethan. 2010. "A Virtual World That Breaks Real Barriers." *Christian Science Monitor,* September 6, pp. 36–37.

Giordano, Peggy C. 2003. "Relationships in Adolescence." Pp. 257–281 in *Annual Review of Sociology, 2003,* edited by Karen S. Cook and John Hagan. Palo Alto, CA: Annual Reviews.

———, Stephen A. Cernkovich, and Alfred DeMaris. 1993. "The Family and Peer Relations of Black Adolescents." *Journal of Marriage and Family* 55 (May): 277–287.

Giroux, Henry A. 1988. *Schooling and the Struggle for Public Life: Critical Pedagogy in the Modern Age.* Minneapolis: University of Minnesota Press.

Gitlin, Todd. 2002. *Media Unlimited: How the Torrent of Images and Sounds Overwhelms Our Lives.* New York: Henry Holt.

Glascock, Anthony P. 1990. "By Any Other Name, It Is Still Killing: A Comparison of the Treatment of the Elderly in American and Other Societies." Pp. 44–56 in *The Cultural Context of Aging: Worldwide Perspective,* edited by Jay Sokolovsky. New York: Bergen and Garvey.

Glater, Jonathan D. 2003. "Legal Research? Get Me Sushi with Footnotes." *New York Times,* October 22, p. A1.

Glazer, Susan. 2010. "Evaluating Microfinance." *LQ Global Research* 4 (April).

Glenn, David. 2007. "Anthropologists in a War Zone: Scholars Debate Their Role." *Chronicle of Higher Education* 54 (September 30):A1, A10–A12.

Global Alliance for Workers and Communities. 2003. *About Us.* Accessed April 28 (www.theglobalalliance.org).

Goering, Laurie. 2008a. "Women Urge Larger Role in Easing World's Ills." *Chicago Tribune,* March 11, p. 11.

———. 2008b. "Outsourced to India: Stress." *Chicago Tribune,* April 20, pp. 1, 18.

Goffman, Erving. 1959. *The Presentation of Self in Everyday Life.* New York: Doubleday.

———. 1961. *Asylums: Essays on the Social Situation of Mental Patients and Other Inmates.* Garden City, NY: Doubleday.

———. 1963. *Stigma: Notes on Management of Spoiled Identity.* Englewood Cliffs, NJ: Prentice Hall.

Goldstein, Greg. 1998. "World Health Organization and Housing." Pp. 636–637 in *The Encyclopedia of Housing,* edited by Willem van Vliet. Thousand Oaks, CA: Sage.

Goldstein, Melvyn C., and Cynthia M. Beall. 1981. "Modernization and Aging in the Third and Fourth World: Views from the Rural Hinterland in Nepal." *Human Organization* 40 (Spring):48–55.

Goldstone, Jack. 2010. "The New Population Bomb: The Four Megatrends That Will Change the World." *Foreign Affairs* (January/February): 31–43.

Gonzalez, David. 2003. "Latin Sweatshops Pressed by U.S. Campus Power." *New York Times,* April 4, p. A3.

Gooding, Caroline. 1994. *Disability Laws, Enabling Acts: Disability Rights in Britain and America.* Boulder, CO: Westview Press.

Goodstein, Laurie. 2008. "India, Exporter of Priests, May Keep Them Home." *New York Times,* December 30, p. A1.

Google. 2010. "Explore Flu Trends and the World." Accessible at google.org/Flutrends.

Gottdiener, Mark, and Joe R. Feagin. 1988. "The Paradigm Shift in Urban Sociology." *Urban Affairs Quarterly* 24 (December):163–187.

——, and Ray Hutchison. 2011. *The New Urban Sociology.* 4th ed. Boulder, CO: Westview Press.

Gottfredson, Michael, and Travis Hirschi. 1990. *A General Theory of Crime.* Palo Alto, CA: Stanford University Press.

Gottlieb, Lori. 2006. "How Do I Love Thee?" *Atlantic Monthly* (March):58, 60, 62–68, 70.

Gould, Elise. 2007. "The Health-Finance Debate Reaches a Fever Pitch." *Chronicle of Higher Education,* April 13, pp. B14, B15.

Gould, Larry A. 2002. "Indigenous People Policing Indigenous People: The Potential Psychological and Cultural Costs." *Social Science Journal* 39:171–188.

Government Accountability Office. 2003. "Women's Earnings: Work Patterns Partially Explain Difference between Men's and Women's Earnings." Washington, DC: U.S. Government. Printing Office.

Grady, Sarah, Stacy Bielick, and Susan Aud. 2010. *Trends in the Use of School Choice: 1993 to 2010.* Washington, DC: U.S. Government Printing Office.

Gramsci, Antonio. 1929. *Selections from the Prison Notebooks.* Edited and translated by Quintin Hoare and Geoffrey Nowell Smith. London: Lawrence and Wishort.

Grazian, David. 2010. *Mix It Up: Popular Culture, Mass Media, and Society.* New York: Norton.

Greeley, Andrew M. 1989. "Protestant and Catholic: Is the Analogical Imagination Extinct?" *American Sociological Review* 54 (August):485–502.

Greenemeier, Larry. 2010. "Gulf Spillover: Will BP's Deepwater Disaster Change the Oil Industry?" *Scientific American* (June 7). Accessible at http://www.scientificamerican.com/article.cfm?id=molotch-deepwater-environmental-sociology.

Greenhalgh, Susan. 2008. *Just One Child: Science and Policy in Deng's China.* Berkeley: University of California Press.

Greenhouse, Linda. 2008. "D.C. Ban Rejected. Landmark Decision on Covert Meaning of 2nd Amendment." *New York Times,* June 27, pp. A1, A12.

Greenhouse, Steven. 2008a. "Unions Look for New Life in the World of Obama." *New York Times,* December 29, p. B6.

——. 2008b. "Millions of Jobs of a Different Collar." *New York Times,* March 26.

——. 2009. "In America, Labor Has an Unusually Long Fuse." *New York Times,* April 5, Week in Review News, p. 3.

Groening, Chad. 2007. "Media Coverage of Virginia Tech Massacre Shows Anti-Gun Bias, Says Watchdog." Accessed May 16 (www.onenewsnow.com).

Groza, Victor, Daniela F. Ileana, and Ivor Irwin. 1999. *A Peacock or a Crow: Stories, Interviews, and Commentaries on Romanian Adoptions.* Euclid, OH: Williams Custom Publishing.

Grusky, David, and Christopher Wimer. 2010. "Editor's Note." *Pathways* (Summer):2.

Guarino, Mark. 2009. "New Orleans 'Katrina Generation' Struggles with Drugs and Depression." *Christian Science Monitor,* May 13.

——. 2010. "Poverty's New Face: Suburbs." *Christian Science Monitor,* February 14, p. 18.

Guest, Robert. 2011. "Tribes Still Matter." *The Economist* (January 22):17–18.

Guo, Guang, Michael E. Roettger, and Tianji Cai. 2008. "The Integration of Genetic Propensities into Social-Control Models of Delinquency and Violence among Male Youths." *American Sociological Review* 73 (August):543–568.

Gurbuz, Mustafa, and Gulsum Gurbuz-Kucuksari. 2009. "Between Sacred Codes and Secular Consumer Society: The Practice of Headscarf Adoption among American College Girls." *Journal of Muslim Minority Affairs* 29 (September):387–399.

Gutiérrez, Gustavo. 1990. "Theology and the Social Sciences." Pp. 214–225 in *Liberation Theology at the Crossroads: Democracy or Revolution?* edited by Paul E. Sigmund. New York: Oxford University Press.

Guttmacher Institute. 2008. *Facts on Induced Abortion Worldwide.* New York: Guttmacher.

H

Haas, Steven A., David R. Schaefer, and Olga Kornienko. 2010. "Health and the Structure of Adolescent Social Networks." *Journal of Health and Social Behavior* 5 (4):424–439.

Hacker, Andrew. 1964. "Power to Do What?" Pp. 134–146 in *The New Sociology,* edited by Irving Louis Horowitz. New York: Oxford University Press.

Hacker, Helen Mayer. 1951. "Women as a Minority Group." *Social Forces* 30 (October):60–69.

——. 1974. "Women as a Minority Group, Twenty Years Later." Pp. 124–134 in *Who Discriminates against Women?* edited by Florence Denmark. Beverly Hills, CA: Sage.

Hall, Matthew, and Barrett Lee. 2010. "How Diverse Are US Suburbs?" *Urban Studies* 47 (January):3–28.

Hall, Mimi. 2005. "Senators 'to Demand Answers' on Slow Action." *USA Today,* September 6, p. 4A.

Hall-Jones, Peter. 2010. Unionism and Economic Performance. Accessed January 25 (www.newunionism.net/library/member%20contributions/news/unionism%20and%20economic%20performance.htm).

Hallinan, Maureen T. 1997. "The Sociological Study of Social Change." *American Sociological Review* 62 (February):1–11.

Halualani, Rona Tamiko. 2002. *In the Name of Hawaiians: Native Identities and Cultural Politics.* Minneapolis: University of Minnesota Press.

Hamilton, Darrick, and Willam Darity, Jr. 2009. "Race, Wealth, and Intergenerational Poverty." *America Prospect* (September):A10–A11.

Hamm, Steve. 2007. "Children of the Web." *BusinessWeek,* July 2, pp. 50–56, 58.

Hank, Karsten. 2001. "Changes in Child Care Could Reduce Job Options for Eastern German Mothers." *Population Today* 29 (April):3, 6.

Hanson, Ralph E. 2005. *Mass Communication: Living in a Media World.* New York: McGraw-Hill.

Haq, Husna. 2009. "An American Hijabi's View." *Christian Science Monitor,* December 13, pp. 16–17.

——. 2011. "How Marriage Is Faring." *Christian Science Monitor,* February 14, p. 21.

Harding, David J. 2009. "Violence, Older Peers, and the Socialization of Adolescent Boys in Disadvantaged Neighborhoods." *American Sociological Review* 74 (June):445–464.

Harlow, Harry F. 1971. *Learning to Love.* New York: Ballantine.

Harman, Donna. 2009. "Dubai's Glitz Lost in Grim Life." *Christian Science Monitor,* May 3, p. 8.

Harrington, Michael. 1980. "The New Class and the Left." Pp. 123–138 in *The New Class,* edited by B. Bruce Briggs. Brunswick, NJ: Transaction.

Harris, Chauncy D., and Edward Ullman. 1945. "The Nature of Cities." *Annals of the American Academy of Political and Social Science* 242 (November):7–17.

Harrisinteractive. 2008. "Cell Phone Usage Continues to Increase." Accessed January 13 (www.harrisinteractive.com).

Hartmann, Heidi, Ashley English, and Jeffrey Hayes. 2010. *Women and Men's Employment and Unemployment in the Great Recession.* Washington, DC: IWPR.

Hasen, Richard L. 2010. "What the Court Did—and Why." *The American Interest* (July–August): 49–55.

Haub, Carl. 2010. "2010 World Population Data Sheet." Washington, DC: Population Reference Bureau.

Haviland, William A., Harald E. L. Prins, Dana Walrath, and Bunny McBride. 2008. *Cultural Anthropology—The Human Challenge.* 12th ed. Belmont, CA: Wadsworth.

Hay, Andrew. 2009. "Spain's New Middle Classes Slip into Poverty." *Reuters.* April 8. Accessed May 11, 2011 (http://uk.reuters.com/article/email/ioUKTRE537029200904).

Hayden, H. Thomas. 2004. "What Happened at Abu Ghraib." Accessed August 7 (www.military.com).

He, Wan, Manisha Sengupta, Victoria A. Velkoff, and Kimberly A. DeBarros. 2005. "65 + in the United States: 2005." *Current Population Reports,* ser. P-23, no. 209. Washington, DC: U.S. Government Printing Office.

Health Care Financing Administration. 2001. *National Health Care Expenditures Projections.* Accessed August 10 (www.hcfa.gov/stats/NHE-proj/).

Hebel, Sara. 2006. "In Rural America, Few People Harvest 4-Year Degrees." *Chronicle of Higher Education* 53 (November 3):A21–A24.

Heckert, Druann, and Amy Best. 1997. "Ugly Duckling to Swan: Labeling Theory and the Stigmatization of Red Hair." *Symbolic Interaction* 20 (4):365–384.

Hedley, R. Alan. 1992. "Industrialization in Less Developed Countries." Pp. 914–920, vol. 2, in *Encyclopedia of Sociology,* edited by Edgar F. Borgatta and Marie L. Borgatta. New York: Macmillan.

Heilman, Madeline E. 2001. "Description and Prescription: How Gender Stereotypes Prevent Women's Ascent up the Organizational Ladder." *Journal of Social Issues* 57 (4):657–674.

Heisig, Jan Paul. 2011. "Who Does More Housework: Rich or Poor? A Comparison of 33 Countries." *American Sociological Review* 76 (1):74–99.

Hellmich, Nanci. 2001. "TV's Reality: No Vast American Waistlines." *USA Today,* October 8, p. D7.

Helvarg, David. 1994. *The War against Greens: The "Wise Use" Movement, the New Right and Anti-Environmental Violence.* San Francisco: Sierra Club Books.

Hendershott, Ann. 2002. *The Politics of Deviance.* San Francisco: Encounter Books.

Herman, William F. 2009. Comment on *Harvard Business Review* blog. October 6. Accessed April 11, 2010 (http://blogs.hbr.org/npr/

how-to-fix-executive-pay/2009/06/why-high-ceo-pay-is-bad-business.html).

Hertz, Rosanna. 2006. *Single by Chance. Mothers by Choice.* New York: Oxford University Press.

Hewlett, Sylvia Ann, and Carolyn Buck Luce. 2005. "Off-Ramps and On-Ramps: Keeping Talented Women on the Road to Success." *Harvard Business Review* (March):43–53.

Hickman, Jonathan. 2002. "America's 50 Best Corporations for Minorities." *Fortune* 146 (July 8):110–120.

Higgins, Chris A., Linda E. Duxbury, and Sean T. Lyons. 2010. "Coping with Overload in Stress: Men and Women in Dual-Earner Families." *Journal of Marriage and Family* 72 (August):847–859.

Higher Education Research Institute. 2004. *Trends in Political Attitudes and Voting Behavior among College Freshmen and Early Career College Graduates: What Issues Could Drive This Election?* Los Angeles: HERI, University of California, Los Angeles.

Hill, Michael R., and Susan Hoecker-Drysdale, eds. 2001. *Harriet Martineau: Theoretical and Methodological Perspectives.* New York: Routledge.

Hillery, George A. 1955. "Definitions of Community: Areas of Agreement." *Rural Sociology* (2):111–123.

Himes, Christine L. 2001. "Elderly Americans." *Population Bulletin* 56 (December).

Hira, Ron. 2008. "An Overview of the Offshoring of U.S. Jobs." Pp. 14–15 in Marlene A. Lee and Mark Mather. "U.S. Labor Force Trends." *Population Bulletin* 63 (June).

Hirschi, Travis. 1969. *Causes of Delinquency.* Berkeley: University of California Press.

Hirst, Paul, and Grahame Thompson. 1996. *Globalization in Question: The International Economy and the Possibilities of Governance.* Cambridge, UK: Polity Press.

Hitlin, Steven, and Jane Allyn Piliavin. 2004. "Values: Reviving a Dormant Concept." Pp. 359–393 in *Annual Review of Sociology, 2004,* edited by Karen S. Cook and John Hagan. Palo Alto, CA: Annual Reviews.

Hochschild, Arlie Russell. 1990. "The Second Shift: Employed Women Are Putting in Another Day of Work at Home." *Utne Reader* 38 (March–April):66–73.

———. 2005. *The Commercialization of Intimate Life: Notes from Home and Work.* Berkeley: University of California Press.

———, with Anne Machung. 1989. *The Second Shift: Working Parents and the Revolution at Home.* New York: Viking Penguin.

Hodson, Randy, and Teresa A. Sullivan. 1995. *The Social Organization of Work.* 2nd ed. Belmont, CA: Wadsworth.

Hoffman, Lois Wladis. 1985. "The Changing Genetics/Socialization Balance." *Journal of Social Issues* 41 (Spring):127–148.

Holden, Constance. 1980. "Identical Twins Reared Apart." *Science* 207 (March 21):1323–1328.

———. 1987. "The Genetics of Personality." *Science* 257 (August 7):598–601.

Holder, Kelly. 2006. "Voting and Registration in the Election of November 2004." *Current Population Reports,* ser. P-20, no. 556. Washington, DC: U.S. Government Printing Office.

Hollingshead, August B. 1975. *Elmtown's Youth and Elmtown Revisited.* New York: Wiley.

Holmes, Mary. 2009. "Commuter Couples and Distance Relationships: Living Apart Together."

Sloan Work and Family Research Network. Accessible at http://wfnetwork.bc.edu/encyclopedia_entry.php?id=15551&area=all.

Homans, George C. 1979. "Nature versus Nurture: A False Dichotomy." *Contemporary Sociology* 8 (May):345–348.

Home School Legal Defense Association. 2005. "State Laws" and "Academic Statistics on Home-schooling." Accessed May 12 (www.hslda.org).

Hondagneu-Sotelo, Pierrette, ed. 2003. *Gender and U.S. Immigration: Contemporary Trends.* Berkeley: University of California Press.

hooks, bell. 1994. *Feminist Theory: From Margin to Center.* 2nd ed. Boston: South End Press.

Horgan, John. 1993. "Eugenics Revisited." *Scientific American* 268 (June):122–128, 130–133.

Horkheimer, Max, and Theodore Adorno. [1944] 2002. *Dialectic of Enlightenment.* Palo Alto, CA: Stanford University Press.

Horowitz, Helen Lefkowitz. 1987. *Campus Life.* Chicago: University of Chicago Press.

Horrigan, John B. 2007. *A Typology of Information and Communication Technology Users.* Washington, DC: Pew Internet and American Life Project.

Horwitz, Allan V. 2002. *Creating Mental Illness.* Chicago: University of Chicago Press.

Hosokawa, William K. 1969. *Nisei: The Quiet Americans.* New York: Morrow.

Hospice Association of America. 2008. *Hospice Facts and Statistics.* Washington, DC: Hospice Association of America.

Houseman, John. 1972. *Run Through.* New York: Simon and Schuster.

Houser, Trevor, Shashank Mohamad, and Robert Heilmayer. 2009. *A Green Global Recovery? Assessing U.S. Economic Stimulus and the Prospects for International Coordination.* Washington, DC: World Resources Institute of Peterson Institute for International Economics.

Housing and Urban Development. 2010. *The Annual Homeless Assessment Report to Congress.* Washington, DC: U.S. Government Printing Office.

Howard, Alex. 2011. "For Election Info, the Internet a New High-Water Mark." Accessed April 11 (http://radar.oreilly.com/print/2011/03/pew-internet-election-2010.html).

Howard, Judith A. 1999. "Border Crossings between Women's Studies and Sociology." *Contemporary Sociology* 28 (September):525–528.

———, and Jocelyn Hollander. 1997. *Gendered Situations, Gendered Selves.* Thousand Oaks, CA: Sage.

Howard, Michael. 2009. *Modern Wicca: A History from Gerald Gardner to the Present.* St. Paul, MN: Llewellyn Books.

Howard, Michael C. 1989. *Contemporary Cultural Anthropology.* 3rd ed. Glenview, IL: Scott, Foresman.

Howard, Russell D., and Reid L. Sawyer. 2003. *Terrorism and Counterterrorism: Understanding the New Security Environment.* Guilford, CT: McGraw-Hill/Dushkin.

Howden, Lindsay M., and Julie A. Meyer. 2011. *Age and Sex Composition: 2010.* May 2011. 2010 Census Brief BR-03.

Hu, Winnie. 2010. "In a New Role, Teachers Move to Run Schools." *New York Times,* September 7, pp. A1, A20.

Huang, Gary. 1988. "Daily Addressing Ritual: A Cross-Cultural Study." Presented at the annual meeting of the American Sociological Association, Atlanta.

Huff, Charlotte. 2007. "Survival of the Fittest." *American Way,* May 1, pp. 30–35.

Hughes, Everett. 1945. "Dilemmas and Contradictions of Status." *American Journal of Sociology* 50 (March):353–359.

Hughlett, Mike. 2008. "Sitting Pretty." *Chicago Tribune,* September 14, sec. 5, pp. 1, 7.

Human Genome Project. 2010. "Human Genome Project Information." Accessed April 21 (www.ornl.gov/sci/techresources/human_genome/home.shtml).

———. 2011. "Human Genome Project Information." Accessed April 25 (www.ornl.gov).

Human Rights Campaign. 2010. *Equity from State to State 2010.* Washington, DC: Human Rights Foundation.

———. "State Laws." Accessed August 5 at http://www.hrc.org/laws_and_elections/state.asp.

Human Terrain System. 2010. "Welcome to the HTS Home Page." Accessed January 6, 2011 (http://humanterrainsystem.army.mil).

Humes, Karen R., Nicholas A. Jones, and Roberto R. Ramirez. 2011. *Overview of Race and Hispanic Origin: 2010.* 2010 Census Brief BR-02. Accessible at http://www.census.gov/prod/cen2010/briefs/c2010br-02.pdf.

Hundley, Tom, and Margaret Ramirez. 2008. "Young Muslims Put Faith in Facebook." *Chicago Tribune,* February 10, p. 12.

Hunt, Darnell. 1997. *Screening the Los Angeles "Riots": Race, Seeing, and Resistance.* New York: Cambridge University Press.

Hunter, Herbert M., ed. 2000. *The Sociology of Oliver C. Cox: New Perspectives: Research in Race and Ethnic Relations,* vol. 2. Stamford, CT: JAI Press.

Hunter, James Davison. 1991. *Culture Wars: The Struggle to Define America.* New York: Basic Books.

Huntington, Samuel P. 1993. "The Clash of Civilizations?" *Foreign Affairs* 72 (Summer):22–49.

Hurn, Christopher J. 1985. *The Limits and Possibilities of Schooling,* 2nd ed. Boston: Allyn and Bacon.

Hussar, William J., and Tabitha M. Bailey. 2011. *Projections of Education Statistics to 2019.* Washington, DC: National Center for Education Statistics.

Hyde, Janet Shibley. 2005. "The Gender Similarities Hypothesis." *American Psychologist* 60 (6):581–592.

Hymowitz, Carol, and Rachel Emma Silverman. 2001. "Can Work Place Stress Get Worse?" *Wall Street Monitor,* January 16, pp. B1, B4.

Igo, Sarah E. 2007. *The Average American: Surveys, Citizens, and the Making of a Mass Public.* Cambridge, MA: Harvard University Press.

Immervoll, Herwig, and David Barber. 2005. *Can Parents Afford to Work? Childcare Costs, Tax-Benefit Policies and Work Incentives.* Paris: Organisation for Economic Co-operation and Development.

Inglehart, Ronald, and Wayne E. Baker. 2000. "Modernization, Cultural Change, and the Persistence of Traditional Values." *American Sociological Review* 65 (February):19–51.

Innocence Project. 2011. *Facts on Post-Conviction DNA Exonerations.* Accessed March 14 (http://www.innocenceproject.org/Content/351PRINT.php).

Institute for Economics and Peace. 2010. "Global Peace Index." Accessible June 29 (www.visionofhumanity.org/gpi/results/world-map.php).

Institute for Women's Policy Research. 2009. *The Gender Wage Gap: 2008.* Washington, DC: IWPR.

Institute of International Education. 2010. "Open Doors 2010 'Fast Facts.'" Accessed at www.ies.org.

Interbrand. 2010. "Best Global Brands: 2009 Rankings." Accessible at www.interband.com/best_global_brands.aspx.

International Centre for Prison Studies. 2010. "Prison Brief—Highest to Lowest Rates." Accessed February 10 (www.kcl.ac.uk/depsta/law/research/icps/worldbrief/wpb.stats.php?area=all&category=wb_poprate).

Interface Group Report (Virginia Tech). 2007. *Presidential Internal Review.* Blacksburg, Virginia Polytechnic Institute and State University.

International Crime Victim Survey. 2004. *Nationwide Surveys in the Industrialized Countries.* Accessed February 20 (www.ruljis.leidenuniv.nl/group/jfcr/www/icvs).

International Gay and Lesbian Human Rights Commission. 2010. Home Page. Accessed February 11 (www.iglhrc.org).

International Institute for Democracy and Electoral Assistance. 2011. "Voter Turnout Database—Custom Query." Accessed April 11 (http://www/idea.int/vt/viewdata.cfm#).

International Monetary Fund. 2000. *World Economic Outlook: Asset Prices and the Business Cycle.* Washington, DC: International Monetary Fund.

International Organization for Migration. 2011. "Facts and Figures." Accessed April 25 (www.iom.int/jahia/jahia/about.migration/lang/en).

International Trade Union Confederation. 2009. "Davos: World Unions Call for Action Against Corporate Grand Theft." Accessed January 31 (www.ituc-csi.org/spip.php?article2736).

Internet Crime Complaint Center. 2009. "IC3 Annual Report on Internet Crime." Released March 31. (www.ic3.gov/media/annualreport/2008_IC3Report.pdf).

Internet World Stats. 2011. "Usage and Population Statistics" and "Internet World Users by Language." Updated on April 25, 2011. Accessed April 25 (www.internetworldstats.com).

Inter-Parliamentary Union. 2011. *Women in National Parliaments.* March 31. Accessed April 23 (www.ipu.org).

InTouch Health. 2010. "About Us." Accessed April 18 (www.intouchhealth.com).

Isaacs, Julia B. 2007a. *Economic Mobility of Families across Generations.* Washington, DC: Economic Mobility Project, Pew Charitable Trusts.

———. 2007b. *Economic Mobility of Men and Women.* Washington, DC: Economic Mobility Project.

———, Isabel V. Sawhill, and Ron Haskins. 2008. *Getting Ahead or Losing Ground: Economic Mobility in America.* Washington, DC: Pew Charitable Trusts.

Issa, Philip, and Sheila R. Zedlewski. 2011. *Poverty among Older Americans, 2009.* Washington, DC: Urban Institute. Accessible at http://www.retirementpolicy.org.

ITOPF. 2006. "Statistics: International Tanker Owners Pollution Federation Limited." Accessed May 2 (www.itopf.com/stats.html).

Jackson, Philip W. 1968. *Life in Classrooms.* New York: Holt.

Jacobs, Andres. 2010. "As China's Economy Grows, Pollution Worsens Despite New Efforts to Control It." *New York Times,* July 29, p. A4.

Jacobs, Jerry. 2003. "Detours on the Road to Equality: Women, Work and Higher Education." *Contexts* (Winter):32–41.

Jacobs, Tom. 2009. "Hot Men of the Links." *Miller-McCune* (May–June):79.

Jacobsen, Linda A., May Kent, Marlene Lee, and Mark Mather. 2011. "America's Aging Population." *Population Bulletin* 66 (February).

Jaffee, Daniel. 2007. *Brewing Justice: Fair Trade Coffee, Sustainability, and Survival.* Berkeley: University of California Press.

Jain, Saranga, and Kathleen Kurz. 2007. *New Insights on Preventing Child Marriage: A Global Analysis of Factors and Programs.* Washington, DC: International Center for Research on Women.

Janis, Irving. 1967. *Victims of Groupthink.* Boston: Houghton Mifflin.

Jäntti, Markus. 2009. "Mobility in the United States in Comparative Perspectives." *Focus* 26 (Fall).

Jargowsky, Paul A., and Rebecca Yang. 2006. "The 'Underclass' Revisited: A Social Problem in Decline." *Journal of Urban Affairs* 28 (1):55–70.

Jasper, James M. 1997. *The Art of Moral Protest: Culture, Biography, and Creativity in Social Movements.* Chicago: University of Chicago Press.

Jayson, Sharon. 2009. "Holding Up the Value of Marriage." *USA Today,* February 18, pp. D1, D2.

Jenkins, Henry. 2006. *Convergence Culture: Where Old and New Media Collide.* New York: New York University Press.

Jenkins, Matt. 2008. "A Really Inconvenient Truth." *Miller-McCure* 1 (March–April):38–41.

Jenkins, Richard. 1991. "Disability and Social Stratification." *British Journal of Sociology* 42 (December):557–580.

Jensen, Gary F. 2005. "Social Organization Theory." In *Encyclopedia of Criminology,* edited by Richard A. Wright and J. Mitchell Miller. Chicago: Fitzrog Dearborn.

Jervis, Rick. 2008. "New Orleans Homicides up 30% over 2006 Level." *USA Today,* January 3, p. 3A.

Jesella, Kara. 2008. "Blogging's Glass Ceiling." *New York Times,* July 27, Style section, pp. 1, 2.

Jimenez, Maria. 2009. *Humanitarian Crisis: Migrant Deaths at the U.S.–Mexico Border.* San Diego: ACLU of San Diego and Imperial Counties.

Joas, Hans, and Wolfgang Knöbl. 2009. *Social Theory: Twenty Introductory Lectures.* Cambridge: Cambridge University Press.

Johnson, Benton. 1975. *Functionalism in Modern Sociology: Understanding Talcott Parsons.* Morristown, NJ: General Learning.

Johnson, David. 2010. "Progress toward Improving the U.S. Poverty Measure: Developing the New Supplemental Poverty Measure." *Focus* 27 (Winter):1–3.

Johnson, Richard A. 1985. *American Fads.* New York: Beech Tree.

Johnson, Will. 2009. "Genie: The Wild Child." Accessed August 4, 2010 (http://knol.google.com/k/genie-the-wild-child-chapter-2#).

Jones, Del, and Barbara Hansen. 2009. "CEO Pay Packages Sink with Economy." *USA Today,* May 4, pp. B1–B2.

Jones, Jeffrey M. 2011. "Americans Increasingly Prioritize Economy over Environment" March 17. Accessed May 25 (http://www.gallup.com/poll/146681/Americans-Increasingly-Prioritize-Economy-Environment.aspx).

Jones, Jo. 2009. "Who Adopts? Characteristics of Women and Men Who Have Adopted Children." *NCHS Data Brief* (12).

Jopling, John, and Reilly Morse. 2010. "The BP Oil Disaster and Its Disproportionate Impacts on Minorities and Communities of Color." *Focus* 36 (October–November):12–14.

Jordan, Miriam. 2009. "As U.S. Job Opportunities Fade, More Mexicans Look Homeward." *Wall Street Journal,* February 13, p. A14.

Joseph, Jay. 2004. *The Gene Illusion: Genetic Research in Psychiatry and Psychology under the Microscope.* New York: Algora Books.

Jost, Kenneth. 2005. "Right to Die." *CQ Researcher,* May 13.

———. 2008. "Women in Politics." *CQ Researcher* 18 (March 21).

Juhasz, Anne McCreary. 1989. "Black Adolescents' Significant Others." *Social Behavior and Personality* 17 (2):211–214.

Kahn, Joseph. 2003. "Made in China, Bought in China." *New York Times,* January 5, sec. 3, pp. 1, 10.

———. 2006. "Where's Mao? Chinese Revise History Books." *New York Times,* September 1, pp. A1, A6.

Kahn, Scott D. 2011. "On the Future of Genomic Data." *Science* (February 11):728–729.

Kaiser Family Foundation. 2005. *Sex on TV4.* Santa Barbara, CA: Kaiser Family Foundation.

———. 2007. "Parents Say They're Getting Control of Their Children's Exposure to Sex and Violence in the Media—Even Online." Accessed January 2, 2008 (www.kff.org/entmedia/entmedia061907nr.cfm).

Kalleberg, Arne L. 2009. "Precarious Work, Insecure Workers: Employment Relations in Transition." *American Sociological Review* 74 (February):1–22.

Kalmijn, Matthijs. 1998. "Intermarriage and Homogamy: Causes, Patterns, Trends." *Annual Review of Sociology* 24:395–421.

Kambayashi, Takehiko. 2008. "Japanese Men Shout the Oft-Unsaid 'I love you.'" *Christian Science Monitor,* February 13.

Kamenetz, Anya. 2006. *Generation Debt.* New York: Riverhead.

Kandel, William. 2005. "Rural Hispanics at a Glance." *Economic Information Bulletin* (December).

Kang, K. Connie. 1996. "Filipinos Happy with Life in U.S. but Lack United Voice." *Los Angeles Times,* January 26, pp. A1, A20.

Karides, Marina. 2010. "Theorizing the Rise of Microenterprise Development in Caribbean Context." *Journal of World-Systems Research* 16 (2):192–216.

Karney, Benjamin R., and John S. Crown. 2007. "Families under Stress: An Assessment of Data, Theory, and Research on Marriage and Divorce in the Military." Santa Monica, CA: RAND.

Kasarda, John D. 2011. Aerotropolis.com. Accessed May 28.

——— and Greg Lindsay. 2011. *Aerotropolis: The Way We'll Live Next.* New York: Farrar, Straus and Giroux.

Katovich, Michael A. 1987. Correspondence. June 1.

Katz, Michael. 1971. *Class, Bureaucracy, and the Schools: The Illusion of Educational Change in America.* New York: Praeger.

520

Kaufman, Sarah. 2006. "The Criminalization of New Orleanians in Katrina's Wake." Accessed April 4 (www.ssrc.org).

Kaufman, Sharon R., and Lynn M. Morgan. 2005. "The Anthropology of the Beginnings and Ends of Life." *Annual Review of Anthropology* 34:317–341.

Kavada, Anastasia. 2005. "Exploring the Role of the Interest in the 'Movement for Alternative Globalization': The Case of the Paris 2003 European Social Forum." *Westminster Papers in Communication and Culture* 2 (1):72–95.

Keeter, Scott, and Courtney Kennedy. 2006. "The Cell Phone Challenge to Survey Research." Washington, DC: Pew Research Center.

Kelley, Eileen, and Emily Bazar. 2010. "Teen Girls Sought in Bank Robery." *USA Today,* January 7, p. A3.

Kelly, Timothy A. 2009. *Healing the Broken Mind: Transforming America's Failed Mental Health System.* New York: New York University Press.

Kennickell, Arthur B. 2009. *Ponds and Streams: Wealth and Income in the U.S., 1989 to 2007.* Washington, DC: Federal Reserve Board.

Kenny, Charles. 2009. "Revolution in a Box." *Foreign Policy* (November):68–74.

Kent, Mary M., and Carl Haub. 2005. "Global Demographic Divide." *Population Bulletin* 60 (December).

Kent, Mary Mederios. 2010. "Large Wealth Gap among U.S. Racial and Ethnic Groups." Accessed September 9 (http://www.prb.org/Articles/2010/usnetworth.aspx?p=1).

Kentor, Jeffrey, and Yong Suk Jang. 2004. "Yes, There Is a (Growing) Transnational Business Community." *International Sociology* 19 (September):355–368.

Kerbo, Harold R. 2006. *World Poverty: The Roots of Global Inequality and the World System.* New York: McGraw-Hill.

———. 2009. *Social Stratification and Inequality.* 7th ed. New York: McGraw-Hill.

Kerr, Richard A., and Eli Kinitisch. 2010. "Climatologists Feel the Heat as Science Meets Politics." *Science* 330 (December 17):1623.

Kershaw, Sarah. 2009. "Rethinking the Older Woman–Younger Man Relationship." *New York Times,* October 15.

Kesmodel, David, and Danny Yadron. 2010. "E-Cigarettes Spark New Smoking War." *Wall Street Journal,* August 25, pp. A1, A12.

Kessler, Ronald C., Emil F. Coccaro, Maurizio Fava, Savina Jaeger, Robert Jin, and Ellen Walters. 2006. "The Prevalence and Correlates of DSM-IV Intermittent Explosive Disorder in the National Comorbidity Survey Replication." *Archives of General Psychiatry* 63 (June):669–678.

Killian, Caitlin. 2003. "The Other Side of the Veil: North Africa Women in France Respond to the Headscarf Affair." *Gender and Society* (August 17):576–590.

Kim, Kwang Chung. 1999. *Koreans in the Hood: Conflict with African Americans.* Baltimore: Johns Hopkins University Press.

Kimmel, Michael S. 2006. "A War against Boys?" *Dissent* (Fall):65–70.

———. 2008. *The Gendered Society.* 3rd ed. New York: State University of New York at Stony Brook.

King, Gary. 2011. "Ensuring the Data-Rich Future of the Social Sciences." *Science* (February 11):719–721.

King, Leslie. 1998. "France Needs Children: Pronatalism, Nationalism, and Women's Equity." *Sociological Quarterly* 39 (Winter):33–52.

King, Meredith L. 2007. *Immigrants in the U.S. Health Care System.* Washington, DC: Center for American Progress.

King, Sharon A. 1999. "Mania for 'Pocket Monsters' Yields Billions for Nintendo." *New York Times,* April 26, pp. A1, A18.

Kingsbury, Alex. 2008. "Q and A: Sudhir Venkatesh." *US News and World Report,* January 21, p. 14.

Kinsey, Alfred C., Wardell B. Pomeroy, and Paul H. Gebhard. 1953. *Sexual Behavior in the Human Female.* Philadelphia: Saunders.

———, ———, and Clyde E. Martin. 1948. *Sexual Behavior in the Human Male.* Philadelphia: Saunders.

Kiper, Dmitry. 2008. "GodTube.com Puts Christian Worship Online." *Christian Science Monitor,* February 6.

Kiser, Edgar. 1992. "War." Pp. 2243–2247 in *Encyclopedia of Sociology,* edited by Edgar F. Borgatta and Marie L. Borgatta. New York: Macmillan.

Kitchener, Richard F. 1991. "Jean Piaget: The Unknown Sociologist." *British Journal of Sociology* 42 (September):421–442.

Klein, Naomi. 1999. *No Logo: Money, Marketing, and the Growing Anti-Corporate Movement.* New York: Picador (St. Martin's Press).

Kleiner, Art. 2003. "Are You In with the In Crowd?" *Harvard Business Review* 81 (July):86–92.

Kleinknecht, William. 1996. *The New Ethnic Mobs: The Changing Face of Organized Crime in America.* New York: Free Press.

Klinenberg, Eric. 2002. *Heat Wave: A Social Autopsy of Disaster in Chicago.* Chicago: University of Chicago Press.

Kluger, Jeffrey. 2010. "Trapped." *Time,* September 26, pp. 61–63.

Knopman, J., L. C. Krey, J. Lee, M. E. Fino, A. P. Novestsky, and N. N. Noyes. 2010. "Monozygotic Twinning: An Eight-Year Experience at a Large IVF Center." *Fertility and Sterility* 94 (July):502–510.

Knudsen, Morten. 2010. "Surprised by Method—Functional Method and System Theory." *Forum: Qualitative Social Research* 11 (September): article 12.

Kochhar, Rakesh. 2006. "Growth in the Foreign-Born Workforce and Employment of the Native Born." Washington, DC: Pew Hispanic Center.

———. 2008. *Latino Workers in the Ongoing Recession: 2007–2008.* Washington, DC: Pew Hispanic Center.

Kohut, Andrew, et al. 2005. *American Character Gets Mixed Reviews: 16-Nation Pew Global Attitudes Survey.* Washington, DC: Pew Global Project Attitudes.

———, et al. 2007. *Global Unease with Major World Powers: Rising Environmental Concern in 47-Nation Survey.* Washington, DC: Pew Global Project Attitudes.

Kokmen, Leyla. 2008. "Environmental Justice for All." *Utne Reader* (March–April):42–46.

Kolata, Gina. 2008. "Study Finds Strong Social Factor in Quitting Smoking." *New York Times,* May 22, pp. A18, A24.

Kornblum, Janet. 2007. "Meet the 'Tech-No's': People Who Reject Plugging into the Highly Wired World." *USA Today,* January 11, pp. A1, A2.

Korzeniewicz, Roberto Patricio, and Timothy Patrick Moran. 2009. *Unveiling Inequality: A World Historical Perspective.* New York: Russell Sage Foundation.

Kosmin, Barry A., and Ariela Keysar. 2009. *American Religious Identification Survey.* Hartford, CT: Trinity College.

Kottak, Conrad. 2011. *Anthropology: Appreciating Human Diversity.* 14th ed. New York: McGraw-Hill.

Kraft Foods. 2009. "Hoaxes and Rumors." Accessed February 4 (http://brands.kraftfoods.com/oscarmayer/hoaxes_rumors).

Krane, Jim. 2009. *Dubai: The Story of the World's City.* London: Atlantic Books.

———. 2010. "To Spend or Not to Spend." Interviewed on Al Jazeera television, March 26. Accessed April 20 (http://english.aljazeera.net/programmes/countingthecost/2010/03/201032510494187263.html).

Krauss, C. 1993. "Marine Leader Contritely Admits He Erred on 'Singles Only' Order." *New York Times,* August 12, p. A1.

Kraybill, Donald. 2001. *The Riddle of Amish Culture.* Rev. ed. Baltimore: Johns Hopkins University Press.

Kreider, Rose M. 2010. "Increase in Opposite-Sex Cohabiting Couples from 2009 to 2010 in the Annual Social and Economic Supplement (AEFC) to the Current Population Survey (CPS)." Working Paper. Washington, DC: U.S. Bureau of the Census.

———, and Renee Ellis. 2011. "Living Arrangements of Children: 2009." *Current Population Reports,* ser. P70, no. 126. Washington, DC: U.S. Government Printing Office.

Kriesberg, Louis. 1992. "Peace." Pp. 1432–1436 in *Encyclopedia of Sociology,* edited by Edgar F. Borgatta and Marie L. Borgatta. New York: Macmillan.

Kristof, Nicholas D. 1998. "As Asian Economies Shrink, Women Are Squeezed Out." *New York Times,* June 11, pp. A1, A12.

Kroll, Luisa, and Matthew Miller. 2010. "The World's Billionaires." Accessed May 11 (www.forbes.com).

Kronstadt, Jessica. 2008a. "Genetics and Economic Mobility." Washington, DC: Economic Mobility Project. Also accessible at www.economicmobility.org/reports_and_research/literature_reviews?id=0004.

———, and Melissa Favreault. 2008. "Families and Economic Mobility." Washington, DC: Economic Mobility Project. Also accessible at www.economicmobility.org/reports_and_research/literature_reviews?id=0004.

Kübler-Ross, Elisabeth. 1969. *On Death and Dying.* New York: Macmillan.

Kunzig, Robert. 2011. "Seven Billion." *National Geographic* (January):40–69.

Kwong, Jo. 2005. "Globalization's Effects on the Environment." *Society* 42 (January–February):21–28.

Ladner, Joyce. 1973. *The Death of White Sociology.* New York: Random Books.

Laermer, Richard. 2002. *Trendspotting: Think Forward, Get Ahead, and Cash in on the Future.* New York: Penguin.

Lahey, Joanna. 2006. *Age, Women, and Hiring: An Experimental Study.* Boston: Center for Retirement Research, Boston College.

Accessed at http://escholarship.bc.edu/retirement_papers/134.

Lalli, Nica. 2009. "No Religion? No Problem." *USA Today,* April 6, p. A15.

Landale, Nancy S., and R. S. Oropesa. 2007. "Hispanic Families: Stability and Change." *Annual Review of Sociology* 33:381–405.

Landler, Mark, and Michael Barbaro. 2006. "No, Not Always." *New York Times,* August 2, pp. C1, C4.

———, and David E. Sanger. 2009. "World Leaders Pledge $1 Trillion to Tackle Crisis." *New York Times,* April 3, pp. A1, A11.

Landtman, Gunnar. [1938] 1968. *The Origin of Inequality of the Social Class.* New York: Greenwood (original edition 1938, Chicago: University of Chicago Press).

Lang, Ilene H. 2010. "Have Women Shattered Corporate Glass Ceiling? No." *USA Today,* April 15, p. A11.

Lansprey, Susan. 1995. "AAAs and 'Naturally Occurring Retirement Communities' (NORCs)." Accessed August 4, 2003 (www.aoa.gov/housing/norcs.html).

Lasswell, Harold D. 1936. *Politics: Who Gets What, When, How.* New York: McGraw-Hill.

Lau, Yvonne M. 2006. "Re-Visioning Filipino American Communities: Evolving Identities, Issues, and Organizations." Pp. 141–153 in *The New Chicago,* edited by John Koval et al. Philadelphia: Temple University Press.

Lauer, Robert H. 1982. *Perspectives on Social Change.* 3rd ed. Boston: Allyn and Bacon.

Laumann, Edward O., John H. Gagnon, and Robert T. Michael. 1994a. "A Political History of the National Sex Survey of Adults." *Family Planning Perspectives* 26 (February):34–38.

———, ———, ———, and Stuart Michaels. 1994b. *The Social Organization of Sexuality: Sexual Practices in the United States.* Chicago: University of Chicago Press.

Lavrakas, Paul J., Charles D. Shuttles, Charlotte Steel, and Howard Fienberg. 2007. "The State of Surveying Cell Phone Numbers in the United States: 2007 and Beyond." *Public Opinion Quarterly* 71 (5):840–854.

Lawler, Edward J., Shane R. Thye, and Jeongkou Youn. 2008. "Social Exchange and Micro Social Order." *American Sociological Review* 73 (August):519–542.

Lawson, Sandra. 2008. *Girls Count.* New York: Goldman Sachs.

Lazarsfeld, Paul, Bernard Beretson, and H. Gaudet. 1948. *The People's Choice.* New York: Columbia University Press.

———, and Robert K. Merton. 1948. "Mass Communication, Popular Taste, and Organized Social Action." Pp. 95–118 in *The Communication of Ideas,* edited by Lymon Bryson. New York: Harper and Brothers.

Leavell, Hugh R., and E. Gurney Clark. 1965. *Preventive Medicine for the Doctor in His Community: An Epidemiologic Approach.* 3rd ed. New York: McGraw-Hill.

Lee, Alfred McClung. 1983. *Terrorism in Northern Ireland.* Bayside, NY: General Hall.

Lee, Barrett A., Kimberly A. Tyler, and James D. Wright. 2010. "The New Homelessness Revisited." *Annual Review of Sociology* 30:501–521.

Lee, Raymond M. 2010. "The Secret Life of Focus Groups: Robert Merton and the Diffusion of a Research Method." *American Sociologist* 41:115–141.

Lehne, Gregory K. 1995. "Homophobia among Men: Supporting and Defining the Male Role." Pp. 325–336 in *Men's Lives,* edited by Michael S. Kimmel and Michael S. Messner. Boston: Allyn and Bacon.

Leland, John. 2008. "In 'Sweetie' and 'Dear,' a Hurt Beyond Insult for the Elderly." *New York Times,* October 7, pp. A1, A22.

Lengermann, Patricia Madoo, and Jill Niebrugge-Brantley. 1998. *The Women Founders: Sociology and Social Theory, 1830–1930.* Boston: McGraw-Hill.

Lenhart, Amanda. 2009. "Pew Internet Project Data Memo: Adults and Social Network Websites." Accessible at www.pewinternet.org/PPF/r/272/report_display.asp.

Lenski, Gerhard. 1966. *Power and Privilege: A Theory of Social Stratification.* New York: McGraw-Hill.

Leonard, Koren Isaakser. 2003. *Muslims in the United States: The State of Research.* New York: Russell Sage Foundation.

Leonhardt, David. 2004. "As Wealthy Fill Top Colleges Concerns Grow over Fairness." *New York Times,* April 22, pp. A1, A12.

Lerach, William S. 2007. "Guilty: Why Is Wall Street So Bullish on Bad CEOs?" *Washington Post National Weekly Edition,* November 19, p. 29.

Levin, Jack, and William C. Levin. 1980. *Ageism.* Belmont, CA: Wadsworth.

Levine, Nancy. 1988. *The Dynamics of Polyandry: Kinship, Domesticity, and Population on the Tibetan Border.* Chicago: University of Chicago Press.

Levine, Susa. 2006. "Culturally Sensitive Medicine." *Washington Post National Weekly Edition* 23 (March 26):31.

Levinson, Daniel J. 1978. *The Seasons of a Man's Life.* With Charlotte N. Darrow et al. New York: Knopf.

———. 1996. *The Seasons of a Woman's Life.* With Judy D. Levinson. New York: Knopf.

Levitt, Peggy, and B. Nadya Jaworsky. 2007. "Transnational Migration Studies: Past Developments and Future Trends." *Annual Review of Sociology* 33:129–156.

Levitt, Steven D., and Stephen J. Dubner. 2006. *Freakonomics: A Rogue Economist Explores the Hidden Side of Everything.* Revised and expanded edition. New York: Morrow.

———, and Sudhir Venkatesh. 2000. "An Economic Analysis of a Drug-Selling Gang's Finances." *Quarterly Journal of Economics* (August):775–789.

Levy, Becca R., Martin D. Slade, Suzanne R. Kunkel, and Stanislav V. Kasl. 2002. "Longevity Increased by Positive Self-Perceptions of Aging." *Journal of Personality and Social Psychology* 83 (2):261–270.

Lichtblau, Eric. 2009. "Telecom Companies Win Dismissal of Wiretap Suits." *New York Times,* June 4, p. A14.

Lieberson, Stanley. 2000. *A Matter of Taste: How Names, Fashions, and Culture Change.* New Haven, CT: Yale University Press.

Light, Donald W. 2004. "Dreams of Success: A New History of the American Health Care System." *Journal of Health and Social Behavior* 45 (Extra issue):1–24.

Light, Paul C. 2005. "Katrina's Lesson in Readiness." *Washington Post,* September 1.

Lim, Louisa. 2007. "Digital Culture: China's 'Gold Farmers' Play a Grim Game." May 14, 2007 broadcast on NPR. Accessible at www.npr.org.

Lindner, Eileen, ed. 2011. *Yearbook of American and Canadian Churches, 2011.* Nashville: Abingdon Press.

Link, Michael W., Ali H. Mokad, Herbert F. Stockhouse, and Nicole T. Flowers. 2006. "Race, Ethnicity, and Linguistic Isolation as Determinants of Participation in Public Heath Surveillance Surveys." *Presenting Chronic Disease* 3 (January).

Linn, Susan, and Alvin F. Poussaint. 1999. "Watching Television: What Are Children Learning about Race and Ethnicity?" *Child Care Information Exchange* 128 (July):50–52.

Lino, Mark. 2010. *Expenditures on Children by Families, 2010.* Washington, DC: U.S. Department of Agriculture, Center for Nutrition Policy and Promotion.

Lipka, Sara. 2009. "Do Crime Statistics Keep Students Safe?" *Chronicle of Higher Education* 55 (January 30):A15–A17.

Lipson, Karen. 1994. "'Nell' Not Alone in the Wilds." *Los Angeles Times,* December 19, pp. F1, F6.

Liptak, Adam. 2006. "The Ads Discriminate, but Does the Web?" *New York Times,* March 5, p. 16.

———. 2008. "From One Footnote, a Debate over the Tangles of Law, Science and Money." *New York Times,* November 25, p. A13.

———. 2010. "Study Finds Questioning of Nominees to Be Useful." *New York Times,* June 28, pp. A10, A11.

Liska, Allen E., and Steven F. Messner. 1999. *Perspectives on Crime and Deviance.* 3rd ed. Upper Saddle River, NJ: Prentice Hall.

Livingstone, Sonia. 2004. "The Challenge of Changing Audiences." *European Journal of Communication* 19 (March):75–86.

Llana, Sara Miller. 2009. "Mexico: Safety Comes in Park Taxes." December 24. Accessible at www.csmonitor.com.

Loeb, Susanna, Bruce Fuller, Sharon Lynn Kagan, and Bidemi Carrol. 2004. "Child Care in Poor Communities: Early Learning Effects of Type, Quality, and Stability." *Child Development* 75 (January–February):47–65.

Lofland, John. 1981. "Collective Behavior: The Elementary Forms." Pp. 441–446 in *Social Psychology: Sociological Perspectives,* edited by Morris Rosenberg and Ralph Turner. New York: Basic Books.

———. 1985. *Protests: Studies of Collective Behavior and Social Movements.* Rutgers, NJ: Transaction.

Lofland, Lyn H. 1975. "The 'Thereness' of Women: A Selective Review of Urban Sociology." Pp. 144–170 in *Another Voice,* edited by M. Millman and R. M. Kanter. New York: Anchor/Doubleday.

Logan, John R., Richard D. Alba, and Werquan Zhang. 2002. "Immigrant Enclaves and Ethnic Communities in New York and Los Angeles." *American Sociological Review* 67 (April):299–322.

Lohr, Steve. 2008. "For a Good Retirement, Find Work. Good Luck." *New York Times,* June 22, p. 3.

Long, Sharon K., and Paul B. Masi. 2009. *Access to and Affordability of Care in Massachusetts as of Fall 2008: Geographic and Racial/Ethnic Differences.* Washington, DC: Urban Institute.

Longhofer, Wesley, and Evan Schofer. 2010. "National and Global Origins of Environmental Association." *American Sociological Review* 75 (4):505–533.

References

Lopez, Mark Hugo. 2010. *The Latino Vote in the 2010 Elections.* Washington, DC: Pew Hispanic Center.

Lorber, Judith. 2005. *Breaking the Bowls: Degendering and Feminist Change.* New York: Norton.

Lublin, Joann S. 2010. "The Corner Office, and a Family." *Wall Street Journal,* October 18, p. B9.

Lucas, Edward. 2008. "The Electronic Bureaucrat." *The Economist* 186 (February 16, special report).

Ludwig, Jens, and Isabell Sawhill. 2007. *Success by Ten: Interviewing Early, Often, and Efficiently in the Education of Young Children.* Washington, DC: Brookings Institution.

Lukacs, Georg. 1923. *History and Class Consciousness.* London: Merlin.

Lundquist, Jennifer Hickes. 2006. "Choosing Single Motherhood." *Contexts* 5 (Fall):64–67.

Luo, Michael. 2008. "What Happens to Public Financing, When Obama Thrived without It?" *New York Times,* November 3, p. A17.

Luster, Tom, Kelly Rhoades, and Bruce Haas. 1989. "The Relation between Parental Values and Parenting Behavior: A Test of the Kohn Hypothesis." *Journal of Marriage and the Family* 51 (February):139–147.

Luttinger, Nina, and Gregory Dicum. 2006. *The Coffee Book: Anatomy of an Industry from Crop to the Last Drop.* Revised and updated. New York: New Press.

Lyall, Sarah. 2002. "For Europeans, Love, Yes; Marriage, Maybe." *New York Times,* March 24, pp. 1–8.

Lynas, Mark. 2008. *Six Degrees: Our Future on a Hotter Planet.* Washington, DC: National Geographic.

Lynn, Barry C. 2003. "Trading with a Low-Wage Tiger." *American Prospect* 14 (February):10–12.

MacDonald, G. Jeffrey. 2007. "Go in Search of a Church by Way of the Web." *USA Today,* October 17, p. D8.

MacDorman, Marian F., and T. J. Mathews. 2009. Behind International Rankings of Infant Mortality: How the United States Compares with Europe. *NCHS Date Brief* (No. 23, November).

MacFarquhar, Neil. 2008. "Resolute or Fearful, Many Muslims Turn to Home Schooling." *New York Times,* March 26, p. A1.

Mach, Annie, and Laura Blumenthal. 2010. "Health Insurance Coverage of Children under 19: 2008 and 2009." 2009–2011 Census Brief BR-09-11. Accessible at http://www.census.gov/prod/2010pubs/acsbr09-11.pdf.

Machalek, Richard, and Michael W. Martin. 2010. "Evolution, Biology and Society: A Conversation for the 21st-Century Sociology Classroom." *Teaching Sociology* 38 (1):35–45.

Mack, Mick G. 2003. "Does Exercise Status Influence the Impressions Formed by College Students?" *College Student Journal* 37 (December).

Mack, Raymond W., and Calvin P. Bradford. 1979. *Transforming America: Patterns of Social Change.* 2nd ed. New York: Random House.

Mackey, John. 2009. "Why Sky-High CEO Pay Is Bad Business." *Harvard Business Review* blog, June 17. Accessed April 11, 2010 (http://blogs.hbr.org/hbr/how-to-fix-executive-pay/2009/06/why-high-ceo-pay-is-bad-business.html).

Mackun, Paul, and Steven Wilson. 2011. *Population Distribution and Change: 2000 to 2010.* March 2011. 2010 Census Brief BR-01.

MacLeod, Calum. 2010. "Chinese Use Internet to Show Dissent." *USA Today,* December 29, p. 31.

MacLeod, Scott, and Vivienne Walt. 2005. "Live from Qatar." *Time,* bonus section, June, pp. A6–A8.

Maestretti, Danielle. 2009. "Information Overload." *Utne Reader* (July–August):22–23.

Magga, Ole Henrik. 2006. "Diversity in Sami Terminology for Reindeer, Snow, and Ice." *International Social Science Journal* 58 (March):25–34.

Magnier, Mark. 2004. "China Clamps Down on Web News Discussion." *Los Angeles Times,* February 26, p. A4.

Mahbub ul Haq Human Development Centre. 2000. *Human Development in South Asia 2000.* Oxford, UK: Oxford University Press for Mahbub ul Haq Human Development Centre.

Malaby, Thomas M. 2009. *Making Virtual Worlds: Linden Lab and Second Life.* Ithaca, NY: Cornell University.

Malcolm, Andrew H. 1974. "The 'Shortage' of Bathroom Tissue: A Classic Study in Rumor." *New York Times,* February 3, p. 29.

Malcolm X, with Alex Haley. [1964] 1999. *The Autobiography of Malcolm X.* Revised with Epilogue by Alex Haley and Afterword by Ossie Davis. New York: One World, Ballantine Books.

Males, Mike, and Meda-Chesney Lind. 2010. "The Myth of Mean Girls." *New York Times,* April 2, p. A21.

Malhotra, Neil, and Yotam Margalit. 2009. "State of the Nation: Anti-Semitism and the Economic Crisis." *Boston Review* (May–June). Accessible at http://bostonreview.net/BR34.3/malhotra_margalit.php.

Malthus, Thomas Robert, Julian Huxley, and Frederick Osborn. [1824] 1960. *Three Essays on Population.* Reprint. New York: New American Library.

Margolis, Mac. 2009. "The Land of Less Contrast: How Brazil Reined in Inequality. *Newsweek,* November 28.

Mark, Gloria, Victor M. Gonzalez, and Justin Harris. 2005. "No Task Left Behind? Examining the Nature of Fragmented Work." Paper presented at CHI 2005, Portland, Oregon.

Markson, Elizabeth W. 1992. "Moral Dilemmas." *Society* 29 (July–August):4–6.

Marosi, Richard. 2007. "The Nation: A Once-Porous Border Is a Turning-Back Point." *Los Angeles Times,* March 21, pp. A1, A20.

Marquis, Julie, and Dan Morain. 1999. "A Tortuous Path for the Mentally Ill." *Los Angeles Times,* November 21, pp. A1, A22, A23.

Marr, Phebe. 2003. "Civics 101, Taught by Saddam Hussein: First, Join the Paramilitary." *New York Times,* April 20.

Marshall, Brent K., and J. Steven Picou. 2008. "Postnormal Science, Precautionary Principle, and Worst Cases: The Challenge of Twenty-First-Century Catastrophes." *Sociological Inquiry* 78 (May):230–247.

Martin, Dominique, Jean-Luc Metzger, and Philippe Pierre. 2006. "The Sociology of Globalization: Theoretical and Methodological Reflections." *International Sociology* 21 (July):499–521.

Martin, Joyce A., Brady E. Hamilton, Paul D. Sutton, Stephanie J. Ventura, Fay Menacker, Sharon Kirmeyer, and T. J. Mathews. 2009. "Births: Final Data for 2006." *National Vital Statistics Reports* 57 (January 7).

Martin, Karin A. 2009. "Normalizing Heterosexuality: Mothers' Assumptions, Talk, and Strategies with Young Children." *American Sociological Review* 74 (April):190–207.

Martin, Marvin. 1996. "Sociology Adapting to Changes." *Chicago Tribune,* July 21, sec. 18, p. 20.

Martin, Susan E. 1994. "Outsider within the Station House: The Impact of Race and Gender on Black Women Politics." *Social Problems* 41 (August):383–400.

Martineau, Harriet. [1837] 1962. *Society in America.* Edited, abridged, with an introductory essay by Seymour Martin Lipset. Reprint. Garden City, NY: Doubleday.

———. [1838] 1989. *How to Observe Morals and Manners.* Philadelphia: Leal and Blanchard. Sesquentennial edition, edited by M. R. Hill, Transaction Books.

Martinez, Elizabeth. 1993. "Going Gentle into That Good Night: Is a Rightful Death a Feminist Issue?" *Ms.* 4 (July–August):65–69.

Marubbio, M. Elise. 2006. *Killing the Indian Maiden: Images of Native American Women in Film.* Lexington: University Press of Kentucky.

Marx, Earl. 2009. "How Will Fair Fare?" *Christian Science Monitor,* April 19, pp. 30–31.

Marx, Karl. [1844] 1964. "Contribution to the Critique of Hegel's Philosophy of Right." In *On Religion,* Karl Marx and Friedrich Engels. New York: Schocker Books.

———, and Friedrich Engels. [1847] 1955. *Selected Work in Two Volumes.* Reprint. Moscow: Foreign Languages Publishing House.

Maryanski, Alexandra R. 2004. "Evaluation Theory." Pp. 257–263 in *Encyclopedia of Social Theory,* edited by George Ritzer. Thousand Oaks, CA: Sage.

Mason, J. W. 1998. "The Buses Don't Stop Here Anymore." *American Prospect* 37 (March):56–62.

Massey, Douglas S. 1998. "March of Folly: U.S. Immigration Policy after NAFTA." *American Prospect* (March–April):22–23.

———. 2007. *Categorically Unequal: The American Stratification System.* New York: Russell Sage Foundation.

———. 2008. "A Mexican Apartheid." Pp. 55–57, vol. 2, in *Encyclopedia of Race, Ethnicity, and Society,* edited by Richard T. Schaefer. Thousand Oaks CA: Sage.

———, and Nancy A. Denton. 1993. *American Apartheid: Segregation and the Making of the Underclass.* Cambridge, MA: Harvard University Press.

———, and Margarita Mooney. 2007. "The Effects of America's Three Affirmative Action Programs on Academic Performance." *Social Problems* 54 (1):99–117.

Masuda, Takahiko, Phoebe C. Ellsworth, Batja Mesquita, Janxin Leu, Shigehito Tanida, and Ellen Van de Veerdonk. 2008. "Attitudes and Social Cognition: Placing the Face in Context: Cultural Differences in the Perception of Facial Emotion." *Journal of Personality and Social Psychology* 94 (3):365–381.

Masud-Piloto, Felix. 2008. "Cuban Americans." Pp. 357–359, vol. 1, in *Encyclopedia of Race, Ethnicity, and Society,* edited by Richard T. Schaefer. Thousand Oaks, CA: Sage.

Mathews, T. J., and Marian MacDorman. 2011. "Infant Mortality Statistics." *National Vital Statistics Reports* 59 (6).

Maynard, Micheline. 2010. "At Toyota, a Cultural Shift." *New York Times,* June 3, pp. B1, B6.

Mazumder, Bhashkar. 2008. *Upward Intergenerational Economic Mobility in the United States.* Washington, DC: Economic Mobility Project.

McChesney, Robert W. 2008. *The Political Economy of Media: Enduring Issues, Emerging Dilemmas.* New York: Monthly Review Press.

McCormack, Mark. 2010. "Changing Masculinities in Youth Cultures." *Qualitative Sociology* 33:111–115.

McDonald, Michael P. 2008. "The Return of the Voter: Voter Turnout in the 2008 Presidential Election." *Forum* 6(4): Article 4.

———. 2009a. "Voter Turnout." Accessed April 8 (http://elections.gmu.edu/voter_turnout.htm).

———. 2009b. "2008 Current Population Survey Voting and Registration Supplement." Accessed April 16 (http://elections.gmu.edu/CPS_2008.html).

McDowell, Linda, Adina Batnitzky, and Sarah Dyer. 2009. "Precarious Work and Economic Migration: Emerging Immigrant Divisions of Labor in Greater London's Service Sector." *International Journal of Urban and Regional Research* 31 (March):3–25.

McFalls, Joseph A., Jr. 2007. *"Population: A Lively Introduction."* 5th ed. Washington, DC: Population Reference Bureau.

McFarland, Andrew S. 2007. "Neopluralism." *Annual Review of Political Science* 10:45–66.

McGirk, Tim. 2009. "Postcard: Dubai." *Time,* October 19, p. 6.

McGlynn, Clare, and Vanessa E. Munro, eds. 2010. *Rethinking Rape Law: International and Comparative Perspectives.* London: Routledge-Cavendish.

McGue, Matt, and Thomas J. Bouchard, Jr. 1998. "Genetic and Environmental Influence on Human Behavioral Differences." Pp. 1–24 in *Annual Review of Neurosciences.* Palo Alto, CA: Annual Reviews.

McGuire, Thomas G., and Jeanne Miranda. 2008. "New Evidence Regarding Racial and Ethnic Disparities in Mental Health: Policy Implications." *Health Affairs* 27 (2):393–403.

McGurty, Eileen Maura. 2000. "Warren County, NC, and the Emergence of the Environmental Justice Movement: Unlikely Coalitions and Shared Meanings in Local Collective Action." *Society and Natural Resources* 13:373–387.

McIntosh, Peggy. 1988. "White Privilege and Male Privilege: A Personal Account of Coming to See Correspondence through Work and Women's Studies." Working Paper No. 189, Wellesley College Center for Research on Women, Wellesley, MA.

McKinlay, John B., and Sonja M. McKinlay. 1977. "The Questionable Contribution of Medical Measures to the Decline of Mortality in the United States in the Twentieth Century." *Milbank Memorial Fund Quarterly* 55 (Summer):405–428.

McLanahan, Sara, and Christine Percheski. 2008. "Family Structure and the Reproduction of Inequalities." *Annual Review of Sociology* 38:257–276.

McLuhan, Marshall. 1964. *Understanding Media: The Extensions of Man.* New York: New American Library.

———. 1967. *The Medium Is the Message: An Inventory of Effects.* New York: Bantam Books.

McNeil, Donald G., Jr. 2002. "W.H.O. Moves to Make AIDS Drugs More Accessible to Poor Worldwide." *New York Times,* August 23, p. D7.

———. 2004. "When Real Food Isn't an Option." *New York Times,* September 3, pp. A1, A5.

McPhail, Clark. 1991. *The Myth of the Madding Crowd.* New York: De Gruyter.

———. 1994. "The Dark Side of Purpose in Riots: Individual and Collective Violence." *Sociological Quarterly* 35 (January):i–xx.

———. 2006. "The Crowd and Collective Behavior: Bringing Symbolic Interaction Back In." *Symbolic Interaction* 29 (Issue 4):433–464.

———, and David Miller. 1973. "The Assembling Process: A Theoretical Empirical Examination." *American Sociological Review* 38 (December):721–735.

———. 2008. "Crowd." *Contexts* (Spring):78–79.

Mead, George H. 1934. In *Mind, Self and Society,* edited by Charles W. Morris. Chicago: University of Chicago Press.

———. 1964a. In *On Social Psychology,* edited by Anselm Strauss. Chicago: University of Chicago Press.

———. 1964b. "The Genesis of the Self and Social Control." Pp. 267–293 in *Selected Writings: George Herbert Mead,* edited by Andrew J. Reck. Indianapolis: Bobbs-Merrill.

Mead, Margaret. [1935] 2001. *Sex and Temperament in Three Primitive Societies.* New York: Perennial, HarperCollins.

Mehl, Matthias R., Simine Vazire, Nairán Ramírez-Esparza, Richard B. Slatcher, and James W. Pennebacker. 2007. "Are Women Really More Talkative than Men?" *Science* 317 (July 6):82.

Meichtry, Stacy. 2011. "Italian Mammas Put Meals on Wheels, Say 'Mangia!' to Faraway Offspring." *Wall Street Journal,* March 31, pp. A1, A14.

Mendes, Elizabeth. 2010. "New High of 46% of Americans Support Legalizing Marijuana." October 28. Accessible at http://www.gallup.com/poll/144086/New-High-Americans-Support-Legalizing-Marijuana.aspx?version=print.

Mendez, Jennifer Bickman. 1998. "Of Mops and Maids: Contradictions and Continuities in Bureaucratized Domestic Work." *Social Problems* 45 (February):114–135.

Merton, Robert. 1948. "The Bearing of Empirical Research upon the Development of Social Theory." *American Sociological Review* 13 (October):505–515.

———. 1968. *Social Theory and Social Structure.* New York Free Press.

———, and Alice S. Kitt. 1950. "Contributions to the Theory of Reference Group Behavior." Pp. 40–105 in *Continuities in Social Research: Studies in the Scope and Methods of the American Soldier,* edited by Robert K. Merton and Paul L. Lazarsfeld. New York: Free Press.

Merton, Robert K., and Patricia L. Kendall. 1946. "The Focused Interview." *American Journal of Sociology* 51 (May):541–557.

Messner, Michael A. 2002. "Gender Equity in College Sports: 6 Views." *Chronicle of Higher Education* 49 (December 6):B9–B10.

———, and Cheryl Cooky. 2010. *Gender in Televised Sports: News and Highlights Shows, 1989–2009.* Los Angeles: Center for Feminist Research, University of Southern California.

———, Margaret Carlisle Duncan, and Nicole Williams. 2006. "This Revolution Is Not Being Televised." *Contexts* 5 (Summer):34–38.

Meston, Cindy M., and David M. Buss. 2007. "Why Humanoids Have Sex." *Archives of Sexual Behavior* 36 (August).

Meyer, Karen. 2011. "Match the Disability." June 22. Unpublished paper. Chicago: DePaul University.

———. 2008. "Americans with Disabilities Act." In *Encyclopedia of Race, Ethnicity, and Society,* edited by Richard T. Schaefer. Thousand Oaks, CA: Sage.

Michals, Jennifer M. 2003. "The Price We Pay to Get Richer: A Look at Student Indebtedness." Unpublished M.A. paper, DePaul University, Chicago, IL.

Michels, Robert. 1915. *Political Parties.* Glencoe, IL: Free Press (reprinted 1949).

Microfinance Information Exchange. 2011. "MIX Market." Accessed May 24 (www.themix.org).

Miles, James. 2009. "A Wary Repeat: A Special Report on China and America." *The Economist* (October 24):1–16.

Milgram, Stanley. 1963. "Behavioral Study of Obedience." *Journal of Abnormal and Social Psychology* 67 (October):371–378.

———. 1975. *Obedience to Authority: An Experimental View.* New York: Harper and Row.

Miller, Dan E. 2006. "Rumor: An Examination of Some Stereotypes." *Symbolic Interaction* 28 (4):505–519.

Miller, David L. 2000. *Introduction to Collective Behavior and Collective Action.* 2nd ed. Prospect Heights, IL: Waveland Press.

———, and JoAnne DeRoven Darlington. 2002. "Fearing for the Safety of Others: Disasters and the Small World Problem." Paper presented at Midwest Sociological Society, Milwaukee, WI.

Miller, Jacqueline W., Timothy S. Naimi, Robert D. Brewer, and Sherry Everett Jones. 2007. "Binge Drinking and Associated Health Risk Behaviors among High School Students." *Pediatrics* 119 (January):76–85.

Miller, Laura. 2008. "The Rise of the Superclass." Accessed in *Salon* May 2 (www.salon.com/books/review/2008/03/14/superclass/print.html).

Miller, Reuben. 1988. "The Literature of Terrorism." *Terrorism* 11 (1):63–87.

Mills, C. Wright. [1959] 2000a. *The Sociological Imagination.* 40th anniversary edition. New Afterword by Todd Gitlin. New York: Oxford University Press.

———. [1956] 2000b. *The Power Elite.* New edition. Afterword by Alan Wolfe. New York: Oxford University Press.

Miner, Horace. 1956. "Body Ritual among the Nacirema." *American Anthropologist* 58 (June):503–507.

Minnesota Center for Twin and Family Research. 2010. "Research at the MCTFR." Accessed January 24 (http://mctfr.psych.umn.edu/research/).

Minyard, Jeremy, and Tim Ortyl. 2009. "Reflected Appraisals." *Context* 8 (November):6–7.

Miyata, Kakuko, and Tetsuro Kobayashi. 2008. "Causal Relationship between Internet Use and Social Capital in Japan." *Asian Journal of Social Psychology* 11:42–52.

Mizruchi, Mark S. 1996. "What Do Interlocks Do? An Analysis, Critique, and Assessment of Research on Interlocking Directorates." Pp. 271–298 in *Annual*

Review of Sociology, 1996, edited by John Hagan and Karen Cook. Palo Alto, CA: Annual Reviews.

Moeller, Philip. 2009. "Unique Havens for an Aging America." *US News and World Report* (October):62–68.

Moeller, Susan D. 1999. *Compassion Fatigue.* London: Routledge.

Mogelonsky, Marcia. 1996. "The Rocky Road to Adulthood." *American Demographics* 18 (May):26–29, 32–35, 56.

Mohai, Paul, David Pellow, and J. Timmons Roberts. 2009. "Environmental Justice." *Annual Review of Environmental Research* 34:405–430.

——, and Robin Saha. 2007. "Racial Inequality in the Distribution of Hazardous Waste: A National-Level Reassessment." *Social Problems* 54 (3):343–370.

Mol, A. J. 2010. "Ecological Modernization as a Social Theory of Environmental Reform." Pp. 63–71 in *The International Handbook of Environmental Sociology,* 2nd ed., edited by Michael R. Redcraft and Graham Woodgate. Cheltenham, UK: Edward Elgar.

——, and D. A. Sonnenfeld, eds. 2000. *Ecological Modernization around the World.* Portland, OR: Frank Cass.

——, ——, and G. Spaargaren, eds. 2009. *The Ecological Modernization Reader.* London: Routledge.

Molotch, Harvey. 1970. "Oil in Santa Barbara and Power in America." *Sociological Inquiry* 40 (Winter):131–144.

Mollen, Milton. 1992. *"A Failure of Responsibility": Report to Mayor David N. Dinkins on the December 28, 1991, Tragedy at City College of New York.* New York: Office of the Deputy Mayor for Public Safety.

Momigliana, Anna. 2010. "Italy: Over 30 and Still Living with Mom." *Christian Science Monitor,* January 27. Accessible at www.csmonitor.com/layout/set/print/content/view/print/275435.

Monaghan, Peter. 1993. "Sociologist Jailed Because He 'Wouldn't Snitch' Ponders the Way Research Ought to Be Done." *Chronicle of Higher Education* 40 (September 1):A8, A9.

Moncarz, Roger J., Michael G. Wolf, and Benjamin Wright. 2008. "Service-Providing Occupations, Offshoring, and the Labor Market." *Monthly Labor Review* (December):71–86.

Money. 1987. "A Short History of Shortages." 16 (Fall, special issue):42.

Montgomery, Marilyn J., and Gwendolyn T. Sorell. 1997. "Differences in Love Attitudes across Family Life Stages." *Family Relations* 46:55–61.

Moore, Molly. 2006. "Romance, but Not Marriage." *Washington Post National Weekly Edition,* November 27, p. 18.

Moore, Wilbert E. 1967. *Order and Change: Essays in Comparative Sociology.* New York: Wiley.

Morin, Rich. 2009. "Most Middle-Aged Adults Are Rethinking Retirement Plans." May 28. Accessed January 26, 2010 (http://pewresearch.org/pubs/1234/the-threshold-generation).

Morris, Aldon. 2000. "Reflections on Social Movement Theory: Criticisms and Proposals." *Contemporary Sociology* 29 (May):445–454.

Morrison, Denton E. 1971. "Some Notes toward Theory on Relative Deprivation, Social Movements, and Social Change." *American Behavioral Scientist* 14 (May–June):675–690.

Morrison, Peter A., and Thomas M. Bryan. 2010. "Targeting Spatial Centers of Elderly Consumers in the U.S.A." *Population Research Policy Review* 29:33–46.

Morse, Arthur D. 1967. *While Six Million Died: A Chronicle of American Apathy.* New York: Ace.

Moskos, Peter. 2008. *Cop in the Hood: My Year Policing Baltimore's Eastern District.* Princeton NJ: Princeton University Press.

Mosley, J., and E. Thomson. 1995. Pp. 148–165 in *Fatherhood: Contemporary Theory, Research and Social Policy,* edited by W. Marsiglo. Thousand Oaks, CA: Sage.

Mueller, G. O. 2001. "Transnational Crime: Definitions and Concepts." Pp. 13–21 in *Combating Transnational Crime: Concepts, Activities, and Responses,* edited by P. Williams and D. Vlassis. London: Franklin Cass.

Mufson, Steven. 2007. "Turning Down the Heat." *Washington Post National Weekly Edition* 24 (July):6–8.

Muñoz, José A. 2008. "Protest and Human Rights Networks: The Case of the Zapatista Movement." *Sociology Compass* (April):1045–1058.

Murdock, George P. 1945. "The Common Denominator of Cultures." Pp. 123–142 in *The Science of Man in the World Crisis,* edited by Ralph Linton. New York: Columbia University Press.

——. 1949. *Social Structure.* New York: Macmillan.

——. 1957. "World Ethnographic Sample." *American Anthropologist* 59 (August):664–687.

Murphy, Caryle. 2009. "Behind the Veil." *Christian Science Monitor,* December 13, pp. 12–15.

Murphy, Dean E. 1997. "A Victim of Sweden's Pursuit of Perfection." *Los Angeles Times,* September 2, pp. A1, A8.

Murray, Velma McBride, Amanda Willert, and Diane P. Stephens. 2001. "The Half-Full Glass: Resilient African American Single Mothers and Their Children." *Family Focus* (June):F4–F5.

N

NAACP. 2008. *Out of Focus—Out of Sync Take 4.* Baltimore: NAACP.

NACCRRA (National Association of Child Care Resource and Referral Agencies). 2010. "Parents and the High Cost of Child Care: 2010 Update." Accessible at http://www.naccrra.org/docs/Cost_Report_073010-final.pdf.

Nakao, Keiko, and Judith Treas. 1994. "Updating Occupational Prestige and Socioeconomic Scores: How the New Measures Measure Up." *Sociological Methodology* 24:1–72.

NARAL Pro-Choice America. 2011. "Who Decides? Restrictions on Low-Income Women's Access to Abortion." Accessed March 17 (www.prochoiceamerica.org/what-is-choice/maps-and-charts/map.jsp?mapID=4).

Nash, Manning. 1962. "Race and the Ideology of Race." *Current Anthropology* 3 (June):285–288.

National Advisory Commission on Criminal Justice. 1976. *Organized Crime.* Washington, DC: U.S. Government Printing Office.

National Alliance for Caregiving. 2009. *Caregiving in the U.S.: Executive Summary.* Washington, DC: NAC and AARP.

National Alliance for Public Charter Schools. 2010. *Measuring Charter Performance: A Review of Public Charter School Achievement Studies.* 6th ed. Washington, DC: NAPCS.

——. 2011. Number of Charter Schools 2009–2010 and 2010–2011. Communication to Schaefer from NAPCS. June 30.

National Alliance on Mental Illness. 2008. "What Is Mental Illness?" Accessed May 24, 2011 (www.nami.org).

National Alliance to End Homelessness. 2011. "Total Homelessness by State—State of Homelessness 2011." Accessible at http://www.endhomelessness.org/content/article/detail/3656.

National Center for Education Statistics. 2009. *Homeschooled Students.* Accessed May 31 (http://nces.ed.gov/programs/coe/2009/section1/indicator06.asp).

——. 2010. *Digest of Education Statistics 2009.* Accessible at http://nces.ed.gov/pubs2010/2010013.pdf.

——. 2011. *Average Undergraduate Tuition and Fees.* Accessed March 29 (http://nces.ed.gov/programs/digest/d09/tables/dt09_335.asp).

National Center on Addiction and Substance Abuse at Columbia University. 2007. *Wasting the Best and the Brightest: Substance Abuse at America's Colleges and Universities.* New York: NCASA at Columbia University.

National Conference of State Legislatures. 2011. "Same-Sex Marriage, Civil Unions and Domestic Partnerships" and "Civil Unions & Domestic Partnership Statutes." Accessed March 21 (http://www.ncsl.org).

National Council on Disability. 2004. *Righting the ADA.* Washington, DC: NCD.

National Education Association. 2009. *Rankings and Estimates: Rankings of the States 2009 and Estimates of School Statistics 2010.* Accessible at http://www.nea.org.assets/docs/010rankings.pdf.

National Gay and Lesbian Task Force. 2008. "Anti-Adoption Laws in the U.S. (as of November 4)." Accessed March 21, 2011 (www.theTaskForce.org).

National Geographic. 2005. *Atlas of the World.* 8th ed. Washington, DC: National Geographic.

National Indian Child Welfare Association. 2010. "ICWA Online Training Course." Accessed January 15 (www.nicwa.org/ica_course).

National Institute of Justice. 2005. *Sexual Assault on Campus: What Colleges and Universities Are Doing about It.* Washington, DC: National Institute of Justice.

National Institute on Aging. 1999. *Early Retirement in the United States.* Washington, DC: U.S. Government Printing Office.

National Law Center on Homelessness and Poverty. 2009a. "Homes Not Handcuffs: The Criminalization of Homelessness in U.S. Cities." Accessible at www.nationalhomeless.org.

——. 2009b. "Maryland 1st to Protect Homeless from Hate Crimes." Accessed May 8 (www.nlchp.org/news.cfm?id=98).

National Organization for Men Against Sexism. 2011. Home Page. Accessed March 17 (www.nomas.org).

National Organization of Mothers of Twins Clubs. 2010. Home Page. Accessed January 24 (www.nomotc.org).

National Vital Statistics Reports. 2010. "Births, Marriages, Divorces, and Deaths: Provisional Data for March 26, 2010." *National Vital Statistics Reports* 58 (March 26).

Navarro, Mireya. 2005. "When You Contain Multitudes." *New York Times*, April 24, pp. 1, 2.

———. 2009. "In Environmental Push, Looking to Add Diversity." *New York Times*, March 10, p. A13.

Nelson, Emily. 2004. "Goodbye, 'Friends'; Hello, New Reality." *Wall Street Journal*, February 9, pp. B6, B10.

Neuman, Lawrence W. 2009. *Understanding Research*. Boston: Allyn and Bacon.

Neuwirth, Robert. 2004. *Shadow Cities: A Billion Squatters, a New Urban World*. New York: Routledge.

Newman, William M. 1973. *American Pluralism: A Study of Minority Groups and Social Theory*. New York: Harper and Row.

Newport, Frank. 2009. *On Darwin's Birthday, Only 4 in 10 Believe in Evolution*. February 11. Accessible at www.gallup.com.

———. 2010a. *In U.S., 64% Support Death Penalty in Cases of Murder*. November 8. Accessible at http://www.gallup.com/poll/144284/Support-Death-Penalty-Cases-Murder.aspx.

———. 2010b. *In U.S., Increasing Number Have No Religious Identity*. Accessed March 28, 2011 (www.gallup.com).

———. 2010c. "Americans' Global Warming Concerns Continue to Drop." March 11. Accessed April 27 (www.gallup.com/poll/126560/Americans-global-warming-concerns-continue-drop.aspx).

———, and Lydia Saad. 2011. *Gallup Review: Public Opinion Context of Tucson Shootings*. January 10. Accessed April 25 (http://www.gallup.com/poll/145526/Gallup-Review-Public-Opinion-Context-Tucson-Shootings.aspx?version=print).

Newsday. 1997. "Japan Sterilized 16,000 Women." September 18, p. A19.

New Unionism Network. 2011. "State of the Unions." Accessed February 10 (http://www.newunionism.net/State_of_the_Unions.htm).

New York Times. 2007. "University Officials Accused of Hiding Campus Homicide." June 24, p. 19.

———. 2008. "Law and Order." January 6, pp. 10–11.

NICHD. 2007. "Children Who Complete Intensive Early Childhood Program Show Gains in Adulthood: Greater College Attendance, Lower Crime and Depression." Accessed January 7, 2008 (www.nichd.nih.gov/news.releases/early_interventions_082107.cfm).

Nielsen Company. 2009. "The Nielsen Company's Guide to Super Bowl XLIII." Accessed February 7, 2010 (http://en-us.nielsen.com/main/news/news_releases/2009/january/the_nielsen_company0).

Nielsen, Joyce McCarl, Glenda Walden, and Charlotte A. Kunkel. 2000. "Gendered Heteronormativity: Empirical Illustrations in Everyday Life." *Sociological Quarterly* 41 (2):283–296.

Niemi, Richard G., and Michael J. Hanmer. 2010. "Voter Turnout among College Students: New Data and a Rethinking of Traditional Theories." *Social Science Quarterly* 91 (June):301–323.

Niesse, Mark. 2008. "Hawaiian Sovereignty Seekers Take Over Historic Iolani Palace in Honolulu." *News from Indian Country* (May 12):3.

———. 2011. "Native Hawaiian Self-Government May Be Set Up by State." *News from Indian Country* (March):3.

Niezen, Ronald. 2005. "Digital Identity: The Construction of Virtual Selfhood in the Indigenous Peoples' Movement." *Comparative Studies in Society and History* 47 (3):532–551.

Nixon, Darren. 2009. "'I Can't Put a Smiley Face On': Working-Class Masculinity, Emotional Labor and Service Work in the 'New Economy.'" *Gender, Work and Organization* 16 (3):300–322.

Nixon, Howard L., II. 1979. *The Small Group*. Englewood Cliffs, NJ: Prentice Hall.

Noam, Eli. 2009. *Media Ownership and Concentration in America*. Cambridge, MA: Oxford University Press.

Nolan, Patrick, and Gerhard Lenski. 2009. *Human Societies: An Introduction to Macrosociology*. 11th ed. Boulder, CO: Paradigm.

Noonan, Rita K. 1995. "Women against the State: Political Opportunities and Collective Action Frames in Chile's Transition to Democracy." *Sociological Forum* 10:81–111.

NORC. 2010. "General Social Surveys, 1972–2008. Number of Memberships." Accessed February 6 (www.norc.org/GSS+Website/Browse+GSS+Variables/Mbemonic+Index/).

Nordhaus, Ted, and Michael Shellenberger. 2007. *Break Through: From the Death of Environmentalism to the Politics of Possibility*. Boston: Houghton Mifflin.

Nordholt, Eric Schulte, Marijke Hartgers, and Rita Gircour, eds. 2004. "The Dutch Virtual Census of 2001." *Analysis and Methodology*. Voorburg: Statistics Netherlands.

NORML. 2010. "Active State Medical Marijuana Programs." Accessed December 9 (http://norml.org/index.cfm?Group_ID=3391).

Norris, Poppa, and Ronald Inglehart. 2004. *Sacred and Secular: Religion and Politics Worldwide*. Cambridge: Cambridge University Press.

North Carolina Department of Environmental and Natural Resources. 2008. "Warren County PCB Landfill Fact Sheet." Accessed April 9 (www.wastenotnc.org/WarrenCo_Fact_Sheet.htm).

NPD Group. 2008. "Wired Baby Boomers Going Digital, Visiting Social Networks and Watching Videos on the Web." Accessed March 18 (www.npd.com/press/releases/press_080909.html).

Nussbaum, Bruce. 2006. "Can Wal-Mart Make It in India?" November 28. Accessed January 23, 2007 (www.businessweek.com).

O

Oberschall, Anthony. 1973. *Social Conflict and Social Movements*. Englewood Cliffs, NJ: Prentice Hall.

O'Connor, Anne-Marie. 2004. "Time of Blogs and Bombs." *Los Angeles Times*, December 27, pp. E1, E14–E15.

O'Donnell, Mike. 1992. *A New Introduction to Sociology*. Walton-on-Thames, UK: Thomas Nelson and Sons.

Office of Immigration Statistics. 2008. "2007 Yearbook of Immigration Statistics." Washington, DC: U.S. Department of Homeland Security.

Ogburn, William F. 1922. *Social Change with Respect to Culture and Original Nature*. New York: Huebsch (reprinted 1966, New York: Dell).

———, and Clark Tibbits. 1934. "The Family and Its Functions." Pp. 661–708 in *Recent Social Trends in the United States*, edited by Research Committee on Social Trends. New York: McGraw-Hill.

O'Hare, William P., and Brenda Curry-White. 1992. "Is There a Rural Underclass?" *Population Today* 20 (March):6–8.

O'Harrow, Jr., Robert. 2005. "Mining Personal Data." *Washington Post National Weekly Edition*, February 6, pp. 8–10.

Okano, Kaori, and Motonori Tsuchiya. 1999. *Education in Contemporary Japan: Inequality and Diversity*. Cambridge: Cambridge University Press.

Oliver, Melvin L., and Thomas M. Shapiro. 2006. *Black Wealth/White Wealth: New Perspectives on Racial Inequality*. 2nd ed. New York: Routledge.

Omi, Michael, and Howard Winant. 1994. *Racial Formation in the United States*. 2nd ed. New York: Routledge.

Onishi, Norimitso. 2003. "Divorce in South Korea: Striking a New Attitude." *New York Times*, September 21, p. 19.

OpenNet Initiative. 2011. Home Page. Accessed April 11 (http://opennet.net).

Orfield, Gary, and Chungmei Lee. 2007. *Historic Reversals, Accelerating Resegregation, and the Need for New Integration Strategies*. Los Angeles: Civil Rights Project, UCLA.

Organisation for Economic Co-operation and Development. 2008. *Growing Unequal? Income Distribution and Poverty in OECD Countries*. Geneva: OECD.

———. 2009a. *OECD Factbook*. Paris: OECD. Accessed February 20, 2010 (http://titania.sourceoecd.org/pdf/factbook2009/3020090 11e-12-02-02.pdf).

———. 2009b. "Green at Fifteen? How 15-Year-Olds Perform in Environmental Sciences and Geosciences in PISA 2006." PISA, OECD Publishing. Accessible at http://dx.doi.org/10.1787/9789264063600-en.

———. 2011. *Statistics on Resource Flows to Developing Countries*. Geneva: OECD. Accessible at http://www.oecd.org/dataoecd/53/43/47137659.pdf.

Ormond, James. 2005. "The McDonaldization of Football." Accessed January 23, 2006 (http://courses.essex.ac.uk/sc/sc111).

Orum, Anthony M., and John G. Dale. 2009. *Political Sociology: Power and Participation in the Modern World*. 3rd ed. New York: Oxford University Press.

Outside the Classroom. 2009. "College Students Spend More Time Drinking than Studying." Accessed March 11 (www.outsidetheclassroom.com).

Oxford Poverty and Human Development Initiative. 2011. "Multidimensional Poverty Index." Accessed March 15 (www.ophi.org.uk).

P

Pace, Richard. 1993. "First-Time Televiewing in Amazonia: Television Acculturation in Gurupa, Brazil. *Ethnology* 32:187–205.

———. 1998. "The Struggle for Amazon Town." Boulder, CO: Lynne Rienner.

Pacific Institute. 2010a. *Cleaning the Waters: A Focus on Water Quality Solutions*. Nairobi, Kenya: Pacific Institute.

———. 2010b. "Water Conflict Chronology." Accessed April 19 (www.worldwater.org/chronology.html).

Padilla, Efren N. 2008. "Filipino Americans." Pp. 493–497 in vol. 1, *Encyclopedia of Race*,

Ethnicity, and Society, edited by Richard T. Schaefer. Thousand Oaks, CA: Sage.

Page, Charles H. 1946. "Bureaucracy's Other Face." *Social Forces* 25 (October):89–94.

Page, Jeremy. 2011. "China's One-Child Plan Faces New Fire." *New York Times,* April 29, pp. A1, A12.

Pager, Devah. 2007. *Marked: Race, Crime, and Funding Work in an Era of Mass Incarceration.* Chicago: University of Chicago Press.

———, Bruce Weston, and Bart Bonikowski. 2009. "Discrimination in a Low-Wage Labor Market: A Field Experiment." *American Sociological Review* 74 (October):777–799.

Pampel, Fred C., Patrick M. Krueger, and Justin T. Denney. 2010. "Socioeconomic Disparities in Health Behaviors." *Annual Review of Sociology* 36:349–370.

Park, Robert E. 1916. "The City: Suggestions for the Investigation of Human Behavior in the Urban Environment." *American Journal of Sociology* 20 (March):577–612.

———. 1922. *The Immigrant Press and Its Control.* New York: Harper.

———. 1936. "Succession, an Ecological Concept." *American Sociological Review* 1 (April):171–179.

Parker, Ashley. 2010. "Where Parties Look for an Audience." *New York Times,* October 30.

Parker, Suzi. 2010. "A Famous Case, DNA Evidence, and New Security." *Christian Science Monitor,* November 22, p. 19.

Parsons, Talcott. 1951. *The Social System.* New York: Free Press.

———. 1966. *Societies: Evolutionary and Comparative Perspectives.* Englewood Cliffs, NJ: Prentice Hall.

———. 1975. "The Sick Role and the Role of the Physician Reconsidered." *Milbank Medical Fund Quarterly Health and Society* 53 (Summer):257–278.

———, and Robert Bales. 1955. *Family: Socialization and Interaction Process.* Glencoe, IL: Free Press.

Passel, Jeffrey S., and D'Vera Cohn. 2011. "Unauthorized Immigrant Population National and State Trends, 2010." Washington, DC: Pew Research Center.

Passero, Kathy. 2002. "Global Travel Expert Roger Axtell Explains Why." *Biography* (July):70–73, 97–98.

Patterson, Thomas E. 2005. "Young Voters and the 2004 Election." Cambridge, MA: Vanishing Voter Project, Harvard University.

Pattillo-McCoy, Mary. 1999. *Black Picket Fences: Privilege and Peril among the Black Middle Class.* Chicago: University of Chicago Press.

Pear, Robert. 1997. "Now, the Archenemies Need Each Other." *New York Times,* June 22, sec. 4, pp. 1, 4.

———. 2009. "Congress Relaxes Rules on Suits over Pay Inequity." *New York Times,* January 28, p. A14.

Pendergrast, Mark. 1999. *Uncommon Grounds: The History of Coffee and How It Transformed Our World.* New York: Basic Books.

Pennington, Bill. 2008. "College Athletic Scholarships: Expectations Lose Out to Reality." *New York Times,* March 10, pp. A1, A15.

Perez, Evan. 2010. "Violent Crime Falls Sharply." *Wall Street Journal,* May 25, p. A23.

Perlman, Janice. 2010. *Favela: Four Decades of Living on the Edge in Rio de Janeiro.* London: Oxford University Press.

Perry, Tony. 2007. "Study: Deployment Does Not Increase Divorce." *Los Angeles Times,* April 16.

Peter, Laurence J., and Raymond Hull. 1969. *The Peter Principle.* New York: Morrow.

Petersen, John L. 2009. "How 'Wild Cards' May Reshape Our Future." *Futurist* (May–June):19–20.

Petersen, William. 1979. *Malthus.* Cambridge, MA: Harvard University Press.

Peterson, Karen S. 2003. "Unmarried with Children: For Better or Worse." *USA Today,* August 18, pp. 1A, 8A.

Petrášová, Alexandra. 2006. *Social Protection in the European Union.* Brussels: European Union.

Pew Forum on Religion and Public Life. 2008. *U.S. Religious Landscape Survey.* Washington, DC: Author.

———. 2010a. *U.S. Religious Knowledge Survey.* Washington, DC: Pew Forum. Accessible at http://pewforum.org.

———. 2010b. *Religious Knowledge Query.* Accessed March 23, 2011 (http://pewforum.org/Uploaded-Files/Topics/Belief-and-practices/religious-knowledge-quiz-handout.pdf).

Pew Global Attitudes Project. 2007. *Global Unease with Major World Powers.* Washington, DC: Pew Global.

Pew Internet and American Life Project. 2009. *Barriers to Broadband Adoption.* Accessed July 7 (http://www.pewinternet.org/Reports/2009/10-Home-Broadband-Adoption-2009/5-Barriers-to-broadband-adoption.aspx).

Pew Internet Project. 2009. "Demographics of Internet Users." Accessed February 4 (www.pewinternet.org/trends/User_Demo_Jan_2009.htm).

———. 2010. "Demographics of Internet Users." November 16. Accessible at www.pewinternet.org/Static-Pages/Trend-Data/Whos-Online.aspx.

Pew Research Center. 2009. "Americans Now Divided Over Both Issues: Public Takes Conservative Turn on Gun Control, Abortion." News release. Washington, DC: Pew Research Center.

———. 2010. *Marrying Out.* Washington, DC: PRC.

Pfeifer, Mark. 2008. "Vietnamese Americans" Pp. 1365–1368, vol. 3, in *Encyclopedia of Race, Ethnicity, and Society,* edited by Richard T. Schaefer. Thousand Oaks, CA: Sage.

Phelan, Jo C., Bruce G. Lint, and Parisha Tehranifar. 2010. "Social Conditions as Fundamental Causes of Health Inequalities: Theory, Evidence, and Policy Implications." *Journal of Health and Social Behavior* 51 (5):528–540.

Phillips, E. Barbara. 1996. *City Lights: Urban–Suburban Life in the Global Society.* New York: Oxford University Press.

Phillips, Susan A. 1999. *Wallbangin': Graffiti and Gangs in L.A.* Chicago: University of Chicago Press.

Piaget, Jean. 1954. *Construction of Reality in the Child.* Translated by Margaret Cook. New York: Basic Books.

Picca, Leslie Houts, and Joe R. Feagin. 2007. *Two-Faced Racism: Whites in Backstage and Frontstage.* New York: Routledge.

Pickert, Kate. 2009. "Getting Well While You Shop." *Time,* June 22, pp. 68–70.

Pincus, Fred L. 2003. *Reverse Discrimination: Dismantling the Myth.* Boulder, CO: Lynne Rienner.

———. 2008. "Reverse Discrimination." Pp. 1159–1161, vol. 3, in *Encyclopedia of Race, Ethnicity, and Society,* edited by Richard T. Schaefer. Thousand Oaks, CA: Sage.

Pinderhughes, Dianne. 1987. *Race and Ethnicity in Chicago Politics: A Reexamination of Pluralist Theory.* Urbana: University of Illinois Press.

Pinderhughes, Raquel. 2008. "Green Collar Jobs." Accessed June 29 (www.urbanhabitat.org/node/528).

Piven, Frances Fox, and Richard A. Cloward. 1996. "Welfare Reform and the New Class War." Pp. 72–86 in *Myths about the Powerless: Contesting Social Inequalities,* edited by M. Brinton Lykes, Ali Banuazizi, Ramsay Liem, and Michael Morris. Philadelphia: Temple University Press.

Plomin, Robert. 1989. "Determinants of Behavior." *American Psychologist* 44 (February):105–111.

Plüss, Caroline. 2005. "Constructing Globalized Ethnicity." *International Sociology* 20 (June):201–224.

Pogash, Carol. 2008. "Poor Students in High School Suffer Stigma from Lunch Aid." *New York Times,* March 1, pp. A1, A14.

Polletta, Francesca, and James M. Jasper. 2001. "Collective Identity and Social Movements." Pp. 283–305 in *Annual Review of Sociology, 2001,* edited by Karen S. Cook and Leslie Hogan. Palo Alto, CA: Annual Reviews.

Pontin, Jason. 2007. "First, Cure Malaria. Next, Global Warming." *New York Times,* June 3, p. 3.

Popenoe, David, and Barbara Dafoe Whitehead. 1999. *Should We Live Together? What Young Adults Need to Know about Cohabitation before Marriage.* Rutgers, NJ: The National Marriage Project.

Population Reference Bureau. 1996. "Speaking Graphically." *Population Today* 24 (June/July).

Portes, Alejandro, Cristina Escobar, and Renelinda Arana. 2008. "Bridging the Gap: Transnational and Ethnic Organizations in the Political Incorporation of Immigrants in the United States." *Ethnic and Racial Studies* 31 (September 6):1056–1090.

Powell, Brian, Catherine Bolzendahl, Claudia Geist, and Lola Carr Steelman. 2010. *Counted Out. Same-Sex Relationships and Americans' Definitions of Family.* New York: Russell Sage Foundation.

Powell, Gary N. 2010. *Women and Men in Management.* 4th ed. Thousand Oaks, CA: Sage.

Prehn, John W. 1991. "Migration." Pp. 190–191 in *Encyclopedia of Sociology,* 4th ed. Guilford, CT: Dushkin.

Preston, Jennifer, and Brian Stelter. 2011. "Cellphone Cameras Become World's Eyes and Ears on Protests across the Middle East." *New York Times,* February 19, p. A7.

Priest, Dana. 2008. "Soldiers on the Edge." *Washington Post National Weekly Edition* 25 (February 4):8–9.

Prince, Martin, Vikram Patel, Shekhar Saxena, Mario Maj, Johanna Maselko, Michael Phillips, and Atif Rahman. 2007. "No Health without Mental Health." *The Lancet* 370 (September 8):859–877.

Proulx, Nichole, Sanfra L. Caron, and Mary Ellin Logue. 2006. "A Look at the Implications of Age Differences in Marriage." *Journal of Couple and Relationship Therapy* 5 (October):43–64.

Provasnik, Stephen, and Michael Planty. 2008. *Community Colleges: Special Supplement to the Condition of Education 2008.* Washington, DC: U.S. Government Printing Office.

Pryor, John H., Sylvia Hurtado, Victor B. Saenz, José Luis Santos, and William S. Korn. 2007. *The American Freshman: Forty Year Trends.* Los Angeles: Higher Education Research Institute, UCLA.

———, ———, Linda DeAngelo, Laura Palucki Blake, and Serge Tran. 2010. *The American Freshman: National Norms Fall 2010.* Los Angeles: Higher Education Research Institute, UCLA.

Quadagno, Jill. 2008. *Aging and the Life Course: An Introduction to Social Gerontology.* 4th ed. New York: McGraw-Hill.

———. 2011. *Aging and the Life Course: An Introduction to Social Gerontology.* 5th ed. New York: McGraw-Hill.

Quarantelli, Enrico L. 1957. "The Behavior of Panic Participants." *Sociology and Social Research* 41 (January):187–194.

———, and Russell R. Dynes. 1970. "Property Norms and Looting: Their Patterns in Continuity Crises." *Phylon* (Summer):168–182.

———, and James R. Hundley, Jr. 1975. "A Test of Some Propositions about Crowd Formation and Behavior." Pp. 538–554 in *Readings in Collective Behavior,* edited by Robert R. Evans. Chicago: Rand McNally.

Quillian, Lincoln. 2006. "New Approaches to Understanding Racial Prejudice and Discrimination." *Annual Review of Sociology* 32:299–328.

Quinney, Richard. 1970. *The Social Reality of Crime.* Boston: Little, Brown.

———. 1974. *Criminal Justice in America.* Boston: Little, Brown.

———. 1979. *Criminology.* 2nd ed. Boston: Little, Brown.

———. 1980. *Class, State and Crime.* 2nd ed. New York: Longman.

Rabikovitch, Shelley, and James Lewis, eds. 2004. *The Encyclopedia of Modern Witchcraft and New Paganism.* New York: Citadel Press.

Rainie, Lee. 2005. *Sports Fantasy Leagues Online.* Washington, DC: Pew Internet and American Life Project.

Rajan, Gita, and Shailja Sharma. 2006. *New Cosmopolitanisms: South Asians in the US.* Stanford, CA: Stanford University Press.

Ramet, Sabrina. 1991. *Social Currents in Eastern Europe: The Source and Meaning of the Great Transformation.* Durham, NC: Duke University Press.

Rampell, Catherine. 2010. "The Growing Underclass: Jobs Gone Forever." *New York Times* Online. Accessed March 5, 2011 (http://economix.blogs.nytimes.com/2010/01/28/the-growing-underclass-jobs-gone-forever/?pagemode=print).

Ramirez, Eddy. 2002. "Ageism in the Media Is Seen as Harmful to Health of the Elderly." *Los Angeles Times,* September 5, p. A20.

RAND. 2007. "RAND Study Finds Divorce among Soldiers Has Not Spiked Higher Despite Stress Created by Battlefield Deployments." News release. April 12 (www.rand.org).

———. 2010. "Retail Medical Clinics Perform Well Relative to Other Medical Settings." *RAND Review* (Winter 2009–2010). Accessed January 25 (www.rand.org/publications/randreview/issues/winter2009/news.html#medclinics).

Rangaswamy, Padma. 2005. "Asian Indians in Chicago." In *The New Chicago,* edited by John Koval et al. Philadelphia: Temple University Press.

Ratha, Dilip, Sanket Mohaptra, and Ani Silwat. 2010. "Outlook for Remittance Flows 2010–2011." *Migration and Development Brief,* World Bank.

Ravitch, Diane. 2010. *The Death and Life of the Great American School System: How Testing and Choice Are Undermining Education.* New York: Basic Books.

Rawlinson, Linnie, and Nick Hunt. 2009. "Jackson Dies, Almost Takes Internet with Him." Accessed July 1 (www.cnn.com/2009/TECH/06/26/michael.jackson.internet/).

Ray, Raka. 1999. *Fields of Protest: Women's Movement in India.* Minneapolis: University of Minnesota Press.

Raybon, Patricia. 1989. "A Case for 'Severe Bias.'" *Newsweek* 114 (October 2):11.

Reinharz, Shulamit. 1992. *Feminist Methods in Social Research.* New York: Oxford University Press.

Reitzes, Donald C., and Elizabeth J. Mutran. 2006. "Lingering Identities in Retirement." *Sociological Quarterly* 47:333–359.

Religion News Service. 2003. "New U.S. Guidelines on Prayer in Schools Get Mixed Reaction." *Los Angeles Times,* February 15, p. B24.

Religion Watch. 2006. "Hinduism Shaping India's Pragmatic Use of Biotechnology." April.

Rennison, Callie. 2002. *Criminal Victimization 2001. Changes 2000–01 with Trends 1993–2001.* Washington, DC: U.S. Government Printing Office.

Renzulli, Linda A., and Vincent J. Roscigno. 2007. "Charter Schools and Public Good." *Contexts* 6 (Winter):31–36.

Reschovsky, Clara. 2004. *Journey to Work: 2000.* Census 2000 Brief C2KBR-23. Washington, DC: U.S. Government Printing Office.

Reuters. 2009. "Terrorism Suspect Wins Police Brutality Claim." Accessed May 18 (http://uk.reuters.com).

———. 2010. "Geoghegan Replaces Feinberg as Pay Czar." September 10. Accessed March 5, 2011 (http://www.reuters.com/assets/print?aid=USTRE6894ZH20100910).

Revkin, Andrew C. 2007. "Wealth and Poverty, Drought and Flood: Report from Four Fronts in the War on Warming." *New York Times,* April 3, pp. D4–D5.

Rice, Ronald E. 2008. *Media Ownership: Research and Regulation.* Cresskill, NJ: Hampton Press.

Rideout, Victoria K., Ulla G. Foehr, and Donald F. Roberts. 2010. Generation M: Media in the Lives of 8–18 Year-Olds. Kaiser Family Foundation. Accessible at www.kff.org/entmedia/mh012010pkg.cfm.

Riding, Alan. 1998. "Why 'Titanic' Conquered the World." *New York Times,* April 26, sec. 2, pp. 1, 28, 29.

———. 2005. "Unesco Adopts New Plan against Cultural Invasion." *New York Times,* October 21, p. B3.

Rieker, Patricia R., and Chloe E. Bird. 2000. "Sociological Explanations of Gender Differences in Mental and Physical Health." Pp. 98–113 in *Handbook of Medical Sociology,* edited by Chloe Bird, Peter Conrad, and Allan Fremont. New York: Prentice Hall.

Rifkin, Jeremy. 1995. *The End of Work; The Decline of the Global Labor Force and the Dawn of the Post-Market Era.* New York: Tarcher/Putnam.

———. 1996. "Civil Society in the Information Age." *The Nation* 262 (February 26):11–12, 14–16.

Riley, Matilda White, Robert L. Kahn, and Anne Foner. 1994a. *Age and Structural Lag.* New York: Wiley InterScience.

———, Robert L. Kahn, and Anne Foner, in association with Karin A. Mock. 1994b. "Introduction: The Mismatch between People and Structures." Pp. 1–36 in *Age and Structural Lag,* edited by Matilda White Riley, Robert L. Kahn, and Anne Foner. New York: Wiley InterScience.

Rimer, Sara. 1998. "As Centenarians Thrive, 'Old' Is Redefined." *New York Times,* June 22, pp. A1, A14.

Ritzer, George. 1977. *Working: Conflict and Change.* 2nd ed. Englewood Cliffs, NJ: Prentice Hall.

———. 2000. *The McDonaldization of Society.* New Century Edition. Thousand Oaks, CA: Pine Forge Press.

———. 2002. *McDonaldization: The Reader.* Thousand Oaks, CA: Pine Forge Press.

———. 2004. *The Globalization of Nothing.* Thousand Oaks, CA: Pine Forge Press.

———. 2008. *The McDonaldization of Society 5.* Thousand Oaks, CA: Sage.

———. 2011. *McDonaldization of Society 6.* Thousand Oaks, CA: Sage.

Robelon, Erik W. 2007. "'Moment-of-Silence' Generates Loud Debate in Illinois." *Education Week,* October 24.

Roberts, J. Timmons, Peter E. Grines, and Jodie L. Mañale. 2003. "Social Roots of Global Environmental Change: A World-Systems Analysis of Carbon Dioxide Emissions." *Journal of World-Systems Research* 9 (Summer):277–315.

Roberts, Sam. 2010. "Extended Family Households Are on the Rise, Census Finds." *New York Times,* March 19.

Robertson, Roland. 1988. "The Sociological Significance of Culture: Some General Considerations." *Theory, Culture, and Society* 5 (February):3–23.

Robinson, Kristopher, and Edward M. Crenshaw. 2010. "Reevaluating the Global Digital Divide: Socio-Demographic and Conflict Barriers to the Internet Revolution." *Sociological Inquiry* 80 (February):34–62

Robison, Jennifer. 2002. "Feminism—What's in a Name?" Accessed February 25, 2007 (www.galluppoll.com).

Rodman, George. 2011. *Mass Media in a Changing World.* 3rd ed. New York: McGraw-Hill.

Rogan, Eugene. 2009. "Sand, Sea and Shopping." *Guardian Weekly,* October 16, pp. 38–39.

Roman, John, Aaron Chalfin, Aaron Sundquist, Carly Knight, and Askar Darmenov. 2008. *The Cost of the Death Penalty in Maryland.* Washington, DC: Urban Institute.

Rootes, Christopher. 2007. "Environmental Movements." Pp. 608–640 in *The Blackwell Companion to Social Movements,* edited by David A. Snow, Sarah A. Sovle, and Hanspeter Kriesi. Malden, MA: Blackwell.

Roscigno, Vincent J. 2010. "Ageism in the American Workplace." *Contexts* (Winter):15–21.

Rose, Arnold. 1951. *The Roots of Prejudice.* Paris: UNESCO.

Rose, Peter I., Myron Glazer, and Penina Migdal Glazer. 1979. "In Controlled Environments: Four Cases of Intense Resocialization." Pp. 320–338 in *Socialization and the Life Cycle,* edited by Peter I. Rose. New York: St. Martin's Press.

Rosen, Eva, and Sudhir Alladi Venkatesh. 2008. "A Perversion of Choice: Sex Work Offers Just Enough in Chicago's Urban Ghetto." *Journal of Contemporary Ethnography* (August):417–441.

Rosenberg, Douglas H. 1991. "Capitalism." Pp. 33–34 in *Encyclopedic Dictionary of Sociology,* 4th ed., edited by Dushkin Publishing Group. Guilford, CT: Dushkin.

Rosenberg, Howard. 2003. "Snippets of the 'Unique' Al Jazeera." *Los Angeles Times,* April 4, pp. E1, E37.

Rosenfeld, Jake. 2010. "Little Labor." *Pathways* (Summer):4–6.

Rosenfeld, Michael J. 2010. "Meeting Online: The Rise of the Internet as a Social Intermediary." Accessed April 2 (www.stanford.edu/~mrosenfe/Rosenfeld_How_Couples_Meet_PAA_updated.pdf).

Rosenthal, Robert, and Lenore Jacobson. 1968. *Pygmalion in the Classroom.* New York: Holt.

———. 1992. *Pygmalion in the Classroom: Teacher Expectations and Pupils' Intellectual Development.* Newly expanded edition. Bancyfelin, UK: Crown House.

Ross, John. 1996. "To Die in the Street: Mexico City's Homeless Population Booms as Economic Crisis Shakes Social Protections." *SSSP Newsletter* 27 (Summer):14–15.

Rossi, Alice S. 1968. "Transition to Parenthood." *Journal of Marriage and the Family* 30 (February): 26–39.

———. 1984. "Gender and Parenthood." *American Sociological Review* 49 (February):1–19.

Rossi, Peter H. 1987. "No Good Applied Social Research Goes Unpunished." *Society* 25 (November–December):73–79.

Rossides, Daniel W. 1997. *Social Stratification: The Interplay of Class, Race, and Gender.* 2nd ed. Upper Saddle River, NJ: Prentice Hall.

Roszak, Theodore. 1969. *The Making of a Counterculture.* Garden City, NY: Doubleday.

Rothkopf, David. 2008. *Superclass: The Global Power Elite and the World They Are Making.* New York: Farrar, Straus and Giroux.

Roy, Donald F. 1959. "'Banana Time': Job Satisfaction and Informal Interaction." *Human Organization* 18 (Winter):158–168.

Rubin, Alissa J. 2003. "Pat-Down on the Way to Prayer." *Los Angeles Times,* November 25, pp. A1, A5.

———, and Sam Dagher. 2009. "Election Quotas for Iraqi Women Are Weakened, Provoking Anger as Vote Nears." *New York Times,* January 14, p. A13.

Ruebain, David. 2005. "Disability Discrimination Act of 1995 (United Kingdom)." Pp. 420–422 in *Encyclopedia of Disability,* edited by Gary Albrecht. Thousand Oaks, CA: Sage.

Ryan, William. 1976. *Blaming the Victim.* Rev. ed. New York: Random House.

Rymer, Russ. 1993. *Genie: An Abused Child's Flight from Science.* New York: HarperCollins.

S

Saad, Lydia. 2004. "Divorce Doesn't Last." *Gallup Poll Tuesday Briefing.* March 30. Accessible at www.gallup.com.

———. 2010a. "Public Agrees with Court: Campaign Money Is 'Free Speech.'" January 22. Accessed April 13 (www.gallup.com).

———. 2010b. "Parties Even in Congressional Midterm Preferences." April 7. Accessed April 16 (www.gallup.com).

———. 2010c. "Americans Firm in Prioritizing Economy over Environment." March 18. Accessible at www.gallup.com.

———. 2011. "Americans' Worries about Economy, Budget Top Other Issues." March 21. Accessible at www.gallup.com.

Sabol, William J., Heather C. West, and Matthew Cooper. 2009. "Prisoners in 2008." *Bureau of Justice Statistics Bulletin* (December).

Sachs, Jeffrey D. 2005. *The End of Poverty: Economic Possibilities for Our Time.* New York: Penguin.

Sacks, Peter. 2007. *Tearing Down the Gates: Confronting the Class Divide in American Education.* Berkeley: University of California Press.

Sagarin, Edward, and Jose Sanchez. 1988. "Ideology and Deviance: The Case of the Debate over the Biological Factor." *Deviant Behavior* 9 (1):87–99.

Saguy, Abigail, and Rene Almeling. 2008. "Fat in the Fire? Science, the News Media, and the 'Obesity Epidemic.'" *Sociological Forum* 23 (March):53–83.

Said, Edward W. 2001. "The Clash of Ignorance." *Nation,* October 22.

Sale, Kirkpatrick. 1996. *Rebels against the Future: The Luddites and Their War on the Industrial Revolution* (with a new preface by the author). Reading, MA: Addison-Wesley.

Salem, Richard, and Stanislaus Grabarek. 1986. "Sociology B.A.s in a Corporate Setting: How Can They Get There and of What Value Are They?" *Teaching Sociology* 14 (October):273–275.

Sampson, Robert J., and W. Byron Graves. 1989. "Community Structure and Crime: Testing Social-Disorganization Theory." *American Journal of Sociology* 94 (January):774–802.

Samuels, Robert. 2010. "A Suicide Reminds Gulf Coast of Oil Spill." *Miami Herald,* June 28. Accessible at http://www.mcclatchydc.com/2010/06/28/96665/a-suicide-reminds-gulf-coast-of.html.

Samuelson, Paul A., and William D. Nordhaus. 2010. *Economics.* 19th ed. New York: McGraw-Hill.

Sanday, Peggy Reeves. 2002. *Women at the Center: Life in a Modern Matriarchy.* Ithaca, NY: Cornell University Press.

———. 2008. Home Page. Accessed March 15 (www.sas.upenn.edu/psanday/).

Sandefur, Rebecca L. 2008. "Access to Civil Justice and Race, Class, and Gender Inequality." *Annual Review of Sociology* 34:339–358.

Sanders, Edmund. 2004. "Coming of Age in Iraq." *Los Angeles Times,* August 14, pp. A1, A5.

Sanderson, Warren, and Sergei Scherbov. 2008. "Rethinking Age and Aging." *Population Bulletin* 63 (December).

Santos, José Alcides Figueiredo. 2006. "Class Effects on Racial Inequality in Brazil." *Dados* 2:1–35.

Sanua, Marianne R. 2007. "AJC and Intermarriage: The Complexities of Jewish Continuity, 1960–2006." Pp. 3–32 in *American Jewish Yearbook 2007,* edited by David Singer and Lawrence Grossman. New York: American Jewish Committee.

Sanyal, Paromita. 2009. "From Credit to Collective Action: The Role of Microfinance in Promoting Women's Social Capital and Normative Influence." *American Sociological Review* 74 (August):529–550.

Sapir, Edward. 1929. "The State of Linguistics as a Science." *Language* 5 (4):207–214.

Saporito, Bill. 2007. "Restoring Wal-Mart." *Time* 170 (November 12):46–48, 50, 52.

Sassen, Saskia. 2005. "New Global Classes: Implications for Politics." Pp. 143–170 in *The New Egalitarianism,* edited by Anthony Giddens and Patrick Diamond. Cambridge: Polity.

Sawhill, Isabel, and Ron Haskins. 2009. "If You Can Make It Here . . ." *Washington Post National Weekly Edition,* November 9, p. 27.

———, and John E. Morton. 2007. *Economic Mobility: Is the American Dream Alive and Well?* Washington, DC: Economic Mobility Project, Pew Charitable Trusts.

Sayer, Liana C., Suzanne M. Bianchi, and John P. Robinson. 2004. "Are Parents Investing Less in Children? Trends in Mothers' and Fathers' Time with Children." *American Journal of Sociology* 110 (July):1–43.

Scarce, Rik. 2005. "A Law to Protect Scholars." *Chronicle of Higher Education,* August 12, p. 324.

Schadler, Ted. 2009. *US Telecommuting Forecast, 2009–2016.* Accessible at www.forester.com.

Schaefer, Peter. 2008. "Digital Divide." Pp. 388–389, vol. 1, in *Encyclopedia of Race, Ethnicity, and Society in the United States,* edited by Richard T. Schaefer. Thousand Oaks, CA: Sage.

Schaefer, Richard T. 1998. "Differential Racial Mortality and the 1995 Chicago Heat Wave." Presentation at the annual meeting of the American Sociological Association, August, San Francisco.

———. 2008a. "Australia, Indigenous People." Pp. 115–119, vol. 1, in *Encyclopedia of Race, Ethnicity, and Society,* edited by Richard T. Schaefer. Thousand Oaks, CA: Sage.

———. 2008b. "'Power' and 'Power Elite.'" In *Encyclopedia of Social Problems,* edited by Vincent Parrillo. Thousand Oaks, CA: Sage.

———. 2011. *Race and Ethnicity in the United States.* 12th ed. Census Update. Upper Saddle River, NJ: Prentice Hall.

———. 2012. *Racial and Ethnic Groups.* 13th ed. Upper Saddle River, NJ: Pearson.

———, and William Zellner. 2011. *Extraordinary Groups.* 9th ed. New York: Worth.

Scharnberg, Kirsten. 2007. "Black Market for Midwives Defies Bans." *Chicago Tribune,* November 25, pp. 1, 10.

Scherer, Ron. 2009. "Job Migration to Suburbs: An Unstoppable Flow?" *New York Times,* April 6.

———. 2010a. "A Long Struggle to Find Jobs." *Christian Science Monitor,* January 31, pp. 18–19.

———. 2010b. "For Jobless, Online Friends Can Be Lifelines." *Christian Science Monitor,* March 25, p. 21.

Scherer/Owings, Michael. 2010. "The Permanent Campaign." *Time* 173:48.

Schleifer, Yigal. 2009. "In Turkey, Surfing for Brides." *Christian Science Monitor,* July 5, p. 14.

Schlesinger, Traci. 2011. "The Failure of Race-Neutral Policies: How Mandatory Terms and Sentencing Enhancements Increased Racial Disparities in Prison Admission Rates." *Crime & Delinquency* 57 (January):56–81. Published online 2008 (http://cad.sagepub.com/pap.dtl).

Schmeeckle, Maria. 2007. "Gender Dynamics in Stepfamilies: Adult Stepchildren's

Views." *Journal of Marriage and Family* 69 (February):174–189.

———, Roseann Giarrusso, Du Feng, and Vern L. Bengtson. 2006. "What Makes Someone Family? Adult Children's Perceptions of Current and Former Stepparents." *Journal of Marriage and Family* 68 (August):595–610.

Schnaiberg, Allan. 1994. *Environment and Society: The Enduring Conflict.* New York: St. Martin's Press.

Schneider, Friedrich. 2010. "Dues and Don'ts." *The Economist* (August 14):62.

Schonfeld, Erick. 2010. "Costolo: Twitter Now Has 190 Million Users Tweeting 65 Million Times a Day." Accessible at TechCrunch at http://techcrunch.com/2010/06/08/twitter-190-million-users/.

Schram, Sangord F., Ruhard C. Fording, Joe Soss, and Linda Houser. 2009. "Deciding to Discipline: Race, Choice and Punishment at the Frontlines of Welfare Reform." *American Sociological Review* 74 (June):398–422.

Schull, Natasha Dow. 2005. "Digital Gambling: The Coincidence of Desire and Design." *Annals of the American Academy of Political and Social Science* 597 (1):65–81.

Schulman, Gary I. 1974. "Race, Sex, and Violence: A Laboratory Test of the Sexual Threat of the Black Male Hypothesis." *American Journal of Sociology* 79 (March):1260–1272.

Schur, Edwin M. 1965. *Crimes without Victims: Deviant Behavior and Public Policy.* Englewood Cliffs, NJ: Prentice Hall.

———. 1968. *Law and Society: A Sociological View.* New York: Random House.

———. 1985. "'Crimes without Victims': A 20-Year Reassessment." Paper presented at the annual meeting of the Society for the Study of Social Problems.

Schwartz, Howard D., ed. 1994. *Dominant Issues in Medical Sociology.* 3rd ed. New York: McGraw-Hill.

Schwartz, Mattathias. 2006. "The Hold-'Em Holdup." *New York Times Magazine,* June 11.

Schwartz, Shalom H., and Anat Bardi. 2001. "Value Hierarchies across Cultures: Taking a Similarities Perspective." *Journal of Cross-Cultural Perspective* 32 (May):268–290.

Schwartzman, Paul. 2009. "Nowhere to Go but Down." *Washington Post National Weekly Edition,* August 10, pp. 13–14.

Scotch, Richard. 1989. "Politics and Policy in the History of the Disability Rights Movement." *The Milbank Quarterly* 67 (Suppl. 2):380–400.

———. 2001. *From Good Will to Civil Rights: Transforming Federal Disability Policy.* 2nd ed. Philadelphia: Temple University Press.

Scott, Alan. 1990. *Ideology and the New Social Movements.* London: Unwin Hyman.

Scott, Gregory. 2001. "Broken Windows behind Bars: Eradicating Prison Gangs through Ecological Hardening and Symbolic Cleansing." *Corrections Management Quarterly* 5 (Winter):23–36.

Scott, W. Richard, and Gerald F. Davis. 2007. *Organizations and Organizing: Rational, Natural and Open Systems Perspectives.* New York: Pearson.

Search Engine Watch. 2011. "comScore: Bing Grows for Sixth Straight Year." March 16. Accessible at http://searchenginewatch.com/3642049.

Seccombe, Karen. 2011. "So You Think I Drive a Cadillac?" Boston: Allyn and Bacon.

Secretan, Thierry. 1995. *Going into Darkness: Fantastic Coffins from Africa.* London: Thames and Hudson.

Security on Campus. 2008. "Complying with the Jeanne Clery Act." Accessed January 13 (www.securityoncampus.org/crimestats/index.html).

Seidman, Steven. 1994. "Heterosexism in America: Prejudice against Gay Men and Lesbians." Pp. 578–593 in *Introduction to Social Problems,* edited by Craig Calhoun and George Ritzer. New York: McGraw-Hill.

Sellers, Frances Stead. 2004. "Voter Globalization." *Washington Post National Weekly Edition,* November 29, p. 22.

Selod, Saher Farooq. 2008a. "Muslim Americans." Pp. 920–923, vol. 2, in *Encyclopedia of Race, Ethnicity, and Society,* edited by Richard T. Schaefer. Thousand Oaks, CA: Sage.

———. 2008b. "Veil." Pp. 1359–1360, vol. 3, in *Encyclopedia of Race, Ethnicity, and Society,* edited by Richard T. Schaefer. Thousand Oaks, CA: Sage.

Sengupta, Somini. 2004. "For Iraqi Girls, Changing Land Narrows Lines." *New York Times,* June 27, pp. A1, A11.

———. 2006. "Report Shows Muslims Near Bottom of Social Ladder." *New York Times,* November 29, p. A4.

———. 2009. "An Empire for Poor Working Women, Guided by a Gandhian Approach." *New York Times,* March 7, p. A6.

Senior Action in a Gay Environment. 2010. Home Page. Accessed March 21 (www.sageusa.org).

Sernau, Scott. 2001. *Worlds Apart: Social Inequalities in a New Century.* Thousand Oaks, CA: Pine Forge Press.

Settersten, Richard, and Barbara Ray. 2011. *Not Quite Adults: Why 20-Somethings Are Choosing a Slower Path to Adulthood, and Why It's Good for Everyone.* New York: Bantam.

Shachtman, Tom. 2006. *Rumspringa: To Be or Not to Be Amish.* New York: North Point Press.

Shah, Anup. 2009. "Climate Justice and Equity." October 4. Accessed December 12 (www.globalissues.org/print/articles/231).

Shane, Scott. 2010. "Wars Fought and Wars Googled." *New York Times,* June 27, pp. PWK1–5.

Shapiro, Joseph P. 1993. *No Pity: People with Disabilities Forging a New Civil Rights Movement.* New York: Times Books.

Shapiro, Thomas M., Tatjana Meschede, and Laura Sullivan. 2010. "The Racial Wealth Gap Increases Fourfold." Research and Policy Brief, Institute on Assets and Social Policy, Brandeis University.

Shapley, Dan. 2010. "4 Dirty Secrets of the Exxon Valdez Oil Spill." Accessed May 3 (www.thedailygreen.com).

Sharkey, Patrick. 2009. *Neighbors and the Black-White Mobility Gap.* Washington, DC: Economic Mobility Project.

Sharma, Hari M., and Gerard C. Bodeker. 1998. "Alternative Medicine." Pp. 228–229 in *Britannica Book of the Year 1998.* Chicago: Encyclopaedia Britannica.

Sharp, Jeff S., and Jill K. Clark. 2008. "Between the Country and the Concrete: Rediscovering the Rural-Urban Fringe." *City and Community* 7 (March):61–77.

Shaw, Claude, and Henry D. McKay. 1942. *Juvenile Delinquency and Urban Areas.* Chicago: University of Chicago Press.

Sheehan, Charles. 2005. "Poor Seniors Take On Plans of Condo Giant." *Chicago Tribune,* March 22, pp. 1, 9.

Sherman, Arloc. 2007. *Income Inequality Hits Record Levels, New CBO Data Show.* Washington, DC: Center on Budget and Policy Priorities.

Shibutani, Tamotshu. 1966. *Improvised News: A Sociological Study of Rumor.* Indianapolis: Bobbs-Merrill.

Shin, Hyon B., and Rosalind Bruno. 2003. "Language Use and English-Speaking Ability: 2000." *Census 2000 Brief,* C2KBR-29. Washington, DC: U.S. Government Printing Office.

Shogren, Elizabeth. 1994. "Treatment against Their Will." *Los Angeles Times,* August 18, pp. A1, A14–A15.

Shostak, Arthur B. 2002. "Clinical Sociology and the Art of Peace Promotion: Earning a World without War." Pp. 325–345 in *Using Sociology: An Introduction from the Applied and Clinical Perspectives,* edited by Roger A. Straus. Lanham, MD: Rowman and Littlefield.

Sicular, Terry, Ximing Yue, Bjorn Gustafsson, and Shi Li. 2006. "The Urban-Rural Income Gap and Inequality in China." Research Paper No. 2006/135, United Nations University—World Institute for Development Economic Research.

Sieber, Renée E., Daniel Spitzberg, Hannah Muffatt, Kristen Brewer, Blanka Füleki, and Naomi Arbit. 2006. *Influencing Climate Change Policy: Environmental Non-Governmental Organizations (ENGOs) Using Virtual and Physical Activism.* Montreal: McGill University.

Siegel, Paul, Elizabeth Martin, and Rusalind Bruno. 2001. "Language Use and Linguistic Isolation: Historical Data and Methodological Issues." Paper presented at the Statistical Policy Seminar, Bethesda, MD.

Silver, Ira. 1996. "Role Transitions, Objects, and Identity." *Symbolic Interaction* 10 (1):1–20.

Silverman, Rachel Emma. 2009. "As Jobs Grow Scarce, Commuter Marriages Rise." Accessed March 31, 2010 (http://blogs.wsj.com/juggle/2009/01/16/as-jobs-grow-scarce-commuter-marriages-rise/).

Silverstein, Ken. 2010. "Shopping for Sweat: The Human Cost of a Two-Dollar T-shirt." *Harpers* 320 (January):36–44.

Simmel, Georg. [1917] 1950. *Sociology of Georg Simmel.* Translated by K. Wolff. Glencoe, IL: Free Press (originally written in 1902–1917).

Simmons, Tavia, and Martin O'Connell. 2003. "Married-Couple and Unmarried-Partner Households: 2000." *Census 2000 Special Reports,* CENBR-5. Washington, DC: U.S. Government Printing Office.

Simon, Stephanie. 2007. "It's Easter; Shall We Gather at the Desktops?" *Los Angeles Times,* April 8, p. A13.

Sisson, Carmen K. 2007. "The Virtual War Family." *Christian Science Monitor,* May 29.

Sjoberg, Gideon. 1960. *The Preindustrial City: Past and Present.* Glencoe, IL: Free Press.

Skinner, E. Benjamin. 2008. "People for Sale." *Foreign Policy* (March–April).

Slack, Jennifer Daryl, and J. Macgregor Wise. 2007. *Culture + Technology.* New York: Peter Lang.

Slackman, Michael. 2008. "9/11 Rumors That Harden into Conventional Wisdom." *New York Times,* September 9, p. A16.

530

Slavin, Barbara. 2007. "Child Marriage Rife in Nations Getting U.S. Aid." *USA Today*, July 17, p. 6A.

Slavin, Robert E., and A. Cheung. 2003. *Effective Reading Programs for English Language Learners: A Best-Evidence Synthesis.* Baltimore: Johns Hopkins University, Center for Research on the Education of Students Placed at Risk.

Sloan, Allan. 2009. "What's Still Wrong with Wall Street." *Time*, November 9, pp. 24–29.

Slug-Lines.com. 2008. "A Unique Commuter Solution." Accessed January 9, 2009 (www.slug-lines.com).

Smart, Barry. 1990. "Modernity, Postmodernity, and the Present." Pp. 14–30 in *Theories of Modernity and Postmodernity*, edited by Bryan S. Turner. Newbury Park, CA: Sage.

Smeeding, Timothy M. 2008. "Poorer by Comparison: "Poverty, Work, and Public Policy in Comparative Perspective." *Pathways* (Winter):3–5.

Smelser, Neil. 1962. *Theory of Collective Behavior.* New York: Free Press.

———. 1963. *The Sociology of Economic Life.* Englewood Cliffs, NJ: Prentice Hall.

———. 1981. *Sociology.* Englewood Cliffs, NJ: Prentice Hall.

Smith, Aaron. 2009. *The Internet's Role in Campaign 2000.* Washington, DC: Pew Internet and American Life Project.

Smith, Christian. 1991. *The Emergence of Liberation Theology: Radical Religion and Social Movement Theory.* Chicago: University of Chicago Press.

———. 2007. "Getting a Life: The Challenge of Emerging Adulthood." *Books and Culture: A Christian Review* (November–December).

———. 2008. "Future Directions of the Sociology of Religion." *Social Forces* 86 (June): 1564–1589.

Smith, Craig S. 2006. "Romania's Orphans Face Widespread Abuse, Group Says." *New York Times*, May 10, p. A3.

Smith, Dan. 1999. *The State of the World Atlas.* 6th ed. London: Penguin.

Smith, David A. 1995. "The New Urban Sociology Meets the Old: Rereading Some Classical Human Ecology." *Urban Affairs Review* 20 (January):432–457.

———, and Michael Timberlake. 1993. "World Cities: A Political Economy/Global Network Approach." Pp. 181–207 in *Urban Sociology in Transition*, edited by Ray Hutchison. Greenwich, CT: JAI Press.

Smith, David M., and Gary J. Gates. 2001. *Gay and Lesbian Families in the United States: Same-Sex Unmarried Partner Households.* Washington, DC: Human Rights Campaign.

Smith, Denise, and Hava Tillipman. 2000. "The Older Population in the United States." *Current Population Reports*, ser. P-20, no. 532. Washington, DC: U.S. Government Printing Office.

Smith, Michael Peter. 1988. *City, State, and Market.* New York: Basil Blackwell.

Smith, Peter. 2008. "Going Global: The Transnational Politics of the Debt Movement." *Globalizations* 5 (March):13–33.

Smith, Tom W. 2003. *Coming of Age in 21st Century America: Public Attitudes toward the Importance and Timing of Transition to Adulthood.* Chicago: National Opinion Research Center.

———. 2009. *Religious Change around the World.* Chicago: NORC/University of Chicago.

Snow, David A., Louis A. Zurcher, Jr., and Robert Peters. 1981. "Victory Celebrations as Theater: A Dramaturgical Approach to Crowd Behavior." *Symbolic Interaction* 4:21–42.

Snyder, Thomas D. 1996. *Digest of Education Statistics 1996.* Washington, DC: U.S. Government Printing Office.

Somavia, Juan. 2008. "The ILO at 90 Working for Social Justice." *World of Work* 64 (December):4–5.

Sorokin, Pitirim A. [1927] 1959. *Social and Cultural Mobility.* New York: Free Press.

Southern Poverty Law Center. 2010. "Active 'Patriot' Groups in the United States in 2009." Accessed November 5 (www.splcenter.org/patriot).

Spalter-Roth, Roberta, and Nicole Van Vooren. 2008a. "What Are They Doing with a Bachelor's Degree in Sociology?" Washington, DC: American Sociological Association. Accessible at http://asanet.org/galleries/research/ASAresearchbrief_corrections.pdf.

———. 2008b. "Skills, Reasons and Jobs. What Happened to the Class of 2005." Washington, DC: American Sociological Association. Accessible at http://asanet.org.

———. 2010. *Mixed Success: Four Years of Experiences of 2005 Sociology Graduates.* Washington, DC: American Sociology Association.

Speak, Suzanne, and Graham Tipple. 2006. "Perceptions, Persecution and Pity: The Limitations of Interventions for Homelessness in Developing Countries." *International Journal of Urban and Regional Research* 30 (March):172–188.

Spencer, Nancy. 2008. "Title IX." Pp. 1308–1310, vol. 3, in *Encyclopedia of Race, Ethnicity, and Society*, edited by Richard T. Schaefer. Thousand Oaks, CA: Sage.

Spitzer, Steven. 1975. "Toward a Marxian Theory of Deviance." *Social Problems* 22 (June):641–651.

Sprague, Joey. 2005. *Feminist Methodologies for Critical Research: Bridging Differences.* Lanham, MD: AltaMira Press.

Squires, Gregory D., ed. 2002. *Urban Sprawl: Causes, Consequences and Policy Responses.* Washington, DC: Urban Institute.

Stahler-Sholk, Richard. 2008. "Zapatista Rebellion." Pp. 1423–1424, vol. 3, in *Encyclopedia of Race, Ethnicity, and Society*, edited by Richard T. Schaefer. Thousand Oaks, CA: Sage.

Stanley, Alessandra. 2007. "Deadly Rampage and No Loss for Words." *New York Times*, April 17.

Stark, Andrew. 2011. "The Price of Moral Purity." *Wall Street Journal*, February 4.

Stark, Rodney. 2004. *Exploring the Religious Life.* Baltimore: Johns Hopkins University Press.

———, and William Sims Bainbridge. 1979. "Of Churches, Sects, and Cults: Preliminary Concepts for a Theory of Religious Movements." *Journal for the Scientific Study of Religion* 18 (June):117–131.

———, and ———. 1985. *The Future of Religion.* Berkeley: University of California Press.

Starr, Paul. 2010. "The Next Health-Reform Campaign." *American Prospect* (September):A3, A5–A7.

Staton, Ron. 2004. "Still Fighting for National Hawaiian Recognition." *Asian Week*, January 22, p. 8.

Steel, Emily. 2010. "Some Data-Miners Ready to Reveal What They Know. *Wall Street Journal*, December 3, pp. B1, B2.

Steffen, Alex, ed. 2008. *World Changing: A User's Guide for the 21st Century.* New York: Harry N. Abrams.

Stein, Leonard I. 1967. "The Doctor-Nurse Game." *Archives of General Psychology* 16:699–703.

Stenning, Derrick J. 1958. "Household Viability among the Pastoral Fulani." Pp. 92–119 in *The Developmental Cycle in Domestic Groups*, edited by John R. Goody. Cambridge, UK: Cambridge University Press.

Stevick, Richard A. 2007. *Growing Up Amish: The Teenage Years.* Baltimore: Johns Hopkins University Press.

Stewart, Robb M. 2010. "Wal-Mart Sets African Offer." *Wall Street Journal*, November 30, p. B2.

Stockard, Janice E. 2002. *Marriage in Culture.* Belmont, CA: Thomson Wadsworth.

Stolberg, Sheryl Gay. 1995. "Affirmative Action Gains Often Come at a High Cost." *Los Angeles Times*, March 29, pp. A1, A13–A16.

———. 2008. "Richest Nations Pledge to Halve Greenhouse Gas." *New York Times*, July 9, pp. A1, A13.

Stone, Andrea, and Marisol Bello. 2009. "Mom's Plight Shows Army Strain." *USA Today*, March 4, p. 3A.

Stoner, Madeleine R. 2008. "Homelessness." pp. 641–644, vol. 2, in *Encyclopedia of Race, Ethnicity, and Society*, edited by Richard T. Schaefer. Thousand Oaks, CA: Sage.

Strassman, W. Paul. 1998. "Third World Housing." Pp. 589–592 in *The Encyclopedia of Housing*, edited by Willem van Vliet. Thousand Oaks, CA: Sage.

Strauss, Gary. 2002. "'Good Old Boys' Network Still Rules Corporate Boards." *USA Today*, November 1, pp. B1, B2.

———. 2011. "$228,000 for a Part-Time Job? Apparently, That's Not Enough." *USA Today*, March 4, p. A1.

Street, Marc D. 1997. "Groupthink: An Examination of Theoretical Issues, Implications, and Future Research Systems." *Small Group Research* 28 (February):72–93.

Subramaniam, Mangala. 2006. *The Power of Women's Organization: Gender, Caste, and Class in India.* Lanham, MD: Lexington Books.

Suitor, J. Jill, Staci A. Minyard, and Rebecca S. Carter. 2001. "'Did You See What I Saw?' Gender Differences in Perceptions of Avenues to Prestige among Adolescents." *Sociological Inquiry* 71 (Fall):437–454.

Sullivan, Harry Stack. [1953] 1968. *The Interpersonal Theory of Psychiatry.* Edited by Helen Swick Perry and Mary Ladd Gawel. New York: Norton.

Sullivan, Kevin. 2006. "Bridging the Digital Divide." *Washington Post National Weekly Edition* 25 (July 17):11–12.

Sum, Andrew, Paul Harrington, and Ishwar Khatiwada. 2006. *The Impact of New Immigrants on Young Native-Born Workers, 2000–2005.* Washington, DC: Center for Immigration Studies.

Sumner, William G. 1906. *Folkways.* New York: Ginn.

Sunstein, Cass. 2002. *Republic.com.* Rutgers, NJ: Princeton University Press.

SustainAbility. 2006. *Brazil—Country of Diversities and Inequalities.* London: SustainAbility.

Sutch, Richard, and Susan B. Carter. 2006. *Historical Statutes of US: Earliest Time to the Present.* Cambridge: Cambridge University Press.

Sutcliffe, Bob. 2002. *100 Ways of Seeing an Unequal World.* London: Zed Books.

Sutherland, Edwin H. 1937. *The Professional Thief.* Chicago: University of Chicago Press.

———. 1940. "White-Collar Criminality." *American Sociological Review* 5 (February):1–11.

———. 1949. *White Collar Crime.* New York: Dryden.

———. 1983. *White Collar Crime: The Uncut Version.* New Haven, CT: Yale University Press.

———, Donald R. Cressey, and David F. Luckenbill. 1992. *Principles of Criminology.* 11th ed. New York: Rowman and Littlefield.

Swatos, William H., Jr., ed. 1998. *Encyclopedia of Religion and Society.* Lanham, MD: AltaMira.

Sweet, Kimberly. 2001. "Sex Sells a Second Time." *Chicago Journal* 93 (April):12–13.

Swidler, Ann. 1986. "Culture in Action: Symbols and Strategies." *American Sociological Review* 51 (April): 273–286.

Swift, Mike. 2011. "Facebook Gaining Overseas as Growth in U.S. Users Slows." *Chicago Tribune,* January 24, p. 19.

Szasz, Andrew. 2007. *Shopping Our Way to Safety: How We Changed from Protecting the Environment to Protecting Ourselves.* Minneapolis: University of Minnesota Press.

Szasz, Thomas. 2010. *The Myth of Mental Illness: Foundations of a Theory of Personal Conduct.* 50th Anniversary Edition. New York: Harper Perennial.

Tabuchi, Hiroko. 2010. "For Some of Japan's Jobless, New Homes Just 5 Feet Wide." *New York Times,* January 2, pp. A1, A3.

Tanielian, Terri. 2009. "Assessing Combat Exposure and Post-Traumatic Stress Disorder in Troops and Estimating the Costs to Society." Testimony presented before the House Veterans' Affairs Committee, Subcommittee on Disability Assistance and Memorial Affairs, March 24.

Tannen, Deborah. 1990. *You Just Don't Understand: Women and Men in Conversation.* New York: Ballantine.

Tatchell, Jo. 2009. *A Diamond in the Desert: Behind the Scenes in the World's Richest City.* London: Hodder and Stoughton.

Taylor, Verta. 1999. "Gender and Social Movements: Gender Processes in Women's Self-Help Movements." *Gender and Society* 13:8–33.

———. 2004. "Social Movements and Gender." Pp. 14348–14352 in *International Encyclopedia of the Social and Behavioral Sciences,* edited by Neil J. Smelser and Paul B. Baltes. New York: Elsevier.

———, Leila J. Rupp, and Nancy Whittier. 2009. *Feminist Frontiers.* 8th ed. New York: McGraw-Hill.

Tedeschi, Bob. 2006. "Those Born to Shop Can Now Use Cellphones." *New York Times,* January 2.

Telles, Edward E. 2004. *Race in America: The Significance of Skin Color in Brazil.* Princeton, NJ: Princeton University Press.

Therborn, Göran. 2010. Review of "Unveiling Inequality." *Contemporary Sociology* 39 (5):585–586.

Third World Institute. 2007. *The World Guide.* 11th ed. Oxford: New Internationalist Publications.

Thomas, Evan, and Pat Wingert. 2010. "Understanding Charter Schools." *Newsweek* 155 (June 21):46.

Thomas, Gordon, and Max Morgan Witts. 1974. *Voyage of the Damned.* Greenwich, CT: Fawcett Crest.

Thomas, R. Murray. 2003. "New Frontiers in Cheating." In *Encyclopaedia Britannica 2003 Book of the Year.* Chicago: Encyclopaedia Britannica.

Thomas, William I. 1923. *The Unadjusted Girl.* Boston: Little, Brown.

Thomasrobb.com. 2007. "WhitePride TV." Accessed May 7 (http://thomasrobb.com).

Thompson, Clive. 2005. "Meet the Life Hackers." *New York Times Magazine,* October 16, pp. 40–45.

Thompson, Ginger. 2001. "Why Peace Eludes Mexico's Indians." *New York Times,* March 11, sec. WK, p. 16.

Thompson, Neil B. 1972. "The Mysterious Fall of the Nacirema." *Natural History* (December).

Thompson, Tony. 2005. "Romanians Are Being Paid to Play Computer Games for Westerners." *Guardian Weekly,* March 25, p. 17.

Threadcraft, Shatema. 2008. "Welfare Queen." In *Encyclopedia of Race, Ethnicity and Society,* edited by Richard T. Schaefer. Thousand Oaks, CA: Sage.

Thurm, Scott. 2010. "Oracle's Ellison: Pay King." *Wall Street Journal,* July 27, pp. A1, A16.

Thurow, Lester. 1984. "The Disappearance of the Middle Class." *New York Times,* February 5, sec. 5, p. 2.

Tibbles, Kevin. 2007. "Web Sites Encourage Eating Disorders." *Today,* February 18. Accessed May 7 (www.msabc.msn.com).

Tierney, John. 1990. "Betting the Planet." *New York Times Magazine,* December 2, pp. 52–53, 71, 74, 76, 78, 80–81.

Tierney, Kathleen J. 2007. "From the Margins to the Mainstream? Disaster Research at the Crossroads." *Annual Review of Sociology* 33:503–525.

———. 1980. "Emergent Norm Theory as 'Theory': An Analysis and Critique of Turner's Formulation." Pp. 42–53 in *Collective Behavior: A Source Book,* edited by Meredith David Pugh. St. Paul, MN: West.

Tierney, William G., and Karri A. Holley. 2008. "Intelligent Design and the Attack on Scientific Inquiry." *Cultural Studies Critical Methodologies* 8 (February): 39–49.

Tigay, Chanan. 2011. "Women and Sports." *CQ Researcher* 21 (March 25).

Tilly, Charles. 1964. *The Vendée.* Cambridge, MA: Harvard University Press.

———. 1993. *Popular Contention in Great Britain 1758–1834.* Cambridge, MA: Harvard University Press.

———. 2003. *The Politics of Collective Violence.* New York: Cambridge University Press.

———. 2004. *Social Movements, 1768–2004.* Boulder, CO: Paradigm.

———. 2007. "Trust Networks in Transnational Migration." *Sociological Forum* 22 (March):3–24.

Timmerman, Kelsey. 2009. *Where Am I Wearing?* Hoboken NJ: Wiley.

Toensing, Gale Country. 2009. "Akaka Bill Gets Obama Approval." *Indian Country Today* (August 19):1, 2.

Tonkinson, Robert. 1978. *The Mardudjara Aborigines.* New York: Holt.

Tönnies, Ferdinand. [1887] 1988. *Community and Society.* Rutgers, NJ: Transaction.

Toossi, Mitra. 2009. "Employment Outlook: 2008–2018." *Monthly Labor Review* (November):30–51.

Toppo, Greg. 2011. "The Search for a New Way to Test Schoolkids." *USA Today,* March 18, p. A4.

Toro, Paul A. 2007. "Toward an International Understanding of Homelessness." *Journal of Social Issues* 63 (3):461–481.

Torres, Lourdes. 2008. "Puerto Rican Americans" and "Puerto Rico." Pp. 1082–1089, vol. 3, in *Encyclopedia of Race, Ethnicity, and Society,* edited by Richard T. Schaefer. Thousand Oaks, CA: Sage.

Touraine, Alain. 1974. *The Academic System in American Society.* New York: McGraw-Hill.

Transactional Records Access Clearinghouse. 2009. "TRAC Monthly Bulletins by Topic, September 2009." Accessed February 11, 2010 (www.trac.syr.edu/tracreports/bulletins/white_collar_crime/monthly_sep09/fil).

Traynor, Ian. 2008. "Europe Expects a Flood of Climate Refugees." *Guardian Weekly,* March 14, p. 1–2.

Trotter III, Robert T., and Juan Antonio Chavira. 1997. *Curanderismo: Mexican American Folk Healing.* Athens: University of Georgia Press.

Truman, Jennifer L., and Michael R. Rand. 2010. "Criminal Victimization, 2009." Bureau of Justice Statistics Bulletin (October).

Trumbull, Mark. 2006. "America's Younger Workers Losing Ground on Income." *Christian Science Monitor,* February 27.

Tschorn, Adam. 2010. "Parkour Ready to Launch." *Chicago Tribune,* July 25, sec. 6, pp. 20–21.

Tuchman, Gaye. 1992. "Feminist Theory." Pp. 695–704 in *Encyclopedia of Sociology,* vol. 2, edited by Edgar F. Borgatta and Marie L. Borgatta. New York: Macmillan.

Tucker, Robert C. (ed.) 1978. *The Marx-Engels Reader.* 2nd ed. New York: Norton.

Ture, Kwame, and Charles Hamilton. 1992. *Black Power: The Politics of Liberation.* With new Afterword by authors. New York: Vintage Books.

Turkle, Sherry. 2004. "How Computers Change the Way We Think." *Chronicle of Higher Education* 50 (January 30):B26–B28.

———. 2011. *Alone Together: Why We Expect More from Technology and Less from Each Other.* New York: Basic Books.

Turner, Bryan S., ed. 1990. *Theories of Modernity and Postmodernity.* Newbury Park, CA: Sage.

Turner, Ralph, and Lewis M. Killian. 1987. *Collective Behavior.* 3rd ed. Englewood Cliffs, NJ: Prentice Hall.

Turner, S. Derek, and Mark Cooper. 2006. *Out of the Picture: Minority and Female TV Station Ownership in the United States.* Washington, DC: Free Press.

UNAIDS. 2010. *Global Report: UNAIDS Report on the Global AIDS Epidemic 2010.* Geneva: UNAIDS.

UNHCR. 2010. *UNHCR Statistical Yearbook 2009.* Geneva: UNHCR.

UNICEF. 2010. "Child Marriage." Accessed January 15 (www.unicef.org/progressfprchildren/2007n6/index_41848.htm?q=printme).

United Nations. 2005. *The Millennium Development Goals Report.* Washington, DC: United Nations.

532

———. 2009. *International Migration Report 2006: A Global Assessment.* New York: United Nations, Economic and Social Affairs.

United Nations Development Fund for Women. 2009. *Who Answers to Women?* New York: UNIFEM.

United Nations Development Programme. 1995. *Human Development Report 1995.* New York: Oxford University Press.

———. 2000. *Poverty Report 2000: Overcoming Human Poverty.* Washington, DC: UNDP.

———. 2009. *Overcoming Barriers: Human Mobility and Development.* New York: Palgrave Macmillan.

United Nations Economic and Social Council. 2010. "Review of the Implementation of the Beijing Declaration." New York: Economic and Social Council.

United Nations Framework Convention on Climate Change. 2010. Home Page. Accessed April 19 (http://unfcc.int).

United Nations Office on Drugs and Crime. 2005. "The United Nations Convention against Transnational Organized Crime and Its Protocols." Accessed March 18 (www.unodc.org).

United Nations Population Division. 2007. *World Abortion Policies 2007.* New York: UNPD.

United Nations Statistics Division. 2008. "Singulate Mean Age at Marriage." Accessed March 1, 2009 (http://data.un.org/search.aspx?q=marriage).

———. 2009. *Demographic Yearbook 2007.* Accessed April 1, 2010 (http://unstats.un.org/unsd/demographic/products/dyb/dyb2.htm).

United Way of King County. 2010. "Community Assessment." Accessed January 18 (www.uwkc/printver.asp?ref=kcca/data/languages/isolation.asp).

University of Michigan. 2003. *Information on Admissions Lawsuits.* Accessed August 8 (www.umich.edu/urel/admissions).

Urban Dictionary. 2010. "Urban Amish." Accessed April 28 (www.urbandictionary.com/define.php?term=urban%20amish).

Urbina, Ian. 2002. "Al Jazeera: Hits, Misses and Ricochets." *Asia Times,* December 25.

U.S. English. 2010. "Making English the Official Language." Accessed January 17 (www.us-english.org/inc/).

U.S. Surgeon General. 1999. *Surgeon General's Report on Mental Health.* Washington, DC: U.S. Government Printing Office.

U.S. Trade Representative. 2007. "Trade Promotion Authority Delivers Jobs, Growth, Prosperity, and Security at Home." January 31 Fact Sheet. Accessed February 19 (www.ustr.gov).

V

Vaidhyanathan, Siva. 2008. "Generational Myth: Not All Young People Are Tech-Savvy." *Chronicle of Higher Education,* September 19, pp. B7–B9.

Vamosi, Robert, Mary Monahan, and Rachel Kim. 2010. *2010 Identity Fraud Survey Report.* Pleasanton, CA: Javelin Strategy.

van den Berghe, Pierre. 1978. *Race and Racism: A Comparative Perspective.* 2nd ed. New York: Wiley.

Van Gennep, Arnold. [1909] 1960. *The Rites of Passage.* Translated by Monika B. Vizedom and Gabrielle L. Caffee. Chicago: University of Chicago Press.

van Vucht Tijssen, Lieteke. 1990. "Women between Modernity and Postmodernity." Pp. 147–163 in *Theories of Modernity and Postmodernity,* edited by Bryan S. Turner. London: Sage.

Vargas, Jose Antonio. 2007. "YouTube Gets Serious with Links to Candidates." *Washington Post,* March 2, p. C1.

Vasagar, Jeeran. 2005. "'At Last Rwanda Is Known for Something Positive." *Guardian Weekly,* July 22, p. 18.

Vaughan, R. M. 2007. "Cairo's Man Show." *Utne Reader* (March–April):94–95.

Veblen, Thorstein. [1899] 1964. *Theory of the Leisure Class.* New York: Macmillan. New York: Penguin.

———. 1919. *The Vested Interests and the State of the Industrial Arts.* New York: Huebsch.

Velásquez, Carmen, and P. Rafael Hernández-Arias. 2009. *Voices from the Communities: Community Health Assets and Needs Assessment.* Chicago: Alivio Medical Center and Stearns Center for Community-Based Service Learning.

Velasquez-Manoff, Moises. 2009. "Could Water Scarcity Cause International Conflict?" *Christian Science Monitor,* October 26.

Venkatesh, Sudhir Alladi. 2006. *Off the Books: The Underground Economy of the Urban Poor.* Cambridge, MA: Harvard University Press.

———. 2008. *Gang Leader for a Day: A Rogue Sociologist Takes to the Streets.* New York: Penguin Press.

Vernon, Glenn. 1962. *Sociology and Religion.* New York: McGraw-Hill.

Villarreal, Andrés. 2004. "The Social Ecology of Rural Violence: Land Scarcity, the Organization of Agricultural Production, and the Presence of the State." *American Journal of Sociology* 110 (September):313–348.

Vincent, Grayson, and Victoria A. Velkoff. 2010. "The Next Four Decades." *Current Population Reports,* ser. P-25, no. 138. Washington, DC: U.S. Government Printing Office.

Viramontes, Helena Maria. 2007. "Loyalty Spoken Here." *Los Angeles Times,* September 23, p. R7.

Visitability. 2009. "Visitability: Becoming a National Trend." Accessed May 5 (www.visitability.org).

Visser, Jelle. 2006. "Union Membership Statistics in 24 Countries." *Monthly Labor Review* (January):38–49.

W

Wachtendorf, Tricia. 2002. "A Changing Risk Environment: Lessons Learned from the 9/11 World Trade Center Disaster." Presentation at the Sociological Perspectives on Disasters, Mt. Macedon, Australia, July.

Waelde, Lynn C., Madeline Uddo, Renee Marquett, Melanie Ropelato, Sharifa Freightman, Adit Pardo, and Jacqueline Salazar. 2008. "A Pilot Study of Meditation for Mental Health Workers Following Hurricane Katrina." *Journal of Traumatic Stress* 21 (5):497–500.

Wages for Housework Campaign. 1999. *Wages for Housework Campaign.* Circular. Los Angeles.

Wagley, Charles, and Marvin Harris. 1958. *Minorities in the New World: Six Case Studies.* New York: Columbia University Press.

Waite, Linda. 2000. "The Family as a Social Organization: Key Ideas for the Twentieth Century." *Contemporary Sociology* 29 (May):463–469.

Waitzkin, Howard. 1986. *The Second Sickness: Contradictions of Capitalist Health Care.* Chicago: University of Chicago Press.

Walder, Andrew. G. 2009. "Political Sociology and Social Movements." *Annual Review of Sociology* 35:393–412.

———, and Giang Hoang Nguyen. 2008. "Ownership, Organization, and Income Inequality: Market Transition in Rural Vietnam." *American Sociological Review* 73 (April):251–269.

Waldman, Amy. 2004a. "India Takes Economic Spotlight, and Critics Are Unkind." *New York Times,* March 7, p. 3.

———. 2004b. "Low-Tech or High, Jobs Are Scarce in India's Boon." *New York Times,* May 6, p. A3.

———. 2004c. "What India's Upset Vote Reveals: The High Tech Is Skin Deep." *New York Times,* May 15, p. A5.

Walker, Andrea C., and David E. Balk. 2007. "Bereavement Rituals in the Muscogee Creek Tribe." *Death Studies* 31:633–652.

Walker, Edward. 2010. "Activism Industry-Driven." *Contexts* (Spring):43–49.

Walker, Marcus, and Roger Thurow. 2009. U.S., Europe Are Ocean Apart on Human Toll of Joblessness. *Wall Street Journal,* May 7, pp. A1, A14.

Wallace, Nicole. 2010. "Gifts for Oil Spill Total $4 Million, but More Is Needed." *The Chronicle of Philanthropy* 24 (14):1.

Wallace, Ruth A., and Alison Wolf. 1980. *Contemporary Sociological Theory.* Englewood Cliffs, NJ: Prentice Hall.

Wallerstein, Immanuel. 1974. *The Modern World System.* New York: Academic Press.

———. 1979a. *Capitalist World Economy.* Cambridge: Cambridge University Press.

———. 1979b. *The End of the World as We Know It: Social Science for the Twenty-First Century.* Minneapolis: University of Minnesota Press.

———. 2000. *The Essential Wallerstein.* New York: New Press.

Wallis, Claudia. 2008. "How to Make Great Teachers." *Time* 171 (February 25):28–34.

Walmart. 2010. "The Ten-foot Attitude." Accessed January 17 (www.wal-martchina.com/english/walmart/rule/10.htm).

Wang, Feng. 2011. "The Future of a Demographic Overachiever: Long-Term Implications of the Demographic Transition in China." *Population and Development Review* 37 (Suppl.):173–190.

———. and Cai Yong. 2011. "China's One-Child Policy at 39." May 31. Washington, DC: Brooking Institution.

Wang, Meiyan, and Fand Cai. 2006. "Gender Wage Differentials in China's Urban Labor Market." Research Paper No. 2006/141. United Nations University World Institute for Development Economics Research.

Watson, Paul. 2005. "Defying Tradition." *Los Angeles Times,* April 24, p. 56.

Wattenberg, Martin P. 2008. *Is Voting for Young People?* New York: Pearson Longman.

Weber, Max. [1904] 1949. Methodology of the Social Sciences. Translated by Edward A. Shils and Henry A. Finch. Glencoe, IL: Free Press.

———. [1913–1922] 1947. *The Theory of Social and Economic Organization.* Translated by A. Henderson and T. Parsons. New York: Free Press.

———. [1916] 1958. *The Religion of India: The Sociology of Hinduism and Buddhism.* New York: Free Press.

Wechsler, Henry, J. E. Lee, M. Kuo, M. Seibring, T. F. Nelson, and H. Lee. 2002. "Trends in College Binge Drinking during a Period of Increased Prevention Efforts: Findings from Four Harvard School of Public Health College Alcohol Surveys: 1993–2001." *Journal of American College Health* 50 (5):203–217.

———, Mark Seibring, I-Chao Liu, and Marilyn Ahl. 2004. "Colleges Respond to Student Binge Drinking: Reducing Student Demand or Limiting Access." *Journal of American College Health* 52 (4):159–168.

The Week. 2009. "First Assisted-Suicide Death." (June 5):7.

———. 2010a. "The Mystery of Falling Crime Rates." (July 16):13.

———. 2010b. "They're Watching You." (September 17):15

———. 2011. "Fighting over Food." (March 4):15.

Weeks, John R. 2008. *Population: An Introduction to Concepts and Issues.* 10th ed. Belmont, CA: Wadsworth.

———. 2012. *Population: An Introduction to Concepts and Issues.* 11th ed. Belmont, CA: Cengage.

Weinberg, Daniel H. 2004. *Evidence from Census 2000 About Earnings by Detailed Occupation for Men and Women.* CENSR-15. Washington, DC: U.S. Government Printing Office.

———, 2007. "Earnings by Gender: Evidence from Census 2000." *Monthly Labor Review* (July–August):26–34.

Weinraub, Bernard. 2004. "UPN Show Is Called Insensitive to Amish." *New York Times,* March 4, pp. B1, B8.

Weinstein, Henry. 2002. "Airport Screener Curb Is Regretful." *Los Angeles Times,* November 16, pp. B1, B14.

Weitz, Rose. 2007. *The Sociology of Health, Illness, and Heath Care.* 4th ed. Belmont, CA: Thomson.

Welch, William M. 2011. "More Hawaii Residents Identify as Mixed Race." *USA Today,* February 28.

Wells-Barnett, Ida B. 1970. *Crusade for Justice: The Autobiography of Ida B. Wells.* Edited by Alfreda M. Duster. Chicago: University of Chicago Press.

Wentling, Tre, Elroi Windsor, Kristin Schilt, and Betsy Lucal. 2008. "Teaching Transgender." *Teaching Sociology* 36 (January):49–57.

Wentz, Laurel, and Claire Atkinson. 2005. "'Apprentice' Translators Hope for Hits All Over Globe." *Advertising Age,* February 14, pp. 3, 73.

West, Candace, and Don H. Zimmerman. 1987. "Doing Gender." *Gender and Society* 1 (June):125–151.

Westergaard-Nielsen, Niels. 2008. *Low-Wage Work in Denmark.* New York: Russell Sage Foundation.

Wheller, Kellie. 2009. "After Listening to This Story." Accessed August 20 (www.npr.org/templates/story/story.php?storyId=1119880383).

White, David Manning. 1950. "'The Gatekeeper': A Case Study in the Selection of News." *Journalism Quarterly* 27 (Fall):383–390.

White House. 2011. "Faith-Based Office Convening on Global Hunger Gets Glowing Reviews from National Leaders." Accessed March 28 (http://www.whitehouse.gov/blog/2011/01/21/faith-based-office-convening-global-hunger-gets-glowing-reviews-national-leaders).

Whitlock, Craig. 2005. "The Internet as Bully Pulpit." *Washington Post National Weekly Edition* 22 (August 22):9.

Whittaker, Stephanie. 2006. "Who Would You Prefer to Work For?" *Gazette* (Montreal), November 4, p. 1.

Whyte, William Foote. 1981. *Street Corner Society: Social Structure of an Italian Slum.* 3rd ed. Chicago: University of Chicago Press.

Whyte, William H., Jr. 1952. "Groupthink." *Fortune* (March):114–117, 142, 146.

Wilford, John Noble. 1997. "New Clues Show Where People Made the Great Leap to Agriculture." *New York Times,* November 18, pp. B9, B12.

Wilgoren, Jodi. 2005. "In Kansas, Darwinism Goes on Trial Once More." *New York Times,* May 6, p. A14.

Wilkes, Rima, and John Iceland. 2004. "Hypersegregation in the Twenty-First Century." *Demography* 41 (February):23–36.

Williams, Carol J. 1995. "Taking an Eager Step Back." *Los Angeles Times,* June 3, pp. A1, A14.

Williams, Christine L. 1992. "The Glass Escalator: Hidden Advantages for Men in the 'Female' Professions." *Social Problems* 39 (3):253–267.

———. 1995. *Still a Man's World: Men Who Do Women's Work.* Berkeley: University of California Press.

Williams, David R., and Chiquita Collins. 2004. "Reparations." *American Behavioral Scientist* 47 (March):977–1000.

Williams, Kristine N., Ruth Herman, Byron Gajewski, and Kristel Wilson. 2009. "Elderspeak Communication: Impact on Dementia Care." *American Journal of Alzheimer's Disease and Other Dementias* 24 (March):11–20.

Williams, Robin M., Jr. 1970. *American Society.* 3rd ed. New York: Knopf.

———, with John P. Dean and Edward A. Suchman. 1964. *Strangers Next Door: Ethnic Relations in American Communities.* Englewood Cliffs, NJ: Prentice Hall.

Wills, Jeremiah B., and Barbara J. Risman. 2006. "The Visibility of Feminist Thought in Family Studies." *Journal of Marriage and Family* 68 (August):690–700.

Wilson, Edward O. 1975. *Sociobiology: The New Synthesis.* Cambridge, MA: Harvard University Press.

———. 1978. *On Human Nature.* Cambridge, MA: Harvard University Press.

———. 2000. *Sociobiology: The New Synthesis.* Cambridge, MA: Belknap Press, Harvard University Press.

Wilson, John. 1973. *Introduction to Social Movements.* New York: Basic Books.

Wilson, William Julius. 1980. *The Declining Significance of Race: Blacks and Changing American Institutions.* 2nd ed. Chicago: University of Chicago Press.

———. 1987. *The Truly Disadvantaged: The Inner City, the Underclass and Public Policy.* Chicago: University of Chicago Press.

———. 1996. *When Work Disappears: The World of the New Urban Poor.* New York: Knopf.

———. 1999. *The Bridge over the Racial Divide: Rising Inequality and Coalition Politics.* Berkeley: University of California Press.

———. 2009. *More Than Just Race: Being Black and Poor in the Inner City.* New York: Norton.

———, J. M. Quane, and B. H. Rankin. 2004. "Underclass." In *International Encyclopedia of Social and Behavioral Sciences.* New York: Elsevier.

———, and Richard P. Taub in collaboration with Reuben A. Buford May and Mary Pattillo. 2006. "Groveland: A Stable African American Community." Pp. 128–160 in *There Goes the Neighborhood* by William Julius Wilson and Richard P. Taub. New York: Knopf.

Winant, Howard B. 1994. *Racial Conditions: Politics, Theory, Comparisons.* Minneapolis: University of Minnesota Press.

———. 2006. "Race and Racism: Towards a Global Future." *Ethnic and Racial Studies* 29 (September):986–1003.

Wines, Michael. 2005. "Same-Sex Unions to Become Legal in South Africa." *USA Today,* December 2, p. A6.

Winickoff, Jonathan P., Joan Friebely, Susanne E. Tanski, Cheryl Sherrod, George E. Matt, Mebourne F. Hovell, and Robert C. McMillen. 2009. "Beliefs about the Health Effects of 'Third-hand' Smoke and Home Smoking Bans." *Pediatrics* 123 (January):74–79.

Winter, J. Allen. 2008. "Symbolic Ethnicity." Pp. 1288–1290, vol. 3, in *Encyclopedia of Race, Ethnicity, and Society,* edited by Richard T. Schaefer. Thousand Oaks, CA: Sage.

Wirth, Louis. 1928. *The Ghetto.* Chicago: University of Chicago Press.

———. 1931. "Clinical Sociology." *American Journal of Sociology* 37 (July):49–60.

———. 1938. "Urbanism as a Way of Life." *American Journal of Sociology* 44 (July):1–24.

Wolf, Naomi. 1992. *The Beauty Myth: How Images of Beauty Are Used against Women.* New York: Anchor Books.

Wolfe, Alan. 2008. "Pew in the Pews." *Chronicle of Higher Education,* March 21, pp. B5–B6.

Women's Flat Track Derby Association. 2011. "Women's Flat Track Derby Association." Accessible at http://www.wftda.com/about.html.

Women's Sports Foundation. 2011. *Title IX.* Accessed March 29 (http://www.womenssportsfoundation.org/Issues-And-Research/Title-IX.aspx).

Wong, Morrison G. 2006. "Chinese Americans." Pp. 110–145 in *Asian Americans: Contemporary Trends and Issues,* 2nd ed., edited by Pyong Gap Min. Thousand Oaks, CA: Sage.

Working Women's Forum. 2010. Home Page. Accessed April 28 (www.workingwomensforum.org).

Workman, Thomas A. 2008. "The Real Impact of Virtual Worlds." *Chronicle of Higher Education,* September 19, pp. B12–B13.

World Bank. 2001. *World Development Report 2002. Building Instructions for Markets.* New York: Oxford University Press.

———. 2003. *World Development Report 2003: Sustainable Development in a Dynamic World.* Washington, DC: World Bank.

———. 2007. *World Development Indicators 2007.* Washington, DC: World Bank.

———. 2009. *World Development Indicators 2009.* Washington, DC: World Bank.

———. 2010a. *World Development Indicators 2010.* Washington, DC: World Bank.

———. 2010b. *World Development Report 2010: Development and Climate Change.* Washington, DC: World Bank.

———. 2011. *Development Indicators 2011.* Washington, DC: World Bank.

World Development Forum. 1990. "The Danger of Television." 8 (July 15):4.

World Economic Forum. 2010. "The Global Competitiveness Report 2010–2011." Geneva: WEF. Accessible at http://www.weforum.org/en/initiatives/gcp/Global%20Competitiveness%20Report/index.htm.

World Health Organization. 2000. *The World Health Report 2000. Health Systems: Improving Performance.* Geneva: WHO.

———. 2009. "Biotechnology (GM Foods)." Accessed May 11 (www.who.int/foodsafety/biotech/en/).

———. 2010. "Suicide Prevention." Accessed October 31 (http://www.who.int/mental_health/prevention/en/).

World Public Opinion. 2008. "World Publics Reject Torture." Accessed January 18, 2010 (www.worldpublicopinion.org/pipa/articles/btjustice-human_rightsra/496.php?nid=&id=&pnt=496).

Worth, Robert F. 2008. "As Taboos Ease, Saudi Girl Group Dares to Rock." *New York Times,* November 24, pp. A1, A9.

Wortham, Robert A. 2008. "DuBois, William Edward Burghardt." Pp. 423–427, vol. 1, in *Encyclopedia of Race, Ethnicity, and Society,* edited by Richard T. Schaefer. Thousand Oaks CA: Sage.

Wray, Matt, Matthew Miller, Jill Gurvey, Joanna Carroll, and Ichiro Kawachi. 2008. "Leaving Las Vegas: Exposure to Las Vegas and Risk of Suicide." *Social Science and Medicine* 67:1882–1888.

Wright, Charles R. 1986. *Mass Communication: A Sociological Perspective.* 3rd ed. New York: Random House.

Wright, Erik Olin, David Hachen, Cynthia Costello, and Joy Sprague. 1982. "The American Class Structure." *American Sociological Review* 47 (December):709–726.

Wright, Eric R., William P. Gronfein, and Timothy J. Owens. 2000. "Deinstitutionalization, Social Rejection, and the Self-Esteem of Former Mental Patients." *Journal of Health and Social Behavior* (March).

Wu, Tim. 2010. *The Master Switch.* New York: Knopf.

Wyatt, Edward. 2009. "No Smooth Ride on TV Networks' Road to Diversity." *New York Times,* March 18, pp. 1, 5.

Y

Yamagata, Hisashi, Kuang S. Yeh, Shelby Stewman, and Hiroko Dodge. 1997. "Sex Segregation and Glass Ceilings: A Comparative Statistics Model of Women's Career Opportunities in the Federal Government over a Quarter Century." *American Journal of Sociology* 103 (November):566–632.

Yap, Kioe Sheng. 1998. "Squatter Settlements." Pp. 554–556 in *The Encyclopedia of Housing,* edited by Willem van Vliet. Thousand Oaks, CA: Sage.

Yardley, William. 2009. "A 2nd State Lets Doctors Lend Help in Suicide." *New York Times,* March 5, p. A15.

Yinger, J. Milton. 1970. *The Scientific Study of Religion.* New York: Macmillan.

York, Richard, Eugene A. Rosa, and Thomas Dietz. 2010. "Ecological Modernization Theory: Theoretical and Empirical Challenges." Pp. 77–90 in *The International Handbook and Environmental Sociology,* 2nd ed., edited by Michael R. Redclift and Graham Woodgate. Cheltenham, UK: Edward Elgar.

Yunus, Muhammad. 2010. *Building Social Business.* New York: Perseus.

Z

Zang, Xiaowei. 2002. "Labor Market Segmentation and Income Inequality in Urban China." *Sociological Quarterly* 43 (1):27–44.

Zarembo, Alan. 2004a. "A Theater of Inquiry and Evil." *Los Angeles Times,* July 15, pp. A1, A24, A25.

———. 2004b. "Physician, Remake Thyself: Lured by Higher Pay and Heavy Recruiting, Philippine Doctors Are Getting Additional Degrees and Starting Over in the U.S. as Nurses." *Los Angeles Times,* January 10, pp. A1, A10.

Zeitzen, Miriam Koktvedgaard. 2008. *Polygamy: A Cross-Cultural Analysis.* Oxford, UK: Berg.

Zellner, William M. 1995. *Counter Cultures: A Sociological Analysis.* New York: St. Martin's Press.

Zernike, Kate. 2002. "With Student Cheating on the Rise, More Colleges Are Turning to Honor Codes." *New York Times,* November 2, p. A10.

Zhang, Xiaodan. 2009. "Trade Unions Under the Modernization of Paternalists Rule in China." *Journal of Labor and Society* 12 (June):193–218.

Zi, Jui-Chung Allen. 2007. *The Kids Are OK: Divorce and Children's Behavior Problems.* Santa Monica, CA: RAND.

Zia, Helen. 2000. *Asian American Dreams: The Emergence of an American People.* New York: Farrar, Straus and Giroux.

Zimbardo, Philip G. 2004. "Power Turns Good Soldiers into 'Bad Apples.'" *Boston Globe,* May 9. Also accessible at www.prisonexp.org.

———. 2007a. "Revisiting the Stanford Prison Experiment: A Lesson in the Power of the Situation." *Chronicle of Higher Education* 53 (March 20):B6, B7.

———. 2007b. *The Lucifer Effect: Understanding How Good People Turn Evil.* New York: Random House.

———, Robert L. Johnson, and Vivian McCann. 2009. *Psychology: Core Concepts.* 6th ed. Boston: Allyn and Bacon.

Zimmerman, Ann, and Emily Nelson. 2006. "With Profits Elusive, Wal-Mart to Exit Germany." *Wall Street Journal,* July 29, pp. A1, A6.

Zimmerman, Seth. 2008a. "Globalization and Economic Mobility." Washington, DC: Economic Mobility Project. Also accessible at www.economicmobility.org/reports_and_research/literature_reviews?id=0004.

———. 2008b. *Labor Market Institutions and Economic Mobility.* Washington, DC: Pew Charitable Trusts.

Zipp, Yvonne. 2009. Courts Divided on Police Use of GPS Tracking. *Christian Science Monitor,* May 15.

Zittrain, Jonathan, and John Palfrey. 2008. "Reluctant Gatekeepers: Corporate Ethics on a Filtered Internet." Pp. 103–122 in *Access Denied,* edited by Ronald Deibert, John Palfrey, Rafal Rohozinski, and Jonathan Zittrain. Cambridge, MA: MIT Press.

Zogby. 2010. "Zogby Interactive: 54% Support Ethnic & Religious Profiling; 71% Favor Full-Body Scans." February 4. Accessed July 2, 2011 (http://www.zogby.com/news/2010/02/04/zogby-interactive-54-support-ethnic-religious-profiling-71-favor-full-body-scans/).

Zola, Irving K. 1972. "Medicine as an Institution of Social Control." *Sociological Review* 20 (November):487–504.

———. 1983. *Socio-Medical Inquiries.* Philadelphia: Temple University Press.

Zoroya, Gregg. 2009. "Military Divorces Edge Up as War Takes Its Toll." *USA Today,* November 11.

Zweigenhaft, Richard L., and G. William Domhoff. 2006. *Diversity in the Power Elite: How It Happened, Why It Matters.* 2nd ed. New York: Rowman and Littlefield.

Zywica, Jolene, and James Danowski. 2008. "The Faces of Facebookers: Investigating Social Enhancement and Social Compensation Hypotheses; Predicting Facebook and Offline Popularity from Sociability and Self-Esteem, and Mapping the Meanings of Popularity with Semantic Networks." *Journal of Computer-Mediated Communication* 14:1–34.

acknowledgments

Chapter 1

page 4: Quotation from Kelsey Timmerman. 2009. *Where Am I Wearing? A Global Tour to the Countries, Factories, and People that Make Our Clothes.* © 2009. Reproduced with permission of John Wiley & Sons, Inc.

page 19: Cartoon by Jim Morin, Miami Herald, Cartoon Arts International Inc.

Chapter 2

page 28: Quotation from Patricia A. Adler and Peter Adler. 2007. "The Demedicalization of Self-Injury: From Psychopathology to Sociological Deviance," *Journal of Contemporary Ethnography* 36, Issue 5, (October 2007):537–570. Copyright © 2007. Reprinted by permission of SAGE Publications.

page 33: Figure 2-4 from Author's analysis of *2009 General Social Survey* in DeNavas-Walt et al. 2009. National Opinion Research Center.

page 34: *Doonesbury* © 1989 G. B. Trudeau. Reprinted with permission of Universal Uclick. All rights reserved.

page 36: Cartoon by F MINUS © 2007 Tony Carrillo. Reprinted by Universal Uclick for UFS. All rights reserved.

page 38: Figure from BabyNameWizard.com, used by permission.

page 42: Figure 2-5 from Henry J. Kaiser Family Foundation. November 2005. Sex on TV 4, Executive Summary; a Biennial Report of the Kaiser Family Foundation (#7399). This information was reprinted with permission from the Henry J. Kaiser Family Foundation. The Kaiser Family Foundation is a non-profit private operating foundation, based in Menlo Park, California, dedicated to producing and communicating the best possible analysis and information on health issues.

page 44: Figure 2-7 from The Gallup poll, October 28, 2010, "New High of 46% of Americans Support Legalizing Marijuana," by Elizabeth Mendes. Copyright © 2010 Gallup, Princeton, NJ. All rights reserved. Reprinted with permission.

page 44: Figure 2-8 from The Gallup poll, October 28, 2010, "New High of 46% of Americans Support Legalizing Marijuana," by Elizabeth Mendes. Copyright © 2010 Gallup, Princeton, NJ. All rights reserved. Reprinted with permission.

Chapter 3

page 52: Quotation from Horace Miner. 1956. "Body Ritual among the Nacirema." *American Anthropologist*, vol. 58 (3), 1956: pp. 503–504. © 1956 American Anthropological Association.

page 56: Figure 3-1 adapted in part from "The State of the World's Children 2009," UNICEF, and in part from "Progress for Children: A World Fit for Children Statistical Review," Number 6, December 2007, UNICEF global databases, UNICEF, NY.

page 65: Figure 3-2 from John H. Pryor, Sylvia Hurtado, Linda DeAngelo, Laura Palucki Blake, and Serge Tran. 2010. *The American Freshman: National Norms for Fall 2007, 2010.* UCLA Higher Education Research Institute. © 2010 The Regents of the University of California. All rights reserved.

page 67: Figure 3-3 adapted from Views on Torture, "World Public Opinion on Torture," June 24, 2008. Reprinted by permission.

Chapter 4

page 76: Quotation from Mary Pattillo-McCoy. 1999. *Black Picket Fences: Privilege and Peril among the Black Middle Class*: 100–102. Copyright 1999. Reprinted by permission of University of Chicago Press.

page 78: Figure 4-1 from Susan Curtiss. 1977. *Genie: A Psycholinguistic Study of a Modern-Day "Wild Child,"* p. 275. Copyright Academic Press 1977. Reprinted with permission of Elsevier.

page 82: Quotation from Daniel Albas and Cheryl Albas. 1988. "Aces and Bombers: The Post-Exam Impression Management Strategies of Students." *Symbolic Interaction,* University of California Press–Journals. Reproduced by permission of the authors.

page 82: Cartoon by Scott Arthur Masear. Reprinted by permission of www. CartoonStock.com.

page 86: Table 4-3 adapted from Jill Suitor, Staci A. Minyard, and Rebecca S. Carter. 2001. "Did You See What I Saw? Gender Difference in Perceptions of Avenues to Prestige among Adolescents," *Sociological Inquiry* 71 (Fall 2001):445, Table 2. University of Texas Press. Wiley-Blackwell Publishing Ltd.

page 87: Cartoon by STAHLER © 2010 Jeff Stahler. Reprinted by Universal Uclick for UFS. All rights reserved.

page 87: Figure 4-2 from Henry J. Kaiser Family Foundation. 2010. Victoria J. Rideout et al., "Generation M^2: Media in the Lives of 8- to 18-Year-Olds," January 2010 (#8010). This information was reprinted with permission from the Henry J. Kaiser Family Foundation. The Kaiser Family Foundation is a non-profit private operating foundation, based in Menlo Park, California, dedicated to producing and communicating the best possible analysis and information on health issues.

page 90: Table 4-4 from Tom Smith. 2003. "Coming of Age in 21st Century America: Public Attitudes Toward the Importance and Timing of Transition to Adulthood." Based on the 2002 General Social Survey of 1,398 people. Used by permission of National Opinion Research Center.

Chapter 5

page 98: Quotation from Philip G. Zimbardo. 2007. *The Lucifer Effect: Understanding How Good People Turn Evil.* Copyright © 2007 by Philip G. Zimbardo, Inc. Used by permission of Random House, Inc. and by the Random House Group Ltd.

page 107: Screen shot from Second Life. Second Life® is a trademark of Linden Research, Inc. Certain materials have been reproduced with the permission of Linden Research, Inc.

page 108: © Dean Vietor/The New Yorker Collection/www.cartoonbank.com.

page 112: Cartoon by Daryl Cagle. © 2004 Daryl Cagle, MSNBC, and PoliticalCartoons.com.

Chapter 6

page 118: Quotation from George Ritzer. 2010. *The McDonaldization of Society 6.* Copyright © 2010 by Sage Publications, Inc. Books. Reproduced with permission of Pine Forge Press, a Division of Sage Publications, Inc. via Copyright Clearance Center.

page 120: © Robert Weber/The New Yorker Collection/www.cartoonbank.com.

Chapter 7

page 136: Quotation from David Grazian. 2010. *Mix It Up: Popular Culture, Mass Media, and Society.* Copyright © 2010 by W. W. Norton & Company, Inc. Used by permission of W. W. Norton & Company, Inc.

page 138: Table 7-1 adapted from John B. Horrigan, *A Typology of Information and Communication Technology Users,* May 7, 2007, p. 5–11, www.pewinternet.org/Reports/2007/A-Typology-of-Information-and-Communication-Technology-Users.aspx. Pew Internet & American Life Project.

page 138: Logo used by permission of New York City Department of Health and Mental Hygiene.

page 142: Cartoon by Dana Summers. © Tribune Media Services, Inc. All Rights Reserved. Reprinted with permission.

page 145: Table from World Economic Forum. 2010. *The Global Competitiveness Report 2010–2011.* World Economic Forum, Switzerland. Copyright © 2010 by the World Economic Forum.

page 146: Figure 7-2 adapted from Michael A. Messner, Margaret Carlisle Duncan, and Nicole William. 2006. "The Revolution Is Not Being Televised," *Contexts,* vol. 5, no. 3 (Summer 2006), p. 35. American Sociological Association. © 2006 by SAGE Publications. Reprinted by permission of SAGE Publications.

page 148: Figure 7-4 adapted from Demographics of Internet Users. Based on a November–December 2009 national survey released January 6, 2009, accessed February 7, 2010 at www.pewinternet.org/static-pages/trend-data/whos-online.aspx. Pew Internet & American Life Project.

page 153 :Cartoon by Harley Schwadron. Reprinted with permission.

Chapter 8

page 158: Quotation from Peter Moskos. 2008. *Cop in the Hood: My Year Policing Baltimore's Eastern District.* © 2008 by Princeton University Press. Reprinted by permission of Princeton University Press.

Acknowledgments

page 164: Figure from Henry Wechsler et al. 2002. "Trends in College Binge Drinking During a Period of Increased Prevention Efforts," *Journal of American College Health,* 2002, vol. 50(5). Reprinted by permission of the publisher, Taylor & Francis Ltd. http://www.tandf.co.uk/journals.

page 166: Figure 8-1 adapted from NORML 2010. Used by permission of the National Organization for the Reform of Marijuana Laws (NORML).

page 167: Table 8-1 from Robert K. Merton. 1968. *Social Theory and Social Structure,* Revised and Enlarged Edition. Adapted by permission of The Free Press, a Division of Simon & Schuster, Inc. Copyright © 1967, 1968 by Robert K. Merton. Copyright renewed 1985 by Robert K. Merton. All rights reserved.

page 174: Cartoon by Sidney Harris. © ScienceCartoonsPlus.com.

Chapter 9

page 186: Quotation from Barbara Ehrenreich. 2009. "Is It Now a Crime to Be Poor?" *New York Times,* August 9, 2009. From *The New York Times,* © 2009 The New York Times All rights reserved. Used by permission and protected by the Copyright Laws of the U.S. The printing, copying, redistribution, or retransmission of this Content without express written permission is prohibited. And reprinted by permission of International Creative Management, Inc. Copyright © 2009 by Barbara Ehrenreich.

page 191: Cartoon © 2008 Pat Bagley, The Salt Lake Tribune, and Political Cartoons.com.

page 196: Table 9-3 from James. A. Davis and Tom W. Smith. 2009. *General Social Surveys, 1972–2008.* Used by permission of the National Opinion Research Center.

page 204: Cartoon by Matt Davies. © Tribune Media Services, Inc. All Rights Reserved. Reprinted with permission.

page 205: Figure 9-5 from Bhashkar Mazumder. 2008. *Upward Intergenerational Economic Mobility in the United States.* Washington, DC: Economic Mobility Project, An initiative of the Pew Charitable Trusts. Used by permission of Dr. Bhashkar Mazumder.

page 207: Nick Anderson Editorial Cartoon used with the permission of Nick Anderson, the Washington Post Writers Group and the Cartoonist Group. All rights reserved.

Chapter 10

page 214: Quotation from Paul Collier. 2007. *The Bottom Billion: Why the Poorest Countries Are Failing and What Can Be Done About It.* © 2007 Paul Collier. Used with permission of Oxford University Press, UK.

page 215: Figure 10-1 adapted from Bob Sutcliffe. 2002. *100 Ways of Seeing an Unequal World,* Fig 1, p. 18. London: Zed Books. Reprinted by permission.

page 217: Figure 10-2 adapted in part from John R. Weeks. 2012. *Population* 11e. © 2012 Wadsworth, a part of Cengage Learning Inc. Reproduced by permission of www.cengage.com/permissions. And adapted in part from Carl Haub. 2010. *2010 World Population Data Sheet.* Used by permission of Population Reference Bureau.

page 220: Figure 10-4 adapted from World Development Indicators 2010 by the World Bank 2010. Copyright 2010. Used by permission of the International Bank for Reconstruction and Development/World Bank via Copyright Clearance Center.

page 221: Figure 10-5 from Chronic Poverty Research Centre. 2009. Administered by Institute for Development Policy and Management, School of Environment and Development, University of Manchester, UK. Used by permission.

page 222: Figure 10-6 OECD Statistics on Resource Flows to Developing Countries (Feb 2011), Table 1, p. 2. www.oecd.org/dataoecd/53/43/47137659.pdf.

page 224: Figure adapted from Edward Telles. 2004:108. *Race in Another America: The Significance of Skin Color.* Princeton University Press. Reprinted by permission of Princeton University Press.

page 225: Figure 10-7 World Bank. 2010. W*orld Development Indicators 2010.* Copyright 2010. Used by permission of the International Bank for Reconstruction and Development/World Bank via Copyright Clearance Center.

Chapter 11

page 236: Quotation from Helen Zia. 2000. *Asian American Dreams: The Emergence of an American People.* Copyright © 2000 Helen Zia. of Published by Farrar, Straus & Giroux, LLC.

page 240: Nick Anderson Editorial Cartoon used with the permission of Nick Anderson, the Washington Post Writers Group and the Cartoonist Group. All rights reserved.

page 255: Figure 11-6 © 2010 Arab American Institute.

page 260: Cartoon by STEIN © 2006. Reprinted with permission by UNIVERSAL UCLICK for UFS. All rights reserved.

Chapter 12

page 266: Quotation from Nancy J. Finley. 2010. "Skating Femininity: Gender Maneuvering in Women's Roller Derby," *Journal of Contemporary Ethnography,* 39(4):359-360, 371–372, 377. Reprinted by permission of SAGE Publications.

page 268: Table 12-1 from Joyce McCarl Nielsen, et al. 2000. "Gendered Heteronormativity: Empirical Illustrations in Everyday Life," *Sociological Quarterly* 41 (no. 2):287. © 2000. Blackwell Publishing. Reprinted by permission.

page 280: Figure 12-5 from NARAL Pro-Choice America Foundation 2011. Used by permission of NARAL, Washington, DC.

Chapter 13

page 288: Quotation from Ted C. Fishman. 2010. Reprinted with the permission of Scribner, a Division of Simon & Schuster, Inc., from *Shock Of Gray: The Aging Of The World's Population And How It Pits Young against Old, Child against Parent, Worker against Boss, Company against Rival, and Nation against Nation* by Ted C. Fishman. Copyright © 2010 by Ted C. Fishman. All rights reserved.

page 294: © Barbara Smaller/The New Yorker Collection/www.cartoonbank.com.

page 294: Figure 13-2 © AARP. 2006. *Attitudes Toward Work and Job Security.* Washington, DC: AARP, 2006.

page 297: Figure 13-3 from Linda Jacobsen, Mary Kent, Marlene Lee, and Mark Mather, America's Aging Population," *Population Bulletin* 66 (Feb):3. Used by permission of Population Reference Bureau.

Chapter 14

page 306: Quotation from Andrew J. Cherlin. 2009. *The Marriage-Go-Round: The State of Marriage and the Family in America Today.* Copyright © 2009 by Andrew J. Cherlin. Used by permission of Alfred A. Knopf, a division of Random House, Inc.

page 319: Signe Wilkinson Editorial Cartoon used with the permission of Signe Wilkinson, the Washington Post Writers Group and the Cartoonist Group. All rights reserved.

page 323: Cartoon by Harley Schwadron. Reprinted with permission.

Chapter 15

page 330: Quotation from Nikki Bado-Fralick and Rebecca Sachs Norris. 2010. *Toying with God: The World of Religious Games and Dolls,* pp. 7–8, 29–30. © 2010. Reprinted by permission of Baylor University Press.

page 333: Figure 15-1 from The Pew Forum on Religion and Public Life, Religious Knowledge Quiz, September 28, 2010, http://features.pewforum.org/quiz/us-religious-knowledge. Pew Internet & American Life Project.

page 337 Cartoon © 2007 Riber Hansson, www.PoliticalCartoons.com.

page 344: Cartoon © 2005 Sandy Huffaker, www.PoliticalCartoons.com.

Chapter 16

page 350: Quotation from Diane Ravitch. 2010. *The Death and Life of the Great American School System: How Testing and Choice are Undermining Education.* Copyright © 2010 Diane Ravitch. Reprinted by permission of Basic Books, a member of the Perseus Books Group.

page 352: Google logo © Google Inc.

page 354: Cartoon by Kirk Anderson. Used by permission of Kirk Anderson, www.kirktoons.com.

page 364: Figure 16-7 from National Alliance for Public Charter Schools. (2011). *The Public Charter Schools Dashboard.* Washington, DC: NAPCS.

Chapter 17

page 370: Quotation from Martin P. Wattenberg. 2008. *Is Voting for Young People?* pp. 1–2, 3. Copyright © 2008 by Pearson Education, Inc. Reprinted by permission. Users may not reproduce copies without permission of Pearson Education.

page 372: Figure 17-1 adapted from OpenNet Initiative 2011. Copyright © The OpenNet Initiative 2011. All rights reserved.

page 378: Figure 17-3 adapted from Inter-Parliamentary Union (IPU), 2011, Women in National Parliaments, www.ipu.org/wmn-e/classif.htm. Used by permission.

page 379: Figure 17-4 (right) from G. William Domhoff. 2010. *Who Rules America,* 6e. © 2010 by The McGraw-Hill Companies, Inc. Reproduced by permission.

page 382: Figure 17-5 Military and National Defense from The Gallup Poll. Copyright © 2009 The Gallup Organization, Princeton, NJ. All rights reserved. Reprinted with permission.

page 383: Figure 17-6, 2010 Global Peace Index, Institute for Economics and Peace.

page 386: Cartoon by STEIN © 2010 Ed Stein. Reprinted with permission by UNIVERSAL UCLICK for UFS. All rights reserved.

Chapter 18

page 392: Quotation from John Bowes (ed.). 2011. *The Fair Trade Revolution,* pp. ix, 2–3, 231–232, Pluto Press. Reprinted by permission of Pluto Press.

page 396: Figure from S. Acharya. 2000. In Mahbub ul Haq Human Development Centre, *Human Development in South Asia 2000: The Gender Question,* p. 54. Oxford University Press, Karachi.

page 398: Cartoon by Mike Thompson, Detroit Free Press.

page 401: Quotation from Sheryl Stolberg. 1995. "Affirmative Action Gains Often Come at a High Cost," *Los Angeles Times,* March 29, 1995:A14. Copyright © 1995 Los Angeles Times. Reprinted by permission.

page 401: Cartoon © 2003 Mike Keefe, The Denver Post, www.PoliticalCartoons.com.

Chapter 19

page 410: Quotation from Andrew Szasz. 2007. *Shopping Our Way to Safety.* University of Minnesota Press. Copyright 2007 by the Regents of the University of Minnesota.

page 412: Figure 19-1 from Carl Haub. 2010. *World Population Data Sheet 2010.* Used by permission of Population Reference Bureau.

page 416: Figure 19-2 from UNAIDS. 2010. Adapted from Global report: UNAIDS report on the global AIDS Epidemic 2010. Copyright © 2010 Joint UN Program on HIV/AIDS (UNAIDS). All rights reserved. Courtesy UNAIDS, Geneva, Switzerland.

page 419: © Michael Maslin/The New Yorker Collection/www.cartoonbank.com.

page 426: Signe Wilkinson Editorial Cartoon used with the permission of Signe Wilkinson, the Washington Post Writers Group and the Cartoonist Group. All rights reserved.

page 427: Quotation from Neil B. Thompson. 1972. Reprinted from *Natural History,* December 1972; copyright © Natural History Magazine, Inc. 1972.

page 428: Cartoon by Joseph Farris. Reprinted by permission of Miller-McCune and Joseph Farris. www.josephfarris.com.

page 429: Figure 19-6 from the Washington Post © 2007 The Washington Post. All rights reserved. Used by permission and protected by the Copyright Laws of the U.S. The printing, copying, redistribution, or retransmission of the Material without express written permission is prohibited. http://www.washingtonpost.com.

page 431: Figure 19-7 from Jeffrey M. Jones. 2011. "Americans Increasingly Prioritize Economy Over Environment," March 17, 2011, from The Gallup Poll. Copyright © 2011 The Gallup Organization, Princeton, NJ. All rights reserved. Reprinted with permission.

page 431: Figure 19-8 Adapted from OECD. 2009. "Green at Fifteen?: How 15-Year-Olds Perform in Environmental Science and Geoscience in PISA 2006," p. 40, www.oecd.org/pisa.

Chapter 20

page 438: Quotation from John D. Kasarda and Greg Lindsay. 2010. *Aerotropolis: The Way We'll Live Next.* New York: Farrar, Straus & Giroux.

page 440: Cartoon by Manny Francisco © 2008 www.PoliticalCartoons.com.

page 448: Table 20-2 Based on Gideon Sjoberg. 1960. *The Preindustrial City: Past and Present*:323–328. Adapted with permission of The Free Press, a Division of Simon & Schuster Adult Publishing Group. Copyright © 1960 by The Free Press. Copyright © renewed 1968 by Gideon Sjoberg. All rights reserved. And based on E. Barbara Phillips. 1996. *City Lights: Urban-Suburban Life in the Global Society,* 2/e. Copyright © 1981 by E. Barbara Phillips and Richard T. LeGates, 1996 by E. Barbara Phillips. Oxford University Press. Used by permission.

page 449: Figure 20-4 adapted from *National Geographic Atlas of the World,* 8e. National Geographic Society, 2005. National Geographic Society, 2005. NG Maps/National Geographic Stock.

page 449: Figure 20-5 adapted from Chauncy Harris and Edward Ullmann. 1945. "The Nature of Cities," *Annals of the American Academy of Political and Social Science,* 242 (November):13. Reprinted by permission of American Academy of Political and Social Science, Philadelphia.

Chapter 21

page 462: Quotation from Gary Alan Fine and Bill Ellis. 2011. *The Global Grapevine: Why Rumors of Terrorism, Immigrations, and Trade Matter,* Oxford University Press. © 2011 Gary Alan Fine and Bill Ellis. Used with permission of Oxford University Press, UK.

page 472: Illustration reprinted by permission of the publisher from John B. Christiansen and Sharon N. Barnartt, *Deaf President Now! The 1988 Revolution at Gallaudet University* (Washington, DC: Gallaudet University Press, 1995), p. 22. Copyright 1995 by Gallaudet University.

page 477: Table 21-3 adapted from Karen Meyer, "Match the Disability." April 30, 2007. Chicago: DePaul University. Reproduced with permission.

Chapter 22

page 484: Quotation from Nick Bilton. 2010. *I Live in the Future & Here's How It Works: Why Your World, Work, and Brain are Being Creatively Disrupted.* Copyright © 2010 by Nick Bilton. Used by permission of Crown Business, a division of Random House, Inc.

page 491: Cartoon by Baloo, from *The Wall Street Journal,* permission Cartoon Features Syndicate.

page 496: Figure 22-1 adapted from *National Geographic Atlas of the World,* 8e. National Geographic Society, 2005. National Geographic Society, 2005. NG Maps/National Geographic Stock.

Trendspotting

Chapter 2, page 33: Bureau of the Census 2004b; El Nasser and Overburg 2009; Nordholt et al. 2004. Chapter 3, page 61: American Community Survey 2010, Table 1602; Link et al. 2006; Siegal et al. 2001; United Way of King County 2010. Chapter 4, page 79: Knopmen et al 2010; Martin et al. 2009; National Organization of Mothers of Twins Clubs 2010. Chapter 5, page 106: Economist 2010a; Facebook 2011; Haub 2010; Schonfeld 2010. Chapter 6, page 125: Bonikowski and McPherson 2006; NORC 2010. Chapter 7, page 147: Rainie et al. 2003; Pew Internet and American Life Project 2009. Chapter 8, page 165: Bureau of Justice Statistics 2010; International Centre for Prison Studies 2010; Sabol et al. 2009. Chapter 9, page 198: Cauchon 2009; Hartmann et al. 2010; Institute for Women's Policy Research 2009. Chapter 10, page 216: Bureau of the Census 2008b; *The Economist* 2011a; *The Week* 2011. Chapter 11, page 242: Alliance for Board Diversity 2008. Chapter 12, page 278: Bureau of the Census 2009a:378. Chapter 13, page 299: Bureau of Labor Statistics 2008b, 2010, Toossi 2009. Chapter 14, page 312: Kershaw 2009; Minyard and Ortyl 2010; Proulx et al. 2006. Chapter 15, page 332: Baker and Smith 2009; Kosmin et al. 2009; Lalli 2009. Chapter 16, page 355: Aud et al. 2010. Chapter 17, p. 374: Freedom House 2011. Chapter 18, page 393: Bureau of Labor Statistics 2009. Chapter 19, page 420: InTouch Health 2010; Laermer 2002:191–195. Chapter 20, page 452: J. Goldstone 2010. Chapter 21, page 469: Newport and Saad 2011. Chapter 22, page 488: Arias 2010: Table 12; Bureau of the Census 2010a: Table 102.

photo credits

FRONT MATTER: Page xiv: © Photodisc/Getty Images; p. xv(top): © Comstock/Corbis; p. xv(bottom): © TRBfoto/Getty Images; p. xvi(top): © Rubberball/Punchstock; p. xvi(center): © Ingram Publishing/Fotosearch; p. xvii: © Resort/PhotoDisc/Getty Images; p. xviii: Siede Preis/Getty Images; p. xix(top): © Rubberball/Getty Images; p. xxvi(top): © John A. Rizzo/Getty Images; p. xxvi(bottom): © Getty Images/Stockbyte; p. xxvii: © Jeppe Wikstrüm/Photolibrary; p. xxviii(top): Fancy Photography/Veer; p. xxviii(bottom): Photodisc/Getty Images; p. xxix(top): Tim Pannell/Corbis; p. xxix(center): Brand X Pictures/PunchStock: p. xxix(bottom): Vladyslav Danilin/Cutcaster

CHAPTER 1: Opener: © Ira Block/National Geographic Stock; p. 4: Book cover of *Where Am I Wearing? A Global Tour to the Countries, Factories, and People that Make Our Clothes* by Kelsey Timmerman. © 2008 reprinted with permission of John Wiley & Sons, Inc.; p. 6(top): © Bob Daemmrich/The Image Works; p. 6(bottom): © Michael Laughlin/AP Images; p. 8: © Getty Images/Digital Vision; p. 9: © Spencer Arnold/Getty Images; p. 10: © R-bit Co Ltd./A. Collection/Getty Images; p. 11(left): © Bibliotheque nationale de France; p. 11(center left): © Granger Collection; p. 11(center right): © Alfredo Dagli Orti/Corbis; p. 11(right): © Granger Collection; p. 12: © Seven Settlements Database of Photos/University of Illinois Chicago; p. 14: © Earl & Nazima Kowall/Corbis; p. 15(top): © Department of Special Collections, The University Library, The University of Illinois at Chicago; p. 15(bottom): © Elmer Martinez/AFP/Getty Images; p. 17: © Dave Martin/AP Images; p. 18: © John Moore/Getty Images; p. 20: © John Foxx/Imagestate Media/Imagestate; p. 21: © Mike Segar/Reuters/Corbis; p. 22: © Stockbyte/PunchStock

CHAPTER 2: Opener: © US Census Bureau; p. 28: © Scott Camazine/PhotoTake; p. 30: © Jason Lindsey/Alamy; p. 32: © Stephano Maccari/iStockphoto.com; p. 33: © Jerry Koch/iStockphoto.com; p. 33(inset): © David Brabyn/Corbis; p. 34: © SuperStock; p. 36: © Department of Defense photo by Staff Sgt. Michael L. Casteel, US Army; p. 40(top): Courtesy of Richard Schaefer; p. 40(bottom): © John Gaps III/AP Images; p. 41: © Lorena Ros/Panos Pictures; p. 42: © Carnegie Mellon University

CHAPTER 3: Opener: © F. Poelking/Age Fotostock; p. 52: © Royalty-Free/Corbis; p. 53(left): © Mandel Ngan/AFP/Getty Images; p. 53(right): © Paul Chiasson, The Canadian Press/AP Images; p. 55: © Sue Bennett/Alamy; p. 57: © Olivia Arthur/Magnum Photos; p. 59(top): © Robert Laberge/Getty Images; p. 59(bottom): © Christine Pemberton/The Image Works; p. 60: © Ty Cacek/Redux Pictures; p. 61: Courtesy of the Oneida Indian Nation; p. 61(inset): © Mike Hollingshead/Science Faction/Corbis; p. 62: © Carmen K. Sisson; p. 63: © I Love Images/Alamy; p. 63(inset): © Liquidlibrary/PictureQuest; p. 64: © Karim Sahib/Getty Images; p. 66: © Eric Audras/PhotoAlto Agency RF Collections/Getty Images

CHAPTER 4: Opener: © Asia Zimmerman/Photolibrary; p. 78(top): P. 274 from *Genie: A Psycholinguist Study of a Modern Day "Wild Child"* by Susan Curtis. © 1977 reprinted with permission from Elsevier; p. 78(bottom): © TongRo Image Stock/Jupiterimages; p. 79: Photo by Charles Robinson; p. 79(inset): © Nicole Hill/Getty Images; p. 80: © Margot Granitsas/The Image Works; p. 84(top): © David H. Wells/The Image Works; p. 84(bottom): © Carlos Osorio/AP Images; p. 85: © Dennis MacDonald/Age Fotostock; p. 86: Courtesy of Rakefet Avramovitz; p. 87: © Dan Wilton/iStockphoto.com; p. 88: © Bridget Clyde/Stock Shot/Alamy; p. 89: © Paul Chesley/Getty Images; p. 90: © A. Ramey/PhotoEdit; p. 91: Courtesy of Communicare, Perth, Australia

CHAPTER 5: Opener: © Robert Goodman/National Geographic Stock; p. 98: Book cover of *The Lucifer Effect* by Philip G. Zimbardo. © 2007 used by permission of Random House, Inc.; p. 99(top): Courtesy of Phil Zimbardo, Stanford University; p. 99(bottom): © CMCD/Getty Images; p. 100: © Photodisc/Getty Images; p. 101: © Dennis MacDonald/Alamy; p. 102: © Peter R. Hvizdak/The Image Works; p. 103(top): Courtesy of Danielle Taylor; p. 103 (bottom): © China Photos/Getty Images; p. 104: © Luis M. Alvarez/AP Images; p. 106: From N. A. Christakis and J. H. Fowler. July 26, 2007, "The Spread of Obesity in a Large Social Network Over 32 Years." *New England Journal of Medicine.* 357:370–379. © 2007, Massachusetts Medical Society. All Rights Reserved; p. 106(inset): © John Birdsall/Age Fotostock; p. 107(top): © Digital Vision; p. 107(bottom right): © Twentieth Century-Fox Film Corporation/Kobal Collection; p. 110: © Mike Goldwater/Alamy; p. 111: © Photo Japan/Alamy

CHAPTER 6: Opener: © Marnie Crawford Samuelson/Aurora Photos; p. 118: Book cover of *The McDonaldization of Society 6* by George Ritzer. © 2011 by Pine Forge Press, an imprint of Sage Publications, Inc.; p. 119: © Viviane Moos/Corbis; p. 120: © Stan Honda/Getty Images; p. 121: © CBS/Photofest; p. 122(top): © Getty Images; p. 122(bottom): © AP Images/Chile's Presidency; p. 123: © Linda Nylind/Guardian News & Media Ltd.; p. 124(top): © Dinodia Images/Alamy; p. 124(bottom): © Brand X Pictures/PunchStock; p. 125: © Alan Petersime, The Indianapolis Star/AP Images; p. 126: © PunchStock/Digital Vision; p. 127: © Koichi Kamoshida/Getty Images; p. 128: © Image Source/PunchStock; p. 129: Courtesy of Sarah Levy

CHAPTER 7: Opener: © Paul Nicklen/National Geographic Stock; p. 136: Book cover of *Mix It Up: Popular Culture, Mass Media, and Society* by David Grazian. © 2010 by W. W. Norton & Company, Inc. Used by permission of W. W. Norton & Company, Inc. Designer: Wes Youssi. Photo: Paul Bradbury/Getty Images; p. 139(left): © Dirck Halstead/Time Life Pictures/Getty Images; p.139(center left): © People Magazine © 2009 Time Inc. All Rights Reserved.; p. 139(center right): © Vince Bucci/Getty Images; p. 139(right): Cover photo by Herb Ritts from Rolling Stone, June 15, 1989. © Rolling Stone LLC 1989. All Rights Reserved. Reprinted by Permission; p. 140: © Summit Entertainment/PhotoFest; p. 142: © Gerald Herbert/AP Images; p. 143: © Kami/Arabianeye; p. 144: © Jordan Althaus/© The CW/Courtesy of Everett Collection; p. 147: © CostinT/iStockphoto.com; p. 149: © Cover photo by Kwaku Alston from *Us Weekly*, February 9, 2009 © Us Weekly LLC 2009. All Rights Reserved. Reprinted by Permission; p. 150(left): © Ben Rose/WireImage/Getty Images; p. 150(right): © RubberBall Productions; p. 151: © Hamid Jalaudin/AP Images; p. 152: © Noah Flanigan 2009

CHAPTER 8: Opener: © John Munson/Star Ledger/Corbis; p. 158: Book cover of *Cop in the Hood* by Peter Moskos. © 2008 Princeton University Press, reprinted by permission of Princeton University Press; p. 159: © Koichi Kamoshida/Getty Images; p. 160: © Paul Drinkwater/NBCU Photo Bank via AP Images; p. 161(left): © Jussi Nukari/Lehtikuva; p. 161(right): © John Smierciak/Chicago Tribune/MCT via Getty Images; p. 162: Courtesy of Mrs. Alexandra Milgram. © 1965 by Stanley Milgram. From the film *Obediance*, distributed by Penn State, Media Sales; p. 163: © Albany Herald, Joe Bell/AP Images; p. 165: © David McClain/Aurora Photos; p. 165(inset): © Comstock/PunchStock; p. 168(top): © Stockbyte/PunchStock; p. 168(bottom): © Frank Wiese/AP Images; p. 170: © Fox Searchlight Pictures/Photofest; p. 171: © David Pollack/Corbis; p. 172: © Ingram Publishing/Fotosearch; p. 173: © Afton Almaraz/Getty Images; p. 175: © Photodisc/Getty Images; p. 177: Courtesy of the United States Secret Service

CHAPTER 9: Opener: © Kumar Sriskandan/Alamy; p. 186: © Norbert von der Groeben/The Image Works; p. 190(top): Courtesy of Jessica Houston Su; p. 190(bottom): © Roger Ball; p. 191: © Alex Slobodkin/iStockphoto.com; p. 192: © William Campbell/Sygma/Corbis; p. 193: © Gopal Chitrakar/Reuters; p. 194: © Ken Woroner/History Channel/The Kobal Collection; p. 197: © Ivan Bajic/iStockphoto.com; p. 198: © PhotoAlto/Alamy; p. 200: © Comstock Images/Alamy; p. 201: © Spike Mafford/Getty Images; p. 203: © Bob Croslin/Getty Images; p. 205: © Stockbyte/Getty Images; p. 206: © Jennifer Graylock/AP Images

CHAPTER 10: Opener: © Mike Greenslade/Alamy; p. 214: Book cover of *The Bottom Billion* by Paul Collier. © 2007 reprinted by permission of Oxford University Press, Inc.; p. 215(globe): © Jan Rysavy/iStockphoto.com; p. 215(scale): © Rafael Laguillo/iStockphoto.com; p. 215(bottom left): © Nati Harnik/AP Images; p. 215(bottom right): © Photofusion Picture Library/Alamy; p. 216: © Ingram Publishing/Alamy; p. 218: © Imaginechina via AP Images; p. 219: © Photodisc/Getty Images; p. 222: © Photodisc/Getty Images; p. 223: The commercial titled "Jeans" was done by Springer & Jacoby Werbung advertising agency for Against Child Labour (a UNICEF company) in Germany. Copywriter: Sven Keitel. Art Director: Claudia Todt. Creative Director: Timm Weber/Bettina Olf; p. 225: © Stuart Franklin/Magnum Photos; p. 227: © Frances Stéphane/Hemis/Alamy; p. 229: © Pascal Saez/Alamy

Chapter 11: Opener: © David R. Frazier Photolibrary, Inc./Alamy; p. 238(top): © Library of Congress Prints and Photographs Division [LC-USZC2-1745]; p. 238(bottom): © Ken Usami/Getty Images; p. 239(center left): © John Lund/Sam Diephuis/Getty Images; p. 239(center right): © Motofish Images/Corbis; p. 239(bottom): © Artville/Photodisc/PunchStock; p. 241: © Bob Daemmrich; p. 242: Jay Freis/Getty Images; p. 243: © Enigma/Alamy; p. 244: Courtesy of Prudence Hannis; p. 245: © Jack Delano/The Granger Collection, New York; p. 246: © Tony Savino/The Image Works; p. 247: © Gaizka Iroz/AFP/Getty Images; p. 249: © Barbara Penoyar/Getty Images; p. 251(top): © Michael Jensen/Auscape/The Image Works; p. 251(bottom): © Bram Belloni/Hollandse Hoogte/Redux Pictures; p. 253: © New Line Cinema/PhotoFest; p. 254: © George Rose/Getty Images; p. 255: Courtesy of Sigma Pi Alpha Sorority, Inc.; p. 256: © Tom Grill/Corbis; p. 257: Photo by David Bohrer © 2002, Los Angeles Times. Reprinted with permission; p. 258: © David L. Moore–Oregon/Alamy; p. 259: © Pixhook/iStockphoto.com

CHAPTER 12: Opener: © Michael Powell/Alamy; p. 266: © Charlie Riedel/AP Images; p. 268(top): © Craig Sjodin/ABC via Getty Images; p. 268(center): Picture provided by Harrison G. Pope, Jr., adapted from *The Adonis Complex* by Harrison G. Pope, Jr., Katherine Phillips, and Roberto Olivardia. The Free Press, © 2000; p. 269(top): © Gideon Mendel/Corbis; p. 269(bottom): © Katharine Andriotis Photography, LLC/Alamy; p. 270: © Jose Castañares/AFP/Getty Images; p. 271: © Bob Daemmrich/The Image Works; p. 272: © Inti St. Clair/Getty Images; p. 274: © John Birdsall/The Image Works; p. 276: © Thinkstock/Photolibrary; p. 277: © Stefano Lunardi/Alamy; p. 278: © Steve Cole/Getty Images; p. 279: Courtesy of Abigail E. Drevs

CHAPTER 13: Opener: © Gary Pearl/StockShot/Alamy; p. 288: Book cover of *Shock of Gray: The Aging of the World's Population and How It Pits Young against Old, Child against Parent, Worker against Boss, Company against Rival, and Nation against Nation* by Ted C. Fishman. Reprinted with permission by Simon & Schuster, Inc.;

name index

subject index